BATTLE
JUTLAND

30TH MAY TO 1ST JUNE 1916

OFFICIAL DESPATCHES WITH APPENDICES

ADMIRALTY 1920

Ex Libris

John
Jones

Published by

The Naval & Military Press Ltd

Unit 10, Ridgewood Industrial Park,

Uckfield, East Sussex,

TN22 5QE England

Tel: +44 (0) 1825 749494

Fax: +44 (0) 1825 765701

www.naval-military-press.com

CONTENTS.

APPENDICES.

TABLE OF CHARTS.

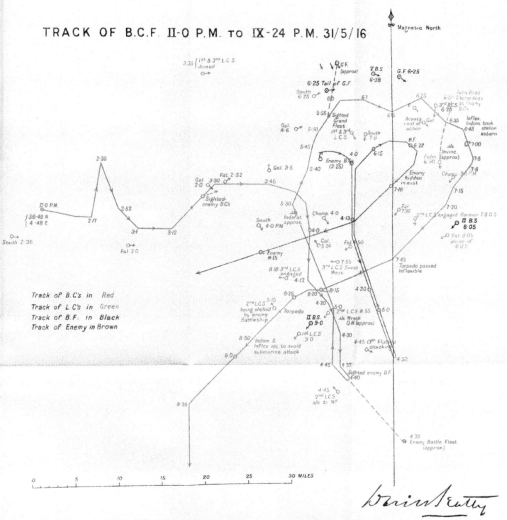

TRACK OF B.C.F. II·0 P.M. TO IX·24 P.M. 31/5/16

Plate II

Magnetic North

Track of B.C's in   Red
Track of L.C's in   Green
Track of B.F. in   Black
Track of Enemy in Brown

0   5   10   15   20   25   30 MILES

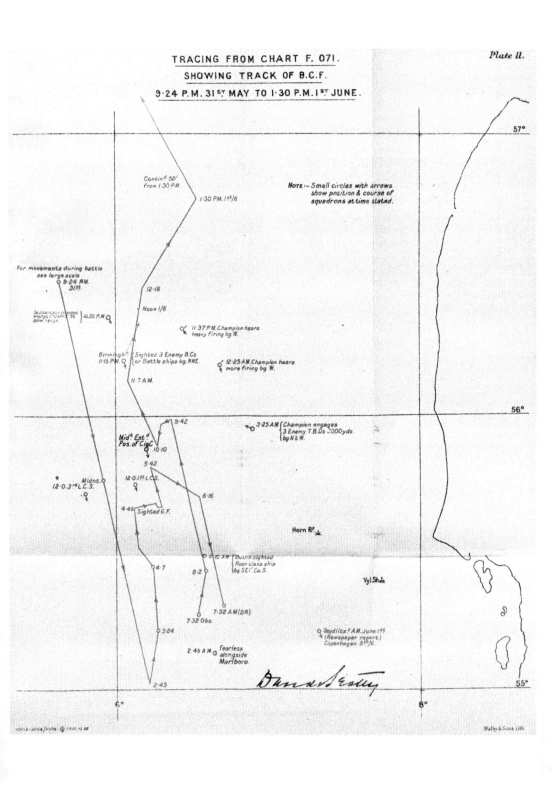

TRACING FROM CHART F. 071.

SHOWING TRACK OF B.C.F.

9·24 P.M. 31ˢᵀ MAY TO 1·30 P.M. 1ˢᵀ JUNE.

Plate II.

NOTE:— *Small circles with arrows show position & course of squadrons at time stated.*

57°

Contin⁴ 50′ from 1·30 P.M.

1·30 P.M. 1ˢᵗ/6

For movements during battle see large scale
9·24 P.M. 31ˢᵗ

12·16

Noon 1/6

Sevs annexl crosses enectys Cruisers at close range. 10.20. P.M.

11·37 P.M. Champion hears heavy firing bg. W.

Birming⁵ᵗ Sighted 3 Enemy B.Cs.
11·15 P.M. or Battle ships bg. NNE.

12·25 A.M. Champion hears more firing bg. W.

11·7 A.M.

56°

9·42

3·25 AM Champion engages 3 Enemy T.B.Ds 3000yds. bg. N b W.

Mid⁵. Est⁴ Pos. of C͟i͟gC

10·10

5·42

12·0 1ˢᵗ L.C.S.

Midnt.
12·0.3ʳᵈ L.C.S.

6·16

4·46 Sighted G.F.

Horn R͟f͟.

4·10 A.M. Dublin sighted Roon class ship bg SE¹ Co. S.

4·7

8·2

Vyl.Sh.

7·32 AM (DR)

7·32 Obs.

3·24

Seydlitz? A.M. June 1ˢᵗ (Newspaper report) Copenhagen 5ᵗʰ/6.

2·45 A.M. Fearless alongside Marlboro.

2·45

Malby & Sons Lith.

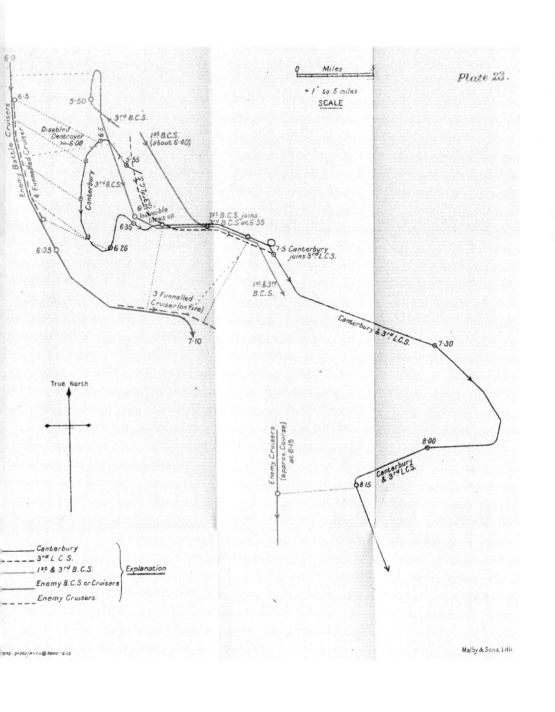

Plate 23.

Miles
0 _____ 5
= 1" to 5 miles.
SCALE

Canterbury
3rᵈ L.C.S.
1ˢᵗ & 3rᵈ B.C.S.
Enemy B.C.S or Cruisers
Enemy Cruisers.
} Explanation

True North

Malby & Sons, Lith.

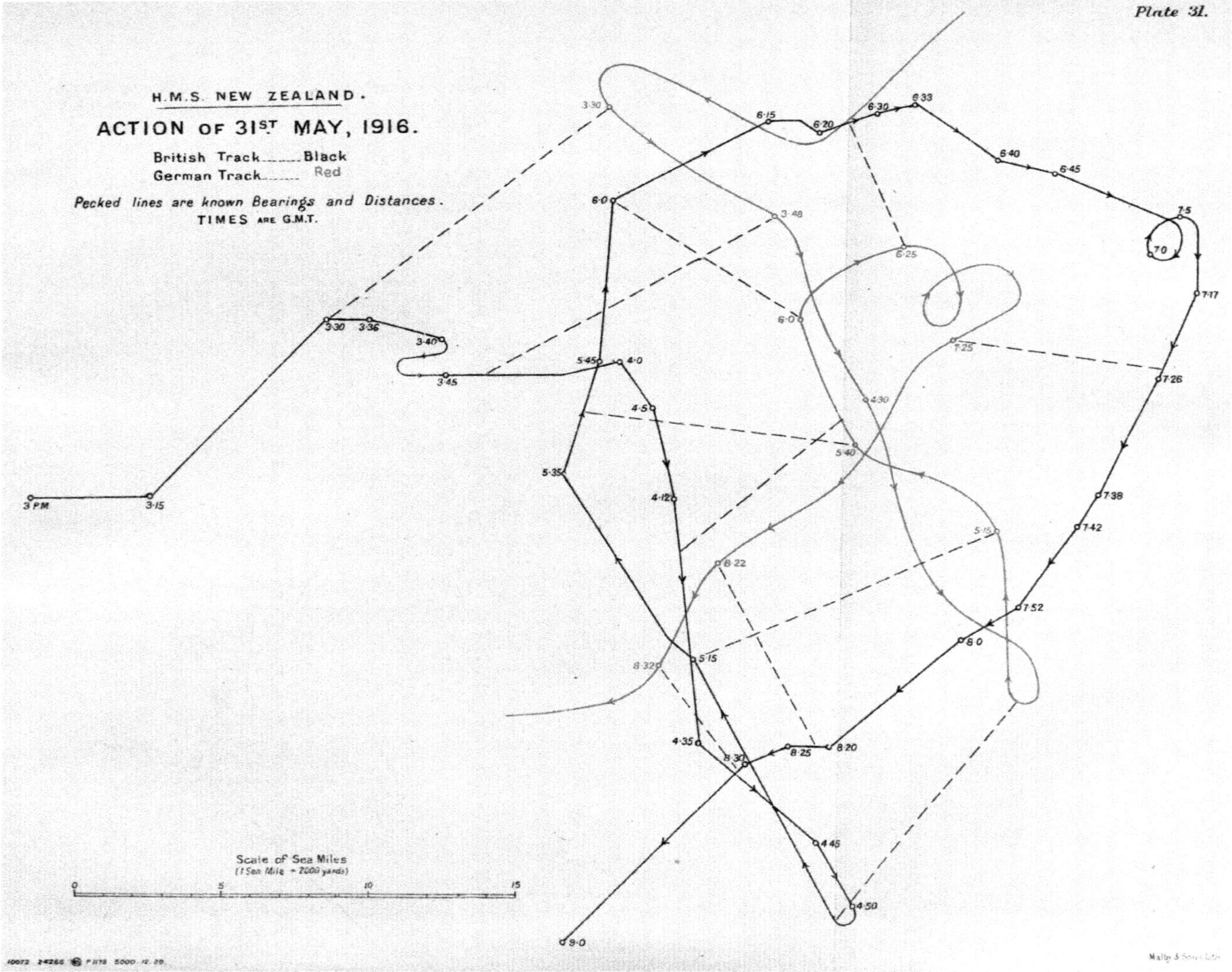

Plate 31.

H.M.S. NEW ZEALAND.

ACTION of 31st MAY, 1916.

British Track......Black
German Track....... Red

Pecked lines are known Bearings and Distances.
TIMES are G.M.T.

Scale of Sea Miles
(1 Sea Mile = 2000 yards)

BATTLE OF JUTLAND.

OFFICIAL DESPATCHES.

DESPATCH FROM THE COMMANDER-IN-CHIEF.

No. 1396/H.F. 0022.

"Iron Duke,"

SIR,   18th June 1916.

BE pleased to inform the Lords Commissioners of the Admiralty that in accordance with the instructions contained in their Lordships' telegram No. 434 of 30th May, Code time 1740, the Grand Fleet proceeded to sea on 30th May 1916.

2. The instructions given to those portions of the fleet that were not in company with my flag at Scapa Flow were as follows :—

To Vice-Admiral Sir Thomas Jerram, with Second Battle Squadron at Invergordon :—

" Leave as soon as ready. Pass through Lat. 58° 15′ N., Long. 2° 0′ E., meet me 2.0 p.m. to-morrow 31st, Lat. 57° 45′ N., Long. 4° 15′ E. Several enemy submarines known to be in North Sea."

Acknowledge.
1930 (Code time)."

To Vice-Admiral Sir David Beatty, Commanding the Battle-cruiser fleet at Rosyth, with the Fifth Battle Squadron, Rear Admiral Hugh Evan-Thomas in company :—

" Urgent, Priority.
Admiralty telegram 1740.

Available vessels, Battle-cruiser Fleet, Fifth Battle Squadron and T.B.D.s including Harwich T.B.D.s proceed to approximate position Lat. 56° 40′ N., Long. 5° 0′ E. Desirable to economise T.B.D.'s fuel. Presume you will be there about 2.0 p.m. tomorrow 31st. I shall be in about Lat. 57° 45′ N., Long. 4° 15′ E. by 2.0 p.m. unless delayed by fog.

Third Battle Cruiser Squadron, " Chester " and " Canterbury " will leave with me. I will send them on to your rendezvous.

If no news by 2.0 p.m. stand towards me to get in visual touch.

I will steer for Horn Reef from position Lat. 57° 45′N., Long 4° 15′ E.

Repeat back rendezvous.
1937 (Code time)."

3. I felt no anxiety in regard to the advanced position of the force under Sir David Beatty, supported as it was by four

ships of the Fifth Battle Squadron as this force was far superior
in gun power to the First Scouting Group and the speed of the
slowest ships was such as to enable it to keep out of range of
superior enemy forces.

4. The operation, however, showed that the ships of the
Third Squadron of the High Sea Fleet possess an unexpected
turn of speed for at any rate a short period.   The " Queen
Elizabeth " class are nominally 25-knot vessels.   The official
Quarterly Return of British and Foreign War Vessels gives the
" König " and " Kaiser " classes a designed speed of 20·5 knots.
I have always expected that they might reach 22 knots for a
short distance, but the fact that the Fifth Battle Squadron was
unable to increase its distance from the German ships when
steaming at their utmost speed comes as an unpleasant surprise
and will have considerable effect on the conduct of future
operations.   It is quite evident that all German ships possess
a speed much in excess of that for which they are nominally
designed.

5. When Sir David Beatty sighted the enemy battle-cruisers
he adopted the correct and only possible course in engaging
and endeavouring to keep between the enemy and his base.
Whether the First Scouting Group was supported or not, his
duty would be to engage and keep touch with the enemy vessels
of similar class to his own, so long as he was not in manifestly
inferior force.   In this case he had a great superiority, and there
could be no question as to his action.

6. The disturbing feature of the battle-cruiser action is the
fact that five German battle-cruisers engaging six British vessels
of this class, supported after the first twenty minutes, although
at great range, by the fire of four battleships of the " Queen
Elizabeth " class, were yet able to sink the " Queen Mary " and
" Indefatigable." It is true that the enemy suffered very heavily
later, and that one vessel, the " Lützow," was undoubtedly
destroyed, but even so the result cannot be other than unpalatable.
The facts which contributed to the British losses were, *first*,
the indifferent armour protection of our battle-cruisers, particularly as regards turret armour and deck plating, and, *second*,
the disadvantage under which our vessels laboured in regard to
the light.   Of this there can be no question.

But it is also undoubted that the gunnery of the German
battle-cruisers in the early stages was of a very high standard.
They appeared to get on to their target and establish hitting
within two or three minutes of opening fire in almost every case,
and this at very long ranges of 18,000 yards. The German
vessels appear to use some such system of fire as the Petravic
method as the guns do not go off exactly together, and it
unquestionably gives excellent results. The " spread " for
both direction and elevation is very small and the rapidity of
fire very great.

7. Once we commence hitting, the German gunnery falls off, but—as shown by the rapidity with which the "Invincible" was sunk at a later stage—their ships are still able to fire with great accuracy even when they have received severe punishment.

8. The fact that the gunnery of the German battlefleet when engaged with our battlefleet did not show the same accuracy must not, I think, be taken as showing that the standard is not so high as with their battle-cruisers, as I am inclined to the opinion that we then had some advantage in the way of light, although it was very bad for both sides.

9. The German organisation at night is very good. Their system of recognition signals is excellent. Ours is practically nil. Their searchlights are superior to ours and they use them with great effect. Finally, their method of firing at night gives excellent results. I am reluctantly compelled to the opinion that under night conditions we have a good deal to learn from them.

10. The German tactics during the action were those which have always been anticipated, and for which provision has been made so far as is possible in my Battle Orders. The "turn away" of the enemy under cover of torpedo boat destroyer attacks is a move most difficult to counter, but which has been closely investigated on the Tactical Board. Vice-Admiral Sir Doveton Sturdee has rendered me much assistance in the study of this particular movement and in devising a counter to it. There is no real counter. Nothing but ample time and superior speed can be an answer, and this means that unless the meeting of the fleets takes place fairly early in the day it is most difficult, if not impossible, to fight the action to a finish. In this particular case, thanks to the fact that the enemy did not, as far as can be seen, expect to find our whole fleet present, there was no time for him to lay a prepared mine area, and not much time to place his submarines, although many submarines were present. It is unlikely that in future operations we shall be so favoured in this respect, and the element of time will therefore be still more important. I foreshadowed in my letter of Oct. 30th, 1914, No. 339/HF/0034, in which their Lordships expressed concurrence, A.L. of November 7th, 1914, M.03177/14,[1] the possibility of it being actually necessary purposely to delay bringing the fleet to close action for some time on account of the possibilities which the mine and submarine give for preparing a trap on a large scale, and it should be understood that this possibility still exists and will be increased as the enemy gets stronger in submarines.

11. It was unnecessary for me to give any special orders to the flag officers during the action. Events followed the course that was expected. All squadrons and flotillas took up their stations as directed in the Battle Orders with most commendable

---

[1] *See* Appendix IV.

accuracy under very difficult circumstances. The torpedo attacks launched by the enemy were countered in the manner previously intended, and practised, during exercises, and the fleet was manœuvred to close again after these attacks by the method which had been adopted for this purpose. The handling of the large fleet was immensely facilitated by the close co-operation and support afforded me by the flag officers.

12. One of the features of the action was the large number of torpedoes that crossed our line without taking effect on any ship except the " Marlborough." Sir Cecil Burney estimates that at least twenty-one torpedoes were seen to cross the line of his squadron. All were avoided by skilful handling, except that single one, and it is notable that the " Marlborough " herself evaded seven. Similarly the Fifth Battle Squadron, in rear of the First Battle Squadron, avoided a considerable number and other squadrons had similar experiences.

It is of supreme importance to keep from the knowledge of the enemy the fact that ships were able to avoid torpedoes by seeing the track, as it would not be beyond the ingenuity of the Germans to devise a means of preventing any track being left.

13. The experience and results of the action, particularly the knowledge we now have of the speed of the enemy's Third Squadron, must exercise considerable influence on our future dispositions and tactics. It will, for instance, not be advisable in future to place our Fifth Battle Squadron in a position removed from support. I have these questions under consideration and will submit my conclusions to their Lordships.

14. A narrative of the action is enclosed.

I am, Sir,
Your obedient Servant,
J. R. JELLICOE,
Admiral.

The Secretary of the Admiralty.

ACTION WITH THE GERMAN HIGH SEA FLEET,
31 MAY–1 JUNE, 1916.

Schedule of Enclosures in Home Fleets, Letter No. 1396/H.F. 0022, dated 18 June, 1916.

Enclosure No.	*Subject.*
3.	(i) Battle Plan showing position of the respective Fleets.[1] (ii) Plan of Battle.[2] (iii) Track of Operations.[3] (iv) Tracks of Vessels of H.M. Fleet.[3]
4.	List of Enemy Vessels sunk.
5.	Extract from Captain (S.'s)report to the Chief of the War Staff, No. 0157 of 7 June, 1916, relative to Explosions in the Minefield laid by "Abdiel," 31 May–1 June, 1916.

Enclosure No. 1 in H.F. letter No. 1,396, dated 18th June 1916.

NARRATIVE.

31st May.

At. 9.30 p.m., "Iron Duke," First and Fourth Battle Squadrons, Third Battle-Cruiser Squadron, Second Cruiser Squadron, Fourth Light-Cruiser Squadron, Commodore (F), Fourth and Twelfth Flotillas, and four destroyers of Eleventh Flotilla, "Canterbury" and "Chester" left Scapa.

At 10 p.m., the Second Battle Squadron, First Cruiser Squadron and remainder of the Eleventh Flotilla left Cromarty.

At 10 p.m., "Lion," First and Second Battle-Cruiser Squadrons, First, Second and Third Light-Cruiser Squadrons, "Fearless" and nine boats of First Flotilla, "Champion" and ten of Thirteenth Flotilla, eight destroyers of Harwich force and "Engadine," left Rosyth.

At 10.40 p.m., the Fifth Battle Squadron (four ships) left Rosyth.

A complete list of the ships present is given in Home Fleet's letter,[4] No. 1,395, of 18th June 1916, and in Enclosure No. 2 to this despatch.

Disposition of the Fleet during the early portion of 31st May.

31st May.

Disposition of the Scapa force at 6 a.m. on 31 May :—

Battle fleet in divisions, line ahead, disposed abeam to starboard, in the order—3rd, 4th, 5th, 6th (Fifth Organisation),

---

[1] Plate 1.   [2] Plate 1a.

[3] NOTE.—Sub-enclosures (iii) and (iv) to Enclosure 3 were amended in October 1916 by the Commander-in-Chief in order to bring the positions at 9 p.m. shown thereon into conformity with those shown on the revision of Sub-Enclosure (ii) that he submitted on the 29th August, 1916 (Plate 4a). The amended versions are printed in Plates 2a and 3a. They are identical with the original versions except that they commence from a slightly altered geographical position. *See* page 51.

[4] Above letter not printed. The despatch published in the Third Supplement, dated Thursday, 6th July 1916, to the "London Gazette," of Tuesday, 4th July 1916, was substituted for it by the Commander-in-Chief, Grand Fleet. For list, however, *see* pp. 43–47.

screened by the Fourth and Twelfth Flotillas; Fourth Light-Cruiser Squadron three miles ahead of First and Fourth Battle Squadrons; Second Cruiser Squadron and four destroyers spread five miles apart ten miles ahead of the battle squadrons.

Battlefleet and Third Battle-Cruiser Squadron :—

The Scapa and Cromarty forces proceeded for the 2 p.m. rendezvous ordered by the Commander-in-Chief in latitude 57° 45′ N., longitude 4° 15′ E., but actually met at 11.15 a.m. in latitude 58° 13′ N., longitude 2° 42′ E. The Rosyth force proceeded for their 2 p.m. rendezvous in latitude 56° 40′ N., longitude 5° E.

At 2 p.m. on 31 May, the "Dreadnought" battlefleet was in latitude 57° 57′ N., longitude 3° 45′ E., in Organisation No. 5, divisions in line ahead disposed abeam to starboard in the order—1st, 2nd, 3rd, 4th, 5th, 6th, divisions screened by the Fourth Eleventh and Twelfth Flotillas; Fourth Light-Cruiser Squadron three miles ahead of the battlefleet; cruisers and destroyers sixteen miles ahead of the battlefleet, spread eight miles apart on a line of direction N. 40° E., and S. 40° W., in the order from East to West :

"Cochrane," "Shannon," "Minotaur," (centre of "Defence," "Duke of "Black
"Hampshire,"   screen) "Warrior," Edinburgh," Prince."

attached cruisers on the flanks; Third Battle-Cruiser Squadron "Chester " and "Canterbury" about twenty miles ahead; the whole steering S. 50° E., zig-zagging, with a speed of advance of fourteen knots.

Battle-Cruiser Fleet and Fifth Battle Squadron :—

At 2 p.m., in latitude 56° 46′ N., longitude 4° 40′ E., course N. by E., speed 19½ knots.

Order :—

"Lion " and First Battle-Cruiser Squadron in single line ahead, screened by "Champion " and ten destroyers of Thirteenth Flotilla ("Nestor," "Nomad," "Narborough," "Obdurate," "Petard," "Pelican," "Nerissa," "Onslow," "Moresby," "Nicator," "Turbulent," and "Termagant ").

Second Battle-Cruiser Squadron in single line ahead, three miles E.N.E. of "Lion," screened by six destroyers of the Harwich force ("Lydiard," "Liberty," "Landrail," "Laurel," "Moorsom," and "Morris ").

Fifth Battle Squadron, in single line ahead, five miles N.N.W. of "Lion," screened by "Fearless " and nine destroyers of First Flotilla ("Acheron," "Aerial," "Attack," "Hydra," "Beaver," "Goshawk," "Defender," "Lizard," and "Lapwing ").

Light-Cruiser Squadrons forming a screen astern, eight miles S.S.E. from "Lion," ships spread on a line of direction E.N.E. and W.S.W., five miles apart, in the order from West to East :

"Southampton," "Nottingham," "Falmouth," "Birkenhead," "Inconstant," "Galatea,"
"Birmingham," "Dublin,"   "Gloucester," "Cordelia," "Phaeton."

"Engadine," seaplane carrier, was stationed between "Gloucester" and "Cordelia."

"Yarmouth" acted as linking ship between "Lion" and Light-Cruiser screen.

The following is an extract from a report received from the Vice-Admiral Commanding Battle Cruiser Fleet, and explains clearly the course of the action until they joined forces with the battlefleet :—

*   *   *   *   *

At 2.20 p.m. reports were received from "Galatea" indicating the presence of enemy vessels to the E.S.E., steering to the Northward. The direction of advance was immediately altered to S.S.E., the course for Horn Reef, so as to place my force between the enemy and his base. "Galatea" reported at 2.35 .p.m., that she had sighted a large amount of smoke as from a fleet, bearing E.N.E. This made it clear that the enemy was to the Northward and Eastward, and that it would be impossible for him to round the Horn Reef without being brought to action. Course was accordingly altered to the Eastward and North Eastward, the enemy being sighted at 3.31 p.m. They appeared to be the 1st Scouting group of five Battle-Cruisers.

After the first report of the enemy, the 1st and 3rd Light Cruiser Squadrons changed their direction and without waiting for orders spread to the East, thereby forming a screen in advance of the Battle Cruiser Squadrons and Fifth Battle Squadron by the time we had hauled up to the course of approach. They engaged enemy Light Cruisers at long range. In the meantime the 2nd Light Cruiser Squadron had come in at high speed and was able to take station ahead of the Battle Cruisers by the time we turned to E.S.E., the course on which we first engaged the enemy. In this respect the work of the Light Cruiser Squadrons was excellent and of great value.

From a report from "Galatea" at 2.25 p.m., it was evident that the enemy force was considerable and not merely an isolated unit of Light Cruisers, so at 2.45 p.m. I ordered "Engadine" to send up a seaplane and scout to N.N.E. This order was carried out very quickly, and by 3.8 p.m., a seaplane with Flight Lieutenant F. J. Rutland, R.N., as Pilot, and Asst. Paymaster G. S. Trewin, R.N., as Observer, was well under way; her first reports of the enemy were received in "Engadine" about 3.30 p.m. Owing to the clouds it was necessary to fly very low, and in order to identify four enemy Light Cruisers the seaplane had to fly at a height of 900 ft., within 3,000 yards of them, the Light Cruisers opening fire on her with every gun that would bear. This in no way interfered with the clarity of their reports, and both Flight Lieutenant Rutland and Asst. Paymaster Trewin are to be congratulated on their achievement, which indicates that seaplanes under such circumstances are of distinct value.

At. 3.30 p.m., I increased speed to 25 knots and formed line of battle, the Second Battle Cruiser Squadron forming astern of the First Battle Cruiser Squadron, with destroyers of the 13th and 9th Flotillas taking station ahead. I turned to E.S.E., slightly converging on the enemy, who were now at a range of 23,000 yards, and formed the ships on a line of bearing to clear the smoke. The Fifth Battle Squadron, who had conformed to our movements, were now bearing N.N.W., 10,000 yards. The visibility at this time was good, the sun behind us and the wind S.E. Being between the enemy and his base, our situation was both tactically and strategically good.

At 3.48 p.m., the action commenced at a range of 18,500 yards, both forces opening fire practically simultaneously. Both appeared to straddle the target early, and at 3.51 p.m., " Lion " received her first hit. Course was altered to the Southward, and subsequently at intervals, to confuse the enemy's fire control; the mean direction was S.S.E., the enemy steering a parallel course distant about 18,000 to 14,500 yards. For the next ten minutes the firing of the enemy was very rapid and effective. " Lion " was hit repeatedly, the roof of " Q " turret being blown off at 4 p.m. Immediately afterwards " Indefatigable " was hit by three shots falling together. The shots appeared to hit the outer edge of the upper deck in line with the after turret. An explosion followed, and she fell out of the line sinking by the stern. Hit again by another salvo near " A " turret she turned over and disappeared.

At 4.8. p.m. the Fifth Battle Squadron came into action and opened fire at a range of 20,000 yards. The enemy's fire now seemed to slacken. It would appear that at this time we passed through a screen of enemy submarines. In evidence of this a torpedo was sighted passing astern of " Lion " from starboard to port. The destroyer " Landrail " of 9th Flotilla, who was on our Port beam trying to take station ahead, sighted the periscope of a submarine on her Port quarter, and at the same time the track of a torpedo which passed under her and crossed the line of the Battle Cruisers between " Tiger " and " New Zealand." Though causing considerable inconvenience from smoke, the presence of " Lydiard " and " Landrail " undoubtedly preserved the Battle Cruisers from closer submarine attack. " Nottingham " also reported a submarine on the Starboard beam.

" Eight destroyers of the 13th Flotilla, " Nestor," " Nomad," " Nicator," " Narborough," " Pelican," " Petard," " Obdurate," " Nerissa," with " Moorsom " and " Morris " of 10th Flotilla, " Turbulent " and " Termagant " of the 9th Flotilla, having been ordered to attack the enemy with torpedoes when opportunity offered, moved out at 4.15 p.m. simultaneously with a similar movement on the part of the enemy. The attack was carried out in a most gallant manner and with great determination. Before arriving at a favourable position to fire torpedoes, they intercepted an enemy force consisting of a Light Cruiser and 15 Destroyers. A fierce engagement ensued at close quarters, with

the result that the enemy were forced to retire on their Battle
Cruisers, having lost two destroyers sunk, and having their torpedo attack frustrated. Our destroyers sustained no loss in
this engagement, but their attack on the enemy Battle Cruisers
was rendered less effective owing to some of the destroyers
having dropped astern during the fight. Their position was
therefore unfavourable for torpedo attack.

"Nestor," "Nomad" and "Nicator," gallantly led by
Commander The Hon. E. B. S. Bingham, of "Nestor," pressed
home their attack on the Battle Cruisers and fired two torpedoes
at them at a range of 6,000 and 5,000 yards, being subjected to
a heavy fire from the enemy's secondary armament. "Nomad"
was badly hit, and apparently remained stopped between the
lines. Subsequently "Nestor" and "Nicator" altered course
to the S.E., and in a short time the opposing Battle Cruisers,
having turned 16 points, found themselves within close range
of a number of enemy battleships. Nothing daunted, though
under a terrific fire, they stood on, and their position being
favourable for torpedo attack, fired a torpedo at the second
ship of the enemy line at a range of 3,000 yards. Before they
could fire their fourth torpedo "Nestor" was badly hit, and
swung to starboard, "Nicator" altering course inside her to
avoid collision, and thereby being prevented from firing the
last torpedo. "Nicator" made good her escape, and subsequently rejoined the Captain (D), 13th Flotilla. "Nestor"
remained stopped, but was afloat when last seen. "Moorsom"
also carried out an attack on the enemy's battle fleet.

"Petard," "Nerissa," "Turbulent" and "Termagant" also
pressed home their attack on the enemy battle-cruisers, firing
torpedoes at a range of 7,000 yards after the engagement with
enemy destroyers. "Petard" reports that all her torpedoes
must have crossed the enemy's line, while "Nerissa" states that
one torpedo appeared to strike the rear ship. These destroyer
attacks were indicative of the spirit pervading His Majesty's
Navy, and were worthy of its highest traditions. I propose to
bring to your notice a recommendation of Commander Bingham
for the Victoria Cross, and other officers for some recognition of
their conspicuous gallantry.

From 4.15 to 4.43 p.m., the conflict between the opposing
Battle-Cruisers was of a very fierce and resolute character. The
Fifth Battle Squadron was engaging the enemy's rear ships,
unfortunately at very long range. Our fire began to tell, the
accuracy and rapidity of that of the enemy depreciating
considerably. At 4.18 p.m., the third enemy ship was seen to
be on fire. The visibility to the North-Eastward had become
considerably reduced, and the outline of the ships very
indistinct. This, no doubt, was largely due to the constant
use of smoke balls or charges by the enemy, under cover of which
they were continually altering course or zigzagging.

At 4.26 p.m., there was a violent explosion in " Queen Mary "; she was enveloped in clouds of grey smoke, and disappeared. From the evidence of Captain Pelly, of " Tiger," who was in station astern, corroborated by Rear-Admiral Brock in " Princess Royal " ahead, a salvo pitched abreast of " Q " turret, and almost instantaneously there was a terrific upheaval and a dense cloud of smoke through which " Tiger " passed barely 30 seconds afterwards. No sign could be seen of " Queen Mary." Eighteen of her officers and men were subsequently picked up by " Laurel."

At 4.38 p.m., " Southampton " reported the enemy's Battle-fleet ahead. The destroyers were recalled, and at 4.42 p.m. the enemy's battlefleet was sighted S.E. Course was altered 16 points in succession to starboard, and I proceeded on a Northerly course to lead them towards the Grand Fleet. The enemy Battle-cruisers altered course shortly afterwards, and the action continued. " Southampton," with the Second Light Cruiser Squadron, held on to the Southward to observe. They closed to within 13,000 yards of the enemy battlefleet, and came under a very heavy but ineffective fire. " Southampton's " reports were most valuable. The Fifth Battle Squadron were now closing on an opposite course, and engaging the enemy battle-cruisers with all guns. The position of the enemy battlefleet was communicated to them, and I ordered them to alter course 16 points. Led by Rear-Admiral Hugh Evan-Thomas, M.V.O., in " Barham," this Squadron supported us brilliantly and effectively.

At 4.57 p.m., the Fifth Battle Squadron turned up astern of me and came under the fire of the leading ships of the enemy battlefleet. " Fearless," with the destroyers of the First Flotilla joined the Battle-cruisers and, when speed admitted, took station ahead. " Champion " with 13th Flotilla took station on the Fifth Battle Squadron. At 5.0 p.m., the First and Third Light-Cruiser Squadrons, which had been following me on the Southerly Course, took station on my starboard bow; the Second Light-cruiser Squadron took station on my port quarter.

The weather conditions now became unfavourable, our ships being silhouetted against a clear horizon to the westward, while the enemy were for the most part obscured by mist, only showing up clearly at intervals. These conditions prevailed until we had turned their van at about 6.0 p.m. Between 5.0 and 6.0 p.m., the action continued on a Northerly course, the range being about 14,000 yards. During this time the enemy received very severe punishment, and undoubtedly one of their Battle-cruisers quitted the line in a considerably damaged condition. This came under my personal observation, and was corroborated by " Princess Royal " and " Tiger." Other enemy ships also showed signs of increasing injury. At 5.5. p.m., " Onslow " and " Moresby," who had been detached to assist " Engadine," with the seaplane, rejoined the Battle-cruiser Squadrons and took station on the starboard (engaged) bow of "Lion." At 5.10 p.m., "Moresby," being 2 points before the beam of the leading enemy ship at a range of 6,000 to 8,000 yards, fired a long range torpedo at the third in their line. Eight minutes later she observed a hit with a torpedo on what she judged to be the sixth ship in the line. Later analysis of the director setting indicated a probability of this result. "Moresby" then passed between the lines to clear the range of smoke and rejoined "Champion." In corroboration of this "Fearless" reports having seen an enemy heavy ship heavily on fire at about 5.10 p.m., and shortly afterwards a huge cloud of smoke and steam, similar to that which accompanied the blowing up of "Queen Mary" and "Indefatigable."

At 5.35 p.m. our course was N.N.E., and the estimated position of the Grand Fleet was N. 16 W., so we gradually hauled to the North Eastward, keeping the range of the enemy at 14,000 yards. He was gradually hauling to the Eastward, receiving severe punishment at the head of his line, and probably acting on information received from his Light-Cruisers which had sighted and were engaged with the Third Battle-Cruiser Squadron (*vide* "Indomitable's" report). Possibly Zeppelins were present also. At 5.50 p.m., British Cruisers were sighted on the port bow, and at 5.56 p.m., the leading battleships of the Grand Fleet bearing North 5 miles. I thereupon altered course to East and proceeded at utmost speed. This brought the range of the enemy down to 12,000 yards. I made a visual report to the Commander-in-Chief that the enemy Battle-Cruisers bore South East. At this time only three of the enemy Battle-Cruisers were visible, closely followed by battleships of the "Konig" class.

At about 6.5 p.m., "Onslow," being on the engaged bow of "Lion," sighted an enemy Light-Cruiser at a distance of 6,000 yards from us, apparently endeavouring to attack with torpedoes. "Onslow" at once closed and engaged her, firing 58 rounds at a range of from 4,000 to 2,000 yards, scoring a number of hits. "Onslow" then closed to within 8,000 yards of the enemy Battle-Cruisers, and orders were given for all torpedoes to be fired. At this moment she was truck amidships by a heavy shell, with the result that only one torpedo was fired. Thinking that all his torpedoes had gone, the Commanding Officer proceeded to retire at slow speed. Being informed that he still had three torpedoes, he closed the Light-Cruiser previously engaged and torpedoed her. The enemy's Battle-Fleet was then sighted at a distance of 8,000 yards, and the remaining torpedoes were fired at them ; having started correctly, they must have crossed the enemy's track. Damage in her feed tank then caused "Onslow" to stop.

*   *   *   *   *

General Position.

At 5 p.m., the position of affairs was as follows :—

"Iron Duke's" position :—
> latitude 57° 24′ N.,
> longitude 5° 12′ E.,
> course S.E. by S.
> speed 20 knots,

in company with the main battlefleet force, cruisers spread, destroyers screening.

"Lion's" position (to "Iron Duke's" reckoning) :—
> lat. 56° 42′ N.,
> long. 5° 44′ E.,
> course N.N.W.,
> speed 25 knots,

in company with the Fifth Battle Squadron and First and Second Battle-Cruiser Squadrons. Enemy battle-cruisers bearing from "Lion" approximately E.S.E. seven miles; enemy battlefleet from "Barham" about S.S.E. nine miles.

Weather Conditions.

Up to 6 p.m. the weather conditions were wholly in favour of the enemy. The horizon to the eastward was entirely obscured by haze, and from the Fifth Battle Squadron when engaging enemy battleships and battle-cruisers only the flashes of the enemy guns could be made out. On the other hand, a strong light to the westward enabled the British ships to be distinguished clearly by the enemy.

This is indicated by the photograph[1] enclosed, taken from "Malaya" by Midshipman Gerald W. Norman. The photograph was taken at about 5.15 p.m. towards the western horizon, the enemy at the same time being to the eastward. Our destroyers shown silhouetted against the bright horizon were at least eight miles distant. The splashes seen in the photograph are from "overs" fired at "Malaya" by the enemy's battlefleet.

Movements of the Fifth Battle Squadron.

At 3.30 p.m., when the Battle-Cruiser Fleet formed line of battle, the Fifth Battle Squadron, consisting of "Barham," "Valiant," "Warspite" and "Malaya," in single line in the order named, were five miles from the Battle-Cruiser Fleet, bearing from them N.N.W. and conforming to their movements.

At 3.56 p.m. fire was opened at some enemy light-cruisers before the port beam steering about S.S.E. After two or three salvoes these enemy light-cruisers turned away eight points and disappeared out of sight.

---

[1] Not reproduced.

At 4.02 p.m. the British battle-cruisers altered course gradually to the south-eastward, the enemy battle-cruisers also turned to the south-eastward. This turn enabled the Fifth Battle Squadron to gain, and at 4.06 fire was opened by pairs, concentrating on the two rear ships at a range of approximately 18,000 yards.

At 4.21 p.m. the enemy battle-cruisers opened fire on the Fifth Battle Squadron, " Barham " being hit shortly after.

At 4.40 p.m., by which time the Fifth Battle Squadron was heavily engaged with the enemy battle-cruisers, enemy destroyers were observed to be attacking, and were driven off by our light-cruisers and destroyers attached to the Battle-Cruiser Fleet. The squadron was turned away by Preparative-flag, and torpedoes were observed to cross the line, one ahead and one astern of " Valiant."

At 4.50 p.m. our battle-cruisers, having previously turned to the northward, crossed the line of fire.

At 4.53 the Fifth Battle Squadron turned sixteen points to starboard in succession by signal from the " Lion " (the enemy battle-cruisers having also turned to the northward).

At 4.55 the enemy's battlefleet was sighted, bearing S.S.E., steering to the Northward, distant about 17,000 yards.

" Barham " and " Valiant " continued to engage the enemy Battle-Cruisers while " Warspite and " Malaya " fired at the head of the enemy's battlefleet.

At about 5.25 p.m., the squadron increased to full speed. During this period the light was very much in favour of the enemy and firing from the Fifth Battle Squadron was very intermittent, whereas a heavy but ineffective fire was received from the leading enemy battleships.

At 6.06 p.m., " Marlborough " was sighted, and the Fifth Battle Squadron turned to form astern of the line at 6.18 p.m.

Up to this time " Barham " had been hit six times by battle-cruisers, " Valiant " was not hit. " Warspite " had been hit twice by either battle-cruisers or battleships. " Malaya " had been hit seven times all by battleships.

Progress of the Action.

Continuous reports were received in " Iron Duke " of the above reported movements. The Fleet was informed that the enemy battlefleet was coming North, and a wireless signal made to the Admiralty that a fleet action was imminent.

Movements of the Third Battle-Cruiser Squadron.

Turning now to the movements of the Third Battle-Cruiser Squadron. This squadron was originally stationed twenty miles ahead of the battlefleet, " Chester " (Captain Robert N. Lawson) acting as linking ship between the squadron and the cruiser line, " Canterbury " (Captain Percy M. Royds) being abreast of the squadron.

At 4.5 p.m., the Commander-in-Chief ordered the Rear-Admiral Commanding, Third Battle-Cruiser Squadron, to support the battle-cruiser fleet in action sixty miles to the southward in position latitude 56° 53′ N., longitude 5° 33′ E., the Rear-Admiral being informed that the enemy's course was reported to be S. 55° E., at 3.50 p.m. The Third Battle-Cruiser Squadron was at the time to the eastward, having turned to intercept the enemy vessels reported by the First Light-Cruiser Squadron at 2.45 p.m., as steering North from position latitude 56° 52′ N., longitude 5° 35′ E. The Third Battle-Cruiser Squadron altered course to S. by E. and worked up to full speed.

At 5.30 p.m., " Chester," which was five miles N. 70° W. of the Third Battle-Cruiser Squadron, reported to " Invincible " by searchlight that she had heard firing and seen flashes of gunfire to the southwestward and turned to investigate. At 5.36 p.m., " Chester " observed a three-funnelled enemy light-cruiser with destroyers. An engagement ensued at about 6,000 yards, the enemy being reinforced by two, or possibly three, more light-cruisers. " Chester " turned to N.E., chased by the enemy ships, which had obtained the range and were inflicting considerable damage on her.

At 5.40 p.m., the Third Battle-Cruiser Squadron, which until then had been steering about S. by E. sighted enemy cruisers to the westward and turned to about W.N.W. It is apparent that the Rear-Admiral Commanding, Third Battle-Cruiser Squadron, was misled by the difference in reckoning between the battlefleet and battle-cruiser fleet and had gone too far to the eastward, actually crossing ahead of the two engaged battle-cruiser squadrons until meeting the enemy advanced cruisers. At 5.52 p.m., the Third Battle-Cruiser Squadron and " Canterbury " engaged three enemy light-cruisers which were then administering heavy punishment to " Chester," " Shark " (Commander L. W. Jones), " Acasta " (Lieutenant-Commander J. O. Barron), " Ophelia " (Commander L. G. E. Crabbe) and " Christopher " Lieutenant-Commander F. M. Kerr), and at 6 p.m., one of the enemy light-cruisers was observed by all three ships of the Third Battle-Cruiser Squadron to blow up. During the engagement, " Shark " was sunk, and " Acasta " severely damaged.

At about 6.10 p.m., the Third Battle-Cruiser Squadron sighted the battle-cruiser fleet, and at 6.21 p.m., took station ahead of the Vice-Admiral Commanding, Battle-Cruiser Fleet, in " Lion," the " Chester " then taking station astern of the Second Cruiser Squadron and remaining with that squadron for the night.

On taking station ahead of " Lion," the Third Battle-Cruiser Squadron engaged the enemy's leading battle-cruiser, which vessel returned the fire, and at 6.36 p.m. " Invincible " (Captain Arthur L. Cay, flying the flag of Rear-Admiral the Hon. Horace L. A. Hood) blew up. The cause was possibly the same as that suggested in the case of " Indefatigable." " Lion," proceeding at full speed, drew ahead, the Vice-Admiral, ordering the Third Battle-Cruiser Squadron to take station astern of his line.

Disposition and Movements of the British Battlefleet and Cruiser Squadrons.

At 5.4 p.m., the attached cruisers were ordered to take up approach stations.

The cruiser line at this time was sixteen miles ahead of the battlefleet, the ships being stationed from port to starboard as follows :—

" Cochrane," " Shannon," " Minotaur," " Defence," " Duke of Edinburgh," " Black Prince " " Warrior,"

" Hampshire " (linking ship).

cruisers in the screen being eight miles apart, centre of the screen bearing S.E. by S.

At 5.40 p.m., heavy firing was heard ahead by " Minotaur," and soon afterwards ships were seen in the mist and were challenged by " Minotaur." " Cochrane " and " Shannon " were recalled by the Rear-Admiral Commanding, Second Cruiser Squadron, and formed into line, the signal being made to engage the enemy. The conditions were exceedingly difficult for making out ships, but the strange vessels on replying to the challenge were ascertained to be the Third Battle-Cruiser Squadron (Rear-Admiral the Hon. Horace L. A. Hood).

At 5.52 p.m., Rear-Admiral Sir Robert Arbuthnot, in " Defence," signalled that the battlefleets would shortly be engaged. Rear-Admiral Herbert L. Heath, in " Minotaur," with the Second Cruiser Squadron, made a sweep to the eastward to ensure that no enemy minelayers were at work in that direction, and proceeded to take up deployment station two points on the engaged van of the battlefleet, being joined there by " Duke of Edinburgh " at 7.17 p.m.

At 5.50 p.m., the cruisers on the right flank of the cruiser line had come in contact with the enemy cruisers. A large three-funnelled enemy light-cruiser was engaged and disabled by " Defence " and " Warrior." She drifted down between the lines, being fired on by the battlefleet, and was subsequently seen to sink by several independent observers.

" Defence " and " Warrior " of the First Cruiser Squadron, which vessels had turned to starboard during the engagement with the light-cruisers, passed between our own and the enemy battle-cruisers and battlefleet, and the two ships found themselves within comparatively short range of the enemy's heavy ships. At 6.16 p.m., " Defence " was observed to be heavily hit and blew up; " Warrior " was badly hit and disabled, but reached the rear of the battlefleet and was taken in tow by " Engadine." It is probable that Rear-Admiral Sir Robert Arbuthnot did not realise the proximity of the German battle fleet, and coming across it at short range in the mist was unable

to extricate his squadron before his flagship was sunk and the
" Warrior " disabled.

Arrival of the Battlefleet.

At 5.45 p.m., " Comus " (Captain Alan G. Hotham), of the
Fourth Light-Cruiser Squadron, then three miles ahead of the
battlefleet, reported that heavy gunfiring was heard from a
direction south. The flashes of guns were shortly afterwards
observed S.S.W., and at 5.56 p.m., some vessels, subsequently
seen to be the British battle-cruisers, were seen bearing S.S.W.
from " Marlborough," steering E., heavily engaged with an
unseen enemy.

At 6.0 p.m., " Iron Duke's " position was latitude 57° 11' N.,
longitude 5° 39' E., course S.E. by S., speed twenty knots;
battlefleet in divisions in line ahead disposed abeam to
starboard (Organisation No. 5), columns eleven cables apart.

It was apparent on meeting that the reckoning of the battle-
cruiser fleet was about twelve miles to the eastward of " Iron
Duke's " reckoning. In consequence of this the enemy were
sighted on the starboard bow instead of ahead, and some
twenty minutes earlier than was anticipated.

At 6 p.m., the Vice-Admiral Commanding, Battle-Cruiser
Fleet, reported enemy battle-cruisers bearing S.E., and at
6. 14 p.m., in reply to a signal, he reported the enemy battlefleet
in sight, bearing S.S.W.

Owing to the uncertainty as to the position of the enemy
battlefleet, it had not been possible to redispose the guides of
columns on any different bearing. Consequently, the deployment
was carried out under some disadvantage, and, indeed, it was
not easy to determine the correct direction of deployment until
the battlefleets were almost in contact.

At this stage it was not clear whether the enemy battlefleet
was ahead of our battlefleet or on the starboard beam, as heavy
firing was proceeding from ahead to the starboard beam and the
cruisers ahead were seen to be hotly engaged. In order to take
ground to starboard a signal was made at 6.2 p.m., to alter
course by 9 pendant to South, but it was then realised that the
enemy battlefleet must be in close proximity, either ahead or on
the starboard side, and the fleet was turned back by 9 pendant
to S.E. preparatory to deployment to port.

The Flotillas were directed to take up destroyer disposition
No. 1 at 6.8 p.m.

At 6.16 p.m., line of battle was formed by the main battlefleet
by Equal Speed pendant on the port wing division; course
S.E. by E. Speed had been reduced at 6.02 p.m., to eighteen
knots to admit of ships closing up, and it was further reduced to
fourteen knots on deployment to allow the battle-cruisers, which
were before the starboard beam, to pass ahead.

The Rear-Admiral Commanding, Fifth Battle Squadron,
having sighted " Marlborough " at 6.6 p.m., and other ships of

the fifth and sixth divisions at 6.19 p.m., turned his squadron to port at 6.20 p.m., to form astern of the sixth division. During this turn the ships of the Fifth Battle Squadron came under a heavy fire from the enemy's leading battleships, but the shooting was not good and few hits were made. At this time " Warspite's " helm unfortunately jammed, causing her to continue to turn towards the enemy's battlefleet. By good handling, although hit several times, " Warspite " was enabled to get away to the northward. The Rear-Admiral Commanding, Fifth Battle Squadron, subsequently ordered her to proceed to Rosyth on receipt of a report of her damage. By 6.30 p.m., the Fifth Battle Squadron (less " Warspite "), was formed astern of " Agincourt " in the battle line.

At 6.33 p.m., speed was increased to seventeen knots, which speed was maintained until the Fleet left the scene for its bases on 1st June. Enclosure No. III. shows the order of the battlefleet, etc., at 6.40 p.m.

Battlefleet Action.

The First Battle Squadron, at the rear of the battle line and the furthest to the westward during deployment, came into action almost immediately the deployment signal had been hauled down. At 6.15 p.m., a salvo pitched short of and over the forecastle of " Hercules," deluging the bridge and conning tower with water. The enemy at this time were made out by our rear ships to be in single line, steering to the eastward, their battle-cruisers leading, followed by four " Königs," four or five " Kaisers " and four " Helgolands," the remainder of the line being invisible owing to the large overlap we had established, and to the converging course. " Marlborough " and her division opened fire at 6.17 p.m. on one of the " Kaiser " class. " Hercules " opened fire at 6.20 p.m. on the second " Kaiser." " Colossus " and her division opened fire at 6.30. The practice from the First Battle Squadron was very satisfactory under the conditions and severe punishment was administered to the enemy. " Marlborough " continued her fire with great success even after the ship had assumed a considerable list after being torpedoed; " Agincourt's " powerful armament was used with good effect, and other ships were also observed to be scoring frequent hits.

" Iron Duke " opened fire at 6.23 p.m. at a three-funnelled light-cruiser passing down the line. This cruiser was engaged by other ships, was heavily hit, and was observed to sink by several eye-witnesses at the end of the line.

At 6.25 p.m. " Falmouth " and " Yarmouth " of the Third Light-Cruiser Squadron, stationed on the starboard bow of " Lion " fired torpedoes at the leading enemy battle-cruiser. The Third Light-Cruiser Squadron then attacked the enemy ships with gunfire.

The battle-cruisers were well ahead by 6.30 p.m. and had reduced to eighteen knots, gradually closing the enemy van and concentrating a heavy fire on the leading ship.

At 6.30 " Iron Duke " shifted her fire to the leading battle-ship (one of the " König " class) bearing S.W., range 11,000 yards. and hit her several times in the third and fourth salvoes at 6.33 p.m. The remainder of the third division also opened fire on the leading enemy battleships of " König " class. " Ben-bow " and the fourth division opened fire at 6.30 p.m., and " Orion " and certain ships of the Second Battle Squadron also opened fire at this time on the rear enemy battle-cruisers and leading battleships. At 6.40 p.m. the second " König " was seen to be heavily hit and to be ablaze fore and aft, then to turn 16 points to starboard, the original third ship passing her. The ship then settled by the stern and was observed to blow up by independent witnesses in " Thunderer," " Benbow," " Barham," " Marne," " Morning Star," and " Magic," at 6.50 p.m.

At this time the visibility was about 12,000 yards, and for ranges about 9,000 yards. The light was, however, extremely baffling, partly due to misty clouds appearing and dissolving, and partly due to layers of smoke from funnels and ships firing. The direction of the wind was W.S.W., force 2.

At 6.55 p.m. the course of the Fleet was altered by divisions to south, conforming to the movements of the battle-cruiser squadrons and with a view to closing the enemy.

Firing was general in the battlefleet, but the use of distribu-tion of gunfire signals was out of the question, only three or four ships being in sight at a time from the van and centre, although more were visible from the rear. Ships fired at what they could see, while they could see it. Hitting had by this time become general.

At 6.54, the Vice-Admiral Commanding, First Battle Squad-ton, in " Marlborough," reported that his flagship had been struck by a torpedo or mine. Later evidence pointed to it being a torpedo, possibly discharged from a submarine. This is supported by the report of " Revenge." Officers in the transmitting station, " A " and " Y " shell rooms, the director tower and spotting tower all felt a shock as if the ship had struck something. A few minutes after the " Marlborough " was torpedoed. A large patch of oil, with an upheaval in the middle and portions of wreckage, came to the surface. " Revenge," on seeing " Marlborough " struck, had hauled out of the line to port about a cable and probably struck and sank a submarine.

At this time the destroyer " Acasta " was passed in a disabled condition. She signalled that she was holed fore and aft and unable to move her engines. In spite of her condition her ship's company were observed to be cheering as the battlefleet passed.

At 6.55 p.m. " Iron Duke " passed the wreckage of " Invin-cible." The ship was split in two, the bow and stern standing out of the water, the centre part resting apparently on the bottom. The position of the wreck was latitude 57° 6' N., longitude 5°02' E. " Badger " was picking up survivors.

In order to guard against the risk of secret documents being recovered by the enemy should the position of the wreck be located by remaining above water, a submarine was sent from Blyth to search for and if necessary, sink the wreck. She was unable to find it, and there is no doubt that the vessel sank.

At 7.10 p.m. " Marlborough " and several other ships were firing at the second of the three of the remaining " Konig " class (" Marlborough " fired fourteen salvoes). At 7.18 a ship turned out of the line very low in the water aft and sinking. An Officer in the torpedo control tower in " Colossus " saw this ship sink at 7.30 p.m., his evidence being confirmed by " Benbow," " Superb," " Colossus," and " Malaya."

At 7.12 p.m. enemy battle-cruisers also emerged from the mist at 10,000 yards range on the starboard beam of the " Colossus " division, which opened fire on them. A ship of the " Derfflinger " class was observed to be hit several times by " Colossus " and " Neptune," and listed over and passed out of sight obscured by heavy smoke and mist. " Colossus " was hit, but only suffered trifling damage. At the same time a ship of the " Seydlitz " class was also fired at and hit by " Collingwood." " Revenge " also fired at and hit a battle-cruiser supposed to be " Von Der Tann," which then turned away.

Attacks by Enemy Flotilla on Battlefleet.

At about 7.10 p.m. a flotilla of enemy destroyers supported by a cruiser was seen approaching " Iron Duke," bearing from " Iron Duke " S. 50° W. (60° green). The Fleet was turned away two points by the " Preparative " and subsequently another two points, fire being opened on the flotilla with 4-in., 6-in., and turret guns at a range of about 10,000 to 8,000 yards. When at about 8,000 yards range, the destroyers fired their torpedoes, turning towards the rear of their line and disappearing in a smoke screen. No torpedoes hit. One destroyer was observed to sink.

At about 7.25 p.m. another enemy's destroyer attack was observed approaching the rear of the battle line from a bearing about 120° green, 9,000 yards from " Iron Duke," and was heavily engaged by the four rear divisions of the battlefleet and Fifth Battle squadron. The Eleventh Flotilla and Fourth Light-Cruiser Squadron had advanced to counter the former enemy destroyer attack and were in a favourable position to counter the second attack during which at 7.22 p.m. they sank an enemy destroyer. They were recalled at 7.40 p.m. In addition, the third destroyer from the left was observed to sink, and the left-hand one to be struck and turned bottom up approximately at 7.35 p.m. At 7.45 p.m. a division of the Twelfth Flotilla, consisting of " Obedient," " Mindful," " Marvel," and " Onslaught," proceeded to attack, and sink an enemy

"V"-class destroyer flying a Commodore's pendant near the rear of the Fifth Battle Squadron.

Line had again been formed at 7.33 p.m. on a S. by W. course and at 7.41 p.m. course was altered to the S.W.

At 7.30 p.m. the Second Light-Cruiser Squadron, having previously turned towards the German line to keep in touch with the enemy's rear, observed the enemy alter course to S. by W. At 8.30 "Southampton" and "Dublin" attacked an enemy destroyer and hit her heavily amidships. She was shortly afterwards seen to sink.

At 8 p.m. firing had practically ceased except towards the rear of the line, where some of the ships of the First and Fifth Battle Squadrons were still engaged.

Whilst the battlefleet had been turned away from enemy torpedo attacks, the Vice-Admiral Commanding, Battle-Cruiser Fleet, had continued engaging the head of the enemy line, gradually hauling round to S.W. by S. and then S.W. to keep in touch. At 7.32 p.m. "Lion's" course was S.W., speed eighteen knots, the leading enemy battleship bearing N.W. by W. The battle-cruiser fleet were inflicting considerable punishment on the enemy, so much so that the enemy torpedo-boat destroyers were called upon to cover the capital ships by emitting volumes of grey smoke. Under cover of this smoke, the enemy were lost sight of at 7.45 p.m.

At 7.58 p.m. the Vice-Admiral Commanding Battle-Cruiser Fleet ordered the First and Third Light-Cruiser Squadrons to sweep to the westward and locate the head of the enemy's line. The British battlefleet also turned to the westward.

At 8.30 p.m. the Vice-Admiral Commanding, Battle-Cruiser Fleet, again sighted the enemy and engaged the leading enemy battle-cruiser at a range of 10,000 yards—only two were sighted. This battle-cruiser was struck by two salvoes and burst into flames and smoke. Heavy explosions took place on board and the ship turned away with a heavy list. "Princess Royal" set fire to a three-funnelled battleship. "New Zealand" and "Indomitable" report that the third ship of the line which they engaged heeled over and was on fire. The enemy was last seen by "Falmouth" steaming to the westward.

At 8.40 p.m. all battle-cruisers felt a heavy shock, as if struck by a mine, torpedo, or sunken wreckage. It seems probable that, in view of the condition in which the enemy were last seen the shock indicated the blowing up of one of their heavy vessels.

Night Disposition.

Darkness was now rapidly setting in, the mist was increasing and it became necessary to decide on the future course of action. The British Fleet was between the enemy and his base. Each side possessed a considerable number of destroyers, it being most probable that the enemy was largely superior in this respect, in numbers, as it was logical to assume that every available torpedo-boat destroyer and torpedo-boat had been ordered out as soon as contact between the fleets became probable.

I rejected at once the idea of a night action between the heavy ships, as leading to possible disaster owing, first, to the presence of torpedo craft in such large numbers, and, secondly, to the impossibility of distinguishing between our own and enemy vessels. Further, the result of a night action under modern conditions must always be very largely a matter of pure chance. I was loth to forego the advantage of position, which would have resulted from an easterly or westerly course, and I therefore decided to steer to the southward, where I should be in a position to renew the engagement at daylight, and should also be favourably placed to intercept the enemy should he make for his base by steering for Heligoland or towards the Ems and thence along the north German coast.

Further, such a course enabled me to drop my destroyer flotillas astern, thus at one and the same time providing the battlefleet with a screen against attack by torpedo craft at night, and also giving our flotillas an opportunity for attacking the enemy's heavy ships should they also be proceeding to the southward with the object of regaining their bases.

Accordingly, at 9 p.m., the fleet was turned by divisions to south (speed seventeen knots) the second organisation being assumed, and the fleet formed in divisions line ahead disposed abeam to port, columns one mile apart, the object of the close formation being that the divisions should remain clearly in sight of each other during the night, in order to prevent ships mistaking each other for enemy vessels.

At 9.24 p.m., the Vice-Admiral Commanding, Battle-Cruiser Fleet, in latitude 56° 29′ N., longitude 5° 27′ E., turned to south.

At 9.27 p.m., the destroyer flotillas were ordered to take station five miles astern of the battlefleet.

At 9.32 p.m., " Abdiel " was directed to lay mines in wide zig-zags from a position fifteen miles 215° from the Vyl light-vessel in a mean direction 180°, ten mines to the mile. This operation was successfully accomplished without observation, and " Abdiel " then proceeded to Rosyth to replenish with mines.

At 10 p.m., " Iron Duke's " position was :—

latitude, 56° 22′ N.,
longitude, 5° 47′ E.,
course, south,
speed, 17 knots,

the order of the fleet from west to east being as follows :—

Battle-Cruiser Fleet ;
Cruiser Squadrons ;
Battlefleet (in divisions, disposed abeam to port, columns
one mile apart, in Organisation No. 2) ;

First Light-Cruiser Squadron four miles one point before
the starboard beam of the Battle-Cruiser Fleet;
Second Light-Cruiser Squadron astern of the Fifth Battle
Squadron and Second Battle Squadron;
Third Light-Cruiser Squadron on starboard bow of the
Battle-Cruiser Fleet;
Fourth Light-Cruiser Squadron ahead of the Battlefleet;
Destroyer Flotillas—five miles astern of the Battlefleet
in the order, west to east—Eleventh, Fourth, Twelfth,
Ninth,[1] Tenth,[1] Thirteenth.

At 10.20 p.m., the Second Light-Cruiser Squadron engaged
five enemy ships, apparently a cruiser and four light-cruisers,
which concentrated on " Southampton " and " Dublin " and
severely damaged both of them. The enemy, however, were
beaten off.

No enemy ship was seen by the battlefleet during the night,
except by " Active " astern of the Second Battle Squadron.
Firing was heard astern, searchlights were seen in use, and a
fair number of star shells were fired by the enemy, which gave
out a brilliant illumination, and it was evident that our destroyer
flotillas and light-cruiser squadrons were in action.

From reports received subsequently it is fairly certain that
the German battlefleet and battle-cruisers crossed astern of the
British battlefleet and made for the Horn Reef channel. In
crossing the rear of the British battle line, the enemy fleet came
in contact with the British flotillas, which seized the opportunity
to deliver a series of brilliant and gallant attacks. The estimated
course of the enemy fleet was S.E. ½ E., and the estimated time
of the last battle squadron passing the Horn Reef light-vessel
abeam, eighteen miles distant, was 3.45 a.m. Submarine E55,
on the bottom to the west of the Horn Reef light-vessel, heard
eleven explosions between 2.15 and 5.30 a.m. on the 1st June.
The estimated time of the last of the enemy's heavy ships
passing over " Abdiel's " minefield is 5 a.m.

PROCEEDINGS OF FLOTILLAS.

ELEVENTH FLOTILLA.

The Commodore (F), in " Castor," with the Eleventh Flotilla,
at 10.4 p.m. was on the right flank in position five miles distant
and about seven points abaft the starboard beam of the Second
Battle Squadron. The Fourth Flotilla was in the centre astern
of the Fourth Battle Squadron, and the Twelfth Flotilla was
on the east flank astern of the First Battle Squadron.

" Castor " and Eleventh Flotilla came in contact with enemy
battle-cruisers at 10.5 p.m., the enemy consisting of three or

---

[1] Destroyers detached from Harwich Force.

more vessels. Fire was opened on "Castor," which vessel returned it at a range of 2,000 yards, and "Castor" "Magic" and "Marne" each fired a torpedo and turned to port. A violent detonation was heard in the engine rooms of three destroyers. The remaining destroyers, with "Castor" were uncertain whether the ships firing at "Castor" were really enemy vessels and thought a mistake had been made. They, therefore, withheld their torpedo fire. "Castor's" W/T and signalling gear having been disabled by the enemy's fire, the Commodore (F) was unable to signal to the destroyers to attack. The enemy disappeared and the flotilla proceeded south.

At 0.15 a.m. a German torpedo boat destroyer was sighted on the starboard bow of "Castor." She received the fire of all "Castor's" guns at point blank range and was not seen again, either by "Castor" or the torpedo boat destroyers following. It appears certain that she was sunk.

FOURTH FLOTILLA.

"Tipperary," "Broke" and the Fourth Flotilla came in contact with enemy cruisers at 11.30 p.m., the enemy being on a southeasterly course; a heavy fire was opened on the flotilla resulting in "Tipperary" being set on fire forward; she sank at 2.0 a.m. "Broke" was badly hit, and her steering gear and engine room telegraphs disabled, and before she could be got under control she rammed "Sparrowhawk." Both vessels were under a very heavy fire, and "Sparrowhawk's" injuries were such that her crew were taken off and she was sunk on the following morning. "Broke" reached the Tyne.

One four funnelled enemy cruiser was torpedoed by "Spitfire" (next astern of "Tipperary") and took a heavy list, and appeared to be in a sinking condition. "Spitfire" also rammed a light-cruiser and carried off 29 feet of her skin plating. She had two cranes and three funnels, a red band being painted on each of the latter.

The remainder of the flotilla altered course to the eastward and then southeastward, and at midnight came in contact with an enemy battle squadron consisting of ships of the Deutschland class. One enemy ship was torpedoed, either by "Ardent," "Ambuscade" or "Garland," and was observed to list over considerably. It is probable that she was sunk. "Fortune" was sunk during this attack. The flotilla was eventually driven off by gunfire and obliged to retire to the northward.

Shortly after turning off "Ardent" sighted four more large German ships crossing her bows and steering N.N.E. "Ardent" attacked and fired a torpedo, but could not observe the result as a devastating fire was opened on her, and she sank with colours flying after a gallant fight, her commanding officer (Lieutenant-Commander Arthur Marsden) being picked up by "Marksman" on the following morning after being five hours in the water.

TWELFTH FLOTILLA.

The Twelfth Flotilla formed astern of the First Battle
Squadron, which was on the port flank and somewhat astern of
station owing to " Marlborough's " speed being reduced by
damage, although by revolutions she was steaming at seventeen
knots.

At 11.30 p.m. the flotilla was obliged to alter course to clear
another flotilla—probably the Fourth Flotilla—which was crossing
on a southeasterly course, and this alteration caused the Twelfth
Flotilla to be about five miles to the eastward and ten miles to
the northward of the First Battle Squadron by midnight.

At 1.45 a.m. an enemy battle squadron was sighted on the
starboard bow, steering S.E., consisting of six ships, the first four
of which were thought to be of the Kaiser class (it is interesting
to note that this points to there being only six ships of the
enemy's Third Battle Squadron left, thus confirming the evidence
already given that two were sunk during the day action).

The Captain (D), Twelfth Flotilla, altered to a parallel course
and increased to 25 knots, leading round in order to attack on a
northwesterly course.   The attack was carried out most successfully, torpedoes being fired at 2 a.m., at a range of about 3,000
yards, at the second and third ships of the line, the latter vessel
being particularly conspicuous by a torpedo boat being stationed
close under the quarter.   Torpedoes took effect on the third
ship, which blew up, the magazine having apparently exploded.
Enemy cruisers astern of the battle line attacked the flotilla and
obliged the Captain (D) to alter course to north.   The cruisers
were shaken off and the flotilla altered round to south to resume
its course after the battlefleet.

The following signal was made to the Commander-in-Chief
by the Captain (D) :—

> Enemy battlefleet steering S.E., approximate bearing
> S.W.   My position ten miles astern of First Battle Squadron.
> 0152.

This signal was unfortunately not received in the battlefleet
owing to telefunken interference.

Whilst the main torpedo attack by the Twelfth Flotilla was
being made, " Maenad " (Commander John P. Champion),
having anticipated that the attack on the enemy would be made
with tubes bearing to starboard, was not ready when the turn
was made and port tubes brought to bear.   He, therefore, held
on the southeasterly course and turned later to fire one torpedo
from the port side when the tube was trained.   He then trained
both tubes to starboard, turned and went ahead, closing in again
to between 4,000 and 5,000 yards from the enemy and firing
two more torpedoes.   The second torpedo struck the fourth ship
in the line.   There was a heavy explosion, the flames topping
the mast heads, and the ship was not seen again, though those

ahead and astern were distinctly visible. The time of this attack was twenty-five minutes later than the main attack. It seems therefore certain that two battleships were hit and there is considerable probability that both were sunk by the Twelfth Flotilla. It is to be noted that six ships were observed by the Captain (D) at the commencement of the attack—only five were seen by "Maenad" when "Maenad's" attack was made, and only four were visible after "Maenad's" attack. The report from "Maenad" was sent to me from Rosyth, before her commanding officer had seen the Captain (D), Twelfth Flotilla, or knew that he had reported having blown up one of the battleships.

NINTH AND TENTH FLOTILLAS.

At 7.30 p.m. the destroyers of the Ninth and Tenth Flotillas under the commanding officer of "Lydiard," took station on the port beam of the "Champion" astern of the battlefleet.

At about 11.30 p.m fire was opened on them by a line of large ships, which were at first mistaken to be a British squadron. Shortly afterwards the "Champion" went ahead and the destroyers lost touch except "Obdurate" and "Moresby."

At 6.0 a.m. it was discovered that the destroyers of the Thirteenth Flotilla and "Morris" were astern. The commanding officer of "Lydiard" detached "Narborough" with the M-class destroyers to join the battle-cruiser fleet, and then proceeded to Rosyth with the L-class destroyers, which were short of fuel.

FIRST FLOTILLA.

"Fearless," not being able to keep up with the flotilla, formed astern of "Agincourt" at 6 p.m., the destroyers remaining with the battle-cruiser fleet during the night.

Shortly after midnight "Fearless" observed what appeared to be a German battleship pass down the starboard side. Reports from ships of the First Battle Squadron confirm this. As ships ahead did not open fire no action was taken, as her course led directly to the destroyers following astern. A heavy explosion was observed not long after, which coincides with the Fourth Flotilla attack on ships of the "Deutschland" class.

THIRTEENTH FLOTILLA.

The Thirteenth Flotilla took station astern of the battlefleet. During the night all except "Obdurate" and "Moresby" lost touch with "Champion." At 2.30 a.m. course was altered to north and "Marksman" and "Nomad" joined.

At 3.25 a.m. four enemy destroyers were sighted, steering to the southeastward, and at 3.30 a.m. were engaged at a range of approximately 3,000 yards The enemy passed and disappeared in the mist, after firing torpedoes at "Champion."

At 4.30 a.m. " Obdurate " picked up two survivors from the " Ardent."

At 5.0 a.m. two rafts were sighted and " Moresby " rescued seven men and " Maenad " eleven men, survivors from the " Fortune."

" Marksman " was detached to the assistance of the " Sparrowhawk " at 6.0 a.m. and the flotilla proceeded to Rosyth.

At 0.30 a.m. the destroyers which had become detached and were then under the orders of " Narborough " came under heavy fire from an enemy ship, which was at first mistaken for one of our light-cruisers or a ship of " Warrior " class. The " Turbulent " was rammed and sunk by gunfire. At daylight the remainder attached themselves to the force under the commanding officer of " Lydiard."

At 11.0 p.m. " Active," astern of " Boadicea," astern of Second Battle Squadron, saw a German light-cruiser come up astern. A ship on the starboard quarter of " Active " switched on searchlights and opened fire. The light-cruiser was heavily hit, stern cocked up in the air, and it was thought that the ship went down. It seems possible that " Active " witnessed the sinking of a German lightcruiser by a German battle-cruiser.

At 11.15 p.m. " Active " struck a submerged object, removing about fifteen feet of her starboard bilge keel. The position in which this occurred was well clear of the scene of the action, and it is possible that the object in question was an enemy submarine.

PROCEEDINGS OF THE FLEET AFTER MIDNIGHT 31 MAY–1 JUNE 1916.

At 2.0 a.m. a report was received from the Vice-Admiral Commanding, First Battle Squadron, that " Marlborough " had been obliged to ease to twelve knots on account of stress on bulkheads at the higher speeds. The remainder of the divisions continued at seventeen knots. The Commander-in-Chief ordered " Marlborough " to proceed to the Tyne or Rosyth by " M " channel. The Vice-Admiral Commanding, First Battle Squadron, called the " Fearless " alongside " Marlborough," shifted to " Revenge " in the " Fearless," and detached " Fearless " to escort the " Marlborough."

The weather was very misty at daylight, visibility being only three to four miles, and I deemed it advisable to disregard the danger from submarines due to a long line of ships and to form line of battle at once in case of meeting the enemy battle-fleet before I had been able to get in touch with my cruisers and destroyers. The battlefleet accordingly altered course to north at 2.47 a.m. and formed line of battle. The Fourth Light Cruiser Squadron was in company, but the sixth division of the battle-fleet comprising the " Revenge," " Hercules " and " Agincourt " had lost touch owing to " Marlborough's " reduction in speed and was broad on the eastern flank of the fleet during the day.

At 3.44 a.m. course was altered to west, heavy firing being heard in that direction. At 4.0 a.m. a Zeppelin was bearing S.E. She approached the fleet, but was driven off by gunfire. At 4.10 a.m. the battlefleet formed divisions in line ahead disposed abeam to starboard.

The Vice-Admiral Commanding, Battle Cruiser Fleet, in accordance with orders, closed the Commander-in-Chief at 5.40 a.m. and was directed to sweep to the northward and eastward, whilst the Commander-in-Chief swept with the battle-fleet first to the southward and eastward and then northward.

At 3.0 a.m. the "Sparrowhawk" was lying disabled in approximately lat. 55° 54′ N., Long. 5° 59′ E., when a German light-cruiser with three high straight funnels equally spaced, two masts and a straight stem (probably "Kolberg") was sighted two miles East steaming slowly to the northward; after being in sight about five minutes she gradually heeled over and sank slowly bows first.

The Commodore (T) with the Harwich force had been ordered at 3.20 a.m. by the Admiralty to proceed to join the Commander-in-Chief to replace vessels requiring fuel. The Commander-in-Chief gave directions for four torpedo boat destroyers to be detached to screen "Marlborough," whose 4.30 a.m. position was Lat. 55° 30′ N., Long. 6° 3′ E., course S.W., speed fourteen knots.

At 9.0 a.m. the Commander-in-Chief ordered the Vice-Admiral Commanding, Battle Cruiser Fleet, who was to eastward of the battlefleet, on a northerly course, to sweep as far as Lat. 57° 30′ N., Long. 5° 45′ E.

At 9.36 a.m. the Admiralty directed the Third Battle Squadron and Third Cruiser Squadron to return to harbour and revert to usual notice.

At 10.31 a.m. the Fifth Battle Squadron joined up with the remainder of the battlefleet.

At 1.15 p.m. the battlefleet, having swept out the area south of the scene of the action, proceeded N.W. for Scapa, the battle-cruiser fleet and "Valiant" proceeding to Rosyth.

At 3.40 p.m. the Commander-in-Chief ordered the Vice-Admiral Commanding, Tenth Cruiser Squadron, and "Donegal" to take up the Muckle Flugga patrol, to look out for "Moewe" and another raider, which were possibly attempting to break out into the Atlantic.

At 4.0 p.m. the Commander-in-Chief informed the Commodore (T) that the Admiralty had been told that there was nothing left for the Harwich force to do. He was ordered to strengthen "Marlborough's" screen by two destroyers and return to Harwich.

At 10.0 p.m. the Commander-in-Chief directed the Vice-Admiral Commanding, Orkneys and Shetlands, to send out at daylight any destroyers available to meet and screen the fleet, approaching on a bearing 82° from Pentland Skerries.

The Commodore (T) reported his 8 p.m. position on 1st June as Lat. 56° 7′ N., Long. 4° 37′ E., course N. 77° W., speed fourteen knots, and that he proposed turning back to intercept the enemy at daylight on the meridian of Long. 4° 30′ E.

The battlefleet, Fourth Light Cruiser Squadron, Fourth, Eleventh and Twelfth Flotillas arrived at Scapa between 10.30 a.m. and noon on 2nd June.

On arrival " Titania " was directed to send a submarine as soon as the weather permitted to sink by torpedo, gunfire, or explosive charge, the portion of wreck of " Invincible " in approximately Lat. 57° 06′ N., Long. 6° 02′ E., if still showing above water. " G. 10 " sailed at 3.0 a.m. 3rd June, and returned to Blyth at 9.20 p.m., 6th, reporting that after searching for forty-eight hours nothing could be found.

At 9.45 p.m. the Commander-in-Chief reported to the Admiralty that the battlefleet was again ready for action and at four hours' notice.

NARRATIVE OF EVENTS RELATING TO DISABLED SHIPS.

" MARLBOROUGH."

At 2 a.m. on 1st June, " Marlborough " reported that her speed was reduced to 12 knots and at 2.30 a.m. she was directed by Commander-in-Chief to proceed to Tyne or Rosyth by " M " channel.

At 3.0 a.m. Vice-Admiral Commanding, First Battle Squadron was directed to send his division to join Commander-in-Chief, keeping one ship as escort if necessary.

He reported that he had transferred to " Revenge " and that " Marlborough " was proceeding with " Fearless " in company.

At 7.0 a.m. Commander-in-Chief ordered Commodore (T) to detach four destroyers to screen " Marlborough," her 4.30 a.m. position being in latitude 55° 30′ N., longitude 6° 3′ E. Course S.W., speed 14 knots.

At 6.50 p.m. 1st June " Marlborough " reported—All compartments between 78 and 111 stations starboard from outer bottom to middle or main deck probably flooded. All double bottom compartments between these stations on starboard side vertical keel damaged and probably double bottom compartments vertical to 2nd longitudinal on port side also damaged. Boilers, auxiliary machinery in " A " boiler room not damaged, except air blower and Diesel engine oil pump. " A " boiler room partially flooded but water is being kept under.

At 9.30 p.m. Admiralty directed " Marlborough " to proceed to Rosyth for temporary repairs.

At midnight 1st–2nd June " Marlborough " reported her position to be in latitude 54° 40′ N., longitude 0° 53′ E., and that she was making for Flamborough Head. Owing to bad weather the water was gaining.

The Commander-in-Chief requested the Senior Naval Officer Humber to send powerful tugs to her and also directed " Canterbury," who was proceeding to Harwich, to proceed to her assistance.

" Canterbury " sighted " Marlborough " off the Humber at 7.30 a.m. 2nd June, when she was informed that her assistance was not required.

At 4.0 a.m. " Marlborough " reported her position to be in latitude 54° 10′ N., longitude 0° 2′ E., course South, speed 11 knots ; water was being kept under control.

" Marlborough " arrived in the Humber at 8.0 a.m. 2nd, screened by " Fearless " and 8 destroyers from Harwich, having been unsuccessfully attacked by enemy submarines whilst en route.

" WARSPITE."

At 9.0 p.m. 31st May, " Warspite " reported that the damage reduced her speed to 16 knots. The Commander-in-Chief ordered her to proceed to Rosyth.

At 6.10 a.m. 1st June, " Warspite " reported to the Commander-in-Chief that she had many holes from shellfire, that the ship was tight and on an even keel. Several compartments were full, but the bulkheads were shored. The ship was being steered from the engine room.

At 9.0 a.m. 1st June the Commander-in-Chief asked the Commander-in-Chief, Rosyth, to send local destroyers to screen " Warspite."

She arrived at Rosyth at 3.0 p.m. on 1st June having been unsuccessfully attacked by enemy submarines en route.

" BROKE."

At 11.24 a.m. 1st June the Commodore (F) reported that " Broke's " midnight position was in latitude 57° 49′ N., longitude 3° 50′ E., course N.W. speed 7 knots; that she was damaged forward and would like escort if available.

At 1.30 a.m. 2nd June, " Active " was dropped astern of fleet and proceeded to search for " Broke." She was informed that two destroyers would be sent as soon as " Broke " had been located.

At 5.0 a.m. the Commander-in-Chief directed the Commodore Commanding, Fourth Light-cruiser Squadron, to detail one light cruiser to assist " Active " in search for " Broke." " Constance " proceeded at 5.30 a.m. 2nd June.

At 6.30 a.m. 2nd June the Rear-Admiral Commanding, Second Cruiser Squadron was ordered to abandon the search for " Warrior " and sweep to find " Broke."

At 9.15 p.m. 2nd June orders were given for the search to be continued next day to the South and S.W. of the area already searched.

At 1.0 a.m. 3rd June "Constance" and "Active" were ordered to return to Scapa.

At 3.0 a.m. 3rd June "Broke" reported her position to be in latitude 56° 21' N., longitude 0° 12' E., course West, speed 6 knots, and the Vice-Admiral Commanding, Battle Cruiser Fleet, was ordered to send four destroyers to meet and screen her. They sailed at 8.0 a.m. 3rd June.

The Second Cruiser Squadron was ordered to return to the base. This squadron arrived at 6.30 p.m. the same day.

The "Broke" arrived in Tyne at 6.0 p.m. 3rd June.

"WARRIOR."

At 8.0 p.m. 31st May "Engadine" took "Warrior" in tow in about latitude 57° 10' N., longitude 5° 45' E., steering W.N.W.

"Warrior" was abandoned at 7.45 a.m. 1st June in approximately latitude 57° 34' N., longitude 2° 56' E., "Engadine" proceeding alongside to take the crew off. The latter arrived at Rosyth at 1.35 a.m. 2nd June with 35 officers, 681 men, 25 cot cases and two walking cases from "Warrior."

At 8.45 a.m. 1st June the Commander-in-Chief, not having received information that "Warrior" was abandoned, informed the Commander-in-Chief, Rosyth, that she was in tow of "Engadine," completely disabled, in latitude 57° 18' N., longitude 3° 54' E., course W.N.W., speed 7 knots, and requested that tugs should be sent.

At 9.55 a.m. 1st June, the Rear-Admiral, Invergordon, informed the Commander-in-Chief that yacht "Albion," in charge of two tugs, had been ordered to leave Peterhead and proceed to the assistance of "Warrior."

"Engadine's" 11.0 p.m. position on 31st May was in latitude 57° 10' N., longitude 2° 17' E.

At 1.45 p.m. 2nd June, the Rear-Admiral, "Cyclops," reported that yacht "Albion III." with three tugs had been unable to find "Warrior."

At 4.30 p.m. the Commander-in-Chief informed the Rear-Admiral Commanding, Second Cruiser Squadron, of the state of affairs about "Warrior" and directed him to search for her and if impossible to salve, to sink her. If the tugs sent out from Peterhead were not required for "Warrior" they were to be sent to tow "Acasta," who was in tow of "Nonsuch," a little to the Eastward of "Warrior's" position.

At 2.30 p.m. the Commander-in-Chief directed Unit 42 from Peterhead to be diverted to search for "Warrior."

At 3.0 p.m., the Rear-Admiral Commanding, Second Cruiser Squadron, reported no sign of "Warrior" in area 17 miles south of and 40 miles north, west and east of her last position given.

Good visibility. Wind, N.W., 6 to 7. Somewhat heavy sea. Second Cruiser Squadron's position at 3.0 a.m., 57° N., 2° 45′ E.

At 8.0 p.m., 2nd June, Third Light-Cruiser Squadron and three destroyers sailed from Rosyth to join in the search for "Warrior."

At 11.30 p.m. Commander-in-Chief informed the Vice-Admiral Commanding, Battle Cruiser Fleet, that the Second Cruiser Squadron had searched area North of 57° 10′ N. and west of longitude 4° 10′ E., and was now searching N.W. of this area for "Broke." He suggested that light-cruisers from Rosyth should search area south of this latitude and east of longitude 3° 50′ E.

At 9.30 a.m., 4th June, Rear-Admiral Commanding, Third Light-Cruiser Squadron, reported his position in 56° 15′ N., longitude 3° 0′ E., and proposed abandoning search at 8.0 p.m. and return to harbour. This was approved and squadron arrived at Rosyth 6.0 a.m., 5th June.

Captain of "Warrior" reported by telegraph that cypher and signal books in use were thrown overboard when ship was abandoned.

*　*　*　*　*

When abandoned, the stern of the ship was two or three feet above water. Stem about normal draught, every sea washing over upper deck. At least two feet of water on main deck. Decks and bulkheads terribly shattered by shell fire and no longer watertight; ship settling down and stability gone. No chance of ship remaining afloat in increasingly heavy weather prevailing.

"CHESTER."

Ordered by Rear-Admiral Commanding, Second Cruiser Squadron, at daylight, 1st to proceed to Humber.

She arrived at the Humber at 5.0 p.m., 1st, and reported her damage.

Three guns out of action, much damage to upper works and holed four places above water line. Engines, boilers and all machinery almost intact. No serious damage below water-line.

"SPARROWHAWK."

"At 7.30 a.m., "Marksman" reported to the Commander-in-Chief that he was endeavouring to tow "Sparrowhawk" stern first.

At 8.5 a.m. "Marksman" reported that hawser had parted, and on receipt of approval from Vice-Admiral Commanding, First Battle Squadron, "Sparrowhawk" was sunk in 56° 8′ N. 6° 10′ E.

---

1 The deletion refers to disposal of secret documents only.

" NONSUCH " AND " ACASTA."

("Acasta" was with "Shark," "Ophelia" and "Christopher" screening Third Battle-Cruiser Squadron.)

At 9.45 a.m., "Nonsuch" reported to Commodore (F) that he was escorting "Acasta" to Aberdeen at 10 knots, the latter being badly damaged.

"Nonsuch" reported later that she had taken "Acasta" in tow about noon in position 57° 16' N., longitude 4° 8' E., course W. ½ N., speed about 6 knots.

"Nonsuch" reported her 7.0 p.m. position on 1st, in 57° 8' N., 2° 33' E., speed about 7·5 knots, all well.

At 8.40 p.m., 1st, Rear-Admiral, Peterhead, was requested to send a trawler unit to screen "Nonsuch" and "Acasta" to Aberdeen, and at 6.30 a.m. 2nd, he was requested to direct "Albion" and tugs which were searching for "Warrior," to proceed to assist "Acasta" in tow of "Nonsuch."

"Nonsuch's" position at 5.0. p.m., 20 miles East of Aberdeen, speed 8 knots, all well.

"Nonsuch" arrived Aberdeen at 8.0 p.m., and "Acasta" at 9.15 p.m.

"ONSLOW" AND "DEFENDER."

"Defender" took "Onslow" in tow between 7.15 and 8.0 p.m., 31st May, "Defender's" maximum speed being 10 knots.

They arrived at Aberdeen at 1.0 p.m. on 2nd June.

Flotillas.

At 7.33 a.m., 1st June, Commodore (F) reported that all destroyers of Eleventh and Twelfth Flotillas and "Sparrowhawk" were in company.

The wreckage of "Ardent" was passed at 8.20 a.m., 1st, in latitude 55° 58' N., 6° 8' E.

At 9.45 a.m., Commodore (F) reported having passed some bodies and lifebuoy marked "Turbulent" at 8.0 a.m., 1st.

At 8.58 a.m., lat. 56° 3' N., long. 6° 4' E., "Orion" reported she had passed considerable wreckage and floating bodies, apparently foreigners.

"Dublin," which was with the Battlefleet until 10.0 a.m., reported that at 6.0 a.m., in Lat. 55° 51' N., long. 5° 53' E., she picked up a stoker from "Tipperary."

J. R. JELLICOE,
Admiral,
19 June 1916.

Enclosure No. 2 in H.F. letter No. 1396/0022, dated 18th June 1916.

LIST OF SHIPS AND ORGANISATIONS OF FLEET
DREADNOUGHT BATTLE FLEET.

1st Division
Organisation No. 2.
2nd Battle Squadron.

- 1st Division Organisation No. 5.
  - KING GEORGE V.
  - AJAX. *Vice Admiral Sir*
  - CENTURION. *Thomas Jerram KCB*
  - ERIN.
- 2nd Division. Organisation No. 5.
  - ORION.
  - MONARCH. *Rear Admiral*
  - CONQUEROR. *Arthur C*
  - THUNDERER. *Leveson CB*

2nd Division
Organisation No. 2.
4th Battle Squadron.

- 3rd Division Organisation No. 5.
  - IRON DUKE. *Rear Admiral*
  - ROYAL OAK.
  - SUPERB. *Alexander Duff CB*
  - CANADA.
  - BENBOW. *Vice Admiral Sir*
- 4th Division Organisation No. 5.
  - BELLEROPHON. *Doveton*
  - TEMERAIRE. *Sturdee Bt.*
  - VANGUARD. *KCB CVO CMG*

3rd Division
Organisation No. 2.
1st Battle Squadron.

- 6th Division Organisation No. 5. *Rear Admiral Ernest FA Count CMG*
  - MARLBOROUGH.
  - REVENGE.
  - HERCULES.
  - AGINCOURT
  - COLOSSUS.
- 5th Division. Organisation No. 5.
  - COLLINGWOOD.
  - NEPTUNE
  - ST. VINCENT

Attached cruisers
- BOADICEA.
- BLANCHE.
- BELLONA.
- ACTIVE.

Attached
- OAK.
- ABDIEL.

Vice Admiral Sir Cecil Burney KCB, KCMG

L.A. Hood CV MVO DSO

Rear Admiral Horace Hon

5TH BATTLE SQUADRON.

Rear Admiral Hugh Evan Thomas MVO

- BARHAM.
- VALIANT.
- WARSPITE.
- MALAYA.

Rear Admiral William C Pakenham CB MVO

Vice Admiral Sir David Beatty KCB MVO DSO

BATTLE CRUISERS.

1st Battle Cruiser Squadron.	2nd Battle Cruiser Squadron.	3rd Battle Cruiser Squadron.
LION.	NEW ZEALAND.	INVINCIBLE.
PRINCESS ROYAL.	INDEFATIGABLE.	INFLEXIBLE.
QUEEN MARY.		INDOMITABLE.
TIGER		

Rear Admiral Osmond de Brock CB

LIGHT CRUISERS

1st Light Cruiser Squadron.	2nd Light Cruiser Squadron.	3rd Light Cruiser Squadron.
GALATEA.	SOUTHAMPTON.	FALMOUTH.
PHAETON.	BIRMINGHAM.	YARMOUTH.
INCONSTANT.	NOTTINGHAM.	BIRKENHEAD.
CORDELIA.	DUBLIN.	GLOUCESTER.
		CHESTER.

Rear Admiral T.D.W. Napier DSO MVO

BATTLE OF JUTLAND:

CRUISER SQUADRONS.

Rear Admiral Sir Robert Arbuthnot Bt MVO

1st Cruiser Squadron.	*2nd Cruiser Squadron.*
DEFENCE.	MINOTAUR.
WARRIOR.	HAMPSHIRE.
DUKE OF EDINBURGH.	COCHRANE.
BLACK PRINCE.	SHANNON.

Rear Admiral Herbert L Heath MVO

LIGHT CRUISER SQUADRON.

4th Light Cruiser Squadron.

CALLIOPE.
CONSTANCE.
COMUS.
CAROLINE.
ROYALIST.

LIGHT CRUISER. CANTERBURY.

DESTROYER FLOTILLAS.

12th Flotilla.	*11th Flotilla.*	*4th Flotilla.*
FAULKNOR.	CASTOR.	TIPPERARY.
MARKSMAN.	KEMPENFELT.	BROKE.
OBEDIENT.	OSSORY.	ACHATES.
MAENAD.	MYSTIC.	PORPOISE.
OPAL.	MOON.	SPITFIRE
MARY ROSE.	MORNING STAR.	UNITY.
MARVEL.	MAGIC.	GARLAND.
MENACE.	MOUNSEY.	AMBUSCADE.
NESSUS.	MANDATE.	ARDENT.
NARWHAL.	MARNE.	FORTUNE.
MINDFUL.	MINION.	SPARROWHAWK.
ONSLAUGHT.	MANNERS.	CONTEST.
MUNSTER.	MICHAEL.	SHARK.
NONSUCH.	MONS.	ACASTA.
NOBLE.	MARTIAL.	OPHELIA.
MISCHIEF.	MILBROOK.	CHRISTOPHER.
		OWL.
		HARDY.
		MIDGE.

1st Flotilla.	*13th Flotilla.*
FEARLESS.	CHAMPION.
ACHERON	NESTOR.
ARIEL.	NOMAD.
ATTACK	NARBOROUGH.
HYDRA.	OBDURATE.
BADGER.	PETARD.
GOSHAWK.	PELICAN.
DEFENDER.	NERISSA.
LIZARD	ONSLOW.
LAPWING.	MORESBY.
	NICATOR

Harwich Destroyers.

LYDIARD.
LIBERTY.
LANDRAIL.
LAUREL.
MOORSOM.
MORRIS.
TURBULENT
TERMAGANT

SEAPLANE CARRIER

ENGADINE

———

Enclosure No. 4 in H.F. Letter No. 1396, dated 18th June 1916.

SINKING OF ENEMY SHIPS.

Battleships or Battle Cruisers.

6.50 p.m. 31 May, '16.	1 Battleship of "KÖNIG" class.	Chief Witness Mate Arthur G. Boyce, "Benbow" Station G.C.T.—8 power glasses.

At 6.40 p.m., 3 "KÖNIGS" then being in sight the second "KÖNIG" was seen to be heavily hit, then to turn 16 points to starboard, the original third ship passing her. He saw

CERTAIN.

this ship settle by the stern, his attention being called to the angle her mainmast was making to the horizon.

Witness then gave a very good description of a ship sinking first by the stern and then capsizing to port, a large amount of smoke and steam coming from foremost funnel. (When last seen she had not actually disappeared.)

Confirmed by 6.33 p.m., report of "THUNDERER," (ship in this case designated as a "KAISER"). Hit by "THUNDERER" very heavily. Ship ablaze fore and aft. Talks of two ships overlapping each other.

Copy of "THUNDERER'S" report :—

Two "KAISER" class were now overlapping each other. Fire was opened, 2nd salvo seen to hit, ditto 3rd. Enemy was

CERTAIN.

blazing for whole length of quarter deck. Enemy firing salvoes at first came down to slow fire with one turret.

6.50 p.m. (approx.)	1 enemy ship in line blown up.	Lieutenant-Commander George B. Hartford, H.M.S "MARNE."
		An enemy ship of the line was seen to blow up at 6.50 p.m., (20 minutes after "INVIN-CIBLE" blew up). Flame was
CERTAIN.		of a purple colour, otherwise explosion was similar to "INVIN-CIBLE." He had no doubt whatever that ship sank.

Confirmed by Lieutenant Charles C. D. Lees, H.M.S. "MORNING STAR," and Sub-Lieutenant Francis D. Butt, H.M.S. "MAGIC." Also by report from H.M.S. "BARHAM."

Probably all above are the same ship.

7.30 p m. 31 May, '16.	1 enemy Battleship or Battle Cruiser.	At 7.10, "MARLBOR-OUGH" opened fire on a ship of "KÖNIG" class of three,
PROBABLE.		and fired 14 salvos. Distinct hits were seen.
		At 7.19, ship turned out of the line very low in the water aft and sinking and object was shifted to the *left hand ship*.

Mr. Charles Trenchard, Boatswain, "COLOSSUS."

| | 1 enemy Battle Cruiser. | This Officer was in torpedo control tower and was watching action carefully. At 7.36 p.m. he saw the second Battle Cruiser, |
| PROBABLE. | | apparently "DERFFLINGER" from silhouette, on fire after being hit by a salvo. Water came up to quarter deck, then over funnels, and he saw the water close over her. The after turret was the last to fire. |

Confirmed by Lieutenant Douglas G. W. Curry, "SUPERB."

"BENBOW" confirms this to a certain extent by talking of a ship with two masts and two funnels showing above water at 7.35 p.m.

Also reported by 2nd Battle Squadron, rear division.

| 7.20 p.m. 31 May. | 1 enemy ship. | "MALAYA." One enemy ship very low in the water dropped astern and, according to two Officers, she suddenly disappeared without an explosion. |

The three foregoing reports possibly all refer to the same ship.

| 0.15 a.m. 1 June. | 1 ship of "DEUTSCHLAND" Class. | At midnight, "GARLAND" in company with "ARDENT," "FORTUNE" and "AMBUS-CADE" sighted a line of German Battleships on starboard bow. Leading Battleship (one of "DEUTSCHLAND" class) opened fire. "GARLAND" turned to port and fired a torpedo at this ship. Range about 800 yards. Torpedo hit and was |

CERTAIN.

seen to explode abreast of the two foremost funnels. Ship took up a heavy list to port.

Confirmed by "ARDENT" as to time, enemy leading ship switching on lights, etc., Commanding Officer states he fired a torpedo at leading enemy ship from a very favourable position, 2,000 yards on her port beam. Torpedo hit, explosion seen, ship's foremost searchlights went out and she turned to starboard.

"AMBUSCADE" fired at centre ship and observed red flash and searchlights go out.

"MALAYA" confirms this and felt 3 explosions between 0.15 and 0.47 a.m. and at end of last attack a brilliant flare lit up the whole sky.

2.0 am.

Battleship of 'KAISER" Class.

At 1.45 a.m., "FAULK-NOR," in company with 12th Flotilla, sighted enemy Battleships on starboard bow steering South East. Altered course parallel to enemy and increased to 25 knots, and, when ahead, led first division ("OBEDIENT," "MINDFUL," "MARVEL," "ONSLAUGHT") round to a North Westerly course to attack. Sighted enemy again immediately.

CERTAIN.

At 2.0 a.m. fired two torpedoes from port tubes, one at second and one at third ship. When third ship was two points abaft beam a very heavy explosion took place and ship seen to blow up. Flames and debris went up to a great height. On firing, altered course to North North West, and proceeded down enemy line, six ships in all, first four being "KAISERS." Thinks last two were "KAISERS" also (but probably "KÖNIGS.")

One Destroyer close under port quarter of third enemy Battleship.

Confirmed by "ONSLAUGHT" — fired four torpedoes, hit second "KAISER" —flames to 400 ft.

Confirmed by "OBEDIENT," "MARVEL," "MINDFUL."

Explosion was so great that magazine probably blew up; flames went up higher than

		mast. It is considered that ship undoubtedly blew up and sank.
.28 a.m. 1 June.	Battleship of " KAISER " class.	H.M.S. " MAENAD " reports :—

After sighting enemy's Battleships at 2.0 a.m., with others of 12th Flotilla, he did not turn with remainder, as tubes were not trained to port but held on, turned some time later and carried out two attacks, one to port and second to starboard. At the second attack the fourth ship was hit amidships, which caused a terrific explosion—apparently of her magazine—the flames topping her mastheads.

PROBABLE.

Though the ship ahead and that astern were seen after this, the ship hit was not seen. The Captain of " MAENAD " is certain there were five Battleships when he fired and only four afterwards. He is certain of the time (taken by deckwatch), and that there were no other British ships visible at the time.

LIGHT CRUISERS.

6.40 p.m. 31 May.	One enemy Light Cruiser CERTAIN.	5.50 p.m. " DEFENCE " and " WARRIOR " fired on Light Cruiser of Russian type. Ship disabled drifted down between the lines, was fired upon by the Battle Fleet and seen to sink at 6.40 p.m. by Lieutenant Douglas G. W. Curry of "SUPERB."
5 52 p m. (approx.) 31 May.	One enemy Light Cruiser. CERTAIN.	Fired on by 3rd Battle Cruiser Squadron and " CANTERBURY " at 5.52 p.m. All ships of 3rd Battle Cruiser Squadron speak of this Light Cruiser as having blown up and sunk.
10.15 p.m.	One enemy 3 funnelled Cruiser. CERTAIN.	" CASTOR " and 11th Flotilla sighted three enemy Cruisers at 10.15 p.m. " CASTOR " attacked with guns and torpedoes. " MARNE " with torpedoes. Torpedo hit one of the Cruisers. Detonation occurred.

Confirmed by Lieutenant Charles C. D. Lees, " MORNING STAR " and Sub-Lieutenant Francis D. Butt, " MAGIC."

11.40 p.m. 31 May.	An enemy ship 3 or 4 funnels	At 11.40 p.m. " SPITFIRE " in company with " TIPPERARY " and 1st half of 4th Flotilla, torpedoed and sank an enemy large ship 3 or 4 funnels

Following evidence from Captain of "MALAYA": At 11.40 3 points abaft starboard beam, observed an attack by our Destroyers on some enemy big ships, steering the same way as us, two of which used searchlights. One of our Destroyers ("TIPPERARY") was on fire, but not before they had hit the second ship in sight. This was seen by the column of smoke and also the explosion was distinctly heard and felt. The leading ship of the enemy, which was seen by the flash of the explosion and glare from the burning "TIPPERARY," had two masts, two funnels and a conspicuous crane and was without doubt one of the "NASSAU" class.

CERTAIN.

It appears very possible that the ship "SPITFIRE" sank was a Battleship of the "HELGOLAND" Class (in the same Squadron as the "NASSAU" Class) and not a Light Cruiser as first reports appeared to indicate.

Heavy ship or Light Cruiser.

Shortly afterwards, "SPITFIRE" rammed and carried away 20 feet of the side plating of an enemy three-funnelled Cruiser. Latter had one red band on each funnel and two derricks.

3.5 a.m.
1 June.

One enemy Light Cruiser.

At 3.0 a.m. "SPARROWHAWK" was lying disabled in approximately Lat. 55° 54' N., Long. 5° 59' E., when a German Light Cruiser, three high straight funnels equally spaced, two masts and a straight stem, (probably "KOLBERG") was sighted about two miles East, steaming slowly to the Northward; after being in sight about five minutes she gradually heeled over and sank slowly, bows first.

CERTAIN.

DESTROYERS.

4.30 p.m.
31 May.

2 enemy T.B.D.s

These two enemy T.B.D.s were sunk by Destroyers from the 13th, 9th and 10th Flotillas.

CERTAIN.

7.15 p.m.
31 May.

1 enemy T.B.D.

Midshipman Arthur B. Shepherd-Cross of H.M.S. "NEPTUNE" 4" control Officer, in fore superstructure, was firing

CERTAIN.

at 7.10 p.m. with 4″ at second from left of enemy Destroyers attacking. Hit with 4″ which appeared to do no damage, but shortly after hit by a larger shell, after which there was a large flame and when splash had subsided the Destroyer had sunk.

Confirmed by " IRON DUKE " and Commander Edward O.B.S. Osborne, H.M.S. " CONQUEROR."

Midshipman Robert T. Young, H.M.S. " BENBOW."

Lieutenant Christopher M. Merewether, H.M.S. " CONQUEROR."

Lieutenant Oliver R. Wace, of H.M.S. " CONSTANCE."

Lieutenant Henry C. Phillips, H.M.S. " CALLIOPE."

7.22 p.m. 31 May. CERTAIN.	One enemy T.B.D.	H.M.S. " CALLIOPE " and 4th Light Cruiser Squadron ordered out to attack enemy T.B.D.s. Opened fire at leading Destroyer and sank her.
7.26 p.m. 31 May. CERTAIN	One enemy T B D.	Lieutenant Russel R. J. Pound and Lieutenant Lawrence B. Hill of H.M.S. " BELLE- ROPHON " saw an enemy Destroyer hit by, apparently, a 12″ shell. This was the third Destroyer from the left of those attacking and was quite clear, as none of them had started to make a smoke screen. There was a large flash when . shell exploded and the Destroyer was seen to sink.
7.35 p.m. 31 May. CERTAIN. ·	One enemy T.B.D.	At 7.35, the left hand De- stroyer of those attacking was hit apparently by " CANADA," and after spray had cleared, was seen to have turned over and to be bilge up, finally sinking 10 minutes or a quarter of an hour later. This was confirmed. by about half the Fleet.
7 50 p.m. 31 May CERTAIN.	One enemy T.B.D.	At 7.43 p.m Captain D. 12th Flotilla, ordered " OBE- DIENT," "MINDFUL," "MARVEL" and "ON- SLAUGHT " to attack an enemy Destroyer bearing West. The enemy destroyer was attacked and sunk at 7.50 p.m. She was of the " V " class, the letter being seen, but the number having been shot away. She was flying a Commodore's pendant. H.M.S. " VALIANT " con- firms.
8.30 p.m. 31 May;	One enemy T.B D.	Fired on by " SOUTHAMP- TON " and " DUBLIN," who hit her heavily amidships. She

PROBABLE.

0.15 a.m.
1 June.

One enemy
T.B.D.

was afterwards sunk by a division of our Destroyers.

At 0.15 a.m. "CASTOR" sighted a Torpedo Boat on the starboard bow. As soon as it was distinguished as an enemy craft, "CASTOR" turned to ram her and opened fire. The Torpedo Boat was too quick on the helm and just avoided being rammed, but received the fire of all guns at point blank range and was not seen again. There would appear to be no doubt that she was sunk, as she was not seen by any of the Destroyers who passed the spot where she was fired on by "CASTOR."

PROBABLE

SUBMARINES.

6.50 p m
31 May.

One enemy
Submarine.

A few minutes after "MARLBOROUGH" had been struck by a torpedo, Officers in Transmitting Room, A and Y Shell Rooms, Director Tower and Spotting Top of H.M.S. "REVENGE" felt a shock as if the ship had hit something. The Officer of "Y" Turret, Captain Evan Jukes Hughes, R.M.L.I., and the Torpedo Officer, Lieut.-Commander Walter K. E. Conlon, R.N., looked over the side and observed a large patch of oil with an upheaval in the middle with portions of wreckage coming to the surface.

CERTAIN.

Reports of H.M. Ships running over submerged objects that may possibly have been Submarines and could not have been wreckage from any vessel sunk during the action, by reason of the position of the ship at the time.

11.15 p.m.
31 May.

POSSIBLE.

"ACTIVE" was felt to bump something heavily. Subsequent investigation showed that some 15 feet of the starboard bilge keel had been torn back.

11.30 p.m.
31 May.

POSSIBLE.

"COLOSSUS." The ship unmistakably passed over some object. The noise as of something scraping along the bottom was heard and felt by officers in the Fore Transmitting Station, Ward Room, and Engine Room. On examination the following damage was found:—

Starboard outer propeller—A piece 16" by 6" broken off one blade; another blade fractured and twisted 6" by 6".

Starboard Inner Propeller— One blade tip broken off 2″ by 12″; another blade tip bent forward 12″ by 3″; remaining blade edge jagged.

4.0 a.m.
1 June.

POSSIBLE.

"MALAYA" reports that Officers in armoured director tower and engine room state that the ship struck some object submerged on the starboard side which scraped along under the bottom. Ship has been damaged under water between 38–48 stations and the Chief Constructor at Invergordon reports that the damage cannot possibly have been caused by shell fire.

The enclosed barograph record[1] from Commander Stanley T. H. Wilton, R.N., of "MALAYA," shows the shock caused by explosions (presumably from the torpedoes fired by our flotillas at enemy ships) during the night of 31st May–1st June. It will be seen that there are four or five distinct separate explosions. The "MALAYA" was in a good position for recording these explosions.

J. R. Jellicoe,
ADMIRAL.
19th June, 1916.

Enclosure No. 5 in H.F. letter No. 1396/0022, dated 18 June, 1916.

Extract from Captain (S.) report to The Chief of the War Staff, No. 0157 of 7 June 1916 *re* explosions on minefield laid by H.M.S. "ABDIEL," 31 May–1 June 1916

Vide Narrative, page 22.

Submarines E. 55, E. 26 and D. 1 left Harwich at 7 p.m. (G.M.T.) on the 30th May, and spread on a line 270° from Vyl Light Vessel, E. 55 4 miles, E. 26 12 miles, and D. 1 20 miles from it.

2. E. 55 sighted Horn's reef at 0.5 a.m. on the 1st June. At 0.20 a.m., a Zeppelin, flying low, approached and E. 55 went to the bottom to the West of Horn's Reef. At 0.45 a.m. a noise was heard as of a sweep passing very close to the Submarine.

Between 2.15 and 5.30 a.m., 11 explosions of varying intensity were heard.

Nothing was seen throughout the day, except a destroyer at 8.25 a.m., steering N.W. It turned back to the S.E. before coming into range.

*   *   *   *

---

[1] Not reproduced.

LIST OF SHIPS AND NAMES OF COMMANDING OFFICERS.

A.

In company with the Commander-in-Chief :—

"Iron Duke" - Captain Frederic C. Dreyer, C.B. (Flying the Flag of the Commander-in-Chief).

"Marlborough" - Captain George P. Ross (Flying the Flag of Vice-Admiral Sir Cecil Burney, K.C.B. K.C.M.G.; Captain E. Percy F. G. Grant, Chief of the Staff).

"Colossus" - Captain Alfred D. P. R. Pound (Flying the Flag of Rear-Admiral Ernest F. A. Gaunt, C.M.G.).

"Hercules" - Captain Lewis Clinton-Baker.

"Neptune" - Captain Vivian H. G. Bernard.

"Collingwood" - Captain James C. Ley.

"Revenge" - Captain Edward B. Kiddle.

"Agincourt" - Captain Henry M. Doughty.

"St. Vincent" - Captain William W. Fisher, M.V.O.

"Bellona" - Captain Arthur B. S. Dutton.

"King George V" Captain Frederick L. Field (Flying the Flag of Vice-Admiral Sir Thomas Jerram, K.C.B.).

"Orion" - Captain Oliver Backhouse, C.B. (Flying the Flag of Rear-Admiral Arthur C. Leveson, C.B.).

"Centurion" - Captain Michael Culme-Seymour, M.V.O.

"Conqueror" - Captain Hugh H. D. Tothill.

"Erin" - Captain The Hon. Victor A. Stanley, M.V.O., A.D.C.

"Thunderer" - Captain James A. Fergusson.

"Monarch" - Captain George H. Borrett.

"Ajax" - Captain George H. Baird.

"Boadicea" - Captain Louis C. S. Woollcombe, M.V.O.

"Benbow" - Captain Henry Wise Parker (Flying the Flag of Vice-Admiral Sir Doveton Sturdee, Bt., K.C.B., C.V.O., C.M.G.).

"Superb" - Captain Edmond Hyde Parker (Flying the Flag of Rear-Admiral Alexander L. Duff, C.B.).

"Canada" - Captain William C. M. Nicholson.

"Bellerophon" - Captain Edward F. Bruen.

"Temeraire" - Captain Edwin V. Underhill.

"Vanguard" - Captain James D. Dick.

"Royal Oak" - Captain Crawford Maclachlan.

"Blanche" - Captain John M. Casement.

"Minotaur" - Captain Arthur C. S. H. D'Aeth (Flying the Flag of Rear-Admiral Herbert L. Heath, M.V.O.).

" Hampshire " - Captain Herbert J. Savill.
" Cochrane " - Captain Eustace La T. Leatham.
" Shannon " - Captain John S. Dumaresq, M.V.O.
" Defence " - - Captain Stanley V. Ellis (Flying the Flag of Rear-Admiral Sir Robert Arbuthnot, Bt., M.V.O.).
" Duke of Edin-burgh." Captain Henry Blackett.
" Black Prince " - Captain Thomas P. Bonham.
" Warrior " - - Captain Vincent B. Molteno.
" Invincible " - Captain Arthur L. Cay (Flying the Flag of Rear-Admiral The Hon. Horace L. A. Hood, C.B., M.V.O., D.S.O.).
" Indomitable " - Captain Francis W. Kennedy.
" Inflexible " - Captain Edward H. F. Heaton-Ellis, M.V.O.
" Calliope " - - Commodore Charles E. Le Mesurier.
" Caroline " - - Captain H. Ralph Crooke.
" Comus " - - Captain Alan G. Hotham.
" Constance " - Captain Cyril S. Townsend.
" Royalist " - Captain The Hon. Herbert Meade, D.S.O.
" Canterbury " - Captain Percy M. R. Royds.
" Chester " - - Captain Robert N. Lawson.
" Active " - - Captain Percy Withers.
" Castor " - - Commodore (F) James R. P. Hawksley, M.V.O.
" Tipperary " - Captain (D) Charles J. Wintour.
" Broke " - - Commander Walter L. Allen.
" Shark " - - Commander Loftus W. Jones.
" Acasta " - - Lieutenant-Commander John O. Barron.
" Spitfire " - - Lieutenant-Commander Clarence W. E. Trelawny.
" Sparrowhawk " - Lieutenant-Commander Sydney Hopkins.
" Achates " - - Commander Reginald B. C. Hutchinson, D.S.C.
" Ambuscade " - Lieutenant-Commander Gordon A. Coles.
" Ardent " - - Lieutenant-Commander Arthur Marsden.
" Fortune " - - Lieutenant-Commander Frank G. Terry.
" Porpoise " - Commander Hugh D. Colville.
" Unity " - - Lieutenant-Commander Arthur M. Lecky.
" Garland " - - Lieutenant-Commander Reginald S. Goff.
" Christopher " - Lieutenant-Commander Fairfax M. Kerr.
" Contest " - - Lieutenant-Commander Ernald G. H. Master.
" Owl " - - Commander Robert G. Hamond.
" Hardy " - - Commander Richard A. A. Plowden.
" Midge " - - Lieutenant-Commander James R. C. Cavendish.
" Ophelia " - - Commander Lewis G. E. Crabbe.
" Kempenfelt " - Commander Harold E. Sulivan.
" Ossory " - - Commander Harold V. Dundas.

" Martial "	- -	Lieutenant-Commander Julian Harrison.
" Magic "	- -	Lieutenant-Commander Gerald C. Wynter.
" Minion "	- -	Lieutenant-Commander Henry C. Rawlings.
" Mystic "	- -	Commander Claud F. Allsup.
" Mons "	-	Lieutenant-Commander Robert Makin.
" Mandate "	-	Lieutenant-Commander Edward McC. W. Lawrie.
" Michael "	- -	Lieutenant-Commander Claude L. Bate.
" Marne "	-	Lieutenant-Commander George B. Hartford.
" Milbrook "	-	Lieutenant Charles G. Naylor.
" Manners "	-	Lieutenant-Commander Gerald C. Harrison.
" Moon "	-	Commander (Acting) William D. Irvin.
" Mounsey "	-	Lieutenant-Commander Ralph V. Eyre.
" Morning Star "	-	Lieutenant-Commander Hugh U. Fletcher.
" Faulknor "	-	Captain (D) Anselan J. B. Stirling.
" Marksman "	-	Commander Norton A. Sulivan.
" Obedient "	-	Commander George W. McO. Campbell.
" Mindful "	-	Lieutenant-Commander John J. C. Ridley.
" Marvel "	-	Lieutenant-Commander Reginald W. Grubb.
" Onslaught "	-	Lieutenant-Commander Arthur G. Onslow D.S.C.
" Maenad "	-	Commander John P. Champion.
" Narwhal "	-	Lieutenant-Commander Henry V. Hudson.
" Nessus "	-	Lieutenant-Commander Eric Q. Carter.
" Noble "	-	Lieutenant-Commander Henry P. Boxer.
" Opal "	-	Commander Charles G. C. Sumner.
" Nonsuch "	-	Lieutenant-Commander Herbert I. N. Lyon.
" Menace "	-	Lieutenant-Commander Charles A. Poignand
" Munster "	-	Lieutenant-Commander Spencer F. Russell.
" Mary Rose "	-	Lieutenant-Commander Edwin A. Homan.
" Mischief "	-	Lieutenant-Commander The Hon. Cyril A. Ward, M.V.O.
" Oak "	- -	Lieutenant-Commander Douglas Faviell M.V.O.
" Abdiel "	-	Commander Berwick Curtis.

B.

In company with Vice-Admiral Sir David Beatty, K.C.B., M.V.O., D.S.O. :—

" Lion "	- -	Captain Alfred E. M. Chatfield, C.V.O. (Flying the Flag of Vice-Admiral Sir <u>David Beatty, K.C.B., M.V.O., D.S.O.</u>; Captain Rudolf W. Bentinck, Chief of the Staff).
" Princess Royal "		Captain Walter H. Cowan, M.V.O., D.S.O. <u>(Flying the Flag of Rear-Admiral Osmond de B. Brock, C.B.).</u>
" Tiger "	- -	Captain Henry B. Pelly, M.V.O.
" Queen Mary "	-	Captain Cecil I. Prowse.

"New Zealand" - Captain John F. E. Green (Flying the Flag of Rear-Admiarl William C. Pakenham, C.B., M.V.O.).

"Indefatigable" - Captain Charles F. Sowerby.

"Southampton" - Commodore William E. Goodenough, M.V.O., A.D.C.

"Nottingham" - Captain Charles B. Miller.

"Birmingham" - Captain Arthur A. M. Duff.

"Dublin" - Captain Albert C. Scott.

"Galatea" - Commodore Edwyn S. Alexander-Sinclair, M.V.O.

"Inconstant" - Captain Bertram S. Thesiger, C.M.G.

"Phaeton" - Captain John E. Cameron, M.V.O.

"Cordelia" - Captain Tufton P. H. Beamish.

"Falmouth" - Captain John D. Edwards (Flying the Flag of Rear-Admiral Trevylyan D. W. Naper, M.V.O.).

"Birkenhead" - Captain Edward Reeves.

"Gloucester" - Captain William F. Blunt, D.S.O.

"Yarmouth" - Captain Thomas D. Pratt.

"Barham" - Captain Arthur W. Craig (Flying the Flag of Rear-Admiral Hugh Evan-Thomas, M.V.O.).

"Warspite" - Captain Edward M. Phillpotts.

"Valiant" - Captain Maurice Woollcombe.

"Malaya" - Captain The Hon. Algernon D. E. H. Boyle, C.B., M.V.O.

"Champion" - Captain (D) James U. Farie.

"Nestor" - Commander The Hon. Edward B. S. Bingham.

"Nomad" - Lieutenant-Commander Paul Whitfield.

"Narborough" - Lieutenant-Commander Geoffrey Corlett.

"Obdurate" - Lieutenant-Commander Cecil H. H. Sams.

"Petard" - Lieutenant-Commander Evelyn C. O. Thomson.

"Pelican" - Lieutenant-Commander Kenneth A. Beattie.

"Nerissa" - Lieutenant-Commander Montague G. B. Legge.

"Onslow" - Lieutenant-Commander John C. Tovey.

"Moresby" - Lieutenant-Commander Roger V. Alison.

"Nicator" - Lieutenant Jack E. A. Mocatta.

"Fearless" - Captain (D) Charles D. Roper.

"Acheron" - Commander Charles G. Ramsey.

"Ariel" - Lieutenant-Commander Arthur G. Tippet.

"Attack" - Lieutenant-Commander Charles H. N. James.

"Hydra" - Lieutenant Francis G. Glossop.

"Badger" - Commander C. A. Fremantle.

"Goshawk" - Commander Dashwood F. Moir.

"Defender" - Lieutenant-Commander Lawrence R. Palmer.

"Lizard" - Lieutenant-Commander Edward Brooke.

" Lapwing "	-	Lieutenant-Commander Alexander H. Gye.
" Lydiard " -	-	Commander Malcolm L. Goldsmith.
" Liberty " -	-	Lieutenant-Commander Philip W. S. King.
" Landrail " -	-	Lieutenant-Commander Francis E. H. G. Hobart.
" Laurel "	-	Lieutenant Henry D. C. Stanistreet.
" Moorsom "	-	Commander John C. Hodgson.
" Morris " -	-	Lieutenant-Commander Edward S. Graham.
" Turbulent "	-	Lieutenant-Commander Dudley Stuart.
" Termagant "	-	Lieutenant-Commander Cuthbert P. Blake.
" Engadine "	-	Lieutenant-Commander Charles G. Robinson.

LETTER FORWARDING REPORTS FROM FLAG OFFICERS.

No. 1415/H.F.0022.

" Iron Duke,"

SIR, 20 June 1916.

WITH reference to my letter No. 1396/H.F. 0022 of 18 June 1916, relative to the action with the German High Sea Fleet on 31 May—1 June 1916, be pleased to lay before the Lords Commissioners of the Admiralty the enclosed reports which have been received from Flag and Commanding Officers who took part in the action.

I am, Sir,
Your obedient Servant,
C. E. MADDEN,
for ADMIRAL.

The Secretary
of the Admiralty.

Schedule of inclosures in letter from Commander-in-Chief, Home Fleets, No. 1415/H.F. 0022, of 20 June, 1916.

Number.

1. " IRON DUKE," 3 June, 1916, No. 153.

2. Vice-Admiral Commanding, First Battle Squadron, 10 June, 1916, No. 021.

    Sub-inclosures.—(1) Track of " MARLBOROUGH " and enemy's vessels engaged.[1]
    (2) " MARLBOROUGH "—Gunnery report.
    (3) " HERCULES," 4 June, 1916, No. 197.

3. Vice-Admiral Commanding, First Battle Squadron, 11 June, 1916, No. 021.

    Sub-inclosures.—(1) R.A. 1st B.S., 10 June, W.16.
    (2) " COLOSSUS," 10 June, No. 658.
    (3) " REVENGE," 2 June, B.111/2.
    (4) " BELLONA," 2 June, 1916.
    (5) " NEPTUNE," 10 June, No. 08.

[1] Plates 3 and 7a.

Number.

       (6) " AGINCOURT," 10 June, 171/02.
       (7) " ST. VINCENT," 10 June, E. 106.
       (8) " COLLINGWOOD," 10 June.
       (9) " ROYAL OAK," 10 June.

4. Vice-Admiral Commanding, First Battle Squadron, 13 June, 1916, No. 457.[1]

  Sub-inclosure.—" MARLBOROUGH " 9 June, 1916.

5. Vice-Admiral Commanding, Second Battle Squadron, 5 June, 1916, No. 149/47.D.

6. Vice-Admiral Commanding, Fourth Battle Squadron, 4 June, 1916, No. 0131, forwarding summary of Fourth Battle Squadron reports.

7. Vice-Admiral Commanding, Fourth Battle Squadron, 5 June, 1916, No. 0131.

  Sub-inclosure.—Rear-Admiral, 4th Battle Squadron, 1st and 4th June, No. 017.

8. Vice-Admiral Commanding, Fourth Battle Squadron, 10 June, 1916, No. 94.

  Sub-inclosure.—" BENBOW," 8 June, C.85.

9. Vice-Admiral Commanding, Battle-Cruiser Fleet, 12 June, 1916, B.C.F.01.

  Sub-inclosures :—

       (1) " LION," 4 June, 1916, No. 115.
       (2) Rear-Admiral, 1st B.C.S., 3 June, No. 011.
       (3) Rear-Admiral, 1st B.C.S., 3 June, No. 011, forwarding report by senior unwounded surviving officer of " QUEEN MARY."
       (4) " PRINCESS ROYAL," 8 June, No. 1/125.
       (5) " TIGER," 6 June, F.61/5.
       (6) Rear-Admiral, 2nd B.C.S., 3 June, No. 513.
       (7) Rear-Admiral, 2nd B.C.S., 6 June, No. 513A, forwarding report of " NEW ZEALAND," 2 June, No. 96/A.4.
       (8) " INDOMITABLE," 2 June, No. 363/16.
       (9) " INDOMITABLE," 3 June, No. 20.S, forwarding report from " INFLEXIBLE," 2 June, 1916, No. 199.W, and report from senior surviving officer of " INVINCI-BLE," dated 2 June.
     (10) Commodore, 1st L.C.S., 2 June, No. 30, forwarding report from " INCONSTANT," 2 June, C.141/46.
     (11) Commodore, 2nd L.C.S., 2 June, No. 037/5.
     (12) Commodore, 2nd L.C.S., 5 June, No. 037/7.
     (13) Commodore, 2nd L.C.S., 6 June, No. 037/8, forwarding reports from " NOTTINGHAM," 2 June, No. 66; " BIRMINGHAM," 2 June, No. 309/10; " DUBLIN," 2 June, 1916.
     (14) Rear-Admiral, 3rd L.C.S., 5 June, No. 0447.
     (15) " CHESTER," 2 June, 1916.
     (16) Rear-Admiral, 5th B S., 9 June, No. 024.A, inclosing reports from " BARHAM," 6 June, No. 181; " WAR-SPITE," 4 June; " VALIANT," 3 June and 5 June; " MALAYA," 6 June, Nos. 88/14 and 89/14.
     (17) Captain (D.), 13th Flo., 3 June, No. 60, inclosing report from " NARBOROUGH," 2 June, 1916.[2]

---

[1] Not printed, as referring solely to personnel, in no way bearing on course of action.

[2] This report from " Narborough " will be found in Enclosure (19); it was not forwarded in Enclosure (17).

(18) Captain (D.), 13th Flo., 7 June, No. 60.

(19) Captain (D.), 13th Flo., 9 June, No. 60, inclosing reports from " NICATOR," 4 June; " PETARD," 2nd June; "NARBOROUGH," 2 June; "OBDURATE," 3 June; " MORESBY," 3 June; " NERISSA," 5 June; " PELICAN," 4 June; " ONSLOW," 2 June.

(20) Captain (D.), 1st Flo., 2 June, No. 013.

(21) Captain (D.), 1st Flo., No. 013, inclosing reports from " ATTACK," 3 June; " DEFENDER," 3 June; [1] extracts from reports of proceedings of " ACHERON," " ARIEL," " BADGER "; report from " LIZARD," 2 June, 1916.

(22) Captain (D.), 1st Flo., No. 013.B.

(23) Commodore (T.), 10 June, No. 00101, forwarding reports from " LYDIARD," 3 June; " LAUREL," 9 June; " LANDRAIL," 9 June; " LIBERTY," 9 June; " MOORSOM," 6 June; " MORRIS," 1 June; " TERMAGANT " 11 June.

(24) " ENGADINE," 2 June, 1916.

(25) " CANTERBURY," 2 June, 1916.

10. Rear-Admiral Commanding, Second Cruiser Squadron, 4 June 1916, No. 110/001/13.

Sub-inclosures :—
- (1) " MINOTAUR," 3 June, No. 274/14.
- (2) " HAMPSHIRE," 3 June, No. 7.B/83.
- (3) " COCHRANE," 2 June, No. 143/B.W
- (4) " SHANNON," 4 June, M.6/1.
- (5) " MINOTAUR "—Extracts from log.
- (6) " MINOTAUR "—Track chart.[2]

11. Rear-Admiral Commanding, Second Cruiser Squadron, 5 June, 1916, No. 111/001/13, forwarding report of " DUKE OF EDINBURGH," 4 June, No. 1/32.

12. Captain V. B. Molteno, late of " WARRIOR," 31 May, 16.

13. Captain V. B. Molteno, late of " WARRIOR," 7 June, 16.

14. Captain V. B. Molteno, late of " WARRIOR," 8 June, 16.

15. Commodore Commanding, Fourth Light-Cruiser Squadron, 3 June 1916, C.14.

16. Commodore Commanding, Fourth Light-Cruiser Squadron, 8 June, 1916, C.17/1, forwarding report from " ABDIEL," 7 June, 1916.

17. " IRON DUKE," 10 June, No. 0/13, forwarding report from " OAK," 9 June, 1916.

18. Vice-Admiral Commanding, First Battle Squadron, 9 June, 1916, forwarding report from " ACTIVE," 9 June, 1916.

19. " ACTIVE," 10 June, 1916.

20. Commodore (F.), 3 June, 1916, No. 0017/2.

21. Commodore (F.), 6 June, 1916, No. 0017/2.

Sub-inclosures :—
- (1) " SPITFIRE," 3 June.
- (2) Copy of telegram 2240 of 4 June, S.N.O., Tyne, to " CYCLOPS."
- (3) Copy of telegram 1630 of 3 June, S.N.O. Aberdeen to R.A. Longhope.
- (4) " ACASTA," 3 June.
- (5) Copy of telegram 1520 of 4 June, S.N.O. Tyne to " CYCLOPS."

---

[1] Not printed. *See* note page 244.   [2] Plates 24 and 25.

(6) " ACHATES," 3 June.

(7) " AMBUSCADE," 3 June.

(8) Report of Lieut.-Commr. Marsden, 3 June, of loss of " ARDENT."

(9) " PORPOISE," 3 June.

(10) " UNITY," 3 June.

(11) " CHRISTOPHER," 2 June.

(12) " GARLAND," 2 June.

(13) " OPHELIA," 3 June.

(14) " OWL," 2 June.

(15) Rear-Admiral, East Coast of England, 3 June, No. 696/W.962 (Narrative of survivors of " SHARK ").

(16) Report from Lieut-Commr. S Hopkins of loss of " SPARROWHAWK."

(17) " BROKE," 3 June.

(18) " BROKE," 8 June.

22. Commodore (F.), 14th June. 1916, No. 0017/2

Sub-inclosures :—

(1) Report of Act.-Sub-Lt. N. J. W. William-Powlett, 8 June, of loss of " TIPPERARY."

(2) " SPITFIRE," 4 June.

(3) " PORPOISE," 6 June.

(4) Lt.-Commr. Hopkins of " SPARROWHAWK," 5 June.

23. Commodore (F.), 4 June, 1916, No. 0017/2A.

Sub-inclosures :—

(1) " FAULKNOR," 3 June, No. 0017/2.

(2) " MAENAD," 5 June.

(3) " ONSLAUGHT," 3 June.

24. H.M.S. " IRON DUKE," 1 track, 30 May–2 June.[1]

25. H.M.S. " IRON DUKE," 1 track, 6–9 p.m., 31 May.[2]

26. H.M.S. " KING GEORGE V," 1 track, 6–9 p.m., 31 May.[3]

27. H.M.S. " ORION," 1 track, 6–10 p.m., 31 May.[4]

28. H.M.S. " THUNDERER," 1 track, 6–8.30 p.m., 31 May[5].

29. H.M.S. " DUKE OF EDINBURGH," 1 track, 5.30–8 p.m., 31 May.[6]

30. Fourth Light-Cruiser Squadron, 1 track, 4 p.m., 31 May–1.30 p.m. 1 June.[7]

31. Battle-Cruiser Fleet, 1 track, 9.24 p.m., 31 May–1.30 p.m., 1 June.[8]

32. Battle-Cruiser Fleet. 1 track, 2 p.m.–9.24 p.m., 31 May.[9]

---

[1] Plate 6a.   [2] Plate 2.   [3] Plate 8.
[4] Plate 29.   [5] Plate 30.   [6] Plate 11a.
[7] Plate 12a.   [8] Plate 11.   [9] Plate 10.

ENCLOSURE No III BATTLE PLAN

Showing the Approximate positions of the Grand Fleet and German High Sea Fleet at 6.40.P.M. on 31st May 1916.

J. R. Jellicoe
Admiral.
19 June 1916

1st Scouting Group

Falmouth
Yarmouth
Birkenhead
Gloucester

Ophelia
Christopher Canterbury

Lion
Princess Royal
Tiger
New Zealand
Inflexible
Indomitable

Goshawk
Lapwing
Lizard

Acheron
Ariel
Attack
Hydra

Badger

Calliope
Constance
Comus
Caroline
Royalist

Castor
Ossory
Martial
Magic
Minion

King George V
Ajax
Centurion
Erin

Acasta

Owl
Hardy
Mischief
Midge

Moon
Mounsey
Morning
Star

Marne
Morris
Milbrook
Manners
Mandate
Michael

Kempenfelt

Tipperary

Broke
Porpoise
Unity
Sparrowhawk
Contest
Garland
Spitfire
Nomad

Achates
Ambuscade
Ardent
Fortune

Minotaur
Cochrane
Shannon
Duke of Edinburgh
Hampshire
Chester

Active

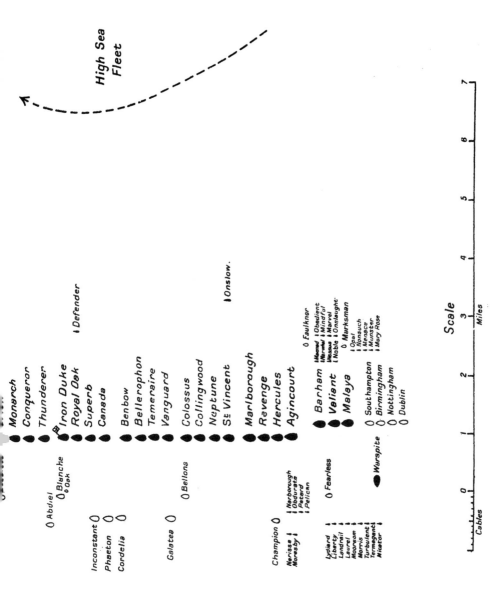

LETTER FROM COMMANDER-IN-CHIEF FORWARDING TRACINGS.

No. 1985/H.F.0022.

                                       " Iron Duke,"

SIR,   –   29 August 1916.

    WITH reference to Admiralty letter M. 05697 of 8 July 1916, enclosing a proof of the Narrative of the action with the German High Sea Fleet on 31 May–1 June 1916, be pleased to inform the Lords Commissioners of the Admiralty that the proof has been corrected and is returned herewith.

    2. The plan of the battle was found to require amendment and a revised tracing [1] is therefore enclosed, together with an additional tracing showing the order of the Battlefleet.[2]

                         I am, Sir,
                         Your obedient Servant,
                         J. R. JELLICOE,
The Secretary of the   Admiral.
    Admiralty.

    Note.—Admiral of the Fleet Viscount Jellicoe is of opinion from later consideration of all the evidence that the original Plan (Plate 1*a*), forwarded with his Despatch of 18th June 1916, is more correct than the revised Plan referred to in the above letter of the 29th August 1916 (Plate 4*a*).

---

       [1] Plate 4*a*.   [2] Plate 5*a*.

CAPTAIN'S REPORT.—H.M.S. "IRON DUKE."

Enclosure No. 1 to Submission No. 1415/0022 of 20/6/16 from
C.-in-C. Home Fleets.

No. 153.

H.M.S. "Iron Duke,"

3rd June 1916.

Sir,

    I HAVE the honour to submit the attached brief report of the part taken by your Flagship, H.M.S. "Iron Duke" during the Action with the German High Sea Fleet off the Coast of Jutland on the 31st May 1916.

    2. As no casualties occurred on board "Iron Duke," which was not hit by the Enemy's fire, no strain was thrown on the Ship's personnel or organization and, consequently, I am not specially mentioning the services of particular Officers and Men.

    The bearing of all was in every way admirable.[1]

I have the honour to be,

Sir,

Your obedient Servant,

FRED. C. DREYER,

The Commander-in-Chief,   Captain.
    H.M. Ships and Vessels,
      Home Fleets.

BRIEF ACCOUNT OF THE ACTION OFF JUTLAND OF 31ST MAY 1916.

    The attached Notes on the Action by the following Officers are forwarded as they are of interest, not only in describing events, but also any difficulties they had to cope with.

Commander (G) Geoffrey Blake, R.N. - In Gun Control Tower.
                                        —Principal Control Officer.

Lieut.-Commander Thomas F. P. In "B" Turret.
Calvert, R.N.

Lieut. Richard Shelley, R.N.   -   · In 13·5-in. Transmitting Station—In Charge.

Mr. Herbert D. Jehan, Gunner R.N. - In 6-in. Control Top, aloft. 6-in. Control Officer.

Mr. Francis W. Potter, Gunner, R.N. · In 13·5-in. Director Tower Aloft—13·5-in. Director-Gunner.

    All times given are G.M.T. All Courses Magnetic.

    I was in the Conning Tower with Captain Oliver E. Leggett, Master of the Fleet, and Lieutenant Commander (T) Edward W.

---

[1] Plates 2 and 6a.

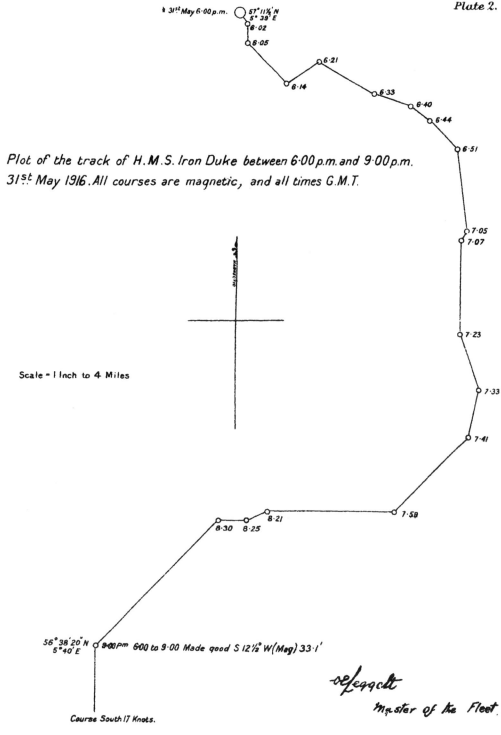

Plate 2.

Plot of the track of H.M.S. Iron Duke between 6·00 p.m. and 9·00 p.m. 31st May 1916. All courses are magnetic, and all times G.M.T.

Scale = 1 Inch to 4 Miles

31st May 6·00 p.m. — 57° 11½' N 5° 39' E

8·02
8·05
6·21
6·14
6·33
6·40
6·44
6·51
7·05
7·07
7·23
7·33
7·41
7·58
8·21
8·30   8·25

56° 38' 20" N 5° 40' E — 9·00 Pm   6·00 to 9·00 Made good S 12½° W (Mag) 33·1'

Course South 17 Knots.

Master of the Fleet.

10072.24266/P1173 (58) 5000.12.20.

Malby & Sons. Lith.

MacKichan, R.N., throughout the Action, and had a very good view of the whole situation.

The Communications worked very well.

The Navyphones were noticeably better than Voicepipes, the former requiring no shouting, but it is fully realised that Voicepipes possess the great advantage of reliability—in fact, they have to be blown away before being out of action.

Very interesting [handwritten marginal note]

The Light was bad, the weather being misty, the visibility varying during the actual firing from 10,000 to about 16,000 yards.

At 4.0 p.m.—" Action " was sounded, the Hands having had Tea, and the Decks having been cleared up.

All preparations for Immediate Action were then made.

At 6.0. p.m.—Course was S.E.—20 knots.

At 6.2 p.m.—Altered Course by 9 Pendant to S.—18 knots.

At 6.5 p.m.—Altered Course by 9 Pendant to S.E.

At 6.14 p.m.—Formed Line of Battle to Port by Equal Speed Pendant. Co. S.E. by E. " Iron Duke " being " straddled " at this time by two Enemy's Heavy Projectiles, with large " spread."

Our Battle Cruisers, which had shortly before come in sight on a Southerly bearing, firing to South Westward, rapidly cleared the Battle Line, disclosing a German 3-funnelled Cruiser somewhat like the " Kolberg " Class, but with larger Funnels, she was apparently stopped and on fire.

6.23 p.m. —Opened Fire with the Turrets on the 3-funnelled Cruiser. Bearing about 80 Green. Range, 11,000. Fall of Shot very easy to observe. The 3rd Salvo Straddled. After the 4th Salvo—Ceased Fire.

6.25 p.m.—Speed 15 knots.

6.30½ p.m.—Opened Fire on a Battleship of " König " Class. Bearing 70 Green—Range, 12,000. The 2nd, 3rd, and 4th Salvoes hitting her, with a total of at least 6 Hits. Enemy Steaming in the same direction as " Iron Duke " on a slightly converging course:

6.33 p.m.—Course S. 71° E. 17 knots. The Bearing of the Enemy was now S. 14° W. The Bearing of the Sun was N. 54° W. The Enemy was lit up by the Sun, whereas " Iron Duke " was probably invisible to them in the mist. However that may be, the " König " Battleship did not return " Iron Duke's " Fire, although heavily hit. 9 Salvoes, comprising a total of 43 rounds, were fired at her in 4 minutes 50 seconds.

At 6.40 p.m.—Course S. 56° E.

At 6.44 p.m.—Course S. 46° E.

At 6.51 p.m.—Course S. 8° E.

At 7.05 p.m.—Course S.W. by S.

At 7.07 p.m.—Course South.

7.11 p.m.—6-in. Opened Fire on Enemy T.B.D.'s attacking the Battle Fleet. Green, 63°. About 10,000 yds., and sank one Enemy T.B.D., and fired on another.

7.13 p.m.—Opened Fire with Turrets on Enemy Battleship, Green, 74. Range 15,400 yards. Enemy steaming nearly directly away.

4 Salvoes Fired, no hits were observed.

7.18 p.m.—Ceased Fire, as Enemy was hidden by a very good Smoke Screen made by his Destroyers.

7.20 p.m.—Trained Turrets on Enemy Battle Cruiser bearing 99 Green, but before Fire could be opened she also was hidden by a Smoke Screen made by attending Enemy's T.B.D.'s.

At 7.23 p.m.—Course S. 19° E.

At 7.24 p.m.—6-in. Opened Fire on Enemy's T.B.D.'s attacking Battle Fleet. Green 115. Range, 10,000.

At 7.27 p.m.—Turrets opened fire, Green 110, Range 9,600 yards, on Enemy's T.B.D.'s which were attacking the Battle Fleet.

One Salvo fired, which the Director Gunner states blew up an Enemy T.B.D.

At 7.31 p.m.—Ceased Firing.

Total ammunition fired—13·5-in.—90 rounds.

                        6-in.—50 rounds.

H.M.S. " Oak " reports that " at *about* 7.35 p.m. the track of a Torpedo was observed to cross the track of our ships, about 200 yards ahead of ' Iron Duke,' Torpedo was travelling slowly. Track finished about 2,000 yards on the Port side of the Line, and the Torpedo sank. Direction of the track was S.E."

Another Torpedo was also reported by " Benbow " which was 4th ship astern of " Iron Duke," at 8.31 p.m. " It is believed that the Torpedo passed ahead of ' Iron Duke,' " but this was not seen by " Iron Duke," although two signalmen were specially stationed under a Signal Officer aloft, to look out for Torpedoes.

It is quite possible that this is due to the difficult light conditions rendering the track invisible from " Iron Duke."

During the night, in view of the proximity of Heavy Enemy's Ships, the Hands remained at Action Stations, the Guns' Crews at their Guns, but being allowed to sleep in turn.

The Corned Beef and Biscuits provided at the Quarters were served out. Cocoa was provided from 9.30 p.m. onwards, and Breakfast brought to the Quarters at 7.30 a.m.

1 *   *   *   *   *

---

[1] Part omitted here, referring solely to personnel, recommendations *i.e.*, in no way bearing on the course of the action.

The Turrets were fired throughout by Director, which system possesses enormous advantages over any other in Action.

1   *   *   *   *

The close study which has been made of the Silhouettes of German ships enabled those sighted to be recognised, except a Battle Cruiser with very large square Funnels, which might have been the " Lutzow."

The Rangefinders obtained very good results, notwithstanding the bad light, and were of the greatest assistance in keeping the range.

The Rangetakers reported that the Enemy's Pole Masts were easier to Range on than those of our own ships.

1   *   *   *   *

No Torpedoes were fired as the large number of our own ships which from time to time crossed the space between the Battle Fleets rendered it inadvisable to fire the slow E.R. Torpedoes, and the Enemy were out of Range for the 30 knot Setting.

The Engine Room Department experienced no difficulties during the action.

FRED. C. DREYER,

Captain.

NOTES MADE BY LIEUTENANT RICHARD SHELLEY, R.N., ON " IRON DUKE'S " 13·5-IN. TRANSMITTING STATION.

G.M.T.

P.M.

5.55.	Heavy firing on the Starboard bow.
	Stand by to load.
	Director firing.
	B.C.F. are heavily engaged on the Starboard bow bearing about 65 Green.
5.59.	Load.
6. 4.	Green 40.
6.23.	All left Guns to the "Ready."
6.25.	Straddle.
6.25½.	Check fire.
6.29½.	70 Green Inclination 100 to the left.
6.30½.	Open fire. Spotting corrections, * * *1 No correction; Straddle no correction; Enemy on fire; * * *1
6.37.10.	No spotting correction.
6.37.40.	Check Fire. 90 Green.
	For information Enemy was straddled and badly hit twice, a fire broke out under " A " and " B " Turrets. Enemy a/c 14 points and disappeared in the mist.
	Passed sunken ship on starboard side.
	Train 60 Green follow the Director.

G.M.T.

P.M.

7. 6.   Target 28 green. " Q ", " X " and " Y " train 40 Green and stand by to pick up the target.

Ship altering course to Port.

7.14.   " Ready."

7.14.20.   Open fire.

7.17.30.   Fired   *   *   *[1]

7.19.10.   Five guns   *   *   *[1] No correction for range.

7.21.20.   Target shifted train 99 green. Range 14,000.

7.23.   Check Fire.

7.24.45.   6-in. opened fire.

7.26.   Destroyer, train 136 green. Check bearing 110 green.

7.27.50.   Open fire 5 guns.

7.26.50.   Check Fire (Director reports target has gone).

7.40.   All Turrets train 90 Green.

7.42.   Ammunition expended :—

        " A " 18 rds. Common ⎫

        " B " 17 rds. Common ⎪

        " Q " 18 rds. Common ⎬ No breakdowns.

        " X " 19 rds. Common ⎪

        " Y " 18 rds. Common ⎭

8.10.   Turrets load cages with Lyddite A.P. Shell.

8.20.30.   Battle Fleet is deploying into line of Battle again.

8.23.   Heavy firing ahead.

8.30.   Train 60 Green.

8.32.50.   70 Green.

8.41.   Enemy's Battle Fleet is somewhere on the Starboard beam, a light cruiser has just been engaging them.

9. 9.   Heavy firing on starboard beam. All turrets train 90 Green.

11.55.   Train 90 Red, follow the Director, stand fast " B " turret.

1st *June*, 1916.

A.M.

1. 4.   Light on Port beam (From Director).

2.30.   Train 40 Green.

2.35.   Alter course to Starboard.

2.37.   Alter course to Port, to original course (166 Gyro).

2.45.   Lined up for training. Read off elevation receivers. Put range on range transmitter.

2.46.   Make certain that all rangefinders and periscopes are clean.

2.55.   Cages are to be kept loaded with Common. Train fore and aft.

3.22.   For information, Firing right ahead.

3.52.   Firing on Port beam. Stand by to open fire.

3.56.   96 Green a Zeppelin.

---

[1] *See* note on p. 381.

G.M.T.

A.M.

4. 1½.	Zeppelin altered course to Starboard, rate 900 opening.
4. 3.	Do not load cages with shrapnel. Zeppelin is apparently retiring.
4.15.	All Turrets are to be ready to load with Common.
5.48.	Turrets train 60 Green.
6. 7.	Turrets train 80 Red follow the Director.
10.46.	Cooks of Messes fallen out to prepare dinner.
12. 0.	" A ", " Q " and " Y " Turrets Crews to Dinner.

P.M.

1. 0.	" B " and " X " to Dinner.
2.23.	Secure.

NOTES MADE BY SHORTHAND IN " B " TURRET OF
H.M.S. " IRON DUKE " AT THE DICTATION OF
LIEUTENANT COMMANDER T. F. P. CALVERT, R.N.,
    DURING THE ACTION OF 31st MAY 1916.

G.M.T.

P.M.

5.55.	Stand By to load.
5.58.	Ship 19 knots.
6. 0.	Battle Cruiser, Starboard Bow, 64 Green. Turrets load—Belay.
6. 2.	Turrets load.
6. 3.	Both Guns loaded.
6. 5.	Stand by to train 40 Green.
6. 6.	White smoke on Upper Deck of " Lion " Port side.
6. 8.	Ship 18 knots.
6.10.	Turrets train 90 Green. " Lion " still on fire.
6.12.	Big shot just short of a destroyer bearing 50 Green. Firing with flashes this way bearing also about 50 Green.
6.13.	Shot fell about 4,000 yds. over on our beam.
6.14.	Fleet deployed to port.
6.15.	11,000.
6.16.30.	Enemy ship, very much on fire, only white smoke, apparently stopped.
6.16.50.	" Lion " " A " and " B " fire 2 gun salvo.
6.17.10.	Next ship to " Lion " fired a salvo.
6.18.	More enemy ships about.
6.18.25.	They are right on our beam, 10° right of where we are.
6.18.45.	Two enemy shots fell between " Lion " and 4 funnelled cruiser on her port beam.
6.19. 4.	Battle Cruiser, " Inflexible " class, fired salvo.
6.19.30.	Ship alter course to starboard.
6.19.50.	Enemy ship apparently blown up. (This must have been " Defence.")
6.20.	Speed of ship 15 knots.
6.20.22.	Ship steady bearing 83 Green.

G.M.T.

P.M.

6.20.35.	Ship alter course.
6.20.50.	We are 9th ship of line bearing 88 Green.
6.21. 5.	Another enemy ship—right on her now—3 funnels, 2 masts.
6.22.10.	Speed of ship 17.
6.23.30.	Opened fire. 1st salvo, 3 shots spotted short; 2nd salvo, Straddle; 3rd Salvo, over; 4th salvo, Not spotted.
6.25.40.	Check fire.
6.25.50.	Ship ahead opened fire.
6.26.10.	Steam escaping amidships.
6.26.15.	British Destroyer passing, 2 black balls up, Not under control, 2 men on forecastle.
6.26.20.	Target 70 Green.
6.30.25.	Opened fire, 1st Salvo shots fell right and short.
6.31.	2nd Salvo, all over. Not sighted at all.
6.31.40.	3rd salvo not spotted.
6.32.10.	Ship alter course to port.
6.32.30.	4th salvo straddle over.
6.33.	Rapid salvoes. 5th salvo not spotted.
6.33.25.	6th salvo enemy on fire.
6.33.48.	7th salvo short.
6.34.25.	8th salvo not spotted.
6.35.13.	9th salvo not spotted.
6.35.55.	10th salvo not spotted.
6.36.	Enemy alter course to starboard 300 opening.
6.36.15.	Check fire.
6.39.10.	Ship 15.
6.40.10.	Ship alter course to Starboard.
6.42.50.	Passed another British destroyer not under control with " 39 " on her stern.
6.43.30.	Destroyer has collision mat over port bow and fire abaft after funnel.
6.45.10.	Very misty, cannot see any enemy ships.
6.48.45.	All turrets train 90 Green.
6.50.	Ship on starboard bow, broken in half.
7. 0.30.	Wing Battleship has just opened fire with a salvo and the second ship.
7. 4.10.	9,300 Turned, went off the target.
7. 5.35.	Target 28 Green.
7. 6.10.	11,400.
7. 6.50.	Ship alter course to port. Target is the left-hand ship.
7. 7.48.	11,000.
7. 8.10.	10,600.
7. 8.40.	12,000.
7. 9.	11,900.
7.10.	13,500.
7.10.40.	14,100.
7.11.	14,800.

G.M.T.

P.M.

7.11.20.	Our 6-in. fired.
7.11.45.	15,300 One Destroyer on this bearing stopped, and one turning in circles.
7.12.10.	Our 6-in. fired.
7.12.30.	Enemy 18.
7.12.35.	15,500.
7.12.50.	Our 6-in. opened heavy fire on enemy destroyers.
7.13.	15,400—400 closing.
7.13.10.	All left guns ready.
7.13.40.	1st salvo, shots fell right.
7.14.25.	15,500.
7.14.40.	15,000.
7.14.45.	2nd salvo, still right.
7.15.5.	15,700.
7.15.50.	Enemy reduced to 10 knots. Range 14,900.
7.16.	Inclination 40 to the left.
7.16.18.	15,500.
7.16.40.	15,600.
7.16.50.	Ship alter course to starboard slowly.
7.16.55.	3rd salvo. 20 Starboard.
7.17. 5.	15,300.
7.17.30.	125 opening.
7.17.45.	Enemy destroyers making a smoke screen.
7.18.30.	4th salvo. One of enemy ships got hit all right.
7.18.25.	16,200.
7.20.32.	Target shifted 99 Green.
7.20.45.	Enemy 17, 11,300.
7.21.	12,200.
7.21.10.	11,900.
7.21.25.	12,000.
7.21.35.	12,200.
7.21.50.	12,500.
7.22.10.	Ship alter course to port.
7.22.15.	Two enemy destroyers about 9,000.
7.23.15.	Check fire.
7.23.50.	Six enemy destroyers within range.
7.24.	6-in. opened fire on enemy destroyers short, * * *[1]
7.24.50.	6-in. fired on destroyers 135 Green.
7.25.25.	8,900.
7.25.30.	Bring left guns to ready.
7.25.40.	8,700.
7.25.48.	Enemy 17.
7.26. 5.	9,000.
7.26.20.	Ship altering course to port.
7.26.30.	9,000.
7.27. 3.	1st salvo, short.
7.28.13.	Check fire.

---

[1] See note on p. 381.

G.M.T.

P.M.

7.30.40.   Four Light Cruisers and flotilla going after enemy destroyers, one has stopped.

7.32.10.   Passed something floating in water.
8.25.30.   Nine heavy ships ahead.
8.29.40.   Ship 15.
8.29.50.   Turrets train 80 Green.
8.31. 5.   Ship 16.
8.31.50.   Train 70 Green.
8.33.30.   Ship 17.
9.07.00.   Train 90 Green.
9.14.00.   Star shell burst on starboard beam.

NOTES MADE IN THE 13·5-IN. GUN CONTROL TOWER TO THE DICTATION OF COMMANDER (G) G. BLAKE, R.N., IMMEDIATELY AFTER THE ACTION OF 31ST MAY 1916.

Heavy Firing first heard about 70 Green.

Shortly after, Battle Cruiser Fleet were made out steering across Bow, firing well on an extreme forward starboard bearing.

The Ships seen were " Lion," " Princess Royal," " Tiger," and " New Zealand."

Afterwards 4 Ships of the 5th B.S. were sighted, coming obliquely towards Battle fleet from Starboard Wing, they joined Battle Fleet.

Battle Fleet deployed to Port, into Line of Battle.

About this time, a German three-funnelled Cruiser was observed badly damaged and in a sinking condition.

" Iron Duke " to clear bores of Guns, fired four Salvoes.

No hits were observed, although straddled.

All other ships within Range were firing at her, especially a Cruiser (" Shannon " Class) which got in front of Battle Line, made a large quantity of smoke and obscured everything on firing side, eventually drawing off towards the rear of the line.

After Battle Cruisers had passed, 3 or 4 German Battleships of " König " Class appeared in the mist, about 70 Green.

* * * *[1]   Range, 11,000. * * *[1]

First Salvo Short.

Second Salvo Straddle—3 Hits.

Third Salvo, 1 Hit—Straddle over.

Fourth Salvo, 2 Hits.

Then enemy altered course about 12 Points, and was lost in the mist and smoke, two more salvoes were fired and appeared to be falling short.

Check fire.

---

[1] *See* note on p. 381.

An enormous explosion occurred on the starboard quarter, sending up a column of white smoke about 1,000 ft. high.

Passed sunken Ship, which proved to be " Invincible."

We then sighted what appeared to be a Battleship very much like the " Queen Elizabeth " Class, but with two thin pole masts, evidently an enemy ship; several of our own ships were firing at her.

We opened fire at her, at a range of about 16,000 yards, * * *[1] shots fell * * *[1] to the right, and by the time the deflection was corrected, and about four salvoes fired, she had disappeared in the mist.

She apparently had a number of Destroyers around her.

Fire was checked, and shortly afterwards another Battleship came into sight, but before fire could be opened on her, she was obscured by smoke, her bearing was about 93 Green. She was probably the " Lützow."

Nothing happened for some time, but eventually a Destroyer attack developed, and the 6-in. were firing continuously for about ten minutes to a quarter of an hour.

The results were not seen.

Shortly after Turrets were directed on to Destroyer bearing 110 Green, and one Salvo was fired.

The Director Gunner states Destroyer fired at disappeared.

No more firing was carried out.

This was the last occasion of engaging the Enemy.

Heavy firing was observed on the Starboard Bow, and " Calliope " was seen to be hit amidships; the flash lit up the whole of the Main Deck. She, however, continued to proceed.

When it got dark, Course was altered to South, and we appeared to have got well ahead of High Sea Fleet, which have been firing at intervals right aft on the Starboard Quarter.

The turrets fired 18 rounds per turret, Capped Powder, Common Shell.

NOTES MADE IN THE 13·5-in. GUN DIRECTOR TOWER ALOFT, AT THE DICTATION OF Mr. F. W. POTTER, GUNNER, R.N., OF H.M.S. " IRON DUKE," DURING THE ACTION OF 31st MAY 1916.

(Times and Bearings, Approximate.)

At 4 p.m., Action being sounded, I repaired to the 13·5-in. Director Tower, and Tested all Circuits. I then received information from T.S. that our Destroyers were engaging the Enemy's Battle Cruisers, and that we should probably be in action in about one hour's time.

Also that 4 ships of the 5th Battle Squadron were engaging the enemy, and the German High Sea Fleet were standing North.

---

[1] *See* note on p. 381.

At about 5.25, I observed flashes from Guns, bearing about Green 60, and about 6 p.m. the Battle Cruisers could be seen heavily engaged with the enemy.

6.25 we opened fire at a three-funnelled Cruiser, which looked like the " Augsburg " Class, Range 11,500.

The first was short, the second over, and the third straddled.

After this the shooting appeared to be good, but unfortunately the enemy got obscured by smoke.

About this time three Battleships of the " König " Class appeared bearing Green 70.

I then received the order to train Green 70, Battleship of the " Koenig " Class, and fire was opened on her.

About six hits were obtained in the vicinity of " A " and " B " Turrets, one salvo causing a big fire on the fore part of the ship. The last salvo fired was a straddle short, as I distinctly saw one shot hit the ship's side and explode.

The enemy now turned away and were obscured by the mist, and the order " check fire " was given.

One of our Destroyers was observed, badly damaged, and a little later we passed a sunken ship which afterwards was reported to be the " Invincible." There were a good many men in the water, and a Destroyer was standing by, picking them up.

After this we passed what appeared to be a ship bottom upwards, which I reported to the Commander.

I was then shifted to another ship, which disappeared in the mist after a few salvoes had been fired at her.

A large Cruiser of the " Moltke " Class came into view, accompanied by about seven Destroyers.

I was put on to the Cruiser, which made a splendid Target, but she was very soon screened by the Destroyer's smoke, so I reported the Enemy obscured. It seemed that as soon as she saw the Fleet she turned about and disappeared.

I then received the order to Train Green 110 a Destroyer, followed by the order " Green 120, a Destroyer." After Ranging for a few moments, the order " Open Fire " was given.

The only Salvo was a straddle short.

When the splash cleared, the Destroyer had disappeared altogether.

The order " Check Fire " was given at about 7.30.

Several bearings were given to me during this time, but no further firing took place.

After the Fleet turned to port, heavy firing was heard, and gun flashes were seen well off the starboard quarter.

At about 8.45 p.m. a star light was seen falling off the starboard beam, which lit up the rear end of the Second Battle Squadron.

At 9.5 p.m., and at various intervals, heavy firing was heard astern.

Nothing more transpired until the following morning, 1st June, when at 4. a.m. I reported a Zeppelin well off the port quarter.

The Fleet now deployed to starboard, and I received orders to stand by to fire at the Zeppelin.

The director was trained and layed on to the Zeppelin, but unfortunately the smoke from our own funnels continually obscured her. Also a hoist of flags blew right across the telescope.

All firing was carried out with the main director circuit,

1 *   *   *   *   *

The crew of the director tower carried out their work in a very cool manner.

NOTES ON THE FIRING OF THE "IRON DUKE'S" 6-IN. GUNS DURING THE ACTION OF 31ST MAY 1916, BY THE 6-IN. CONTROL OFFICER ALOFT— MR. HERBERT D. JEHAN, GUNNER, R.N.

A Destroyer attack was observed coming towards the Fleet, starboard bow.

The order was given by the Captain from Conning Tower "Destroyer 63 Green, Open fire when ready."

The Guns were given the Bearing of the Leading Destroyer at an estimated range of 10,000 yards, and 600 closing, fire was opened by salvoes, first salvo was over and out for line. This was corrected 1 *   *   *   the next salvo being short, and the third salvo straddled, *the fourth hit the Destroyer which appeared to stagger and Independent was ordered. No less than four hits were observed and the Destroyer sank.*

The 6-in. were ordered to Check Fire and shift to another Destroyer bearing 84 Green, Range 9,000. This Destroyer appeared to be hit once by the 6-in., but not disabled, and turned away. Range increased rapidly to extreme Gun Range, and the 6-in. were ordered to Check Fire.

The second attack came from aft, the order given by the Captain from Conning Tower was "Destroyers 135 Green, Open Fire when ready." This was passed to Battery, and 10,000 put on the Sights. "Salvoes Commence" being ordered. The guns appeared to be a long time before opening fire. One Gun fired, and I could not see the Fall of Shot.

A Check Bearing was given 115 Green, and it appeared to me as if the after guns were on the second Destroyer, and the foremost guns on the leading Destroyer.

I did not check fire, as I thought it would be waste of time.

It was most difficult to spot through the firing of the ships.

1 *   *   *   *   *

There seemed to be one Destroyer put out of action, but not by the 6-in.

---

1 *See* note on p. 381.

When, eventually, the remaining Destroyers turned away and formed a smoke screen, range was increased the same way, and check fire was ordered when extreme gun range was reached.

Transmitting Station reported that range went as low as 7,600 to extreme 12,000.

During the first attack spotting was fairly easy, but during the second it was most difficult.

1*   *   *   *   *

No Submarines were sighted, although on several occasions the wash from the Light Cruisers and Destroyers looked like the feather of a Submarine.

VICE-ADMIRAL'S REPORT, 1st BATTLE SQUADRON.[2]

Enclosure No. 2 to Submission No. 1415/0022 of 20/6/16 from C.-in-C. Home Fleets.

No. 021.

" Royal Oak,"

SIR,   10th June, 1916.

I HAVE the honour to report that the First Battle Squadron and " Bellona " left the Northern Base in accordance with your orders at 9.30 p.m. 30th May, 1916, my Flag being in " Marlborough," and proceeded in company with your Flag to the Southeastward.

2. The first intimation of the enemy being at sea was received in " Marlborough " about 2.30 p.m. 31st May, a signal being intercepted from " Galatea " to Senior Officer, Battle Cruiser Fleet, reporting enemy cruisers bearing E.S.E.

Further enemy reports were received from various units of the Battle Cruiser Fleet, and at 3.55 a signal was made by Senior Officer, Battle Cruiser Fleet, that he was engaging the enemy.

At 4.0 p.m., Senior Officer, 2nd Light Cruiser Squadron, reported enemy battle-fleet in sight steering East, and at 5.0 p.m. that they had altered course to North.

The situation as it developed was reported by visual signal from time to time to the ships under my command.

About 5.30 p.m. heavy gun firing was heard on the starboard bow and a little later flashes were clearly seen.

At 5.45 p.m., " Lion," " Princess Royal," " Tiger " and " New Zealand " were sighted on starboard bow heavily engaged with the enemy, whose flashes could now be seen to the Southward, this being reported to Flag at 6.0 p.m., at which time our battle-cruisers were bearing S.S.W. 3 to 4 miles, steering East, " Lion," the leading ship. The 5th Battle Squadron then came in sight bearing S.W., also heavily engaged.

3. At 6.2 p.m., " Marlborough's " position was Lat. 57.04 N., Long. 5.29 E., course being altered by 9 pendant to South, speed

---

[1] *See* note on p. 381.   [2] Plates 3 and 7a.

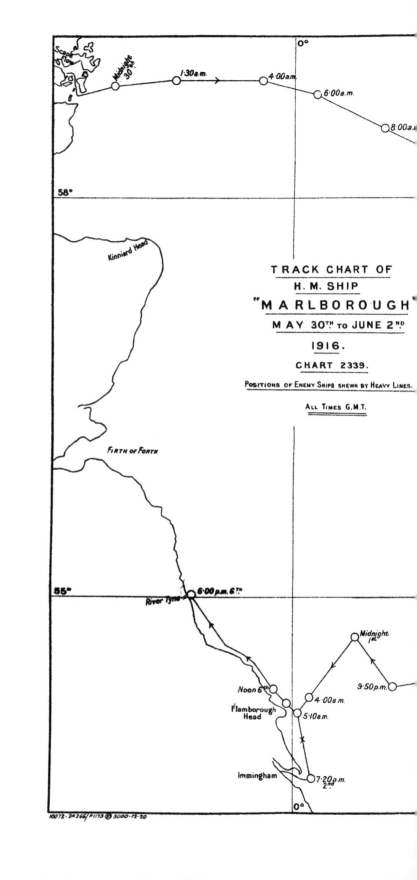

Plate 3.

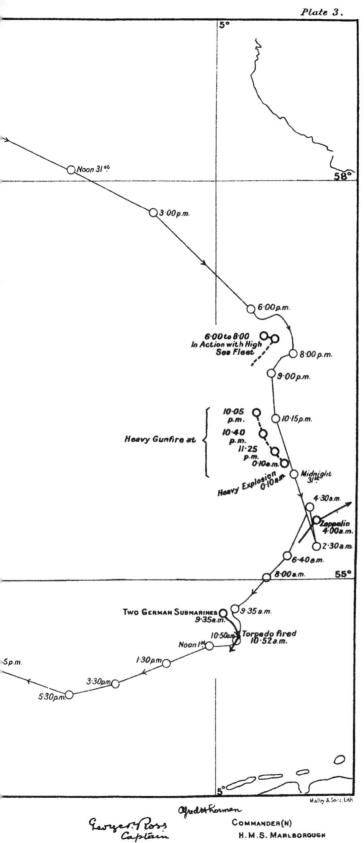

5°

58°

Noon 31st

3·00 p.m.

6·00 p.m.

*6·00 to 8·00
In Action with High
Sea Fleet*

8·00 p.m.

9·00 p.m.

*10·05
p.m.*

10·15 p.m.

Heavy Gunfire at
*10·40
p.m.*
*11·25
p.m.*
0·10 a.m.

Heavy Explosion 0·10 a.m.

*Midnight
31st*

4·30 a.m.

*Zeppelin
4·00 a.m.*

2·30 a.m.

6·40 a.m.

8·00 a.m.

55°

*Two German Submarines
9·35 a.m.*

9·35 a.m.

10·50 a.m.

*Torpedo fired
10·52 a.m.*

Noon 1st

5 p.m.

1·30 p.m.

3·30 p.m.

5·30 p.m.

5°

Malby & Sons, Lith.

Alfred H Norman

*George H Ross
Captain*

COMMANDER (N)
H.M.S. MARLBOROUGH

18 knots, and at 6.6 p.m. course was again altered to S.E. by 9 pendant.

6.15 p.m., Signal was received to form line of battle S.E. by E. by equal speed pendant, enemy bearing E.S.E. from " Barham."

4. About this time the Battle-cruisers, who appeared to be ahead of the leading division, turned to starboard as if to cross the enemy's T.

5. One of our armoured cruisers, probably " Warrior," was observed passing down the engaged side, making for her position in rear of the line. When near the end of the line she turned up parallel to it and engaged the enemy at short range. Heavy enemy salvoes were observed to fall all round her; she then turned about 14 points to port, a salvo struck her and a large flame was seen to burst from her quarter deck and she then passed astern.

6. A salvo of 5 shots fell ahead of the " Hercules " about 6.15 p.m. As the Battle-cruisers drew ahead and their smoke cleared, the German line could be more easily seen and 4 Kaisers and 4 Helgolands could be dimly made out. " Marlborough " opened fire at 6.17 p.m. at a battleship of the Kaiser class— range 13,000 yards, about Green 110.

" Marlborough " fired 7 salvoes and hits were observed in 5th and 7th salvoes, the remainder of the squadron opening fire as a target became visible.

7. At 6.20 p.m., speed of 14 knots was ordered by general signal. Shortly after this there was much bunching up of ships in the rear of the line, " Marlborough " and other ships had to reduce to 8 knots and " St. Vincent " had to stop for a short time. Owing to haze and the enemy's smoke, organised distribution of fire was out of the question; individual ships selected their own targets.

8. As the action developed and disabled ships of both sides passed down between the lines, great difficulty was experienced in distinguishing the enemy's from our own ships.

9. " Marlborough " now shifted fire to a three funnelled ship, and at 6.34 p.m. formed up astern of the line and opened fire on a battle ship of the Kaiser class.

10. At 6.45 p.m. " Marlborough " altered course to avoid a torpedo. At 6.54 p.m. a heavy explosion was experienced under the Fore bridge, the ship taking up a list of 8 degrees to starboard. The torpedo had struck the ship abreast of No. 1 dynamo room and hydraulic room, both of which were flooded, the 2 men stationed in the former being killed. Water was also reported up to the floor plates in " A " boiler room and it was considered necessary to draw the fires in that boiler room, but as a speed of 17 knots could be maintained I decided that " Marlborough " should maintain her position in the line and continue to lead her division. The list remained steady and it

was reported in less than an hour that the water was being kept under.

11. Shortly after being struck, " Marlborough " opened fire on an enemy cruiser passing down the line which was suspected of having fired the torpedo. The 3rd and 4th salvoes both hit and appeared to open up her side, as a deep red flame could be seen inside her hull. A torpedo was fired at her at 7.10 p.m. During this time the " Acasta " was passed disabled on the port side, and " Marlborough " avoided 3 more torpedoes by the use of the helm.

12. " Marlborough " then engaged a ship of the König class, firing 14 salvoes. Distinct hits were seen in four salvoes. (The gunnery difficulties experienced by the ship after she was torpedoed are reported in the ship's gunnery report.) This ship finally turned out of the line, very low in the water aft, and was apparently sinking. A destroyer was observed to place herself on her engaged side, and make a dense smoke in order to screen her.

13. Shortly after this a heavy smoke screen was observed at what appeared to be the head of the enemy battlefleet, and it was soon apparent that the destroyers were attacking under its cover.

I immediately hoisted the signal " NM," informing our flotillas astern that the enemy flotillas were making an attack. At the same time the preparative was hoisted, and I turned my division away.

As far as I could judge the whole squadron opened fire on the attacking destroyers with the whole of the secondary and some of the main armament, and the attack was checked, and they turned away, but not before they were able to fire some of their torpedoes, which, however, were avoided.

Two of the enemy's destroyers were observed to be hit by " Marlborough's " 6-inch gun fire alone, and there must have been others as the fire was so intense.

14. As the destroyer attack developed the enemy battlefleet in sight were observed to turn at least 8 points until their sterns were towards our line. They ceased fire, declined further action, and disappeared into the mist.

Our destroyers in rear of the line proceeded out to attack the enemy destroyers and sink any disabled craft.

15. During the action at one period the enemy appeared to be firing steady, well drilled salvoes, by some form of director such as the Petravic system, but their rangefinding and range keeping appear to have been at fault when they were hit, although the firing on our armoured cruisers was remarkable for its accuracy.

Many of their salvoes were seen to fall over and it was not till late in the action that they apparently found the range when the " Colossus " was straddled by 4 successive salvoes, correct for elevation.

16. As the action progressed their fire became more feeble. A certain number of shell of 4-in. or 6-in. calibre were seen to burst on the water just short of " Marlborough " and other ships of the First Battle Squadron, some leaving a cloud of light green vapour, and others a heavy grey vapour which spread over the surface of the water.

17. During the action many reports of submarines were made, some being undoubtedly authentic, and course was altered to attack them and avoid their torpedoes.

Shortly before " Marlborough " was torpedoed, a heavy shock was felt on board " Revenge " in the transmitting room and other places, and two independent officer witnesses saw quantities of oil float to the surface and wreckage come up astern.

18. The tracks of torpedoes approaching the ship were clearly seen from the top and reported in good time so that they were avoided, with the exception of the one which struck the ship, and therefore it is considered to be probable that it came from a submarine.

19. It is estimated that at least 21 torpedoes passed through the First Battle Squadron, only one taking effect.

20. Before, during, and after the action the wireless telegraphy communication throughout the squadron were entirely satisfactory and invaluable for manœuvring and action signals, especially in the case of the repeating ship (" Bellona "), who was often unable to distinguish the flag signals. No damage to aerials or instruments was sustained except in " Marlborough," whose auxiliary aerial was partially shot away, and an inter- mittent earth on the main aerial feeder, which could not be traced for three quarters of an hour, interrupted the reception of distant signals. In " Colossus " the internal buzzer communication between Main office and signal tower was shot away.

No enemy signalling was heard on auxiliary, and though they continually attempted to jamb the main installation signals from ships in company were easily overread.

21. After the enemy disappeared in the haze the First Battle Squadron conformed to the movements of your flag, but though " Marlborough " went the revolutions for 17 knots I estimate the speed over the ground was only approximately 15·8 owing to the damage. Consequently the 6th division fell some way astern during the night.

22. Four night attacks were observed during the night, the first on the starboard beam, the others taking place in succession towards the stern. Several explosions were heard and 2 very large ones with flames shooting up into the sky were seen : star shell were seen.

E 2

23. About midnight, smoke was observed ahead of " Marlborough," which crossed from starboard to port and back again from port to starboard, and then came down the starboard side.

It appeared to be a large ship and was challengd by " Revenge," who was answered by 2 letters, though they were not the correct ones. She then disappeared.

24. At 2.30 a.m., 1st June, it was reported to me that the bulkhead in " A " boiler room of " Marlborough " would not stand the speed, namely, revolutions for 17 knots, and that it was advisable to reduce to 10 or 12 knots.

In consequence of this " Marlborough " was hauled out of line and the remainder of the division continued. I signalled " Fearless," who was observed to be astern of " Agincourt," to come alongside " Marlborough," and I and my Staff transferred to " Revenge " in her, and then sent her back to escort " Marlborough," who was subsequently ordered to Rosyth *viâ* " M " Channel.

25. Shortly after arriving in " Revenge " a Zeppelin was sighted, evidently scouting. Fire was opened on her which caused her to dip and she quickly disappeared. She looked a remarkably easy target if shrapnel had been available.

26. At daylight, owing to the very low visibility and to the fact that the Division had dropped so far astern during the night (as explained above) and also to the transfer of my Flag to " Revenge," the remainder of the Fleet was out of sight.

I shaped course as necessary to affect a junction.

At 3.40 a.m., " Faulknor " with " Obedient " and " Marvel " joined my Flag and reported the 12th Flotilla had attacked a Division of the German Battlefleet during the night, and that one battleship had been blown up.

27. At 5.15 a.m., " Revenge " passed through the wreckage of a German battleship or battle-cruiser, judging from the size of the floating powder cases.

At 6.30 a.m., what appeared to be the wreckage of the " Black Prince " was passed through, and a little later 2 rafts were observed with three men on them. I ordered " Obedient " to take them off, but she reported on rejoining that before she got there they had been taken off by a Dutch steamer, whose Captain protested against their being taken off his steamer, and so the Captain of " Obedient " left them.

At 8.35 a.m., passed " Sparrowhawk " abandoned with " Marksman " close to. " Marksman " reported she was unable to tow her. She had attempted to do so, but the hawsers had parted. I, therefore, ordered her to sink her. She did so and then joined my Flag.

Nothing else of interest occurred and I rejoined your Flag that evening.

29. The following ammunition was fired by the First Battle Squadron :—

	Main Armament.	Secondary Armament.	Torpedoes.
" Marlborough " - - -	162	60	2
" Revenge " - - - -	102	87	1
" Hercules " - - -	98	—	—
" Agincourt " - - -	144	111	—
" Colossus " - - -	93	16	—
" Collingwood " - - -	84	35	—
" Neptune " - - -	48	48	—
" St. Vincent " - - -	98	—	—
	829	357	3

30. I would like to bring to your notice the conduct of the crew of the " Acasta," as mentioned in the report from the Captain of " Hercules "; although badly damaged and apparently in a hopeless state, they cheered the " Hercules " as the latter passed.

I have the honour to be,
Sir,
Your obedient Servant,
CECIL BURNEY,
Vice-Admiral Commanding
First Battle Squadron.

The Commander-in-Chief,
Grand Fleet.

GUNNERY REPORT, H.M.S. " MARLBOROUGH."

H.M.S. " Marlborough,"
4th June 1916.
GUNNERY REPORT.

Number of Rounds fired.

Gun.	No. of Rds. fired.	A.P. Lyddite.	Common.
13·5	162	138	24
		Lyddite Comm.	
6-in.	60	55	5

Breakdowns, Accidents, &c.

(1) Right gun of " A " turret had inner " A " tube and jacket cracked, a large portion of jacket being broken off. This occurred about the 5th round fired by this gun, and it is considered that a premature must have occurred, although the damage to the rifling is comparatively small. A.P. lyddite was being fired.

(2) After the ship was struck by a mine or a torpedo, it took up a list of about 7° to starboard. Due to this list, difficulty was experienced in all turrets due to shell slipping forward as it rolled out of main cage into waiting position and fouling driving band with shell brake. Four turrets had to unship brake.

(3) Due to heavy list, all firing generators in turrets flooded, and it was necessary to disconnect pipe and allow water to drain away.

1 *   *   *   *   *

Missfires.—Nil.

Control and method of fire.

Controlled from fore top; firing by director. No difficulty was experienced in distinguishing own shots or in spotting *overs* or shorts, and hits could be easily distinguished by a deep red flame and clouds of grey and white smoke; occasionally when shell burst well inside ship no flame could be seen, but only a large amount of greyish smoke.

Without the director, it would have been almost impossible to keep gunlayers on correct object; there was so much confusion amongst enemy's ships, one ship was passing another; smoke from cruisers on fire often obliterated the object; own ship was continually altering course small amounts; the above made it difficult to keep on the same object for any length of time.

Description of firing.

With objects fired at. All times are Greenwich mean times. Only hits that were actually seen and confirmed by two or more persons are given.

Time.

6.10 p.m. Sighted British battle cruisers engaging enemy's ships.

6.12 Red 7, cruiser, four funnels, one mast (disappeared in smoke and mist before fire could be opened).

6.15 After deploying to port. Battleship, two funnels widely separated, two masts (probably " Kaiser " class) estimated range 10,000 yards, rangefinders could not get a range.

6.17 Opened fire. Seven salvoes were fired in 4 minutes; 5th and 7th were clearly seen to hit. In the 5th salvo a deep red flame could be seen and salvo struck, in the 7th salvo a large volume of grey smoke appeared.

6.21. Ceased firing, as enemy was hidden by cruiser on fire (Roon class).

6.24. Green 98, a cruiser, 3 funnels (Roon, one funnel gone) ? range by rangefinder 10,500 yards.

---

[1] *See* note on p. 381.

p.m.

6.25. Opened fire. 5 salvoes were fired. Hits could not be distinguished for certain, as two or three ships were firing at same object.

6.27. 6-in. guns opened fire at same object. It was during this firing that right gun of " A " turret was severely damaged and put out of action, cause not known for certain, but probably due to premature. It was about the fifth round fired by the gun, A.P. Lyddite was used. Inner " A " tube is cracked all round about half way along gun. A large portion of jacket is broken off, and a crack extends 15 ft. along jacket.

6.29. Checked fire. There was a pause of ten minutes, during which the ship was altering course, and enemy were hidden by smoke.

6.39. Object a battleship of Kaiser class. Range 13,000 yards ; one salvo was fired, and enemy turned away and disappeared.

6.42 to ⎫ Ship was altering course, and enemy's movements
6.54. ⎭ were very difficult to follow.

6.54. " Marlborough " was hit by a torpedo or mine in Diesel engine room. The shock was sufficient to shake off switches on lever power board, and some fuses in telephone circuits. These were very quickly replaced, and all control instruments were found to be in step.

7.0. Passed destroyer " Acasta " on port hand flying 6 flag and with collision mat over starboard quarter. Green 90 a cruiser of Roon class, stopped, range by rangefinder 9,800 yards.

7.3. Opened fire. Fired four salvoes in two minutes, the 3rd and 4th both hit and appeared to open up her side, as a deep red flame could be seen inside her hull.

7.5. Ceased fire, as she appeared completely disabled and sinking fast.

7.6. Object shifted, a battleship, two funnels widely separated, left hand ship of three (Markgraf class). Range by R.F. 10,750.

7.12. Opened fire. Fired 14 salvoes in 6 mins., the 6th, 12th, 13th and 14th were all distinct hits. In the 6th salvo, a large cloud of grey and white smoke appeared near the foremast. In the 12th salvo two hits could be clearly seen under bridge and rather low.

7.18. Checked fire.

7.19. Enemy hauled out of line and turned away, lost in smoke ; object shifted, one ship to the left that was not fired at.

7.20.	Enemy destroyer attack took place between the lines.
7.22.	6-in. guns opened fire. Turrets fired one salvo into the brown. After this, no more was seen of the enemy. During the night a lot of firing could be heard astern.

At about 4.0 a.m. a lot of firing could be heard to the southward, and shortly after a Zeppelin was sighted crossing astern and steering approximately east. Three-in. H. A. gun open fire and fired 12 rounds. " X " and " Y " turrets opened fire with A.P. shell, which was already in the guns, and two rounds of common which was in G.L. cage. Four rounds were fired. The nose of the Zeppelin was observed to dip very suddenly at one period, but it could not be ascertained for certain whether she was hit. Range varied between 5,000 and 10,000 yards.

If ship had not been disabled, rendering it undesirable to " A " and " B " turrets, it would have been worth while turning so as to get full broadside bearing.

CAPTAIN'S REPORT, H.M.S. " HERCULES."

No. 197.

H.M.S. " Hercules,"

Sir,
4th June 1916.

I have the honour to report the following circumstances with regard to the action on Wednesday, 31st May 1916.

2. The Ship's company, having fallen out from Action Stations to get tea, closed up again on hearing gun-firing on the starboard bow—5.50 p.m.

3. The Battle Fleet, less 5th Battle Squadron, were then in divisions ahead disposed abeam to starboard, 10 cables. Course— S.E. by S.; Speed—19 knots.

4. At 5.55 p.m., our Battle Cruisers were sighted on starboard bow, through the mist, in action. Range of " Tiger "—11,000 yards. Enemy's shots were falling occasionally between our Battle Cruisers and our Battle Fleet and shortly afterwards appeared to hit " Tiger."

At 6.0 p.m., our Battle Cruisers began to draw across our bows from starboard to port, the " Lion " being slightly on fire on her forecastle, port side.

6.5 p.m.—Turned in succession to South by " 9 " pendant.

6.13 p.m.—Formed line of Battle S.E. by E.

6.15 p.m.—As " Hercules " started to deploy a salvo, with a small spread, of some five shots straddled our forecastle and deluged the Fore Bridge, Conning Tower and Fore Top—a mass of heavy water falling on board.

From a fragment of shell picked up on the forecastle the projectile would appear to be an A.P., nearly 15-in.

After this deluge I wondered where this salvo had come from as only the flashes of some four or five of the enemy's ships beyond our Battle Cruisers could be seen from the Bridge. I then noticed that the rear of our Battle line must have afforded a fine silhouette for the enemy, as some of our ships on the reverse side of us were clearly visible against the bright sunlit sky. I remarked to Captain Schoultz [1] at the time—" What a fine target our ship must be for the enemy as we can see nothing of him."

6.20 p.m.—" Hercules " fired her first salvo at an enemy ship —four funnels—apparently of " Roon " class. She was noticed to be already disabled and stopped.

About this time the " Barham " and her ships were edging across and forming astern of " Agincourt," firing continuously.

At about 6.30 p.m., three of enemy's Battleships of " Kaiser " class were seen indistinctly through the mist, and seven or eight salvoes were fired at that ship which appeared most visible. Fire was continually checked owing to the haze.

About this time, one of our four-funnelled cruisers to the Southward was being heavily hit. The after magazine exploded, the flame reaching above her mast; then, after a short interval, her foremost magazine blew up, and no more was seen of her.

6.40 p.m.—Ship of " Warrior " class, bearing S.E., 3–4,000 yards, was observed attempting to escape from the enemy's fire, a great many shots falling all around her. She was steaming at full speed and zigzagging all the time.

6.45 p.m.—Deployment finished as far as " Hercules " was concerned. Course, S.E. by divisions.

6.47 p.m.—One of enemy's ships (" Roon " ?) on our starboard side badly on fire. (Vide 6.20 p.m.)

6.55 p.m.—" Marlborough " struck by a mine or torpedo on starboard side. She listed quickly to starboard but continued firing. From this time a speed of 16 knots was never exceeded by our 6th Division.

6.56 p.m.—" Acasta," with " 6 " flag flying and " not under control " signal up, was passed; she cheered " Hercules " while drifting past.

7. 5 p.m.—Altered course together 3 points to starboard.

7. 9 p.m.—Altered course back 3 points to port.

7.10 p.m.—Several enemy Battle Cruisers to left of the " Kaiser " class ships were now clearly visible. The lefthand Battle Cruiser observed was a " Derfflinger " or a " Lützow "; the second was " Seydlitz " or " Moltke "; the third appeared to be also a Battle Cruiser, but was obscured by smoke. Approximate course of these ships—S.E.

7.12 p.m.—Turned together to South and opened fire at second Battle Cruiser from the left; hits were made with Lyddite Common at the fifth and sixth salvoes. Range about 9,000 yards.

---

[1] Russian Navy.

First hit—abaft the foremost funnel; second hit—abreast main-mast. The enemy did not reply to our fire until after the third salvo and then appeared to be firing " individual." They usually fired about five seconds after " Hercules."

Lieutenant Commander (T) observed the leading ship also hit during this time and that two or three of the enemy's shots fell 100 yards short between " Hercules " and " Agincourt," and one near " Revenge's " starboard quarter. This one burst.

The enemy Battle Cruisers then disappeared from view.

7.20 p.m.—Passed on port side at a distance of about two miles a ship with a broken back and bow and stern portions out of water to a height of about 50 ft. Undoubtedly a man-of-war, painted red bottom colour and grey topsides. Men were observed on the after portion of the wreck and one of our three-funnelled light cruisers passed within 100 yards of her.

7.24 p.m.—Turned away 2 points—S.S.E.—by Sub-divisions.

7.31 p.m.—Observed much smoke made by enemy. Received signal " Enemy torpedo craft are approaching." A few salvoes with 12-in. guns were fired at attacking destroyers, which fell among them—Range, 6,000 yards; they then withdrew. " Agincourt " certainly made one direct hit.

7.35 p.m.—Altered course by Sub-divisions to S. by W.

Shortly after this turn two tracks of torpedoes were observed from the Fore Top approaching from starboard. Turned " Hercules " 6 points away and two torpedoes passed ship—one along starboard side and 40 yards across bow; the other under the stern, very close.

7.40 p.m.—Squadron formed line ahead by signal. Course, S.W.

During the next half hour ships in " Marlborough's " division signalled sighting submarines and ships altered course as neces-sary. " Hercules " saw none, but conformed to movements of the other ships.

By about 8.30 p.m., " Marlborough's " division had dropped considerably astern of the 5th Division.

9.5 p.m.—Squadron now proceeded to Southward at 17 knots —6th Division, 15¾ knots—for the night. Weather misty; visibility, 2 to 5 miles.

From 10.15 p.m. to 12.30 a.m., 1st June, five separate engage-ments appear to have occurred. Each lasted about 5–10 minutes. On the first occasion searchlights were observed and attack bore N.W. by W. The attacks gradually worked round the stern to N. by E., and in the third a star shell was fired. During the third or fourth, a big explosion took place in the middle of the gun flashes. Very approximate position of explosion Lat. 56° 13' N., Long. 6° 5' E.

2.20 a.m.—" Marlborough " hauled out of the line, and fell astern.

2.55 a.m.—Altered course to North.

3. 8. a.m.—12 knots. Flag transferred to " Revenge."

3.30 a.m.—17 knots astern of " Revenge."

3.37 a.m.—Altered course to 205°.

3.45 a.m.—Heard firing ahead.

3.50 a.m.—Zeppelin on starboard bow. Fired 4-in. and 3-pdr. without effect. Course, 345°. Zeppelin disappeared 2 points abaft starboard beam.

3.53 a.m.—Course 205°, 19 knots.

4.45 a.m.—Passed floating mine.

4.57 a.m.—Passed one of the 5th Battle Squadron, and one Cruiser, Green 105°, Course 347°.

5.20 a.m.—Passed wreckage; drums, life-buoys, &c., to port (German ?). Lat. 55° 52′ N., Long. 6° 5′ E.

6.30 a.m.—Passed wreckage, including two 6-in. ammunition cases (British). Lat. 56° 15′ N., Long. 5° 56½′ E.

6.40 a.m.—Altered course to S.S.E.

7.34 a.m.—Altered course to N.N.W.

7.44 a.m.—Sighted destroyer, bearing S.E. by S., and two four-funnelled cruisers.

7.45 a.m.—21 knots.

8.35 a.m.—Passed large triangular object, apparently portion of ship, on port side, 5–6,000 yards distant, also a capsized boat near by, and other wreckage together with oil. Lat. 56° 11′ N., Long. 6° 3′ E., 22 fathoms (possibly same place as explosion occurred during third or fourth night attack).

8.42 a.m.—Sighted a flotilla leader N. by E., and challenged.

8.44 a.m.—Sighted destroyer in crippled condition (" Sparrowhawk ").

9.7 a.m.—Altered course to N.W. to clear " Texel."

9.9. a.m.—Passed four Dutch Merchant vessels round two men clinging to wreckage. S.S. " Texel," " Thames Tug," " Kangean " and " Zuiderdilk." " Texel " signalled " All's well." Lat. 56° 21′ N., Long. 5° 50′ E.

5. Ammunition expended :—

> 12 Common Filled Powder.
> 4 A.P. Filled Lyddite.
> 82 Common Filled Lyddite.

6. Torpedoes were not fired as no opportunities occurred.

I have the honour to be,
Sir,
Your obedient Servant,
L. CLINTON BAKER,
Captain.

The Vice-Admiral Commanding
First Battle Squadron.

Enclosure No. 4 to Submission No. 1415/0022 of 20/6/16 from
C.-in-C. Home Fleets.

From—THE VICE-ADMIRAL COMMANDING, FIRST BATTLE
SQUADRON.

To—THE COMMANDER-IN-CHIEF, GRAND FLEET.

Date—11th June 1916.

No. 021.

IN compliance with your signal 1132 of to-day's date,
I have the honour to forward herewith reports from the Rear-
Admiral, 1st Battle Squadron, and the following Ships on the
action of 31st May :—

" Colossus."
" Revenge."
" Bellona."
" Neptune."
" Agincourt."
" St. Vincent."
" Collingwood."
" Royal Oak."
" Active."

CECIL BURNEY,
Vice-Admiral.

REAR-ADMIRAL'S REPORT, FIRST BATTLE SQUADRON.

From—The Rear Admiral, First Battle Squadron.
To—The Vice Admiral Commanding the First Battle Squadron.
No.—W. 16.
Date—10th June 1916.

The accompanying report of Flag Captain A. D. Pound,
Royal Navy, records the action of my Flagship.

Her movements were followed by the Fifth Division except
for occasional turns away to avoid torpedoes.

The Ships of the Fifth Division were well handled and signals,
which there was no difficulty in transmitting by either visual or
wireless, were promptly obeyed.

That the " Colossus " received a larger proportion of the
enemy's fire than the remainder of the Division appears to be
due to the enemy emerging from the mist opposite to her and
possibly to her being recognised as a Flagship.

2. The diary section of the attached report is compiled from
the notes of times and occurrences supplied by my Secretary,
Mr. Harold Foot, who was stationed on the Fore Bridge with
a watch and note book. As he is an observant Officer unlikely
to be disturbed by any occurrence they may be taken as being
correct.

3. Whatever circumstances may have constrained the Battle
Cruiser Fleet to fall back upon the Battle Fleet in the manner it

did, the result was unfortunate. The Fifth Division was unable to open fire upon the enemy owing to the Battle Cruisers being in between, and when they cleared from the Battleships it made it extremely difficult to ascertain whether Ships coming into view through the mist were friend or foe.

4. The Division's firing was well carried out. There was probably wastage of ammunition owing to many Ships firing at the one nearest object, but there was no time to correct this by signal, and if ships commenced leaving her to other ones she might have been left unfired at by any.

5. The visibility was extremely baffling, partly due to misty clouds appearing and dissolving and partly to the layers of smoke from funnels and Ships firing.

E. F. A. GAUNT,
Rear Admiral.

CAPTAIN'S REPORT, H.M.S. "COLOSSUS."

No. 658.

H.M.S. "Colossus,"
1st Battle Squadron,

SIR, 10th June 1916.

THE report of the action of 31st May, as far as it affected H.M. Ship under my command, has been divided up as follows :—

(a) Diary of events.

(b) Tracing, showing rough relative positions of targets engaged.[1]

(c) Appendix I, giving details of action with a Battle Cruiser (either " Lützow " or " Derfflinger ").

(d) Appendix II, giving details of damage to propellors through passing over wreckage or a submarine.

(e) Copy of report of Officers and Men commended.[2]

(f) List of Casualties.[2]

Generally speaking, the action from the point of view of this ship was a most tantalising one, as the presence of the enemy was obvious from the flashes of his guns, but only for a short period did an opportunity occur of getting into action with any of the enemy's capital ships.

The conduct of the Officers and Men was excellent, and such as one had always hoped it would be.

I have the honour to be,
Sir,
Your obedient Servant,

A. D. POUND,
Captain.

The Vice-Admiral Commanding,
    1st Battle Squadron
        (through R.A. 1st B.S.).

---

[1] Plate 4.   [2] Not printed.

CHRONOLOGICAL ORDER OF EVENTS, 31st MAY–1st JUNE 1916, AS OBSERVED FROM "COLOSSUS."

5.40 p.m.—Conditions : Visibility, 6 miles, overcast.
    Sea, calm.
    Wind, S.W., light.
    Heavy firing heard 4 points on Starboard Bow.

5.48 p.m.—Passed Norwegian Barque on Starboard Hand.

5.50 p.m.—1 Cruiser and 4 Light Cruisers closing in from Starboard Bow.

5.50 p.m.—Our Battle Cruisers in sight Starboard Bow, firing.

5.51 p.m.—Enemy Battleships ("Helgoland" and others) reported in sight on Starboard Bow. They only showed up for about half a minute.

5.54 p.m.—Light Cruiser on Port Bow of Battle Cruisers, firing.

5.57 p.m.—Reported that Enemy Battle Fleet had altered course to North.

5.59 p.m.—Speed of Battle Fleet, 18 knots.

6. 1 p.m.—Battle Cruiser Fleet 1 point on our Starboard Bow firing intermittently.

6. 2 p.m.—Enemy Battle Fleet is sight indistinctly.

6. 4 p.m.—First Battle Cruiser Squadron right ahead—2 miles—firing. Destroyers take up screening positions.

6. 5 p.m.—First Battle Cruiser Squadron altered course 4 points to Starboard.

6. 6 p.m.—"Lion"—steam coming from abreast fore turret, port side.

6. 7 p.m.—Sun coming out. Visibility ahead and on Starboard Bow bad owing to smoke and mist.

6. 8 p.m.—Enemy in sight to S.S.E. (Flashes of guns only visible.)

6. 9 p.m.—First Battle Cruiser Squadron altering. Resultant course 1 point to Starboard of ours.

6.10 p.m.—Fifth Battle Squadron on Starboard Beam. "Barham" opened fire. First Battle Cruiser Squadron altering to Port.

6.11 p.m.—Enemy's salvoes falling round First Battle Cruiser Squadron.

6.12 p.m.—Battle Fleet deployed by equal speed pendant to S.E. by E.

6.13 p.m.—Large projectile ricochetted over.

6.15 p.m.—5th Battle Squadron astern and under fire. 1st Battle Cruiser Squadron on Starboard Bow.

6.16 p.m.—One Cruiser ("Defence" class) starboard quarter, on fire and partially blown up. Fire right fore and aft, result of hit by salvo.

6.18 p.m.—Salvo 200 short and left of "Colossus."

6.19 p.m.—A second Cruiser of "Defence" class hit and blown up—major part of explosion aft. "Marlborough" opened fire.

Plate 4.

H.M.S. COLOSSUS.

COURSE AND DISPOSITION OF FLEET FROM
VI·0·P.M. – VIII·39 P.M. ON 31.5.16.

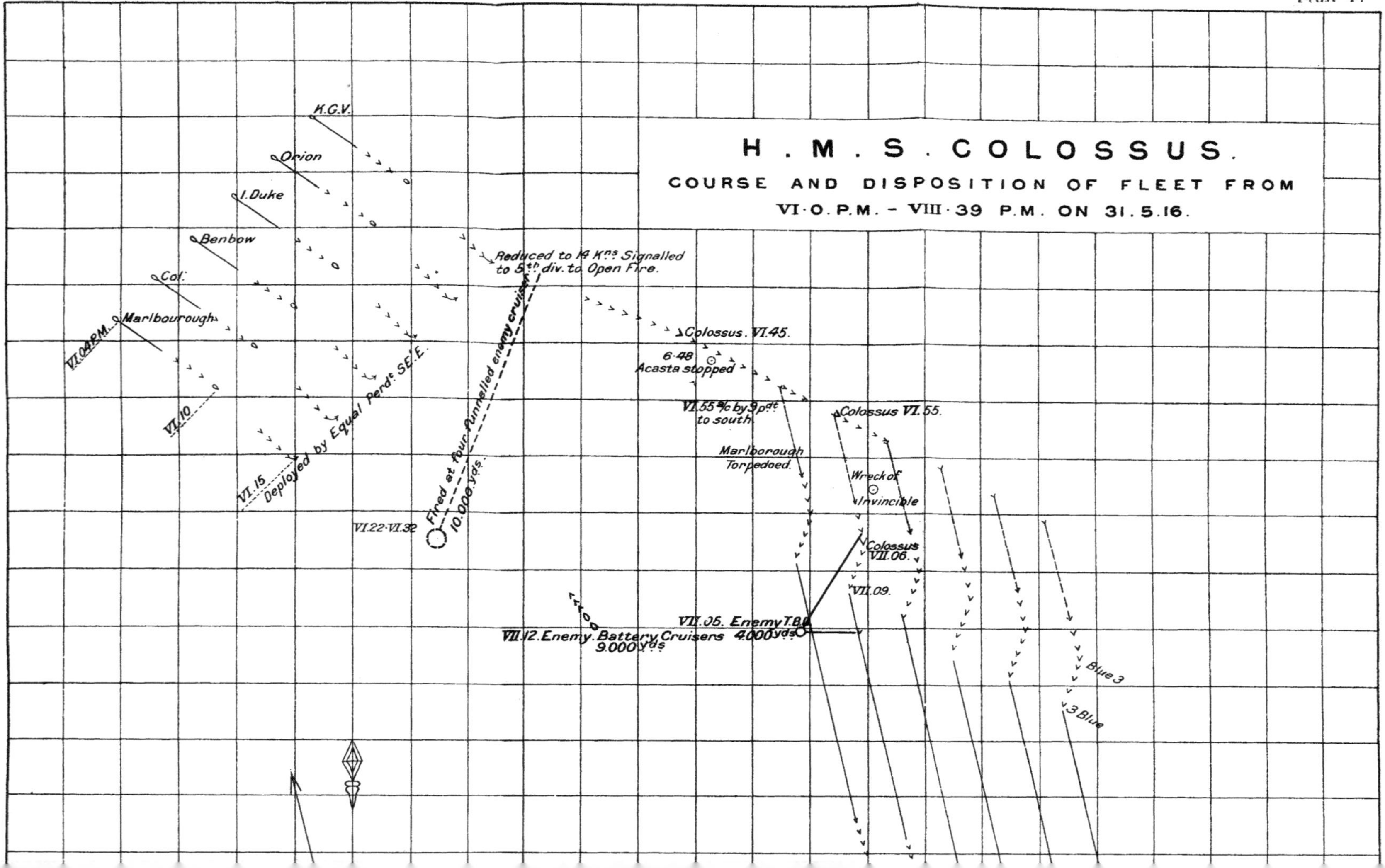

Blue 3

3 Blue

Colossus VI.55

Wreck of Invincible

Colossus VII.06

VII.09

Colossus. VI.45.

6·48 Acasta stopped

VI.53 % by 9 deg to south

Marlborough Torpedoed

VII.35. Enemy TBs 4,000 yds

VII.12. Enemy Battery Cruisers 9,000 yds

Reduced to 14 Kn.s Signalled to 5th div. to Open Fire.

Fired at four funnelled enemy cruiser

10,000 yds

VI.22–VI.32

K.G.V.

Orion

I. Duke

Benbow

Col.

Marlbourough

VI.04 P.M.

VI.10.

VI.16 Deployed by Equal Speed S.E.

3.35 Speed Equal Pend.: S.E.

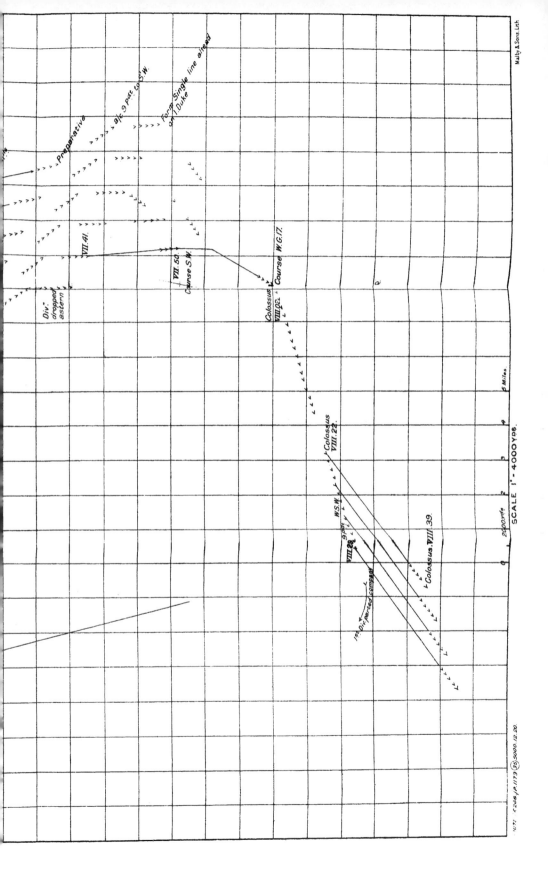

Preparative

a/c 3 pct to S.W.

Form Single line ahead
on Duke

VII. 41.

Div^n dropped
astern

VII. 50.

Course S.W.

Colossus
VIII. 02 — Course W.G. 17.

a

Colossus
VIII. 22.

W.S.W.
9 pct

VIII 28

1st Div. pented company

Colossus. VIII. 39

SCALE 1" = 4000 YDS.

2000 yds   0   1   2   3   4   5 Miles

Malby & Sons. Lith.

6.20 p.m.—5th Battle Squadron Starboard Quarter.

6.21 p.m.—Heavy Shell just over.

6.22 p.m.—Enemy vessel (4 funnels) on fire and apparently disabled on Starboard Beam, 12,000.

Enemy Battle Line apparently Starboard Quarter.

6.25 p.m.—1 ship ahead and 3 astern firing.

6.30 p.m.—" Colossus " fired 3 deliberate salvoes at enemy Battle Fleet, which was difficult to see.

6.32 p.m.—Shifted fire on to enemy 4-funnelled cruiser Starboard Beam opposite course (? stopped).

4 salvoes fired at minute interval.

one of our Destroyers (G. 09) on fire on Starboard Bow.

6.37 p.m.—Nothing clearly in sight.

Intermittent firing from Battle Fleet at one enemy vessel, apparently broken down, 10,000 yards (4 funnels).

6.45 p.m.—Firing practically ceased. Altered course to S.E., 15 knots. Nothing clearly in sight.

6.48 p.m.—Passed " Acasta " on Starboard Hand, disabled.

6.50 p.m.—Course S.

6.53 p.m.—" Revenge " hauling out of line to port.

7. 0 p.m.—Opened fire on enemy 3-funnelled cruiser (*ex* "Greek") steaming opposite course on Starboard Beam, 9,700. Other ships of Battle Fleet also firing. Fired 3 salvoes.

7. 2 p.m.—Passed wreck of " Invincible " port hand. Broken in two pieces. " Oak " standing by. Two survivors in sight near propellers.

7. 3 p.m.—" Benbow " firing 6-in. on enemy Destroyer Starboard Bow.

3 points to Starboard together.

7. 5 p.m.—Battle Cruiser Fleet opened fire Starboard Bow. Ships not actually in sight.

Opened fire 12-in. and 4-in. on enemy Destroyer coming down on Starboard Bow, 4,000 yards. Hit Destroyer, which disappeared apparently sunk. " A " turret also fired on several Destroyers further off.

7.10 p.m.—Altered course 3 points to Port together.

7.12 p.m.—Suddenly observed " Derfflinger " class ship emerge from mist 10,000 yards Starboard Beam accompanied by two (possibly more) Battle Cruisers.

Attention of ships generally concentrated on enemy Destroyer.

Immediately shifted to leading Battle Cruiser and opened fire at 9,000 yards range, closing at 7.16 p.m. to 8,400.

7.16 p.m.—" Colossus " hit in superstructure just abaft funnel (foremost) by 12-in. shell which exploded and caused fire in port gun decks and signal deck. Cordite chief cause of fire, extinguished in a few minutes. Another 12-in. shell hit sounding platform on Port Signal Deck, but apparently passed overboard without bursting.

7.17 p.m.—Heavy shell burst 30 yards short abreast " A " turret. Splinters penetrated foremost funnel and unarmoured parts of ship in about 20 places and wrecked S. 1 Searchlight, burst fire main in Captain's Cabin Flat and caused unimportant damage. Rangetaker fore Upper Bridge severely wounded, one Marine look-out same position slightly wounded. Leading Signalman in Fore Top severely wounded.

(For details of this action, see Appendix I.)

7.18 p.m.—Hit in Fore part of ship by splinters from heavy shell, which burst short.

7.15 p.m.⎫ Fired 5 salvoes at " Derfflinger " (or " Lützow ") on
to ⎬ beam, steering same course, 8,000–9,000 yards
7.20 p.m.⎭ range. Observed at least 4 direct hits (4th and 5th salvoes) (2 hits on water line). Enemy vessel obscured by heavy smoke and mist, but just previously observed to have listed.

7.25 p.m.—Firing ceased.

7.35 p.m.—" Colossus " turned to port to avoid torpedo coming from Starboard, hoisted Black Pendant.

7.40 p.m.—Speed, 20 knots.

7.42 p.m.—Battle Fleet Line ahead, course S.W., formed on " Iron Duke."

8. 0 p.m.—Divisions line ahead disposed quarterly to Starboard. Course, W.; speed, 14.

8.15 p.m.—Firing taking place right ahead. Altered course to W.S.W.

8.23 p.m.—Passed a lot of dead fish.

8.24 p.m.—Altered course to S.W. by 9 pdt. 3 ships of 5th Battle Squadron in company 5 miles Starboard Quarter.

8.32 p.m.—Altered course to W. by 9 pdt.

8.55 p.m.—Our Light Cruisers in action on Starboard Beam presumably engaging enemy Destroyers. " Benbow " also opened fire (6-in.).

8.58 p.m.—Altered course to S. Light cruisers still firing.

9. 5 p.m.—Light now bad. Range for the night, 3,000. Firing heard and seen Starboard Bow.

9.20 p.m.—Observed large star signal.

9.48 p.m.—Commander-in-Chief's reference position, 36.26 N. 5.57 E., course S., 17 knots.

10.35 p.m.—Firing Starboard Quarter lasting about 10 minutes. One of our Destroyers apparently on fire.

10.10 p.m.—Firing on Starboard Beam lasting 4 minutes.

11.30 p.m.—Passed over wreckage or submarine.

(For damage to propellers, *see* Appendix II.)

11.40 p.m.—Rapid and continuous firing for 15 minutes right astern.

1st June 1916.

2.15 a.m.—General Quarters.

" Marlborough's " Division } absent.
" King George's " Division }

Conditions : Visibility, 2 miles, misty, overcast; sea calm ; wind light, S.W.

2.28 a.m.—" King George's " Division in sight Starboard Beam.

2.30 a.m.—Course, N. 1 pdt. A. BD 5.

2.48 a.m.—" King George " take guide of Fleet.

3 ships of 5th Battle Squadron in company.

3.17 a.m.—2 heavy salvoes heard just abaft Port Beam.

3.30 a.m.—More heavy firing port quarter.

3.38 a.m.—Altering course by Divisions to W.

3.40 a.m.—Speed, 15 knots.

3.43 a.m.—Zeppelin sighted Port Quarter steering N., range, 16,000 yards.

3.47 a.m.—Speed, 17 knots.

3.50 a.m.—Line ahead, course N.

3.55 a.m.—Two or three shots (12-in.) from Fleet at Zeppelin. Zeppelin rising turned away.

4. 0 a.m.—" King George " take guide of Fleet.

4. 8 a.m.—Formed Divisions in line ahead disposed to Starboard.

4.30 a.m.—Visibility, 2½ miles.

4.40 a.m.—" Lützow " reported (by signal) ahead damaged.

4.50 a.m.—Commander-in-Chief guide of Fleet.

5. 8 a.m.—3 ships of 5th Battle Squadron taking station Starboard Beam, 11 cables.

5.15 a.m.—5 Armoured Cruisers Starboard Bow.

5.30 a.m.—2nd Light Cruiser Squadron coming up astern.

6. 7 a.m.—Course, S.E.

7.15 a.m.—Course, N. Visibility, 4 miles.

8.18 a.m.—Passed a lot of wreckage with large Carley raft and lifebuoy with " EN." on it.

8.40 a.m.—Course, S.S.W. Speed, 17 knots.

9.30 a.m.—Submarine reported by " Barham."

9.43 a.m.—Sighted " Lion " and Battle Cruisers Port Quarter.

9.40 a.m.—Destroyers taking up screening positions.

9.50 a.m.—Battle Cruiser Fleet forming on Port Wing.

9.57 a.m.—Course, N. by W.

10.30 a.m.—BJ 1.

APPENDIX 1.

ACTION WITH BATTLE CRUISER (EITHER " LÜTZOW " OR " DERFFLINGER ")

At 7.15 p.m., " Colossus " was engaged (with both Main and Secondary Armament) in driving off a destroyer attack on the Starboard Bow, when an enemy battle cruiser appeared on the Starboard Beam, at a range of between 10,000 and 9,000 yards.

This enemy's ship was immediately engaged.

It was not possible to obtain any range before opening fire.

Five salvoes in all were fired—2 short, 1 over, and 2 straddled. Out of the last two salvoes, four direct hits were obtained with armour-piercing lyddite. Two of these hits were on the water-line, whilst the other two were on the fore part, where they caused a fire.

After the first salvo, which straddled, the enemy turned away, and was observed with a considerable list in the smoke screen formed by their destroyers.

The leading enemy battle cruiser (either " Lützow " or " Derfflinger ") did not engage " Colossus."

The second ship in the enemy's line engaged " Colossus," and four salvoes dropped close to the ship ; two direct hits only were received, but a certain amount of damage was received from shell bursting short. Of the shell which hit short, some burst on impact with the water, whilst others ricochetted over the ship without bursting.

Of the direct hits, one entered the foremost superstructure on the starboard side, and burst on the port side of the lower gun deck, at a distance of about 24 ft. from the point at which it entered. Two Starboard 4-in. guns were manned at the time.

This shell was a 12-in. H.E. Shell, detonation appears to have been complete, but its action was very local. (*See* photographs marked " A."[1])

The whole of No. 5 gun's crew were knocked down by the blast, and two men were wounded by splinters from the superstructure.

2 *   *   *   *   *

No. 5 4-in. port gun was temporarily put out of action, two pieces of the driving band of the 12-in. shell having caused the sight to jamb. The cam of the sight was untouched. A hole was made in the oil bath casing covering the training rack, and small pieces of metal falling in rendered the training stiff.

A splinter entered the left slit in the O.L.O. hood of " P " turret, and fractured the left front window of the rangefinder. Apparently the prisms are uninjured, and a test, using the " internal adjustment," showed the rangefinder to be in good adjustment. Damp, however, entered from the broken window.

The down-take to " A " Boiler room was just under where the shell burst, and the fumes were sucked down by the fans, which caused inconvenience until the fans were stopped.

These gases were not poisonous.

The blast which penetrated to the stokehold through the downtake, temporarily put the fire engine out of action.

The second direct hit was on the sounding machine platform, on the port signal deck, but the shell did not burst in the ship. (*See* photograph marked " B."[1])

The shells which burst short caused damage as follows :—

About 20 holes in the side plating in the fore part of the ship.
Small hole in funnel.

---

[1] Not reproduced.   [2] *See* note on p. 381.

Severed fire-main in Captain's Cabin Flat.

Besides other minor damage.

As a rule, the flying splinters could be seen and avoided in the fore-top, but, as a rule, the personnel will be too occupied to notice them.

A shell, bursting short, wounded two men in the top, and a further splinter made a hole about 3 in. in diameter in the support for the roof. The 1-in. side plates were hardly dented when struck by splinters.

A. D. POUND,
Captain.

APPENDIX II.

STRIKING OF WRECKAGE OR SUBMARINE.

At 11.30 p.m., on 31st May, the ship unmistakably passed over something. The noise as of something scraping along the bottom was heard and felt by Officers in the Fore Transmitting Station, Ward Room, and Engine Room. On examination of the ship's bottom and propellers by divers, the following damage was found :—

Ship's Bottom.—Nil.

Starboard Outer Propeller.—One blade—a piece broken off to a depth of 2½ to 3 in. for a length of 16 in. Another blade—fractured and twisted to a depth of 6 in. for a length of 6 in.

Starboard Inner Propeller.—One blade—Tip broken off to a depth of 2 in. and length of 12 in. Another blade—Tip bent forward to a depth of 3 in. for a length of 12 in. Remaining blade—edge jagged.

A. D. POUND,
Captain.

CAPTAIN'S REPORT, H.M.S. " REVENGE."

From.—The Commanding Officer, H.M.S. " Revenge."

To.—Vice Admiral Commanding, First Battle Squadron.

Date.—2nd June 1916. No. B. 111/2.

Subject.—Action of 31st May and 1st June 1916.

Former.—

H.M.S. " Revenge,"
2nd June 1916.

SIR,

In accordance with your signal 1603 of to-day, Friday, 2nd June 1916, I have the honour to forward the following general account of the action of 31st May and 1st June 1916 as observed from " Revenge."

6. 5 p.m.—Fleet in 2nd Organisation. Course, South. Speed 18 knots. Observed British Battle Cruiser Fleet of 4 ships in line ahead, engaged with enemy battle cruisers; latter could not be distinguished.

6. 8 p.m.—Observed flashes of enemy's guns.

6. 9 p.m.—Observed " Lion " hit on forecastle and on fire; soon extinguished.

6.10 p.m.—Reports of enemy Battle Fleet S.S.E.

6.15 p.m.—5th Battle Squadron observed firing on enemy Battle Fleet.

6.17 p.m.—Shots falling round ship. Deployed to port, S.E. by E.

6.25 p.m.—Cruisers who had deferred taking up battle stations till too late now found themselves under heavy fire from enemy Battle Fleet. "Black Prince"(?) observed to be struck aft and then forward; magazines evidently exploded and she disappeared.

At the same time "Warrior" was very badly damaged, and "Minotaur" or "Shannon" had miraculous escape, being straddled frequently.

6.30 p.m.—Reduced to 14 knots.

6.42 p.m.—Increased to 17 knots.

During this time, fire was maintained by Director method against enemy's battleships, which were very indistinct. (No ranges being obtainable.) Also on a four funnelled cruiser between the lines, apparently damaged and stopped.

6.48 p.m.—Divisions separately altered course to S.E.

About this time "Marlborough" was struck by a torpedo.

With regard to this at—

6.50 p.m.—Officers in Transmitting Room, "A" and "Y" Shell Rooms, Director Tower and Spotting Top all felt a shock as if the ship had struck something. The Officer of "Y" Turret, Captain Evan Jukes-Hughes, Royal Marine Light Infantry, and the Torpedo Officer, Lieutenant-Commander Walter K. Conlon, Royal Navy, looked over the side and observed a large patch of oil, with an upheaval in the middle, with portions of wreckage coming to the surface. A few minutes previous to this I had myself observed "Marlborough" struck by mine or torpedo. At the time I thought the former, but since I think she was torpedoed by a submarine, who then dived and attempted to go under the battleship line. "Revenge" on seeing "Marlborough" struck, hauled out to port about a cable, and my belief is, struck and sunk the submarine.

About 6.55 p.m.—A light cruiser passed down between the lines, apparently making a torpedo attack. She was not fired at for some time, being possibly mistaken for British. Eventually "Marlborough" with 13·5-in. and "Revenge" and ships astern with 6-in., opened fire on her, and she was soon apparently a wreck, stopped, with 2 funnels gone and on fire. She was not observed to sink.

6.56 p.m.—Passed " Acasta," disabled. She signalled " holed fore and aft. Unable to move engines."

6.59 p.m.—Squadron turned, leading ships together and remainder in succession to South.

7. 9 p.m.—3 points to starboard together.

About 7.15 p.m. a torpedo was fired at the " Von der Tann." Range, 9,000 yards. The torpedo was observed to run true.

On the Fleet first deploying, fire was opened on the leading ship of the Second Squadron. Some salvoes were fired, unspotted. Fire was then checked as the enemy was too indistinct. Subsequently, as our line turned to the southward, converging on the enemy, the leading division, consisting of 5 battle cruisers, came clearly into sight. Fire was opened on the leading ship. Hits were obtained with the second salvo, and bursts of flame were observed on the quarterdeck. Hitting was continued for 2 salvoes. As it was evident that several ships ahead were firing at this target, and that this enemy's ship was seriously damaged, fire was shifted to the 4th ship in the line, apparently the " Von der Tann," and hits were obtained and burst of flame noticed aft.

Two Turret Officers are of the opinion that she was sunk by the second of two salvoes, of which three shots are believed to have struck and caused the ship to blow up. Fire was continued until a flotilla of destroyers, passing through the Battle Cruiser line, made a most efficient smoke screen, entirely obscuring the target. At this period the enemy fleet turned 8 points to starboard and rapidly drew out of sight.

7.22 p.m.—The destroyers made a determined torpedo attack, but were stopped by the 6-in. guns of our ships.

At the same time our own light cruisers and destroyers from the van and rear were observed attacking them.

It was observed that the destroyers flew a long, red pendant, as mentioned in the " AX " papers. One destroyer was observed disabled, and they all disappeared after the enemy fleet, using a smoke screen.

7.10 p.m.—Fleet turned back 3 points to port together.

7.16 p.m.—Turned together to South.

About 7.17 p.m. observed the two ends of a German light cruiser sticking up out of the water. Apparently had been blown in two parts.

7.28 p.m.—Turned away 2 points from the enemy, by subdivisions, to avoid torpedo attack.

7.35 p.m.—" Revenge " altered course to port to avoid two torpedoes. One passed about 10 yards ahead and one about 20 yards astern.

7.37 p.m.—Leading ships together and remainder in succession to South-West.

7.43 p.m.—" Revenge " altered course to port to avoid torpedoes, two passing astern.

7.54 p.m.—Single line ahead, course S.W.

8. 4 p.m.—Divisions separately alter course in succession to West, speed 17 knots.

9. 0 to 9.15 p.m.—Heard and observed heavy firing to the Eastward, apparently a destroyer attack.

10.40 p.m.—Observed flashes of heavy firing and two heavy explosions lighting up the sky in that direction.

At the time my impression was that some ship had blown up.

About 12.30., what was at first taken for destroyers approaching was observed and 6-in. guns turned on them and the order had been given to open fire, when it was seen that the object was a large ship. She was challenged and made reply " PL " and rapidly disappeared astern. She had the appearance of a Battle Cruiser and resembled our own.

1 a.m., 1st June.—

Firing and an explosion was heard right astern.

Nothing more of interest occurred during the night, until

2.45 a.m., June 2nd.—Vice Admiral Sir Cecil Burney, Royal Navy, hoisted his flag in " Revenge."

3.35 a.m.—A Zeppelin was observed about 4,000 to 5,000 yards off, and 2 rounds of 15-in. were fired, besides fire from 3-in. H.A. gun. The tail was observed to dip, as if the 15-in. shell had passed fairly close, and it had the effect of driving the Zeppelin off at once.

5.15 a.m.—Passed through the wreckage of a German battleship or battle cruiser judging from the size of the floating powder cases.

6.30 a.m.—Passed wreckage of H.M.S. " Black Prince," including Carley raft and life buoy with name of ship.

Observed 2 rafts with 3 men. Destroyer " Obedient " found them being picked up by a Dutch steamer. They were German seamen, very exhausted; ship not known, but from size of rafts, " Obedient " estimated at least a light cruiser.

8.35 a.m.—Passed " Sparrowhawk " abandoned. (Later sunk by " Marksman ")

Rough diagrams of the various phases are attached.[1]

I have the honour to be,
Sir,
Your obedient Servant,
E. B. KIDDLE,
Captain.

---

[1] Plates 5 and 6.

Plate 5.

6.5 P.M. MAY 31.

Position of British Fleet when we sighted our Battle Cruisers firing at an enemy on their Starboard Bow.

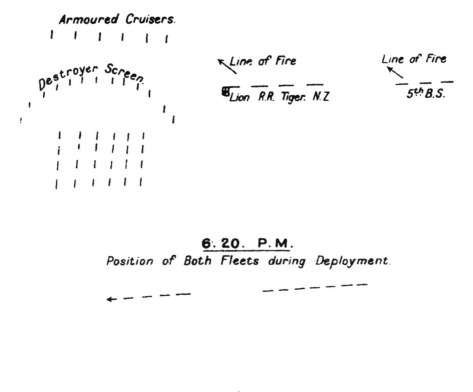

Armoured Cruisers.

Destroyer Screen.

Line of Fire

Lion. R.R. Tiger. N.Z.

Line of Fire

5ᵗʰ B.S.

6.20. P.M.

Position of Both Fleets during Deployment.

Armoured Cruisers under very heavy fire trying to take up position astern.

B.C.S.

5ᵗʰ B.C.S.

British Battle Fleet

R

Visibility about 12,000 yards, and for Ranges about 9,500 yards.

Plate 6.

POSITION AT ABOUT 6.30. P.M.

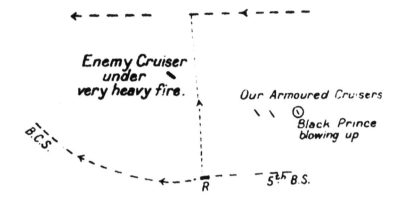

POSITION AT FROM 6.55 TILL 7.22 P.M.

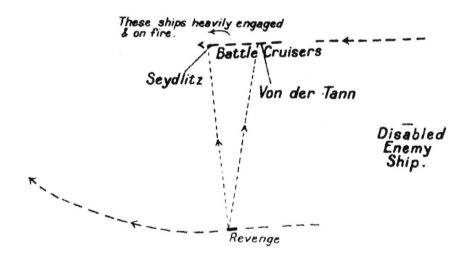

Malby & Sons Lith

H.M.S. " Revenge,"

SIR,   4th June 1916.

IN accordance with your signal 0900 of 4th June, I have
the honour to report that the wreckage was supposed to be that
of H.M.S. " Black Prince " from the lifebuoy with name of ship
on it, 2 Carley Rafts, Cordite Cases, Seamen's Life Saving Jackets,
Gratings, and Wooden débris. The position was Latitude
56° 2′ North, Longitude 5° 57′ East, worked from " Iron Duke's "
positions.

I have the honour to be,
Sir,
Your obedient Servant,
E. B. KIDDLE,
Captain.

The Commander-in-Chief,
Grand Fleet
(through the Vice-Admiral Commanding
1st Battle Squadron).

CAPTAIN'S REPORT, H.M.S. " BELLONA."

H.M.S. " Bellona,"

SIR,   2nd June 1916.

WITH reference to your signal No. 1550 of to-day I have
the honour to report as follows : though I fear my remarks will
be of little value, as I felt at the end of the action that owing
to the length of the line and the low visibility, I had gathered
but little of what had happened.

2. As regards H.M.S. " Bellona's " special duty of repeating
signals : The signals appeared to me to be comparatively few,
simple, and such as might be expected, and I imagine they got
through with rapidity and accuracy.

3. H.M.S. " Bellona " lay from ¾ of a mile to a mile on the
off side of the 5th Division, in this position I had expected to
get a fair share of " overs " round about me; but as a matter
of fact only one large shell fell close (about 50 yards over), and
it seemed to me that the enemy was firing mostly short. There
was, of course, never any great volume of fire.

4. His salvoes seemed to cover an extraordinarily small area,
a thing which has struck me before.

5. It seemed to me that we had the better visibility, and I
expect the enemy was hampered by smoke.

6. I was not able to get much idea of what our own shooting
was like. During the whole action I only saw two of the enemy's
big ships. I did see our shots hit the enemy twice, but beyond
that it seemed to me that we also were shooting short.

7. I saw no Zeppelin or air craft of any description ; I did
not expect a Zeppelin attack, but I certainly thought they
would have them there for reporting our movements, &c.

8. I only observed one effort by hostile torpedo craft, and that only seemed to be made by three boats.

9. I could not understand the action of certain of our 4 funnelled cruisers. They seemed to me to be not only uselessly exposing themselves to the enemy's heavy ships, but also getting in the way of our torpedoes, and hampering our line with their smoke. I naturally know nothing of the reason for their action, and merely give this as an impression.

I have the honour to be,
Sir,
Your obedient Servant,
ARTHUR B. S. DUTTON,
Captain.

The Vice-Admiral Commanding
　　First Battle Squadron,
　　　　H.M.S. " Revenge."

H.M.S. " NEPTUNE."—CAPTAIN'S REPORT OF ACTION WITH GERMAN FLEET ON 31ST MAY 1916.

No. 08.

H.M.S. " Neptune,"
10th June 1916.

SIR,

　　I HAVE the honour to forward the following report on the action with the German fleet on 31st ultimo.

At 5.46 p.m., when steering S. 50° E. in columns of divisions line ahead, disposed abeam, one mile apart, (Organisation No. 5) flashes from gun-fire were observed on Starboard bow.

5.51 p.m.—Gun-fire heard on Starboard bow.

5.56 p.m.—One of our cruiser squadrons, either First or Second, was observed on Port bow, engaging enemy, the latter being out of sight of " Neptune."

6. 1 p.m.—Signal " 9 Pdt. E—G.18 " was hauled down.

6. 6 p.m.—The inspiring signal—
　　　　" Remember the traditions of the glorious First of June—avenge Belgium "
　　was received and transmitted to all on board.

About this time the First Battle Cruiser Squadron (3 in number) and one " New Zealand " were observed steering to the Eastward across our bow. They were engaging an enemy invisible to " Neptune." The Fifth Battle Squadron appeared some distance astern of them.

The signal " Equal speed Pdt. C.L." (S.E. by S.) was hoisted.

6.16 p.m.—Signal hauled down. Formed into line.

About this time the flashes of enemy's guns were seen on Starboard beam and quarter, and the splashes of his projectiles were observed on Starboard side.

Enemy appeared to be firing on our cruisers, some of which appeared out of the mist. One of " Warrior " class was seen to be badly hit and set on fire; she passed across to Port quarter. Another cruiser, appearently " Defence," was observed to be hit, and was reported to have blown up.

A third cruiser of same type, though surrounded with shells, managed to make her escape.

6.32 p.m.—" Collingwood " opened fire. About this time 5th division got somewhat bunched up, and " St. Vincent " came up on " Neptune's " beam, masking her fire and interfering with view of enemy. " St. Vincent " opened fire, which now became general in our line.

6.40 p.m.—" St. Vincent " having dropped astern, " Neptune " opened fire on one of enemy's battleships, which appeared to be unfired on. Owing to the mist, enemy could only be indistinctly seen. Fire was opened at 11,000 yards, but after two salvoes, both of which appeared to be short; owing to the impossibility of spotting and gradual disappearance of the target firing was discontinued. Enemy appeared to fire one or two salvoes in our direction and then to discontinue.

6.44 p.m.—Course altered to S.E.

6.50 p.m.—Passed " Acasta " hove to and putting collision mats over two holes, one on Starboard quarter and one on Port bow.

6.55 p.m.—" 9 Pdt. E.—G. 17 " hauled down.

About this time a three-funnel cruiser (" Moraves " class), apparently disabled, was observed to come out of the mist on Starboard beam. She possibly fired the torpedo which hit " Marlborough."

First Battle Squadron opened fire on her. " Neptune " fired one salvo at her, but as so many other ships were firing at this cruiser, I ceased fire. She was observed to be hit several times, and was lost sight of astern. She did not return the fire.

About 7.4 p.m.—" Neptune " opened fire on the leading of two battle cruisers, " Lützow " class. The first salvo was fired at a range of 10,200 yards and fell over. * * * [1]—fire." Salvo short. " Up * * * [1] " Straddle and hit. " Up * * * [1] " and hit again. They then turned away, the leader on fire aft, and rapidly disappeared in a cloud of smoke.

An enemy light cruiser was now seen steering to Northward. She was soon hit, while turning to Port, by a salvo from one of our ships. She appeared to stop and to settle down in the water. Believed to have sunk.

---

[1] *See* note on p. 381.

7.10 p.m.—About six or eight German destroyers commenced an
            attack on our line from a position about 2 points
            before the Starboard beam. A salvo from 12-in.
            was fired at them while 4-in. guns were being
            manned. " Neptune " opened fire with 4-in. guns
            on one destroyer, which was not being fired at,
            and hit her three times, then opened fire on another
            (the second in the line) and she was hit too, believed
            by " Neptune," but might have been by another
            ship. Both are believed to have sunk. The
            remaining destroyers were driven off, but not
            without torpedoes being fired at our line. The
            tracks of three torpedoes were clearly seen from
            the fore-top, one of which passed very close to
            " Neptune," and was avoided by use of helm.

Two submarines—one on the surface about three miles on
Starboard quarter, and the other in diving trim about two miles
a point before the Starboard beam—are believed to have been
seen from fore-top about this time.

About 7.5 p.m. a badly damaged vessel, apparently a German
light cruiser, was passed about a mile on Port beam.   She was
very badly crumpled up, with waist below water, and bow and
stern above the surface. She seemed to have been abandoned.
From subsequent information this appears to have been
" Invincible."

Invincible

About 10.40 p.m. heavy firing, apparently from an engagement
between light cruisers and destroyers, was observed to the North-
West, about four or five miles off.   One ship appeared to be set
on fire.

Flashes were observed to the Northward at intervals during
the night.

About 3.45 a.m. on 1st instant a Zeppelin was observed on
Port quarter. She passed over to Starboard beam. A round
was fired at her from " X " turret, after which she turned away
and made off.

The white ensign flown by our ships did not seem to stand
out clearly at a distance in the white misty weather, nor the
union jack either.

It is not known why the red ensign was abandoned, but it is
considered that red shows up better than any other colour against
any background likely to be met with, and a large red flag,
flown in a conspicuous position, such as the foretopmast head,
is recommended.

In the case of most of the Officers and men of " Neptune,"
this was the first occasion on which they had been in any kind
of an action. It had an exhilarating and beneficial effect, the
opportunity of coming in contact with the enemy being much
appreciated.

The behaviour of all during the short and disappointing engagement was most creditable, all orders being rapidly and accurately carried out without undue excitement.

Separate reports giving names of Officers and men recommended are being forwarded.

I have the honour to be, .

Sir,

Your obedient Servant,

V. H. G. BERNARD.

The Vice-Admiral Commanding   Captain.

First Battle Squadron.

H.M.S. "AGINCOURT," CAPTAIN'S REPORT OF ACTION.

No. 171/02.   H.M.S. "Agincourt,"

SIR,   10th June 1916.

IN accordance with your signal, I have the honour to submit the following report on the action of 31st May, as far as H.M.S. "Agincourt" was concerned.

At 6. 0 p.m.—The ship's position was Lat. 57° 7' N., Long. 5° 41' E.; course, 134°; speed, 20 knots.

6. 8.   Altered course to 122°.

6.17.   Altered course to 45°—thereby deploying into line : "Agincourt" now being rear ship of the line.

At 6.12 p.m.—Our Battle Cruisers and flashes of enemy's guns came into sight from just on the port bow to the starboard bow, crossing from right to left. Shortly after this, the 5th Battle Squadron was seen following our Battle Cruiser Squadron and firing at the enemy, but the flashes of these enemy ships' guns only came into sight through the mist one at a time.

The "Lion" was noted to have a fire on board, which was apparently put out.

Our Light Cruisers and Destroyers appeared to hang about just in front of the 6th Division, and thus came in for some of the enemy's projectiles not apparently intended for them.

A clear view of the enemy could not be obtained, but from general opinion the enemy ships first fired on were Battle Cruisers.

6.14.   Enemy shots falling near the ship.

6.16.   Salvo straddled "Hercules" while deploying.

6.17.   Turned into line after "Hercules."

6.18.   "Marlborough" opened fire; but the range was not yet clear of our own ships for "Agincourt."

6.24.   Opened fire on enemy Battle Cruiser; range, 10,000 yards. Target could just be made out, but her number in their line could not be stated with accuracy. Hits had been obtained on this ship when the smoke from our own Armoured Cruisers blotted out the enemy vessels, one of which was very heavily hit.

6.25.   Speed by signal—14 knots.

6.32.   Opened fire again on same ship. Another hit was observed, but mist made it impossible to be certain of fall of shot.

Our own line of fire was now blocked by our own Destroyers. Fore Control observed a Battle Cruiser, apparently crippled, heading in the opposite direction and flashing FU by searchlight. Fire was then opened on enemy four-funnelled Cruiser, thought to be the " Roon."

6.34.   Lost sight of enemy.

6.36.   Course, 111°.

6.48.   Course, 104°.

6.55.   Observed "Marlborough" struck by torpedo or mine on the starboard side. A few minutes after, the periscope of a submarine was seen passing the ship on starboard side. This could be seen from the Control Top and not from the Bridge or Conning-tower.

7. 0.   Course, 168°; speed, 18 knots.

7. 4.   Turrets opened fire again on enemy three-funnelled Cruiser. "Marlborough" was firing at her. She was apparently already disabled and on fire, but was floating when she passed out of sight.

7. 6.   Four enemy Battleships, apparently their 5th Division, appeared out of the mist, two of which showed clearly against the mist. Opened fire on one of these: range, 11,000 yards; at least four straddles were obtained and effective hits seen.

7. 8.   Enemy torpedo just missed astern. It had been reported from aloft, and course was altered. This was probably fired by a submarine.

7.17.   Enemy fire straddled ship. Enemy destroyers were now observed approaching from enemy's lines.

7.18.   6-in. guns opened on them. When five hits had been observed on the first one fire was shifted to another; two hits were observed on her before she was lost in the mist. Enemy destroyers made a smoke screen which hampered the turrets firing during the time enemy ships turned away.

7.35.   Track of two torpedoes running parallel observed approaching. Course altered to avoid torpedoes; passed ahead.

7.41.   Submarine reported starboard side; turned away to avoid.

7.45.	Course, 185°; speed, 15 to 17 knots.
7.50.	Passed a wreck on port hand.
8. 3.	Course, 258°; 17 knots.
8.25.	Torpedo track on starboard side; turned at full speed; torpedo broke surface about 150 yards on starboard bow.

During the night three distinct sets of firing occurred : the first being on starboard quarter; the second two points on quarter; the third right astern.

A ship or Destroyer closed " Agincourt " at high speed during the night, her track very visible. I did not challenge her, so as not to give our Division's position away. She altered course and steamed away.

2.30.	Vice-Admiral shifted his Flag to " Revenge."
3.52.	Zeppelin in sight. Opened with 6-in. guns and 3-in. anti-aircraft. Apparently no hits were obtained on Zeppelin; she went away towards the East.

T.N.T. common were used throughout the action.

Rounds fired :—

12-in. guns - - -	144 rounds.
6-in. guns - - - - -	111 ,,
Anti-aircraft guns - - -	7 ,,

I have much pleasure in reporting the smooth working of everything on board and the happy alacrity and discipline of all hands. No direct hits were made on " Agincourt," but several splinters came on board, doing very minor damage.

I have the honour to be,
Sir,
Your obedient Servant,
H. M. DOUGHTY,
Captain.

The Vice-Admiral Commanding
First Battle Squadron.
H.M.S. " Royal Oak."

CAPTAIN'S REPORT, H.M.S. " ST. VINCENT."

E.106.

H.M.S. " St. Vincent,"
Sir, 10th June 1916.

I HAVE the honour to forward the following report of the action of 31st May 1916, as far as it concerned " St. Vincent."

In the approach " St. Vincent " was rear ship of the 5th Division, i.e., the next division to port of the starboard wing Division led by " Marlborough."

On forming line of battle to port, " St. Vincent," therefore, became the fifth ship from the rear. The weather was very misty—visibility extreme about 5½ miles. Sea smooth.

The first enemy seen, at which fire could be opened, was a three-funnelled cruiser two points before the starboard beam, heading the opposite way to our line, and apparently stopped. Range, 11,000 yards. " St. Vincent " gave her a few salvoes, as did every other ship of the squadron apparently, but she making no reply, and being evidently in a sinking condition, cease fire was ordered.

Ten minutes later (about 6.54 p.m.) three large ships came into view near the starboard beam, steering a roughly similar course. (At times a fourth was seen, and also another Division, very faint indeed, beyond these ships.)

The leading ship that I looked at carefully, I took to be a " Kaiser " class battleship, but her funnels were short, neat and square. Arrangement of them with regard to masts was similar to " Kaiser " class. Also their distance apart was great. It is possible that this ship may have been " Lützow," but was not thought to be so at the time. The German ships opened fire with quick ripples almost simultaneously with " St. Vincent's " first broadside, which was directed against their third ship considered to be a " Kaiser." The third ship was chosen as there were many ships ahead of " St. Vincent " who could attack the two leading ships. And this was clearly done, all ships being continuously surrounded by splashes.

Rangefinders on " St. Vincent's " target agreed closely, gun range varying from 10,000 yards at start to 9,500 yards at the end. Rate very small, about 50 closing. Only small spotting corrections of up or down 50 occasionally necessary to change from 1 short to 2 short. German fire, which was brisk and regular at the start, very soon declined in rate and accuracy.

" St. Vincent's " fire was by Director, and the target was held closely till 7.26 p.m. (32 minutes in all), when the enemy had turned 8 or 10 points away, disappearing into the mist and with a smoke screen made by Destroyers to cover them as well.

Total rounds fired, 96 (88 A.P. Lyddite and 8 Common Lyddite).

To avoid enemy torpedoes crossing the track of the First Battle Squadron all ships were frequently under helm, and this led to a little bunching, but mutual understanding and consideration prevented embarrassment—e.g., " Neptune " turns sharply to avoid torpedo—" St. Vincent," next astern, wishes to keep steady for gunfire and is not threatened by that torpedo— " St. Vincent " must overlap " Neptune " for a short time.

The Director was, of course, invaluable under the conditions obtaining.

I have the honour to be,

Sir,

Your obedient Servant,

W. W. FISHER,

Captain.

The Vice Admiral Commanding
   First Battle Squadron,
      H.M.S. " Royal Oak."

CAPTAIN'S REPORT, H.M.S. " COLLINGWOOD."[1]

H.M.S. " Collingwood,"

SIR,   10th June 1916.

In accordance with your signal 0600 of to-day, I have the honour to submit the following report of the action of 31st May 1916.

2. At 3.15 p.m., enemy reports between the Light Cruiser Squadrons and Battle Cruisers and the Commander-in-Chief began to be received. The Grand Fleet was steering S.E. by S. in columns of divisions, line ahead to starboard, 19 knots, " Collingwood " being second ship of " Colossus " division (No. 5).

3. At 4.50 p.m., the Flag signalled that the enemy's Battle Fleet were coming North.

Our Battle-Cruisers pass to Eastward.

4. At about 6.15 p.m., our Battle Cruiser Squadron, consisting of two " Lions," " Tiger," and " New Zealand," appeared to the Southward, steering about E.N.E., and engaging with starboard guns. The weather was thick, visibility about 4 miles, and nothing was at first seen of the enemy, but soon afterwards the flashes of their guns was observed.

Grand Fleet Deploys.

5. At 6.23 p.m., deployed to S.E. by E., by equal speed method, and speed of fleet reduced to 14 knots.

6. At 6.28 p.m., " Colossus " signalled for fire to be opened at the enemy as soon as seen, and soon afterwards a cruiser was observed to the southward apparently stopped, and fire was opened on her, at a range of about 9,000 yards. The bearing was approximately abeam.

Gun Flashes only visible.

7. From time to time after this, the flashes of the guns of the enemy's ships beyond the cruiser were observed, but insufficiently clearly to lay the director or guns on, and at no time could the enemy's hulls be seen from the fore conning tower or director tower.

Enemy Searchlight Signals observed.

8. An Officer in the after director tower, Lieutenant J. U. P. Fitzgerald, Royal Navy, informed me afterwards that, on one occasion for a few moments, he was able to make out dimly the hulls of three or four ships—he thought of the " Helgoland " and " Nassau " classes—and later that he saw the enemy's line, or some ships of them, turn away apparently together. He saw a signal " FU " made by searchlight by some ships in the enemy's line, several times just before they appeared to turn away. The

[1] Plate 7.

signalman in " Collingwood's " foretop also saw this, and, about five minutes earlier, our " Compass sign " made about five times. It struck him that these signals were being made to the enemy cruiser at which heavy fire was at the time being directed.

9. The hull of one ship, thought to be " Kaiser " class, was seen once in the foretop for a few moments, but disappeared before the guns could be laid on her.

10. It is to be noted here that the times of the various prominent incidents of the battle observed were not specially noted, and those given in this report (other than alterations of course taken from the signal book) are not reliable.

11. The " Defence " and " Warrior " (or " Black Prince ") were observed, it is thought, about 6.40 p.m., between our line and the enemy's, steering towards our rear, firing vigorously, and themselves on fire and repeatedly struck, and the former ship was observed to be blown up.

First Destroyer attack on our Line.

12. A torpedo attack by an unknown but small number of destroyers was directed on our rear from the beam direction soon after fire was opened, and the 5th Division turned away two points by " Preparative." Fire was opened with 4-in. guns at a destroyer which approached more nearly than the others. It is believed that this attack accounted for the torpedo which struck " Marlborough."

13. Speed was increased by signal to 17 knots.

14. At 6.57 p.m., course was altered to south.

" Colossus " struck by heavy shell.

15. " Colossus " was observed to be struck forward, it is thought about 7.10 p.m. ; but, with this exception, the splashes of enemy shot about our line appeared to be infrequent. One or two salvoes were observed to fall over " Collingwood," and a spent heavy yellow-coloured projectile, striking short, ricochetted and burst on striking the water between us and " Colossus." (Some apparently medium calibre projectiles were falling short at the beginning of the action, but " Collingwood " was not struck.)

Another (?) Enemy Cruiser observed.

16. Soon after this, another damaged enemy cruiser of " Rostock " class was observed about abeam, and fire was opened on her with lyddite common shell. I am, myself, in some doubt as to whether this was, in fact, another ship, or the same one as was being fired at previously, the fleet having, perhaps, brought her again into view by alteration of course to starboard. An Officer in the after conning tower considers that the first cruiser was sunk, and that this was certainly a different and larger one.

17. At 7.22 p.m., speed was reduced by signal to 15 knots.

Plate 7.

H.M.S. COLLINGWOOD.

TRACK CHART OF NAVAL ACTION 31ST MAY.

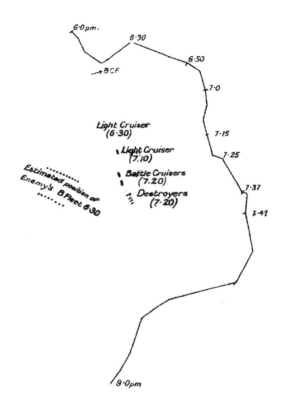

6.0 pm Position Lat 57·11 N. Long 5° 28 E.

6·0 pm.

6·30

6·50

→ BCF

7·0

Light Cruiser (6·30)

7·15

Light Cruiser (7.10)

7·25

Estimated position of Enemy's B Fleet 6·30

Battle Cruisers (7.20)

7·37

Destroyers (7.20)

7·41

TRUE MERIDIAN

9·0 pm

Scale 8 Miles = 1 Inch.

10072. 24266/P 1173 (20) 5000. 12. 29.

Captain

10·6·16

Malby & Sons, Lith.

Enemy's Battle-Cruisers and Destroyers appear.

18. About 7.20 p.m. (?), an enemy's battle cruiser, taken by me to be " Seydlitz," appeared on starboard beam (turned to same direction as our fleet), shortly followed by another. Other officers considered she was a " Derfflinger," and the question remains in doubt, though my impression of the central funnel is a fairly clear one. She presented a clear target, range about 8,000 yards, and fire was shifted to her. Unfortunately, the guns were loaded with lyddite common shell. She was struck at once by two salvoes which started fires and silenced all but her fore turret guns. She very shortly (and before A.P. shell could arrive at the guns) disappeared in dense smoke which was being made by a number of destroyers (not more than six) which were attacking from about 2 points before our beam. The general impression is that these destroyers turned round to starboard (*i.e.*, towards course of our fleet) to fire their torpedoes at a range of about 9,000 yards.

While approaching, and after turning, they made dense clouds of smoke into which the battle cruisers disappeared. It occurs to me that the latter were accompanying the flotilla, probably fired torpedoes themselves, and then took cover in the smoke of the destroyers.

19. At 7.26 p.m., a general signal to turn away 2 points was made.

Torpedoes cross our Line.

20. " Colossus " now signalled the approach of a torpedo and turned away. Immediately afterwards a torpedo track was seen about 20° abaft " Collingwood's " beam, coming straight at the ship. I am under the impression that the ship was at the time already under helm. Large helm was put on and the torpedo passed very close astern. At the same time, another was observed to pass about 30 yards ahead. It is thought that the ship had turned about 4 or 5 points when these torpedoes crossed the line.

21. Fire was continued at a damaged destroyer on the quarter with 12-in. guns for a few minutes and then ceased, no hostile craft being seen afterwards.

General Remarks.

22. On one or two occasions, fires were distinguished on board enemy's ships. It is to me remarkable that, notwithstanding the very weak attacks of the German destroyers (for whose operations the weather conditions were admirable) and the great range (about 9,000 yards) at which their torpedoes were fired, so large a number of their torpedoes passed through the rear of our line. The smooth water helped my foretop lookouts to distinguish the tracks of the torpedoes.

It is obvious to me that the fact that all but one missed is principally providential. The loss suffered by these destroyers appeared to be small; only one was observed by " Collingwood " to be put out of action. The great value of this form of attack on a line of ships is, to me, an outstanding feature of the battle fleet action.

The apparently concerted torpedo attack by battle cruisers and destroyers covered by dense smoke, and the remarkably close range to which the battle cruisers approached, is noteworthy.

Conduct of Officers and Men.

23. All ranks and ratings performed their duties to my complete satisfaction. There was a complete absence of excitement in all departments, and I am convinced that, had " Collingwood " suffered damage, the behaviour of Officers and Men would have proved to be entirely in accordance with the best traditions of His Majesty's Navy.

I have the honour to be,
Sir,
Your obedient Servant,
JAMES LEY,
Captain.

The Vice-Admiral Commanding,
    First Battle Squadron.

CAPTAIN'S REPORT, H.M.S. " ROYAL OAK."

H.M.S. " Royal Oak,"

Sir,   10th June 1916.

With reference to your signal of to-day, I have the honour to submit the following report on the action of 31st May —1st June.

P.M.

5.47. Firing first heard.

5.49. Flashes distinctly visible. Green 65 to S. Westward.

6.12. Formed line of Battle.

6.15. Heavy firing observed to the Southward.

6.25. " Iron Duke " opened fire on 3 funnelled cruiser.

6.29. " Royal Oak " opened fire with 15-in. guns on the same 3 funnelled cruiser. Fired 4 salvoes, the first salvo fired was seen to have straddled the target. The hit was observed on after part of the ship with the 3rd salvo. Range about 10900 yards from the plot.

6.33. " Royal Oak " opened fire with 6-in. guns. Two or 3 salvoes fired on above target, all apparently straddling. " Royal Oak " was straddled once.

6.35. " Royal Oak " checked fire, enemy cruiser being no longer visible. When last seen was burning fiercely. There was a large amount of spray from shots in front of her at this time.

1 *   *   *   *   *

---

¹ *See* note on p. 381.

P.M.

Observed cruisers heavily engaged on the starboard bow, two of our cruisers seemed to be badly damaged.

6.45. Enemy Battle fleet faintly visible on the starboard beam. Order passed to " open fire " but could not be carried out owing to mist enveloping them. From spotting top the four engaged ships looked like " Königs " or " Kaisers."

6.50. Passed wreck of ship on starboard beam, broken in two pieces, believed to be " Invincible." Speed varied from 15 to 18 knots.

Invincible again [margin note]

7.9. " Royal Oak " and " Benbow " opened fire, with 6-in. guns on enemy destroyers. Bearing Green 65 to the Westward.

7.11. " Marlborough " reported she had been struck by a mine or a torpedo.

7.15. Observed 3 enemy battle cruisers to Westward on starboard beam. Opened fire with 15-in. guns on leading enemy's battle cruiser " Derfflinger " class. Atmosphere much clearer for a few moments.

7.16. Enemy ship fire at was observed to be hit several times aft. Opening range 14,000 yards. Speed of own ship 15 knots. Enemy turned away into mist. Fire was shifted to the next ship, a few rounds only could be fired as she was soon lost in the mist. All 6-in. guns were meanwhile firing on the enemy Destroyers on starboard beam, who were zigzagging frequently.

7.28. Eenmy destroyers, making a very effective smoke screen, turned away to starboard, our own destroyers coming down from ahead and chasing them off.

7.30. Altered course, leading ships together, rest in succession to S. by W. " Royal Oak " was not in action again. The total expenditure of ammunition being 15-in.--39; 6-in.--84.

7.44. Heavy firing heard from rear of British line, enemy ships very faintly visible on starboard quarter. Shots seen falling fairly close to " Benbow."

7.50. Speed 15 knots.

7.51. Heavy firing observed on green 125.

7.55. Increased speed.

8.17. Firing observed on port bow.

8.20. 3 light cruisers of " Calliope " class under heavy fire; observed a hit on starboard quarter of rear cruiser abreast 2nd gun from aft. Apparently did not affect the ship.

8.55. Observed firing apparently a heavy destroyer engagement on starboard quarter. A big flare was seen lasting quite 15 seconds.

P.M.

At 10.12 and 10.45 firing again broke out in this direction, in the latter of these a battleship division was apparently engaged, ships being occasionally silhouetted against searchlights.

A.M.

2.20. " Iron Duke " fired a gun at cruiser on starboard bow, who did not answer challenge.

3.20. Heard heavy firing.

3.45. Altered course to port. Speed 15 knots.

3.52. Rear battle ship of division fired at a Zeppelin, red 150. Got ranges of Zeppelin as 19,000–20,000 yards. " Iron Duke " fired 13·5-in. at her, she turned away and disappeared, behind a cloud, and was not again sighted.

There were no mishaps with the exception of one missfire with a 15-in. gun, and this was immediately rectified.

I have the honour to be,

Sir,

Your obedient Servant,

C. MACLACHLAN,

The Vice Admiral Commanding,   Captain.
    3rd Battle Squadron.

CAPTAIN'S REPORT, H.M.S. " MARLBOROUGH."

Sub-Enclosure to Enclosure No. 4 to Submission No. 1415/0022 of 20/6/16 from C.-in-C. Home Fleets.

H.M.S. " Marlborough,"
9th June 1916.

SIR,

I HAVE the honour to report that at 6.54 p.m. on the 31st May, the ship was struck by a torpedo in the Diesel engine room. At the same time a periscope was observed by witnesses about 1,000 yards on the starboard beam. No track of this torpedo was observed, though looked for by several observers immediately after the explosion.

The explosion caused a list to starboard of seven degrees, and flooded the Diesel Engine Room, Hydraulic Engine Room, and water was reported to be entering " A " boiler room, the biggest leak being between the framing of the watertight door to the lower bunker 100–111, and the bulkhead to which it is secured, which had parted. I then telephoned orders to draw fires in " A " boiler room. Speed was now reduced to 17 knots.

" Marlborough " continued in the line, and at 7.0 p.m. three torpedoes were reported on the starboard beam and bow. Course was immediately altered to starboard and then to port; two torpedoes passed ahead and one astern of the ship.

The T.B.D. "Acasta," lying disabled, was then passed one cable on the port beam. At 7.0 p.m. fire was reopened on a disabled enemy ship, range 9,800 yards, four salvoes were fired, and the third and fourth were observed to hit. Ceased fire at 7.07 p.m.

At 7.10 p.m. fired a torpedo at a disabled German ship with three funnels. This may have been the same ship. At 7.12 p.m. opened fire on battleship of "Markgraf" class, one point before the starboard beam, distant 10,200 yards, steering south. Fourteen salvoes in six minutes were fired at this ship, and the sixth, twelfth, thirteenth, and fourteenth were observed to hit. The speed was now 15 knots Ceased firing at 7.18 p.m.

At 7.19 a T.B.D. flotilla was sighted attacking on the starboard bow, opened fire at them with range 11,000 yards. Course was altered away two points to S.S.E., and at 7.22 the flotilla scattered in a dense cloud of funnel smoke, two boats being hit. At 7.24, altered course to S.E. by S., and fired a torpedo at a battleship of the "Markgraf" class. At 7.33 three torpedoes were observed on starboard beam and bow, course was immediately altered to starboard and then to port, one passed ahead, one astern, and the other very close astern or under the ship.

Ship was steadied on course S. by W., and at 7.52 to S.S.W. At 8.0 p.m. course was altered to West and speed to 17 knots, a report also was made to the Commander-in-Chief that "Marlborough's" maximum speed was reduced to 17 knots.

At 8.20, altered course to S.W., 9.0 to S. 4 E., and 9.15 to S. 7 W. At 10.5 p.m. there was gunfire on the starboard beam and again at 10.40, abaft the starboard beam, distant about 8 miles.

At 11.44 p.m. gunfire heavy on starboard quarter, and again at 00.10 a.m. about 7 points abaft starboard beam. A very heavy explosion was observed, evidently a ship blowing up.

At about 2 a.m. 1st June, Commander Currey reported to me that the water was gaining, and that he and Engineer Commander Toop considered that it was dangerous for the ship to steam any longer at a speed of 17 knots, so with great regret I immediately informed you that speed must be reduced. Speed was then reduced to 15 knots, and "Marlborough" hauled out of line, the "Revenge," "Hercules," and "Agincourt" proceeding at 17 knots.

At 2.15 a.m. speed was reduced to 13 knots and "Fearless" ordered alongside port side. Engines were stopped at 2.30 a.m. "Fearless" came alongside, embarking you and your staff.

At 3.0 a.m. I proceeded N. 4 E., and later on the "Fearless" joined as escort. A Zeppelin was sighted at 4.0 a.m. passing astern and steering to the Eastward. Two common and two A.P. shells from 13·5-in. guns and twelve H.E. shell from H.A. gun were fired, and the Zeppelin was observed to dip suddenly, but proceeded on its course.

Orders were now received from the Commander-in-Chief to proceed to Tyne or Rosyth *viâ* M channel, so at 4.30 a.m. course was altered to S. 38 W., 14 knots. Owing to the deep draught of the ship I decided to proceed to Rosyth.

At 9.30 a.m. two submarines were observed, bearing west about 8 miles off and steering towards "Marlborough" with conning towers showing. Five minutes later they dived, so course was altered away from them, course being resumed at 10.50 a.m. to S. 56 W. At 10.52 a.m. an oily patch was observed about 2 miles astern, and the track of a torpedo over-hauling the ship, the torpedo passed along the port side, two cables off. At 11.10 a.m. course was altered to westward, and at 1.45 p.m. Commodore (T) with Harwich Flotillas was sighted bearing S.E. T.B.D.'s "Lark," "Lance," "Lysander," and "Lassoo," and shortly afterwards "Laforey," "Lookout," "Lawford," and "Laverock" joined as escort. At 4.0 p.m. T.B.D.s "Ness" and "Albatross" joined.

At 8.0 p.m. the wind was freshening from the S.W., force 5, and by 10.0 p.m. W.S.W., force 6, with a rising sea.

About 10.0 p.m. the water was rising in "A" boiler room through the suction of the ash expeller pump and submersible pump continually choking and the canvas hose of the ejector bursting. At midnight the water was still gaining, and was now about 4 feet below the grating around the top of the boilers. Commander Currey reported that matters were serious below, and asked that a salvage tug might be signalled for. I then altered course to S.W. by W. reduced, to 10 knots, and steered for the lee of Flamborough Head, which was distant about 50 miles, stationed the "Fearless" one and a half cables to windward of the fore bridge as the sea was breaking over the starboard side of the upper deck. At the same time I informed the Commander-in-Chief of the state of affairs, and asked the S.N.O., Tyne, to send tugs to meet me off Flamborough Head I also warned destroyers to be prepared to come alongside lee side.

The "Laforey" and "Lookout" then asked if they could be of use in laying an oil track ahead of "Marlborough." At 2 a.m. "Lance's" division was ordered to lay oil track ahead, and to windward of "Marlborough." This proved most success-ful, and I was very grateful to the destroyers for the suggestion. My wireless messages were intercepted by the Admiralty and a signal was received from the Admiralty to proceed to the Humber. In the meantime in "A" boiler room, Stoker Petty Officer Ackerman was sent down in a diving dress and cleared the suctions of the pumps, and at 1 a.m. the water was stopped from rising. Speed was increased to 12 knots at 3 a.m.

At about 4.30 a.m. the steam ejector was repaired and the boiler room was cleared of water well below the floor plates at about 5.15 a.m. As the land was closed the weather improved, and at 5.30 a.m. the destroyers stopped making oil track.

"Marlborough" passed Spurn Light Vessel at 7.35 a.m., and secured to No. 3 buoy off Immingham at 10 a.m.

When the ship was torpedoed, Stoker William Rustage, Official Number K. 20,877, and Stoker Edgar G. Monk, Official Number K. 4,266, who were on duty in the Diesel room, were instantly killed.

[1]   *   *   *   *   *

I have the honour to be,

Sir,

Your obedient Servant,

GEORGE P. ROSS,

The Vice-Admiral Commanding,   Captain.

First Battle Squadron.

ENGINEERING REPORT.

H.M.S. "MARLBOROUGH" IN ACTION.

31st May 1916.

The explosion distorted the bulkhead on starboard side of "A" Boiler Room between Boiler Room and Lower Bunkers 90–111. The forward athwartships bulkhead at 92 station was also distorted. The firebars and fire of No. 1 Boiler Room fell into Ash Pans. The Boilers and steam pipes remained intact and there was no escape of steam. Water came into the Boiler Room, the biggest leak being between the framing of the water-tight door to lower bunker 100–111, and the bulkhead to which it is secured. Electric and secondary lighting was not interfered with in "A" Boiler Room.

The fire and bilge pump, steam ejector, and ash expeller pump were put on the bilge in a most expeditious manner, but water continued to rise and put out fires in Nos. 1 and 6 boilers within a few minutes of the explosion, ten minutes after the explosion the water put the fires out in Nos. 2 and 5 boilers—as fires were put out boilers were shut off; water continued to rise, when fires were drawn in Nos. 3 and 4 boilers, and the main steam system in "A" Boiler Room was then isolated. All efforts were directed to clear the boiler room of water, special attention being given to keeping suctions clear of ashes and dirt. This was successful and at about 7.30 the water was at the level of the floor plates and was kept there until the following day.

All coal and oil fuel necessary for "B" and "C" Boiler Rooms was taken from the Starboard side and coal was trimmed from starboard upper outer bunkers to lower and oil fuel pumped from starboard tanks to Port emergency tanks; no compartments were flooded for trimming purpose.

From the time the explosion on the 31st May until arrival of the vessel in the Humber about 8.30 a.m. on 2nd June the heel of vessel to starboard at no time exceeded $7\frac{1}{2}$ degrees.

[1]   *   *   *   *   *

---

[1] Part omitted here, referring solely to personnel, recommendations, &c., in no way bearing on the course of the action.

REPORT OF WORK DONE AFTER EXPLOSION OF TORPEDO IN
DIESEL ENGINE ROOM, 31ST MAY, 6.54 G.M.T.

During the afternoon enemy vessels were reported, and
great excitement prevailed amongst the ship's company at the
chance of getting a shot at the enemy. Signal was made by
Flag to prepare for immediate action. Shortly after this was
completed, distant firing was heard and signals were coming in
from various ships engaging the enemy.

At 4.15 sounded off action stations. I then ordered the
forward wreckage party and Canteen Assistants to throw overboard all bacon and Canteen gear stowed in the boat-deck
storeroom and the men returned to their stations.

At 6.18 opened fire, I went round the main deck and saw
all the men at their stations. All went smoothly until at 6.54,
ship was struck by a torpedo. I was just stepping out of lower
conning tower door when the torpedo exploded, and it felt
uncomfortably close. I saw the oil fuel come out between angle
iron and the deck, and then it closed up and stopped completely.
No one in the lower conning tower was even slightly damaged,
or in the switchboard room. I got no answer from upper conning
tower for about ½ minute after challenging, and they then
challenged " correct." I then went out of the conning tower
and found thick fumes of oil fuel on the main deck. The lights
were all out in the immediate vicinity of the explosion, and
they came on again about ½ minute after I got up there. I saw
a man come out of the Hydraulic Room, Forrard starboard side,
and I saw the oil fuel on the main deck, and oil fuel in the Diesel
room escape. I ordered the sliding shutters to be closed, also
the vent doors to escapes, and the sliding shutters and ventilating
valves. I ascertained that two men were in Diesel room, but as
trunk was full there was no doubt they were killed by explosion.

I then ordered the Medical Distributing Station to be shored up,
and the 6-in. magazine (this magazine was reported badly dented).

I received a message that " A " boiler room was flooding,
and could not keep the water under. I reported to upper
conning tower and then went down in " A " boiler room myself,
but found the bulkhead on fore end and bunker bulkhead,
starboard side, badly dented and a lot of water coming out of
starboard after bunker door. I found the men in the stokehold
working in splendid style. The water had put out the fires in
the four starboard boilers, and they were stoking four port
boilers with water almost up to their knees as if nothing was
going on. Their coolness and courage is deserving of great praise.

I left the boiler room and went down to 6-in. magazine and
" B " space to see the damage there. I found 6-in. magazine
very slight leakage, but there was a large dent in the side plating.
There was also a slight leak in starboard aft corner of 6-in. shell
room. There was no leakage in " B " space, magazine, or shell
room. Water was gaining in fore medical distributing station,
and I had the deck shored up, which was showing signs of
weakness, and I took the forward medical party and kept the

small hand fire pump going. I then went down to my station, and the report came through that the water in " A " boiler room was under control, and that fires were being primed and topped.

The ship now had a list to starboard of about 8 degrees. The ship was still steaming as fast as possible with " B " and " C " boiler rooms, about 17 knots. At about 8 p.m. I again went round the damage in " A " boiler room, water the starboard side was just up to floor plates. There was a heavy stream coming through between the starboard after bunker door framing and bulkhead. A moderate stream from both ends of electric lead passage, a smaller stream through the Diesel engine exhaust, but the ash expeller was keeping the water under. I then went up on the main deck, starboard side, between 90 and 111 bulkheads, and found oil fuel coming out of the deck and gaining slowly. I could find no puncture anywhere, so assumed the deck was leaking at the angle iron. I then ordered the pump keeping the medical distributing station clear to shift to the main deck and pump out, and to alternate between the two. At about midnight I got up the five-ton portable electric pump from " Y " space, which worked well, and was sufficient to keep the water under in the medical distributing station and the main deck. The glands for the electric leads on the starboard bulkhead of the lower conning tower flat now began to give trouble. I got a small punch and caulked with white lead and yarn. I cut off some leads and carefully screwed on a blank flange, and in cases of leakage between bulkhead and glands shored up with small shores. This enabled two hands to keep the flat dry with buckets. I next opened electricians' workshop (66–78) and found water coming up slowly through the deck, showing compartments below were flooded. I set up the door with shores which had been shaken, and this almost stopped the leakage. There were no signs of water leaking in any other compartments I examined.

At about 1 a.m. I went below to " A " boiler room again, and I consider that the fore and aft starboard bulkhead and starboard forward corner of athwartship bulkhead was gradually coming in, so I ordered the carpenter to put up some more shores on the weakening parts, and I went aft to see the Engineer-Commander and discuss the situation. I told him I considered it unsafe to continue with this high speed. He said he was using fuel entirely from the starboard side; this was not bringing the ship upright, but it prevented the list getting worse. This made me assume that water was gaining on us in other compartments we could not see, and he agreed with me that he did not consider it safe to continue. He also stated he thought the fire of " A " and " B " turrets would probably bring down the shores. If this happened, I did not consider the bulkheads would hold, so I came on the bridge and reported the matter to the Captain. At about 2 a.m. H.M.S. " Fearless " came alongside the ship and took the Vice-Admiral and Staff away. The ship proceeded at 11 knots. I then went round and found that at this speed the flow of water had not increased, and the bulkhead did not get any worse. I reported to the Captain, and speed was gradually increased to 13 knots. I then went aft and discussed the subject of flooding port side aft abreast wing engine room with the Engineer-Commander to bring the ship back to nearly upright, but we came to the conclusion that it would be better to keep the ship with 8 degrees list than to make her heavy, as in the event of being hit with another torpedo she would have plenty of reserve buoyancy, an 8 degrees' list being no danger to the ship. The flooding could be done quickly if necessary to put her on an even keel for gunfire, so I did not submit the question to the Captain to flood the port wings. The electric lead glands were getting worse, but by taking them in hand at once the water was kept from gaining. In the compartments inside the damage I had a hand stationed at all bulkheads to report any increase of water through leaky glands or rivets. About 6 a.m. I took Chief Stoker Bond down to " D " pump, and we tried the 2nd–4th longitudinal as far aft as 78, and it was tight, no water being in the compartment. Abaft 78 it was open to the sea. The starboard bath-rooms were all practically empty. A rivet hole was found on the boundary angle of the war signal station, through which the oil fuel was leaking on to the main deck. This was plugged with a wooden plug, and in about half an hour's time the main deck between 90 and 111 bulkheads, starboard side, began to buckle upwards in large blisters. I shored it down with mess tables and stools.

The bunker plate on the mess deck was also leaking badly, so I shored one of the small collision mats over this and stopped it. At about 11 a.m. the submersible pump (100 tons), supplied for trial, was placed down the starboard aft of " A " boiler room, and started about noon. This pump was of great value and worked very well, and throws a good head of water. It works better under water than pulling and heaving, as it keeps cooler.

The afternoon and early evening passed quietly, then the wind and sea arose. This was a most anxious time, as the ship began to work, and I did not know what might happen. I placed two extra shores inside by the centre of the boilers half way along each boiler. At about 10.45 the carpenter reported water gaining in " A " stokehold. I went down to see what could be done. I found Engr. Lieut.-Commr. Cunninghame down below assisting with the pumps. The working of the ship had disturbed the dirt in the bottom, and the suction of the ash expeller and submersible pump were continually choking. The ejector was tried, but the canvas hose burst, a spare hose was shipped and blew away from the joint. The Engineer-Commander gave orders for three bands to be made to secure the end connection (the ejector was completed at 4.30 a.m.). About 11.30 the submersible was shifted to clear its suction, and in so doing the roll of the ship took it against the shores of the door and knocked them away. This increased the flow of water, as they could not be replaced owing to the depth of water in the boiler room. At midnight the water was still gaining, and was now about 4 ft. below the grating around the tops of the boilers. I considered the situation serious, and reported the matter to the Captain, I also informed him I considered salvage tugs should be asked for, as in the event of "A" boiler room flooding, it was impossible to say where such a large volume of water may find its way, and it was quite possible it might be necessary to stop the engines. I came down from the bridge and got up the diving gear. Stoker Petty Officer Ackerman went down in the diving dress and kept the suctions clear, and at 1 a.m. the water was stopped from rising. At about 4.30 a.m. the steam ejector was repaired and the boiler room was cleared of water well below the floor plates about 5.15, and the situation became in hand.

On arrival in the Humber, Commander Ward came on board to ascertain the damage and what was required. One 6-in. and two 3-in. petrol motor salvage pumps were sent on board in the afternoon, and the tug "Englishman" with a large pump was sent alongside on arrival. During the afternoon a large number of shores and planks were sent off to the ship. Captain Pomeroy of the Liverpool Salvage Association came on board about noon, and his professional advice about shores and stopping leaks was very valuable. He advised about placing additional shores, and what he considered the ship could stand. The ship was brought to an even keel by flooding the wing compartments abreast port wing engine room and pumping more oil over to the port side. The Boatswain's Stores forward, the Paint Store, sand, and all heavy weights from forward were brought aft, and placed on the quarter deck and in the Admiral's lobby. "A" and "B" and 6-in. magazines and shell rooms were cleared into lighters, sheet anchor and cables were landed. Starboard provision and flour rooms were cleared and placed over the port side. There was 2 ins. of water in the flour room, due to leaky electric glands. On Saturday evening, about 6.45, the starboard fore and aft bulkhead in "A" boiler room began to give slightly. More additional shores were then placed, and the bulkhead was made quite safe about midnight Saturday–Sunday. The salvage vessel "Linnet" came alongside at 8 a.m. Sunday, and placed an 8-in. submersible pump in "A" boiler room. Sunday evening the ship was on an even keel, drawing 33 ft. 6 ins. forward and 31 ft. 6 ins. aft. The ship did not proceed to sea on Monday owing to weather. Tuesday ship proceeded to sea and made good 10 knots. Rounding Flamborough Head at noon the ship ran into a heavy swell, which continued until 5 p.m., but no shores gave way, and the ship stood it well.

1　　＊　　　＊　　　＊　　　＊　　　＊

H. SCHOMBERG CURREY,
Commander.

---

1 Part omitted here, referring solely to personnel, recommendations, &c. in no way bearing on the course of the action.

VICE-ADMIRAL'S REPORT, 2nd BATTLE SQUADRON.

Enclosure No. 5 to Submission No. 1415/0022 of 20/6/16 from
C.-in-C. Home Fleets.

No. 149/47 D.

"King George V.,"

SIR,   5th June 1916.

I HAVE the honour to forward herewith a summary of the
events occurring during the recent action, compiled from reports
made by ships of the Second Battle Squadron, accompanied by
plans sent in by " King George V.,"[1] " Erin,"[2] " Orion,"[3]
" Monarch,"[2] and " Thunderer,"[4] and a diary of events before,
during, and after the action, kept on board " King Geogre V."

2. I am unable to supply much detail from personal
observation, as it was impossible to gather any general idea of
the action, only momentary glimpses of the enemy being
obtained.

As leading ship, in addition to the hazy atmosphere, I was
much hampered by what I imagine to have been cordite fumes
from the battle-cruisers after they passed us, and from other
cruisers engaged on the bow; also by funnel gases from small
craft ahead, and, for a considerable time, by dense smoke from
" Duke of Edinburgh," who was unable to draw clear.

3. There is some evidence that submarines were close;
" Duke of Edinburgh " three times made the signal of their
presence, and my Flag Lieutenant-Commander is certain that
he saw the two periscopes of one vessel.

On the other hand, it was obvious to me that a good deal of
" Duke of Edinburgh's " fire was directed not at a submarine
but at the wake of vessels ahead.

The right gunlayer and trainer of " Y " turret in " King
George V. " state that they saw a torpedo break surface
400 yards short of " King George V."

4. I should like to mention specially that about 9 p.m.
I negatived an attack with Whitehead torpedoes ordered by
" Caroline," as I was certain that the vessels seen on our
starboard beam were our own battle-cruisers. The Navigating
Officer of my Flagship, who has just come from the battle-cruiser
fleet, was also certain that they were ours, and saw them
sufficiently clearly to give their approximate course, which I
reported to you.

Shortly afterwards, I told " Caroline " to attack if he was
quite certain they were enemy ships, as he was in a better position

---

[1] Plate 8.

[2] No trace of receipt at Admiralty of plans by " Erin " or " Monarch."

[3] Plate 29.   [4] Plate 30.

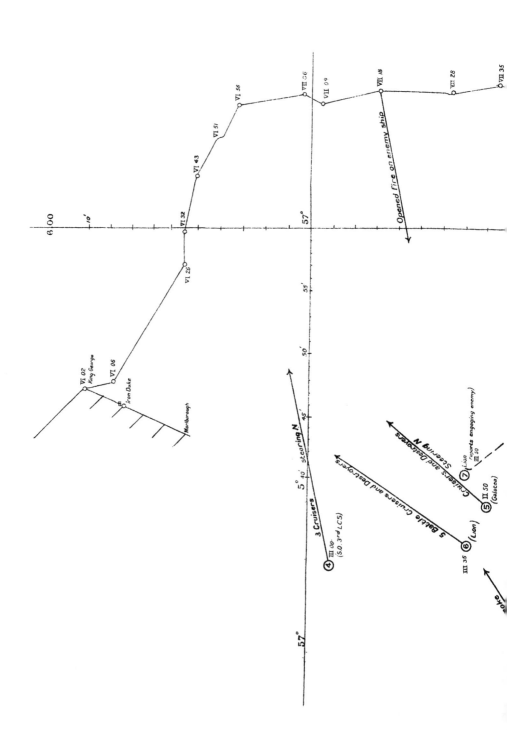

Plate 8

⑧

VII 39
VII 41
VII 47
VII 53
VIII 01
VIII 04

—50′

⑩ VIII 20
(S.O 2ⁿᵈ L C S)
reports snapping cruisers

VIII 16

⑨ IV 45
(Lion)

Sighted enemy Battle Fleet.

VIII 26.

Task of King George V.

⑪ VIII.45
(S.O 3ʳᵈ L C S)

Enemy Battle Cruisers

IX.03.

② II 35
(Galatea)

① II 20
(Galatea)

2 Cruisers Stopped

5 Columns
of Smoke

⑤ III 22
(Nottingham)

Plan showing Track of H.M.S. George V.

VI p.m. to IX p.m. May 3ʳᵈ 1916.

Large circles show cruiser reports of enemy

The VI.02 p.m. position was obtained from observations
of the Sun, and Venus on the meridian at 2.30 p.m.

Scale. 3 Miles = 1 Inch.
(in Lat 57° N)

Malby & Sons, Lith.

10072. 2×266 P4173 ⊕ 5000 12 20

to see them than I was, but I do not know whether an attack was made.

If they were enemy ships and no attack was made, the fault is mine, and not that of " Caroline."

I have the honour to be,
Sir,
Your obedient Servant,
T. H. M. JERRAM,
Vice-Admiral,
Commanding Second Battle Squadron.

The Commander-in-Chief,
H.M. Ships and Vessels,
Grand Fleet.

ACTION OF 31st MAY, 1916.

SUMMARY OF REPORTS FROM SECOND BATTLE SQUADRON.

Time.	Ship Reporting.	Observations.	Remarks.
5.40 p.m.	"King George V."	Observed battle cruisers in action, probably about 30° green.	
6.15 p.m.	" Orion " -	Trained on an enemy cruiser, apparently of " Kolberg " class already on fire aft and stopped, steam escaping from funnels, foremast shot away. Range, 12,400 yards. Did not open fire, as blanked by a ship of 1st Cruiser Squadron.	
6.15 p.m.	" Monarch "	Enemy hidden from us by our battle cruisers. Two four - funnelled British cruisers retiring towards rear end of our battle fleet. One disappeared in a cloud of steam. One surrounded by splashes but appeared to emerge undamaged.	
6.17 p.m.	"Thunderer"	1st Cruiser Squadron under heavy fire, being straddled frequently. They were seen to damage a German cruiser severely, setting her on fire aft. This was thought to be either "Prinz Adalbert " or " Friedrich Karl."	As these vessels are believed to have been sunk some time ago, probably it was "Kolberg"class.

Time.	Ship Reporting	Observations.	Remarks
6.20 p.m.	" Orion "	Observed one of our battle cruisers heavily engaged before starboard beam. Ricochets falling near us.	
6.25 p.m.	"Thunderer"	" Iron Duke " opened fire on damaged cruiser. " Thunderer " also opened fire, followed by " Conqueror."	This was probably same ship of " Kolberg " class referred to previously by " Thunderer " and " Orion."
6.25 p.m.	"Thunderer"	Four enemy ships—" Kaiser " class and battle cruisers—hove in sight. Guns were laid on one of these, but we were masked by " Conqueror " before we could fire. Ranges of 22,000 were obtained in the fore top.	
6.30 p.m. (approx.)	" Erin " -	2nd Battle Squadron's view of enemy obscured by smoke of " Duke of Edinburgh." Enemy's battle fleet must then have turned 16 points, our battle cruiser fleet about this time passing between us and them and being joined by the 3rd Battle Cruiser Squadron.	
6.30 p.m.	" Monarch "	Opened fire on enemy light cruiser of " Kolberg " class stopped. Range, 10,400. Fired three salvoes; first missed right, second missed right, third appeared to straddle.	Probably same ship previously referred to by " Orion " and " Thunderer."
6.31 p.m.	"Conqueror"	Opened fire on " Markgraf " class; rough range, 12,000 yards. This ship quickly disappeared in the haze, and fire was shifted to a three-funnelled cruiser (probably the late " Maravev Amurski," vide Sheet " D," 959—War Vessels); rough range, 10,000 yards.	It seems probable that this also refers to " Kolberg " class vessel under fire from several ships.
6.32 p.m.	" King George V."	Ship bearing S.E. blew up; it is not known what this vessel was, but it was thought to be an enemy light cruiser. Also passed shortly after this " Acasta " badly damaged placing collision mat, and another British de-	One was observed there shortly before heavily on fire, probably " Stettin " class.

Time.	Ship Reporting.	Observations.	Remarks.
6.32 p.m.	" Orion "	stroyer apparently with disabled engines. Sighted ship of " Kaiser " class, 105 green, range, 11,100 yards; fired four salvoes by director, first two short, third over, fourth hit with 13,300 on sights. Large flames observed near enemy's after turret when fourth salvo fell. Enemy then obscured.	R.A. " Orion " personally observed the hits.
6.33 p.m.	" Monarch "	Sighted five battleships, 95 green, three " Königs " and two " Kaisers," range 12,000 yards. Opened fire on leading " König," two salvoes, first right and over, second appeared to straddle quarter deck. These ships disappeared from view, but we fired one salvo at one of " Kaisers," the result not being seen.	
About 6.33 p.m.	" Thunderer "	Two " Kaiser " class (apparently) were now overlapping each other showing between " Iron Duke " and " Royal Oak," and fire was opened through the interval; first salvo was over, second salvo straddled in line with foremast, and two or three large bursts with black smoke were observed (" Thunderer " was using powder filled common). A third salvo was fired with no correction, and a similar result obtained. The enemy was blazing for the whole length of her quarter deck. A.P. shell was then ordered, but " Iron Duke " masked the fire. Enemy was firing rapidly by salvoes at first, but shortly came down to *slowish fire from one turret.*	Apparently same ships as those observed by " Monarch."
6.37 p.m.	" Orion "	" Orion " ceased fire, enemy out of sight.	
6.51 p.m.	" King George V."	" King George V." had to alter course to starboard to avoid collision with 4th Light Cruiser Squadron in the van.	

Time.	Ship Reporting.	Observations.	Remarks.
7.09 p.m.	" Orion "	Sighted ship apparently battle cruiser of " Derfflinger " class, 60° green, accompanied by a large number of destroyers, approaching and then turning on approximately parallel course.	
7.10 p.m. (approx.)	" Ajax "	Fired one salvo which fell short at an enemy battle-cruiser, range 19,000 yards. 4th Light Cruiser Squadron then crossed line of fire and obscured the view.	Probably same ship as observed by " Orion."
7.12 p.m.	" Conqueror "	A destroyer attack developed from starboard beam. Fire was opened at 10,000 yards. Destroyers turned away obscuring themselves with smoke screen.	
7.14 p.m.	" Monarch "	Opened fire at " König " class escorted by destroyers, 76° green. Fired five salvoes, the last two appearing to straddle. Range 17,350–18,450 yards. Enemy commenced zigzagging after third salvo.	
7.15 p.m.	" Orion "	Opened fire on battle cruiser of " Derfflinger " class. Fired six salvoes, the last two straddling. Enemy turned away about the fourth salvo. Range, 19,000 yards.	Same ship as that seen at 7.09 p.m.
7.15 p.m.	" Erin "	A three-funnelled enemy ship was observed to be heavily on fire just abaft the beam.	
7.16 p.m.	" Centurion "	Fire opened on apparently a " Kaiser " class vessel, going very slowly or stopped, and surrounded by destroyers. Range, 17,500 yards. Shots did not hit.	Seems likely to have been same ship as observed by " Monarch " at 7.14 p.m., though one reported as being " König " class, and the other as " Kaiser."
7.17 p.m.	" King George V."	" King George V." opened fire on leading enemy ship. Range on sights, 12,800 yards; salvo fell short. Target was either leading German battleship or " Lützow " class with three	

Time.	Ship Reporting.	Observations.	Remarks.
		destroyers on engaged side making a smoke screen.	
7.17 p.m.	" Monarch "	Ship observed heavily on fire. 95° green.	
7.19 p.m.	" Monarch "	Sighted battle cruiser " Derfflinger " class. 110 green. Range, 16,000 yards. Also battle cruiser (" Seydlitz " or " Moltke ") behind and beyond her. Trained on enemy but director missfired and then ships disappeared in haze.	
7.20 p.m.	" Monarch "	Three enemy destroyers, 95° green (approx.) being fired at by 4th Battle Squadron.	
7.21 p.m.	" Orion " -	Sighted enemy battleship (" Markgraf " or " Kaiser " class). 98° green, on approximately parallel course, apparently the leading ship of a column, as others could be seen astern of her. Range, 14,800 yards. " Orion " then altered course by signal, which prevented fire being opened.	*See* King George V's report at 7.17 p.m.
7.25 p.m.	"Centurion" "Conqueror" " Orion " " Monarch " "Conqueror"	Several ships report destroyers approaching to attack and " Conqueror " opened fire. Range, 11,000 yards. Shortly afterwards one enemy destroyer seen to be floating bottom up.	
7.27 p.m.	" King George V."	" King George V." had to alter course to starboard to avert collision with light craft in the van. " Duke of Edinburgh " much in the way and making a lot of smoke.	
8.20 p.m.	" Erin " -	A sharp action observed on starboard beam between the 3rd Light Cruiser Squadron and some enemy cruisers.	
8.30 p.m.	"King George V." " Monarch "	Saw flashes of enemy guns on starboard bow and flashes from our battle cruisers ahead.	
8.40 p.m. (approx.)	" Monarch "	" Calliope " hit, 1,000 yards on starboard beam.	
9.00 p.m.	"King George V."	Sighted British battle cruisers W.N.W. steering S.W.	
9.07 p.m.	" King George V."	" Caroline " made signal " Attack with Whitehead	

Time.	Ship Reporting.	Observations.	Remarks.
		torpedoes " V.A. II. B.S. made, " Negative attack, those ships are our battle cruisers." " Caroline " then made, " These appear to be enemy ships." V.A. II. B.S. replied, " If you are quite sure attack. " Caroline " was about six points on starboard bow, about 1–2 miles distant, but was not seen to attack.	
9.15 p.m.	" King George V."	Heavy firing on starboard quarter.	
9.20 p.m. (very approx.)	" King George V."	Saw a white fire ball, very brilliant, 110 green.	
9.30 p.m.	" Erin " -	Firing seen astern and one German three - funnelled vessel was seen to be on fire fore and aft.	
10.30 p.m. (approx.)	" Thunderer "	An enemy cruiser challenged three times, switching on and off four red lights horizontal above four green horizontal. Fire was not opened as it was considered inadvisable to show up battle fleet unless obvious attack was intended. Our destroyers shortly after attacked this cruiser and a hot engagement followed. She was seen to be hit many times ; she eventually turned to port.	
10.30 p.m.	" Boadicea "	After taking up night station astern of " Thunderer," a large cruiser challenged with four red lights horizontal, and four green horizontal immediately afterwards. After challenging she sheered off to starboard.	Same ship as reported by " Thunderer."
10.50 p.m.	" Boadicea "	Two or three enemy cruisers engaged a ship about 4,000 yards astern. A fire started on our ship, and a hit or explosion was seen on enemy cruiser. This action lasted about 4 minutes.	
1st June. 4.00 a.m.	" King George V."	Sighted Zeppelin about 80° green. " Thunderer " fired one salvo.	

Time.	Ship Reporting.	Observations.	Remarks.
7.00 a.m.	"King George V."	Passed wreckage of foreign origin, apparently a number of large German cordite cases.	
8.45 a.m.	"King George V."	Passed wreckage and dead bodies, undoubtedly British.	

GENERAL REMARKS.

"Ajax" - - It appeared that each enemy ship was accompanied by a destroyer which emitted dense volumes of smoke with the idea of obscuring the target.

"Centurion" - Submarines were reported on several occasions, and Lieutenant Peet has no doubt that he sighted a submarine with double periscope at 7.40 p.m., bearing 60° green, 2,000 yards.

"Orion" - Firing was by director, which was invaluable.

"Thunderer" Just before opening fire there was a very large explosion on starboard quarter, apparently beyond Fifth Battle Squadron; a column of water and debris was thrown up.

No enemy shots fell nearer than 400 yards (short).

Objects came into view and disappeared again in about 3 minutes, a quick R.F. reading, used immediately, was the only practicable method. Most of the ranges taken were about 11,000 yards, but for a short period ranges 22,000 to 18,000 were obtained in the fore top.

Powder filled common excellent to commence with, i.e., till straddling is well established, the bursts being easy to distinguish.

NOTES MADE ON BOARD "KING GEORGE V."

Battle-fleet was in divisions in line ahead columns disposed abeam to starboard, 8 cables apart, steering S. 50 E.

31st May, p.m.

(1) 2.24. Signal received form "Galatea" 2 cruisers probably hostile, in sight (56 — 48 N., 5 — 26 E.), bearing E.S.E. stopped, later report course of enemy S.S.E. chased at 2.38 p.m. (1420 and 1422.)

31st May, p.m.

(2)	2.40.	" Galatea " reported a large quantity of smoke bearing E.N.E. (56.50 N., 5.27 E.). Speed of fleet, 17 knots. (1435.)
	2.45.	Guides of columns ordered to bear N.E. by N.
	2.52.	18 knots.
(3)	3.00.	Altered course, leaders together, to S.E. by S.
		" Galatea " reported smoke appeared to be from 7 vessels—Destroyers and cruisers steering North 56.52 N., 5.38 E. (1450.)
(4)	3.07.	S.O. 3rd L.C.S. reported 3 cruisers bearing E. steering N. 56,—59 N., 5.33 E. (1500.)
	3.08.	Cruisers took up cruising disposition No. 1.
	3.13.	S.O. 1st L.C.S. reported enemy altered course to N.W. Columns opened to 1°. (1507.)
	3.17.	19 knots.
(5)	3.25.	" Nottingham " reported sighting 5 columns of smoke bearing E.N.E., 56.46 N., 5.20 E. (1522.)
(6)	3.40.	S.O. B.C.F. reported 5 Battle Cruisers and large number of destroyers bearing N.E., 56.53 N., 5.35 E. Course of enemy, S.E. (1535.)
	3.50.	S.O. B.C.F. reported course of enemy S. 55 E.
	3.55.	20 knots.
(7)	3.57.	S.O. B.C.F. reported that he was engaging the enemy (56.53 N., 5.40 E.); it was later ascertained that 5th B.S. were also engaging the enemy. (1550.)
(8)	4.40.	S.O. 2nd L.C.S. reported having sighted enemy battle-fleet bearing S.E. course North, 56.34 N., 6.26 E. (1636.)
	4.46.	Enemy Battle-fleet course reported to be E.N.E (Single line ahead.) (1630.)
	4.55.	Enemy battle fleet course reported to be North.
(9)	5.16.	S.O. B.C.F. reported sighting enemy's battle fleet bearing S.E. (56.36 N., 6.9 E.) (1645.)
	5.40.	Observed cruisers in action.
	5.45.	2nd L.C.S. reported enemy's battle fleet altered course N.N.W. (1740.)
	5.54.	2nd L.C.S. reported enemy's battle fleet altered course N. (1750.)
	6.02.	Altered course leaders together, remainder in succession to South, 19 knots.
	6.06.	Altered course leaders together rest in succession to S.E.
	6.13.	Equal speed S.E. by E.
	6.20.	Reduced to 14 knots.
	6.26.	Altered course to port.
	6.32.	Increased to 17 knots, battleships in rear opened fire.

31st May, p.m.

6.32. Ship bearing S.E. blew up; it is not known what this vessel was, but it was thought to be an enemy light cruiser; also passed shortly after this " Acasta " badly damaged, placing collision mat, and another destroyer apparently with disabled engines.

One of our four-funnelled cruisers observed to be heavily hit.

6.51. " King George V." had to alter course to starboard to avoid collision with 4th L.C.S. in the van.

6.56. Altered course to South. This was done just previous to a signal being made.

7.02. " Marlborough " reported being hit by a torpedo. Altered course 3 points to starboard.

7.09. Course South.

7.12. 2nd B.S. ordered to take station ahead.

7.17. " King George V." opened fire on leading enemy ship; range on sights 12,800 yards, salvo fell short. Remainder of 2nd B.S. had opened fire shortly before. Target ship was either leading German battleship or " Lützow " class battle cruiser with three destroyers on engaged side making a heavy smoke screen.

7.20. Altered course 4 points to port together by signal.

7.22. Target obscured by smoke screen and haze; ceased fire.

7.27. " King George V." had to alter course to starboard to avert collision with light craft in the van. " Duke of Edinburgh " much in the way and making a lot of smoke.

7.42. Formed single line ahead on " Iron Duke."

(10) 8.26. 2nd L.C.S. reported they were engaging enemy cruisers, 56.47 N., 5.56 E.   (2020.)

11) 8.52. 3rd L.C.S. reported Battle Cruisers probably hostile bearing N. steering W.S.W., 56.42 N., 5.41 E. (2045.)

8.56. " Warrior " reported both engines disabled and in tow of " Engadine," 56.10 N., 5.50 E.   (2103.)

9.03. Course South.

9.03. 2nd L.C.S. reported being attacked by enemy destroyers from the West; these were driven off to N.W. (2055.)

9.07. " Caroline " made signal " Attack with Whitehead torpedoes." V.A. II made " Negative attack, these ships are our battle cruisers." " Caroline " then made " These appear to be enemy ships." V.A. II replied " If you are quite sure, attack." " Caroline " was about six points on the starboard

31st May, p.m.

> bow, about 1–2 miles distant, but was not seen to attack.

9.11.   Sighted our battle cruisers bearing W.N.W. steering S.W.

9.30.   Assumed second organisation, divisions in line ahead, course South, columns 1 mile apart, destroyers astern of battle fleet 5 miles.

10.45. Eleventh flotilla reported having been engaged with enemy cruisers. (2240.)

11.36. " Birmingham " reported battle cruisers, probably hostile, bearing N.E. steering South, 56.26 N., 5.46 E.

11.40. 2nd L.C.S. reported engaged with enemy cruisers, 10.15 p.m. (2240.)

June, a.m.

3.47.   3rd L.C.S. reported engaging Zeppelin (0335.)

3.57.   Battle fleet opened fire on Zeppelin.

4.30.   " Dublin " reported one cruiser and two destroyers, probably hostile, bearing East, course South. (0430.)

4.47.   Ordered to look out for " Lützow," damaged (ahead).

8.55.   " Castor " and eleventh flotilla joined up.

9. 0.   Informed C.-in-C. we had passed wreckage of foreign origin at 7 a.m. and of obviously English origin at 8.45 a.m.

VICE-ADMIRAL'S REPORTS, 4TH BATTLE SQUADRON.

Enclosure No. 6 to Submission No. 1415/0022 of 20/6/16 from C.-in-C. Home Fleets.

From : The Vice-Admiral Commanding, Fourth Battle Squadron, H.M.S. " Benbow."

To : The Commander-in-Chief, Grand Fleet, H.M.S. " Iron Duke."

Date : 4th June 1916.

No. : 0131.

The attached summary of the reports from the Fourth Battle Squadron on the action of the 31st May is submitted in continuation of the rough personal reports already forwarded.

A more detailed report will be submitted separately.

F. C. D. STURDEE,

Vice-Admiral.

ACTION ON 31ST MAY.—SUMMARY OF REPORTS FROM SHIPS OF FOURTH BATTLE SQUADRON.

Time.	" Benbow."	" Canada."	" Bellerophon."	" Temeraire."	" Vanguard."
P.M. 5.55	—	—	—	—	Ship on bow flashed I A R.
6.10	—	—	—	—	British Armoured Cruiser blew up.
6.14	Range of enemy's ship in damaged condition, 13,000–14,000	—	—	—	—
6.15	—	—	Sighted some grey misty objects.	—	—
6.20	—	—	—	—	British Armoured Cruiser blew up.
6.22	—	Two salvoes at German ship which had suffered heavily.	British Armoured Cruiser blew up. —	—	—
6.25	—	—	Opened fire. Control Officer given free hand. Impossible to count enemy	—	—
6.28	Director on German ship, " Lützow " class, 16,000 yards.	—	—	—	—

Time.	" Benbow."	" Canada."	" Bellerophon."	" Temeraire."	" Vanguard."
P.M.					
6.30	Opened fire. Shots lost in haze.	—	—	—	—
6.32	—	—	—	—	Opened fire at 3-funnelled cruiser (?) " Freya," 11,000. Hit fourth salvo.
6.34	—	—	—	Opened fire on Cruiser. Hit third salvo.	—
6.35	Fired again with A and B turrets.	—	—	—	German cruiser (?) " Freya " stopped, disabled.
6.38	Fired again with A and B. Target then obscured by ship on fire drifting between ship and enemy.	—	—	—	—
6.40	Fire again opened, 12,500 Target crossed after second salvo. Mist then obscured.	—	Checked fire. No enemy in sight.	—	—
6.45	—	—	—	—	Checked fire. (?) " Freya " out of sight.
6.48	Observed enemy turn away.	—	—	—	—
7.0	—	—	—	—	German Battle Cruiser " Lützow " on fire.
7.9	Fired at T.B.D.'s. (6-in)	—	A. Turret and 4-in. at Destroyers. Hit.	—	—
7.11	German T.B.D. on fire.	—	—	—	—
7.15	—	Engaged T.B.D.'s. before beam.	—	—	—
7.17	Opened fire A. and B. ? " Lützow."	—	Opened fire at Battle Cruiser, 11,000. Straddled.	Opened fire at enemy Battle Cruiser 12,000, 7 salvoes.	—
7.19	Opened with all turrets.	—	—	—	—
7.20	—	Four salvoes at Battleship or Battle Cruiser.	—	—	Fired a few 12-in. at torpedo craft.

Time.	" Benbow."	" Canada."	" Bellerophon."	" Temeraire."	" Vanguard."
P.M.					
7.20	Hit seen on German Battle Cruiser. Mean R.F. range same as on sights at this salvo.	—	—	—	—
7.25	—	Engaged destroyers with 6-in.	—	—	Few salvoes at T.B.D.'s.
7.28	Ceased fire. Smoke screen	—	—	—	—
7.30	—	Three salvoes of 14-in on T.B.D. Hit.	—	—	Fired at Enemy Light Cruiser, Disabled.
?	—	—	—	4-in. on T. B. D.'s. also two 12-in. salvoes.	—
7.32	German T.B.D. sunk.	—	—	—	—
7.34	German T.B.D. sunk. German T.B.D. observed to capsize.	—	—	—	—
7.35	6-in. on T.B.D.'s. Enemy's Battle Cruiser reported still afloat. Two funnels and two masts showing above water.	—	—	—	—
8.57	One salvo, 6-in. at T.B.D.	—	—	—	—
10.35	—	—	—	Destroyer Leader glow from shell bursts.	Destroyer Leader disappeared or sunk.

Enclosure No. 7 to Submission No. 1415/0022 of 20/6/16 from C.-in-C. Home Fleets.

No. 0131.   " Benbow,"

SIR,   5th June 1916.

I HAVE the honour to report that, in the battle of 31st May 1916, off the Jutland Coast the Fourth Battle Squadron was in the centre of the Battle Line with the " Blanche " acting as repeating ship on the off side.

The " Emperor of India " and " Dreadnought " were not present, being away refitting.

The Flag of Rear-Admiral Alexander L. Duff, C.B., was hoisted in the " Superb."

2. The ships under my direct command were the " Benbow," " Bellerophon," " Temeraire," and " Vanguard," they formed the Fourth Division of the Battle Fleet, with the " Benbow " leading.

The " Superb " and " Canada " were in the Third Division under the immediate command of the Commander-in-Chief who led that Division in the Fleet Flagship " Iron Duke."

3. The Fourth Division being placed in the centre of the Fleet conformed generally to the movements ordered by the Commander-in-Chief.

4. On one occasion only was any separate action necessary, when at 7.10 p.m. a Destroyer attack was observed. The Fourth Division were then ordered to turn away by Sub-Divisions two points in succession in conformity with the Grand Fleet Battle Orders.

The attack was soon repelled by the gun fire of the ships, and the Division ordered to turn back to the course of the Fleet forming astern of the Third Division.

5. At 8.31. p.m., the track of a torpedo was seen passing ahead. " Benbow " turned towards it. It is believed that the torpedo passed ahead of " Iron Duke."

6. The attached summary shows the principal points noted by the four ships of the Fourth Division.

7. Our ships were not seriously under fire, but, considering the youth of the ships' companies and the fact that it was their first time under fire, it is most satisfactory to be able to report on the keenness and cool behaviour of the Officers and men of all the ships. No apprehension was shown.

8. The general gunnery efficiency seemed to be good, and no breakdowns were reported.

The conditions of light and haze did not give the ships much opportunity for using their guns and the restraint from firing when the enemy was hidden by haze reflects credit on the control.

The rapid manner in which the Destroyers were made to turn away promptly showed good control and effective fire.

9. None of the ships were struck nor were there any casualties.

10. The visibility was low and variable, the maximum range obtained being 13,500 yards, which was recorded in " Benbow " at 6.14 p.m., as the range of an enemy capital ship.

The average range obtainable was about 11,000 yards.

11. Owing to the haze and low visibility the targets were few and consisted of a Light Cruiser at moderate range, a Battle Cruiser at longer range and Destroyers approaching to attack.

12. Firing commenced on an enemy's Battle Cruiser at 6.30 p.m., and due to the varying visibility, was intermittent up to 7.28 p.m., when the enemy retired behind a smoke screen.

At 7.18 p.m., a big fire was observed in this ship.

13. There was considerable difficulty in distinguishing friend from foe owing to these large Fleets meeting in varying visibility.

14. The following ammunition was expended from the main armament :—

"Benbow"   - 40 rounds   "Vanguard"   - 80 rounds
"Bellerophon"   62 rounds   "Temeraire" - 72 rounds

15. Rear-Admiral Duff's report is attached.

I have the honour to be,
Sir,
Your obedient Servant,
F. C. D. STURDEE,
Vice-Admiral.

The Commander-in-Chief,
H.M. Ships and Vessels,
Grand Fleet.

REAR-ADMIRAL'S REPORT, 4TH BATTLE SQUADRON.

From—The Rear-Admiral Fourth Battle Squadron.

To—The Vice Admiral Commanding Fourth Battle Squadron.

Date—4th June 1916.   *No.*—017.

Submitted. The enclosed report was written before arriving in harbour on June 2nd. It was not sent in at the time as not being in command of a Division the report of the Captain of "Superb" would practically cover all the points coming under my observation.

A. L. DUFF,
Rear-Admiral.

Report on action of 31st May 1916.

No. 017.

"Superb,"
SIR,   1st June 1916.

IN accordance with your signal 1835 of 1st instant, I have the honour to make the following report.

2. Owing to weather conditions under which the action was fought, and knowing little of the general situation preceding the arrival of the Battle Fleet on the scene of action, or, in fact, at any time, necessarily limits the scope of my remarks to what I actually saw take place.

3. The main features of the action appeared to be :—

(*a*) The low visibility;

(*b*) The difficulty of distinguishing between friend and foe, owing to the weather conditions. This was accentuated through ignorance of the disposition of the Rosyth force, already in action, presumably with the enemy Battle Cruisers but possibly with his Battle Fleet as well;

(c) The Cruiser line being caught under a heavy fire before being able to take up their Battle station on the flanks of the Battle Fleet.

4. The scene immediately before and during deployment of the Battle Fleet was an interesting one. To the right, in the haze, our Battle Cruisers could be distinguished hotly engaged, but with what portion of the enemy's forces could not be seen. In front, and between us and the enemy whose position was only denoted by the flash of his guns, were our Cruisers endeavouring to take up their after-deployment station on the flanks under a heavy fire.

A Cruiser of the " Minotaur " class was observed to be badly damaged and I was informed that she was observed to blow up. Another of the " Warrior " class was being literally smothered in salvoes; and a Light Cruiser, after being hidden from view by columns of water, seemed to have disappeared.

5. At 6.14 p.m. (G.M.T.) the Fleet was deployed by " equal speed pendant " to S.E. by E., and line of battle was formed with the Second Battle Squadron leading. At 6.45, the firing appeared to be general in our Battle Fleet.

6. During the engagement, the Third Sub-division was never under fire of the enemy and the few shots that fell in our vicinity were either ricochets or " overs." Only two ships of the enemy were seen with sufficient distinctness to enable fire to be opened on them. These ships I believe to have been the " Derfflinger " and a Cruiser of the " Prinz Heinrich " type. Identification was an extraordinarily difficult matter, but I am fairly sure that neither were Battleships, and that the only indication I saw of the enemy line of battle was from smoke and the flash of guns.

7. The ship believed to be a Cruiser of the " Prinz Heinrich " type came under a very heavy fire and was apparently disabled and her guns silenced. The " Derfflinger " at first was firing from four turrets, but latterly it seemed from only one. A fire was seen to break out aft. I thought it was followed by an explosion.

8. *Visibility.*—At the time the signal for deployment was made (6.14 p.m.—G.M.T.) I estimated the visibility at about 5 to 6 miles. By 6.45 p.m. it had somewhat decreased and the light was becoming bad. From then on, the visibility varied, but was not, I think, ever more than 12,000 yards. The direction of the wind was S.W. by S.—Light.

9. *Destroyer Attack.*—At 7.10 p.m., the course of the Fleet being South, enemy Destroyers were observed approximately abeam, attempting under cover of a smoke screen to deliver an attack on the centre and rear of the Fleet. The attack was neither made with dash nor was it pressed home, whether on

account of the fire from the 6-in. guns of our ships or the threat of a counter-attack from our Light Cruisers, I do not know. The Destroyers, however, before they retired, were well within long-range distance, and possibly the attack might have proved effective, had the Fleet not been turned away by the " Preparative."

10. The weather conditions were very favourable to Torpedo attack, and it is an interesting fact that the enemy made so little effective use of this weapon against our Battle Line. Possibly he was reserving his Destroyers in the hope of making more effective use of them after dark.

11. As the result of turning away, touch was lost with the enemy Battle Fleet and was not regained before darkness necessitated drawing the Fleet off for the night.

12. Of the enemy's Battle formation and movements, I was unable to form any definite idea.

13. The enemy had much to be thankful for to the weather conditions, which, it seems to me, alone saved him from being cut off from his base, and denied the British Fleet the satisfaction of fighting a decisive battle.

14. The steaming of the " Superb " during the afternoon of the 31st was highly satisfactory, and reflects great credit on the Engine Room Department.

15. The incidents as affecting the " Superb " are dealt with in the report of her Commanding Officer.

I have the honour to be,
Sir,
Your obedient Servant,
A. L. DUFF,
Rear-Admiral.

The Vice-Admiral Commanding,
Fourth Battle Squadron.

Enclosure No. 8 to Submission No. 1415/0022 of 20/6/16 from
C.-in-C. Home Fleets.

CAPTAIN'S REPORT, H.M.S. " BENBOW."

No. C. 85.

H.M.S. " Benbow,"
SIR, 8th June 1916.
I HAVE the honour to forward the following report on the action with the German High Sea Fleet on 31st May 1916, and a simple narrative of events as they appeared from the Control Officer's point of view in the Gun Control Tower. * * *1

(1) Very great difficulty was experienced in getting the Director on to the target, and fire could not be opened as soon as it ought to have been, the enemy could be seen from the Gun Control Tower and Conning Tower when using Zeiss Glasses, but not from the Gun Telescope on the bearing plate.

1 See note on page 381.

*   *   *   *   *1

At 6.38 nearly all turret Officers thought that we opened fire on the enemy cruiser drifting down between the lines, whereas we were firing at one of the " Kaiser " class beyond her.

*   *   *   *   *2

Attached also are some extracts from reports of officers from their several positions.

I have the honour to be,
Sir,
Your obedient Servant,
H. W. PARKER,
Captain.

The Vice Admiral Commanding
  Fourth Battle Squadron.

II.

No. 94.

COMMANDER IN CHIEF,

SUBMITTED in continuation of former reports.

F. C. D. STURDEE,

10th June 1916.   Vice-Admiral.

EXTRACTS FROM OFFICERS' REPORTS.
H.M.S. " BENBOW."

Spotting Officer in the Top.—The difficulties of spotting on this occasion were very great.

With the mist varying in intensity, enemy ships coming into sight for a few seconds and then disappearing, I found it extremely hard to be certain that I was spotting on to the same ship as that indicated (through the voice pipe) by the Control Officer.

The difficulty of being certain that one was spotting on to the ship fired at was even more marked.

For some seconds after each salvo my vision was blanked by smoke, my glasses shaken off the object, and owing to the short range and consequent short time of flight in which to recover (to say nothing of the fact that between the moment of firing and the fall of shot there was often a small change of helm) it was practically impossible to be certain that one was spotting on the ship fired at.

The position was galling and trying to the last degree; but I had no alternative on more than one occasion but to inform the Control Officer that I could not observe the fall of shot (this being probably due to my spotting on the wrong ship).

---

[1] *See* note on p. 381.

[2] Part omitted here, referring solely to personnel, recommendations, &c., in no way bearing on the course of the action.

*   *   *   *   *[1]

2. *Director Layer.*—Little difficulty was experienced due to smoke from our own guns, but great difficulty due to the short range of visibility.

Great difficulty was experienced in getting on to the object at which the Control Officer wished to fire, due to the distance of the Control Officer from Director Tower.

When aloft, the Control Officer has the same condition of light as Director Layer, when below, either may see the object, whereas the other may not be able to do so.

(3) *Spotting.*—Was extremely difficult owing to the poor visibility. It was useless attempting to use the high power glasses, and with binoculars it was not easy to get on the correct bearing.

(4) *Respirators.*—The respirators supplied are unsuitable. The small ones are easily displaced, and the " sausage " ones are awkward and frail. Two came to pieces during handling in the T.S.

(5) It was particularly noticed with regard to the enemy's salvoes that in all cases one projectile fell well to the left (our left) of the remainder, and that whereas the single shell invariably exploded on striking the water, the remainder did not.

REPORT OF ENGAGEMENT WITH THE GERMAN HIGH SEA FLEET ON 31st MAY 1916.

NARRATIVE OF EVENTS FROM A GUNNERY POINT OF VIEW.

Wednesday.

G.M.T.

P.M.

5.59. Observed Battle Cruisers engaged on Starboard Bow. Observed flashes of enemy's guns.

6. 4. Sighted enemy ships right ahead.

6.14. Obtained ranges of an enemy ship with 3 funnels (13,000–14,000 yards) bearing Green 60, apparently in a damaged condition. Probably " Helgoland " Class. Trained guns on, but did not fire.

6.26. " Iron Duke " opened fire.

6.29. After great difficulty owing to the haze and smoke, succeeded in getting Director on to a German ship; apparently of the " Kaiser " class, obtaining two ranges from " X " turret, mean of 16,000 yards.

6.30. Opened fire with " A " and " B " turrets, Green 73. Shots lost in haze.

---

[1] *See* note on p. 381.

G.M.T.
P.M.

6.35. Fired again with " A " and " B " turrets. Object obscured by haze.

6.36. " A " and " B " turrets fired.

6.38. " A " and " B " turrets fired, object was then obscured by smoke from an enemy ship on fire drifting down between " Benbow " and the enemy. This ship was apparently an enemy cruiser with three or four funnels.
    Several of " Benbow's " rangefinders were apparently taking ranges of this ship instead of the ship actually fired at.

6.40. Fire was again opened with " A " and " B " turrets, at a range of 12,500 yards, the target was crossed after the second salvo, and the order " Control " was given by the Control Officer. The Cease Fire Gong was then rung, mist and smoke obscuring the target.

6.48. The enemy were observed turning away to Starboard.

6.54. Ship turned to Southward.

7. 2. Passed wreck of " Invincible."

7. 9. 6-in. opened fire on Destroyers bearing Green 56, at 8,000 yards. *   *   *1

7.11. One destroyer observed to be on fire.

7.17. Opened fire with " A " and " B " turrets on enemy ship, " Lützow " class, Green 132 (about).

7.19. Spotted down   *   *   *1 and opened fire with all turrets.

7.20. Hit observed near after turret by several observers.

    *   *   *   *   *1

7.28. Ceased fire. Enemy destroyers making smoke screen. 6-in. ceased fire about this time.

7.32. German destroyer observed to sink.

7.34. German destroyer making smoke observed to sink.

7.34. German destroyer observed to capsize.

7.35. 6-in. opened fire on two lots of Destroyers. Enemy Battle Cruiser reported to be still afloat, 2 masts and 2 funnels showing above water.

7.47. Trembling shock felt in T.S.

7.49. Collected reports of rounds fired :—

" A " turret	-	12
" B "	,,	-	12
" Q "	,,	-	4
" X "	,,	-	5
" Y "	,,	-	5

        Total rounds fired   38

7.57. Turrets, stand easy.

8.24. Heavy firing heard right ahead.

---

1 *See* note on p. 381.

G.M.T.

P.M.

8.27. Altered course 4 points to Port.

Top reported track of torpedo right ahead, crossing " Iron Duke's " bows.

8.34. Course S.W. by S.

8.57. 6-in. firing on destroyers, one salvo (short).

9. 2. Altered course 4 points to Port.

9.14. Observed star shell on starboard bow.

Thursday.

Observed Zeppelin on Port quarter passing astern P. or S.

Opened fire with " Y " turret, 1 round.

    ,,   ,,   6-in., 1 round.

VICE-ADMIRAL'S REPORT, BATTLE CRUISER FLEET.

Enclosure No. 9 to Submission No. 1415/0022 of 20/6/16 from C.-in-C. Home Fleets.

B.C.F. 01.   " Lion,"

SIR,   12th June 1916.

I HAVE the honour to report that at 2.37 p.m. on 31st May 1916, being in Lat. 56.47 N., Long. 4.59 E., I altered course to the Northward to join the Commander-in-Chief, in accordance with previous orders.

2. The force under my command was as follows :—

" Lion " (Captain A. E. M. Chatfield, C.V.O.) flying my flag, " Princess Royal " (Captain W. H. Cowan, M.V.O., D.S.O.) flying the Flag of Rear-Admiral O. de B. Brock, C.B., " Tiger " (Captain H. B. Pelly, M.V.O.), " Queen Mary " (Captain C. I. Prowse), " New Zealand " (Captain J. F. E. Green) flying the Flag of Rear-Admiral W. C. Pakenham, C.B., M.V.O., " Indefatigable " (Captain C. F. Sowerby), " Southampton," flying the Broad Pennant of Commodore W. E. Goodenough, M.V.O., " Nottingham " (Captain C. B. Miller), " Birmingham " (Captain A. A. M. Duff), " Dublin " (Captain A. C. Scott), " Galatea," flying the Broad Pennant of Commodore E. S. Alexander Sinclair, M.V.O., " Inconstant " (Captain B. S. Thesiger, C.M.G.), " Phaeton " (Captain J. E. Cameron, M.V.O.), " Cordelia " (Captain T. P. H. Beamish), " Falmouth " (Captain J. D. Edwards), flying the Flag of Rear-Admiral T. D. W. Napier, M.V.O., " Birkenhead " (Captain E. Reeves), " Gloucester " (Captain W. F. Blunt, D.S.O.), " Yarmouth " (Captain T. D. Pratt), " Champion " (Captain J. U. Farie, Captain D, 13th Destroyer Flotilla), with Destroyers " Nestor " (Commander Hon. E. B. S. Bingham), " Nomad " (Lieut.-Commander P. Whitfield), " Narborough " (Lieut.-Commander G. Corlett),

" Obdurate " (Lieut.-Commander C. H. Sams), " Petard " (Lieut.-
Commander E. D. O. Thomson), " Pelican " (Lieut.-Commander
K. A. Beattie), " Nerissa " (Lieut.-Commander M. C. B. Legge),
" Onslow " (Lieut.-Commander J. C. Tovey), " Moresby " (Lieut.-
Commander R. V. Alison), " Nicator " (Lieut. in Command
J. E. A. Mocatta), " Fearless " (Captain C. D. Roper, Captain D,
1st Destroyer Flotilla), with Destroyers " Acheron "　(Com-
mader C. G. Ramsey), " Ariel " (Lieut.-Commander A. G. Tippet),
" Attack " (Lieut.-Commander C. H. N. James), " Hydra "
Lieut. F. G. Glossop), " Badger " (Commander C. A. Fremantle),
" Goshawk " (Commander G. H. Knowles), " Defender " (Lieut.-
Commander L. R. Palmer), " Lizard " (Lieut.-Commander
E. Brooke), " Lapwing " (Lieut. H. W. D. Griffith), Destroyers
from the Harwich force temporarily attached to my command,
" Lydiard " (Commander M. L. Goldsmith), " Liberty " (Lieut.-
Commander P. W. S. King), " Landrail " (Lieut.-Commander
F. E. H. G. Hobart), " Laurel " (Lieut. H. D. Stanistreet),
" Moorsom " (Commander J. C. Hodgson), " Morris " (Lieut.-
Commander E. S. Graham), " Turbulent " (Lieut.-Commander
J. L. C. Clark), " Termagant " (Lieut.-Commander C. P. Blake),
and Seaplane Carrier " Engadine " (Lieut.-Commander C. G.
Robinson).

The Battle Cruiser Fleet was accompanied by four ships
of the 5th Battle Squadron under the command of Rear-Admiral
H. Evan-Thomas, M.V.O., flying his Flag in " Barham " (Captain
A. W. Craig). The other three ships were " Warspite " (Captain
E. M. Phillpotts), " Valiant " (Captain M. Woollcombe), and
" Malaya " (Captain Hon. A. D. E. H. Boyle, C.B.).

3. The force was disposed as follows : 5th Battle Squadron
N.N.W. 5 miles from " Lion," screened by " Fearless " and 9
Destroyers of 1st Flotilla. The 2nd Battle Cruiser Squadron was
stationed E.N.E. 3 miles from " Lion," screened by 6 Destroyers
of the Harwich Force. " Lion " and 1st Battle Cruiser Squadron
were screened by " Champion," 10 Destroyers of 13th Flotilla,
" Turbulent " and " Termagant." Squadrons were in single
line ahead, steering N. b E. Light Cruisers were in L.S. 6,
centre of screen bearing S.S.E., line of direction of screen E.N.E.
and W.S.W., " Engadine " was stationed between B and C.

4. At 2.20 p.m. reports were received from " Galatea "
indicating the presence of enemy vessels to the E.S.E., steering
to the Northward. The direction of advance was immediately
altered to S.S.E., the course for Horn Reef, so as to place my
force between the enemy and his base. " Galatea " reported at
2.35 p.m. that she had sighted a large amount of smoke as from
a fleet, bearing E.N.E. This made it clear that the enemy was
to the Northward and Eastward, and that it would be impossible
for him to round the Horn Reef without being brought to action.
Course was accordingly altered to the Eastward and North-Eastward, the enemy being sighted at 3.31 p.m. They appeared to
be the 1st Scouting group of five Battle Cruisers.

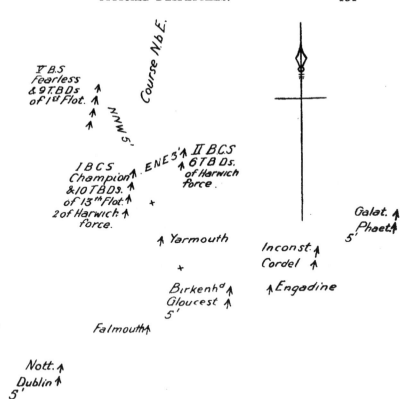

5. After the first report of the enemy the 1st and 3rd Light Cruiser Squadrons changed their direction and without waiting for orders spread to the East, thereby forming a screen in advance of the Battle Cruiser Squadrons and 5th Battle Squadron by the time we had hauled up to the course of approach. They engaged enemy Light Cruisers at long range. In the meantime the 2nd Light Cruiser Squadron had come in at high speed and was able to take station ahead of the Battle Cruisers by the time we turned to E.S.E., the course on which we first engaged the enemy. In this respect the work of the Light Cruiser Squadrons was excellent and of great value.

6. From a report from " Galatea " at 2.25 p.m. it was evident that the enemy force was considerable and not merely an isolated unit of Light Cruisers, so at 2.45 p.m. I ordered " Engadine " to send up a seaplane and scout to N.N.E. This order was carried out very quickly, and by 3.8 p.m. a seaplane with Flight-Lieutenant F. J. Rutland, R.N., as Pilot, and Asst. Paymaster G. S. Trewin, R.N., as Observer, was well under way; her first reports of the enemy were received in " Engadine " about 3.30 p.m. Owing to clouds it was necessary to fly very low, and in order to identify 4 enemy Light Cruisers the Seaplane

had to fly at a height of 900 ft. within 3,000 yards of them, the Light Cruisers opening fire on her with every gun that would bear. This in no way interfered with the clarity of their reports and both Flight-Lieutenant Rutland and Asst. Paymaster Trewin are to be congratulated on their achievement, which indicates that seaplanes under such circumstances are of distinct value.

7. At 3.30 p.m. I increased speed to 25 knots and formed Line of Battle, the 2nd Battle Cruiser Squadron forming astern of the 1st Battle Cruiser Squadron, with Destroyers of the 13th and 9th Flotillas taking station ahead. I turned to E.S.E., slightly converging on the enemy, who were now at a range of 23,000 yards, and formed the Ships on a line of bearing to clear the smoke. The 5th Battle Squadron, who had conformed to our movements, were now bearing N.N.W., 10,000 yards. The visibility at this time was good, the sun behind us and the wind S.E. Being between the enemy and his base, our situation was both tactically and strategically good.

8. At 3.48 p.m. the action commenced at a range of 18,500 yards, both forces opening fire practically simultaneously. Both appeared to straddle the target early, and at 3.51 p.m. "Lion" received her first hit. Course was altered to the Southward, and subsequently at intervals, to confuse the enemy's fire control; the mean direction was S.S.E., the enemy steering a parallel course distant about 18,000 to 14,500 yards. For the next ten minutes the firing of the enemy was very rapid and effective. "Lion" was hit repeatedly, the roof of Q turret being blown off at 4 p.m. Immediately afterwards "Indefatigable" was hit by three shots falling together. The shots appeared to hit the outer edge of the upper deck in line with the after turret. An explosion followed, and she fell out of the line sinking by the stern. Hit again by another salvo near A turret she turned over and disappeared.

9. At 4.8 p.m. the 5th Battle Squadron came into action and opened fire at a range of 20,000 yards. The enemy's fire now seemed to slacken. It would appear that at this time we passed through a screen of enemy submarines. In evidence of this a torpedo was sighted passing astern of "Lion" from Starboard to Port. The Destroyer "Landrail" of 9th Flotilla, who was on our Port beam trying to take station ahead, sighted the periscope of a Submarine on her Port quarter, and at the same time the track of a torpedo which passed under her and crossed the line of the Battle Cruisers between "Tiger" and "New Zealand." Though causing considerable inconvenience from smoke, the presence of "Lydiard" and "Landrail" undoubtedly preserved the Battle Cruisers from closer Submarine attack. "Nottingham" also reported a Submarine on the Starboard beam.

10. Eight Destroyers of the 13th Flotilla, "Nestor," "Nomad," "Nicator," "Narborough," "Pelican," "Petard,"

" Obdurate," " Nerissa," with " Moorsom " and " Morris " of 10th Flotilla, " Turbulent " and " Termagant " of the 9th Flotilla, having been ordered to attack the enemy with torpedoes when opportunity offered, moved out at 4.15 p.m. simultaneously with a similar movement on the part of the enemy. The attack was carried out in the most gallant manner and with great determination. Before arriving at - a favourable position to fire torpedoes, they intercepted an enemy force consisting of a Light Cruiser and 15 Destroyers. A fierce engagement ensued at close quarters, with the result that the enemy were forced to retire on their Battle Cruisers, having lost two Destroyers sunk, and having their torpedo attack frustrated. Our Destroyers sustained no loss in this engagement, but their attack on the enemy Battle Cruisers was rendered less effective owing to some of the Destroyers having dropped astern during the fight. Their position was therefore unfavourable for torpedo attack.

11. " Nestor," " Nomad," and " Nicator " gallantly led by Commander Hon. E. B. S. Bingham of " Nestor," pressed home their attack on the Battle Cruisers and fired two torpedoes at them at a range of 6,000 and 5,000 yards, being subjected to a heavy fire from the enemy's secondary armament. " Nomad " was badly hit and apparently remained stopped between the lines. Subsequently " Nestor " and " Nicator " altered course to the S.E. and in a short time, the opposing Battle Cruisers having turned 16 points, found themselves within close range of a number of enemy Battleships. Nothing daunted, though under a terrific fire, they stood on, and their position being favourable for torpedo attack, fired a torpedo at the 2nd ship of the enemy line at a range of 3,000 yards. Before they could fire their fourth torpedo, " Nestor " was badly hit and swung to Starboard, " Nicator " altering course inside her to avoid collision and thereby being prevented from firing the last torpedo. " Nicator " made good her escape and subsequently rejoined the Captain D, 13th Flotilla. " Nestor " remained stopped, but was afloat when last seen. " Moorsom " also carried out an attack on the enemy's Battle Fleet.

12. " Petard," " Nerissa," " Turbulent," and " Termagant " also pressed home their attack on the enemy Battle Cruisers, firing torpedoes at a range of 7,000 yards after the engagement with enemy Destroyers. " Petard " reports that all her torpedoes must have crossed the enemy's line, while " Nerissa " states that one torpedo appeared to strike the rear ship. These Destroyer attacks were indicative of the spirit pervading His Majesty's Navy, and were worthy of its highest traditions. I propose to bring to your notice a recommendation of Commander Bingham for the Victoria Cross, and other officers for some recognition of their conspicuous gallantry.

13. From 4.15 to 4.43 p.m. the conflict between the opposing Battle Cruisers was of a very fierce and resolute character. The 5th Battle Squadron was engaging the enemy's rear ships,

unfortunately at very long range. Our fire began to tell, the accuracy and rapidity of that of the enemy depreciating considerably. At 4.18 p.m. the 3rd enemy ship was seen to be on fire. The visibility to the North-Eastward had become considerably reduced and the outline of the ships very indistinct. This, no doubt, was largely due to the constant use of smoke balls or charges by the enemy, under cover of which they were continually altering course or zig-zagging.

14. At 4.26 p.m. there was a violent explosion in " Queen Mary "; she was enveloped in clouds of grey smoke and disappeared. From the evidence of Captain Pelly, of " Tiger," who was in station astern, corroborated by Rear-Admiral Brock in " Princess Royal " ahead, a salvo pitched abreast of Q turret, and almost instantaneously there was a terrific upheaval and a dense cloud of smoke through which " Tiger " passed barely 30 seconds afterwards. No sign could be seen of " Queen Mary." Eighteen of her Officers and Men were subsequently picked up by " Laurel."

15. At 4.38 p.m. " Southampton " reported the enemy's Battle Fleet ahead. The Destroyers were recalled, and at 4.42 p.m. the enemy's Battle Fleet was sighted S.E., Course was altered 16 points in succession to Starboard, and I proceeded on a Northerly course to lead them towards the Grand Fleet. The enemy Battle Cruisers altered course shortly afterwards, and the action continued. " Southampton " with the 2nd Light Cruiser Squadron held on to the Southward to observe. They closed to within 13,000 yards of the enemy Battle Fleet and came under a very heavy but ineffective fire. " Southampton's " reports were most valuable. The 5th Battle Squadron were now closing on an opposite course and engaging the enemy Battle Cruisers with all guns. The position of the enemy Battle Fleet was communicated to them, and I ordered them to alter course 16 points. Led by Rear-Admiral Hugh Evan-Thomas, M.V.O., in " Barham," this Squadron supported us brilliantly and effectively.

16. At 4.57 p.m. the 5th Battle Squadron turned up astern of me and came under the fire of the leading ships of the enemy Battle Fleet. " Fearless " with the Destroyers of 1st Flotilla joined the Battle Cruisers and, when speed admitted, took station ahead. " Champion " with 13th Flotilla took station on the 5th Battle Squadron. At 5 p.m. the 1st and 3rd Light Cruiser Squadrons, which had been following me on the Southerly course, took station on my Starboard bow; the 2nd Light Cruiser Squadron took station on my Port quarter.

17. The weather conditions now became unfavourable, our ships being silhouetted against a clear horizon to the Westward, while the enemy were for the most part obscured by mist, only showing up clearly at intervals. These conditions prevailed until we had turned their van at about 6 p.m. Between 5 and 6 p.m. the action continued on a Northerly course, the

range being about 14,000 yards. During this time the enemy received very severe punishment, and undoubtedly one of their Battle Cruisers quitted the line in a considerably damaged condition. This came under my personal observation, and was corroborated by " Princess Royal " and " Tiger." Other enemy ships also showed signs of increasing injury. At 5.5 p.m. " Onslow " and " Moresby," who had been detached to assist " Engadine " with the Seaplane, rejoined the Battle Cruiser Squadrons and took station on the Starboard (engaged) bow of " Lion." At 5.10 p.m. " Moresby," being 2 points before the beam of the leading enemy ship at a range of 6,000 to 8,000 yards, fired a long-range torpedo at the 3rd in their line. Eight . minutes later she observed a hit with a torpedo on what was judged to be the 6th Ship in the line. Later analysis of the director setting indicated a probability of this result. " Moresby " then passed between the lines to clear the range of smoke, and rejoined " Champion." In corroboration of this, " Fearless " reports having seen an enemy heavy ship heavily on fire at about 5.10 p.m., and shortly afterwards a huge cloud of smoke and steam similar to that which accompanied the blowing up of " Queen Mary " and " Indefatigable."

18. At 5.35 p.m. our course was N.N.E. and the estimated position of the Grand Fleet was N. 16 W., so we gradually hauled to the North-Eastward, keeping the range of the enemy at 14,000 yards. He was gradually hauling to the Eastward, receiving severe punishment at the head of his line, and probably acting on information received from his Light Cruisers which had sighted and were engaged with the 3rd Battle Cruiser Squadron (*vide* " Indomitable's'" report). Possibly Zeppelins were present also. At 5.50 p.m. British Cruisers were sighted on the Port Bow, and at 5.56 p.m. the leading Battleships of the Grand Fleet bearing North 5 miles. I thereupon altered course to East and proceeded at utmost speed. This brought the range of the enemy down to 12,000 yards. I made a visual report to the Commander-in-Chief that the enemy Battle Cruisers bore South-East. At this time only 3 of the enemy Battle Cruisers were visible, closely followed by Battleships of the " König " class.

19. At about 6.5 p.m. " Onslow," being on the engaged bow of " Lion," sighted an enemy Light Cruiser at a distance of 6,000 yards from us, apparently endeavouring to attack with torpedoes. " Onslow " at once closed and engaged her, firing 58 rounds at a range of from 4,000 to 2,000 yards, scoring a number of hits. " Onslow " then closed to within 8,000 yards of the enemy Battle Cruisers and orders were given for all torpedoes to be fired. At this moment she was struck amidships by a heavy shell, with the result that only one torpedo was fired. Thinking that all his torpedoes had gone, the Commanding Officer proceeded to retire at slow speed. Being informed that he still had three torpedoes, he closed the Light Cruiser pre-

viously engaged and torpedoed her. The enemy's Battle Fleet was then sighted at a distance of 8,000 yards, and the remaining torpedoes were fired at them; having started correctly, they must have crossed the enemy's track. Damage in her feed tank then caused " Onslow " to stop.

20. At 7.15 p.m. " Defender," whose speed had been reduced to 10 knots, while on the disengaged side of the Battle Cruisers, by a 12-in. shell which damaged her foremost boiler, but failed to explode, closed " Onslow " and took her in tow. Shell were falling all round them during this operation, which, however, was successfully accomplished. During the heavy weather of the ensuing night the tow parted twice, but was re-secured. The two struggled on together until 1 p.m., 1st June, when " Onslow " was transferred to tugs. I consider the performance of these two destroyers to be gallant in the extreme, and I am recommending Lieut.-Commander J. C. Tovey of " Onslow " and Lieut.-Commander Palmer of " Defender " for special recognition. " Onslow " was possibly the Destroyer referred to by the Rear-Admiral Commanding the 3rd Light Cruiser Squadron as follows :—" Here I should like to bring to your notice the action of a Destroyer (name unknown, thought to be marked with the number ' 59 ' ?" Acasta " which we passed close in a disabled condition soon after 6 p.m. She apparently was able to struggle ahead again and made straight for the " Derfflinger " to attack her. The incident appeared so courageous that it seems desirable to investigate it further, as I am unable to be certain of the vessel's identity."

21. At 6.15 p.m. " Defence " and " Warrior " crossed our bows from Port to Starboard, necessitating our hauling to Port to clear. They were closely engaging an enemy Light Cruiser, but immediately after clearing us they came under the fire of enemy heavy ships, and passed down between us and the enemy on opposite courses.

22. At 6.20 p.m. the 3rd Battle Cruiser Squadron, consisting of " Invincible " (Captain A. L. Cay) flying the flag of Rear-Admiral Hon. H. L. A. Hood, C.B., M.V.O., D.S.O., " Indomitable " (Captain F. W. Kennedy), and " Inflexible " (Captain E. H. F. Heaton-Ellis, M.V.O.) appeared ahead, steaming South towards the enemy's van. I ordered them to take station ahead, which was carried out magnificently, Rear-Admiral Hood bringing his Squadron into action ahead in a most inspiring manner, worthy of his great naval ancestors. At 6.25 p.m. I altered course to the E.S.E. in support of the 3rd Battle Cruiser Squadron, who were at this time only 8,000 yards from the enemy's leading ship. They were pouring a hot fire into her and caused her to turn to the Westward of South. At the same time I made a visual report to the Commander-in-Chief of the bearing and distance of the enemy Battle Fleet. At 6.33 p.m. " Invincible " was struck by a complete salvo about Q turret and immediately blew up.

23. After the loss of " Invincible," the Squadron was led by " Inflexible " until 6.50 p.m.   By this time the Battle Cruisers were clear of our leading Battle Squadron then bearing about N.N.W. 3 miles, and I ordered the 3rd Battle Cruiser Squadron to prolong the line astern and reduced to 18 knots.   The visibility at this time was very indifferent, not more than 4 miles, and the enemy ships were temporarily lost sight of.   It is interesting to note that after 6 p.m., although the visibility became reduced, it was undoubtedly more favourable to us than to the enemy. At intervals their ships showed up clearly, enabling us to punish them very severely, and establish a definite superiority over them.   The damage received by our ships during this period, excepting the destruction of " Invincible," was slight.   From the reports of other ships and my own observation it was clear that the enemy suffered severely, Battle Cruisers and Battleships alike.   The head of their line was crumpled up, leaving Battle-ships as targets for the majority of our Battle Cruisers.   Before leaving us the 5th Battle Squadron were also engaging Battle-ships.   The report of Rear-Admiral Evan-Thomas shows that excellent results were obtained, and it can be safely said that his magnificent Squadron wrought great execution.

24. From the report of Rear-Admiral T. D. W. Napier, M.V.O., the 3rd Light Cruiser Squadron, which had maintained its station on our Starboard bow well ahead of the enemy, at 6.25 p.m. attacked with the torpedo at a range of 6,000 yards.   " Falmouth" and " Yarmouth " both fired torpedoes at the leading enemy Battle Cruiser, and it is believed that one torpedo hit, as a heavy under-water explosion was observed.   The 3rd Light Cruiser Squadron then gallantly attacked the heavy ships with gun-fire, with impunity to themselves, thereby demonstrating that the fighting efficiency of the enemy had been seriously impaired. Rear-Admiral Napier deserves great credit for his determined and effective attack.   " Indomitable " reports that about this time one of the " Derfflinger " class fell out of the enemy's line.

25. At 7.6 p.m. I received a signal from the Commander-in-Chief that the course of the Fleet was South.   Subsequently signals were received up to 8.46 p.m., showing that the course of the Grand Fleet was to the South-Westward.   Between 7 and 7.12 p.m. we hauled round gradually to S.W. by S. to regain touch with the enemy, and at 7.14 p.m. again sighted them at a range of about 15,000 yards.   The ships sighted at this time were two Battle Cruisers and two Battleships, apparently of the " König " class.   No doubt more continued the line to the Northward, but that was all that could be seen. The visibility having improved considerably as the sun descended below the clouds, we re-engaged at 7.17 p.m. and increased speed to 22 knots.   At 7.32 p.m. my course was S.W., speed 18 knots, the leading enemy Battleship bearing N.W. by W. Again after a very short time the enemy showed signs of punishment, one ship being on fire while another appeared to

drop right astern. The Destroyers at the head of the enemy's line emitted volumes of grey smoke, covering their capital ships as with a pall, under cover of which they undoubtedly turned away, and at 7.45 p.m. we lost sight of them.

26. At 7.58 p.m. I ordered the 1st and 3rd Light Cruiser Squadrons to sweep to the Westward and locate the head of the enemy's line, and at 8.20 p.m. we altered course to West in support. We soon located two Battle Cruisers and Battleships, and were heavily engaged at a short range of about 10,000 yards. The leading ship was hit repeatedly by " Lion " and turned away 8 points, emitting very high flames and with a heavy list to Port. " Princess Royal " set fire to a 3-funnelled Battleship; " New Zealand " and " Indomitable " report that the 3rd Ship, which they both engaged, hauled out of the line heeling over and on fire. The mist which now came down enveloped them, and " Falmouth " reported they were last seen at 8.38 p.m. steaming to the Westward.

27. At 8.40 p.m. all our Battle Cruisers felt a heavy shock as if struck by a mine or torpedo, or possibly sunken wreckage. As, however, examination of the bottoms reveals no sign of such an occurrence, it is assumed that it indicated the blowing up of a great vessel. This seems a very probable explanation in view of the condition in which the enemy was last seen.

28. I continued on a South-Westerly course with my Light Cruisers spread until 9.24 p.m. Nothing further being sighted, I assumed that the enemy were to the North-Westward, and that we had established ourselves well between him and his base. " Minotaur " was at this time bearing North 5 miles, and I asked her the position of the leading Battle Squadron of the Grand Fleet. Her reply was that it was not in sight, but was last seen bearing N.N.E. 5 miles at 8.10 p.m. My position, course, and speed had been made to the Commander-in-Chief at 7.30, 8.40, and 9 p.m., the latter signal giving the bearing of the enemy as N. by W., steering S.W. by S., which as near as could be judged was correct. At 9.16 p.m. I received a signal from the Commander-in-Chief that the course of the Fleet was South.

29. In view of the gathering darkness and for other reasons, viz. : (a) Our distance from the Battle Fleet; (b) The damaged condition of the Battle Cruisers; (c) The enemy being concentrated; (d) The enemy being accompanied by numerous Destroyers; (e) Our strategical position being such as to make it appear certain that we should locate the enemy at daylight under most favourable circumstances, I did not consider it desirable or proper to close the enemy Battle Fleet during the dark hours. I therefore concluded that I should be carrying out the Commander-in-Chief's wishes by turning to the course of the Fleet, reporting to the Commander-in-Chief that I had done so.

30. My duty in this situation was to ensure that the enemy Fleet could not regain its base by passing round the Southern flank of our forces. I therefore turned to South at 9.24 p.m. at 17 knots, and continued this course until 2.30 a.m., with the 1st and 3rd Light Cruiser Squadrons spread to the Southward and Westward. My intention was to ask permission to sweep S.W. at daylight, but on receiving a signal that the Commander-in-Chief was turning to North, and ordering me to conform and close, I proceeded accordingly, and rejoined the Commander-in-Chief at 5.20 a.m.

31. The movements of the Light Cruiser Squadrons and Flotillas are described in detail in their own reports. " Champion" and most of the 13th Flotilla were in visual touch after the Destroyer attack on the enemy line at 4.40 p.m. on 31st May, but they became detached later and stationed themselves at the rear of the Battle Fleet for the night. At .0.30 a.m. on 1st June a large vessel crossed the rear of the Flotilla at high speed. She passed close to " Petard " and " Turbulent," switched on searchlights and opened a heavy fire which severely damaged " Petard " and disabled " Turbulent." At 3.30 a.m. " Champion " was engaged for a few minutes with 4 enemy destroyers. " Moresby " reports 4 ships of " Deutschland " class sighted at 2.35 a.m., at whom she fired one torpedo. Two minutes later an explosion was felt by " Moresby " and " Obdurate." On investigation I find the " Moresby " was in station with " Obdurate " astern of " Champion." Some of the strange vessels were sighted by " Champion " and " Obdurate," who took them to be some of our own Light Cruisers. This was impossible, and it is very much to be regretted that "Champion " did not take steps to identify them. If, as was probable, they were the enemy, an excellent opportunity was missed for an attack in the early morning light. More important still, a portion of the enemy might have been definitely located.

32. " Fearless " and the 1st Flotilla were very usefully employed as a submarine screen during the earlier part of the 31st May, but their limited speed made it almost impossible for them to regain their proper stations when the Battle Cruisers altered course. At 6.10 p.m. when joining the Battle Fleet, " Fearless " was unable to follow the Battle Cruisers without fouling the Battleships, so turned 32 points and took station at the rear of the line. She sighted during the night a Battleship of the " Kaiser " class steaming fast and entirely alone. She was not able to engage her, but believes she was attacked by destroyers further astern. A heavy explosion was observed astern not long after. The incident could be identified by the fact that this ship fired a star shell. By midday on 1st June all the 1st Flotilla were getting short of fuel and had to be detached in pairs to make their base at 15 knots.

33. The 1st and 3rd Light Cruiser Squadrons **were almost** continuously in touch with the Battle Cruisers, one or both

Squadrons being usually ahead. They were most valuable as a submarine screen when no destroyers were present; they very effectively protected the head of our line from Torpedo attack by Light Cruisers or Destroyers, and were prompt in helping to regain touch when the enemy's line was temporarily lost sight of. The 2nd Light Cruiser Squadron was at the rear of our Battle line during the night, and at 9 p.m. assisted to repel a Destroyer attack on the 5th Battle Squadron. They were also heavily engaged at 10.20 p.m. with 5 enemy Cruisers or Light Cruisers, " Southampton " and " Dublin " suffering severe casualties during an action lasting about 15 minutes. " Birmingham," at 11.30 p.m., sighted 2 or more heavy ships steering South. A report of this was received by me at 11.40 p.m. as steering W.S.W. They were thought at the time to be Battle Cruisers, but it is since considered that they were probably Battleships.

34. The work of " Engadine " appears to have been most praiseworthy throughout, and of great value. Lieut.-Commander C. G. Robinson deserves great credit for the skilful and seamanlike manner in which he handled his ship. He actually towed " Warrior " for 75 miles between 8.40 p.m., 31st May, and 7.15 a.m., 1st June, and was instrumental in saving the lives of her Ship's Company.

35. I have not referred to " Chester " as she did not come under my personal command or observation. Her report shows that she fought gallantly and successfully against superior forces and suffered considerably in casualties and damage.

36. It is impossible to give a definite statement of the losses inflicted on the enemy. The visibility was for the most part low and fluctuating, and caution forbade me to close the range too much with my inferior force.

A review of all the reports which I have received, however, leads me to form the following estimate of the enemy's losses during the course of the operations described in this report :—

> 3 Battle Cruisers,
> 2 Battleships (" König " or " Kaiser " class)
> 1 " Pommern " class,   } Sunk.
> 2 Light Cruisers,
> 3 Destroyers.

> 2 Battle Cruisers,   } Severely
> Several Light Cruisers and Destroyers, } damaged.

This is eloquent testimony to the very high standard of Gunnery and Torpedo efficiency of His Majesty's Ships. The Control and drill remained undisturbed throughout, in many cases despite heavy damage to material and personnel. Our superiority over the enemy in this respect was very marked, their efficiency becoming rapidly reduced under punishment, while ours was maintained throughout.

37. As was to be expected, the behaviour of the Ships' Companies under the terrible conditions of a modern sea battle was magnificent without exception. The strain on their moral was a severe test of discipline and training. Officers and men were imbued with one thought, the desire to defeat the enemy. The fortitude of the wounded was admirable. A report from the Commanding Officer of " Chester " gives a splendid instance of devotion to duty. Boy, 1st Class, John Travers Cornwell, of " Chester " was mortally wounded early in the action. He nevertheless remained standing alone at a most exposed post, quietly awaiting orders till the end of the action, with the gun's crew dead and wounded all round him. His age was under 16½ years. I regret that he has since died, but I recommend his case for special recognition in justice to his memory, and as an acknowledgment of the high example set by him.

Awarded the Victoria Cross

Our casualties were very heavy, and I wish to express my deepest regret at the loss of so many gallant comrades, Officers, and Men. They died gloriously.

38. Exceptional skill was displayed by the Medical Officers of the Fleet. They performed operations and tended the wounded under conditions of extreme difficulty. In some cases their staff was seriously depleted by casualties, and the inevitable lack of such essentials as adequate light, hot water, &c., in ships battered by shell fire, tried their skill, resource, and physical endurance to the utmost.

39. As usual, the Engine Room Departments of all ships displayed the highest qualities of technical skill, discipline, and endurance. High speed is a primary factor in the tactics of the Squadrons under my command, and the Engine Room Departments never fail.

40. I have already made mention of the brilliant support afforded me by Rear-Admiral H. Evan-Thomas, M.V.O., and the 5th Battle Squadron, and of the magnificent manner in which Rear-Admiral Hon. H. L. A. Hood, C.B., M.V.O., D.S.O., brought his Squadron into action. I desire to record my great regret at his loss, which is a national misfortune. I would now bring to your notice the able support rendered to me by Rear-Admiral W. C. Pakenham, C.B., and Rear-Admiral O. de B. Brock, C.B. In the course of my report I have expressed my appreciation of the good work performed by the Light Cruiser Squadrons under the command respectively of Rear-Admiral T. D. W. Napier, M.V.O., Commodore W. E. Goodenough, M.V.O., and Commodore E. S. Alexander-Sinclair, M.V.O. On every occasion these Officers anticipated my wishes and used their forces to the best possible effect.

41. I desire also to bring to your notice the skill with which their respective ships were handled by Captains F. W. Kennedy (" Indomitable "), who commanded the 3rd Battle Cruiser

Squadron after the loss of Rear-Admiral Hood, C. F. Sowerby
(" Indefatigable "), H. B. Pelly, M.V.O. (" Tiger "), J. F. E.
Green (" New Zealand "), W. H. Cowan, M.V.O., D.S.O.
(" Princess Royal "), C. I. Prowse (" Queen Mary "), A. L. Cay
("Invincible "), E. H. F. Heaton-Ellis, M.V.O. (" Inflexible "),
C. B. Miller (" Nottingham "), A. E. M. Chatfield, C.V.O.
(" Lion "), on whom lay special responsibility as commanding
my Flagship, J. D. Edwards (" Falmouth "), A. A. M. Duff
(" Birmingham "), E. Reeves (" Birkenhead "), W. F. Blunt
(" Gloucester "), T. D. Pratt (" Yarmouth "), A. C. Scott
(" Dublin "), B. S. Thesiger (" Inconstant "), R. N. Lawson
(" Chester "), J. U. Farie (" Champion "), (Captain D, 13th
Flotilla), J. E. Cameron, M.V.O. (" Phæton "), T. P. H. Beamish
(" Cordelia "), and C. D. Roper (" Fearless "), (Captain D,
1st Flotilla).   With such Flag Officers, Commodores and Captains
to support me, my task was made easier.   The Destroyers of
the 1st and 13th Flotillas were handled by their respective
Commanding Officers with skill, dash and courage.   I desire to
record my very great regret at the loss of Captains C. F. Sowerby
(" Indefatigable "), C. I. Prowse (" Queen Mary "), and A. L. Cay
(" Invincible "), all Officers of the highest attainments who can
be ill-spared at this time of stress.

42. I wish to endorse the report of the Rear-Admiral
Commanding the 5th Battle Squadron as to the ability displayed
by Captains E. M. Phillpotts (" Warspite "), M. Woollcombe
(" Valiant "), Hon. A. D. E. H. Boyle (" Malaya "), and A. W.
Craig (" Barham ").

43. In conclusion, I desire to record and bring to your notice
the great assistance that I received on a day of great anxiety
and strain from my Chief of the Staff, Captain R. W. Bentinck,
whose good judgment was of the greatest help.   He was a tower
of strength.   My Flag Commander, Hon. R. A. R. Plunkett,
was most valuable in observing the effect of our fire, thereby
enabling me to take advantage of the enemy's discomfiture,
my Secretary, F. T. Spickernell, who made accurate notes of
events as they occurred, which proved of the utmost value in
keeping the situation clearly before me; my Flag Lieutenant,
Commander R. F. Seymour, who maintained efficient communications under the most difficult circumstances despite the fact
that his signalling appliances were continually shot away.   All
these Officers carried out their duties with great coolness on
the manœuvring platform, where they were fully exposed to
the enemy's fire.

44. In accordance with your wishes, I am forwarding in
a separate letter a full list of Officers and Men whom I wish to
recommend to your notice.

45. I enclose the reports rendered to me by Flag Officers
Commodores and Commanding Officers regarding their proceedings

Plate 9.

DIAGRAMS SHOWING PHASES 31.5.16.

Diagrams are not to Scale. Margin of paper is approximately N. (Mag).

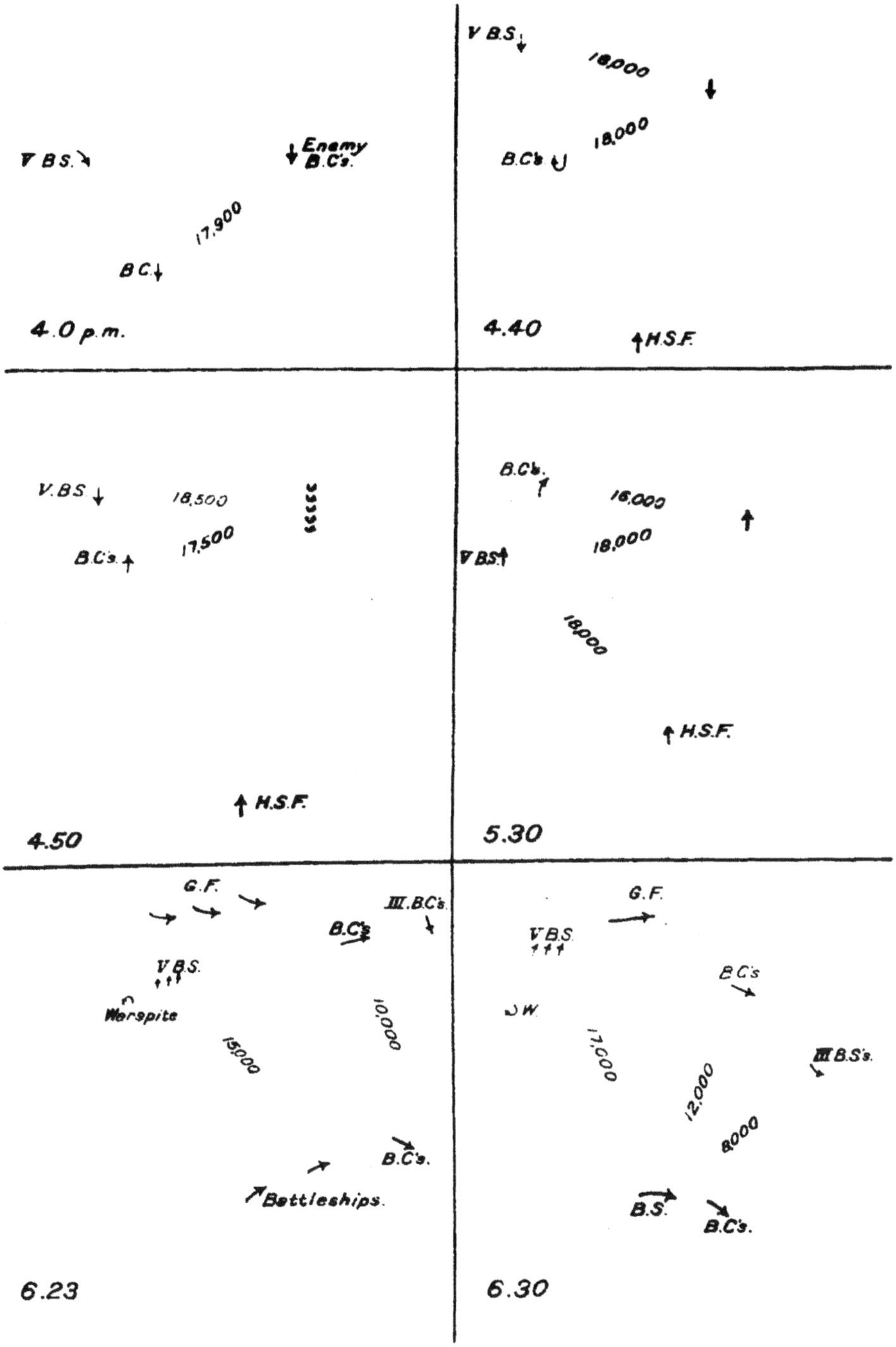

V B.S. ↓

18,000

↓

B.Cs ↺

18,000

V BS. ↘

↓ Enemy
B.C's.

B.C. ↺

17,900

B C ↓

4.0 p.m.

4.40

↑H.S.F.

V. BS ↓

18,500

B.C's. ↑

17,500

B.Cs. ↑

16,000

↑

V BS. ↑

18,000

18,000

↑ H.S.F.

↑ H.S.F.

4.50

5.30

G.F. →

→ → →

III. BC's.

B.C's ↗

↓

V B.S.
↑↑↑

Warspite

15,000

10,000

6.23

G.F. →

V B.S.
↑↑↑

B.C's ↘

J W

17,000

III B.C's. ↗

12,000

8,000

B.S. →

B.C's. ↘

6.30

B.C's. ↗

↗ Battleships.

Malby & Sons. Lith

16:20ʰʳˢ German battle cruisers formed line ahead;

Lützow
Derfflinger
Seydlitz
Moltke
Von der Tann

during the period under review.   A sheet of diagrams is attached ;[1]
a track chart has already been forwarded.[2]

I have the honour to be,

Sir,

Your obedient Servant,

DAVID BEATTY,

Vice-Admiral.

Commander-in-Chief,
Grand Fleet.

Note.—On 17th July 1916 a Plan of Battle, prepared from all
available data, was forwarded by Vice-Admiral Beatty to the
Commander-in-Chief Grand Fleet.   *See* Plate 8a.

CAPTAIN'S REPORT, H.M.S. " LION."

Enclosure No. 1 to Battle Cruiser Fleet.   Letter No. B.C.F. 01
of 12/6/16.

No. 115.

H.M.S. " Lion,"

4th June 1916.

Sir,

I have the honour to report that on 31st May 1916,
H.M. Ship under my command, flying your flag, was in action
with the enemy under the following circumstances.

At 3.25 p.m., G.M.T., enemy ships were reported on the
starboard bow, bearing E. by N.

At 3.30 p.m., enemy ships were in sight from " Lion " and
a range of 23,000 yards obtained.

At 3.44 p.m., the enemy, who were rapidly closing, were
identified as 5 German Battle Cruisers.

2. Enemy opened fire at 3.47 p.m., " Lion " replying half
a minute later, the range being 18,500, course E.S.E.

" Lion " was twice hit by heavy shell at 3.51 p.m.   At
4.0 p.m. a shell disabled " Q " turret, and shortly afterwards
" Indefatigable " was seen to be blown up, evidently by a
magazine explosion.

3. At 4.2 p.m. the range was 14,600 and as the enemy appeared
to have our range, course was altered on 2 or 3 occasions 1 point
to throw him out.

The enemy appeared to be hit several times by our shell.
" Lion " was firing at the leading ship, which was either
" Lützow " or " Derfflinger."

4. At 4.12 p.m. our course was S.S.E. and range 21,000
and course was altered to S.E. to close the enemy.

At this period more than one enemy ship was firing at " Lion "
and she was hit several times, but no important damage was

---

[1] Plate 9.   [2] *i.e.,* in two portions, *see* Plates 10 and 11.

done though several fires were started, and there was a large
number of killed and wounded, chiefly from a shell that exploded
on the Mess Deck in the Canteen Flat.

5. At 4.26 p.m. a very great explosion was seen in the " Queen
Mary " and she entirely disappeared.

6. At 4.38 p.m. the enemy Battle Fleet was sighted ahead,
and course was altered 16 points to North, enemy Battle
Cruisers responding so as to take station ahead of their Battle
Fleet.

7. " Lion " reopened fire at 4.38 p.m. re-engaging enemy
leading ship (" Von Der Tann " ?) shortly after we passed
wreckage of " Queen Mary," with survivors in water and a
destroyer.

The ship was now hit several times, the range being 15,000
yards. The ship had fires in several places, including a cordite
case in the starboard 4-in. battery, which I ordered the 4-in.
crews to extinguish, but this could not immediately be done
owing to their extent and to the pressure on the fire mains being
lost from perforations. All fires were eventually got under.

8. About this time, a fire which had been smouldering in
" Q " turret ignited the charges still in the trunks : this killed
all the Magazine and Shell Room parties and reached to the
Mess Deck, where it burnt some of the Ship's Company. The
Magazine doors being shut, however, saved a more serious
explosion.

A fire was also reported in " X " Magazine, but this proved
to be an error due to smoke penetrating down from a heavy
shell burst in the Sick Bay, which killed a large number of men
in the vicinity.

9. At 5.1 p.m. fire was shifted to " Lützow " class again,
range 15,000 yards. " Lion " was hit twice by big shell, one
of which wrecked the ship's galley compartment.

At 5.12 p.m. " Lion " ceased fire owing to the enemy being
obscured, and did not reopen until 5.41 p.m. The visibility
at this time was decreasing, and when fire was reopened on
a ship that appeared to be of the " König " class Battleship,
the range was 14,000 yards, the enemy being just visible.

Ship's course was now N.E. by N.

10. At 5.46 p.m. the range was 14,000 yards and the enemy
was observed to be hit by two salvoes, causing him to alter
course to starboard and to cease fire.

11. At 5.56 p.m. the Battlefleet was in sight on the port
bow. Altered course to N.E. by E., and at 6.4 p.m. to East,
the enemy Battle Cruisers bearing S.E.

12. " Defence " and " Warrior " now crossed " Lion's " bow
and were engaging a Light German Cruiser, who was seriously
injured by them. This caused " Lion " to cease fire and to
lose touch with the enemy.

13. At 6.21 p.m. the Third Battle Cruiser Squadron was sighted, and took station ahead, and " Lion " reopened at distant ships on the starboard beam (" König " class ?).

At 6.29 p.m. course was E. by S. and at 6.32 p.m. enemy heavy ships again came into view and opened fire on the 3rd B.C.S. At 6.36 p.m. " Invincible " blew up.

14. Course was continued to be altered to starboard to close the enemy, and at 6.37 p.m. was altered to E.S.E.; at 6.44 to S.E., and 6.48 p.m. to S.S.E.

At 6.53 p.m. speed was reduced to 18 knots to keep station on the Battlefleet, who were leading away to port owing to a Destroyer attack.

" Lion " continued to engage the leading ship of enemy, occasionally ceasing fire when he became invisible.

Very few hits were made on the ship subsequent to this, the enemy's fire appreciably slackening.

15. The ship continued to circle to starboard.

At 7.3 p.m. our course was altered to S.S.E., and at 7.6 p.m. to South; at 7.9 p.m. to S.S.W. and at 7.11 p.m. to S.W. by S.

16. Fire was reopened on the leading ship of the enemy at 15,000 yards at 7.15 p.m., and speed was increased to 22 knots; at 7.25 p.m. to 24 knots.

At 7.19 p.m. the enemy's leading Destroyers made a heavy screen of black smoke to protect their ships from our gunfire.

At 7.32 p.m. course was S.W., and 7.50 p.m. W.S.W. The enemy was still not sufficiently visible to open fire, and this continued until 8.21 p.m., when the flashes of his guns were again seen on our starboard beam.

At 8.23 p.m. " Lion " opened fire with rapid salvoes on his leading ship, either " Lützow " or " König " class. Our shooting appeared to be very effective, and the enemy appeared on fire at 8.27 p.m.

17. The enemy now turned away more to starboard, and the light was failing.

" Lion " ceased fire at 8.30 p.m., our course then being N. 35° W.

18. At 8.40 p.m., a heavy bump was felt on the starboard side. This appeared to me like a heavy hit on the water-line but this was not the case, and it has not yet been ascertained what was the cause. It is possible " Lion " may have run over a sunken ship, and divers are examining her bottom.

Shortly afterwards, " Indomitable " hauled out of line and reported she had been torpedoed, which she subsequently negatived, which seems to imply that she had the same experience as " Lion."

19. The enemy was not sighted again.

Damage :—

20. The damage to the ship is not serious, except that " Q " turret is wrecked, but is repairable.

The ship was hit altogether 12 times by enemy heavy shell, but the damage, which I have already reported to you separately, does not seriously affect our sea-worthiness or fighting efficiency, and the ship is now ready for sea.

Conduct of Officers and Men :—

21. The conduct of the Officers and Ship's Company was in every detail magnificent.

The ship has been in commission for so long, and the men are so highly trained, and have such a fine spirit, that even in action they can do almost anything without their officers.

The unnerving sights that occurred, with the heavy casualties which amounted to 95 killed and 49 wounded, mostly in the first two hours of the action, were a tremendous strain on the strongest discipline, yet there was never the least sign of wavering in the least degree from their duty.

On visiting the Mess Deck twice during the action while the ship was temporarily disengaged, I observed nothing but cheerful determination, zeal to succour the wounded, and thoughtfulness for the good safety of the ship to keep her efficient.

1   *   *   *   *   *

I have the honour to be,
Sir,
Your obedient Servant,
A. E. M. CHATFIELD.
Captain.

The Vice-Admiral Commanding
Battle Cruiser Fleet.

REAR-ADMIRAL'S   REPORT.—1ST   BATTLE   CRUISER SQUADRON.

Enclosure No. 2 to Battle Cruiser Fleet Letter No. B.C.F. 01 of 12/6/16.

No. 011.

"Princess Royal,"
SIR,   3rd June 1916.

I BEG to forward a narrative of events of the engagement of 31st May; the times given and the sequence are approximate only. A track chart is also attached.[2] The First Battle Cruiser Squadron followed the "Lion" during the engagement and conformed to her movements.

2. During the greater part of the engagement the conditions of light were most unfavourable, the German Fleet were

---

[1] Part omitted here, referring solely to personnel, recommendations, &c., in no way bearing on the course of the action.
[2] Plate 12.

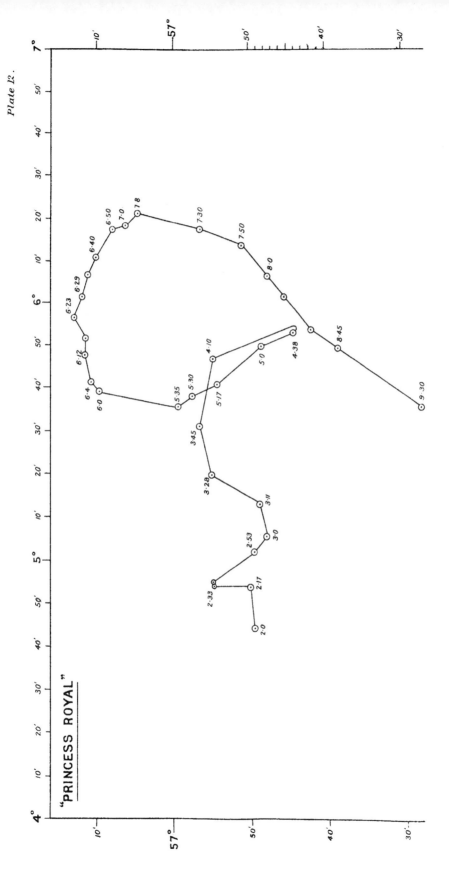

Plate 12.

"PRINCESS ROYAL"

partially obscured by mist which made spotting very difficult, whereas our own line were showing up against a clear horizon.

3. The " Queen Mary " was hit by a plunging salvo near " Q " turret which apparently penetrated the armoured deck and ignited the magazine. A bright flame was observed to shoot up as she was hit, followed almost immediately by a mass of cordite smoke in which the ship disappeared. I deeply regret the loss of Captain Prowse and an exceptionally fine company of Officers and men.

4. Further reports on the damage sustained, lists of killed and wounded will be forwarded.

I have the honour to be,
Sir,
Your obedient Servant,
O. DE B. BROCK,
Rear-Admiral.

The Vice-Admiral Commanding
    Battle Cruiser Fleet.

NOTES ON ACTION—31st MAY 1916.

The first news of the enemy being in the vicinity was a report from the Commodore Commanding First Light Cruiser Squadron, at 2.25 p.m., who reported two Cruisers. He then reported a large amount of smoke, bearing E.S.E., at 2.40 p.m., and at 3.0 p.m. " Galatea " further reported that the smoke appeared to be from 7 vessels, besides Destroyers and Cruisers, and that they had turned to the Northward. Fleet then altered course, leading ships together, remainder in succession, to S.E.

At 2.59. Altered course to East.

At 3.10. Altered course to N.E., speed increased to 23 knots.

At 3.16. " Galatea " reported that enemy had altered course to N.W., his own course being N.N.W.

At 3.23. " Princess Royal " called attention to E. by N., from which direction Enemy were first sighted.

At 3.26. Ships were ordered to action stations, and at 3.30 speed increased to 26 knots.

At 3.42. The Vice-Admiral Commanding, Battle Cruiser Fleet, reported the enemy to the Commander-in-Chief.

At 3.45. Battle Cruisers were formed on a compass line of bearing N.W., and S.O., 1st L.C.S., reported he was leading enemy to the N.W.

At 3.45. Concentration of fire signal was made : " Leading pair engage right-hand ship of enemy."

At 3.50. Enemy opened fire and missed over, which was returned by the Battle Cruisers at 3.51 p.m.

The action then became general, the enemy rate of fire being greater than ours due to the conditions of light and wind. " Lion " was hit at 3.55 p.m. and " Princess Royal " at 3.56, putting main control out of action. Enemy fire then became short, spread

K 2

of salvoes being very small, and error for direction practically nil.

At 3.59, Hits were observed on enemy No. 3 in line. Spotting became difficult owing to smoke from Destroyers.

At 4.11. Torpedo missed " Princess Royal."

At 4.16. Argo Tower was repaired and ship fired with main control again.

At 4.21. A heavy explosion occurred in " Queen Mary," and ship sank immediately.

At 4.23. The leading ship of enemy was hit.

At 4.27. And again at 4.32 " Princess Royal " was hit.

At 4.40. Our Destroyers attacked Enemy's Destroyers, who appeared to be getting into a position for attacking the Battle Cruisers.

At 4.40. Altered course 16 points to Starboard and reopened fire at 4.50 p.m.

At 5. 0. Passed an " L " class Destroyer picking up survivors from " Queen Mary."

Shortly afterwards, about 4.45 p.m., 5th Battle Squadron came down on an opposite course and were ordered by " Lion " to turn 16 points by Compass Pendant. They were then heavily engaged by the Battle Cruisers and a Division of the Enemy Battle Fleet. After about $\frac{1}{4}$ of an hour, " Warspite " hauled out of line.

At 5.35. Course was altered to N.N.E., and at 5.40 p.m. fire was reopened at which time leading divisions of our Battlefleet were sighted on the port beam. Armoured Cruisers and Light Cruisers and Destroyers were close to, taking station for deployment. The Third Battle Cruiser Squadron came into action ahead of the " Lion," and apparently the " Invincible " was shortly afterwards hit, as her wreck was noticed with the stern and bow standing out of the water. About this time a torpedo was noticed to pass under the ship from port to starboard from the direction of our own Fleet.

At 6. 5. The First Cruiser Squadron was apparently engaging a Light Cruiser, and stood out across the " Lion's " bows, necessitating an alteration of course of Battle Cruisers to port.

" Onslow " then approached the light cruiser at full speed and apparently fired a torpedo, but was driven off and hit by enemy's heavy ships.

Leading Battle Cruisers' fire was then masked by First Cruiser Squadron who were very heavily engaged by the enemy. Enemy appeared to be firing shrapnel at times.

This movement of the First Cruiser Squadron appeared to cause a division of the enemy's Battlefleet who had been directing their fire on the Battle Cruisers to concentrate on the First Cruiser Squadron.

At 6.22. Destroyer was hit near after funnel by an over.

What appeared to be an over at First Cruiser Squadron put " Princess Royal's " " X " turret out of action.

At this time the leading four enemy battleships appeared to concentrate on " Lion " and " Princess Royal."

At 6.40. A torpedo passed " Princess Royal " from starboard to port.

At 7.15. Enemy ship on fire, and remainder of enemy Battle Cruisers apparently had enough, making a very successful smoke screen. Ceased fire.

At 7.28. Enemy's Destroyers appeared to be launching an attack, and were driven off by Battle Fleet.

At 8.26. Enemy opened fire, " Princess Royal " engaged what appeared to be a 3-funnelled Battleship. Hits were undoubtedly obtained and fire observed.

About 8.32 " Lion " and " Princess Royal " were again hit.

At 8.32. " Princess Royal " fired a torpedo.

At 8.40. Ship gave two very distinct shudders, which were at first thought to be a torpedo. This was afterwards ascertained to be incorrect.

Three-funnelled Battleship had three bands round after funnel.

What appeared to be " Hindenburg " had two massive funnels, wide apart and painted dull red.

A German recognition sign. Lützow had one red funnel.

Enclosure No. 3 to Battle Cruiser Fleet Letter No. B.C.F. 01 of 12/6/16.

REPORT OF LOSS OF " QUEEN MARY " IN ACTION ON 31st MAY 1916.

No. 011.

II.

Vice-Admiral Commanding
    Battle Cruiser Fleet,

The attached report from Midshipman J. L. Storey, R.N., the senior uninjured survivor from H.M.S. " Queen Mary," is submitted for information.

" Princess Royal,"   O. DE B. BROCK,
        3rd June 1916.   Rear-Admiral.

                                H.M.S. " Crescent,"
SIR,   3rd June 1916.

I DEEPLY regret to report that H.M.S. " Queen Mary," commanded by Captain C. I. Prowse, R.N., was completely destroyed when in action with the German Fleet at 5.25 p.m. on Wednesday, the 31st May.

The total number of Officers and men saved was 18.

1 *   *   *   *   *

The circumstances of the loss of the Ship are, as far as I know, as follows :—

At 4.20 p.m. the " Queen Mary " was third ship in the line of the 1st B.C.S., and action was sounded, and at 4.45 the order was given " load all guns." At 4.53 fire was opened on the third ship of the enemy's line, the range being about 17,000 yards.

The fire was maintained with great rapidity till 5.20, and during this time we were only slightly damaged by the enemy's fire. At 5.20 a big shell hit " Q " Turret and put the right gun out of action, but the left gun continued firing. At 5.24 a terrific explosion took place which smashed up " Q " Turret and started a big fire in working chamber and the Gun House was filled with smoke and gas. The Officer on the Turret, Lieutenant Commander Street, gave the order to evacuate the Turret. All the unwounded in the Gun House got clear and, as they did so, another terrific explosion took place and all were thrown into the water. On coming to the surface nothing was visible except wreckage, but thirty persons appeared to be floating in the water.

At 5.55, H.M.S. " Laurel " saw the survivors in the water and lowered a whaler and rescued seventeen. When this number had been picked up, H.M.S. " Laurel " received orders to proceed at full speed, being in grave danger of the enemy's ships.

All Officers and men were treated with the greatest kindness by the Officers and men of H.M.S. " Laurel," and were landed at Rosyth at about 8 p.m., 1st June.[2]

I have the honour to be,
Sir,
Your obedient Servant,
J. L. STOREY,
Midshipman, R.N.

CAPTAIN'S REPORT.—H.M.S. " PRINCESS ROYAL."

Enclosure No. 4 to Battle Cruiser Fleet Letter No. B.C.F. 01 of 12/6/16.

No. 1/125.

H.M.S. " Princess Royal,"

SIR,   8th June 1916.

I HAVE the honour to report that " Princess Royal," flying your Flag, was in company with " Lion," First and Second

---

[1] Part omitted here, referring solely to personnel, recommendations, &c., in no way bearing on the course of the action.

[2] It will be noted that the above times are " Summer time " and not G.M.T.

Battle Cruiser Squadrons, less "Australia," on the afternoon of the 31st May, when the Enemy's Fleet was sighted bearing N.E., our position being Lat. 56° 51 N., Long. 5° 16 E., and course N.E. Fire was opened by the enemy at 3.46 p.m. and immediately returned by us, "Lion" and "Princess Royal" concentrating on the leading ship (of "Derfflinger" type), the opening range being 16,000 yards. She was straddled at the third salvo, and a hit was observed at 3.54 p.m. Course was gradually altered to southward.

Lützow

2. The hit forward at 3.56 p.m. caused the electric training of the Argo Tower to fail, and the hand gear was found to be set up. Control was turned over to "B" turret for ten minutes, and then resumed by the Argo Tower, of which the rangefinder was out of action. At 4.11 a torpedo missed the Ship, passing under the midship section from starboard to port. The shooting of "Lion" and "Princess Royal" appeared good for some time before the enemy turned away at 4.26 p.m.

3. Shortly afterwards, the High Sea Fleet came in sight, and our course was altered to the northward (4.38 p.m.). On picking up the enemy again, their right-hand ship was seen to be enveloped in smoke and steering away. Four salvoes were fired at a three-funnelled cruiser steering southwards, and fire at 4.50 was opened on the second ship in the line, as "Lion's" smoke interfered with our view of the leading ship; she resembled the "Seydlitz." The "Lion's" smoke becoming better, fire was shifted at 4.56 to the leading ship again (also of the "Seydlitz" or similar type). At 5.8 the enemy could no longer be seen and fire was checked.

4. At 5.41 p.m. fire was opened on the left-hand ship which at 5.48 was seen to be on fire. The wreck of the "Invincible" was passed at 6.36 p.m. on the starboard hand. The course of the Squadron was gradually altered to the eastward. At 6.4 fire was checked, the enemy not being visible.

5. Fire was reopened at 6.12, the target being apparently a battleship (two funnels wide apart). Course had to be altered slightly to the N.E. at 6.15 to allow the First Cruiser Squadron to cross our front; the original course was afterwards resumed and then gradually worked round to the southward, and half an hour later to the south-westward.

6. The Ship came, about this time, under a heavy fire, possibly from the battleships of the "König" class, which were seen abaft the beam. "X" Turret was put out of action by this fire, and the ship was holed in the starboard after reserve bunker by another shot of the same salvo, which wrecked the after engine-room casings before exploding against the upper deck on the port side. Fire was checked at 6.22 p.m., the enemy being invisible owing to smoke, and advantage was taken of the lull to check the instruments. At 6.40 p.m. a torpedo missed the Ship, passing from port to starboard under the middle section again.

7. Fire was reopened at 7.14 p.m. for three minutes on an enemy ship which was on fire amidships, having been hit by " Lion."

About 8.40 p.m. a very heavy shock was felt, and everyone thought a torpedo had hit us, but this was not so, however; and therefore we must have struck and passed over a very heavy object, possibly a submarine or a sunken vessel.

8. At 8.21 p.m. fire was reopened on the leading battle cruiser, which could now be seen without any interference from " Lion " smoke, and good ranges could be obtained for the first time. She was repeatedly hit until 8.30, when she dropped astern on fire and was hidden by destroyer smoke screen. Fire was resumed at 8.33 on a three-funnelled battleship of the " Helgoland " or " Pommern " type, and hits were obtained with the second and third salvoes. Fire was checked at 8.36, the target being obscured by the smoke screen.

9. Nothing more was seen of the enemy after this.

10. After the turn northwards at 4.38 p.m. the enemy was always on the starboard side.

11. The only electrical defect which developed in the course of the action affecting the fighting efficiency was the failure of the electrical training of the Argo Tower at the beginning of the action, caused by the blowing of the fuzes in No. 1 starboard and port pipe passages (caused by the explosion of the shell which hit at 3.56 p.m.). These were replaced and the Argo Tower Motor worked correctly.

12. The gunnery interruptions were :—

" A " Turret—Right Gun.—Retractor lever bent, causing missfires. Turret Armourer and Chief Armourer away on advance leave, and considerable delay caused.

Left Gun.—Crank pinion axis broke with breech in closed position. Breech could not be opened for 11 hours. Gun out of action.

" B " Turret.—Turret armour hit without internal damage. Tubes occasionally missfired—bad tubes.

" Q " Turret.—Right gun hit on muzzle, cracked inner " A " tube for 2 ins. and caused scoring of right trunnion bush.

" X " Turret.—12-in. hit on armour which was badly distorted. Large piece thrown through gunhouse, killing left gun's crew, damaging sliding shaft to breech and destroying all pressure pipes on left side. Turret jambed and out of action.

Gun Control Tower.—Two 12-in. shell striking forward caused vibration which put training gear temporarily out of action and jammed transmitter gear of Argo Range-finder. Slight damage by splinters to 4-in. gun circuits, &c. repaired by Ship's Staff.

Voice-pipes.—Captain's, on Compass Platform to Argo Tower and between Argo Tower and Director Tower both cut by fragments of the first salvo which hit the ship. All voice-pipes in both struts and auxiliary director circuit destroyed by shell.

Rounds Fired.—

" A " Turret	- -	34
" B " Turret	- -	78
" Q " Turret	- -	78
" X " Turret	- -	40

13. The main engines and boilers were not affected by hits. and steam was easily maintained for all services.

Examination of the propellers by divers shows that a very small piece has been removed from one blade, and a cone from a propeller nut has come off. This may have been caused by the collision referred to in para. 7.

The explosion of the shell which came through the starboard after reserve bunker and wrecked the casings of the after engine rooms, filled them with dense smoke, some of which penetrated to the starboard forward engine room, but this dispersed after the fire was subdued, the hole on the port side of the after deck facilitating the dispersion.

14. The electric light on the upper and main decks was cut off at the switchboard previous to the action to prevent probable causes of fire through short-circuiting of leads.

15. " Princess Royal " was hit by approximately nine heavy shell, besides a constant stream of shell fragments. The principal damage was—

(*a*) Caused by shell exploding against upper deck in Admiral's Port cabin over " B " Turret Flat, which wrecked the cabin, killed and wounded many of the Fore 4-in. guns' crews and salvage party, put the Fore Distributing Station out of action till it could be cleared of smoke, partially gassed the men in the Transmitting Station and Lower Conning Tower, and started several fires, which were very difficult to put out owing to gas and darkness.

(*b*) Hole through base of No. 1 Funnel.

(*c*) Hole through armour in port forward reserve bunker, by which the fire main pipe and the gearing of the flood valve to " B " port magazine were shot away.

(*d*) Gunhouse of " X " Turret.

(*e*) Shell through starboard after reserve bunker, which wrecked the after engine room casings and exploded on the port side of the main deck, killing and wounding many of the After 4-in. guns' crews and salvage party, breaking the fire main and brine system, and causing several fires.

The fires were subdued in a minimum of time but under much difficulty, due to the lack of electric light, the failure of the oil lighting, the breaking of fire mains and valves, and the heavy smoke and gases caused by the explosions and fires.

The two holes in the Ship's side were plugged as soon as it was possible to get at them after the fires were dealt with.

16. Soon after opening fire, a shell burst in " B " Turret Flat, putting out the lights, jambing the hatch to the Fore Distributing Station, and filling the air with thick clouds of smoke, which were very irritating to the eyes and throat, especially the latter. Respirators were immediately put on, and were found most useful. Goggles were used but were found to get dimmed. The gases, being heavy, hung about in the Distributing Station for hours afterwards. The effects of the gas on the system also became obvious by nausea, giddiness and vomiting, so that the Station was evacuated and the Port Fore 4-in. Battery used. The removal of wounded, as anticipated, proved slow and very difficult. After the action was over, the Fore Distributing Station was used for operations.

The Port After Mess Deck, the Distributing Station and the Issue Room were used for the treatment of the wounded aft.

The greater proportion of the injuries consisted of burns about the face and arms, which proved serious and led in a few hours to much swelling of mouth and eyes, and great shock.

The conduct of the wounded was steady, no complaint being heard.

¹ *   *   *   *   *

I have the honour to be,
Sir,
Your obedient Servant,
WALTER COWAN,

The Rear-Admiral Commanding.   Captain.
First Battle Cruiser Squadron.

CAPTAIN'S REPORT.—H.M.S. " TIGER."

Enclosure No. 5 to Battle Cruiser Fleet Letter No. B.C.F. 01
of 12/6/16.

No. F. 61/5.   H.M.S. " Tiger,"
SIR,   6th June 1916.

In accordance with your signal 0945 of 2nd June 1916 I have the honour to submit herewith report of proceedings of 31st May 1916.

I have the honour to be,
Sir,
Your obedient Servant,
H. B. PELLY,

The Vice-Admiral Commanding   Captain.
Battle Cruiser Fleet,
(Through R.A.C., 1st B.C.S.)

---

¹ Part omitted here, referring solely to personnel, recommendations, &c., in no way bearing on the course of the action.

G.M.T.

P.M.

3.44. Enemy reported in sight from " Lion."

3.45. Observed enemy Battle Cruisers, 5 in number, which appeared to be " Hindenburg," " Lützow," " Derfflinger," " Seydlitz," and " Moltke," in the order named from right to left, bearing North and on the Port Beam.

Weather was misty in patches with varying visibility.

3.46. Target given, 4th ship from the left, probably " Seydlitz."

3.49. Enemy opened fire; first salvo about 2,000 yards short.

3.50. " Lion "opened fire.

3.51. " Tiger " opened fire. Smoke from our own T.B.D.s on engaged side which were proceeding to take station ahead caused considerable interference.

Range, 18,500 yards.

1st salvo missed for direction. 2nd over.

3.52. " Tiger " hit on Forecastle.

" Tiger's " salvoes apparently short and hitting.

Increased rate of fire.

3.55. " Q " turret hit and " X " turret hit.

3.56. Hit under P. 6 6-in. gun.

It is of interest to note here that after 3.56 p.m. " Tiger " was apparently not hit again by heavy shell. Several minor hits were registered but no appreciable damage was done.

4. 4. Observed " Indefatigable " sinking.

4.10. T.B.D.s ordered to attack enemy. A desultory action was continued, but the enemy's fire appeared to be wild and uncertain.

4.24. I observed a salvo pitch abreast " Q " turret of " Queen Mary " (this was the first time I had seen " Queen Mary " hit) and almost instantaneously there was a terrific upheaval and a dense cloud of smoke. This could not altogether be avoided as " Tiger " was close up (about 2 cables) from " Queen Mary."

As " Tiger " passed through the cloud there was a heavy fall of material on her decks, but no sign whatever could be seen of the " Queen Mary." She must have sunk instantaneously.

4.25. Shifted target to 3rd ship from the left, apparently the " Derfflinger."

4.26. Established hitting.

4.34. Enemy Torpedo Boats were observed to turn and attack. Opened fire on them with 6-in. battery and appeared to find their range after three salvoes. Range 11,000 yards.

4.39. Checked fire.

4.42. Altered Course in succession 16 points to Starboard on observing 8 enemy Battleships of the " König " class.

G.M.T.
P.M.

4.45. 5th Battle Squadron opened fire.

4.50. Recommenced firing at opposite number (" Derfflinger "). Long range, 18,000 yards, and enemy very indistinct. Only two salvoes fired.

4.58. Altered Course to Port. Recommenced fire at same ship (" Derfflinger "). Light conditions improved and hitting seemed to be established and maintained. " Derfflinger " appeared to be down by the stem and to leave the line.

5.10. Enemy obscured. Speed 24 knots.

5.42. Enemy Battle Cruisers reappeared (only 4).

5.44. Engaged 3rd ship from the left, apparently " Seydlitz." 5th Battle Squadron were also engaging the Battle Cruisers.

5.56. Checked fire as unable to spot and 5th Battle Squadron appeared to be engaging the Enemy Battle Cruisers.

6. 5. Sighted Battleships of Grand Fleet.

6. 7. 6-in. battery opened fire on Light Cruiser of " Kolberg " class on Starboard bow and hit her. This Cruiser eventually drifted between the lines and 6-in. battery fired several salvoes at her and she was last seen sinking by the stern at 6.19.

6.19 to 6.29. Firing a few salvoes at opposite number, but spotting was not possible and fall of shot lost.

6.25. The " Defence " class made a fine entry across the " Lion's " bow into the battle, but they were met by a very heavy fire and suffered disaster. I did not actually observe their loss.

6.36. Enemy developed a very heavy smoke screen and under cover launched a T.B.D. attack on the Battle Fleet. Opened fire with 6-in. guns. The shooting appeared to be good and so the attack was not pressed home. The heavy smoke clouded fall of shot, but apparently several hits were made. Under cover of smoke the enemy turned away.

6.37. Cease Fire.

6.37 to 6.39. About this time three torpedoes passed close to the stern of the ship. Course was altered for one of them, but the others were passing clear.

6.40 to 7.17. Nothing in sight.

7.17. Enemy squadron of four ships appeared, of which two were Battle Cruisers, but I am not sure of the other two.

7.19. Opened fire on opposite number. She appeared to drop astern past Number 4 ship.

7.23. Ceased fire.

G.M.T.
P.M.

7.27. Much smoke observed on Starboard bow, and apparently T.B.D. attack developing. Opened fire with 6-in.

7.31. Ceased Fire.

8.21. Enemy sighted, apparently Battle Ship with 3 funnels. Opened fire and hitting established.

8.29. Enemy altered away.

8.37. Felt a very heavy shock and had no doubt that ship had been torpedoed. Enquiries gave no result, so I concluded that the ship must have struck something under water.

8.40. Cease Fire.

Reports are attached which were written by various Officers in accordance with my directions, also a report in detail of the damage done.

These consist of—

Enclosure No.   I.—Report by Commander A. G. Craufurd, R.N.

Enclosure No. II.—Report by Lieutenant-Commander W. N. Lapage, R.N., Torpedo Officer.

Enclosure No. III.—Report by Lieutenant-Commander P. Macnamara, R.N., Gunnery Officer.

Enclosure No. IV.—Report by Engineer Commander C. H. A. Bermingham, R.N.

Enclosure No.   V.—Report in detail of damage sustained during action.[1]

A separate report of recommendations is also forwarded.

REPORT OF REAR-ADMIRAL SECOND BATTLE CRUISER SQUADRON.

Enclosure No. 6 to Battle Cruiser Fleet Letter No. B.C.F. 01 of 12/6/16.

2nd Battle Cruiser Squadron.

No. 513.   " New Zealand,"
                                          3rd June 1916.

SECOND BATTLE CRUISER SQUADRON.

REPORT ON ACTION OF 31ST MAY 1916.

SIR,

HEREWITH I have the honour to submit observations on the engagement between British and German Fleets, on 31st May 1916. Time table in Appendix I. was compiled by

---

[1] Enclosures detached 12/6/16 and not forwarded by V.A.C. Battle Cruiser Fleet.

Captain and officers of " New Zealand " and is believed to be reliable. From this table and tracing of courses steered[1] the action of the Battle Cruiser Fleet can be reconstructed.

2. On sighting the enemy, Second Battle Cruiser Squadron was ordered to form astern of First Battle Cruiser Squadron, a position retained throughout the action. Fire opened steadily, both sides using simultaneous firing. The director proved invaluable. Though the merit of German salvoes was unequal, yet many pitched all shots together. As fire continued, concentrated falls became less frequent; later on, whenever shots again began to fall together, it was taken as a sign that a fresh enemy was being encountered.

3. Steep angles of descent reduced ricochet and splash. Visibility was generally good, though I was never able personally to identify the enemy vessel under fire. Her position in the line was the most I could make out. Smoke and spray interference were slight.

4. Within a few minutes of entering action, two or three shots falling together hit " Indefatigable " about outer edge of upper deck in line with after turret. A small explosion followed, and she swung out of line, sinking by the stern. Hit again almost instantly near " A " turret by another salvo, she listed heavily to port, turned over and disappeared.

5. As the number of ships in each line was now equal, " New Zealand " shifted target from the fourth to the rear ship. Deterioration in enemy fire was remarked, though one of his ships, probably the third, was still delivering salvoes, close in fall and apparently containing a full number of projectiles. Soon splashes other than those due to fire of " New Zealand " could be seen round her target, thus showing Fifth Battle Squadron was within range. " New Zealand " accordingly resumed fire at the fourth enemy ship, a change recommended also by the catastrophe to " Queen Mary."

6. In the Battle Cruiser Fleet it had been constantly assumed that German battle cruisers would never be found far from adequate support, and thus no surprise was felt when their battle fleet was sighted. This was the moment when the aid of a powerful fighting force was indispensable if the Battle Cruiser Fleet was to be able to avoid engagement with the battle fleet. Here the Fifth Battle Squadron played its part nobly, and as elsewhere during the action it proved itself a tower of strength.

7. After this disengagement the fleets again came together, both steering northerly, fighting as obscuration and range allowed, but with the British always bearing heavily on the head of the opposite line. The Third Battle Cruiser Squadron dashing gallantly into action ahead of " Lion," increased pressure on enemy leaders, checking their advance and compelling them continually to turn away. Thus when the Grand Fleet was

---

[1] Plates 9a and 31.

observed to port, turning to parallel course and with rear apparently well engaged, it was felt that decision was at hand.

8. Nothing now remained but for the Battle Fleet to reap the fruits of a situation brilliantly prepared by the Battle Cruiser Fleet and by the Fifth Battle Squadron. Jointly, this body had performed a magnificent feat of arms. Its position relative to the enemy could not have been improved. It had inflicted severe punishment upon him, and was ready to supplement the frontal attack of the principal forces. For such an attack light was necessary; and visibility had already begun to fail. The Germans may have used smoke screens; but from whatever cause or causes, the atmosphere was thickening, and this, together with the turning away of the enemy fleet, resulted in touch being lost. Hope remained that the decisive operation had only been deferred until the morrow. Here fresh disappointment awaited us, but as search was conducted under orders from Grand Fleet, account is unnecessary.

9. It was evident the Germans had suffered severely, but their full loss could only slowly become known. The British felt that although an unlimited success had been earned, only a limited one had been obtained. The Germans had more cause to rejoice, as they had escaped annihilation. From such a point of view they might well congratulate themselves; but in its nature such success is essentially different from victory, even though some of the benefits of victory accompany it. By the many who have ignorantly believed that any and every meeting of the fleets must prelude a sweeping British victory, the inconclusive nature of this battle will be deeply felt; yet inconclusive actions are the rule in naval warfare, and of all the greater military events recorded in history, the least common has been the naval victory in which the whole force of the enemy has been obliterated.

I have the honour to be,
Sir,
Your obedient Servant,
W. C. PAKENHAM,
Rear-Admiral.

The Vice-Admiral Commanding
Battle Cruiser Fleet.

APPENDIX I. TO REPORT FROM REAR-ADMIRAL COMMANDING SECOND BATTLE CRUISER SQUADRON, DATED 2ND JUNE 1916.

ACTION OF 31ST MAY 1916.

TIME TABLE COMPILED BY CAPTAIN AND OFFICERS OF H.M.S. "NEW ZEALAND."

G.M.T.

P.M.

2.20. Course N. by E. 19½ knots.
2.30. Sounded off action.

G.M.T.

P.M.

2.35. Course S.S.E. 19½ knots gradually increasing to 25 knots.

3. 0. Course E.

3.13. Altered to N.E.

3.24. Observed smoke of five ships bearing starboard 40.

3.30. Made out five enemy battle cruisers escorted by destroyers, bearing E.N.E., steering N.W. course. We altered course to E., speed 26 knots.

3.36. Altered to take station astern of 1st Battle Cruiser Squadron.

3.45. In station astern of " Tiger," course E.

3.49. Enemy altered course about 16 points to starboard (away).

3.51. Our speed 25 knots. " Lion " altered course to starboard to parallel course of enemy. Formed on line of bearing N.W.

3.54. Speed 26 knots. Enemy, " Lion," and 1st Battle Cruiser Squadron opened fire. Range 19,000 yards.

3.57. " New Zealand " opened fire, 18,000 yards on fourth ship from the right.

4. 0. Our course S.S.E. 25 knots. Straddled enemy. Commenced lyddite common.

4. 8. " Indefatigable " blew up.

4.10. Shifted fire on the fifth (rear) battle cruiser. Our course S.

4.22. Altered course a little to port.

4.26. " X " turret reported hit, but still in action. Ship now straddling.

4.32. " Queen Mary " blew up.

4.37. " Lion " kept away to starboard.

4.44. Sighted enemy battle fleet ahead on port bow.

4.45. Altered course 16 points to starboard in succession. Enemy battle fleet opened fire on us. Our course N. by W. 25 knots.

4.52. Unable to fire though being heavily fired at, owing to being unable to get enough elevation on. Range 19,000 yards.

5. 0. Fifth Battle Squadron passed us on our port hand and turned to northward soon after under heavy fire from enemy's battle fleet.

5.42. Observed flashes of firing from enemy's battle cruisers.

5.47. Opened fire on battle cruiser (second from left, all that were visible). Range 17,200 yards.
Firing till 5.58. Intermittent firing owing to mist and smoke.

5.56. Sighted Grand Fleet bearing N. by E. Our course and speed being N.N.E., 25 knots.

6. 8.⎫ Altered to E.N.E., 24 knots. Enemy gradually turning
  to ⎬ away.
6.30.⎭ Heavy fire from enemy battle cruisers and battle fleet. " Invincible " sunk. " Defence " and " Warrior " crossed ahead and under very heavy fire passed down starboard side of Battle Cruiser Fleet. Firing as continuously as mist and smoke allowed.

6.30. Altered course to S.E., 26 knots.

6.41. Ceased fire. Enemy obscured. Passed wreck of " Invincible."

6.45. Commenced to circle gradually to starboard.

6.52. Submarine reported on starboard bow, hauled out of line and then back.

6.59. " Indomitable " and " Inflexible " took station astern. Speed 18 knots. Gradually circling round to starboard. Enemy out of sight or screened by mist and smoke.

7.10. Course S. 18 knots.

7.28. Enemy destroyers attacked, bearing starboard 80. Our course S.S.W. Range 17,800 yards. Fired two salvoes at them, and then 4th Light Cruiser Squadron (I think) went out at them and drove them off.

8.20. Course altered to W. 17 knots. Sighted enemy battle cruisers, five ships, starboard 60.

8.21. Opened fire on third ship. Range 13,000 closing.

8.31. She appeared to be hit and heeling over, on fire and hauled out of line. Then shifted fire on to the fourth ship.

8.41. " New Zealand " appeared to strike something under water, but no damage. Observed what appeared to be a burst of air under water about 50 yards on starboard beam.
Ceased fire. Enemy obscured.

9.35. Course S. 17 knots.

CAPTAIN'S REPORT ON ACTION OF 31st MAY 1916. " H.M.S " NEW ZEALAND."

Enclosure No. 7 to Battle Cruiser Fleet Letter No. B.C.F. 01 of 12/6/16.

No. 96/A. 4.

H.M.S. " New Zealand,"

SIR,   2nd June 1916.

    I HAVE the honour to make the following report on the action which took place on Wednesday, 31st May 1916, between our fleet and the German Fleet.

2. The day was hazy and fine with practically no wind. I should put the visibility down as between 7 and 10 miles, varying in patches. Smoke also added occasionally to the haziness, but I was rather impressed by the little smoke interference there was.

3. Range-taking and Spotting were difficult. It was very difficult to distinguish hits, but occasional bursts of smoke with a salvo seemed to denote a hit.

4. The firing of the enemy was extremely good, their salvoes having very little spread, and they seemed to pick up the range quickly and correctly, and their salvoes were rapid.

5. We were fortunately only hit once by a heavy projectile, about 1 foot above the deck on the port side of " X " Turret (the after turret) which punched a hole about 2 feet in diameter. It also went through the tongue of the towing slip which was secured round the turret. The shell must have burst on deck as there were sputterings round about there. It also damaged the deck, cutting through it and through the deck below into the Engineer's Workshop.

6. I attach a timed account of the various incidents as they occurred. All these times are G.M.T. and are, I consider, absolutely reliable, as they come from 3 different sources.

7.[1]   *   *   *   *   *

8. I consider that the Battle Cruiser described at 8.31 p.m. to be heeling over and on fire, was in a sinking condition when she hauled out of line. The different reports received by Officers in this ship agree that our last 2 or 3 salvoes fired at her hit her heavily. She appeared to be a " Seydlitz " class.

[2]   *   *   *   *   *

I have the honour to be,

Sir,

Your obedient Servant,

JOHN F. E. GREEN,

The Rear-Admiral Commanding   Captain.
    Second Battle Cruiser Squadron,
    H.M.S. " New Zealand."

No. 513a.

" NEW ZEALAND "—ACTION OF 31st MAY 1916.

Vice-Admiral Commanding
    Battle Cruiser Fleet,

Submitted.

W. C. PAKENHAM,

" New Zealand,"   Rear-Admiral.
    6th June 1916.

---

[1] *See* note on p. 381.

[2] Part omitted here referring solely to personnel, recommendations, &c., in no way bearing on the course of the action.

REPORT OF SENIOR OFFICER 3RD BATTLE CRUISER SQUADRON.

Enclosure No. 8 to Battle Cruiser Fleet Letter No. B.C.F. 01 of 12/6/16.

No. 363/16.

H.M.S. " Indomitable,"

Sir,   2nd June 1916.

I HAVE the honour to report that H.M. Battle Cruisers " Invincible," " Indomitable," and " Inflexible," H.M. Light Cruisers " Chester," and " Canterbury " and H.M. Destroyers " Christopher," " Ophelia," " Shark," and " Acasta " left the Pentland Firth at 9.35 p.m. on 30th May 1916, just ahead of the Grand Fleet, with which visual touch was kept by the late Rear-Admiral Commanding Third Battle Cruiser Squadron, The Honourable Horace Lambert Alexander Hood, C.B., M.V.O., D.S.O., through " Chester " till we were in Latitude 57.49 N., Longitude 4.42 E. at 2.23 p.m. on 31st May.

2. At 2.23 p.m. we received from " Galatea " our first intimation that the enemy were actually at sea; we were then steering 115°, speed of advance 14 knots; the speed of advance during the night had been 16.8 knots. Telefunken signals of strength 10 had just previously been heard. From then onwards many signals giving various positions of the enemy were received. At 3.13 p.m. the Rear-Admiral Commanding 3rd Battle Cruiser Squadron increased speed to 22 knots; at 3.18 p.m. he ordered ships to " Action Stations "; 3.45 p.m. he altered course to 137°, the squadron was then in single line ahead with " Canterbury " ahead distant 5 miles, " Chester " on starboard side bearing 256° to 212° distant 5 miles and the four destroyers ahead of the Battle Cruisers as a submarine screen. By 4.12 p.m. we were steaming at full speed.

3. As usual, the positions of the enemy received in the W/T signals did not agree, but they all pointed to the enemy steering 345° or 298°, and it is evident that the late Rear-Admiral acted on this; at 3.57 p.m. we received signals from the Senior Officer, Battle Cruiser Fleet : " Am engaging enemy 1500." At 5.30 p.m. the sound of gunfire was plainly heard. At this time the visibility greatly decreased owing to the mist, the density of which was various degrees; for, on some bearings, one could see 16,000 yards, whilst on others only 2,000 yards. From then till dark the visibility ranged from 14,000 to 5,000 yards, which was, in my opinion, a great handicap to us, the attacking force; in fact much more of a handicap to the attacker then the defenders.

At 5.40 p.m. flashes of gunfire were seen on a bearing about 215°, but I could not distinguish any ships. The Rear-Admiral, " Invincible," altered course to starboard without signal, turning about 9 points, thus bringing the engaged vessels and " Chester " on the port bow of the 3rd Battle Cruiser Squadron, and leaving our destroyers off our port quarter; after a short time we made

out the engagement to be between the enemy's light cruisers
and "Chester." The Rear-Admiral led the squadron between
"Chester" and the enemy's light cruisers whom we engaged;
at 5.55 p.m. we opened fire on the enemy with our port guns.
Shortly afterwards some more of the enemy's cruisers were seen
following at some distance astern of the light cruisers which we
were engaging, and I observed our destroyers developing an
attack on them. At the same time these enemy vessels opened
a heavy fire on our destroyers, and I am afraid that "Acasta"
and another destroyer were either sunk or damaged for I only
saw two of them afterwards, nor did I again see either "Chester"
or "Canterbury." I desire to record the fact that, when I saw
them, they were heading to make a determined attack. At
this moment my attention was called to the enemy's light
cruisers turning 16 points; they were at that time under a
heavy gunfire from the 3rd Battle Cruiser Squadron, and a few
minutes later one was seen to be heavily on fire and apparently
she blew up. There was also observed amongst them a four-
funnelled cruiser, apparently of the "Roon" class. She was
observed to lose two funnels, to be steaming and firing very slowly
and heavily on fire amidships.

4. The First Battle Cruiser Squadron was then sighted on
our port bow, heavily engaged with some enemy whom I could
not see owing to the mist. At 6.13 p.m. "Invincible" turned
to starboard, apparently stopped, and large quantities of steam
were observed to be escaping from her escape pipes. At the
same moment "Inflexible" turned to port and tracks of
torpedoes were observed by "Indomitable" coming from
the enemy's light cruisers with whom we had been engaged.
The range at which I engaged them was about 12,000 yards.
I turned away from the torpedoes and increased to full speed.
One torpedo actually ran alongside this ship at a distance of
about 20 yards, which we managed to outrun. As we turned,
two torpedoes passed close to the stern of the ship, but they
had run their distance, for I managed to turn ahead of them
and resume my place in the Squadron as did "Inflexible"
astern of "Invincible," which ship was then again going ahead,
having turned to about 153°. In all about 5 torpedoes' tracks
were seen coming from the enemy's light cruisers.

At 6.14 p.m. "Invincible," while steam was escaping, hoisted
the "Disregard," but hauled it down at once and followed it
by hoisting 1 flag and the squadron got into proper order again.
About 6.20 p.m. at a range of 8,600 yards the leading ship of
the enemy's battle cruisers was seen firing at the 3rd Battle
Cruiser Squadron. They were promptly engaged, and I realised
that "Invincible" could have sustained little or no damage
from a torpedo, as I had thought she had when she stopped
at 6.13 p.m., for I had to go 20 knots to regain station in the
line; 6.32 p.m. shells were falling about "Indomitable" from
the enemy's battle cruisers, which were distant about 8,000 yards.

At 6.33 p.m. " Invincible " was straddled by a salvo and was hit in the after part; 6.34 p.m. a salvo or one shot appeared to hit her about " Q " turret, and she immediately blew up. Wreckage, &c. was thrown about 400 feet in the air. She appears to have broken in half immediately, for, when the smoke cleared and we had got to the position, the bows were standing upright about 70 feet out of the water and 50 yards away the stern was standing out of the water to a similar height, while in a circle round was wreckage and some few survivors. The visibility, which I have before said was sometimes up to 14,000 yards, was now generally much less than that.

5. The positions of affairs, when I took charge of the 3rd Battle Cruiser Squadron on the lamentable death of Rear-Admiral Hood, appeared to me to be as follows :—

We were steering 153°, as shown on attached chart.[1] The enemy's battle cruisers were disappearing out of sight, but were still firing on " Indomitable " and " Inflexible." The Director Gunner, Mr. James H. Moore, reported that about this time one of the " Derfflinger " class fell out of enemy's line and he saw her sink. The Lieutenant-Comander (G) in the Control top at same period remarked that she was very low in the water. The 1st and 2nd Battle Cruiser Squadrons were coming up astern of " Indomitable "; " Inflexible " being about 3 cables ahead of latter. When " Invincible " blew up, " Inflexible " turned sharply to port, and I did the same and eased the speed as I wanted to continue the action in the same direction as previously and wished, if " Inflexible " turned 8 or more points to port, to turn possibly under her stern, or, at all events, to get the 3rd Battle Cruiser Squadron to resume their original course and then alter it further to starboard in order to continue the action. However, " Inflexible " quickly turned to starboard and continued to turn towards the enemy. By being compelled to ease my speed I had dropped astern of " Inflexible." I made no signal to her as she was turning as I desired. You then ordered the 3rd Battle Cruiser Squadron to prolong your line, which we did. Shortly after this I saw the Grand Fleet astern of us bearing about 340°.

6. Until 7.20 p.m. none of the enemy could be distinguished owing to the mist; but at that time it commenced to lift, and at 7.26 p.m. " Indomitable " reopened fire on the enemy's rear ship, the range being about 14,000 yards and decreasing. Towards the head of the enemy's line dense quantities of grey smoke could be seen and out of this came a destroyer attack, which was beaten off but caused our battlefleet astern to turn away from the enemy. At 7.40 p.m. our fire was checked owing to lack of visibility. At 8.26 p.m. ranges could again be got on the enemy, and " Indomitable " engaged the 2nd ship from the enemy's rear, which, as the range decreased, appeared to be " Seydlitz." The enemy very quickly straddled us and

---

[1] Plate 13.

continued to do so, even after we ceased firing. I believe that "New Zealand" was also firing on this ship; at all events. "Seydlitz" turned away heavily damaged, and her fire lessened. At 8.42 p.m. we ceased fire the enemy bearing 307°, but we could not see to spot.

7. The only damage sustained by "Indomitable" was a small hole in her middle funnel, though many splinters from shells fell on the deck, but no one was injured. At 8.44 p.m. "Indomitable" received so severe a shock that I was knocked off the compass platform. I thought that the ship had been mined or hit by a torpedo, but no damage has so far been discovered. I assume that we either hit some wreckage or a submarine.

8. From then onwards I conformed to your orders and nothing further of importance occurred with the exception that at 3.12 a.m. on 1st June a Zeppelin was sighted on the starboard quarter coming up from the Southward. At 3.17 a.m. fire was opened by "A" and "X" turrets, the Zeppelin then turned 101°, but had not been damaged in any way. At 3.21 a.m. she turned to 10° and continued her course astern of us, but at too great a range to justify a further expenditure of ammunition. Several light cruisers stationed on our port quarter engaged the Zeppelin, but apparently without causing her any damage.

1   *   *   *   *   *

11. The following is amount of ammunition expended by this ship during the action :—

> 98 rounds of A.P. Lyddite, 12-in.
> 66 rounds of Common Lyddite, 12-in.
> 10 rounds of Powder Common, 12-in.

12. I desire to emphasize the fact that, when "Invincible" blew up and sank, the Captain of "Inflexible"—Captain Edward Henry Fitzhardinge Heaton-Ellis, M.V.O.—without warning such as he would have had in the case of a wounded ship, found himself leading the squadron, and he at once followed the highest traditions of our Service by closing the enemy.

. 13. As the Officer left as Senior Officer of the 3rd Battle Cruiser Squadron, I desire to record the sincere sorrow of all the Officers and men of the 3rd Battle Cruiser Squadron in the loss that the Nation has sustained in the death of Rear-Admiral The Hon. Horace L. A. Hood, C.B., M.V.O., D.S.O., Captain Arthur Lindesay Cay, Royal Navy, and the Officers and men of H.M.S. "Invincible," many of whom were personally known to me and friends of mine.

Of Rear-Admiral Hood's attainments it is not for me to speak, but he drew from all of us our love and respect. The Officers and men of "Invincible" had previously been our chums in the Mediterranean.

---

1 Part omitted here, referring solely to personnel, recommendations &c., in no way bearing on the course of the action.

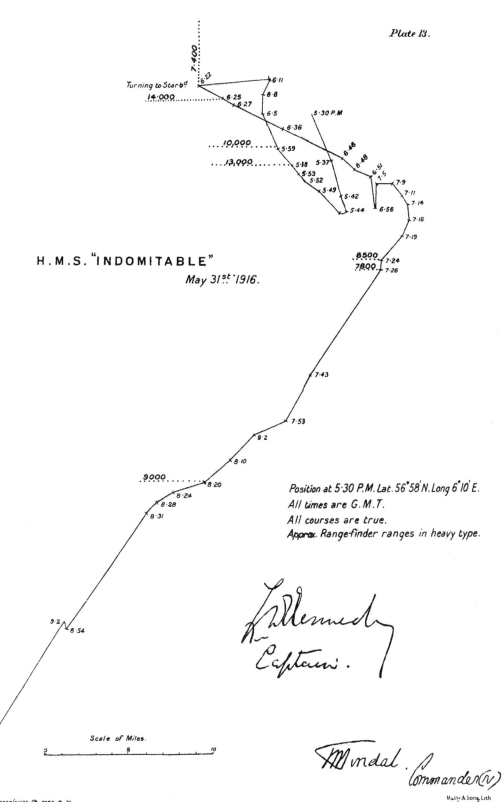

Plate 13.

H.M.S. "INDOMITABLE"

May 31st 1916.

Turning to Starbd

Position at 5·30 P.M. Lat. 56°58'N. Long 6°10'E.
All times are G.M.T.
All courses are true.
Approx. Rangefinder ranges in heavy type.

Scale of Miles.

Mathy & Sons, Lith.

10072 24266/P1173 Ⓒ 5000 12·20.

13. Since compiling the above report, I have seen Commander Hubert E. Dannreuther, who was the Gunnery Commander of H.M.S. "Invincible" on 31st May. He states that the cause of "Invincible" stopping at 6.30 p.m. was that her helm jammed when put "hard-a-port."

I have the honour to be,
Sir,
Your obedient Servant,
F. W. KENNEDY,
Captain and Senior Officer,
3rd B.C. Squadron.

The Vice-Admiral Commanding,
Battle Cruiser Fleet.

Enclosure No. 9 to Battle Cruiser Fleet Letter No. B.C.F. 01
of 12/6/16.

REPORTS OF THE 3RD BATTLE CRUISER SQUADRON ON THE ACTION OF 31ST MAY 1916.

No, 20 S.

Submitted.

2. I concur in the attached reports as far as was seen and known in "Indomitable."

3. I know that the late Rear-Admiral Commanding, 3rd Battle Cruiser Squadron, had a high opinion of Commander Dannreuther's abilities and zeal.

F. W. KENNEDY,
Captain and Senior Officer of
3rd Battle Cruiser Squadron.

The Vice-Admiral Commanding,
Battle Cruiser Fleet.

REPORT OF SENIOR SURVIVING OFFICER, H.M.S. "INVINCIBLE."

H.M.S. "Crescent,"
SIR, 2nd June 1916.

I DEEPLY regret to report that H.M.S. "Invincible," commanded by Captain A. L. Cay, R.N., and flying the flag of Rear-Admiral the Hon. Horace L. Hood, Rear-Admiral Commanding the Third Battle Cruiser Squadron, was blown up and completely destroyed when in action with the enemy at 6.34 p.m. on Wednesday the 31st May.

The total number of officers and men on board at the time was 1,031. Of these only six survived. The names of the survivors are as follows :—

> Commander H. E. Dannreuther, R.N.
> Lieutenant C. S. Sanford, R.N.
> Chief P.O. (P.T.I.) Thompson.
> Yeo. Signals Pratt (Walter Maclean), 216963.
> Able Seaman Dandridge (Ernest George), 239478.
> Gunner Gasson, R.M.A.

Of the above, all are free from injury with the exception of Gunner Gasson, who was severely burnt about the head and arms. They are now accommodated in this ship except Gunner Gasson, who is in the Hospital Ship " Plassy."

The circumstances of the destruction of the ship are briefly as follows :—

The " Invincible " was leading the 3rd B.C.S. and at about 5.45 p.m. first came into action with an enemy light cruiser on the port bow. Several torpedoes were seen coming towards the ship, but were avoided by turning away from them. " Invincible's " fire was effective on the light cruiser engaged, and a heavy explosion was observed. A dense cloud of smoke and steam from this explosion appeared to be in the same position some minutes later.

" Invincible " then turned and came into action at about 6.15 p.m. with the leading enemy battle cruiser, which was thought to be the " Derfflinger." Fire was opened at the enemy at about 8,000 yards, and several hits were observed.

A few moments before the " Invincible " blew up Admiral Hood hailed the Control Officer in the Control Top from the fore bridge : " Your firing is very good, keep at it as quickly as you can, every shot is telling." This was the last order heard from the Admiral or Captain who were both on the bridge at the end.

The Ship had been hit several times by heavy shell, but no appreciable damage had been done when at 6.34 p.m. a heavy shell struck " Q " turret and, bursting inside, blew the roof off. This was observed from the control top. Almost immediately following there was a tremendous explosion amidships indicating that " Q " magazine had blown up. The ship broke in half and sank in 10 or 15 seconds.

The survivors on coming to the surface saw the bow and stern of the ship only, both of which were vertical and about 50 feet clear of the water.

The survivors were stationed as follows prior to the sinking of the ship :—

> Commander Dannreuther (Gun
>   Control Officer) -   -   -
> C.P.O. Thompson -   -   - }Fore Control Top.
> A.B. Danbridge -   -   -

Yeo. Signals Pratt - -	Director Tower platform.
Lieutenant (T) Sandford -	Fore Conning Tower, hatch of which was open.
Gunner Gasson - - -	" Q " turret, at the range-finder.

There was very little wreckage, the six survivors were supported by a target raft and floating timber till picked up by H.M.S. " Badger " shortly after 7 p.m.

Only one man besides those rescued was seen to come to the surface after the explosion, and he sank before he could reach the target raft.

The " Badger " was brought alongside the raft in a most expeditious and seamanlike manner, and the survivors were treated with the utmost kindness and consideration by the officers and men.

I have the honour to be,
Sir,
Your obedient Servant,
H. E. DANNREUTHER,
Captain Francis W. Kennedy, R.N.,   Commander.
H.M.S. " Indomitable."

CAPTAIN'S REPORT.—H.M.S. " INFLEXIBLE."

ENGAGEMENT ON 31st MAY 1916.

No. 199 W.

" Inflexible,"
SIR,   2nd June 1916.

  I HAVE the honour to inform you that " Inflexible " left Scapa Flow at 9 p.m. on Tuesday, 30th May 1916, in company with " Invincible " (flying the Flag of Rear-Admiral the Hon. Horace L. A. Hood, C.B., M.V.O., D.S.O.), " Indomitable " (Captain Francis W. Kennedy), " Chester," " Canterbury," and the four destroyers " Ophelia," " Christopher," " Shark," and " Acasta." This Squadron, which left in advance of the main fleet, which sailed shortly after, under the command of the Commander-in-Chief, was stationed 10 miles ahead of the armoured cruiser screen ; speed of advance of fleet was 17 knots.

  2. At noon on Wednesday, 31st May, the position of the Third Battle Cruiser Squadron was 58° 7' North, 3° 55' East. At 2.20 p.m., the first reports of the enemy were intercepted by W/T.

  3. At 3.15 p.m. speed of Squadron was increased to 22 knots and at 4.0 p.m. to 24 knots, gradually working up to full speed, course being altered as necessary by " Invincible," presumably with the idea of joining up with the Battle Cruiser

Fleet, reports having been intercepted that " Lion " was engaging the enemy.

At about 5.30 p.m. firing was heard ahead, and at 5.40, four hostile light cruisers were sighted on the port bow, apparently engaging the " Chester." On seeing the battle-cruisers, these ships turned away ; fire was opened on the second light cruiser from the right at a range of 8,000 yards, but was checked at 6 o'clock as the ship fired at was enveloped in a high column of smoke and was not seen again ; it is presumed that she blew up. Fire was re-opened on the next cruiser, but after one salvo was fired she disappeared in the mist. Meanwhile the four destroyers in company had left the Squadron in order to attack the enemy and were last seen hotly engaged.

4. At 6.15 p.m., two tracks of torpedoes were observed ; course was altered to avoid one which was seen to pass down the port side at a distance of about 20 ft. (the torpedo was going very slowly—apparently near the end of its run) ; the other torpedo passed astern.

At about this time another torpedo was observed to pass underneath the ship, and emerge the other side.

5. At 6.20 p.m., enemy's heavy ships were observed ahead, course was altered about 8 points to port and fire was opened at a range of about 8,000 to 9,000 yards. Owing to the haze and smoke only one ship was visible, apparently a battleship of the " Kaiser " or " König " class, and some direct hits were considered to have been obtained on this vessel. At 6.30 p.m., the " Invincible " blew up, apparently owing to being hit amidships abreast " Q " turret by a salvo. About 6.35 p.m., enemy disappeared in the mist and firing ceased.

During this engagement, " Inflexible " was continuously fired at, and was straddled repeatedly, but the enemy ship fired at could not be determined owing to the mist. " Inflexible " was now leading the line and having passed the wreck of " Invincible," altered course two points to starboard, fire having ceased, in order to close the enemy. At 6.45 p.m., " Inflexible " altered a further four points to starboard, when orders were received from " Lion " for " Indomitable " and " Inflexible " to prolong the line by taking station astern.

6. At 7.25 p.m., enemy's torpedo craft approached to attack, but were driven back by gunfire ; the track of a torpedo passed 150 yards astern of the ship.

7. At 8.20 p.m., action was resumed at 6,000 yards range with the enemy's armoured ships—believed to be of the " Kaiser " Class. At 8.30, fire was checked, the enemy's ships disappearing in the mist.

At 8.35 p.m., the track of a torpedo was observed across the bows of " Inflexible."

At 8.40, a violent shock was felt underneath the ship and a large swirl of oil was observed about 100 yards on the starboard beam : this violent shock was presumably caused by the ship coming into collision with wreckage.

8. " Inflexible " remained in company with the Vice-Admiral Commanding until arrival in the Forth A.M. the 2nd June.

At 2.24 p.m., 1st June, " Inflexible " passed a whaler of German pattern marked " V. 29," and later, in about latitude 57° 2′ N., Longitude 6° 13′ E., passed large numbers of German bodies in lifebelts and a lifebuoy marked " S.M.S. —— " (the name of the ship being covered by a body lying over it).

9. Except for the collision mentioned in paragraph 7, which must have caused an indentation of the outer skin, no damage has been sustained, and no casualties have occurred on board " Inflexible " during the recent engagement, but the right gun of " Q " turret, which was cracked for a length of 30 ft. during calibration, was used and this appears to have enlarged the crack.

1 *   *   *   *   *

I have the honour to be,
Sir,
Your obedient Servant,
EDW. HEATON ELLIS.
Captain.

Captain Francis William Kennedy, Royal Navy,
Senior Officer, Third Battle Cruiser Squadron.

---

1 Part omitted here, referring solely to personnel, recommendations, &c , in no way bearing on the course of the action.

COMMODORE'S REPORT.—1st LIGHT CRUISER SQUADRON.

Enclosure No. 10 to Battle Cruiser Fleet Letter No. B.C.F. 01 of 12/6/16.

No. 30.

"Galatea,"

SIR,   2nd June 1916.

I HAVE the honour to report for your information the part taken by the First Light Cruiser Squadron in the recent action and afterwards.

2. At 6.7 p.m. on 31st May, owing to damage to the port after forced draught fan, "Galatea's" speed was reduced to 18 knots for a time, but after temporary repairs had been made a speed of 24 knots was attained. "Inconstant" was placed in charge of "Phaeton" and "Cordelia" until "Galatea" was able to rejoin next morning. Report from Captain of "Inconstant" covering that period is enclosed.

3. At 2.18 p.m. on 31st May in latitude 56° 52' N., longitude 5° 21' E., "Galatea" and "Phaeton" being in the Port Wing position of the Light Cruiser Screen, course and speed of Battle Cruiser Fleet being S.E., 20 knots, attention was drawn by a steamer, bearing S. 72 E. about 12 miles, blowing off steam and the masts and two funnels of a war vessel were made out in her vicinity. This was reported by "Galatea," who in company with "Phaeton," closed at high speed. It was then found that two German Destroyers had stopped the steamer and that a squadron of Cruisers and Torpedo-boat Destroyers were a little to the North-eastward apparently steaming in various directions which made it difficult to send an adequate report.

4. At 2.28 p.m. "Galatea" and "Phaeton" opened fire on the two destroyers who proceeded to the Northward at speed.

5. At 2.32 p.m. a three-funnelled cruiser opened fire at 15,000 yards, salvoes falling both sides of "Galatea" and "Phaeton," but only one 5·9-in. shell hit "Galatea"; this did not burst.

On the approach of the other enemy cruisers the First Light Cruiser Squadron—"Inconstant" and "Cordelia" were closing —proceeded to the North-west in extended order keeping just out of gun range, the Vice-Admiral Commanding Battle Cruiser Fleet, who was to the West-south-westward about 15 miles, having signalled that he was steering east, and it was hoped by drawing the enemy North-west the Battle Cruisers would be able to get in behind them, but shortly afterwards the Battle Cruisers were seen in action with the enemy's heavy ships.

6. At 3.35 p.m. the enemy's Light Cruisers turned to the South-eastward and the 1st and 3rd Light Cruiser Squadrons, the latter having come up, followed on a parallel course.

7. At 3.45 p.m. the Battle Cruisers were sighted about South-south-east in action with an enemy to the South-eastward.

About 4.0 p.m. the Fifth Battle Squadron was sighted to the South-west and opened fire on the enemy's Light Cruisers, which turned to the Northward under cover of smoke bombs. 1st and 3rd Light Cruiser Squadrons followed them.

8. At 4.15 p.m. the enemy's Light Cruisers turned again to the South-east and course was altered to steam parallel.

9. At 5.1 p.m. the Battle Cruisers were sighted to the Southward steering about North-west, and course was altered to North-west.

10. At 5.27 p.m. a signal was received from "Lion" to keep touch with enemy's Battle Cruisers; these were not in sight, but course was altered to Northward and shortly after the enemy's Battle Cruisers were made out steering in the same direction about 16,000 yards on Starboard beam. The Squadron continued in this direction.

11. At 5.50 p.m. a signal was received from "Lion" for Light Cruisers to attack with torpedoes; speed was increased to get into position, but, shortly after, the advance Cruisers of our Battle Fleet were met steering a South-easterly course and the leading ships of the latter turned to port when quite close, but almost immediately turned 12 points to starboard and it appeared that the Battle Fleet was going to deploy in that direction.

12. At 6.7 p.m. course was altered to the Westward and then to the Northward between the 4th and 5th Divisions of the Battle Fleet to get out of the way.

At this time the port forced draught fan broke down and speed had to be reduced. "Inconstant" was directed to go on with "Phaeton" and "Cordelia" to the head of the line, "Galatea" following and taking station at the head of the Battle Fleet clear of Fourth Light Cruiser Squadron and Destroyers by 8 p.m., remaining in that position for the night.

13. At 2.35 a.m. on 1st June, on the Battle Cruisers being sighted, "Galatea," who was then able to steam 24 knots, rejoined the First Light Cruiser Squadron.

14. During the action several metal cylinders about the size of a picket boat's funnel were passed, these had been thrown overboard by enemy Light Cruisers with material in them to make smoke.

15. On the 1st June, in latitude 56° 25' N., longitude 6° 21' E., several bodies with life-belts which did not appear to be British were seen and shortly afterwards two pear-shaped blue and white mines were passed; it was thought that these and the bodies must have belonged to a German destroyer.

16. At 7.30 p.m. on the 31st May in latitude 57° 0' N., longitude 6° 23' E., the wreck of what is believed to be "Invincible" was passed, the bow and stern standing out of the water. As "Galatea" passed the stern sunk. There was practically

no wreckage about and none of the crew were seen at the time, but on passing the same spot next day three or four bodies in life-belts were seen in the vicinity. The above position was verified on the second day.

About 7 miles 331 degrees from the wreck of "Invincible" a large amount of heavy oil and a great deal of wreckage was seen; this did not appear to have come from "Invincible."

I have the honour to be,
Sir,
Your obedient Servant,
E. S. ALEXANDER SINCLAIR,
Commodore Commanding
First Light Cruiser Squadron.

The Vice-Admiral Commanding,
　　Battle Cruiser Fleet.

CAPTAIN'S REPORT.—H.M.S. "INCONSTANT."

C. 141/46.

H.M.S. "Inconstant,"
2nd June 1916.

SIR,
　　I HAVE the honour to report as follows with regard to my movements after receiving your signal to go on with the 1st L.C.S. at 6.27 p.m. on 31st May.

2. I proceeded full speed on an Easterly and then Southerly Course passing round the Battle Fleet. Owing to the necessity of keeping on the far side of the Repeating Light Cruisers of the various Battle Squadrons and to the fact that the Battle Fleet was continually altering course to starboard, I had to go on the outside of a circle and it was not until about 7.25 p.m. that I reached the head of the Battle Fleet line.

3. On arrival at the head of the Battle Line, I found the 5 ships of the 4th L.C.S. with at least one complete Destroyer Flotilla, a Light Cruiser and also four or five Cruisers.

4. The Battle Cruisers were at this time about 4 miles ahead of the Battle Fleet, and I moved up and placed the three ships of the 1st L.C.S. on the engaged quarter of the Battle Cruisers, from where we could prevent a Destroyer attack coming down from the bow on to our Battle Fleet, and at the same time afford some protection to the rear of the Battle Cruiser Line.

5. At about 8.0 p.m. the ship struck or was struck by something. "Cordelia" has since reported that she struck something at about the same time, so it is assumed we struck some submerged wreckage.

6. At about 8.15 p.m. the Battle Cruisers became engaged, apparently with the Enemy's Battle Fleet, and the 3rd L.C.S., who were ahead of the Battle Cruiser Line, went on at full speed and became engaged, but I could not see against whom. Owing

to this the Battle Cruisers had no Light Cruisers at the head of their line, and so I proceeded there at full speed.

7. At 8.29 p.m. all three ships of the Squadron sighted a submarine breaking surface on the Port Side. This was reported by W/T.

8. Owing to the overs, I passed about 2,000 yards on the dis-engaged side of the line and formed on the engaged bow of the Battle Cruiser Fleet. By the time I got there, the 3rd L.C.S. had ceased firing.

9. In order to prevent having too many independent Squadrons, just before dark, I took station with the 1st L.C.S. astern of the 3rd L.C.S.

10. At 9.57 p.m. I received a signal from the S.O., B.C.F., to take station W. by S. 4 miles from "Lion. "Lion's" estimated position at this time was about 12 miles N.E.

11. I picked up the Battle Cruisers at daylight, steering South. At 2.35 a.m. "Lion" signalled "Course N.", and again at 3.10 a.m., "Course N.E."

12. At 4.10 a.m. "Lion" signalled, "Spread well to Westward and endeavour to locate enemy. Keep linking ships in visual touch."

Whilst spread in this manner, "Galatea" rejoined and took command of 1st L.C.S.

I have the honour to be,
Sir,
Your obedient Servant,
B. S. THESIGER,
Captain.

The Commodore Commanding,
    First Light Cruiser Squadron.

COMMODORE'S REPORTS.—2ND LIGHT CRUISER SQUADRON.

Enclosure No. 11 to Battle Cruiser Fleet Letter No. B.C.F. 01 of 12/6/16.

No. 037/5.

"Southampton,"
Sir,   2nd June 1916.

    I HAVE the honour to submit the following report of the proceedings of the Second Light Cruiser Squadron, consisting of H.M. Ships "Southampton" (wearing my Broad Pendant), "Nottingham" (Captain Charles B. Miller), "Birmingham" (Captain Arthur A. M. Duff), and "Dublin" (Captain Albert C. Scott) during the operations on 31st May and 1st June :—

31st May.

2. The enemy were reported by the Senior Officer, 1st Light Cruiser Squadron, between 2.23 and 2.56 p.m.

3. At 4.40 p.m. "Southampton" sighted and reported enemy's battle fleet bearing S. by E., steering N. The Second Light Cruiser Squadron closed to within 13,000 yards to observe enemy's battle fleet, and came under very heavy fire.

At 5.00 p.m. the Second Light Cruiser Squadron turned Northwards and followed our battle cruisers and 5th battle squadron. The Second Light Cruiser Squadron were at this time practically in line with the rear ship of the 5th battle squadron, and came under a very heavy fire from time to time until about 6.05 p.m.; no damage, however, resulted.

4. At 6.15 p.m. our battle fleet was sighted right ahead.

5. At 6.35 p.m. "Warspite" suddenly turned South and ran in towards the German line, coming under heavy concentrated fire.

"Warspite" shortly afterwards rejoined the line at the rear. During this time the Second Light Cruiser Squadron occupied position "N" (in accordance with Grand Fleet Battle Orders, page 41).

6. At about 6.40 p.m. the action appeared to become general.

7. At 6.47 p.m. the Second Light Cruiser Squadron turned in towards the German line partly to finish off a disabled battleship, but more to observe the enemy's rear more clearly, their course being in doubt. Enemy's turn to E.S.E. was reported by "Southampton" at 7.04 p.m.

The Squadron now came under heavy fire from the German battle fleet, and it became necessary to return to the rear of our battle line.

Between 6.55 and 7.05 p.m. water and spray was constantly coming on board "Southampton" from enemy's salvoes, which were dropping all round the ship.

8. At 7.30 p.m. the Germans altered course together to S. by W., and their destroyers made an effective smoke screen, as the German fleet was now in bad light.

9. At about 8.30 p.m. a German destroyer was sighted and fired on by "Southampton" and "Dublin," who hit her heavily amidships. She was afterwards sunk by a division of our destroyers.

10. At 9.00 p.m. the enemy's destroyers attempted to attack our 5th battle squadron from the North-West. They were driven off by the Second Light Cruiser Squadron; one destroyer was observed to have been hit.

11. At 10.20 p.m. the Squadron was engaged with five enemy ships, apparently a cruiser and four light cruisers, who concentrated on "Southampton" and "Dublin" at very short range. The action was very sharp while it lasted (about 15 minutes), and the casualties in "Southampton" were heavy. Detailed lists of killed and wounded in "Southampton" and "Dublin" have been forwarded separately.[1]

---

[1] Not printed.

Three fires broke out on board "Southampton" during the action; these were promptly extinguished, though the hoses had been very much cut up by shell fire.

12. On the enemy retiring, "Southampton," "Nottingham," and "Birmingham" proceeded and remained astern and on starboard quarter of the centre of the battle fleet during the night, as it was not known what protection they had against destroyer attack. Firing astern was heard at intervals between 10.30 p.m. and 2.00 a.m.

H.M.S. "Dublin" became detached from the Squadron during the night, and did not rejoin till 10.00 a.m. the next day.

1st June.

13. Squadron, except "Dublin," regained touch with our Battle Cruiser Fleet at 4.30 a.m., and proceeded as ordered.

"Southampton" passed a mine, with horns, at 4.25 a.m. in Latitude 55° 25' N., Longitude 6° 11' E.

14. The behaviour of all ranks and ratings of "Southampton" while the ship was in the trying position of receiving a heavy fire from 11 and 12-in. guns without being able to return it, and also during the night action with fires breaking out on board was in every way in accordance with the best and highest traditions of the Service.

1   *   *   *   *   *

15. A track chart[2] of movements of "Southampton" is enclosed (Enclosure 2).

I have the honour to be,
Sir,
Your obedient Servant,
W. E. GOODENOUGH,

The Vice-Admiral Commanding,   Commodore,
     Battle Cruiser Fleet,   Second Light Cruiser Squadron.
     H.M.S. "Lion."

Enclosure No. 12 to Battle Cruiser Fleet.
Letter No. B.C.F. 01 of 12/6/16.

No. 037/7.

                         "Southampton,"
SIR,   5th June 1916.

IN continuation of my letter No. 037/5 of 2nd June, I have the honour to report that from a piece of shell found on board "Southampton" it appears that one of the cruisers engaged with the Second Light Cruiser Squadron at 10.20 p.m. on 31st May was armed with 9·4-in. guns, probably the "Roon" or "Fürst Bismarck."

---

[1] Part omitted here, referring solely to personnel, recommendations, &c., in no way bearing on the course of the action.

[2] There is no trace of this chart at the Admiralty.

The course of the enemy squadron was S.S.E., and position at 10.20 p.m. Latitude 56° 10′ Nl., Longitude 6° 11′ E. When beaten off, they appeared to retire to the westward.

One torpedo (high speed setting) was fired at close range by "Southampton" at 10.21 p.m. It is worth observing that when passing within about a mile of the spot, by reckoning, at 11.30 a.m. the next day, the sea was covered by oil, for an area of about a square mile.

1 *   *   *   *   *

I have the honour to be,
Sir,
Your obedient Servant,
W. E. GOODENOUGH,

The Vice-Admiral Commanding,   Commodore,
Battle Cruiser Fleet,   2nd Light Cruiser Squadron.
H.M.S. "Lion."

Enclosure No. 13 to Battle Cruiser Fleet Letter No. B.C.F. 01 of 12/6/16.

No. 037/8.

"Birmingham,"
SIR,   6th June 1916.

    I HAVE the honour to submit the enclosed reports of proceedings on 31st May and 1st June, which have been received from H.M. Ships "Nottingham," "Birmingham," and "Dublin."

I have the honour to be,
Sir,
Your obedient Servant,
W. E. GOODENOUGH,

The Vice-Admiral Commanding,   Commodore.
Battle Cruiser Fleet, ·
H.M.S. "Lion."

CAPTAIN'S REPORT.—H.M.S. "BIRMINGHAM."

No. 309/10.

H.M.S. "Birmingham,"
SIR,   2nd June 1916.

    I HAVE the honour to report that during the operations on 31st May 1916 and 1st June 1916 I was in the immediate presence of your broad pendant except for a few hours during the night 31st May 1916–1st June 1916, and I therefore only mention a few points that may be of interest together with an account of my proceedings during the time I was separated from you.

    2. About 4.35 p.m. G.M.T. on Wednesday, 31st May 1916, H.M.S. "Birmingham" was under heavy fire from 11-in. or 12-in. guns of the enemy's battle fleet, and on one or two other occasions later in the evening.

---

¹ Part omitted here, referring solely to personnel, recommendations, &c., in no way bearing on the course of the action.

On all these occasions the shells were falling all round the ship so close that a good many pieces of the shells as they burst came on board and also a good deal of water thrown up by them. The fact that the ship was not actually hit appeared extraordinary, and I attribute it in a great measure to the fact that on each occasion when fire was opened the ship at once steered away at full speed, and on each salvo falling near the ship, course was at once altered 2 points one way or another. As a result of this, although the next salvo appeared correct for range it was generally well clear to the right or left. But there was also a large element of good fortune in it, as when there was more than one ship firing at us it was impossible to avoid them all and many fell all round the ship.

It was noticed that just before they ceased firing on account of the ship getting out of range, the time of flight was 40 seconds, which appeared also to be the time between the salvoes.

3. About 7.0 p.m. G.M.T. on 31st May 1916 fire was opened on a disabled battleship or large cruiser with the remainder of the squadron, and the shooting appeared to be good, the bursts of the shell on her being quite obvious.

4. I was unable to fire on the destroyer that the rest of the squadron fired at later in the evening owing to being blanketed by some of our own destroyers.

5. During the attack on the enemy's cruisers about 10.15 p.m. G.M.T. it was impossible, owing to the smoke made by the three ships that were ahead of me in the line, to see anything until the enemy's ships switched on their searchlights when fire was opened on the rear ship. From the same cause it was then so difficult to see that I could not distinguish what class of ships they were. The enemy ship returned the fire and the shot fell very close round the ship.

6. After the squadron turned to the Eastward together I found myself approaching our 5th Battle Squadron, who were steering to the Southward, and was obliged to turn to the northward to avoid the two rear ships, thus losing touch with the remainder of the 2nd Light Cruiser Squadron. As I could not see any destroyers or light cruisers guarding the 5th Battle Squadron from enemy destroyer attack in that direction, I remained during the dark hours on the starboard quarter of the rear ship from where I could act in the event of an attack on them. At daylight I sighted " Southampton " and " Nottingham " on my starboard bow and rejoined.

7. At about 11.30 p.m. G.M.T. on 31st May 1916 I observed two or more large enemy ships switch on their searchlights and open fire on some of our destroyers or light cruiser and destroyers, astern. At the time I was convinced from their appearance and the speed they were going that they were the enemy battle cruisers, but I have since ascertained that they were probably battleships.

M 2

8. Soon after midnight 31st May–1st June 1916 I observed heavy firing some distance away to the North-eastward.

9. When under fire of the battle fleet the engines were put to full speed and subsequently kept at it for two hours in order to regain station. During this period the revolutions averaged 381, or 14 higher than the ship has done since she was in commission. The work of the engine-room department under Engineer Commander John B. Hewitt was most satisfactory throughout a very arduous day.

I have the honour to be,

Sir,

Your obedient Servant,

A. DUFF,

The Commodore Commanding,   Captain.
    Second Light Cruiser Squadron,
        H.M.S. " Southampton."

CAPTAIN'S REPORT.—H.M.S. " DUBLIN."

H.M.S. " Dublin,"

SIR,   2nd June 1916.

    I HAVE the honour to report that the proceedings of H.M. Ship under my command during 30th–31st May and 1st June were as follows :—

Tuesday Night, 30th May.

At 9.30 p.m.   Proceeded to sea with 2nd Light Cruiser Squadron. When clear of May Island, took up usual screen ahead of Battle Cruisers, 2nd L.C. Squadron on Starboard wing position.

31st May.

At 2.30 p.m.   " Galatea " reported enemy's Cruisers in sight.

At 3.40 p.m.   Sighted 5 enemy Battle Cruisers and several destroyers with them.

At 3.50 p.m.   " Lion " opened fire on enemy's Battle Cruisers.

At 4. 4 p.m.   " Indefatigable " blew up.

At 4.12 p.m.   Ordered by Commodore of 2nd L.C. Squadron to support our Destroyers in a Torpedo attack. " Dublin " at the time being about 5 cables on disengaged bow of " Lion " and, proceeding at " Full speed," it was found impossible to cross the bows of the " Lion " to take up position, also our smoke would have much interfered with the " Lion " if I could have crossed her bows.

4.30 p.m.   " Queen Mary " blew up and sank.

4.35 p.m.   2nd Light Cruiser Squadron 'in " Single Line ahead."

4.40 p.m.   Our Battle Cruisers altered course 16 points to Starboard, 2nd Light Cruiser Squadron now to rear.

4.43 p.m.   Enemy's Battle Fleet sighted—steering to the Northward.

4.56 p.m.   2nd Light Cruiser Squadron under very heavy shell fire from enemy's Battle Fleet, salvoes falling very close, but the ship did not receive a direct hit, although many pieces of 12-in. shell came inboard, the Navigating Officer, Lieutenant Percy Strickland, being hit by a small piece which did no harm. He was standing by my side at the time, on the Upper Bridge.

4.58 p.m.   A 12-in. shell struck the water a few yards on Starboard beam and 4 shells passed just over the bridge.

5.15 p.m.   Observed one of our " M " class Torpedo Boat Destroyers sinking.

5.47 p.m.   " Opened fire " on damaged enemy ship.

6.22 p.m.   Ship bearing N.E. blew up.

6.23 p.m.   " Warspite " hauled out of line and enemy's Battle Fleet concentrated their fire on her, but she had regained her position in line by 6.45 p.m.

7.20 p.m.   Our Battle Fleet " opened fire " on enemy's Battle Fleet.

7.45 p.m.   Observed two enemy destroyers on Starboard Beam, " opened fire " on same.

8. 6 p.m.   Lost sight of enemy's Battle Fleet.

8.56 p.m.   Observed two enemy torpedo boat destroyers on Starboard bow and " opened fire " on same, and they disappeared in a cloud of smoke.

9.10 p.m.   Heard heavy firing S.W.

10.40 p.m.   Sighted enemy's vessels on Starboard Beam, it being quite dark and rather misty. Directly enemy " switched on " searchlights " Dublin " opened a very rapid fire on an enemy ship on the Beam, but it was impossible to distinguish what ship it was.

10.45 p.m.   Lieutenant Percy Strickland. Navigating Officer, was killed as he was stepping on to the Upper Bridge, ship was being hit many times, and on a fire starting on the Seamen's Mess Deck the ship was hauled out 3 points, which made enemy's shells fall short.

10.55 p.m.   Resumed course of 2nd Light Cruiser Squadron.

11.0 p.m.   All firing ceased, and in total darkness hauled
About   over 3 points to Port as " Southampton " appeared to be doing so.

11.20 p.m.   Resumed Course and Speed of 2nd Light Cruiser
Squadron, but lost sight of them.

From 11.0 p.m. until 2.0 a.m. on 1st June,
observed continuous flashes of guns to the
Northward.

At daylight, no vessel in sight but visibility low;
I think the shell which passed through the
Chart House and then exploded must have
affected the Standard Compass, otherwise the
ship must have been in close touch with
2nd Light Cruiser Squadron.

4. 0 a.m.   Course North. Nothing in sight. Weather very
misty. Impossible to work up a "dead
reckoning," as Navigating Officer is dead
and his records gone, and the charts in Chart
House badly damaged.

The wireless trunk having been shot away, it
was some considerable time before the main
aerials were connected up; in the meanwhile
the Battle aerial was connected up and signals
were received.

4.10 a.m.   Sighted about one mile off some enemy's vessels,
one of which resembled the "Roon," the
others were too indistinct to make out what
class of vessel they belonged to, they were
steering a southerly course at a high rate of
speed.

In a few seconds the enemy was lost in the fog,
the ship was turned with the object of chasing
and shadowing them, but the existing conditions of weather made this impossible. Course
was therefore shaped for a position where it was
hoped to meet with and join up with the
2nd Light Cruiser Squadron. The Commander-
in-Chief was informed of sighting the enemy.
The Commodore, 2nd Light Cruiser Squadron,
was asked for course and speed of Squadron.

5.30 a.m.   Passed a lot of oil fuel and rescued a man on
a piece of wood who turned out to be George
T. A. Parkyn, Stoker 1st class of H.M.S.
"Tipperary," who had been in the water for
about 5 hours, and stated his ship had been
sunk by shell fire at night. (His statement
is enclosed.)

The ship had previous to this passed through a
large number of dead bodies.

6. 0 a.m.   Sighted Torpedo Boat Destroyer "Sparrowhawk " in a very damaged condition, bows
crumpled up to the Bridge and stern badly
damaged. Destroyer Leader "Marksman "

standing by to take men from her; helped
" Marksman " by giving her a lee, and
when I parted company with " Marksman "
she was attempting to tow " Sparrowhawk,"
but I saw·it was a hopeless case, and an
intercepted signal later stated that " Sparrowhawk " had been sunk.

At 8. 5 a.m. Joined the Flag of the Commander-in-Chief.

During the night action the ship was struck by 13 shells,
about half of which did not explode.

I would like to mention the cool behaviour of all Officers and
Men during the time when the 12-in. shell were falling thickly
around the ship by day, and also, when the ship was under
heavy fire at night.

1 * * * * *

I have the honour to be,
Sir,
Your obedient Servant,
A. C. SCOTT,
The Commodore Commanding,   Captain.
2nd Light Cruiser Squadron.

STATEMENT OF GEORGE THOS. AUG. PARKYN, STOKER 1st CLASS, EX " TIPPERARY." RESCUED AT SEA ON THE MORNING OF 1st JUNE 1916.

I was at work in No. 3 Stokehold, and at about 11.0 p.m.
(31st May 1916) I learnt that we were in action with German
Torpedo Craft. We had been in action about ¼ of an hour
when the Bridge caught fire from shells.

The vessel kept afloat for some time after this, going down
about break of day, 1½ hours or 2 hours after being hit.

When abandoning the ship the Motor Boat was tried, the
only boat left, but sank as soon as it touched water.

Some men had previously got away on a small raft, and
about 17 men got on to the larger raft. I saw neither of these
after.

" Tipperary " plunged suddenly, going down by the Bows.
I saw no other survivors while in the water.

GEORGE THOMAS AUGUSTUS PARKYN,
Stoker 1st Class.

CAPTAIN'S REPORT.—H.M.S. " NOTTINGHAM."

No. 66.

H.M.S. " Nottingham,"
SIR,   2nd June 1916.
I HAVE the honour to report the proceedings of H.M. Ship
under my command, during the Action on 31st May 1916.

---

¹ Part omitted here, referring solely to personnel, recommendations,
&c., in no way bearing on the course of the action.

2. At 2.55 p.m. a signal was received from Senior Officer, Battle Cruiser Fleet, to 2nd Light Cruiser Squadron : " Prepare to attack the van of the enemy."

3. " Nottingham " was at that time on " Lion's " starboard bow and took up a position a shade on her port bow as far ahead as possible, in order to break up any attack from Enemy Torpedo Craft, and to support our own Torpedo Boat Destroyers of 13th Flotilla.

4. The enemy Torpedo Boat Destroyers started to attack about 4.0 p.m., and " Nottingham " opened fire upon them, which fire appeared to be effective, and the attack was not pressed home.

5. As " Lion " was gradually opening the range, " Nottingham " altered to starboard to prevent getting in her way, and when " Nottingham " could no longer support the T.B.D.'s, she took station on Commodore 2nd Light Cruiser Squadron, which station she maintained during the remainder of the action.

6. About 4.40 p.m., " Nottingham " fired an E.R. Torpedo at Enemy Battle Fleet; the range being about 16,500 yards, the Battle Fleet being in line ahead. No other opportunity for firing torpedoes presented itself.

7. The ship was steaming at high speed from 3.0 p.m. until 8.0 p.m., and from 4.0 p.m. to 6.0 p.m. the engines were running at a mean speed of 377 revolutions, the greatest S.H.P. developed being 28,156.

8. No defects were brought to light except an increased leakage of oil fuel from after tanks into reserve feed tanks in After Engine Room, caused probably by the vibration.

9. I would submit that this performance is most creditable to the whole of the Engine Room Staff especially in that Engineer Commander Gerald Moore, R.N., was able to receive no assistance from the Senior Engineer Lieutenant, he and 14 Engine Room Ratings (including seven chief or P.O.'s) being out of the ship at the time.

10. I enclose a tracing showing the rough track of " Nottingham " between 3.0 p.m. and 10.30 p.m.[1] This track was plotted by a trained rating working in the Lower Conning Tower.

11. " Nottingham " sustained no damage and no direct hits from heavy shell, although she was frequently straddled and fragments of heavy shell bursting in the water close to the ship struck the sides and fell about the upper deck.

12. The behaviour of both Officers and Ship's Company was everything that could be desired.

I have the honour to be,
Sir,
Your obedient Servant,
CHARLES B. MILLER,
Captain.

The Commodore Commanding,
   Second Light Cruiser Squadron,
     H.M.S. " Southampton."

---

[1] Plate 14.

TRACING OF THE APPROXIMATE COURSES STEERED BY
H.M.S "NOTTINGHAM" FROM III·0 P.M. TO X·30 P.M
MAY 31st

Plate 14.

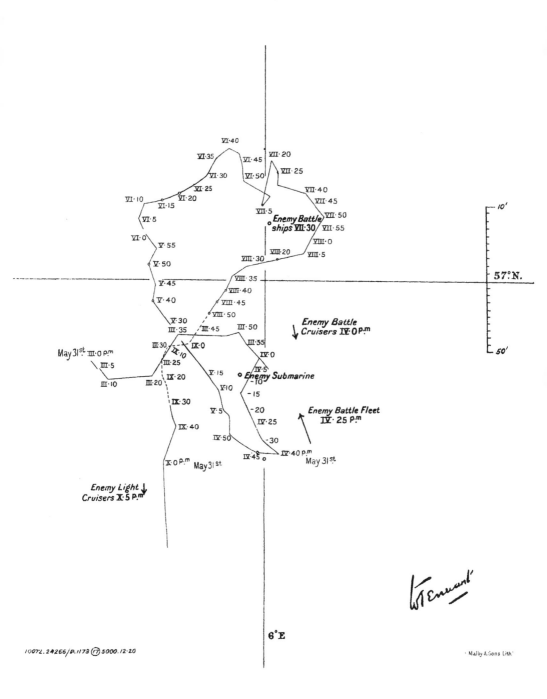

VI·40

VI·35 VI·45 VII·20

VI·30 VI·50 VII·25

VI·25 VII·40

VI·10 VI·20 VII·45

VI·15 VII·5

VI·5 *Enemy Battle* VII·50

ships VII·30 VII·55

VI·0 V·55 VIII·0

V·50 VIII·20 VIII·5

VIII·30

57°N.

V·45 VIII·35

V·40 VIII·40

VIII·45

V·30 VIII·50

III·35 III·45 III·50 *Enemy Battle*

Cruisers IV·0 P.m

III·30 III·55

IX·0

May 31st III·0 p.m IX·10 IV·0

III·5 III·25 IV·5

III·10 III·20 IX·20 V·15 *Enemy Submarine* –10

V·10 –15

IX·30 *Enemy Battle Fleet*

V·5 –20 IV·25 p.m

IX·40 IV·25

IV·50 –30

X·0 p.m May 31st IV·45 IV·40 p.m

May 31st

Enemy Light ↓

Cruisers X·5 p.m

6°E

10'

57°N.

50'

10072.24266/P.1173 (17) 5000.12·20

Malby & Sons Lith.

REAR-ADMIRAL'S REPORT.—3RD LIGHT CRUISER
SQUADRON.

Enclosure No. 14 to Battle Cruiser Fleet, Letter No. B.C.F. 01
of 12/6/16.

No. 0447.

"Falmouth,"

SIR,   5th June 1916.

I HAVE the honour to submit the following report of the
proceedings of the Third Light Cruiser Squadron under my
command during the action on 31st May 1916.[1]

2. At 2.23 p.m., the Light Cruiser Screen being then spread
in an E.N.E. direction, the centre bearing S.S.E. from "Lion,"
and the course just being altered to N. by E., "Galatea's"
report of enemy Cruisers was received, and the First Light
Cruiser Squadron proceeded in an E.S.E. direction at full speed,
and the Third Light Cruiser Squadron closed in support, also
at full speed.

3. I directed "Engadine" to take cover near our Battle
Cruisers.

4. At 2.45 p.m., we sighted two or three enemy Cruisers,
about 12 miles E.S.E., firing at the First Light Cruiser Squadron,
and the shots falling mostly short. Being far outranged, we
endeavoured to keep touch without closing much, and to lead
the enemy round to the direction of our Battlefleet (N.W.),
whilst the Battle Cruisers were steering to the eastward to cut
them off.

5. At 3.33 p.m., the enemy altered to about E.S.E. and
the First and Third Light Cruiser Squadrons did the same. At
this time splashes were falling close ahead.

6. At 4.32 p.m., we passed a quantity of what looked like
large brass cartridge cases of twelve to fifteen inches diameter,
but have since been considered to have probably been smoke
boxes, as the enemy had already been much obscured by whitish
clouds of smoke.

7. We then endeavoured (at 4.30 p.m.) with the First Light
Cruiser Squadron to engage the four enemy cruisers which
appeared to be detached to the northward of the enemy's main
body, but at 4.50 p.m. we sighted our own Battle Cruisers
ahead and steering towards us (W.N.W.), and engaged with
the enemy Battle Cruisers to starboard. We accordingly altered
to keep ahead of our Battle Cruisers, and twenty minutes later
passed the wreckage of a sunken ship.

8. At 5.33 p.m., we sighted two or three cruisers approaching
from the N.W., which were the first portion of our own Battlefleet screen, and we altered round gradually and joined in with
the Battlefleet screen steering about S.E.

9. Here we were much restricted for room, the First Cruiser
Squadron, Fourth Light Cruiser Squadron and Destroyer Screen

---

[1] Plate 15.

all moving in the same direction with us. The First Light Cruiser Squadron managed to turn away and get clear and thus eased the crowding.

10. We then, in common with other ships, engaged a large 3-funnelled Light Cruiser, I think "Elbing," from 9,700 to 4,600 yards; and she was soon brought to a standstill. "Falmouth" fired a torpedo at her at about 5,000 yards, but the result is unknown.

11. Fire was then shifted to two other Light Cruisers who were firing at our destroyers; and after a short time they turned away and were lost to view.

12. Two enemy Battle Cruisers then appeared detached from the others, and steering about east, thought to be "Derfflinger" and one other (possibly "Lützow").

They were from 6,000 to 5,000 yards on our starboard beam, and were engaged by the Third Battle Cruiser Squadron, who joined from the north and turned to the eastward about 2,000 yards on our port beam.

13. No other target presenting itself, fire was directed at the leading Battle Cruiser from 5,200 to 6,100 yards, and fire was returned by the Battle Cruisers with 6-in.

14. "Falmouth" and "Yarmouth" both fired torpedoes at her, and it is believed that "Falmouth's" torpedo hit, as an underwater explosion was distinctly visible.

15. About 6.30 p.m., "Invincible" blew up in approx. 57° 8′ N., 6° 17′ E. My impression is that it was the result of a shot into her magazine. There was certainly so sign of water in the explosion.

16. Soon after, the enemy Battle Cruisers turned away to westward, and were were left without an enemy to engage.

17. Here I should like to bring to your notice the action of a destroyer (name unknown, thought to be marked with the number "59,"? "Acasta"?) which we passed close in a disabled condition soon after 6.0 p.m. She apparently was able to struggle ahead again and made straight for the "Derfflinger" to attack her. The incident appeared so courageous that it seems desirable to investigate it further, as I am unable to be certain of the vessel's identity.

18. "Canterbury" joined my squadron at 7.0 p.m., and being ahead of our Battle Cruisers we kept that position, steering about W.S.W., and at 7.36 p.m. reduced to 18 knots by signal from "Lion."

19. At 7.50 p.m. I was directed by "Lion" to sweep to the westward and to locate the head of the enemy's line before dark; and I formed the Light Cruisers on a line of bearing South, course West, 24 knots.

20. Five enemy cruisers were sighted W. by N. and fire was opened at 8.18 p.m., at 9,600 yards, closing to 6,000; the enemy replied, but their fire was erratic. At 8.25 p.m. the course was

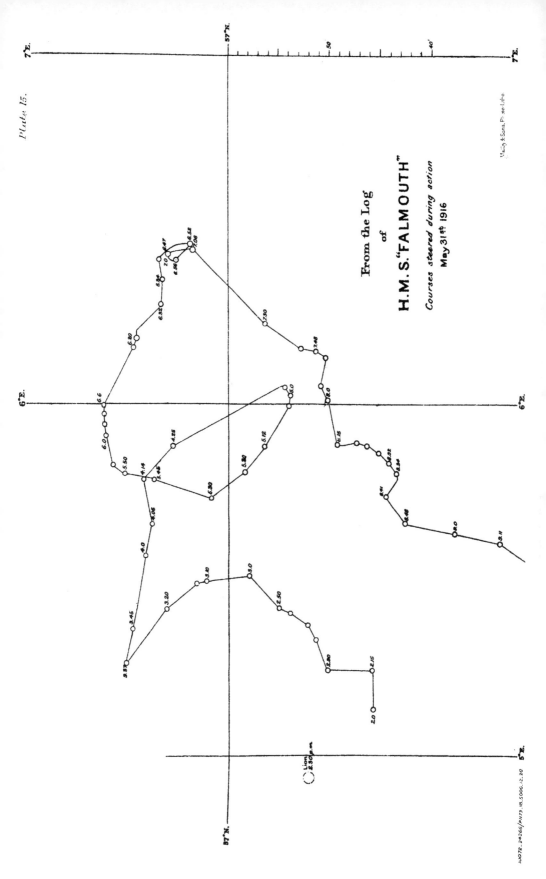

Plate 15.

From the Log
of

H.M.S. "FALMOUTH"

Courses steered during action
May 31ᵗʰ 1916

Malby & Sons, Photo-Litho.

Lion
2.30 p.m.

11.072 - 24266/P1173. 18,5,000. 12.20

S.W., 25 knots. At 8.32 the course was W.S.W. and the enemy altered 8 points together away from us.

21. Our course was altered to West and W.N.W., but at 8.38 p.m. we lost sight of the enemy in the mist, and fire was checked.

22. We then found ourselves drawing across the bows of the enemy's Battle Cruisers, who I think were being engaged by our Battle Cruisers, and we turned to about W.S.W., and then S.S.W. to regain our position ahead of our Battle Cruisers.

23. During the night we kept on the starboard bow of our Battle Cruisers and Battle ships, steering South, and altering to N. by E. at daylight.

24. At 3.15 a.m. a Zeppelin was following the rear of our Fleet, observing, and we drove it off with shrapnel fire, although unable to bring it down at the range, which was 14,000 yards.

It is interesting to note that Naval Airship " L. 24 " in a badly damaged condition succeeded in reaching the coast of Schleswig on 1st June, but then came down, and broke in two pieces " (D.A.R. No. 83 of 3rd June 1916).

25. The remainder of the second day was spent sweeping to the Northward with our Battle Cruisers without sighting any enemy, and at night we returned with them to our base.

26. Although the Squadron was under fire during the afternoon and evening of the 31st May, no ships received any direct hits except " Falmouth " whose fore top communications were out.

Ships were occasionally struck by shrapnel and small pieces of shell.

There were no casualties.

I have the honour to be,
Sir,
Your obedient Servant,
T. D. W. NAPIER,
Rear-Admiral.

The Vice-Admiral Commanding,
Battle Cruiser Fleet.

CAPTAIN'S REPORT.—H.M.S. " CHESTER."

Enclosure No. 15 to Battle Cruiser Fleet Letter No. B.C.F. 01 of 12/6/16.

H.M.S. " Chester,"
2nd June 1916.

SIR,

IN confirmation of my telegram 1700 and 0830 of June 1st, I have the honour to make the following preliminary report on the circumstances in which H.M.S. " Chester " went into action on May 31st.

2. From daylight on May 31st " Chester " was attached to 3rd B.C.S. and stationed as a linking ship between the armoured cruiser screen of the Battlefleet and the three ships of the

3rd B.C.S., to pass signals visually, W/T not being in use except in cases of emergency.

3. The distance between the Battle cruisers and the cruiser screen varied during the day from about 18 to 12 miles, " Chester " keeping a midway position. The mean course was about S. 50 E. after 5.20 a.m. and the Battle cruisers were from a point to two points on the Port bow of the battle fleet. At noon they were about 30 miles apart. Check bearings and distances were passed through " Chester " twice during the day. " Chester's " noon position was Lat. 58·8 N., Long. 3·36 E.

4. At 3.26 p.m. the battle cruisers increased speed and steered E.S.E. and " Chester " had to turn towards the " Minotaur " (S.O. of Armoured cruisers) to pass to her the signal reporting Battle Cruisers alteration of course and speed, the visibility having slightly decreased, perhaps to 8 miles. Having passed the signal, " Chester " followed Battle cruisers (which were then just visible) at full speed.

5. A W/T from C.-in-C. to 3rd B.C.S. was intercepted at 4.15 p.m. ordering the squadron to re-inforce B.C.F. At about this time a large number of reports, some apparently contradictory, were being intercepted, relative to position, course, and speed of enemy sighted and engaged by various units of the Fleet.

6. Third B.C.S. steered to the Southward at about 4.15 p.m. (their mean course was apparently S. by E.) to carry out C.-in-C.'s signal, proceeding at a high speed. " Chester " turned with them. The bearing and distance of 3rd B.C.S. from " Chester " was then about S. 70 E. 8 miles. On a S. by E. course " Chester " at full speed was very slowly overhauling 3rd B.C.S. The distance was gradually decreased to about 6 miles, and the bearing kept about the same. The visibility was rapidly decreasing.

7. At 2.23 p.m., intercepted reports indicated that enemy ships were in the close vicinity. Visibility to the Westward was rather less, I think, than to the Eastward.

8. At 5.30 p.m. the sound of gunfire to the S.W. was heard and flashes of guns were seen in this direction. This was reported to " Invincible " by searchlight, and " Chester " turned to S.W. to investigate.

9. At 5.36 one 3-funnelled light Cruiser with one (or perhaps two—opinions differ) destroyers was sighted dimly a little on Starboard bow. She was challenged and made no reply. " Chester " altered course to about West. The appearance of the destroyer made it most probable that the ship was an enemy. (The light cruiser had, I think, been firing at some ships to the westward of her, but her target was not in sight from " Chester "). As the " Chester's " course laid her open to torpedo attack by the destroyer at once, course was altered to starboard from about West to about North (the approximate course of enemy)

bringing enemy well abaft the port beam. The approximate position at this time was Lat. 57·10 E., Long. 5·42 E.

10. While turning two more light cruisers were sighted astern of the other. The leading light cruiser opened fire on "Chester" at about the time of the completion of the turn to Northward, and "Chester's" first salvo was fired at her at about the same time as her (the leading light cruiser's) second salvo.[1] The range was about 6,000 yards. After "Chester's" third salvo, the fourth salvo (about) of the enemy disabled No. 1 gun portside, and killed or wounded a large proportion of the guns' crews of Numbers 1, 2, and 3 Port. The appearance of two more light cruisers made it desirable to increase the range rapidly. "Chester" turned to N. Eastward, her speed and rapid alteration of course making any effective firing from "Chester" impracticable. The after gun continued firing steadily in local control. By the time "Chester" had steadied on a North Easterly course all enemy ships had apparently opened fire and obtained an accurate range. In about the first five minutes of the action most of "Chester's" casualties occurred and the three guns, No. 1 Port, and Nos. 1 and 2 starboard were, I believe, disabled during the same period. There were several small cordite fires in the first few minutes; they were not serious, except for damage to personnel. The personnel of all guns' crews was also seriously reduced.

12. Enemy ships turned together to North Eastward soon after "Chester's" turn, bringing the enemy leading ship astern of "Chester" and the two other slightly on starboard quarter. The 3rd B.C.S. had approached from the Eastward, and when first noticed by me were on a North Westerly course to Eastward of "Chester."

13. From the time of altering course to the N.E. my attention was given to dodging enemy's salvoes by steering towards the last fall of shot; thus maintaining the mean course to the N. Eastward, and keeping enemy's salvoes falling alternately on either side, on account of the constantly changing deflections. This was apparently successful, as regards saving the ship from a large amount of further serious damage. In the last few minutes I believe she was seldom hit, but the changes of ship's course rendered it impossible for the after guns to make effective shooting, even if the guns' crews had been in a fit state and sufficient numbers to do so. But it was obvious to me that "Chester" was smothered with enemy's fire, and I considered only the best way of getting out of action, withour further heavy loss, by zigzagging and taking shelter to the North Eastward of the Battle Cruisers.

---

[1] The Commanding Officer H.M.S. "Chester" on 13th June 1916, reported that it appeared "that the leading German Light Cruiser fired two salvoes before 'Chester' fired.'" He also stated that "it appears likely that the three enemy Light Cruisers concerned were the 'Wiesbaden,' 'Frankfurt,' and 'Pillau.'"

14. After 19 minutes under fire, as observed in the transmitting station, " Chester " crossed the bows of " Invincible " and took station on her starboard bow. The last enemy salvo was fired about the time " Chester " passed " Invincible," and took station on her starboard bow. The Battle cruisers opened fire on enemy light cruisers shortly before this.

15. " Chester " remained to North Eastward of 3rd B.C.S. for a short time, and when they went into heavy action shortly afterwards, took station astern of " Minotaur's " squadron further to the Eastward, remaining with them. I reported condition of ship and casualties to R.A. " Minotaur " during the night, and was ordered to Humber by signal from him at daylight, June 1st.

16. My opinion is that all enemy salvoes were fired by director. Considering that there were three enemy ships, the rate of fire was perhaps not great. Spread for both elevation and direction was small. Range was thoroughly well maintained, but correction for deflection was evidently difficult. I do not estimate the rate of fire of any one ship higher than one salvo every 45 secs., and if three ships were not firing all the time, it was slower than this. There were usually four or five shots per salvo.

17. The behaviour of officers and ship's company was admirable. I propose to forward a fuller report on this and other matters when I have had further opportunity of consulting with officers of the ship.

18. The principal items of serious damage to material are :—
   1. Three guns disabled.
   2. After control destroyed.
   3. Whaler and one cutter smashed, and some other boats damaged.
   4. Forecastle deck holed and splintered in many places.
   5. Large amount of electrical circuits and voice pipes (including fire control) damaged.
   6. All funnels holed, foremost funnel very badly.
   7. Forebridge considerably damaged.
   8. All rigging in a bad state.
   9. Three holes in armour, and damage to frames behind these.
   10. Two holes in side above armour.
   11. E.R. ventilation trunks wrecked, and forecastle deck fittings generally much damaged.
   12. Two boilers, slight damage to tubes from splinters.
   13. Number of small steam and water pipes holed and shot away.

19. Since drafting the above, I am informed that Commander Forbes (seriously wounded and in hospital) stated that he is

sure that there was a fourth enemy light cruiser engaged, besides one destroyer. I am not yet able to confirm this.

I have the honour to be
Sir,
Your obedient Servant,

The Secretary to the
    Admiralty.

ROB. N. LAWSON.
Captain.

Submitted for information.

Copies of this letter have been forwarded to Admiralty, C.-in-C. H.F., and R.A. Falmouth.

Vice-Admiral Commanding,
    Battle Cruiser Fleet.

ROB. N. LAWSON,
Captain,
5th June 1916.

REAR-ADMIRAL'S REPORT.—5TH BATTLE SQUADRON.

Enclosure No. 16 to Battle Cruiser Fleet Letter No. B.C.F. 01
of 12/6/16.

No. 024A.

"Queen Elizabeth,"

SIR,   9th June 1916.

I HAVE the honour to forward herewith report on the
Action of the 31st May, together with reports from ships of the
5th Battle Squadron.

2. My recommendations of Officers and Men will be forwarded
later when reports are received from H.M. Ships "Malaya"
and "Barham."

I have the honour to be,
Sir,
Your obedient Servant,
HUGH EVAN THOMAS,

The Commander-in-Chief,   Rear Admiral.
The Grand Fleet.

No. 024.

"Queen Elizabeth,"

SIR,   9th June 1916.

I HAVE the honour to report that, on 31st May 1916,
when in Latitude 57° N., Longitude 4° 45′ 30″ E., at 2.23 p.m.,
the Fifth Battle Squadron, consisting of "Barham" (Captain
Arthur W. Craig) bearing my Flag, "Valiant" (Captain Maurice
Woollcombe), "Warspite" (Captain Edward M. Phillpotts), and
"Malaya" (Captain the Hon. Algernon D. E. H. Boyle, C.B.,
M.V.O.), in single line ahead in the order named, and accompanied
by the "Fearless" (Captain Charles D. Roper), "Defender"
(Lieut.-Commander Lawrence R. Palmer), "Acheron" (Com-
mander Charles G. Ramsey), "Ariel" (Lieut.-Commander Arthur
G. Tippet), "Attack" (Lieut.-Commander Charles H. Neill
James), "Hydra" (Lieutenant Francis G. Glossop), "Badger"
(Commander Theodore E. J. Bigg), "Lizard" (Lieut.-Commander
Edward Brooke), "Goshawk" (Commander George H. Knowles),
"Lapwing" (Lieutenant Hubert W. D. Griffith), was five miles
N.N.W. of the First Battle-cruiser Squadron, steering N. by E.,
when a W/T signal was intercepted from "Galatea"—"Enemy
in sight," upon which the Battle-cruiser Fleet and Fifth Battle
Squadron were turned to S.S.E. by signal from the Vice Admiral
Commanding the Battle-cruiser Fleet and speed increased to
25 knots.

2. At 3.50 p.m., some light cruisers were sighted before the
port beam, steering about S.S.E.; these were made out to be
enemy vessels, but not without difficulty owing to mist. The
"Fearless" and destroyer screen were stationed astern, not

having speed to go ahead, and when the range was clear a signal was made to open fire at 3.56 p.m. After two salvoes short, one cruiser appeared to be straddled—range 19,000—upon which the enemy turned away about 8 points and, after one or two more salvoes had been fired, were not seen again.

3. About this time the battle-cruisers in line ahead were heavily engaged with what afterwards proved to be the enemy battle-cruisers.

4. At 4.02 p.m., the " Indefatigable " blew up, the remaining ships altering course gradually to the South-eastward; the enemy also turned to the South-eastward, which enabled the Fifth Battle Squadron to gain on them, and at 4.06 fire was opened at an estimated range of 19,000 yards. At 4.08, a signal was made for Fifth Battle Squadron to concentrate in pairs on the two rear enemy ships.

5. The light was very difficult, the targets being constantly obscured, and seldom were more than one or two ships visible at a time. Often only the flashes of the enemy's guns could be seen, while to the South-westward—the direction of Fifth Battle Squadron from the enemy—the destroyers, which were trying to get ahead some distance off, were silhouetted against a clear horizon.

6. About this time two distinct explosions were seen, and a second battle-cruiser, ahead of the Fifth Battle Squadron, blew up (ascertained to be " Queen Mary ").

7. At 4.21 p.m., the enemy opened fire on the Fifth Battle Squadron, " Barham " being hit at 4.23.

8. From 4.21 p.m. to 4.40 p.m., firing was intermittent, owing to the great difficulty in seeing the enemy.

9. At 4.40 p.m., enemy destroyers were observed to be attacking, and were driven off by our light cruisers and destroyers attached to the battle-cruiser fleet. The Squadron was turned away by " Preparative Flag," and torpedoes were observed to cross the line—one ahead and one astern of " Valiant," the second ship.

10. About this time the Fifth Battle Squadron was heavily engaged with the enemy battle-cruisers. " Licn " and battle-cruisers were observed to have turned to the Northward, and the enemy battle-cruisers to have turned away.

11. At 4.50 p.m., " Lion " approached the Fifth Battle Squadron steering to the Northward, with the signal flying to the Fifth Battle Squadron—" Turn 16 points in succession to starboard "; this turn was made after our battle-cruisers had passed at 4.53, and the Fifth Battle Squadron altered course a little further to starboard to follow and support the battle-cruisers. During this turn, it appears that " Malaya," the last ship of the line, sighted the enemy's battle fleet; it was sighted by " Barham " approximately S.S.E. a few minutes after she had steadied on her Northerly course.

12. At 4.56 p.m., " Barham's " auxiliary W/T office was wrecked by the explosion of a shell on the main deck, and the Warrant Telegraphist and all the operators killed.

13. The enemy's battle-cruisers appeared to have turned again to the Northward at about the same time as the Fifth Battle Squadron.

14. " Barham " and " Valiant " continued to engage the enemy's battle-cruisers, while " Warspite " and " Malaya " fired at the head of the enemy's battle fleet, at a guessed range of 17,000 yards, which proved to be about 19,000 yards.

15. At about 5.25 p.m., the signal was made to increase to utmost speed, and course was altered a little to starboard to support the battle-cruisers. The enemy ships were constantly obscured by mist and were only seen at intervals.

16. At 5.00 p.m., " Barham's " main W/T was put out of action by the explosion of a shell which cut the feeders.

17. At 6.06 p.m., " Marlborough " was sighted on the port bow, steering E.S.E., but no other ships were seen for some minutes, and then only those astern of her. It was therefore concluded that this was the head of our battle line, and that the Fifth Battle Squadron would be able to form ahead of the battle fleet.

18. At 6.19 p.m., however, other ships were sighted, and it was observed that the Grand Fleet was deploying to the North-east, the sixth division being the starboard wing column. It therefore became necessary to make a large turn to port to form astern of the "Marlborough's " division, and to prevent masking the fire of the battle fleet. This was done without signal, and all ships were exceedingly well handled by their Captains, and came into line by turning with " Barham " in the quickest possible time.

19. During this turn ships came under a heavy fire from the enemy's leading battleships, but the shooting was not good and very few hits were made. At this time " Warspite's " helm jambed, causing her to continue her turn straight towards the enemy's battle fleet. However, by good handling, although hit several times while approaching the enemy's line, she was enabled to get away to the Northward. I subsequently ordered her to proceed to Rosyth on receipt of report of her damage.

20. At 6.30 p.m., the Fifth Battle Squadron (less " Warspite ") was formed astern of " Agincourt " and in the battle line.

21. Up to this time, " Barham " had been hit six times, all by battle-cruisers. " Valiant," no hits. " Malaya," seven hits, probably three by battle cruisers and four by battleships. " Warspite " had been hit twice before her helm jambed, and she turned towards the enemy's line.

22. With regard to the damage done to the enemy up to the time of joining the Grand Fleet, it is difficult to be definite owing to the thick haze to the Eastward. The enemy battle-cruisers were frequently straddled, as reported by all ships.

After forming astern of our battle line,

"Malaya" reports, at 7.20 p.m., one enemy's ship dropped astern obscured in smoke—range, 10,400 yards. "Prepared to open fire on an enemy's battleship very low in the water and dropping astern. According to two officers, she suddenly disappeared without an explosion." At 7.40 p.m., an enemy destroyer was seen to sink.

"Valiant" reports at 6.25 p.m., four enemy ships on fire at the head of the line, one enemy Dreadnought stopped and disabled. At 6.41 p.m., three heavy columns of smoke seen on the starboard bow. At 7.08 p.m., enemy ship of "Roon" class heavily hit. At 7.18, enemy's leading ship on fire.

"Barham" reports the rear battle-cruiser ("Seydlitz"?) was damaged before "Barham" opened fire, and was straddled once by "Barham." The fore-top director officer reports that a hit was obtained at this straddle.

The second battle-cruiser ("Moltke") was frequently straddled, but only hits with common shell (three to five) were made out with certainty.

Three enemy battleships were observed to be under a heavy fire in the last stage of the action—one was hit simultaneously by two shells, and another was on fire amidships.

At this time several of the control party in the fore-top independently observed an enemy battleship blow up, and a gap in the line after it. "Barham" obtained at least three hits on a battleship of the "Kaiser" class.

An enemy cruiser ("Roon" class?) was disabled and under a heavy fire from many ships about 6.15 to 6.30 p.m.

23. After joining the Grand Fleet the Fifth Battle Squadron conformed to the movements of the Commander-in-Chief, engaging the rear ships of the enemy's battle fleet until they turned away and went out of sight, all ships apparently covering themselves with artificial smoke.

24. At about 7.18 p.m., observed "Marlborough" hit by torpedo. The squadron turned away to the Northward, avoiding a torpedo, which passed ahead of "Barham."

At 7.42 p.m., altered course by signal, leading ships of divisions together to the South, "Marlborough's" division on the port beam. At 8.00 p.m., turned to the Westward to increase distance from "Marlborough."

At 10.00 p.m., observing that we had gone a long way ahead of "Marlborough," the squadron was turned round to regain station on her, again resuming the course at 10.08. It was observed, however, that "Marlborough" was going very slowly, and fearing that the Fifth Battle Squadron would be too far astern of the fleet in the morning, speed was increased to regain station.

25. At 10.15 p.m., observed heavy firing a little abaft the starboard beam, which I surmised to be attacks by enemy destroyers and light craft on our light cruisers and destroyers.

As destroyers were reported crossing our bow some distance ahead, the squadron was turned to starboard gradually, and eventually right round to the course again.

At 10.39, heavy firing was observed on the starboard quarter, and destroyers appeared to be attacking the cruisers. At 11.35, a further attack was seen farther off nearly right astern.

26. No further incident occurred until the Second Battle Squadron was observed ahead about three to five miles at early dawn. When the fleet was turned to the Northward, the Fifth Battle Squadron kept station on the Second Battle Squadron until ordered by the Commander-in-Chief to take station on the beam of the starboard wing division.

27. Track charts are enclosed, also diagrams, to show as nearly as possible the relative positions of the Fifth Battle Squadron and the enemy at twelve different phases of the action, as well as the rough position of our battle-cruisers; but the distances between our battle-cruisers and the enemy are not known, so the diagram must not be taken to represent their true position.

28. Recommendations of officers and men whom I wish to bring to your notice are being made the subject of a separate letter.

I have the honour to be,

Sir,

Your obedient Servant,

HUGH EVAN THOMAS,

Rear Admiral Commanding

Fifth Battle Squadron.

The Vice Admiral Commanding
  Battle-cruiser Fleet.

No. 024.

" Queen Elizabeth,"

SIR,   18th June 1916.

WITH reference to paragraph 21 of my report on the action of 31st May 1916, the statement "Malaya" was hit seven times, probably three by battle-cruisers and four by battleships," is not correct.

2. This statement was based on the impression I received when going round "Malaya" on her arrival at Scapa Flow.

3. "Malaya" now reports that all her hits were from the enemy's battle fleet; it is therefore submitted that the words in the third line of paragraph 21 of my report between "hits" and the second "by" may be deleted, and the word "all" substituted.

I have the honour to be,

Sir,

Your obedient Servant,

HUGH EVAN THOMAS,

Rear Admiral Commanding

Fifth Battle Squadron.

The Commander-in-Chief,
    Grand Fleet.

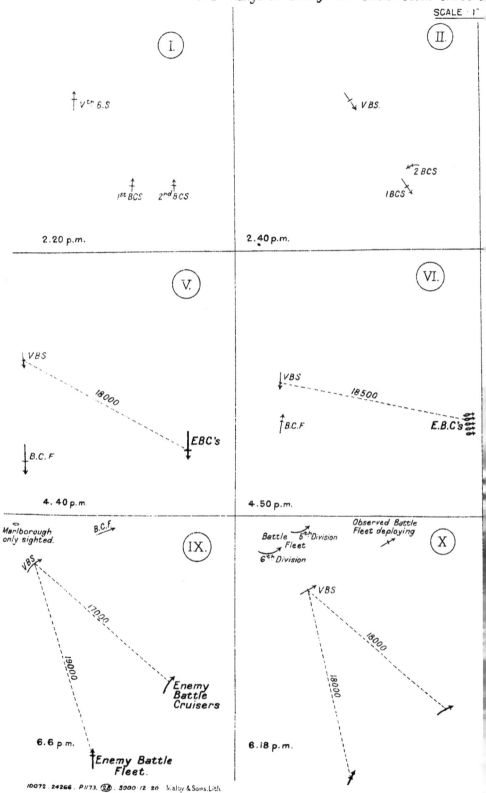

DIAGRAM ILLUSTRATING TWELVE

NOTE:- Range of Enemy from British Battle Cruisers

SCALE · 1"

I.

† V^{ce} B.S

1st BCS   2nd BCS

2.20 p.m.

II.

V BS.

2 BCS

1 BCS

2.40 p.m.

V.

↓ VBS

18000

↓ B.C.F

↓ EBC's

4.40 p.m.

VI.

↓ VBS

18500

↑ B.C.F

E.B.C's

4.50 p.m.

IX.

Marlborough only sighted.

B.C.F.

VBS

17000

19000

Enemy Battle Cruisers

6.6 p.m.

Enemy Battle Fleet.

X

Observed Battle Fleet deploying

Battle   5th Division
Fleet
6th Division

VBS

18000

18000

6.18 p.m.

10072.24266. P1173. 28. 5000·12 20   Malby & Sons. Lith.

ot known. – Position of British Battle Cruisers approximate only.

0 8000 YDS.

III.

19000

VBS.

Enemy
Battle
Cruisers

B.C.F

.0 p.m.

IV.

VBS

17000

EBCs

B.C.F.

4.20 p.m.

VII.

BCF

VBS   19000

Enemy's
Battle Cruisers

19000

Enemy's
Battle Fleet

.0 p.m.

VIII.

B.C.F.

VBS   18000

Enemy
Battle
Cruisers

18500

Enemy's
Battle Fleet

5.30 p.m.

XI

4th Div.
5th Div.
6th Div.

VBS

W

16000
16000

15000
15000

EsB.C's

E's B.F

.23 p.m.

XII.

Br B.F.

VBS

Warspite

17000

11000

E.B.F.

Hugh Evan Thomas

6.30

SCHEDULE OF ENCLOSURES TO FIFTH BATTLE SQUADRON SUBMISSION No. 024 of 9TH JUNE 1916 TO THE VICE-ADMIRAL COMMANDING BATTLE-CRUISER FLEET.

1. Track charts (2).[1]
2. Diagram.[2]
3. "Barham's" report of the action dated 6th June with track chart[3] and two enclosures.
4. "Warspite's" report of the action with track chart.[4]
5. "Valiant's" report of the action dated 3rd June with track chart[5] (triplicate only—original and duplicate forwarded direct to Vice-Admiral Commanding Battle-cruiser Fleet).
6. "Valiant's" letter of 5th June 1916—Gunnery and Torpedo Notes.
7. "Malaya's" report on the action dated 6th June with six enclosures A to F (including track chart).[6]

CAPTAIN'S REPORT.—H.M.S. "BARHAM."

No. 181.

H.M.S. "Barham,"

SIR,   6th June 1916.

I HAVE the honour to forward herewith a report on the action of 31st May 1916, in which H.M. Ship under my command flying your flag took part.

2. The recording of details is not so full or accurate as I should have wished. This is partly due to the fact that Lieutenant Reginald Edward Blyth, R.N., Assistant Navigator, who was in the lower conning tower for the purpose, was mortally wounded about 1 hour after the engagement opened. Mr. Alec Edward Dodington, Midshipman, R.N., who worked with him, was afterwards entirely occupied in keeping the reckoning, which he did in a highly creditable manner under difficult circumstances.

3. Whilst the general trend of the action remains clearly fixed in the memory, it is impossible to reconstruct it strategically or tactically, owing to the difficulty of seeing the enemy, and to the lack of knowledge of the movements or positions of our own squadrons.

It is considered of great importance that in a squadron flagship, an Assistant Navigating Lieutenant should be permanently borne who will be able not only to keep an accurate reckoning continuously, but also to note tactical data. The importance of a reliable position after action cannot be overestimated, and during action a continuous plot of our own and the enemy's tracks may be invaluable in avoiding mines or in deciding in a tactical or strategical movement.

---

[1] Receipt cannot be traced at the Admiralty.   [2] Plate 16.
[3] Plate 10a.   [4] Plate 17.   [5] Plate 18.   [6] Plate 19

4. Although the "Barham" received considerable structural damage from the enemy's shells, and the casualties were fairly heavy, the ship was in a thoroughly efficient fighting condition, and had all guns in action and fire control practically intact at the end of three hours' engagement. This reflects great credit on the Officers responsible for the upkeep of the propelling machinery and of the guns' mountings and electrical equipment.

5. During the engagement, the behaviour of the Officers and men was entirely praiseworthy, and their duties were carried out in a cool and intelligent manner, under, in some cases, very trying situations.

1 *   *   *   *   *

I have the honour to be,
Sir,
Your obedient Servant,
A. W. CRAIG,
Captain.

Rear Admiral Commanding
    Fifth Battle Squadron.

ENCLOSURE TO "BARHAM'S" LETTER No. 181 OF 6TH JUNE 1916.

REPORT OF ACTION OF 31ST MAY 1916.

Disposition and courses prior to Action.
Noon position 56° 49′ 5 N., Long. 3° 28′ E.

Fifth Battle Squadron ("Barham," "Valiant," "Warspite," "Malaya") 5 miles astern of 1st B.C.S. ("Lion," "Princess Royal," "Queen Mary," "Tiger").

2nd B.C.S. ("New Zealand," "Indefatigable") some distances on Port Beam of 1st B.C.S.

Course S. 81 E. advancing 18 knots.

2.15 p.m. course N. by E. 5th B.C.S. 5 miles ahead of "Lion," ordered to look out for advanced Cruisers of Grand Fleet.

2.38 p.m. S.S.E. 22 knots in consequence of 1st L.C.S. reporting enemy cruiser S.S.E. at 2.35 p.m.

The Battle Cruiser Squadron turned rather before the 5th Battle Squadron and were out of sight for some time.

Hauled round gradually to N.E. following motions of Battle Cruiser Fleet, and then back to eastward, the enemy Light Cruisers being sighted at 3.50 on this course, and shortly after, two Battle Cruisers all steering to S.E. Speed now 24 knots.

2. Our Destroyer escort on the enemy side attempting to pass ahead of "Barham" prevented fire being opened until 3.58, when the two enemy Light Cruisers (Kolberg type) were engaged, range 17,000. These turned away 8 points after the third salvo and it is not thought that they were hit.

----

¹ Part omitted here, referring solely to personnel, recommendations, &c., in no way bearing on the course of the action.

3. At 4.11, fire was opened with director salvoes on the rear (left hand) Battle Cruiser, which had smoke issuing from her, and seemed damaged, bearing 35°, Red, Range 19,000. This ship was straddled, but hits could not be seen with certainty.

4. Fifth Battle Squadron were now following the 1st and 2nd Battle Cruiser Squadrons, about 5 miles astern of them and gradually hauled round to the southward, bringing enemy Battle Cruisers nearly abeam. About 4.16 " Barham " shifted to second ship from the left ("Moltke") and the squadron were ordered to concentrate in pairs on the two left-hand ships. The enemy presented a fair target at range of 18,000–17,000 yards, and was frequently straddled. Three certain hits only were seen, but after we started using A.P. Lyddite, hits could not be seen. This would naturally be the case, however, and it was noted that the enemy hits on " Barham," though doing great internal damage, did not show outside the ship.

1*　　　*　　　*　　　*　　　*

6. Towards the latter part of the southerly run, the visibility of the enemy got considerably worse, the ships being the same colour as the background. Two terrific explosions were seen amongst our Battle Cruisers ahead at about 4.10 and 4.24 respectively, and the wreckage of these vessels (" Indefatigable " and " Queen Mary ") was passed about ten to twelve minutes later, with a number of men in the water which were being rescued by Destroyers.

During this part of the Action " Barham " was under a steady fire from the enemy, but was only hit twice, one below the water line, doing practically no damage.

7. About 4.45 p.m. the 1st and 2nd Battle Cruiser Squadrons turned in succession 16 points to Port, and it was seen that the enemy Battle Cruisers had turned also, and that some of the German's 3rd Squadron were coming up astern of them. The " Lion " turned 16 points to Port, the other three Battle Cruisers following her and Vice Admiral Battle Cruiser Fleet ordered 5th Battle Squadron to turn 16 points in succession to starboard. This was done at 4.53 and the squadron hauled in again astern of the Battle Cruisers about two miles.

8. The range was now about 19,000 to 20,000, but the enemy could rarely be seen, though the flashes of his salvoes were very bright. These salvoes were very rapid ripples (almost simul· taneous), and it was not possible to lay on them, as they were gone before the sights were on the spot. Our fire was therefore intermittent, and any enemy which showed up for long range enough to lay on was selected. On the other hand, it appeared. looking at the horizon and sky behind us, that we should be very clear to the enemy and offer at times a splendid target.

---

1 *See* note on p. 381.

9. Shortly after turning, the ship was hit by a heavy shell which entered the glacis before No. 1 6-in. gun starboard and abreast the after end of " B " turret redoubt armour. This shell burst at the main deck over the Medical Store, completely wrecking the Auxiliary W/T Office and the Medical Store, and putting the starboard forward Hydraulic Pump out of action. The bulk of the Medical Stores, stretchers, &c., were destroyed, and heavy casualties occurred amongst the Medical Party and the Wireless Staff. The 6-in. Hand Ups and Dredger Hoist starboard, and the Dredger Hoist Port were penetrated, and the flash of the shell passed up to the battery deck and ignited some cartridges in S. 2 casemate, causing severe casualties.

Large pieces of the shell also penetrated the middle deck, and a piece entering the Lower Conning Tower mortally wounded Lieutenant Blyth, Assistant Navigating Officer. The Platform Deck, forming the roof of the forward 6-in. Magazine was also pierced, and the 6-in. Magazine and Shell Room filled with smoke. There were three other heavy hits during this part of the Action, but the first is described in detail, as it was much more vital than the remainder, and might have easily put the Lower Conning Tower out of Action. As it was, it put the Auxiliary W/T and starboard fore Hydraulic Pump out of Action and cut a number of fire control voice pipes, and the pipes to the port steering engine Telemotor.

10. " Barham " was now without wireless communication as the Auxiliary Office was completely wrecked, and the Main W/T feeder and Action feeder had gone, consequently the position of our Battlefleet was not known until a part of them were sighted before the Port Beam shortly after 6 p.m. This turned out to be the 1st Battle Squadron who were on the right wing of the Battlefleet, and as they deployed to starboard on an easterly course, 5th Battle Squadron hauled round to a parallel course, following the Battle Cruisers. The 5th Battle Squadron were now blanking the range for 1st Battle Squadron, and it was a question as to whether 5th Battle Squadron should endeavour to follow the Battle Cruisers to the head of the line or form astern of " Marlborough's " Division. The Rear-Admiral decided on the latter alternative, and " Barham " led in turning about 8 points to port and reducing speed. The leading enemy Battle Squadron (" Königs ") seeing this, opened a terrific fire on the turning point, and " Barham " was surrounded by a hailstorm of splashes, but no hits of importance were made. The " Warspite " was now seen to be dropping astern and reported that she had been holed several times under water and was steering from engine-room.

It should be mentioned that just before turning into line astern of our Battle Fleet, the Armoured Cruisers " Defence " and " Black Prince " came down at high speed between the 5th Battle Squadron and the enemy and about 1 mile from 5th Battle Squadron steering in the opposite direction. " Defence " was hit by two heavy salvoes in succession, and blowing up, sank in a few minutes. " Black Prince " was heavily hit aft and turned out of Action, apparently in a sinking condition.

11. " Barham " formed astern of " Agincourt " and opened fire again, first at a partially disabled enemy ship believed to be a three-funnel Cruiser, and then at an enemy Battleship of " König " type, second from right of those visible. The range was partly obscured by smoke from our own Battleships' guns and funnels, and it was only possible to sight the enemy intermittently, and spotting was very difficult. It appeared, however, that several hits were obtained on a ship of the " Kaiser " class. During this period, at least four torpedoes passed through the line close to " Barham," and were avoided by turning away. A submarine also attacked and was fired on by the 6-in. guns. The attack apparently failed. Enemy Destroyers made an attack from the head of their line, and fire was opened on them from 6-in. guns. One was apparently hit.

About 6.50 p.m. the enemy were lost to view, and fire ceased.

Fifth Battle Squadron then stood to the westward on the right wing of the Battle Fleet, and eventually turned to the southward, astern of the line.

During the night there appeared to be constant attacks by Torpedo Craft on ships, first to the westward and then to the northward, and about 0.45 a.m. an immense explosion was seen to the N.N.E. No attack was made on 5th Battle Squadron.

A tracing showing the " Barham's " track[1] during the Action with notations of the principal events is forwarded herewith. It is proposed to forward as soon as possible a detailed account of the damage received, and further details of the Action, together with proposals for the future, based on the experience of this Action. Also the names of Officers and men who especially distinguished themselves, or who are recommended for meritorious conduct.

A. W. CRAIG,
Captain.

ENCLOSURE No. 2 TO " BARHAM'S " LETTER No. 181 OF 6TH JUNE 1916.

NOTES ON DAMAGE TO THE ENEMY.

1. Rear Battle Cruiser, " Seydlitz." ?	This ship was damaged before " Barham " opened fire, and was straddled once by " Barham." The foretop director officer reports that a hit was obtained at this straddle.
2. Second Battle Cruiser, " Moltke."	This ship was frequently straddled, but only hits with common shell (3 to 6) were made out with certainty.

[1] Plate 10a.

3. Enemy Battleships - 3 of these were observed to be under a heavy fire in the last stage of the action—one was hit simultaneously by 2 shells, and another was on fire amidships.

At this time several of the control party in fore-top independently observed an enemy battleship blow up, and a gap in the line after it. " Barham " obtained at least three hits on a battleship of " Kaiser " class.

4. Enemy Cruiser,   Disabled and under heavy fire from " Roon " class (?).   many ships about 6.15 to 6.30 p.m.

CAPTAIN'S REPORT.—H.M.S. " WARSPITE."

H.M.S. " Warspite,"
SIR,   4th June 1916.

I HAVE the honour to submit the following combined diary of events and report on action of Wednesday, 31st May, and Thursday, 1st June, 1916 :—

2. The enemy was sighted at 3.50 p.m. at the time when the engagement commenced between the battle cruiser fleets.

3. On the signal being received from " Barham " to open fire " Warspite " waited to see at which ship " Barham " was firing, and at 4.2 p.m. fire was opened on the second light cruiser from the van (second from the right)—range, 18,500 yards. She was straddled and turned away either on fire or using smoke protection. On the signal to attack the enemy's battle cruisers, and concentration signal 2P being received, fire was shifted to the rear battle cruiser; range, 19,500; she was straddled several times, turned away, and eventually got out of range.

Fire was then shifted to another battle cruiser; result unknown.

4. As the 5th Battle Squadron turned to the northward at 4.55 p.m. the enemy's battle squadron was sighted, and as their battle cruisers were very bad targets owing to visibility, the leading ship of the enemy's battle fleet was engaged ; range 17,000. Only a few salvoes were fired, but it is believed that she was straddled after the second salvo; the target was then right aft and fire was checked.

5. For the next half hour fire was intermittent and ineffective on the enemy battle cruisers owing to low visibility causing great difficulty in selection of target.

6. At 6 p.m. the Grand Fleet was sighted, and course was altered to the south eastward in the wake of " Barham."

At 6.18 p.m. course was altered to the northward, following the motions of " Barham " and " Valiant," but as we were apparently closing " Malaya " I ordered Port 20°, and then the steering gear commenced to give trouble.

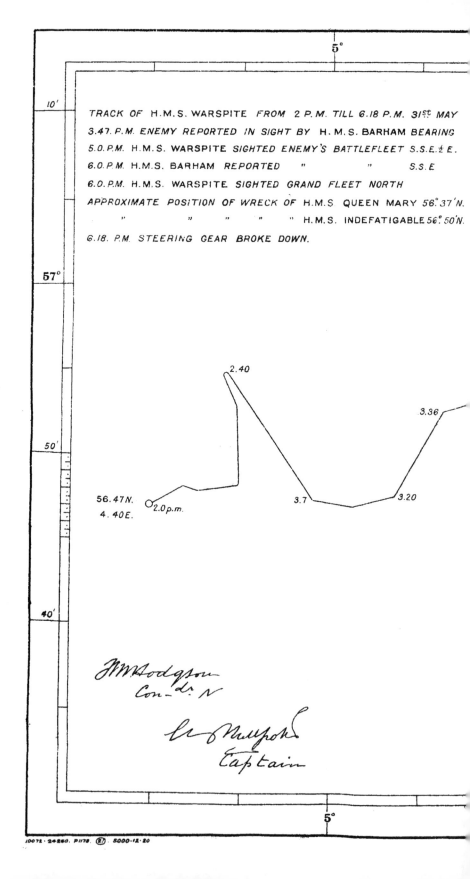

TRACK OF H.M.S. WARSPITE FROM 2 P.M. TILL 6.18 P.M. 31ᵗ MAY

3.47. P.M. ENEMY REPORTED IN SIGHT BY H.M.S. BARHAM BEARING

5.0. P.M. H.M.S. WARSPITE SIGHTED ENEMY'S BATTLEFLEET S.S.E.¼ E.

6.0. P.M. H.M.S. BARHAM REPORTED " " S.S.E

6.0. P.M. H.M.S. WARSPITE SIGHTED GRAND FLEET NORTH

APPROXIMATE POSITION OF WRECK OF H.M.S. QUEEN MARY 56°.37′N.

" " " " " H.M.S. INDEFATIGABLE 56°.50′N.

6.18. P.M. STEERING GEAR BROKE DOWN.

2.40

3.36

56.47N.
4.40E.   2.0 p.m.   3.7   3.20

J.M. Hodgson
Com—dr N

M G Mullows
Captain

Plate 17.

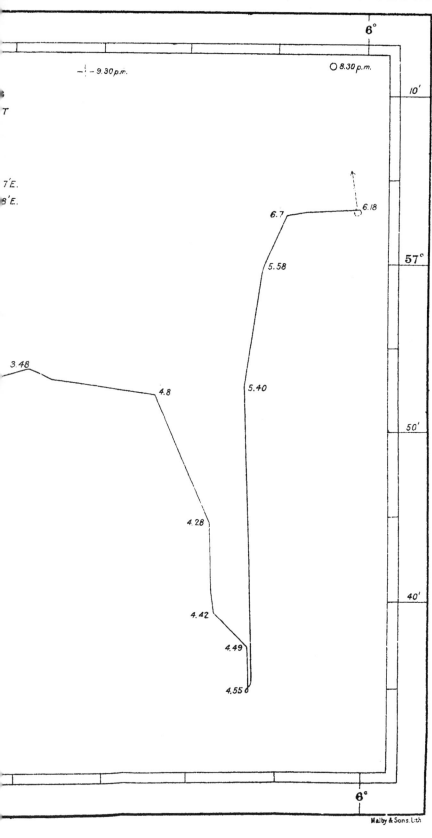

7. I have been unable to ascertain the exact cause of the trouble, as subsequent events followed rapidly in succession, and " Warspite " closed the enemy's battle fleet so rapidly that she came under a very heavy fire. However, after careful investigation I have elucidated the following facts :—

(a) The thrust bearing on the steering engine heated, probably owing to the ship having been hit about this time, but it was impossible to distinguish in the Conning Tower between hits and shell falling close alongside.

The result of this was a slowing up of the steering engine.

(b) Taking into consideration that the ship was steaming 25 knots at the time, the helm was put over far too quickly.

(c) The telemotor gearing from the lower conning tower to engine room was bent, probably as a result of (a) and (b) above.

8. " Warspite " shaved close under " Valiant's " stern, and every attempt was made by helm and engines to bring her head back to port with the dire result that she only closed the head of the enemy's battle fleet at decreasing speed. I then decided to go full-speed ahead, and continued the turn to starboard ; I am unable to give further details, except that I managed to get away to the northward after practically turning two circles under the concentrated fire of several of the enemy's battleships.

During this time centralised control was impossible, but fire was kept up by all turrets on local control. Closest range was estimated to be about 12,000 yards, and the ship was badly damaged by shell fire, but not completely disabled.

I then attempted to take station astern of " Malaya," but before arriving at 5 cables distance I realised that the ship was still unmanageable, so I withdrew to the northward to shift over steering gear to some other position. The after steering compartment was reported flooded, so the steering position at the engine itself was adopted.

8. A rough survey of the damage by gunfire was made, and I considered that owing to the danger of flooding the engine rooms a moderate speed only was safe for the time ; I consequently reported to the Senior Officer 5th Battle Squadron that " Warspite " could steam 16 knots and requested the position of the battle fleet. I received orders to proceed to Rosyth.

9. I shaped course accordingly at 8.30 p.m., steaming 16 knots, and every endeavour was made to plug holes and shore bulkheads.

Speed was gradually increased until 9.35 a.m. 1st June, when, whilst zigzagging at 19 knots, two torpedoes passed close to the ship, one on either side ; but no periscope was seen, as owing to a southerly breeze there were many " white horses " on the surface of the water. Speed was then increased to 21 knots and subsequently to 22 knots, and a signal was made to the Commander-in-Chief, Rosyth, that " Warspite " had been attacked by two submarines, and was proceeding to Rosyth without escort.

An escort of torpedo boats and destroyers was sent, but just as the first two were sighted at 11.42 a.m., another submarine showed her periscope close under the bows. Orders were given to increase to full speed, and to put the helm over to ram her, but owing to the length of time required to transmit the orders to the engine-room steering position she was missed by a few yards.

I then zigzagged at full speed from the spot where the periscope was last seen, and saw no more of the submarine.

9. This increase of speed necessitated re-shoring up, and consequently speed was reduced at 0.20 p.m., when escort had joined up.

10. "Warspite" arrived at Rosyth at 3.15 p.m., and proceeded straight into dock.

1 *   *   *   *   *

I have the honour to be,
Sir,
Your obedient Servant,
E. M. PHILLPOTTS,
Captain.

The Rear-Admiral Commanding
Fifth Battle Squadron.

H.M.S. " Valiant," c/o G.P.O., London,
Sir,   3rd June 1916.

I HAVE the honour to forward herewith a report which I have to-day transmitted to the Vice-Admiral Commanding Battle Cruiser Fleet, in compliance with his signal of 2nd June 1916. The report was forwarded to the Vice-Admiral in duplicate.

I have the honour to be,
Sir,
Your obedient Servant,
M. WOOLLCOMBE,
The Rear-Admiral Commanding   Captain.
Fifth Battle Squadron.

CAPTAIN'S REPORT, H.M.S. " VALIANT.

H.M.S. " Valiant," c/o G.P.O., London,
2nd June 1916.
Sir,

IN compliance with your signal of to-day, 2nd June, 1 have the honour to report as follows on the action of 31st May 1916. All times shown in this report are G.M.T., and all courses are true.

---

¹ Part omitted, here referring solely to personnel, recommendations, &c., in no way bearing on the course of the action.

2. About 3.30 p.m., from the reports of our own light cruisers and the increasing strength of the enemy's wireless signals, it became evident that we were in close contact with some part of the German Fleet. By 3.45 p.m. hands were closed up at their quarters and ready to open fire.

3. At 4.0 p.m. my D.R. position was Lat. 56° 59′ N., Long. 5° 31′ E., course 95°, speed 23 knots.

4. The Fifth Battle Squadron was then in single-line ahead, with our Battle Cruiser Squadron slightly off our starboard bow, distant about 4 miles, steering Easterly, and turning in succession to the Southward. The enemy, consisting of four or five Battle Cruisers, were bearing Red 40° from "Valiant," range about 22,000 yards. Our Light Cruiser Squadrons were 6 points on our port bow, distant about 8,000 yards.

5. At 4.1 p.m. H.M.S. "Valiant" opened fire on the enemy, who were steering approximately south-east, using the second ship from the right as a target. Shortly after opening fire the signal was received, "Concentrate in pairs from the rear." "Valiant" then shifted her fire on to second ship from the left.

6. At 4.2 p.m. a big explosion was observed on the starboard bow, and one of our Battle Cruisers disappeared—probably H.M.S. "Queen Mary"; about five minutes later a similar explosion was witnessed in the rear of our Battle Cruiser Squadron, and what was probably H.M.S. "Indefatigable" blew up. This ship did not appear to be undergoing heavy punishment from gun-fire and, in the opinion of Lieutenant-Commander May and two other Officers, there were two separate explosions at short intervals, probably caused by mines or torpedoes.

7. At 4.6 p.m. our course was altered to 110°.

8. Altered course to 155°.

9. At 4.14 p.m. "Warspite" opened fire.

10. At 4.17 p.m. altered course 140°.

11. At 4.21 p.m. the enemy opened fire on the Fifth Battle Squadron for the first time, and straddled H.M.S. "Barham."

12. At 4.23 p.m. altered course 164°, and at the same time "Barham," was hit.

13. At 4.29 p.m. "Valiant," who was slightly on the starboard quarter of "Barham," was ordered to take station astern.

14. At 4.31 p.m. altered course 121°.

15. At 4.32 p.m. ship swinging to starboard, course 170°.

16. At 4.37 p.m. ship swinging slowly to port, course 156°.

17. At 4.41 p.m. we observed an attack on the enemy from ahead by our light cruisers and destroyers. Result unknown.

18. At 4.45 p.m. the Fifth Battle Squadron was heavily engaged.

19. At 4.46 p.m. the ship was severely shaken by one salvo, which burst just short on the port side aft, and plunging projectiles may have hit the ship below the water line. On examination

on arrival in harbour, it was ascertained that no internal damage had been caused.

20. At 4.47 p.m. ship turning to starboard, course 172°.

21. At 4.48 p.m. the enemy's salvoes falling astern of " Valiant."

· 22. At 4.50 p.m. observed our Battle Cruiser Squadron on Port bow, steering North.

23. At 4.51 p.m. passed one of our " L " class destroyers picking up survivors from scattered wreckage of a big ship. She was not being fired on at the moment, but possibly a good many shorts, intended for the Fifth Battle Squadron, fell around her shortly afterwards.

24. At 4.54 p.m. ceased fire *pro tem.*, our Battle Cruisers blanking us on the Port side.

25. At 4.57 p.m. the Fifth Battle Squadron altered course 16 points to starboard in succession, course 360°, following in rear of our Battle Cruiser Squadron.

26. At 5.2 p.m. " Barham " was hit amidships between the funnels.

27. At 5.6 p.m. " Valiant " reopened fire at enemy's Battle Cruisers, target most indistinct on the starboard beam, the light at this period of the action was very favourable to the enemy, silhouetting our ships against the bright sky of the western horizon, the sun being obscured by clouds at this time. " Valiant " was now firing at the second ship from the right, but due to mist and smoke this ship was occasionally obscured and the plainest target had to be fired at.

28. At 5.9 p.m. altered course 348°. " Barham " hit astern.

29. At 5.11 p.m. the enemy's Battle Squadron appeared 2 points abaft the starboard beam, consisting of about eight Dreadnoughts, but it was very difficult to determine the exact number. " Barham " again hit, amidships at this time.

30. At 5.12 p.m. " Valiant " straddled forward and aft, and the whole of the Fifth Battle Squadron was under heavy fire from the greatly superior forces of the enemy.

31. At 5.13 p.m. " Valiant " altered course to port and took up a position on the port quarter of the " Barham," as the Fifth Battle Squadron at this time was altering course slowly to port to get astern of our Battle Cruisers, and it was observed that a very accurate fire was being concentrated on the turning point. By so doing, the next four salvoes intended for " Valiant " missed her by 10 yards ahead. At this period the enemy was keeping up a very rapid and accurate fire, very small spread of from 50 to 100 yards, range most accurate, but in most cases missing for direction. It was observed that the splashes from the big shells were extremely small, seldom rising above the level of the hull of the ship.

32. At 5.14 p.m. course was now 295° after the turn to port.

Plate 18.

TRACK OF "H.M.S. VALIANT", 31ST MAY 1916.

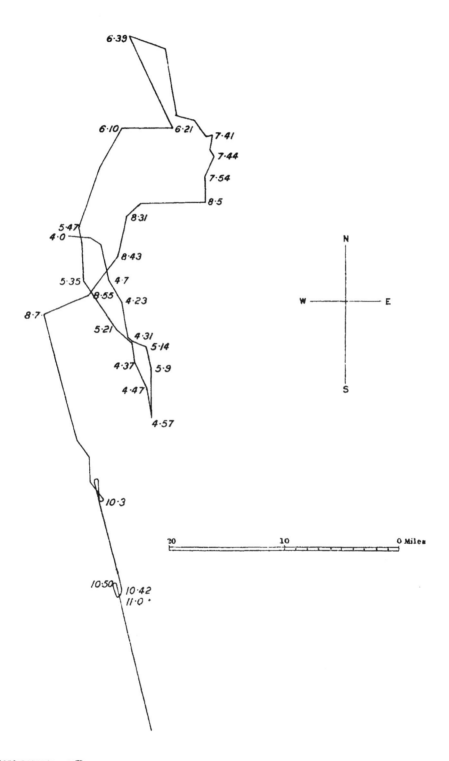

33. At 5.17 p.m. the enemy was now on the starboard quarter. The Fifth Battle Squadron was now proceeding " all out " at 25 knots, but the enemy still appeared to be keeping up with us.

34. At 5.17½ p.m. altered course 310°.

35. At 5.21 p.m. altered course 325°.

36. At 5.23 p.m. " Barham " signalled " Proceed at utmost speed."

37. At 5.24 p.m. enemy was now very indistinct, the sun shining brightly on our port bow.

38. At 5.26 p.m. the action was gradually being broken off.

39. At 5.29 p.m. one salvo landed just short of " Valiant " and one just over.

40. At 5.35 p.m. altered course 355°. It was observed that enemy was now in port quarter line bearing 135° Green.

41. At 5.37 p.m. altered course 360°.

42. At 5.40 p.m. " Valiant " engaging about fourth ship from the right, being the only ship which was sufficiently visible to fire at.

43. At 5.43 p.m. our Battle Cruiser Squadron on starboard bow had now altered course 16 points to the southward and re-engaged the enemy at long range.

44. At 5.44 p.m. altered course 355°.

45. At 5.47 p.m. the Fifth Battle Squadron altered course to Starboard, course 20°, with the idea of re-engaging.

46. At 5.48 p.m. there was a lull in the action, target most indistinct. Lined up Director, which had got out of step.

47. At 5.53 p.m. light much improved; re-engaged, one enemy's salvo landed just over " Valiant."

48. At 5.56 p.m. our Battle Cruiser Squadron was now observed turning to the Eastward with the apparent idea of heading off the enemy and crossing his " T."

49. At 6.0 p.m. fired one torpedo from starboard after tube at German Battlefleet, bearing 140° green, result unknown.

50. At 6.1 p.m. range 19,000 increasing. Altered course 30°.

51. At 6.1½ p.m. lost sight of the enemy in the mist.

52. At 6.2 p.m. our Battle Cruiser Squadron altered course to the E.S.E. Lull in action.

53. At 6.5 p.m. observed distant firing on starboard bow.

54. At 6.6 p.m. enemy reappeared, bearing Green 130°.

55. At 6.7 p.m. the Grand Fleet in sight. Observed " Marlborough " leading First Division, bearing Red 10° about three miles.

56. At 6.10 p.m. altered course 90°.

57. At 6.13 p.m. the Fifth Battle Squadron altering course to starboard, enemy bearing Green 38°.

58. At 6.14 p.m. " Barham " reopened fire.

59. At 6.15 p.m. " Valiant " reopened fire, action resumed, enemy firing at our Battle Cruiser Squadron.

60. At 6.17 p.m. enemy bearing Green 50°, range 19,000, visibility now very good.

61. At 6.19 p.m. observed Grand Fleet deploying to port to the North-East, weather B.C., very little mist.

62. At 6.20 p.m. Fifth Battle Squadron came under heavy fire; our Battle Fleet opened fire on the enemy at the same time. Observed our first and second Cruiser Squadrons crossing from our port to our starboard bow. As H.M. Ships " Defence," " Warrior " and " Black Prince " came within range of the enemy, they received a concentrated and extremely hot fire; the shot were falling at regular intervals, grouped in salvoes, forming a danger zone of from 1,000 to 1,500 yards. H.M.S. " Defence " was smothered in shell fire, the after magazine appeared to blow up, shortly followed by the foremost one. All the ammunition then appeared to explode, and the ship blew up and sank. H.M.S. " Warrior " also entered the danger zone. Shortly afterwards she came between us and the enemy and was overwhelmed; but, in this case, some of the enemy's shooting was bad and about 2,000 over. A large explosion took place at one end of the ship and clouds of very dense black smoke poured out, which undoubtedly screened us but also prevented our seeing the enemy. H.M.S. " Black Prince," although under the same hot fire, appeared to come through with but little damage.

63. At 6.21 p.m. altered course to port, course 335°.

64. At 6.22 p.m. " Warspite " was observed in difficulties on the starboard quarter, steering gear evidently broken down.

65. At 6.24 p.m. several salvoes landed just over " Valiant," who was also under hot fire from enemy's shrapnel bursting short, the fore-top, ship's side and funnel being hit.

66. At 6.25 p.m. the Grand Fleet was now fully engaged and head of the line altering course to starboard with the idea of closing the range. Several fires now broke out simultaneously at the head of the enemy's battle line, four battleships and battle cruisers observed heavily on fire. An enemy Dreadnought was also observed to be stopped and disabled on the engaged side of the enemy's line; this was probably a German Flagship, as a light cruiser was seen to go alongside her. Commander (N) saw one big salvo fall exactly between these two ships just as the light cruiser ranged up alongside.

67. At 6.26 p.m. reduced to 18 knots; Fifth Battle Squadron forming astern of our Battle Fleet, now deploying.

68. At 6.30 p.m. reduced to 14 knots.

69. At 6.32 p.m. " Warspite " hauled out of the line to port.

70. At 6.33 p.m. increased to 16 knots.

71. At 6.34 p.m. decreased to 12 knots.

72. At 6.35 p.m. bad kink in rear of our line of battle; altered course slowly to port.

73. At 6.30 p.m. increased to 14 knots.

74. At 6.39 p.m. altering course slowly to starboard.

75. At 6.40 p.m. line straightened, course 105°.

76. At 6.41 p.m. observed three heavy columns of smoke on starboard bow, enemy bearing green 16° and now very indistinct.

77. At 6.42 p.m. "Valiant" very close up to "Barham," hauled out on latter's port quarter and reduced to slow speed.

78. At 6.49 p.m. increased to 12 knots.

79. At 6.50 p.m. increased to 15 knots.

80. At 6.50½ p.m. increased to 18 knots, course 110°. One enemy ship observed bearing green 93°.

81. At 6.56 p.m. "Preparative" signalled. Altered course two points to port.

82. At 6.57 p.m. increased to 20½ knots.

83. At 6.58 p.m. "Warspite" rejoined the line.

84. At 7.0 p.m. reduced to 18 knots.

85. At 7.2 p.m. altered course 175°, action recommenced.

86. At 7.3 p.m. enemy in sight bearing green 7°.

87. At 7.5 p.m. passed H.M.S. "Acasta" close to on port side, evidently badly holed, with collision mat over starboard side and some one standing by her. H.M.S. "Galatea" proceeding alongside to her assistance. Enemy reopened fire.

88. At 7.6 p.m. course 170°.

89. At 7.8 p.m. armoured cruiser bearing green 60° observed to be heavily hit. It is thought that this was a German ship of "Roon" class, but she appeared to be receiving fire of both friend and foe alike.

90. At 7.9 p.m. the Grand Fleet altered course, leaders together to south (magnetic).

91. At 7.10 p.m. "Valiant" reopened fire.

92. At 7.15 p.m. passed wreck of what was apparently a Dreadnought ship on port beam, about 3,000 yards distant. She appeared to be broken in half, resting on the bottom with her bow and stern about 100 yards apart, cocked up at right angles out of the water. She was painted pale grey, red bottom colour, ram bow, overhung stern and balance rudder.

93. At 7.18 p.m. "Marlborough" hit by torpedo. Leading enemy's ship observed to be on fire.

94. At 7.22 p.m. reduced to 10 knots.

95. At 7.23 p.m. enemy's Battlefleet now altered course together away from us, and broke off the action, sending out a low cloud of smoke which effectually covered their retreat and obscured them from further view.

96. At 7.24 p.m. increased to 12 knots.

97. At 7.25 p.m. increased to 13 knots.

98. At 7.27 p.m. an attack was made by eight enemy destroyers, bearing on our starboard bow, on the First and Fifth Battle Squadrons. Two enemy destroyers were detached and cut off by our light cruisers and destroyed. Of the six remaining, three were beaten off and returned to the South-East, two are believed to have been sunk and one severely crippled by the rapid fire from our starboard 6-in. battery. Altered course 2 points to port, course 105°, to avoid this attack.

99. At 7.28 p.m. opened fire with starboard 6-in. battery as before mentioned.

100. At 7.30 p.m. increased to 20 knots.

101. At 7.33 p.m. altered course 140°. Destroyer attack beaten off.

102. At 7.35 p.m. transferred 6-in. fire to large destroyer or Flotilla Leader. Observed her to be hit at least twice and straddled frequently. This ship was shortly afterwards engaged by our light cruisers and destroyers when on our starboard quarter, and on the evidence of Chief Petty Officer Webster (aloft director layer) this vessel was observed to founder. Reduced to 18 knots, enemy battlefleet now out of sight.

103. At 7.37 p.m. altered course 80°.

104. At 7.41 p.m. altered course 190°.

105. At 7.44 p.m. altered course 152°.

106. At 7.45 p.m. our light cruisers were observed to finish off three disabled German destroyers.

107. At 7.49 p.m. altered course 205°.

108. At 7.50 p.m. reduced to 15 knots.

109. At 7.54 p.m. altered course 180°.

110. At 8.5 p.m. altered course 270°.

111. At 8.7 p.m. increased to 17 knots.

112. At 8.25 p.m. altered course, leaders together, to W.S.W. (magnetic). Remainder of Grand Fleet on port bow and beam.

113. At 8.30 p.m. observed firing one point on port bow, probably our Battle Cruisers engaging retiring enemy.

114. At 8.31 p.m. altered course 195° with Fifth Battle Squadron.

115. At 8.43 p.m. altered course 218° and increased to 20 knots.

116. At 8.55 p.m. altered course 247°.

117. At 8.56 p.m. submarine on starboard bow. Altered course as requisite. Second Light Cruiser Squadron, coming up from astern on our starboard side, all opened fire with their starboard guns, apparently on the submarine in question.

118. At 9.7 p.m. altered course south (magnetic) with Fifth Battle Squadron.

119. At 9.35 p.m. reduced to 18 knots.

120. At 9.40 altered course S.S.E. (magnetic).

121. At 9.47 p.m. altered course S. by W. (magnetic), 16 knots.

122. At 9.55 p.m. altered course S.S.E. (magnetic).

123. At 10.3 p.m. altered course 18 points to starboard. Course North (magnetic).

124. At 10.8 p.m. altered course 16 points to port. Course south (magnetic), 20 knots. First Division of First Battle Squadron now bearing 1 mile on port beam.

125. At 10.15 p.m. observed heavy firing on starboard beam about 10 miles distant, which lasted for five minutes. One big explosion was noticed.

126. At 10.24 p.m. passed drifter with nets out on starboard side.

127. At 10.29 p.m. reduced to 17 knots.

128. At 10.39 p.m. observed heavy firing on starboard quarter. From the evidence of various officers and the Chief Yeoman of Signals, who were on the Bridge at this time, this appeared to be a night attack by one of our light cruisers and four of our destroyers on a column of enemy's ships. Our light cruiser was observed to be hit by three successive salvoes from a four-funnelled German Cruiser. Also two of our attacking Destroyers were seen to be badly hit. This attack took place on the enemy's port side and they appeared to be steaming south. Several shots from this action fell close to " Valiant."

129. At 10.42 p.m. altered course S.W. (magnetic).

130. At 10.45 p.m. altered course 340°.

131. At 10.49 p.m. one light cruiser (" Southampton " class) passed us on port side.

132. At 10.50 p.m. altered course 16 points to starboard, course South (magnetic).

133. At 11.35 p.m. observed heavy night action on starboard quarter. From the evidence we surmised that there appeared on this occasion to be two German Cruisers with at least two funnels and a crane amidships, apparently steering to the eastward at a high speed. These cruisers then evidently sighted an unknown small number of British ships ahead of them, possibly a light cruiser and a few destroyers in station about two miles astern of " Malaya " (rear ship of the Fifth Battle Squadron). Both Germans switched on top searchlights and opened a very rapid and extraordinarily accurate independent fire on our light cruiser. She replied, but was soon in flames fore and aft. The enemy, after five minutes, ceased fire and switched off.

134. With reference to night attacks, it was noticed that on each occasion German ships fired a white star shell which opened up like a parachute, before switching on their searchlights. Searchlights were already trained on the ship before being switched on.

135. At 11.38 p.m. increased to 20 knots.

136. Midnight. Reduced to 17 knots.

137. At 0.12 a.m., 1st June, heavy firing was observed astern in the distance.

138. An enemy's torpedo was observed by Lieutenant Glenny to pass 100 yards ahead of " Valiant " about 1 hour after the beginning of the action. " Warspite " reports that another torpedo also missed " Valiant " astern by 20 yards; time not known.

139. This concludes my record of the action as no further incidents of note occurred before our return to harbour.

1 *   *   *   *   *

I have the honour to be,
Sir,
Your obedient Servant,
M. WOOLLCOMBE,
Captain.

The Vice-Admiral Commanding
Battle Cruiser Fleet.

GUNNERY AND TORPEDO NOTES ON ACTION OF 31ST MAY 1916. H.M.S. "VALIANT,"

H.M.S. " Valiant," c/o G.P.O., London,
5th June 1916.

SIR,

I HAVE the honour to forward herewith Gunnery and Torpedo notes on the action of 31st May 1916.

I have the honour to be,
Sir,
Your obedient Servant,
M. WOOLLCOMBE,
Captain.

The Rear-Admiral Commanding
Fifth Battle Squadron.

GENERAL GUNNERY REMARKS ON ACTION OF 31ST MAY 1916.

Control.—Was carried out from the 15-in. G.C.T., the light was extremely bad, the target most difficult to be seen. During the whole of the action it was only possible in isolated cases to definitely state the nature of ship fired at. Most of the time it was simply a case of seeing a number of patches of smoke and it was not even possible to distinguish funnels, masts, &c.

The actual spotting was difficult only from the point of view of knowing at which target the Director Layer had fired, and whenever the control officer was observing the ship actually fired at, it was easy to see if the splashes were short, right or left; overs were not seen. Many hits were plainly visible.

2 *   *   *   *   *

At about 5.30 such great difficulty was experienced in distinguishing any of the enemy's ships that the control was temporarily turned over to the control officer in the Fore Top and the Gunnery Lieutenant went aloft, but after about five minutes he returned and took over the control in the 15-in. G.C.T. as the conditions aloft were even more difficult.

---

1 Part omitted here, referring solely to personnel, recommendations, &c. in no way bearing on the course of the action.
2 *See* note, page. 381.

During the first part of the action, from 3.30 G.M.T. till about 4.30, good ranges were obtained, but fire was actually opened on an estimated range and in consequence a correction Down was given, but after the next salvo, which went short, as good ranges were being obtained, a correction Up was applied, and this again went short, another Up gave a visible hit.

The Range Finders were a very great help and on three or four occasions on calling down straddle to the T.S., they reported gun range 300 to 400 yards less than Rangefinder range.

Range Finding—Was extremely difficult except at the commencement.

1 *　　　*　　　*　　　*　　　*

The target fired at had to be shifted a large number of times due to—concentration signal, altering course, engaging Battle Fleet in lieu of Battle Cruisers, and frequently due to proper target being obscured by smoke and haze.

The Range Finder Glasses (especially those of the after turrets) became covered with cordite smoke, and in the case of " Y " turret a Boy 1st Cl. was employed sitting on the top of the turret cleaning them.

After the first half hour, sufficient ranges were not obtained to give a rate, but isolated groups of ranges were obtained, which were of great value for checking the range on sights.

Director Fire—Was used throughout the action, it would have been impossible for individual to have been used; great difficulties being experienced in getting a Director Gunlayer on to the right set of flashes. Turret gunlayers .could not see sufficiently plainly through their periscopes.

The left gun of " A " turret went out of step, firing was carried out by Director by means of checking with the right gun. The fault : wire partially carried away from the left elevating receiver.

" X " turret training went out of step. The Director was lined up twice during the action, during a lull, thus overcoming the trouble.

Enemy's Splashes.—Although the ship was straddled many times and a large number of shots were only just short, the splashes appeared to be very small and did not rise much above the hull of the ship; no water came on board and no trouble was experienced with spray on glasses.

Due to this the control officers experienced no additional difficulties when ship was being heavily fired at than when receiving no fire.

The additional noise was much less than expected and the control appeared to run smoothly, orders being always able to

---

[1] *See* note on p. 381.

be got through telephones, the only difficulty being the aloft Director voice pipe due to wind.

Rate of Fire.—The fire was kept slow and deliberate due to the same difficulty of getting on to the right target, on four or five occasions rapid bursts were carried out when it was seen that hitting was established. There were several long lulls when firing did not take place :—

(1) When our Battle Cruiser Fleet steamed between us and the enemy and their smoke obscured the target.
(2) When the " Defence " was sunk, smoke obscured the target.
(3) When the " Warrior " was heavily hit and poured out volumes of black smoke.
(4) At 5.30 and 6.45 when smoke and mist obscured the enemy.

Breakdowns.

Director—With the exceptions above stated, worked extremely well and was in step at the end.

Control Instruments and Communications.—Nil.

Turrets.—All turrets fired most satisfactorily and had no breakdowns of any importance; all turret officers reported that they were easily at the ready and only missed a total of three salvoes, *i.e.,* " B " three failures to fire, two tubes balanced very high, one cause unknown.

1 *   *   *   *   *

6-in. Control.—6-in. firing was carried out, starboard side, at extreme range against German Destroyers and a Light Cruiser.

Control was from fore-top through the G.C.T.

Firing was very accurate and destroyer attack was beaten off.

Three failures to fire occurred, two being tubes and one cause unknown.

No other delays or accidents.

The firing of the 6-in. guns did not inconvenience the control of the 15-in. guns.

In accordance with Gunnery Order No. 56 of 1st April 1915, the Director Gunlayer's eyesight was tested and his eyes showed no ill-effects whatever.

1 *   *   *   *   *

Number of Rounds fired.

					Right.	Left.
" A " -	-	-	-	-	36	35
" B " -	-	-	-	-	39	36
" X " -	-	-	-	-	40	34
" Y " -	-	-	-	-	35	33
Starboard 6-in. -	-	-			76	

[1] *See* note on p. 381.

GENERAL TORPEDO REMARKS ON ACTION OF 31st MAY 1916. " H.M.S. VALIANT."

The enemy was not sufficiently visible throughout the action for ranges to be taken with the torpedo rangefinder.

The visibility was generally low and observations from the Torpedo Control Tower were much hampered by waste steam coming up the engine-room exhaust.

2. In the first period of the action, from about 4.10 to 4.50 p.m., the enemy was before the port beam and the range was long. There was no opportunity to fire torpedoes.

3. After becoming engaged on the starboard side one or two chances occurred for firing torpedoes, but they involved considerable risk of hitting our own ships; at 6.0 p.m. an opportunity presented itself to fire at the enemy's battlefleet. The course was estimated as parallel to our own ships, range 14,000 and bearing 140 Green. A 28-knot torpedo was used and started correctly from the starboard after tube. Result of shot not known.

4. No further opportunity presented itself, partly owing to the long range and partly owing to risk to our own ships.

5. The enemy fleet appeared to take great care not to get within torpedo range when on a bearing exposing him to torpedo fire.

6. One torpedo was seen to cross " Valiant's " bows and another is understood to have been seen from " Warspite " to cross our stern. Times not known with any accuracy.

7. The ship was not hit and electrical gear was not severely tested. There was difficulty in getting No. 4 Tube dynamo to take its load, but this did not affect the electrical supply generally. All breakers stood the concussion without coming off.

All communications, gyro compass, &c., were intact. Navy-phones could be used at all times in spite of shell bursting close to the ship.

8. The two after searchlight barrels and mirrors, which were left up in case of fog, were damaged by blast. One of the 24-in. mirrors, though broken, was held together by the lead backing and wire netting and was quite fit for use. This is the only mirror in the ship so fitted.

CAPTAIN'S REPORT.—H.M.S. " MALAYA."

No. 88/14.

H.M.S. " Malaya,"

SIR,   6th June 1916.

IN reporting events, besides a few general remarks, I cannot do better than forward the attached diary of events collected from various sources. The times and principal items were taken by Assistant Paymaster Keith M. Lawder in the spotting top, and, as he was unfettered by other duties, can be considered reliable.

2. Considering the vast amount of ammunition expended on us, I attribute the small number of hits to the very small spread of the German salvoes; though the firing was good and range-taking good they appeared to use very small spotting corrections.

3. The speed of the High Sea Fleet appeared to be very high and was estimated to be over 21 knots.

4. Our firing at enemy Battle Cruisers at long range appeared to be good, but it is difficult to say what was the result, though the fourth salvo was a distinct hit. When firing at the High Sea Fleet after turning 16 points, owing to the haze and light rendering spotting exceedingly difficult, the fall of some salvoes could not be seen.

5. Several tracks of torpedoes were reported, but none were actually verified.

6. The E.R. Torpedo in the foremost submerged flat could not be fired as the bar was jambed owing to the ship being struck below the water line on the starboard side forward. One torpedo was fired from the after tube.

7. The conduct of the men was all that could be desired, and I wish to bring to your notice several cases for special mention, principally in connection with the fire on the Gun Deck. This will form the subject of a separate letter.

8. Suggestions for preventing the spread of fire on the Gun Deck in future will be forwarded later.

9. The following Enclosures are attached :—

> A. Diary of events.
> B. Track of "Malaya."
> C. Gunnery notes, accidents, &c.
> D. Torpedo notes, accidents, &c.
> E. Remarks from Engine Room Department.
> F. Damage sustained.

I have the honour to be,

Sir,

Your obedient Servant,

A. D. BOYLE,

The Rear-Admiral Commanding,   Captain.
    Fifth Battle Squadron.

Plate 19.

TRACING SHEWING THE TRACK OF H.M.S. "MALAYA"
During the Engagement on May 31st 1916,
between 3.50 p.m. and 9.45 p.m.

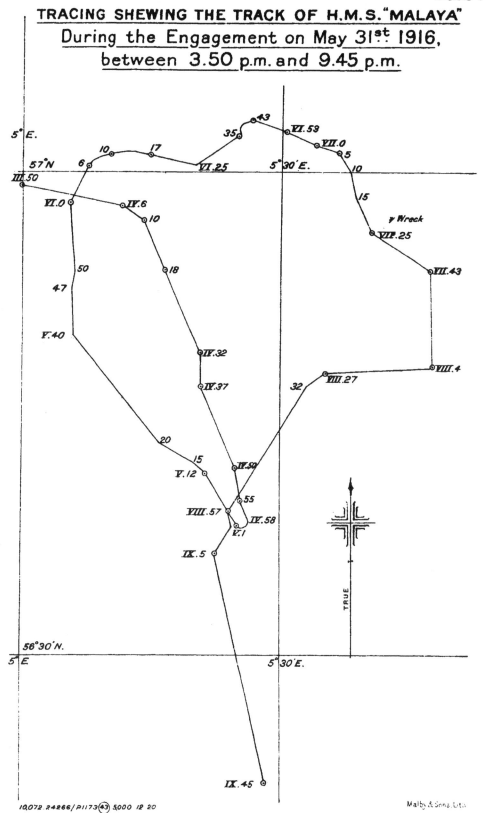

Enclosure " A " to " Malaya's " No. 88/14 of 6 June 1916.

DIARY OF EVENTS, MAY 31 TO JUNE 1, FROM NOTES MADE BY ASSISTANT PAYMASTER LAWDER IN THE SPOTTING TOP, COMBINED WITH MY OWN, LIEU-TENANT-COMMANDER (G)'S, AND OTHER OFFICERS' OBSERVATIONS. " H.M.S. MALAYA."

(All times are G.M.T.)

P.M.

4.00. " Barham " opened fire. Our Battle Cruisers were on starboard bow, we not having turned, and two enemy Light Cruisers on port bow.

4. 2. " Valiant " opened fire at apparently Light Cruisers.

4. 5. " Warspite " opened fire. Observed enemy Battle Cruiser about Red 5°, steering to southward.

4. 6. Altered course to starboard.

4.10. Altered course to starboard.

4.15. Opened fire on rear enemy Battle Cruiser (" Seydlitz," we thought). Range, 18,500; fell short.

Between 4.00 and 4.15 p.m. (actual times not noted) one of our Battle Cruisers was observed to blow up, a vast column of smoke and nothing more was seen.

Shortly after another big explosion was heard from the direction of our Battle Cruisers.

4.20. ⎫ Our Destroyer Flotilla fell back to starboard quarter.
to ⎬ First salvo : short and left. Second salvo : ahead
4.32 ⎭ and still short. Third salvo : over. Fourth salvo (4.32) : straddled and apparently hit in line with foremast. Range, 19,200. Enemy soon after altered course to port together. (Armoured Director had been used up to now, but shifted to Aloft Director

1 *   *   *   *   *

4.35. Enemy turned to port together. Enemy's Destroyers sighted on port bow.

4.45. Enemy's salvo fell just ahead of us, followed by several more. Our range, 21,000.

4.50. Passed one of our Destroyers with boats lowered picking up survivors among some wreckage.

Soon after our Battle Cruisers passed us on engaged side on opposite course. Only four present—" Lion," " Princess Royal," " Tiger," and " New Zealand."

Shortly after our Battle Cruisers passed observed enemy's Battle Fleet on port bow in three or four columns heading straight for us. (Aloft reported three columns, the fourth column seen from below may have been cruisers in the haze very hard to distinguish.)

4.57. Altered course 16 points (in succession) to starboard and followed our Battle Cruisers. Enemy's Battle Fleet opened fire on the turn, so " Malaya " turned short.

¹ *See* note page 381.

P.M.

4.59. Enemy's salvo 50 yards over.

5.00. Increased to full speed (25 knots).

After turning could see a four funnel cruiser ahead of enemy's Battle Fleet, which by this time had deployed. Opened fire at guessed range of 17,000 at what appeared to be a "König" class. Spotting very difficult now owing to haze.

5. 5. Enemy has our range exactly, so hauled out a little to port.

5.12 ⎫
to ⎬ Enemy's salvoes straddled "Valiant" and "Malaya." At this time we were outlined against a bright yellow
5.30 ⎭ horizon, but enemy were nearly obscured by mist, and we were under a very heavy constant fire from at least four ships of the High Sea Fleet. Only flashes were visible, and six salvoes were falling round the ship per minute, and at one time, counting some which were probably meant for "Warspite," *nine* salvoes fell in rapid succession.

Shifted target to what appeared to be the leading enemy Battleship, and as soon as a short salvo was obtained broke into rapid Director as it was realised that "Malaya" was presenting a good target.

It had been decided to fire the 6-in. guns short to make a screen, but before this was done the whole starboard battery was put out of action by shell bursting there.

5.14. Enemy's salvo fell close over our port bow, sending spray well over the spotting top and black water into the conning tower, &c.

5.17. Altered course two points to port together.

5.20. Shell struck ship on starboard side forward about water line, shaking the ship very heavily indeed.

5.25. Splinter cut steampipe to starboard syren, escape of steam rendering communication with top impossible for a few minutes till shut off.

5.27. Shell struck ship aft (roof of " X " turret).

5.30. Shell struck starboard side of upper deck just above S. 3 six-inch gun, followed by another in the same place, wrecking the 6-in. battery and causing a fire for a short time.

5.35. Shell struck somewhere along starboard side.

5.37. Two shell fell just over and abreast of port forward 6-in. gun. The officers aloft saw the shell and state that they fell within a few feet of the ship's side.

5.45. Ship had now a list of about 4° to starboard, and for a short time guns were firing at nearly extreme elevation. From the top oil could be seen coming from our starboard side abreast of after 6-in. gun.

6.00. Course, N.N.E. Enemy's rate of fire at us much reduced.

P.M.

6. 5. Fired long range torpedo at third ship of enemy's Battle Fleet, four points abaft the beam, range, approximately 12,900 yards.

6. 6. Sighted some of the Grand Fleet ahead of us coming towards us.

6.15. Altered course to starboard. We were now past the sun, and not such a good target.

6.20. " Defence " coming down on starboard bow blew up, and " Warrior " also on starboard bow was severely damaged. Heavy firing all along the line.

6.23. " Warspite " hauled out of line and turned to starboard in a circle. Enemy concentrated on her. " Warspite " replied rapidly, but seemed to stop after turning about 24 points.

6.26. Eased from full speed.

6.32. Fifth Battle Squadron altered course to port so as to take station astern of rear ships of First Battle Squadron. Very congested at this point, many destroyers and Light Cruisers being mixed up with us and enemy firing rapidly, but no hits were observed.

6.35. Altering course in succession to starboard.

6.45. A lull in the firing.

7.15. Firing general again and enemy more distinct.

7.20. Opened fire on what appeared to be rearmost ship of enemy line (range, 10,400). That ship was under fire of several of our ships and was shortly after obscured by smoke and dropped astern.

Prepared to open fire on a Battleship which was very low in the water and dropping astern. According to two Officers she suddenly disappeared without an explosion. She had two short fat funnels.

7.25 to 7.40 Enemy destroyers made an attack. Opened fire with the two remaining 6-in. guns of starboard battery and also fired two 15-in. salvoes at a range of 8,000 yards. Other ships were firing on the destroyers as well, which retired. One at least was seen to sink, and this was the last of the enemy seen in daylight owing to the Battle Fleet having turned away.

7.40. Light Cruisers and Destroyers astern of us turned to starboard, apparently to attack enemy's light craft. Ceased firing—enemy out of sight.

8.30. Some firing heard right ahead some distance off.

10.20. Firing observed on starboard beam. In the flashes one of our " Dublin " class could be distinguished, and was apparently hit twice. Enemy Destroyers were beyond her, and used a form of Very's Light. It appeared as if one of enemy's Destroyers was well on fire and sank.

11.40. Three points abaft starboard beam observed what appeared to be an attack by our Destroyers on some enemy big ships steering the same way as ours, two of which used searchlights. One of our Destroyers, with three funnels (appearance of " Termagant " class), was set on fire, but not before she had hit the second ship. This was seen by the column of smoke, and also the explosion was distinctly heard and felt.

The leading ship of the enemy, which was seen by the flash of the explosion, had two masts, two funnels, and a conspicuous crane (apparently " Westfalen " class).

A.M.   *June 1st.*

0.17 ⎫ Two attacks some way astern of us. We distinctly felt
to   ⎬ three explosions, and at end of last attack a brilliant
0.45 ⎭ flare lit up the whole sky.

2.15. Some firing a long way off astern.

4.00 Some shots, apparently 6-in. or larger calibre, fell near ship, but no flashes could be seen, and it was afterwards concluded from W/T that they came from ships firing at enemy Zeppelins.

                                 A. D. BOYLE.

Enclosure " C " to " Malaya's " No. 88/14 of 6 June 1916.

" MALAYA." GUNNERY REMARKS.

1. The enemy's Battle Cruisers when we were engaging them appeared to be zig-zagging at very short intervals.

1 *   *   *   *   *

The ranges obtained and reports showed that gun range was being kept, so it would appear that this zig-zag was quite a constant one, and that they were never far off the mean course.

2. 1 *   *   *   *   *

3. When the High Sea Fleet were engaging us heavily it appeared that some were using Director and others Individual.

4. " X " turret was the only turret which developed defects.

" A " turret had no accidents.

" B " turret had no accidents of a serious nature. One of the dogs on the main cage of the right gun became bent and had to be removed. Whilst this was being done the auxiliary shell hoist was being used, and there was no delay in the firing.

" X " turret.—A heavy shell (12-in.) struck the centre of the roof rear end, bulging the roof, without exploding. All the securing bolts were sheared and the roof was started up clear of the walls of the turret. The only damage done inside the turret was to put the rangefinder out of action, Kilroy danger signal right gun, and the foresight of the open director sight. During the action it was found impossible to load the main cage

-----

[1] *See* note, page 381.

from the shell bogie on the foremost side of the trunk when the turret was trained on the beam bearing, and the auxiliary shell hoist had to be used for the gun affected. This was due to the fixed rack having come up 5/16 in. on the foremost side of the trunk in the fore and aft line. The same trouble, but to a much lesser extent, has been reported before, but it was not then sufficient to prevent the working of the bogie after additional clearance had been cut on the underneath side of the traversing trolley.

" Y " turret had no accidents of a serious nature. Trouble was experienced with the cordite trays of the left gun loading cage, but it was put to rights without delaying the firing.

Owing to the list of the ship the port pumps could not get enough water, so sea water had to be admitted to the system.

There was no failure of Director, or any other electrical gear.

There was one missfire, due to a defective tube.

Enclosure " D " to " Malaya's " No. 88/14 of 6 June 1916.

TORPEDO AND ELECTRICAL REMARKS.

Torpedo.—Fired one torpedo, from starboard after flat at 6.5 p.m. Range of torpedo, 10,750; range of enemy, 12,900 approximately. Gyro angle, 20° left. Bearing of third ship, at which ship torpedo was fired, was four points abaft the beam. Torpedo appeared to run correctly.

Starboard forward tube. The bar jambed owing to a hit on the armour close to the Flat.

Electrical Breakdowns. — Communications. — None, except where circuits were cut or burnt in the starboard battery.

Lighting and Power.—None, except where circuits were cut or burnt in the starboard battery.

Gyro Compass.—Masters remained on meridian. The repeaters got out of step when our guns fired. After the action, remained in step when the compass platform repeater was isolated, an earth having developed on this circuit in the starboard battery.

Enclosure " E " to " Malaya's " No. 88/14 of 6 June 1916.

REMARKS FROM ENGINE ROOM DEPARTMENT.

About 6.00 p.m., G.M.T., several sprayers in " A " boilers were extinguished by water which had become mixed with the oil fuel in the starboard inner bunkers. These inner bunkers were shut off and oil fuel for the sprayers was obtained from the port side. It was subsequently discovered that the water in the inner bunkers was due to leakage from the outer bunkers in which two shells had exploded.

Several compartments forward on starboard side were hit below the water line and flooded ; the consequent list to starboard deprived the port hydraulic tanks of water for a few minutes and recourse was had to salt water supply.

The ship was gradually brought to the correct trim by pumping oil fuel across from the starboard to the port bunkers. It was thus possible to avoid any increase in the draught other than that due to the flooded compartments.

During the shell explosion on the starboard gun deck, flame and debris passed down the starboard air supply trunk to " A " boiler room, damaging fittings and slightly burning one Stoker Petty Officer on duty near the boilers.

Enclosure " F " to " Malaya's " No. 88/14 of 6 June 1916.

DAMAGE SUSTAINED.—EIGHT HITS.

Stations 36–60.—Two hits, one indenting the upper armour plate, the other indenting and tearing the ship's plating below the armour.

The wing compartments 29–36, 36–52 lower deck, and Chief Petty Officers' bathroom 36–52 middle deck, were flooded.

At 52–56 the angle at the bottom of the armour on the main deck is sprung off the plates, several rivets are sheared, gussets and Z bars are distorted and a few armour bolts are slackened.

The steam pipe to the syren was fractured by an indirect hit.

Also at 52 a heavy shell struck the plates above the water line, pushing the plating back.

Stations 82–109.—Two hits. The Gun Deck was depressed several inches, several seams were opened out, the hatch was distorted. The galley, canteen, drying room and fittings on the gun deck were wrecked by a large shell passing through the forecastle deck and exploding in the 6-in. gun battery.

No. 3 six-inch gun starboard damaged and the mounting wrecked.

Cordite on this deck set fire to and destroyed all electric cables, &c.

Below W.L.—Two hits. There is a large hole at 92–94 below the armour apparently caused by two projectiles. The inner and outer oil bunkers 82–100 and wing compartments 82–109 were flooded; the seamen's bathroom 91–100 middle deck was flooded, and there were leaks into adjacent compartments.

" X " *Turret.*—A heavy shell struck the centre of the roof rear end, bulging and perforating the roof slightly, without exploding. All the securing bolts were sheared and the roof started. The only damage done in the turret was that the rangefinder was put out of action, as was the Kilroy danger signal to the right gun.

It was found that the main cage at the bottom could not be loaded from the shell bogie on the foremost side of the trunk when the turret was abeam. This was due to the fixed rack having come up 5/16 in. on the foremost side of the trunk.

No. 89/14.

H.M.S. " Malaya,"

SIR, 6 June 1916.

IN continuation of my previous report of Events, I beg to report that early on the morning of June 1st (about 4.0 a.m.), officers in the armoured director tower and engine room report that the ship struck something submerged on the starboard side which scraped along under the bottom.

I purposely refrained from claiming or reporting anything until the damage below had been examined by experts.

2. The Chief Constructor came on board to-day and informed me that the lower damage, 38–48, could not possibly have been done by a shell, but had been caused by striking something submerged, and that, in view of the depth below the water line, he thought it most likely was a submarine.

In view of the distance from the scene of the action it could not have been any of the wreckage, besides which nothing was seen above the water, and it seems more than probable that we struck a submarine.

I have the honour to be, Sir,
Your obedient servant,
A. D. BOYLE,

The Rear-Admiral Commanding, Captain.
Fifth Battle Squadron.

Commander-in-Chief.

Submitted.

HUGH EVAN-THOMAS,

10 June 1916. Rear-Admiral.

LETTER OF PROCEEDINGS OF CAPTAIN (D), 13TH FLOTILLA.

Enclosure No. 17 to Battle Cruiser Fleet, Letter No. B.C.F. 01
of 12/6/16.

No. 60. H.M.S. " Champion,"

SIR, 3rd June 1916.

I HAVE the honour to forward the following report of
Proceedings of H.M.S. " Champion " and 13th Destroyer Flotilla
during the recent action of the 31st May–1st June 1916.

2. At 2.50 p.m., 31st May, H.M.S. " Onslow " and " Moresby "
were detached to join H.M.S. " Engadine," but attacked enemy
Battle Cruiser Fleet with remainder of Flotilla, as described in
paragraph 5.

3. At commencement cf action station was taken up on the
starboard bow of H.M.S. " Lion," Destroyers in company
being :—

" Nestor "	-	Commander	Hon. Edward B. S. Bingham.
" Nomad "	-	Lieut. Commander	Paul Whitfield.
" Narborough "-	,,	,,	Geoffrey Corlett.
" Obdurate "	- ,,	,,	Cecil H. H. Sams.
" Petard "	- ,,	,,	Evelyn C. O. Thomson.
" Pelican "	- ,,	,,	Kenneth A. Beattie.
" Nerissa "	- ,,	,,	Montague C. B. Legge.
" Onslow "[1]	- ,,	,,	John C. Tovey.
" Moresby "[1]	- ,,	,,	Roger V. Alison.
" Nicator "	-	Lieutenant Jack E. A. Mocatta.	
" Termagant "	-	Lieut. Commander Cuthbert P. Blake.	
" Turbulent "	-	,, ,,	Dudley Stuart.

(The last two named Destroyers being temporarily attached.)

4. At 4.30 p.m. Enemy's Battle Fleet was sighted by
" Champion " and reported to you.

5. At 4.15 p.m. the whole Flotilla was ordered to attack
Enemy Battle Cruiser Fleet. This attack was well carried out,
and it is thought that at least two Enemy Destroyers were sunk.
I regret to state that H.M.S. " Nestor " (Commander Hon.
E. B. S. Bingham) and H.M.S. " Nomad " (Lieutenant Commander
Paul Whitfield) did not return from this action, and must be
considered to have been sunk.

6. At 7.45 p.m. H.M.S. " Onslow " was reported unable to
steam, and was taken in tow by H.M.S. " Defender."

7. No further opportunity of attacking Enemy occurred
during the day.

8. At night station was taken astern of Battle Fleet, course
South. About 11.30 p.m. heavy firing was opened on our
starboard beam, apparently at some of our Destroyers between

---

[1] Attached to " Engadine."

the 13th Flotilla and the enemy. I hauled out to the eastward as I was unable to attack with any of our own Flotilla, our own forces being between me and the Enemy. I then resumed course South; firing was observed at intervals during the night on our starboard beam. Destroyers of the 13th Flotilla, with the exception of H.M.S. " Obdurate " and " Moresby," lost touch with me during the night. H.M.S. " Narborough " as Senior Officer, reports that he took charge of the remainder, and rejoined the Fleet at 9.45 a.m. on the 1st instant.

H.M.S. " Marksman " and " Maenad " joined me at about 2.30 a.m. At 2.50 a.m. course was altered to North to conform with signal received from the Commander-in-Chief.

9. At 3.25 a.m. four Destroyers, steering southward, were sighted; owing to the mist I was uncertain at first who they were; but at 3.30 a.m. I made them out to be the enemy, and opened fire, range about 3,000 yards. Two torpedoes were fired at " Champion," the first one passing under our bows, the second just missing close astern. Enemy passed on opposite course, and when ship had been steadied after avoiding torpedoes, the enemy had disappeared in the mist, and I resumed my same course.

10. At 4.30 a.m. H.M.S. " Obdurate " picked up two survivors, and H.M.S. " Marksman " one survivor, from H.M.S. " Ardent."

At 5 a.m. two rafts were sighted, and H.M.S. " Moresby " rescued seven men, and H.M.S. " Maenad " eleven men, survivors from H.M.S. " Fortune."

11. At about 6 a.m. H.M.S. " Marksman " was detached to examine vessel to westward, which appeared to be a disabled Destroyer, and lost touch with me. Nothing further occurred, and I returned to base, by your orders, arriving at 3.30 p.m., 2nd June 1916.

12. Letter of Proceedings from H.M.S. " Narborough," the Senior Officer surviving from Destroyer attack, is attached. Reports have been called for from remainder of 13th Flotilla, and an addendum to this letter will be forwarded when the reports have been collected.

13. In addition to loss of H.M.S. " Nestor " and " Nomad," H.M.S. " Turbulent " (Lieutenant-Commander Dudley Stuart) is reported by H.M.S. " Narborough " to have been lost sight of at 0.30 a.m. on the 1st instant, and was probably rammed, or sunk by gunfire.

Total casualties and names have not yet been ascertained.

I have the honour to be,
Sir,
Your obedient Servant,
J. U. FARIE,
13th Flotilla.

The Vice-Admiral Commanding
Battle Cruiser Fleet, H.M.S. " Lion."

Enclosure No. 18 to Battle Cruiser Fleet, Letter No. B.C.F. 01
of 12/6/16.

ADDENDUM TO LETTER OF PROCEEDINGS NO. 60 OF 3RD JUNE 1916.

No. 60.   H.M.S. " Champion."
SIR,   7th June 1916.
     WITH reference to paragraph 12 of my letter of proceedings
No. 60 of 3rd June 1916, I have the honour to forward this
addendum, containing extracts from reports received from
destroyers of 13th Flotilla, who were engaged in the action,
31st May–1st June 1916.

H.M.S. " Obdurate," dated 3rd June 1916.

     On receiving the signal to carry out torpedo attack on enemy
battle cruiser fleet, " Obdurate " turned towards the enemy
and soon became engaged with their destroyers and one light
cruiser.   Range varied from 6,000 to 3,000 yards, and during the
destroyer action one of the enemy's destroyers was blown up
and two others badly damaged; probably one of these two sank
as the guns firing at her lost sight of her.
     The enemy destroyers and light cruiser were driven back to
the protection of their big ships, and " Obdurate " was then too
far astern to deliver a torpedo attack.   " Obdurate " was hit
twice by a 4·1 shell, but suffered no casualties.

H.M.S. " Petard," dated 2nd June 1916.

     On receiving the signal to attack with torpedoes, I attacked
with H.M.S. " Turbulent."   The first torpedo fired was set for
high speed, six feet deep, and was aimed at the head of the
German destroyer flotilla, which was crossing over to meet our
attack.   The track was closely followed, and tube's crew state
that they undoubtedly saw it hit a German Destroyer about
amidships and explode.   I opened fire with my gun on this
destroyer a few minutes later, and she was then lying stopped,
with her upper deck awash and obviously sinking.
     " Petard " then took part in the general engagement with
the German Destroyers, and the three remaining torpedoes were
fired at a range of about 7,000 yards on the bow of the German
Battle Cruiser Fleet.   All these torpedoes must have crossed
the track of the German line.
     At 12.15 a.m. course was altered to S.W. by W., and ten
minutes later the line crossed ahead of a division of German
Battleships.   I sighted the leading battleship about six points
on my starboard bow steering S.E. at about 400 or 500 yards.
This ship switched on recognition lights, consisting of two red
over one white light and, as some destroyer ahead of me in the
line then switched on her " fighting lights," I think the Germans
at once knew we were enemy.   As " Petard " had no torpedoes

left I could not attack, so I increased to full speed, and altered course slightly to port to avoid being rammed. I passed about 200 yards ahead of the German ship, who appeared to be one of the " Wittelsbach " class. As soon as we were clear of her stem, she illuminated us with searchlights, and we came under a heavy fire from her and the next ship in the line. Two salvoes seemed to strike us, and, in all, I think, we received six hits.

I regret that I never saw " Turbulent," who was in station astern of " Petard," after passing the German Squadron ; according to the evidence of some of my Ship's Company, I am afraid she must have been rammed and sunk.

H.M.S. " Pelican," dated 4th June 1916.

" Pelican " was unable to fire torpedoes owing to the other two divisions being engaged by enemy torpedo craft between the fleets, and by a division of the 9th Flotilla, who were coming up in the opposite direction.

At about 10.35 p.m. there was heavy firing in N. Westerly direction, and destroyers were seen in the searchlight rays of attacking ships. Shortly afterwards there was a huge explosion in that direction. At 0.40, June 1st, when on a course S.W., speed 30 knots, I observed two ships on starboard quarter, which were at first taken to be our Light Cruisers. They switched on three vertical lights, the upper two being red and lower green, at the same time " Pelican's " stem was lit up by a searchlight which was immediately transferred to " Petard " and " Turbulent," who were astern. When sighted position was unfavourable for attack.

H.M.S. " Nerissa," dated 5th June 1916.

4.30 p.m., commenced attack on a northerly course, owing to enemy turning 16 points, this attack had eventually to be carried out on a southerly course, which I did in company with " Termagant," but firing two torpedoes, range 7,000 yards. Just previous to this attack " Nomad " was observed quite close, stopped and apparently badly damaged in the engine room. One torpedo apparently took effect on rear ship.

H.M.S. " Onslow," dated 2nd June 1916.

At about 6.5 p.m., sighting an enemy Light Cruiser, class uncertain, with 3 funnels, with topgallant forecastle only about 6,000 yards from 1st B.C.S., I decided to attack her. All guns engaged enemy Light Cruiser, and 58 rounds were fired at a range of 2,000 to 4,000 yards ; undoubtedly a large number of hits were scored, as they were easily spotted at this range. I then gave orders for all torpedoes to be fired. I saw the first torpedo leave the ship, and immediately was struck by a big shell amidships the starboard side. There was a big escape of steam, completely enveloping both torpedo tubes. Sub-Lieutenant Moore, Leading Signalman Cassin, also several other ratings and myself saw the torpedo hit Light Cruiser below conning tower, and explode.

Owing to two shells having exploded in No. 2 Boiler room, and badly damaged main feed tank and all the water in the reserve feed tank being now used, at 7.0 p.m. ship stopped and electric current was lost. At 7.15 p.m. "Defender" closed "Onslow" and asked if assistance was required. On learning "Defender" could only steam 10 knots, I asked to be taken in tow whilst endeavouring to effect repairs; this "Defender" did under very trying circumstances, and with large enemy ships rapidly approaching. In tow of "Defender" I then proceeded W. by N. Using salt-water feed, Engineer Lieutenant Commander Foulkes raised speed for slow speed to enable me to use steering engine, and when weather got worse to lessen strain on towing hawser. Owing to ship's condition I decided to make for the nearest port—Aberdeen—arriving there about 1.0 p.m. the 2nd June.

H.M.S. "Moresby," dated 3rd June 1916.

At 5.0 p.m. an enemy Dreadnought squadron then observed steering Northward was attacked. At 5.10 p.m., being two points before the beam of the leading ship 6–8,000 yards, a long range torpedo was fired at the third ship. About 8 minutes later I observed an upheaval due to a torpedo, and am informed it was on the 6th ship. This agrees with the director setting. The enemy were then straddling frequently; my smoke was bad; I therefore turned towards the enemy and ran between the lines, in order to clear the range from smoke nuisance.

At about 2.35 a.m., four "Deutschland" class ships were seen bearing West, 4,000 yards. I hauled out to port, firing a H.S. torpedo at 2.37 G.M.T. No more could be fired as left tube was empty, and the fore director was pointed skywards when the sight bore of that tube. Mist and smoke prevented the enemy being seen again.

H.M.S. "Nicator," dated 4th June 1916.

At 4.15 p.m. torpedo attack was carried out. Two torpedoes were fired at a range of about 6,000 yards. During this attack enemy's Destroyers were continually engaged with gunfire, and were observed to be retiring, leaving at least two in a disabled condition. A third torpedo was fired at second ship of enemy's Battle Fleet at a range of about 3,000 yards. "Nestor" and "Nicator" continued to close until within about 2,500 yards, when "Nestor" was hit in the region of No. 1 Boiler Room; she immediately altered course 8 points to starboard, and "Nicator" was obliged to alter inside her to avoid collision, thereby failing to fire a 4th torpedo.

At 3.30 p.m., June 1st, in Lat. 55.50 N., Long. 0.55 W., a torpedo fired by a hostile submarine was observed approaching from abaft the starboard beam at an angle of 30 degrees, running on the surface; helm was at once put hard a starboard and telegraphs to full speed. Torpedo passed ahead. On resuming course a submerged explosion was very distinctly felt all over the ship, but no damage could be found. Submarine was not sighted.

1 *   *   *   *   *

I have the honour to be,
Sir,
Your obedient Servant,
J. U. FARIE,
Captain (D),
13th Destroyer Flotilla.

The Vice-Admiral Commanding
Battle Cruiser Fleet, H.M.S. " Lion."

Enclosure No. 19 to Battle Cruiser Fleet, Letter No. B.C.F. 01 of 12/6/16.

From—Captain (D), 13th Destroyer Flotilla,

To—The Vice-Admiral Commanding Battle Cruiser Fleet.

Date—9th June 1916.

No.—60.

Submitted.

Enclosed are action reports from Destroyers in accordance with your signal of to-day.

J. U. FARIE,
Captain (D),
13th Destroyer Flotilla.

H.M.S. " NARBOROUGH,"
Sir,   2nd June 1916.
I HAVE the honour to report in accordance with your orders the following movements of the 13th Flotilla on 31st May and 1st June 1916.

Previous to action commencing the Flotilla was stationed ahead of Battle Cruiser Squadron. Shortly after the action had commenced Destroyers were ordered to attack with torpedoes, second and third Divisions drew out to Port of " Champion " in accordance with orders signalled to get ahead for attacking. Third Division followed second Division down to the attack, but " Petard " and " Turbulent " were separated by " Nottingham " crossing " Petard's " bows. " Petard " and " Turbulent " proceeded independently.

Previous to turning, the German High Sea Fleet were observed coming up from the Southward.

Before getting into the favourable position to fire Torpedoes, enemy's Light Cruisers and Destroyers, fourteen or fifteen in No., came across towards our Battle Cruiser Squadron, and were

---

¹ Part omitted here, referring solely to personnel, recommendations, &c. in no way bearing on the course of the action.

intercepted by 13th and 9th Flotillas. General firing took place the Third Division were unable to open fire owing to the 9th Flotilla, who had come up in the opposite direction, getting between them and enemy Destroyers. Enemy's flotilla retired to their own Battle Cruiser Squadron after short action. It is thought that at least two enemy Destroyers were sunk.

The position of enemy's Battle Cruiser Squadron was then unfavourable for firing Torpedoes, and in view of enemy's Battle Fleet having been sighted, I decided not to fire Torpedoes at long range at Battle Cruiser Squadron, but to retain all Torpedoes for use pending Fleet action. Accordingly " Narborough " and " Pelican " rejoined " Champion." The remaining Destroyers of the 13th Flotilla rejoined " Champion " except " Nestor " and " Nomad," who had been observed badly damaged.

Proceeded in company of " Champion " from 8 p.m. till midnight. Firing was observed to starboard beam at intervals between 10 and 11 p.m. and a heavy action at 11.30 p.m. Several ships were seen on starboard beam about midnight, but it could not be made out whether hostile.

At 0.30 a.m., 1st June 1916, a large vessel making much smoke was observed crossing the rear of the Flotilla from starboard to port at a fast speed. This vessel was thought to be one of our Light Cruisers or an Armoured Cruiser of the " Warrior " class, one of whom had been on our starboard quarter during the First Watch. When on starboard quarter at about 1,000 yards vessel switched on two red lights over one green for a few seconds, then switched searchlights on to rear boats and opened heavy fire. " Petard " was struck and severely damaged; " Turbulent " was either rammed or heavily shelled and no further note of her was obtained. Vessel was immediately lost sight of owing to heavy smoke.

Flotilla then proceeded to the Westward.

At Daylight it was noticed that Destroyers ahead were not in touch with " Champion." I took charge of Destroyers 13th Flotilla, consisting of " Narborough," " Pelican," " Nerissa," " Nicator," and " Petard," and placed myself under orders of " Lydiard " of 9th Flotilla. " Termagant " had previously rejoined 9th Flotilla.

On receiving orders by W/T to join Battle Cruiser Squadron I proceeded as requisite, rejoining Fleet at 9.45 a.m., having previously despatched " Petard " and " Nicator " to base as they were running short of fuel. At 7 p.m., 13th Flotilla were ordered to join " Badger " and return to base. Arrived base at 2 p.m. 2nd June 1916.

I have the honour to be, ·

Sir,

Your obedient Servant,

To Captain (D) GEOFFREY CORLETT,
　　13th Destroyer Flotilla, Lieutenant-Commander.
　　　　H.M.S. " Champion."

H.M.S. " OBDURATE,"
13th Flotilla,

SIR,   3rd June 1916.

    I BEG to report that at the commencement of the action on 31st May between H.M. Battle Cruisers and the German High Sea Fleet, H.M.S. " Obdurate " was separated from the remainder of the 13th Flotilla, and was about 1,000 yards on the engaged side of H.M.S. " Lion."

    Every endeavour was made to join the flotilla, but this was not accomplished when the signal was made to carry out a Torpedo Attack on the enemy.

    On receiving the Signal, " Obdurate " turned towards the enemy's Battle Cruiser Fleet and soon became engaged with their destroyers and one Light Cruiser, who were apparently approaching to carry out a torpedo attack on our Battle Cruisers.

    Range varied from 6,000 to 3,000 yards, and during the destroyer action one of the enemy's destroyers was blown up, and two others badly damaged ; probably one of those two sank as the guns firing at her lost sight of her.

    The enemy Destroyers and light cruisers were driven back to the protection of their big ships' guns, and the " Obdurate " was then too far astern to deliver a torpedo attack.

    H.M.S. " Obdurate " was hit twice by a 4·1 shell, but suffered no casualties.

    " Obdurate " then rejoined H.M.S. " Champion," and remained with her till ordered to return to base at 1 p.m. on 1st June.

I have the honour to be,
Sir,
Your obedient Servant,

Captain (D),   C. H. HUTTON SAMS,
   13th Flotilla,   Lieut.-Com.
   H.M.S. " Champion."

H.M.S. " PETARD,"
13th Destroyer Flotilla,

SIR   2nd June 1916.

    I HAVE the honour to report the proceedings of H.M. Ship under my command during the action on 31st May.

    2. " Petard " was in company with 13th Flotilla ahead of " Lion " at the commencement of the action, and when destroyers were ordered to attack was in station astern of " Pelican " and " Narborough." Owing to " Nottingham " cutting through flotilla, " Petard " had to reduce speed and pass astern of her, and then being some distance astern of " Pelican," I decided to attack with " Turbulent," and accordingly attacked immediately after " Nestor's " division. The first torpedo fired was set for high speed, six feet deep, and was aimed by Mr. Epworth, Gunner

(T), at the head of the German Destroyer Flotilla, which was crossing over to meet our attack. The track of the torpedo was closely followed, and the tube's crew state they undoubtedly saw it hit a German T.B.D. about amidships and explode. I certainly myself opened fire with my guns on this T.B.D. a few minutes later, and she was then lying stopped, with her upper deck awash and obviously sinking.

3. " Petard " then took part in the general engagement with the German Destroyers, and the three remaining torpedoes were fired at a range of about 7,000 yards on the bow of the German Battle Cruisers. All these torpedoes were fired at about the second or third German Battle Cruiser, and must have crossed the track of the German line.

4. After this, as our Fleet had turned to the Northward, " Petard " proceeded to rejoin, and passing the spot where the hull of H.M.S. " Queen Mary " was lying, picked up the Captain of the after turret of that ship. " Petard " then passed astern of the 5th Battle Squadron and rejoined " Champion." " Petard " remained with the Flotilla, and accompanied it South during the night.

5. At 12.15 a.m. course was altered to S.W. by W., and about ten minutes later the line crossed ahead of a division of German Battleships. I sighted the leading Battleship about six points on my starboard bow, steering S.E. at about 400 or 500 yards. This ship switched on recognition lights, consisting of two red over one white light and, as some destroyer ahead of me in the line then switched on her " fighting lights," I think the Germans at once knew we were enemy. As " Petard " had no torpedoes left, I could not attack, so I increased to full speed and altered course slightly to port to avoid being rammed. I passed about 200 yards ahead of the German ship, who appeared to be one of the " Wittelsbach " class.

6. As soon as we were clear of her stem, she illuminated us with searchlights, and we came under a heavy fire from her and the next ship in the line. Two salvoes seemed to strike us, and in all, I think, we received six hits.

No. 1 was aft on the port side of the Quarterdeck ; this shot disabled the whole after gun's crew and supply party.

No. 2 blew a hole in the ship's side in the Commanding Officer's cabin, about three feet by two, and then wrecked the whole of the Officers' cabins.

No. 3 made a large hole in the upper deck on top of No. 2 stokehold, and then entering the stokehold cut an oil pressure gauge pipe. The oil spurting out of this pipe made a considerable fire.

No. 4 hit below the midship gun platform and did little damage.

No. 5 was, apparently, a shrapnel, and this burst just short of the ship in line with the two foremost funnels, covering the whole of that part of the ship with splinters. Most of the cowls and plates in this part of the ship were penetrated by these.

No. 6 hit a cowl aft and did little damage besides.

If only " Petard " had had some torpedoes left, I am certain a successful torpedo attack could easily have been made.

1 *　　　*　　　*　　　*　　　*

10. I regret that I never saw H.M.S. " Turbulent," who was in station astern of " Petard," after passing this German Squadron. According to the evidence of some of my ship's company I am afraid she must have been rammed and sunk.

11. After this action " Petard " proceeded as fast as possible, and eventually rejoined the Flotilla at daylight. At 6.0 p.m. " Petard " and " Nicator " were detached to return to Rosyth. At 7.0 a.m. " Nicator " transferred Probationary Surgeon Neil MacLeod to " Petard," who carried out his work in a most excellent manner but, I am afraid, was too late to save most of the wounded. Previous to his arrival C.P.O. Thomas Knight, O.N. (165,128), had done his utmost for them.

12. At 3.30 p.m. in Lat. 55.50 N., Long. 0.55 W., " Nicator " reported that she was attacked by a submarine, and a torpedo passed under her stern. " Petard " and " Nicator " eventually arrived at Rosyth at 7.45 p.m.

1 *　　　*　　　*　　　*　　　*

I have the honour to be,
Sir,
Your obedient Servant,
E. C. O. THOMSON,
Lieutenant Commander.

The Captain (D),
　13th Destroyer Flotilla.

H.M.S. " PELICAN."
13th Flotilla,

SIR,　　　　　　　　　　　　　　　　4th June 1916.

I HAVE the honour to report the following proceedings of H.M. Ship under my command during the engagement of 31st May–1st June 1916.

The formation of the fleet was cruising order, course S.S. 1 E., 19½ knots.

The enemy Battle cruisers accompanied by destroyers were sighted at 3.15 p.m. G.M.T.

At 3.45 H.M.S. " Champion " and 13th Flotilla formed single line ahead and took station on starboard bow of the B.C.F.

Fire was opened by the enemy at 3.48 and by our fleet at 3.50.

At 4.20, having received a signal to attack with torpedoes, the 13th Flotilla proceeded in the order 1st, 2nd and 3rd Divs. The 3rd Div., consisting of " Narborough " and " Pelican,"

---

¹ Part omitted here, referring solely to personnel, recommendations, &c. in no way bearing on the course of the action.

were unable to fire torpedoes owing to the other two divisions being engaged by enemy torpedo craft between the fleets and by a division of 9th Flotilla, who were coming up in the opposite direction; we therefore turned to rejoin " Champion."

The flotilla reformed in single line ahead and took station on the disengaged side of 5th Battle Squadron, Course Nly.

At 6.00 the Grand Fleet was sighted steering about S. by E., and fire was opened at 6.15 p.m.

Between 7.10 and 10.20 Courses were South and South-West with speeds varying between 10 and 20 knots, during which time firing was observed on Starboard beam and quarter.

At about 10.35 there was heavy firing in N.Wly. direction, and destroyers were seen in the Search light rays attacking ships. Shortly after there was a huge explosion in that direction.

At 0.40, June 1st, when on a Course S.W., speed 30 knots, observed two ships on Starboard quarter, which were at first taken to be our Light Cruisers. They switched on three vertical lights, the upper two being red and the lower green, at the same time " Pelican's " stern was lit up by a Search light, which was immediately transferred to " Petard " and " Turbulent " who were astern.

When sighted position was unfavourable for attack and, as she was shortly lost sight of, " Pelican " proceeded to regain touch with the flotilla.

At daybreak it was found that the destroyers then in company were as follows :—" Narborough," " Pelican," " Petard," " Nerissa," " Nicator " and a division of 9th Flotilla, led by " Lydiard." These were formed up at 1.30 a.m. and steered N. 70 W. at 15 knots.

At 5.35, having received a signal to rejoin B.C.F., " Narborough," " Pelican " and " Nerissa " proceeded S. 60 E. at 25 knots.

At 9.50 sighted Grand Fleet, and at 10.08 joined Flag " Lion," and took up position for submarine screen, Course N. by W.

At 4.0 p.m. " Pelican " was ordered to return to base to replenish with fuel, where she arrived at 1.30 p.m., 2 June, with 9 tons of oil only remaining on board.

Nothing of importance occurred on the passage back.

The conduct of all officers and men was everything that could be desired under the trying circumstances of waiting to join in the action which I felt confident would be the case, having had the majority of them under my command for over two years.

I have the honour to be,
Sir,
Your obedient Servant,
KENNETH A. BEATTIE,
Lieut.-Commander.

The Captain (D),
13th Flotilla.

H.M.S. " NERISSA,"

SIR,   5th June 1916.

I HAVE the honour to report proceedings of H.M. Ship under my command during recent action in the North Sea on 31st May 1916, and 1st June 1916. Being in company with 1st Battle Cruiser Squadron, " New Zealand," " Indefatigable," " Barham," " Malaya," " Valiant," " Warspite," " Champion," " Fearless," 13th Flotilla, two divisions of first Flotilla, one division of 10th Flotilla, 1st, 2nd and 3rd Light Cruiser Squadrons.

31st May.

P.M.

3. 0.   1st Light Cruiser Squadron reported in action.

3.30.   Sighted enemy's Battle Cruisers, five in number, with destroyers and Light Cruisers. 13th Flotilla took station ahead of 1st Battle Cruiser Squadron, having been screening them previously.

3.44.   Enemy opened fire and action developed.

4. 0.   Sighted High Sea Fleet ahead.

4.30.   13th Flotilla ordered to attack enemy's Battle Cruisers with torpedoes. Took station astern of 3rd division of 13th Flotilla and commenced attack on a Northerly course, owing to enemy turning 16 points, this attack had eventually to be carried out on a Southerly course, which I did in company with " Termagant," firing two torpedoes, range 7,000 yards. Just previous to this attack " Nomad " was observed quite close, stopped and apparently badly damaged in the Engine Room, the enemy's Light Cruisers were firing accurate salvoes during the attack, and this fire was returned, though spotting was very difficult, one torpedo apparently took effect on rear ship. Rejoined " Champion " on disengaged side of Battle Cruisers, steering to the Northward and joined the Grand Fleet, remaining in company with " Champion " throughout the remainder of the action.

9.10.   Altered Course to South 20 knots.

9.36.   Altered Course to S.S.E. 17 knots.

11.40.   Observed firing and searchlights abaft starboard beam, a ship apparently being attacked by destroyers, many salvoes fell between " Nerissa " and " Moresby," who was next ahead.

11.45.   Lost touch with " Moresby " and remained in company with " Lydiard." Course S.E., 25 knots.

1st June.

A.M.

12.28.   Altered Course to S.W., 30 knots.

1.20.   Altered Course to N. 70 W., 25 knots; more firing astern was observed.

A.M.

3. 0.   15 knots.

5.30.   Altered course to N. 70 E., 25 knots, to rejoin Battle
Cruiser Squadron in company with " Narborough "
and " Pelican."

1 *   *   *   *   *

I have the honour to be,

Sir,

Your obedient Servant,

M. G. B. LEGGE,

Lieutenant-Commander.

The Captain (D),
H.M.S. " Champion."

H.M.S. " ONSLOW,"

c/o G.P.O.,

2nd June, 1916.

SIR,

I HAVE the honour to forward the following report of the
part taken by H.M. Ship under my command during the action
of the 31st May, 1916.   During the forenoon and early afternoon
of Wednesday, 31st May, " Onslow," working as a unit of the
13th Flotilla, was screening the 1st Battle Cruiser Squadron.
At 2.50 p.m. " Onslow " and " Moresby " were detached to close
" Engadine."   I took " Moresby " under my orders and proceeded to close " Engadine " at 25 knots course East, at 3.0 p.m.
" Engadine " stopped and hoisted out one seaplane then
steamed N. by E., 20 knots, waiting for seaplane to return,
finally hoisting it in at 3.45 p.m.   At 3.50 p.m. enemy's Battle
Cruisers were sighted steering approximately S.S.E., shortly
afterwards being engaged by the 1st Battle Cruiser Squadron
and 5th Battle Squadron on a nearly parallel course.   I then
asked the Commanding Officer of " Engadine " if he further
required assistance of " Onslow " and " Moresby," and on
receiving reply " No," I proceeded with " Moresby " to close
the nearest squadron, the 5th Battle Squadron, at 30 knots,
course S.S.E. at 4.55 p.m.   I again sighted the 1st Battle Cruiser
Squadron and enemy's Battle Cruisers returning, steering approximately N.N.E.   I turned to N.N.E., taking station about
3 miles on engaged bow of " Lion."   I found that steering
N.N.E. " Onslow " was rapidly opening from " Lion " and
closing enemy's Battle Cruisers about 5 points on their engaged
bow, distant 18,000 yards.   I was unable to see any enemy's
Light Cruisers or Destroyers ahead of their Battle Cruisers, and
deemed it a favourable opportunity to deliver an attack with
torpedoes, and with this idea proceeded to close enemy more.
Shortly afterwards four enemy Light Cruisers appeared ahead of
their Battle Cruisers and closed " Onslow," and opened a heavy
and very accurate fire on both " Onslow " and " Moresby."

---

¹ * Part omitted here, referring solely to personnel, recommendations,
&c., in no way bearing on the course of the action

Realising I should be unable to get within torpedo range, at 5.5 p.m. I retired N.W. in the direction of " Lion," " Moresby," to avoid making a double target with " Onslow," separated and went astern of 1st Battle Cruiser Squadron, " Onslow " taking station astern of 1st Light Cruiser Squadron on engaged bow of " Lion," course N.N.E.	Armoured cruisers of Grand Fleet were sighted at 5.45 p.m.	Grand Fleet Battle Squadron at 5.50 p.m. I had been endeavouring to join up with one of our Destroyer Flotillas, the only one close was the 1st Flotilla on the disengaged beam of 1st Battle Cruiser Squadron.	As I was in a most advantageous position for repelling enemy's Destroyers endeavouring to attack 1st Battle Cruiser Squadron, or delivering an attack myself, I considered it better for me to remain on engaged bow of " Lion."	At about 6.5 p.m. enemy's Battle Cruisers turned to a course about S.E., 1st Battle Cruiser Squadron turned to approximately the same course shortly afterwards.	At this moment sighting an enemy Light Cruiser, class uncertain, with 3 funnels and topgallant forecastle, only about 6,000 yards from 1st Battle Cruiser Squadron, I decided to attack her to endeavour to frustrate her firing torpedoes at our Battle Cruisers.	I gave orders to all guns to engage enemy Light Cruiser, and 58 rounds were fired at a range of 2,000 to 4,000 yards, undoubtedly a large number of hits were scored as they were easily spotted at this range.	While closing this Light Cruiser I saw Enemy Battle Cruisers had again turned, placing " Onslow " 4 points on their port bow about 11,000 yards.	I then gave orders for all torpedoes to be fired at enemy Battle Cruiser line by Gunner T, on receiving a further executive signal from myself on the bridge.	On arriving at 8,000 yards from leading enemy Battle Cruiser I gave this signal and turned the ship to port to bring enemy on my starboard beam.	There appeared to be delay in carrying out the order, and Sub-Lieutenant R. L. Moore ran down to tubes and got astride foremost tube alongside Captain of tube's crew.	On the sights coming on to centre enemy's Battle Cruiser, he gave the order to fire.	I saw this torpedo leave the tube and instantaneously the ship was struck by a big shell amidships the starboard side. Immediately there was a big escape of steam, completely enveloping both Torpedo tubes.	On enquiring I received a report that all torpedoes had been fired and consequently turned away at greatly reduced speed, passing about 3,500 yards from enemy's Light Cruiser previously mentioned.	I sent to Sub-Lieutenant Moore to find out damage done; while doing this he discovered only one torpedo had been fired, and observing enemy's Light Cruiser beam on, and apparently temporarily stopped, fired a torpedo at her.	Sub-Lieutenant Moore, Leading Signalman Cassin, also several other ratings and myself, saw torpedo hit Light Cruiser below conning tower and explode. Sub-Lieutenant Moore then came forward and reported to me we still had two torpedoes left, and at the same time drew my attention to enemy's line of battleships.	" Onslow " was on their port bow about 8,000 yards. Both remaining torpedoes were fired under the supervision of Sub-Lieutenant Moore; they started the run satisfactorily and must have crossed enemy's line. I then proceeded to close H.M.S. "Champion," with the idea of rejoining 13th Flotilla, but owing to two shells having exploded in No. 2 boiler room, and badly damaged main feed tank, and all the water in reserve feed tank being now used at 7.0 p.m., ship stopped, and owing to loss of electric current, I was unable to answer "Champion's" searchlight. At 7.15 p.m. "Defender" closed "Onslow" and asked if assistance was required. On learning "Defender" could only steam ten knots, I asked to be taken in tow whilst endeavouring to effect repairs, this "Defender" did under very trying conditions and with large enemy ships rapidly approaching. In tow of "Defender" I then proceeded W. by N. Using salt water feed, Engineer Lieutenant Commander Foulkes raised steam for slow speed to enable me to use steering engine and when weather got worse, to lessen strain on towing hawser. Owing to the ship's condition, No. 2 boiler room and captain's cabin flat were flooded and a considerable quantity of water also getting into Wardroom and Officers' cabin flat, and weather getting bad, I decided to make for nearest port—Aberdeen—arriving there at 1.0 p.m. the 2nd June.

I have the honour to be,

Sir,

Your obedient Servant,

JACK C. TOVEY,

Lieutenant-Commander.

Captain (D),
    13th Flotilla.

H.M.S. "MORESBY,"

3rd June 1916.

REPORT OF PROCEEDINGS 31st MAY TO 2nd JUNE.

SIR,

I HAVE the honour to report that H.M.S. "Moresby," under my Command, was in company with "Engadine" and "Onslow" at the commencement of the Action. "Onslow's" orders were carried out and at 5 p.m. an enemy "Dreadnought" squadron, then observed steering Northward, was attacked.

1. 5.10 p.m., being two points before the beam of the leading Ship, 6–8,000 yards, a long range torpedo was fired at the third Ship. The enemy bad station did not justify further expenditure in view of the night work expected to follow. About eight minutes later I observed an upheaval due to a Torpedo and am informed it was on the sixth Ship. This agrees with the director setting. The enemy were then straddling frequently —my smoke was bad—I therefore turned towards the enemy and ran between the lines in order to clear the range from smoke nuisance.

The enemy shooting was very good and had they fired double salvoes they would have hit. By observing attentively and using large helm, the Ship was not straddled more than 6 times and only one piece of H.E. was picked up.

The enemy Ships appeared not to fire after a certain bearing, but the fresh Ship starting seemed to straddle with almost the first salvo, though not again.

The deflection was often too much, and simple use of helm avoided the following salvo which would have hit.

2. Passing astern of the 5th B.S. I rejoined " Champion " at 6.30 p.m. Her orders were then carried out.

3. About 2.35 a.m. four " Deutschland " Class Ships were seen bearing West, 4,000 yards. I considered action imperative, hoisted Compass West, hauled out to Port, firing a H.S. Torpedo at 2.37 G.M.T. No more could be fired as the left tube was empty and the fore director was pointed skyward when the sights bore of that tube. This incident and opportunity was over very quickly as the enemy were steaming 18 knots S.E. A concussion shook the Ship about 2 minutes later, it was well marked aft and was felt in the " Obdurate." Mist and smoke prevented the enemy being seen again, but I feel certain the enemy were " Deutschland " and that the Torpedo hit something.

4. At 2.47 a.m. the " Champion " was rejoined and her orders obeyed.

5. At 1.30 p.m., 1st June, orders were received to return to base, due to lack of oil. " Nonsuch " was heard, and a zigzag search was carried out until the uncertainty of my position and lack of fuel caused me to proceed.

6. Four Light Cruisers were met at 3.30 p.m., course N.W. At 4.40 p.m. 5 " Shannons " and one Destroyer steering N. 50 W. Base was reached at 7.30 a.m.

7. Torpedoes were observed at 7.48 p.m., 1st May, 2 in No., one ahead and the second astern.

About 3.35 a.m., 1st June, two more were seen set shallow, one of these was just avoided, it appeared to keep very good depth, but was not a Heater.

1 * * * * *

I have the honour to be,
Sir,
Your obedient Servant,
ROGER ALISON,
Lieutenant-Commander.

Captain (D) 13,
H.M.S. " Champion."

---

¹ Part omitted here, referring solely to personnel, recommendations, &c., in no way bearing on the course of the action.

H.M.S. " NICATOR,"

4th June 1918.

Sir,   War Base.

I HAVE the honour to report in accordance with your order :—

That on signal from V.A. Battle Cruisers to take station ahead being received, " Nicator " took up station as ordered.

On finding it necessary to reduce speed to keep station on " Nomad," who appeared to be dropping astern, permission was requested and approved to pass ahead and take station astern of " Nestor."

At 4.15 p.m. Second Division being ordered to attack, full speed was ordered. At 4.20 p.m. enemy's destroyers appeared to be within gun range and effective fire was opened at 7,000 yards (rate rapidly closing).

At this time " Nestor," with " Nicator " and " Nomad " astern, was steering a course closing enemy's B.C.F. at an inclination of about three points, to attain good position to attack.

On " Nicator " opening fire, second division was subjected to moderately heavy fire from enemy's T.B.D.'s and one Light Cruiser.

On attaining a position five points before beam of leading ship of enemy's B.C.F., " Nestor " turned twelve points (approximately), to Port followed by " Nicator " and " Nomad," thereby steering a roughly reciprocal course, closing enemy's line at an inclination of about two points.

At this time " Second Division " was subjected to a heavy fire from secondary armament of enemy's B.C.F. and one Light Cruiser.

" Nomad " was badly hit and hauled out of line to Port.

Range of enemy's B.C.F. was now estimated at about 6,000 yards, and, position being favourable for attack, a Torpedo was fired. A second Torpedo was fired at 5,000 yards on the same side.

This torpedo was fired as it was considered very unlikely that the ship would escape disablement before another opportunity occurred. During this attack, enemy's T.B.D.'s were continually engaged with gunfire, and were observed to be retiring, leaving at least two in a disabled condition.

When enemy's B.C.F. bore abeam, " Nestor " and " Nicator " altered course about twelve points in succession to Starboard. At the same time enemy's B.C.F. altered course 16 points together; this brought " Nestor " and ",Nicator " still closing enemy about 2 points on a reciprocal course.

The enemy's B.C.F. was now supplemented by a very large number of Battleships in line ahead, astern of B.C.F. " Nestor " and " Nicator " were now subjected to a very heavy fire from secondary armament of enemy's Battle Fleet at a range of about

3,000 yards, and position being favourable, a third Torpedo was fired at second ship of enemy's Battle Fleet.

" Nestor " and " Nicator " continued to close until within about 2,500 yards, when " Nestor " was hit in region of No. 1 boiler room; she immediately altered course 8 points to Starboard and " Nicator " was obliged to alter inside her to avoid collision, thereby failing to fire a fourth Torpedo.

Signal for Destroyers recall being observed " Nicator " altered to West (approx.) and rejoined " Champion " forming single line ahead on her. Whilst returning, " Nomad " was observed to be stopped between the lines.

During Torpedo attack, enemy's T.B.D.'s were passed on a reciprocal course at a range of about 600 yards; their fire appeared to be very poor. Whilst the ship was subject to very heavy fire from enemy's Battle Fleet, course was altered to either side of " Nestor's " wake at frequent intervals to avoid salvoes.

At 6.0 p.m. on signal " Pdts. 1A " being made " Nicator " took station astern of " Termagant," informing " Obdurate " of her having joined First Division. Remained in company with " Champion " for remainder of action.

At about 9.30 p.m. (course S.S.E., 20 knots), in company with " Champion " and T.B.D.'s, heavy firing was heard and seen off Starboard bow.

At 9.50 p.m. a/c South, heavy firing was heard at frequent intervals off the Starboard beam. This was assumed to be a division of enemy's Battleships or Cruisers being attacked by divisions of a T.B.D. Flotilla; vessels attacked appeared at about 12.15 a.m. to be distant $\frac{3}{4}$ mile.

" Nicator " was occasionally in beam of searchlights and several salvoes fell close.

At 12.30 a.m. a/c to S.W., Speed 30 knots (following " Termagant ").

At 1.17 a.m. a/c to W.N.W., 25 knots.

At daylight it was seen that " Termagant " and " Nerissa " were astern of Ninth Flotilla; " Champion," and remainder of First Div. of 13th Flotilla not in sight—(" Turbulent " not in company).

At 5.50 a.m. a/c to N. 70 E., 20 knots.

At 6.15 a.m., on account of shortage of oil, was ordered by " Lydiard " to return to Base in company with " Petard."

At 3.30 p.m., in Lat. 55—50 N., Long. 0—55 W., a Torpedo fired by a hostile submarine was observed approaching from abaft the Starboard beam at an angle of thirty degrees, running on the surface; helm was at once put hard a starboard and telegraphs to full speed. Torpedo passed ahead.

On resuming course a submerged explosion was very distinctly felt all over the ship; no damage could be found.

Submarine was not sighted.
Arrived Queensferry 9.40 p.m., 1st June.

1 *   *   *   *   *

I have the honour to be
Sir,
Your obedient Servant,
JACK E. A. MOCATTA,
Captain (D),   Lieutenant in Command.
H.M.S. " Champion."

REPORTS OF CAPTAIN (D), 1st FLOTILLA.

Enclosure No. 20 to Battle Cruiser Fleet, Letter No. B.C.F. 01
of 12/6/16.

No. 013.   H.M.S. " Fearless,"
SIR,   2nd June 1916.
    I HAVE the honour to forward the following report of my
proceedings during the recent operations in the North Sea.
    2. The first report of the enemy being sighted was received
at 2.30 p.m., G.M.T., on 31st May. The First Flotilla consisting
of " Fearless " and nine destroyers :—

" Acheron,"	" Hydra,"	" Defender,"
" Ariel,"	" Badger,"	" Lizard,"
" Attack,"	" Goshawk,"	" Lapwing,"

was then screening the Fifth Battle Squadron.
    3. The action gradually becoming general, " Fearless " and
destroyers took station on the disengaged side of the Fifth
Battle Squadron. About 4.1 p.m., G.M.T., " Indefatigable "
was seen to blow up, and another big explosion was observed
about 15 minutes later, presumably " Queen Mary."
    4. At 4.45 p.m., G.M.T., our Battle Cruisers were seen steaming
North, and at 4.55 p.m. " Fearless " and First Flotilla altered
course 16 points and steamed North on the disengaged bow of
the First Battle Cruiser Squadron. Although " Fearless " was
steaming at full speed, having received a signal from " Lion "
to close and form Submarine Screen, she was unable to get up,
and gradually dropped back.
    5. Soon after this the Grand Fleet was sighted, and at 6.8 p.m.,
G.M.T., finding that " Fearless " could not get up and was
steaming across the front of the Battle Fleet making heavy
smoke, the ship was turned about 32 points, and station taken
up with other Light Cruisers and Destroyers on the disengaged
quarter of the Battle Fleet.
    6. This position was maintained until the " Acasta " was
found disabled with the signal " In danger of sinking " flying.

---

¹ Part omitted here referring solely to personnel, recommendations,
&c., in no way bearing on the course of the action.

"Galatea" was taking her in tow. "Fearless" relieved "Galatea" and would have taken the destroyer in tow, but the latter reported she was not then in danger of sinking and I did not consider I ought to hamper myself with a disabled vessel in the middle of the action. I therefore proceeded and followed after the Battle Fleet, passing the wreck of a Light Cruiser, upside down and stem out of the water, apparently German, judging by the draught markings.

7. The Battle Fleet was not picked up until after dusk, when a column of ships was sighted ahead and station was taken astern of what was subsequently found to be the First Battle Squadron. Much heavy firing was observed during the night.

8. About midnight, G.M.T., a large vessel, which appeared to be a German Battleship was seen to pass down the starboard side, but as ships ahead did not open fire and it was considered that she must have been seen, it was thought advisable to take no action, as her course led directly to the destroyers following, and, judging from the action which occurred shortly afterwards, they apparently engaged her.

9. When daylight broke "Fearless" was found to be astern of "Agincourt" and was ordered alongside "Marlborough" by the Vice-Admiral, at 2.45 a.m. G.M.T., 1st June, to transfer him to "Revenge," and this was accomplished at 3.10 a.m.

10. Acting under orders received from the Vice-Admiral, "Fearless" then proceeded to join "Marlborough" and escort her.

11. At 4.10 a.m., G.M.T., fire was opened at a Zeppelin, Latitude 55° 20′ N., Longitude 6° 27′ East. "Marlborough" also opened fire, and it retired.

12. At 2.45 p.m., G.M.T., 1st June, 4 destroyers of Harwich force joined "Marlborough" for escort duty, and 4 more later; also 2 patrol destroyers at about 5.0 p.m.

13. "Marlborough" was left off the Bull Lightship in the Humber at 8.0 a.m., G.M.T., on 2nd June, and "Fearless" then returned to base, arriving at 8.0 p.m., G.M.T.

> I have the honour to be,
> Sir,
> Your obedient Servant,
> C. D. ROPER,
> Captain (D.),
> First Flotilla.

The Vice-Admiral Commanding,
　Battle Cruiser Fleet.

Enclosure No. 21 to Battle Cruiser Fleet, Letter No. B.C.F. 01 of 12/6/16.

No. 013.

H.M.S. "Fearless,
SIR,　　　　　　　　　　　　　　　　6th June 1916.

I HAVE the honour to forward herewith the reports of proceedings during the action of 31st May of the Commanding

Officers of H.M. Ships "Attack" and "Defender," together with extracts containing items of interest from the reports of the Commanding Officers of H.M. Ships "Acheron,"[1] "Ariel," and "Badger."

2. Owing to lack of speed "Fearless" was unable to keep up with 1st Flotilla, and at 6.0 p.m., G.M.T., 31st May parted company with the destroyers, who from that time onward were in company with 1st Battle Cruiser Squadron and were not seen again by "Fearless" until return into harbour.

3. The report of the Commanding Officer of "Attack" is forwarded complete.

[2] *   *   *   *   *

I have the honour to be,
Sir,
Your obedient Servant,
C. D. ROPER,

The Vice-Admiral Commanding,   Captain (D),
    Battle Cruiser Fleet.   First Flotilla.

H.M.S. "ATTACK,"

SIR,   3rd June 1916.
    I HAVE the honour to report that on Wednesday, May 31st, at :—

P.M.
3.40.   In Lat. 56.52 N., Long. 5.22 E., Course S. 81 E., Speed 25 Knots, the 5th B.S. signalled "Enemy in sight. "Attack" sighted enemy immediately on receipt of signal. B.C.F. engaged, and shortly afterwards B.C.F. appeared to alter course to the S.E.

---

[1] Extract from "Acheron" omitted as containing solely recommendations of personnel in no way bearing on the course of the action.

[2] Part omitted here, referring solely to personnel, recommendations, &c., in no way bearing on the course of the action.

The 1st Flotilla was formed in No. 3 Submarine Screen on 5th B.S. organisation as follows :—

◯ *Fearless (Captain (D))*

◯ *Defender.*

◯ *Acheron*   ◯ *Badger*

◯ *Ariel*   ◯ *Lizard*

◯ *Attack*   ◯ *Goshawk*

◯ *Hydra*   ◯ *Lapwing*

P.M.

3.50. 1st Flotilla took station in Division Line ahead on Starboard Quarter of 5th B.S.

3.51. " Barham " opened fire.

3.54. " Valiant " opened fire.

3.56. " Warspite " opened fire.

      5th B.S. was generally engaged and altering course to the S.E.

3.58. Large explosion to the S.E'ward was observed amongst B.C.F.

4. 5. 1st Flotilla formed LT2.

4. 6. Enemy returned 5th B.S. fire.

4.15. 5th B.S. and destroyers steering SSE.

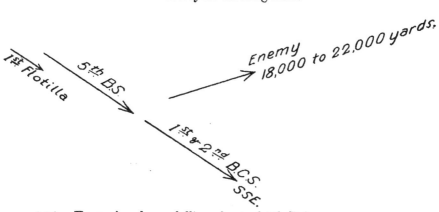

4.16. Enemy's salvoes falling short of 5th B.S.

4.18.   ,,   ,,   ,,   over 5th B.S.

      5th B.S. apparently altered formation to Subdivisions in starboard quarter line.

4.23. Salvo appeared to hit last ship in enemy's line.

4.24. Altered course to SE'ward. Large explosion appeared to take place amongst B.C. Fleet.

4.25. 1st Flotilla forming astern of 5th B.S.

4.30. Enemy's salvoes improving and range decreasing.

4.31. 1st Flotilla ordered to take station ahead of 5th B.S. leaving 5th B.S. on starboard hand.

P.M.

4.38. Small craft on port bow opened fire (this ship was so far off that she was almost undistinguishable).

4.38. Enemy's salvoes falling very close to 5th B.S.

4.42. Destroyers (1st Flotilla) in divisions line ahead astern of 5th B.S.

4.48. Passed British destroyer rescuing survivors, probably from "Queen Mary."

4.50. Battle cruisers—"Lion," "Princess Royal," "Tiger" and "New Zealand" passed 5th B.S. to port on opposite courses.

     1st Flotilla turned 16 points together and took station on port beam of B.C.F. heading N.

4.51. Enemy concentrated heavy fire on B.C.F., overs falling amongst 1st Flotllla.—"Lion" observed to be hit.

4.55. 1st Flotilla taking station astern of B.C.F.

4.59. "Tiger" on fire aft.—"Lion" and "Tiger" being hit.

5. 4. Wireless Office reported that enemy's ships repeatedly making by w/t RA RA RA – – – – – and jambing each other.

5. 5. a/c NW 24 knots. Enemy's fire on B.Cs slackening, apparently enemy is concentrating their fire on B.S. astern.

5. 6. Enemy's salvoes on 5th B.S. observed to be very good.

5. 9. Light cruisers and Destroyers coming up from the Southward.

5.10. More ships observed coming up from the Southward.

5.10. Approx disposition of ships in sight.

Light-cruisers

and destroyers steaming N.W.

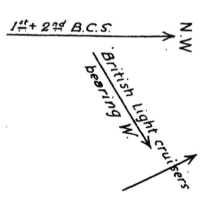

P.M.

5.13. 1st Flotilla formed submarine screen on B. C. Fleet B.C.F. no longer engaged with enemy.

5.15. a/c N.N.W., enemy no longer in sight.

5.25. a/c N.N.E., and received signal from " Lion "—" Prepare to renew action."

5.27. a/c N.E. by N.

5.35. Renewed action with the enemy to the S.W., who appeared to be steaming to the w'ard.

5.45. Fires observed in " Lion " and " Tiger." Enemy's salvoes appeared to be very good.

6. 0. Battle Fleet, 3rd B.C.S., Armoured and Light Cruisers and T.B.D. Flotillas joined up from the N'ard.

B.C. Fleet altered course to E'ard and S.E.

6.10. General engagement.

About this time a Battle Cruiser of the 3rd B.C.S. blew up. Course and speed of 1st B.C.F. S.E., 28 knots.

Nose of 11-in. projectile (A.P. ?) struck " Attack," passed through after shelter, pierced upper deck, and then fell into the Ward Room.

The 1st Flotilla had difficulty in passing through the G.F. Flotillas just joining up; it was not easy to keep " Acheron " in sight, and at the same time avoid the numerous cruisers and destroyers passing through. The enemy's projectiles were falling amongst this mass of T.B.D.'s, and it was remarkable that no one except " Defender " appeared to be seriously damaged.

6.15. Ship of " Defence " class—on starb. quarter—badly on fire and then appeared to blow up.

6.25. " Badger " detached to stand by survivors of " Invincible."

6.30. Approx. disposition of ships in sight.

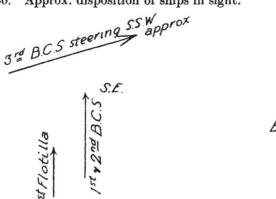

P.M.

6.32. Passed two halves of vessel (red bottom colour) with bow and stern sticking out of the water, and bearing SW.

6.39. Fire of B.C.F. and enemy eased up considerably.

6.43. Firing ceased—speed 18 knots—received signal to take station ahead of Admiral.

6.50. a/c East.

7. 2. a/c SSE and 1st Flotilla formed submarine screen No. 3 on B.C. Fleet, speed 22 knots.

7. 3. Battle fleet engaged to the N.W. B.C. F a/c to SSW and SW.

7.11. B.C. Fleet reengaged the enemy. 1st Flotilla in Division's Line ahead on prto beam of B.C. Fleet.

7.15. Course S.W. and S., speed 24 knots.

7.21. Received signal from " Lion "—" Enemy's torpedo craft approaching." Followed " Acheron," who proceeded to take station ahead of B.C. Fleet. (No attack, however, was delivered by enemy's torpedo craft.)

7.30. B.C. Fleet ceased fire. Battle Fleet still engaged.

7.35. Course S.S.W., speed 28 knots, enemy away to the westward.

8.20. B.C. Fleet again engaged the enemy. Course S.W., enemy bearing N.W. Great number of enemy's overs falling amongst 1st Flotilla, small splinters striking " Attack."

8.30. Light cruisers engaged to the W.S.W. of us. " Badger " rejoined. First Flotilla formed submarine screen No. 3 on B.C.F.

8.40. Firing ceased. Course S.W. 10 knots.

8.50. Speed 17 knots.

9. 0. Large explosion N.

Action ceased as far as B.C. Fleet and 1st Flotilla were concerned. Two balls of flame were noticed to fall from the sky far away astern—time not actually noted, but about 10.0 to 10.30 p.m.

9.18. a/c South, and steamed S. 17 knots until 2.30 a.m. on 1st June, when at 2.35 a/c 16 points.

June 1st.

2.45. a/c N.N.E.

3. 0. Increased to 20 knots.

3.22. a/c N. by E. " Inflexible " and " Indomitable " opened fire on starboard side—nothing visible from " Attack."

4. 0. " Lion's " position 55.26 N.⎱
              6.15 E. ⎰

4. 3. a/c N.N.W.

4.20. a/c N.$\frac{1}{2}$E.

4.40. a/c East.

4.50. a/c South, 15 knots, and passed down between two lines of the Battle Fleet, bound to the N'ard.

4.55. a/c E.S.E.

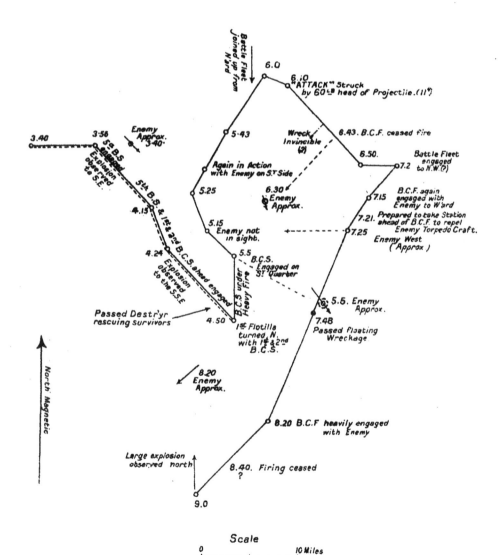

D.R. POSITIONS OF H.M.S. "ATTACK" DURING THE ENGAGEMENT ON WEDNESDAY. MAY 31st 1916.

Plate 20.

3.40 P.M. } D.R. Lat. 56°52′N.
" Long. 5°22′E.

········ 1st FLOTILLA SCREENING 5ª B.S.
———— 1st " " B.C.F.

Battle Fleet joined up from N'ard

6.0

6.10 "ATTACK" Struck by 60ᴸᴮ head of Projectile.(11")

Enemy Approx. 3·40·

3.40   3·56   5ª B.S. sighted   5.43   Wreck Invincible (?)   6.43. B.C.F. ceased fire
        Explosion observed to S'd   6.50.   Battle Fleet engaged to N.W.(?)
        5ᵗʰ B.S. & 1ˢᵗ & 2ⁿᵈ B.C.S.   7.2

Again in Action with Enemy on S.T. Side   B.C.F. again engaged with Enemy to W'ard   7.15

4.15   5.25   6.30 Enemy Approx.   7.21. Prepared to take Station ahead of B.C.F. to repel Enemy Torpedo Craft.
        5.15 Enemy not in sight.   7.25
        Enemy West (Approx)

4.24   5.5 B.C.S. Engaged on S.T Quarter   5.5. Enemy Approx.
        Explosion observed to the S.S.E   7.48 Passed floating Wreckage

Passed Destr'yr rescuing survivors   4.50   1ˢᵗ Flotilla turned N. with 1ˢᵗ & 2ⁿᵈ B.C.S.

North Magnetic

8.20 Enemy Approx.

8.20 B.C.F heavily engaged with Enemy

Large explosion observed north

8.40. Firing ceased ?

9.0

Scale
0   10 Miles

10072 · 24266/P1173 ⒧ 5000 12.20   Malby & Sons. Lith

P.M.

5. 5. a/c N.N.E., speed 18 knots (appeared to be making N.½E. course.)

5.25. Sighted the Battle Fleet, N.¼E., steering N.½E.

5.30. Increased to 20 knots.

5.32. a/c S.E.

6.10. a/c South.

7.25. a/c N.N.E.

8. 0. a/c N.

8.30. B.C.F. formed divisions in line ahead disposed abeam to port.

9. 0. Formed submarine screen No. 5 on " New Zealand."

9.40. a/c W.S.W

9.45. a/c S.½W.

9.50. a/c S.S.W.

9.57. 15 knots.

10. 5. a/c N.N.by W.

11. 0. Received orders from " Badger " to return to base and complete with oil. Course N. 74 W., 15 knots.

> Position 56.03 N. ⎱ 0.45 p.m. " Lizard " took sta-
> 6.22 E. ⎰ tion astern.

> At 0.30 a.m. on 2nd June. Reduced to 13 knots to economise oil, as was running very short. At 2.30 a.m. saw what appeared to be gun flashes bearing West.

7.50 a.m. Passed May Island.

Note.—All times G.M.T. All courses and bearings Magnetic.

(2) Diagram of courses during the action is attached.

(3) On arrival in harbour completed with oil; effected temporary repairs by ship's staff to hole in U.D., and then at 1.0 p.m. reported to " Lion "—" Ready for sea."

I have the honour to be,
Sir,
Your obedient Servant,

Captain (D),   C. H. N. JAMES,
  1st Flotilla.   Lieut.-Comdr.

H.M.S. " DEFENDER,"

Sir,   3rd June 1916.

    I HAVE the honour to report my proceedings during period noon 30th May to noon 3rd June.

Ship was undocked at Leith at 1.00 p.m. 30th, and proceeded to Rosyth, ammunition and fuel taken on board. At 6.00 p.m. I reported to Captain (D). First Flotilla that ship was ready for sea, and requested orders. Orders were given to raise steam and proceed with them. Sailed with them and under orders of " Fearless " screened the 5th B.S.

At about 4.30 p.m. 31st May the action commenced with the enemy, ship then being with 5th B.S. At about 5.30 p.m.

" Lion " ordered First Flotilla to screen ahead of Battle Cruisers;
using our utmost speed endeavoured to do so, and by the time
the 2nd action was in progress ship was 200 yards on the beam
of " Lion " away from the enemy. At 6.30 a 12-in. shell struck
the ship's side in the foremost boiler room, placing that boiler
room out of action, killing a Stoker Petty Officer, and causing an
oil fuel fire. The shell failed to explode, but wrecked a fan, and
other damage to No. 1 boiler, finally lodging in the ashpit. Being
unable to maintain my position in the line, turned 16 points, and
passed between the battle fleets until reached an area of com-
parative calm, when turned again and repaired damage. The
fire having been dealt with, it was found a mat kept the
stokehold dry, my only trouble now being lack of speed. I
looked round for useful employment, and saw a destroyer in
great difficulties, so closed her. She proved to be H.M.S.
" Onslow " (Lieut.-Commander C. J. Tovey) and unable to
steam. Proceeded to take her in tow; meanwhile the action
had developed more in our direction, and stray shells were falling
round us; however, by 7.15 the " Onslow " was in tow, steaming
for Rosyth at 12 knots. During the night No. 2 boiler was got
into use.

At 1.00 a.m. the weather became bad and the tow parted;
" Onslow " was able to steam slowly by herself then, so we went
on slow together. At about 5.00 a.m. had to stop and adjust
bottom lines, which had carried away. It then appeared that
" Onslow " could not make headway, so by his orders took in
tow again, using my wire; managed this, but towing slip parted
shortly afterwards. Using two shackles of cable round the after
bollards and gun, got her in tow again. Proceeded at eight
knots; sea still rising continually; had to reduce speed until
very little headway on.

Unfortunately had hazy idea of position, sounding failed
owing to the sea. The wind, which had been blowing all day
from the S.W., backed suddenly to the North, adding to our
troubles, as it blew hard with a nasty sea.

At 9.30 a.m., 2nd June, land was sighted, and as Aberdeen
was the nearest course, was steered for it, " Onslow " being
transferred to tugs about 1.00 p.m.

" Defender " proceeded to Rosyth, where temporary repairs
to side, shell extracted, were carried out by " Woolwich," orders
were given to proceed to Harwich.

1 *   *   *   *   *

I have the honour to be,
Sir,
Your obedient Servant,

Captain C. D. Roper, R.N.   L. R. PALMER,
H.M.S. " Fearless."   Lieutenant-Commander.

---

¹ Part omitted here, referring solely to personnel, recommendations,
&c., in no way bearing on the course of the action.

H.M.S. "LIZARD,"
1st Flotilla,

SIR,   2nd June 1916.

I HAVE the honour to forward report of proceedings whilst at sea on 31st May, 1st and 2nd June.

P.M.   *30th May.*
10.30. Left harbour and formed JG 3 on 5th B.S. After leaving May Island proceeded on an easterly course.

31st May.
2.50. Received signal that enemy had been sighted. Shortly after
3. 0   several enemy B.C. and light cruisers were sighted ahead on a Southerly course about 12 miles distant. At
3.40   · speed of squadron was increased to 24½ knots, the B.C.S. having already opened fire. At
3.50   destroyers were ordered out of the way and were ordered to form L.T. formation on "Fearless." At this time "Barham" commenced ranging.
4. 0. "Fearless" and First flotilla were ordered to take station astern, and whilst doing so, B.C.S. were observed returning on opposite course. At
5.15   the course being now about North, Destroyers were ordered into JG 3 on "Lion," but were unable to get into position as "Lion" was steaming 24 knots. At
6. 5   course was altered to N.E. by E., and action resumed. The Grand Fleet which had been sighted about 5.30 on Port bow and deployed at this time commenced firing.
6.20. Course E.
6.30. Course S.E. Enemy being apparently out of range, fire now ceased.
7. 0. Formed JG 3 on "Lion's" division. At
8.20   sighted several enemy light cruisers on Starbd. Beam, and "Lion" opened fire, destroyers drawing ahead to avoid being hit.
8.25. Course W.N.W. (towards enemy). Meanwhile the Grand Fleet seemed to be heavily engaged astern and on our Starbd. quarter.
8.27. Course S.W. Received signal that enemy destroyers were advancing to attack, but their attack seemed to be driven off by Light Cruiser squadron, which afterwards appeared to form a screen between us and the enemy. Nothing further happened until about
2.30 a.m., when a Zeppelin was observed at about 5,000 ft. and about 6–7 miles away. A Battle cruiser was observed to fire a salvo at her, and at about
3.30   heavy firing was heard astern. At
11.30   "Lizard" was ordered to return to base and oil.

E. BROOKE,
Lieutenant Commander.

The Vice-Admiral Commanding,
1st B.C.S.

EXTRACT FROM REPORT OF PROCEEDINGS OF H.M.S. " BADGER," 31st MAY–1st JUNE 1916.

" At 6.0 p.m. the 3rd B.C.S. was observed ahead heavily engaged, and shortly afterwards 2 explosions occurred in the ' Invincible,' and she disappeared in a cloud of smoke. When it cleared the bow and stern were seen sticking out of the water surrounded by a quantity of wreckage, and at 6.40 I was ordered by V.A., B.C.F., to return to the ' Invincible ' and pick up survivors. Commander Dannreuther, Lieutenant Sanford, C.P.O. Thompson, Yeo. Sigs. Pratt, A. B. Danbridge, Gunner R.M. Gasson, were picked up, the last-mentioned suffering from severe burns. ' Badger ' then rejoined ' Lion,' passing through the Battle Fleet which was engaged."

EXTRACT FROM REPORT OF PROCEEDINGS OF H.M.S. " ARIEL," 30th MAY TO 2nd JUNE.

" Witnessed the sinking of H.M.S. ' Invincible,' also of an enemy capital ship near the commencement of the action at about the same time that the ' Indefatigable ' was sunk, but was unable to distinguish class or type.

" Continued with B.C.F. till 3.50 p.m., 1st June. At 2.15 p.m., 1st June, when in approximate position 57° 00′ N., 6° 02′ E. passed 20 to 30 bodies of German bluejackets, all supported by black-covered life jackets bearing a name consisting of about six letters commencing with the letter L, the bodies had in all but one case the appearance of having been drowned or having died of exposure, only one appearing to be damaged. A red life belt bearing the lettering S.M.S. ' L—— ' was also seen, also black jolly boat marked ' V—— ' probably from a German Destroyer, it was empty."

Enclosure No. 22 to Battle Cruiser Fleet, Letter No. B.C.F. 01 of 12/6/16.

No. 013B.

H.M.S. " Fearless,"

SIR,   8th June 1916.

WITH reference to your Memorandum No. B.C.F. 01 of 8th June 1916, I have the honour to report as follows :—

2. At about 5.10 p.m. on Wednesday, 31st May, when on a Northerly course, " Fearless " being on the port side of 1st Battle Cruiser Squadron, with the latter heavily engaged, one of the enemy's ships was seen to be heavily on fire aft, and shortly afterwards a huge cloud of smoke and steam, exactly similar to that which accompanied the blowing up of " Indefatigable " and " Queen Mary," was seen to ascend and it was assumed that one of the enemy's ships had blown up.

3. An enemy ship was seen to blow up about 6.30 p.m., though beyond the fact that it was a large ship the class could not be stated.

4. As stated in my report No. 013 of 2nd June, shortly after Midnight when " Fearless " was astern of " Agincourt," an enemy battleship, either of the " Koenig " or " Kaiser " class, was seen to pass down the starboard side. As she was not engaged by the ships ahead no action was taken, it being too late to fire a torpedo when she could be identified as she was then well abaft the beam.

Her course led directly towards the destroyers following astern, and, judging from the action which followed about 10 minutes afterwards, they apparently engaged her. Heavy firing broke out which lasted a few minutes, and then a star shell was fired, and shortly afterwards a very heavy explosion occurred—much too big for any destroyer or Flotilla leader—and this was followed by complete silence, which was taken as eloquent testimony that the one ship had disappeared.

It is considered probable that it was either the 4th or 12th Destroyer Flotilla which engaged this ship.

The fact that this ship fired a star shell should be an easy means of identifying the incident.

It cannot be stated as to whether any other ships observed this incident.

I have the honour to be,

Sir,

Your obedient Servant,

C. D. ROPER,

Captain (D),

First Flotilla.

The Vice-Admiral Commanding,
Battle Cruiser Fleet.

REPORTS OF DESTROYERS FROM HARWICH FORCE ATTACHED TO BATTLE CRUISER FLEET.

Enclosure No. 23 to Battle Cruiser Fleet, Letter No. B.C.F. 01 of 12/6/16.

From.—The Commodore (T).

No.—00101.

Date.—10th June 1916.

To.—The Vice-Admiral Commanding Battle Cruiser Fleet.

Submitted.

In accordance with your telegram of 9th June, timed 11.11, herewith are forwarded reports from the following destroyers on the action of 31st May 1916 :—

" Lydiard."	" Liberty."
" Laurel."	" Moorsom."
" Landrail."	" Morris."

2. H.M.S. "Termagant" is at present detached, but has been directed by telegraph to forward direct to you her report without delay.

3. Copies of these reports are being forwarded to the Commander-in-Chief, Grand Fleet.

R. Y. TYRWHITT,
Commodore (T).

H.M.S. "LYDIARD," [1]

SIR,   3rd June 1916.

I HAVE the honour to report that in the recent action I was in nominal command of the following destroyers detached from the Harwich force :—

" Lydiard."	" Moorsom."	" Turbulent."
" Liberty."	" Morris."	" Termagant."
" Landrail."	" Laurel."	

The first six boats were detailed as submarine screen for " New Zealand " and " Indefatigable " (2nd B.C.S.).

" Turbulent " and " Termagant " worked with 13th Flotilla and 1st B.C.S. (" Lion," &c.).

At 10.40 p.m. May 30th.   Fleet proceeded.

Noon   31st.   56.44 ; 3.45.

3.28   " Enemy in sight, E. by N."

3.33   5 Flag. Destroyers ordered ahead 5 miles.

Owing to lack of speed my division was not able to get ahead, and I therefore had to remain on the engaged side of the B.C.S. or drop astern. I chose to remain where I was rather than lose all chance of making a torpedo attack.

At 3.45.   The action commenced.

3.58.   " Indefatigable " blew up.

4.30.   " Queen Mary " blew up.

A torpedo from a submarine went under " Landrail " and passed between " Tiger " and " New Zealand."

At 4.30.   " Lion " ordered us to go away. I turned 16 points in succession and formed astern of line.

Ordered " Laurel " (who had also failed to keep up) to pick up survivors of " Queen Mary " (she found 17 in all).

Owing to taking up this position the " L " destroyers missed making a torpedo attack with the " M's."

---

[1] Plates 21 and 22.

H.M.S. LYDIARD.
31ST MAY 1916.

Plate 21.

4·35 P.M.

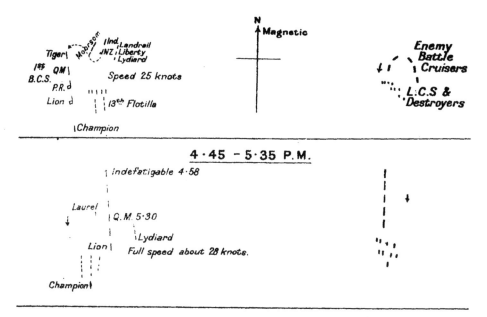

N ↑ Magnetic

Tiger \
IST QM \
B.C.S.
P.R. d
Lion d

Mobson / IInd, Landrail
INZ, Liberty
' Lydiard

Speed 25 knots

13th Flotilla

\ Champion

Enemy
Battle
Cruisers

L.C.S &
Destroyers

4·45 — 5·35 P.M.

Indefatigable 4·58

Laurel

Q.M. 5·30

\ Lydiard

Lion |

Full speed about 28 knots.

Champion

5·40 P.M.

5th B.S.
opened fire

Posn of Q.M's wreckage.

+ Laurel ordered to rescue
survivors.
INZ.

Tiger \ Lydiard

P.R.

Full speed, 28 knots

Lion

Enemy

Champion

13th Flo. attacking.

Malby & Sons Lith

Plate 22.

H.M.S. LYDIARD.
31ST MAY.
6·00 P.M.

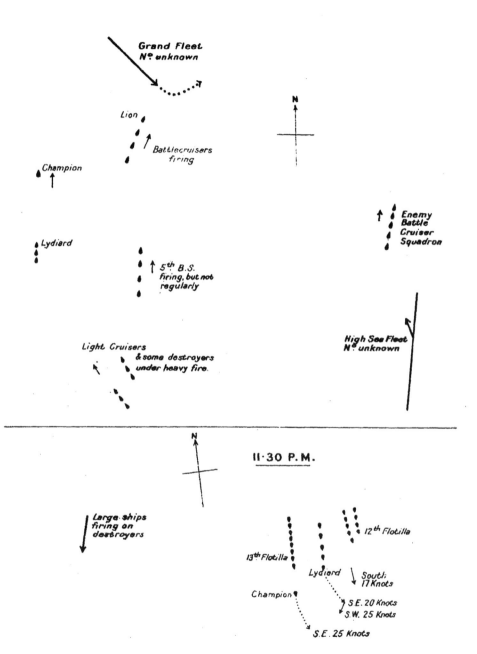

Grand Fleet
Nº unknown

Lion

Battlecruisers
firing

N

Champion

Enemy
Battle
Cruiser
Squadron

Lydiard

5th B.S.
firing, but not
regularly

Light Cruisers
& some destroyers
under heavy fire.

High Sea Fleet
Nº unknown

N

11·30 P.M.

Large ships
firing on
destroyers

12th Flotilla

13th Flotilla

Lydiard

South
17 Knots

Champion

S.E. 20 Knots

S.W. 25 Knots

S.E. 25 Knots

By 5 p.m. B.C.S. had turned N.W. "Champion" and T.B.D.'s were on their port quarter 3–4 miles, and my division was endeavouring unsuccessfully to keep up with them.

The 5th B.S. on our S. beam was engaging to star'd to their great disadvantage (vile background, though standing out clearly against the Western sky themselves).

At 7.30. "Champion" turned south, and I took station on her port beam for the night.

8.30. Position 57.7 N., 6.13 E.

9.57. Ordered "Moorsom" to return to base—holed aft and short of oil.

A great deal of firing was observed to westward about 2 or 3 miles away and at about—

11.30 p.m. Fire was opened on us by a line of large ships which we took to be our own.

"Turbulent" (I learnt next morning) was sunk—and another.

"Champion" suddenly increased to high speed and disappeared to starboard. I continued S. and eventually turned S.W. and W. to get on other side of the big ships—who still spasmodically opened fire towards us.

At 4.15. "Laurel" reported sufficient oil to reach base, and survivors of "Queen Mary" in need of medical aid. Despatched her to Firth of Forth.

At 6 a.m. I discovered what the haze had hitherto hidden from me—that I had a long line of stragglers astern of my division—"Narborough," "Pelican," "Nicator," "Nerissa," "Petard," "Termagant," and "Morris."

Intercepted 4 a.m. position of "Lion." Set course N. 77 E. to meet "Lion," but found "L.'s" had not sufficient oil to reach her and get back to base.

Put "Narborough" in charge of all the "M.'s" and ordered him to rejoin "Lion."

7.30 a.m. Proceeded to Firth of Forth with "Liberty" and "Landrail."

7.10 p.m. Arrived oiler.

1.30 a.m. Proceeded with five boats to escort "Lion" and B.C.S. into Firth of Forth.

In utmost haste to catch "Landrail."

I have the honour to be,
Sir,
Your obedient servant,
M. L. GOLDSMITH,
Commander.

Com. T., H.M.S. "Carysfort."

H.M.S. "LAUREL,"

SIR,   9th June 1916.

IN accordance with your signal 1545 of the 9th June I have the honour to submit the following report :—

When the enemy were sighted "Laurel" was in position E. of Submarine Screen, Figure 4.

Battle Cruisers formed single line ahead and destroyers were ordered to take station ahead of B.C. Squadron.

"Laurel" was on the engaged beam of "New Zealand," after the B.C. Squadron had formed single line ahead, and was going full speed to get ahead into station. Owing to dense smoke from the funnels which would have obscured the range of the Battle Cruisers, and as it is impossible for "Laurel" to proceed at full speed without this dense smoke, it was decided to pass under the stern of the "Indefatigable"; a parallel course was then steered on the disengaged side. A position before the beam of the 4th ship of the line had been reached when 9th Flotilla were ordered astern.

At that time "Laurel" was proceeding towards the wreckage of the "Queen Mary" to pick up survivors and signal was received from "Lydiard" to carry out this operation. Difficulty was experienced owing to the heavy wash caused by the Battle Cruiser and 5th Battle Squadrons passing and re-passing at close range.

While attempting to hoist the whaler after this operation one of the blocks carried away, and as the signal to proceed at utmost speed had been received and the enemy were closing, whaler was cleared and abandoned. Course was steered to re-join 9th Flotilla.

En route it was observed that a light cruiser of the "Birmingham" class was being fired at apparently by enemy battle cruisers; endeavour was made to make a smoke screen between her and the enemy.

"Laurel" rejoined 9th Flotilla, at 7 p.m under the orders of "Champion."

During the night of the 31st May "Laurel" followed astern of "Morris," 9th Flotilla being in single line ahead. The 13th Flotilla was on the starboard and the 11th Flotilla on the port beam columns 1 cable apart.

Course was shaped for "Queensferry" at 4 a.m. 1st June. "Laurel" being sent on ahead with survivors from "Queen Mary."

I have the honour to be,
Sir,
Your obedient servant,
HENRY D. C. STANISTREET,
Lieutenant in Command.

The Commodore (T.),
    H.M.S. "Carysfort."

H.M.S. " LANDRAIL,"
9th Flotilla.

SIR,   9th June 1916.

IN accordance with your orders I forward the following report :—

On the 30.5.16 at 9.35 p.m. Destroyers slipped and proceeded joining the 2nd Battle Cruiser Squadron outside the outer boom Firth of Forth. Having been in company in Night Cruising Order, Submarine Screen No. 4 was formed at 4.37 a.m., on the 31.5.16.

At 2.38 p.m. 31.5.16. Steam was raised for full speed by Battle Cruisers.

At 3.28 p.m. Signal was made, Flag, General, " Enemy in sight, Bearing E. by N."

The Second Battle Cruiser Squadron were in the van and " L " boats were carrying out the Submarine Screen for them.

At 3.30 p.m. Second B.C.S. took station astern of First B.C.S., and " L " boats were in Division line ahead on the engaged side of B.C.S. distance about 5 cables.

3.32 p.m. Course was altered to East, and fire was opened.

3.35 p.m. Destroyers were ordered to take station 5 miles ahead of B.C.S. and full speed was put on the telegraphs.

At that time the " L " boats were on the beam of " Indefatigable " and " New Zealand "

Every endeavour was made to take up the station ordered and to keep smoke from funnels under.

At 3.45 p.m. Signal was received from " Lion " to clear the range and as slow progress was being made in getting ahead the " Lydiard " altered course 16 points to starboard to get astern of B.C.S.

Previous to this signal a torpedo passed under " Landrail " directed at the B.S.C. and passing about 60 yards ahead of " Queen Mary." A periscope was observed on the Port Quarter, and the signal was hoisted to this effect.

On getting clear of B.C.S. to the rear, H.M.S. " Laurel " was detailed to pick up survivors from " Queen Mary."

At 5.5 p.m. Destroyers were ordered to attack, but before the attack could be delivered by the " L " boats the recall was hoisted.

Recall was hoisted at 5.10 p.m. and " L " boats took station on the disengaged side of the " Barham," " Malaya," " Valiant," and " Warspite " about 2 miles.

At 6.40 p.m. Speed was reduced to 20 knots and destroyers joined H.M.S. " Champion."

At 7.5 p.m.   Course was altered to South, and "L" boats proceeded in company with H.M.S. "Lydiard," leader of the Division.

At 11.30 p.m.   Steering south fire was opened to starboard of us; this we took to be our own ships and continued on our course. This fire was continued spasmodically, and during it H.M.S. "Champion" went on to high speed and disappeared without signal.

7.30 a.m., 1st June.   Owing to shortage of oil fuel Division returned to Firth of Forth, where it arrived at 7 p.m., and completed with oil.

At 1.30 a.m. 2nd June.   Proceeded to sea to escort B.C.S. into harbour.

I have the honour to be,

Sir,

Your obedient servant,

F. E. HOBART,

Lieut.-Comdr., R.N.

H.M.S. "LIBERTY,"

9th June 1916.

SIR,

I HAVE the honour to report that in the recent action fought on May 31st, I was in command of H.M.S. "Liberty," her position was Fleet No. 2, in the 1st Div. of 9th Flotilla, astern of H.M.S. "Lydiard."

At 10.40 p.m. May 30th proceeded out of harbour, and formed submarine screen as ordered, the Port side of 2nd B.C.S.

At Noon, May 1st, position approx. 56.44 N., 3. 45 E.

At 3.28 approx. "New Zealand" hoisted "Enemy in sight, E. by N."

At 3.33 approx. "Lion" hoisted "5 flag" destroyers take station 5 miles ahead of B.C. Fleet. 1st Div. was then on the quarter of the rear Battle Cruiser.

Telegraphs were put to full speed, and Division endeavoured to reach their appointed station, passing up the engaged side of our Battle Cruiser line ½ mile inside, a very heavy fire was experienced from the "shorts" of the enemy's Battle Cruisers, but "Liberty" was only hit by splinters and no damage was done.

At 3.45 approx. Fire was opened by the B.C.S.

At 3.50 "Indefatigable" blew up.

At 4.10 approx. "Queen Mary" blew up.

At 4.30, when division was abeam 2nd Battle Cruiser in our line, "Lion" hoisted destroyers clear the range. The Division turned 16 points passed down the engaged side and formed astern of B.C. Line.

At 4.45 approx. the destroyers from the van delivered an attack.

The 1st Div. closed the enemy line, but owing to the position they had come from and the van destroyers attacking from ahead, it was impossible for the attack to get home.

" Lion " hoisted " destroyers recall," and all destroyers returned ahead of B.C.S.

At 5 p.m. B.C.S. turned to N.W. and destroyers passed under their stern, and took station on the disengaged side of the 5th B.S., who were engaging the enemy to starboard.

Division again came under a heavy fire, but no damage was done.

At 6.30 p.m. Division joined up with " Champion " and 13th Flotilla.

At 7.30 approx. " Champion " turned to South and division took station on her port beam. Speed, 15 knots.

At 11.30. Fire was opened on the Flotilla by about 4 heavy ships, who appeared to be 4,000 yards on our port beam. Searchlights were trained on the flotilla, and heavy firing continued. H.M.S. " Turbulent " being sunk.

Speed was increased to 20 knots and course altered away from heavy ships, gradually being altered to round ahead of them to the S.W.

Speed was increased to 25 knots and course S.W. and W. till daylight.

H.M.S. " Liberty " kept close station on " Lydiard " so as not to lose her.

At daylight. 1st Division not having enough oil left to continue, returned to base to oil arriving alongside oiler at 7.30 p.m.

At 1.30 a.m. division proceeded to sea to meet B.C.S. and escort them in.

I have the honour to be,
Sir,
Your obedient Servant,
PHILIP W. KING,
Lieutenant-Commander.

The Vice Admiral,
Battle Cruiser Fleet
(through Com. T.).

H.M.S. " MOORSOM,"
6.6.16.

REPORT OF PROCEEDINGS, 30th MAY–1st JUNE.

Sir,

I have the honour to report that " Moorsom " under orders of " Lydiard " left Queensferry at 9.35 p.m., 30th May, in company with 2nd B.C.S.

At 3.25 p.m., 31st May, Enemy was sighted bearing E. by N.

2nd B.C.S. took station astern of 1st B.C.S. and 9th Flotilla (which included 10th) were ordered to take station ahead of " Lion."

" Moorsom " took station with 13th Flotilla ahead of " Lion."

At 4.10 p.m destroyers were ordered to attack enemy with torpedoes.

"Moorsom" attacked with the leading division of 13th Flotilla; but torpedoes were not then fired, as enemy destroyers attacked simultaneously, and to engage them made position for torpedo attack bad.

When enemy destroyers had been driven off, Battle Cruisers had turned 16 points and enemy's Battle Fleet was coming up astern of their Battle Cruisers. Torpedo attack was made on van of Battle Fleet, two torpedoes being fired.

Ship was shortly afterwards hit aft, but no immediate damage to fighting efficiency was done.

A second torpedo attack on Battle Fleet was then carried out, two torpedoes being fired.

"Moorsom" then rejoined "Lydiard," who was with Capt. "D," 13th Flotilla, on disengaged side of 5th B.S.

No further active part was taken in the action, ship returned to base at 10.15 p.m. in accordance with orders from "Lydiard," as oil fuel was short owing to damage to oil tanks aft.

I have the honour to be,
Sir,
Your obedient Servant,
J. C. HODGSON,
Commander.

To Commodore " T,"
    H.M.S. " Carysfort."

H.M.S. " MORRIS,"
1st June 1916.

Sir,

I have the honour to report that on 31st May 1916 when attached to the 2nd Division of the 9th Flotilla ("Moorsom," "Morris," and "Laurel"), screening the Battle Cruisers, I sighted the German Battle Cruisers (five ships) bearing East by North at 3.35 p.m., G.M.T. As soon as the 1st and 2nd Battle Cruiser Squadrons formed line ahead, I increased to full speed to join the "Moorsom."

At 3.50 p.m., G.M.T., action was joined between the British and German Battle Cruisers. I was then, owing to the position I had been in when acting as submarine screen, one mile astern of the "Moorsom," on the engaged side of the 1st Battle Cruiser Squadron, and steering S. 64° E.

By the time I had drawn ahead to the beam of H.M.S. " Lion," I observed German Destroyers making an attack on our Battle Cruisers. I turned to Port and engaged those nearest me, one of which was sunk and two disabled. The Enemy Destroyers were driven off and did not get within torpedo range of our Battle Cruisers.

Shortly before the end of this Destroyer action, I came within torpedo range of the Enemy Battle Cruisers, but could not fire my torpedoes owing to my range being fouled by our own destroyers. I did not again get within torpedo range of the Enemy.

On rejoining H.M.S. "Moorsom" after the destroyer action, we were on the disengaged quarter of our Battle Cruisers with H.M.S. "Champion" and about 20 to 30 Destroyers of other Flotillas. We took no further active part in the engagement.

H.M.S. "Moorsom," having been hit, returned to the Base at 10.15 p.m., after which I remained with the 9th Flotilla led by H.M.S. "Lydiard" for the remainder of the night.

1 *   *   *   *   *

I have the honour to be,
Sir,
Your obedient Servant,
E. S. GRAHAM,
Lieutenant Commander.

Captain (D.),
10th Flotilla.

"TERMAGANT"—REPORT OF PROCEEDINGS IN ACTION OF 31st MAY–1st JUNE 1916.

III.

No. 83/00101.

Commander-in-Chief,
Grand Fleet.

Submitted in continuation of my submission No. 76/00101 of 10th June 1916.

R. Y. TYRWHITT,
15th June 1916. Commodore (T).

H.M.S. "Termagant,"
Sir, 11th June 1916.
I HAVE the honour to forward herewith a report of proceedings of this ship on 31st May–1st June 1916.

I have the honour to be,
Sir,
Your obedient Servant,
C. P. BLAKE,
Lieutenant-Commander.

The Commodore (T)
(through Captain (D), 10th Flotilla).

---

1 Part omitted here, referring solely to personnel, recommendations, &c. in no way bearing on the course of the action.

II.

No. A/709.

     Commodore (T).

     Submitted.

    A copy has been sent to V.A., Commanding Battle Cruiser Fleet.

WILMOT NICHOLSON,

"Aurora,"   Captain (D), 10th Flotilla.

    12th June 1916.

H.M.S. "TERMAGANT"—REPORT OF PROCEEDINGS, 31ST MAY–1ST JUNE.

30th May.

P.M.

9.45.   Proceeded under orders of "Champion," with 13th Flotilla.

31st May.

A.M.

0. 0.   Formed submarine screen on 1st Battle Cruiser Squadron, speed 18 knots; course, N. 73° E.

1.15.   Co. N. 81° E.

2.35.   Fleet commenced to zig-zag. Co. and speed as requisite for keeping station.

P.M.

3.25.   Co. of Fleet, East; speed, 25 knots. Assumed complete readiness for action.

3.30.   Enemy sighted E. by N.

3.32.   13th Flotilla proceeded to take station ahead of "Lion."

3.42.   13th Flotilla proceeded to take station on starboard bow of "Lion," 2 miles.

3.45.   13th Flotilla proceeded to form Divisions in line ahead.

4.05.   "Lion" ordered destroyers to attack with torpedoes.
Proceeded astern of "Nerissa" to attack.

4.32.   Opened fire on enemy Light Cruiser, range 5,000 yards.
Under fire of enemy Light Cruiser and destroyers.
No suitable opportunity occurred for firing torpedoes.

4.45.   Ceased firing.
Proceeded astern of "Nerissa" to rejoin Flotilla.

5.10.   "Lion" recalled destroyers.

5.30.   "Lion" a/c N.N.E.

6. 0.   Sighted British Battle Fleet.

6.10.   "Champion" formed 13th Flotilla in single line ahead, stationed on port side of British Cruisers. Speed, 25 knots.

6.35   13th Flotilla. Speed, 15 knots.

7.05.   Flotilla a/c S.E.

P.M.

7.45.	Flotilla a/c S., 10 knots.
8.05.	Flotilla a/c W. by S.
8.15.	Flotilla a/c West, 17 knots.
8.27.	Flotilla a/c W.S.W., 17 knots.
8.40.	Flotilla a/c S.W.
9. 0.	Flotilla a/c S., 20 knots.
9.30.	Flotilla reduced to 17 knots.
10.05.	Flotilla reduced to 10 knots.
10.20.	Flotilla increased to 17 knots; firing and searchlight to starboard.
10.45.	Flotilla a/c S.E., 20 knots.
11.40.	Flotilla a/c S.W., 30 knots.

1st June.

A.M.

1. 0.	Flotilla a/c W.N.W., 28 knots.
2.40.	Flotilla reduced to 15 knots.
2.55.	Formed divisions in line abreast. Co., S. 70 W.
	During the night the 9th flotilla joined the 13th flotilla. " Termagant " ordered to join 9th flotilla.
5.20.	13th flotilla a/c N. 77 E., 20 knots.
6.10.	' Lydiard ' ordered " Termagant " to rejoin 13th flotilla. Proceeded 26 knots to search for 13th flotilla.
7.40.	Owing to loss of fresh water, which shortly afterwards necessitated drawing fires in one boiler, and oil running low, not having sighted 13th flotilla, decided to return to base. Shaped course N. 75 West; speed, 18 knots. Arrived Rosyth midnight.

REPORTS FROM COMMANDING OFFICER— H.M.S. " ENGADINE."

Enclosure No. 24 to Battle Cruiser Fleet Letter No. B.C.F. 01 12.6.16.

H.M.S. " Engadine,"
2nd June 1916.

SIR,

I HAVE the honour to make the following report on this Ship's movements on 31st May and 1st June 1916 :—

When in company with the Battle Cruiser Fleet, Seaplane No. 8359 was hoisted out at 3.7 p.m. with Flight Lieutenant F. J. Rutland, R.N. as Pilot, and Assistant Paymaster G. S. Trewin, R.N. as Observer, with orders to scout N.N.E. for hostile Ships, in accordance with your signal received on board at 2.40 p.m. Their reports are attached.

The delay in hoisting out Seaplane was caused through the Ship having to keep clear of the Cruisers.

After the Seaplane was hoisted out, the Ship proceeded in an E.N.E. direction, same direction as the Seaplane and Light Cruisers.

The following signals were received from the Seaplane :—

1530.—Three enemy Cruisers and 5 Destroyers, distance from me 10 miles bearing 90°, steering course to the N.W.

1533.—Enemy's course is South.

1545.—Three enemy Cruisers and 10 Destroyers steering South.

1548.—Four enemy Cruisers and 10 Destroyers steering South.

The last signal was not received in the Ship, which I think was due to Seaplane descending at the time and the amount of other W/T going on. Attempts were made to pass these signals on to H.M.S. "Lion" by searchlight, but this could not be done, as apparently she had already opened fire on the enemy. An attempt was also made to pass them through H.M.S. "Barham," but this failed also for the same reason.

The Seaplane returned at 3.47 p.m. and was hoisted in, and the Ship proceeded then to about 4 miles on the disengaged side of the Battle Cruisers and followed their movements. Two Destroyers who had been told off as our escort were ordered to rejoin their Flotilla at 4.12 p.m.

At 6.40 p.m. I passed H.M.S. "Warrior," who had fallen out of line in a damaged condition and was proceeding W.N.W. I asked her if I could be of any assistance and was ordered to stand by her.

At 8.40 p.m. I took H.M.S. "Warrior" in tow, using her 6½-in. wire, and towed her at 8 knots W.N.W. until 7.15 a.m. (June 1st) (this Ship doing revolutions for 18 knots).

At 7.15 a.m. I was ordered to slip and proceed alongside to take off the Ship's company. This was completed by 8.25 a.m. The position of H.M.S. "Warrior" at this time was Lat. 57° 21' N., 3° 2' E. She was still afloat, but midships and the afterpart of the deck were awash. The Captain stated she was making water fast and would sink in an hour.

H.M.S. "Engadine" then proceeded straight to Rosyth, arriving there at 1.35 a.m. (2nd June), having on board the crew of H.M.S. "Warrior," numbering 743, consisting of 35 officers, 681 men, 25 Cot cases, and 2 walking cases.

The weather at the time the "Warrior" was abandoned was S.W. swell, and wind S.W., force 5, increasing.

When alongside H.M.S. "Warrior" the rubbing streak on the port-side, midships, was torn off to the extent of about 10 ft., and a plate burst on the port side of foremost stokehold, 5 ft.

below the waterline to the extent of about 6 ins. This has been temporarily repaired and is quite water-tight.

1   *   *   *   *   *

> I have the honour to be,
> Sir,
> Your obedient Servant,
> C. G. ROBINSON,
> Lieutenant-Commander, R.N.,
> In Command.

The Vice-Admiral Commanding,
    1st Battle Cruiser Fleet,
      H.M.S. " Lion."

> H.M.S. " Engadine,"
SIR,   31st May 1916.

    I HAVE the honour to make the following report :—

At 2.40 p.m. (G.M.T.), in accordance with signal and your orders, Seaplane No. 8359 was got out and proceeded to scout for enemy ships.

I was hoisted out at 3.7 p.m. (G.M.T.) and was off the water at 3.8 p.m. (G.M.T). (Times were taken on board.)

The last information from Ship which I received was, that the enemy were sighted in a N.N.E. direction, steering North.

I steered N. 10 E., and after about ten minutes sighted the enemy. Clouds were at 1,000 to 1,200 ft., with patches at 900 ft. This necessitated flying very low.

On sighting the enemy it was very hard to tell what they were and so I had to close to within a mile and half at a height of 1,000 ft. They then opened fire on me with anti-aircraft and other guns, my height enabling them to use their anti-torpedo armament.

When sighted they were steering a northerly course. I flew through several of the columns of smoke caused through bursting shrapnel.

When the Observer had counted and got the disposition of the enemy and was making his W/T report, I sheered to about three miles, keeping the enemy well in sight. While the Observer was sending one message, the enemy turned 16 points. I drew his attention to this and he forthwith transmitted it. The enemy then ceased firing at me. I kept on a bearing on the bows, about three miles distant of the enemy, and as the weather cleared a little, I observed the disposition of our Fleet, and judged by the course of our Battle Cruisers, that our W/T had got through.

At 3.45 p.m. (G.M.T.) a petrol pipe leading to the left front carburettor broke and my engine revolutions dropped from 1,200 to 800 and I was forced to descend.

---

1 Part omitted here, referring solely to personnel, recommendations &c., in no way bearing on the course of the action.

On landing I made good the defect with rubber tube and reported to the Ship that I could go on again.

I was told to come alongside and be hoisted in. I was hoisted in at about 4.0 p.m. (G.M.T.).

The visibility at 1,000 ft. was about 4 miles varying to one, and this reduced the advantage of Seaplane's height. Also the Seaplane having to remain so close to the enemy increased the chances of jambing the W/T. The messages, as sent, were received in H.M.S. " Engadine."

I could not keep both our Fleet and the enemy's Fleet in sight, through low lying clouds.

I wish to point out the desirability of having a good arc lamp for this work. I could have signalled direct to any Ship the position of the enemy, if the W/T had been jambed. As it was, it was not known if the messages had been received until our Fleet were sighted and their course observed.

The speed at which things took place prevented any receiving, the Observer being busy coding and sending all the time. The enemy commenced to jam latterly.

The enemy's anti-aircraft firing was fairly good, the shock of exploding shrapnel could be felt ; the explosions taking place about 200 ft. away on one side, in front and astern.

I have the honour to be,

Sir,

Your obedient Servant,

F. J. RUTLAND,

Flight Lieut., R.N.

Commanding Officer,

H.M.S. " Engadine."

H.M.S. " Engadine,"

Sir,   31st May 1916.

With reference to the flight made this afternoon in Seaplane No. 8359, to scout for hostile ships, I have the honour to report as follows :—

2. The clouds were very low, which necessitated low flying, and therefore reduced the range of visibility, which varied from nil to four miles, except for one short spell, when it was about 7–10 miles. During this brief break in the mist clouds, I sighted 3 Cruisers and 5 Destroyers at about 3.20 p.m. We closed this Fleet, and from their position and composition, it appeared to be hostile. When we had closed them to about 1½ miles, flying at a height of 1,000 ft., I saw more Destroyers, and then heard the reports of bursting shell and saw shrapnel bursts around us.

3. In the middle of my sending a W/T message, timed 1530, I saw the hostile Fleet altering course to due South. On completion of that message, I transmitted another, timed 1533, giving their alteration of course. The Seaplane altered course to the

Southward and stood off them about 3 miles, in order to watch their movements and verify their composition, sending messages timed 1545 and 1548.

4. Whilst proceeding to transmit the 1548 signal engine trouble developed and I had to reel in aerial, before actually landing, starting to reel in at a height of 300 feet. Some of our Destroyers then came into sight.

5. Whilst on the water a " Town " Class Cruiser passed us, so I semaphored to her the direction the enemy were steering.

6. The " Engadine " then came into sight and ordered us to be hoisted in-board.

7. From the time of sighting the enemy to the breaking of the petrol pipe, I saw none of our Ships in sight; also as it was essential to get the information through before the enemy jambed the W/T, it was impossible in the short space of time to gauge our bearings from our own Ships.

8. The signals transmitted by me were :—

1530. Three enemy Cruisers and 5 Destroyers, distance from me 10 miles bearing 90°, steering course to the N.W.

1533. Enemy's course is South.

1545. Three enemy Cruisers and 10 Destroyers steering South.

1548. Four enemy Cruisers and 10 Destroyers steering South.
(This signal was not completed owing to enforced descent.)

9. I attempted to call up H.M.S. " Engadine " and a " Town " Class Cruiser, when on the water, with the lamp, but apparently it was not seen.

10. The enemy Cruisers seen had three funnels, like the " Tiger's " funnels (one of the funnels of one Ship painted red), and hulls were about the length of the " Warrior " Class. They did not appear sufficiently large for Battle Cruisers and I could not distinguish their turrets.

I have the honour to be,
Sir,
Your obedient Servant,
G. S. TREWIN,
Observer.
(Assistant Paymaster, R.N.)

Flight Lieut. F. J. Rutland, R.N.,
H.M.S. " Engadine."

CAPTAIN'S REPORT—H.M.S. " CANTERBURY."

Enclosure No. 25 to Battle Cruiser Fleet, Letter No. B.C.F. 01
of 12.6.16.

H.M.S. " Cänterbury,"
Sir,   2nd June 1915.

I HAVE the honour to report proceedings of this ship from
30th May to Friday 2nd June, during which period I was attached
to a portion of your force, viz., first to Third Battle Cruiser
Squadron, and later to Third Light Cruiser Squadron.

Left Scapa Flow in company with 3rd B.C.S. at 9 p.m.
Tuesday 30th May, and took station five miles ahead, " Chester "
being five miles astern. Shaped course as necessary to maintain
position ahead of Grand Fleet, steaming in S. 73 East direction
until 3.45 p.m. 31st, when in latitude 57·40 North, Longitude
5·40 East, course was altered to South South Eeast.

At 2.25 p.m. Wednesday 31st reports of enemy's vessels
commenced to be received, continuing to 5.40 p.m., when in
latitude 56·58 North, 6·14 East, Third B.C.S. turned round to
about N. 30 West. I immediately turned to the same direction
and increased to full speed, quickly closing.

At about 5.52 p.m. Third B.C.S. opened fire to port, and
immediately after, a four-funnelled cruiser of " Roon " class and a
three-funnelled cruiser were sighted on out port bow ahead of
the enemy's battle cruisers, distance about 12,000 yards, steering
in southerly direction.

To follow Third B.C.S. it would mean running past the
battle cruisers, and considering this inadvisable I turned roughly
16 points to port and engaged enemy's light cruisers, who were
then administering heavy punishment to two British destroyers,
one of whom was on fire aft, and the other standing by her :
our approach soon reduced the fire on them—we fired 40 rounds
of 6-in. and 35 rounds of 4-in. at a range of 10,000 yards.

The three-funnelled cruiser was seen to be badly on fire aft,
while this ship although surrounded by falling shot was only
hit once. A 4·1-in. high explosive armour-piercing shell hitting
her in the ship's side just abaft after 6-in. gun, passing through
two bulkheads, the main deck and landing in the fresh water tank
—failing to explode.

I was then joined at about 7.15 p.m. by 3rd Light Cruiser
Squadron, and asked permission to join up under the Rear-
Admiral, taking station next astern of him in Falmouth, and
with 3rd Light Cruiser squadron engaged enemy's head.

I remained under the orders of Rear-Admiral Third Light
Cruiser Squadron until 8.35 p.m. 1st June, when I received orders
to proceed to Harwich to join Commodore (T).

At 3.20 a.m. I received orders from the C.-in-C. to proceed
to the assistance of H.M.S. " Marlborough," and sighted her
off the Humber 2.45 p.m. 2nd June.

During the action the firing of the German light cruisers was all by director, each salvo falling in a space of 30 yards, and being very rapid.

"Invincible" was seen to blow up at 6.35 p.m., a terrible explosion taking place, the ship being split in two, her bow and stern standing on one end entirely separated. In addition to the light cruisers already reported one battle cruiser (No. 2) was seen to be heavily on fire.

Attached a rough track chart of the impression that remains in my mind of the approximate movements.[1]

I have the honour to be,
Sir,
Your obedient Servant,
PERCY ROYDS,
Captain.

Vice-Admiral,
Commanding Battle Cruiser Squadron.

---

[1] Plate 23

REAR-ADMIRAL'S REPORT—2ND CRUISER SQUADRON.

Enclosure No. 10 to Submission No. 1415/0022 of 20 June 1916
from C.-in-C., Home Fleet.

No. 110/001/13.

H.M.S. " Minotaur,"

SIR,   4th June 1916.

I HAVE the honour to report as follows concerning the
movements of the Second Cruiser Squadron in the action with
the German Fleet on 31st May :—

2. The cruiser line was proceeding in disposition L.S. 1–16,
the ships being stationed from port to starboard as follows :—

" Cochrane "   " Shannon "   ⎧ " Minotaur " (flag).
                                       ⎨ " Hampshire."
                                       ⎩ (Linking with C.-in-C.)

⎧ " Defence "   " Duke of Edinburgh "   " Black Prince."
⎨ " Warrior."

3. At 5.40 p.m. heavy firing was heard ahead and soon after
ships were seen in the mist. Ships of Second Cruiser Squadron
were recalled and formed into line, and signal made to engage
the enemy. The conditions were exceedingly difficult; there
appeared to be one enemy cruiser, but the others were doubtful,
but before fire was opened, a reply to the challenge was received
and showed the ships to be our own 3rd B.C.S. The cruiser
was not seen again.

4. At 5.52 p.m. a signal from " Defence " indicated that
battle fleets would shortly be engaged. I therefore proceeded
for my assigned position 2 points on the engaged van of the
battle fleet. A somewhat wide sweep was made and there was
a little delay owing to an alteration of course by the battle fleet,
but correct station was finally assumed and maintained.

5. At 7.17 p.m. " Duke of Edinburgh " joined my flag.

6. At 7.11 p.m. I proceeded with the squadron at 20 knots
to take up station astern of the battle cruiser fleet who were
then engaged with the enemy. Orders were given to open fire
if favourable opportunity occurred. The control officer, however,
quite rightly withheld his fire, as he could see nothing to range
on or to spot by, and considered it would be an absolute waste
of ammunition which might well be required the following
morning. The cruiser squadron was successful, however, in
drawing some of the enemy's fire. One salvo fell short on the
starboard bow of " Minotaur " and some others in close proximity; others near to other ships of the squadron. Later on,
observing that the battle cruiser fleet was altering course away
from the enemy, I followed suit.

7. Throughout the action, only on a very few occasions
were the enemy ships actually seen, and then extremely indistinctly. Even when the salvoes referred to in the preceding

paragraph fell, no more than the flashes of the enemy's guns could be seen, and as the range seemed well outside that of the 9·2-in. and 7·5-in. guns I did not consider it desirable to waste ammunition, and made no signal to open fire.

8. The " Chester " joined my flag before dark and reported her condition. I therefore ordered her at daylight to make the best of her way to the Humber, informing S.O., Battle Cruiser Fleet. There was no particular incident during the night.

9. At about 9.20 a.m. on 1st June the ship passed through extensive oil patches with air bubbles rising from the bottom in position Lat. 56·5 N., Long. 6·11 E. This position may give some clue as to the nationality and class of vessel lying at the bottom.

10. As regards the behaviour of officers and men, I would conclude by observing that the demeanour throughout was fully up to expectations, especially whilst the ship was being fired at and shots dropping close. The one great disappointment was that no opportunity occurred of inflicting damage on the enemy in return.

1   *   *   *   *   *

12. Reports from individual ships, track charts[2] of " Minotaur " and an extract from " Minotaur's " signal log[3] are attached.

I have the honour to be,
Sir,
Your obedient Servant,
H. L. HEATH,
Rear-Admiral.

The Commander-in-Chief,
Home Fleets.

SCHEDULE OF ENCLOSURES IN SUBMISSION No. 110/001/13 of 4th JUNE 1916.

R.A.C. 2ND C.S. TO COMMANDER-IN-CHIEF, H.F.

No.
1. " Minotaur " of 3rd June 1916.
2. " Hampshire " of 3rd June 1916.
3. " Cochrane " of 2nd June 1916.
4. " Shannon " of 4th June 1916.
5. Extracts from Log of " Minotaur."[3]
6. Chart Tracks of " Minotaur."[2]

---

[1] Part omitted here, referring solely to personnel, recommendations, &c., in no way bearing on the course of the action.

[2] Plates 24 and 25.

[3] " Minotaur's " signal log not printed, as matter is embodied in Record of British Messages.

CAPTAIN'S REPORT—H.M.S. "MINOTAUR." ·

No. 274/14.

"Minotaur,"

SIR,   3rd June 1916.

In accordance with your orders, I have the honour to submit the following report covering the period from noon, 31st May, to noon, 1st June 1916 :—

2. At noon we were cruising in "L.S. 1," "Minotaur" occupying position "C," advancing 14 knots. At about 2.30 p.m. reports were received indicating the enemy's presence : steam was ordered for full speed.

3. At 3.30 p.m. the cruiser line was ordered to advance to 16 miles ahead, but as the speed of the Fleet was gradually increased, we never drew more than 12 miles ahead.

4. At about 5.0 p.m. firing was heard on the starboard bow and, later on, flashes of guns were seen.

5. At about 5.50 p.m. several vessels, two of them large, were seen in the mist bearing down on us. On receiving no reply to the challenge, we altered course to Port so as to bring them abaft the beam, and repeated the challenge. Receiving no reply to this, I ordered the starboard battery to open fire, but almost immediately received a report from the top that they could recognise one of the vessels as the "Invincible" class, and almost at the same time a ship came through the mist and I recognised her myself.

7 (*sic*). This turn to Port took us some little way out of our station and out of sight of the Fleet, so we turned to E.S.E.

8. At 6.8 p.m., having received a report that the enemy had deployed to the Eastward, we altered course to the North East to take station on our Fleet, presuming that they were doing likewise, at the same time collecting our squadron and forming line ahead. We very soon discovered, however, that this was taking us further away from the gunfiring and that our Fleet was not deploying to the Eastward, we therefore stood back to pick up our Battlefleet, arriving on their Port, or disengaged, bow with all our destroyers and Light Craft between us and the leading Battleship. This position we maintained for some time as, owing to not having a very great advantage over the Battleships in speed and to their constantly altering course to starboard, we were unable to draw ahead.

8. At 7.10 p.m. the position was as follows :—We were leading the Second Cruiser Squadron in line ahead, being three to four miles on the Port side of the "King George V." gaining on her very slightly, with all the destroyers and Light Craft between us and the "King George V." About four miles distant on our Starboard Bow were the Battle Cruisers. It was now decided that the place for our squadron was on the Quarter of the Battle Cruisers Squadrons, which would be in conformity with the plan of deployment, but this could only be done after

Plate 24.

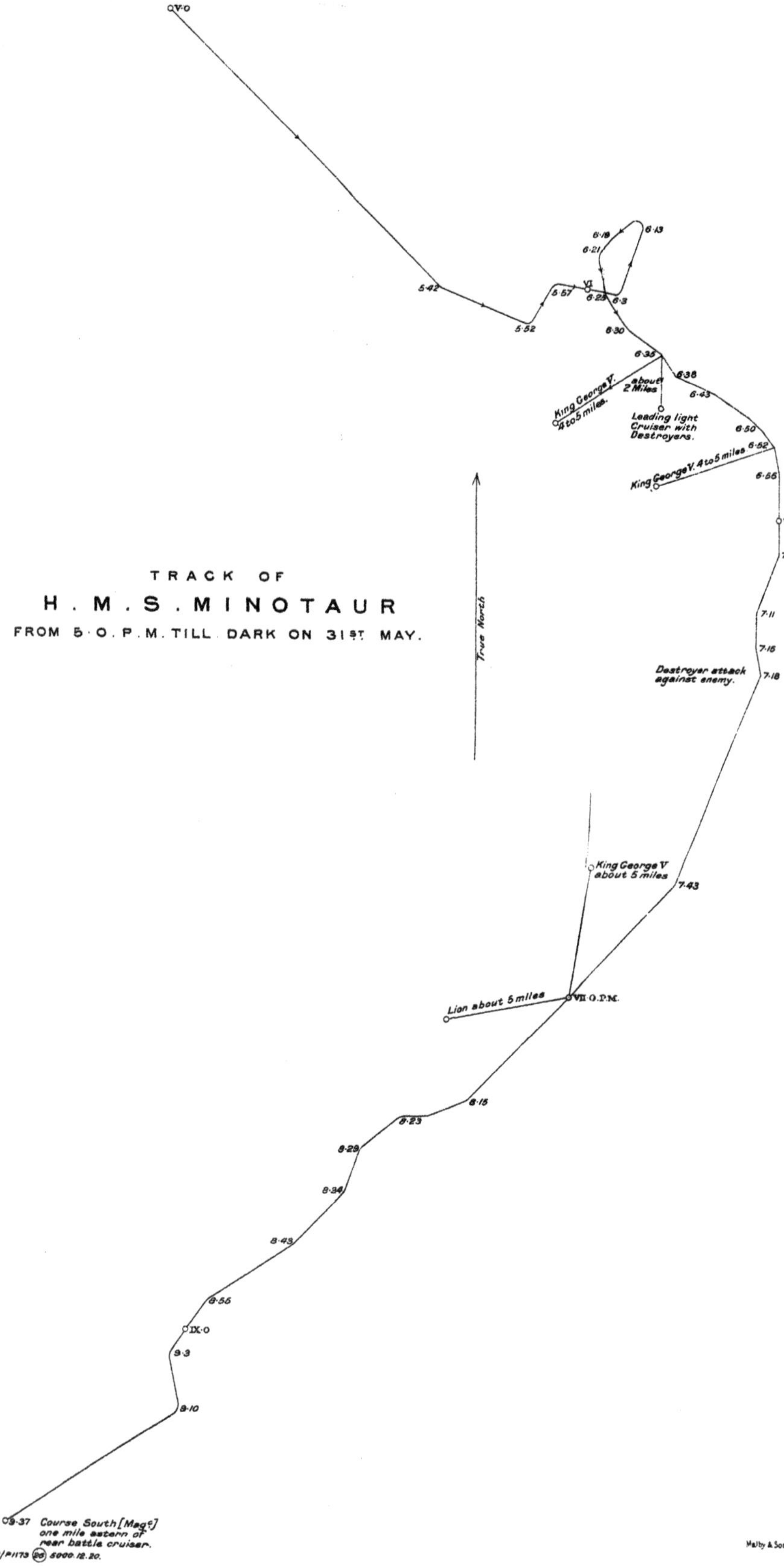

V·0

6·13
6·18
6·21

5·42
5·57   VI
6·25 6·3
5·52
6·30

6·35
6·38
King George V.   about   6·43
4 to 5 miles.   2 Miles.
Leading light   6·50
Cruiser with   6·52
Destroyers.   6·56
King George V. 4 to 5 miles

VII·0

7·6

TRACK OF   7·11

H.M.S.MINOTAUR   7·15

FROM 5·0.P.M. TILL DARK ON 31ST MAY.   7·18
Destroyer attack
against enemy.

True North

King George V
about 5 miles
7·43

Lion about 5 miles   VII 0.P.M.

8·15
8·23
8·29
8·34

8·43

8·55
IX·0
9·3

9·10

9·37 Course South [Magt]
one mile astern of
rear battle cruiser.

'9·24266/P1173 (80) 5000 12.20.   Malby & Sons. Lith

Plate 25.

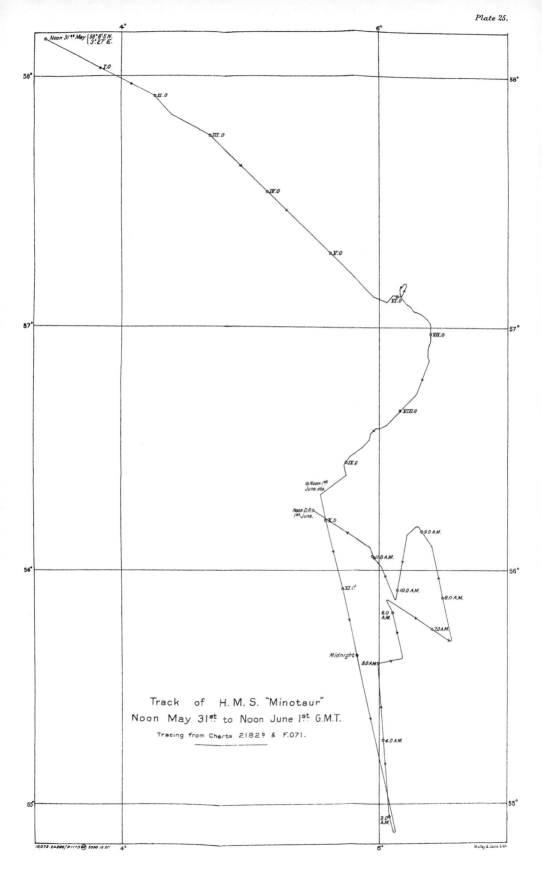

Noon 31st May { 58° 8.5 N.
{ 3° 27' E.

I.0

II.0

III.0

IV.0

V.0

VI.0

VII.0

VIII.0

IX.0

Noon 1st June.obs.

Noon D.R.
1st June. X.0

9.0 A.M.

11.0 A.M.

XI.0°

10.0 A.M.

8.0 A.M.

6.0
A.M.

7.0 A.M.

Midnight

5.0 A.M.

4.0 A.M.

3.0
A.M.

Track of H.M.S. "Minotaur"
Noon May 31st to Noon June 1st G.M.T.

Tracing from Charts 2182b & F.071.

10,072. 24+206/P1173 5000 12 20.

Malby & Sons. Lith.

we had drawn clear of our Battleships, which, I have explained, we were only doing very slowly. When within about three or four miles of our rear Battle Cruiser, we observed them to be heavily engaged. We could occasionally see the firing of the enemy's guns, but that was all.

9. At about 8.30 p.m. salvoes of large calibre fell ahead of us on our starboard bow, and shortly after one salvo fell short abreast of the ship. I asked the Gunnery Lieutenant in the top whether it was any use our opening fire, laying on the flashes of the enemy's guns, and he replied that he thought it would be a waste of ammunition as he would be unable to spot anything but a direct hit, and with this I quite agreed, so we hauled out a couple of points so as not to steam into the salvoes. Shortly after this the firing ceased.

10. The whole night we spent steaming south, keeping on the Port quarter of the Battle Cruisers.

11. At 2.45 a.m. we turned to the Northward. From 5.0 a.m. until noon we were conforming to the movements of the Battle Cruisers, or getting into touch with and forming on the Battlefleet, which movements are best described by the chart tracing enclosed.[1]

I have the honour to be,
Sir,
Your obedient Servant,
A. C. S. HUGHES D'AETH.
Captain.

The Rear-Admiral Commanding,
Second Cruiser Squadron.

CAPTAIN'S REPORT—H.M.S. " HAMPSHIRE."

No. 7B/83.

H.M. Ship " Hampshire,"
SIR,   3rd June 1916.

IN accordance with your signal 1150 of 2nd June 1916, I have the honour to forward the attached report of proceedings from Noon, 31st May, to Noon, 1st June 1916.

I have the honour to be,
Sir,
Your obedient Servant,
H. J. SAVILL,
Captain.

The Rear-Admiral Commanding,
Second Cruiser Squadron.

REPORT OF PROCEEDINGS.

At noon on 31st May, H.M. Ship under my command was in position observed Lat. 58·10 N., Long. 3·20 E. steering S. 50 E.; speed of advance, 14 knots. The special duty of the ship was to act as linking ship between " Minotaur " at position C and " Active " at position J in L.S. 1 diagram.

---

[1] Plates 24 and 25.

At 3. 0 p.m.   Speed of advance increased to 17 knots, and
At 3. 5 p.m.   course altered to S.E. by S., and
At 3.25 p.m.   S. 29 E. and 20 knots.
At 4.10 p.m.   Speed 21 knots.
At 5.10 p.m.   Altered course S. 40 E.
At 5.35 p.m.   Being then hazy, visibility about 5 miles,
                "Defence" from position D asked course and
                speed, and could "Hampshire" see "Mino-
                taur." Course and speed were given, and
                bearing and distance of "Minotaur"—S. 66 E.
                9,000 yards from "Hampshire."

At 5.40 p.m.   Firing was heard bearing south.
At 5.47 p.m.   Flashes of guns could be seen S.S.W., and at
                same time "Defence" was observed firing.
At 5.52 p.m.   A ship was sighted on Starboard Bow steering
                to N.E. and challenged. At the same time
                course was altered to N. 70 E. to conform
                with "Minotaur." The challenged ship replied
                "Zwanzi," and

5.56 p.m.   fire was opened on her at 9,500 yards bearing
                S. ½ E.

This ship appeared to be a three-funnelled
cruiser, probably the "Kolberg" type, and
appeared to be standing to the N.E., and
one, possibly two, more ships (Battle Cruisers?)
appeared in the haze for about two minutes
ahead of her. Four salvoes were fired at her
in three minutes; the first missed to the right,
the second appeared to hit and light smoke

Hampshire 5.56 p.m. Opened fire

Minotaur

North. Mag.ᶜ

Warrior
Defence

Enemy
Cruiser

and steam appeared from the base of the centre funnel. After the second salvo the enemy turned away and were lost in the haze. These ships seemed almost white.

At 6. 2 p.m. Another battle cruiser was sighted, which replied to the challenge correctly.

At 6. 4 p.m. Course was altered to S. 60 E., and

At 6. 7 p.m. to N. 70 E., to conform with " Minotaur."

At 6. 7 p.m. Our Battle Fleet appeared to be deploying to Starboard and it was reported to " Minotaur."

At 6.20 p.m. Ordered to close " Minotaur," and arrived in Station astern of " Shannon " at

6.50 p.m. " Chester " forming astern of " Hampshire." " Duke of Edinburgh " also came up and eventually formed ahead of " Hampshire." Up to this time station had been kept between battle fleet and " Minotaur," the " Active " having been lost sight of.

At this time, 7.0 p.m., squadron was abreast of the van of the Battle Fleet, the 2nd Battle Squadron leading.

At 7.20 p.m. The two leading ships of the squadron passed ahead of the Battle Fleet, but " Hampshire " had to keep to port and eventually got back into station again, when the Battle Fleet altered gradually to S.W.

At 8. 0 p.m. Heavy firing was heard from Battle Cruiser Fleet, which was ahead and to Starboard of our line, and continued for some time.

At 9.42 p.m. Course was altered to S., speed 17 knots for the night.

At 11.35 p.m. The reflection of flashes from guns was observed abaft the Port Beam.

At 3.15 a.m. A Zeppelin was observed over the Battle Cruiser Fleet, bearing S.S.E. and reported to " Minotaur " and " Lion."

From now till noon, 1st June 1916, " Hampshire " remained in close touch with " Minotaur." The report of the Control Officer is included in foregoing.

SUBMARINE REPORTS.

A number of reports from Submarine Look-outs were made, but the following cases appear on investigation to be reliable.

Many of these reports were made due to the extraordinary way in which the water was churned up by the number of vessels at high speed in close proximity.

At 6. 5 p.m. A periscope was reported on port bow and ship was turned towards it and fire opened on it. " Midge " also went towards it. This was undoubtedly a dummy, and was observed very clearly from the Fore Bridge.

At 6.54 p.m.   Fire was opened on a periscope on port beam, and ship turned in that direction. It was seen by Officer of Y Group, Fore Turret, and Control Top. It dived and was not seen again.

At 8.40 p.m.   An unmistakable jar was felt in Fire Control position, Fore Turret, " A " Turret, Fore T.S., Fore Cross Passage, and Fore " A " and " B " Shell Rooms, and a very large swirl as from a submarine almost breaking surface was seen in our wake, and must have passed about 20 yards from Starboard Beam of " Chester." Also the periscope was seen at an angle by at least two observers. The shock was sufficient to knock down a projectile in the Fore Turret, cause the men in the Fore Shell Room to inquire if the Ship had been torpedoed, and nearly knock men in submerged flat off their feet.

CAPTAIN'S REPORT—H.M.S. " COCHRANE."

No. 143/B.W.   H.M.S. " Cochrane,"
SIR,   2 June 1916.
      IN accordance with your Signal 1150 of 2 June 1916, I have the honour to forward an account of the proceedings of H.M.S. " Cochrane " from noon, 31st May, to noon, 1st June.

      2. At noon, 31st May, " Cochrane " was in Lat. 58° 20 N., Long. 3° 47 E., steering to the S.E., speed of advance 16 knots. being the left-hand ship of Cruisers spread in L.S.1—10 miles, Destroyer " Mischief " accompanied " Cochrane." 3rd B.C.S. was occasionally in sight hull down ahead, Battle Fleet (B.F.) on starboard quarter. Visibility to the Sd. not so good as to the E. and N.

      3. At 2.23 p.m. we received, by intercepted W/T Signal, the first intimation of enemy being sighted by the Cruisers from Rosyth—some 70 miles to the Sd. of us. At 2.40 p.m. steam was raised for full speed. Speed of advance was increased to 18 knots at 3.5 p.m., and to 20 at 3.25 p.m. Heavy firing was heard to the Sd. about 4.0 p.m. At 6.0 p.m., Cruisers were closed and formed single line ahead in the order—" Minotaur," " Cochrane," " Shannon," " Hampshire "—course South to close the B.F.

      4. From this time " Cochrane " was astern of " Minotaur " until noon 1st June, so a detailed account of movements is not given, but a short narrative of what occurred.

      5. While we were closing in, the B.F. steered to the S.Ed., then S., and then S.W., the enemy being away to the W. and N. of our battle line. Six of our Battle Cruisers (B.C.F.) were well ahead of our B.F., steering to the S.Wd., and all Battleships

and Battle Cruisers were heavily engaged off and on, the heaviest firing coming as a rule from the van and rear. 5th B.S. was not seen on the 31st, and I presumed they were in the rear with the remaining Battle Cruisers. Our Squadron gradually drew ahead along the disengaged side of the B.F. and reached the van soon after 8.0 p.m., having been joined by the " Duke of Edinburgh " at 7.20 p.m.

6. At about 8.0 p.m. we crossed the bows of the leading Battleship (" King George V ") and made for the disengaged quarter of the B.C.F. At this time the B.C.F. was steering about S.W. and the B.F. had altered course more to the Sd., the gap between them about 4 miles and increasing rapidly. The leading ships of the B.F. were not then engaged. The weather was hazy, visibility about 8 to 10 miles, and owing to this and the smoke from " Minotaur," which entirely blocked our view to starboard most of the time, it was very seldom possible to see anything of the enemy beyond the flashes of their guns. At no time could I distinguish what their ships were. Later the B.F. altered to W., but must have then been out of sight of our B.C.F.

7. The B.C.F., which were on our starboard bow, became heavily engaged about 8.45 p.m., and enemy salvoes could be seen falling amongst the light cruisers and destroyers on their disengaged bow, while one salvo appeared to straddle the rear ship of our line—" Hampshire " or " Duke of Edinburgh." Firing ceased before 10.0 p.m., when it was nearly dark, and by 10 p.m. our Fleet had all turned to Course S., speed 17 knots, for the night.

8. At 2.45 a.m. on 1st June, Course was altered to the N., we being then in Lat. 55° 3 N., Long. 6° 10 E. The morning was very hazy and throughout the forenoon visibility was seldom more than 3 or 4 miles. At 3.40 a.m. a Zeppelin was sighted from the Main Top, South (right astern) a long way off. At 9.0 a.m. there was heavy firing in the direction of the B.F. for about half an hour. Position at noon 1st June was Lat. 56° 16 N., Long. 5° 35 E., Course N.W., speed 20 knots.

9. A short report from the Officer controlling in the Fore Top —Lieutenant-Commander G. C. Dillon, R.N.—is enclosed.

I have the honour to be,
Sir,
Your obedient Servant,
E. LEATHAM,

The Rear Admiral Commanding   Captain.
   Second Cruiser Squadron.

Enclosure to my (" Cochrane's ") Letter No. 143/B.W. of 2 June 1916.

About 4.0 p.m. heard firing on starboard bow.
View, during practically the whole of the action was obscured by funnel smoke of " Minotaur."

Visibility was very variable the whole time.

Battle Fleet opened fire and deployed into single line. No splashes of enemy shots were visible.

Sighted B.C.F. taking station ahead of B.F.

L.C.S. on our starboard beam engaged, supported by B.C.F. Saw occasional glimpses of enemy ships through the smoke, but could not make out details. Our salvoes appeared to be falling close to enemy unit, spread of about 500 yards.

B.C.F. and L.C.S. ceased firing, and L.C.S. took station in rear of B.C.F., Cruiser Squadron being on port quarter of B.C.F. throughout.

Later, B.C.F. engaged enemy at what appeared to be fairly close range. Flashes of enemy guns were visible from " Cochrane."

Enemy salvoes were consistently about 2,000 yards over B.C.F. and appeared very ragged. A number of shell were observed to burst on graze.

B.C.F., L.C.S. and Cruisers turned to port; enemy fired one or two salvoes at rear ship of cruiser line (" Chester ") which fell over. A few minutes later enemy fired a star shell which lit up an area of about 1,000 yards.

About 3.0 a.m. sighted B.C.F. and L.C.S.

About 4.0 a.m. Zeppelin was sighted astern. L.C.S. opened fire at her shortly afterwards.

E. LEATHAM,
Captain.

CAPTAIN'S REPORT—H.M.S. " SHANNON."

No. M. 6/1.

H.M.S. " Shannon,"

SIR,   4th June 1916.

I HAVE the honour to enclose herewith the following :—

(1) Report on the proceedings of H.M.S. " Shannon," including signals received, in company with your Flag during the 24 hours from Noon, 31st May, to Noon, 1st June 1916.

(2) Report by the Officer in the Control Top.

(3) Report by the Squadron Wireless Officer, Lieutenant Charles G. Fothergill, R.M.L.I., who was on board H.M.S. " Shannon."[1]

(4) List of the cyphers received.[1]

I have the honour to be,
Sir,
Your, obedient Servant,
F. DUMARESQ,
Captain.

The Rear Admiral Commanding,
  Second Cruiser Squadron,
    H.M.S. " Minotaur."

---

[1] Not printed.

PROCEEDINGS OF H.M.S. "SHANNON," 2ND CRUISER SQUADRON, DURING THE PERIOD FROM NOON, 31ST MAY, TO NOON, 1ST JUNE 1916.

Dispositions.

The Cruisers were in L.S. 1–12, and were spread in the following order :—

"Cochrane"   "Shannon"   "Minotaur"   "Hampshire." from North to South.

The 1st Cruiser Squadron were spread continuing the line to the southward.

"Chester" and "Canterbury" were stationed about 6 miles ahead of the Cruiser Line.

Noon.

"Shannon's" position Lat. 58·10 N., 3·31 E. Course, S. 50 E., advancing 16 knots.

Positions.

C.-in-C.'s reference position, 58·9 N., 2·59 E.

Weather.

Visibility about 15 miles. Sea calm. Horizon slightly misty.

Full Speed.

Received the C.-in-C.'s general signal to raise steam for Full Speed.

P.M.

2.55.   Cruisers increased to 18 knots.

5.10.   Destroyer "Hardy" screening "Shannon" proceeded to investigate a Norwegian Barque, she was ordered by signal to keep on her course (1710). Time did not permit of investigation.

5.20.   Passed Norwegian Barque "Candace" about five cables on starboard beam steering N.N.W.

Submarines.

5.25.   Opened fire on Periscope on Starboard Quarter. Submarine appeared to come from direction of Barque.

5.27.   Periscope reported on port Quarter. Opened fire. These submarines were apparently waiting near the Barque in case she were boarded.

5.35.   "Hampshire" opened fire on a Periscope and hauled out of line towards it.

5.38.   "Shannon" stationed "Hardy" six cables ahead.

Heavy Firing.

5.40.   Heard heavy firing S.S.W.

5.45.   A Danish Steamer with the Funnel Markings of the Danish United Steamship Company bearing South, crossed ahead from starboard to Port. This ship altered course twice when on port bow and reduced speed. Considered suspicious.

P.M.

5.50. Observed Gun Flashes S.S.W., visibility now was from 4 to 5 miles. Grey ships were observed from the Fore Top.

5.55. Opened Fire on Periscope on starboard quarter. Observed tremendous explosion about this time and bearing S.

6. 5. III. B.C.S. sighted S. 30 E., 5 miles, steering S.W. to join B.C.F.

6. 8. III. B.C.S. at this time altered course to the northward.

6.11. At this time " Cochrane " rejoined from the northward. " Minotaur " now altered course gradually 32 points to port.

6.26. " Minotaur " stationed attached T.B.D.'s one mile on port beam.

6.28. Observed Battle Fleet deploying to S.E. by E.

6.38. Visibility now about six miles.

Observed " Duke of Edinburgh " bearing South between K.G.V. and the enemy. At this time also " Chester " was observed approaching from the Southward to take station in the Cruiser Line having been damaged in action.

6.53. Passed the XIth Flotilla on the starboard beam.

6.58. " Lion " leading Battle Cruisers bearing S. 40 W., 5½ miles.

7.14. " Duke of Edinburgh " joined, coming from the van. " Lion " and Battle Cruisers altered course to port and opened fire to S.W.

7.26. Cruisers trying to cross ahead of van to take up Battle Station. At this time K.G.V. leading the van was six cables distant on the starboard bow of " Shannon." If it had not been for the Battle Fleet reducing to 15 knots, the Cruisers would have been unable to cross ahead.

7.26. XIth and XIIth Flotillas now came up on the beam between K.G.V. and the Cruisers to take station in readiness for attack. At this time the IVth L.C.S. passed through these Flotillas and took station on the engaged bow of K.G.V.

8. 0. Observed " K.G.V. " altering to starboard.

8. 5. At this moment " Shannon " passed a small boat painted grey inside and out, three cables on the starboard beam. This boat looked like a Norwegian Pram.

About 8.15 passed many dead fish floating, also one ammunition case of foreign pattern floating.

8.18. Lost sight of " K.G.V. " at this time on a bearing N. 10 E. Battle Cruisers on the starboard bow opened fire to the westward.

8.30. Observed a salvo of five 12-in. fall about 1,000 yards short of " Minotaur."

About the same time one heavy shell fell about 500 yards beyond " Hampshire."

P,M.	Cruisers then altered course to port together to open the range.
8.40.	"Shannon" struck some object which bumped along under the bottom.
8.45.	"K.G.V." in sight N.N.E. 5 miles. "Lion" and Battle Cruisers bear W. 6 miles.
8.47.	Hauled out to starboard to clear the smoke from "Minotaur" and "Cochrane."
9.37.	Sighted "Lion" and Battle Cruisers on port bow altering to port.
10.15.	About this time the enemy fired a large magnesium light lasting two minutes, bearing N.W.
A.M.	
2.45.	"Lion" and B.C.S. at this time in sight bearing South 6 miles, and the IVth L.C.S. West 6 miles.
3.19.	Heard "Indomitable" firing at Airship. This airship passed to the southward of the Battle Cruisers steering S.W.
5.11.	Sighted Vth B.S. South five miles.
5.20.	Sighted "Colossus" S. 46 W. four miles.
7. 0.	Passed Dutch Fishing Smack.
7. 5.	Passed Dutch Schooner "Europa."
7.40.	Sighted "Agincourt" and rear ships of 1st B.S. with Destroyers N. 18 W., 5 miles.
9. 0.	Heard firing N.N.W. This was most probably "Marksman" sinking "Sparrowhawk."
9.19.	"Minotaur" sent two Destroyers to examine a floating object which looked like the conning tower of a submarine. T.B.D.'s reported it was a capsized ship, probably German Destroyer. Considered most probable this was "Sparrowhawk" not yet completely sunk. This was the position signalled by "Marksman."
9.23.	Observed Steam Trawler on starboard beam steaming fast S.S.W.
9.55.	Passed a large patch of oil on the starboard hand.
10.10.	Sighted IVth L.C.S. and Vth B.S. bearing S. by W.

NOTE.—Signals, being included in record of British Messages, have been omitted from this Enclosure.

A REPORT BY LIEUTENANT-COMMANDER (G) F. W. BENNETT, CONTROL OFFICER STATIONED IN FORE TOP (PRIMARY CONTROL).

H.M.S. "Shannon."

May 31st.

Noon to 3. p.m.—"Shannon" steaming in a South Easterly direction. Half of Anti-T.B. Armanent closed up on Submarine Watch. Half of Main Armament manned.

At 3 p.m.—"Action" Stations. Everything prepared in every way for immediate action with enemy.

Sea calm.   Wind 2–3.   Visibility seven miles and decreasing.

Between 4 and 5.30 p.m.—Periscopes were reported on both quarters (probably 3 submarines in all, one showing two periscopes); all were fired on by 12-pdrs. bearing and 30 rds. of 12-pdr. 18 cwt. Common shell were expended.

From Fore Top none were actually seen, these reports being received from aft; these periscopes are definitely reported by the following Officers :—

> Major Troup, R.M.
> Lieut. Durnford, R.N.
> Lieut. Lambert, R.N.
> Lieut. Williams, R.M.

as well as by a number of Gunlayers, Guns Crews, a signalman, and a Rangetaker.

No direct hits on them are claimed, but many shells burst in their immediate proximity and all appeared to drop astern or dive.

It is noted that during this period when Submarines were undoubtedly present in considerable numbers a large sail, flying a conspicuously new Norwegian Ensign, with name " Candace " " Norge," and two Norwegian Ensigns painted on her starboard side, was also in the vicinity.

I do not think that she had been examined, and under the circumstances it certainly was not possible for Second C.S. to do so.

At about 5.35. " Hampshire," who was at this time next astern of " Shannon," opened fire on a periscope and turned out of line to Port in an endeavour to ram submarine.

At about 5.40 heavy firing was heard on Starboard bow *i.e.*, from a Southerly direction), this was presumed to be our Battle Cruisers and 5th B.S., who had been reported previously as by W/T as being engaged.

At 5.50.—Gun flashes were seen in this direction.   Visibility of Grey ships was at this time about 10,000 yards.

At 5.55.—Our Battle Cruisers were sighted with their Starboard sides engaged with an enemy invisible from us—at about this time a large explosion was seen to occur apparently ahead of and beyond our Battle Cruisers.   The tongue of flame from it appeared to me to reach a height of about 300 ft. and to hang into the air for a very appreciable time (say 20 secs.).   It was a dullish yellow in colour and left no smoke visible from " Shannon " on subsidence.

From this time until about 9.10 p.m. our Battle Cruisers were intermittently engaged.

At 6.30 p.m.—Some of our Battleships were heard to be in Action on Starboard Quarter of " Shannon," but it was not known with whom they were engaged.   No enemy shells appeared to fall close to them.

From this time onward reference is made to the attached sketches[1] made from rough drawings taken at the time by Sub-Lieutenant B. C. Brooke, R.N., who was stationed as Rate keeper in Fore Top of " Shannon."

Fig. (1). Conditions at 6.50 p.m.

" Shannon's " course, S. 40 E.

" Chester " had just come over from Westward and taken station astern.

Battle Fleet apparently engaged with an enemy bearing S.W.

Battle Cruisers were not now engaged.

Fig. (2). Conditions at 7.5 p.m.

" Shannon's " Course S. 10 W.

Second Cruiser Squadron endeavouring to take up station on engaged bow of Battle Fleet.

Battle Fleet still engaged.

Battle Cruisers not engaged and turned slightly to Port.

Fig. (3). Conditions at 7.22 p.m.

" Duke of Edinburgh " had now taken station astern of " Shannon."

Battle Cruisers were engaged, and had wheeled to Starboard. Leading ships of 2nd C.S. starting to cross bows of Battle Fleet from Port to Starboard.

Observed two enemy ships apparently on fire on Starboard beam of centre of Battle Fleet.

Battle Cruisers firing intermittently.

Light Cruisers making way through 11th and 12th Destroyer Flotillas to attack enemy Light Cruisers.

Fig. (4). Conditions at 7.31 p.m.

Battle Cruisers heavily engaged.

Observed a few enemy shells falling short of Battle Cruisers, but the great majority of splashes could not be seen at all from " Shannon."

" Minotaur " and " Cochrane " had crossed bows of K.G.V. from port to starboard.

" Shannon " was unable to do so and had to shear off to Port.

Light Cruiser Squadron engaged bearing N.W. from " Shannon."

At 7.50 p.m. " Shannon " crossed to engaged bow of " K.G.V.", visibility decreasing.

At 8.0 p.m. Battle fleet altered course to starboard to close enemy and by 8.15 were lost to sight bearing about N. by E.

At 8.5 p.m. passed small empty boat, apparently a skiff not of British Naval build.

8.10 to 8.15 p.m. observed many dead fish floating, as if killed by explosion of mine or ship, also one ammunition case of foreign pattern.

---

[1] No trace of receipt at the Admiralty.

Passed another empty boat, looking like cutter of foreign pattern.

At 8.15 p.m.—Battle Fleet out of sight from " Shannon " was heard to be in Action.

British Battle Cruisers re-opened fire on enemy, probably enemy Battle Cruisers, who answered hotly.

Fig. (5). Conditions at 8.27 p.m.

Course of 2nd C.S., West.

" Shannon " was now in a position, for the first time, in which her guns could be trained on to what were considered, it is believed rightly, to have been the enemy's flashes. This was done, and the Gunlayers subsequently reported no great difficulty in taking them as their point of aim. Sights were set to a purely arbitrary range of 15,000 yards and fire could have been opened, though with no possibility of either range-taking or spotting the result might have been of negligible value.

Taking into consideration the desirability of husbanding ammunition for the closer Action which appeared at that time to be imminent, and the fact that no permissive order to open fire had been received, fire was withheld.

A salvo of enemy shell were observed to fall about 1,000 yards short of " Minotaur " and another salvo fell " over " between " Shannon " and " Duke of Edinburgh " and some straggling shots, possibly rico's, also fell close.

At 8.30 " Minotaur " altered course outwards to S. 25 W. " Shannon " followed, and although the Battle Cruisers Action was continued no more enemy flashes or Fall of shot were observed.

Visibility of grey ship was now about 9,000 yards.

At 8.40 p.m.—A report was received from Transmitting station and from Main Top that a submarine had been rammed by " Shannon." Though not seen, this was distinctly felt in Fore Top, and on subsequent inquiry it appears that Officers and men in Engine Rooms, Boiler Rooms, Magazines, and Passages, and in all Turrets noticed and remarked on a loud bumping and grating sound, and considerable shock to the ship at about this time.

At 8.45 p.m.—" King George V." again sighted bearing N.N.E· Visibility had again improved and her range was estimated at 10,000 yards.

Conformed to her course, i.e. S. 75 W. to close enemy.

At 9.10 p.m.—Battle Cruisers reported that they had lost enemy in the mist.

At about 9.30 p.m.—Hands were sent to Night Action Stations and all secondary armament was kept completely manned all night. 9·2-in. Turrets were kept completely manned and 7·5-in. turrets manned with reduced Crews.

The night passed without incident.

June 1st.

At 2.20 a.m.—Hands were sent to Action stations.

Desultory firing was heard from 3.0 till 3.30 a.m. and again for about 15 minutes at 4 a.m.

The remainder of the Morning and Forenoon passed without incident.

At Noon.—Reduced armament to ordinary daily watch-keeping conditions.

FREDERIC BENNETT,
Lieut.-Comdr. (G).

No. 111/001/13.

Commander-in-Chief,
Home Fleets.

Submitted in continuation of my report No. 110/001/13 of 4th June 1916.

H. L. HEATH,
" Minotaur,"   Rear-Admiral.
5th June 1916.

CAPTAIN'S REPORT—H.M.S. "DUKE OF EDINBURGH."[1]

Enclosure No. 11 to submission No. 1415/0022 of 20.6.16.

From C.-in-C., Home Fleets.

NOON 31ST MAY TO NOON 1ST JUNE 1916.

No. 1/32.

H.M.S. "Duke of Edinburgh,"
SIR,   4th June 1916.

I HAVE the honour to report that at Noon on the 31st May 1916 the First Cruiser Squadron was spread ahead of the Battle Squadron in accordance with "Cruising Diagram No. 1" as follows :—"Defence" and "Warrior" in position "D," "Duke of Edinburgh" in position "F," "Black Prince" in position "G," ships five miles apart, Course S. 50° E. advancing 16 knots.

At 1.6 p.m. a destroyer was sighted, bearing South distant about 5 miles, and at 1.33 p.m. the "Black Prince" reported that she was the "Moon."

At 2.21 p.m. the "Galatea's" signal to the Senior Officer, Battle Cruiser Fleet, reporting the presence of hostile cruisers was received.

At 2.40 p.m. the Senior Officer of Cruisers ordered steam to be raised for full speed.

At 3.20 p.m. Cruisers opened out to 8 miles apart in accordance with Signal from the Commander-in-Chief and increased speed of advance to 18 knots.

At 3.56 p.m. Course was altered to S.E. by S. by order of the Senior Officer, Cruisers.

At 4.40 p.m. "Defence" signalled that she was steering S.E. to close the "Minotaur"—presumably on account of the

---

[1] Plate 11*a*.

decrease in visibility. This Signal was passed to " Black Prince,"
and " Duke of Edinburgh " altered course and increased speed
to close " Defence."

By 5.30 p.m. the distance apart of Cruisers was about six
miles and the visibility was slightly greater.

At 5.40 p.m. " Black Prince " signalled by searchlight,
" Light Cruisers, 3, bearing S.S.E., steering N.E., challenged
answered correctly " (which signal was passed to " Defence ").
At the same moment the Light Cruisers were sighted by " Duke
of Edinburgh " and observed to be in action ; the enemy were
invisible except for the flashes of their guns. The Light Cruisers
appeared to be the 2nd Light Cruiser Squadron.

At 5.42 p.m. I altered course to port to close " Defence "
by signal and increased to full speed ; at the same time I observed
that " Black Prince " had turned about 12 points to port. This
was the last I saw of " Black Prince," but at 8.56 p.m. intercepted a signal from her, " Urgent, Submarine on port hand,
Lat. 56° 55 N., Long. 6° 11 E. 2048."

2. The first indication of any proximity of the enemy Fleet
was at 5.40 p.m., when I observed dropping shots falling between
me and the Light Cruisers and in the distance a large amount
of smoke and mist and I presumed that they were being chased
by a superior force.

At 5.50 p.m. the " Defence " and " Warrior " were engaging
a three-funnelled enemy Cruiser, on fire aft, with their starboard
broadsides, having turned about 4 points to port.

At 6.8 p.m. I altered course to Starboard and opened fire
(2 salvoes of port 9·2-in.) at the same disabled Cruiser. I then
observed (on my starboard hand) the van of our Battle Cruiser
Squadron approaching on a Course almost at right angles to my
own, and altered course to port parallel to them. The Battle
Cruisers approached and passed us hotly engaged with the enemy
on their starboard side. Then I observed the " Defence '
followed by the " Warrior " alter course across the bows of the
Battle Cruisers, the latter passing very close to the bows of the
" Lion." Being prevented by the Battle Cruisers from following
the " Defence " I proceeded to take up Station on the engaged
bow of the Battle Fleet. Whilst being passed by the Battle
Cruisers we were also passed by a large number of Light Cruisers
and Destroyers proceeding to take up their position at the head
of the line, and it was at this period that we and they passed
through a zone of the enemy's fire, namely, the overs from the
Battle Cruiser Fleet (heavy projectiles and splinters of H.E.
Shells).

3. The Battle Cruiser Fleet, Light Cruisers and Destroyers
gained on me and I was then left on the starboard bow of the
leading Battleship ; but the volumes of smoke we were making
was masking the van Battleships and I crossed to get ahead,
when in that position I saw the Second Cruiser Squadron and
turned to port to join up with them, and remained with them
until noon on 1st June.

4. Whilst ahead of the Battle Fleet at about 6.47 p.m. the Control Officer aloft—Lieutenant-Commander (G) John K. B. Birch, Royal Navy—observed the track of a Torpedo passing from Starboard to Port, and it was owing to his vigilance in seeing the Torpedo and his promptitude in informing me on the Upper Bridge that I was able to avoid it by putting the helm hard over to port, otherwise it would have undoubtedly struck my starboard side aft.

5. The highest speed worked up to in endeavouring to close ' Defence " and failing that in proceeding to the van of the Battle Line was 136 revolutions—about 22 knots, this is the same number of revolutions steamed on the Contractors' 8 hour Full Power Trial in November 1905. This took about half an hour to work up to.

6. The volume of smoke made by this Class of Ship on all occasions of increasing to full speed is very large and thick and masks the fire of many ships in the vicinity, so that positions different to those originally intended or generally ordered have to be taken up.

1 *   *   *   *   *

I have the honour to be,
Sir,
Your obedient Servant,
HENRY BLACKETT,

The Rear-Admiral Commanding   Captain.
Second Cruiser Squadron.

REPORT OF CONTROL OFFICER ON ACTION OF 31st MAY 1916.

H.M.S. " Duke of Edinburgh,"
Sir,   4th June 1916.

I HAVE the honour to report on the action of the 31st May 1916.

P.M.

5.20. Sighted 2 light cruisers on starboard bow, steaming towards us at high speed and in action. Impossible to see the enemy, only flashes of his guns visible.

5.40. The action closing us rapidly, still very hazy, visibility 6,000 to 8,000 yards, occasional glimpses of enemy.

5.50. Saw what appeared to be two enemy battle cruisers. " Defence " and " Warrior " opened fire with their starboard broadsides. A number of Light Cruisers passing, at close range, between this ship and the enemy prevented us opening fire.

6.00. " Defence " and " Warrior " in action. I noticed the " Defence " was straddled twice by what appeared to be large calibre projectiles.

---

1 Part omitted here, referring solely to personnel, recommendations, &c., in no way bearing on the course of the action.

P.M.

6.08.   Altered course to Starboard; this took us clear of our Light Cruisers and enabled us to open fire on an enemy 3-funnelled cruiser—apparently the " Augsburg." At this time the enemy's heavy ships appear to have turned to the Southward, leaving this Cruiser isolated, and for a short time a number of ships concentrated on her. She received a good deal of punishment, was much reduced in speed, on fire aft, and was struck twice amidships by a heavy projectile. She continued firing her bow gun at intervals.

6.12.   The Battle Cruiser Squadron overtook and passed us, they were engaged with the enemy abaft their beam— the enemy had apparently resumed their original course—and

6.25.   From 6.12 to 6.25 a number of projectiles fell short of and over the ship. I noticed " Defence " and " War-rior " circle to starboard and pass between the Battle Cruisers and enemy, apparently with the intention of forming up astern of the Battle Cruisers. While turning up I observed a fire in " Defence," and also saw an explosion on board " Warrior," which might have been a torpedo on her starboard side and abreast of her foremast.

6.35.   The action drew away, lost sight of the enemy.

6.38.   Passed sunken vessel; she was broken in halves, with the bow and stern out of the water. Upper works painted white or light grey, green stripe, probably at waterline and red bottom colour. The crew were in a small boat, and were going towards a destroyer as we passed.

6.47.   Observed track of a torpedo, approaching from starboard, which was avoided by altering course to Starboard and passed 50 yards clear astern.

6.55.   2nd and 7th Cruiser Squadrons arrived. Took station astern of " Hampshire." The Battle Squadron were now in action. No enemy visible from our position, only flashes of guns.

7.30.   Still endeavouring to get into position ahead of Battle Fleet, our Battle Cruisers altering course to Starboard (approximately S.W. by W.) to head off enemy.

7.55.   Several rounds of 3-pr. fired at submarines reported on our port bow by " Hampshire." I think this was only a school of porpoises; in any case the reported position was one most advantageous to attack us or the Battle Fleet, and though a careful watch was kept, no tracks of torpedoes were seen.

P.M.

8.00.   In position on Battle Fleet.

8.25.⎫ Battle Cruisers engaging again; saw flashes of enemy's
to ⎬   guns. Occasional firing going on, enemy invisible
9.20.⎭ from our position.

9.25.   Star shell fired.

10.00. Too dark for long range firing, went to night Defence
        Stations.

Nothing more seen of the enemy.

I have the honour to be,

Sir,

Your obedient Servant,

J. K. B. BIRCH,

Lieutenant-Commander (G).

Captain Henry Blackett, Royal Navy,
    H.M.S. "Duke of Edinburgh."

CAPTAIN'S REPORTS—H.M.S. "WARRIOR."

Enclosure No. 12 to Submission No. 1415/0022 of 20/6/16
    from C.-in-C., Home Fleets.

H.M.S. "Engadine,"

Sir,   31st May 1916.

I HAVE the honour to report that I abandoned H.M.S.
"Warrior" in Lat. 57° 21' N., Long. 3° 2' E. under the following
circumstances :—

2. "Warrior" and "Defence," after sinking an enemy
Light Cruiser, came under the fire of the enemy's Battle Cruisers.
"Defence" was observed to blow up shortly afterwards, having
been struck by two salvoes in quick succession. "Warrior"
also received pretty severe punishment, both engine rooms being
very soon flooded by hits well below the water line, as well as
by several hits about the water line and through the upper deck.
The engines, however, continued to revolve and carried the
Ship out of action in rear of our line.

3. Every possible step was taken to shore bulkheads, stop
leaks, and cover holes in the deck.

4. H.M.S. "Engadine" at my request, took "Warrior" in
tow at about 8 p.m., and at 9 p.m. I signalled by W/T to the
Commander-in-Chief :—

"Both engines disabled, am in tow of H.M.S. 'Engadine.'
Proceeding to Cromarty."

5. At this time I had every hope of saving the Ship. During
the night the wind freshened from S.S.W. to S.W., and the sea
continued to rise. This made the Ship worse, and, combined
with the seas washing over the decks, flooded the main deck.

6. After obtaining the opinions of the Engineer Commander, Commander, and next Senior unwounded executive Officer, as to the chances of saving the Ship, as well as my own personal inspection, I decided that, as it was impossible to save the Ship under the existing weather conditions, she should be abandoned and the personnel saved.

7. I then ordered the " Engadine " to come alongside, a proceeding involving considerable risk owing to the weather, and transferred the whole ship's company to her, including badly wounded cot cases, one of whom, owing to the motion of the two ships, and in spite of every care, was dropped over board in the operation, but was afterwards recovered dead.

8. After consulting the Officer in Command of " Engadine," I decided he should make for Queensferry, and I directed " Engadine " to report to the Commander-in-Chief the position in which " Warrior " was abandoned. This signal could not be passed owing to W/T congestion till 2.0 p.m.

9. I regret to report the casualties as shown on the attached list. A list of which has been telegraphed to Admiralty.[1]

10. A fuller report will be made as soon as opportunity admits, but I must at once state that all ranks and ratings behaved in accordance with the finest traditions of the Service, and every exertion was made to save the Ship subsequently.

I have the honour to be,
Sir,
Your obedient Servant,
V. B. MOLTENO,

Commander-in-Chief,   Captain.
Home Fleets.

Enclosure No. 13 to Submission No. 1415/0022 of 20/6/16
from C.-in-C., Home Fleets.

H.M.S. " WARRIOR," ACTION OF THE 31ST MAY 1916.

Admiralty,

SIR,   7 June 1916.

IN amplification of my letter of the 1st June (dated in error the 31st May), reporting the abandonment of H.M.S. " Warrior " on 1st June, I have the honour to report as follows :—

GENERAL NARRATIVE OF EVENTS.

At about 5.40 p.m., G.M.T., being in company with " Defence " (5 cables astern) in position D (L.S. 1–10), steering S.E. by S. at 20 knots, flashes were observed about 2 points before the Starboard beam, which I imagined (quite correctly) were our battle cruisers, engaging the enemy's battle cruisers. Our own light cruisers appeared to be on the disengaged bow of our battle

---

[1] List not printed.

cruisers, steering so that I was on their Starboard bow. These light cruisers came in sight at the same time as the more distant flashes of our battle cruisers guns. As our light cruisers approached smaller natures of projectiles were observed to be falling, generally speaking short of them, also heavier natures of projectiles apparently short of the enemy Battle Cruisers, fired by our own Battle Cruisers. These projectiles were seen to be falling before any enemy vessels were seen.

At about 5.47 I observed about 4 points on my Starboard bow (course still S.E. by S.) three, and possibly four, enemy light cruisers.

" Defence " altered course about 3 points to port and brought the second or third light cruiser, which was closer than the others, to the bearing of Green 80. She then signalled " open fire " and " ship interval 12 secs."

This vessel had 3 funnels and appeared to be one of the type building in Germany for Russia of which Lieutenant (G) had obtained a silhouette.

I ordered speed to be increased to 21 knots to close " Defence." Three salvoes were fired by " Defence " and three by " Warrior," but all our shots falling short, I ordered " check fire." " Defence " then altered course to Starboard, bringing the enemy light cruiser almost ahead and shortly after, by another turn to Starboard, to about Red 40. Time noted of making this second alteration of course was 6.1 for " Warrior."

Our light cruisers had now passed under our stern fairly close to us and projectiles of 6-in. and 4-in. guns were falling fairly well round us from the aforementioned light cruiser. At 6.5 Port guns had opened fire on the same enemy. I saw her hit both by " Warrior's " and " Defence's " 2nd salvo, and she appeared to be crippled, and very soon nearly stopped. " Defence " continued to close her to about 5,500 yards before turning away to Starboard at 6.17, and " Warrior " closed to about 3 cables of " Defence " going about 135 revolutions (just 22 knots).

At 6.19 " Warrior " turned to Starboard, and " Defence " was observed to be hit by two salvoes in quick succession. A huge furnace appeared to be under her fore turret for quite an appreciable time (10 secs. perhaps) and then she blew up and disappeared.

From the time of about 6.7 onwards " Defence " and " Warrior " were being straddled by heavy salvoes (11-in. to 14-in.).

At 6.17 I ordered the Lieut.-Commander (N) to work the ship from the conning tower, and entered it myself and continued to work the ship from that position till the action was over, Lieut.-Commander (T) and Signal Bosn. remaining just outside, as there was no room for them inside. A shell a few moments afterwards wrecked the bridge and wounded Lieut.-Commander (T) (Lieut.-Commander Bromley) outside the C.T.

T 2

" Defence " having gone at about 6.20 p.m. and light cruiser Russian type sinking just afterwards, I decided to withdraw and obstruct the fire of the B.C. fleet and 5th B.S. as little as possible, but I noticed that the ship was losing her speed as I turned away, and sent a message to keep the engines going at all costs.

At 6.32 I received a report that Starboard engine room was disabled, and at 6.33 that both engine rooms were disabled, and shortly afterwards that there were two or three fires on the Main Deck, one especially bad round the Ship's and Armament offices, which blocked access to the Engine Rooms. During the whole time the " Warrior " was withdrawing she drew the fire of at least four of the enemy's heavy ships, first they appeared to be Battle Cruisers, but latterly were certainly Battle Ships.

I passed some distance astern of the 5th B.S. except " Warspite," who was considerably astern of the remainder of 5th B.S. and to Starboard (enemy's side) of the line. I should have passed astern of her also had she not turned to Starboard and passed under my stern, thereby screening me from the enemy's fire. This was a particularly gallant act as the " Warspite " had just been having a very severe pounding herself, and she probably saved " Warrior " being sunk then and there.

" Warrior " then passed the rear of our own Battle Fleet and observed one of our armoured cruisers almost astern of the Battle Fleet, about 4 miles away.

Lieut. Sargent, R.N.R., who was stationed in the Main top, reported that he observed a ship of " Black Prince " class blow up about 10 minutes after the " Defence." Owing to officers and men having dispersed, I am unable to get this report confirmed, but I think it quite probable.

After passing the rear of our battle fleet I shaped a course for Kinnaird Head, and almost at once sighted the " Engadine." I directed her to stand by me, as I was badly disabled. Both engine rooms were filled with water to within 10 ft. of the Main Deck, but the engines · continued to revolve, giving the ship a speed of quite 10 to 12 knots.

Having ascertained that there was no possibility of the engines working for more than another hour, at 8 p.m. I directed H.M.S. " Engadine " to take " Warrior " in tow, which she did, and proceeded towing at a speed of 8.2 knots for the first hour, and I had good hopes of saving the ship.

At 7 a.m. next day, speed was about 6 knots, as " Warrior " by then had sunk so low aft.

Officers and men worked most heroically in shoring bulkheads, stopping shell holes and leaks, and manning the hand pumps, but owing to the rising sea and the list to Port which was increasing, it was impossible to keep the water from rising on Main Deck.

At about 7.45 a.m. I decided that unless the ship were abandoned immediately most of the ship's company and all the wounded would perish; I therefore decided to abandon her. However, as I did not know but that a vessel might be close by to tow her, and that the weather might possibly get quite smooth, I closed all the W.T. openings before quitting her. As it turned out the ship was quitted only at the very last moment, after which it would have been impossible for the "Engadine" to get alongside and take off the ship's company.

I consider that two to three hours was the maximum time she could have remained afloat, under the weather conditions that prevailed. Every sea was washing over the upper deck, and her stern was within 3 ft. of the water, and a list of about 6° to Port (Windward).

The position in which "Warrior" was abandoned is estimated to be 15 miles North Magnetic from that given originally, viz., Lat. 57.21 N., Long. 3.2 E. This position is determined after correcting the reckoning when "Engadine" made May Island at 1 a.m. next morning. At the time I signalled Lat. 57.21 N., Long. 3.2 E. this position agreed almost exactly with the reckoning of "Engadine" and the position was only subsequently found to be in error as explained above.

I have already forwarded through the V.A., B.C.F., the action I took in regard to the confidential books and papers on board, and an additional copy is forwarded herewith.[1]

To assist in making out an accurate account of the battle I have drawn out the attached series of plans[2] illustrating the positions of other vessels relative to "Warrior," but, of course, all the vessels that were within the radius of vision are not put down, but those only which I and my Lieut.-Commander (N) and Lieut. (G) can remember observing.

The times were taken by my Clerk, Mr. O. H. Matthews in the lower C.T. with a watch set for G.M.T.

As regards the movements of the other ships of the squadron, just before opening fire I enquired what were the movements of the other two ships of 1st C.S. I was informed that the ship at G was moving to her station on deployment, that at F was trying to follow "Warrior," and as I looked round I saw the ship at F about 2½ miles W. by S. from "Warrior."

I saw neither of them again during the action, but I was informed just as "Warrior" left the action and got out of range, that "Duke of Edinburgh" (but probably this was "Black Prince") had been under very heavy fire during the action. I cannot say who the officer or man was who made this report, but it was not Lieutenant Sargent, R.N.R.

H.M.S. "Engadine" was most skilfully handled, first when taking in tow and subsequently in coming alongside. Her Captain and Officers behaved splendidly in caring for us, and I am making an application for the Royal Humane Society Medal for Flight-Lieutenant Rutland, R.N., who gallantly risked his life to save a wounded man.

---

[1] Not printed.　　　　　[2] Plate 26 a—g.

I am forwarding this incompleted narrative with the attached plans, which are not to scale, in order to give a general idea of what occurred, but I shall forward a further amplifying report in a few days.

All Officers and Men, except those in the following list, have been sent to their respective Depôts to be kitted up, and to have 10 days' leave. The Officers mentioned below I am retaining in London to complete my reports. I have applied for and obtained a room at the Admiralty where we can meet and where I can be communicated with :—

> Commander G. J. P. Ingham.
> Lieutenant-Commander E. J. Birch.
> Engineer-Commander H. W. Kitching.
> Fleet-Paymaster R. W. Walker.
> Lieutenant R. Mends.
> Engineer-Lieutenant G. Morgan.
> Artificer-Engineer A. J. Daniels.
> Mr. Matthews, Clerk.

By orders of the First Sea Lord, who expressed a wish to see me, I am forwarding a copy of this report direct to the Admiralty.

I have the honour to be,
Sir,
Your obedient Servant,
V. B. MOLTENO,

The Secretary of the Admiralty,   Captain.
   and the Commander-in-Chief,
     Grand Fleet.

Enclosure No. 14 to Submission No. 1415/0022 of 20/6/16
from C.-in-C., Home Fleets.

1 *   *   *   *   *

GENERAL OBSERVATIONS, DATED 8TH JUNE 1916.

By CAPTAIN, H.M.S. " WARRIOR."

Visibility was quite 11 miles at 4.0 p.m., but grew steadily less up to 7 p.m., when it was only about 8 miles.

It was much clearer looking to North and West than towards South and East.

The enemy vessel sunk was the only one which could be certainly recognised by me, but I am almost certain of seeing the " Moltke " as well.

The Signal Boatswain is sure of recognising the " König " or " Kaiser " class of ship.

Lieut.-Commander (N) is certain that leading battleship was one of the " Kaiser " class.

---

[1] Part omitted referring only to damage inflicted on " Warrior."

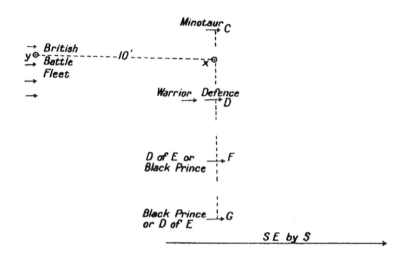

Minotaur C

→ British
y⊙ Battle ----- 10' ----- x⊙
→ Fleet
→

→

Warrior Defence
→   →D

D of E or   F
Black Prince

Black Prince   G
or D of E

S E by S

↖ British Light
↑ Cruiser Squadron
↑ (emerging from mist)
↑ Distant from Warrior
   about 10 miles.

⟨∴⟩ Hereabouts, flashes
    from guns of Battle
    Cruisers, apparently
    firing to South eastward.

Grand Fleet in L S 1 - 10.

*Plate 26*ᵇ

31 - V - 16
5.50 P. M.

Grand Fleet
apparently
commencing
deployment

Warrior → Defence

D of E or
Black Prince ↗

Black Prince
or D of E ↩

Light
Cruiser
Squadron

Enemy Light
Cruiser
(at high speed)

Battle
Cruisers
(firing to SE)

Splashes
apparently
from Battle
Cruisers (British)

SE by S →

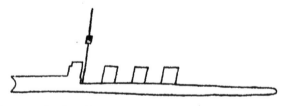

Enemy Light Cruiser as seen from Warrior.

10027· 24260/P1175· (4 ⓘ) 6000·12·20

Malby & Sons. Lith.

Plate 26c

31 - V - 16
5. 56 P. M.

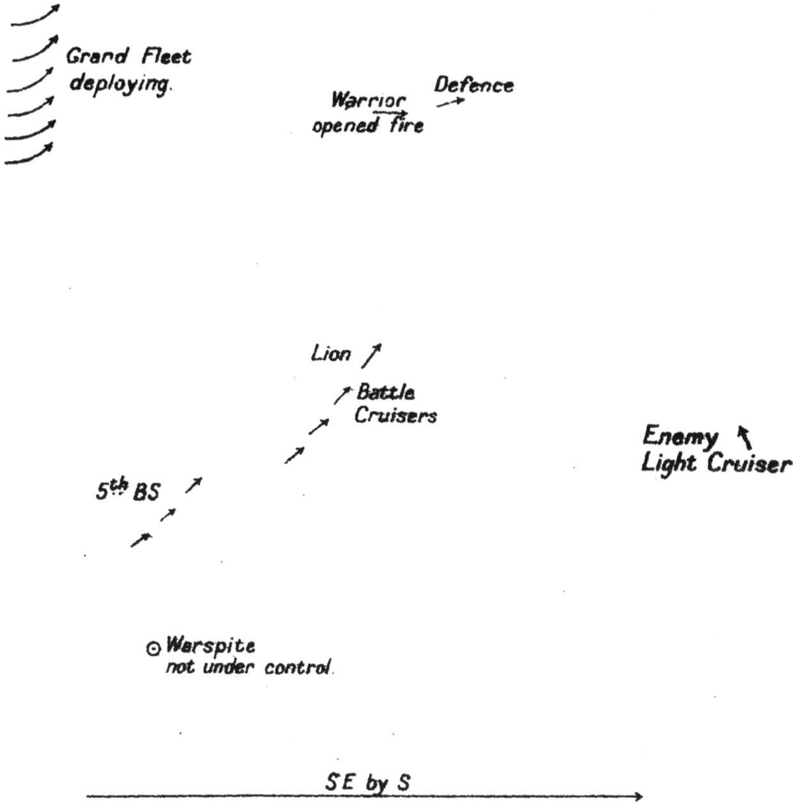

Grand Fleet
deploying.
Warrior
opened fire
Defence
Lion
Battle
Cruisers
Enemy
Light Cruiser
5th BS
Warspite
not under control.
SE by S

10087 · 28288/P1173. (MC). 5000 12·20

Malby & Sons, Lith.

Warrior → _Defence_ ↘

Battle
Cruisers ↑ ↑ ↑ ↑

Enemy
Light Cruiser ↙

5ᵗʰ BS ↑ ↑ ↑

Enemy
Dreadnought ↙

⊙ Warspite

———————— SE by S ————————→

Leading Enemy Dreadnought Kaiser Class.

H027· 2+260/P1173. (4D) 5000·12·20   Malby & Sons.Lith

Battle
Cruisers ↑ ↑ ↑ ↑

↓ Warrior

5.ᵗʰ B S ↑ ↑ ↑

↓ Defence

◎ Warrior

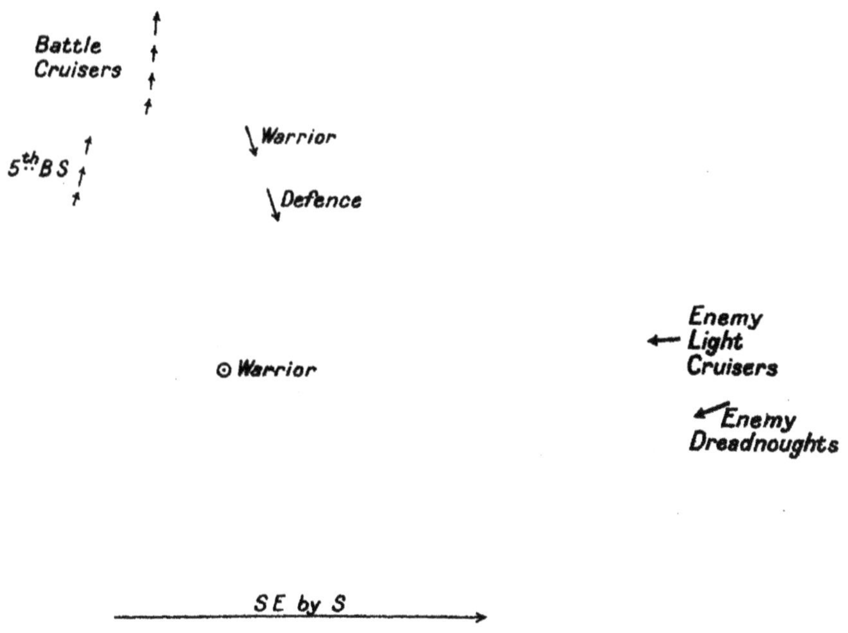

Enemy
← Light
Cruisers

↙ Enemy
Dreadnoughts

SE by S →

10027· 24266/P1173. (M B) 5000·12·20

Malby&Sons.Lith

Plate 26f.

31 - V - 16
6.20 P.M. (about)

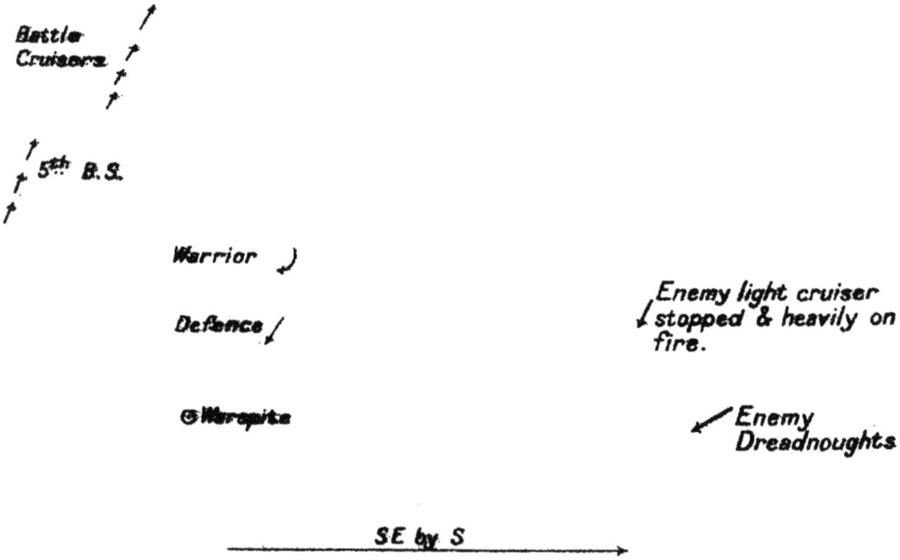

Battle Cruisers
5th B.S.
Warrior
Defence
Warspite
Enemy light cruiser stopped & heavily on fire.
Enemy Dreadnoughts
SE by S

Defence blew up about this time.

[illegible]/PHTO · 2000 · 12 · 20

Malby & Sons. Lith.

Plate 26g

31 - V - 16
6.30 P.M. (about)

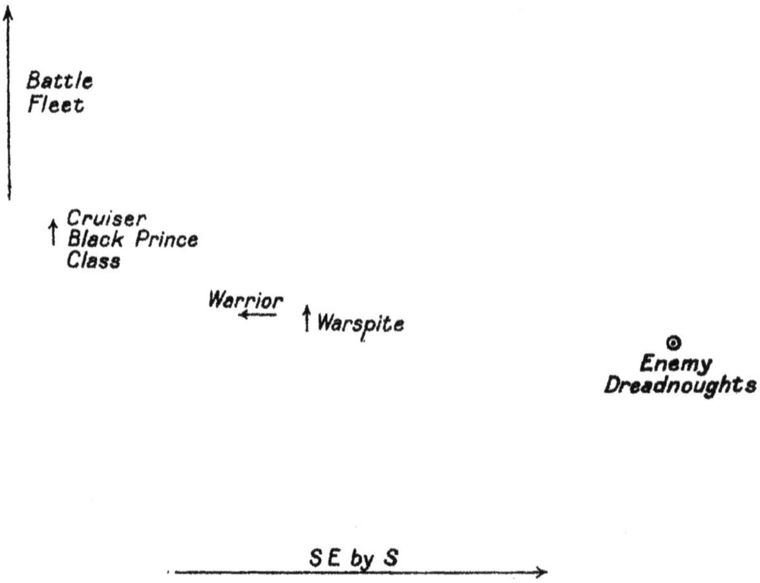
Battle
Fleet
Cruiser
Black Prince
Class
Warrior
Warspite
Enemy
Dreadnoughts
S E by S

Warrior then passed astern of Battle Fleet and was taken in tow by Engadine.

Malby & Sons Lith.

Lieutenant (G) is almost certain of the " Moltke " or " Von der Tann."

Fire from the German heavy ships was by director and very accurate from the first. Salvoes fell close to the ship almost before the enemy could be seen.

Calibration was very close indeed, about 75 yards spread usually.

To the smallness of spread is undoubtedly due the fact that the " Warrior " was not hit more often. The whole salvo missed as a rule. There was practically no spread for direction.

At least three, and probably four, heavy ships were firing at " Warrior " and " Defence " from 6.5 p.m. till 6.40 p.m.

" Warrior " was holed at least fifteen times by 11-in. to 14-in. calibre guns, and about six times by 6-in. or 4-in.; one of the latter hit the fore turret early in the action doing very little damage.

" Warrior " was being hit by 6-in. or 4-in. projectiles before the enemy light cruisers were within range of her guns.

The light cruiser which was sunk was seen to use smoke boxes. These were floating on the water and gave out a large dirty-white cloud which at times completely hid her, and were a great hindrance to the spotting officer.

With regard to spotting, the " over " splashes of a salvo which straddled were usually visible, but this was not the case with shots which fell further over.

Owing to the hazy atmosphere and the great vibration aloft only very low power glasses could be used. The vibration was abnormal owing to rigging being cut.

Spray from splashes fell several times into fore top and put the spotter out of action for about —— (*sic*).

At the time " Warrior " was close to " Warspite " the enemy vessels were no longer visible, but only the flashes of their guns, while " Warspite " and " Warrior " were receiving very heavy fire.

There were 100 casualties, 19 of these were in the engine room, and most of the remainder on the main deck.

V. B. MOLTENO,
Captain.

LETTER OF PROCEEDINGS—FROM COMMODORE,
4TH LIGHT CRUISER SQUADRON.

Enclosure No. 15 to Submission No. 1415/0022 of 20/6/16
from C.-in-C., Home Fleets.

No. C. 14.

" Calliope,"
SIR, 3rd June 1916.

I HAVE the honour to forward herewith, in the form of a diary, the proceedings of the Fourth Light Cruiser Squadron when not actually in station, during the Fleet action of 31st May 1916.

2. The diary has been compiled from the reports and track charts[1] forwarded by ships of the Squadron.

I have the honour to be,
Sir,
Your obedient Servant,
C. E. Le MESURIER,
Commodore,
Fourth Light Cruiser Squadron.

The Commander-in-Chief,
Grand Fleet.

(Enclosure to 4th Light Cruiser Squadron Letter No. C. 14 of 3rd June 1916.)

DIARY OF PROCEEDINGS.

Date, 31st May 1916.　　　　All times G.M.T.

P.M.

5.45.　Heavy firing S.S.W.

6.12.　One Enemy Light Cruiser to Southward, on fire and stopped.

6.13.　4th Light Cruiser Squadron turned to East in line ahead. Battle Cruiser Fleet 2′ South, steering East, engaging enemy Battle Cruisers on parallel course.

6.20.　One enemy four-funnel Light Cruiser observed to sink.

6.22.　" Queen Mary " blew up.

6.32.　" Invincible " blew up.

6.35.　" Acasta " badly hit, passed through Squadron from Southward.

6.35.　Centre and Rear Divisions of Battle Fleet opened fire.

6.45.　Altered course to close " King George V." division. Received signal for deployment.

7.0–7.15.　Took up action station on " King George V."

7.15.　One enemy Battle Cruiser (? " Lutzow ") bearing West surrounded by T.B.D.'s steering slowly to N.W.

7.18.　Two enemy Battle Ships " König " class, engaged by " Orion " division, observed heavily on fire.

7.22.　Ordered by Commander-in-Chief to attack enemy destroyers. Latter—a half flotilla—bearing N.W. by N., steering towards head of " King George V." division. Opened fire 8,000–9,000 yards, leading T.B.D. disappeared, one other disabled.

7.25–7.35.　At least six torpedoes observed in Squadron to pass ahead or through the Squadron's track.

7.36.　Enemy destroyers retired, 4th Light Cruiser Squadron resumed station on " King George V."

---

[1] Plate 12a.

P.M.

8.5.   "Castor" and T.B.D.'s turned to West, a smoke screen observed W.N.W.—1st Division, "Calliope," "Constance," and "Comus" turned to support "Castor."

8.18.   Opened fire on enemy's destroyers, a half flotilla steering towards rear of Battle Cruiser Fleet in direction S.S.W.

8.24.   Enemy destroyers made smoke cloud and retired on own line.

8.26.   Sighted enemy Battle Fleet N.W., 8,000 yards, "Pommern" class centre, "Kaiser" class rear divisions, course south.

8.28.   Enemy Battleships opened fire on Light Cruisers.

8.30.   "Calliope" fired a torpedo at leading ship of "Kaiser" division at 6,500 yards—Light Cruisers retired on "King George V." divisions heavily shelled by three enemy battleships.

8.35.   Enemy ceased firing.

8.38.   An explosion noticed on one "Kaiser" class Battleship.

8.45.   "Calliope" took station on 2nd Battle Squadron. "Constance" and "Comus" proceeded through the line to get ahead of the "King George V."

8.45.   "Caroline" and "Royalist" (ahead of "Castor" and destroyers) who were ahead of "King George V." observed three enemy Battleships—pre-Dreadnoughts N.N.W. closing slowly—leading enemy ship challenged by Searchlight towards "Castor."

9.5–9.10.   "Caroline" fired two torpedoes and "Royalist" fired one torpedo at enemy, mean range 8,000 yards. Enemy opened fire on "Caroline" and "Royalist," also on "Comus"—rejoining "Caroline." Latter and "Royalist" turned away.

9.14.   Enemy ceased firing.

9.17.   Enemy fired one large star shell.

9.35.   "Calliope" reached head of line, 4th L.C.S. formed astern of her. Squadron closed on "King George V." at 2.0 a.m. 1st June.

REPORT FROM COMMANDING OFFICER— H.M.S. "ABDIEL."

Enclosure No. 16 to Submission No. 1415/0022 of 20/6/16 from C.-in-C., Home Fleets.

H.M.S. "Abdiel,"

SIR,   7th June 1916.

I HAVE the honour to forward herewith report of "Abdiel's" proceedings during the action with the German Fleet on 31st May and until arrival at Queensferry, 8 p.m., on 1st June.

During the day and until coming in contact with the enemy at 5.40 p.m., "Abdiel" was in company with the 4th Light Cruiser Squadron, who were acting as a screen from four to five miles ahead of the Battle Fleet and spread ¾ of a mile apart to starboard; "Abdiel" being ¾ of a mile on the port beam of the Commodore's ship—"Calliope"—the port wing ship.

P.M.

5.45. Steering S.E. by S. at 19½ knots, observed ships in action bearing South and steering East.

Closed "Calliope" on her ordering the 4th L.C.S. to close and form single line ahead.

Remained close the "Calliope," conforming as far as possible to the movements of the Squadron without geeting in their way until the Battle Fleet had deployed at about 6.15 p.m., when I proceeded to the centre of the disengaged side of the Fleet according to orders, and remained there during the action.

10.15. Having received orders by W/T from C.-in-C. to lay mines as directed in Operation Memo. "M" of 31st May, proceeded S.S.E. at 31 knots.

A.M.   1st June.

0.30. Sighted Horns Reef Light Ship; bearing E. by S.

1.24. Arrived at a position 15 miles 215° from Vyl Lightship; reduced speed and ran a line of 80 mines, 10 to the mile, set for 15 ft. deep at low water, steering S. 9 E. (mag.) for the first 40 and S. 34 W. (mag.) for the remainder, zig-zagging on each course.

2. 4. Finished laying mines and proceeded North at 30 knots.

2.20. A/c to N. 77 W.

2.55. A/c to S. 79 W.

3.50. Heard heavy firing S.W. about 10 miles off.

4.30. Reduced to 25 knots.

7.40. A/c to N. 46 W., having passed round the South of Area 1 Minefield according to orders.

4.40. Passed four of 8th Flotilla Patrol and arrived at Queensferry at 8 p.m., having met or seen nothing else.

While laying the mines the lights of 3 Fishing Vessels were seen, but I am of opinion that they did not observe "Abdiel" or what she was doing, as it was not daylight and visibility was very low owing to drizzling rain and overcast sky.

No mines were seen to remain on the surface.

The ship was not hit during the action.

I have the honour to be,

Sir,

The Commander-in-Chief,   Your obedient Servant,

Grand Fleet,   B. CURTIS,

H.M.S. "Iron Duke."   Commander in Command.

C17/1.   II.

Commander-in-Chief, Grand Fleet.

Submitted.

C.E.C.M.,

Commodore, 4th Light Cruiser Squadron.

H.M.S. " OAK "—REPORT OF PROCEEDINGS DURING THE ACTION
OF 31ST MAY, 1916.

No. 0/13.

Commander-in-Chief,
Home Fleets.

Forwarded.

H.M.S. " Iron Duke,"   FRED C. D. DREYER,
10th June 1916.   Captain.

Enclosure No. 17 to Submission No. 1415/0022 of 20/6/16
from C.-in-C., Home Fleets.

. H.M.S. " Oak,"
SIR,   9th June 1916.

I HAVE the honour to make the following report on the
movements of H.M.S. " Oak," and of the observations from
that vessel, of the action fought on 31st May and of the night
action which followed.

At 5.55 p.m. " Oak " took up her station for the approach
2 cables astern of H.M.S. " Canada," and at 6.04 p.m. the fleet
deployed to port, to South, and speed was reduced to 18 knots.
" Oak " turned so as to keep about 2,500 yards on the disengaged
beam.

A very widely-spread salvo, from the enemy, here straddled
the " Iron Duke," the nearest shot being about 1,000 yards
over.

At 6.08 p.m. " Iron Duke " opened fire at what appeared to
me to be a battleship of the " Koenig " class. She had two tall
funnels. The first salvo was short, the second over, and the
third straddled with, I think, two hits. Each subsequent salvo
appeared to me to straddle, with varying hits between 1 and 3
from each salvo.

At 6.12 p.m. course was altered to S.E. by S. The above
enemy ship was last seen by me, enveloped in a mist of steam
or white smoke, with occasional bursts of flame coming from her.

During this period I gradually increased the distance from
the line to 3,500 yards, as a few overs had begun to pitch about
2,500 to 3,000 over. These were all isolated shots, and the return
fire from the enemy at the 4th and 1st Battle Squadrons, appeared
to me to be very wild. Salvoes were badly spread, which is not
usual with German fire, and most of them were pitching very
badly short. It struck me that the enemy's *morale* was already
badly shaken. The only hit seen by me on our battle line was
one, on a vessel of the " Hercules " class. No shots were
observed to be fired at the 2nd B.S.

Also during this period the 1st cruiser squadron, which had
been on a beam bearing from the " Iron Duke," turned to

starboard and engaged the enemy at close range, on an opposite course, apparently about 6 to 7 thousand yards. Enemy's fire at these ships was fairly good, but even these salvoes were observed to be badly spread out, usually about 800 to 1,000 yards. Shots from one salvo were seen to hit "Defence" aft, and the after magazine exploded. The flame and smoke from this explosion rose at least a 1,000 feet into the air. The ship, however, continued to steam on, but a second salvo hit her and she then disappeared. The actual sinking of the "Defence" and "Black Prince" was not observed.

At 6.22 p.m. speed was reduced to 14 knots, and shortly after course was altered by divisions to S.S.E. The leading ships then ran into a heavy bank of mist, in which the visibility was reduced to about 4,000 yards.

At 6.30 p.m. course was altered by divisions to South.

An enemy Battle-Cruiser of the latest type was then observed bearing about West, heading S.S.E. and making very little way through the water. She had two funnels spaced very far apart, the visible section of which appeared to be almost square. At that range no masts could be seen, so they must have been of the light pole variety, or else they had been shot away. Ships opened on her in succession and she was badly punished; she still continued to fire, however, but their fall was only occasionally seen. One salvo from "Iron Duke" was observed to start a very big fire in her just abaft the after superstructure and before the after turret. The ship was evidently doomed, and to screen her from further damage, or perhaps to enable her crew to be rescued, a division of enemy T.B.'s were observed to close our line, heading about S.S.E. and laying a smoke screen. "Iron Duke" opened fire with 6-in., and the leading boat shortly disappeared behind the splash of a salvo. A heavy salvo—I think from "Benbow"—accounted for another boat. The salvo pitched with a percentage of shots short, and pieces of the T.B. were observed in the air. When the splash subsided the boat could not be seen. The remaining boats then made off.

At about 7.35 p.m. the track of a torpedo was observed to cross the track of our ships, about 200 yards ahead of "Iron Duke." Torpedo was travelling slowly. Track finished about 2,000 yards on the port side of the line and the torpedo sank. Direction of the track was S.E.

No more enemy ships were seen after this. "Oak" conformed to the movements of the battle line until 9.15 p.m., when she was ordered to keep close to "Iron Duke" during the night. Station was taken up 2 cables 2 points before the Port beam.

After this actions were observed to be taking place on a bearing S.W. and also between the bearings N.W. to N. by E between 9.30 and midnight. A few smaller rounds were seen to be fired in the early part of the middle watch right astern of the fleet. No signals were received however, which would have indicated the nature of the action which was going on to Northward.

When daylight broke, station was taken up 5 cables on the port bow of " Iron Duke."

I have the honour to be,
Sir,
Your obedient Servant,
The Commander-in-Chief, DOUGLAS FAVIELL,
Home Fleets. Lieut.-Commander.
(Through the Flag-Captain
H.M.S. " Iron Duke.")

CAPTAIN'S REPORTS, H.M.S. " ACTIVE."

Enclosure No. 18 to Submission No. 1415/0022 of 20/6/16
from C.-in-C., Home Fleets.

H.M.S. " Active,"
SIR, 9th June 1916.

I HAVE the honour to report that at about 11.15 p.m. on May 31st H.M. Ship under my command was felt to strike something. No damage was apparent from the inside of the ship, and no leak developed.

On June 8th divers were sent down, and it was found that some 15 feet of the Starboard Bilge Keel had been torn back, and was projecting about 4 feet from the ship's side.

A sketch is attached showing the extent of the damage.[1]

It is submitted, that as a temporary measure, the Bilge Keel be cut, as shown by the dotted red line in the sketch, and any ragged edges removed from the fracture.

The ship's approximate position at 11.15 p.m. May 31st was Lat. 56° 1′ N., Long. 5° 55′ E., Course South, Speed 17 knots, following astern of the 2nd Battle Squadron.

I have the honour to be,
Sir,
Your obedient Servant,
PERCY WITHERS,
The Vice Admiral Commanding Captain.
1st Battle Squadron,
H.M.S. " Royal Oak."

COMMANDER IN CHIEF,

SUBMITTED. I requested Lieut. Catto to examine the Bilge Keel and he reports that he can cut off the pieces if he has the loan of the pneumatic tools and divers from " Iron Duke."

CECIL BURNEY,
Vice Admiral Commanding
9th June 1916. First Battle Squadron.

---

[1] Not reprinted.

Enclosure No. 19 to Submission No. 1415/0022 of 20/6/16
from C.-in-C., Home Fleets.

H.M.S. " Active,"

SIR,   10th June 1916.

IN accordance with your signal 0800 of to-day's date,
I have the honour to report that :—

(1) H.M.S. " Active " during the advance was acting as
linking ship in position " J."

(2) At about 6.0 p.m. an enemy Cruiser, apparently of the
" Wiesbaden " class was sighted on the starboard bow, and
engaged by H.M.S. " Shannon " and one other Cruiser, which
were between " Active " and the enemy. As, owing to the
misty weather, it was not possible to get an accurate range,
two salvos were fired. These fell a long way short, and cease
firing was sounded. The signal to deploy being then made, no
opportunity of closing the vessel occurred.

(3) The Fifth Battle Squadron not being present, and not
having the speed of the 4th L.C.S., I took station on the
disengaged beam of the leading Battle Squadron, and repeated
signals.

(4) When the Fleet formed up for the night, " Active " took
station astern of 2nd Battle Squadron.

(5) At about 10.15 p.m. an action took place lasting for from
5 to 10 minutes, just abaft the starboard beam, about 3 miles
distant.

(6) At about 11.0 p.m. a squadron of what appeared to be
Light Cruisers opened fire from the starboard quarter at a ship
about a mile astern of " Active." The After Control Officer
describes this vessel as having four funnels, and two masts, the
mainmast having a large top, and having shown a red light over
a green just before the action commenced. One funnel was
apparently shot away during the action, which lasted about
10 minutes. The ship burst into flames and appeared to sink,
the fires suddenly going out. Fire was not opened, as there
were doubts as to which were hostile ships, in addition to which
I did not feel justified in indicating the position of the Battle
Fleet.

(7) At about 11.15 p.m. the ship was felt to bump something
heavily, subsequent investigation revealing the fact that some
15 ft. of the Starboard Bilge Keel has been torn back. This
has formed the subject of a separate report.

(8) Several actions subsequently took place, but so far astern,
that only the flashes in the sky could be seen.

I have the honour to be,

Sir,

Your obedient Servant,

PERCY WITHERS,

Captain.

The Vice Admiral Commanding
1st Battle Squadron,
H.M.S. " Royal Oak."

REPORTS OF COMMODORE (F).

Enclosure No. 20 to Submission No. 1415/0022 of 20/6/16
from C.-in-C., Home Fleets.

N. 0017/2.   H.M.S. " Castor,"
SIR,   3rd June 1916.

I HAVE the honour to forward the following report of my
movements on the night of 31st May–1st June.

At about 8.30 p.m. on 31st May the Enemy's Destroyers
were sighted on starboard bow of our van, and the " Castor "
and Half Flotilla proceeded to attack, the Commodore of 4th
Light Cruiser Squadron detaching 3 ·Cruisers to support.

2. The enemy destroyers did not develop their attack, and
" Castor " returned to her position ahead of the Fleet, course S.W.

3. At about 9.0 p.m. the Battle Fleet turned, leaders
together, to South, the Flotilla remaining on Starboard bow of
Second Battle Squadron, and a line of Battle Cruisers was then
sighted on the Starboard quarter closing Fleet. They appeared
very much like enemy Battle Cruisers, but by an intercepted
signal from Vice-Admiral 2nd B.S. to the Commodore, 4th L.C.S.,
the Vice-Admiral 2nd B.S. was apparently satisfied they were
our own.

Soon after sighting them these Battle Cruisers opened fire on
two of the 4th L.C.S. ahead of the Flotilla.

I turned the Flotilla away from the Battle Cruisers, and
expected the Fleet to open fire on them.

The leading Battle Cruiser then fired a star shell, which
appeared to justify the opinion that they were enemy ships;
but as' the Fleet still held their fire I could not attack, as it was
not dark enough to make an attack unsupported by fire from
the Fleet.

The Battle Cruisers turned off to starboard and were lost
sight of.

4. At 9.45 p.m. Flotillas were ordered to take station astern
of Battle Fleet.

5. At about 10.5 p.m., when on the starboard quarter of the
Fleet, ships were sighted on the starboard bow.

They challenged us by the first two signs of the challenge of
the day.

They then made T, followed by R.

When about 2,500 yards away the two leading ships switched
on search lights and opened fire on " Castor."

" Castor " opened fire, and was seen hitting with range on
guns of 2,000 yards. The bursting of shells from the 6-in. guns
-was the most noticeable.

" Castor " then fired a torpedo, high speed setting, and turned
to Port.

6. With regard to the eight Destroyers which " Castor " was
leading, two destroyers fired torpedoes, but the remainder of
them which were near " Castor " say they were so blinded by

" Castor's " guns they could not see anything, and the others were so certain in their own minds that a mistake had been made, and that we were being fired on by our own ships that they decided not to fire their torpedoes.

7. Three Captains of Destroyers inform me that their Engineer Lieutenants reported feeling a violent detonation under water at the time " Castor " " Magic " and " Marne " fired their torpedoes, and that they themselves observed the lights of the second ship go out and the glow of an explosion on her side; but this was not felt in " Castor," probably as she was receiving other shocks at the time.

8. The Flotilla then proceeded South after the Battle Fleet, my object being to be within reach of the Fleet at daybreak should the Fleet have found the enemy and a Fleet action take place.

9. At about 12.15 a.m. I sighted a Torpedo Boat on the starboard bow. As soon as it was distinguished as an enemy craft, " Castor " turned to ram her and opened fire.

The torpedo boat was too quick on the helm, and just avoided being rammed, but received the fire of all guns at point blank range, and was not seen again.

A flare, probably from shell explosion was seen on her deck aft.

Believing her to be sunk, " Castor " turned again to South to follow the Fleet.

There would appear to be no doubt that she was sunk, as she was not seen by any of the destroyers who passed the spot where she was fired on by " Castor."

10. With reference to paragraph 5, the Enemy consisted of three or more cruisers, of which the leading ship appeared to be a large cruiser.

Their firing was not really very good, and though " Castor " was straddled by the first salvo this was not remarkable considering the range.

" Castor " drew the whole fire of the two cruisers, and it is unfortunate that this element of doubt existed in the minds of the Captains of the Destroyers as to whether the ships were enemy, as a good opportunity of firing torpedoes was lost.

" Castor " could make no signals to the destroyers, as her communication and wires were cut and W/T temporarily out of action.

The handling of the destroyers was remarkably good, considering no signals could be made.

1 * *   *   *   *

14. I would mention that some ship ahead of the Second Battle Squadron at about 9.0 p.m. made the signal by searchlight : " Please give me the Challenges and Replies for the day, as I have lost mine."

---

[1] Part omitted here referring solely to personnel, recommendations, &c., in no way bearing on the course of the action.

I did not see a reply made, but evidently the signal was taken in by one of our ships, and the Captain of the " Manners " informs me he saw the reply being made.

It is possible that this was one of the enemy's ships asking, and may account for " Castor " being challenged by at any rate part of the correct challenge for the day.

15. The effect of fire on " Castor " was as follows :—A large hole, 4 ft. by 4 ft. 6 in. Starboard side under No. 2 4-in. gun, evidently high explosive shell which burst in the heads, splinters passing through the bulkhead into the Recreation Space, destroying Fire Main service, Ventilation service, and Voice Pipes to 4-in. guns.

Two men were killed in the heads, and three of the ammunition supply party in Recreation Space.

(2) One shot passed through Upper Mess Deck just above the water line, cut through an iron ladder, and passed out through the Port side, evidently exploding whilst passing out.

(3) Three shells struck Fore Bridge, doing extensive damage to bridge, cutting all electric circuits and damaging Bridge Steering Gear (which was not being used). Five men were killed on the Bridge.

(4) One shell exploded on the Forecastle, killing two men but not doing any material damage to speak of.

(5) Several shells hit the ship's side on the armoured plating, fragments passing up and causing damage to after 4-in. guns, Funnels, After Control, Casings and Boats.

(6) One shell struck Motor Boat, which set her on fire and completely shattered her.

(7) In all there were 23 wounded. These men were chiefly forward ammunition supply parties, and others consisted of men stationed at foremost and after 4-in. Guns and First Aid Party.

I have the honour to be,
Sir,
Your obedient Servant,
J. R. P. HAWKSLEY,
Commodore (F).

The Commander-in-Chief,
Grand Fleet.

Enclosure 21 to Submission No. 1415/0022 of 20/6/16 from C.-in-C., Home Fleets.

From—The Captain (D), 4th Destroyer Flotilla.

To—The Commodore (F), Grand Fleet Flotillas.

No. 0110.

Date—6th June 1916.

Submitted with reference to your general signal 1800 of 2nd instant, I attach reports which have been received from Destroyers of 4th Flotilla relative to the action with the enemy on 31st May and 1st June 1916.

The report from H.M.S. " Broke " will be forwarded as soon as it has been received.

E. O. GLADSTONE,
Captain (D).
4th Destroyer Flotilla.

" Hecla."

II.

No. 0017/2.
Commander-in-Chief,
        Grand Fleet.
    Submitted.

J. R. P. HAWKSLEY,
Commodore (F).

" Castor,"
        6th June 1916.

H.M.S. " SPITFIRE,"
3rd June 1916.

SIR,

I HAVE the honour to report that I observed the following damage to enemy ships on night of 31st May, between 11.0 and 11.40 p.m.

1. " Spitfire " torpedoed a 4-funnelled cruiser, class not determinable, but she had 4 very tall funnels.   She was observed to heel over immediately on being struck and appeared to be in a sinking condition.

2. " Spitfire " was rammed by and rammed (port bow to port bow) a cruiser of " Freya " class (presumably).   20 feet of her skin plating from upper deck to below scuttles is now in " Spitfire."

3. A battle-cruiser of " Moltke " type passed close astern of " Spitfire " at about the same time.   She was going very fast, but appeared to be on fire between her funnels and on her fore mess deck, but there was no flame—only smoke.

I have the honour to be,
Sir,
Your obedient Servant,
C. TRELAWNY,
Lieut.-Comdr.

The S.O., 4th Flotilla.

COPY OF NAVAL SIGNAL CONTAINING SUMMARY OF
REPORTS OF CERTAIN DESTROYERS.

From—The Naval Depôt, North Shields.

To—R.A. " Cyclops " for " Hecla," 4 a.m.

" Spitfire " reports position unknown owing to loss of Bridge times approximate was next astern " Tipperary " about 11 p.m. 31st May when attacked by four enemy's Cruisers from North West which sank " Tipperary " (stop) " Spitfire " fired torpedo at second in line seen to hit (stop).   Had noticed list badly, believed sunk (stop)   Had four very tall funnels (stop)   " Spitfire " rammed port bow to port bow enemy's cruiser with

3 perpendicular funnels 1 red band on every funnel 2 crane (stop) " Spitfire " carried off 20 feet of enemy's side plating (stop) About 11.30 p.m. enemy Battle Cruiser with 2 funnels far apart passed close astern of " Spitfire " steering between South and West observed on fire between funnels and on girdle (?) (stop) " Porpoise " reports saw one large ship blow up at 3 a.m. 1st June position unknown (stop) " Contest " reports Blank (?) (stop) Report of " Broke " will follow to-morrow Sunday.

(2240)
4th June 1916.

COPY OF TELEGRAM—CLAIM BY " ACASTA."

From—S.N.O. Aberdeen.

To—R.A. Longhope.

Date—3rd June, 1916.

For " Hecla." Considered that torpedo hit leading Enemy's Battle Cruiser at 6.14 p.m. (G.M.T.).

Explosion seen, unable to assess damage caused by gunshot. " Acasta." (1630.)

H.M.S. " ACASTA,"

SIR, 3rd June 1916.

I HAVE the honour to forward the following report of action on 31st May.

In company with " Shark," " Ophelia " and " Christopher " screening 3rd Battle Cruiser Squadron.

P.M.

5.50. Steering N.W. in line ahead on port quarter of Battle Cruiser Squadron. Enemy Light Cruisers and Destroyers sighted ahead, opened fire at 5,000 yards. Enemy course Westerly.

6. 0 (approximately). Altered course to East.

6. 5. Enemy turned 16 points.

6.10. Division altered to port and " Shark " stopped, so I returned to " Shark's " assistance as she was badly hit. While doing so " Acasta " was holed forward and aft.

6.12 to 6.18. Fired foremost tube at leading enemy battle Cruiser which apparently hit as explosion was observed by independent witnesses—range 4,500 approximately.

" Acasta " was badly hit in engine room, which burst several steam pipes and caused five casualties, one of whom was Engineer-Lieutenant J. Forrest, and engine-room had to be evacuated. Steering gear was shot away and I was unable to steer or stop the engines until 6.30.

Ship was under extremely heavy fire from enemy Light
Cruisers and Destroyers and a Battle Cruiser from
6.5 to 6.25.

The moral of the ship's company was excellent.

At 9.0 p.m. a Cruiser, apparently German, was observed heavily
on fire to the S.W. and subsequently seen again after
2 a.m.

1 *   *   *   *   *

At noon, 1st June, " Nonsuch " took me in tow until 2.30 p.m.,
2nd June; his assistance was invaluable as I had no
oil left and met heavy weather.

I have the honour to be,
Sir,
Your obedient Servant,
·JOHN O. BARRON,

Captain (D),   Lt.-Comdr.
4th Flotilla.

COPY OF TELEGRAM—REPORT BY " CONTEST."

From —Naval Depôt, North Shields.

To—" Cyclops," for " Hecla."

Date—4th June, 1916.

" Contest " now reports she fired Torpedo at large 3 funnelled
ship 11.35 p.m., seen to hit. (1520).

H.M.S. "ACHATES."

SIR,   3rd June 1916.
I HAVE the honour to forward an account of " Achates' "
part in the action on the night of Wednesday, 31st May.

Orders having been received, shortly after 10 p.m., for
4th Flotilla to take station 5 miles astern of the Battle Squadron,
single line ahead in the following order was assumed at about
10.50 p.m. :—*1st Half Flot.* : " Tipperary," " Spitfire," " Sparrowhawk," " Garland " and " Contest "; followed by *2nd Half
Flot.* : " Broke," " Achates," " Ambuscade," " Ardent,"
" Fortune," " Porpoise " and " Unity."

Our course was then South, speed 18 knots. Position (approx.)
at 11.15 : Lat. 55° 48′ N., Long. 6° 23′ E.

At approx. 11.30 p.m., heavy firing was observed on our starbd.
bow and directed towards the head of our line, and shortly
afterwards the " Tipperary " was observed to haul out of the
line to starboard, badly hit and burning furiously. Shortly after
this the " Broke " hauled out of the line, apparently hit and
not under control, and " Achates," narrowly avoiding collision

---

¹ Part omitted here, referring solely to personnel, recommendations
&c., in no way bearing on the course of the action.

with her, endeavoured to join up with 1st Half Flotilla. Firing at this time was general in the enemy's line on our starbd. bow and beam and the range close, the order to fire was passed to the tubes as sights came on. I subsequently cancelled the order to fire torpedoes being under the impression that our Cruisers were engaging the enemy between us and the enemy's line and fearing that my torpedoes would cross the line of our own ships.

I respectfully submit that in future the maximum amount of information may be given to destroyers as to the disposition of our own forces, observing the difficulty of recognition by night.

At approx. midnight the " Achates " and " Ambuscade " were chased by enemy's cruisers to the Eastward, and failing to cross ahead of the enemy's line (Enemy's course appeared to be S.E.), I worked round to the North and eventually West and South passing in rear of their line and endeavouring to join Commodore (F).

I lost touch with " Ambuscade " about 12.30 a.m. and continued to search until 5 a.m., when I intercepted a signal from " Porpoise " that he required assistance, and I endeavoured to join him. " Porpoise " was eventually joined by " Garland," and as I was by this time running short of fuel, I proceeded to Rosyth, arriving there at 4 a.m., 2nd June, and after fuelling returned to this base arriving at 9 p.m., 2nd June.

I wish to bring to your notice the excellent manner in which all destroyers of my division were handled during the day and night action on the 31st, and I am of the opinion that the Commanding Officer of " Ambuscade " in particular, who was more immediately under my notice, by skilful handling, brought his ship undamaged out of action.

I have the honour to be,
Sir,
Your obedient Servant,
R. B. C. HUTCHINSON,
Commander.

Captain (D.),
4th Flotilla.

H.M.S. " AMBUSCADE,"

Sir,   3rd June.

I have the honour to forward the account of " Ambuscade's " part in the night action between the 4th Flotilla and the enemy's Battle Fleet on the night of 31st May.

The flotilla was in single line ahead, the 1st half under " Tipperary " leading, followed by " Broke," " Achates," " Ambuscade," " Ardent," " Fortune," " Porpoise " and " Unity," steering South, five miles astern of the second Battle Squadron.

At 11.30 p.m. enemy cruisers were observed on the starboard bow steering South-east at high speed. " Tipperary " drew enemy's fire, and was passed about 5 cables on starboard beam, apparently in a sinking condition.

I attacked with 2 torpedoes, and from a violent explosion shortly afterwards, consider a hit may have been obtained. It is believed " Fortune " was sunk about this time.   I then hauled off to the Eastward, following " Achates," eventually turning South.

At about 11.55 p.m. we encountered enemy's Battle Fleet steering South East.   The third torpedo was fired at ships whose fire was concentrated on " Ardent."   A red flah was observed at water line between searchlights of centre ship, and these momentarily went out, giving the possibility of a hit, observing that, though improbable, " Ardent " may also have been able to fire.   The " Ardent " was not seen after this.

All torpedoes were now discharged, and by smoke screen, and continual alteration of helm, I got away to the Eastward, and failing to keep in touch with the " Achates," turned North, and eventually South, joining Commodore (F) at 3.0 a.m. on June 1st.

The enemy's fire and working of searchlights was extremely accurate, while their use of star shells rendered a surprise torpedo attack almost impossible.

1 *   *   *   *   *

I have the honour to be,
Sir,
Your obedient Servant,
GORDON A. COLES,
Lieut. Commander.

REPORT OF COMMANDING OFFICER, H.M.S. " ARDENT."

M.F.A. " China,"
Hospital Ship No. VI,
Sir,   3rd June 1916.

I REGRET to report the loss through enemy gunfire of H.M.S. " Ardent " at about 12.30 a.m. (G.M.T.) June 1st. Single line ahead was formed astern of the Battle Fleet after dark on 31st May.   As far as I could judge, the line " Ardent " was in consisted of :   " Achates," " Ambuscade," " Ardent," " Fortune," and several other Torpedo Boat Destroyers in rear, Course South, speed 17 knots.   " Tipperary's " line appeared to be well out to the Starboard of us.

2. Various other ships were seen dimly and much firing going on, on either side until just after midnight, when four large ships appeared closing in on our Starboard hand, Course about S. by E. The leader challenged by switching on and off several groups of Green and Red lamps.   Almost immediately they switched on Searchlights, picked up " Fortune " and opened fire.   " Fortune " was hit at once.   I altered to Starboard and endeavoured to assist " Fortune," and from a very favourable position from about 2,000 yards on her port beam fired a torpedo at the leading enemy's ship, which undoubtedly scored a hit, the explosion was

---

¹ Part omitted here referring solely to personnel, recommendations, &c., in no way bearing on the course of the action.

seen, and the enemy ship's foremost searchlights' went off and she turned to Starboard. The second Ship in the line then fixed her searchlights and opened fire on " Ardent," so I increased speed and turned away to Port. I could see the " Fortune " badly hit, on fire, and apparently sinking, but still firing her guns in a most gallant manner at her big adversary.

A few minutes after this I altered course to South to try to pick up " Ambuscade," steered for what I thought was her smoke, to find I was rapidly closing four large German Ships crossing my bows from Starboard to Port, course about N.N.E. at a high speed. It was too late to get away, so I attacked immediately and fired a torpedo from a favourable position at the leader, I could not see if it hit, as at once a most devastating fire was poured in on the " Ardent " from the two leading Ships, who both had their searchlights on us. This bombardment continued for about five minutes when the enemy ceased fire and switched off, after which period the Ship was a total wreck, and appeared to be sinking. I then sank the Secret books, etc., and went aft to try and make a Raft, all our boats, Carley floats, &c. being smashed to bits. At this moment the enemy recommenced firing from point blank range, I gave the order " save yourselves," and about forty survivors jumped into the sea, with no support beyond lifebelts, waistcoats, &c., and shortly after the Ship sunk with her colours flying.

I was in the water about five hours before being picked up by " Marksman," and regret that up to date have heard of no more survivors. It is perhaps unnecessary for me to add that the Officers and Ship's company of the " Ardent " behaved according to the highest traditions of the British Navy. All Ranks and Ratings fought the Ship until every gun was out of action with the utmost determination.

When all did their duty it is impossible for me to name any individual for special recommendation.

I have the honour to be,

Sir,

Your Obedient Servant,

A. MARSDEN,

Lieut. Commander, H.M.S. " Ardent."

The Captain (D),
Fourth Flotilla,
H.M.S. " Hecla."

H.M.S. " PORPOISE,"

3rd June.

REPORT ON FLEET ACTION.[1]

SIR,

I HAVE the honour to report the following :—

The various phases of the action and actions can be better ascertained from large ship accounts up to 9.47 p.m. 31st, when

---

[1] Plate 27.

4th Flotilla was steering N. and N.N.E. 18 knots in 2 columns—
" Tipperary," " Spitfire," " Sparrowhawk," and " Garland,"
" Contest," to starboard; " Broke," 2nd division, " Porpoise "
and " Unity." Course, South, 18 knots.

At 10.54. D 4 ordered 2nd half flotilla to take station astern
of 1st half flotilla, at same time " Porpoise " and " Unity "
reported enemy destroyers astern, steering east.

About midnight, actions were going on all round us, chiefly
to westward. An enemy armoured cruiser came up abaft the
starboard beam, challenged, opened fire on " Fortune " and
" Porpoise." " Fortune " was at once hit badly. I had to starboard my helm to clear her and was hit by an 8-in. projectile
which hit base of the after funnel, killed one man at midship
gun, stunning gun's crew, killing the L.T.Ò. at Foremost tube,
wounding No. 2. The air chamber of spare torpedo exploded,
blowing the deck in and bending and bursting main steam pipe.
The forebridge wheel and telegraphs having gone, I went aft,
and from the top of E.R. hatch got the helm to starboard from
its being 10° to port. H.M.S. " Fortune " was lying between
" Porpoise " and the enemy, emitting clouds of smoke and
steam, both ships being shelled, but enemy searchlights being
somewhat screened by " Fortune's " smoke and steam. We
connected after steering position and telegraphs and got ship's
head N. by W., steaming about 100 revolutions, but losing water
rapidly, so stopped main engines with ½-in. in boiler gauge glasses
and ½ ton in R.F.W.T. We plugged exhaust pipe and ran down
Nos. 3 and 4 boilers to R.F.W.T. and eventually got under way,
gradually working up from 100 revs. to 145 revs. in the course
of the day and following night.

Fell in with H.M.S. " Garland " and " Contest " in Lat.
56.40 N., 3.50 E. at 11 a.m. who escorted " Porpoise " to the
Tyne. H.M.S. " Contest " having a broken stem, H.M.S.
" Garland " (Lieut.-Comdr. Goff) took " Porpoise " alongside and
took her up the River Tyne in a most seamanlike manner.

²∗   ∗   ∗   ∗   ∗

I have the honour to be,
Sir,
Your obedient Servant,
H. D. COLVILLE,
Commander.

H.M.S. " UNITY,"
SIR,   3rd June 1916.

I HAVE the honour to report the part taken by H.M.S.
" Unity " in the night action on 31st May–1st June and
subsequent proceedings :—

At about 10 p.m. on 31st May, when in company with
4th Flotilla, station was taken 5 miles astern of Battle Fleet,

---

² Part omitted here, referring solely to personnel, recommendations,
&c., in no way bearing on the course of the action.

Plate 27.

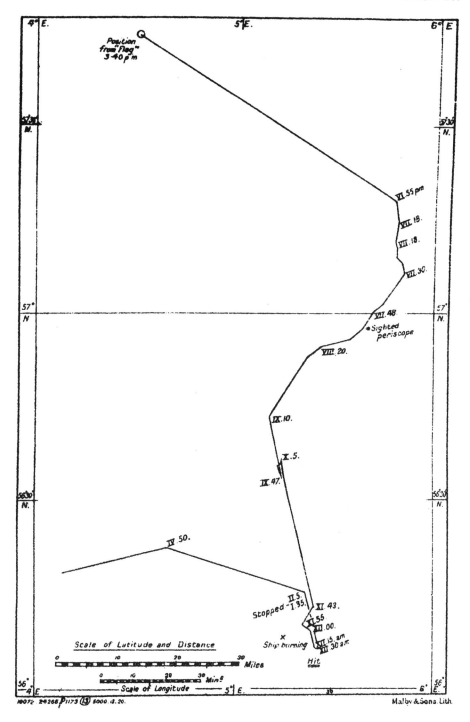

Position
from Flag
3·40 p.m.

4° E.   5° E.   6° E.

57°30′ N.   57°30′ N.

VI·55 pm

VII·19.

VII·18.

VII·30.

57° N.   57° N.

VII·48.
* Sighted periscope

VIII·20.

IX·10.

X·5.

IX·47.

56°30′ N.   56°30′ N.

IV·50.

Stopped — II·5.   II·5. 1·35.   XI·43.

XII·55

XII·00.

× Ship burning   XII·15. am
XII·30 am

Hit

Scale of Latitude and Distance

0   10   20   30   Miles

0   10   20   30   Min.s

Scale of Longitude   5° E.   6° E.

56° 4° E.   5° E.   56° 6° E.

Course South, speed 18 knots. "Unity" was the last ship in the line of 12 destroyers.

At 10.45 p.m. observed three enemy destroyers approaching on the starboard quarter; the leading boat fired a torpedo and immediately altered course away. I avoided the torpedo by going full speed and turning towards it, using full helm.

At 11.30 p.m. sighted two enemy destroyers on starbd. beam; fire was opened on them and they turned away.

About the same time "Tipperary" and leading destroyers of our line appeared to be in action with large ships. I observed the destroyers ahead alter course to port on a S.Ely course, and therefore increased speed to get into position for a torpedo attack.

About midnight I realised I was following a strange British Flotilla, and having lost sight of my own, decided to remain with them.

At 1 a.m., 1st June, course was altered to S.W. by the leading T.B.D. and speed increased to 28 knots. No large vessels were seen at any time which I could have attacked.

At daylight I found myself in company with "Lydiard" and 10 destroyers of the 9th and 13th Flotillas. I parted company at 5.45 a.m. to look for the fleet as the other destroyers were apparently returning to their base to oil. At 7.45 a.m. I searched for "Achates," but as I could not find her, and being short of oil, decided to make for Aberdeen to complete.

Arrived Aberdeen at 10 p.m., 1st June, and proceeded at 3 a.m., 2nd June, after oiling, to make further search for the Fleet, in the event of being required for screening duty.

Owing to bad weather, returned at 5 p.m., 2nd June, to Aberdeen for further instructions.

I sailed again at 6 a.m., 3rd June, and returned to the Northern Base.

I have the honour to be,
Sir,
Your obedient Servant,
A. M. LECKY,
Lieut.-Commander.

The Captain "D,"
4th Destroyer Flotilla.

H.M.S. "CHRISTOPHER,"
2nd June 1916.

REPORT OF PROCEEDINGS ON 31st MAY 1916.

In accordance with orders received, H.M.S. "Christopher" left Scapa at 8.50 p.m. on the 30th May, forming screen for 3rd Battle Cruiser Squadron.

At 5.45 p.m. on the 31st May, being then in position on port quarter of 3rd Battle Cruiser Squadron, steering North, the enemy were sighted on the port bow, consisting of three light cruisers (three funnels) and a destroyer flotilla with a Flotilla Cruiser. The division then attacked destroyer flotilla, coming under heavy fire from light cruisers and destroyer flotilla, and shortly afterwards from three Battle Cruisers. The division then turned sixteen points to regain position ahead of 3rd Battle Cruiser Squadron. Thirty rounds were fired, but the range was about 10,000 yards and visibility low and no direct hits could be observed. The enemy destroyers turned away, " Christopher " and " Ophelia " then took station ahead of Battle Cruisers. Only one opportunity of firing a torpedo at the leading Battle Cruiser occurred, but range was then masked by light cruisers. H.M.S. " Christopher " again came under fire at 8.30 p.m. from three Battle Cruisers while screening engaged side of Battle Cruisers (" New Zealand "). No damage was sustained and no casualties occurred. H.M.S. " Christopher " remained screening 1st Battle Cruiser Squadron, and no further action took place.

I have the honour to be,

Sir,

Your obedient Servant,

F. M. KERR,

Lieutenant-Commander.

H.M.S. " GARLAND,"

2nd June 1916.

Sir,

I beg to forward the following report of my proceedings on the night of 31st May–1st June :—

P.M.

9. 2.   Sighted 4 German T.B.D.'s, ship was in the midst of a 16 pt. turn at the time. Germans closed and showed recognition lights. Then red lights vertical. I at once opened fire on them. The two leaders turned, fired a torpedo each and made off at full speed to westward. The torpedoes missed me astern. I at once reported German T.B.D.'s presence to Captain " D."

10.35.   Sighted a German Cruiser of " Graudenz " class bearing W., course S., estimated speed, 17 knots. This was reported to Captain " D."

11.25.   A line of German ships appeared on starboard beam of flotilla, on a slightly converging course and opened fire on Destroyers. We returned their fire.

11.28.   Being in a favourable position, I turned and fired torpedo from after tube at a 3 funnelled Cruiser, the third ship in enemy's line. Torpedo was seen to explode abreast of Cruiser's mainmast, but as I was thereafter engaged in avoiding collision with other Destroyers, I did not see if vessel sank and was unable to find her again later.

11.40.   Closed " Tipperary," whose fore part was burning previously, in order to render her assistance ; but as soon as I eased down close astern of her, two enemy cruisers steamed across her bows at close range and opened fire on both of us, so I had to leave her and was chased away to eastward.

P.M.

11.55. Joined up with "Achates," " Fortune " and " Porpoise."

12. 0. Sighted a line of German Battleships on stbd. bow, steering south.

Leading Battleship switched on recognition lights and then searchlights and opened fire on us.

12. 5. Turned to port and fired torpedo from fore tube at leading ship, which appeared to be one of the " Deutschland " class. Range about 800 yards. Torpedo hit and was seen to explode abreast of the two foremost funnels, ship was seen to take on a heavy list to port, but whether she sank or not I was unable to ascertain as I was chased to the N.E.

I was unable, after this, to again find remainder of flotilla, but later, fell in with " Contest," who could only steam 20 knots. We sighted several German T.B.D.'s, who all made off at full speed on seeing us.

2.25. Sighted four German T.B.D.'s heading S.S.E. at full speed. Altered course to cross their bows and opened fire at about 5,000 yards. Germans at first began to turn on to a parallel course and returned our fire, and then thought better of it and turned away. At least one shot was seen to take effect on the stern of one German T.B.D.

As there was now no possibility of finding rest of Flotilla, I shaped course for Tyne, with " Contest," and later searched for and found " Porpoise," both of whom I escorted to the Tyne.

With the exception of one boat, which was hit by a 6-in. shell, no damage was sustained and no casualties.

1 * * * * *

I have the honour to be,
Sir,
Your obedient Servant,
R. S. GOFF,
Lieut.-Comdr.

The Captain " D,"
4th Destroyer Flotilla.

H.M.S. " OPHELIA,"

SIR,   3rd June 1916.

I HAVE the honour to report that H.M.S. " Ophelia " was in action on May 31st.

H.M.S. " Ophelia " left Scapa in company with H.M. Ships " Shark," " Acasta," and " Christopher," " Shark " being Senior

---

¹ Part omitted here, referring solely to personnel, recommendations, &c.. in no way bearing on the course of the action.

Officer, on May 30th at 9 p.m. to screen 3rd Battle Cruiser Squadron.

About 6 p.m. May 31st a German Light Cruiser and about ten T.B.D.'s were sighted off port bow. " Shark," followed by " Acasta " " Ophelia," and " Christopher," altered course to engage them. The Enemy were steaming in a Nly. direction and we were steaming in a Wly. direction.

About 6.15 p.m. " Shark " altered course 16 points to port and at the time was being heavily fired on by enemy's light cruiser, I altered course before arriving in " Shark's " wake so as to avoid enemy's fire.

Shortly after altering course " Shark " was put out of action, and I retired towards our light cruisers under the enemy's superior fire, continually altering course to avoid enemy's salvoes.

The enemy soon altered course to the Southward and I proceeded at full speed to attack enemy's Battle Cruiser, and at 6.29 p.m. fired torpedo at about 8,000 yards, afterwards proceeding to join Light Cruisers.

Some few minutes after firing torpedo an upheaval of water was observed by enemy's port quarter.

Subsequently I rejoined 3rd Battle Cruiser Squadron.

There were no casualties and damage to ship was immaterial.

I consider great credit is due to Eng. Lieut.-Comdr. George D. Campbell and C.E.R.A. Jesse Wadham for the way the Ship steamed at high speed.

This being the first time under way except for passage from Sunderland to Scapa.

No Torpedo or Gunnery Practices have been carried out by " Ophelia," and crew of " Hardy " have not yet turned over to her.

I have the honour to be,

Sir,

Your obedient Servant,

L. E. CRABBE,

Commander.

H.M.S. " OWL,"

SIR,   June 2nd.

I HAVE the honour to report in accordance with Commodore F.'s signal, that at 9.30 a.m. on June 1st, in about Lat. 56° 11′ N., Long. 6° 10′ E. " Owl " passed wreckage and the bows of a torpedo craft, about 6 feet floating stem up. It looked as if she had been rammed and cut in two and that her fore part floated. It is thought this was a German craft as there was no ring in bows for the towing wire as fitted in our Boats, also several lifebuoys painted red were observed.

I have the honour to be,

Sir,

Your obedient Servant,

R. G. HAMOND,

Captain " D."   Comdr.

REPORTS OF SURVIVORS OF H.M.S. "SHARK."

Office of Rear-Admiral Commanding,
East Coast of England,
No. 696/W. 962. Immingham Dock, Grimsby.

SIR, 3rd June 1916.

I HAVE the honour to report the following survivors of H.M.S. "Shark" were picked up by the Danish S.S. "Vidar" about 10.0 p.m. on Wednesday the 31st May, about 70 miles from the Danish coast :—

*William Charles Richard Griffin, Petty Officer 1st class, official number 201404—Portsmouth.

*Joseph Owen Glendower Howell, A.B., official number 230192—Portsmouth.

Charles Filleul, Stoker Petty Officer—Portsmouth.

Charles Cleeberg Hope, A.B., S.G., official number 238376—Portsmouth.

Charles Smith, A.B., S.T., official number J. 13416—Portsmouth.

Thomas Walton Swan, A.B., Portsmouth.

(The two marked * are in naval hospital in Hull, suffering from wounds and shock, the remainder are in R.N. Depôt, Immingham, and will be sent to Portsmouth Barracks on 3rd June.)

2. The survivors state that they were in company with the following vessels :—"Acasta," "Ophelia," "Contest" or "Christopher" or "Cockatrice," and at 6 p.m. they engaged a four-funnel German cruiser. "Shark" fired one torpedo at her, which Charles Smith, who was stationed at the after tube, states that he saw hit the cruiser and explode, and he further states that the ship stopped and seemed to be on fire.

3. At this time "Invincible," "Indomitable" and "Inflexible" were from two to four cables on the starboard beam. They also fired at the German cruiser.

4. About 6.15 the ship eased down and stopped owing to the pipes to the oil suctions having been damaged. The fore steering gear was also put out of action at this time and shortly afterwards was shot away altogether.

5. Two enemy destroyers now attacked "Shark," who had been left behind by the other vessels. One of them was driven off by gunfire from the midship gun (the only gun left in action), and the second was also hit, but succeeded in firing two torpedoes at "Shark" from a range of about 1,500 to 1,800 yards, one of which hit "Shark" abreast the after funnel. The enemy destroyers were painted light grey.

6. "Shark" took a heavy list and sank almost immediately. This was about 7 p.m.

7. Stoker Petty Officer Filleul reports that before the ship was torpedoed the Captain gave orders for all men not engaged at the guns to lie down on the deck.   He states that " Shark " at this time was between the opposing Battle Fleets and that shrapnel was being fired at them.   This is confirmed by the fact that the two wounded men are suffering from shrapnel wounds—not severe.

8. The boats were all riddled and useless, but two Carley Floats floated off and 14 or 15 men got into each.

9. While they were in the water about ten or more enemy battle cruisers or battleships passed about 5 miles off, followed by a large number of our battle ships within a mile who were engaging the enemy heavily.   A lot of enemy shells were falling " over " our ships.

10. The water was very cold and the survivors gradually succumbed until at about 10 p.m., when they were picked up, only seven were alive.   The seventh, Chief Stoker (Pensioner) Francis Newcombe, O. No. 155192 died after getting on board S.S. " Vidar," and his body was taken to Hull.   The survivors were treated very well by the Captain and crew of the " Vidar."

11. The Captain of the " Vidar " told the survivors that a little while before he picked them up he saw what looked like the bow of a big German Man-of-War standing out of the water ; the draft marks were in metres.

12. After being picked up they passed a large (presumably German) Man-of-War heavily on fire.

13. The following information relative to the officers of " Shark " has been given :—

The Captain, Commander Loftus Jones, had his left leg shot away before the vessel sank, and although he had a life-belt cannot have survived long.

Sub-Lieutenant P. H. G. I. Vance was killed before the ship sank.

Midshipman Thomas Smith, R.N.R., was seen after the ship was torpedoed, but not at all in the water.

No definite information can be given as regards the other officers.

14. It is considered that the men mentioned in paragraph 1 are the sole survivors.

It is submitted that the kind action of the Master of the Danish S.S " Vidar " (now at Hull) should be suitably recognised.

I have the honour to be,
Sir,
Your obedient Servant,
STUART NICHOLSON,
Rear-Admiral Commanding,
East Coast of England.

The Secretary,
of the Admiralty.

No.—953/W. 962.

Subject.—H.M.S. " Shark." Report by Torpedo Coxswain.

The Secretary of the Admiralty.

29th July 1916.
With reference to my submission No. 696/W. 962 of 3rd June 1916,. the attached report of William Charles Richard Griffin, P.O. 1st Class, Official Number, 201404, late Torpedo Coxswain of H.M.S. " Shark," is submitted.

He was the senior of the ratings saved from H.M.S. " Shark," but was not interviewed at the time of writing my previous letter as he was in hospital.

2. This Petty Officer has now practically recovered. Able Seaman Howell, the other survivor from H.M.S. " Shark," who was sent to hospital in Hull, will probably not be fit to travel for six to eight weeks.

STUART NICHOLSON,
Rear-Admiral Commanding,
East Coast of England.

TO REAR-ADMIRAL COMMANDING EAST COAST OF ENGLAND.

Sir,
I, Wm. Griffin, Torpedo Coxswain, will endeavour to give you the information to the best of my knowledge of the action and sinking of the H.M.S. " Shark." We were in company with the Battle Cruisers " Invincible," &c., also four destroyers (including the " Shark "); during the day 31st of May we were told by the Captain that we would probably meet the enemy. During the afternoon, about 3 o'clock, I should say, the report of the enemy was sighted, which was in great number, and action stations was rung on the alarm bell. We then proceeded at a speed of 25 knots. The signal was made open fire, in which we altered course to Port, the course being N.E., the Starboard guns being used. Again we altered course to Port, the course being N., it was. then that our steering was hit, I report steering gear gone, Sir, which the captain gave orders to me to man the after wheel, it was then that I got wounded in the head and over the right eye, we then went to Starboard making use of our guns on the Port side, this was when the Forecastle gun's crew were completely blown away, gun and all; about this time the " Acasta " arrived, and the captain of the " Acasta " asked if he could assist us, and the captain replied don't get sunk over us, we then with our steering gear and engines out of action, she was helpless and with only one gun firing which was the midship gun, and the captain came off the bridge and spotted for the midship gun, during that time he gave me orders for the boats and rafts to be lowered and got out, but the boats was useless, he also gave orders for the collision mat to be got out, which was done ;

all this time the enemy's Light Cruisers and destroyers were constantly shelling us; several of the enemy destroyers came very close to us in line formation, the range being about 600 yards, we were still firing our only gun, by this time the gun's crew consisted of three men, the Midshipman, T. Smith, R.N.R., J. Howell, A.B., Gunlayer II., and C. Hope, A.B. The captain was then wounded slightly in the leg, but he managed to control the gun, myself remaining there for orders from the captain. I must say that during the first part of the action the foremost and after torpedo were fired, and the spare torpedo was just hoisted up in line with the tube when a shell hit the air chamber and exploded. We were about half an hour in action when our engines stopped, she was battered about by shell, and began to settle down at the bows. At this time the gunlayer, J. Howell, A.B., was wounded in the left leg, it was about a minute afterward, the captain had his leg shot away, the shell not exploding. C. Hope, A.B., left the gun and assisted the captain, doing what he could to it. It was about five minutes afterwards that the ship sunk. Captain gave orders to save yourselves, the two rafts were filled up (the third raft could not be got out owing to shell fire), and as time went on the men began to gradually die away with exposure, the water being very cold. While we were in the water we saw a number of our ships and destroyers pass us at full speed chasing the enemy. At 10 o'clock (old time) we were picked up by the Danish steamer, S.S. " Vidar," bound for Hull, there was seven of us, one, Ch. Sto. Newcombe, who died on board. Nearly everyone on board wore lifebelts or life-saving collars, which proved a great success, and the rafts were also of great service to us, carrying about twelve. This is the best account I can give.

Your obedient Servant,
Wm. GRIFFIN,
Torpedo Coxswain,
Late H.M.S. " Shark,"

REPORTS OF COMMANDING OFFICER, H.M.S. " SPARROWHAWK."

H.M.S. " Onslaught,"
Sir,   5th June.
I HAVE the honour to report the proceedings and loss of H.M.S. " Sparrowhawk " on night and morning of 31st May–1st June.

After dark on 31st, the flotilla was in following order: " Tipperary," " Spitfire," " Sparrowhawk " and remainder of 4th Flotilla in company with Captain (D) in single line ahead, Course South, 17 knots, 5 miles astern of 2nd B.S.

About 11.30 vessels were sighted on the Starboard quarter overtaking the flotilla and apparently steering the same Course, except that the leading ship had 3 funnels, they could not be distinguished, the night, though light, being hazy.

When the leading Ship was abreast of " Tipperary," she switched on her searchlights and immediately opened fire, at the same time showing recognition signals of red and green lights. I ordered torpedoes to be fired at 3rd Ship in the line; one torpedo was fired, the estimated range being inside 1,000 yards, and it is thought a hit may have been obtained as an explosion was observed by men aft. The " Tipperary " was now well on fire; next ahead could not be seen. I hauled out of line to port, the enemy about this time putting out his searchlights. I found " Broke " just clear of the line, and not seeing any other destroyers, took station astern of her. Within a few minutes fire was opened on " Broke " from the Starboard bow and she altering course to port, I altered at the same time to avoid turning in her wake. The enemy then ceased fire.

" Broke " appeared to be steadied on a course about East. A destroyer was then sighted on Port Bow, steering across my bows, and to give her more room, I ordered port 10°, but ship had hardly started to swing, when " Broke " was observed to be turning to port very rapidly, helm was put hard a starboard, but before this had any effect, " Broke " hit " Sparrowhawk " just before forebridge, cutting halfway into the ship and locking the 2 ships together; whilst in this position, a destroyer, name unknown, rammed " Sparrowhawk " in the stern, cutting off about 5 feet and ramming rudder hard a port.

The 2 ships now drifted apart and endeavour was made, by working screws, to make to the westward but progress was very slight.

About 2 a.m. a three funnelled German Cruiser, apparently " Mainz " class, was seen to sink.

Survivors of " Tipperary " were picked up about 3 a.m.

" Dublin " and " Marksman " were sighted about 4 a.m., and in accordance with orders of Captain of " Marksman," the Ship having been prepared for towing, officers and men were taken on board " Marksman," and endeavour was made to tow " Sparrowhawk " stern first, but owing to resistance caused by stern being off and helm hard-a-port, wire parted, and in accordance with orders from V.A., 1st B.S. " Sparrowhawk " was sunk by gunfire. All Confidential Books and documents were burned with the exception of General Signal Book Standard and Service Call Signs, which were brought back, and the Vocabulary Signal Book, which was in use in W/T office at the time of collision and could not be found afterwards, as W/T office was badly wrecked, it may have gone over board then, or been thrown in a corner which could not be searched.

I have the honour to be,
Sir,
Your obedient Servant,
S. HOPKINS,
Lt. Comder.

The Captain (D),
4th Flotilla.

Chewton Lodge,
Highcliffe,
Sir,[1]   Hants.

IN accordance with orders from the Admiralty I have this day forwarded by express delivery to Admiralty preliminary report of sinking of enemy's cruiser on morning of 1st June, for repetition by telegram to Commander-in-Chief, and I beg to confirm this report by letter.

In the early morning of 1st June "Sparrowhawk" was lying disabled in practically the same position she was in at midnight, when she was 5 miles astern of 2nd Battle Squadron. Position cannot be given by Latitude and Longitude as charts and other documents were either destroyed or went down in the ship.

About 3 a.m. a vessel was sighted bearing East about 2 miles, steaming slowly North, after being in sight for about 10 minutes she gradually healed over and sank bows first. Ship had 3 high funnels equally spaced with little or no rake, 2 masts on which I thought I could make out searchlight platforms and, as far as I could see, a straight stem, but details were difficult to make out owing to mist. I considered her to be a German cruiser of "Augsburg" or similar class.

I have the honour to be,
Sir,
Your obedient Servant,
S. HOPKINS,
The Commander-in-Chief,   Lieut.-Comdr.
Grand Fleet.

H.M.S. "BROKE,"
Sir,   3rd June 1916.
I HAVE the honour to report as follows regarding the proceedings of H.M.S. "Broke," from 9.15 p.m. 31st May to 5.0 p.m. 3rd June 1916.

2. At 9.15 p.m., 31st May, the 4th Flotilla was in L.T. 2 formation ahead of "King George V." Course South, 17 knots.

3. At 9.50 Flotilla turned 16 Points and took station 5 Miles astern of Battle Fleet, passing through the lines.

4. At 10.6 resumed Course South, 17 knots. "Broke's" half Flotilla joining astern of "Tipperary's" by signal.

5. From about 10.30 intermittent heavy firing was observed on the Starboard Bow, and a signal was intercepted "D. XI to C. in C., Have been engaged by enemy destroyers."

6. At about 1040 a large explosion as of a Ship blowing up was observed S. by E. Shortly afterwards I observed two ships on the Starboard side of "Tipperary" make the correct reply to the "Challenge." I thought they were two of our cruisers but was not certain. I then observed, certainly, one of our Armoured Cruisers pass ahead on our Port Side.

---

[1] This letter was sent to the Commander-in-Chief as an enclosure to Commodore (F.)'s letter dated 14th June 1916, printed on page 326.

7. Soon afterwards, about 11.0 p.m., three cruisers, rather before the Starboard Beam, standing about S.S.W., switched searchlights on " Tipperary " and leading destroyers and opened fire; " Tipperary " was observed to burst into flame. " Broke," not having been illuminated, turned to Port and fired Starboard After Torpedo Tube at the rear Cruiser. The results of this shot is unknown. " Broke " swung as far as S.E. and then resumed her course South, no destroyers at that time being visible ahead.

8. About 5 minutes later (11.30 p.m.) a large Ship was sighted about two points before " Broke's " Starboard Beam standing about S.S.W. I gave the order to challenge, but immediately the stranger challenged by a green light system, followed by switching on searchlights and opening fire. The order was given to fire the remaining Starboard Tube, full speed ahead both, and fire was opened by " Broke," and after a slight pause for the firing of the Torpedo I gave the order Hard a Starboard. The No. 1 of the Tube has since reported that his sights never came on, of which I was unaware at the time, and did not know that the Torpedo had not been fired.

9. Almost immediately after turning to Port a Destroyer (" Sparrowhawk ") was sighted on the Port side. I then gave the order Hard a Port; not getting any reply the Navigating Officer went down to the Lower Bridge and found all hands killed and the Helm jammed hard a starboard. I, in the meantime, had given the order full steam astern. The Port Telegraph moved one revolution but the Starboard Telegraph and Wheel were completely jammed, having been put out of action at the second or third round.

10. The Ship then struck " Sparrowhawk " on her Starboard Bow abreast the bridge. Owing to damage to No. 1 Stokehold and large escape of steam no communication could be established with the Engine Room for a considerable time. The Engineer Lieutenant Commander coming on deck and being informed that the fore part of the Ship and all Officers had gone, stopped the engines.

11. I told the 1st Lieutenant to go aft and stop the engines. He reported that he could not get aft, but subsequently managed to, and was shortly followed by the Lieutenant (N) and myself. The after steering position was connected and the engines put to astern to clear " Sparrowhawk."

12. The condition of neither ship was accurately known, but I considered " Sparrowhawk," not having been under fire, was in the better condition of the two.

13. The Enemy Ship ceased fire and was not again seen after the collision, but during the short time of engagement accounted for heavy casualties and damage to forward Stokehold, Guns' crews and Bridge.

14. At Midnight course was shaped North at slow speed, three enemy ships being subsequently sighted and passed without apparently noticing " Broke."

15. At about 1.15 a.m., 1st June, two destroyers closed " Broke," the leader making a Challenge which appeared to commence with letter " K." " Broke " made challenge and was answered by a Searchlight and fire by the leading destroyer about 2 cables distant on port quarter. " Broke " turned away firing Port after Gun, the only one immediately available, owing to casualties and difficulty of communication with the fore part of the Ship. No Searchlight was available.

16. After about half a dozen rounds, 2 striking the ship amidships, the destroyers sheered off, " Broke " turning back to the Northward. Course was then shaped up the North Sea as far as state of wind and sea permitting.

17. " Broke " passed through 57.45 N., 4 . 0 E, 58.20 N., 1.10 E. with the intention of making Cromarty or Scapa, but at 4.0 a.m., 2nd June, owing to a strong N.W. Breeze springing up it was found necessary to keep away to South, and subsequently, as the wind permitted, course was altered to the Westward and Tyne being made at 5.0 p.m., June 3rd.

18. W/T Communication was established with " Marvel " on the night of 1st–2nd June, but owing to Main W/T being out of action, was soon lost, the subsequent alteration of course to the Southward (due to N.W. wind and Sea) could not therefore be reported.

19. All forward Mess Decks and Storerooms were flooded owing to the collision and effect of shell fire. The three forward boilers were put out of action, the forward stokehold leaking considerably. There was no damage at all abaft the after funnel.

20. " Broke's " casualties, lists of which are forwarded,[1] amounted to :—42 Killed, 6 Missing, 14 severely wounded, 20 slightly wounded. Total, 82.

21. Some time after clearing " Sparrowhawk," 23 of her ratings, 5 of which were wounded, were discovered on " Broke's " forecastle, some of these stating that they had been thrown off the fore bridge.

22. I would mention that at about 10.30 p.m. on 31st May, the Ship appeared to pass over some submerged object, a considerable shock being distinctly felt both on the Bridge and in the Engine Room.

I have the honour to be,

Sir,

Your obedient Servant,

WALTER L. ALLEN,

Commander.

The Commander in Chief,
    Grand Fleet.

H.M.S. " BROKE,"

SIR,   8th June 1916.

I HAVE the honour to submit the following addition to my report, dated 3rd June, on the proceedings of H.M.S. " Broke " on the night of 31st May–1st June.

---

[1] Not printed.

This addition is the result of careful investigation and sifting of evidence of members of the Ship's Company stationed aft, whom I was unable to properly interview before.

Paragraph 7.

It is not certain whether there were two or three cruisers attacking " Tipperary."

> Leading Seaman Belsey (who fired the Torpedo),
> Electrical Artificer Weeks,
> Stoker P.O. Sleight (Fire Brigade),

and Stoker Jackson,

reliable men who were in good positions to see, are all of them quite clear and convinced on the following points :—

(1) There were 2 Cruisers, the rear one, only burning searchlights, the van one doing most of the firing.

(2) They saw or heard the After Torpedo fired, watched it as far as possible, saw the explosion against a 3 straight-funnelled ship, apparently a cruiser. Stoker P.O. Sleight described the funnels in detail, and particularly the bands such as are evident in the photographs " Braunschweig " and " Bremen " classes, on pages 127, 135 " Jane's Fighting Ships, 1915."

On the other hand, the No. 2 of this tube saw no explosion.

The Torpedo Gunner's Mate at the forward tube did not consider the opportunity sufficiently favourable to justify a shot, and therefore did not fire.

The training of the forward tube was 10 Degrees Before; that of the after tube abeam. This would account for the after tube having more time.

Paragraph 8.

The T.G.M. at the forward tube having previously adjusted the Director by order, for " similar courses," considered the enemy to be standing in the opposite direction, and altered his Director accordingly, and consequently lost what would otherwise have been a possible shot.

A considerable amount of latitude is allowed to the Nos. 1 of the tubes, on account of their scattered positions, distance from the bridge, and unreliable means of communication.

The ship that engaged the " Broke " was a 2 funnelled ship, and cranes were observed.

The reason why I reported previously that it was not considered that " Broke " had seriously damaged an enemy ship, was as follows :—

On the return passage I had too much to attend to, to interrogate others than officers; and the Gunner, though he informed me that some people thought that the torpedo had hit, did so in such a manner as to lead me to believe that the evidence was of little value.

1 *   *   *   *   *

I regret that this report is so late, but the pressure of work connected with the ship prevented me completing a thorough investigation earlier.

I have the honour to be,

Sir,

Your obedient Servant,

WALTER L. ALLEN,

Commander.

The Commader-in-Chief,
    H.M. Ships and Vessels,
        Grand Fleet.

Enclosure 22 to Submission No. 1415 of 20/6/16
from C.-in-C., Home Fleets.

From—The Commodore (F), Grand Fleet Flotillas, H.M.S. " Castor."

To—The Commander-in-Chief, Grand Fleet.

Date—14th June 1916.

Number 0017/2.

Herewith are submitted reports from the Captain (D) Fourth Destroyer Flotilla, concerning :—

" Tipperary,"
" Spitfire,"
" Porpoise,"
" Onslaught,"
" Broke."

J. R. P. HAWKSLEY,

Commodore (F).

REPORT OF LOSS OF H.M.S. " TIPPERARY."

SIR,   8th June 1916.
    I HAVE the honour to report, as the only surviving Executive Officer of H.M.S. " Tipperary," the circumstances of the loss of that Ship, to the best of my recollection.

On the night of Wednesday the 31st of May H.M.S. " Tipperary " was leading the 1st Division of the 4th Flotilla in. line ahead with the 2nd Division of that Flotilla on her Port beam. The course, to the best of my knowledge, was about South. The night was dark and Sea fairly calm.

The Captain (D) (Captain C. J. Wintour) was on the Bridge with Lieutenant (N) E. N. G. Maton amd the Signal Boatswain (Mr. A. W. Phillips); the First Lieutenant (Lieutenant J. A Kemp) was in the Crows Nest, from which he controlled the

---

¹ Part omitted here, referring solely to personnel, recommendations, &c., in no way bearing on the course of the action.

Guns. The Flotilla Lieutenant (G) (Lieutenant G. T. C. Collins) was on the lower Bridge; Lieutenant (T) (R. I. Collier) with the Gunner (T) (J. Oates) was at the Torpedo Tubes, but the former was seen to go on the Bridge just before the action commenced; my own station as Sub-Lieutenant was at the after Guns, the position being on the Platform just aft of the Auxiliary W/T Office. I could not, therefore, see forward.

About 11.30 p.m. I saw some Ships on the Starboard Beam and reported these to the Bridge, but I could not make out what they were. Soon afterwards I saw smoke and a slight glare from another Ship apparently going in the same direction as us. I asked what this was, but got no reply from the Bridge. I took her to be a friend.

About 11.50 a Ship on our Starboard Beam fired one Gun. Several men say this was a Star Shell, and that our Port Searchlight was switched on. No orders were passed aft. I thought it was one of our ships firing on us by mistake; but immediately afterwards the Ship fired a Salvo which hit us forward. I opened fire with the After Guns. A shell then struck us in a steam-pipe, and I could see nothing but steam, but both our Starboard Torpedoes were fired.

The firing appeared to last about three minutes during which time we were continually hit forward.

When the steam died away I found that the Ship was stationary and badly on fire foreward. The enemy were not to be seen; nearly everybody amidships was either killed or wounded; the boxes of cartridges for the fore-guns were exploding one after the other. I closed down aft.

A Ship on our Port Bow then fired a few rounds but did not hit us. The First Lieutenant arrived aft, very shaken; also probationary Surgeon (G. Blurton, R.N.V.R.,) hit in the leg. The Engineer Commander (W. D. Colquhoun) was also on the Quarter-deck, I asked him if he thought we could do anything with the fire, but he appeared to be quite dazed; as a Shell had struck the Engine-room he was probably suffering from Concussion. All the boats were smashed, but both Carley Floats were got into the Water.

About 1 a.m. two enemy Ships appeared off our Port Beam; one seemed to be a Destroyer (two funnels), the other rather smaller and may have been a Submarine on the surface. These Ships closed us and asked, in English, "What Ship we were." They did not open fire.

One of the Carley Floats, which had left the Ship, may have been picked up by them.

Two small fires occurred down aft, but were soon put out.

By this time most of the wood and Boats from amidships had been thrown overboard, and the wounded got aft on to Quarter-deck.

The confidential Books were got up and those not in the Safes were put in an Ammunition Box and weighted. The Port Torpedoes were fired to prevent explosion.

About 1.45 the First Lieutenant gave the order " Everybody aft," and the Confidential books were thrown overboard. The Ship soon afterwards heeled over to Starboard and the Bows went under. The First Lieutenant gave the order " Everybody for themselves." The Ship sank in about one minute, the Stern going right up into the Air. I did not see the First Lieutenant after we were in the Water.

About half an hour later two German pulling Boats passed quite close, one about the size of a 14-oared cutter, with about 12 men in her, and the other, about the size of a Whaler full of men.

After about an hour in the Water, I got on to the Carley Float. We were afterwards sighted by H.M.S. " Sparrowhawk," who picked us up soon after 5 a.m. There were originally 30 Men on the Float. Four died, I think from exposure, before we got to the " Sparrowhawk," and another four on board. All the times mentioned above are very rough. I had no watch.

We were afterwards transferred from H.M.S. " Sparrowhawk " to H.M.S. " Marksman."

1 *   *   *   *   *

I am,
Sir,
Your obedient Servant,
N. J. W. WILLIAM-POWLETT,
Acting Sub-Lieutenant R.N.

" SPITFIRE'S " REPORT OF 4TH JUNE.

H.M.S " Spitfire,"
4 June 1916.

SIR,

I HAVE the honour to report the proceedings of H.M. ship under my command in action with the enemy on the night of 31st May. The charts, notebooks, &c., in use at the time were unfortunately lost or destroyed, so it is impossible to state times and positions accurately.

2. The formation of the 4th Flotilla at dusk was L.T. 1 ahead of Battle Fleet. At dusk Flotilla was ordered to take station astern, and the formation at about 9.30 p.m. was single line ahead, course South, speed 17 knots.

" Tipperary " was leading followed by 1st division—" Spitfire," " Sparrowhawk," " Garland," " Contest "; 2nd division—" Achates," " Ambuscade," " Ardent," " Fortune," " Broke " and 2nd half Flotilla.

The position at this time was, to the best of my recollection, about 50 miles N.N.W. of Horn's Riff. The exact formation of the Fleet was not known.

---

1 Part omitted here, referring solely to personnel, recommendations, &c., in no way bearing on the course of the action.

3. During the movements denoted in paragraph 2 enemy T.B.D.s and submarines were reported and fired at by " Garland," " Contest," and " Fortune." These were not seen from " Tipperary " apparently, but I believe I saw the T.B.D. which " Garland " fired at, but as course was being altered at the time I lost sight of her.

4. Shortly after 9.30 p.m. heavy firing was observed S.W., apparently an enemy torpedo attack. Firing lasted some considerable time and then died away.

5. About 10.45 p.m. enemy cruisers came up from the starboard quarter (N.W.). These were reported from, I believe, " Garland " by W/T, and at the same time they opened fire from starboard beam at " Tipperary," who also opened fire practically at the same moment.

I fired my after torpedo at the 2nd ship in the line which was a cruiser with four tall funnels. The torpedo struck her between the 2nd funnel and mainmast. She appeared to catch fire fore and aft simultaneously and heeled right over to starboard and undoubtedly sank.

The 2nd torpedo was fired a few seconds later than the first, but I do not know its effect as I turned away immediately. Meanwhile " Tipperary " had received the full force of the enemies' fire and was ablaze forward, her forebridge and superstructure burning fiercely.

I fired a number of rounds at the enemy to try and distract their concentration on " Tipperary," and then turned away after 2nd torpedo had gone, to reload.

6. Course till turning away was South, and after that West, till I very soon got close to our next flotilla. Switched on fighting and navigation lights for a few seconds and turned to South again. Then having as I hoped given sufficient time to reload, I turned back to attack an enemy cruiser who had her searchlight on " Tipperary." Unfortunately the torpedo davit was struck in three places and the gunner, T.G.M. and L.T.O. all wounded, which prevented the last torpedo being got into its tube. I fired a few rounds at the enemy searchlight which went out, and then closed " Tipperary," but immediately came in sight of two enemy cruisers close to, steering to South-Eastward. The nearer or more Southern one altered course to ram me apparently. I therefore put my helm hard-a-port and the two ships rammed each other, port bow to port bow. Those aft noted that the enemy cruiser had 3 funnels with a red band on each. The funnels were similar in appearance to those of H.M.S. " Canada," though, of course, not so large. She also had a crane each side amidships similar to " Triumph's." I consider I must have considerably damaged this cruiser as 20 feet of her side plating ($\frac{1}{4}$-in. F.) was left on my forecastle. The plating was an upper strake, the top part having part of the gutter way and deck plating adhering to it, and the lower part had some side scuttle holes. By the thickness of the coat's paint (3/32-in.) she would not appear to have been a very new ship.

The effect of the collision on " Spitfire " was to completely demolish the bridge and searchlight platform, and the mast and foremost funnel were brought down, whaler, dinghy, and davits torn away. The cruiser also fired a large calibre gun at point-blank range, the projectile passing through the starboard bridge screens without exploding. Another projectile of the same calibre (probably 8-in.) passed through the bottom of the 2nd funnel from port fore side to starboard after side, grazing the top of the boiler, but fortunately without exploding. This may have been at a different time, or just before colliding.

The forecastle was torn open from stem to abreast the galley above water, and from stem to the 2nd bulkhead below water. On the fore mess deck no side plating was left from stem to as far as the capstan engine from deck level to tops of lockers. Some water got into the store rooms between 2nd and 3rd bulkheads, but the 3rd bulkhead (foreside of No. 1 oil tank) held well, and there was never any water in fore magazines or shell-rooms or on lower mess deck. Of those on the bridge, 3 were killed and 3 severely wounded. I myself was only slightly hurt. One of FX gun's crew was lost overboard.

7. Just after getting clear of this cruiser an enemy battle cruiser grazed past our stern at a high speed, and I think she must have intended to ram us. She was steering about N.W. and was emitting large volumes of smoke amidships. From her appearance she was either of the " Moltke " type and on fire amidships, or else a 3-funnelled battle cruiser with the centre funnel shot away. Lights were flickering underneath her forecastle as if she was on fire forward.

8. The extent of the damage to " Spitfire " seemed so great and the possibility of steaming for long at any speed so small that I decided not to endeavour to rejoin the fleet, but to make for port.

Meanwhile, until I had extricated myself from the wreckage forward the 1st lieutenant had taken charge, and having noted the course to be N.W. just before the collision he steered from aft and continued on that course.

At this period I considered it advisable to throw overboard the steel chest and despatch box of confidential and secret books. When I again took charge I found fires on forebridge and at base of midship funnel being extinguished by the engineer officer, C.E.R.A. and C.P.O. Smith, and others, the majority of the ordinary fire party having been wounded.

Having found ship was making no water forward aft of the damage and that 3 boilers were still in use, I shaped course and speed to make the least water and the most progress towards the land. The wind and sea got up considerably and at one period the wind suddenly shifted 8 points, so that I was unable to make the Tyne until noon on June 2nd—the mutual ramming having occurred about 11.40 p.m. on 31st May.

9. Ship was docked in Middle Dock on June 3rd and the crew sent on leave with the exception of a small care and maintenance party. It is understood that the Captain Superintendent will make arrangements as to their relief.

1 *   *   *   *   *

I have the honour to be,
Sir,
Your obedient Servant,

The Captain (D.),
4th Flotilla,
H.M.S. " Hecla."

C. TRELAWNY,
Lieutenant-Commander.

H.M.S. " Porpoise,"
Sir,   6th June.
I HAVE the honour to forward the attached track chart [2] of this ship on the night of 31st May for information.

I have the honour to be,
Sir,
Your obedient Servant.
H. D. COLVILLE,
Commander.

Enclosure No. 23 to Submission No. 1415/0022 of 20/6/16 from C.-in-C., Home Fleets.

REPORT OF MOVEMENTS, &c., OF CAPTAIN (D), TWELFTH DESTROYER FLOTILLA, DURING THE NIGHT OF 31st MAY–1st JUNE.

No. 0017/2a.
Commander-in-Chief,
      Grand Fleet.
    Submitted.

J. R. P. HAWKSLEY,
" Castor,"   Commodore (F).
    4th June 1916.

No. 0017/2.   H.M.S. " Faulknor,"
Sir,   3rd June 1916.
IN accordance with your signal Number 1800 of 2nd June, I have the honour to report as follows :—

31st May.

On Fleet deploying, Twelfth Flotilla in L.T. took station on beam of 5th Division of Battle Fleet, dropping back gradually

---

[1] Part omitted here, referring solely to personnel, recommendations, &c., in no way bearing on the course of the action.
[2] Plate 27.

abeam of Fifth Battle Squadron who were prolonging the line.

At 7.35 p.m.—"Faulknor" opened fire on a single enemy destroyer, about 5,000 yards on starboard beam.

At 7.43 p.m.—Ordered first division to attack destroyer and then rejoin. First Division ("Obedient," "Mindful," "Marvel," "Onslaught") then attacked and at 8.6 p.m. rejoined "Faulknor," "Obedient" reporting that enemy destroyer had been sunk. "Obedient" reported that this destroyer was flying a Commodore's pennant.

At 9.35 p.m.—Flotilla was in station astern of Fifth Division of Battle Fleet, 2 cables astern of "Agincourt," course South, speed 17 knots.

At 9.45 p.m.—Reduced to 12 knots.

At 10.45 p.m.—Increased to 17 knots, flotilla then being 5 miles astern of 5th division of Battle Fleet.

At 11.30 p.m.   Being forced off course, to port, by one of our own Flotillas led by a cruiser (believed to be "Champion"), increased to 20 knots, course S.S.E. Cruiser kept pressing us to port and eventually our course was N.E. Reduced to 15 knots to let cruiser and destroyers astern of her pass ahead.

1st June.

At 12.15 a.m.—Strange Flotilla having passed ahead, altered course to South, speed 17 knots. These alterations of course and speed were estimated to have put us 5' to east of our original position and to have dropped us to 10' astern of Fleet.

1.45 a.m.—Sighted strange ships on starboard bow steering S.E. On closing they were seen to be battleships of the "Kaiser" class. Altered course parallel to enemy and increased to 25 knots. Ordered first division (who were on my starboard quarter) to attack.

1.50 a.m.   "Obedient" reported that enemy were out of sight. Ordered first division to take station astern and led round to attack on a N.W. course. Ordered flotilla to follow round and attack enemy. Sighted enemy again, almost immediately, still steering S.E.

About 2.0 a.m.   Fired two torpedoes from port tubes, the first one at second ship in line, and the second one at third ship in line. When third ship was about 2 points abaft our beam, there was a very heavy explosion and she was seen to blow up. The flames and *débris* appeared to go up a great height. On firing, altered course to N.N.W. and proceeded down enemy line, six battleships in all. The first four of which were certainly " Kaiser " class, and I think the last two were of the same class. I am, however, not absolutely positive about the class of the last two. One destroyer was stationed close under port quarter of third enemy battleship. Controlled fire was opened on the enemy's battleships and continued as we passed down the line. As we neared end of battle line, cruisers were observed (three, apparently " Rostock " class) behind battleships, and standing towards us, opening fire heavily on us as they approached. Altered away N. by E. and increased to full speed. After a short time cruisers altered back towards their own Fleet and continued to attack the destroyers astern of us. Altered course back to S.W. and gradually to South at 2.20 a.m., with the intention of keeping in touch.

2.25 a.m.   Again sighted enemy, who appeared to be one cruiser standing towards us. Altered course to west. Lost sight of enemy and altered course back to south. After this we did not again sight enemy. When enemy line was last seen at about 2.10 a.m. they appeared to be steering S.S.W.

The following reports were made to Commander-in-Chief :—

0152.   Enemy's battlefleet steering S.E., approximate bearing S.W. My position 10′ astern of first battle squadron.

0212.   Enemy steering S.S.W.

Both above signals were made twice on power and were not answered.

Flotilla was ordered to work round to South after making their attack, but most of them appeared to have been cut off by the cruisers, as only " Obedient " and " Marvel " were with " Faulknor " when attack was completed.

Note.—There is no doubt that enemy battlefleet turned away, probably 8 points directly after we first sighted them, but they must have turned back to S.E. almost immediately. Their speed was estimated to be 16–18 knots, and the range on torpedoes being fired was about 3,000 yards.

3.30 a.m.   Passed " Marlborough " steering North.

3.40 a.m.   Joined 5th division of Battlefleet and took station on quarter of " Agincourt."

3.55 a.m.   Opened fire on a Zeppelin, but I do not think we
          hit 'her.

1 *   *   *   *   *

I have the honour to be,
Sir,
Your obedient Servant,
A. J. B. STIRLING,

The Commodore (F.),   Captain (D),
   Grand Fleet Flotillas.   Twelfth Destroyer Flotilla.

Enclosure to Captain (D), 12th Flotilla's Report No. 0017/2,
dated 3/6/16.

H.M.S. " NARWHAL,"
12th Destroyer Flotilla,
SIR,   3rd June 1916.
     I HAVE the honour to report that at 2.10 a.m. on 1st June
1916, when steaming South at 17 knots in company with
" Faulknor " and 12th Flotilla, I sighted enemy's Battle Fleet
about 1 mile on Starboard bow, steering approximately S.S.E.
     Course was altered to port to conform to movements of
" Faulknor," and signal was received from Capt. (D). to attack.
     I increased to full speed and followed " Maenad," who after
getting ahead of enemy altered to starboard to come in to the
attack.
     At 2.20 I sighted the first three ships of enemy's line, and
at 2.21 fired first torpedo at third ship, a Battleship of " Kaiser "
class, estimated range about 3,000 yards. A large explosion
was observed in her direction about three minutes later.
     At about 2.25 a second torpedo was fired at what appeared
to be the last ship in the enemy's line, class of vessel not
distinguishable.
I have the honour to be,
Sir,
Your obedient Servant,
H. V. HUDSON,

The Captain (D),   Lieut.-Commander, R.N.
   12th Destroyer Flotilla.

From—The Commanding Officer, His Majesty's Ship " Maenad."

Dated—5 June 1916.

To—Captain D, H.M.S. " Faulknor."

Submitted :—

     Attached is approximately the same report as one I was
ordered to send to Captain D, XIII. Flotilla, when at Queensferry,
marked " copy " of one to you.

---

     [1] Part omitted here, referring solely to personnel, recommendations,
&c., in no way bearing on the course of the action.

At the time it was written it was not known if any other ships had seen the explosion referred to or not.

I would point out that the time, viz. 2.28 G.M.T. by deck watch, was noted by my orders and checked just afterwards by my 1st Lieut., and that as nearly all other times appear to be 2.10 a.m., while my attack took place when nearly daylight and after the remainder by at least 10 minutes, the point is of importance, and would seem to indicate a distinct possibility of two ships having been sunk.

J. P. CHAMPION,
Commander.

H.M.S. " MAENAD,"
3rd June 1916.

SIR,

I HAVE the honour to report that at 2.28 a.m. on 1st June after attacking enemy's line of Dreadnought battleships of the " Kaiser " class with torpedoes, one of them, the fourth in the line, was hit amidships, which caused a terrific explosion apparently of her magazines, the flames topping her mastheads. Though the ships ahead and astern of her were seen after this, the ship hit was not seen again, and I consider there is little doubt that she was sunk.

No other British ships were visible to me at this time.

The details of my attack were as follows :—

After sighting the enemy's battleships about 2 a.m. and getting your signal to attack, I trained both tubes to starboard anticipating that you intended closing and firing starboard side.

When you turned to starboard therefore I was not ready and held on my course, turning later to fire one torpedo from the port side when the tube was trained.

I then trained both tubes to starboard and went ahead, closing in again to between 4 and 5,000 yards, when I fired two more torpedoes with different settings on the director.

The second torpedo struck the target with the above result.

The enemy turned away from 2 to 3 points after firing the third torpedo tho' a two point turn had been allowed for.

During this third attack, Sub-Lt. Hon. A. Stuart opened fire on the ship abeam with the after 4-in. gun and obtained three hits on her upper works with 6,000 yards on his sights. This ship did not open fire on " Maenad," tho' she was straddled several times by the ship astern until the latter blew up, when the firing ceased. The ship was not struck in spite of many close shots both short and over.

Shortly after this I met the " Marksman " and " Champion," who ordered me to join him, and I remained in her company till arrival at Queensferry on 2nd June 4 p.m.

At 3 a.m. two passing German destroyers were engaged on opposite courses in a few minutes, but were lost in the mist and not followed by " Champion."

At 5 a.m. 10 survivors of " Fortune " were picked up, also one body from " Ardent " for identification purposes.

I have the honour to be,
Sir,
Your obedient Servant,

Captain D.
    H.M.S. " Faulknor,"
    XII. Flotilla.

J. P. CHAMPION,
Comd.

II.

Forwarded :—

" Faulknor,"
6.6.16.

It appears more than probable that a *second* ship of the " Kaiser " class was destroyed by " Maenad's " torpedo. In connection with the attached report it is pointed out that this report was made out when " Maenad " was at Rosyth, and I did not see either " Maenad " or Comdr. Champion from time of my attack until I met him in Commodore Halsey's cabin in " Iron Duke." Commander Champion asserts that there were only 5 ships in enemy line, whereas I distinctly saw and counted 6.

A. J. B. STIRLING,
Captain (D),
12th Flotilla.

Commander-in-Chief.
    (Through Com. F.)

H.M.S. " ONSLAUGHT,"

Sir,

3rd June 1916.

I have the honour to submit the following report of the action of June 1st.

At about 2.30 a.m. on June 1st we received the signal from " Faulknor " to attack the enemy.

The telegraphs were put on to full ahead, all hands being at action stations, except the foremost gun's crew (gun out of action), who were distributed as necessary for ammunition supply, &c. The enemy appeared in single line ahead ; our own course and the enemy's being convergent, with tubes bearing to starboard.

Owing to mist no torpedoes were fired as the target was not clear.

The ship was then turned 4 points to Port and then 2 minutes later 16 points to port, when she was again heading for the enemy on a convergent but opposite course.

The order was passed to tubes : " Fire when your sights are on."

The two after torpedoes being set for short range, were fired by the Gunner (T), and the two foremost ones by the T.G.M., set for long range ; the first of these latter two hit the second ship of the line (apparently one of the " Kaiser " class).

A big explosion ensued, the flames mounting to about 400 ft. All torpedoes having been fired "Onslaught" turned 8 points to starboard; meanwhile a 3-funnelled ship, next astern of the one torpedoed opened fire and shell burst against the port side of the chart house and fore bridge, igniting a box of cordite, causing a fire in the chart house, completely wrecking the fore bridge and destroying nearly all navigational instruments.

At the time there were on Fore Bridge :—the Captain, First Lieutenant, Torpedo Coxwain, 2 Quartermasters, and both Signalmen and the Gunner on his way up the Bridge ladder. I had just been sent down to tell the Engine Room to make black smoke, in order to screen our movements, and had only got to the bottom of the ladder from the forecastle deck to the upper deck. I went back to the bridge and finding everything wrecked, Captain mortally wounded, and the First Lieutenant killed, I assumed command and gave orders for the after steering position to be connected, which was done very smartly. The fire having been got under, I took station astern of the "Mindful." In view of the fact that all torpedoes had been fired, one gun out of action, and that amongst our casualties were all the principal people, as regards the working of the ship, I considered that the ship was not in a condition to again give action.

No other means of signalling being available a Wireless was sent to "Castor" ("Faulknor" not answering) asking permission to proceed back to harbour, which was approved later. At 5.15 a.m. a position was obtained from "Mindful," and a course set N. 60 W., 30 knots. The glass top of the after compass was broken, and it was checked by boats' compass. The conditions were such on the bridge that the Doctor considered it necessary to remove the Captain to shelter; this was done. At 10.0 a.m. speed was reduced to 15 knots owing to the state of the sea. At 12.30 p.m. the Captain died.

At 2.0 p.m. increased speed to 25 knots.

About 4.0 p.m. a signal was made to Inchkeith that I expected to arrive off May Island at 7.0 p.m., and that I had no means of long-distance signalling and the private signals had been destroyed by fire.

At 7.0 p.m. sighted Arbroath during a rain squall and altered course to S. by W. increasing speed to 30 knots.

I signalled my 7.0 p.m. position to Inchkeith.

Off May Island, Torpedo Boat No. 34 signalled me to stop and take stations astern. She escorted "Onslaught" as far as the Forth Bridge, and when abreast of H.M.S. "Woolwich" I anchored.

The dead and wounded were taken charge of by the Staff Surgeon of "Woolwich," and sent ashore in Hospital Lighter.

I remained at anchor during the night and in the morning acting under orders of Captain of "Woolwich," weighed and secured to No. 39 buoy.

The behaviour of the Ship's Company during the whole action and afterwards deserves the highest praise.

1   *   *   *   *   *

I have the honour to be,
Sir,
Your obedient Servant,
H. KEMMIS,
Sub-Lieutenant.

The Captain (D),
12th Destroyer Flotilla.

II.

No. 0017/2.

Commodore (F),
Grand Fleet Flotillas.

With reference to my report No. 0017/2 dated 3rd June 1916, the attached report from " Onslaught " is submitted.

A. J. B. STIRLING,
Captain (D),
Twelfth Destroyer Flotilla.

" Diligence,"
8th June 1916.

III.

No. 0017/2.

Commander-in-Chief,
Grand Fleet.

Submitted.

J. R. P. HAWKSLEY,
Commodore (F).

" Castor,"
9th June 1916.

Enclosure to Captain (D), 12th Flotilla's Report, No. 0017/2, dated 3/6/16.

REPORT OF 1st DIVISION, 12TH DESTROYER FLOTILLA.

H.M.S. " Obedient,"
3rd June 1916.

With reference to Commander (F), Signal 1800, of 2nd June 1916. The following is consolidated report of 1st Division, after meeting held on board H.M.S. " Obedient." H.M.S. " Onslaught " absent :—

P.M.
5.45.   Enemy in sight to the South.
British Battle Cruisers steering N.E. heavily engaged.
Battle cruisers and Flotilla crossed bows of 12th Flotilla.

---

¹ Part omitted here, referring solely to personnel, recommendations, &c., in no way bearing on the course of the action.

P.M.

6. 0. 5th Battle Squadron passed this Flotilla and deployed, flotilla under heavy fire from enemy Battle fleet.

" Marvel " struck by 12-in. shell.

Flotilla formed in L.T. and took up cruising station on flank of Battle fleet.

6.15. " Defence " blew up astern of Flotilla.

6.30. Enemy Battle cruiser totally disabled bearing S.W.

7.38. 1st Division opened fire on enemy Destroyer bearing West.

7.45. 1st Division · parted company, attacked enemy T.B.D. and sank her.

Division straddled by Salvoes from T.B.D.'s further to the west.

7.59. Rejoined Captain (D) in accordance with signal.

Report to (D) 12, T.B.D. sunk was of the " V " class, the letter seen but number shot away. She was flying Commodore's pendant.

8.30. Course S.W., 17 knots.

9. 0. Course South.

9.20. Course S.S.E., 20 knots.

10.30. Destroyers were attacked on Starboard beam, ship observed on fire.

11.20. Observed one of our flotillas attack enemy Battle fleet on our starboard bow. Three torpedoes were seen to explode, ship also observed to be on fire.

A.M.

12.10. Flotilla received heavy gunfire from the direction of the Starboard beam.

12.18. Course E., 17 knots.

12.30. N.E., being chased. Then turned round to South.

1.43. " Obedient," D 12. Enemy S.W.

1.45. 1st Division proceeded to attack.

1.50. Enemy turned away, 1st Division rejoined D 12.

2. 0. Commenced second attack, enemy clearly visible to Port. Dreadnought battleships leading, pre-Dreadnoughts astern of them steering E.S.E.

2. 5. " Obedient " fired torpedo at Kaiser class battleship.

2. 9. Approximately. Torpedo exploded between her funnels, clearly lighting her up. Explosion was so great, that magazine probably blew up, flames went up higher than mast. It is considered that ship undoubtedly blew up and sank.

2.10. " Obedient " fired 2nd torpedo at pre-Dreadnoughts.

Between 2.5 and 2.8 " Marvel " fired four torpedoes. At this time division was being straddled by a heavy fire, noise of guns and bursting shells was too great to allow of certain observations as to results of latter torpedoes, it is not considered that their explosion could have been heard, unless their magazines had gone up as in first case. " Mindful " only having two boilers attempted to go straight for enemy, Sighting them on Starboard bow, and turned to fire, but was masked by " Onslaught," which was following in wake of " Obedient," and again by another T.B.D., name unknown.   " Mindful " was obliged to turn away to avoid being rammed on both occasions.

" Onslaught " fired torpedoes, one of which was observed to hit an enemy Dreadnought.

" Mindful " and " Onslaught " under heavy fire.   " Onslaught " hit within a few seconds of firing torpedoes.

2.20.	Flotilla worked round to the South. " Mindful " and " Onslaught " placed themselves under orders of " Opal."
3.25.	Observed " Marlborough " steering North. Slight list to Starboard.
3.35.	Joined " Revenge."
3.55.	Zeppelin in sight. " Revenge " fired 15-in. salvoes at her.
8.45.	Observed British destroyer with bows gone.
9.10.	Observed men on rafts, informed D 12.
9.25.	Parted company with D 12 and returned to pick up men on rafts. They had already been picked up by Dutch steamer. Men were German Bluejackets, and it is believed belonged to German cruiser seen to sink by " Sparrowhawk."

" Obedient "   G. McOWEN CAMPBELL,
Commander.

" Marvel " - R. WATKINS GRUBB,
Lieut.-Commander.

" Mindful " - J. C. RIDLEY,
Lieut.-Commander.

HARWICH FORCE.

DIARY OF EVENTS FOR PERIOD TUESDAY, 30TH MAY, TO SATURDAY, 3RD JUNE, 1916.

(Forwarded by Commodore Tyrwhitt on 19 July 1916.)

Tuesday, 30th May.

" Lucifer " sailed at 8.0 a.m. (G.M.T.) for the Humber to refit.

" Manly " returned to Harwich on completion of refit at the Humber.

Admiralty directed that destroyers detached at Dover should return to Harwich. " Loyal," " Lennox," " Lassoo," " Lark," " Miranda," " Mastiff " and " Matchless " arrived from Dover about 5.0 p.m. (G.M.T.). (" Meteor " was detained there by defects).

At 6.20 p.m. Admiralty directed that Harwich Force should be ready to sail at daylight if required. Informed Admiralty that the probable strength of the Squadron would be 5 Light Cruisers, 2 flotilla leaders, and 21 destroyers, including eight detailed for the 3rd Battle Squadron.

Wednesday, 31st May.

" Hornet," " Ferret," " Druid," " Sandfly," " Beaver," " Hind," " Lennox " and " Mastiff " left Harwich at 2.0 a.m. to join the Vice-Admiral, 3rd Battle Squadron in the Swin.

Remainder of Harwich force was kept at one hour's notice.

" Lennox " returned with defects and was replaced by " Matchless," who sailed at 4.20 a.m.

" Lookout " and " Laforey " returned to Harwich from Chatham on completion of defects.

" Meteor " arrived at Harwich from Dover at 5.0 p.m.

Intercepted W/T signals during the afternoon showed that an action was being fought between the British and German Fleets. At 4.45 p.m. requested instructions from the Admiralty, and at 5.12 p.m. the Harwich Force proceeded to sea so as to be ready to carry out any orders received. At 5.40 p.m. the Admiralty ordered the force to return to harbour and wait orders. Arrived at base at 6.30 p.m.

Thursday, 1st June.

At 3.9 a.m. received directions from the Admiralty to proceed to join the C.-in-C. Grand Fleet. Following ships sailed at 3.50 a.m. : " Carysfort," " Cleopatra," " Conquest," " Aurora," " Undaunted," " Nimrod," " Lightfoot,"

" Laforey,"	" Lance,"	" Loyal,"	" Manly,"
" Lookout,"	" Lassoo,"	" Leonidas,"	" Murray,"
" Lawford,"	" Lysander,"	" Mentor,"	" Milne,"
" Laverock,"	" Lark,"	" Miranda,"	" Myngs."

At 6.20 a.m. informed the C.-in-C., Grand Fleet, that the Harwich Force was proceeding to Lat. 55–30 N., Long. 6–0 E.

At 8.36 a.m. received orders from the C.-in-C. to send a division to escort " Marlborough." Detached " Laforey," " Lookout," " Lawford " and " Laverock " for this purpose at 9.20 a.m.

At 1.53 p.m. sighted " Marlborough," and despatched " Lance," " Lassoo," " Lysander " and " Lark " to escort her.

At 5.35 p.m. received directions from the C.-in-C., Grand Fleet, and at 7.2 p.m. from the Admiralty, to return to base.

Friday, 2nd June.

The Squadron arrived at Harwich at 7.30 p.m.

" Canterbury " was in harbour on arrival, having taken part in the action of 31st May–1st June and proceeded direct to Harwich.

" Laforey," " Lookout," " Lawford," " Laverock," " Lance," " Lassoo," " Lysander," " Lark," arrived at Harwich at 11.0p.m. on completion of escort duty with " Marlborough."

Saturday, 3rd June.

Nothing to report.

BRITISH SUBMARINES.—REPORT FROM CAPTAIN (S).

From—The Captain (S), H.M.S. "Maidstone."
To—The Chief of the War Staff, Admiralty.
Date—7th June, 1916.
No.—0157.

Submitted :

Submarines "E.55," "E.26" and "D.1" left Harwich at 7.0 p.m. (G.M.T.) on the 30th May, to spread on a line 270° from Vyl Light Vessel, "E.55" 4 miles, "E.26" 12 miles, and "D.1" 20 miles from it.

2. "E.55" sighted Horn's Reef at 0.5 a.m. on the 1st June. At 0.20 a.m., a Zeppelin, flying low, approached and "E.55" went to the bottom to the west of Horn's Reef. At 0.45 a.m. a noise was heard as of a sweep passing very close to the Submarine.

Between 2.15 and 5.30 a.m., 11 explosions of varying intensity were heard.

Nothing was seen throughout the day, except a Destroyer at 8.25 a.m., steering N.W. It turned back to the S.E. before coming into range.

On the 2nd, at 1.25 p.m., a German Submarine passed out of range, steering to the Southward. At 6.13 p.m., another Submarine was sighted zigzagging to the S.E., and a Torpedo was fired at her just as she was turning away. There was a loud explosion and an upheaval of water on her Port bow, but the Submarine was able to continue her course to the South. The Torpedo evidently struck the Port forward hydroplane.

On the 3rd June, a Submarine was sighted at 7.20 a.m., which dived 2 miles away, and at 3.0 p.m., another, which passed out of range, steering to the South.

3. Submarine "E.26" sighted Horn's Reef at 11.35 p.m. on the 31st, and Vyl Light Vessel at 1.0 a.m., going to the bottom on her billet between 2.0 a.m. and 3.0 a.m.

Nothing was sighted throughout the 1st June.

On the 2nd June, a Submarine, steering South, was sighted at 11.30 a.m., but she passed out of range.

At 0.20 a.m. on the 3rd, while charging on the surface, flashing was seen very close and approaching rapidly, and it was answered by five other vessels, which appeared to be Destroyers in line ahead, steering to the S.E. "E.26" had just time to make a rapid dive before they passed.

4. Submarine "D.1" arrived on her station and dived at 4.30 a.m. on the 1st June. Nothing was sighted throughout her patrol.

5. All three Submarines left their stations after dark on June 3rd, and returned to Harwich.

A. K. WAISTELL,
Captain (S).

(Copy to Commander-in-Chief, Grand Fleet,
      and Commodore (S)).

REPORTS FROM INTERNED OFFICERS.

Interned Prisoner of War,
Bella Vista,
Scheveningen, Holland,

SIR,   14th May 1918.

I BEG to forward herewith the following reports with reference to the action of 31/5/16 off Jutland, under three headings :—

A.—Report of the proceedings of the 2nd Division of the 13th Flotilla under my command.

B.—Report of the proceedings of H.M.S. " Nestor " under my command and her subsequent loss with attached appendices.

C.—Commander P. Whitfield's report on loss of H.M.S. " Nomad."

    1. Recommendations for recognition of the Officers and men concerned.[1]

    2. Track chart of H.M.S. " Nestor's " operations.[2]

    3. A letter written by Petty Officer C. J. Lewis.

I have the honour to be,
Sir,
Your obedient Servant,
E. B. S. BINGHAM,
Commander Royal Navy,
(late H.M.S. " Nestor ").

To
    The Secretary to the Admiralty,
    Whitehall, London.

REPORT " A."—THE PROCEEDINGS OF THE 2ND DIVISION OF 13TH FLOTILLA AFTER 4.0. P.M. ON THE 31ST MAY 1916.

Composition of the Division.

The 2nd Division consisted of the following T.B.D.s :—

    " Nestor " (Commander Honble. E. B. S. Bingham, R.N.).

    " Nomad " (Lieut.-Commander Paul Whitfield, R.N.).

    " Nicator " (Lieutenant J. Mocatta).

    H.M.S. " Onslow " was previously detached on special service with H.M.S. " Engadine " and, therefore, does not enter into my report.

2nd Division ordered to attack.

Shortly after 4.0 p.m. the signal was made by Captain " D," H.M.S. " Champion," to the 2nd Division under my command to attack enemy's Battle Cruisers with torpedoes.

Proceeding to the attack.

I therefore hoisted the signal " Proceed at Full Speed " and shaped a course two points to Port of our own Battle Cruisers

---

[1] Recommendations not printed.   [2] *See* opposite page.

course in order to reach an advantageous position on the starboard bow of the enemy Battle Cruiser line from whence my attack would be subsequently launched; at the same time I observed the enemy's T.B.D.s carrying out a similar manœuvre.

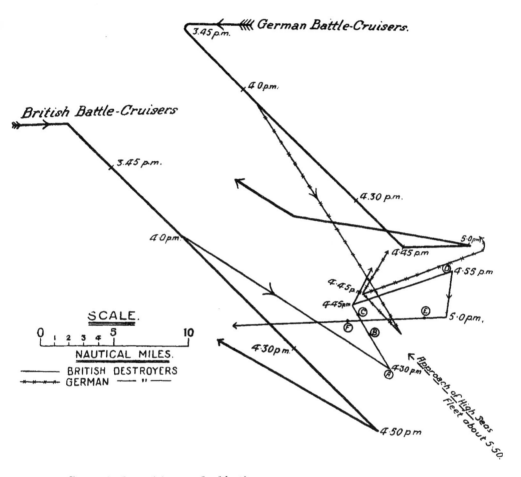

Strategical position and objectives.

This position A (*see* plan) was reached after half an hour's steaming, and appeared to me to be a suitable point to turn and carry out the following objectives :—

    1. Frustrate the intended attack by the enemy's T.B.D.s on our own Battle Cruisers by engaging them with gunfire.

    2. Press home our own torpedo attack on enemy's Battle Cruisers.

With this in mind I turned my division approximately 14 points in succession, the remainder of the British Flotilla conformed with this movement in their respective turn.

Destroyer action.

Fire was then opened at extreme range 10,000 on enemy's
T.B.D.s (15 in number) and we rapidly closed them. After
proceeding somewhat over five minutes on this North-Westerly
course, the "Nomad" hauled out of line and stopped
(position B), having received damage to her machinery.

The "Nicator" then took station a cable astern of "Nestor"
and a vigorous action ensued at close range between the two
opposing lines of destroyers. Before long two enemy's T.B.D.s
were observed to sink, and a 3rd to be heavily damaged steaming
at very slow speed; the remainder retired on their B.C. line,
dividing themselves into two portions.

Observations during action.

During this action, which came to very close quarters, I was
able to observe good results from the "Nestor's" salvo fire,
which, with that of the "Nicator," was, undoubtedly, responsible
for the sinking of their leading destroyer.

"Nestor" fires two torpedoes at enemy's B.C. line.

At position C, "Nestor" fired two torpedoes from the
starboard beam, both appearing to run well, as a result of which
the enemy's B.C.s were observed to alter course four points to
port in succession.

*Enemy's T.B.D.s retire.—"Nestor" and "Nicator" press home
torpedo attack.*

As related, the enemy's destroyers then retired, some of
which made back for the head of their B.C. line hotly pursued
by "Nestor" and "Nicator," the remainder shaped course
towards the rear of their B.C. line chased by the remaining two
divisions of British destroyers.

It will be seen in plan that "Nestor" and "Nicator" now
driving a portion of the enemy's T.B.D.s before them on an
E.N.E course, were at the same time rapidly closing the enemy's
B.Cs.; here we were subjected to the heaviest shell fire from the
secondary armament of most of their B.C.s, but we pressed on
fully determined to drive home our torpedo attack at the closest
possible range; when within 3 to 4,000 yards and on the beam of
the leading B.C., the "Nestor" fired her third torpedo
(position D).

"Nestor" and "Nicator" withdraw, the former hit.

Then, having accomplished my two objectives, I turned back
followed by "Nicator" to rejoin Captain "D," H.M.S.
"Champion." Shortly after this turn, however, an enemy's
light cruiser, believed to be their flotilla cruiser, issuing from the
disengaged side of the German B.C. line, took us under heavy
fire and shortly before 5 p.m. one of her shells hit No. 1 boiler;
six minutes later No. 2 boiler was also hit.

Between the positions E and F the " Nestor " was only able to steam at slow speed, and eventually came to a standstill at position F.

" Nestor " refuses assistance.

Before reaching the final position F, H.M.S. " Petard," Lieut-Commander E. C. O. Thomson, closed to within hailing distance of me offering assistance and a tow; this I was obliged to refuse, for I could not see my way to involving a 2nd destroyer in a danger which properly only applied to one, for at the time we were still under fire and able to steam slowly. In the light of subsequent events I am convinced that my decision was justified.

" Nicator " rejoins Captain " D."

" Nicator," who had so gallantly supported me all through the attack, succeeded in making good her escape and, I understand, rejoined Captain " D."

1 *   *   *   *   *

REPORT " B."—THE LOSS OF H.M.S. " NESTOR."

Details of the proceedings of H.M.S. " Nestor " up to the time she was stopped in the final position " F," have already been given in report " A."

High Sea Fleet observed to the S.E.

No sooner had the two B.C. lines disappeared to the N.W. hotly engaged than the German High Sea Fleet was observed approaching from the S.E. following on the course of their B.C.s. It became obvious that they would pass within three or four miles of our position. At this time " Nomad " was lying stopped E.S.E., one and a half miles from " Nestor."

The High Sea Fleet opened heavy fire on " Nomad " and she sank after a few minutes.

Preparation to abandon ship.

From the time that we realised that our destruction was imminent, all preparations were made with a view to saving as many lives as possible, and all confidential matter was thrown overboard and seen to sink.

The motor boat and whaler were lowered to the water's edge and the wounded were later placed in the motor boat. The Carley floats were hoisted out and placed alongside, the dinghy being damaged by shell fire was useless, the cables were got ready on the F'xle in the unlikely event of a tow being forthcoming; this was done on the suggestion of Lieutenant M. J. Bethell with a view to keeping the minds of the men occupied.

---

1 Part omitted here referring solely to personnel, recommendations, &c., in no way bearing on the course of the action.

" Nestor " shelled by High Sea Fleet.

The High Sea Fleet then drew up and we were very soon straddled, not before, however, we had fired our fourth and remaining torpedo. The " Nestor " now occupied the undivided attention of the H.S. Fleet and was hit in many places, principally aft and rapidly commenced sinking by the stern. Immediately I saw that she was doomed I gave my last order " Abandon Ship."

Abandon ship, " Nestor " sinks.

This was carried out in perfect order and discipline; the boats and Carley boats worked their way clear of the ship, which all the time was being subjected to a tornado of fire, and a few minutes afterwards she reared up in a perpendicular position and sank by the stern. Three cheers were given for the " Nestor " and " God save the King " was sung.

As Your Lordships are aware, the greater part of the Officers and men were saved, they being distributed in the motor boat and two Carley floats, but a few were obliged to remain in the water with their lifebelts on. The whaler, which had been damaged by shell fire, shoved off with a party including myself, but she sank after a few strokes and their occupants swam to the motor boat, where they supported themselves holding on to the gunwhale.

Enemy's T.B.D.s close, pick up, and make Prisoners of war of " Nestor's " crew.

After a period of about twenty minutes a division of enemy's T.B.D.s were detached from the H.S. Fleet and, closing us rapidly, picked up all the survivors and hoisted our motor boat inboard. Thus we found ourselves prisoners of war on board S.M.T.B.D. " S 16 "; the " Nestor's " Officers and men were promptly separated, the former being placed below in the Captain's cabin, the wounded in the Wardroom, and the men in the stokeholds and engine-room.

Survivors, 2 stokers from H.M.S. " Indefatigable."

At 8.30 p.m. two stokers from the " Indefatigable," unconscious and covered in oil, were picked up and treated by Surgeon probationer A. Joe, of " Nestor."

Conjectural movement of S.M. " S.16."

The subsequent movements of this T.B.D. can only be a matter of conjecture; from statements made to me by Dr. Joe, who was called forward to attend on " Indefatigable's " men, and from further statements made to me by my ships' company, I have reason to believe that we escorted a badly damaged B.C. until noon on first of June; whether or not this B.C. reached harbour I am unable to say, as the division of destroyers to which we belonged parted company with her and proceeded

direct to Wilhelmshaven, arriving there at about four thirty p.m.
Arrival at Wilhelmshaven.

1　　*　　　　*　　　　*　　　　*　　　　*

REPORT " C."

Bella Vista,
14 Van Stockweg,
Scheveningen.

SIR,

I HAVE the honour to report the circumstances leading to
the sinking of H.M.S. " Nomad " under my command, by
gunfire of the enemy during the battle of Jutland on May 31st,
1916.

On May 30th, " Nomad " and " Nicator," in company with
" Birmingham," were carrying out a night patrol, and during
that night received orders to join H.M.S. " Lion " and Battle
Cruiser Squadron off May Island in the morning.

At about 5 a.m. we sighted the fleet, and I received orders
to join up with Captain " D " of 13th Flotilla, in " Champion."

During the afternoon of May 31st we heard many wireless
messages on the German Telefunken note, which was reported
to be gettting closer and closer.

All preparations were made for Action, and the hands sent
to their Action Stations, and allowed to fall out again when
everything was found correct.

The signal was then received for " Champion " and the
13th Flotilla to take station one mile ahead of the 1st B.C.s,
and " Champion " and the three divisions of the 13th Flotilla
at once went on ahead, forming in " L.T." formation, with
" Nestor," " Nomad " and " Nicator " on the port wing.

The enemy were soon sighted, and the hands sent to Action
Stations. Very soon the B.C.s were engaging the Battle
Cruisers of the enemy, and at this early stage it would appear
that " Nomad " was hit somewhere aft, as a great noise was
heard in the region of the main bearings.

At about 4 p.m. the " Lion " ordered destroyers to attack,
and led by Commander Bingham in H.M.S. " Nestor," " Nomad "
and " Nicator " followed. As these ships developed full speed,
it became apparent that something was wrong in the main
bearings of " Nomad," as she was losing ground on " Nestor,"
and " Nicator " drew up on our beam. To keep the close
formation of the division, I ordered " Nicator " to pass me, and
myself took " Nicator's " position of third ship of the line.
I sent for the Engineer Officer and enquired if anything was
wrong, and he replied that he was finding out and that there
was a great noise in the main bearings. Flange joints had
started to leak and after these were tightened up the ship was
able to maintain the speed of the division.

---

1 Part omitted here, referring solely to personnel, recommendations,
&c., in no way bearing on the course of the action.

The Division having steamed sufficiently ahead to enable an attack to be made, "Nestor" turned towards the enemy and, followed by "Nicator" and "Nomad," commenced the attack.

At this moment about 15 enemy destroyers advanced to intercept us, and I ordered fire to be opened on the third destroyer of the line.

It would seem that the enemy considerably underestimated the speed of our division, as the "Nomad" was soon being badly hit, while the "Nestor" and "Nicator" seemed to suffer less. A shell close by the bridge brought down the wireless gear, and at the same time dislocated the searchlight.

Firing at the enemy's destroyers was carried with precision, resulting in the turning of the enemy's destroyers and rendering at least two out of action.

During this encounter, and before being close enough to fire our torpedoes with good effect, a shell entered the Engine Room, tearing up the deck for about 8 feet and bursting in the Engine Room, shattered the Starboard Bulkhead valve, and destroyed all the steampipes in the vicinity. I regret that this shell killed Eng. Lt.-Commdr. Benoy and severely wounded E.R.A. Willis, whose ultimate fate was never known.

Steam poured into the Engine Room, and the main engines and auxiliary engines came to a standstill. The emergency gear shutting off steam to the Engine Room having been rendered useless, I gave orders to shut off from the boilers. It was then reported to me by the Senior E.R.A., T. C. Dickson, that the stokeholds reported that they could not get water and I ordered the upper deck emergency valves to the oil burners to be shut. It was later discovered that the feed tanks had been shot through.

With the ship stopped, firing at the enemy was continued, and one enemy destroyer was seen to sink.

By this time the fleets had turned 16 points and the foremost 4-in. gun reported that it could no longer bear on the enemy. This report was immediately followed by a similar report from the midship 4-in. gun.

The after 4-in. gun continued firing for a while, but, being continually enveloped in clouds of steam, had to cease firing.

My attention was drawn by the signalman to a torpedo coming straight for the ship from the starboard quarter. I, at that moment, was watching the trail of another torpedo coming straight under the bridge from the starboard bow. Happily both torpedoes passed under the ship without hitting.

I ordered the ship to be prepared for being towed, and when this was done, observing that the ship's list to port had visibly increased and that she was slowly sinking by the stern, I ordered the confidential books, papers, and charts to be destroyed.

Proceeding aft to destroy the confidential books in my cabin, I observed an enemy's battle squadron on the horizon on the starboard quarter, but too far aft to allow of my torpedoes being fired. It seemed to be a question whether this squadron would arrive on a possible bearing before the ship had listed to such an extent as to make the firing of torpedoes impossible. As it turned out, the enemy came on the bearing just in time, the torpedoes only just clearing the tube, and the last torpedo, I consider, damaged its tail on clearing, so great was the list. I then, with Able Seaman W. Read, went aft to complete the destruction of the confidential books.

Immediately after this was done, out of the haze appeared another of the enemy's battle squadrons. "Nomad" was lying directly in their course, and firing was opened by them on the already crippled and sinking ship. The squadron firing at us were four ships, of which the "Thuringen" and "Posen" were two.

The ship was soon again being badly hit and rapid salvoes were being fired at us.

Seeing the ship could not float much longer, and with a view to saving as much life as possible, I ordered the ship to be abandoned. During this time the fore magazine was hit and blew up and No. 2 boiler was hit.

I went round the ship and, ascertaining that her life was a matter of minutes, left her. Firing was continued at her up to a range of 500 yards, and a salvo was fired at her after she sank, about a minute and a half after my leaving her.

¹   *   *   *   *   *

I have the honour to be,
Sir,
Your obedient Servant,
PAUL WHITFIELD,
Commander, R.N.

Commander Hon. E. B. S. Bingham, V.C., R.N.

APPENDIX 3.

To Commander Bingham, V.C., R.N.

On the 2nd of June 1916, whilst a prisoner in the German Naval Barracks at Wilhelmshaven, I received the following information from a German Bluejacket—a survivor from the German Battle Cruiser "Ludzow," who, for 15 years previous to the war, had lived in Australia and served on Merchant Ships engaged in the coast trade. He stated that he came to Germany for a holiday just before the war and explained that was the excuse all Germans were obliged to give for returning to the Fatherland about that time. He commissioned the "Ludzow" new 10 months before this date and had taken part in the Lowestoft raid.

On the morning of 31st May 1916 they were at sea when on board his ship the order was passed to issue respirators to the crew; it then became evident that they were likely to go into action; in the course of the day they were informed that in company with their High Seas Fleet they would engage the English Battle Cruiser Squadron and some of the

---

¹ Part omitted here, referring solely to personnel, recommendations &c., in no way bearing on the course of the action.

King Edward the Seventh Class. After the action had been on some time and the British Destroyers came out to attack the German Cruisers, he was ordered with the remainder of the Guns' Crews on the side of the ship where his gun was stationed to supply ammunition to the light guns on the opposite side to repel the attack, but he said owing to lack of cover many were killed and the light guns' crews disorganised by hits from the British ships, mostly in the superstructure; shortly afterwards the ship was torpedoed by one of the British destroyers and she listed but continued to steam with the Fleet, her speed gradually decreasing, when one of the " Barham " Class made a dead set at her and literally tore her to pieces with 15-in. shells. He explained one shell struck a Turret, the 2nd from forward, and lifted the top right off, killing everyone inside. After this he was ordered to assist in the fore dressing station, but stated it was impossible to remain there as the Doctors were killed and the numerous wounded that had been taken there for treatment were nothing but a mass of arms and legs caused by shells penetrating the hull of the ship. He then proceeded to the after dressing station, but did not go down, as the upper deck in places was awash and the firing had ceased. Shortly after, the order to abandon the ship was given, and destroyers that were standing by came alongside and took off the remains of the crew. He said you can take it from me when I left that ship there were five hundred dead on board. Our full crew were fourteen hundred, for we had on board about a crew and a half to fill up the places of wounded and killed. He also stated the Germans had no intention of coming into action with the British Grand Fleet, their idea was to sink the Battle Cruisers and the King Edward class that accompanied them, then return to their base before the Grand Fleet could come up and engage them, as both Fleets had been constantly shadowed all day by Zeppelins. He told me it was a great surprise to the Germans when they found instead of the King Edward class that came out of the fog behind the Cruisers, they had the " Barham " class with 15-in. guns to deal with.

I wish to state this man could speak perfect English and I had no fear of misunderstanding him.

I have the honour to remain, Sir,
Your obedient Servant,
Petty Officer CHARLES JUBILEE LEWIS,
O.N. 225,059,
Late of H.M.S. " Nestor."

SUPPLEMENTARY REPORTS. [1]

R 3/2747.

H.M.S. " Benbow,"
SIR,   3rd June 1916.

I HAVE the honour to forward herewith a narrative of events which occurred during the action of 31st May 1916.

I have the honour to be,
Sir,
Your obedient Servant,
H. W. PARKER,
The Vice Admiral Commanding,   Captain.
Fourth Battle Squadron,
H.M.S. " Benbow."

CAPTAIN'S REPORT.—H.M.S. " BENBOW."

H.M.S. " Benbow,"
3rd June 1916.

NARRATIVE OF EVENTS DURING ENGAGEMENT WITH THE GERMANS ON MAY 31ST, 1916.

G.M.T.   *Wednesday.*

P.M.

5.59 Observed Battle Cruisers engaged on Starboard Bow. Observed flashes of enemy's guns.

6. 4 Sighted enemy's ships right ahead.

6.14 Obtained ranges of an enemy ship with 3 funnels (13,000–14,000 yards), bearing Green 60, apparently in a damaged condition. Trained guns on, but did not open fire.

6.26 " Iron Duke " opened fire.

6.29 After great difficulty, owing to the haze and smoke, succeeded in getting Director on to a German ship, apparently of the " Lützow " Class, obtaining two ranges from " X " turret, mean of 16,000 yards.

6.30 Opened fire with " A " and " B " turrets. Green 73. Shots lost in haze.

6.35 Fired again with " A " and " B " turrets. Object obscured by haze.

6.38 " A " and " B " turrets fired ; object was then obscured by smoke from a ship on fire drifting down between " Benbow " and enemy. This ship was apparently an enemy cruiser with 3 or 4 funnels. ·

---

[1] The reports in this section were called for and received in the Admiralty in 1919.

G.M.T.

P.M.

6.40 Fire was again opened with " A " and " B " turrets, at a range of 12,500 yards; the target was crossed after the second salvo, and the order " Control " was given by the Control Officer.

The cease-fire gong was then rung, mist and smoke obscuring the target.

6.48 The enemy were observed turning away to Starboard.

6.54 Ship turned to Southward.

7. 2 Passed wreck of " Invincible."

7. 9 6-in. opened fire on Destroyers, bearing Green 56, at 8,000 yards.   Asked permission to open fire with turrets.

7.11 One Destroyer observed to be on fire.

7.17 Opened fire with " A " and " B " turrets on enemy ship probably " Lützow," Green 132 (about).

7.19   *   *   * 1   opened fire with all turrets.

7.20 Hit observed near after turret by several observers.

1 *   *   *   *   *

7.28 Ceased fire. Enemy Destroyers making smoke screen. 6-in. ceased fire about this time.

7.32 German Destroyer observed to sink.

7.34 German Destroyer making smoke observed to sink.

German Destroyer observed to capsize.

7.35 6-in. opened fire on 2 lots of Destroyers. Enemy Battle Cruiser reported to be still afloat, 2 masts and 2 funnels showing above water.

7.47 Trembling shock felt in Transmitting Station.

7.49 Collected reports of rounds fired :—

" A " turret -	-	- 12
" B " ,,	-	- 12
" Q " ,,	-	- 4
" X " ,,	-	- 5
" Y " ,,	-	- 5
Total rounds fired -	-	- **38**

7.57 Turrets stand easy.

8.24 Heavy firing heard right ahead.

8.27 Altered course 4 points to Port.

Top reported track of torpedo right ahead, crossing " Iron Duke's " bows.

8.34 Course, S.W. by S.

8.57 6-in. firing on Destroyers, one salvo (short).

9. 2 Altered course 4 points to Port.

9.14 Observed star shell on starboard bow.

---

1 *See* note on p. 381.

Thursday.

Observed Zeppelin on Port Quarter passing astern P. or S.
Opened fire with " Y " turret, 1 round.
Opened fire with 6-in., 1 round.

H. W. PARKER,

The Vice-Admiral Commanding,   Captain.
    Fourth Battle Squadron,
      H.M.S. " Benbow."

CAPTAIN'S REPORT.—H.M.S. " CANADA."

H.M.S. " Canada,"

SIR,   2nd June 1916.

IN compliance with your signal 1835 of 1st instant,
I have the honour to report as follows :—

2. On 31st May at 5.10 p.m., the Fleet steaming S.E. by S.
in organization 5 disposed to Starboard, the signal was made
for Light Cruisers to take up position for approach. At 6.6 p.m.
the Fleet altered course to S.E., the Battle Cruisers being then
before the Starboard beam engaging the enemy heavily. At
6.10 the signal was made to 3rd and 8th Flotillas : " Take up
position for approach."

3. At 6.15 formed Line of Battle, S.E. by E., speed being
then 18 knots.

At 6.22 three Armoured Cruisers, probably 2nd Cruiser
Squadron, were abaft our starboard beam, steaming in a N.N.W.
direction, when one of them blew up.

At 6.38 " Canada " fired two salvoes at German Ship, which
had apparently suffered heavily, and was much obscured by
smoke and the splash of other ships' fire. Object extremely
indistinct. Neither of these salvoes were seen to fall for certain.
At 6.45 ceased firing.

About 7.15 engaged destroyers about a point before the
beam. These turned away, using smoke screen.

4. At 7.20 fired four salvoes at battleship or battle-cruiser
on starboard beam, very indistinct, probably " Kaiser " class.
Range of first salvo was 13,000 yards, which was very short.
Third and fourth salvoes appeared to straddle, but conditions
were such as to make it impossible to be certain. This ship then
disappeared in dense smoke, probably a smoke screen.

5. At 7.25 signal was made to turn 2 points away from enemy,
followed 2 minutes later by a second 2 points.

At 7.25 engaged destroyers attacking abaft starboard beam
with our 6-inch. Broadside was divided between left-hand or
leading boat and the right-hand boat. At 7.30 fired three
salvoes of 14-in. on leading attacking destroyer abaft starboard
beam. Third salvo appeared to hit. This destroyer vanished
in smoke and is believed to have sunk. The right-hand destroyer
was also straddled by 6-in. and was lost sight of.

From 7.20 to 7.25 " Canada " appeared (from direction) to be fired at by a battleship of " Kaiser " class, or the " Derfflinger," on starboard quarter.   Shots fell a long way short.

7.35, ceased firing.

7.40, signal was made : " Single Line ahead, course S.W."

6. H.M.S. " Canada " was not struck during the action, and there are, therefore, no casualties to report.

I have the honour to be,
Sir,
Your obedient Servant,
W. C. M. NICHOLSON,

The Vice Admiral Commanding   Captain.
     Fourth Battle Squadron.

H.M.S. " Vanguard,"
2nd June 1916.

SIR,

I HAVE the honour to report on the action of 31st May, the details of which, so far as they came under my observation, are given in the enclosed narrative of events, and general remarks on the action.

2. Although H.M. Ship " Vanguard " was not hit and sustained no casualties, the conditions were a sufficiently severe test of morale to justify a word of commendation of the ship's company. All officers and men did their duty thoroughly well and with a cool and cheerful demeanour which it was a pleasure to observe. Men, organisation, machinery and material in general stood the test well.

1 *   *   *   *   *

3. I beg to draw special attention to item in narrative of events timed 5.55 p.m. From this it would appear the enemy must have a knowledge of Vocabulary Signal Book Number 2, although it has only very recently been brought into use.

I have the honour to be,
Sir,
Your obedient Servant,
J. D. DICK,

The Vice Admiral Commanding   Captain.
     Fourth Battle Squadron,
          H.M.S. " Benbow."

---

¹ Part omitted here referring solely to personnel, recommendations, &c., in no way bearing on the course of the action.

H.M.S. " Vanguard,"
2nd June 1916.

ACTION OF 31st MAY 1916. H.M.S. "VANGUARD."

GENERAL NARRATIVE OF EVENTS.

P.M.

5.52   Battle Fleet being in Columns of Divisions (Organisation No. 5), Course South, Speed 12 knots. Gunfire and flashes were observed between the bearing S. by W. and W.S.W. About this time our Battle Cruisers could be distinguished—" Lion " bearing S. by W.— and the Fifth Battle Squadron bearing W.S.W. with some of our four-funnelled armoured cruisers on about the same bearing as the 5th Battle Squadron. Visibility at this time about 9,000 yards, although flashes of guns could be seen further than the ships producing them.

5.55   A ship on starboard bow (probably German) flashing by signal " IAR " (" Stop engines ")—Vocabulary Signal Book No. 2. She continued repeating this for some time.

5.50   Heard gunfire on port bow—bearing S.S.E.

6.00   Our cruisers coming in.

6.13⎫
to ⎬ Forming line of battle. Course, S.E. by E. During this period our Battle Cruisers with the 5th Battle Squadron and four-funnelled cruisers were hotly engaged
6.22⎭ with enemy Battle Cruisers. During the period 6.15 to 6.25, enemy's shell were falling close to " Vanguard," mostly short, some of them ricochets, but one or two salvoes whistled overhead falling about 300 yards over.

6.10   One of our four-funnelled cruisers struck by an enemy salvo blew up and disappeared.

6.20   Another of our four-funnelled cruisers struck by enemy's salvo blew up and disappeared.

6.24   One of our four-funnelled cruisers surrounded by splashes of enemy shell, zig-zagging to escape, which she did, but apparently badly hit.

6.26   " Iron Duke " opened fire.

6.32   " Vanguard " opened fire, using director, at a three-funnelled enemy cruiser with swan bow (? " Freya "). Range about 11,000 yards. Hit her at 4th salvo. (This was the first target that presented itself. Enemy Battle cruisers had been visible earlier but were blanketted by our Battle Cruisers and 5th Battle Squadron). Continued firing at this cruiser.

6.35   (?) " Freya " apparently stopped (disabled).

P.M.

6.45   Divisions' 9 Pendant turn to S.E.

6.45   (?) " Freya " out of sight—checked fire, no target being visible.

6.50   Passed " Acasta " disabled (two cables on starboard beam).

6.54   Division's 9 Pendant turn to S.

7.00   Observed a German Battle Cruiser (? " Lützow ") badly on fire aft. She showed up very clearly against western horizon, but could not fire at her, being blanketted by " Colossus."

7.10   Passed wreck of " Invincible " (2 cables on port beam). A destroyer standing by.

7.10   Turned together to South. About this time enemy destroyers advanced making a heavy screen of black smoke which, drifting to leeward (i.e., towards our line), hid enemy ships from view and also formed a very effective screen for the T.B.Ds. themselves. Altered course 2 points away from enemy by sub-divisions.

7.18   Speed, 13 knots.

7.20   Fired a few 12-in. salvoes into the advancing enemy flotillas. Also fired a few rounds of 4-in. at them. One of the enemy T.B.Ds. drifted disabled out of the smoke screen.

It is presumed that enemy destroyers fired their torpedoes about this time, but nothing was seen of tracks.

7.25   Speed, 15 knots. Fired a few salvoes at another group of enemy T.B.Ds.

7.30   Fired at an enemy light cruiser, which was apparently disabled. 9 Point turn to S. by W.

7.50   Forming single line ahead on " Iron Duke." Course S.W.

8.00   Divisions separately alter course W. Speed, 17 knots.

8.25   Divisions separately alter course to S.W.

9.00   Divisions separately alter course to South. About this time, a white star shell was fired bearing west— evidently by a German destroyer preparatory to torpedo attack.

10.10 Torpedo attack on 2nd Battle Squadron—then on starboard beam of " Vanguard," one to two miles distant.

10.35 Torpedo attack on 2nd Battle Squadron—then on starboard quarter of " Vanguard " and from one to two miles distant.

" Vanguard " could have fired on this attack without using searchlights as enemy craft were visible in the beams of 2nd Battle Squadron searchlights. Considered it better not to take any action revealing presence of 4th Battle Squadron, of which enemy T.B.Ds. appeared to be ignorant.

This attack made apparently from astern seemed to suffer a good deal by 2nd Battle Squadron's gunfire. An enemy Flotilla Leader was observed to be struck several times by shell, making her glow fiercely for several seconds on each occasion. She was probably badly damaged.

(A diagram is attached[1] showing approximate courses throughout the Day Action, together with insets indicating the order of the Battle Fleet, as the principal changes occurred, also making reference to some of the principal events as they occurred.)

J. D. DICK,
Captain.

GENERAL REMARKS.

(1) Four targets were fired at :—

1st. Enemy cruiser, 3 funnels, swan bow (? " Freya ")·
About 9 salvoes (each of four guns). She was hit at fourth salvo and several times subsequently and is believed to have been badly damaged.
Range, 10,000 to 11,000.

2nd. A single T.B.D. lying between the lines apparently disabled, but in a position to fire a torpedo.
2 salvoes—8,300. Hit her, second salvo.

3rd. Enemy flotilla coming out of cloud of oil fuel smoke and turning in succession.
About 3 salvoes fired. Shell fell amongst them, but did not see any definite hits.
Range about 8,000 to 9,000.

4th. Enemy light cruiser similar to No. 1 target, but straight bow. About 3 salvoes.
She was hit. Fire ceased as she became obscured in smoke. She was not firing.
Range, 9,000 to 10,000.

Total rounds fired :—

12-in. Capped Common -	-	-	-	15
12-in. H.E. ,,	-	-	-	42
4-in. Common -	-	-	-	5
4-in. H.E. Common -	-	-	-	5

(2) Director Firing (aloft position) in conjunction with primary control from Fore Top was used throughout, and with

---

[1] No trace of receipt at Admiralty.

the exception of one small breakage (which was quickly repaired)
it worked very well. A few mishaps occurred in the working of
gun machinery and mechanisms, but nothing to cause material
delay.

¹ *　　　　*　　　　*　　　　*　　　　*

(4) Except for the thick weather, the gunnery conditions
were favourable for us—*i.e.*, the lee position and the best of the
light.

(5) Two matters contributed to save the enemy Battle
Cruisers from receiving the full fire of our battle line, viz. :—

> Thick weather and the fact that the line of fire was
> masked to a considerable extent by our Battle Cruisers
> and the 5th Battle Squadron. So far as " Vanguard "
> is concerned there was a difficulty in finding an enemy
> ship not masked by one of our own.
>
> It is not known whether the enemy Battle Fleet was
> present or not. They were not seen by " Vanguard."

(6) The employment by the enemy of a destroyer smoke
screen appeared to be skilful and well timed, and it
probably saved one of their heavy ships (? " Lützow) " from
destruction by hiding her from view.

(7) The position of the wreck of " Invincible " is such that
it is likely to invite the enemy's attention in the way of diving
for secret books, &c.

One of our submarines in the vicinity might do some good
work.

J. D. DICK,

H.M.S " Vanguard,"　　　　　　　　　　　　　　　　　Captain.
　2nd June 1916.

CAPTAIN'S REPORT—H.M.S. " BELLEROPHON."

" Bellerophon," 4th B. Squadron,

SIR,　　　　　　　　　　　　　　　　Saturday, 3rd June 1916.

I HAVE the honour to forward the following report of the
action fought on 31st May off the Horn Reef between the Grand
Fleet and the German High Sea Fleet, or parts of those Fleets.

2. The weather on the afternoon of the Battle was misty,
with a light southerly breeze and smooth sea ; the visibility was
very variable and deceptive, it did not often exceed four or five
miles, but sometimes and during part of the engagement, it
reached ten miles or more.

3. The Commander-in-Chief had informed the Fleet by signal
of the main events of the afternoon, how the 1st Light Cruiser
Squadron had sighted and chased two of the German Destroyers
until their Battle Cruisers were sighted, and then turned and

---

¹ *See* note, page 381.

led them to the N.W.; and then that the enemy's Battle Fleet were coming North and that the Battle cruiser fleet and 5th Battle squadron were engaging them.

4. Meanwhile the 1st, 2nd and 4th Battle squadrons, less " Emperor of India," " Royal Sovereign " and " Dreadnought," with the Attached cruisers, 4th Light Cruiser squadron and Destroyers were steaming S.E. by S. at full speed, a nominal 20 knots and actually a little more.

5. At about 5.50 G.M.T. the sound of distant firing was heard, and at 6.03 some British four-funnel cruisers were sighted coming in from ahead, and shortly afterwards the " Lion " " Tiger," " Princess Royal " and " New Zealand," but no enemy could be distinguished, though all these ships were firing briskly, and receiving the enemy's fire.

6. The Battle Fleet altered course to South by 9 Pdt. at 6 o'clock G.M.T., but went back to S.E. at 6.8 and at 6.15 we sighted some grey misty outlines through the intervals in the Battle cruisers and their smoke that appeared to be the enemy.

7. At 6.20 G.M.T. the position of the Fleet was very complicated. The Battle Fleet from divisions in line ahead steering S.E. by S. was forming line of battle to S.E. at 14 knots; the Battle Cruisers having come in from about S.S.W. were crossing between the battle line and the enemy to get ahead of the former; the Cruiser squadrons were steering roughly North and bearing about West, ahead of the enemy, on the Starboard quarter of the Battle Fleet; Light Cruiser squadrons were steaming about at high speed in various directions, and the Destroyers were taking up their positions for action on the battle line. The Battle Cruisers were firing with moderate rapidity and had evidently been hit here and there by the enemy, the Cruiser Squadrons were under a heavy fire, and at 6.22 one was seen to receive a salvo on her Fore turret and then to blow up and disappear.

8. As the " Bellerophon " turned into the line to S.E. the enemy became more plain, and with a clear range to them I ordered " Commence " at 6.25 G.M.T. It was impossible to count down the line from the bridge, sometimes one ship was in sight and sometimes another, so I contented myself with pointing out the enemy line to the Control Officer and left him to fire at any of them that he could see at the time. At 6.40 fire was checked as no enemy could be seen. At 6.45 passed the " Acasta " with 6, flag flying and engines stopped. At 6.35 altered course by 9 Pdt. to South. At 7.4 passed the wreck of the " Invincible," a Destroyer in attendance with a boat down. Just about this time several projectiles fell near the ship, and the " Colossus " in the next division was seen to receive a hit from a big shell.

10. The weather was now clearer, but the absence of wind caused the smoke from funnels, guns and shell, and from some

ships on fire to hang about on the water and obscure the view. Just at this time too the enemy employed some Destroyers to run a smoke screen between the Fleets which completely hid them and their movements for a time. An enemy cruiser or battleship of the " Deutschland " class was the centre of a heavy fire from the British line, but so many ships were concentrating on her that it was impossible to spot, and the fire did not appear very effective.

11. The High Sea Commander seemed to wish to have as little to do with the British battle line as he could, and confined his attention to the detached elements such as the 5th Battle squadron, Battle cruiser, and Cruiser squadrons. But his Light cruisers and Destroyers made one or two bids to attack the Battle line, but were driven off by gunfire, and though they must have been within 9,000 yards I saw no track of a torpedo, though a special lookout was kept for it. I directed both A turret and 4-in. guns to fire on the German torpedo craft when they were seen turning towards us ; the Officer of the turret claims a hit on one of them, as his shell burst on her and she was not seen again.

12. At about 7.17 G.M.T. the " Bellerophon " was firing at a Battle cruiser leading a division at a range of 11,000 yards and certainly straddled her more than once.

13. Between 7.0 and 7.40 several small turns were made and the Preparative was used to evade the attacks of Torpedo craft. At 7.40 the Battle line reformed on the " Iron Duke," course S.W. and at 8.0 divisions turned separately to West in succession, thus cutting in between the enemy and his base, but he was still going away to the Northward and was soon out of sight, and the action was discontinued.

14. I am perfectly satisfied with the conduct of everyone on board the Ship I have honour to command, everything worked smoothly and well in all departments. During the afternoon the ship steamed as she had never done before, and had a little in hand for keeping station. During the action there were no accidents and the only delay was caused by a box of faulty tubes which was soon discarded.

I have the honour to be,

Sir,

Your obedient Servant,

E. F. BRUEN,

Captain.

To the Vice-Admiral Commanding
    4th Battle Squadron.

CAPTAIN'S REPORT.—H.M.S. " TEMERAIRE."

No. 84/3.

H.M.S. " Temeraire,"

SIR, 2nd June 1916.

I HAVE the honour to make the following report on the Action of 31st May and 1st June 1916, in accordance with General Signal No. 1835 of 1st June 1916.

The actual time of the commencement of the action was not noted, but the first thing seen from " Temeraire " was the flash from the guns of our Battle Cruisers on the starboard bow. About the same time the Armoured Cruisers, Light Cruisers, and Destroyers were seen steaming in from their positions ahead of the Battle Fleet, to take up their Battle Stations.

There was considerable mist, which reduced the visibility to about 12,000, and nothing could be seen of the enemy, except the flash of his guns.

As the Armoured Cruisers approached the Battle Fleet, they were seen to be under a heavy fire, evidently from guns in the nature of 12-in., they were replying rapidly. They were probably about 1½ mile nearer the enemy than the Battle Fleet, and so able to see him. Only one Armoured Cruiser was observed to be badly hit, and she received a heavy shell about abreast of the after turret, which sent up a huge flash and much smoke; shortly afterwards she was still more heavily hit, probably by several guns of a salvo, and she disappeared in the smoke. What became of her was not seen, as the smoke took some time to clear, by which time no one was looking her way. It was reported that between the first hit and the second she fired a salvo.

The Battle Fleet deployed to S.E. by E. at 6.20 p.m., the enemy still being invisible, except for flashes.

The Battle-Cruiser Fleet came up from the quarter, and passed between the Battle Fleet and the enemy. They were about 2 miles nearer the enemy and heavily engaged. It could be seen that the " Lion " had been hit, as smoke was coming from a hole in her side a little before " A " turret, but no hits were seen to take place as they passed, although the fall of shot seemed very close.

After the Battle-Cruisers had passed, an enemy cruiser, probably the " Roon," was observed in a disabled condition. The " Iron Duke " opened fire at her, followed by other ships and " Temeraire " opened fire at 6.34 p.m. Director was used, and firing was slow on account of the number of ships firing. The first salvo was over, the second short, and the third was seen to hit with at least two rounds, and probably three, this salvo being fired at 8,000 yards. The enemy as now obscured by smoke and splashes from the other ships firing, and, as it was considered certain that she was out of action, fire was checked in order to save waste of ammunition. She appeared again a minute or two later in a less damaged condition than had been expected, and two more salvos were fired at her.

About 7.15 p.m. the enemy's Battle-Cruisers were sighted, the leading ship being only just clear of the bows of the " Colossus." " Temeraire " opened fire shortly after sighting them with a range of about 12,500, and seven salvos were fired. It is thought that they were all spotted and distinguished from those of other ships, but whether any hits were obtained cannot be said. The enemy was handled in a way which made fire-control difficult. She was showing the whole of her port side when fire was opened, then turned away until stern on, continuing to come round to starboard, and disappeared in the mist. She was observed to be heavily hit on several occasions.

Shortly after ceasing fire on the Battle-Cruiser, a flotilla of enemy's destroyers was sighted, a little before the starboard beam. They were making a large amount of smoke, probably to screen their Battle-Cruisers. The 4-in. guns were manned and opened fire, and, as the position of the enemy seemed so favourable for an attack, the main armament was also put on to them. Three boats were seen, just to the left of the smoke screen, steering in different directions, and a salvo was fired just as they all came in a bunch. It was spotted as going very close to them, and perhaps among them, but it is not known whether any hits were made. Two more salvoes were fired at places where the boats seemed thickest, and then fire with the main armament was checked, as the enemy appeared to sheer off and it was desired to avoid waste of ammunition. The range used was about 9,000.

The 4-in. fired 40 rounds. The control and gunlaying were hindered by the smoke from the 12-in. and the difficulty in getting the gunlayers on to a definite target. It appears, however, that the gunlayers were rather over-careful about their exact target, and sometimes held their fire when it would have been permissible to fire into the " brown."

During the night there was very heavy firing for a short time, from what appeared to be our Light Cruisers and Destroyers driving off an attack on the rear of the Fleet. One enemy craft appeared to have got fairly close up, but she was receiving a very heavy fire and being constantly hit, until she disappeared or sank. Nothing could be made out as to what she was, and all that could be seen were the bursts of the shells hitting her and that she was heavily on fire.

Heavy firing was heard again at early dawn, sounding like big guns.

Soon after daylight, a Zeppelin was sighted on the port quarter, abaft the bearing of " A " turret. The Director Layer was able to get his sight to come on with a range of 10,000 set. One Director salvo was fired the port side, and then the Fleet turned and brought the starboard side to bear, roughly on the beam. Two more salvos were fired on this side. It was unfortunate that as the guns were loaded with lyddite they had to be fired before loading with shrapnel.

The " Temeraire " was not hit, but a few shots fell close, notably one passed close to the main mast and one hit the water about 500 yards short on starboard bow. passing over the forecastle.

All arrangements for action in " Temeraire " worked satisfactorily ; the behaviour of the ship's company was all that could be desired, they were cheerful and eager for the fight.

I have the honour to be,
Sir,
Your obedient Servant,
EDWIN V. UNDERHILL,

The Vice-Admiral Commanding,   Captain.
   Fourth Battle Squadron.

ACTION ON 31st MAY 1916. H.M.S. "SUPERB."

No. 104.

H.M.S. " Superb,"
Fourth Battle Squadron,

SIR,   3rd June 1916.

     IN compliance with your orders, I have the honour to forward the following report of the action of the 31st May 1916. All times are G.M.T.

2. Gun firing was first heard about 5.30 p.m., apparently on starboard bow in a direction about South. Course and speed of the fleet then was S.E. by S., 19 knots. Later (about 5.50 p.m.) firing was seen about S.S.W. (flashes only), which eventually turned out to be our Battle Cruiser Fleet with Light Cruisers engaged with an unseen enemy to the Southward and to Starboard of our course.

6.05.   Course, South.

6.08.   Course, S.E. Our Armoured Cruisers, Light Cruisers, with some destroyers were observed about this time heavily engaged and apparently falling back on the Battle Fleet. As we were deploying, they seemed to turn to port.

6.12.   Deployed by Equal Speed Pt. to S.E. by E. and sighted Ships to Southward indistinctly—probably enemy ; too misty and indistinct to open fire. About this time a few projectiles were dropping in our vicinity but none very close. One appeared to pass between

"Iron Duke" and "Royal Oak" at 6.14, about 300 over, and burst on striking water, emitting a pale grey smoke.

Our Battle Cruisers on deployment seemed to be between us and the enemy and steaming at high speed on a course a few points to port of that of the fleet. "Lion" was observed to have a small fire nearly abreast her fore turret on the Port side, some white smoke appeared to be coming through her forecastle deck. They eventually passed ahead of us and disappeared in the mist. "Lion" was seen to be straddled once or twice. Two of our Armoured Cruisers appeared now to be continually straddled and struck by heavy projectiles. One salvo was seen by certain Officers to strike one of them (four funnels), and immediately afterwards she blew up with a heavy explosion and red flames. Another Officer also states that about this time he saw another vessel (three funnels) blow up.

6.26. "Iron Duke" opened fire, followed by "Royal Oak" and a three-funnelled enemy ship, "Kolberg" class, was observed steaming an opposite course.

6.26–50. "Superb" opened fire, green 80, range about 10,400 yards. First two salvoes out for deflection (enemy apparently stopped or reduced to slow speed, not at first realised). Third and fourth salvoes straddled and hit. Ship seen flaming fiercely amidships and aft. She disappeared in a dense cloud of white smoke. The Commander (G) and other Officers thought she sank, but I find she was seen later by ships astern of us. About this time the Navigating Officer states he saw another large German ship, but not for long. Two of our T.B.Ds. were also seen on fire, one at fore end, and one at after end, both heading on opposite course to fleet nearly.

7. 0. Passed wreck of "Invincible"; it was not known at the time what ship it was. A T.B.D. was standing by her with a boat down.

About 7.20. Observed certain enemy ships in line with some destroyers ahead, a large ship resembling the "Derfflinger" was clearly seen, but opinions differ as to how many were seen astern of her, some say two, some say three, of which one is described as resembling the "Helgoland" class. Personally I think they were Battle Cruisers. "Superb" opened fire on the supposed "Derfflinger" at 7.20, steaming apparently nearly parallel to us. We could not get a range, so opened fire at 11,000 yards without Deflection correct,

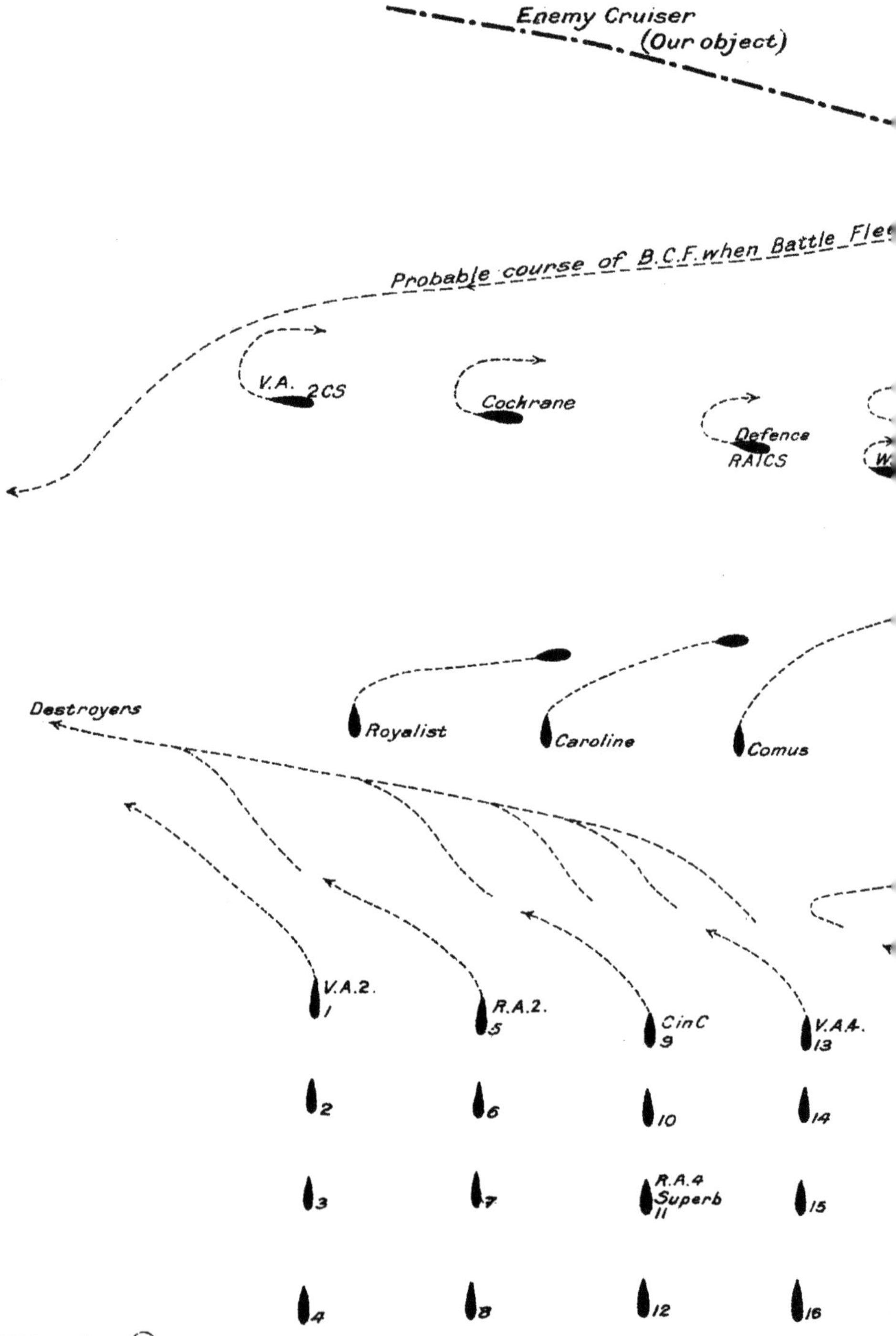

Enemy Cruiser
(Our object)

Probable course of B.C.F. when Battle Fleet

V.A. 2CS

Cochrane

Defence
RA1CS

W

Royalist

Caroline

Comus

Destroyers

V.A.2.
1

R.A.2.
5

CinC
9

V.A.4.
13

2

6

10

14

3

7

R.A.4
Superb
11

15

4

8

12

16

10072.24266/P.1179. 34 5000.12.20.

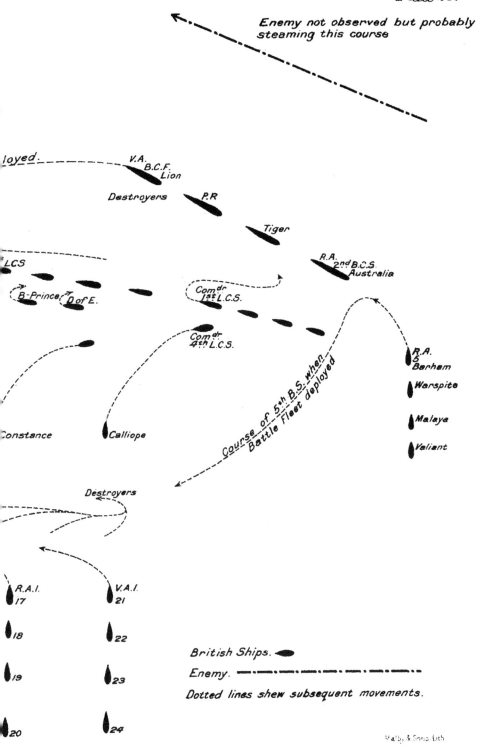

Plate 28.

Enemy not observed but probably
steaming this course

loyed.
V.A.
B.C.F.
Lion

Destroyers   P.R

Tiger

R.A. 2nd B.C.S.
Australia

LCS

B-Prince D of E.

Com dr
1st L.C.S.

Com dr
4th L.C.S.

R.A.
5
Barham

Warspite

Malaya

Constance   Calliope

Valiant

Course of 5th B.S. when
Battle Fleet deployed

Destroyers

R.A.I.   V.A.I.
17   21

18   22

British Ships.

Enemy.

19   23   Dotted lines shew subsequent movements.

20   24

Malby & Sons. Lith

but first salvo short. She was hit with the third and fourth salvoes, and then turned away heavily on fire aft. Some Officers say the destroyers ahead turned and made a smoke screen to hide these ships. I cannot personally confirm this, but they passed out of sight. " Superb " fired by director, which in such misty weather was invaluable. Control Officer had no difficulty in getting director on correct object, and no difficulty was found in distinguishing our own salvoes Chief difficulty throughout action was making certain between friend and foe.

7.23 and 7.26. Two turns of two Pts. to Port by Preparative. These turns are assumed to have been due to an abortive destroyer attack by the enemy which never developed, partly to excellent 6-in. firing from " Royal Oak " (perhaps also " Iron Duke ") and to the approach of our Light Cruisers and destroyers to engage them.

7.36. Course, S. by W. Formed single line.

7.43. Course, S.W.
Course and speed was subsequently altered at 8.3, 8.25, and 8.29 to West, 17 knots, W.S.W. and S.S.W. respectively.

9. 5. Course south for the night and about this time destroyers took station astern.

10.13. Much firing on Starboard Quarter, apparently a destroyer action; direct flashes seen and some large red fire-balls or something of that sort.
About this time a vessel on port hand passed showing bright white lights at irregular intervals.

11.30 and 11.43. Firing observed right astern, but no direct flashes seen, only the glare of gun flashes.

1st June.

0.25. Ditto on port quarter.

2.45. Turned to West and shortly afterwards to North.

3.35. Heard heavy gun firing about W.S.W.

3.50. Sighted a Zeppelin S.E. Several Officers seem to think she was signalling with a searchlight, and the Lieutenant (T) observed trailing from her what he took to be a trailing Earth for her W/T.

Nothing more of the enemy was seen after this.

Throughout the whole action it was misty and very difficult to see objects distinctly.

I attach a rough sketch of the wreck of the " Invincible " taken at the time by Lieutenant Curry (T) from several points of view.   Also a rough plan[1] of the movements of ships before deployment, as they appeared to Sub-Lieutenant Paul in the fore-top.

I have the honour to be,

Sir,

Your Obedient Servant,

E. HYDE PARKER,

Captain.

The Vice-Admiral Commanding
    Fourth Battle Squadron,
        H.M.S. " Benbow."

CAPTAIN'S REPORT.—H.M.S. " BLANCHE."

H.M.S. " Blanche,"

2nd June 1916.

SIR,

IN accordance with your signal 1825 of 1st June 1916, I have the honour to forward herewith the following report on the action of the 31st May 1916.

The presence of the enemy was first indicated by a wireless message from H.M.S. " Galatea," stating that two cruisers, probably hostile, were in sight bearing E.S.E. " Galatea's " position at that time, i.e., 2.25 p.m., being 56.48 N., 5.21 E. A signal was then made by " Iron Duke "—" Raise steam for full speed." The vessels reported by " Galatea " eventually proved to be enemy T.B.Ds. and were chased by her. At 3.4 p.m. course of Battle Fleet was altered to S.E. by S. (position 57.52 N., 4.17 E.).

At 3.22 p.m. speed was increased to 19 knots. At 3.26 p.m. H.M.S. " Nottingham " reported sighting smoke of five columns bearing E.N.E. Her position then was 56.46 N., 5.15 E. At 3.52 S.O.B.C.F. reported course of enemy S. 55 E. His position then was 56.53 N., 5.36 E. At 4.0 p.m. speed was increased to 20 knots. S.O.B.C.F. reported " Am engaging enemy " (position 56.53 N., 5.34 E.).

At 4.20 p.m. S.O. 3rd B.C.S., who was in position 57.32 N., 5.44 E., was ordered to reinforce Battle Cruiser Fleet. At 5.0 p.m. information was received that enemy's Battle Fleet was coming north. At 5.7. p.m. a signal was made to take up the position for approach.

5.47 p.m. enemy's Battle Fleet reported as having altered course to N.N.W.

6.9 p.m. Our Battle Fleet altered course by 9 pendant to S.E. (position 57. 09 N., 5.40 E.).

6.15. Altered course by equal speed pendant to S.E. by E. and reduced to 14 knots. Observed violent explosion on board a vessel bearing about S.W. " Blanche " took up position for repeating signals, 12 cables from " Canada."

---

[1] Plate 28.

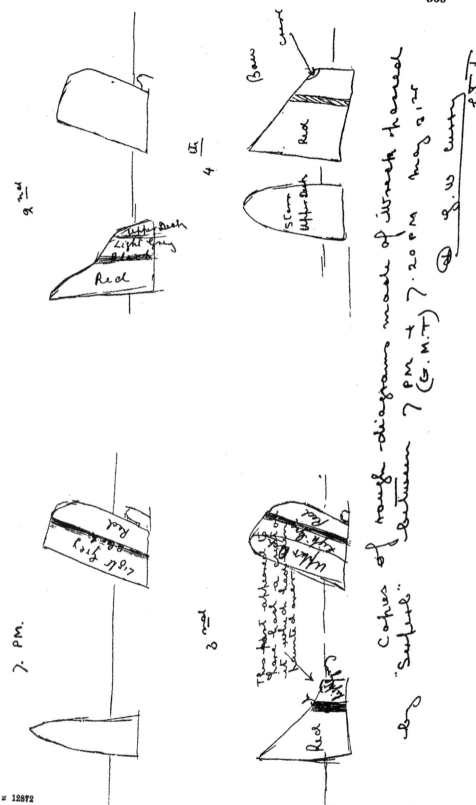

6.20. A second explosion was observed on board another vessel in the same vicinity.

6.25. Our Battle Fleet opened fire. 6.40. Our Battle Fleet ceased fire, except at rear of line.

6.50. Observed " Acasta " with signal flying " Am in danger of sinking through damage received by gun-fire."

6.56. Altered course to S. by 9 pendant.

7.0. Passed sunken ship, apparently a Light Cruiser. The stem and stern were showing out of water and a T.B.D. was standing by her.

7.12. Battle Fleet opened fire. 7.20. Battle Fleet ceased fire. Light Cruisers and T.B.Ds. engaged enemy's Torpedo craft in the van.

7.24. Altered course to S.S.E.

7.32. Destroyers were recalled.

7.35. Altered course to S. by W.

7.40. Altered course to S.W. by S.

7.48. Altered course to S.W.

8.3. Altered course to W.

8.28. Altered course to S.W.

9.3. Altered course to S. " Blanche " closed to 6 cables from " Canada." This course was maintained till 3.15 a.m. 1st June.

The " Blanche " at first took up her position approximately 12 cables on port beam of " Canada." At about 7.0 p.m. it became difficult to distinguish signals, owing to smoke interference, and " Blanche " closed on " Iron Duke," dropping back after the action was finished.

Owing to the misty weather and smoke interference, also the fact that " Blanche " was 12 cables further away from the enemy, and affords a very poor observation platform owing to low freeboard, it was very difficult to distinguish the enemy, and only on one occasion could the funnels and masts of the enemy be seen.

The general impression was that the enemy was engaging the rear end of our line, and very few shell splashes were observed near ships in our vicinity.

It is not known whether " Marlborough " was torpedoed by submarine or not, but the almost entire absence of enemy submarines and mines during the action leads one to believe that the enemy were either unaware of the presence of our Battle Fleet or, owing to the inferior force at first opposed to them (consisting of the B.C.F. and 5th B.S.), were led to abandon their well-known intention of leading our fleet to a spot where both of these were in readiness.

That some action was expected is shown by the large number of submarines reported off our east coast immediately before and after the action. The apparent futility of the enemy's T.B.Ds. as far as could be seen from the " Blanche " would lead one to believe that our cruisers, Light Cruisers, T.B.D.s had the upper hand. Their failure to attack the Battle Fleet during the night is unaccountable, unless it is assumed that they did not realise the position of our Battle Fleet.

Having got between the enemy and his base it was only the atmospheric conditions and the absence of air-craft on our side which prevented the enemy Battle Fleet being located on the morning of the 1st June, and possibly brought to a decisive engagement. The presence of the enemy Zeppelin may have assisted them in their escape.

I have the honour to be,
Sir,
Your obedient Servant,

The Vice-Admiral Commanding,   J. M. CASEMENT,
Fourth Battle Squadron,   Captain.
   H.M.S. " Benbow."

The Vice-Admiral Commanding, 2nd Battle Squadron.
(Through Rear-Admiral.)

3rd June 1916.   **25**

Report on Action of 31st May 1916.

V.A.'s Signal No. 1815 of 2nd June 1916.

The attached report on the Action of 31st May 1916 is submitted in accordance with the above-quoted signal.

O. BACKHOUSE.

CAPTAIN'S REPORT.—H.M.S. " ORION."

P.M.   H.M.S. " Orion."

6.15. Deployed S.E. by E.

Trained on an enemy cruiser apparently of Kolberg class already on fire aft and stopped, steam escaping from funnels. Foremast shot away.

Range from foretop rangefinder, 12,400.

Did not open fire as blanked by a ship of the 1st Cruiser Squadron. Fire opened by other ships of the 2nd Division.

About this time one of the 1st Cruiser Squadron on starboard quarter blew up and totally disappeared.

6.20. Observed one of the Battle Cruisers heavily engaged before starboard beam. Ricochets falling near ship.

6.32. Sighted ship of Kaiser class bearing 105° green on slightly diverging course, range by rangefinder, 11,100 yards.

6.33. Opened fire by director. Fired four salvoes. First two short. Third over and fourth hit with 13,300 on sights. Large flames observed near enemy's after turrets when fourth salvo fell. Immediately after this, enemy lost sight of in spray and mist resulting from a short salvo from another ship.

6.37. Ceased fire, enemy out of sight.

A a 2

7.00. Passed wreck of what appeared to be British battle
         cruiser, 3,000 on starboard side. Bow and Stern showing
         above water.

7.09. Sighted ship, apparently battle cruiser of Derfflnger
         class bearing 60° green, accompanied by a large number
         of destroyers approaching and then turning on approxi-
         mately parallel course.

7.15. Opened fire by director on her. Range, 19,800. Fired
         six salvoes of which the last two were seen to straddle.
         Other ships of the 2nd Division also firing at same
         enemy.
         Enemy turned away about the fourth salvo.

7.20. Ceased fire, enemy drawing out of range, and becoming
         indistinct.

7.21. Sighted enemy battleship (Markgraf or Kaiser class)
         coming out of smoke bearing green 98° on approxi-
         mately parallel course, apparently the leading ship
         of a column, as others could be seen astern of her.
         Range by Foretop rangefinder, 14,800, but before
         director could be steadied on target ship, ship turned
         4 points to port to follow 1st Division in avoiding a
         destroyer attack.
         Enemy then lost sight of in the smoke from enemy
         destroyers advancing from head of column.
         Fire not opened on enemy destroyers as own light cruisers
         and destroyers advanced and blanked the range.
         No further enemy ships seen after this time.

Firing was by director throughout, and the control was
carried out from aloft.

1   *   *   *   *   *

Director was invaluable.
There was no interference with spotting by the fire of other
ships.

1   *   *   *   .*   *

Number of rounds fired—51 A.P. Lyddite; accidents and
delays—nil.
As the ship did not come under fire there are no other points
calling for special mention.
Tracing is attached showing track of ship and of enemy's
ships observed with times of events.[2]

O. BACKHOUSE.

---

[1] *See* note, page 381.   [2] Plate 29.

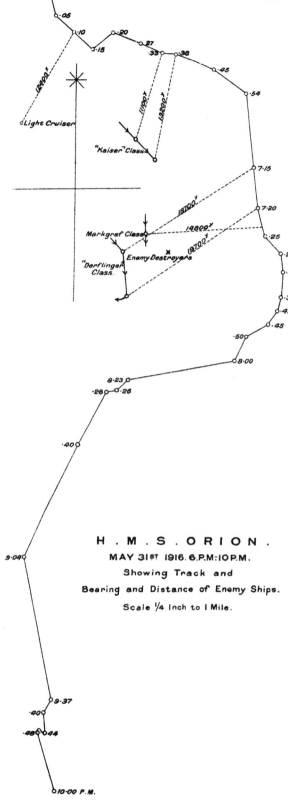

Plate 29.

6·00
·05
·10
·20
·15
·27
·33
·38
·45
·54

12400ʸ

Light Cruiser

11100ʸ
13200ʸ

"Kaiser" Class

15700ʸ

7·15
7·20
·25
·29
·33
·39
·42
·45

14800ʸ
13700ʸ

Markgraf Class

Enemy Destroyers

"Derflinger" Class

·50
8·00
8·23
·26
·26
·40

9·04

H . M . S . O R I O N .
MAY 31ˢᵗ 1916. 6.P.M:10 P.M.
Showing Track and
Bearing and Distance of Enemy Ships.
Scale ¼ Inch to 1 Mile.

9·37
·40
·48
·44

10·00 P.M.

NOTES TAKEN IN H.M.S. "MONARCH" DURING THE ACTION OFF JUTLAND, 31ST MAY 1916.

1758.   Light Cruisers opened fire, bearing ahead, course S.E. by S.

1802.   Altered course South. Sighted Battle Cruiser Force in action on Starboard Bow. 4-funnelled cruiser in action ahead (" Defence ").

1806.   Altered course S.E. Battle Cruiser Force commenced to cross between Battle Fleet and enemy. Cruisers heavily engaged.

1815.   Battle Fleet deployed to form line of battle S.E. by E. Battle Cruiser Force blanking us from enemy. Two 4-funnelled cruisers (" Defence " and " Warrior ") retiring towards rear end of our Battle Fleet. " Defence " disappeared in cloud of steam. " Warrior " obscured by splashes, but appeared to emerge safely.

1822.   Formed astern of 1st Division, course S.E. by E.

1830.   Opened fire on enemy light cruiser (" Kolberg " class) apparently stopped, heading about N.N.W., bearing 75° Green. Fired three salvoes, range 10,400. 1st missed right, 2nd just missed right, 3rd straddled.

1833.   Sighted five battleships about 95 Green, 3 " Königs " and 2 " Kaisers," 12,000 yards. Opened fire on leading " König " (2 salvoes). 1st over and right. 2nd appeared to straddle Quarter Deck. Shifted to ship of " Kaiser " class, 1 salvo, result not seen. Battleships disappeared. Ceased fire.

1845.   Altered course S.E.

1853.   Altered course South.

1905.   Altered course S.W. by S. to form ahead of " Iron Duke."

1908.   Altered course South.

1914.   Opened fire at Battle Cruiser (probably " Lützow ") escorted by Destroyers, bearing 76° Green. Fired five salvoes. 1st Short. Up. 2nd over, down * * *[1]. 3rd short, up. 4th and 5th straddled, but hits could not be seen for certain owing to smoke. Ship lost to sight in spray and smoke. She commenced zig-zagging after 3rd salvo. Range 17,300 to 18,450.

1916.   Ship observed heavily on fire, bearing 95 Green.

1919.   Observed Battle Cruiser of " Derfflinger " class bearing 110 Green. Also " Seydlitz," " Moltke " and " Von der Tann " behind and astern of her. They were very much scattered and appeared to have no formation. Trained on to " Derfflinger," but she disappeared behind smoke screen before " Monarch " could open fire.

1922.   Altered course S.E. 4th Battle Squadron firing at enemy destroyers about 95 green. 4th Light Cruiser Squadron attacked and drove off enemy destroyers.

---

[1] *See* note, p. 381.

1927. Altered course South.
1935. Altered course S.W.
1942. Altered course S.W. by W. ½ W.
2000. Altered course West.
2022. Altered course W.S.W.
2026. Altered course West.
2028. Altered course S.W.
2030. Heavy firing ahead.
2040. " Calliope " hit. Could only see flashes of German guns.
2102. Altered course South.

Throughout the action and during the night " Monarch " kept station on " Orion " and did not act independently at any time.

The following incidents occurred during the night of 31st May—1st June :—

About 2130, a German star shell was fired on our starboard beam.

About 2200, a Division of German battleships was in action with one of our destroyer flotillas on our starboard quarter.

A little later, another destroyer attack took place astern of us.

About 0330 a Zeppelin was sighted on our starboard beam when we were steering North. Trained turrets on to her, but did not fire as she was outside the range.

Steamed through a good deal of wreckage during the morning of 1st June and noticed one of the " Fortune's " lifebuoys.

CAPTAIN'S REPORT—H.M.S. " THUNDERER."

From—The Commanding Officer H.M.S. " Thunderer."

To—The Vice-Admiral Commanding Second Battle Squadron.

Date—3rd June 1916. No. 149.

Subject—Action of 31st May.

This account is almost entirely compiled from notes taken in the foretop by Commander St. Aubyn E. Wake; the view from conning tower and bridge was very limited by smoke and haze.

For the above reason I had to trust entirely to statements from aloft as to target, being able to distinguish nothing clearly myself.

P.M.
5.30. Heavy firing ahead.
5.52. Sighted our armoured cruisers, 1st or 2nd C.S., heavily engaged.
6.00. Deployed to port. Cruisers above mentioned under heavy fire, being straddled frequently. They were seen severely to damage a German cruiser, setting her on fire aft.

P.M.

6.17. This was thought to be· either " Adalbert " or " Karl Friedrich."

Enemy shooting at our battle cruisers appeared to be very good and rapid, many hits being observed. Could only see flashes of enemy's guns.

6.25. " Iron Duke " opened fire on damaged cruiser, followed at 6.28 p.m. by " Thunderer," then by " Conqueror " and others. Range about 11,800 yards, rate 0.

This was possibly the cruiser above mentioned.

Spotting difficult owing to the number of ships concentrating.

1 *   *   *   *   *

Four enemy ships now hove in sight, " Kaiser " class and battle cruisers. Guns were layed on one of these, but we were masked by " Conqueror " before we could fire. The weather had cleared considerably at this time and ranges of 22,000 yards–18,000 yards were obtained in the foretop.

On dropping clear of " Conqueror " we were masked by " Iron Duke." This target was, therefore, not fired at by " Thunderer " at all.

Two " Kaiser " (apparently) class were now observed overlapping each other, showing between " Iron Duke " and " Royal Oak." As there was a good gap between the two latter, I ordered fire to be opened through the interval.

The first salvo fell over owing to the range of the last object being used in error. This was at once corrected and the range from the foretop rangefinder (13,000 yards) put on.

The second salvo straddled in line with her foremast. Two or three large bursts with black smoke were observed, the shell used being powder filled common.

A third salvo was fired with no correction and a similar result obtained. This enemy was blazing for the whole length of her quarter deck.

" Iron Duke " was hitting this enemy, as was probably " Royal Oak."

A.P. Shell was now ordered, but before we could fire had to check fire owing to " Iron Duke " again masking us. By the time we had cleared, enemy had disappeared in the smoke. She was firing rapidly by salvoes at first, but shortly came down to slowish fire from one turret.

No further object presented itself, though rear of line was firing for some time after this.

Remarks.

(1) Just before opening fire there was a very large explosion on our starboard quarter, apparently beyond 5th Battle Squadron ; a column of water and debris was thrown up.

(2) No shots fell nearer to " Thunderer " than 400 yards (short). One was observed to fall over " Conqueror." Several salvoes and single shots fell short of " Iron Duke."

---

1 *See* note, page 381.

(3) Objects came into view and disappeared again in about 3 minutes. A quick R.F. reading, used immediately, was the only practicable method.

Most of the ranges taken were about 11,000 yards, but for a short period ranges 22,000 to 18,000 were obtained in the foretop.

(4) [1] *   *   *   *   *

(5) Firing was by Director throughout.

(6) No delays or mishaps occurred.

(7) Passed 2 British T.B.D.s on fire, one flying 6 flag. 6.59 p.m., passed also a cruiser broken in two, bow and stern showing above water. This was thought to be a light cruiser, but nationality was not distinguished. "Badger" standing by her.

(8) Battlefleet ceased firing about 8.30 p.m.

Shortly afterwards observed 3 of our light cruisers on our starboard bow. They were under a heavy fire, one with two funnels being hit 6 or 8 times in a few minutes. Enemy flashes were seen.

(9) 9.15 p.m., heavy firing on starboard quarter.

(10) About 10.30 p.m. an enemy cruiser challenged three times, switching on and off 4 red lights horizontal above 4 green horizontal.

Fire was not opened as it was considered inadvisable to show up battlefleet unless obvious attack was intended. Our destroyers shortly after attacked this cruiser and a hot engagement followed. She was seen to be hit many times. She eventually turned to port.

(11) Desultory firing was heard through the dark hours at intervals.

(12) About 3.0 a.m., 1st June, heavy firing to westward.

Shortly after this a Zeppelin hove in sight. "Thunderer" fired a salvo of common at it—range about 12,000 yards.

(13) 9.15 a.m.–10.15 a.m., passed wreckage, bodies, etc., among other things a short gig with brass sailing horse—a cask painted stone colour with red, white and black bands. Bodies had cork lifebelts in some cases and Kapok waistcoats in others.

Copy of signals[2] during action and track[3] of "Thunderer" attached. A comparison of these may be interesting.

J. A. FERGUSSON,
Captain.

H.M.S. "CONQUEROR."

H.M.S. "Conqueror,"
23rd March 1919.

Submitted,

With reference to Admiralty Letter M. 0962/19 of the 8th March 1919, the following is the report made by the Commanding Officer, at that time Captain Tothill, as to the part taken by H.M.S. "Conqueror" in the Battle of Jutland.

---

[1] *See* note, page 381·   [2] Not forwarded to Admiralty.   [3] Plate 30.

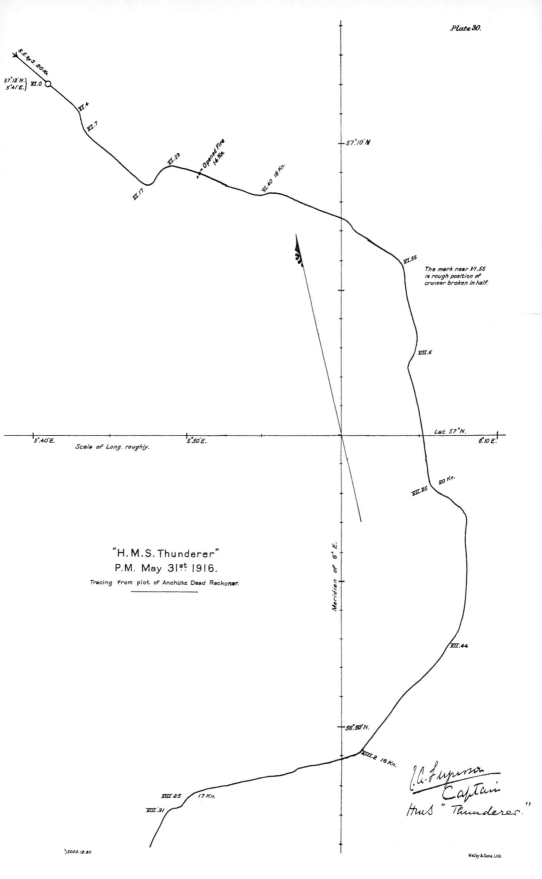

Plate 30.

57°.12'N.
5°.41'E. VI.0.

S.E. by S. 20 Kn.

VI.4

VI.7

VI.29

VI.17

Opened Fire
14 Kn.

VI.40 18 Kn.

57°.10'N

VI.55

The mark near VI.55
is rough position of
cruiser broken in half.

VII.6

Lat. 57°N.

5°.40'E.

Scale of Long. roughly.

5°.50'E.

6°.10'E.

20 Kn.

VII.25

"H.M.S. Thunderer"
P.M. May 31st 1916.

Tracing from plot of Anchütz Dead Reckoner.

Meridian of 6° E.

VII.44

56°.50'N.

VII.2 18 Kn.

VIII.25   17 Kn.

VIII.31

E.A. Ferguson
Captain
Hms "Thunderer."

5000.12.20

Malby & Sons. Lith.

"The enemy was first observed at 6.25 p.m. and at 6.31 p.m.,
" fire was opened on one of the 'Markgraf' class—rough range,
" 12,000 yards. This ship quickly disappeared in the haze, and
" fire was shifted to a three-funnelled cruiser (probably the late
" 'Maravev-Amurski,')—rough range, 10,000 yards—shortly
" afterwards this ship dropped astern and passed out of sight.

"No other ship presented a visible target until after 7.0 p.m.,
" but at 7.12 p.m. a destroyer attack developed from the
" starboard beam. Fire was therefore opened on these
" destroyers—rough range, 10,000 yards—and they turned
" away, obscuring themselves behind a smoke-screen.

"At 7.25 p.m. another torpedo attack was observed to
" develop from the starboard quarter, and fire was opened on
" these destroyers—rough range, 11,000 yards. These destroyers
" also turned away, making use of a smoke-screen, but shortly
" afterwards one was observed to be floating bottom up.

J. R. SEGRAVE,

The Vice-Admiral Commanding,   Captain."
  2nd Battle Squadron,
   H.M.S. " King George V."

From—The Commanding Officer H.M.S. " Ajax."

Date—2nd June, 1916. No. CR. 118/11.

To—The Vice-Admiral Commanding 2nd Battle Squadron.

Former—V.A. 2nd B.S. Signal (1815) of 2.6.16.

REMARKS ON ACTION OF 31st MAY, 1916.
H.M.S. "AJAX."

With reference to your signal (1815) of to-day, Friday, I have practically nothing to report. Until shortly after 7.0 p.m. the enemy were not seen, due to smoke and funnel gas of ships proceeding to the head of the line.

2. Shortly after 7.0 p.m. a clearer view was obtained, and one salvo was fired at an enemy battle-cruiser at 19,000 yards. This fell short.

3. The 4th Light Cruiser Squadron then crossed the line of sight proceeding to attack, and again obscured the view, so I ordered cease firing.

4. After that nothing was seen but patches of dense smoke at too far a distance for any hope of effective fire.

5. It appeared to me that each enemy ship was accompanied by a Destroyer which emitted dense volumes of smoke with the idea of obscuring the target.

GEO. H. BAIRD,
Captain.

FURTHER REPORT FROM CAPTAIN, H.M.S. " BLANCHE."

H.M. Gunnery School,
R.N. Barracks, Devonport,
Sir,   26th April 1919.
        In accordance with Admiralty Letter M. 0962/19, I have
the honour to forward a report of the proceedings of H.M.S.
" Blanche " during the Battle of Jutland, 1916.
        2. H.M.S. " Blanche " left Scapa Flow in company with
Battle Fleet at 10.10 p.m. on Tuesday, 30th May, taking station
astern of 3rd Sub.
        3. When Pentland Skerries bore S. 56 W. 2'.0 at 11.54,
course was shaped N. 82 E. 17 knots.   At 12.27 altered course
S. 78 E.

1.50 a.m.	Altered course S. 73 E.
3.30	" Blanche " took station 2'.5 astern of centre of Battle Fleet.
5. 8	Altered course S. 50 E.
6. 0	Opened to 3'.0 from Battle Fleet. Zig-zagged 2 points every 10 minutes.
9. 5	Speed of advance 16 knots.
10.30	Closed to 2'.5 from Battle Fleet.
	Observed position at noon 58.08 N., 2.58 E.
Noon.	Reduced to 15 knots.
2.43 p.m.	Increased to 17 knots.
2.50	Increased to 18 knots.
3. 9	Altered course S.E. by S.
	Opened to 4'.0 from Battle Fleet.
3.30	In station, speed 19 knots.
4. 0	Increased to 20 knots.
5.15	Took up station for the Approach, i.e., 5 cables astern of centre of line joining rear ships of two centre divisions.
5.30	Heard gun-fire to Southward.
6. 0	Battle Fleet deployed into line. " Blanche " altered round gradually to take up her station as repeating ship, keeping from 8 to 10 cables from " Iron Duke " and steering a parallel course.
6.25	Battle Fleet opened fire.
6.40	Battle Fleet ceased fire.
7.12	Fire was resumed.
7.20	Fire ceased again.
7.30	Our Battle Fleet lost touch with enemy Battle Fleet.
	From 6 p.m. to 8 p.m. D.R. in " Blanche " was kept by Shore's D.R. Calculator, giving Course and distance made good S. 17 E. 25'.0.
8. 0	Course S.W., 17 knots.
8. 3	Altered course West.
8.28	Altered course S.W., 14 knots.

8.47 p.m.	17 knots.
9. 3	Altered course S. Reduced to 13 knots to drop into station as Repeating Ship to 2nd Division.
9.30	In station. Speed, 17 knots.
10.40	Observed numerous flashes and heavy firing to the Northward.
11.20	Ship apparently struck some obstacle, a glancing blow.

1st *June.*

2.45 a.m.	Fleet altered course to North into single line ahead. " Blanche " proceeded as requisite to follow round and take up station as repeating ship on Port side of 4th B.S.
3.30	Heard gun-fire on Port beam.
3.43	Altered course West, 15 knots.
3.50	Sighted Zeppelin bearing S.E.
3.54	Altered course North, 17 knots.
4.23	Altered course S. 85 W., 12 knots.
4.30	Altered course N. by E., 18 knots.
4.48	Altered course North, 17 knots.
6. 3	Altered course S.E.
6.15	Altered course S. 55 E.
6.25	Altered course S.E.
6.30	Altered course S.E. by S.
7.12	Passed horned mine floating.
7.15	Course North. In station 5 cables astern of Battle Fleet.
8.30	Passed a small waterlogged boat containing a body.
8.54	Altered course S.S.W.
9.36	Altered course W.S.W.
9.48	Altered course S.S.W.
10. 5 a.m.	Altered course N. by W.
11.10	Altered course N. 45 W. In station 5 cables astern of Battle Fleet.

Observed position at noon : Lat. 56.20 N., Long. 5.22 E.
The remainder of passage to Scapa Flow was uneventful.

I have the honour to be,
Sir,
Your obedient Servant,
J. M. CASEMENT,

The Commander-in Chief,   Captain.
  H.M. Ships and Vessels,
     Devonport.

II.

No. 1014/0147.
Admiralty.

Forwarded in continuation of Plymouth Letter No. 685/0147 of 18th March 1919.

CECIL F. THURSBY,

26th April 1919.   Admiral.

REPORT (FROM MEMORY) OF PROCEEDINGS OF H.M.S. "BOADICEA" IN ACTION AT BATTLE OF JUTLAND, 1916.

(Admiralty Letter M. 0962/19 of 8.3.19.)

Original Report forwarded to Vice-Admiral Sir Thomas H. M. Jerram, K.C.B., K.C.M.G.

SIR,

H.M.S. "Boadicea" was attached to your Squadron as repeating ship during the day action, and no points of interest occurred which are not already known to you.

2. During the night of 31st May–1st June I was stationed $2\frac{1}{2}$ cables astern of "Thunderer"—the rear battleship. At about 10.30 p.m. a large ship was seen approaching about two points abaft the starboard beam at high speed. She challenged with 4 green lights horizontal, followed by 4 red when under helm, turning away. Thirty seconds was the time estimated during which the ship was in sight.

3. Directions were given for firing the starboard torpedo; but the time of enemy ship being in sight did not permit of this being done. At about 11 p.m. an action took place several miles astern of "Boadicea," lasting for several minutes, but no details of ships engaged could be made out.

I have the honour, etc.,

L. C. WOOLLCOMBE,

Captain.

APPENDIX I.

INFORMATION FROM GUNNERY RECORDS.

NOTE BY ADMIRALTY.

To supplement the foregoing despatches such extracts of gunnery reports received at the Admiralty a few months after the Battle of Jutland as contain information of interest in regard to the general course of the action are published.

Portions of the original reports received have been deleted, but only as far as plots from Fire Control Tables or references to fire control methods are concerned, these Tables and Methods being secret.

Whilst the records contained in the following pages supplement the despatches (which, indeed, in some cases contain similar gunnery reports, *e.g.*, " Iron Duke," page 52), it should be noted that the information was compiled in some cases from notes taken on the bridge during the Battle, or under other conditions which militated against accuracy in the estimation of ranges, resulting sometimes in a conflict of opinion between the entries of adjacent ships.

All ships did not furnish plots, transmission station records or other notes : reasons are explained in some of the following letters.

BATTLE OF JUTLAND.

From—Commanding Officer, " H.M.S. " Revenge."
To—Admiral Commanding, First Battle Squadron.
Date—18th November 1916.
No. D. 36/8.

SIR,

In accordance with Admiralty Letter G. 03934/16 of 20th October 1916, I have the honour to forward the following further remarks on the Battle of Jutland.

*   *   *   *   *

3. The information given below is obtained from notes by various Officers, taken down as soon as practicable after the action and not from records kept on the spot.

4. *Bearings and Ranges of Enemy Battleships.*—No bearings are available.

Ranges.—6.15 to 6.45 p.m.—Intermittent salvoes only were fired No hits were observed and no ranges are available.

7.0 to 7.30 p.m.—At 7.5 p.m. approximately, after altering course, fire was opened on the leading ship (left hand ship), thought to be one of the " Kaiser " class. Initial range 11,000 yards. A spotting correction of " Down 800 " gave a straddle, " Rapid Director " was ordered and several hits were obtained on this ship. As it was evident that several ships were firing at this target, fire was shifted to No. 4 ship from the left, one of the " Kaiser " Class, and rapid salvoes fired, several hits being observed. Fire was continued until the enemy turned away together and were lost in the mist and smoke screen about 7.30. 16 salvoes were fired at the two ships. The final range obtained was 9,500 yards.

*   *   *   *   *

I have the honour to be,
Sir,
Your obedient Servant,
E. B. KIDDLE,
Captain.

H.M.S. " Hercules,"
30th October 1916.

SIR,

WITH reference to H.F. Memo. 1187/84 of the 23rd October 1916 and Admiralty Letter G. 03934/16 of the 20th October 1916, I have the honour to report that I was in command of H.M.S. " Benbow " during the action of 31st May 1916 and forward the following extracts from the Navigating Officer's Note Book (Commander G. P. Bigg-Wither) of that ship and some extracts from notes taken by the Gunnery Officer of that ship (Lt.-Commander F. Elliott); there is no other information in H.M.S. " Hercules " other than that forwarded by my predecessor :—

Extracts from Navigating Officer's Note Book.

6.41 p.m.—4 enemy ships in open order visible on Starboard beam steering similar course to " Benbow " (S.E.) " Kaiser " class ?

6.44 p.m.—3-funnelled enemy ship (" Helgoland " class ?) bows one apparently stopped with destroyers round her bearing Green, 90°. (" Benbow's " course S.E.)

6.45 p.m.—Four 2-funnelled ships and one 4-funnelled ship bearing Green 100°–120° when they turned away. (" Benbow's " course S.E.)

7.10 p.m.—Enemy destroyers (6) bearing about 70° 8,000 yards. (" Benbow's " course S.E.)

7.16 p.m.—Fire observed in Enemy ship.

7.26 p.m.—Enemy destroyers on starboard beam. Our Light Cruisers attacking them.

Extracts from Gunnery Lieutenant's Notes.

6.14 p.m.—Obtained ranges of an enemy ship with 3 funnels, 13,000-14,000 yards bearing Green 60°, apparently in a damaged condition. (" Benbow's " course N.E. by E.)

6.30 p.m.—Ship of " Lutzow " or " Kaiser " class bearing Green 73°, 16,000 yards (" Benbow's " course S.E. by E.)

6.40 p.m.—Fire re-opened range 12,500 yards. No bearing taken.

7.17 p.m.—Opened fire on enemy ship " Lutzow " class, bearing about Green 132. (" Benbow's " course S.S.E.)

. 7.19 p.m.—Spotted down 1,600 yards, and opened fire with all turrets.

7.20 p.m.—Hit observed near after turret by several observers.

I have the honour to be,
Sir,
Your obedient Servant,
H. W. PARKER,
Captain.

The Vice-Admiral Commanding,
Fourth Battle Squadron.

From—The Commanding Officer, H.M.S. " Ajax."

To—The Secretary of the Admiralty (through Vice-Admiral Commanding Second Battle Squadron).

30th September 1916.

No. E. 68/14.

Subject.—Plot contained in the action of the 31st May 1916.

Former.—H. F. Memorandum 1187/68 of 24th September 1916.

H.M.S. " Ajax."

In accordance with the above quoted Memorandum, I have the honour to forward the plot of the period of time in which H.M. Ship under my command was in sight of the enemy.

2. Owing to the mist and smoke this was all that could be obtained.

GEORGE H. BAIRD,
Captain.

From—The Commanding Officer, H.M.S. " Ajax."

To—The Secretary of the Admiralty.

Date.—30th October 1916.

No. E. 74/7.

Subject.—Further information of the action of 31st May 1916.

Former.—Admiralty Letter of 20th October 1916, G. 03934/16.

H.M.S. " Ajax."

With reference to the above quoted Order, the following particulars are forwarded :—

1. Range on Sights at Open Fire, 18,700.

*   *   *   *   *

3. Rough Bearing was 87 Green—a Battle Cruiser. . . . . The trainer in Gun Control Tower had very great difficulty in seeing the object.

GEO. H. BAIRD,
Captain.

From—The Commanding Officer, H.M.S. " Erin."

To—The Vice-Admiral Commanding, Second Battle Squadron.

3rd October 1916, No. 49.

Subject—Rangefinding Plot of Action, 31st May 1916.

Former—H.F. 1187/68 of 24th September 1916.

H.M.S. " Erin."

Submitted,

WITH reference to H.F. 1187/68 of 24th September 1916, only six ranges were taken altogether, at considerable intervals and no value could be obtained from them.

The roll containing this information was therefore not kept and has since been destroyed.

V. A. STANLEY,
Captain.

H.M.S. " Monarch,"

SIR,   29th October 1916.

WITH reference to Admiralty Letter G. 03934/16 of 20th October 1916 the following is submitted for information of their Lordships :—

*   *   *   *   *

6.30 p.m.—Opened fire on ship of " Kolberg " class, Bearing 75 Green. Enemy on opposite course, but apparently stopped. .

6.33 p.m.—Sighted 5 Battleships (" Königs " and " Kaisers ") about 95 Green. Opened fire.

7.14 p.m.—Opened fire at Battleships of " König " class escorted by destroyers, bearing 76 Green.

7.16 p.m.—Ship observed heavily on fire, bearing 95 Green.

7.19 p.m.—Sighted Battle Cruiser of " Derflinger " class, bearing 110 Green, also Battle Cruiser (appeared to be " Seydlitz ") beyond " Derflinger."

G. BORRETT,
Captain.

The Secretary,
    of the Admiralty.

From—Commanding Officer, H.M.S. " Conqueror."

To—The Vice Admiral Commanding, Second Battle Squadron.

2nd October 1916. No. 103.

Subject.—Dreyer table plotting charts—31st May 1916.

Former.—H.F. 1187/68 of 24th September 1916.

H.M.S. " Conqueror."

Herewith Dreyer Table Plotting Chart for action during daylight of 31st May 1916.

Very few ranges were taken.

Remarks outside of plot are those passed from Foretop to Transmitting Station.

H. H. D. TOTHILL,
Captain.

No. 274/001/2.

"Bellerophon,"
Sir,   10th October 1916.
WITH reference to H.F. Memorandum 1187/68 of 24th September 1916, ordering Dreyer Table plotting charts of the action of the 31st May 1916 to be sent to the Admiralty, I have the honour to report that very few ranges were obtained and though a small plot was made,   *   * *   *   * the record has not been kept.

I have the honour to be,
Sir,
Your Obedient Servant,
HUGH WATSON,
The Vice Admiral Commanding,   Captain.
Fourth Battle Squadron.

No. R. 1/68.

H.M.S. "Calliope,"
Sir,   15th October 1916.
IN accordance with H.F. Memorandum 1187/68 of 24/9/16, I have the honour to forward herewith a synopsis of what range and bearing records were taken in "Calliope," when in sight of enemy vessels on the evening of 31st May 1916.

(a) 6.12 p.m.—One enemy Light Cruiser S.S.E., 11,000 yards, engaged by two armoured cruisers.
    "King George V." bearing from "Calliope," N.W. by N. 3'.

(b) 6.13 p.m.—Enemy Battle Cruisers. South 13,000 yards, engaged by Battle Cruiser Fleet.
    "Lion" bearing from "Calliope," South 2'.

(c) 6.20 p.m.—One Enemy Light Cruiser (4 funnels) bearing (approximately) S. by E. from "Calliope," 12,000 yards seen to sink.

(d) 6.35 p.m.—Enemy Capital Ships, class not distinguished, bearing West from "Calliope," engaged by Centre and Rear Divisions (IV. and I. Battle Squadrons) of Battle Fleet.

(e) 7.00 p.m.—Fourth Light Cruiser Squadron took station 2' on starboard bow "King George V."—latter bearing N.N.E. Course South. One enemy Battle Cruiser ("Lutzow"?) bearing West steering slowly to N.W. with destroyer screen.

(f) 7.28 p.m.—Enemy destroyers, half flotilla, observed N.W. by N. threatening van of Battle Fleet. Rear Battle Cruiser— "Indomitable"—then bore S.E. 2,000' yards and "King George V" N.E. by E. 7,000 yards from "Calliope." Fourth Light Cruiser Squadron closed to engage: two enemy destroyers sunk at approx. 8,000 yards. Enemy destroyers retired. 7.36 p.m. Squadron resumed station at Van.

(g) 8.05 p.m.—Smoke Screen observed W.N.W.

(h) 8.10 to 8.15 p.m.—"Calliope," "Constance," "Comus," moved out N.W. to support "Castor" and XI. Flotilla. Engaged enemy destroyers W.N.W. Steering S.S.W.

(i) 8.24 p.m.—Enemy destroyers made smoke screen and retired.

(j) 8.26 p.m.—Sighted main body enemy Battle Fleet, N.W. 8,000 yards, Six or seven Capital Ships made out—two (three) "Heligoland"?. (Note—3 tall funnels, no boat cranes): four "Kaiser" class—approximate course S.W., speed 18–20 knots. Enemy opened fire with secondary armament.

(*k*) 8.30 p.m.—" Calliope " fired a torpedo. Target leading Ship,
"Kaiser" division, bearing W. by N. 6,500 yards
"Calliope," "Constance," "Comus" retired towards
our Battle Fleet.

(*l*) 8.38 p.m.—Distinct explosion observed in one "Kaiser" class
battleship.

(*m*) 8.40 p.m.—Lost touch with enemy Battle Fleet who ceased firing,
bearing W. by S.

I have the honour to be,
Sir,
Your obedient Servant,
C. E. LE MESURIER,
Commodore.

The Secretary of the Admiralty,
Whitehall, S.W.

Reg. No. 836/114.

H.M.S. " Constance,"

Sir,   3rd October 1916.

WITH reference to memorandum H.F. 1187/68 of the 24th September 1916 I have the honour to report as follows; though all times,
bearings, and distances are approximate :—

1. 6.00 p.m.—Enemy light cruisers bearing 50' Green—10,000 yards.
   ("Constance" masked by "Defence" and "Warrior.")
2. 6.30 p.m.—Enemy Battle Cruisers, bearing 100' Green—14,000
   yards.
3. 7.10 p.m.—Enemy Destroyers, right ahead, 7,500 yards.
4. 7.30 p.m.—Enemy 3rd Battle Squadrons, bearing 80' to 110' Green
   —12,000 yards.
5. 8.15 p.m.—Enemy Destroyers right ahead at extreme visibility.
6. 8.25 p.m.—Four "Kaiser's" and ? three "Helgolands," bearing
   70' to 80' Green—8,000 yards.

I have the honour to be,
Sir,
Your obedient Servant,
C. S. TOWNSEND
Captain.

The Commodore Commanding,
4th Light Cruiser Squadron,
H.M.S. " Calliope."

No. 156/2.

H.M.S. " Malaya,"

Sir,   5th October 1916.

IN accordance with Memorandum H.F. 1187/68 of 24th September
1916 I have the honour to forward a range-plot comprising a period of
thirty-three minutes, which is the plot taken between 4.0 p.m. and
4.33 p.m., G.M.T., during the action against the German Battle Cruisers.
During the later stages of the action with the High Sea Fleet, ranges were
few and isolated owing to low visibility.

*   *   *   *   *

The ranges from 3m.–30s. to 8m.–30s. were taken of what then
appeared to be the rear enemy battle cruiser, on which "Malaya" was
ordered to concentrate with "Warspite." "Malaya" never opened fire
as a fifth enemy battle cruiser ("Seydlitz") made its appearance some
way astern, and object was shifted immediately.

First gun was fired at 15m.–0s. (*i.e.*, 4,15 p.m., G.M.T.). Straddled
at 17m–30s.

When enemy turned away after being hit, few ranges were obtained
for the following minute or so as enemy smoke interfered.

*   *   *   *   *

The gun range reached 21,500 yards.

Enemy altered back again to form astern of leading enemy battle cruisers.

*   *   *   *   *

At 30m–0s the enemy altered course away and was lost in the increasing haze.

I have the honour to be,
Sir,
Your obedient Servant,
A. D. BOYLE,
Captain.

The Rear-Admiral Commanding,
    Fifth Battle Squadron.

No 2.

H.M.S. " Malaya,"

SIR,   30th October 1916.

WITH reference to Admiralty Letter G. 03934/16 of the 20th instant, I have the honour to forward the following additional remarks on the Action of 31st May :—

(i) No additional information is available.

(ii) At 4.15 p.m. the first salvo was fired at the rear German Battle Cruiser (" Seydlitz ") at a range of 18,600 yards.

*   *   *   *   *

I have the honour to be,
Sir,
Your obedient Servant,
A. D. BOYLE,
Captain.

The Secretary of the Admiralty.

From—The Commanding Officer, H.M. Ship " Warspite.'

To—The Rear-Admiral Commanding, Fifth Battle Squadron.

The Secretary of the Admiralty,
Whitehall, London,
9th October 1916.

Submitted, with reference to Memorandum H.F. 1187/68, dated 24th September 1916, neither the Dreyer Table chart nor any range and bearing records have been retained . . .; it has not therefore been possible to comply with the above order to forward charts and records to the Admiralty.

(Signed)   E. M. PHILLPOTTS,
Captain,
125/D.

H.M.S. " PRINCESS ROYAL."

FORE T.S. RECORD OF ACTION, 31ST MAY 1916.

3–27.	Train Green 40.
3–30.	Red 30.
23.	23.
34–45	5 Enemy Battle Cruisers in sight.
39–20	Red 20
42–30	Right hand ship (" Lutzow " Class).
47–35	16000.
48– 5	Red 42.
48–53	14600.
49–36	14700.
50– 5	Red 78.
15	14200.
51–15	13200.

```
    52- 0   Red 89.
    53- 0   Red 108.
       45   12800.
    55- 5   Red 115.
       15   12800.
 4- 1-20   Red 130.
    6-50   19100.
   15-28   18500.
   15-50   18500.
   18- 5   18500.
   18-45   18500.
   19-50   18500.
   21-28   17700.
   22- 0   17000.
   24-15   16000.
   24-40   15900.
   25-20   14900.
   31-15   13000.
           13800.
   33-00   15000.
   34-15   15800.
   35-40   Enemy Battle Fleet ahead.
   37-28   Red 65.
   46-45   Green 99.   Three-funnelled cruiser.
   47-45   15000.
   48-15   Green 94.
   49- 6   15300.
   49-11   15300.
   51- 8   Green 105.   Right hand, Battle Cruiser steering to the left
   52-45   17000.
   53-35   17200.
   54-50   17800.
   56- 5   Green 110.   Leading Battle Cruiser.
   57-12   18000.
   58- 9   17925.
   58-24   17900.
 5- 2-40   19400.
   34- 5   18000.
   38-45   14000.
   44-34   15300.
 5-46-00   Change target.   Left hand ship.
 6- 0-30   Try 15000.
    1-30   14900.
    2-55   12000.   Green 40.   A Light Cruiser.
    7-30   Put 16000 on.
    9-45   Battle Cruiser.
   11-45   14000.
   16-40   13000.
   19-45   Green 98.
   19-55   12000.   Battle Cruiser.
   29-35   Green 102.
   30- 3   12000.   Battleship ( ?).
 7-14-10   18000.   Battle Cruiser.
 8-18-00   12000.   Green 60.   Leading Battle Cruiser.
   19-50   10000.
   20-30    9000.
   21-50    9400.
   22-33    9350.
   24-30    9500.
   25-15    9625.
   31- 5    9500.   Three funnelled ship.
   32-47    9850.
```

H.M.S. " Princess Royal,"
SIR, 3rd November 1916.

WITH reference to H.F. 1187/84 of 23rd October 1916, I have the honour to report that the ranges given in my letter 1/257 of 6th October are those on the transmitter whilst actually firing. All times are G.M.T. except in paragraph six of the letter where for " Argo at 8.52 " read " Argo at 8.22 p.m. G.M.T."

2. In ship's letter of proceedings dated 8th June 1916, 1/125, the following times are incorrect and should be amended as follows :—

Paragraph 4.—Time of passing wreck of " Invincible '" should be 6.38 p.m., G.M.T.

Paragraph 6.—Time of coming under fire from battleships was 6.18 p.m., G.M.T.

Paragraph 7.—Time heavy shock was felt was 8.34 p.m., G.M.T.

Paragraph 8.—First time should be 8.19 p.m., G.M.T.
Second time should be 8.28 p.m., G.M.T.
Third time should be 8.30 p.m., G.M.T.
Fourth time should be 8.34 p.m., G.M.T.

I have the honour to be,
Sir,
Your obedient Servant,
WALTER COWAN,
Captain.

The Rear-Admiral Commanding,
First Battle Cruiser Squadron.

GUNNERY RECORDS DURING ACTION OF 31st MAY 1916

No. 7.

H.M.S. " Tiger,"
SIR, 10th October 1916.

IN compliance with Memorandum No. H.F. 1187/68, dated 24th September 1916, I have the honour to forward herewith a record of gun range, target fired at and remarks for every minute the ship was in action on 31st May 1916. Bearings are noted whenever there is any record of them, but no regular record of gun bearings was taken during the action.

This record was compiled within four days of the action from all available records, but the data were only incidentally noted during the general scheme of control and their accuracy cannot be guaranteed

*   *   *   *   *

I have the honour to be,
Sir,
Your obedient Servant,
RUDOLPH BENTINCK,
Captain.

The Rear Admiral Commanding,
First Battle Cruiser Squadron.

GUNNERY REMARKS DURING ACTION OF 31ST MAY 1916.

G.M.T.	Gun Range.	Object.	Remarks.
3.44	—	—	Enemy reported in sight from " Lion."
3.45	—	—	Sighted enemy B.C.S. apparently 3, " Derflinger," " Seydlitz," and " Moltke."

GUNNERY REMARKS DURING ACTION OF 31ST MAY 1916—*cont.*

G.M.T.	Gun Range.	Object.	Remarks.
3.48	—	—	Enemy opened fire.
3.50	—	—	" Lion " opened fire.
3.51	18,500	4th ship from right, " Seydlitz " class.	Considerable interference from own T.B.D.'s' smoke.
3.52	18,200	,,	" Tiger " hit on forecastle.
3.53	16,900	,,	* * *
3.54	15,700	,,	" Q " and " X " turrets hit and temporarily out of action.
3.54½	15,200	,,	
3.55	13,900	,,	Interference from T.B.D. smoke.
3.55½	13,900	,,	Hit under " P. 6 " near after 6-in. magazine and fire.
3.56	13,800	,,	
3.56½	13,200	,,	
3.57	11,400	,,	
3.57½	11,200	,,	
3.58	11,400	,,	Interference enemy shorts and T.B.D. smoke.
3.58½	11,100	,,	
3.59	10,700	,,	
4.00	10,750	,,	
4.00½	10,500	,,	
4.01	11,200	,,	
4.01½	11,100	,,	
4.01¾	11,000	,,	
4.02	11,700	,,	
4.02¾	12,400	,,	
4.03½	11,800	,,	
4.03¾	12,200	,,	" Indefatigable " sinking.
4.05¼	12,300	,,	Salvoes appeared ragged.
4 05½	12,700	,,	Ordered " individual." Line up director.
4.06¼	12,000	,,	
4.06½	12,100	,,	
4.07	13,000	,,	
4.07½	14,100	,,	
4.07.55	14,200	,,	Straddle.
4.08.5	14,300	,,	
4.08.40	14,800	,,	
4.09¼	13,900	,,	
4.09.45	16,900	,,	Straddle.
4.10	17,000	,,	
4.10.5	17,900	,,	Director lined up correct. " X " in individual " Director."
4.10.55	17,700	,,	
4.11.5	18,000	,,	Straddle ?
4.11.20	17,500	,,	* * *
4.12.20	17,800	,,	
4.12.50	18,000	,,	
4.13.35	17,300	,,	
4.14.20	17,400	,,	
4.14.30	17,800	,,	
4.14.50	17,300	,,	Gun range and rangefinder same.
4.15.50	17,300	,,	Hitting.

GUNNERY REMARKS DURING ACTION OF 31ST MAY 1916—*cont.*

G.M.T.	Gun Range.	Object.	Remarks.
4.16.25	17,300	" Seydlitz " class, 4th ship from right.	——
4.16.40	17,300	,,	Over.
4.17.10	18,100	,,	——
4.18.10	17,500	,,	——
4.19.00	17,900	,,	——
4.20	18,300	,,	——
4.21	17,500	,,	——
4.21.40	17,500	,,	——
4.21.50	16,800	,,	Straddle.
4 22	16,800	,,	——
4.23.50	17,400	,,	Salvo ragged, " individual."
4.23.05	17.400	,,	Line up. Gun and mean range same.
4.24.10	16,600	3rd ship from left, " Derflinger " class.	" Queen Mary " blew up. Smoke passed " Tiger."
4.25	15,800	,,	——
4.25.30	15,800	,,	Enemy on port bow hitting " Tiger," chiefly in funnels.
4.25.50	16,200	,,	Straddle.
4.26.40	16,200	,,	Director.
4.27.30	16,000	,,	——
4.27.55	15,600	,,	Straddle.
4.28.15	15,500	,,	——
4.28.45	15,000	,,	——
4.28.55	14,800	,,	——
4.29.45	14,000	,,	——
4.30.15	13,900	,,	——
4.30.45	13,700	,,	One gun of " X " primary loading.
4.30.55	13,400	,,	——
4.31.15	12,400	,,	Straddle ?
4.31.35	12,300	,,	Gun and mean range same.
4.32.15	12,000	,,	" Red 123."
4.33	12,000	,,	——
4.33.30	11,800	,,	——
4.34.45	11,900	,,	6-in. opened fire on German T.B.D. attack.
4.35.20	13,000	,,	——
4.36.05	13,600	,,	——
4.36.25	14,500	,,	——
4.37.25	15,300	,,	——
4.37.55	15,500	,,	——
4.38.25	16,400	,,	——
4.39.25	17,500	,,	Enemy out of sight, check fire.
4.40	—	—	" Lion " altered course 16 points to starboard.
4.43	—	—	Lined up, speed of ship 28 knots.
4.51	—	Bearing, green 90.	Director Increased elevation.
4.55.30	18,000	3rd B.C. from left, " Derflinger."	——
4.57.15	18,000	,,	Ship altered course to port, enemy very misty and then seen to alter course 16 points.

GUNNERY REMARKS DURING ACTION OF 31ST MAY 1916—*cont.*

G.M.T.	Gun Range.	Object.	Remarks.
5.01.50	20,000	3rd B.C. from left, " Derfflinger."	——
5.02.05	18,000	,,	——
5.03.05	18,500	,,	——
5.04.10	19,300	,,	——
5.05.05	18,800	,,	——
5.05.35	18,800	,,	Straddle, very certain.
5.06.20	19,000	,,	——
5.06.35	19,000	,,	——
5.07.00	18,800	,,	——
5.08.30	18,400	2nd B.C. from left	3rd ship appeared to lose station and drop out of line burning.
5.09.00	18,500	,,	——
5.09.45	17,800	,,	Check fire. Report ammunition. Right gun of " A " out of action with fracture R.I. and O, cut off valve ram. Lined up.
5.43	—	—	Enemy re-appeared.
5.44	—	3rd ship from left, green 105.	——
5.46	15,000	,,	——
5.48	13,000	,,	——
5.48.25	14,000	,, Green 100	——
5.49	15,000	,,	——
5.50	14,500	,,	——
5.51	14,500	,,	——
5.52	14,500	,,	Straddle.
5.53	14,800	,,	——
5.53.20	13,600	,,	——
5.54.55	13,800	,, Green 85	Gun and mean R.F same, 2 rangefinders.
5.55.55	15,100	3rd ship from left, green 105.	Big deflection spotting correction to get salvo clear of apparently 15-in. salvoes falling short and in line.
5.58	14,300	,, Green 75.	——
5.59	14,700	,,	——
6.00	15,100	,,	Interference from 15-in.
6.02.20	16,300	,,	——
6.04	16,900	,,	——
6.05	15,400	,,	Check fire.
6.07	—	—	6-in. fired at L.C. " Kölberg " class.
6.12	—	—	6-in. ceased fire, continued again at 6.19 to 24.
6.17	15,000	3rd ship from left	——
6.18	15,400	,,	——
6.21	8,000	,, Green 85	——
6.21.35	8,000	,,	——
6.22.15	6,200	,,	——
6.23	6,300	,,	Gun range 1,500 below Argo R.F.
6.24.10	5,900	,,	——
6.25	7,700	,,	Straddle.
6.25.15	7,500	,,	Straddle.

GUNNERY REMARKS DURING ACTION OF 31ST MAY 1916—*cont.*

G.M.T.	Gun Range.	Object.	Remarks.
6.25.55	7,000	3rd ship from left	——
6.26.30	6,300	,,	——
6.27.20	6,900	,,	——
6.29	—	—	Check fire.
6.36	—	—	6-in. fired at T.B.D. attack on battle fleet, 13·5-in. lined up, check ammunition.
7.16	19,800	,, Green 70	——
7.16.40	19,750	,,	——
7.20	20,200	,,	Enemy turned away. Check fire. Tested director on L.C. on port bow.
8.21	7,900	Right hand of two 3-funnel B.S.	Apparently " Helgoland " class.
8.21.30	8,900	,,	——
8.22.30	8.400	,, Green 76	——
8.23.15	7,900	,,	——
8.24.30	7,900	,,	——
8.25.10	6,900	,,	Straddle.
8.26	6,900	,,	——
8.26.45	7,400	,.	——
8.27.20	7,900	,,	——
8.28	7,900	,.	——
8.30	10,900	,,	Gun and mean range R.F. same.
8.31	10,300	,,	Straddle.
8.31.30	10,700	,,	——
8.32	·11,100	,,	Straddle.
8.32.15	11,200	,,	——
8.33.45	10,600	,,	——
8.34.40	10,300	,,	——
8.35.30	9,500	,,	——
8.36.30	7,600	,,	Check fire.

H.M.S. " New Zealand,"
8th June 1916.

ACTION WITH GERMAN FLEET, 31ST MAY 1916.

RECORD OF RANGES, &C., COMPILED FROM TRANSMITTING STATION AND CONTROL TOP RECORDS.

All times are Rough G.M.T.

Time.	Remarks, &c.	Gun Range.
3.51	Commenced ranging on 4th Ship from right -	—
3.52	. . . .	—
3.53	. . . .	
3.57	Opened fire - - - - -	18,100
3.57½	. . . . . .	17,000
3.58	. . . . . .	15,800
3.58½	. . . . . .	—

RECORD OF RANGES, &c.—*cont.*

Time.	Remarks, &c.	Gun Range.
3.58½	- - - - - - -	14,600
3.59	- - - - - - -	13,400
3.59½	- - - - - - -	13,000
4.0	- - - - - - -	12,500
4.1	- - - - - - -	12,300
4.1½	- - - - - - -	11,000
4.2	- - - - - - -	10,800
4.2½	- - - - - - -	11,100
4.3	- - - - - - -	11,400
4.3½	- - - - - - -	11,400
4.4	- - - - - - -	11,600
4.4½	- - - - - - -	11,600
4.5½	- - - - - - -	12,000
4.6	a/c to Star. - - - - -	12,300
4.6½	- - - - - - -	13,200
4.7	- - - - - - -	13,800
4.9	Shifted fire to 5th (rear) Ship - - -	—
4.10	- - - - - - -	14,100
4.10½	- - - - - - -	—
4.11	- - - - - - -	14,800
4.12	- - - - - - -	—
4.12½	- - - - - - -	16,000
4.13	- - - - - - -	16,400
4.14	- - - - - - -	16,400
4.16	- - - - - - -	17,100
4.17	- - - - - - -	16,900
4.19	- - - - - - -	17,400
4.20	- - - - - - -	—
4.21	- - - - - - -	18,100
4.21½	- - - - - - -	—
4.22	- - - - - - -	17,600
4.22½	Shifted to 4th Ship, 5th ship obscured -	—
4.23	- - - - - - -	18,100
4.24	- - - - - - -	17,600
4.25½	- - - - - - -	18,000
4.26	- - - - - - -	17,850
4.26½	- - - - - - -	17,450
4.29	- - - - - - -	17,800
4.30½	- - - - - - -	17,750
4.31	- - - - - - -	17,450
4.32	- - - - - - -	—
4.33	- - - - - - -	16,400
4.34	- - - - - - -	15,100
4.36	- - - - - - -	14,500
4.36½	- - - - - - -	14,800
4.37	- - - - - - -	15,200
4.38½	- - - - - - -	—
4.39½	- - - - - - -	—
4.41	- - - - - - -	17,350
4.42	Enemy out of range - - - -	18,850
4.58	Right hand Battle Cruiser. Set sight to longest range at which it would bear.	18,000
5.0	Enemy out of range - - - -	18,600
5.46	Green 76 a Battle Cruiser - - -	18,000 (estimated).

RECORD OF RANGES, &C.—*cont.*

Time.	Remarks, &c.	Gun Range.
5.47		17,000
5.48		15,700
5.50		14,600
5.51		—
5.51½		—
5.52		14,500
5.53		15,450
5.55		15,000
5.56		14,300
5.58	Enemy nearly lost in smoke and mist; spotting very difficult.	14,300
6.4	Enemy obscured	—
6.6	Starb. 71 the leading Battleship. Fired 3 salvoes. Enemy obscured.	16,000
6.19	Left-hand Battleship	17,000
6.19½		16,000
6.20	a/c to Port	—
6.21½	Green 90. 2nd Ship from left	9,700
6.22		10,500
6.22		10,350
to 6.25		10,100
6.26		10,300
6.27		9,500
6.27½	Checked fire	—
8.24	Green 60. 3rd Ship from right	11,500 (estimated).
8.25		10,400
8.26		9,200
8.26½		9,600
8.27		9,500
8.28		9,100
8.29		9,400
8.30	Enemy on fire forward and hauling out of line, listing heavily.	—
8.36		10,700
8.38	Impossible to see fall of shot	—
8.39	Checked fire	—

H.M.S. "Inconstant,"

SIR,

12th October 1916.

WITH reference to the Commander-in-Chief's Memorandum H.F. 1187/68 of 24th September 1916, I have the honour to forward herewith the only records that were taken during the action of 31st May last. * * *

I have the honour to be,
Sir,
Your obedient Servant,
B. S. THESIGER,

The Secretary of the Admiralty,
London, S.W.

Captain.

H.M.S "INCONSTANT."

RECORDS TAKEN DURING ACTION OF 31ST MAY 1916.

Time.	Object.	Bearing	Range.	Own Course
4.35	Three - funnelled Light	—	20,150	
4.39	Cruiser and four De-	—	19,250	
4.45	stroyers.	Red 38	18,750	S.S.E.
4.46		106 True	17,500	
4.47				
5.59*	Large Cruiser (Class un-certain).	Green 60	13,750	Rough E.N.E.
6.7	Light Cruiser - - -	Green 45	13,000	Rough E.N.E.
6.8			13,200	

* Bearing of enemy and own course are very approximate at this time.

EVENTS DURING ACTION.

No. 428

"Falmouth,"

SIR,   9th June 1916.

IN accordance with the Vice-Admiral Commanding Battle Cruiser Fleet's signal No. 2105 of the 7th instant, I have the honour to report that no consecutive records were kept in either control or transmitting stations, but notes were made when possible of ranges, rates, &c., as shown in the following table, which has been compiled from these notes and gives the approximate hitting ranges at the time, ship fired at, &c. The times given are taken from notes taken from the Bridge.

Time (approx.)	Bearing.	Range.		Deflection.		Remarks.
		From	To	From	To	
Object—Light Cruiser.						
6.7 p.m. -	Bow	9,700	8,100	12R.	28R.	
	Before beam.	8,100	5,800	28R.	38R.	Disabled and stopped.
	On beam	5,800	4,600	38R.	28R.	
	Abaft beam.	4,600	5,400	28R.	22R.	Enemy in sinking condition. Ceased fire.
Object—Battle Cruiser.						
6.15 p.m.	Beam	6,000	6,600	8R.	Zero	
Object—Light Cruiser.						
6.30 p.m.	Before beam.	6,000	9,100	Zero	8R.	Fire observed aft. Enemy driven off, and disappeared in mist.

EVENTS DURING ACTION—*cont.*

Time (approx.)	Bearing.	Range.		Deflection.		Remarks.
		From	To	From	To	
Object—Battle Cruiser.						
6.15 p.m. to 6.30 p.m.	Abaft beam.	5,200	6,100	Zero	8R.	Enemy turned away and was lost to sight.
Object—Light Cruiser Z1.						
8.18 p.m.	Beam	9,600	6,000	Zero	8L.	Very indistinct owing dusk.
	Beam	6,000	9,300	8L.	Zero	
Object—Light Cruiser Z2.						
	Beam	9,300	9,600	Zero	Zero	
Object—Light Cruiser Z1.						
8.38 p.m.	Beam	9,800	10,200	Zero	10R.	Enemy turned away and disappeared.

C. 87/108.

I have the honour to be,
Sir,
Your obedient Servant,
J. D. EDWARDS,
Captain.

The Rear Admiral Commanding,
Third Light Cruiser Squadron.

No. 226.

H.M.S. " Birkenhead,"
8th October 1916.

SIR,
WITH reference to H.F. 1187/68 of 24th September 1916, I have the honour to report that the following are the Range and Bearing records during the daylight period of 31st May 1916.

Time.	" Birkenhead's " Course.	Class of Enemy Ships.	Bearing of Enemy.	Course of Enemy.	Distance.
5.50	N. 35° E.	Light Cruiser (" Wiesbaden ").	S.	Stopped	7,500
6.25	S.E.	Two Battle Cruisers (" D e r f l i n g e r,") " Seidlitz ").	S. 55° W. (approx.)	E. (approx.).	8,000
7.15	S. 55° W.	Battleships - -	N. 80° W.	W.S.W.	—
8.35	N. 70° W.	Smoke of Enemy ships	N.	Westerly	10,000 (approx.)

I have the honour to be,
Sir,
Your obedient Servant,
E. REEVES,
Captain.

The Rear Admiral Commanding,
Third Light Cruiser Squadron.

APPENDIX II.

RECORD OF MESSAGES BEARING ON THE OPERATION.

Messages are arranged in chronological order of "Time of Despatch," all times being G.M.T. Complete reliance, however, cannot be placed on the *absolute accuracy* of these times owing to the differences of ships' clocks and the difficulties experienced in logging signals in action.

2. The following types have been used for printing :—

Messages to or from Com.-in-Chief. - - Clarendon.

Messages between Senior Officers of Squadrons (other
 than the Commander-in-Chief) and their Squadrons } *Italics.*
 and between ships of the same squadron - - -

All other messages . . . . - Roman.

On 30th May 1916 the Admiralty received news which pointed to early activity on the part of the German Fleet. The Commander-in-Chief, Grand Fleet, and the Vice-Admiral Commanding Battle Cruiser Fleet were informed accordingly by telegram. The Admiralty also informed the Commander-in-Chief that eight enemy submarines, which they had reason to believe had recently sailed from German ports, were probably in the North Sea.

Admiralty telegram No. 434 of 30th May 1916, time of origin 1740, sent to the Commander-in-Chief and repeated to the Vice Admiral Commanding Battle Cruiser Fleet, contained the following instructions :—

"You should concentrate to Eastward of Long Forties ready for eventualities."

Date, Time of Despatch.	From	To	System.	Message.	Time of Origin.
MAY 30th					
11.58 a.m.	Admiralty .	V.A. Dover -	L/T	Harwich Destroyers return there at once. Recall Belgian coast patrol temporarily.	1158
12.5 p.m.	Admiralty .	R.A. East Coast.	L/T	Recall minesweeping sloops - - -	1205
12.17 —	Admiralty .	S.O. 3rd B.S., S.O. 3rdC.S., C.-in-C.Nore	L/T	3rd B.S. and 3rd C.S. should have steam at short notice by daylight to-morrow, and 3rd C.S. should proceed to Swin to-day.	1217
12.33 —	**S.O.M.S.** .	**C.-in-C.** .	W/T	**Position 58° 45′ N., 2° 15′ W. Torpedo fired at Gentian missed.**	**1230**
12.37 —	Admiralty .	Captain S., Maidstone.	L/T	Have all Submarines ready for sea at short notice.	1237
2.37 — recd.	Comdr. (T) .	S.O.B.C.F. -	L/T	5 Light Cruisers, 15 Destroyers, ready for service.	1230
4.35 —	**C.-in-C.** .	**General** .	Sem.	**If the fleet goes to sea under present conditions, Royal Oak will take station in 3rd sub-division, order of which will be Iron Duke, Royal Oak, Superb, Canada. Active will go with Cruisers and take position J. The Cruisers are to leave in one group and take route A. 3rd B.C.S. Canterbury and Chester will be ordered out independently ahead of Cruisers and will follow route B. The D.T. signal not applying to this squadron, the 4 T.B.Ds. for this squadron meeting them off Hoxa obstruction.**	**1615**
5.35 —	Owl .	C.-in-C. A.C.O. & S. Captain D4.	W/T	Urgent. Trawler Dunpedril reports Submarine, 3.45 p.m., Lat. 58° 35′ N., Long. 2° 35′ W.	1700
5.40 —	S.O. 2nd B.S.	General .	Flags	Preparatory signal for leaving Cromarty -	—

* *Note.*—The "Remarks" appearing in the "Message Column" appeared in the Remarks Column of the Signal Log.

Date, Time of Despatch.	From	To	System.	Message.	Time of Origin.
30 MAY	*—cont.*				
5.40 p.m.	C.-in-C.	General	Flags	Preparatory signal for leaving Scapa, negative Royal Sovereign and Menelaus.	1735
5.43 —	C.-in-C.	Royal Oak	Sem.	Return to Fleet Anchorage and anchor in A6.	1735
5.43 —	C.-in-C.	S.O. 4th B.S.	Sem.	Please send Menelaus over to North shore and delay experiments for the present.	1740
5.45 —	S.O. B.C.F.	B.C.F. 5th B.S. 1st, 9th, 13th Flotilla.	Flags	Raise steam for 22 knots and report when ready to proceed.	—
5.54 —	C.-in-C.	Marksman	W/T	Return at once with your Destroyers	1535
5.49 — (recd.)	C.-in-C.	S.O.B.C.F.	L/T	Urgent. Raise steam	1740
5.55 —	Admiralty	C.-in-C.	L/T	3rd B.S., 3rd C.S., 5th L.C.S. and Harwich Destroyers will not be sent out until more is known.	—
5.55 —	C.-in-C.	Commodore F. and Dundee.	Tel.	Trident will pass through patrols from East after midnight to-night.	1700
6.0 —	C.-in-C.	S.O. 4th L.C.S. Caroline, Constance.	Sem.	Caroline and Constance are to return to Y line by sunset.	1800
6.1 —	*S.O. 3rd L.C.S*	*3rd L.C.S.*	*Sem.*	*Steam should be raised as soon as possible and report now when you expect to be ready for 15 knots and 22 knots. Falmouth will be ready at 7.45 and 8 p.m.*	*1800*
6.4 —	*Commodore F.*	*Captain D12*	*Sem.*	*Recall patrols*	*1800*
6.4 —	*Commodore F.*	*Onslaught*	*W/T*	*Return to harbour*	*1800*
6.5 —	S.O. 2nd B.S.	General	Flags	Raise steam for 18 knots and report when ready to proceed.	—
6.7 —	S.O. B.C.F.	General	Flags	Commanders of squadrons to report the time at which their squadrons will be ready to proceed. Reply: 5th B.S. ready to proceed at 9.40 p.m., 1st B.C.S. ready to proceed 8.45 p.m., 2nd B.C.S. will be ready to proceed at 9 p.m., 1st L.C.S. ready to proceed at 8.23 p.m., 2nd L.C.S. ready to proceed 9 p.m., 3rd L.C.S. ready to proceed 8 p.m., 9th Flotilla 8.30 p.m., 1st Flotilla 9 p.m., Engadine 9.45 p.m.	—
6.7 —	C.-in-C.	S.O. 2nd C.S. and Commodore F.	Sem. and Tel.	My 1615. Additional four Destroyers are to be detailed for 2nd C.S.	1754
6.10 —	Commodore F.	C.-in-C.	Tel.	Achates defect completed	1805
6.11 —	C.-in-C.	S.O.M.S.	W/T	Keep Sloops out to-night, Tuesday. Fleet may come out.	1750

6.12 —	*S.O. 3rd L.C.S*	*3rd L.C.S.*	*Sem.*	*L.C.'s. diagram No. 1.*
				  Falmouth, Yarmouth C
				  Birkenhead, Gloucester D
				If Engadine joins she will leave harbour astern of Gloucester.
					1812

Date, Time of Despatch.	From	To	System.	Message.	Time of Origin.
30 MAY 6.14 —	*—cont.* *Captain D12*	Commodore F.	Tel.	*Should Marksman be recalled ?* *Reply : C.-in C. has already ordered Marks- man and Destroyers to return.*	*1815* *1816*
6.18 —	*Captain D12-*	*Mischief, Narwhal, Mary Rose.*	Tel.	*Proceed into harbour and complete with oil fuel.*	*1800*
6.20 —	Admiralty -	Commodore T.	L/T	Light Cruisers and Destroyers should be ready to sail at daylight if required. Report your probable strength ? Reply : Probable strength will be five Light Cruisers, two Flotilla leaders, 21 Destroyers, including eight detailed for 3rd B.S.	— 1940
6.25 —	C.-in-C. -	3rd B.C.S. Chester, Canterbury.	Flags Sem.	**Raise steam for 22 knots. At what time will 3rd B.C.S. be ready to sail ? Reply: 8.15 p.m.** **At what time will Chester and Canterbury be ready to sail ? Reply: 8.30 p.m.**	—
6.25 —	C.-in-C. -	Commodore F.	Tel.	**Nymphe will not leave if Fleet goes out. The four Destroyers for 3rd B.C.S. screen to raise steam for 22 knots.**	1820
6.28 —	S.O. B.C.F. -	Leda - -	W/T	Gunboats raise steam - - - Reply : Gunboats ready to proceed -	1800 1915
6.30 —	Admiralty -	S.O. 5th B.S.	L/T	Very urgent. Raise steam - - -	—
6.30 —	*Gloucester* -	*Falmouth* -	Sem.	*What key memorandum is in force ?* *Reply : Key memorandum No. 12, S.W. C.B. 01160.*	*1819* *1825*
6.34 —	C.-in-C. -	Nymphe -	Tel.	**Bank fires. Steam at four hours' notice -**	—
6.35 —	Admiralty -	Captain S., Maidstone.	L/T	Urgent. Three Submarines detailed in accordance with C.-in-C.'s orders should proceed to position ordered by him and remain till night of 3rd June.	—
6.37 —	C.-in-C. -	Campania, Blanche.	Sem. and S.L.	**Campania will follow Blanche and be last to leave.**	1832
6.37 —	*Commodore F.*	*Captain D4* -	Sem.	*The four Destroyers for 3rd B.C.S. screen to raise steam for 22 knots.*	*1835*
6.40 —	C.-in-C. -	A.C.O. & S. Shannon, 2nd and 7th C.S.	Sem.	**Flag of V.A. Sir Somerset Gough Calthorpe is to be shifted to Leander to-night and hauled down at sunset to-morrow, Wed- nesday. R.A. Minotaur will take com- mand of 2nd and 7th C.S. at sunset to-night, Tuesday.**	1826
6.44 —	Admiralty -	C.-in-C. S.O. B.C.F.	L/T	**Three Harwich Submarines for vicinity of Vyl Light Vessel, proceed to-night instead of to-morrow morning.**	1844
6.45 —	*Captain D., 1st Flotilla.*	*1st Flotilla* -	Sem.	*Organisation as follows : 1st Division, Acheron, Ariel, Attack, Hydra ; 2nd Division, Badger, Lizard, Goshawk, Lapwing. Defender to keep station astern of Fearless.*	*1840.*
6.48 —	*Captain D4* -	*Commodore F.*	Sem.	*Hardy will join Group 8 in place of Paragon not yet arrived.*	*1846*

Date, Time of Despatch.	From	To	System.	Message.	Time of Origin.
30 MAY —cont. 6.55 p.m.	Admiralty	R.A. East Coast, Captain-in-Charge, Lowestoft.	L/T	Recall auxiliary patrols by secret word	—
6.58 —	Erin	S.O. 2nd B.S.	Sem.	Immediate. I should like to fill up with coal if possible, as amount short, about 100 tons, makes it rather awkward for centre boiler room. Reply : Collier has been ordered.	1902
7.0 —	S.O. 2nd B.S.	2nd B.S., 1st C.S., Boadicea.	W/T	2nd B.S. assume W/T organisation J 8.40 p.m.	1856
7.0 —	S.O. B.C.F.	Nottingham	W/T	Destroyers are to economise fuel as much as possible.	1855
7.0 —	C.-in-C.	Cruisers and Destroyers.	Flags & Tel.	Raise steam for 20 knots	1900
7.2 —	Commodore F.	General Neg. Nymphe.	Flags	Raise steam for 22 knots	—
7.3 —	Admiralty	R.A. East Coast ; Captain-in-Charge, Lowestoft ; Commodore, Harwich ; C.-in-C. Nore.	L/T	Weather permitting, Aircraft should scout to seawards at daylight to-morrow.	1903
7.5 —	C.-in-C.	Battlefleet Neg. R. Sovn.	Flags	Raise steam for 19 knots	—
7.7 —	S.O. 1st C.S.	S.O. 2nd B.S.	S.L.	1st C.S. will be ready to proceed 18 knots at 10 p.m.	1900
7.10 —	S.O. B.C.F.	B.C.s and 5th B.S.	Flags	Raise steam for working cables at 8 p.m.	—
7.11 —	C.-in-C.	Campania	Flags and S.L.	Raise steam for full speed	—
7.14 —	Commodore F.	Oak	Sem.	Raise steam for 22 knots	1908
7.18 —	C.-in-C.	Titania	L/T	Available T.B.Ds. and Submarines prepare for sea.	1918
7.20 —	Commodore F.	General 11th Flotilla, Captain's D4 and D12.	Sem.	Reference screening groups, dated 29th May. Group 8 will only consist of four Destroyers, three from 4th Flotilla and one from 12th Flotilla.	—
7.20 —	C.-in-C.	S.O. 7th C.S., S.O. 4th L.C.S.	Sem.	Will Cruisers and 4th L.C.S. be ready to leave 9.30 p.m. ? Reply : Yes.	1915
7.20 —	Commodore F.	Captain D4 and Captain D12.	Sem.	Report names of Destroyers detailed for Group 8.	—
7.22 —	Commodore F.	Marksman	Sem.	Are all Destroyers returning ? Reply : All have been told to return, but as they were spread I did not wait to collect them.	1920
7.25 —	C.-in-C. Rosyth.	Admiralty	L/T	Nottingham, Nomad, Nicator, sailed for dark night patrol.	—
7.27 —	C.-in-C.	S.O. 2nd B.S.	W/T	Priority. How soon can you have steam for 19 knots?	1915
7.30 —	C.-in-C.	S.O. 2nd B.S.	L/T	Leave as soon as ready, pass through Lat. 58 15′ N., Long. 2 0′ E., meet me 2 p.m. to-morrow, 31st, Lat. 57° 45′ N., Long. 4° 15′ E. Several Enemy Submarines known to be in North Sea.	1930

Date, Time of Despatch.	From	To	System.	Message.	Time of Origin.
30 MAY	*—cont.*				
7.30 p.m.	S.O. B.C.F. -	Nottingham -	W/T	What course did you steer after leaving Isle of May ?	1925
				Reply : 63° for 10 miles then to 111° -	1948
7.35 —	*Shannon* -	*S.O. 7th C.S.* -	Flags	*2nd C.S. ready to proceed at 9.30 p.m.* -	—
7.36 —	*S.O. 7th C.S.*	*Hampshire* -	Sem.	*Can you move off at 9.30 p.m. ? Reply : Yes.*	1935
7.45 —	S.O. 2nd B.S.	General - -	Flags	Raise steam for 19 knots with all dispatch and report when ready to proceed.	—
7.46 —	**S.O. 4th B.S.**-	**C.-in-C.** -	Flags	**4th B.S. ready to proceed 9.45 p.m.** -	—
7.49 —	**S.O. 1st B.S.** -	**C.-in-C.** -	Sem.	**1st B.S. will be ready to proceed at 9.45 p.m.**	1945
7.50 —	S.O. 2nd B.S.	General -	Flags	Unmoor, weigh western anchor. Shorten in to three shackles.	—
7.50 —	**C.-in-C.** -	**Commodore F.**	Tel.	**T.B.Ds. for B.Cs. Cruisers and 1st B.S. to meet squadrons off Swona. Those for 4th B.S. off Hoxa obstruction. B.Cs. will be leaving at 9 p.m.**	1945
7.50 —	*Oak* - -	*Castor* - -	W/T	*Ready to proceed* - - - -	1935
7.54 —	*Leda* - -	S.O. B.C.F. -	W/T	*Request instructions* - - - -	1930
7.55 —	S.O. B.C.F. -	*Leda* - -	W/T	Priority. Proceed and sweep Y Channel from Isle of May. Look out for signals to clear fleet, which will be sailing about 9.30 p.m. Ascot out of action. Paddle steamers will not join you.	1947
7.55 —	*Commodore F.*	*Captains D4 and D12.*	Sem.	*Inform Group 8 that the group consists of Owl, Midge, Hardy, Mischief. They are to meet 2nd C.S. outside Hoxa when fleet proceeds.*	1952
7.55 —	Admiral Supt. Glasgow.	Commodore F.	Tel.	With reference to your message 1450, Napier and Mameluke will not be completed until to-morrow, Wednesday. Will sail 1st June.	1805
7.57 —	S.O. 2nd B.S.	Kempenfelt -	Tel.	Direct Moon to proceed to Peterhead to fuel.	1955
8.0 —	S.O. B.C.F. -	B.Cs. 5th B.S. and Engadine	Flags	Unmoor, weigh western anchor. Shorten in to three shackles.	—
8.0 —	**C.-in-C.** -	**General** -	Sem.	**Until further orders Royal Oak, Fleet No. 10, Superb 11, Canada 12, ships named show Fleet Nos.**	1930
8.2 —	**C.-in-C.** -	**S.O. 3rd B.C.S. Chester, Canterbury.**	Flags	**S.O. 3rd B.C.S. take Chester and Canterbury under your orders.**	—
8.7 —	*S.O. 2nd C.S.*	*2nd and 7th C.S.*	Sem.	*Following organisation when signal Cruisers assume 2nd organisation is hoisted.* *1st Division :—* *Minotaur, Fleet No. 1.* *Hampshire, Fleet No. 2.* *2nd Division :—* *Cochrane, Fleet No. 3.* *Shannon, Fleet No. 4.* *In L.S. 1, Cochrane goes to A, Shannon B, Minotaur, Hampshire, C.*	2000
8.7 —	**C.-in-C.** -	**General** -	Flags	**Fleet will leave by D.T.3 method at 9.30 p.m., negative Royal Sovereign and Menelaus.**	—
8.10 —	**S.O. 2nd C.S.**-	**C.-in-C.** -	Sem.	**Following organisation of 2nd and 7th C.S.** **1st Division:—** **Minotaur, Hampshire.** **2nd Division:—** **Cochrane, Shannon.** **In L.S. 1, Cochrane to A, Minotaur and Hampshire C.**	2000

Date, Time of Despatch.	From	To	System.	Message.	Time of Origin.
30 MAY 8.15 p.m.	*—cont.* C.-in-C.	R.A. Cyclops	Tel.	Gate to be opened at 9.30 for fleet leaving	1900
8.15 —	C.-in-C.	R.A. Cyclops	Tel.	Light Groups I, II, III, from 10.30 p.m.	2010
8.15 —	C.-in-C.	General	Sem.	Fleet will leave to-night by D.T.3 method, ships in close order. All squadrons pass East of Swona and North of Skerries, except 4th L.C.S., which is to go West of Swona and South of Skerries. Routes modified as follows : squadrons for route A to pass through Lat. 58 47′ N., Long. 2 37′ W., squadrons for route B to pass through Lat. 58 45′ N., Long. 2 37′ W., then all squadrons steer 84 . Routes to be followed : Cruisers route A, 4th L.C.S. route B, 1st B.S. route A, 4th B.S. route A. Battlefleet will alter to 90 at 1.30 a.m., Cruisers conforming. Rear subdivisions of battlefleet to remain one mile astern of leading subdivision until daylight. Cruisers assume L.S. 1—10, but not to spread until daylight.	2010
8.15 —	*Commodore F.*	*Captains D4 and D12.*	Sem.	*Group 7 to leave harbour 8.50 p.m.*	*2010*
8.15 — (recd.)	C.-in-C.	S.O.B.C.F.	L/T	Admiralty telegram 1740. Available vessels of B.C.F., 5th B.S. and Destroyers, including Harwich Destroyers, proceed to approximate position Lat. 56° 40′ N., Long. 5 E. Desirable to economise Destroyers' fuel. Presume that you will be there about 2 p.m. to-morrow, Wednesday, 31st May. I shall be in about 57 45′ N., 4 15′ E. by 2 p.m. unless delayed by fog. 3rd B.C.S, Chester and Canterbury will leave with me. I may send them on to your rendezvous. If no news by 2 p.m. stand towards me to get in visual communication. I will steer for Horn Reef from position Lat. 57 45′ N., Long. 4 15′ E. Repeat back rendezvous	1937
8.17 —	*S.O. 2nd C.S.*	*2nd C.S. and 7th C.S.*	Flags and Sem.	*Have steam for working cables, 8.50 p.m.*	*2000*
8.17 —	S.O. 3rd L.C.S	Commodore Galatea.	Sem.	Have you got any orders about weighing yet ? Reply : No orders.	2015
8.20 —	S.O. B.C.F.	B.Cs. and 5th B.S.	Flags	Have steam for 15 knots at half-an-hour's notice. Have steam for 22 knots at one hour's notice.	—
8.20 —	**S.O.M.S.**	C.-in-C.	W/T	**My position with 12 sloops 8 p.m. 58 30′ N., 2 38′ W. zigzagging in the vicinity.**	2010
8.23 —	S.O. B.C.F.	L.C.S. and Destroyers.	Flags	Have steam for 22 knots at half-an-hour's notice. Have steam for 15 knots now.	—
8.25 —	S.O. B.C.F.	S.O. 5th B.S., S.O. 2nd B.C.S., Captains D1 and 13.	Sem.	Fearless and 1st Flotilla are to precede 5th B.S. out of harbour and screen them. Champion and 13th Flotilla are to precede Lion and 1st B.C.S. out of harbour and screen them. Two of 9th Flotilla are to join 13th Flotilla. Lydiard and remainder of 9th Flotilla are to precede and screen 2nd B.C.S.	2015

Date, Time of Despatch.	From	To	System.	Message.	Time of Origin.
30 MAY *—cont.*					
8.27 p.m.	S.N.O. Harwich.	Admiralty	L/T	Submarines D1, D6, E26, E31, E53, E55, sailed.	—
8.27 —	S.O. 2nd B.S.	General	Flags	Proceed out of harbour in D.T.3. at 9.45 p.m. 18 knots.	—
8.30 —	*S.O. 2nd B.S.*	*Erin*	Sem.	*Collier will not go alongside you*	2025
8.31 —	S.O. 2nd B.S.	R.A. Invergordon.	W/T	Request gate may be opened by 9.15 p.m.	2019
8.36 —	S.O. 2nd B.S.	Kempenfelt	Tel.	Gate will be opened at 9.15 p.m.	—
8.39 —	**S.O.B.C.F.**	**C.-in-C.**	L/T	**Your 1937 has been received and understood. My rendezvous 2 p.m., 31st May, Lat. 56° 40′ N., Long. 5° E. Your rendezvous Lat. 57° 45′ N., Long. 4° 15′ E.**	2030
8.40 —	S.O. 2nd B.S.	Captain D., Kempenfelt.	Tel.	Arrange to screen both divisions of Battle Squadron when outside. The two divisions will be four miles apart.	2039
8.40 —	**C.-in-C.**	**3rd Sub.**	Sem.	**C.-in-C. will lead 3rd Sub. out**	2031
8.45 —	*Kempenfelt*	*11th Flotilla*	Flags	*Slip*	—
8.50 —	*S.O.3rd B.C.S*	*3rd B.C.S., Chester and Canterbury.*	Flags	*Weigh*	—
8.50 —	S.O. B.C.F.	General	S.L.	Proceed out of harbour 9.30 p.m.	2015
8.51 —	Commodore F.	R.A. Cyclops	Sem.	Request main Switha Gate from 9.45 p.m.	2050
8.52 —	Admiral Chatham.	Admiralty	L/T	R.A.C. 3rd C.S. in Roxburgh, left Sheerness with Devonshire for Swin Channel.	1943
8.52 —	**C.-in-C.**	**S.O.M.S.**	W/T	**Fleet leaving 9.30 p.m. to 10.30 p.m. steering 84° from Pentland Skerries. Keep clear.**	2038
8.53 —	**Longhope**	**C.-in-C.**	W/T	**Duke of Clarence to C.-in-C. and Dundee. Drifter reports sighted Submarine 5 p.m. S.E. by S. from Pentland Skerries on surface, but submerged on Drifter approaching.**	2025
8.55 —	R.A. 1st B.S.	6th Subdivision	Sem.	*6th Subdivision are to be underway and pointed to E. by N. by 10 p.m.*	2050
8.55 —	S.O. 1st C.S.	1st C.S.	Sem.	*Ships are to be underway and heading to Eastward by 9.45 p.m. without further signal. Defence will go ahead 12 knots at 9.45 p.m. without further signal. Form in single line ahead in sequence of Fleet Nos. close order. Speed will be increased to 14 knots at outer obstruction and to 18 knots just before reaching Whistle Buoy, both increases by signal.*	2055
8.55 —	Iron Duke	—	—	Remarks : 3rd B.C.S., Canterbury and Chester proceeding.	—
8.55 —	*Commodore F.*	*Castor and Captain D12.*	S.L.	*Prepare to slip 10.15 p.m.*	—
8.55 —	*Commodore F.*	*Captain D12*	S.L.	*Unless otherwise ordered Castor and 11th Flotilla will follow 4th B.S. to sea and therefore leave Gutter Sound last.*	2050
8.55 —	*S.O. 3rd L.C.S*	*3rd L.C.S.*	Sem.	*3rd L.C.S. will leave at 9.20 p.m.*	2055

Date, Time of Despatch.	From	To	System.	Message.	Time of Origin.
30 MAY *—cont.* 8.55 p.m.	**C.-in-C.**	**All Ships**	W/T	W/T organisation S. will be adopted 9.30 p.m. Ships addressed are to take W/T guard on the wave length denoted from the time specified until further orders. Revenge Q., St. Vincent, German interception. Benbow stand by S., Superb W., Hercules X.	2050
8.56 —	*S.O.1st L.C.S.*	*1st L.C.S.*	Sem.	*Be underway and pointed by 9.15 p.m.*	*2055*
8.56 —	**C.-in-C.**	**General**	Flags	Fleet will leave by D.T.3 method at 9.30 p.m., speed 17 knots after passing obstruction.	—
8.58 —	S.O. 3rd L.C.S.	Engadine	S.L.	3rd L.C.S. will pass bridge at 9.35 p.m., form astern of Gloucester, 4th ship.	2058
9.0 —	*S.O.3rd B.C.S.*	*3rd B.C.S., Chester and Canterbury.*	Flags	*Form single line ahead in sequence of fleet numbers. Admiral intends to proceed at 12 knots.*	—
9.0 —	S.O. B.C.F.	General	Sem.	Summary of N.C.I. Submarine, 7.50 to-day, 56° 17′ N., 1° 30′ W.	2056
9.0 —	**C.-in-C.**	**Admiralty**	L/T	Priority. Fleet leaving 9.30 p.m. to-day, Tuesday.	—
9.2 —	S.O. B.C.F.	Ships in Company.	W/T	Ships denoted to take W/T guard on wave length denoted at 2115. Lion S.D.X., Princess Royal X., Queen Mary W., Tiger Q., Indefatigable U.	2054
9.3 —	*S.O.3rd L.C.S.*	*3rd L.C.S.*	Sem.	*Have steam for 22 knots*	—
9.6 —	*S.O. 1st B.S.*	*5th Sub. and Bellona.*	F.L.	*Marlborough will slip from the buoy and come to head of D. line ready to lead subdivision out and will go ahead at 12 knots on the Easterly course at 9.55 p.m.*	*2047*
9.7 —	Commodore F.	C.-in-C.	S.L.	All Destroyers returned. Screen for Battle Cruiser Squadron leaving.	2105
9.9 —	S.O. 2nd B.S.	R.A. Invergordon.	W/T	Request Covesea Light may be shown from 10.30 p.m. to 11.30 p.m.; Kinnaird Light from 1 a.m. to 1.45 a.m.	2052
9.9 —	S.O. B.C.F.	S.O. 3rd L.C.S.	F.L.	Signal for steam for Light Cruisers and Destroyers is cancelled by signal D.T.	2100
9.10 —	*S.O.2nd L.C.S*	*2nd L.C.S.*	Flags	*Weigh*	—
9.10 —	*S.O. Cruisers*	*Cruisers*	Flags	*Weigh*	—
9.10 —	S.O. B.C.F.	S. O. 5th B.S.	F.L.	Follow 1st B.C.S. out of harbour and take station five miles astern.	2105
9.10 —	**S.O. 4th L.C.S.**	**C.-in-C.**	Sem.	Distribution A.B. completed	2115
9.15 —	Lydiard	S.O. 2nd B.C.S.	F.L.	Organisation of 9th Flotilla :— 1st Subdivision—Lydiard, Liberty, Landrail. 2nd Subdivision—Moorsom, Laurel, Morris.	2115
9.15 —	S.O. B.C.F.	Light Cruisers	Flags	Raise steam for 22 knots	—
9.15 —	*S.O.2nd L.C.S*	*2nd L.C.S.*	Flags	*Turn together to S.E.*	—
9.15 —	*Commodore F.*	*Mischief*	S.L.	*Proceed with all despatch*	*2115*

Date, Time of Despatch.	From	To	System.	Message.	Time of Origin.
30 MAY	—*cont.*				
9.15 p.m.	*S.O.3rd L.C.S.*	*Yarmouth* -	S.L.	*What is delay in weighing ? Reply : Anchor came up foul of port cable. I had to let go again.*	—
9.15 —	*S.O. Cruisers*	*Cruisers* -	Flags	*Turn together to E.* - - - -	—
9.15 —	**C.-in-C.** -	**S.O. Sweepers**	W/T	**Is the weather clear ?** - - - -	**2112**
9.16 —	Moon - -	Peterhead -	W/T	*Inform Aberdeen and P.W.S.S. Arrive 10.30 p.m. Require oil fuel immediately on arrival.*	2045
9.17 —	*S.O. Cruisers*	*Cruisers* -	F.L.	*Assume 2nd organisation. Show fleet numbers. Reply : Fleet numbers—Minotaur 1, Hampshire 2, Cochrane 3, Shannon 4.*	—
9.20 —	*S.O.2nd C.S.*	2nd and 7th C.S.	Flags	*Comprise 2nd Cruiser Squadron* - -	—
9.22 —	*S.O. 2nd C.S.*	2nd C.S. -	Sem.	*Minotaur will move off at 12 knots at 9.30 p.m.*	2120
9.23 —	*S.O.3rd L.C.S.*	*Gloucester* -	F.L.	*Increase speed* - - - - -	—
9.23 —	S.O. B.C.F. -	S.Os. of Squadrons. All Captain D.'s in company other than Port Defence Vessels.	W/T	Pass N. of May Island, then steer 66°. Speed from outer gate 18 knots.	2110
9.24 —	*S.O. 4th B.S.*	4th B.S., Royal Oak, Blanche.	Sem.	*Shorten in to three shackles at 9.30 p.m. Benbow will go ahead about 10 p.m. Blue stern lights to be shown to-night, Tuesday.*	2100
9.25 —	*S.O.2nd L.C.S.*	2nd L.C.S. -	Flags	*Form single line-ahead in sequence of fleet numbers. Admiral intends to proceed at 12 knots.*	—
9.25 —	*S.O.2nd C.S.* -	2nd C.S. -	Flags	*Form single line-ahead in sequence of fleet numbers. Admiral intends to proceed at 12 knots.*	—
9.27 —	**S.O. 4th L.C.S.**	C.-in-C. -	F.L.	**4th L.C.S. ready to proceed** - - -	—
9.28 —	*S.O.3rd L.C.S.*	3rd L.C.S. -	F.L.	*Admiral intends to proceed at 12 knots* -	—
9.30 —	Rosyth -	S.O. B.C.F. -	W/T	*Priority. From Naval Centre. With reference to my message 1940. Message appears to be correct and is from Trident, who was apparently in 56° 0′ N., 1° 28′ W., at 8.15 p.m.*	2115
9.30 —	*S.O.3rdB.C.S.*	3rd B.C.S., Chester and Canterbury.	Sem.	*3rd B.C.S. is to be 10 miles ahead of Cruiser line, Chester to be five miles astern of 3rd B.C.S., Canterbury five miles ahead of Invincible. Modified route B will be followed. At dawn Chester to be in visual touch with Cruiser line. Canterbury in visual touch with Invincible. Speed of advance 17 knots. Zigzag during early hours.*	2110
9 30 —	*S.O.3rdB.C.S.*	3rd B.C.S., Chester and Canterbury.	Flags	*Admiral intends to proceed at 19 knots* -	—
9.30 —	*R.A.2nd B.S.*	2nd Division -	Flags	*Weigh* - - - - - -	—
9.30 —	*S.O. 4thL.C.S.*	4th L.C.S. -	F.L.	*Weigh* - - - - - -	—

Date, Time of Despatch.	From	To	System.	Message.	Time of Origin.
30 MAY —*cont.*					
9.31 p.m.	S.O. B.C.F. -	Lydiard -	F.L.	Slip and follow Light Cruisers. Wait for 2nd B.C.S. at outer gate.	2125
9.31 —	Nottingham -	C.-in-C. and S.O. B.C.F. -	W/T	Urgent. Trident reports attacked by Submarine, 56° N., 1° 31′ W., at 6.45 p.m.	2120
9.34 —	*S.O.4th L.C.S.*	*4th L.C.S.* -	F.L.	*Alter course together to E. by N.* - -	—
9.35 —	*S.O.2nd B.C.S*	*2nd B.C.S.* -	Flags	*Weigh* - - - - - -	—
9.35 —	Cyclops -	Commodore F.	S.L.	Switha main gate open - - -	2135
9.38 —	S.O.3rd B.C.S.	Destroyers -	Flags	Take station for Submarine screen now as previously arranged by diagram No. 5.	—
9.38 —	S.O.3rd L.C.S.	Engadine -	F.L.	18 knots after passing outer gates without further signal.	2135
9.38 —	*S.O.4th L.C.S.*	*4th L.C.S.* -	F.L.	*Form single line-ahead in sequence of fleet numbers, speed 12 knots.*	—
9.38 —	C.-in-C. -	S.O. 4th L.C.S.	F.L.	Abdiel has been ordered to close you -	2130
9.40 —	Rosyth -	S.O. B.C.F. -	W/T	From Naval Centre. Intercepted message from Hull received, indicates some vessels were attacked by Submarine at 7.45 p.m., 30th, in Lat. 56° 15′ N., Long. 1° 30′ W. Message not clear. Am obtaining verification and making other inquiries.	1940
9.40 —	*S.O.2nd B.S.*	*1st Division* -	Flags	*Weigh* - - - - - -	—
9.40 —	*S.O.3rd L.C.S.*	*3rd L.C.S.* -	F.L.	*Admiral intends to proceed at 11 knots* -	—
9.43 —	*S.O. 2nd B.C.S*	*2nd B.C.S* -	Flags	*Point ship* - - - - -	—
9.43 —	S.O. B.C.F. -	S.O.s of Squadrons. All Captain D.s in company other than Port Defence Vessels.	W/T	Light Cruisers form L.S.6 on passing May Island. Lion will steer 66° from May Island for 20 miles, then shape course for Lat. 56° 40′ N., Long. 5° 0′ E.	2125
9.47 —	*R.A. 2nd B.S.*	*2nd Division* -	Flags	*Admiral intends to proceed at 12 knots*	—
9.48 —	*Captain D4* -	*3rd Division, Oak.*	W/T	*Slip* - - - - - -	—
9.48 —	S.O. B.C.F. -	W/T Guards -	W/T	Cease communication by W/T except on sighting the Enemy or replying to the Admiral after passing May Island.	2141
9.49 —	R.A. Invergordon.	S.O. 2nd B.S. -	Sem.	Following from Naval Centre, Rosyth Reports. Submarine at 7.45 p.m. to-day, Tuesday, in Lat. 60° 27′ N., Long. 4° 10′ W. Ends. No further particulars.	2135
9.50 —	*S.O.3rd B.C.S*	*3rd B.C.S., Chester and Canterbury.*	Flags	*Alter course in succession to S. 73° E.* -	—
9.50 —	S.O. B.C.F. -	*S.O. 2nd B.C.S.*	F.L.	*2nd B.C.S. maintain your station five miles ahead during dark and drop back at daylight.*	2150

Date, Time of Despatch.	From	To	System.	Message.	Time of Origin.
30 MAY —*cont.*					
9.50 p.m.	*S.O. B.C.F.*	*1st B.C.S.*	F.L.	*Weigh*	—
9.50 —	*S.O.2nd B.C.S*	*2nd B.C.S.*	Flags	*Form single line-ahead in sequence of fleet numbers. Admiral intends to proceed at 12 knots.*	—
9.50 —	Iron Duke	—	—	Remarks : 4th Sub. underway	—
9.50 —	**Broughness**	**C.-in-C.**	Tel.	**Visibility three miles**	2145
9.52 —	*S.O.3rd L.C.S.*	*3rd L.C.S., Engadine.*	S.L.	*From S.O. B.C.F. to S.O.s of Squadrons. Pass North of May Island then steer 66°. Speed from outer gate 18 knots.*	2150
9.54 —	*S.O. B.C.F.*	*1st B.C.S.*	F.L.	*Point ship*	—
9.55 —	*S.O.3rd B.C.S*	*3rd B.C.S., Chester, Canterbury.*	Flags	*Admiral intends to proceed at 20 knots*	—
9.55 —	Rosyth	S.O. B.C.F.	W/T	From N.C. Danish s.s. Robert from Frederikshavn on 27th inst., in 56° N., 1° 42′ E., reports that she sighted supposed German Submarine steering E., about 150 feet long, low forward and aft, raised deck amidships, conning tower on top painted grey, letter U on bow—no number, guns fore and aft. No periscope seen or other distinguishing marks. Submerged on sighting fishing trawler to the Eastward. At noon in 56° 29′ N., 0° 26′ W., Submarine was sighted steering N. on the surface, too distant to obtain particulars.	—
9.55 —	*Capt. D4*	*3rd Division,- Oak.*	W/T	*Form single line-ahead in sequence of fleet numbers. Speed 10 knots.*	—
9.55 —	*S.O. 1st C.S.*	*1st C.S.*	F.L.	*Admiral intends to proceed at 14 knots*	—
9.55 —	*S.O.3rdL.C.S.*	*3rd L.C.S.*	F.L.	*Admiral intends to proceed at 17 knots*	—
9.55 —	S.O.4th L.C.S.	Abdiel	F.L.	Abdiel take station astern of Royalist. Speed 14 knots.	—
9.55 —	*S.O.4th L.C.S.*	*4th L.C.S.*	F.L.	*Admiral intends to proceed at 14 knots*	—
9.57 —	**C.-in-C.**	**3rd Sub.**	F.L.	**Weigh. Point ship**	—
9.58 —	*S.O. 2nd B.S.*	*1st Division*	F.L.	*Form single line-ahead in sequence of fleet numbers. Admiral intends to proceed at 14 knots.*	—
9.58 —	S.O. 2nd C.S.	Active	S.L.	Leave room for four Destroyers to take station astern of Shannon.	2155
9.58 —	*S.O.4th L.C.S.*	*4th L.C.S.*	F.L.	*Abdiel has been ordered to take station astern of Royalist.*	2158
9.59 —	*S.O. B.C.F.*	*Leda*	W/T	If too dark for sweeping to-night patrol between 90° and 180° from May Island, 10 miles to the Eastward, and sweep Y Channel at daylight.	2131
10.0 —	*R.A. 2nd B.S.*	*2nd Division*	Flags	*Admiral intends to proceed at 14 knots*	—
10.0 —	**C.-in-C.**	**Ships in company.**	W/T	**Cease W/T communication except on sighting the Enemy or replying to the Admiral. W/T guards may use auxiliary in case of necessity.**	2200

Date, Time of Despatch	From	To	System.	Message.	Time of Origin.
30 MAY —*cont.*					
10.2 p.m.	*S.O. 1st C.S.*-	*1st C.S.* -	F.L.	*Admiral intends to proceed at 18 knots* -	—
10.2 —	Benbow -	—	—	Remarks : Benbow underway· -	—
10.3 —	*S.O. B.C.F.*-	*1st B.C.S.*	F.L.	*Form single line-ahead in sequence of fleet numbers. Speed 12 knots.*	—
10.3 —	*S.O. 2nd B.S.*	*Erin* - -	F.L.	*Inform gate trawler you are the last ship* -	2200
10.7 —	*S.O. 5th B.S.*	*5th B.S.* -	F.L.	*Weigh* - - - - - -	—
10.7 —	*R.A. 1st B.S.*	*6th Subdivision*	F.L.	*Form single line-ahead in sequence of fleet numbers. Speed 12 knots.*	—
10.7 —	*S.O. 4th L.C.S.*	*4th L.C.S.* -	F.L.	*Admiral intends to proceed at 17 knots* -	—
10.9 —	*S.O. 1st C.S.*-	*1st C.S.* -	F.L.	*Alter course in succession to E. by N.* -	—
10.9 —	*S.O. 3rd L.C.S*	*3rd L.C.S.* -	F.L.	*Admiral intends to proceed at 18 knots* -	—
10.10 —	*S.O. 5th B.S.*	*5th B.S.* -	F.L.	*Form single line-ahead in sequence of fleet numbers. Speed 12 knots. Preserve open order.*	—
10.11 —	*S.O. 2nd B.C.S*	*2nd B.C.S.* -	F.L.	*Admiral intends to proceed at 15 knots* -	—
10.11 —	*Commodore F.*	*General* -	F.L.	*Slip* - - - - - -	—
10.12 —	*S.O. 3rd B.C.S*	*3rd B.C.S., Chester and Canterbury.*	F.L.	*Alter course in succession to S. 85° E.* -	—
10.12 —	S.O. 2nd C.S.	8th Group Destroyers.	F.L.	My speed 17 knots. I am passing North of Pentland Skerries.	—
10.13 —	S.O. 4th L.C.S.	Narwhal -	F.L.	I intend to pass you, leaving you on my starboard hand. Keep out of the way.	—
10.14 —	*Captain D12*-	*Commodore F., Captain D4.*	F.L.	*2nd C.S. just passed gate* - - - -	2210
10.17 —	Commodore F.	General - -	F.L.	*Form single line ahead 12 knots* - -	—
10.18 —	*Caroline* -	*S.O. 4th L.C.S.*	F.L.	*Steering gear has broken down. Reply : Rejoin when ready.*	—
10.20 —	*S.O. 2nd B.C.S*	*2nd B.C.S.* -	F.L.	*Admiral intends to proceed at 18 knots* -	—
10.20 —	C.-in-C. -	3rd Sub. -	F.L.	**Form single line-ahead in sequence of fleet numbers. Admiral intends to proceed at 12 knots.**	—
10.20 —	Owl - -	Minotaur -	S.L.	Will you please give me names of ships in 2nd C.S. ? Reply : Minotaur, Hampshire, Cochrane, Shannon, in that order. Are you S.O. of Group 8 ? Reply : Yes.	2215
10.21 —	S.O. 2nd B.S.	2nd B.S., 1st C.S., Boadicea, Kempenfelt.	W/T	Raise steam for 20 knots by 2 a.m. tomorrow, Wednesday.	2221
10.22 —	*R.A. 2nd B.S.*	*2nd Division and Destroyers.*	F.L.	*Alter course in succession to N. 79° E.* -	—
10.25 —	*S.O. 1st L.C.S.*	*1st L.C.S.* -	F.L.	*Spread for L.S.6 when May Island is abeam. Galatea steer 60° for 20 miles, then 79°.*	2220
10.25 —	*R.A. 2nd B.S.*	*2nd Division and Destroyers.*	F.L.	*Admiral intends to proceed at 18 knots* -	—

Date, Time of Despatch.	From	To	System.	Message.	Time of Origin.
30 MAY *—cont.*					
10.30 p.m.	*S.O. B.C.F.*	*1st B.C.S.*	W/T	*Admiral intends to proceed at 15 knots*	—
10.30 —	*S.O. 2nd B.S.*	*1st Division*	F.L.	*Admiral intends to proceed at 18 knots*	—
10.30 —	*S.O. 3rd B.C.S.*	*3rd B.C.S., Chester and Canterbury.*	F.L.	*Canterbury take station ahead five miles of Invincible.*	—
10.31 —	*S.O. 1st B.S.*	*5th Subdivision*	S.L.	*Alter course in succession to S. 3° W. Admiral intends to proceed at 17 knots.*	—
10.31 —	**Campania**	**C.-in-C.**	W/T	**Ready to proceed**	**2130**
10.32 —	*Commodore F.*	*11th Flotilla*	F.L.	*Stop engines, show no lights at all*	—
10.32 —	**C.-in-C.**	**Blanche**	F.L.	**Campania has been ordered to take station astern of you. Show shaded stern light.**	**2230**
10.32 —	*S.O. 4th L.C.S.*	*4th L.C.S.*	F.L.	*Admiral intends to proceed 18 knots. Keep closed up.*	—
10.34 —	*S.O. 3rd B.C.S*	*3rd B.C.S., Chester and Canterbury.*	F.L.	*Alter course in succession to S. 79° E.*	—
10.34 —	*Commodore F.*	*Marne*	S.L.	*I am stopped (Pass down line). Pass through gate before stopping.*	—
10.35 —	Admiralty	Commodore T.	L/T	Eight Destroyers should be sent to join 3rd B.S. in Swin after daylight. Remainder of your force should be kept at one hour's notice after daylight.	—
10.37 —	S.O. B.C.F.	Captain D13	W/T	Admiral intends to proceed at 18 knots	—
10.38 —	*S.O. 2nd B.S.*	*1st Division*	F.L.	*Alter course in succession to N. 78° E.*	—
10.40 —	*Inconstant*	*Cordelia*	F.L.	*I shall steer N. 80° E. for 1 hour and seven minutes after May Island is abeam and then alter to S. 82° E. without signal.*	2240
10.40 —	*S.O. B.C.F.*	*1st B.C.S.*	W/T	*Admiral intends to proceed at 18 knots*	—
10.42 —	*S.O. 5th B.S.*	*5th B.S.*	F.L.	*Admiral intends to proceed at 18 knots*	—
10.45 —	*R.A. 1st B.S*	*6th Subdivision*	F.L.	*Admiral intends to proceed at 17 knots*	—
10.47 —	*S.O. 2nd B.C.S.*	*2nd B.C.S. and Screen.*	F.L.	*Alter course in succession to E.N.E.*	—
10.47 —	*Captain D4*	*4th Flotilla, Oak.*	W/T	*Course for the night. ' Pass through Lat. 58° 47' N., Long. 2° 37' W., and then 84° until 1.30 a.m., then 90°.*	2213
10.50 —	S.O. 2nd C.S.	Destroyers, Group 8.	F.L.	My course N. 80° E. Destroyers take station five cables astern of Shannon	—
10.54 —	**C.-in-C.**	**Campania**	F.L.	**Take station astern of Blanche**	—
10.54 —	*S.O. 2nd C.S.*	*2nd C.S.*	F.L.	*Course N. 80° E. Ships in column to be in open order. Destroyers take station five cables astern of Shannon.*	—
10.55 —	*S.O. 3rd L.C.S.*	*3rd L.C.S. and Engadine.*	F.L.	*After passing May Island assume L.S.6, East by South, North by East, Engadine follow Falmouth and Yarmouth, who will steer N. 83 E., 28 miles at 18 knots, then S. 79° E.*	2250

Date, Time of Despatch.	From	To	System.	Message.	Time of Origin.
30 MAY —*cont.* 10.56 p m.	*S.O. 1st C.S.* -	*1st C.S.* -	F.L.	*Alter course in succession to E. ¼ N.*	—
10.57 —	*S.O. 1st B.S.*	*5th Subdivision and Faulknor.*	F.L.	*Alter course in succession to S. 82° E.*	—
11.0 —	*S.O.3rd B.C.S.*	*3rd B.C.S., Chester and Canterbury.*	F.L.	*Admiral intends to proceed at 17 knots*	—
11.0 —	*Captain D4 Flotilla.*	*Broke* -	F.L.	*Proceed* -	2255
11.0 —	S.O. B.C.F. -	Captain D13 -	W/T	Alter course in succession to E. by N.	—
11.1 —	S.O. B.C.F. -	S.O.s. of Squadrons.	W/T	Lion will be abeam of May Island at 0005	2301
11.2 —	*S.O.2nd B.C.S*	*2nd B.C.S. and Screen.*	F.L.	*Alter course in succession to N. 82° E.*	—
11.2 —	*S.O. 5th B.S.*	*5th B.S.* -	F.L.	*Ships in column to be three cables apart*	—
11.3 —	*S.O. B.C.F.* -	*1st B.C.S.* -	F.L.	*Alter course in succession to E. by N.*	—
11.6 —	Ebro -	S.O. 10th C.S.	W/T	Boarded Dutch s.s. Ngihok. to Belfast. Green Customs Clearances. Allowed to proceed. 59° 13′ N., 13° 30′ W. Course 247°.	2103
11.8 —	*S.O. 1st C.S.* -	*1st C.S.* -	F.L.	*Alter course in succession to S. 72° E. Admiral intends to proceed at 18½ knots.*	—
11.9 —	*S.O. 1st B.S.*	*5th Subdivision*	F.L.	*Alter course in succession to N. 83° E.*	—
11.10 —	*R.A. 1st B.S.*	*6th Subdivision*	F.L.	*Alter course in succession to S. 83° E.*	—
11.10 —	*Commodore F.*	*11th Flotilla* -	F.L.	*Admiral intends to proceed at 17 knots. Keep closed up.*	—
11.15 —	*S.O. 5th B.S.*	*5th B.S. Fearless.*	F.L.	*Alter course in succession to N. 76° E.*	—
11.16 —	S.O. B.C.F. -	Captain D13 -	W/T	You should screen Lion and 1st B.C.S.	2312
11.19 —	*Commodore F.*	*11th Flotilla* -	F.L.	*Admiral intends to proceed at 19 knots*	—
11.20 —	*R.A. 2nd B.S.*	*2nd Division and Destroyers.*	F.L.	*Alter course in succession to S. 72° E.*	—
11.20 —	Blanche -	Commodore F.	F.L.	Can you see Campania ? Reply : No, 1 am asking last Destroyer.	—
11.20 —	*S.O. 4th L.C.S.*	*4th L.C.S.* -	F.L.	*Alter course in succession to S. 78° E.*	—
11.20 —	**C.-in-C.** -	**Admiralty** -	W/T	**11th Submarine Flotilla now ready for sea. Submit Admiralty may give it orders as situation develops. Inform me by " I " method.**	2245
11.23 —	*Commodore F.*	*Mons* -	F.L.	*Can you see Campania ? Reply : No* -	—
11.30 —	*Commodore F.*	*11th Flotilla* -	F.L.	*Admiral intends to proceed at 17 knots*	—
11.30 —	*Falmouth* -	*Birkenhead* -	F.L.	*Falmouth will go 28 miles at 16 knots and then increase to 18 knots.*	2325
11.35 —	S.O. 5th B.S.	Fearless -	W/T	One hour and seven minutes after passing May Island course will be altered to 85°.	2320
11.35 —	*S.O. 2nd B.S.*	*1st Division* -	F.L.	*Alter course in succession to S. 72° E.*	—
11.38 —	*S.O.3rd L.C.S.*	*Yarmouth and Engadine.*	F.L.	*Course N. 83° E. Speed 16 knots* -	—

Time Time of Despatch.	From	To	System.	Message.	Time of Origin.
30 MAY —*cont.*					
11.40 p.m.	S.O.B.C.F. -	Nottingham -	W/T	B.C.F. sailed. Lion will pass North of May Island about midnight and then steer 66° for 20 miles. Light Cruisers in L.S.6. Course will then be shaped for 56° 40′ N., 5° 0′ E., speed of advance 18 knots. Take up your station on screen at daylight. Destroyers join Champion, who is with me. (Passed to S.O.L.C.S. for information.)	2215
11.43 —	S.O.3rd L.C.S.	S.O. 1st L.C.S.	F.L.	My course is N. 83° E., 16 knots till 1.10 then S. 79° E., 18 knots.	2340
11.44 —	*Commodore F.*	*11th Flotilla* -	F.L.	*Marne and Manners take station on port quarter. Michael and Mons close up.*	—
11.45 —	*S.O. 1st B.S.*	*5th Subdivision and Faulknor*	F.L.	*Alter course in succession to S. 78° E.* -	—
11.45 —	R.A. Invergordon.	Admiralty -	L/T	2nd Battle Squadron, 1st Cruiser Squadron, Boadicea, Kempenfelt and nine Destroyers sailed 10.15 p.m.	2220
11.46 —	*S.O.3rd L.C.S.*	*Yarmouth* -	F.L.	*Can you see Engadine? Reply: Yes, astern of us.*	*2345*
11.52 —	C.-in-C., Rosyth.	Admiralty -	L/T and W/T	Battle Cruiser Fleet, Engadine and Destroyers sailed at 10 p.m. (*Received in Iron Duke 12.17 a.m.*)	2220
11.55 —	**R.A. Scapa** -	**R.A. Invergordon.**	W/T	From C.-in-C. Rosyth for C.-in-C. Trident reports attacked at 7.45 p.m. by Submarine 56° 17′ N., 1° 30′ W.	2145
11.58 —	**Blanche** -	**C.-in-C.** -	F.L.	**Castor reports that Destroyers can see no sign of Campania.**	2358
11.59 —	**C.-in-C.** -	**Campania** -	W/T	**Speed from obstruction 17 knots. Course from Skerries 84° until 1.30 a.m., then 90°.**	2316
12.0 midnight.	*S.O. B C.F.*-	*1st B.C.S.* -	F.L.	*Alter course in succession to N. 83° E.* -	—
MAY 31st					
12.4 a.m.	S.O. 5th B.S.	Fearless -	W/T	Course from May Island abeam, 66° -	2355
12.5 —	*S.O.2ndL.C.S.*	*Birmingham* -	F.L.	*Take position F* - - - -	—
12.9 —	S.O. B.C.F. -	Champion -	F.L.	Alter course in succession to N. 83° E. -	—
12.10 —	*S.O.2ndL.C.S.*	*Southampton, Dublin.*	F.L.	*Alter course in succession to S.E. by E. Admiral intends to proceed at 20 knots.*	—
12.11 —	S.O. B.C.F. -	Champion -	F.L.	I shall alter course at 1.15 a.m. to S. 81° E., speed 18 knots.	0010
12.12 —	Naval Depot, North Shields.	Admiralty -	L/T	A.P. Vessels have been recalled into harbour by code word.	2140
12.16 —	*S.O.4th L.C.S.*	*Caroline* -	W/T	*My position, course, and speed at 11.30 p.m. 58° 44′ N., 2° 33′ W. 84°, 18 knots.*	*0000*
12.20 —	Captain D1 -	Captain D13 -	W/T	Course 1 hour 7 minutes after May Island abeam, 66° true.	0015
12.26 —	**C.-in-C.** -	**Destroyer Screen.** -	F.L.	**Alter course in succession to S. 78° E.** -	—
12.30 —	*S.O. 5th B.S.*	*5th B.S.* -	F.L.	*Alter course in succession to N. 83° E.* -	—
12.40 —	C.-in-C. Rosyth.	Admiralty -	L/T	5th B.S., four ships sailed at 10.40 p.m. - (*Passed to C.-in-C. by Interception. Received 2.31 a.m.*)	2205

Date, Time of Despatch.	From	To	System.	Message.	Time of Origin.
31 MAY —*cont.*					
12.40 a.m.	*S.O. 5th B.S.*	*5th B.S.* -	F.L.	*Course will be altered to 85° true at 1.37 a.m. without further signal.*	—
12.42 —	**C.-in-C.** -	2nd i/c 4th B.S., S.O. 4th B.S., S.O. 1st B.S., 2nd i/c 1st B.S., Iron Duke, Campania.	W/T	6th Subdivision alter course in succession to 90° at 1.30 a.m. without further signal. Remaining subdivisions conform.	0006
1.0 —	*S.O.2ndB.C.S.*	*2nd B.C.S.* -	F.L.	*Alter course in succession to E. by S.* -	—
1.10 —	**C.-in-C.** -	Cyclops - -	W/T	Order boarding steamers to proceed South of bearing 90° from Pentland Skerries and burn navigation lights.	2333
1.12 —	*S.O.3rd L.C.S*	*3rd L.C.S.* - *Engadine.*	F.L.	*Alter course in succession to S. 79° W. Speed of advance 18 knots.*	—
1.15 —	**C.-in-C.** -	S.O. 1st, 4th B.S., R.A. 1st, 4th B.S., Commodore F., Captain D's. 4, 11, 12.	W/T	At dawn Battlefleet form divisions line-ahead disposed abeam to starboard. Columns eight cables apart. Organisation number five.	2356
1.15 —	**R.A. Scapa** -	R.A. Invergordon.	W/T	A.18. For C.-in-C., following message from Aberdeen W/T Station. Begins— W.234 from R.A. Peterhead. Large Submarine reported by motor launch, seen stationary on the surface, submerged 11.15 a.m., Tuesday, 30th May, 57° 10′ N., 0° 40′ W. Submarine reappeared 2 p.m., steering N.E. on the surface 57° 20′ N., 0° 40′ W. Motor launch fired two rounds, whereupon Submarine submerged. Submarine was dark in colour, two masts, very large conning tower.	2215
1.15 —	*S.O.2ndL.C.S.*	*Southampton, Dublin.*	S.L.	*Alter course in succession to S. 80° E. Speed 18 knots.*	—
1.15 —	*S.O. B.C.F.*-	*1st B.C.S. and Champion.*	F.L.	*Alter course in succession to S. 81° E.* -	—
1.17 —	S O. B.C.F. -	Champion -	F.L.	Correct positions of screening Destroyers on port hand.	0115
1.22 —	*Commodore F.*	*General* - -	F.L.	*Admiral intends to proceed at 21 knots* -	—
1.22 —	**C.-in-C.** -	Admiralty -	W/T	Battlefleet is proceeding to 57° 45′ N., 4° 15′ E., B.C.F. to 56° 40′ N., 5° 0′ E., both by 2 p.m., to-morrow 31st May.	0122
1.22 —	S.O. 2nd C.S.	Destroyers -	F.L.	Take station ahead of Minotaur - -	—
1.23 —	*S.O. 2nd C.S.*	*2nd C.S.* -	F.L.	*Ships in column to be in close order* - -	—
1.25 —	S.O.3rd L.C.S.	Engadine -	F.L.	Pass ahead of Falmouth ready to take up cruising station between B. and C. Falmouth is in C. Inconstant in B.	0121
1.26 —	**R.A. Scapa** -	R.A. Inver- - gordon.	W/T	From S.N.O. Blyth to C.-in-C. Submarine G1. Arrived 11 p.m. Nothing to report.	2330
1.30 —	Yarmouth -	S.O. 2nd B.C.S.	F.L.	What is position of Lion from you, please ? Reply : We are four miles ahead of Lion.	0225
1.30 —	*R.A. 1st B.S.*	*6th Subdivision and Marksman.*	F.L.	*Alter course in succession to S. 73° E.* -	—
1.30 —	*S.O.4th L.C.S.*	*4th L.C.S.* -	F.L.	*Admiral intends to proceed at 17 knots* -	—

Date, Time of Despatch.	From	To	System.	Message.	Time of Origin.
31 MAY	*—cont.*				
1.33 a.m.	*S.O. 2nd B.S.*	*1st Division*	F.L.	*Admiral intends to proceed at 19 knots*	—
1.33 —	S.O. B.C.F.	Champion	F.L.	There appear to be no Destroyers between you and the one on my port beam. You had better screen my port bow until Destroyers are in station.	0132
1.35 —	S.O. 1st B.S.	Faulknor	F.L.	Alter course in succession to S. 73° E.	—
1.45 —	R.A. Cyclops	Admiralty	L/T and W/T	Campania sailed (*Received in Iron Duke 2.0 a.m.*)	0120
1.47 —	*S.O. 2nd B.S.*	*2nd B.S.*	W/T	*Form divisions in line-ahead disposed abeam to starboard. Columns to be six cables apart.*	—
1.47 —	*S.O. Cruisers*	*All Cruisers*	F.L.	*Take up cruising disposition No. 1 distance between X and Y, 10 miles, my course S. 73° E., speed of advance 17 knots.*	—
1.50 —	*S.O. 4thL.C.S.*	*4th L.C.S.*	F.L.	*Alter course in succession to S. 72° E.*	—
1.51 —	S.O. 2nd B.S.	Kempenfelt	F.L.	Divisions in line ahead to starboard six cables apart will be formed at 2 a.m. Adjust screen accordingly.	0150
1.53 —	S.O. 2nd B.S.	Boadicea	W/T	Take station-ahead one mile	0152
1.58 —	*S. O.2nd B.S.*	*R.A. 2nd B. S.*	W/T	*My speed is 19 knots*	*0151*
2.0 —	**C.-in-C.**	**3rd Sub. and Screen.**	F.L.	**At 1.55 course will be altered to S. 73 E. without further signal.**	**0135**
2.0 —	S.O. 2nd C.S.	Destroyers	F.L.	Destroyers join their respective Cruisers	—
2.7 —	R.A. Cyclops	Admiralty	L/T	Iron Duke, 1st B.S., 4th B.S., less E. of I. and Dreadnought, 3rd B.C.S., 2nd C.S., except Achilles, 7th C.S., less Donegal, 4th L.C.S., Revenge, Royal Oak, Bellona, Blanche, Active, Canterbury, Chester, Abdiel, Oak, Castor, Tipperary, Faulknor, Broke, Marksman, 4th Flotilla, 11th Flotilla, 12th Flotilla sailed.	—
2.10 —	Benbow	—	—	Remarks : Sighted 1st B.S. ahead	—
2.11 —	*S.O. 1st C.S.*	*1st C.S.*	F.L.	*Alter course in succession to S. 87° E.*	—
2.15 —	S.O. 2nd B.S.	S.O. 1st C.S.	W/T	Spread as soon as you are clear of minefield. Keep 10 miles ahead of me. My speed of advance will be 18 knots.	0201
2.17 —	*S.O. 2nd B.S.*	*R.A. 2nd B.S.*	F.L.	*Guides to bear S. 3° W.*	—
2.17 —	S.O. 3rd L.C.S.	Engadine	F.L.	Take up cruising position. I am going to zigzag.	0215
2.18 —	*R.A. 2nd B.S.*	*2nd Division*	F.L.	*Alter course in succession to S. 72° E. Speed 19 knots.*	—
2.18 —	*S.O. 3rd L.C.S.*	*Yarmouth*	F.L.	*Take station as repeating ship and report position of Lion when sighted.*	*0215*
2.20 —	*S.O. Cruisers*	*All Cruisers*	S.L.	*Zigzag when in station*	—
2.20 —	**R.A. Scapa**	**R.A. Invergordon.**	W/T	**From S.N.O. Aberdeen for C.-in-C. Moon arrived.**	**2250**
2.22 —	*Yarmouth*	*S.O. 3rd L.C.S.*	F.L.	*2nd B.C.S. bears W. by S. about three miles*	*0226*
2.23 —	*S.O.3rd L.C.S.*	*Yarmouth*	F.L.	*They are probably still five miles ahead of Lion.*	*0223*

Date, Time of Despatch.	From	To	System.	Message.	Time of Origin.
31 MAY —cont.					
2.26 a.m.	S.O.2nd C.S.	Hampshire	F.L.	Take your Destroyer with you and keep visual touch Minotaur C and Active at J. Report bearing and distance of Iron Duke as soon as you obtain it. Zigzag when in station.	0220
2.30 —	S.O. B.C.F.	General	Flags	Alter course together two points to port	—
2.30 —	S.O.3rd B.C.S.	3rd B.C.S., Chester and Canterbury.	Flags	Alter course in succession to S. 73° E.	—
2.30 —	R.A 1st B.S.	5th Division	Flags	Alter course together one point to port	—
2.30 —	S.O. B.C.F.	General	Flags	Commence zigzagging	—
2.34 —	S.O.3rd B.C.S.	3rd B.C.S., Chester and Canterbury.	Flags	Alter course together two points to port	—
2.34 —	S.O. 4th B.S.	Porpoise	F.L.	Examine steamer passing on starboard side	0230
2.35 —	**C.-in-C.**	**General**	Flags	**Alter course together two points to starboard.**	—
2.35 —	S.O. 3rd B.C.S.	Chester	Flags	Take station astern five miles	—
2.35 —	S.O.2nd L.C.S.	Southampton, Dublin.	S.L.	Zigzag, speed of advance 18 knots. Assume open order.	—
2.35 —	S.O. 2nd C.S.	Hampshire	F.L.	Active on my port quarter	0235
2.36 —	S.O. 2nd B.S.	General	Flags	Alter course leading ships together the rest in succession to S. 87° E.	—
2.36 —	S.O. 2nd C.S.	Active	F.L.	Can you see Battlefleet ? You should be in position J about five miles W. of us and five miles ahead of Iron Duke and in signal touch with Iron Duke.	0230
2.37 —	S.O. 3rd B.C.S.	Chester	F.L.	Are you in touch with Cruisers ? Reply : No	0230 0245
2.38 —	Commodore F.	General	Flags	Alter course together two points to starboard	—
2.40 —	Shannon	S.O. 2nd C.S.	F.L.	Please say what kind of zigzag you are doing	0240
2.40 —	S.O.3rd B.C.S.	3rd B.C.S., Chester and Canterbury.	Flags	Alter course together four points to starboard	—
2.40 —	S.O. B.C.F.	General	Flags	Alter course together four points to starboard.	—
2.40 —	S.O.5th B.S.	5th B.S.	Flags	Admiral intends to proceed at 19½ knots	—
2.45 —	S.O.2nd B.C.S.	2nd B.C.S.	Flags	Form in single line-abreast to starboard	—
2.45 —	S.O.2nd B.S.	2nd B.S.	F.L.	Alter course together two points to starboard	—
2.45 —	**C.-in-C.**	**General**	Flags	**Alter course together two points to port**	—
2.45 —	S.O. B.C.F.	General	Flags	Admiral intends to proceed at 19½ knots	—
2.46 —	S.O. 4th B.S.	4th Division	Flags	Alter course together three points to port. Speed 16 knots.	—
2.47 —	S.O.2nd B.C.S.	9th Flotilla	Flags	Take up Submarine screen as denoted in diagram 8.	—
2.47 —	R.A. 1st B.S.	5th Division	Flags	Alter course together two points to port	—
2.50 —	S.O. B.C.F.	General	Flags	Alter course together four points to port	—
2.50 —	S.O.3rd B.C.S.	3rd B.C.S., Chester and Canterbury	Flags	Alter course together four points to port	—

Date, Time of Despatch.	From	To	System.	Message.	Time of Origin.
31 MAY —*cont.*					
2.50 a.m.	*S.O. 2nd B.S.*	*2nd B.S.*	Flags	*Alter course together two points to port* .	—
2.50 —	*S.O. 2nd C.S.*	*2nd C.S.*	F.L.	*Zigzag will be as follows : Two points each side of the normal every 10 minutes counting from the hour. At the hour the alteration will be to starboard, at 10 minutes past to port, and so on.*	0247
2.50 —	*S.O. B.C.F.*	*2nd B.C.S.*	F.L.	Take station on a line of bearing N. 9 E. three miles. Speed of advance 18 knots.	—
2.50 —	*S.O. 5th B.S.*	*5th B.S.*	Flags	*Alter course together two points to port* .	—
2.50 —	*S.O. 2nd C. S.*	*Calliope*	F.L.	What is bearing and distance of Iron Duke ? Reply : Iron Duke is not visible, am dropping back to close her.	0252
2.51 —	*S.O.2nd B.C.S.*	*2nd B.C.S.*	Flags	*Ships in column to be five cables apart* .	—
2.53 —	*Yarmouth*	*S.O. 3rd L.C.S.*	F.L.	*Lion bears N. 50 W. four miles. As 2nd B.C.S. are in the position I should be, I am taking station ahead of them.*	0245
2.53 —	*S.O. 4th B.S.*	*4th Division*	Flags	*Alter course together six points to starboard.*	—
2.54 —	*R.A. 1st B.S.*	*5th Division*	Flags	*Alter course together three points to starboard*	—
2.55 —	*S.O. 1st B.S.*	Ships in Company.	Flags.	Alter course in succession nine points to starboard.	—
2.55 —	**C.-in-C.**	**General**	Flags	**Alter course together two points to port**	—
2.57 —	*S.O. 1st C.S.*	*1st C.S.*	Sem.	*When L.S.1—10 is made Warrior to B, Defence C, Duke of Edinburgh D, Black Prince F. Zigzag ¾ of a point each side of course, when in station advance 18 knots.*	—
2.58 —	*R.A. 1st B.S.*	*5th Division*	Flags	*Alter course together three points to starboard.*	—
2.59 —	*S.O.2nd B.C.S.*	*2nd B.C.S.*	Flags	*Admiral intends to proceed at 18 knots* .	—
3.0 —	*S.O. 2nd B.S.*	*2nd B.S.*	Flags	*Alter course together two points to port* .	—
3.0 —	*S.O. 3rd B.C.S.*	*3rd B C.S., Chester and Canterbury.*	Flags	*Alter course together four points to starboard*	—
3.0 —	*S.O. B.C.F.*	General	Flags	Alter course together four points to starboard.	—
3.0 —	Lion	—	—	Remarks : 2nd B.C.S. in sight ahead, 5th B.S. in sight astern.	—
3.0 —	*S.O. 5th B.S.*	*5th B.S.*	Flags	*Alter course together four points to starboard*	—
3.0 —	*Commodore F.*	*11th Flotilla*	Flags	*Admiral intends to proceed at 17 knots* .	—
3.2 —	*S.O. 3rd L C.S.*	*S.O. B.C.F.*	F.L.	Nottingham and two Destroyers joined up	0253
3.5 —	**C.-in-C.**	**General**	Flags	**Alter course together two points to starboard.**	—
3.5 —	*S.O. 3rdL.C.S.*	*Nottingham*	F.L.	Screen is in L.S.6. I am in position C and zigzagging.	0303
3.5 —	*Hampshire*	*S.O. 2nd C.S.*	F.L.	*Active reports cannot see Iron Duke.* Reply : Drop back on bearing West until you get touch with 4th L.C.S.	0305
3.5 —	*S.O. 5th B.S.*	*Warspite*	Flags	*Take up appointed station* . . .	—
3.5 —	*S.O.3rd B.C.S.*	*3rd B.C.S., Chester and Canterbury.*	Flags	*Resume the original course together* . .	—

Date, Time of Despatch.	From	To	System.	Message.	Time of Origin.
31 MAY	—*cont.*				
3.5 a.m.	R.A. 1st B.S.	5th Division -	Flags	*Alter course together three points to port* -	—
3.7 —	S.O. 5th B.S.	5th B.S. -	Sem.	Barham is using 10° of helm and not increasing speed on the turn.	0305
3.7 —	S.O. 1st B.S.	Ships in Company.	Flags	Alter course in succession nine points to port.	—
3.8 —	S.O. 4th B.S.	4th Division -	Flags	*Alter course together six points to port* -	—.
3.10 —	S.O. B.C.F.	1st B.C.S. -	Flags	*Alter course together four points to port* -	—
3.10 —	S.O.3rdB.C.S.	3rd B.C.S., Chester and Canterbury.	Flags	*Alter course in succession 16 points to starboard.*	—
3.10 —	S.O. 2nd B.S.	2nd B.S. -	Flags	*Alter course together two points to starboard*	—
3.10 —	S.O. B.C.F. -	Champion -	F.L.	2nd B.C.S. are taking station three miles on port beam of Lion.	0305
3.10 —	S.O.4thL.C.S.	S.O. 2nd C.S.	S.L.	Iron Duke bears S. 60° W. - - -	0310
3.10 —	S.O. 2nd C.S.	Armed Boarding Steamers	F.L.	Keep to the Southward clear of the fleet	0309
3.10 —	Lion - -	—	—	Remarks : Nottingham, Nomad and Nicator rejoined.	—
3.12 —	S.O. 5th B.S.	5th B.S. -	Flags	*Alter course together four points to port* -	—
3.14 —	Nottingham	S.O. 3rd L.C.S.	F.L.	What is bearing and direction of screen? Reply : E. by S. and N. by E.	0316
3.15 —	S.O. 1st C.S.	1st C.S. -	Flags	*Spread in accordance with cruising diagram No. 1. Distance between X and Y 10 miles.*	—
3.15 —	Calliope -	—	—	Remarks : Sighted two armed boarding steamers on port beam.	—
3.15 —	S.O.4thL.C.S.	4th L.C.S. -	Flags	*Admiral intends to proceed at 15 knots* -	—.
3.16 —	S.O. Cruisers	Cruisers -	S.L.	*Speed of advance 16 knots* - - -	—
3.18 —	S.O. 2nd B.S.	General -	Flags	Admiral intends to proceed at 18 knots -	—
3.18 —	S.O. 5th B.S.	5th B.S. -	Flags	*Admiral intends to proceed at 18 knots* -	—
3.18 —	**R.A. Scapa** -	**Aberdeen** -	W/T	**For C.-in-C. Moon completed with oil fuel.**	0215
3.19 —	S.O.3rdL.C.S.	Yarmouth -	S.L.	What is bearing and distance of Lion now? Reply : N. 65 W. five miles.	0315
3.20 —	S.O.3rdB.C.S.	3rd B.C.S., Chester and Canterbury.	Flags	*Alter course in succession 16 points to starboard.*	—
3.20 —	S.O.4th L.C.S.	4th L.C.S. -	Flags	*Alter course together two points to port* -	—.
3.20 —	S.O. B.C.F.	General -	Flags	Alter course together four points to starboard.	—
3.20 —	R.A. 1st B.S.	5th Division -	Flags	*Alter course together three points to port* -	—
3.22 —	S.O.3rdB.C.S.	3rd B.C.S., Chester and Canterbury.	Flags	*Admiral intends to proceed at 18½ knots* -	—
3.22 —	R.A. 1st B.S.	5th Division -	Flags	*Alter course together four points to starboard*	—.
3.22 —	S.O. 4th B.S.	4th Division -	Flags	*Alter course together four points to port* -	—
3.23 —	S.O. 5th B.S.	5th B.S. -	Flags	*Alter course together four points to starboard*	—.

Date, Time of Despatch.	From	To	System.	Message.	Time of Origin.
31 MAY	—*cont.*				
3.25 a.m.	*S.O. 4th B.S.*	*4th Division*	Flags	*Alter course together seven points to starboard.*	—
3.25 —	*Hampshire*	*S.O. 2nd C.S.*	S.L.	*4th L.C.S. S.W. 2½ miles. Have lost touch with Active.*	*0320*
3.26 —	*R.A. 1st B.S.*	*5th Division*	Flags	*Alter course together four points to starboard*	—
3.28 —	*S.O.3rdL.C.S.*	Birkenhead, Engadine, Inconstant, Southampton	S.L.	I am moving three miles to port to get on my bearing from Lion.	0325
3.29 —	*R.A. 1st B.S.*	*5th Division*	Flags	*Alter course together four points to port*	—
3.30 —	*S.O. B.C.F.*	General	Flags	Alter course together four points to port	—
3.30 —	*S.O.3rdB.C.S.*	*3rd B.C.S.*	Flags	*Alter course together two points to port*	—
3.30 —	*S.O. 4th B.S.*	*4th Division*	Flags	*Alter course together three points to starboard*	—
3.30 —	*S.O.4thL.C.S.*	*4th L.C.S.*	Flags	*Alter course together four points to starboard*	—
3.31 —	*S.O 2nd C.S.*	*Hampshire*	S.L.	*If you cannot get touch with Active endeavour to obtain bearing and distance of Iron Duke through 4th L.C.S.*	*0330*
3.32 —	*S.O 5th B.S.*	*5th B.S.*	Flags	*Alter course together four points to port*	—
3.34 —	*S.O.3rdB.C.S.*	Chester	S.L.	Keep touch between Cruisers and myself	*0325*
3.35 —	*S.O 4th B.S.*	*4th Division*	Flags	*Alter course together six points to port*	—
3.40 —	*S.O.3rdB.C.S.*	*3rd B.C.S.*	Flags	*Alter course together four points to starboard.*	—
3.40 —	S.O. B.C.F.	General	Flags	Alter course together four points to starboard.	—
3.40 —	*S.O. 4th B.S.*	*4th Division*	Flags	*Alter course together five points to starboard*	—
3.40 —	Porpoise	S.O. 4th B.S.	S.L.	Danish steamer Danæ reports that she was boarded last night waiting for daylight bound for Kirkwall. She was flying black and white striped cone. *(Passed to C.-in-C. 4.10 a.m.)*	—
3.40 —	*S.O.4thL.C.S.*	*4th L.C.S.*	Flags	*Alter course together four points to port*	—
3.42 —	*S.O. 5th B.S.*	*5th B.S.*	Flags	*Alter course together four points to starboard*	—
3.42 —	*S.O.3rdL.C.S.*	*S.O. B.C.F.*	S.L.	Engadine is in cruising station between B and C.	*0340*
3.43 —	*S.O.4thL.C.S.*	*4th L.C.S.*	Flags	*Alter course together four points to starboard*	—
3.44 —	*S.O.4thL.C.S.*	*4th L.C.S.*	Flags	*Form single line-ahead in sequence in which ships now are.*	—
3.45 —	*S.O. 1st B.S.*	*6th Division*	Flags	*Alter course in succession to S. 73° E.*	—
3.45 —	*S.O 4th B.S.*	*4th Division*	Flags	*Alter course together three points to port*	—
3.46 —	*S.O. 4th B.S.*	*4th Division*	Flags	*Admiral intends to proceed at 17 knots*	—
3.50 —	S.O. B.C.F.	General	Flags	Alter course together four points to port	—
3.50 —	*S.O.3rdB.C.S.*	*3rd B.C.S.*	Flags	*Alter course together four points to port*	—
3.50 —	**C.-in-C.**	**Commodore F.**	S.L.	**Reinforce port wing of screen**	**0350**

Date, Time of Despatch.	From	To	System.	Message.	Time of Origin.
31 MAY	—cont.				
3.50 a.m.	Active	S.O. 2nd C.S.	S.L.	In touch with 4th L.C.S. and Iron Duke, bearing from Iron Duke W. ½ S.	0345
3.52 —	S.O. 5th B.S.	5th B.S.	Flags	Alter course together four points to port	—
3.55 —	S.O. 4th L.C.S.	4th L.C.S.	Flags	Alter course together to S. 72° E. Speed 17 knots. Ships in column to be five cables apart.	—
3.55 —	Galatea	S.O. B.C.F.	S.L.	Have just been fired at by Submarine	0350
3.55 —	S.O. 2nd C.S.	Hampshire	S.L.	What is Hampshire's bearing and distance from Iron Duke? Reply: W.S.W. two miles.	0352
3.55 —	Commodore F.	11th Flotilla	Flags	Form single line-ahead. Ships to be in open order.	—
3.58 —	S.O. 4th B.S.	4th Division	Flags	Alter course together one point to starboard	—
3.59 —	S.O. 2nd B.S.	R.A. Invergordon.	W/T	For Moon. Join at 2 p.m. rendezvous	0303
3.59 —	S.O. 2nd C.S.	Hampshire	S.L.	Repeat bearing and distance from Iron Duke. Reply: Active bears from 4th L.C.S. W.S.W. two miles. Active's distance from Iron Duke five miles.	0339
3.59 —	S.O. 2nd B.S.	R.A. Invergordon.		For 0303 Moon. Join me Lat. 57° 45′ N., 4° 15′ E. at 2 p.m. to-day, Wednesday.	—
4.0 —	S.O. 2nd B.S.	General	Sem.	It is known there are several Submarines in the North Sea. Two ships have been attacked during the last 24 hours. An especially vigilant look-out should be kept.	0400
4.0 —	S.O. 3rd B.C.S.	3rd B.C.S.	**Flags**	Alter course together four points to starboard	—
4.0 —	S.O. 2nd B.C.S.	2nd B.C.S.	Flags	Form in single port quarter-line, ships to be six points abaft each others beam.	—
4.0 —	S.O. 2nd B.S.	2nd B.S.	Flags	Alter course together two points to starboard	—
4.0 —	S.O. B.C.F.	General	Flags	Admiral intends to proceed at 19 knots	—
4.0 —	S.O. 4th L.C.S.	4th L.C.S.	Flags	Caroline and Royalist exchange stations in the fleet.	—
4.0 —	C.-in-C.	General	Flags	Alter course together two points to starboard.	—
4.1 —	C.-in-C.	Destroyers	Flags	Form Submarine screen	—
4.2 —	S.O. 4th B.S.	4th Division	Flags	Alter course together two points to starboard	—
4.2 —	S.O. 5th B.S.	5th B.S.	Flags	Alter course together four points to starboard	—
4.3 —	R.A. 1st B.S.	5th Division	Flags	Alter course together three points to starboard.	—
4.3 —	S.O. 1st B.S.	6th Division	Flags	Alter course together three points to starboard.	—
4.4 —	S.O. B.C.F.	General	Flags and S.L.	Alter course together two points to starboard.	—
4.5 —	S.O. 5th B.S.	5th B.S.	Flags	Alter course together two points to starboard	—
4.5 —	S.O. 3rd L.C.S.	L.C.'s and Engadine.	S.L.	Falmouth is in station now	0405
4.5 —	S.O. 4th L.C.S.	Abdiel	S.L.	Take station on port beam of Calliope	—
4.6 —	S.O. 2nd B.C.S.	S.O. B.C.F.	S.L.	What is present course? Was signal Blue 2 zigzagging? Reply: Galatea has just been fired at by Submarine, have turned together to S. 36 E.	0403

Date, Time of Despatch.	From	To	System.	Message.	Time of Origin.
31 MAY *—cont.*					
4.7 a.m.	*S.O.4thL.C.S.*	*4th L.C.S.* -	Flags	*Ships in column to open out to ¾ of a mile*	—
4.8 —	S.O. B.C.F.	S.O. 5th B.S.	S.L.	Port wing Light Cruiser Galatea has just been fired at by Submarine.	0355
4.8 —	**C.-in-C.** -	**S.O. 4th B.S.**	S.L.	**Has 1st B.S. been in sight during night, if so, what time? Reply : One point on starboard bow at 2.10 a.m.**	**0405**
4.10 —	*S.O. 2nd B.S.*	*2nd B.S.* -	Flags	*Alter course together two points to port* -	—
4.10 —	*S.O.3rdB.C.S.*	*3rd B.C.S.* -	Flags	*Alter course together four points to port* -	—
4.10 —	*S.O.4thL.C.S.*	*4th L.C.S.* -	Flags	*Alter course together two points to starboard*	—
4.10 —	S.O. B.C.F.	Light Cruisers	Flags	Alter course together to S. 35° E. - -	—
4.10 —	*Commodore F.*	*Captain D4* -	Flags	*What screen have you ordered? Reply : JG9 adjusted for two columns.*	—
4.10 —	**C.-in-C.** -	**General** -	Flags	**Alter course together two points to port**	—
4.17 —	*S.O.4thL.C.S.*	*4th L.C.S.* -	Flags	*Admiral intends to proceed at 16 knots* -	—
4.20 —	*S.O.3rdB.C.S.*	*3rd B.C.S.* -	Flags	*Alter course together four points to starboard*	—
4.20 —	S.O. B.C.F.	General -	Flags	Alter course together two points to port	—
4.20 —	*S.O. 2nd B.S.*	*2nd B.S.* -	Flags	*Alter course together two points to port* -	—
4.21 —	*R.A. 1st B.S.*	*5th Division* -	Flags	*Alter course together three points to port* -	—
4.22 —	S.O.2ndB.C.S.	Destroyers -	Sem.	Screen in line-ahead - - - -	—
4.22 —	*S.O. 1st B.S.*	*6th Division* -	Flags	*Alter course together three points to port* -	—
4.22 —	S.O. B.C.F.	General -	Flags	Alter course together to S. 81° E. - -	—
4.22 —	*Hampshire* -	*S.O. 2nd C.S.*	S.L.	*Iron Duke bears W. by S. seven miles from Hampshire. This is based on Active's reports that Iron Duke bears W. by S. five miles from Active.*	*0420*
4.25 —	*S.O. 5th B.S.*	*5th B.S.* -	Flags	*Alter course together to S. 81° E.*	—
4.25 —	*Commodore F.*	*General* -	Flags	*Take station for Submarine screen No. 9* -	—
4.26 —	*R.A. 1st B.S.*	*5th Division* -	Flags	*Alter course together four points to port* -	—
4.26 —	*Commodore F.*	*11th Flotilla* -	Flags	*Take up positions B—C—D—T, Castor take position A.*	—
4.26 —	*S.O. Cruisers*	*Cruisers* -	S.L.	*Speed of advance 17 knots* - - -	—
4.28 —	*S.O.4thL.C.S.*	*4th L.C.S.* -	Flags	*Alter course together two points to port* -	—
4.28 —	S.O. B.C.F.	Tiger, Barham.	Sem.	Tiger repeat all signals between Admiral and 5th B.S.	0426
4.30 —	*S.O.3rdB.C.S.*	*3rd B.C.S.* -	Flags	*Alter course together four points to port* -	—
4.30 —	S.O. B.C.F.	General -	Flags	Alter course together four points to starboard.	—
4.30 —	*S.O. 2nd B.S.*	*2nd B.S.* -	Flags	*Alter course together two points to starboard*	—
4.30 —	*S.O.4thL.C.S.*	*4th L.C.S.* -	Flags	*Zigzag one point, first turn to port, conforming with wing ships.*	—

Date, Time of Despatch.	From	To	Sys-tem.	Message.	Time of Origin.
31 MAY	—cont.				
4.30 a.m.	Commodore F.	Captain D4 -	Flags	Take up positions E—F—G—H. Please arrange them.	—
4.32 —	S.O. B.C.F.	Petard,Pelican	Sem.	What is your station? Reply : Petard G, Pelican F.	0430
4.33 —	S.O. 1st B.S.	6th Division -	Flags	Alter course together three points to port -	—
4.35 —	S.O. B.C.F.	S.O.2nd B.C.S.	S.L.	Continue zigzagging - - - -	0430
4.35 —	S.O. B.C.F.	Princess Royal	Sem.	Lion has none of those signals mentioned. Use auxiliary buzzer as requisite.	0432
4.35 —	S.O. 5th B.S.	5th B.S.	Flags	Form single line-ahead - - - -	—
4.37 —	S.O. 2nd B.S.	Kempenfelt -	Sem.	With reference to my 1955 of yesterday. Why has Moon gone to Aberdeen?	0434
				Reply : Moon was sent to Aberdeen in accordance with orders re ZX.	0453
	S.O. 2nd B.S.	Kempenfelt -	Sem.	Your 0453. Why did you send Moon to Aberdeen when my 1955 ordered her to go to Peterhead?	0657
				Reply :—Following signal was made to Moon. Proceed to Peterhead to fuel 2000.	—
				Following reply from Moon. Signal 2000 received. I am proceeding to Aberdeen to fuel 2040.	—
				I did not countermand this order as I did not suppose there was fuel at Peterhead and I knew there was at Aberdeen, observing that Moon has had experience at Peterhead.	0700
4.37 —	C.-in-C. -	Campania -	W/T	Return to base - - - - -	0421
4.39 —	Biarritz -	Princetown	W/T	Operation complete - - - -	0410
4.40 —	R.A. 1st B.S.	5th Division -	Flags	Alter course together four points to star-board.	—
4.40 —	S.O.3rdB.C.S.	3rd B.C.S. -	Flags	Alter course together four points to star-board.	—
4.40 —	S.O. B.C.F.	General -	Flags	Alter course together four points to port	—
4.40 —	S.O. 2nd B.S.	2nd B.S. -	Flags	Alter course together two points to starboard	—
4.42 —	S.O.3rdL.C.S.	Yarmouth -	S.L.	What is bearing and distance of Lion? Reply : S. 84° W., 4½ miles.	0440
4.43 —	S.O. 5th B.S.	5th B.S. -	Flags	Alter course together two points to port -	—
4.44 —	S.O. 1st B.S.	6th Division -	Flags	Alter course together three points to star-board.	—
4.47 —	C.-in-C. -	S.O.3rdB.C.S., S.O. 1st B.S., S.O.4th L.C.S., S.O. 7th C.S., R.A. 1st B.S.	W/T and S.L.	I intend to steer South 50° East at 5 a.m., advancing 16 knots; conform.	0430
4.47 —	C.-in-C. -	General -	Flags	Guides to bear North 40° East from Guide of Fleet.	—
4.48 —	S.O.4thL.C.S.	4th L.C.S. -	Flags	Negative zigzag - - - - -	—
4.50 —	S.O.3rdB.C.S.	3rd B.C.S. -	Flags	Alter course together four points to port -	—
4.50 —	S.O. B.C.F.	General -	Flags	Alter course together four points to star-board.	—

Date, Time of Despatch.	From	To	System.	Message.	Time of Origin.
31 MAY *—cont.*					
4.50 a.m.	Commodore T.	Admiralty	L/T	Urgent. No orders have been received for Harwich force yet. Reply : Orders are to remain at one hour's notice. See my 22.	0450
4.50 —	R.A. 1st B.S.	5th Division	Flags	*Alter course together 12 points to starboard*	—
4.50 —	S.O. 2nd B.S.	2nd B.S.	Flags	*Alter course together two points to port*	—
4.52 —	S.O. 1st B.S.	6th Division	Flags	*Alter course in succession 16 points to starboard.*	—
4.52 —	S.O.4thL.C.S.	4th L.C.S.	Flags	*Alter course together 16 points to starboard*	—
4.59 —	R.A. 1st B.S.	5th Division	Flags	*Alter course together 16 points to starboard*	—
5.0 —	S.O.3rdB.C.S.	3rd B.C.S.	Flags	*Alter course together four points to starboard*	—
5.0 —	S.O. 2nd B.S.	2nd B.S.	Flags	*Alter course together two points to port*	—
5.0 —	**C.-in-C.**	**Marlborough**	S.L.	**Are you in touch with Cruisers? Reply: Yes.**	0455
5.0 —	S.O.3rdL.C.S.	Engadine	S.L.	I am dropping a mile. Do not get outside your distance.	0455
5.0 —	S.O.4thL.C.S.	4th L.C.S.	Flags	*Alter course together one point to starboard*	—
5.0 —	**C.-in-C.**	**General**	Flags	**Alter course leading ships together the rest in succession to South 50° East.**	—
5.0 —	S.O. 5th B.S.	5th B.S.	Flags	*Alter course together four points to starboard*	—
5.3 —	R.A. 1st B.S.	5th Division	Flags	*Alter course in succession to S. 50° E.*	—
5.5 —	S.O 1st B.S.	6th Division	Flags	*Alter course in succession 16 points to starboard.*	—
5.5 —	S.O.3rdL.C.S.	Birkenhead	S.L.	*Pass to Southampton. Galatea was fired at by Submarine 0350.*	*0505*
5.5 —	S.O. B.C.F.	Champion, Fearless.	Sem.	Use every endeavour to economise fuel in Destroyers. Sudden changes in speed are to be avoided.	0500
5.7 —	S.O. 1st B.S.	Calliope	S.L.	Following received : My course at 5 a.m. is S. 50° E., conform.	—
5.7 —	S.O.4thL.C.S.	4th L.C.S.	Flags	*Alter course together 15 points to starboard*	—
5.9 —	S.O.4thL.C.S.	4th L.C.S.	Flags	*Alter course in succession to S. 50° E.*	—
5.10 —	S.O.4thL.C.S.	4th L.C.S.	Flags	*Zigzag one point, first turn to port. Conform with wing ships.*	—
5.10 —	S.O. B.C.F.	General	Flags	Alter course together four points to port	—
5.10 —	S.O.3rdB.C.S.	3rd B.C.S.	Flags	*Alter course together four points to port*	—
5.10 —	S.O. 2nd B.S.	2nd B.S.	Flags	*Alter course together two points to starboard*	—
5.10 —	S.O. B.C.F.	Princess Royal	Sem.	Are any messages intercepted, addressed S.O. B.C.F.? Reply : No.	0506
5.11 —	S.O. 5th B.S.	5th B.S.	Flags	*Alter course together four points to port*	—
5.15 —	S.O. Cruisers	Cruisers	S.L.	*My course S. 50 E. Speed of advance 16 knots.*	—
5.15 —	S.O.3rdB.C.S.	3rd B.C.S.	Flags	*Form astern and follow in the wake of your divisional Guides.*	—
5.15 —	S.O.3rdB.C.S.	3rd B.C.S., Chester and Canterbury.	Flags	*Alter course in succession to S. 50° E.*	—

Date, Time of Despatch.	From	To	System.	Message.	Time of Origin.
31 MAY *—cont.*					
5.15 a.m.	S.O.4thL.C.S.	4th L.C.S.	Flags	*Form single line-abreast to starboard on Comus in sequence of Calliope, Constance, Comus, Royalist and Caroline. Ships to be five cables apart.*	—
5.16 —	S.O. 1st B.S.	6th Division	Flags	*Alter course in succession to S. 50° E. Admiral intends to proceed at 16 knots.*	—
5.19 —	S.O.3rdB.C.S.	3rd B.C.S., Chester and Canterbury.	Flags	*Admiral intends to proceed at 17½ knots*	—
5.20 —	S.O. B.C.F.	General	Flags	Alter course together four points to starboard.	—
5.20 —	S.O.3rdB.C.S.	3rd B.C.S.	Flags	*Alter course together two points to starboard*	—
5.20 —	S.O. 2nd B.S.	2nd B.S.	Flags	*Alter course together two points to starboard*	—
5.20 —	S.O. 1st B.S.	Bellona	S.L.	*Take up cruising disposition No. 1, 10 miles from centre of Battlefleet.*	—
5.20 —	Campania	Cyclops	W/T	Preparatory signal for entering Scapa via Hoxa Sound. One ship wishes to enter, expecting to arrive Nevi Skerry Gate 8.45 a.m.	0502
5.20 —	S.O.4thL.C.S.	4th L.C.S.	Flags	*Speed of advance 16 knots*	—
5.21 —	S.O. Cruisers	Cruisers	S.L.	*Alter course together 16 points to starboard*	—
5.22 —	S.O. 5th B.S.	5th B.S.	Flags	*Alter course together four points to starboard*	—
5.26 —	S.O. Cruisers	Active	S.L.	What is course of fleet? Reply : S. 50° E.	0525
5.30 —	S.O. B.C.F.	General	Flags	Alter course together four points to port	—
5.30 —	S.O. 2nd B.S.	2nd B.S.	Flags	*Alter course together two points to port*	—
5.31 —	S.O. 5th B.S.	5th B.S.	Flags	*Alter course together four points to port*	—
5.32 —	S.O.3rdB.C.S.	3rd B.C.S.	Flags	*Form astern and follow in the wake of your divisional Guides.*	—
5.32 —	Hampshire	S.O. Cruisers	S.L.	*Active appears to be steering S. 50° E.*	—
5.34 —	S.O.3rdB.C.S.	3rd B.C.S., Chester and Canterbury.	Flags	*Alter course in succession to S. 38° E.*	—
5.35 —	S.O. Cruisers	Cruisers	S.L.	*Alter course together 16 points to starboard*	—
5.35 —	S.O.4thL.C.S.	4th L.C.S.	Flags	*Admiral intends to proceed at 15½ knots*	—
5.36 —	S.O. Cruisers	Cruisers	S.L.	*Speed of advance 17 knots*	—
5.37 —	S.O.3rdL.C.S.	Inconstant	S.L.	Can you see Engadine? Reply : Yes, bearing E.S.E.	0536
5.40 —	S.O.3rdB.C.S.	3rd B.C.S.	Flags	*Alter course together two points to starboard*	—
5.40 —	S.O. B.C.F.	General	Flags	Alter course together four points to starboard.	—
5.40 —	S.O. 2nd B.S.	2nd B.S.	Flags	*Alter course together two points to port*	—
5.40 —	S.O. Cruisers	Cruisers	S.L.	*Speed of advance 16 knots*	—
5.41 —	S.O. 5th B.S.	5th B.S.	Flags	*Alter course together four points to starboard.*	—
5.43 —	S.O.3rdB.C.S.	3rd B.C.S.	Flags	*Form astern and follow in the wake of your divisional Guides.*	—

Date, Time of Despatch.	From	To	System.	Message.	Time of Origin.
31 MAY *—cont.*					
5.44 a.m.	*S.O. 2nd C.S.*	*Hampshire* -	S.L.	*What is Hampshire's bearing and distance from Iron Duke? Reply : N.E. by E. 7¼ miles.*	*0542*
5.45 —	Hampshire -	Active - -	S.L.	What is Active's bearing and distance from Iron Duke? Reply : S. 60° E. five miles.	0545
5.45 —	*S.O. 3rd B.C.S.*	*3rd B.C.S., Chester and Canterbury.*	Flags	*Alter course in succession to S. 50° E.* -	—
5.45 —	**C.-in-C.** -	**General** -	Flags	**Admiral intends to proceed at 17 knots**	—
5.50 —	*S.O. 3rd B.C.S.*	*3rd B.C.S.* -	Flags	*Alter course together two points to port* -	—
5.50 —	S.O. B.C.F.	General -	Flags	Alter course together four points to port	—
5.50 —	*S.O. 2nd B.S.*	*2nd B.S.* -	Flags	*Alter course together two points to starboard*	—
5.52 —	*S.O. 3rd L.C.S.*	*Engadine* -	S.L.	Keep within easy signalling distance -	0550
5.52 —	*S.O. 5th B.S.*	*5th B.S.* -	Flags	*Alter course together four points to port* -	—
5.55 —	*S.O. 3rd B.C.S.*	*Chester* -	S.L.	At 6.30 a.m. report what Cruisers are in sight and their bearing. Reply : Minotaur and two T.B.Ds. W.N.W., Shannon N.W.	0530 / 0640
5.58 —	*S.O. 4th L.C.S.*	*4th L.C.S.* -	Flags	*Admiral intends to proceed at 16 knots* -	—
6.0 —	S.O. B.C.F.	General -	Flags	Alter course together four points to starboard.	—
6.0 —	*S.O. 3rd B.C.S.*	*3rd B.C.S.* -	Flags	*Alter course together four points to starboard*	—
6.0 —	*S.O. 2nd B.S.*	*2nd B.S.* -	Flags	*Alter course together two points to starboard*	—
6.0 —	*S.O. Cruisers*	*Cruisers* -	S.L.	*Speed of advance 17 knots* - - -	—
6.0 —	**C.-in-C.** -	**General** -	Flags	**Alter course together two points to port**	—
6.1 —	*S.O. 5th B.S.*	*5th B.S.* -	Flags	*Alter course together two points to starboard*	—
6.3 —	**R.A. Scapa** -	**R.A. Invergordon.**	W/T	**From Admiralty. For C.-in-C. Swedish steamer Boren sailed from Philadelphia on the 16th May for Stockholm with petroleum. Should be brought in if met.**	0306
6.5 —	**C.-in-C.** -	**S.O. 2nd C.S.**	S.L.	**Are Cruisers in touch with 3rd B.C.S.? Reply : Not since 5.15 a.m. Canterbury and Chester were in touch till then.**	0602 / 0622
6.10 —	*S.O. 3rd B.C.S.*	*3rd B.C.S.* -	Flags	*Alter course together four points to port* -	—
6.10 —	S.O. B.C.F.	General -	Flags	Alter course together four points to port	—
6.10 —	*S.O. 2nd B.S.*	*2nd B.S.* -	Flags	*Alter course together two points to port* -	—
6.11 —	*S.O. 5th B.S.*	*5th B.S.* -	Flags	*Alter course together four points to port* -	—
6.12 —	Moon - -	R.A. Invergordon.	W/T	Moon proceeding to rendezvous 57° 45′ N., 4° 15′ E., 2 p.m.	0615
6.14 —	Felixstowe -	Admiralty -	L/T	4.40 a.m. intercepted Maidstone from Submarine E. 37. Arrive Cork L.V. about 9 a.m. Have nothing to communicate. (*Group corrupt.*)	—
6.20 —	*S.O. 3rd B.C.S.*	*3rd B.C.S.* -	Flags	*Alter course together four points to starboard.*	—

Date, Time of Despatch.	From	To	System.	Message.	Time of Origin.
31 MAY —*cont.*					
6.20 a.m.	*S.O. 2nd B.S.*	*2nd B.S.* -	Flags	*Alter course together two points to port* -	—
6.20 —	S.O. B.C.F.	General -	Flags	Alter course together four points to starboard.	—
6.20 —	*S.O.2ndB.C.S.*	*2nd B.C.S.* -	Flags	*Admiral intends to proceed at 19¼ knots* -	—
6.20 —	**C.-in-C.** -	**General** -	Flags	**Alter course together two points to starboard.**	—
6.20 —	*S.O.4thL.C.S.*	*4th L.C.S.* -	Flags	*Admiral intends to proceed at 15½ knots* -	—
6.21 —	*S.O. 5th B.S.*	*5th B.S.* -	Flags	*Alter course together four points to starboard.*	—
6.21 —	Trident -	Longhope -	W/T	Arriving Hoxa Sound 6.45 a.m. - -	0610
6.22 —	*S.O. Cruisers*	*Cruisers* -	S.L.	Report Yes or No whether you can see *Battle Cruisers?* Replies : *Shannon—No.* *Cochrane—No.*	0620 0628 0630
6.25 —	*S.O.4thL.C.S.*	*4th L.C.S.* -	Flags	*Admiral intends to proceed at 16 knots* -	—
6.30 —	*S.O.3rdB.C.S.*	*3rd B.C.S.* -	Flags	*Alter course together four points to port* -	—
6.30 —	S.O. B.C.F.	General -	Flags	Alter course together four points to port	—
6.30 —	*S.O.2nd B.S.*	*2nd B.S.* -	Flags	*Alter course together two points to starboard*	—
6.30 —	**C.-in-C.** -	**General** -	Flags	**Alter course together two points to starboard.**	—
6.30 —	*S.O. Cruisers*	*Cruisers* -	S.L.	*Speed of advance 16 knots* - - -	—
6.30 —	S.O. 5th B.S.	5th B.S. -	Flags	*Alter course together four points to port* -	—
6.40 —	*S.O.3rdB.C.S.*	*3rd B.C.S.* -	Flags	*Alter course together four points to starboard*	—
6.40 —	S.O. B.C.F.	General -	Flags	Alter course together four points to starboard.	—
6.40 —	*S.O.2nd B.S.*	*2nd B.S.* -	Flags	*Alter course together two points to starboard*	—
6.40 —	*S.O. 5th B.S.*	*5th B.S.* -	Flags	*Admiral intends to proceed at 20 knots* -	—
6.42 —	*S.O. 5th B.S.*	*5th B.S.* -	Flags	*Alter course together four points to starboard*	—
6.42 —	Defence -	S.O. 2nd B.S.	W/T	Dutch steamer in path of Fleet, Lat. 58° 8′ N., Long. 1° 44′ E.	0624
6.45 —	B.C.F. -	S.O. B.C.F. -	—	Coal remaining— Oil remaining— Lion 3115 Tons 605 Tons Princess Royal 3071 ,, 597 ,, Queen Mary 3148 ,, 634 ,, Tiger 3010 ,, 793 ,, New Zealand 2685 ,, 462 ,, Indefatigable 2745 ,, 464 ,, Falmouth 1150 ,, 235 ,, Birkenhead 1016 ,, 323 ,, Gloucester 1213 ,, 235 ,,	—
6.45 —	**C.-in-C.** -	**General** -	Flags	**Alter course together two points to port**	—
6.48 —	S.O. 1st C.S.	S.O. 2nd B.S.	W/T	1st C.S. from left to right: Warrior, Defence, Duke of Edinburgh, Black Prince.	0635
6.50 —	*S.O.3rdB.C.S.*	*3rd B.C.S.* -	Flags	*Alter course together four points to port* -	—
6.50 —	S.O. B.C.F.	General -	Flags	Alter course together four points to port	—

Date, Time of Despatch.	From	To	System.	Message.	Time of Origin.
31 MAY —*cont.*					
6.50 a.m.	S.O. 2nd B.S.	2nd B.S. -	Flags	*Alter course together two points to port* -	—
6.51 —	S.O. 5th B.S.	5th B.S. -	Flags	*Alter course together four points to port* -	—
6.54 —	Shannon -	S.O. 2nd C.S.	S.L.	*Chester bearing S.E.* - - - -	0650
6.54 —	S.O.4thL.C.S.	4th L.C.S. -	Flags	*Admiral intends to proceed at 15½ knots* -	—
6.56 —	S.O. 2nd C.S.	Chester -	S.L.	Are you in touch with B.C.S.? Reply : Yes.	0655
7.0 —	S.O.3rdB.C.S.	3rd B.C.S. -	Flags	*Alter course together four points to starboard*	—
7.0 —	S.O. B.C.F.	General -	Flags	Alter course together four points to starboard.	—
7.0 —	S.O. 2nd B.S.	2nd B.S. -	Flags	*Alter course together two points to port* -	—
7.0 —	S.O.4thL.C.S.	4th L.C.S. -	Flags	*Admiral intends to proceed at 16 knots* -	—
7.0 —	S.O. 5th B.S.	5th B.S. -	Flags	*Alter course together four points to starboard*	—
7.2 —	**S.O. 2nd C.S.**	**C.-in-C.** -	S.L.	**Your 0602. Minotaur now in touch through Chester.**	0700
7.5 —	**C.-in-C.** -	**General** -	Flags	**Alter course together two points to port**	—
7.9 —	**C.-in-C.** -	**All Cruisers** -	S.L. and Flags	**My course is S. 50 E. Take up cruising disposition No. 1, centre of screen, 12 miles from Battlefleet.**	0700
7.10 —	S.O.3rdB.C.S.	3rd B.C.S. -	Flags	*Alter course together four points to port* -	—
7.10 —	S.O. B.C.F.	General -	Flags	Alter course together four points to port	—
7.10 —	S.O. 2nd B.S.	2nd B.S. -	Flags	*Alter course together two points to starboard*	—
7.10 —	S.O. 5th B.S.	5th B.S. -	Flags	*Alter course together four points to port* -	—
7.15 —	Yarmouth -	S.O. B.C.F. -	S.L.	Trawler flying British colours, standing W.S.W. Brisbane H 252.	0705
7.16 —	R.A. Invergordon.	S.O. 2nd B.S.	W/T	Moon has sailed from Aberdeen 5.25 a.m. to-day, Wednesday.	0545
7.20 —	S.O.3rdB.C.S.	3rd B.C.S. -	Flags	*Alter course together four points to starbaord*	—
7.20 —	S.O. 2nd B.S.	2nd B.S.	Flags	*Alter course together two points to starboard*	—
7.20 —	S.O. B.C.F.	General -	Flags	Alter course together four points to starboard.	—
7.20 —	S.O. Cruisers	Cruisers -	S.L.	*My course is S.E. Speed of advance 18 knots*	—
7.20 —	S.O. 5th B.S.	5th B.S. -	Flags	*Alter course together four points to starboard.*	—
7.20 —	**C.-in-C.** -	**General** -	Flags	**Alter course together two points to starboard.**	—
7.30 —	S.O.3rdB.C.S.	3rd B.C.S. -	Flags	*Alter course together four points to port* -	—
7.30 —	S.O. B.C.F.	General -	Flags	Alter course together four points to port	—
7.30 —	S.O. 2nd B.S.	2nd B.S. -	Flags	*Alter course together two points to port* -	—
7.30 —	**C.-in-C.** -	**General** -	Flags	**Alter course together two points to starboard.**	—
7.30 —	S.O. 5th B.S.	5th B.S. -	Flags	*Alter course together four points to port* -	—

Date, Time of Despatch.	From	To	System.	Message.	Time of Origin.
31 MAY —*cont.*					
7.40 a.m.	*S.O.3rdB.C.S.*	*3rd B.C.S.* -	Flags	*Alter course together four points to starboard.*	—
7.40 —	S.O. B.C.F.	General -	Flags	*Alter course together four points to starboard.*	—
7.40 —	*S.O. 2nd B.S.*	*2nd B.S.* -	Flags	*Alter course together two points to port* .	—
7.40 —	*S.O. B.C.F.*	*Princess Royal*	Sem.	*Am trying to get you on auxiliary reduced power.*	*0730*
7.40 —	*S.O. 5th B.S.*	*5th B.S.* -	Flags	*Alter course together four points to starboard.*	—
7.45 —	*S.O. 1st C.S.*	*1st C.S.* -	S.L.	*Alter course in succession to East* - -	—
7.45 —	S.O. B.C.F.	Ships in company.	Sem. and S.L.	Should fog come down or visibility be less than two miles, L.Cs. are to turn to course of advance and to reduce to speed of advance. B.C. Squadrons and 5th B.S. will form astern of their Guides, turn to course of advance and reduce to speed of advance by signal. A general signal as to course and speed will be made by buzzer as soon as possible. Destroyers to take station as laid down in G.F.B.O. Art. IIc, para. 9.	0725
7.47 —	Warrior -	—	—	Remarks : Sighted Battlefleet - -	—
7.50 —	*S.O.3rdB.C.S.*	*3rd B.C.S.* -	Flags	*Alter course together four points to port* -	—
7.50 —	S.O. B.C.F.	General -	Flags	Alter course together four points to port	—
7.50 —	*S.O. 2nd B.S.*	*2nd B.S.* -	Flags	*Alter course together two points to starboard.*	—
7.50 —	*S.O. 5th B.S.*	*5th B.S.* -	Flags	*Alter course together four points to port* .	—
7.50 —	**C.-in-C.** -	**General** -	Flags	**Alter course together two points to port**	--
7.52 —	*S.O. 1st C.S.*	*1st C.S.* -	Flags	*Alter course in succession to S. 87 E.* -	—
7.55 —	Chester -	S.O.3rdB.C.S.	S.L.	Invincible is about 18 miles distant from Minotaur.	0750
8.0 —	*S.O.3rdB.C.S.*	*3rd B.C.S.* -	Flags	*Alter course together four points to starboard.*	--
8.0 —	S.O. 2nd B.S.	Kempenfelt -	Sem.	Moon sailed from Aberdeen 6.30 a.m. to-day.	0750
8.0 —	*S.O. B.C.F.*	General -	Flags	Alter course together four points to starboard.	--
8.0 —	*S.O. 2nd B.S.*	*2nd B.S.* -	Flags	*Alter course together two points to starboard*	---
8.0 —	**C.-in-C.** -	**General** -	Flags	**Alter course together two points to port**	--
8.0 —	**C.-in-C.** -	**General** -	Flags	**Reference position at 8 a.m., 58 28' N., 1 17' E.**	--
8.0 —	*S.O. 5th B.S.*	*5th B.S.* -	Flags	*Alter course together four points to starboard*	---
8.0 —	*S.O. 5th B.S.*	*5th B.S.* -	Sem.	*Attention is called to B.C. Orders No. 11, readiness for fighting, which are to be complied with.*	0755
8.2 —	S.O.3rdL.C.S.	Inconstant -	S.L.	Use Cordelia to divide the distance if necessary.	0800
8.5 —	Admiralty -	R.A.,EastCoast and Naval Base, Lowestoft.	L/T	Auxiliary patrols may proceed out, keeping within 30 miles of coast.	0805

Date, Time of Despatch.	From	To	System.	Message.	Time of Origin.
31 MAY 8.6 a.m	—*cont.* Falmouth -	Engadine -	S.L.	Should visibility become less than two miles, Light Cruisers will turn to course of advance and reduce to speed of advance.	0800
8.10 —	*S.O. 3rd B.C.S.*	3rd B.C.S. -	Flags	*Alter course together four points to port* -	—
8.10 —	*S.O. 2nd B.S.*	2nd B.S. -	Flags	*Alter course together two points to port* -	—
8.10 —	S.O. B.C.F.	General -	Flags	Alter course together four points to port	—
8.10 —	S.O. 5th B.S.	5th B.S. -	Flags	*Alter course together four points to port* -	—
8.13 —	*Benbow, Captain.*	*Bellerophon* -	Sem.	*Our Gyro Compass has gone wrong, our steering, I am afraid, is erratic.*	*0805*
8.15 —	*S.O. 3rd B.C.S.*	3rd B.C.S. -	Flags	*Resume the original course together* - -	—
8.15 —	S.O. B.C.F.	General -	Flags	Resume the original course together -	—
8.15 —	**S.O. 2nd C.S.**	**C.-in-C.** -	**S.L.**	**2nd C.S. in assigned position** - - -	—
8.17 —	Champion -	S.O. B.C.F. -	Flags	Yarmouth sighted Submarine on starboard side.	—
8.19 —	Yarmouth -	S.O. B.C.F. -	S.L.	Passed Submarine bearing N.E., course unknown, steering N. *(Passed to S.O. 3rd L.C.S., 8.26 a.m.)*	0810
8.20 —	S.O. 1st C.S.	S.O. 2nd B.S.	S.L.	Sailing vessels in sight, S.E. by E. and E. by N.	0802
8.20 —	*Warrior* -	*S.O. 1st C.S.* -	S.L.	*Cruiser bearing N. 28° E. Light Cruiser and Battlefleet bearing N. 10° W.*	—
8.20 —	*S.O. 3rd B.C.S.*	3rd B.C.S. -	Flags	*Alter course together 16 points to starboard*	—
8.20 —	*S.O. 2nd B.S.*	2nd B.S. -	Flags	*Alter course together two points to port* -	—
8.20 —	**C.-in-C.** -	**General** -	Flags	**Alter course together two points to starboard.**	—
8.20 —	*S.O. Cruisers*	*Cruisers* -	S.L.	*My course S. 50° E. Speed of advance 16 knots.*	—
8.20 —	*S.O. 5th B.S.*	5th B.S. -	Flags	*Alter course together four points to starboard*	—
8.22 —	S.O. B.C.F.	General -	Flags	Alter course in succession eight points to port.	—
8.22 —	*S.O. 3rd B.C.S.*	Chester, Canterbury, and Screen.	Flags	Preserve compass bearings and distances	—
8.25 —	**Commodore F.**	**C.-in-C.** -	**S.L.**	**Percentage of fuel in T.B.Ds. :—** **11th Flotilla 89, least 87 per cent.** **12th „ 89, „ 88 „** **4th „ 88, „ 85 „**	**0820**
8.25 —	*S.O. 2nd B.S.*	2nd B.S. -	Flags	*Indicate percentage of principal fuel remaining aboard at 8 a.m. Replies :—* *King George V. 81 per cent.* *Ajax 82 „* *Erin 89 „* *Orion 77 „* *Centurion 77 „* *Monarch 75 „* *Conqueror 79 „* *Thunderer 75 „* *Boadicea 90 „* *Kempenfelt 99 „*	—
8.25 —	*S.O. 5th B.S.*	5th B.S. -	Flags	*Alter course together eight points to port* -	—

Date, Time of Despatch.	From	To	System.	Message.	Time of Origin.
31 MAY —*cont.* 8.26 a.m.	S.O. 2nd B.S.	Kempenfelt -	Sem.	Would 20 knots be an economical speed for Moon to proceed at, and would going two or three knots faster greatly increase her expenditure? Reply :	0825
				Twenty knots is economical but an increase over that is not. Over 22 knots, expenditure begins to go up very quickly.	0830
8 26 —	S.O. B.C.F.	S.O. 5th B.S.	S.L.	Yarmouth ahead of Lion reported Submarine.	0825
8.30 —	*S.O. 2nd B.S.*	*2nd B.S.* -	Flags	*Alter course together two points to starboard*	—
8.30 —	*S.O.3rdB.C.S.*	*3rd B.C.S.* -	Flags	*Alter course together 16 points to starboard*	—
8.30 —	**C.-in-C.** -	**General** -	Flags	**Alter course together two points to starboard.**	—
8.30 —	*S.O. Cruisers*	*Cruisers and Destroyers.*	S.L. and Flags.	*Indicate percentage of principal fuel remaining on board :—* *Minotaur* *74 per cent.* *Hampshire* 90 ,, *Shannon* 92 ,, *Cochrane* 91 ,, *Mischief* 90 ,, *Owl* 84 ,, *Hardy* 80 ,, *Midge* 86 ,, *(Passed to C.-in-C. via Hampshire 9.35 a.m.)*	—
8.30 —	Minotaur -	—	—	Remarks : Cruisers on starboard beam -	—
8.30 —	*S.O. 5th B.S.*	*5th B.S.* -	Flags	*Alter course together two points to port* -	—
8.35 —	*S.O.3rdB.C.S.*	*3rd B.C.S.* -	Flags	*Alter course together two points to port* -	—
8.35 —	S.O. 2nd B.S.	S.O. 1st C.S.	S.L.	I intend to steer S. 54° E. at 9.20 a.m. -	—
8.35 —	Minotaur -	—	—	Remarks : 3rd B.C.S. on port bow - -	—
8.35 —	S.O. B.C.F.	Yarmouth -	S.L.	Where is Submarine now? - - -	0830
			S.L.	Reply : Lost sight of periscope almost at once.	0835
	S.O. B.C.F.	Yarmouth -	S.L.	You hoisted green flag and then reported Submarine on a bearing which made to port of you, which was correct?	0840
			S.L.	Reply : Bearing was correct, ship had port helm on, periscope last seen astern when flag was hoisted. Green flag was supposed position of Submarine then a little on starboard side.	—
8.36 —	S.O. 1st C.S.	S.O. 2nd B.S.	S.L.	Battlefleet bearing N. 10° W., Cruiser bearing N. 28° E., Light Cruiser bearing N. 10° W.	0810
8.36 —	S.O. B.C.F.	Champion -	S.L.	When you hoisted green flag what did you see?	0832
				Reply : We were repeating Yarmouth's signal and showed her pendants at the dip. Champion saw nothing.	0839
	S.O. B.C.F.	Champion -	S.L.	Reply : Pendants were hoisted in a position in which they could not be seen.	0850
8.37 —	*Shannon* -	*S.O. Cruisers*	S.L.	*Three Battle Cruisers S. 60° E.* - -	*0830*
8.38 —	*S.O. 1st C.S.*	*1st C.S.* -	S.L.	*My course S. 53° E. at 8.50 a.m. Preserve relative bearings and distances.*	—

Date, Time of Despatch.	From	To	System.	Message.	Time of Origin.
31 MAY	—*cont.*				
8.40 a.m.	*S.O.3rdB.C.S.*	*3rd B.C.S.*	- Flags	*Alter course together four points to starboard*	—
8.40 —	S.O. B.C.F.	General	- Flags	Alter course in succession eight points to starboard	—
8.40 —	*S.O. 2nd B.S.*	*2nd B.S.*	- Flags	*Alter course together two points to starboard*	—
8.45 —	C.-in-C. Nore	Admiralty	- L/T	Immediate. Your 130, 30th May. Aircraft from Felixstowe, Isle of Grain and Westgate have returned from scouting. Nothing to report.	0731
8.45 —	**R.A. Scapa** -	**Aberdeen**	- W/T	**For C.-in-C.** Trident arrived and proceeded	**0830**
8.45 —	Indomitable	—	—	Remarks : Sighted 2nd and 7th C.S. on starboard quarter.	—
8.47 —	*S.O. 5th B.S.*	*5th B.S.*	- Flags	*Alter course together eight points to starboard.*	—
8.48 —	**C.-in-C.** -	**Cruisers**	- S.L.	**My speed of advance will be 15 knots at 9 a.m.**	—
8.50 —	*S.O.3rdB.C.S.*	*3rd B.C.S.*	- Flags	*Alter course together four points to port*	-
8.50 —	S.O. B.C.F.	General	- Flags	Alter course together two points to port	—
8.50 —	*S.O. 2nd B.S.*	*2nd B.S.*	- Flags	*Alter course together two points to port*	-
8.50 —	**C.-in-C.** -	**General**	- Flags	**Alter course together two points to port**	—
8.50 —	Minotaur -	—	—	Remarks : Sighted one Cruiser and one Destroyer starboard bow.	—
8.50 —	*S.O. Cruisers*	*Cruisers*	- S.L.	*Take up cruising disposition No. 1, distance between X and Y 12 miles. My course S. 50° E. Speed of advance 16 knots*	—
8.51 —	S.O.3rdL.C.S.	Engadine	- S.L.	Am dropping a mile to keep touch - -	0850
8.55 —	**C.-in-C.** -	**General**	- Sem. and S.L.	**Unit 42 of Peterhead patrol engaged and sank, 27th inst., large Enemy Submarine carrying two guns. No casualties amongst our vessels.**	—
8.55 —	S.O. B.C.F.	Yarmouth	- S.L.	Correct the station of Cruiser line - -	0850
8.55 —	*S.O. 5th B.S.*	*5th B.S.*	- Flags	*Alter course together two points to port*	-
8.57 —	*S.O. 5th B.S.*	*5th B.S.*	- Flags	*Attention is called to amount of smoke issuing from your funnels.*	—
8.57 —	S.O. B.C.F.	General	- S.L.	Have steam for full speed at half an hour's notice by noon.	—
8.57 —	*Malaya* -	*Warspite*	- Sem.	*If convenient will you please exercise intercommunication between control positions.*	*0850*
9.0 —	*S.O.3rdB.C.S.*	*3rd B.C.S.*	- Flags	*Alter course together four points to starboard.*	—
9.0 —	S.O. B.C.F.	General	- Flags	Alter course together four points to starboard.	—
9.0 —	*S.O. 2nd B.S.*	*2nd B.S.*	- Flags	*Alter course together two points to starboard*	—
9.0 —	*S.O. 5th B.S.*	*5th B.S.*	- Flags	*Alter course together four points to starboard.*	—
9.0 —	**C.-in-C.** -	**General**	- Flags	**Alter course together two points to port**	—
9.2 —	*Commodore F.*	*11th Flotilla* -	Flags	*Take up appointed station* - - -	—
9.2 —	*Kempenfelt* -	*Moon* -	- W/T	*Economise fuel and do not exceed 20 knots*	*0845*

Date, Time of Despatch.	From	To	System.	Message.	Time of Origin.
31 MAY *—cont.* 9.5 a.m.	**C.-in-C.** -	**General** -	Flags	**Admiral intends to proceed at 16 knots** -	—
9.5 —	*S.O. 5th B.S.*	*5th B.S.* -	Flags	*Have steam for full speed at half hour's notice by 12 noon.*	—
9.6 —	*Shannon* -	*S.O. Cruisers*	S.L.	*Sailing ship S.E. from Chester* - -	*0803*
9.6 —	*Commodore F.*	*Marne* - -	S.L.	*Too far ahead. Check your position with Castor.*	—
9.8 —	*Turbulent* -	*S.O. B.C.F.* -	Flags	Turbulent sighted Submarine 14 points from right ahead on starboard side.	—
9.8 —	*Commodore F.*	*Mons* - -	S.L.	*Too far out* - - - - - -	—
9.9 —	*S.O. B.C.F.*	*Tiger* - -	Sem.	*Did you pass Submarine report to Barham? Reply : Yes.*	*0908*
9.10 —	*S.O 3rd B.C.S.*	*3rd B.C.S.* -	Flags	*Alter course together four points to port* -	
9.10 —	S.O. B.C.F.	General -	Flags	Alter course together four points to port	—
9.10 —	*S.O. 2nd B.S.*	*2nd B.S.* -	Flags	*Alter course together two points to port* -	—
9.10 —	*S.O. 5th B.S.*	*5th B.S.* -	Flags	*Alter course together four points to port* -	—
9.12 —	**C.-in-C.** -	**St. Vincent** -	S.L.	**Did you hear any Telefunken between 6 and 8 a.m.? Reply : No.**	0918
9.13 —	*Centurion* -	*S.O. 2nd B.S.*	Flags	*Light Cruisers N. by E., Destroyers N. by W.*	—
9.13 —	S.O. 2nd B.S.	General -	Flags	Guides to bear S. 36° W. from Guide of fleet.	—
9.15 —	**Marlborough**	**C.-in-C.** -	S.L.	**From Bellona. 2nd B.S. bearing south** -	C910
9.16 —	S.O. B.C.F. -	Turbulent -	Sem.	What did you see when you reported Submarine ? Reply : Very distinct periscope steering south on port quarter.	0915 0920
9.16 —	**R.A. Scapa** -	**R.A. Inver-Gordon.**	W/T	**For C.-in-C. 828. Weather reports at 6 a.m. Ramsgate, wind W. 1.5, Bar. 30.17. Rosyth, wind W., light, fine, misty, sea smooth. Shotley, 7 a.m., Bar. 30.20, temperature 59, wind and sea moderate.**	0900
9.17 —	**S.O. Cruisers**	**C.-in-C.** -	S.L.	**1st C.S. now joining Cruiser line** -	0900
9.20 —	S.O. 2nd B.S.	General -	Flags	Alter course leading ships together, rest in succession to S. 54° E.	—
9.20 —	S.O. B.C.F.	General -	Flags	Alter course together four points to starboard.	—
9.20 —	*S.O.3rd B.C.S.*	*3rd B.C.S.* -	Flags	*Alter course together four points to starboard.*	—
9.20 —	**C.-in-C.** -	**General** -	Flags	**Alter course together two points to starboard.**	—
9.20 —	*Commodore F.*	*Manners* -	Flags	*Take up appointed station* -	—
9.21 —	*Commodore F.*	*Manners* -	Sem.	*You are ahead of station* -	—
9.22 —	*S.O.3rd B.C.S.*	*3rd B.C.S., Chester and Canterbury.*	Flags	*Admiral intends to proceed at 16½ knots* -	—
9.25 —	*Bellona* -	*S.O. 1st B.S.* -	S.L.	*I have had to stop my port engine. Expect to be about an hour with starboard engine only.*	*0915*
9.25 —	S.O. 2nd B.S.	General -	Flags	Admiral intends to proceed at 18 knots -	—

Date, Time of Despatch.	From	To	System.	Message.	Time of Origin.
31 MAY *—cont.*					
9.25 a.m.	*S.O. 5th B.S.*	*5th B.S.* -	Flags	*Alter course together four points to starboard.*	—
9.27 —	S.O. B.C.F.	Turbulent -	Sem.	Why did you hoist green flag if sighted on port hand? Reply : It had passed to starboard by the time signal was made.	0925
9.28 —	*Commodore F.*	*Michael* -	Flags	*Take up appointed station* - - -	—
9.30 —	*S.O.3rd B.C.S.*	*3rd B.C.S.* -	Flags	*Alter course together four points to port* -	—
9.30 —	S.O. B.C.F.	General -	Flags	Alter course together four points to port	—
9.30 —	**R.A. Scapa** -	**Aberdeen** -	W/T	**For C.-in-C. Campania arrived** - -	0915
9.30 —	S.O. Cruisers	Owl -	S.L.	Examine sailing vessel S. by E. - -	—
9.30 —	*Commodore F.*	*Manners* -	Sem.	*When on normal course you should be about 1,200 yards 7½ points abaft my port beam.*	—
9.30 —	*S.O. 5th B.S.*	*5th B.S.* -	Flags	*Alter course together four points to port* -	—
9.30 —	**C.-in-C.** -	**General** -	Flags	**Alter course together two points to starboard.**	—
9.32 —	*Thunderer* -	*S.O. 2nd B.S.*	Sem.	*Battlefleet bearing North by West* - -	—
9.35 —	*S.O. 5th B.S.*	*Valiant* -	Flags	*Attention is called to the smoke issuing from your funnels.*	—
9.36 —	*Commodore F.*	*Michael* -	Sem.	*What is your lettered position on diagram? Reply : Position D.*	—
9.36 —	*Shannon* -	*S.O. 2nd C.S.*	S.L.	*Two sailing ships S.S.E. (From Chester)* -	0929
9.37 —	S.O. 2nd B.S.	S.O. 1st C.S.	S.L.	My speed of advance 17 knots - -	0925
9.40 —	*S.O.3rd B.C.S.*	*3rd B.C.S.* -	Flags	*Alter course together four points to starboard.*	—
9.40 —	S.O. B.C.F.	Yarmouth -	S.L.	Is Light Cruiser line in correct station? Reply : Falmouth bears N.E. four miles.	0940
9.40 —	S.O. B.C.F.	General -	Flags	Alter course together four points to starboard.	—
9.40 —	*S.O. 2nd B.S.*	*2nd B.S.* -	Flags	*Alter course together two points to port* -	—
9.40 —	*Yarmouth* -	*S.O.3rd L.C.S.*	S.L.	*Lion bears W. by N. four miles* - -	—
9.40 —	*S.O. 5th B.S.*	*5th B.S.* -	Flags	*Alter course together four points to starboard.*	—
9.43 —	Captain (S.), Maidstone.	Admiralty -	L/T	Four Submarines returning from Terschelling have reported by W/T.	—
9.45 —	*Commodore F.*	*Manners* -	Flags	*Distance should be about 1,500 yards, not 1,200.*	—
9.45 —	S.O. 5th B.S.	Fearless -	S.L.	Try and keep down smoke as much as possible.	0935
9.45 —	*S.O. 1st C.S.*	*1st C.S.* -	S.L.	*Speed of advance 17 knots* - - -	—
9.45 —	**C.-in-C.** -	**S.O. 2nd B.S.**	S.L.	**My course S. 50° E. Speed 16 knots, zigzagging two points. Form divisions in line-ahead disposed abeam to starboard. Columns eight cables apart. Reference position 8 a.m., 58° 28′ N., 1° 17′ E.**	—
9.45 —	*S.O.3rd L.C.S.*	*Light Cruisers*	S.L.	*Am keeping on port zigzag for an hour to correct station.*	—
9.48 —	*Commodore F.*	*Michael* -	Sem.	*You should be about 800 yards astern of Manners when on normal course.*	—

Date, Time of Despatch.	From	To	System.	Message.	Time of Origin.
31 MAY —*cont.*					
9.50 a.m.	**C.-in-C.** -	**General** -	Flags	**Alter course together two points to port** -	—
9.50 —	S.O.3rd B.C.S.	Chester -	S.L.	Are you in touch with fleet? - - - Reply : With Armoured Cruiser line only	0950 1007
9.50 —	*S.O.3rdB.C.S.*	*3rd B.C.S.* -	Flags	*Alter course together four points to port* -	—
9.50 —	S.O. B.C.F.	General -	Flags	Alter course together four points to port	—
9.50 —	*S.O. 2nd B.S.*	*2nd B.S.* -	Flags	*Alter course together two points to starboard*	—
9.50 —	Engadine -	S.O.3rd L.C.S.	S.L.	Sea suitable for getting off but not for landing, but impossible to distinguish where mist ends and water begins in coming down to sea. Will be alright if horizon clears. (*Passed to S.O. B.C.F. via Yarmouth at 11 a.m.*)	0945
9.50 —	*S.O. 5th B.S.*	*5th B.S.* -	Flags	*Alter course together four points to port* -	—
9.50 —	S.O. 2nd C.S.	S.O. 1st C.S.	S.L.	2nd C.S. disposed as follows : Minotaur (Flag), Hampshire position C, Shannon B, Cochrane A. Request disposition 1st C.S.	0950
9.55 —	Chester -	S.O. 2nd C.S.	S.L.	Steamer S. ½ W. from Chester - -	0940
10.0 —	S.O.3rdB.C.S.	Chester -	S.L.	Ask Minotaur for bearing of Iron Duke? - Reply : Iron Duke bears N. 65° W. 13 miles from Minotaur. Minotaur bears S.W. eight miles from Chester.	1000 1025
10.0 —	*S.O.3rdB.C.S.*	*3rd B.C.S.* -	Flags	*Alter course together four points to starboard.*	—
10.0 —	S.O. B.C.F.	General -	Flags	Alter course together four points to starboard.	—
10.0 —	*S.O. 2nd B.S.*	*2nd B.S.* -	Flags	*Alter course together two points to port* -	—
10.0 —	**C.-in-C.** -	**General** -	Flags	**Alter course together two points to port** -	—
10.0 —	*S.O. 5th B.S.*	*5th B.S.* -	Flags	*Alter course together four points to starboard.*	—
10.0 —	*S.O. B.C.F.*	*1st B.C.S.* -	Flags	*Attention is called to the smoke issuing from your funnels.*	—
10.1 —	*Shannon* -	*S.O. 2nd C.S.*	S.L.	*Have ordered Hardy to board sailing vessel. If suspicious, to send crew below while fleet passes and send her in.*	1000
10.5 —	S.O. 2nd B.S.	General -	Flags	Admiral intends to proceed at 17 knots -	—
10.5 —	S.O. B.C.F.	Light Cruisers	S.L.	Take up cruising disposition No. 6. Centre to bear E. by S. Line of direction N.E.	—
10.5 —	**C.-in-C.** -	**Cruisers** -	Flags	**Take up cruising disposition No. 1. Centre of screen to be 10 miles from Battlefleet.**	—
10.7 —	**S.O. Cruisers**	**C.-in-C.** -	S.L.	**Three small sailing trawlers ahead of Fleet. They are being examined by Destroyers.**	0925
10.10 —	*S.O.3rdB.C.S.*	*3rd B.C.S.* -	Flags	*Alter course together four points to port* -	—
10.10 —	*S.O. 2nd B.S.*	*2nd B.S.* -	Flags	*Alter course together two points to starboard* -	—
10.10 —	S.O. B.C.F.	General -	Flags	Alter course together four points to port	—

Date, Time of Despatch.	From	To	System.	Message.	Time of Origin.
31 MAY 10.10 a.m.	*—cont.* S.O. B.C.F.	5th B.S. and 2nd B.C.S.	Flags	5th B.S. take station on compass bearing N.W. five miles. 2nd B.C.S. take station on compass bearing N.E. three miles.	—
10.10 —	*S.O. 5th B.S.*	*5th B.S.* -	Flags	*Alter course together four points to port* -	—
10.10 —	S.O. 5th B.S.	S.O. B.C.F. -	S.L.	Can you inform me what speed Lion is going through the water to make speed of advance 18 knots? Reply : 19½ knots.	1000
10.11 —	*S.O.2ndB.C.S.*	*2nd B.C.S.* -	Flags	*Resume the original course together* - -	—
10.12 —	S.N.O. Harwich.	Admiralty -	L/T	Following reconnaissance carried out from Felixstowe : (1) E.S.E. 45 miles turning N., returned over middle buoy Inner Gabbard ; (2) Steered S.S.E. 2½ hours ; (3) Steered E. for about 60 miles ; (4) Steered S. 40° E. one hour. Nothing to report.	—
10.15 —	S.O. 1st C.S.	S.O. 2nd C.S.	S.L.	1st C.S. are in cruiser disposition No. 1. Distance between X and Y 10 miles on 2nd B.S. Warrior, Defence, Duke of Edinburgh, Black Prince at B, C, D, F respectively.	1000
10.15 —	**C.-in-C.** -	**S.O. of Cruisers.**	S.L.	**Report sequence of Cruisers** - - -	**1010**
10.15 —	**S.O. 2nd C.S., via Calliope.**	**C.-in-C.** -	S.L.	**2nd B.S. in sight bearing from Minotaur S.W. by W., eight miles.** (*Not passed to C.-in-C. by Calliope, vide 1007.*)	**1010**
10.15 —	**Calliope** -	**C.-in-C.** -	S.L.	**2nd B.S. bearing S.S.E.** - - -	**1007**
10.18 —	*S.O.3rdL.C.S.*	*Yarmouth* -	S.L.	*What is bearing and distance of Lion?* - *Reply : West four miles* - - - -	*1010* *1025*
10.19 —	*S.O.2ndB.C.S.*	*2nd B.C.S.* -	Flags	*Admiral intends to proceed at 20 knots* -	—
10.20 —	*S.O.3rdB.C.S.*	*3rd B.C.S.* -	Flags	*Alter course together four points to starboard.*	—
10.20 —	S.O. B.C.F.	General -	Flags	Alter course together four points to starboard.	—
10.20 —	*Bellona* -	*S.O. 1st B.S.*	S.L.	*Port engine correct* - - - - -	—
10.20 —	*S.O. 2nd B.S.*	*2nd B.S.* -	Flags	*Alter course together three points to port* -	—
10.20 —	**C.-in-C.** -	**General** -	Flags	**Alter course together two points to starboard.**	—
10.20 —	Admiralty -	Captain S. Titania, Blyth.	L/T	Send one Destroyer and four Submarines to Lat. 54° 30′ N., Long. 4° 0′ E., to wait orders by wireless. Above position will be called rendezvous 01, and Submarines may be ordered to new positions described by true bearing and distance from it. In absence of further orders Destroyer and Submarines should return after being 24 hours at rendezvous.	—
10.24 —	*S.O.4thL.C.S.*	*4th L.C.S.* -	S.L.	*If 2nd Battle Squadron comes in from ahead alter course as necessary to starboard to clear, without waiting for a turning signal.*	*1020*
10.27 —	*S.O. 5th B.S.*	*5th B.S.*	Flags	*Alter course together four points to starboard.*	—
10.30 —	*S.O.3rdB.C.S.*	*3rd B.C.S.* -	Flags	*Alter course together four points to port* -	—
10.30 —	S.O. B.C.F.	General -	Flags	Alter course together four points to port	—

Date, Time of Despatch.	From	To	Sys tem.	Message.	Time of Origin.
31 MAY	—*cont.*				
10.30 a.m.	*S.O. 2nd B.S.*	2nd B.S. -	Flags	*Alter course together three points to starboard.*	—
10.30 —	**C.-in-C.** -	**General** -	Flags	**Alter course together two points to starboard.**	—
10.30 —	*S.O. 5th B.S.*	5th B.S. -	Flags	*Alter course together four points to port* -	—
10.35 —	*S.O. 5th B.S.*	5th B.S. -	Flags	*Admiral intends to proceed at 19½ knots* -	—
10.39 —	*S.O. 1st C.S.*	1st C.S. -	S.L.	*Spread in accordance with cruising diagram No. 1, distance between X and Y 10 miles, on C.-in-C., whose course is S. 50° E., 16 knots. Zigzag two points. Defence and Warrior at D, Duke of Edinburgh at F, Black Prince at G.*	*1030*
10.40 —	S.O. B.C.F.	General -	Flags	Alter course together four points to starboard.	—
10.40 —	*S.O. 3rd B.C.S.*	3rd B.C.S. -	Flags	*Alter course together four points to starboard.*	—
10.40 —	*S.O. 2nd B.S.*	2nd B.S. -	Flags	*Alter course together four points to port* -	—
10.40 —	**C.-in-C.** -	**St. Vincent** -	S.L.	**Keep a sharp look-out for Telefunken in about half an hour's time.**	1035
10.40 —	*S.O. 5th B.S.*	5th B.S. -	Flags	*Alter course together four points to starboard.*	—
10.45 —	S.O. 2nd B.S.	Mystic - -	Flags	Close Boadicea - - - -	—
10.45 —	*Nottingham* -	*S.O. 2nd.L.C.S.*	S.L.	*I am closing in* - - - -	*1045*
10.46 —	Minion -	S.O. 2nd B.S., Kempenfelt.	W/T	Mine in sight - - - - -	1030
10.47 —	S.O. 2nd B.S.	Boadicea -	Sem.	Examine strange ship bearing E.S.E. Am sending a Destroyer to assist you.	1046
10.47 —	S.O. B.C.F.	Champion -	S.L.	Am sending Destroyer to examine trawler	1045
10.48 —	S.O. B.C.F.	Onslow -	Flags	Investigate strange ship passing through fleet and report results.	—
10.49 —	Engadine -	S.O. B.C.F. -	S.L.	Trawler flying Dutch colours trawling -	1030
10.49 —	S.O. 2nd B.S.	General -	Flags	Alter course leading ships together the rest in succession, to S. 50° E. Columns to be eight cables apart.	—
10.50 —	*S.O. 3rd B.C.S.*	3rd B.C.S. -	Flags	*Alter course together four points to port* -	—
10.50 —	S.O. B.C.F.	General -	Flags	Alter course together four points to port	—
10.50 —	*S.O. 2nd B.S.*	2nd B.S. -	Flags	*Alter course together four points to starboard.*	—
10.50 —	Benbow -	—	—	Remarks : 2nd B.S. ahead - - -	—
10.50 —	*S.O. Cruisers*	*Cruisers* -	S.L.	*Alter course together 32 points to starboard*	—
10.50 —	*S.O. 5th B.S.*	5th B.S. -	Flags	*Alter course together four points to port* -	—
10.50 —	**C.-in-C.** -	**General** -	Flags	**Alter course together two points to port**	—
10.50 —	Yarmouth -	S.O. B.C.F. -	S.L.	Name of trawler Arie - - - -	1045
10.55 —	S.O. 2nd B.S.	General -	Flags	Guides to bear on starboard beam of Guide of fleet.	1030
10.55 —	*Shannon* -	*S.O. Cruiser* -	S.L.	*Chester reports steamer S.S.E.* - - -	—

Date, Time of Despatch.	From	To	System.	Message.	Time of Origin.
31 MAY —*cont.*					
11.0 a m.	*S.O.3rdB.C.S.*	3rd B.C.S.	Flags	*Alter course together four points to starboard.*	—
11.0 —	S.O. B.C.F.	General	Flags	Alter course together four points to starboard.	—
11.0 —	*S.O.2ndB.C.S.*	2nd B.C.S.	Flags	*Admiral intends to proceed at 19½ knots (Commenced zigzagging with Lion)*	— —
11.0 —	S.O. 2nd B.S.	General	Flags	Alter course together eight points to port	—
11.0 —	S.O. 1st C.S.	S.O. 2nd C.S.	S.L.	1st C.S. disposed as follows : Defence and Warrior at D, Duke of Edinburgh at F, Black Prince at G. What is your speed of advance?	1100
11.0 —	Owl	S.O. 2nd C.S.	S.L.	Three Dutch fishing vessels from Schisnengen. All correct.	1045
11.0 —	2nd L.C.S.	S.O. B.C.F.	S.L.	Coal Water Oil remaining. remaining. remaining. 8 a.m. :— Southampton— 1,105 Tons. 12 Tons 240 Tons Dublin— 1,190 ,, 14 ,, 255 ,, Nottingham— 953 ,, 10 ,, 186 ,, Birmingham— 1,099 ,, 15 ,, 211 ,,	—
11.0 —	**C.-in-C.**	**General**	Flags	**Alter course together two points to starboard.**	—
11.0 —	*S.O. 5th B.S.*	5th B.S.	Flags	*Alter course together four points to starboard.*	—
11.2 —	*Shannon*	*S.O. 2nd C.S.*	S.L.	*Steamer flying Dutch colours*	*1055*
11.2 —	*S.O.4thL.C.S.*	4th L.C.S.	Flags	*Admiral intends to proceed at 16½ knots*	—
11.5 —	S.O. 2nd B.S.	General	Flags	Alter course together eight points to port	—
11.5 —	S.O. 2nd B.S.	General	Flags	Thunderer take Guide of fleet	—
11.5 —	*S.O.4thL.C.S.*	4th L.C.S.	Flags	*Alter course together two points to starboard.*	—
11.5 —	*S.O. 5th B.S.*	5th B.S.	Flags	*Alter course together four points to port*	—
11.5 —	S.O.4thL.C.S.	Abdiel	Sem.	Keep clear of 2nd B.S.	—
11.10 —	**C.-in-C.**	**General**	Flags	**Alter course together two points to port**	—
11.10 —	*S.O.3rdB.C.S.*	3rd B.C.S.	Flags	*Alter course together four points to port*	—
11.10 —	S.O. B.C.F.	General	Flags	Alter course together four points to port	—
11.10 —	*S.O.4thL.C.S.*	4th L.C.S.	Flags	*Alter course together two points to port*	—
11.10 —	Commodore F.	11th Flotilla	Flags	Assume 2nd organisation screen in J G 9 1st Div. A, B, C, T positions, 2nd Div. F, G, H, U.	—
11.10 —	S.O. 2nd C.S.	S.O. 1st C.S.	S.L.	Flag of V.A.Cruisers was hauled down last night. 2nd and 7th C.S. have been amalgamated and form 2nd C.S. Flag flying in Minotaur.	1100
1.10 —	*S.O. 5th B.S.*	5th B.S.	Flags	*Alter course together four points to starboard.*	—
11.11 —	**C.-in-C.**	**S.O. 2nd B.S.**	S.L.	**Flagship is on normal course now**	—

Date, Time of Despatch.	From	To	System.	Message.	Time of Origin.
31 MAY —cont.					
11.11 a.m.	S.O. 2nd C.S.	S.O. 1st C.S.	S.L.	My course S. 50° E., speed of advance 15 knots.	—
11.13 —	Boadicea	S.O. 2nd B.S.	S.L.	Dutch trawler Cleara Vlaardinger out since May 1st. No W/T or pigeons.	1012
11.15 —	S.O. 2nd B.S.	2nd B.S.	Flags	Alter course together 16 points to starboard	—
11.15 —	S.O. 5th B.S.	5th B.S.	Flags	Alter course together four points to port	—
11.18 —	Commodore F.	Kempenfelt	Flags	Take station 1,000 yards ahead of position I	—
11.18 —	S.O. 4th L.C.S.	4th L.C.S.	S.L.	Carry on zigzagging	1115
11.19 —	S.O. 2nd B.S.	Thunderer	Sem.	Haul down 4 Pendant	—
11.19 —	**S.O. 2nd C.S.**	**C.-in-C.**	S.L.	**Disposition of Cruisers : Cochrane at A, Shannon at B, Minotaur and Hampshire at C, Defence and Warrior at D, Duke of Edinburgh at F, Black Prince at G.**	1105
11.20 —	S.O. 3rd B.C.S.	3rd B.C.S.	Flags	Alter course together six points to starboard	—
11.20 —	S.O. B.C.F.	General	Flags	Alter course together four points to starboard.	—
11.20 —	S.O. 5th B.S.	5th B.S.	Flags	Alter course together four points to starboard.	—
11.22 —	**St. Vincent**	**C.-in-C.**	S.L.	**Following signal intercepted on W.L. 2300 without call sign, in plain language, in English. Begins : Coupling is 3 inches. Spark is good. We have had a little engine trouble, but it is running well now at 1900 R.P. 17. Clouds are numerous and rather low. The W.L. by station tests is 425 metres. We hope you are receiving our signals clearly. Engine and set working very well. Extra column " Daily Mail." The Northumberland magistrates at Newcastle yesterday decided to refer Berwick for compensation. No. Ends. Note very high. Strength 5.**	1120
11.22 —	Commodore F.	Boadicea	S.L.	What position are you taking? Reply : One mile ahead of King George V.	—
11.22 —	Iron Duke	—	—	Remarks : 2nd B.S. in station	—
11.23 —	Admiral, Devonport.	Admiralty	L/T and W/T	Australia sailed with escort (Received in Iron Duke 12.30 p.m., in Lion 12.40 p.m.)	1012
11.25 —	**C.-in-C.**	**S.O. 2nd B.S.**	S.L.	**Have you sent any T.B.Ds. with 1st C.S.?** Reply : No, as I was so short.	1122
11.25 —	**C.-in-C.**	**2nd B.S.**	Flags	**Manœuvre well executed**	—
11.25 —	Engadine	S.O. B.C.F.	S.L.	Conditions suitable for large and small machines.	1120
11.30 —	S.O. 3rd B.C.S.	3rd B.C.S.	Flags	Alter course together three-quarters of a point to port.	—
11.30 —	S.O. B.C.F.	General	Flags	Alter course together four points to port	—
11.30 —	**C.-in-C.**	**General**	Flags	**Alter course together two points to starboard.**	—
11.30 —	Commodore F.	Captain D4	Flags	Am occupying positions up to L inclusive and not position S.	—
11.30 —	Shannon	S.O. 2nd C.S.	S.L.	From Hardy, boarding report. Industrie, fishing vessel of Rotterdam, not suspicious. Hardy now dealing with Dutch trawler.	—

Date, Time of Despatch.	From	To	Sys tem.	Message.	Time of Origin.
31 MAY *—cont.* 11.30 a.m.	S.O. 5th B.S.	5th B.S.	Flags	*Alter course together four points to port* -	—
11.30 —	Queen Mary	S.O. B.C.F. -	Sem.	*Following received : Long Hope to S.O. 10th C.S., code time 1045. With reference to Admiralty message timed 0305, Borden has arrived at Kirkwall.*	*1115*
11.30 —	Onslow -	S.O. B.C.F. -	Sem. and S.L.	She was Dutch iron-built ketch Arie Holland, port of registry Maaslins, letters K N P.	—
11.31 —	S.O. 1st C.S.	Warrior -	Flags	*Take station astern five cables* - - -	—
11.33 —	S.O. B.C.F.	Onslow - -	S.L.	How many men did she have on board? —they appeared very numerous. Reply : 16, which is about the number I have always found.	1128
11.34 —	Shannon -	S.O. 2nd C.S.	S.L.	*Dutch trawler N.W. is not clear of the fleet. Hardy has orders to send crew below if required.*	*1115*
11.35 —	Shannon -	S.O. 2nd C.S.	S.L.	*Two small sailing vessels bearing S. and S.S.W. from Chester.*	*1115*
11.35 —	Shannon -	S.O. 2nd C.S.	S.L.	*Sailing ship S. 84° E. from Chester* -	*1057*
11.35 —	Kempenfelt -	Commodore F.	S.L.	*All Destroyers present except Moon, who has been detailed to oil at Aberdeen.*	*1115*
11.35 —	**S.O. 2nd B.S.**	**C.-in-C. and Commodore F.**	S.L.	**Moon left Aberdeen at 5.30 a.m. this morning. I have directed her to rejoin at 2 p.m. rendezvous, but she will probably be late.**	1123
11.36 —	**C.-in-C.** -	**St. Vincent** -	S.L.	**Can you give me any idea where intercepted signal comes from? Reply : Have no idea of origin of signal, but fragments of similar message have just been received with call sign N.D.**	1135
11.40 —	S.O. 3rd B.C.S.	3rd B.C.S. -	Flags	*Alter course together to S. 50° E.* - -	—
11.40 —	S.O. B.C.F.	General -	Flags	Alter course together four points to starboard.	—
11.40 —	S.O. 5th B.S.	5th B.S. -	Flags	*Alter course together four points to starboard.*	—
11.46 —	Commodore F.	Destroyers -	Sem.	*Preparatory fog positions : 1st Div. port quarter and 2nd Div. astern of Castor, 3rd Div. astern of Kempenfelt, 4th Div. starboard quarter of Kempenfelt.*	*1145*
11.48 —	**Revenge** -	**C.-in-C.** -	S.L.	**Auxiliary W/T set out of action. Cause at present unknown.**	1135
11.50 —	S.O. 3rd B.C.S.	3rd B.C.S. -	Flags	*Alter course together two points to port* -	—
11.50 —	S.O. B.C.F.	General -	Flags	Alter course together four points to port	—
11.50 —	Shannon -	S.O. 2nd C.S.	S.L.	*Danish sailing vessel bearing N.W., two sailing trawlers bearing E.S.E.*	*1130*
11.50 —	**C.-in-C.** -	**General** -	Flags	**Alter course together two points to port**	—
11.50 —	S.O. 5th B.S.	5th B.S. -	Flags	*Alter course together four points to port* -	—
11.55 —	Shannon -	S.O. 2nd C.S.	S.L.	*Following from Chester : What is bearing of Iron Duke ?*	—
11.58 —	**St. Vincent** -	**C.-in-C.** -	S.L.	**German coded message received from IZ to IB. Strength 3. W.L. 2100 feet. Telefunken. German naval procedure used.**	1156

Date, Time of Despatch.	From	To	System.	Message.	Time of Origin.
31 MAY *—cont.*					
12.0 noon	S.O. 3rd B.C.S.	3rd B.C.S.	Flags	*Alter course together four points to starboard.*	—
12.0 —	S.O. B.C.F.	General	Flags	Alter course together four points to starboard.	—
12.0 —	S.O. Cruisers	Cruisers	S.L.	*My speed of advance 16 knots*	—
12.0 —	S.O. B.C.F.	General	Flags and S.L.	Indicate noon position :— Lion 56.44 N. 3.45 E. Princess Royal 56.46 3.38 Queen Mary 56.46 3.39 Tiger 56.45 3.40 New Zealand 56.48 3.38 Indefatigable 56.49 3.35	—
12.0 —	C.-in-C.	Cruisers	S.L.	**My speed of advance 14 knots**	—
12.0 —	C.-in-C.	General	Flags	**Admiral intends to proceed at 15 knots**	—
12.0 —	C.-in-C.	General	Flags	**Alter course together two points to port**	—
12.0 —	S.O. 5th B.S.	5th B.S.	Flags	*Alter course together four points to starboard.*	—
12.6 p.m.	S.O. 2nd C.S.	Chester	S.L.	Iron Duke bears N. 65° W., 13 miles from Minotaur.	1206
12.6 —	S.O.4thL.C.S.	Abdiel	S.L.	Clear trawler out of the way	1205
12.7 —	Shannon	S.O. 2nd C.S.	S.L.	*From Cochrane : Danish vessel is Gimbira of Croense.*	1145
12.8 —	Shannon	S.O. 2nd C.S.	S.L.	*From Hardy. Trawler Maria Josepha of Vlessingen bound for fishing ground Zealand.*	—
12.10 —	S.O.3rdB.C.S.	3rd B.C.S.	Flags	*Alter course together four points to port*	—
12.10 —	S.O. B.C.F.	General	Flags	Alter course together four points to port	—
12.10 —	S.O. 2nd B.S.	2nd B.S.	Flags	*Let fires die out in boilers not required for 19 knots*	—
12.10 —	Shannon	S.O. 2nd C.S.	S.L.	*From Cochrane : Two trawlers, Dutch, steering S.S.W.*	1150
12.10 —	S.O. 5th B.S.	5th B.S.	Flags	*Alter course together four points to port*	—
12.11 —	S.O.2ndL.C.S.	Dublin	Sem.	*At 12.20 Southampton will zigzag three points each way to regain station.*	1210
12.13 —	Chester	Minotaur	S.L.	One steamer and five sails bearing between S.W. and S.E.	1220
12.15 —	Chester	S.O.3rdB.C.S.	S.L.	At 1205 Iron Duke bore N. 65° W., 13 miles from Minotaur. Minotaur bore N. 62° W., 10 miles from Chester.	1215
12.20 —	C.-in-C.	General	Flags	**Alter course together two points to starboard.**	—
12.20 —	C.-in-C.	Cruisers	S.L.	**Battle Cruiser Fleet will probably be sighted later and is to be reported by visual.**	1215
12.20 —	S.O. B.C.F.	General	Flags	Alter course together four points to starboard.	—
12.20 —	Kempenfelt	Boadicea	Sem.	I am taking station between T and Battlefleet.	—
12.20 —	S.O.4thL.C.S.	Abdiel	S.L.	Three sails S.E. Be ready to go ahead and get them clear.	1215
12.20 —	S.O. 5th B.S.	5th B.S.	Flags	*Alter course together four points to starboard.*	—
12.20 —	S.O. 3rdB.C.S.	3rd B.C.S.	Flags	*Alter course together four points to starboard.*	—

Date, Time of Despatch.	From	To	System.	Message.	Time of Origin.
31 MAY *—cont.*					
12.22 p.m.	*S.O. 3rd B.C.S.*	3rd B.C.S.	Flags	*Admiral intends to proceed at 15½ knots*	—
12.25 —	S.O. 4th L.C.S.	Abdiel	S.L.	Proceed in execution of previous orders	—
12.26 —	*S.O. 2nd C.S.*	Shannon	S.L.	Reports of trawlers boarded need not be passed to R.A. unless they are found suspicious or any action is necessary.	1225
12.28 —	*S.O. Cruisers*	Cruisers	S.L.	*Speed of advance 14 knots at 12.30 p.m.*	—
12.28 —	S.O. 2nd C.S.	Owl	S.L.	Examine sailing vessels South	—
12.30 —	*S.O. 3rd B.C.S.*	3rd B.C.S.	Flags	*Alter course together four points to port*	—
12.30 —	S.O. B.C.F.	General	Flags	Alter course together four points to port	—
12.30 —	S.O. B.C.F.	Turbulent	S.L.	Report total amount of fuel carried and consumption per hour at this speed?	1230
				Reply : 236 tons, consumption per hour at present speed 4 tons per hour.	1245
12.30 —	**C.-in-C.**	**General**	Flags	**Alter course together two points to starboard.**	—
12.30 —	*S.O. 5th B.S.*	5th B.S.	Flags	*Alter course together four points to port*	—
12.40 —	*S.O. 3rd B.C.S.*	3rd B.C.S.	Flags	*Alter course together four points to starboard.*	—
12.40 —	S.O. B.C.F.	General	Flags	Alter course together four points to starboard.	—
12.40 —	*S.O. 5th B.S.*	Warspite	Flags	*Attention is called to smoke issuing from your funnels.*	—
12.40 —	**C.-in-C.**	**General**	Flags and S.L.	**Reference position at noon, 58° 9′ N., 2° 59′ E.**	—
12.40 —	**S.O. 2nd C.S.**	**C.-in-C.**	S.L.	**There are a good many steam and sailing trawlers, Dutch, in sight. Nothing suspicious has yet been reported by Destroyers.**	1230
12.40 —	*S.O. 5th B.S.*	5th B.S.	Flags	*Alter course together four points to starboard*	—
12.42 —	S.O. B.C.F.	Moresby	Flags and S.L.	Recall	—
12.43 —	S.O. 3rd L.C.S.	Inconstant	S.L.	If Engadine should stop to hoist out planes keep at least two miles clear of her on account of wash.	1245
12.50 —	*S.O. 3rd B.C.S.*	3rd B.C.S.	Flags	*Alter course together four points to port*	—
12.50 —	S.O. B.C.F.	General	Flags	Alter course together four points to port	—
12.50 —	**C.-in-C.**	**General**	Flags	**Alter course together two points to port**	—
12.50 —	*S.O. 5th B.S.*	5th B.S.	Flags	*Alter course together four points to port*	—
12.55 —	Iron Duke	—	—	Remarks : 12.55 passed Dutch sailing trawler S. Ch. 325, Make Linerum, and Dutch sailing trawler M.A. 63.	—
1.0 —	*S.O. 3rd B.C.S.*	3rd B.C.S.	Flags	*Alter course together four points to starboard*	—
1.0 —	S.O. B.C.F.	General	Flags	Alter course together four points to starboard.	—
1.0 —	S.N.O. Blyth	Admiralty	L/T	Urgent. Your 1020. Position Lat. 54° 30′ N., Long. 4° 0′ E., rendezvous 01, Talisman detailed.	1140

Date, Time of Despatch.	From	To	System.	Message.	Time of Origin.
31 MAY —cont.					
1.0 p.m.	Commodore F.	Destroyers	Sem.	W/T silence is to be kept except for reporting Enemy or answering the Admiral. Buzzer communication may be used for manœuvring.	1300
1.0 —	C.-in-C.	General	Flags	Alter course together two points to port -	—
1.0 —	S.O 5th B.S.	5th B.S.	Flags	Alter course together four points to starboard	—
1.2 —	S.O.2ndL.C.S.	Dublin -	Sem.	At 1.10 p.m. Southampton will zigzag two points.	1300
1.3 —	S.O.3rdB.C.S.	3rd B.C.S.	Flags	Indicate noon positions:— Invincible Lat. 58° 6' N., Long. 3° 51' E. Indomitable Lat. 58° 3' N., Long. 3° 52' E. Inflexible Lat. 58° 8' N., Long. 3° 55' E.	—
1.5 —	C.-in-C.	Leading Ships of Division.	Flags	Indicate Lat. and Long. at noon:— Iron Duke 58° 09' N. 2° 59' E. Benbow 58° 07' N. 2° 59' E. Colossus 58° 05' N. 3° 03' E. Marlborough 58° 05' N. 2° 59' E. Orion 58° 05' N. 3° 05' E. K. G. V. 58° 04' N. 3° 09' E.	
1.10 —	S.O.3rdB.C.S.	3rd B.C.S.	Flags	Alter course together four points to port -	—
1.10 —	S.O. B.C.F. -	General	Flags	Alter course together four points to port -	—
1.10 —	S.O.4thL.C.S.	4th L.C.S.	Flags	Admiral intends to proceed at 15 knots -	—
1.10 —	S.O. 5th B.S.	5th B.S.	Flags	Alter course together four points to port -	—
1.14 —	R.A. Scapa -	R.A. Invergordon.	W/T	For C.-in-C. Weather reports based on observations at 7 a.m. Anticyclone over England, depression approaching N.W. coast. Rain Ireland. Fog Straits of Dover. Forecast—Districts J, H, G and East Scotland: wind at surface moderate or fresh, between S. and W., some rain and mist, fair intervals. England S. and East Coast: wind at surface moderate, W., fair generally.	1212
1 15 —	Duke of Edinburgh.	C.-in-C. - S.O. Cruisers.	S.L.	H.M.S. Moon south five miles from position F. (Received by Iron Duke as position D.)	1250
1.15 —	Hampshire -	C.-in-C. -	S.L.	Trawlers have nets out to eastward -	1245
1.15 —	S.O. 4th L.C.S.	C.-in-C. -	S.L.	Fishing nets passed - - - -	—
1.15 —	Felixstowe -	Admiralty -	W/T	31st, 11.5 a.m., intercepted. Lurcher from Maidstone. German Submarine attacked British Seaplane 40 miles E. of Outer Gabbard L.V. Are you in touch with all three Submarines ?	1100
1.20 —	S.O.3rdB.C.S.	3rd B.C.S. -	Flags	Alter course together four points to starboard	—
1.20 —	S.O. B.C.F.-	General	Flags	Alter course together four points to starboard.	—
1.20 —	C.-in-C. -	General	Flags	Alter course together two points to starboard.	—
1.20 —	S.O. 5th B.S.	5th B.S. -	Flags	Alter course together four points to starboard	—
1.21 —	R.A. Cyclops	Aberdeen -	W/T	From Leda for S.O., B.C.F., Y channel completed, nothing found.	0950
1.30 —	S.O.3rdB.C.S.	3rd B.C.S. -	Flags	Alter course together four points to port -	—

Date, Time of Despatch.	From	To	System.	Message	Time of Origin.
31 MAY —*cont.*					
1.30 p.m.	S.O. B.C.F. -	General -	Flags	Alter course together four points to port-	—
1.30 —	*S.O. 5th B.S.*	*5th B.S* -	Flags	*Alter course together four points to port*	—
1.30 —	S.O. B.C.F. -	5th B.S.	Flags	Take station on compass line of bearing N.N.W. five miles.	—
1.30 —	S.O. B.C.F. -	Light Cruisers	Flags	Take station according to look-out diagram No. 6, Centre of screen to bear S.S.E. Line of direction E.N.E.	—
1.30 —	S.O. B.C.F.	2nd B.C.S. -	Flags	Take station on compass line of bearing E.N.E. three miles.	—
1.31 —	*S.O.2ndB.C.S.*	*2nd B.C.S.*	Flags	*Resume original course together. Admiral intends to proceed at 20 knots.*	
1.31 —	Falmouth -	Engadine -	S.L.	Close - - - -	—
1.35 —	**C.-in-C.** -	**General** -	Flags	**Alter course together two points to starboard.**	
1.35 —	**C.-in-C.** -	**Commodore F.**	S.L.	**Following from Duke of Edinburgh: Moon, South, five miles from position D.**	1250
1.38 —	*S.O. 5th B.S.*	*5th B.S.* -	Flags	*Alter course together two points to starboard*	—
1.40 —	*S.O. 3rdB.C.S.*	*3rd B.C.S.*	Flags	*Alter course together four points to starboard*	—
1.40 —	S.O. B.C.F. -	General -	Flags	Alter course together four points to starboard.	—
1.40 —	*S.O.4th L.C.S.*	*4th L.C.S.*	S.L.	*Admiral intends to proceed at 14 knots* -	—
1.45 —	*S.O.2ndB C.S.*	*2nd B.C.S*	Flags	*Admiral intends to proceed at 20 knots* - *(Commenced zigzagging with Lion.)*	—
1.48 —	**Commodore F.**	**C.-in-C.** -	S.L.	**Moon rejoined** - - - -	1340
1.50 —	*S.O.3rdB.C.S.*	*3rd B.C.S.*	Flags	*Alter course together four points to port* -	—
1.50 —	S.O. B.C.F. -	General -	Flags	Alter course together four points to port-	—
1.50 —	*Shannon* -	*S.O.2nd C.S.* -	S.L.	*Norwegian barque Remonstrant bearing E. ½ N., two more sailing ships bearing N.E. ½ N.*	*1300*
1.50 —	*S.O. 5th B.S.*	*5th B.S.* -	Flags	*Admiral intends to proceed at 20 knots* -	—
1.55 —	**C.-in-C.** -	**Battlefleet** -	Sem.	**When Interrogative Pendant is hoisted, indicate by numeral signal, rate per hour at which ships can oil Destroyer alongside :—**	1352
				Iron Duke 100 K.G. V 40	
				Royal Oak 150 Ajax 20	
				Superb 50 Centurion 50	
				Canada 100 Erin 60	
				Benbow 50 Orion 60	
				Bellerophon 100 Monarch 50	
				Temeraire 60 Conqueror 50	
				Vanguard 50 Thunderer 45	
				Marlborough 40 Revenge 120	
				Hercules 35-40 Neptune 40	
				Colossus 40 Collingwood 50	
				Agincourt 100 St. Vincent 30	
1.55 —	**C.-in-C.** -	**General**	Flags	**Alter course together two points to port** -	—
1.55 —	*S.O.5th B.S.* -	*5th B.S.* -	Flags	*Alter course together two points to port* -	—
2.0 —	*S.O.3rdB.C.S.*	*3rd B.C.S.* -	Flags	*Alter cours together four points to starboard*	—

Date, Time of Despatch.	From	To	System.	Message.	Time of Origin.
31 MAY *—cont.*					
2.0 p.m	S.O. B.C.F.-	General	Flags	Alter course togetner four points to starboard.	—
2.0 —	**C.-in-C.**	**General**	Flags	**Alter course together two points to port** -	—
2.0 —	Nottingham -	S.O. 2nd L.C.S	S.L.	*Am on port zigzag to correct bearing.*	*1400*
2.4 —	S.O. 5th B.S.	5th B.S.	Flags	*Alter course together four points to starboard*	—
2.5 —	Admiralty -	All Ships	W/T	Mines are suspected just Eastward of Corton Light Vessel. This vicinity is to be avoided until swept.	1340
2.5 —	S.O. 3rd L.C.S.	Engadine	S.L.	Your new cruising station 5½ miles S. 50° E. from Falmouth.	—
2.6 —	S.O. B.C.F. -	General	Flags	Resume original course together -	—
2.8 —	S.O. B.C.F. -	Destroyers	Flags	Take up position as Submarine screen when course is altered to N. by E.	—
2.10—	Galatea	S.O. B.C.F. -	S.L.	Two-funnelled ship has stopped steamer bearing E.S.E., eight miles, am closing.	1410
2.10—	S.O.3rdB.C.S.	3rd B.C.S.	Flags	*Alter course together four points to port* -	—
2.10—	S.O. 5th B.S.	5th B.S.	Flags	*Alter course together four points to starboard*	—
2.13—	S.O. 5th B.S.	5th B.S.	Flags	*Form single line-ahead ships in column to be three cables apart.*	—
2.13—	S.O.2nd L.C.S.	Nottingham	S.L.	*Who is alter course signal from ?* Reply : *To Light Cruisers from Lion, stop was omitted by Nottingham in order to get subsidiary signal through as rapidly as possible.*	*1408*
2.15—	S.O B.C.F. -	General	S.L.	Alter course leading ships together the rest in succession to N. by E.	1351
2.15—	S.O. B.C.F. -	S.O. 5th B.S.-	S.L.	When we turn to Northward look out for advanced Cruisers of Grand Fleet.	1412
2.15—	C. in-C.	Cruisers	S.L.	**My course S.E. by S. at 3 p.m. Raise steam for full speed with all despatch.** *(Time of despatch shown was logged in Iron Duke but records cannot be found of such a signal at the time stated in any other ship's log.)*	—
2.17—	C.-in-C.	S.O. 2nd C.S. -	S.L.	**Are you in touch with Battle Cruisers ?** - Reply : **Not since 1 o'clock.** - -	**1416** **1440**
2.17—	S.O. 5th B.S.	5th B.S.	Flags	*Alter course in succession to N. by E.* -	—
2.20—	S.O.3rd B.C.S.	3rd B.C.S.	Flags	*Alter course together four points to starboard*	—
2.20—	Galatea	General	Flags	Enemy in sight - - - - -	—
2.20—	Engadine -	—		Remarks : Sighted two Enemy Cruisers bearing East.	—
2.20—	Galatea	S.O. B.C.F. -	W/T	Urgent. Two Cruisers, probably hostile, in sight bearing E.S.E., course unknown, My position Lat. 56°48′ N., Long.5° 21′ E. *(Received in Iron Duke 2.18 p.m.)*	1420
2.20—	C.-in-C.	General	Flags	**Alter course together two points to starboard**	——
2.21—	S.O. 5th B.S.	5th B.S.	Flags	*Admiral intends to proceed at 19½ knots* -	—
2.22—	S.O.4th L.C.S.	Abdiel -	Sem.	Sail South, be ready to go ahead to clear her away.	1420
2.23—	**R.A. Cyclops-**	Aberdeen	W/T	**For C.-in-C. from S.N.O. Blyth, Talisman and Submarines G2, 3, 4, 5 sailed noon for rendezvous 54° 30′ N., 4° 0′ E. in accordance with orders received from Admiralty.**	1400
2.25—	S.O. B.C.F. -	Destroyers	Flags	Take up position as Submarine screen when course is altered to S.S.E.	—

Date, Time of Despatch.	From	To	System.	Message.	Time of Origin.
31 MAY *—cont.*					
2.28 p.m.	**St. Vincent**	**C.-in-C.**	Sem.	**German coded message intercepted from DZ to DR. Strength 9. 2,600 feet wave. Telefunken.**	**1415**
2.30 —	Galatea	S.O. B.C.F.	W/T	Urgent. My 1420. Cruisers are stopped. *(Received in Iron Duke 2.25 p.m.)*	1422
2.30 —	*S.O.3rd B.C.S.*	*3rd B.C.S.*	Flags	*Alter course together four points to port*	—
2.30 —	**C.-in-C.**	**General**	Flags	**Alter course together two points to starboard.**	—
2.30 —	Inconstant	S.O. 3rd L.C.S.	S.L.	Am keeping touch with Galatea	1425
2.31 —	S.O. 3rd L.C.S.	Lion	S.L.	Am closing 1st L.C.S.	1430
2.31 —	Falmouth	Engadine	S.L.	Close Battle Cruisers	1430
2.32 —	*S.O. 5th B.S.*	*5th B.S.*	Flags	*Alter course together two points to port*	—
2.32 —	S.O. B.C.F.	General	Flags	Alter course leading ships together the rest in succession to S.S.E.	—
2.33 —	*Indomitable*	*S.O.3rd B.C.S.*	Sem.	*Have just heard Telefunken signals very loud.*	*1430*
2.33 —	S.O. B.C.F.	General	Flags	Admiral intends to proceed at 22 knots	—
2.33 —	S.O. B.C.F.	General	Flags	Raise steam for full speed and report when ready to proceed.	—
2.34 —	Galatea	S.O. B.C.F.	W/T	Urgent. Enemy ships reported in my 1420 are two Destroyers. Am chasing. *(Received in Iron Duke 2.34 p.m.)*	1430
2.34 —	Galatea	S.O. B.C.F.	W/T	Urgent. One Cruiser, probably hostile, bearing E., steering S.S.E. My position Lat. 56° 50' N., Long. 5° 19' E. *(Received in Iron Duke 2.30 p.m.)*	1430
2.35 —	**C.-in-C.**	**General**	Flags	**Raise steam for full speed and report when ready to proceed.**	—
2.35 —	**Admiralty**	**C.-in-C.**	W/T	**Talisman with four Blyth Submarines has been ordered to rendezvous 01 in Lat. 54° 30' N., Long. 4° 0' E., to remain there 24 hours waiting orders.**	**1435**
2.35 —	*S.O. 5th B.S.*	*5th B.S.*	Sem.	*Length of line is 12 cables instead of nine. Take up appointed station.*	*1435*
2.37 —	*Nottingham*	*S.O.2nd L.C.S.*	S.L.	*Have increased speed to 23 knots*	*1438*
2.37 —	S.O.3rd L.C.S.	Engadine	S.L.	Two Enemy Cruisers sighted about East. Take cover near Battle Cruisers.	1435
2.38 —	S.O. B.C.F.	General	Flags	The hands are to be stationed at action stations constantly throughout the day.	—
2.39 —	Galatea	S.O. B.C.F.	W/T	Urgent. Have sighted large amount of smoke as though from a fleet bearing E.N.E. My position Lat. 56° 50' N., Long. 5° 19' E. *(Received in Iron Duke 2.35 p.m.)*	1435
2.40 —	*S.O. 5th B.S.*	*5th B.S.*	Flags	*Alter course in succession to S.S.E. Speed 22 knots.*	—
2.40 —	*S.O.3rd B.C.S.*	*3rd B.C.S., Chester and Canterbury.*	S.L.	*Raise steam for full speed and report when ready to proceed.*	—
2.40 —	*S.O.3rd B.C.S.*	*3rd B.C.S.*	Flags	*Alter course together four points to starboard*	—
2.43 —	**C.-in-C.**	**General**	Flags	**Alter course together two points to port. Speed 17 knots. Guides to bear N.E. by E. from Guide of fleet.**	—

Date, Time of Despatch.	From	To	System.	Message.	Time of Origin.
31 MAY *—cont.*					
2.43 p.m.	*Cordelia* -	*Inconstant* -	Sem.	*How many ships can you make out ?—I can only make out one. Reply : One ship and two Destroyers.*	—
2.44 —	*S.O.3rd B.C.S.*	*3rd B.C.S.* -	Flags	*The hands are to be stationed at action stations constantly throughout the day.*	—
2.45 —	**C.-in-C.** -	**Cruisers**	S.L.	**My speed of advance 17 knots** - -	**1425**
2.45 —	*S.O. Cruisers*	*Cruisers* -	S.L.	*Speed of advance 16 knots* - - -	
2.45 —	Galatea -	S.O. B.C.F. -	S.L.	Enemy apparently turned North - -	1445
2.46 —	S.O. B.C.F. -	Champion -	Sem.	Send two Destroyers to Engadine - -	1445
2.47 —	S.O. B.C.F. -	Engadine -	S.L.	Send up Seaplanes to scout N.N.E. Am sending two Destroyers to you.	1445
2.48 —	R.A. Scapa -	Princetown -	W/T	From C.-in-C., Rosyth. Leda, Shipjack and Jason arrived.	1139
2.50 —	R.A. Scapa -	Princetown -	W/T	Following message received from Naval Depot, North Shields. Negro left North Shields.	1445
2.50 —	*S.O.3rd B.C.S*	*3rd B.C.S.* -	Flags	*Alter course together four points to port* -	—
2.51 —	Galatea -	S.O. B.C.F. -	W/T	Urgent. My 1435. Smoke seems to be seven vessels besides Destroyers and Cruisers. They have turned North. My position Lat. 56° 52' N., Long. 5° 33' E. (*Received in Iron Duke 2.51 p.m.*)	1445
2.52 —	**St. Vincent** -	**C.-in-C.**	S.L.	**German coded signal received. 2,300 feet wave. Strength 10. Telefunken used.**	**1445**
2.52 —	S.O. 1st L.C.S.	S.O. B.C.F. -	S.L.	1st L.C.S. are under fire - - -	1450
2.52 —	S.O. B.C.F. -	General -	Flags	Alter course leading ships together the rest in succession to S.E.	—
2.55 —	*S.O. 1st L.C.S.*	*Inconstant* -	S.L.	*Where are our Battle Cruisers ? Reply : Bearing W.S.W., just hull down, apparently steering S.E.*	—
2.55 —	**C.-in-C.** -	**General**	Flags	**Admiral intends to proceed at 18 knots** -	—
2.57 —	**C.-in-C.** -	**General**	Flags	**Raise steam for full speed with all despatch**	—
3.0 —	**C.-in-C.** -	**Destroyers**	Flags	**Destroyers bank fires in boilers not required for 21 knots.**	—
3.0 —	*S.O. Cruisers*	*Cruisers* -	S.L.	*My course and speed, S.E. by S., advancing 18 knots. Assume stations for immediate action.*	
3.0 —	**C.-in-C.** -	**Cruisers**	Flags	**My course is S.E. by S. at 3 p.m.** - -	—
3.0 —	Lion - -	—	—	Remarks : Seaplane left Engadine - -	—
3.0 —	S.O. B.C.F. -	2nd L.C.S.	S.L.	Prepare to attack the van of the Enemy -	—
3.0 —	**C.-in-C.** -	**General** -	Flags	**Assume complete readiness for action in every respect.**	—
3.0 —	*S.O.3rd B.C.S.*	*3rd B.C.S.* -	Flags	*Alter course together four points to starboard*	—
3.1 —	S.O. B.C.F. -	General -	Flags	Alter course leading ships together the rest in succession to E.	—
3.2 —	**C.-in-C.** -	**General**	Flags	**Alter course leading ships together the rest in succession to S.E. by S.**	—
3.3 —	S.O. 5th B.S. -	5th B.S. -	Flags	*Ships in column to be 3½ cables apart* -	—
3.4 —	Engadine	—	—	Remarks : Seaplane 59 hoisted out -	—

Date, Time of Despatch.	From	To	System.	Message.	Time of Origin.
31 MAY—*cont.*					
3.5 p.m.	Galatea -	S.O. B.C.F. -	S.L.	Several Cruisers and Destroyers bearing E., steering various courses. My position Lat. 56° 54' N., Long. 5° 21' E. Am keeping touch. Course N., 25 knots. Enemy Cruisers have altered to N.W.	1505
3.5 —	S.O. B.C.F. -	Engadine -	S.L.	Tell Seaplanes Enemy have turned N. -	1500
3.5 —	*S.O. 5th B.S.*	*5th B.S.* -	Flags	*Alter course in succession to E.S.E.-* -	—
3.5 —	**Falmouth** -	**S.O. B.C.F., C.-in-C.**	W/T	**Urgent. Three Cruisers, probably hostile, in sight, bearing E., course N. My position Lat. 56° 59' N., Long. 5° 31' E.**	1500
3.8 —	Galatea -	S.O. B.C.F. -	W/T	Urgent. Enemy ships reported have altered course N.W., my course is N.N.W. My position Lat. 56° 59' N., Long. 5° 27½' E. *(Received in Iron Duke 3.8 p.m.)*	1507
3.10 —	**C.-in-C.** -	**Cruisers** -	S.L.	**Take up cruising disposition No. 1. Centre of screen 16 miles from B.F. Speed of advance 18 knots. Assume complete readiness for action.**	—
3.10 —	Engadine -	Seaplane 8089	S.L.	Enemy has turned North - -	—
3.10 —	**St. Vincent** -	**C.-in-C.** -	S.L.	**Five coded German messages received. Call signs DR DR IB AR IH OD IY JV. Strength 8-12. 2,300 feet wave. Telefunken.**	1510
3.10 —	*S.O. 4th L.C.S*	*4th L.C.S* -	Flags	*Admiral intends to proceed at 18 knots* -	—
3.10 —	*S.O. 3rd B.C.S*	*3rd B.C.S.* -	Flags	*Alter course together four points to port* -	—
3.10 —	**Admiralty** -	**C.-in-C.** -	W/T	**At 2.31 p.m. directionals placed Enemy Light Cruiser in Lat. 56° 57' N., Long. 6° 9' E., and Enemy Destroyer in Lat. 56° 57', Long. 5° 43' E.** *(Received in Lion 3.29 p.m.)*	1510
3.10 —	*S.O. 1st C.S.-*	*1st C.S.* -	S.L.	*Zigzag ¾ of a point each side of normal* -	1455
3.11 —	*S.O. 3rd B.C.S*	*3rd B.C.S.* -	Flags	*Form astern and follow in the wake of your divisional Guides.*	—
3.12 —	S.O. B.C.F. -	General -	Flags	Admiral intends to proceed at 23 knots -	—
3.13 —	S.O. B.C.F. -	General -	Flags	Alter course leading ships together the rest in succession to N.E.	—
3.13 —	*S.O. 3rd B.C.S.*	*3rd B.C.S.* -	Flags	*Admiral intends to proceed at 22 knots* -	—
3.14 —	*S.O. 5th B.S.*	*5th B.S.* -	Flags	*Alter course in succession to E., speed 22 knots.*	—
3.15 —	New Zealand	—	—	Remarks: Sighted five Enemy ships on starboard bow.	—
3.15 —	**S.O. 3rd B.C.S.**	**C.-in-C.** -	S.L.	**Priority. My course E.S.E., 22 knots** -	1510
3.16 —	**C.-in-C.** -	**General** -	Flags	**Columns to be one mile apart** - - -	—
3.18 —	**C.-in-C.** -	**General** -	Flags and S.L.	**Admiral intends to proceed at 19 knots** -	—
3.18 —	*S.O. 3rd B.C.S*	*3rd B.C.S.* -	Flags	*Assume complete readiness for action in every respect.*	—
3.20 —	S.O. 3rd B.C.S.	Chester and Canterbury.	S.L.	Keep a good look out - - - -	1522

Date, Time of Despatch.	From	To	System.	Message	Time o. Origin
31 MAY —*cont.* 3.20 p.m.	S.O. B.C.F. -	General -	Flags	Admiral intends to proceed at 24 knots	—
3.21 —	**S.O. B.C.F. -**	**S.O.s of Squadrons.**	W/T	**My position Lat. 56° 48′ N., Long. 5° 17′ E., course N.E., speed 23 knots.** (*Received by C.-in-C. N. 40° E.*)	1515
3.21 —	*S.O. 5th B.S.*	*5th B.S.* -	Flags	*Alter course in succession to N.E., speed 23 knots.*	—
3.22 —	**C.-in-C.** -	**Destroyers** -	Flags	**Raise steam for full speed** - -	—
3.22 —	Galatea -	S.O. B.C.F. -	S.L. and W/T	Urgent. Am leading Enemy N.W., they appear to be following. My position Lat. 57° 02′ N., Long. 5° 23′ E. (*Received in Iron Duke 3.29 p.m.*)	1520
3.23 —	*P. Royal* -	*S.O. B.C.F.* -	Flags	*Attention is called to E. by N.-* - -	—
3.23 —	*S.O. Cruisers-*	*Cruisers* -	S.L.	*My course and speed are S. 29° E., 20 knots*	—
3.24 —	**Nottingham -**	**C.-in-C., S.O. B.C.F.**	W/T	**Urgent. Have sighted smoke bearing E.N.E. five columns. My position Lat. 56° 46′ N., Long. 5° 14′ E.**	1522
3.25 —	Galatea -	S.O. B.C.F. -	W/T	Urgent. Have sighted smoke on bearing E.S.E., apparently squadron astern of Cruisers steering W.N.W. bearing E.S.E. (*Received in Iron Duke 3.27 p.m.*)	1515
3.25 —	**C.-in-C.** -	**Cruisers** -	S.L.	**My speed of advance is 19 knots** - -	1520
3.25 —	Lion - -	—	—	Remarks : Enemy in sight on starboard bow.	—
3.25 —	*Nottingham -*	*S.O. 2nd L.C.S.*	S.L.	*Sighted smoke on bearing E.N.E., five columns.*	—
3.25 —	*S.O. Cruisers*	*Cruisers* -	S.L.	*Negative zigzag* - - - -	—
3.27 —	**C.-in-C.** -	**S.O. B.C.F.** -	W/T	**My position at 1515, 57° 50′ N., 4° 15′ E., course S.E. by S., speed 19 knots.**	1526
3.27 —	S.O. B.C.F. -	General -	Flags	Assume complete readiness for action in every respect.	—
3.30 —	*S.O. 5th B.S.*	*5th B.S.* -	Flags	*Assume complete readiness for action in every respect.*	—
3.30 —	Onslow -	Engadine -	Sem.	Onslow and Nestor have been told off to stand by you. Can you please give me any idea of what you are likely to do ? Reply : Am keeping close to Battle Cruisers. Course N.N.E. Seaplane has gone out E.N.E. and am keeping look out for return. If you are detailed to work with me, please open out to one mile on either side, and when picking up planes should like you to keep at least a mile off. Circle round at 10 knots. My present speed is 20 knots.	—
3.30 —	S.O. B.C.F. -	General	Flags	Alter course leading ships together, the rest in succession to E., speed 25 knots.	—
3.30 —	**R.A. Scapa -**	**R.A. Invergordon.**	W/T	**For C.-in-C. Weather report from Rosyth, Immingham and Harwich respectively. Wind S.E. 1-3, dull, c. and o., misty, rain 29.98. Based on observation at 1 p.m. : wind S.W., fine, b. and be., barometer 30.19. Based on observations at 1 p.m. : barometer 30.25, rising, temperature 64, wind E.S.E., light.**	1300
3.31 —	**C.-in-C.** -	**S.O.s of, Squadrons.**	Sem.	**Flag Officers inform their divisions of the situation.**	1532

Date, Time of Despatch.	From	To	System.	Message.	Time of Origin.
31 MAY	—cont.				
	Commodore F.	Destroyers ·	Sem.	Enemy's Cruisers and Destroyers, believed hostile, 50 miles ahead, steering North.	1515
	S.O. 4th B.S.	4th Division ·	Sem.	Following is situation at 2.20 p.m. Galatea reported Cruisers in Lat. 57° N., 5° 20′ E., Enemy steering E.S.E. at 2.30 p.m., chasing two T.B.Ds. Further Cruiser reports received : Enemy altered course to N.W. at 2.30, 1st L.C.S. leading Enemy to N.W., Enemy appear to be following in five columns, approximate position Lat. 57° 0′, Long. 5° 25′ E.	1530
	R.A. 1st B.S.	5th Division	Sem.	S.O. 1st L.C.S. reported at 3 p.m., smoke probably consisting of seven vessels besides Destroyers and Cruisers. They have turned N.W. His position Lat. 56° 52′ N., Long. 5° 33′ E. This is the main report. Besides this there are various minor reports of Cruisers and Destroyers.	1535
	S.O. 2nd B.S.	1st Division	Sem.	An Enemy's force, apparently consisting of seven ships besides Destroyers and Cruisers, have been sighted by 1st and 3rd L.C.S. Their course is N.W., which leads them direct to Battlefleet. One Enemy Cruiser is reported steering S.S.E. Position of 1st and 3rd L.C.S. is about S.E. true, 60 miles, at 3 p.m.	1540
	S.O. 4th B.S.	4th Division ·	Sem.	At 3.35 p.m. S.O. B.C.F. reports five Battle Cruisers and large numbers of Destroyers in sight in 57° 12′ N., 5° 40′ E.	1545
	S.O. 1st B.S.	6th Division	Sem.	Galatea is leading the Enemy to the N.W. and they are apparently following her.	1540
	Commodore F.	Destroyers ·	Sem.	Position of forces at 4 p.m. : Battle Cruiser Fleet 56° 56′ N., 5° 45′ E., Enemy bearing from B.C.F. E.N.E., steering E.S.E., being engaged, 1st and 3rd L.C.S. chasing 12 miles astern.	1620
	Commodore F.	Destroyers ·	Sem.	Position of Enemy's Battlefleet at 4.4 p.m. : 56° 30′ N., 6° 30′ E., course N.	1645
	S.O. 4th B.S.	4th Division	Sem.	5th B.S. accompanied by 1st and 2nd B.C.S. engaging Enemy.	—
	S.O. 4th B.S.	4th Division ·	Sem.	At 4.45 p.m. Enemy 26 to 30 ships steering S.E., bearing S.S.E. from Battle Cruisers. Approximate position of Enemy 56° 30′, 6° 30′. Champion ordered to attack with Whitehead torpedoes.	1727
3.31 p.m.	Seaplane N. 82A.	S.O. via Engadine.	W/T	Cruisers three, Destroyers five. Enemy bearing and distance from me E. 10 miles. Enemy course N.W.	1530
3.31 —	**C.-in-C.** ·	**S.O. 2nd C.S.-**	S.L.	**Centre of screen should bear S.E. by S.** ·	**1530**
3.32 —	S.O. B.C.F. ·	General ·	Flags	Alter course leading ships together the rest in succession to East.	—
3.33 —	S.O. B.C.F. ·	Galatea ·	W/T	Indicate bearing of Enemy · ·	1532
3.33 —	S.O. 2nd C.S.	Owl · ·	S.L.	Speed of advance 20 knots · ·	—
3.34 —	S.O. B.C.F. ·	2nd B.C.S. ·	Flags	Prolong the line by taking station astern	—
3.34 —	S.O. B.C.F. ·	Falmouth ·	W/T and S.L.	Are you in visual touch with Galatea ? Report her bearing.	1532
			S.L.	Reply : Enemy bearing E., steering S.E. Galatea N.N.E. two miles. My position Lat. 57° 10′ N., Long. 5° 14′ E.	1538

Date, Time of Despatch.	From	To	System.	Message.	Time of Origin.
31 MAY *—cont.*					
3.34 p.m	S.O. B.C.F. -	13th Flotilla -	Flags	Take station ahead	—
3.35 —	S.O. B.C.F. -	S.O. 5th B.S. -	S.L.	Speed 25 knots. Assume complete readiness for action. Alter course leading ships together the rest in succession to E. Enemy in sight.	—
3.35 —	*S.O. 5th B.S.*	*5th B.S.* -	Flags	*Alter succession in course to E., speed 24 knots.*	—
3.35 —	Engadine -	—	—	Remarks : Endeavoured to pass Seaplane signals 1530, 1532, 1545 to S.O. B.C.F. and S.O. 5th B.S. Broke off visual communication and went into action. (*Remarks : There are no records of Engadine calling up S.O. B.C.F. or S O.5th B.S.*)	—
3.35 —	S.O. B.C.F.	General -	Flags	Admiral intends to proceed at 24 knots -	—
3.35 —	S.O. B.C.F. -	General -	Flags	Enemy in sight bearing E. by N. - -	—
3.35 —	**C.-in-C.** -	**3rd Sub. and Commodore F.**	Sem.	**Enemy Cruisers and Destroyers are being chased to the Northward by our B.C.F. and should be in touch with our Cruisers by 4 p.m.**	**1530**
3.35 —	*S.O. Cruisers*	*Cruisers* -	S.L.	*My course is S.E. by S.* - - -	*1530*
3.36 —	Seaplane N. 82A.	S.O. via Engadine.	W/T	Enemy's course is South - -	1530
3.36 —	*S.O.2nd B.C.S*	*2nd B.C.S.* -	Flags	*Alter course in succession 16 points to starboard.*	—
3.36 —	**S.O. B.C.F.** -	**S.O.s of Squadrons.**	W/T	**Present course and speed E. 25 knots** (*Received in Iron Duke 3.32 p.m.*)	**1530**
3.36 —	S.O.3rd L.C.S.	S.O. 1st L.C.S.	S.L.	They appear to have turned to the East (*This presumably refers to the Enemy.*)	1530
3.37 —	S.O.2ndB.C.S.	9th Flotilla -	Flags	9th Flotilla take station ahead of Lion -	—
3.38 —	S.O.2ndB.C.S.	Destroyers -	Flags	Take station ahead five cables - -	—
3.40 —	**S.O. B.C.F.** -	**C.-in-C.** -	W/T	**Urgent. Enemy Battle Cruisers, five in number, bearing N.E., Destroyers, large number, bearing N.E., course unknown. Position of reporting ship Lat. 56° 53′ N., Long. 5° 28′ E.**	**1535**
3.40 —	*S.O. 5th B.S.*	*5th B.S.* -	Flags	*Admiral intends to proceed at 24½ knots* -	—
3.40 —	**S.O. 2nd C.S.**	**C.-in-C.** -	S.L.	**Chester received course and speed of fleet at 3.20.**	**1538**
3.40 —	**C.-in-C.** -	**General** -	Flags and S.L.	**Reference position 3.30 p.m., 57° 45′ N., 4° 32′ E.**	**1545**
3.42 —	S.O. B.C.F. -	13th Flotilla -	Flags	Take station two points before the starboard beam two miles.	—
3.42 —	S.O. B.C.F. -	9th Flotilla -	—	Take station ahead - - -	—
3.42 —	Fearless -	—	—	Remarks : Sighted two Enemy Cruisers (six sighted at 3.50 p.m.).	—
3.44 —	Galatea -	S.O. B.C.F. -	W/T	Urgent. The Enemy Light Cruisers and Destroyers have altered course to South. I am following. My position Lat. 57° 04′ N., Long. 5° 10′ E. (*Received in Iron Duke 3.41 p.m.*)	1535
3.44 —	Falmouth	S.O. B.C.F. and C.-in-C.	W/T	**Urgent. Enemy bears E. by S. from me, distance unknown, course S.E., speed 21 to 25 knots. My position Lat. 57° 10′ N., Long. 5° 14′ E.**	**1538**

Date, Time of Despatch.	From	To	Sys- tem.	Message.	Time of Origin.
31 MAY *—cont.*					
3.45 p.m.	*S.O. 3rd B.C.S.*	*3rd B.C.S.* -	Flags	*Alter course in succession to S. 26° E.*	—
3.45 —	Seaplane N. 82 A.	Engadine -	W/T	Three Cruisers, 10 Destroyers. Enemy's course is South.	1545
3.45 —	**C.-in-C.** -	**Royal Oak** -	Sem.	**You must steer a steadier course in action or your shooting will be bad.**	**1540**
3.45 —	*S.O. B.C.F.* -	*Battle Cruisers*	Flags	*Form on a line bearing N.W.*	—
3.45 —	**S.O. B.C.F.** -	**C.-in-C.** -	W/T	**Urgent. Course of Enemy S. 55° E. My position Lat. 56° 53′ N., Long. 5° 33′ E.**	**1545**
3.45 —	S.O. B.C.F. -	General	Flags	Alter course together to E.S.E. -	—
3.46 —	*S.O. B.C.F.* -	*Battle Cruisers*	Flags	*Lion and Princess Royal concentrate on Enemy's leading ship.*	—
3.47 —	Engadine -	—	—	Remarks : Seaplane returned -	—
3.47 —	Lion - -	—	—	Remarks : Enemy opened fire -	—
3.47 —	*S.O. 5th B.S.*	*5th B.S.* -	Flags	*Enemy in sight bearing E.* -	—
3.47 —	S.O. B.C.F. -	General -	Flags	Open fire and engage the Enemy -	—
3.47 —	Lion - -	—	—	Remarks : Lion opened fire -	—
3.50 —	*S.O. 1st L.C.S.*	*1st L.C.S.* -	S.L.	*Am working up to full speed* -	*1550*
3.50 —	Galatea -	S.O. 3rd L.C.S.	S.L.	Do you know relative position, course and speed of our Battle Cruisers ? Am I right in trying to lead Enemy ?	—
3.50 —	Warspite -	—	—	Remarks : Barham opened fire -	—
3.50 —	Warspite -	—	—	Remarks : Enemy opened fire. Battle Cruisers opened fire.	—
3.50 —	Lion - -	—	—	Remarks : Lion being frequently hit by Enemy. Turret wrecked at 4 p.m.	—
3.55 —	**S.O. B.C.F.** -	**C.-in-C.** -	W/T	**Urgent. Am engaging Enemy. My position Lat. 56° 53′ N., Long. 5° 31′ E.**	**1550**
3.55 —	S.O. B.C.F. -	Captain D13 -	W/T	Opportunity appears favourable for attacking.	—
3.55 —	*S.O. 2nd L.C.S.*	*2nd L.C.S.* -	S.L.	*Spread for look-out duties on a line of bearing N.W. in sequence in which ships now are from Lion.*	—
3.55 —	S.O. Cruisers	Cruisers -	S.L.	My course S.E. by S. -	1550
3.55 —	S.O. B.C.F. -	General -	Flags and W/T	Increase the rate of fire -	1558
3.55 —	*S.O. 4th L.C.S.*	*4th L.C.S.* -	Flags	*Alter course together two points to port* -	—
3.56 —	S.O. 5th B.S.	Destroyers -	Flags	Keep out of the way -	—
3.56 —	S.O. B.C.F. -	Captain D1 and D 13.	Flags	Proceed at your utmost speed -	1548
3.58 —	**C.-in-C.** -	**Cruisers** -	S.L.	**Speed of advance 20 knots** -	—
3.58 —	*Gloucester* -	*S.O. 3rd L.C.S.*	S.L.	*Enemy fleet steering South* -	—
3.59 —	S.O. 5th B.S.	Fearless -	Flags	Fearless take station astern of Malaya -	—
3.59 —	Galatea -	S.O. B.C.F. -	W/T	Urgent. Enemy bearing E.S.E. Course of Enemy E.S.E. My position, course and speed, Lat. 57° 03′ N., Long. 5° 27′ E., E.S.E., 28 knots. *(Lion received course of Enemy South. Received in Iron Duke 3.59 p.m.)*	1555

Date, Time of Despatch.	From	To	System.	Message.	Time of Origin.
31 MAY —*cont.*					
3.59 p.m.	**C.-in-C.**	**General** -	Flags	**Admiral intends to proceed at 20 knots**·	—
4.0 —	*S.O.3rd B.C.S.*	*3rd B.C.S.* -	Flags	*Admiral intends to proceed at 24 knots* -	—
4.0 —	Warspite -	—	—	Remarks : Opened fire - · · ·	—
4.0 —	*S.O. 5th B.S.*	*5th B.S.* -	Flags	*Open fire and engage the Enemy* - ·	—
4.1 —	Lion - -	—	—	Remarks : Indefatigable blew up · ·	—
4.1 —	*Commodore F.*	*11th Flotilla* -	Sem.	*Don't forget black flag in action* - ·	*1600*
4.2 —	*S.O.3rd B.C.S.*	*General* -	Flags	*Alter course in succession to S.S.E.* - ·	—
4.5 —	**C.-in-C.** -	**S.O. 3rd B.C.S.**	W/T	**Proceed immediately to support B.C.F. Position Lat. 56° 53′ N., Long. 5° 31′ E., course S. 55° E. at 3.50 p.m.**	1604
4.5 —	*Birmingham*·	*S.O.2nd L.C.S.*	S.L.	*Ten Destroyers ahead of Enemy's Battle Cruisers.*	—
4.5 —	**C.-in-C.** -	**General** - -	Sem.	**Battle Cruiser Fleet are engaging Enemy's Battle Cruisers**	1605
4.7 —	Falmouth -	S.O. B.C.F. and S.O. 5th B.S.	S.L.	Enemy steering E.N.E. - · · · (*Not logged as having been received by S.O. B.C.F. or S.O. 5th B.S.*)	1600
4.7 —	**S.O. Cruisers**·	**C.-in-C.** -	S.L.	**Chester has again passed out of sight** -	1600
4.8 —	R.A. Invergordon.	Admiralty -	W/T	Biarritz sailed 12.10, repeated to Admiralty, C.-in-C., R.A. Scapa and Captain M.	1430
4.9 —	S.O. B.C.F. -	Champion via Princess Royal.	W/T	Attack the Enemy with torpedoes (*Not logged as having been received by Champion until 5.16 p.m. This signal was passed to Champion by Princess Royal at that time, presumably owing to Lion's W/T being out of action.*)	1602
4.10 —	*S.O. B.C.F.* -	*Princess Royal*	W/T	*Main W/T out of action* - · · ·	*1605*
4.11 —	Lion - ·	—	—	Remarks : Nottingham reports Submarine on starboard side.	—
4.11 —	S.O. B.C.F. -	Destroyers -	S.L.	Clear range - · · · · ·	—
4.12 —	Onslow -	Engadine -	Sem.	Can you dispense with my services ? If so, I will join 5th B.S. Reply : Yes, certainly.	—
4.12 —	S.O.3rd L.C.S.	S.O. 1st L.C.S.	S.L.	What are you going to steer ? Reply : I am steering S.E. Am altering to S.S.E. to go between the Enemy's fleet.	—
4.13 —	**Indomitable** -	**C.-in-C.** -	S.L.	**Have just heard Telefunken signals. Strength 4 at first, now 10.**	—
4.14 —	**C.-in-C.** -	**4th L.C.S.**	Flags	**Negative zigzag** - · · · ·	—
4.15 —	*S.O.2nd L.C.S.*	*Nottingham* -	S.L.	*Support Destroyers* - · · ·	—
4.15 —	**S.O.3rd B.C.S.**	**C.-in-C.** -	W/T	**My position, course and speed : 57° 39′ N., 5° 35′ E., S.S.E., 25 knots.**	1606
4.17 —	*Birmingham*·	*S.O. 2nd L.C.S.*	Sem.	*I am porting a little to give Nottingham and Destroyers room.*	—
4.17 —	**C.-in-C.** -	**S.O. 5th B.S.**·	W/T	**Are you in company with S.O. B.C.F. ?** - **Reply : Yes, I am engaging Enemy** -	1615 1630
4.18 —	*S.O. 5th B.S.*	*5th B.S.* -	Flags	*Ships in column to be three cables apart. Speed 24 knots.*	—
4.19 —	S.O.1st L.C.S.	S.O. 3rd L.C.S.	S.L.	Am I in your way ? Reply : My course S.S.E. Will you steer the same ?	1623

Date, Time of Despatch.	From	To	System.	Message.	Time of Origin.
31 MAY —*cont.*					
4.20 p.m.	Lion	—	—	Remarks : Queen Mary blew up	—
4.20 —	Captain S. Maidstone.	Admiralty	L/T	Lurcher reports being holed slightly aft, after collision with Submarine E. 53. If Submarines are required to remain over to-night, Wednesday, in position allotted, Lurcher can be relieved by Firedrake. Reply : Approved to relieve Lurcher.	—
4.25 —	*S.O.3rdL.C.S.*	3rd L.C.S.	Flags	*Alter course in succession to S.S.E.*	—
4.25 —	*Nottingham*	*S.O.2ndL.C.S.*	S.L.	*Am edging to starboard to keep smoke clear of Lion.*	—
4.25 —	**C.-in-C.**	**Battlefleet**	Sem.	**Keep just clear of wake of next ahead if it helps ships to keep up.**	1620
4.26 —	*S.O. B.C.F.*	*Princess Royal*	W/T	*Keep clear of smoke*	*1625*
4.27 —	S.O. 5th B.S.	Destroyers	Flags	Take station ahead	—
4.30 —	S.O.3rdL.C.S.	Galatea	S.L.	It seems that they are going through Horn Reef and not to Skager-Rack. Reply : Yes, I think so. If all Light Cruisers got together I think we could deal with Northern Squadron. I make them 16000.	1630
4.30 —	*S.O. 5th B.S.*	5th B.S.	Flags	*Subdivisions separately alter course in succession two points away from the Enemy preserving their formation.*	—
4.30 —	**Southampton**	C.-in-C., S.O., B.C.F.	W/T	**Urgent. One Enemy Cruiser bearing S.E., steering N.E. (My position Lat. 56° 38′ N., Long. 6° 07′ E.)**	1630
4.30 —	*Nottingham*	*S.O.2ndL.C.S.*	Sem.	*Two Cruisers S.S.E.*	—
4.30 —	Southampton	B.C.F.	S.L.	Enemy Destroyers attacking	—
4.30 —	*S.O. 5th B.S.*	5th B.S.	Flags	*Alter course together four points to port*	—
4.31 —	*S.O. 5th B.S.*	5th B.S.	Flags	*Negative alter course four points to port*	—
4.32 —	*Birmingham*	*S.O.2ndL.C.S.*	Sem.	*One four-funnelled Cruiser*	*1604*
4.33 —	Southampton	S.O. B.C.F.	S.L.	Battleships S.E.	—
4.34 —	*S.O.3rdL.C.S.*	3rd L.C.S.	Flags	*Form single line-ahead in sequence of fleet numbers. Ships in column open order.*	—
4.35 —	Southampton	—	—	Remarks : Challenged four-funnelled Cruiser bearing S.E. No reply.	—
4.38 —	**Southampton**	C.-in-C., S.O., B.C.F.	W/T	**Urgent. Priority. Have sighted Enemy battlefleet bearing approximately S.E., course of Enemy N. My position Lat. 56° 34′ N., Long. 6° 20′ E.**	1638
4.38 —	**C.-in-C.**	**S.O. 10th C.S.**	W/T	**10th C.S. take up Eastern patrol**	1638
4.38 —	Champion	S.O. B.C.F.	W/T	Course of Enemy's battlefleet is E.N.E. single line-ahead. Van Dreadnoughts. Bearing of centre S.E. My position Lat. 56° 51′ N., Long. 5° 46′ E.	1630
4.40 —	S.O.3rdL.C.S.	S.O. 1st L.C.S.	S.L.	When your squadron have passed me I will edge over.	1637
4.40 —	*S.O. 1st C.S.*	*1st C.S.*	S.L.	*Am steering S.E. to close Minotaur*	*1635*
'.40 —	*S.O. 5th B.S.*	*5th B.S.*	Flags	*Subdivisions separately alter course in succession two points away from the Enemy preserving their formation.*	—

Date, Time of Despatch.	From	To	System.	Message.	Time of Origin.
31 MAY *—cont.*					
4.40 p.m.	*S.O. 5th B.S.*	*5th B.S.* -	Flags	*Concentrate in pairs from the rear* - -	—
4.40 —	S.O. B.C.F.	General -	Flags	Alter course in succession 16 points to starboard.	—
4.41 —	*S.O.3rdL.C.S.*	*3rd L.C.S.* -	Flags	*Admiral intends to proceed at 22 knots* -	—
4.42 —	Lion - -	—	—	Remarks: Sighted Enemy battlefleet ahead	—
4.43 —	*Duke of Edinburgh.*	*Black Prince* -	S.L.	*Am steering S.E. to close Defence* - -	*1640*
4.43 —	S.O. B.C.F.	Destroyers -	Flags	Recall - - - -	—
4.45 —	*S.O.2ndL.C.S.*	*Birmingham* -	S.L.	*Turn* - - - -	—
4.45 —	*S.O. B.C.F.*	*Princess Royal*	Sem.	*Report Enemy's battlefleet to C.-in-C. bearing S.E.*	—
4.45 —	**S.O. B.C.F.** -	**C.-in-C.** via Princess Royal.	W/T	**Urgent. Priority. Have sighted Enemy's battlefleet bearing S.E. My position Lat. 56° 36' N., Long. 6° 04' E.** (*Received by C.-in-C. as 26–30 Battleships, probably hostile, bearing S.S.E., steering S.E.*)	**1645**
4.45 —	Commodore T	Admiralty -	L/T	314. Have you any instructions? - -	1645
4.45 —	*S.O. 5th B.S.*	*5th B.S.* -	Flags	*Form single line-ahead* - - - -	—
4.45 —	S.O. B.C.F.	General -	Flags	Have sighted Enemy battlefleet bearing S.E.	—
4.47 —	**C.-in-C.** -	**General** -	Sem.	**Enemy's battlefleet is coming North** -	**1645**
4.47 —	S.O. B.C.F.	Fearless -	Flags	Pick up men in water round us - -	—
4.48 —	**Southampton**	**S.O. B.C.F., C.-in-C.**	W/T	**Urgent. Priority. Course of Enemy's battlefleet, N., single line-ahead. Composition of van Kaiser class. Bearing of centre, E. Destroyers on both wings and ahead. Enemy's Battle Cruisers joining battlefleet from Northward. My position Lat. 56° 29' N., Long. 6° 14' E.**	**1646**
4.48 —	S.O. B.C.F.	5th B.S. -	Flags	Alter course in succession 16 points to starboard.	—
4.50 —	*S.O.3rdB.C.S.*	*3rd B.C.S.* -	Flags	*Alter course in succession to S. by E.* -	—
4.50 —	Lion - -	—	—	Remarks : Passed 5th Battle squadron steering on opposite course.	—
4.50 —	*Commodore F.*	*Destroyers* -	Sem.	*Destroyers keep an extra look out for Submarines.*	—
4.50 —	S.O. B.C.F.	Destroyers -	Flags	Close and take station ahead - - -	—
4.51 —	**C.-in-C.** -	**Admiralty** -	W/T	**Urgent. Fleet action is imminent** -	**1650**
4.52 —	S.O. B.C.F.	General -	Flags	Admiral intends to proceed at 25 knots -	—
4.52 —	S.O.3rdL.C.S.	S.O. 1st L.C.S.	S.L.	Look out for Enemy battlefleet steering N.	1630
4.55 —	*S.O.4thL.C.S.*	*4th L.C.S.* -	Flags	*Admiral intends to proceed at 19½ knots* -	—
4.55 —	*S.O. 5th B.S.*	*5th B.S.* -	Flags	*Observe attentively the Admiral's motions*	—
4.55 —	S.O. B.C.F.	Captain D., 1st and 13th, via Princess Royal	W/T	Destroyers close nearer Admiral - - (*Received by Champion 5.18 p.m.*)	1650

Date, Time of Despatch.	From	To	System.	Message.	Time of Origin.
31 MAY —*cont.*					
4.56 p.m.	S.O.3rdB.C.S.	S.O. B.C.F.	W/T	What is your position, course and speed?	1655
4.58 —	*S.O.1stL.C.S.*	*Inconstant*	S.L.	*Edge across Falmouth's bows as soon as you can.*	*1640*
5.0 —	*S.O.3rdL.C.S.*	*3rd L.C.S.*	Flags	*Admiral intends to proceed at 25 knots*	—
5.0 —	Lion	—	—	Remarks : Sighted 1st and 3rd L.C.S. on starboard bow.	—
5.0 —	*S.O.2ndL.C.S.*	*2nd L.C.S.*	Flags	*Alter course in succession to N.N.W.*	—
5.0 —	**Admiralty**	**C.-in-C.**	W/T	**At 4.9 p.m. Enemy battlefleet Lat. 56° 27′ N., Long. 6° 18′ E., course N.W. 15 knots.**	**1700**
5.0 —	S.O. 3rd B.S.	Admiralty	W/T	Urgent. I am proceeding to Black Deep light vessel.	1700
5.0 —	**Southampton**	**C.-in-C., S.O. B.C.F.**	W/T	**Enemy's battlefleet is steering N., bearing from me E., 10 to 11 miles distant. Position Lat. 56° 33′ N., Long. 6° 00′ E.**	**1700**
5.1 —	S.O. B.C.F.	5th B.S.	Flags	Prolong the line by taking station astern	—
5.2 —	S.O.3rdL.C.S.	S.O. 1st L.C.S.	S.L.	I am keeping up to keep clear of Battle Cruisers.	1700
5.4 —	**C.-in-C.**	**Attached Cruisers.**	Flags	**Take up station for the approach**	—
5.5 —	*S.O. 5th B.S.*	*5th B.S.*	Flags	*Engage the Enemy's right from 1 to 4*	—
5.5 —	*S.O.3rdL.C.S.*	*3rd L.C.S.*	Flags	*Form single line-ahead in sequence you now are.*	—
5.7 —	*Nottingham*	*S.O. 2nd L.C.S.*	S.L.	*Rear division of Enemy appears to have altered this way.*	*1700*
5.8 —	*Nestor*	*Captain D13*	W/T	*All torpedoes fired, speed reduced to 17 knots*	*1705*
5.10 —	*S.O. B.C.F.*	*General*	Flags	*Admiral intends to proceed at 24 knots*	—
5.10 —	*S.O. 5th B.S.*	*5th B.S.*	Flags	*Admiral intends to proceed at 25 knots*	—
5.12 —	S.O.3rdL.C.S.	S.O. 1st L.C.S.	S.L.	Can you see what Enemy's Cruisers are doing astern of us? Reply : No. I can see nothing of them.	1712
5.12 —	*S.O.3rdL.C.S.*	*3rd L.C.S.*	Flags	*Alter course in succession to N.W. by N.*	—
5.14 —	Warspite	—	—	Remarks : Hit	—
5.15 —	Admiralty	Commodore T.	L/T	Your 314. Complete with fuel. You may have to relieve Light Cruisers and Destroyers in B.C.F. later.	1715
5.15 —	Commodore T.	Admiralty	L/T	315. Priority. Urgent. I am proceeding to sea.	1710
5.16 —	**C.-in-C.**	**S.O. B.C.F.**	W/T	**My position Lat. 57° 25′ N., Long. 5° 12′ E., steering S.E. by S., speed 20 knots.**	**1713**
5.17 —	**C.-in-C.**	**Thunderer**	S.L.	**Can you pass Conqueror? If so, do so**	**1715**
5.20 —	**Canada**	**C.-in-C.**	Sem.	**Have intercepted hoists of code, apparently German. Call signs RA. RA. VT. ZIZ.**	**1710**
5.20 —	S.O. B.C.F.	Destroyers	Flags	Form a Submarine screen	—
5.20 —	Warspite	—	—	Remarks : Sighted Enemy's battlefleet	—
5.20 —	*S.O.3rdL.C.S.*	*3rd L.C.S.*	Flags	*Alter course in succession to N.N.W.*	—
5.21 —	*S.O.3rdL.C.S.*	*Gloucester*	S.L.	*Can you see Enemy Cruisers right astern? Reply : Yes, I think they are firing at us, but are 1,000 yards short.*	*1720*

Date, Time of Despatch.	From	To	System.	Message.	Time of Origin.
31 MAY *—cont.*					
5.22 p.m.	*Tiger* - -	*S.O.1stB.C.S.*	Sem.	*After 6-inch magazine flooded, two guns out of action.*	*1725*
5.25 —	S.O. B.C.F.	General -	Flags	Prepare to renew the action - - -	—
5.25 —	S.O. Cruisers	Owl - -	Flags	Take station on the present bearing five cables.	—
5.30 —	S.O. B.C.F.	S.O.3rdB.C.S.	W/T	Check and repeat 1655. S.O. B.C.F. from S.O. 3rd B.C.S. (*Repeated 5.55 p.m.*)	1655
5.30 —	*S.O.1stL.C.S.*	1st L.C.S. -	Flags	*Ships to be in open order* - - -	—
5.30 —	*S.O. 5th B.S.*	5th B.S. -	Flags	*Proceed at your utmost speed* - - -	—
5.30 —	Admiralty -	C.-in-C. Nore	L/T	With reference to A.L.M. 0782 of 24th February, 1915. Hold tugs in readiness.	1730
5.30 —	Falmouth -	—	—	Remarks : Sighted Cruisers port bow -	—
5.30 —	Admiralty -	C.-in-C.,Rosyth	L/T	With reference to A.L.M. 0782 of 13th February, 1915, hold tugs in readiness. Not necessary to do so at Clyde with reference to A.L.M. 0782 of 24th February 1915.	1730
5.32 —	*Captain D12*	*12th Flotilla* -	Sem.	*If fleet deploys to port L.T. will be formed. 1st and 2nd divisions forming on starboard and port quarter of Faulknor, and 3rd division astern of Marksman. If deployment is to starboard L.T.1 will be formed, order from port to starboard being 1st, 2nd and 3rd Divisions.*	*1745*
5.32 —	Canterbury -	S.O.3rdB.C.S.	S.L.	Can see flashes ahead - - - -	—
5.34 —	Indomitable	—	—	Remarks : Invincible opened fire - -	—
5.35 —	S.O. B.C.F.	General -	S.L.	Alter course in succession to N.N.E. -	—
5.35 —	Admiralty -	Commodore Harwich ; V.A. Dover.	L/T	With reference to Admiralty letter M 07593 of the 3rd February, 1916. Hold tugs in readiness.	1735
5.35 —	Admiralty -	Commodore T.	W/T	Your 315. Return at once and await orders	1725
5.35 —	Indomitable	—	—	Remarks : Sighted ships firing on starboard quarter.	—
5.35 —	S.O.1stL.C.S.	S.O. B.C.F. -	W/T	Submit Submarine passed in Lat. 57° 05' N., Long. 5° 12' E., at 3.40 p.m.	1735
5.35 —	*S.O.2ndL.C.S.*	2nd L.C.S. -	Flags	*Close and form single line-ahead* - -	—
5.36 —	Falmouth -	Black Prince	S.L.	Battle Cruisers engaged to the S.S.W. of me.	1735
5.38 —	S.O.3rdB.C.S.	Destroyers -	Flags	Close - - - - - -	—
5.40 —	Orion - -	—	—	Remarks : Centre ship of 1st C.S. opened fire.	—
5.40 —	Indomitable	—	—	Remarks : 3rd B.C.S. altered course towards Enemy without signal.	—
5.40 —	Inflexible -	—	—	Remarks : Enemy Light Cruisers port bow	—
5.40 —	S.O. B.C.F.	General -	Flags	Open fire and engage the Enemy - -	—
5.40 —	Admiralty -	C.-in-C.Rosyth	L/T	Referring A.L.M. 03287 13th May, 1915, despatch A.P. vessels for patrol as arranged.	1740

Date, Time of Despatch.	From	To	System.	Message.	Time of Origin.
31 MAY 5.40 p.m.	*—cont.* **Minotaur** -	**C.-in-C.** -	S.L.	**Report of guns heard South** - - - (*Reports were also received from Hampshire and Comus.*)	—
5.40 —	**R.A. Scapa** -	Aberdeen -	W/T	From S.N.O. Blyth. For C.-in-C. Submarine patrol are to return p.m. 1st June should they be ordered to remain as no relief at present available. (*Received in Iron Duke, 11.55 p.m.*)	1540
5.40 —	Galatea -	S.O. B.C.F. -	W/T	Enemy Battle Cruisers altering course to starboard. (*Time of receipt not shown in Lion's log.*)	1740
5.40 —	Southampton	C.-in-C., S.O. B.C.F.	W/T	Urgent. Priority. The Enemy's battlefleet have altered course N.N.W. My position Lat. 56° 46′ N., Long. 5° 40′ E.	1740
5.40 —	Admiralty -	S.N.O., Jarrow, R.A. Invergordon, R.A.EastCoast	L/T	With reference to A.L.M. 0782 of 13th February, 1915. Hold tugs in readiness.	1740
5.40 —	*S.O. 2nd C.S.*	*Shannon* -	S.L.	*I think you had better keep your Destroyer within half a mile and give her a position.*	*1736*
5.42 —	*S.O. 1st C.S.*	*1st C.S.* -	Flags	*Close* - - -	—
5.42 —	**Black Prince**	**C.-in-C.** and **S.O. 2nd C.S.**	W/T	Enemy Battle Cruisers bearing South five miles. My position Lat. 56° 59′ N., Long. 5° 24′ E.	1740
5.45 —	S.O. 2nd C.S.	Owl - -	Sem.	Minotaur's position at 5 p.m. 57° 18′, 5° 38′, course S.E. by S., 21 knots.	1740
5.45 —	S.O.2ndL.C.S.	Warspite and Barham.	S.L.	Enemy torpedo craft are approaching from E.S.E.	—
5.45 —	**Admiralty** -	**C.-in-C.** -	W/T	Enemy main force at 4.30 p.m. 56° 31′ N., 6° 5′ E., steering N. 15 knots. (*Received in Iron Duke, 5.53 p.m.*)	1745
5.45 —	Canterbury -	—	—	Remarks : Cruiser Kolberg class and Destroyers starboard bow.	—
5.46 —	**S.O. 1st C.S.**	**S.O. 2nd C.S. C.-in-C.**	W/T and S.L.	Ships in action bearing S.S.W., steering N.E. My position Lat. 57° 07′ N., Long. 5° 38′ E.	1745
5.47 —	S.O. B.C.F.	Light Cruisers	Flags	Attack the Enemy with torpedoes -	—
5.48 —	Falmouth -	S.O. Cruisers	S.L.	Two heavy Enemy ships bearing S.S.E., steering N.E. My position Lat. 57° 07′ N., Long. 5° 45′ E.	1745
5.50 —	**Calliope** -	**C.-in-C.** -	S.L.	**Have observed what appears to be flashes of guns S.S.W.**	—
5.50 —	**S.O. 1st B.S.**	**C.-in-C.** -	Sem.	**Gunflashes and heavy gun firing on starboard bow.**	—
5.50 —	Admiralty -	S.N.O. Invergordon,C.-in-C. Rosyth, Ad. Supt. Tyne.	L/T	Fleet action imminent. All docks should be ready in case they are required for vessels of the fleet.	1750
5.50 —	Southampton	C.-in-C., S.O. B.C.F.	W/T	Urgent. Priority. Enemy battlefleet has altered course to N. Enemy Battle Cruisers bear S.W. from Enemy battlefleet. My position Lat. 56° 50′ N., Long. 5 44′ E.	1750
5.50 —	Duke of Edinburgh.	—	—	Remarks : Defence opened fire at Enemy	—
5.52 —	Canterbury -	—	—	Remarks : Opened fire - -	—
5.53 —	*Captain D12*	*12th Flotilla* -	Sem.	*Keep a good look-out for Enemy Submarines*	—

Date, Time of Despatch.	From	To	System.	Message.	Time of Origin.
31 MAY — *cont.*					
5.53 p.m.	S.O. 1st C.S.	*Warrior* -	Flags	*Open fire and engage the Enemy* ·	—
5.53 —	Benbow ·	—	—	Remarks : Firing reported off starboard bow.	—
5.55 —	Inconstant ·	—	—	Remarks : Battlefleet sighted · · ·	—
5.55 —	S.O. B.C.F.	General ·	Flags	Admiral intends to proceed at 25 knots ·	—
5.55 —	**C.-in-C.** ·	**Marlborough** ·	S.L.	**What can you see? Reply : Our Battle Cruisers bearing S.S.W., steering East, Lion leading ship.**	1800
				Further reply from Marlborough : 5th B.S. bearing S.W.	1805
5.55 —	S.O. 3rd B.C.S.	3rd B.C.S. ·	Flags	*Open fire and engage the Enemy* · ·	—
5.56 —	S.O. B.C.F.	General ·	Flags	*Alter course in succession to N.E. by E. Speed 25 knots.*	—
5.56 —	Indomitable	—	—	Remarks : Inflexible and Indomitable opened fire.	—
5.56 —	Colossus ·	—	—	Remarks : Battle Cruisers (British) sighted starboard bow.	—
5.58 —	S.O.4thL.C.S.	4th L.C.S. ·	Flags	*Close* · · · · · ·	—
5.59 —	**C.-in-C.** ·	**Oak** · ·	Flags	**Take up approach station** · · ·	—
6.0 —	Cordelia ·	—	—	Remarks : Lion appeared on fire forward	—
6.0 —	Indomitable	—	—	Remarks : Enemy three-funnelled Cruiser out of action.	—
6.0 —	R.A. 1st B.S.	5th Division ·	Sem.	*Remember traditions of glorious 1st of June and avenge Belgium.*	1730
6.0 —	Warspite ·	—	—	Remarks : Not under control signal hoisted.	—
6.0 —	Caroline ·	S.O.4thL.C.S.	Sem.	*Smoke bearing South four columns, can hear firing 2nd L.C.S.*	1740
6.0 —	S.O.4thL.C.S.	4th L.C.S. ·	Flags	*Form single line-abreast to starboard, ships to be five cables apart.*	—
6.0 —	S.O. 5th B.S.	5th B.S. ·	Flags	*Enemy in sight. S.S.E. Battlefleet* ·	—
6.0 —	S.O. Cruisers	Cruisers ·	Flags	*Alter course in succession to N.E. Proceed at your utmost speed.*	—
6.0 —	S.O. Cruisers	Cruisers ·	S.L.	*Form single line-ahead in the sequence in which ships now are. Open fire South.*	—
6.0 —	S.O. B.C.F.	General ·	Flags	Alter course in succession to E. · ·	—
6.1 —	**C.-in-C.** ·	**S.O. B.C.F.** ·	S.L.	**Where is Enemy's B.F.?** (*Repeated at 6.10*) **Reply : Have sighted Enemy's battlefleet bearing S.S.W.** (*Received in Iron Duke 6.14 p.m.*)	—
6.2 —	**C.-in-C.** ·	**General** · ·	Flags	**Alter course leading ships together, rest in succession to South. Speed 18 knots.**	—
6.2 —	Captain D, 1st Flotilla.	1st Flotilla ·	Flags	*Close* · · · · · · ·	—
6.2 —	S.O.1stL.C.S.	S.O. 3rd L.C.S.	Sem.	I was told to keep touch with Battle Cruisers. It seems to be getting a bit thick this end. What had we better do ?	1800
6.3 —	Southampton	C.-in-C. and S.O. B.C.F.	W/T	**Urgent. Have lost sight of Enemy's battlefleet. Am engaging the Enemy's Battle Cruisers. My position is Lat. 56° 57′ N., Long. 5° 43′ E., course N.N.E., speed 26 knots.**	1800

Date, Time of Despatch.	From	To	System.	Message.	Time of Origin.
31 MAY —*cont.*					
6.5 p.m.	S.O.3rd B.C.S	3rd B.C.S.	Flags	*Disregard the Admiral's motions*	—
6.5 —	Strange T.B.D.	Engadine	S.L.	Whole Hun battlefleet coming up, steering N. by E.	—
6.6 —	**C.-in-C.**	**General**	Flags	**Alter course leading ships together the rest in succession to S.E.**	—
6.6 —	**Lion**	**C.-in-C.**	S.L.	**Enemy's B.Cs. bearing S.E.**	—
6.6 —	S.O. B.C.F.	S.O. 3rd B.C.S.	W/T	My position is Lat. 55° 58′ N., Long. 5° 37′ E., course E., speed 25 knots.	1805
6.6 —	*S.O.4th L.C.S.*	4th L.C.S.	Flags	*Admiral intends to proceed at 18 knots*	—
6.7 —	*S.O. Cruisers*	*Cruisers*	S.L.	*Cease fire*	—
6.8 —	New Zealand	—	—	Remarks : Sighted Grand Fleet on port bow.	—
6.8 —	**C.-in-C.**	**Destroyers**	Flags	**Take up Destroyer disposition No. 1**	—
6.9 —	Duke of Edinburgh.	—	—	Remarks : Duke of Edinburgh opened fire	—
6.10 —	Indomitable	—	—	Remarks : Sighted battlefleet starboard side.	—
6.10 —	**Barham**	**C.-in-C.**	Flags and W/T	**Enemy's battlefleet S.S.E.**	—
6.10 —	Duke of Edinburgh.	—	—	Remarks : Enemy Cruiser appeared to be hit and on fire.	—
6.10 —	*S.O.4th L.C.S.*	4th L.C.S.	Flags	*Form single line ahead in sequence of fleet numbers.*	—
6.10 —	*Tipperary*	*Commodore F.*	Sem.	*Are you W. or V. ? Reply V.*	—
6.10 —	*S.O. Cruisers*	*Cochrane*	S.L.	*2nd C.S. form single line ahead in sequence of fleet numbers. Admiral intends to proceed at 21 knots. Cease fire.*	—
6.10 —	*S.O. 2nd C.S.*	*Shannon*	Sem.	*I am going round to take up position in the van for Easterly deployment.*	1810
6.11 —	*S.O.4th L.C.S.*	4th L.C.S.	Flags	*Alter course together 16 points to starboard.*	—
6.12 —	*Captain D12*	12th Flotilla	Flags	*Take up cruising order L.T.*	—
6.12 —	S.O.3rd B.C.S.	S.O. 3rd L.C.S.	S.L.	Where is Lion ?	—
6.13 —	*S.O. 2nd C.S.*	*Hampshire*	S.L.	*Can you see our battlefleet, and which way are they steering ?*	1812
6.14 —	*S.O.5th B.S.*	5th B.S.	Flags	*Form single line-ahead in sequence in which ships now are.*	—
6.14 —	*Commodore F.*	11th Flotilla	Flags	*Take up cruising order No. 2, speed 25 knots.*	—
6.15 —	Indomitable	Indomitable and Inflexible.	Flags	*Form single line-ahead in the sequence in which ships now are.*	—
6 15 —	*Indomitable*	—	—	*Remarks : Invincible resumed Guide of fleet*	—
6.15 —	**C.-in-C.**	**General**	Flags and W/T	**The column nearest S.E. by E. is to alter course in succession to that point of the compass, the remaining columns altering course leading ships together the rest in succession so as to form astern of that column, maintaining the speed of the Fleet.**	—
6.15 —	Inflexible	—	—	Remarks : Altered course to avoid torpedo	—
6 15 —	*S.O. 2nd C.S.*	*2nd C.S.*	Flags S.L.	*Form single line-ahead in sequence of fleet numbers. Ships in column to be in open order.*	—

Date, Time of Despatch.	From	To	System.	Message.	Time of Origin.
31 MAY *—cont.* 6.15 p.m.	Fearless	—	—	Remarks: Large explosion seen in Enemy's line. 6.17. Further explosion seen.	—
6.17 —	S.O. 2nd C.S.	Destroyers	Flags	Form Submarine screen -	—
6.17 —	Commodore F.	11th Flotilla	Flags	1st Division take station astern. 2nd Division take station on port quarter.	—
6.18 —	S.O. 5th B.S.	5th B.S.	Flags	Alter course in succession 16 points to port-	—
6.19 —	C.-in-C.	S.Os. in company. (Call sign of S.O. 3rd B.C.S. apparently used.)	W/T	Priority. Present course of fleet S.E. by E.	1815
6.21 —	Commodore F.	Active -	Sem.	Keep out of way of Destroyers -	—
6.21 —	S.O. B.C.F -	General	Flags	Admiral intends to proceed at 26 knots -	—
6.22 —	Hampshire -	S.O. 2nd C.S.-	S.L.	Our battlefleet appears to be standing to the Southward bearing S.W. by.W.	1810
6.22 —	S.O.4th L.C.S.	4th L.C.S.	Flags	Alter course together to S.E. by E. -	—
6.22 —	S.O.4th L.C.S.	4th L.C.S.	Flags	Form single line-ahead in sequence of fleet numbers. Speed 25 knots.	—
6.23 —	C.-in-C.	11th Flotilla -	Flags	Present course of the fleet is S.E. by E -	1815
6.24 —	Southampton	C.-in-C. - S.O. B.C.F.	W/T	Enemy battlefleet bear 10 to 11 miles S.S.E. Course of Enemy battlefleet N.E. My position Lat. 56° 58′ N., Long. 5° 51′ E.	1820
6 24 —	S.O.4th B.S.	4th Division -	Flags	Open fire and engage the Enemy -	—
6.25 —	S.O. 2nd C.S.	Hampshire -	S.L.	Close Minotaur -	—
6.26 —	S.O.3rd B.C.S	3rd B.C.S. -	Flags	Admiral intends to proceed at 20 knots -	—
6.26 —	C.-in-C.	Dreadnought Battlefleet and attached Cruisers.	W/T and Flags	Admiral intends to proceed at 14 knots	—
6.27 —	S.O.1st L.C.S.	Inconstant	S.L.	My speed has been reduced to 18 knots. Go on with 1st L.C.S. and try and get ahead of battlefleet.	—
6.27 —	Lion -	C.-in-C. via van Battleship and 4th L.C.S.	S.L.	Enemy battlefleet in sight bearing South, the nearest ship is distant seven miles.	1818
6.27 —	S.O. 2nd C.S.	Destroyers -	Flags	Form single line-ahead in sequence of fleet numbers. Take station on the port beam of Minotaur, one mile.	—
6.29 —	S.O.3rd B.C.S.	3rd B.C.S. -	Flags	Open fire -	—
6.29 —	C.-in-C.	Dreadnought Battlefleet and attached Cruisers.	W/T and Flags	Subdivisions separately alter course in succession to S.S.E., preserving their formation. (Negatived.)	—
6.29 —	Commodore F.	11th Flotilla -	Flags	Alter course in succession to E.S.E. Speed 20 knots.	—
6.30 —	S.O. 1st L.C.S.	1st L.C.S. -	Flags	1st L.C.S. join Inconstant -	—
6.30 —	R.A. 1st B.S.	5th Division -	Flags	Open fire and engage the Enemy -	—

Date, Time of Despatch.	From	To	System.	Message.	Time of Origin.
31 MAY —*cont.*					
6.30 p.m.	Inflexible -	—	—	Remarks : Invincible blew up -	—
6.33 —	**C.-in-C.** -	**General**	Flags	**Admiral intends to proceed at 17 knots** -	—
6.33 —	Benbow -	—	—	Remarks : Benbow's first gun fired. B turret.	—
6.35 —	Inconstant -	Phaeton and Cordelia.	Flags	Take station astern of Inconstant - -	—
6.35 —	Indomitable -	S.O. B.C.F. -	S.L.	What speed are you going ? Reply : 15 knots.	—
6.35 —	S.O. 2nd C.S.	2nd C.S. -	Sem.	Keep me informed of movements of our own battlefleet.	1830
6.37 —	Commodore F.	11th Flotilla -	Flags	Admiral intends to proceed at 14 knots -	—
6.37 —	Princess Royal.	S.O. B.C.F. -	S.L.	Following received : Present course of fleet is S.E. by E.	—
6.38 —	S.O. Cruisers.	Cruisers -	Flags	Alter course in succession to S.S.E. -	—
6.39 —	Commodore F.	11th Flotilla -	Flags	Admiral intends to proceed at 12 knots -	—
6.39 —	S.O. B.C.F. -	Indomitable -	S.L.	What speed are you going ? Reply : 25	—
6.40 —	S.O. B.C.F. -	Badger - -	S.L.	Pick up men from ship on starboard hand	—
6.40 —	Commodore F.	11th Flotilla -	Flags	Alter course together two points to port -	—
6.40 —	S.O. 1st B.S.-	Colossus -	Sem.	Why are you hauling out of line ? - - (Note.—Made three times, no reply.)	—
6.40 —	Engadine -	—	—	Remarks : Sighted Warrior in damaged condition.	—
6.40 —	Canterbury -	—	—	Remarks : Shark or Fortune hit and on fire.	—
6.40 —	S.O. 4th L.C.S.	4th L.C.S. -	Flags	Admiral intends to proceed at 22 knots -	—
6.40 —	S.O.2nd L.C.S.	Birmingham -	Flags	Close - - - -	—
6.40 —	Benbow -	—	—	Remarks : Acasta in danger of sinking -	—
6.40 —	S.O. B.C.F. -	S.O. 3rd L.C.S.	S.L.	What is bearing of Enemy's Battle Cruisers ? Reply : Last seen 1820. Altered course to W., engaged by 3rd B.C.S.	1845
6.40 —	Hampshire -	S.O. 2nd C.S.-	S.L.	Shall I take station in the line ? Reply : Yes, take station astern of Shannon.	—
6.41 —	Indomitable -	S.O. B.C.F. -	S.L.	Invincible has sunk - - - -	—
6.42 —	Commodore F.	11th Flotilla -	Flags	Alter course together two points to starboard	—
6.42 —	S.O. B.C.F. -	Destroyers -	—	Destroyers take station ahead-	—
6.42 —	S.O. 2nd C.S.	Hampshire -	Flags	Take station 2½ cables astern of Shannon -	—
6.43 —	S.O.4th L.C.S.	4th L.C.S. -	Flags	Admiral intends to proceed at 20 knots -	—
6.43 —	S.O. 2nd C.S.	2nd C.S. -	Flags	Form single line-ahead in the sequence in which ships now are.	—
6.43 —	S.O.4th L.C.S.	4th L.C.S. -	Flags	Alter course together 12 points to starboard-	—
6.44 —	**C.-in-C.** -	**Dreadnought Battlefleet and attached Cruisers.**	W/T and Flags	**Divisions separately alter course in succession to S.E., preserving their formation.**	—

Date, Time of Despatch.	From	To	System.	Message.	Time of Origin.
31 MAY —cont.					
6.45 p.m.	S.O. 1st L.C.S.	Inconstant -	S.L.	All right now. Am coming on at 22 knots. Do not wait for me.	—
6.45 —	Commodore F.	11th Flotilla -	Flags	Alter course together four points to starboard	—
6.45 —	Commodore F.	11th Flotilla -	Flags	Admiral intends to proceed at 22 knots	—
6.45 —	Indomitable -	3rd B.C.S.	Flags	Admiral intends to proceed at 15 knots	—
6.46 —	New Zealand	—	—	Remarks : Sighted 3rd B.C.S. one point on starboard bow.	
6.46 —	S.O. 4th L.C.S	4th L.C.S.	Flags	Admiral intends to proceed at 18 knots	—
6.46 —	Captain D12	12th Flotilla -	Flags	Alter course in succession to S.E., speed 17 knots.	
6.47 —	Commodore F.	11th Flotilla	Flags	Admiral intends to proceed at 25 knots	—
6.48 —	S.O. 4th L.C.S.	4th L.C.S.	Flags	Alter course together 12 points to port	
6.50 —	Marlborough	—	—	Remarks : Marlborough struck starboard side.	—
6.50 —	Commodore F.	11th Flotilla -	Flags	Alter course together two points to port	
6.50 —	S.O. B.C.F. -	General	Flags and S.L.	3rd B.C.S. prolong the line astern -	—
6.51 —	Indomitable	3rd B.C.S.	Flags	Form single line ahead	—
6.51 —	S.O. 4th L.C.S.	4th L.C.S.	Flags	Alter course in succession to S.S.E. -	—
6.52 —	S.O. 4th L.C.S	4th L.C.S.	Flags	Admiral intends to proceed at 22 knots	—
6.52 —	S.O. 4th L.C.S	Champion	S.L.	Am going round starboard bow of King George V.	—
6.53 —	S.O. B.C.F.	General	Flags	Admiral intends to proceed at 18 knots	—
6.53 —	Commodore F.	11th Flotilla	Flags	Form astern and follow in the wake of your divisional Guides.	
6.54 —	C.-in-C.	S.O. B.C.F., S.O. 3rd B.C.S., S.O. 2nd C.S.	W/T	**Present course of fleet is South**	1854
6.54 —	S.O. B.C.F. -	C.-in-C.	W/T	**Submarine in sight in position Lat. 57° 02′ N., Long. 6° 24′ E.**	1845
6.54 —	Commodore F.	11th Flotilla -	Flags	Alter course together four points to starboard	—
6.55 —	Indomitable -	Inflexible	Sem.	Thank you for a good lead	—
6.55 —	Engadine -	Warrior	S.L.	Can I do anything for you ? Reply : Stand by me.	—
6.55 —	C.-in-C.	Dreadnought Battlefleet and attached Cruisers.	W/T and Flags	**Alter course leading ships together the rest in succession to South.**	—
6.55 —	C.-in-C.	S.O. 1st B.S.	S.L.	**Can you see any Enemy Battleships ? Reply : No.**	1850
6.56 —	Commodore F.	11th Flotilla -	Flags	Admiral intends to proceed at 20 knots	—
6.56 —	Captain D13	S.O. 4th L.C.S.	S.L.	You are blanketing me	—
6.57 —	Captain D12	12th Flotilla -	Flags	Alter course in succession two points to port	—

Date, Time of Despatch.	From	To	System.	Message.	Time of Origin.
31 MAY *—cont.* 6.57 p.m.	*Commodore F.*	*11th Flotilla* -	Flags	*Alter course together two points to starboard*	—
6.57 —	**Marlborough**	**C.-in-C.** -	W/T	**Urgent. Have been struck by a mine or torpedo, but not certain which.**	1855
6.58 —	**Marlborough**	**C.-in-C.** -	W/T	**Urgent. Have been struck by a torpedo** -	1857
6.58 —	*S.O.3rd L.C.S*	*3rd L.C.S.* -	Flags	*Form single line-ahead in sequence of fleet numbers.*	—
6.59 —	*Commodore F.*	*11th Flotilla* -	Flags	*Admiral intends to proceed at 25 knots* -	—
7.0 —	**K. G. V.** -	**C.-in-C.** -	S.L.	**There is a Submarine ahead of you** -	1859
7.0 —	Warrior -	Engadine -	S.L.	Both engine rooms are full of steam. Please keep close by me, port quarter.	—
7.0 —	S.O. B.C.F. -	Destroyers -	Flags	Form Submarine screen No. 3 - - -	—
7.0 — (received)	**S.O. B.C.F.** -	**C.-in-C.** -	S.L.	**Enemy are to Westward** - - -	1755
7.0 —	Benbow -	—	—	Remarks : Passed Invincible—Destroyer rescuing survivors.	
7.0 —	*Commodore F.*	*11th Flotilla* -	Flags	*Admiral intends to proceed at 20 knots* -	—
7.0 —	*Commodore F.*	*11th Florilla* -	Flags	*Alter course together two points to starboard*	—
7.0 —	*Captain D12*	*12th Flotilla* -	Flags	*Alter course in succession to South* - -	—
7.0 —	Canterbury -	S.O. 3rd L.C.S.	Sem.	May I join up with you ? Reply : Yes. -	—
7.0 —	*S.O. 4th L.C.S*	*4th L.C.S.* -	Flags	*Admiral intends to proceed at 25 knots* -	—
7.0 —	*S.O. 5th B.S.*	*5th B.S.* -	Flags	*Admiral intends to proceed at 18 knots* -	—
7.1 —	Duke of Edinburgh.	General -	Flags	Submarine on port side, two points from right ahead.	—
7.3 —	**C.-in-C.** -	**Badger** -	S.L.	**Is wreck one of our ships ? Reply : Yes, Invincible.**	—
7.3 —	**Iron Duke** -	—	—	**Remarks : Passed Invincible bottom up. Badger standing by.**	—
7.4 —	Colossus -	—	—	Remarks : Marlborough hauled out of line to starboard.	—
7.4 —	Southampton	S.O. B.C.F. -	W/T	Urgent. Priority. Enemy battlefleet steering E.S.E. Enemy bears from me S.S.W. Number unknown. My position Lat. 57° 02′ N., Long. 6° 07′ E (*Received in Iron Duke 7.0 p.m.*)	1900
7.4 —	*S.O. 4th L.C.S.*	*4th L.C.S.* -	Flags	*Admiral intends to proceed at 20 knots*	—
7.4 —	*Commodore F.*	*11th Flotilla* -	Flags	*Alter course together eight points to port*	—
7.5 —	*Captain D12*	*12th Flotilla* -	Flags	*Alter course together three points to starboard*	—
7.5 —	*Commodore F.*	*11th Flotilla* -	Flags	*Cruising order No. 2. Course South* -	—
7.5 —	**C.-in-C.** -	**Dreadnought Battlefleet and attached Cruisers.**	W/T and Flags	**Alter course together three points to starboard.**	—
7.8 —	Fearless -	—	—	Remarks : Galatea took Acasta in tow. 7.10, Galatea slippped Acasta.	—
7.8 —	*S.O. 4th L.C.S.*	*4th L.C.S.* -	Flags	*Alter course together three points to starboard.*	—

Date, Time of Despatch.	From	To	System.	Message.	Time of Origin.
31 MAY 7.9 p.m.	—*cont.* C.-in-C.	Dreadnought Battlefleet and attached Cruisers.	W/T and Flags	**Alter course together three points to port**	—
7.9 —	*S.O. 4th L.C.S.*	*4th L.C.S.*	Flags	*Alter course together three points to port*	—
7.9 —	Benbow	C.-in-C.	Sem.	**Enemy Destroyers S.W.** (*Received in Iron Duke 7.16 p.m.*)	1908
7.9 —	C.-in-C.	Dreadnought Battlefleet and attached Cruisers.	W/T and Flags	**Alter course together to South**	—
7 10 —	R.A. 1st B.S.	*Collingwood*	Flags	*Follow in the wake of your next ahead*	—
7 10 —	Fearless	Galatea	—	Can I be of any assistance ? Reply : Will you look after Acasta ? Reply : Yes.	—
7 10 —	*Captain D12·*	*12th Flotilla*	Flags	*Alter course together three points to port·*	—
7 10 —	Commodore F.	*11th Flotilla*	Flags	*Alter course together two points to starboard. Speed 25 knots.*	—
7.11 —	*S.O. 4th L.C.S.*	*4th L.C.S.*	Flags	*Alter course together four points to port*	—
7.12 —	C.-in-C.	1st B.S.	S.L.	**Take station astern of 4th B.S.**	—
7.12 —	*S.O.4th L.C.S.*	*4th L.C.S.*	Flags	*Alter course together eight points to starboard*	—
7.12 —	*S.O. B.C.F.·*	*Tiger*	S.L.	*Report state of turrets ? Reply : X and B turrets are out of action.*	—
7.12 —	*S.O. 4th L.C.S.*	*Constance*	Sem.	*Get astern of me*	—
7.13 —	*S.O. 4th B.S.*	*4th Division*	Flags	*Subdivisions separately alter course in succession two points away from the Enemy preserving their formation.*	—
7.13 —	Benbow	—	—	Remarks : 6-inch guns in action	—
7.15 —	S.O. B.C.F.	General	Flags	Admiral intends to proceed at 22 knots	—
7.15 —	Commodore F.	*11th Flotilla*	Flags	*Alter course together two points to port*	—
7.15 —	Duke of Edinburgh.	Hampshire	S.L.	What speed are you going? Reply : 21 knots.	—
7.15 —	*S.O. 4th B.S.*	*4th Division*	Flags	*Speed 13 knots. Alter course together two points to starboard. (Negatived.)*	—
7.16 —	*S.O.4th L.C.S.*	*4th L.C.S.*	Flags	*Alter course together four points to starboard. Admiral intends to proceed at 18 knots.*	—
7.16 —	C.-in-C.	S.O. 2nd B.S.	S.L. and Flags	**2nd B.S. take station ahead**	—
7.18 —	Fearless	Acasta	S.L.	What damage have you sustained? Reply : Holed fore and aft, engines and boilers out of action. Are you making much water? Reply : Not now.	—
7.18 —	C.-in-C.	2nd B.S.	S.L.	**Increase speed of engines**	—
7.18 —	C.-in-C.	2nd B.S.	Flags	**Proceed at your utmost speed**	—
7.20 —	R.A. 1st B.S.	*5th Division*	Flags	*Follow in the wake of your next ahead*	—
7.20 —	Fearless	Champion	S.L.	Have you any Destroyers to spare to stand by Acasta? Reply : No.	—

Date, Time of Despatch.	From	To	System.	Message.	Time of Origin.
31 MAY 7.20 p.m	*—cont.* Warrior -	Engadine -	Sem.	Have a bad list and cannot stop engines	—
7.20 —	C.-in-C. -	Dreadnought Battlefleet and attached Cruisers.	W/T and Flags	**Admiral intends to proceed at 15 knots**	—
7.20 —	S.O. 2nd C.S.	Duke of Edinburgh.	Flags	Take station astern of Hampshire - -	—
7.21 —	C.-in-C. -	2nd B.S. -	Flags	**Alter course together four points to port**	—
7.22 —	C.-in-C. -	Dreadnought Battlefleet and attached Cruisers.	W/T and Flags	**Subdivisions separately alter course in succession two points away from Enemy preserving their formation.**	—
7.22 —	S.O. B.C.F.	General -	Flags	Admiral intends to proceed at 24 knots -	—
7.22 —	C.-in-C. -	S.O. 4th L.C.S.	Flags	**4th L.C.S. prepare to attack the torpedo vessels of Enemy. Proceed at your utmost speed.**	—
7.22 —	*S.O. 4th L.C.S.*	*4th L.C.S.* -	Flags	*Alter course together eight points to port* -	—
7.22 —	*S.O. 4th L.C.S.*	*4th L.C.S.* -	Flags	*Admiral intends to proceed at 20 knots* -	—
7.23 —	S.O. B.C.F.	General -	Sem. S.L.	Enemy's Destroyers are approaching to attack.	—
7.23 —	C.-in-C. -	S.O. 4th L.C.S.	S.L.	**Do not get in the way of firing of Battle Cruisers.**	—
7.25 —	C.-in-C. -	Dreadnought Battlefleet and attached Cruisers.	Flags	**Subdivisions separately alter course in succession two points away from Enemy preserving their formation.**	—
7.25 —	Fearless	Acasta -	Sem.	I must leave you - - - -	—
7.25 —	Inflexible -	—	—	Remarks : Enemy's torpedo boat on starboard beam steering towards us (subsequently altering course to starboard.)	—
7.26 —	*Commodore F.*	*1st Half-Flotilla*	Flags	*Attack Enemy Destroyers bearing W.N.W.*	—
7.27 —	*S.O. Cruisers*	*Cruisers*	Flags	*Form single line-ahead in the sequence in which ships now are. Admiral intends to proceed at 21 knots.*	—
7.27 —	*S.O. 4th L.C.S.*	*4th L.C.S.* -	Flags	*Admiral intends to proceed at 25 knots* -	—
7.28 —	*S.O. 2nd B.S.*	*2nd B.S.* -	Flags	*Admiral intends to proceed at 15 knots* -	—
7.30 —	Indomitable	—	—	Remarks : Struck under fore part. Supposed Submarine starboard side.	—
7.31 —	Marlborough	C.-in-C. -	W/T	**My speed is reduced to 17 knots** - - (*Not logged as having been received in Iron Duke.*)	1932
7.32 —	C.-in-C. -	S.O. 4th L.C.S.	S.L.	**Do not go too near Enemy's battlefleet** -	1931
7.35 —	Warrior -	Engadine -	F.L.	Am now trying to shut off steam in engine room.	—
7.35 —	C.-in-C. -	Dreadnought Battlefleet and attached Cruisers.	W/T and Flags	**Alter course leading ships together rest in succession to S. by W.**	—

Date, Time of Despatch.	From	To	System.	Message.	Time of Origin.
31 MAY —*cont.* 7.35 p.m.	*S.O.3rdL.C.S.*	*3rd L.C.S.* -	S.L.	*Which side are your torpedoes ready?* *Replies : Yarmouth, both tubes loaded with L.R. torpedoes; Gloucester, both sides ; Canterbury, both sides.*	*1930*
7.36 —	*Commodore F.*	*11th Flotilla* -	Flags	*Cruising order No. 2. Course S.S.W.* -	—
7.36 —	*S.O.4thL.C.S.*	*4th L.C.S.* -	S.L.	*Alter course together eight points to port* -	—
7.36 —	*Owl* - -	*S.O. 2nd C.S.*	S.L.	Should Destroyers join up with their own flotillas? Reply : No, remain where you are.	1930
7.36 —	**C.-in-C.** -	**Dreadnought Battlefleet.**	W/T	**Form single line-ahead in sequence of fleet numbers.**	1936
7.38 —	*Commodore F.*	*11th Flotilla* -	Flags	*Alter course in succession to South* - -	—
7.38 —	*Captain D12*	*12th Flotilla* -	Flags	*Open fire, South-West* - - - -	—
7.39 —	*Constance* -	*General* -	Flags	*Torpedo passing from starboard to port* -	—
7.39 —	*Commodore F.*	*11th Flotilla* -	Flags	*Admiral intends to proceed at 22 knots* -	—
7.39 —	*S.O.4thL.C.S.*	*4th L.C.S.* -	Flags	*Submarine port side three points from righ ahead.*	—
7.40 —	*Engadine* -	*Warrior* -	F.L.	What speed are you going? Reply : I don't know. I am trying to shut off steam.	—
7.40 —	*Inflexible* -	*S.O. B.C.F.* -	Flags	*Submarine starboard beam* - - -	—
7.40 —	*S.O. 2nd B.S.*	*2nd B.S.* -	Flags	*Admiral intends to proceed at 18 knots* -	—
7.40 —	**C.-in-C.** -	**S.O. 2nd B.S.**	S.L.	**My course S.W.** •	—
7.40 —	**C.-in-C.** -	**Destroyers** -	S.L.	**Recall** • - • - •	—
7.40 —	*Lion* - -	*C.-in-C.* -	W/T	**Enemy bears from me N.W. by W. distant 10 to 11 miles. My position Lat. 56° 56′ N., Long. 6° 16′ E. Course S.W. Speed 18 knots.**	**1930**
7.40 —	*S.O.4thL.C.S.*	*4th L.C.S.* -	Flags	*Am taking station on battlefleet* - -	—
7.40 —	*Captain D12*	*12th Flotilla* -	Flags	*Attack the torpedo vessels of the Enemy bearing S.W.*	—
7.40 —	*Canterbury* -	—	—	Remarks : Enemy Light Cruiser on fire	—
7.40 —	S.O. B.C.F.	*General* -	Flags	Admiral intends to proceed at 18 knots ·	—
7.42 —	*Indomitable* -	*Inflexible* -	F.L.	*I am going slow. I think I have been hit* -	—
7.42 —	**C.-in-C.** -	**3rd and 4th Divisions.**	Flags	**Form single line-ahead in sequence of fleet numbers. Course S.W.**	—
7.42 —	*Commodore F.*	*11th Flotilla* -	Flags	*Alter course together two points to port* -	—
7.43 —	**C.-in-C.** -	**S.O. B.C.F.** -	W/T	**Present course of fleet S.W.** - - -	**1940**
7.43 —	*S.O.3rdL.C.S.*	*3rd L.C.S.* -	Flags	*Alter course together two points to port* -	—
7.44 —	*S.O.4thL.C.S.*	*4th L.C.S.* -	Flags	*Admiral intends to proceed at 22 knots*	—
7.45 —	*Warrior* -	*Engadine* -	F.L.	Stand by to tow me - • - •	···
7.45 —	**C.-in-C.** -	**Destroyers** -	S.L.	**Tell Castor to come back. Destroyers recalled.**	···

Date, Time of Despatch.	From	To	System.	Message.	Time of Origin.
31 MAY —*cont.*					
7.45 p.m.	Southampton	C.-in-C.	W/T	Urgent. Enemy has detached unknown number of ships, type unknown, which are steering N.W. at 7.15 p.m. My position Lat. 56° 50′ N., Long. 6° 27′ E.	1945
7.45 —	Captain D12	12th Flotilla	Flags	Alter course together four points to port	—
7.45 —	Commodore F.	11th Flotilla	Flags	Alter course together two points to starboard	—
7.45 —	S.O.3rdL.C.S.	3rd L.C.S.	Flags	Admiral intends to proceed at 18 knots. Form single line-ahead in sequence of fleet numbers.	—
7.45 —	Faulknor	S.O. 2nd L.C.S.	S.L.	Am sending a division of Destroyers to attack Destroyers on my starboard beam.	—
7.45 —	S.O. B.C.F.	S.O. 2nd C.S.	S.L.	Pass to leading British Battleship. Leading Enemy Battleship bears N.W. by W., course about S.W. (Note K. G. V. passed to C.-in-C. Received in Iron Duke via K. G. V. 7.59 p.m.)	1945
7.46 —	Commodore F.	11th Flotilla	Flags	Alter course in succession to S.W.	—
7.46 —	Llewellyn	Captain D13, Captain D1.	S.L.	Onslow unable to steam, in tow of Defender. Defender two boilers out of action.	1940
7.47 —	Commodore F.	11th Flotilla	Flags	Admiral intends to proceed at 17 knots	—
7.47 —	**S.O. B.C.F**	C.-in-C.	W/T	Urgent. Submit van of Battleships follow Battle Cruisers. We can then cut off whole of enemy's battlefleet. (Received in Iron Duke, 7.54 p.m.)	1950
7.48 —	S.O.3rdL.C.S.	3rd L.C.S.	Flags	Alter course together two points to starboard.	—
7.49 —	C.-in-C.	Marlborough	S.L.	**Are you alright? Reply : Can only steam 17 knots.**	1945
7.50 —	S.O.4thL.C.S.	4th L.C.S.	Flags	Admiral intends to proceed at 20 knots	—
7.50 —	Commodore F.	S.O. 2nd B.S.	S.L.	What is course and speed of fleet? Reply : S.W. 15 knots.	—
7.50 —	S.O. B.C.F.	Minotaur	S.L.	What ship are you? Reply : H.M.S. Minotaur.	—
7.50 —	S.O. B.C.F.	Battle Cruisers	Sem. and W/T	Indicate state of efficiency of ships as follows : (1) Maximum speed maintainable, (2) Number of guns main armament fit for action, (3) Indicate amount of ammunition remaining, expressed in tenths of the original outfit. Princess Royal—(1) Full speed, (2) Six guns, (3) Eight-tenths. Inflexible—(1) 25 knots, (2) Seven guns, (3) Nine-tenths. Indomitable—(1) Full speed, (2) All guns, (3) Nine-tenths.	1945
	Lion	S.O. B.C.F.	—	Reply : Lion—Q turret out of action. A turret, one gun correct, one hand-loading. B turret correct. X turret, one gun correct and one gun temporarily disabled. 100 rounds per turret remaining. 4-in. guns correct. Two 4 S.A. battery.	—
7.50 —	Captain D12	12th Flotilla	Flags	Alter course together four points to starboard	—
7.51 —	S.O. B.C.F.	Princess Royal	S.L.	Indicate your position? Reply : 8 p.m. position 56° 48′ N., 6° 8′ E. Reply from Lion : Our position is the same as yours.	1950

Date, Time of Despatch.	From	To	System.	Message.	Time of Origin.
31 MAY —*cont.* 7.52 p.m	**C.-in-C.**	**General**	Flags	**Admiral has resumed Guide of fleet**	—
7.52 —	*Commodore F.*	*11th Flotilla*	Flags	*Admiral intends to proceed at 18 knots*	—
7.55 —	*Indomitable*	*Inflexible*	S.L.	*I have had to ease to 14 knots*	—
7.55 —	Duke of Edinburgh.	Hampshire	S.L.	What are you firing at? Reply: Submarine on port quarter.	—
7.55 —	*Tiger*	*S.O. B.C.F. and S.O. 1st B.C.S.*	Sem.	*Q magazine is flooded and I cannot right ship at present. I am taking in considerable water every time helm is put over.*	1950
	S.O. B.C.F.	*Tiger*	Sem.	*Where is water entering ship? Reply: After 6-in. and Q magazine.*	2000
7.56 —	Warrior	Engadine	Sem.	Keep close on my port quarter	—
7.57 —	Duke of Edinburgh.	—	—	Remarks: Opened fire on Submarine port beam.	—
7.57 —	*Indomitable*	*Inflexible*	S.L.	*Am now going 20 knots*	—
7.58 —	*Commodore F.*	*11th Flotilla*	Flags	*Alter course in succession to West*	—
7.58 —	*Captain D12*	*12th Flotilla*	Flags	*Admiral intends to proceed at 12 knots*	—
7.58 —	*S.O.4thL.C.S.*	*4th L.C.S.*	Flags	*Admiral intends to proceed at 18 knots*	—
7.59 —	*Commodore F.*	*11th Flotilla*	Flags	*Admiral intends to proceed at 20 knots*	—
8.0 —	Warrior	Engadine	Sem.	We are nearly stopped. Come and take me in tow.	—
8.0 —	Engadine	S.O. B.C.F.	W/T	Am standing by Warrior. Position, Lat. 57° 10' N., Long. 5° 43' E., steering W.N.W. *(Received in Iron Duke, 8.10 p.m.)*	1920
8.0 —	S.O. B.C.F.	Light Cruisers	S.L.	Sweep to the Westward and locate the head of the Enemy's line before dark. *(Passed to 3rd L.C.S. by S.O. 3rd L.C.S. at 8.14 p.m.)*	2000
8.0 —	*S.O.3rdL.C.S.*	*3rd L.C.S.*	Flags	*Light Cruisers form on a compass line of bearing South, course West.*	—
8.0 —	Badger	S.O.4thL.C.S.	Sem.	Could you please give me present position? Reply: Position at 7.50 p.m., 56° 46' N., 6° 03' E.	—
8.0 —	Minotaur	—	—	Remarks: Hampshire reported Submarine on port side, then starboard side. Hampshire and Shannon opened fire.	—
8.0 —	**C.-in-C.**	**General**	Flags and W/T	**Divisions separately alter course in succession to West preserving their formation. Speed 17 knots.**	—
8.0 —	**C.-in-C.**	**S.O. B.C.F.**	W/T	**Present course of fleet is West**	2000
8.2 —	*S.O. 1st B.S.*	*Revenge*	Sem.	*You must try and not run up on me. I can only go 17 knots.*	—
8.2 —	*S.O.3rdL.C.S.*	*3rd L.C.S.*	Flags	*Ships in column to be one mile apart*	—
8.3 —	*Captain D12*	*12th Flotilla*	Flags	*Alter course in succession to S.W.*	—
8.5 —	*Marksman*	*Opal*	Sem.	*I am going to get into cruising order L.T. again.*	—

Date, Time of Despatch.	From	To	System.	Message.	Time of Origin.
31 MAY 8.7 p.m.	—cont. **C.-in-C.** -	**Marlborough** -	S.L. and W/T	**Is there any reply to my 1945?** - - **Reply: "A" boiler room, dynamo room, starboard hydraulic room flooded. Slight leak in foremost 6-inch magazine. Maximum speed 17 knots. Right gun of "A" turret out of action.**	**2000** **2005**
8.7 —	*Shannon* -	*S.O. Cruisers*	S.L.	*Battlefleet altering to W. by N. ¾ N. 17 knots*	*2000*
8.7 —	*Captain D12*	*12th Flotilla* -	Flags	*Alter course in succession to West* - -	—
8.8 —	*Commodore F.*	*11th Flotilla* -	Flags	*Admiral intends to proceed at 18 knots* -	—
8.8 —	*S.O. 2nd C.S.*	*Cruisers* -	Flags	*Admiral intends to proceed at 19 knots* -	—
8.9 —	*S.O.3rdL.C.S.*	*S.O. B.C.F.* -	Flags	*Ships bearing N. by W.* - - -	*2010*
8.10 —	*S.O. B.C.F.*	*General*	Flags	*Open fire* - - - - -	—
8.10 —	*Princess Royal*	*S.O. B.C.F.* -	Sem.	*Tiger reports two guns put out of action* -	—
8.11 —	*Commodore F.*	*1st Half-Flotilla*	Flags	*Attack Destroyers N.W.* - - -	—
8.12 —	*Commodore F.*	*Kempenfelt* -	F.L.	*Do not follow unless Enemy are in force* -	—
8.14 —	**C.-in-C.** -	**S.O. 2nd B.S.**	S.L.	**2nd B.S. follow our Battle Cruisers** - *(Logged as having been received in King George V. at 8.7 p.m.)*	**2010**
8.14 —	*Commodore F.*	*S.O. 2nd B.S.*	Flags	*Enemy's Destroyers bearing N.W.* - - *(Passed to C.-in-C. 8.26 p.m.)*	—
8.15 —	*Marlborough*	—	—	*Remarks : Marlborough sighted Submarine starboard bow.*	—
8.15 —	*Princess Royal*	*S.O. B.C.F.* -	Sem.	*I think Princess Royal must have run over a Submarine. Ship is not making water. There was a very heavy bump.*	—
8.15 —	*Commodore F.*	*S.O.4thL.C.S. and Kempenfelt.*	F.L.	*12 enemy Destroyers N.W.* - - -	—
8.15 —	*Kempenfelt* -	*3rd Division of Destroyers.*	F.L.	*Take station astern* - - - -	—
8.15 —	*S.O.3rdL.C.S.*	*3rd L.C.S.* -	Flags	*Admiral intends to proceed at 20 knots* -	—
8.15 —	S.O. B.C.F.	*Minotaur* -	S.L.	What is bearing of our leading battleship? Reply : N.N.E. five miles King George V.	2010
8.16 —	*S.O.4thL.C.S.*	*1st Division, 4th L.C.S.*	Flags	*Support Castor* - - - -	—
8.17 —	*S.O. B.C.F.*	*Battle Cruisers*	Flags	*Alter course in succession to W. Admiral intends to proceed at 17 knots.*	—
8.17 —	Falmouth -	—	—	Remarks : Opened fire - - -	—
8.17 —	New Zealand	—	—	Remarks : Enemy opened fire - -	—
8.18 —	*S.O.4thL.C.S.*	*4th L.C.S.* -	Flags	*Proceed at your utmost speed* - -	—
8.18 —	*S.O. 2nd B.S.*	*R.A. 2nd B.S.*	S.L.	*Follow me* - - - - -	—
8.19 —	Falmouth -	—	—	Remarks : Zeppelin in sight, port beam (uncertain).	—
8.20 —	S.O. B.C.F -	*S.O.2ndL.C.S.*	W/T	What is your position, course and speed? Are you in touch with the Enemy?	2015
8.20 —	*S.O.3rdL.C.S.*	*Light Cruisers*	Flags	*Open fire and engage the Enemy* - -	—
8.20 —	Inflexible -	—	—	Remarks : Opened fire - - -	—

Date, Time of Despatch.	From	To	System.	Message.	Time of Origin.
31 MAY	*—cont.*				
8.21 p.m.	S.O. B.C.F.	General -	Flags	Alter course in succession to W.S.W. -	—
8.21 —	**C.-in-C.** -	**Dreadnought Battlefleet and attached Cruisers.**	W/T	**Alter course leading ships together the rest in succession to W.S.W.**	—
8.21 —	**C.-in-C.** -	**S.O. B.C.F.** -	W/T	**Present course of fleet is W.S.W.** - -	2020
8.22 —	*Commodore F.*	*1stHalf-Flotilla*	Flags	*Reform* - - - - -	—
8.25 —	*Caroline* -	*2nd Division, 4th L.C.S.*	Flags	*Admiral intends to proceed at 18 knots* -	—
8.25 —	**Canada** -	**C.-in-C.** -	Sem.	**Have received on D wave 14 groups, apparently German. Call signs RZ RZ RZ.**	2020
8.25 —	S.O. B.C.F.	General -	Flags	Alter course in succession to S.W. - -	—
8 25 —	S.O. 2nd C.S.	8th Group Destroyers.	Flags	Take station ahead of Minotaur - -	—
8.25 —	**C.-in-C.** -	**Dreadnought Battlefleet and attached Cruisers.**	W/T and Flags.	**Alter course leading ships together the rest in succession to West.**	—
8.25 —	*S.O.4thL.C.S.*	*Constance and Comus.*	Sem.	*Get out on quarter and open fire on Destroyers ahead.*	—
8.25 —	*S.O.3rdL.C.S.*	*3rd L.C.S.* -	Flags	*Admiral intends to proceed at 25 knots* -	—
8.26 —	*Commodore F.*	*1st Half-Flotilla*	Flags	*Alter course in succession to S.W.* - -	—
8.27 —	*S.O. Cruisers*	*Cruisers* -	S.L.	*When Minotaur hauls out turn together without further signal.*	2027
8.28 —	*Caroline* -	*2nd Division, 4th L.C.S.*	Flags	*Admiral intends to proceed at 21 knots* -	—
8.28 —	**C.-in-C.** -	**Dreadnought Battlefleet.**	W/T and Flags.	**Alter course leading ships together the rest in succession to S.W.**	—
8.28 —	**Falmouth** -	**C.-in-C. and S.O. B.C.F.**	W/T	**Urgent. Am engaging Enemy's Cruisers. My position Lat. 56° 47′ N., Long. 5° 46′ E.**	2022
8.29 —	*S.O. Cruisers*	*Cruisers*	Flags	*Alter course together two points to port*	—
8.30 —	*S.O.3rdL.C.S.*	*Birkenhead and Yarmouth.*	Sem.	*Form astern* - - - - -	—
8.30 —	S.O. 2ndL.C.S.	S.O. B.C.F. -	W/T	My position Lat. 56° 46′ N., Long. 6° 25′ E., course W.S.W., speed 20 knots, in company with our battlefleet, not in touch with Enemy	2025
8.30 —	**C.-in-C.** -	**S.O. B.C.F.** -	W/T	**Present course of fleet is S.W.** - -	2024
8.31 —	**Royal Sovereign.**	**C.-in-C.** -	W/T	**Permission to join your flag** - -	201
8.31 —	Benbow -	—	—	Remarks : Torpedo passed the ship from port to starboard.	—
8.31 —	*Commodore F.*	*11th Flotilla* -	Flags	*Alter course together four points to port* -	—
8.32 —	*Captain D12*	*12th Flotilla* -	Flags	*Alter course in succession to S.W.* - -	—
8.33 —	**Inconstant** -	**S.O. B.C.F. and C.-in-C.**	W/T	**Submarine, Lat. 56° 56′ N., Long. 6° 06′ E.**	2030
8.34 —	*S.O. Cruisers*	*Cruisers* -	S.L.	*Alter course together two points to starboard*	—
8.35 —	*Caroline* -	*2nd Division 4th L.C.S.*	Flags	*Admiral intends to proceed at 18 knots* -	—

Date, Time of Despatch.	From	To	System.	Message.	Time of Origin.
31 MAY *—cont.*					
8.35 p.m.	Warrior ·	Engadine ·	Sem.	What is your position now ? Reply : 57° 10′ N., 5° 42′ E.	—
8.35 —	*Commodore F.*	*11th Flotilla* ·	Flags	*Alter course together four points to starboard*	—
8.37 —	**Warrior via Engadine.**	C.-in-C. ·	W/T	Both engines disabled. Warrior in tow of Engadine, Lat. 57° 10′ N., Long. 5° 37′ E.	2103
8.38 —	**C.-in-C.** ·	Comus ·	F.L.	Who are you firing at ? Reply : Enemy's B.F. bearing West.	—
8.38 —	*Commodore F.*	*11th Flotilla* ·	Flags	*Take up cruising order No. 2. Speed 22 knots.*	—
8.39 —	*S.O. Cruisers*	*Cruisers* ·	S.L.	*Admiral intends to proceed at 20 knots* ·	—
8.40 —	Engadine ·	—	—	Remarks : Took Warrior in tow. Position 57° 10′ N., 5° 42′ E.	—
8.40 —	Canterbury ·	Chester ·	S.L.	I am coming in ahead of you · · ·	—
8.40 —	S.O. 2nd B.S.	S.O. B.C.F. ·	W/T	Priority. What is your position, course and speed ? Am following you.	2021
8.40 —	Admiralty ·	Australia ·	W/T	Reported from reliable source that commerce raider Moewe has sailed from Wilhelmshaven, also that Niobe was expecting to sail on 1st June from Wilhelmshaven on raiding cruise.	2040
8.40 —	*Tiger* · ·	*S.O. B.C.F.* ·	W/T	*Main W/T can receive only* · ·	2035
8.45 —	*Commodore F.*	*11th Flotilla* ·	Flags	*Admiral intends to proceed at 17 knots* ·	—
8.45 —	**S.O. 2nd B.S.**	C.-in-C. ·	W/T	Urgent. Our Battle Cruisers are not in sight.	2044
8.46 —	**C.-in-C.** ·	S.O. B.C.F. ·	W/T	Indicate the bearing of Enemy · · *(Logged by S.O. B.C.F. as having been received from Galatea. Vide 2100 S.O. B.C.F. to Galatea.)*	2046
8.46 —	**Falmouth** ·	C.-in-C., S.O. B.C.F.	W/T	Battle Cruisers unknown. Bearing of Enemy N. Course of Enemy W.S.W. Position of reporting ship Lat. 56° 42′ N., Long. 5° 37′ E.	2045
8.47 —	*Captain D12* ·	*12th Flotilla* ·	Flags	*Admiral intends to proceed at 20 knots* ·	—
8.50 —	Comus ·	Boadicea ·	F.L.	What is speed of fleet ?· · ·	—
8.50 —	*Caroline* ·	*Royalist* ·	F.L.	*Attack with torpedoes* · · ·	—
8.50 —	*Warspite* ·	*S.O. 5th B.S.* ·	W/T	*Warspite has two big holes abreast engine room. Wing engine room not yet flooded. Warspite can steam 16 knots. Request position of battlefleet.*	2035
8.50 —	**S.O. 2nd L.C.S.**	C.-in-C. ·	S.L.	Enemy's Destroyers are attacking West · *(Not logged as having been received in Iron Duke.)*	—
8.51 —	**Black Prince**	C.-in-C. · ·	W/T	Urgent. Submarine on port hand, Lat. 56° 55′ N., Long. 6° 11′ E.	2045
8.54 —	Inflexible ·	—	—	Remarks : Four Destroyers approaching on port beam.	—
8 55 —	*Inconstant* ·	*1st L.C.S.* ·	F.L.	*Admiral intends to proceed at 18 knots* ·	—
8.55 —	S.O. B.C.F. ·	S.O. 2nd C.S. ·	S.L.	Please give me position of 2nd B.S. Reply : Not in sight. When last seen bearing N.N.E. five miles at 8.10 p.m.	—
8.57 —	*S.O. Cruisers*	*Cruisers* ·	S.L.	*Admiral intends to proceed at 18 knots* ·	—

Date Time of Despatch.	From	To	System.	Message.	Time of Origin.
31 MAY —*cont.*					
8.57 p.m	Southampton	C.-in-C. -	W/T	Urgent. Am engaging Enemy Destroyers. Enemy ships bearing W. from me, number unknown. My position Lat. 56° 38′ N., Long. 6° 09′ E.	2055
8.59 —	Lion - -	C.-in-C. -	W/T	Urgent. Enemy Battle Cruisers and pre-Dreadnought Battleships bear from me N. 34° W., distant 10 to 11 miles, steering S.W. My position Lat. 56° 40′ N., Long. 5° 50′ E., course S.W., 17 knots.	2040
9.0 —	Commodore F.	11th Flotilla -	Flags	*Alter course in succession to South* - -	—
9.0 —	Caroline -	S.O. 2nd B.S.-	F.L.	Three ships bearing N.W. 8,000 yards. May be attacking with torpedoes. Apparently old Battleships. (*Not logged in K. G. V. signal log.*)	2055
9.0 —	S.O. Cruisers	Cruisers -	S.L.	*Keep in the Admiral's wake* - - -	—
9.0 —	Titania -	Talisman -	W/T	Remain on patrol until further orders or p.m. Saturday, 3rd June.	1925
9.0 —	R.A. Scapa -	Aberdeen -	W/T	For C.-in-C. Following weather reports off entrance of Rosyth, Shotley and Immingham respectively. Wind S.W. 3-4—29.82—9 p.m. 30.25 stationary, temperature 66, wind W.N.W. light, 9 p.m., wind S.W. 1-3 fine (mainly b.c.), barometer 30.14. (*Received in Iron Duke 11.35 p.m.*)	2100
9.1 —	C.-in-C. -	Dreadnought - Battlefleet.	W/T and Flags.	Divisions separately alter course in succession to South preserving their formation	—
9.1 —	S.O. B.C.F. -	S.O. 2nd B.S.-	W/T	My position now Lat. 56° 40′ N., Long. 5° 50′ E., course S. 50° W., speed 17 knots.	2040
9.3 —	Benbow -	—	—	Remarks : 6-in. guns opened fire - -	—
9.4 —	Benbow -	—	—	Remarks : " B " turret fired - - -	—
9.5 —	Caroline -	Royalist -	F.L.	*Did you fire any torpedoes ? Reply : Yes, one.*	—
9.5 —	S.O.3rd L.C.S.	Leading Destroyers.	S.L.	What is course and speed ? (No answer.)	2100
9.5 —	King George V.	—	—	Remarks : Caroline apparently made signals to Destroyers to attack.	—
9.5 —	S.O. B.C.F. -	Galatea -	W/T	Your 2046. N. by W. - - - (*Received in Iron Duke 9.4 p.m.*)	2100
9.5 —	**S.O. 1st B.S.**	C.-in-C. -	W/T	Urgent. Enemy Destroyers are attacking Light Cruisers from Westward.	2101
9.5 —	S.O.2nd L.C.S.	2nd L.C.S. -	S.L.	*Admiral intends to proceed at 20 knots* -	—
9.5 —	Badger -	S.O. B.C.F. -	S.L.	Following ranks and ratings were rescued from Invincible. Commander Dannreuther, Lieut. Sandford, C.P.O. Thompson, Yeo. of Sig. Pratt, A.B. Banbridge, Gunner Gasson, R.M.A.	2051
9.6 —	S.O. 2nd B.S.	Caroline -	S.L.	Negative. Those ships are our Battle Cruisers.	—
	Caroline -	S.O. 2nd B.S.-	S.L.	Those are evidently Enemy ships - - (*Also made by Commodore F. at 9.15 p.m.*)	—
	S.O. 2nd B.S.	Caroline -	S.L.	If you are quite sure attack - - -	—
9.7 —	S.O. 5th B.S.	Warspite -	W/T	*Warspite proceed to Rosyth* - - -	2105
9.7 —	Captain D12-	12th Flotilla -	Flags	*Alter course in succession to South* - -	—

Date, Time of Despatch.	From	To	System.	Message.	Time of Origin.
31 MAY—*cont.* 9.7 p.m.	**S.O. 2nd B.S.**	**C.-in-C. -**	W/T	**Urgent. Our Battle Cruisers in sight bearing W.N.W., steering S.W.**	2105
9.10 —	**Southampton**	**C.-in-C.**	W/T	**Enemy reported in my 2055 has been driven to the N.W. My position Lat. 56° 35′ N., Long. 6° 09′ E.**	2112
9.10 —	*S.O. 3rd L.C.S.*	*3rd L.C.S.*	Flags	*Admiral intends to proceed at 17 knots. Alter course in succession to S.W.*	
9.10 —	**C.-in-C. -**	**S.Os. of Squadrons and all Captains D.**	W/T	**Present course of fleet is South -**	2104
9.12 —	**C.-in-C. -**	**Oak -**	F.L.	**Keep close to me during night -**	2100
9.15 —	Minotaur -	—	—	Remarks : White rocket starboard quarter	—
9.15 —	Benbow	—	—	Remarks : Rocket showing stars starboard bow.	—
9.15 —	*Shannon*	*S.O. 2nd C.S.-*	S.L.	*King George V. bears N.N.E. about eight miles.*	2100
9.17 —	**C.-in-C. -**	**Colossus**	W/T	**Keep within visual signal touch -** (*Not logged as having been received by Colossus.*)	2130
9 17 —	**C.-in-C.**	General -	Flags and W/T	**Assume 2nd organisation. Form divisions in line-ahead columns disposed abeam to port. Columns to be one mile apart.**	—
9.17 —	*Captain D12*	*12th Flotilla -*	F.L.	*Alter course in succession to S. by E. ½ E.*	—
9.17 —	Duke of Edinburgh.	Shannon -	F.L.	Your masthead light is burning -	—
9.20 —	Engadine	Warrior -	F.L.	Am going to steer North 70° West- -	—
9.20 —	*Constance -*	*Caroline -*	F.L.	*Calliope on starboard bow of Iron Duke. I think she is damaged.*	—
9.20 —	*Caroline -*	*4th L.C.S. -*	F.L.	*1st Division take station astern of 2nd Division.*	—
9.20 —	**Oak -**	**C.-in-C. -**	F.L.	**You have a bright light before your port fore superstructure.**	—
9.27 —	*Marksman*	*Captain D12 -*	F.L.	*Permission to attack Enemy bearing South*	—
9.27 —	**C.-in-C. -**	**S.Os. of Squadrons, Commanders of Divisions of Battlefleet and Captain D11.**	W/T	**Destroyers take station astern of battlefleet five miles.**	2115
9.28 —	**R. A. Invergordon.**	**R.A. Scapa -**	W/T	**For information of C.-in-C. Following received from Biarritz : Trawler A. 648 reports two Submarines came to surface 40 miles E. of Buchan Ness this morning Wednesday.**	2031
9.29 —	*Inconstant -*	*1st L.C.S. -*	F.L.	*Admiral intends to proceed at 22 knots -*	—
9.30 —	S.O. B.C.F. -	General -	Flags	Alter course in succession to South -	—
9.30 —	Cordelia	—	—	Remarks : Submarine on port bow -	—
9.30 —	Defender -	Warspite -	F.L. F.L.	I will take station astern of you - - Reply : Am steering West 16 knots, compass and steering gear very erratic.	— —
	Defender -	Warspite	F.L. F.L.	Permission to take station astern of you - Reply : Approved.	—

Date, Time of Despatch.	From	To	System.	Message.	Time of Origin.
31 MAY—*cont.* 9.30 p.m.	Moorsom -	Fearless -	F.L.	Can you please give me your rough position ? Reply : Lat. 56° 40′ N., Long. 5° 40′ E.	—
9.30 —	*Captain D12-*	*12th Flotilla -*	F.L.	*Alter course in succession to South. Admiral intends to proceed at 18 knots.*	—
9.31 —	*Caroline* -	*4th L.C.S.* -	F.L.	*Admiral intends to proceed at 18 knots. Form single line-ahead in sequence of fleet numbers.*	—
9.31 —	S.O.3rd L.C.S.	S.O. B.C.F. -	W/T	What is your position, course and speed ? -	2130
9.32 —	*S.O. B.C.F.-*	*Princess Royal*	F.L.	*Please give me challenge and reply now in force as they have been lost. (Challenge and reply passed as requested.)*	—
9.32 —	**C.-in-C.** -	Abdiel - -	W/T	**If there is time before daylight lay mines in position given for operation M and then proceed to Rosyth via S. side of Area 1.** *(Received by Abdiel 10.5 p.m.)*	2132
9.33 —	*S.O.2nd L.C.S*	*2nd L.C.S.* -	S.L.	*Admiral intends to proceed at 21 knots*	—
9.35 —	*Princess Royal*	*S.O. B.C.F.* -	F.L.	*May we have a blue stern light, please ?* -	2130
9.36 —	*S.O. 5th B.S.*	*5th B.S.* -	F.L.	*Admiral intends to proceed at 18 knots* -	—
9.38 —	*Captain D12-*	*12th Flotilla -*	F.L.	*Admiral intends to proceed at 12 knots* -	—
9.38 —	**S.O. B.C.F.** -	**C.-in-C.** -	W/T	**My position now Lat. 56° 35′ N., Long. 5° 41′ E., course S.W., speed 17 knots. Enemy's bearing N. by W., steering W.S.W.** *(Received in Iron Duke 9.41 p.m.)*	2100
9.39 —	*Gloucester* -	*Falmouth* -	S.L.	*Battle Cruisers have altered course to port, appear steering South.*	—
9.39 —	*S.O.2nd L.C.S*	*2nd L.C.S.* -	S.L.	*Admiral intends to proceed at 17 knots* -	—
9.40 —	*Marne* -	*Commodore F.*	F.L.	*Battlefleet are altering course to port* -	—
9.41 —	Inconstant -	Falmouth -	F.L.	Please show your stern light. What is your speed ? Reply : Speed 17 knots.	—
9.41 —	S.O. B.C.F. -	S.O. 1st L.C.S.	W/T	1st L.C.S. take station W. by S. four miles. Keep a good look-out for movements of Enemy bearing N. by W. *(Received by Iron Duke as " Take station N.W.")*	2107
9.41 —	*S.O.3rd L.C.S.*	*3rd L.C.S.* -	S.L.	*Alter course in succession to South-* -	—
9.42 —	*S.O. 2nd C.S.*	*8th Group Destroyers.*	S.L.	*Admiral intends to proceed at 17 knots* -	—
9.43 —	**S.O. B.C.F.** -	**C.-in-C., S.O. 2nd B.S., S.O. 1, 2, 3 L.C.S., Captain D13.**	W/T	**My position Lat. 56° 28′ N., Long. 5° 38′ E., course South, speed 17 knots.**	2135
9.45 —	Bellona -	R.A. 1st B.S.	F.L.	I am taking station astern of St. Vincent	2140
9.45 —	*Commodore F.*	*11th Flotilla -*	F.L.	*Alter course in succession to E.N.E. Take up cruising order No. 4.*	—
9.45 —	Defender -	Warspite -	F.L.	Defender's maximum speed 15 knots. Onslow's speed nothing.	—
9.46 —	*R.A. 1st B.S.*	*6th Subdivision*	F.L.	*Admiral intends to proceed at 17 knots* -	—
9.47 —	*S.O. 5th B.S.*	*5th B.S.* -	F.L.	*Admiral intends to proceed at 16 knots* -	—

Date, Time of Despatch.	From	To	System.	Message.	Time of Origin.
31 MAY—*cont.* 9.48 p.m.	**C.-in-C.**	**S.O. B.C.F., S.Os. of Squadrons, Commander of Divisions and all Captains D.**	W/T	**Reference position 9.45 p.m., 56° 26′ N., 5° 47′ E., course S., speed 17 knots.**	**2145**
9.48 —	Badger	S.O. B.C.F.	F.L.	Please give me your course and speed ? Reply : 17 knots.	—
9.50 —	*Commodore F.*	*11th Flotilla*	F.L.	*Alter course 16 points outwards*	—
9.50 —	Galatea via Caroline.	Calliope	F.L.	Can you manage to keep up with the leading Battleship. I will try to hold on to you then.	2140
9.52 —	Active	Boadicea	F.L.	I propose to take station astern of you. Reply : Right.	—
9.55 —	*Commodore F.*	*11th Flotilla*	F.L.	*Alter course in succession to N.E., speed 22 knots.*	—
9.55 —	**Admiralty**	**C.-in-C.**	W/T	**Three Destroyer flotillas have been ordered to attack you during the night.**	**2105**
9.55 —	Galatea	S.O. 4th L.C.S.	F.L.	My speed is reduced. I have lost my squadron. Shall I be in your way if I remain on your starboard bow ? Suppose you can keep touch with Battleships. Reply : Am reducing to 16 knots to keep touch with King George V. Destroyers have dropped astern.	2153
9.57 —	Badger	S.O. B.C.F.	F.L.	Have ordered 1st Flotilla to screen B.C.F.	2250
9.58 —	*Garland*	*Captain D4*	W/T	*German Destroyers steering S.E.*	—
9.58 —	**Admiralty**	**C.-in-C.**	W/T	**At 9 p.m. rear ship of Enemy B.F. in Lat. 56° 33′ N., Long. 5° 30′ E., on southerly course.** *(Received in Iron Duke 10.23 p.m.)*	**2158**
9.58 —	Talisman	Submarines G.6, E.43.	W/T	Talisman and four Submarines proceeding to position 54° 30′ N., 4° 0′ E. Entering your patrol area at 1 a.m.	2025
10.0 —	*S.O. 4th L.C.S*	*4th L.C.S.*	F.L.	*Admiral intends to proceed at 16 knots*	—
10.0 —	Inconstant	S.O. 3rd L.C.S.	F.L.	Inconstant with 1st L.C.S , less Galatea, are astern of you	2200
10.0 —	*Contest*	*Captain D4*	F.L.	*German Destroyers steering S.E.*	2200
10.1 —	S.O. B.C.F.	Princess Royal and Tiger.	F.L.	*What course do you make us steering now ?* Reply : *Tiger South, Princess Royal South.*	—
10.3 —	*S.O.5th B.S.*	*5th B.S.*	F.L.	*Alter course in succession 16 points to starboard.*	—
10.3 —	*Garland*	*Captain D4*	W/T	*German Submarines astern*	2200
10.3 —	*S.O. B.C.F.*	*Tiger*	F.L.	*What is state of Tiger now ?* Reply : *Water not gaining.*	2201
10.5 —	Princess Royal	—	—	Remarks : Opened fire on Cruisers on starboard beam. 10.20 p.m. ceased firing.	—
10.7 —	*S.O. 5th B.S.*	*5th B.S.*	F.L.	*Alter course in succession 16 points to port*	—
10.8 —	*S.O. 5th B.S.*	*5th B.S.*	F.L.	*Admiral intends to proceed at 18 knots*	—

Date, Time of Despatch.	From	To	System.	Message.	Time of Origin.
31 MAY—*cont.* 10.10 p.m	Chester	Minotaur	F.L.	Am last ship in your line, and have 23 killed and 25 seriously wounded, three guns disabled. Electric circuit partly disabled, gun control disabled. Have no holes below water line and four holes above water line. Can receive on main wireless. State of oil tanks doubtful. Can do 24 knots until 3 p.m. to-morrow. Will report further on state of oil tanks.	2210
10.10 —	S.O. 4th L.C.S.	4th L.C.S.	F.L.	*Report when all ships are in station and all correct. Rear ships report when leading Battleship is sighted.*	2210
	Caroline	S.O. 4th L.C.S.	F.L.	*All ships present and in station. Two torpedoes were expended by Caroline and one by Royalist to-day.* (*Reply from Caroline at 10.55 p.m.*)	—
10.12 —	Benbow	—	—	Remarks : Firing commenced starboard beam.	—
10.20 —	**C.-in-C.**	**Oak**	F.L.	**Who is vessel on your port bow ? Reply : Abdiel.**	—
10.23 —	Galatea	S.O. 4th L.C.S.	F.L.	On second thought I think I had better keep ahead of you. I shall be more out of the way in case of attack. Reply : Thank you, my present speed is 16 knots.	2200
10.25 —	Inconstant	1st L.C.S.	F.L.	*At 10.30 p.m. alter course to S. 48° E. and reduce to 11 knots till 11 p.m., when course will be altered to S. and speed increased to 17 knots without signal.*	2225
10.25 —	**Captain D4**	**C.-in-C.**	W/T	**Submarine five miles North of Dragonfly (?) at 10 p.m.**	**2220**
10.26 —	S.O. 5th B.S.	5th B.S.	F.L.	*Admiral intends to proceed at 17 knots*	—
10.27 —	Contest	Captain D4	F.L.	*Contest fired one round at three German Destroyers astern steering S.E.*	2225
10.30 —	**Canada**	**C.-in-C.**	F.L.	**Contest to Captain D. Urgent. German T.B.D. steering N.E.**	—
10.30 —	Naval Centre, Sheerness.	Admiralty	L.T.	3rd B.S. and 3rd C.S. at anchor Black Deep.	2000
10.30 —	Garland	Commodore F.	F.L.	*Garland fired at Enemy's Destroyers astern*	2225
10.40 —	Boadicea	Thunderer	F.L.	Enemy's ships on starboard beam -	—
10.40 —	Boadicea	—	—	Remarks : Sighted Enemy's Cruisers showing four red and four green lights horizontal. Shown three times.	—
10.41 —	**Admiralty**	**C.-in-C.**	W/T	**At 10.41 p.m. the Admiralty informed the Commander-in-Chief that the enemy was believed to be returning to its base as its course was S.S.E. ¾ E. and speed 16 knots."**	**2241**
10.42 —	Captain D12	12th Flotilla	F.L.	*Admiral intends to proceed at 17 knots*	—
10.42 —	R.A. Invergordon.	Admiralty	L/T	Cromarty tugs in readiness except Dromedary which is under repair. Hope to undock Emperor of India noon to-morrow, Thursday, retaining two tugs for undocking.	2045
10.43 —	Fortune	Captain D4	W/T	*Fortune fired one round at 9.55 p.m. in direction torpedo came from.*	2235
10.45 —	Benbow	—	—	Remarks : Heavy firing on starboard quarter.	—

Date, Time of Despatch.	From	To	System.	Message.	Time of Origin.
31 MAY—*cont.* 10.46p.m.	**C.-in-C.**	**Commodore F.**	W/T	**Urgent. Are you engaging Enemy's Destroyers ? Reply : No.** (*Reply via Kempenfelt.*)	2243 2300
10.48 —	*Contest*	*Captain D4*	W/T	*Destroyers off starboard quarter steering E.*	—
10.50 —	*Commodore F.*	*11th Flotilla*	F.L.	*Alter course 16 points outwards*	—
10.50 —	**Commodore F. via Kempenfelt.**	**C.-in-C.**	W/T	**My position, course and speed South 17 knots, have been engaged by Enemy Cruisers.** (*This signal crossed 2243 from C.-in-C.*)	2240
10.55 —	*Porpoise*	*Captain D4*	W/T	*German Destroyer astern steering East*	2250
11.0 —	*S.O. 4th L.C.S*	*4th L.C.S.*	F.L.	*Admiral intends to proceed at 16 knots*	—
11.0 —	*S.O.4thL.C.S.*	*4th L.C.S.*	F.L.	*Report if all ships in station and speed unimpaired. I intend to drop slowly back until leading Battleship is sighted.*	—
11.0 —	*S.O. Cruisers*	*Cruisers*	F.L.	*Negative signalling except in case of emergency.*	2055
11.1 —	*Captain D4*	*Broke*	F.L.	*Give me manœuvring room. You have lights on fore bridge and forecastle.*	2252
11.5 —	*Warrior*	*Engadine*	F.L.	What speed are you going now ? Reply : We have revolutions for 19 knots and hope we are going seven.	—
11.22 —	*Unity*	*Fortune*	W/T	*Switch off stern light*	—
11.25 —	*Warrior*	*Engadine*	F.L.	By our log we are going 8.2 knots	—
11.26 —	*Captain D4*	*Garland*	W/T	*11th Destroyer flotilla is on our starboard beam.*	2315
11.30 —	*S.O.2ndL.C.S.*	*Nottingham*	F.L.	*My wireless is shot away, answer calls for me and report the action.*	—
11.30 —	*Minotaur*	—	—	Remarks : Observed flashes port quarter, apparently gun fire.	—
11.30 —	**Birmingham**	**C.-in-C., S.O. B.C.F.**	W/T	**Urgent. Priority. Battle Cruisers, unknown number, probably hostile, in sight, N.E. course S. My position Lat. 56° 26' N., Long. 5° 42' E.**	2330
11.31 —	**Commodore F.**	**C.-in-C. via Kempenfelt.**	W/T	**What is the present course and speed of fleet ? Reply : South, 17 knots.**	2341
11.34 —	*Benbow*	—	—	Remarks : Firing reported astern and on port quarter.	—
11.38 —	**S.O. 2nd L.C.S. via Nottingham.**	**C.-in-C., S.O. B.C.F.**	W/T	**Urgent. Have engaged Enemy's Cruisers 10.15 p.m., bearing W.S.W.** (*Received in Iron Duke 11.38 p.m.*)	2240
11.39 —	*Benbow*	—	—	Remarks : Firing port quarter	—
11.45 —	*Benbow*	—	—	Remarks : Firing port quarter (long distance)	—
11.47 —	*Ambuscade*	*Captain D4*	W/T	Have fired two torpedoes and heard one explosion. (*Via Indomitable to S.O. B.C.F.*)	2342
11.55 —	*S.O.2ndL.C.S.*	*2nd L.C.S.*	W/T	*Admiral intends to proceed at 20 knots*	—
JUNE 1st. 12.0 midnight	*Fearless*	—	—	Remarks : Action on port quarter and astern continued till 12.30.	—
12.0 —	*Commodore F.*	*11th Flotilla*	F.L.	*Admiral intends to proceed at 18 knots*	—
12.0 —	*S.O. 5th B.S.*	*5th B.S.*	F.L.	*Admiral intends to proceed at 17 knots*	—

Date, Time of Despatch.	From	To	System.	Message.	Time of Origin.
1 JUNE —*cont.*					
12.4 a.m.	Captain D12-	Commodore F.	F.L.	*1st B.S. is South five miles. Am I to follow you or steer South after fleet ?*	2350
				Reply : Keep in touch with fleet	0015
12.5 —	Captain D12-	12th Flotilla -	F.L.	*Alter course in succession to E.S.E.*	—
12.5 —	Superb	—	—	Remarks : Observed firing astern from 12.5 to 12.15 a.m., also 12.30 large flare astern and firing.	—
12.7 —	Dublin	S.O. 2nd L.C.S.	W/T	*What is present course and speed of Southampton ?*	0005
				Reply : My position, course and speed at midnight, Lat. 55°43′ N., Long. 6°24′E., South, 20 knots.	0015
12.10 —	Achates	Commodore F.	—	*2nd Division of Destroyers 4th Flotilla still steering South, is this correct ?*	0007
				Reply : Yes	0031
12.12 —	**C.-in-C.**	**Royal Oak**	W/T	**You are showing a bright light forward**	**2347**
12.16 —	Captain D12-	12th Flotilla -	F.L.	*Admiral intends to proceed at 17 knots.* Remarks : 12.16 a.m. Enemy Cruiser on either bow opened fire. Flotilla spread.	—
12.30 —	Captain D12-	Commodore F.	W/T	*What is your position, course and speed ?*	0027
12.30 —	Contest	Achates	W/T	*Have lost 1st Division, can only steam 20 knots. Request instructions.*	0016
12.30 —	S.O.2ndL.C.S.	Dublin	W/T	*My speed 17 knots*	—
12.30 —	Captain D12	Commodore F.	W/T	*My course and speed at 12.15 a.m., S., 17 knots.*	0017
12.33 —	Achates	Commodore F.	W/T	*Am being chased to the eastward*	0031
12.35 —	Commodore F.	11th Flotilla -	F.L.	*Admiral intends to proceed at 20 knots*	—
12.37 —	S.O.2ndL.C.S.	2nd L.C.S.	W/T	*Admiral intends to proceed at 17 knots*	—
12.42 —	Garland	Commodore F.	W/T	*I am at present steering S. What shall I steer ?*	0030
12.56 —	Commodore F.	Captain D, 4th and 12th Flotillas, and 4th and 12th Flotillas.	W/T	*My course and speed are S., 18 knots*	0045
1.0 —	Captain D12	12th Flotilla -	F.L.	*Admiral intends to proceed at 18 knots*	—
1.0 —	Fearless	—	—	Remarks : Vessel blown up on starboard quarter.	—
1.0 —	Commodore F.	11th Flotilla -	F.L.	*Admiral intends to proceed at 25 knots*	—
1.15 —	Ambuscade -	Commodore F.	W/T	*What is your position ?*	0100
1.22 —	Achates	Commodore F.	W/T	*Indicate your position*	0000
1.27 —	Commodore F.	11th Flotilla -	F.L.	*Admiral intends to proceed at 20 knots*	—
1.37 —	Inconstant -	1st L.C.S.	F.L.	*Admiral intends to proceed at 20 knots*	—
1.48 —	**Admiralty**	**C.-in-C.**	W/T	**At 1.48 a.m. the Admiralty informed the Commander-in-Chief that enemy submarines were apparently coming out from German ports, and that a damaged enemy ship, probably Lutzow, was in Lat. 56° 26′ N., Long. 5° 41′ E. at Midnight.**	**0148**

Date, Time of Despatch.	From	To	System.	Message.	Time of Origin.
1 JUNE—*cont.*					
1.50 a.m.	*Constance* -	*S.O. 4th L.C.S.*	F.L.	*2nd B.S. bearing East three miles* -	—
1.52 —	*S.O.4thL.C.S.*	*4th L.C.S.* -	F.L.	*Admiral intends to proceed at 18 knots* -	—
1.53 —	*S.O.2ndL.C.S.*	*Nottingham* -	F.L.	*What is in sight astern ? Reply : Nothing in sight astern.*	—
1.56 —	*S.O. 1st B.S.*-	*Revenge*	F.L.	*I must ease down and will haul out of line to starboard, you continue on.*	*0155*
1.56 —	**S.O. 1st B.S.**-	**C.-in-C.** -	W/T	**Obliged to ease to 12 knots. Remainder of Division are continuing at 17 knots.**	0155
1.56 —	**Capt. D12** -	**C.-in-C.** -	W/T	**Urgent. Priority. Enemy's Battleships in sight. My position 10 miles astern of 1st B.S.** (*This signal was incompletely logged in Faulknor's log, and there are no records of it having been received in Iron Duke.*)	0152
2.0 —	*Ambuscade* -	*Commodore F.*	W/T	*Have expended all torpedoes. I am alone. Position 0200, 56° 0' N., 6° 08' E., doubtful, request instructions.*	*0155*
2.0 —	*S.O. 5th B.S.*	*5th B.S.*	F.L.	*Admiral intends to proceed at 18 knots* -	—
2.1 —	*S.O.4thL.C.S.*	*4th L.C.S.* -	F.L.	*Prepare to form in single line-abreast to starboard. Take station ahead. Ships in column to be five cables apart.*	—
2.6 —	**Commodore F.** via Kempenfelt.	**C.-in-C.** -	W/T	**What is your position, course and speed ?**	0200
2.7 —	*Admiralty* -	*Talisman* -	W/T	Detach two Submarines towards Lister Deep, objective—damaged ships. They should remain 48 hours and be careful of other British Submarines.	0207
2.7 —	*S.O.2ndL.C.S.*	*Active* •	S.L.	Who is ahead of you ? Reply : 2nd B.S.	0200
2.8 —	**Captain D12**	**C.-in-C.** -	W/T	**Urgent. Am attacking** - - - - (*There are no records of this signal having been received by any ship.*)	0207
2.10 —	*Commodore F.*	*11th Flotilla* -	F.L.	*Admiral intends to proceed at 25 knots* -	—
2.13 —	**Captain D12**-	**C.-in-C.** -	W/T	**Urgent. Course of enemy S.S.W.** - - (*There are no records of this signal having been received by any ship except Marksman.*)	0212
2.15 —	**C.-in-C.** -	**General** -	F.L.	**At 2.30 a.m. 2nd B.S. alter course to starboard to North. 4th B.S. will follow round. B.F. will form single line-ahead in 5th organisation.**	0200
2.15 —	*S.O.4thL.C.S.*	*4th L.C.S.* -	F.L.	*Keep closed up. Admiral intends to proceed at 20 knots.*	—
2.15 —	*S.O.2ndL.C.S.*	*2nd L.C.S.* -	F.L.	*Report any casualties and damage ? Replies : Nottingham nil, Birmingham nil.*	—
2.15 —	Chester •	S.O. 2nd C.S.-	W/T	Oil will last several days. Dead now number 28, seriously wounded 36, all from upper deck. In view of depletion of numbers and difficulty of fighting ship without trained crews, fire control only one side, possible flooding of lower mess deck in bad weather. Request instructions. (*Received by S.O. 2nd C.S. as—oil will last several hours.*)	0205

Date, Time of Despatch.	From	To	System.	Message.	Time of Origin.
1 JUNE —*cont.*					
2.17 a.m.	*S.O. 1st B.S.-*	*Revenge*	F.L.	*I am going to transfer to you in Fearless*	0215
2.18 —	**King George V.**	**C.-in-C.**	F.L.	**4th L.C.S. is one mile on my starboard beam.**	0210
2.20 —	Captain D13	Marksman	F.L.	Where are Enemy's ships ? Reply : Suspicious ships South.	—
2.20 —	Marksman	—	—	Remarks : Engaged Enemy's Destroyers and Light Cruisers (four Destroyers and two Cruisers).	
2.20 —	*S.O. 4thL.C.S.*	*4th L.C.S.*	F.L.	*Admiral intends to proceed at 17 knots*	—
2.20 —	S.O. 2nd C.S.	Destroyers	Flags	Form Submarine screen	—
2.21 —	S.O. 1st B.S.	Fearless	F.L.	Come alongside my port side. I am going to transfer to Revenge in you.	—
2.22 —	**C.-in-C.**	**S.O. B.C.F. S.O. 4th L.C.S., S.O. 2nd C.S., S.O. 1st C.S., All Captains D.**	W/T	**Priority. My position 2.30 a.m., Lat. 55° 07′ N., Long. 6° 21′ E., altering course N., conform and close.**	0212
2.25 —	**C.-in-C.**	**S.O. 4th L.C.S.**	F.L.	**Battlefleet will alter course to North at 2.30 a.m. Keep ahead.**	0215
2.25 —	Captain D13	Marksman	F.L.	Where is our battlefleet ? Reply : Bearing South.	—
2.25 —	S.O. 2nd C.S.	Destroyers	S.L.	How long will your fuel last ? Reply : At present speed oil fuel will last Owl 40 hours, Hardy 40 hours, Midge 40 hours, Mischief 48 hours.	0225
2.25 —	Falmouth	—	—	Remarks : Sighted Battle Cruisers port bow.	—
2.27 —	S.O. 2nd C.S.	Destroyers	Flags and S.L.	Negative form Submarine screen. We shall be turning 16 points presently.	—
2.27 —	**C.-in-C.**	**Attached Cruisers.**	F.L.	**Take special repeating ship, port side**	—
2.27 —	*Mœnad*	*Captain D12*	W/T	*What is your position ?*	*0225*
2.27 —	*Nottingham*	*S.O. 2nd L.C.S.*	F.L.	*Barham N.E.*	*0225*
2.28 —	S.O. 5th B.S.	Nottingham	F.L.	Indicate bearing of battlefleet ? Reply from Southampton : 2nd B.S. South, two miles.	—
2.28 —	S.O. B.C.F.	S.O. 3rd L.C.S.	S.L.	Is Galatea in sight ? Reply : No	—
2.29 —	*Commodore F.*	*11th Flotilla*	F.L.	*Alter course 16 points outwards*	—
2.29 —	S.O. B.C.F.	Inconstant	S.L.	What Light Cruisers are in company ? Reply : Phaeton, Cordelia. Galatea's speed reduced and told me to take charge of 1st L.C.S. and carry on.	—
2.30 —	S.O. 2nd C.S.	Chester	Sem.	Make the best of your way to the Humber	0228
2.30 —	S.O. B.C.F.	Ships in Company.	Flags	Assume complete readiness for immediate action in every respect.	—
2.30 —	**King George V.**	**C.-in-C.**	F.L.	**Shall I go on ?** Reply : **Wait a minute**	—
2.30 —	Marksman	Captain D13	F.L.	What are ships bearing South ? Reply : Germans, I think.	—
2.30 —	**C.-in-C.**	**Galatea**	F.L.	**I am altering course at 2.30 a.m. to North**	—
2.30 —	*S.O. 3rd L.C.S.*	*Gloucester*	S.L.	*Are there any signs of 1st L.C.S. ?* Reply : *1st L.C.S. on my port quarter.*	—

Date, Time of Despatch.	From	To	System.	Message.	Time of Origin.
1 JUNE—*cont.*					
2.30 a.m.	Southampton	—	—	Remarks : Firing on port bow	—
2.30 —	**R.A. 1st B.S.**	**C.-in-C.**	F.L.	**Marlborough's division is not in visual touch.**	**0230**
2.33 —	Benbow	—	—	Remarks : Iron Duke opened fire	—
2.34 —	S.O. B.C.F.	T.B.Ds.	Flags	Form Submarine screen	—
2.35 —	*Captain D12*	*Marksman*	W/T	*Work round to South*	*0220*
				(Passed to Champion.)	
2.35 —	Marksman	Captain D13	F.L.	Shall I join you ? Reply : Yes	—
2.35 —	**C.-in-C.**	**King George V.**	S.L.	**Carry on when you are a bit straight**	—
2.35 —	*S.O.2ndL.C.S.*	*Nottingham*	F.L.	*Admiral intends to proceed at 20 knots*	—
2.35 —	*S.O.2ndL.C.S.*	*2nd L.C.S.*	F.L.	*Admiral intends to proceed at 22 knots. Negative zigzag.*	—
2.35 —	S.O. 5th B.S.	5th B.S.	Flags	*Admiral intends to proceed at 21 knots*	—
2.36 —	S.O. B.C.F.	General	Flags	Alter course in succession 16 points to starboard.	—
2.36 —	*Onslaught*	*Captain D12*	W/T	*1st Lieut. killed. Captain seriously injured. Fore bridge gone.*	*0230*
2.40 —	*Commodore F.*	*11th Flotilla*	F.L.	*Alter course in succession to N.N.W.*	—
2.40 —	Marksman	Mænad	F.L.	Am joining Champion	—
2.40 —	*S.O.4thL.C.S.*	*4th L.C.S.*	Flags	*Alter course together to N.*	—
2.40 —	S.O. 2nd B.S.	S.O. 4th L.C.S.	F.L.	What ship is that ahead of you ? Keep out of my way when I alter course. Reply : Galatea reported last night reducing speed.	—
2.40 —	*S.O.4thL.C.S.*	*4th L.C.S.*	Flags	*Ships in column to be five cables apart*	—
2.40 —	S.O. B.C.F.	S.O. 1st L.C.S.	W/T	Alter course in succession to N.	0234
2.41 —	*Commodore F.*	*11th Flotilla*	F.L.	*Admiral intends to proceed at 22 knots*	—
2.42 —	*Nottingham*	*S.O. 2nd L.C.S.*	S.L.	*Galatea is other side of battlefleet, reported reducing speed.*	—
2.42 —	*Mænad*	*Captain D12*	W/T	*What is your course and speed ?*	*0238*
2.42 —	*S.O. 2nd B.S.*	*Orion*	F.L.	*Keep straight on*	—
2.43 —	S.O. B.C.F.	S.O. 2nd C.S.	S.L.	Am altering course to North. Are you in sight of battlefleet ? Reply : No. We make our battlefleet N. 38° E., 16 miles from us.	—
2 44 —	*S.O. 5th B.S.*	*5th B.S.*	Flags	*Alter course in succession 16 points to starboard. Admiral intends to proceed 19 knots.*	—
2.45 —	S.O. B.C.F.	General	F.L.	Indicate your position ? Replies : Princess Royal 55° 0′ N., 6° 10′ E. ; New Zealand 54° 55′ N., 6° 7′ E. ; Indomitable 54° 58′ N., 6° 15′ E. ; Inflexible 55° 6′ N., 6° 16′ E.	—
2.45 —	*Nottingham*	*S.O. 2nd L.C.S.*	S.L.	*Birmingham N. by E.*	—
2.45 —	*S.O.4thL.C.S.*	*4th L.C.S.*	Flags	*Admiral intends to proceed at 15 knots*	—
2.45 —	*Onslaught*	*Captain D12*	W/T	*Remainder of casualties not yet ascertained*	*0240*

Date, Time of Despatch.	From	To	System.	Message.	Time of Origin.
1 JUNE—cont.					
2.47 a.m.	Tiger - -	S.O. B.C.F. -	S.L.	Inconstant reports one Light Cruiser S.W. -	0225
2.50 —	S.O. 5th B.S.	S.O. 2nd B.S.-	F.L.	Request bearing of Battle Cruisers? Reply: I do not know where Battle Cruisers are.	—
2.50 —	Hercules -	Revenge -	Sem.	How does your reckoning compare with mine, as reference position made at 9.45 p.m. last night? I make it we are now 12 miles to N.W. of Iron Duke.	0235
				Reply : Working from Iron Duke's reference position of last night, I make our position about N. by E. seven to eight miles.	0300
2.50 —	S.O.4thL.C.S.	4th L.C.S. -	Flags	Zigzag one point. First turn to starboard-	—
2.50 —	S.O. 2nd C.S.	S.O. B.C.F. -	S.L.	Have detached Chester to Humber. She had only oil till 3 p.m.	0250
2.50 —	S.O. 2nd C.S.	2nd C.S. -	Flags	Alter course in succession to N. - -	—
2.50 —	**C.-in-C.** -	**General** -	S.L.	**King George V. take Guide of fleet - -**	—
2.50 —	S.O. B.C.F.-	Tiger - -	S.L.	Where is Inconstant ? - - - -	—
2.51 —	S.O.2ndL.C.S.	Birmingham -	S.L.	Report if battlefleet astern of you alters course.	—
2.52 —	Admiralty -	Commodore T.	L/T	5th L.C.S., 9th and 10th flotillas should join C.-in-C. to replace squadrons or flotillas short of fuel. Proceed towards Lat. 55° 30′ N., Long. 6° 0′ E., until orders are received from C.-in-C.	0252
2.52 —	S.O.3rdL.C.S.	Chester -	S.L.	Are you detached to join me ? Reply : Have orders to proceed to Humber with wounded.	—
2.52 —	S.O. B.C.F. -	General -	Flags	Alter course in succession to N.N.E. -	—
2.52 —	S.O. B.C.F. -	S.O. 2nd C.S.-	S.L.	Can you give me bearing of our battlefleet ? Reply : No. We make our battlefleet N. 38° E., 16 miles from us.	0254
2.54 —	**Abdiel -** -	**C.-in-C.** -	W/T	**Minefield has been accurately laid in accordance with orders.**	0245
2.55 —	Captain D13	Destroyers in Company.	Flags	Alter course in succession to W.N.W. Admiral intends to proceed at 19 knots.	—
2.57 —	**C.-in-C.** -	**Canada -** -	W/T	**Priority. Are you in W/T communication with Captain D, 4th flotilla ? Reply : No.**	—
2.58 —	S.O.2ndL.C.S.	S.O. 1st L.C.S.	S.L.	Do you know where B.Cs. are ? Reply : No, have not seen them since yesterday evening, as my speed has been reduced.	0200
2.59 —	Admiralty -	Commodore T.	W/T	Position of British Submarines. Talisman and two Submarines Lat. 54° 30′ N., Long. 4° 0′ E., and two Submarines proceeding thence towards Lister Deep. Three Submarines W. of Vyl L.V.	0259
3.0 —	**C.-in-C.** -	**Boadicea, Active.**	F.L.	**Pass through line between Iron Duke and Thunderer. Do not come at an acute angle.**	0256
3.0 —	S.O. 5th B.S.	5th B.S. -	Flags	Alter course together two points to port -	—
3.0 —	Unity - -	Commodore F.	W/T	Am with 9th Flotilla. Have all torpedoes. Maximum speed.	0215
3.0 —	S.O. Cruisers	Cruisers -	Flags	Admiral intends to proceed at 19 knots -	—
3.0 —	S.O.2ndL.C.S.	2nd L.C.S -	S.L.	Zigzag. Speed of advance 16½ knots -	—

Date, Time of Despatch.	From	To	System.	Message.	Time of Origin.
1 JUNE—*cont.*					
3.5 a.m.	Captain D13	Marksman -	Sem.	Do you know where the rest of your flotilla is ? Reply : I think to the southward.	—
3.5 —	S.O. B.C.F. -	General -	Flags	Admiral intends to proceed at 20 knots -	—
3.5 —	S.O. B.C.F. -	S.O. 2nd C.S.-	S.L.	Did you get signal from C.-in-C. to close ? Reply : Yes, am proceeding at 20 knots.	0306
3.5 —	*Kempenfelt* -	Commodore F.	S.L.	*I do not think we made our speed on southern course.*	—
3.5 —	*S.O. Cruisers*	Cruisers -	Flags	*Alter course in succession to N. ½ E.* -	—
3.5 —	*S.O. 1st B.S.*	Revenge -	Sem.	*Haul out of line to starboard and stop engines.*	0300
3.6 —	S.O. 2nd L.C.S.	S.O. 4th L.C.S.	S.L.	Do you know where our Battle Cruisers are? Reply : Regret have no idea. Galatea is other side of battlefleet reducing speed.	0240
3.8 —	*S.O. 5th B.S.*	5th B.S. -	Flags	*Alter course together two points to starboard*	—
3.10 —	*S.O. 5th B.S.*	Malaya -	Sem.	*Report nature of damage - - - -* Reply : *Two, if not three, shell-holes below water-line, starboard side, and watertight compartment of submerged tube flooded, also C.P.O.'s bath-room and gunner's store room, and I think that has caused a leak into two oil tanks. Turret hit on top and loading can only be carried out by auxiliary means, owing to bogie jamming. One 6-in. gun completely out of action, three others can be fired by percussion. Casualties heavy on gun deck, all damage starboard side.*	0310 0320
				Further reply : Re previous report of damage, now ascertained to be—(1) All starboard bunkers in A boiler room flooded, (2) The compartment outboard of these bunkers also flooded, and one outboard compartment of B boiler room ; (3) Wing compartments starboard side of submerged flat flooded, as steampipe to capstan engine passes through this it is highly probable that steam cannot be put on capstan ; (4) Chief P.O.'s bathroom flooded ; (5) Water in three other compartments on starboard side of ship ; (6) Starboard fore submerged tube bar jammed ; (7) Ship's company's galley wrecked and wiring for Nos. 1 and 2 groups of starboard 6-in. battery fused. All lighting circuit starboard side should be renewed.	—
3.10 —	S.O. B.C.F.-	Inconstant -	S.L.	Alter course to N.N.E. Admiral intends to proceed at 20 knots.	—
3.10 —	*Gloucester* -	S.O. 3rd L.C.S.	S.L.	*Zeppelin bearing S.E.* - - -	—
3.10 —	Falmouth -	—	—	Remarks : Sighted Light Cruisers port bow, apparently 2nd L.C.S. Passed mine port beam.	—
3.11 —	S.O. B.C.F. -	S.O. 2nd C.S.-	S L.	What course are you steering to head off C.-in-C. ?	0310

Date, Time of Despatch.	From	To	System.	Message.	Time of Origin.
1 JUNE—*cont.* 3.11 a.m.	**C.-in-C.** -	**S.O. 1st B.S.**-	W/T	Marlborough proceed to Tyne or Rosyth by M Channel. Destroyers will be sent when available. You should ask for local Destroyers to convoy you. There are four of our Submarines South of Area 1.	0228
3.12 —	**Admiralty** -	**C.-in-C.** -	W/T	German light Cruiser in 55° 45′ N., 6° 25′ E., damaged, crew taken off, Destroyers standing by 3 a.m.	0312
3.12 —	S.O. Cruisers	Destroyers -	Flags	Form Submarine screen - - -	—
3.12 —	*S.O. Cruisers*	*Cruisers* -	Flags	*Admiral intends to proceed at 20 knots*	—
3.14 —	S.O. 2nd C.S.	S.O. B.C.F. -	S.L.	Aircraft in sight S.S.E. and S.-	—
3.14 —	S.O. 2nd C.S.	S.O. B.C.F. -	S.L.	My course is N. ½ E. - - -	—
3.14 —	S.O.1st L.C.S.	S.O. 2nd L C.S	S.L.	Have you seen anything ? Reply : Not since 10.30 last night when I was heavily engaged with Enemy's Cruisers.	—
3.14 —	**C.-in-C.** -	**Marlborough** -	W/T	Send your division to join me, keeping one ship as escort if necessary What is your position, course and speed ?	0302
3.15 —	**C.-in-C.** -	**S.O. 5th B.S.** -	W/T	Priority. My course 2.30 a.m. is N. -	0310
3.15 —	New Zealand	—	—	Remarks : Sighted Zeppelin starboard quarter.	—
3.15 —	**S.O. 1st B.S.**-	**C.-in-C.** -	W/T	I am now transferring to Revenge. What is your position, course and speed ?	0314
3.15 —	Falmouth -	S.O. B.C.F. -	S.L.	Zeppelin bearing S.E. by S., steering about N.E. by E.	0315
3.15 —	Falmouth -	—	—	Remarks : Zeppelin starboard quarter -	—
3.15 —	Indomitable-	S.O. B.C.F. -	W/T and S.L.	Enemy's Airship in sight to the southward	0315
3.15 —,	*Nottingham* -	*S.O. 2nd L.C.S.*	F.L.	*Can hear signals very strong from drifter on your bow.*	*0315*
3.19 —	Indomitable-	—	—	Remarks : Fired three rounds at Zeppelin	—
3.20 —	**C.-in-C.** -	**Revenge** -	W/T	My course at 2.30 a.m., North, 16 knots. Close me.	0307
3.20 —	S.O.2ndL.C.S.	S.O. 5th B.S.-	S.L.	What is your speed ? Reply : Speed of advance 17 knots.	—
3.20 —	Superb -	—	—	Remarks : Heard firing astern, also at 3.35 a.m. on port quarter.	—
3.20 —	*Opal* -	*Captain D12* -	W/T	*Opal and eight Destroyers. Course S., 16 knots, 15 miles to westward of your 0200 position.*	*0315*
3.20 —	Hydra -	S.O. B.C.F. -	S.L.	Zeppelin bearing South - - - -	—
3.20 —	*Hampshire* -	*S.O. Cruisers* -	S.L.	*Zeppelin bearing South* - - - -	—
3.20 —	Falmouth	—	—	Remarks : Torpedo passed ahead from port to starboard. Commenced firing at Zeppelin.	—
3.20 —	*Onslaught* -	*Commodore F.*	W/T	*All torpedoes fired. Gunner and 1st Lieut. killed. Commanding officer severely wounded. One gun out of action. Permission to return to base.*	*0310*
				Reply : Approved - - - -	*0430*

H h 2

Date, Time of Despatch.	From	To	System.	Message.	Time of Origin.
1 JUNE —*cont.*					
3.20 a.m.	**Admiralty** -	**C.-in-C.** -	W/T	Five Light Cruisers, 13 Destroyers ordered from Harwich towards Lat. 55° 30′ N., Long. 6° 0′ E., to join you and replace vessels requiring fuel.	0320
3.22 —	Canterbury -	—	—	Remarks : Torpedo passed the track from port to starboard.	—
3.22 —	PrincessRoyal	—	—	Remarks : Tiger fired at Zeppelin - -	—
3.24 —	S.N.O. Harwich.	Admiralty -	L/T	Lurcher arrived - - - - -	.—
3.24 —	*Shannon* -	*S.O. Cruisers* -	S.L.	*Hostile Airships bearing S.S.E.* - -	—
3.25 —	*Commodore T.*	*Light Cruisers and Destroyers.*	Flags	*Raise steam for full speed with all despatch and report when ready to proceed.*	—
3.25 —	*Narborough* -	*Captain D13* -	W/T	*Submit I have Pelican, Nicator, Nerissa, Petard, in company with me. Petard can only go 28 knots. Nicator reports serious accident. Request instructions.*	*0305*
3.27 —	*Inconstant* -	*Cordelia* -	S.L.	*Rejoin* - - - - - -	—
3.28 —	S.O. B.C.F. -	General -	S.L. and Flags	Alter course in succession to N. by E. -	—
3.29 —	**Admiralty** -	**C.-in-C.** -	W/T	**Urgent. At 2.30 German Main Fleet in Lat. 55° 33′ N., Long. 6° 50′ E., course S.E. by S., 16 knots.**	0329
3.30 —	*S.O. 5th B.S.*	*5th B.S.* -	Flags	*Alter course together four points to starboard*	—
3.30 —	**Oak** -	**C.-in-C.** -	S.L.	**Report of guns W.S.W.** - - -	—
3.31 —	Marlborough	Faulknor -	S.L.	V.A. has shifted his flag to Revenge. They are about five miles astern of me.	—
3.33 —	*Marlborough* -	*Revenge* -	W/T	*Make to 6th Division. Alter course.*	—
3.34 —	*S.O. 5th B.S.*	*5th B.S.* -	Flags	*Admiral intends to proceed at 18 knots* -	—
3.35 —	**C.-in-C.** -	**S.O. B.C.F.** -	W/T	**Did you get Admiralty telegram 0148 ?** -	0326
3.35 —	*S.O.2ndL.C.S.*	*2nd L.C.S.* -	S.L.	*Speed of advance 17 knots* - - -	—
3.35 —	Badger -	S.O. B.C.F. -	S.L.	Destroyers had about 80 tons of oil fuel at 4 a.m. -	—
3.36 —	**C.-in-C.** -	**S.O. 2nd B.S.** -	S.L.	**Look out for damaged Enemy Battle Cruisers ahead or on either bow, probably with large number of T.B.Ds.**	0330
3.36 —	*S.O. 1st B.S.* -	*1st B.S.* -	Flags	*Admiral intends to proceed at 17 knots* -	—
3.38 —	**S.O. 5th B.S.** -	**C.-in-C.** -	W/T	**Barham, Malaya, Valiant, two miles ahead of 2nd B.S.**	0335
3.40 —	**Benbow** -	**C.-in-C.** -	Sem.	**Heavy firing heard W.S.W. from Benbow** -	0335
3.40 —	*S.O. 5th B.S.*	*5th B.S.* -	Flags	*Alter course together four points to port. Admiral intends to proceed at 17 knots.*	—
3.40 —	*Commodore F.*	*11th Flotilla* -	S.L.	*Alter course in succession 16 points outwards*	—
3.42 —	*Captain D13*	*Destroyers in Company.*	Flags	*Admiral intends to proceed at 16 knots* -	—
3.42 —	Inconstant -	S.O. B.C.F. -	S.L.	Cordelia is sinking a mine - - -	0335
3.42 —	**S.O.3rdL.C.S.**	**S.O. B.C.F., C.-in-C.**	W/T	**Priority. Am engaging Enemy Zeppelin. My position Lat. 55° 17′ N., Long. 6° 08′ E.**	0335

Date, Time of Despatch.	From	To	System.	Message.	Time of Origin.
1 JUNE—*cont.*					
3.42 a.m.	*Unity* - -	*Commodore F.*	W/T	*What is your position, course and speed ?*	*0333*
3.42 —	*S.O. B.C.F.*	*Princess Royal*	Sem.	*What ship is firing ?* - - -	*0342*
3.42 —	**C.-in-C.** -	**General** - -	Flags	**Divisions separately alter course in succession to West preserving their formation. Admiral intends to proceed at 15 knots.**	—
3.44 —	**C.-in-C.** -	**King George V.**	S.L.	**What Battleships are ahead of you ?** Reply : Three ships of 5th B.S.	**0340**
3.45 —	*R.A. 1st B.S.*	*Collingwood* -	Sem.	*Report Zeppelin bearing S.S.E., steering North, to C.-in-C., we have no searchlights.*	*0350*
3.45 —	**C.-in-C.** -	**General** -	Flags	**Admiral resume Guide of fleet -** - -	—
3.45 —	S.O. 1st B.S.	Faulknor -	Flags	Close - - - - - - -	—
3.46 —	*Captain D12-*	*12th Flotilla* -	W/T	*Have joined B.F. Course N., speed 17 knots. Conform.*	*0330*
3.47 —	*S.O.2ndL.C.S.*	*Dublin* - -	W/T	*My position Lat. 55° 19' N., Long. 6° 33' E., course North, speed 17 knots. What is your position, course and speed ?*	*0330*
				Reply : My position approximately 4.30 a.m., 55° 30' N., 6° 32' E.	*0422*
3.48 —	Marksman -	Captain D13 -	S.L.	Are you joining battlefleet ? Reply : Yes.	—
3.48 —	*S.O.3rdL.C.S.*	*3rd L.C.S.* -	Flags	*Admiral intends to proceed at 20 knots* -	—
3.50 —	Captain D12	S.O. 1st B.S. -	Sem.	Flotilla attacked battlefleet, six Kaiser class and three Cruisers at 2 a.m., last seen steering S.E. One Battleship blown up.	0240
				Reply : I congratulate you on the result of your attack last night. Has the information been reported to the C.-in-C.? If not, I will pass it on to him.	1055
3.50 —	*Commodore T.*	*General* -	Flags	*Slip* - - - - - - -	—
3.50 —	*Captain D13*	*Destroyers in Company.*	Flags	*Zigzag. Admiral intends to proceed at 17½ knots.*	—
3.52 —	**C.-in-C.** -	**General** -	Flags	**Alter course leading ships together rest in succession to North. Admiral intends to proceed at 17 knots.**	—
3.52 —	**S.O. 1st B.S.**	**C.-in-C.** - -	W/T	**Marlborough steering North about 12 knots.**	**0330**
3.52 —	**Collingwood** -	**C.-in-C.** -	W/T	**Urgent. Enemy Airship S.S.E.** - -	**0350**
3.53 —	*S.O.4thL.C.S.*	*4th L.C.S.* -	Flags	*Alter course together two points to port* -	—
3.53 —	Benbow -	—	—	Remarks : Zeppelin in sight - - -	—
3.54 —	**Bellona** -	**C.-in-C.** - -	S.L.	**One Airship bearing S.E., steering West -**	—
3.54 —	Iron Duke -	—	—	Remarks : Sighted Airship on port bow -	—
3.55 —	*S.O.2ndL.C.S.*	*2nd L.C.S.* -	F.L.	*Admiral intends to proceed at 22 knots. Negative zigzag.*	—
3.55 —	Benbow -	—	—	Remarks : 5th B.S. in sight on port bow (three ships)	—
3.55 —	*Commodore F.*	*11th Flotilla* -	S.L.	*Alter course together eight points to starboard.*	—
3.55 —	*Nottingham* -	*S.O. 2nd L.C.S.*	F.L.	*Battlefleet altered course to East* - -	—
3.55 —	**C.-in-C.** -	**General**	Flags	**Engage Enemy Airship -** - - -	—

Date, Time of Despatch.	From	To	System.	Message.	Time of Origin.
1 JUNE—*cont.*					
3.57 a.m.	*S.O. 5th B.S.*	*5th B.S.* -	Flags	*Alter course in succession to N.* - -	—
3.58 —	S.O. 5th B.S.	S.O. 2nd L.C.S.	S.L.	Alter course leading ships together the rest in succession to North. Admiral intends to proceed at 17 knots.	—
3.58 —	**C.-in-C.** -	**General** -	Flags	**Cease fire** - - - - - -	—
4.0 —	*S.O. 1st B.S.*	*Marlborough* -	W/T	*Proceed to Tyne or Rosyth by M Channel. Destroyers will be sent when available. You should ask for local Destroyers to convoy you. There are four of our Submarines S. of Area 1.*	0400
4.0 —	**C.-in-C.** -	**General** -	Flags	**King George V. take Guide of fleet** -	—
4.2 —	*Commodore F.*	*Opal* - -	S.L.	*Have you seen anything of battlefleet or Cruisers? Reply: No.*	—
4.3 —	S.O. 5th B.S.	General	S.L.	Alter course leading ships together the rest in succession to North. Admiral intends to proceed at 17 knots.	—
4.4 —	**S.O. B.C.F.** -	**C.-in-C.**	W/T	**When last seen Enemy was to the W., steering S.W., and proceeding slowly. Zeppelin has passed astern of me steering West. Submit I may sweep S.W. to locate Enemy.**	0350
4.4 —	**S.O. B.C.F.** -	**C.-in-C.** -	W/T	**My position Lat. 55° 26′ N., Long. 6° 14′ E., course N. by E., speed 20 knots.**	0400
4.5 —	S.O. B.C.F. -	General -	Flags	Reference position at 4 a.m., 55° 26′ N., 6° 15′ E.	—
4.5 —	Marlborough	—	—	Remarks: Enemy Airship in sight, 4.7 a.m. open fire, 4.12 a.m. cease fire.	—
4.6 —	*S.O. 5th B.S.*	*5th B.S.* -	Flags	*Alter course together two points to port* -	—
4.6 —	*S.O.4thL.C.S.*	*4th L.C.S.* -	Flags	*Close Caroline* - - - - -	—
4.7 —	S.O. B.C.F.	Light Cruisers	S.L.	Spread well to westward and endeavour to locate Enemy. Keep linking ships in visual touch and pass to 3rd L.C.S. My course N.N.W., 20 knots.	0407
4.7 —	*S.O.4thL.C.S.*	*4th L.C.S.* -	Flags	*Admiral intends to proceed at 24 knots* -	—
4.8 —	Fearless -	Marlborough -	Sem.	I have been sent to escort you, shall I proceed in front? Reply: Yes, please.	—
4.8 —	**C.-in-C.** -	**5th B.S.** -	S.L.	**Take station ahead three miles** - -	—
4.10 —	*Achates* -	*Ambuscade* -	W/T	*What is your position, course and speed?*	0320
4.10 —	*S.O. 5th B.S.*	*5th B.S.* -	Flags	*Alter course together two points to starboard*	—
4.11 —	Fearless -	Marlborough -	Sem.	What speed are you going? Reply: 13 knots.	—
4.12 —	*Commodore F.*	*12th Flotilla* -	S.L.	*Alter course together eight points to port* -	—
4.13 —	**C.-in-C.** -	**General** -	Flags	**Form divisions in line-ahead, columns disposed abeam, ships turning to port.**	—
4.13 —	*Commodore F.*	*12th Flotilla* -	S.L.	*Alter course together four points to starboard*	—
4.13 —	*Captain D12.*	*Opal* - -	W/T	*Steer North* - - - - -	0410
4.14 —	*S.O.4thL.C.S.*	*4th L.C.S.* -	Flags	*Form single line-ahead. Alter course in succession to N.N.W.*	—
4.14 —	S.O. B.C.F. -	General -	Flags	Alter course in succession to N.N.W. Ships in column to keep close order.	—

Date, Time of Despatch.	From	To	System.	Message.	Time of Origin.
1 JUNE 4.15 a.m.	Admiralty -	R.A. East Coast	W/T	Send two Destroyers to eastern end of M Channel to escort Marlborough. Reply : Ness and Albatross detailed.	0415
4.16 —	*Marne* -	*Commodore F.*	S.L.	*No signs of Battle squadron. Shall I return ?*	—
4.16 —	*Commodore F.*	*Ossory* -	S.L.	*Could you not have fired torpedoes last night ? Reply : I did not think there was a chance to hit, so did not fire.*	
4.17 —	*S.O. 2nd B.S.*	*1st Division* -	Flags	*Alter course together eight points to port* -	—
4.17 —	*S.O. 1st B.S.*	*1st B.S.* -	Flags	*Admiral intends to proceed at 18 knots* -	—
4.17 —	*Commodore F.*	*12th Flotilla* -	S.L.	*How many casualties have you ?* - -	—
4.18 —	*Commodore F.*	*11th Flotilla* -	S.L.	*Alter course together four points to port* -	—
4.18 —	*Ossory* -	*Commodore F.*	S.L.	*Can you give me an approximate reference position ?*	
4.20 —	*S.O. 5th B.S.*	*Valiant* -	Sem.	*Report nature of damage ? Reply : Nil*	—
4.20 —	Marksman -	S.O. 1st B.S. -	S.L.	Marksman, Mænad with Champion, remainder lost touch with after engaging Enemy. Told them to steer South after me, and at 3.40 a.m. on meeting Revenge told them to steer North and try to pick up fleet.	—
4.20 —	S.O. B.C.F. -	S.O. 2nd C.S.-	S.L.	My position at 4 a.m., 55° 26′ N., 6° 15′ E. What do you make yours ? Reply : 4 a.m., 55° 17′ N., 6° E., 4th L.C.S. bearing S.E. by E.	0419
4.20 —	S.O. 5th B.S.	S.O. 2nd B.S.-	S.L.	Request bearing of Iron Duke ? Reply : S. 40° E.	—
4.20 —	Marksman -	Mænad -	S.L.	Close. It is coming on thick - - -	—
4.20 —	Fearless -	Marlborough -	Sem.	Will you please give me your position? Reply : My position 4.30 a.m., 55° 29′ N., 6° 01′ E.	—
4.20 —	*Achates* -	*Ambuscade* -	W/T	*I am endeavouring to join you* - - -	*0410*
4.22 —	*Commodore T.*	*General* - -	Flags	*Take up night cruising order, columns to be two cables apart. Admiral intends to proceed at 15 knots.*	—
4.22 —	*S.O. 5th B.S.*	*5th B.S.* -	Flags	*Admiral intends to proceed at 17 knots* -	—
4.23 —	**C.-in-C.** -	**5th B.S.** -	S.L.	**Keep in visual touch** - - - -	0421
4.23 —	*S.O. Cruisers*	*Cruisers* -	S.L.	*Keep within visual signalling distance* -	—
4.23 —	*S.O. 1st B.S.*	*5th Subdivision*	Flags	*Alter course together two points to port* -	—
4.25 —	S.O. B.C.F. -	General -	Flags	Alter course in succession to N. ½ E. - -	—
4.25 —	*S.O. 4th L.C.S.*	*4th L.C.S.* -	Flags	*Alter course together two points to port* -	—
4.26 —	Southampton	—	—	Remarks : Mine in sight on port quarter	—
4.26 —	*Commodore T.*	*General* - -	Flags	*Alter course in succession to E.S.E.* - -	—
4.27 —	**C.-in-C.** -	**Marlborough** -	W/T	**What is your position, course and speed ?** - **Reply : My position Lat. 55° 29′ N., Long. 6° 03′ E., course S.W., speed 14 knots.**	0427 0430

Date, Time of Despatch.	From	To	System.	Message.	Time of Origin.
1 JUNE *—cont.*					
4.28 a.m.	*S.O. 4th L.C.S.*	4th L.C.S. -	Flags	*Alter course together two points to port*	—
4.28 —	*S.O. 3rd L.C.S.*	3rd L.C.S. -	Flags	*Admiral intends to proceed at 23 knots*	—
4.30 —	Marlborough	Fearless -	S.L.	My course S.W., speed 14 knots - -	0435
4.30 —	*S.O. B.C.F.-*	*Battle Cruisers*	Sem. and S.L.	*Damage yesterday was heavy on both sides, we hope to-day to cut off and annihilate the whole German Fleet. Every man must do his utmost. Lutzow is sinking and another German Battle Cruiser expected to have sunk.*	—
4.30 —	**C.-in-C. -**	**General**	Flags	**Resume original course together - -**	—
4.30 — (?)	*Ambuscade* -	*Commodore F.*	S.L.	*Have expended all torpedoes. Tipperary and Fortune were blown up.*	—
4.30 —	*S.O. 4th L.C.S.*	4th L.C.S. -	Flags	*Alter course together four points to starboard*	—
4.30 —	*S.O. 1st B.S.*	5th Subdivision	Flags	*Alter course together two points to starboard* -	—
4.31 —	**Dublin -**	**S.O. B.C.F. and C.-in-C.**	W/T	**Urgent. One Cruiser and two Destroyers, probably hostile, in sight. Bearing East, Course S. My position Lat. 55˚ 30′ N., Long. 6′ 33′ E.**	0430
4.32 —	*Commodore F.*	*Ambuscade* -	S.L.	*Form astern of Kempenfelt division. Were flotilla in action last night? Reply: Enemy's Battleships cut through 4th Flotilla. We had one Cruiser and, I think, our other torpedo got home.*	—
4.32 —	**S.O. 2nd L.C.S.**	**C.-in-C. and S.O. B.C.F.**	W/T	**Priority. Mine in sight Lat. 55° 26′ N., Long. 6° 14′ E.**	0425
4.32 —	*S.O. 4th B.S.*	4th Division -	Flags	*Resume original course together - -*	—
4.34 —	S.N.O. Harwich.	Admiralty -	L/T	Carysfort, Undaunted, Conquest, Cleopatra, Aurora, Nimrod, Lightfoot, Laforey, Mentor, Myngs, Murray, Milne, Miranda, Manly, Loyal, Lance, Lasso, Leonidas, Lark, Firedrake, Lookout, Laverock, Lysander, Lawford, sailed.	—
4.34 —	*Dublin -*	*S.O. 2nd L.C.S*	W/T	*My position approximately at 4.30 a.m. Lat. 55′ 30′ N., Long. 6° 32′ E.*	*0432*
4.35 —	*S.O. 4th L.C.S*	4th L.C.S. -	Flags	*Alter course in succession to North. Admiral intends to proceed at 18 knots.*	—
4.35 —	S.O. 2nd C.S.	S.O. 4th L.C.S.	F.L.	Course of Fleet is North - - -	0435
4.36 —	S.O. B.C.F. -	S.O. 2nd L.C.S	S.L.	Close nearer to Admiral - - -	—
4.38 —	*Commodore F.*	*Ambuscade* -	S.L.	*What course have you been steering? Reply: South.*	—
4.38 —	*S.O. 5th B.S.*	5th B.S. -	Flags	*Admiral intends to proceed at 19 knots* -	—
4.38 — (?)	*Commodore F.*	*11th Flotilla* -	S.L.	*Form cruising order. Course S. - -*	—
4.40 —	*Commodore F.*	*Ambuscade* -	S.L.	*Have you seen battlefleet? Reply: No* -	—
4.40 —	**C.-in-C. -**	**S.O. B.C.F. -**	W/T	**Enemy fleet has returned to harbour. Try to locate Lutzow.**	0440
4.40 —	Active -	S.O. 5th B.S.-	S.L.	Am I to take station on 5th B.S.'s bow? Reply: Keep touch with Iron Duke and Barham when we get in station.	0430

Date, Time of Despatch.	From	To	System.	Message.	Time of Origin.
1 JUNE —*cont.*					
4.40 a.m.	*Nonsuch* -	*Captain D12* -	W/T	*Cut off by German Cruisers. Do not know my position. Am steering South. Request instructions.*	*0230*
4.42 —	*S.O. 4th L.C.S.*	*4th L.C.S.* -	Flags	*Zigzag one point. First turn to starboard*	—
4.42 —	*S.O. 2nd L.C.S.*	*Tiger* - -	S.L.	*Our battlefleet S.E.* - - -	*0430*
4.43 —	**King George V.**	**C.-in-C.** -	S.L.	**Battle Cruiser fleet in sight N.N.W.**	**0435**
4.45 —	*S.O. 1st B.S.*-	*Marlborough* -	W/T	*Report which port you decide to go to ?* -	*0440*
				Reply : Rosyth - - - -	*0600*
4.45 —	*Shannon* -	*S.O. 2nd C.S.*-	Sem.	*2nd L.C.S., 5th B.S. and 4th L.C.S. E. by S.*	*0425*
4.45 —	**C.-in-C.** -	**R.A. Invergordon.**	W/T	**Soudan and Berbice to be sent to Scapa** -	**0445**
4.45 —	*S.O. 1st B.S.*-	*5th Subdivision*	Flags	*Alter course together two points to port* -	—
4.45 —	**C.-in-C.** -	**General** -	S.L.	**Leading ships of divisions look out for Lutzow, damaged, ahead.**	**0430**
4.45 —	S.O. B.C.F. -	S.O 1st, 2nd and 3rd L.C.S.	W/T	*My course is East* - - - -	*0445*
4.46 —	S.O. B.C.F. -	General -	Flags	*Alter course in succession to E.* - -	—
4.46 —	**Canada** -	**C.-in-C.** -	W/T	**Following received : Opal to D12. Eight T.B.Ds., course South, 16 knots, 15 miles to westward.**	—
4.50 —	*S.O. 1st B.S.*-	*5th Subdivision*	Flags	*Alter course together two points to port* -	—
4.50 —	**C.-in-C.** -	**General** -	Flags	**Admiral resume Guide of fleet** - -	—
4.50 —	*Commodore T.*	*General* - -	Flags	*Alter course in succession to S.* - -	—
4.50 —	**King George V.**	**C.-in-C.** -	S.L.	**Mine in sight, starboard beam of Centurion**	—
4.50 —	*S.O. 4th L.C.S.*	*4th L.C.S.* -	Flags	*Alter course together four points to starboard*	—
4.50 —	S.O. B.C.F. -	Captain D13, Narborough.	W/T	*My position at 4 a.m. was 55° 26′ N. 6° 15′ E., course N. ⅓ E., speed 20 knots. What is your position, course and speed ?—and join me with destroyers.*	*0440*
4.50 —	*S.O. 3rd L.C.S.*	*Light Cruisers*	Flags	*Spread on a line of bearing South, ships two miles apart.*	—
4.51 —	*Dublin* -	*S.O. 2nd L.C.S.*	W/T	*My 0432. Dublin steering North, 17 knots*	*0445*
4.52 —	*S.O. 4th L.C.S.*	*4th L.C.S.* -	Flags	*Alter course together four points to starboard.*	—
4.52 —	Galatea -	S.O. B.C.F. -	S.L.	My speed is reduced to 18 knots. I can now do 24, with a little time to work up. Propose joining 1st L.C.S. if they are with you.	0445
4.52 —	S.O. B.C.F. -	S.O. 2nd C.S.-	S.L.	Our battlefleet bearing N.E. My course is E.	0450
4.52 —	S.O.2nd L.C.S.	S.O. B.C.F. -	S.L.	What is your speed ? - - - -	—
4.55 —	Obedient -	S.O. 1st B.S. -	Flags	Mine in sight N.W. - -	—
4.55 —	Benbow -	—	—	Remarks : Sounded action - - -	—
4.55 —	S.O. B.C.F. via Minotaur.	S.O. 4th L.C.S.	S.L.	Where is battlefleet please ? Reply : Bearing S.S.E.	—

Date, Time of Despatch.	From	To	System.	Message.	Time of Origin.
1 JUNE —cont.					
4.55 a.m.	S.O. 4th L.C.S.	4th L.C.S.	Flags	Alter course together four points to starboard. Admiral intends to proceed at 24 knots.	—
4.55 —	Captain D13	Destroyers in Company.	Flags	Admiral intends to proceed at 21 knots	—
4.55 —	S.O. 3rd L.C.S.	3rd L.C.S.	Flags	Form single line-ahead in sequence of fleet numbers.	—
4.56 —	Garland	Achates	W/T	My position at 3.30 a.m. 56° 30′ N., 5° 49′ E. Contest in company. Contest cannot steam more than 20 knots. Request instructions.	0410
4.57 —	S.O. 1st B.S.	5th Subdivision	Flags	Admiral intends to proceed at 19 knots	—
4.57 —	S.O. 2nd L.C.S.	S.O. 5th B.S.	S.L.	Our Battle Cruisers N.W.	0455
4.57 —	S.O. B.C.F.	Galatea	S.L.	1st L.C.S. bears W. from me	—
4.58 —	Commodore T.	General	Flags	Alter course in succession to S.E. by S.	—
4.58 —	Marne	Commodore F.	W/T	12th Flotilla bearing S.E. with Cruisers	—
4.58 —	**King George V.**	C.-in-C.	S.L.	**Our Light Cruisers and some T.B.Ds. on port bow. B.C.F. in sight N.W.**	**0453**
4.58 —	Benbow	General	Flags	Mine in sight	—
5.0 —	Mænad	Marksman	Sem.	Please give me your position ? Reply : Estimated position 5 a.m. 56° 2′ N., 6° 8′ E.	—
5.0 —	S.O. B.C.F.	S.O. 2nd L.C.S.	S.L.	What is bearing and distance of C.-in-C. ? Is Dublin in touch with Enemy?	0500
5.0 —	Tiger	S.O. B.C.F.	S.L.	Our battlefleet bears S.E.	—
5.0 —	S.O. B.C.F.	General	Flags	Admiral intends to proceed at 15 knots	—
5.0 —	S.O. 1st B.C.S.	S.O. B.C.F.	Sem.	With reference to men killed, when do you propose burying them ?	0445
5.1 —	**C.-in-C.**	**Commodore F.**	W/T	**My position at 4.45 a.m. is 55° 29′ N., 6° 2′ E., steering N. at 17 knots. What is your position, course and speed?**	**0455**
5.2 —	S.O. 4th L.C.S.	Caroline	S.L.	Keep clear of Active	—
5.2 —	S.O. 4th L.C.S.	4th L.C.S.	Flags	Alter course together to North. Admiral intends to proceed at 20 knots.	—
5.2 —	S.O. 2nd C.S.	2nd C.S.	Flags	Alter course in succession to East	—
5.3 —	**C.-in-C.**	**5th B.S.**	Flags	**Take station on the starboard beam of Colossus, 11 cables distance.**	—
5.3 —	S.O. B.C.F.	General	Flags	Alter course in succession eight points to starboard.	—
5.5 —	S.O. 1st B.S.	5th Subdivision	Flags	Alter course together one point to starboard	—
5.5 —	**C.-in-C.**	**S.O. 5th B.S.**	S.L.	**Ascertain and report Warspite's position, course and speed, and condition.**	**0444**
5.5 —	S.O. B.C.F.	B.C.F.	Flags	Alter course in succession six points to port	—
5.6 —	S.O. 5th B.S.	5th B.S.	Flags	Admiral intends to proceed at 20 knots	—
5.7 —	S.O. 3rd L.C.S.	3rd L.C.S.	Flags	Ships in column to be one mile apart	—
5.7 —	Commodore T.	General	Flags	Alter course in succession to E.S.E.	—
5.7 —	S.O. 4th L.C.S.	4th L.C.S.	Flags	Form single line-ahead in sequence in which ships now are.	—

Date, Time of Despatch.	From	To	System.	Message.	Time of Origin.
1 JUNE *—cont.*					
5.8 a.m.	**C.-in-C. via Engadine.**	**Warrior**	W/T	**What is your position?**	**0505**
5.10 —	*S.O. B.C.F.*	*B.C.F.*	Flags	*Alter course in succession eight points to port. Admiral intends to proceed at 18 knots.*	—
5.10 —	*S.O. 5th B.S.*	*5th B.S.*	Sem.	*5th B.S. is stationed three miles ahead of Iron Duke to look out for damaged German Battle Cruiser Lützow and Destroyers with her.*	—
5.11 —	*Commodore T.*	*General*	Flags	*Admiral intends to proceed at 20 knots*	—
5.12 —	*Cochrane*	*S.O. 2nd C.S.*	Sem.	*5th B.S. on starboard beam*	*0510*
5.12 —	*Commodore F.*	*General*	S.L.	*Admiral intends to proceed at 20 knots*	—
5.13 —	*S.O.3rdL.C.S.*	*3rd L.C.S.*	Flags	*Alter course together to North. Admiral intends to proceed at 20 knots.*	—
5.13 —	*Captain D12*	*Nonsuch*	W/T	*Steer North. Endeavour to join fleet steering N. 18 knots. Otherwise return to base.*	*0500*
5.14 —	*Commodore T.*	*General*	Flags	*Alter course in succession to N. 60° E.*	—
5.14 —	*S.O.2ndL.C.S.*	*S.O. B.C.F.*	S.L.	5th B.S. bears about S.E. three miles	—
5.15 —	*S.O. 2nd C.S.*	*S.O. 5th B.S.*	S.L.	What is bearing and distance of Iron Duke from you ? Reply : West, three miles.	—
5.15 —	*Fearless*	*Marlborough*	S.L.	Mine ahead of you	—
5.15 —	*Marvel*	*S.O. 1st B.S.*	Sem.	Please give me your 4 a.m. position ? Reply : 55° 8′ N., 6° 16′ E.	—
5.15 —	*S.O.4thL.C.S.*	*4th L.C.S.*	Flags	*Form single line-abreast to starboard on Comus in sequence of Calliope, Constance, Comus, Royalist and Caroline. Ships in column to be five cables apart.*	—
5.15 —	*Princess Royal*	*Tiger*	S.L.	*I hope all is well after our busy afternoon ? Reply : Many thanks for kind inquiries, am rather heavy. I hope all is well with you.*	*0515*
5.15 —	*S.O. 1st B.S.*	*5th Subdivision*	Flags	*Alter course together one point to port*	—
5.15 —	**C.-in-C.**	**General**	Flags	**Reference position 4.45 a.m., 55° 29′ N., 6° 02′ E.**	—
5.15 —	Benbow	—	—	Remarks : Battle Cruisers, Light Cruisers and Destroyers sighted on port quarter.	—
5.15 —	S O. B.C.F.	S.O. 2nd L.C.S.	S.L.	Where is Dublin, and is she in touch with Enemy Cruiser reported ? Reply : Dublin last reported position was approximately Lat. 55° 30′ N., Long. 6° 32′ E. at 4.32 a.m. I have not seen her since 10 p.m. last night.	0507 0515
5.16 —	*S.O. 5th B.S.*	*5th B.S.*	Flags	*Admiral intends to proceed at 17 knots*	—
5.17 —	*Commodore F.*	*Mons*	Flags	*Take station one mile on port bow*	—
5.17 —	*S.O.3rdL.C.S.*	*Cordelia*	S.L.	I am going to make a sweep to the northward.	—
5.20 —	*Cochrane*	*S.O. 2nd C.S.*	Sem.	*Battleships bearing S.S.W.*	*0515*
5.20 —	*S.O. Cruisers*	*Cruisers*	Flags	*Alter course in succession to North*	—
5.20 —	*S.O. B.C.F.*	*General*	Flags	Admiral intends to proceed at 20 knots	—

Date, Time of Despatch.	From	To	System.	Message.	Time of Origin.
1 JUNE —*cont.*					
5.20 a.m.	Cordelia -	S.O. 3rd L.C.S.	S.L.	Galatea has rejoined, am passing your signal.	0520
5.20 —	**C.-in-C.** -	**S.O. B.C.F.** -	S.L.	**Where are you going? Reference position 4.45 a.m., 55° 29′ N., 6° 02′ E., course North, speed 17 knots.**	0520
				Reply: I have closed you in accordance with your orders. Am I to locate Cruiser reported by Dublin, probably one of two in sinking condition last night?	0525
				Further reply: Yes, I will take a cast to southward and eastward and then come North again, as I think Lützow must be to eastward.	0535
5.20 —	*S.O. 4th L.C.S.*	*Comus* - -	Flags	*Take station ahead of Iron Duke three miles*	—
5.20 —	S.O. 3rd L.C.S.	Champion -	S.L.	Go between Yarmouth and Birkenhead -	0520
5.21 —	*Commodore T.*	*General* - -	Flags	*Admiral intends to proceed at 22 knots* -	—
5.22 —	Biarritz -	C.-in-C., Nore	W/T	Request instructions as to passage between Newarp Light and Sheerness.	0550
5.23 —	*S.O. Cruisers*	*Cruisers*	Flags	*Admiral intends to proceed at 17 knots* -	—
5.25 —	Hampshire -	S.O. 2nd C.S.-	Sem.	*Battlefleet bearing W.S.W.* - - -	*0515*
5.25 —	S.O. 5th B.S. via Valiant.	Warspite -	W/T	*What is your position, course and speed and condition?*	0518
5.26 —	*S.O. 1st B.S.*	*5th Subdivision*	Flags	*Alter course together one point to port* -	—
5.27 —	*Agincourt* -	*S.O. 1st B.S.* -	Flags	*Mine in sight port side* - - - -	--
5.28 —	S.O. 1st L.C.S.	S.O. 3rd L.C.S.	S.L.	Course of Battle Cruisers North, 18 knots. I have rejoined.	—
5.29 —	*Achates* -	*Ambuscade* -	W/T	*What is your position, course and speed?*	*0445*
5.30 —	*S.O. 3rd L.C.S.*	*3rd L.C.S.* -	Flags	*Ships in column to be two miles apart* -	--
5.30 —	*S.O. 2nd B.S.*	*Boadicea* -	S.L.	*Take station ahead of King George V. one mile.*	*0523*
5.30 —	Dublin -	Marksman -	S.L.	Have you seen battlefleet or anyone?	—
				Reply: No. Champion is with us.	
5.30 —	**Admiralty** -	**C.-in-C.** -	W/T	**Elbing still afloat at 3.47, without crew. Position 3 a.m. 55° 45′ N., 6° 25′ E.**	0530
5.30 —	**C.-in-C.** -	**Captain D12 Flotilla.**	W/T	**Direct Onslaught to return to base** -	0517
5.30 —	S.O. 3rd L.C.S.	S.O. 1st L.C.S.	S.L.	Will you spread between me and Battle Cruisers and keep touch, they are East from me?	0525
				Reply: Certainly. I am taking eastern position as my speed is a little reduced. Lion bears E.	
5.30 —	*S.O. 5th B.S.*	*5th B.S.* -	Flags	*Alter course together two points to port* -	—
5.32 —	*S.O. 3rd L.C.S.*	*3rd L.C.S.* -	Flags	*Alter course together to N.N.W.* - -	—
5.32 —	**S.O. 2nd C.S.**	**C.-in-C.**	W/T	**Minotaur bears from Barham N. 26° E., three miles. Duke of Edinburgh is with squadron.**	0531
5.35 —	Marlborough	Fearless -	Flags	Alter course in succession to S.W. by W.-	—
5.35 —	*S.O. 1st B.S.*	*5th Subdivision*	Flags	*Alter course together one point to starboard*	—

Date, Time of Despatch.	From	To	System.	Message.	Time of Origin.
1 JUNE	*—cont.*				
5.36 a.m.	S.O.5th B.S.	S.O. 2nd C.S.-	S.L.	Following received. Leading ships look out for damaged Battle Cruiser Lützow and Destroyers. (*Minotaur repeated to Cruisers and Destroyers in company.*)	0510
5.37 —	S.O. B.C.F. -	General -	Flags	Admiral intends to proceed at 20 knots -	—
5.37 —	*S.O.4thL.C.S.*	*4th L.C.S.* -	Flags	*Admiral intends to proceed at 17½ knots*	—
5.40 —	S.O.3rdL.C.S.	S.O. 1st L.C.S.	S.L.	Glad to see you back. Anything the matter?	0540
5.40 —	S.O. 5th B.S.	Active -	Flags	Take station astern of Malaya - -	—
5.40 —	**Commodore F.**	**C.-in-C.** -	W/T	**My position approximately at 5 a.m. 55° 48′ N., 6° 22′ E., course N., speed 20 knots.**	0535
5.42 —	*S.O. 5th B.S.*	*5th B.S.* -	Flags	*Admiral intends to proceed at 16 knots* -	—
5.43 —	S.O. B.C.F. -	General -	Flags	Alter course in succession to S.E. - -	—
5.43 —	*S.O.3rdL.C.S.*	*3rd L.C.S.* -	Flags	*Alter course together to S.E.* - - -	—
5.44 —	S.O. B.C.F. -	Captain D13 -	W/T	My position 55° 45′ N., 6° 16′ E., course N., speed 18 knots.	0530
5.44 —	*S.O.3rdL.C.S.*	*3rd L.C.S.* -	Flags	*Admiral intends to proceed at 18 knots* -	—
5.44 —	S.O.3rdL.C.S.	S.O. 1st L.C.S.	S.L.	Can you give bearing and distance of Lion?	0541
5.45 —	*S.O. 1st B.S.*	*5th Subdivision*	Flags	*Alter course together one point to starboard*	—
5.45 —	Warrior -	Engadine -	Sem.	Have you enough coal to get to Cromarty? Reply: Will have 135 tons left at 6 a.m. Consumption per hour 5 tons at present speed revolutions for 15 knots. Reckon our position at 8 a.m. from entrance to Cromarty 210 miles. Calculation of amount of coal is on the right side.	0500
5.45 —	*Commodore F.*	*Ossory* - -	S.L.	*What did you make out those Cruisers were which attacked me last night? Reply: Two three-funnelled Cruisers like Germans. I only saw two, both of which we had seen before, when you challenged them and they did not answer. I do not think they were ours.*	—
5.45 —	*S.O.2ndL.C.S.*	*2nd L.C.S.* -	S.L.	*Admiral intends to proceed at 24 knots* -	—
5.46 —	**C.-in-C.** -	**Warrior** -	W/T	**What is your position, course and speed?**	0505
5.46 —	Marksman -	Captain D13 -	S.L.	Please give me your position? Reply: My position is very doubtful, but is roughly 56° N., 6° 20′ E.	—
5.46 —	*Captain D13*	*Destroyers in Company.*	Flags	*Alter course in succession to N. Admiral intends to proceed at 23 knots.*	—
5.48 —	S.O. B.C.F. -	S.Os. 1st, 2nd and 3rd L.C.Ss, and Captain D13.	W/T	My course S.E., speed 18 knots, position 55° 45′ N., 6° 16′ E.	0530
5.50 —	**C.-in-C.** -	**Colossus** -	S.L.	**Challenge Cruisers ahead of you** - -	0550
5.50 —	Marlborough	Fearless ·	F.L.	Submarines G2, G3, G4, G5, are in a position Lat. 54° 30′ N., Long. 4° 0′ E.	0525

Date, Time of Despatch.	From	To	System.	Message.	Time of Origin.
1 JUNE	—cont.				
5.50 a.m.	S.O. 4th L.C.S.	4th L.C.S. -	S.L.	*Zigzag 1½ points. First turn to starboard*	—
5.54 —	S.O. B.C.F. -	S.O. 2nd L.C.S.	S.L.	I am casting to the S.E. to endeavour to pick up a wounded Battle Cruiser sighted by Dublin. Screen ahead of me. I shall alter course to the southward at 6.15 a.m.	0550
5.55 —	Commodore T.	General - -	Sem.	*If the flotillas are required for special service the flotilla leaders will take charge.*	*0550*
5.55 —	S.O. 1st B.S.	5th Subdivision	Flags	*Alter course together one point to port* -	—
5.55 —	Commodore F.	Destroyers -	Flags	*Alter course together eight points to port* -	—
5.55 —	S.O. 3rd L.C.S.	Light Cruisers	Flags	*Alter course in succession to S.* - -	—
5.55 —	C.-in-C. -	S.O. B.C.F. -	W/T	What do you know of Indomitable's and Inflexible's movements?	0555
				Reply : They are with me - - -	0630
5.55 —	S.O. 5th B.S.	5th B.S. -	Flags	*Alter course together two points to port* -	—
5.57 —	Commodore F.	C.-in-C. -	W/T	My position 56° 9′ N., 6° 15′ E., course W., speed 20 knots.	0600
5.58 —	S.O. 4th B.S.	C.-in-C. -	S.L.	Four Armoured Cruisers in line-ahead, ahead of 5th B.S., steering same course.	0550
6.0 —	Commodore T.	C.-in-C. -	W/T	Am proceeding to Lat. 55° 15′ N., Long. 3° 05′ E., with five Light Cruisers and 18 Destroyers. Request instructions. My position 0515. Sunk L.V., 22 knots.	0540
				Reply : Detach four T.B.Ds. to screen Marlborough proceeding to Rosyth via "M" channel does not require any help. Her position at 4.30 a.m. 55° 30′ N., 6° 3′ E., steering S.W., 14 knots.	0700
6.0 —	S.O. Cruisers	Cruisers -	Flags	*Alter course together one point to port. Admiral intends to proceed at 18 knots.*	—
6.2 —	C.-in-C. -	Light Cruisers	Flags	Preserve compass bearings - - -	—
6.2 —	C.-in-C. -	Colossus -	S.L.	Pass course to Cruisers. Cruisers preserve compass bearings.	—
6.3 —	C.-in-C. -	General	Flags and S.L.	Alter course leading ships together the rest in succession to S.E.	—
6.3 —	S.O. B.C.F. -	S.O.s 1st, 2nd and 3rd L.C.S.	W/T	My course 6.15 a.m. South - - -	0600
6.5 —	C.-in-C. -	Vanguard -	S.L.	Drop back so that I can turn - -	0600
6.6 —	S.O. 3rd L.C.S.	3rd L.C.S. -	S.L.	*Alter course in succession to S.E.* -	—
6.7 —	Shannon -	S.O. 2nd C.S.-	S.L.	*Battlefleet are altering approximately 12 points to starboard.*	*0600*
6.8 —	S.O. 4th L.C.S.	4th L.C.S. -	S.L.	*Alter course together to S.E.* - -	—
6.10 —	Kempenfelt -	Commodore F.	Sem.	*I make my position at 6 a.m. 56° 4′ N., 5° 30′ E.*	—
6.10 —	S.O. 2nd L.C.S.	2nd L.C.S. -	S.L.	*Birmingham take station E., three miles. Nottingham take station W., three miles.*	—
6.11 —	S.O. Cruisers	Cruisers -	Flags	*Reform* - - - - -	—
6.12 —	S.O. Cruisers	Cruisers -	Flags	*Alter course in succession 12 points to starboard.*	—
6.13 —	S.O. 3rd L.C.S.	3rd L.C.S. -	S.L.	*Alter course in succession to South* - -	—

Date, Time of Despatch.	From	To	System.	Message.	Time of Origin.
1 JUNE —cont.					
6.14 a.m.	**C.-in-C.** -	**S.O. B.C.F., S.O. 1st B.S., S.O. 2nd C.S., All Captains D.**	W/T	**My course S.E. Speed 17 knots** -	**0602**
6.15 —	S.O. B.C.F. -	General -	Flags	Alter course in succession to South -	—
6.15 —	S.O. B.C.F. -	Captain D13 -	W/T	What is your position, course and speed?	0615
6.17 —	S O. 4thL.C.S.	4th L.C.S. -	S.L.	*Reform on Comus* -	—
6.20 —	S.O. Cruisers	Cruisers -	Flags	*Admiral intends to proceed at 17 knots* -	—
6.20 —	Vanguard -	S.O. 4th B.S.-	S.L.	Urgent. *Following parts for 12-in. Holstrom breech mechanism damaged during action, 31st May, Urgently required. Lock, electric, one; guide bolt, one; insulating bushes for front end of striker, six. This type of mechanism being unique application to replace through usual channels will only result in delay. Submit therefore a telegraphic demand be made on Admiralty that Vanguard is sending direct to the makers, Coventry Ordnance Works, the following parts for rebushing of tube chamber, namely, vent stalk, one. All this work very urgent, as spare parts have already been used.*	0520
6.30 —	Revenge -	—	—	Remarks : Passing wreckage both sides-	—
6.30 —	Warrior -	Engadine -	Sem.	If I hoist K flag slip the tow and drop alongside, starboard side if possible. This will be an urgent signal to take off ship's company. At night a succession of K's will be made till answered by J. Have a grass line and buoy ready on the end of towing-wire in case it is again required to take ship in tow.	—
6.30 —	Commodore F.	Destroyers -	Flags	*Assume cruising order. Course S.E.* -	—
6.30 —	S.O.4thL.C.S.	4th L.C.S. -	S.L.	*Admiral intends to proceed at 17 knots* -	—
6.31 —	S.O. 1st B.S.	5th Subdivision	Flags	*Alter course together one point to port* -	—
6.31 —	S.O.2ndL.C.S.	S.O. B.C.F. -	S.L.	*Sail right ahead* -	0630
6.33 —	S.O. Cruisers	Cruisers -	Flags	*Alter course together one point to starboard. Admiral intends to proceed at 18 knots.*	—
6.35 —	Commodore F.	Destroyers -	Flags	*Alter course in succession to S.S.E.* -	—
6.35 —	S.O. 5th B.S.	5th B.S. -	Flags	*Alter course together two points to starboard Admiral intends to proceed at 18 knots.*	—
6.39 —	Mentor -	Commodore T.	Flags	*Mine in sight* -	—
6.40 —	**Commodore T.**	**C.-in-C.** -	W/T	**Cancel my message timed 0540 first sentence. I am proceeding to Lat. 55° 30' N., Long. 6° 0' E.**	**0620**
6.43 —	**C.-in-C.** -	**General** -	Flags	**Alter course leading ships together the rest in succession to S.E. by S.**	—
6.43 —	S.O. Cruisers	Cruisers -	Flags	*Alter course together two points to port* -	—
6.44 —	S.O. 5th B.S.	5th B.S. -	Flags	*Alter course together two points to port* -	—

Date, Time of Despatch.	From	To	System.	Message.	Time of Origin.
1 JUNE —cont.					
6.45 a.m.	S.O.3rdL.C.S.	3rd L.C.S. -	Flags	*Alter course in succession to S.E. Admiral intends to proceed at 20 knots.*	—
6.45 —	Dublin -	Marksman -	Sem.	I have picked up a man belonging to Tipperary. Can you tell me what happened to Tipperary and Sparrowhawk ? Reply : Tipperary was sunk.	—
6.45 —	S.O.2ndL.C.S.	2nd L.C.S. -	S.L.	*Admiral intends to proceed at 22 knots*	—
6.46 —	S.O.3rdL.C.S.	Inconstant -	S.L.	Are you in easy signalling touch with the next Light Cruiser? Reply : Yes, with Phaeton.	0645
6.47 —	S.O. 1st B.S.	5th Subdivision	Flags	*Alter course in succession to S.S.E. -*	—
6.48 —	S.O. 5th B.S.	5th B.S. -	Flags	*Alter course together two points to starboard*	—
6.50 —	Dublin -	Marksman -	Sem.	I suppose you will sink Sparrowhawk? Reply : I am trying to take her in tow, but if it cannot be managed, shall sink her.	—
6.51 —	**Marksman** -	**C.-in-C.** -	W/T	**Tipperary sunk. I am getting survivors** -	**0650**
6.52 —	S.O.3rdL.C.S.	Light Cruisers	S.L.	*Alter course in succession to South* • •	—
6.54 —	Captain D13	Marlborough -	W/T	My position 56° 0′ N., 6° 10′ E., course N., 23 knots, at 0545.	0601
6.54 —	S.O. Cruisers	Cruisers -	Flags	*Alter course together two points to starboard*	—
6.55 —	S.O. 5th B.S.	5th B.S. -	Flags	*Alter course together two points to port* •	—
6.57 —	Captain D13	Marlborough -	W/T	My position at 0615 56° 9′ N., 6° 5′ E., course N. ½ W., 20 knots. Please give me yours.	0621
6.58 —	Captain D13	S.O. B.C.F. -	W/T	Joining Marlborough • • • •	0640
7.0 —	**S.O. 5th B.S.**	**C.-in-C.** -	W/T	**Malaya several holes below water. Submerged flat flooded. Hit on top of one turret, necessitating use of auxiliary loading gear. One 6-in. gun out of action. Speed unimpaired. Several casualties. Barham armament and speed unimpaired. Two compartments flooded. Several casualties. Main and auxiliary W/T wrecked. Buzzer still in use. Valiant no damage. Warspite holed twice in wing engine room. Speed reduced to 16 knots.**	**0605**
7.0 —	**C.-in-C.** -	**S.O. B.C.F.** -	W/T	**Abdiel has laid mines 12 miles W. of her last mine field. I will sweep N. on a five mile front from 55° 35′ N., 6° 23′ E. Keep to the Eastward of me.**	**0632**
7.0 —	S.O.2ndL.C.S.	2nd L.C.S. -	S.L.	*Admiral intends to proceed at 21 knots* -	—
7.0 —	**S.O. B.C.F.** -	**C.-in-C.** -	W/T	**If nothing is sighted by 7.30 a.m. propose altering and sweep N.E. Reply ; Approved** - - - -	**0655** **0721**
7.3 —	S.O. 5th B.S.	5th B.S. -	Flags	*Alter course together two points to port* -	—
7.4 —	**C.-in-C.** -	**S.O. 1st B.S., Commodore F**	W/T	**Join me 8.15 a.m. 55° 56′ N., 6° 13′ E.** -	**0638**
				Reply from S.O. 1st B.S. : Cannot reach rendezvous before 8.45 a.m.	**0805**

Date, Time of Despatch.	From	To	System.	Message	Time of Origin.
1 JUNE —cont.					
7.5 a.m.	S.O. Cruisers	Cruisers -	Flags	Alter course together two points to port -	—
7.7 —	S.O. 1st B.S.	5th Subdivision	Flags	Alter course together two points to starboard	—
7.12 —	S.O. 5th B.S.	5th B.S. -	Flags	Alter course together two points to starboard	—
7.15 —	Engadine -	—	—	Remarks : K flag hoisted by Warrior -	—
7.15 —	S.O. Cruisers	Cruisers -	Flags	Alter course together two points to starboard	—
7.15 —	C.-in-C. -	General -	Flags	**Mine in sight** - - - - -	—
7.16 —	C.-in-C. -	General -	Flags	Alter course leading ships together the rest in succession to N.	—
7.16 —	C.-in-C. -	Commodore F.	W/T	Are all your Destroyers in company or in communication? Report names of any you cannot get into communication with.	0658
				Reply : All Destroyers of 11th Flotilla present, also Ambuscade.	0733
7.20 —	C.-in-C. -	Warrior and Warspite.	W/T	What is your position, course and speed?	0703
				Reply from Warspite : position Lat. 56° 32′ N., Long. 0° 44′ E., course W., speed of advance 16 knots.	0730
				(Warrior's reply see 8.2 a.m.)	
7.20 —	C.-in-C. -	S.O. B.C.F., S.O. 1st B.S., S.O. 7th C.S., Captains D4, 11, 12.	W/T	**My course N.** - - -	0715
7.20 —	Warrior -	Engadine -	Sem.	Slip wire, never mind buoying it - -	—
7.20 —	S.O. 4th L.C.S.	4th L.C.S. -	Flags	Alter course together 16 points to starboard-	—
7.20 —	Blanche -	C.-in-C. -	S.L	**Mine on your starboard bow** - -	—
7.20 —	S.O. 2nd B.S.	1st Division -	Flags	Form astern and follow in the wake of your divisional Guide.	—
7.23 —	S.O. 5th B.S.	5th B.S. -	Flags	Alter course together two points to port -	—
7.23 —	S.O. 2nd B.S.	Centurion -	S.L.	I am going to turn to starboard -	—
7.24 —	Canada -	General -	Flags	Mine in sight - - - -	—
7.25 —	S.O. Cruisers	Cruisers -	Flags	Alter course together two points to port -	—
7.25 —	S.O. B.C.F. -	General -	Flags and W/T	Alter course in succession to N.N.E. -	0726
7.25 —	Narborough-	S.O. B.C.F. -	W/T	My 6 a.m. position 56° 10′ N., 4° 4′ E., proceeding from S.E. 25 with Pelican and Forrester.	0652
7.26 —	S.O. B.C.F. -	Destroyers -	Flags	Form Submarine screen - - - -	—
7.27 —	S.O. Cruisers	Cruisers and Destroyers.	Flags	Reform. Alter course in succession to N.-	—
7.27 —	C.-in-C. -	Light Cruisers	Flags	**Preserve compass bearings** - - -	—
7.30 —	S.O. 1st B.S.	C.-in-C. -	W/T	**My position 6.40 a.m. 55° 55′ N., 6° 15′ E., course S.S.E., 19 knots.**	0640
7.30 —	S.O. 3rd L.C.S.	3rd L.C.S. -	S.L.	Alter course in succession to N.N.E. Admiral intends to proceed at 18 knots.	—
7.3 —	S.O. 4th L.C.S.	4th L.C.S. -	Flags	Admiral intends to proceed at 20 knots -	—

Date, Time of Despatch.	From	To	System.	Message.	Time of Origin.
1 JUNE —*cont.*					
7.32 a.m.	S.O. B.C.F. -	S.O. 2nd L.C.S.	S.L.	Indicate numbers of officers and men killed and wounded and rank of officer left in command ? Replies : Southampton, 28 men killed, 35 men seriously injured, one officer and five men less seriously. Nottingham and Birmingham, nil. Dublin, one officer and two men killed and 19 wounded. Southampton has considerable damage to hull and one 6-in. gun and anti-aerial gun out of action.	—
7.32 —	*S.O. 5th B.S.*	*5th B.S.*	Flags	*Admiral intends to proceed at 17 knots* -	—
7.32 —	**S.O. 2nd C.S.**	**C.-in-C.**	S.L.	**Escort Destroyers of Group 8 in company**	0730
7.32 —	*S.O.2ndL.C.S.*	*2nd L.C.S.*	S.L.	*Alter course in succession to N.N.E.*	—
7.33 —	**S.O. 2nd C.S.**	**C.-in-C.**	S.L.	**1st B.S. in sight N.**	0731
7.35 —	*S.O. 5th B.S.*	*5th B.S.*	Flags	*Alter course together four points to starboard*	—
7.35 —	*S.O. 1st B.S.*	*1st B.S.*	Flags	*Alter course together one point to starboard*	—
7.36 —	**Marksman** -	**C.-in-C., Captain D11.**	W/T	**Am endeavouring to tow Sparrowhawk stern first.**	0731
7.36 —	Marlborough-	Captain D13 -	W/T	My position 7.15 a.m. 55° 5′ N., 5° 44′ E., course S.W. by W., speed 14 knots.	0715
7.37 —	*S.O.3rdL.C.S.*	*3rd L.C.S.*	S.L.	*Alter course together 16 points to starboard*	—
7.38 —	S.O. B.C.F. -	S.Os. 1st, 2nd and 3rd L.C.S.	W/T	Course will be altered at 8 a.m. to N.	0735
7.40 —	*S.O. 1st B.S.*	*5th Subdivision*	Flags	*Admiral intends to proceed at 20 knots*	—
7.40 —	*S.O. Cruisers*	*Cruisers*	Flags	*Admiral intends to proceed at 17 knots*	—
7.41 —	*S.O. 1st B.S.*	*5th Subdivision*	Flags	*Alter course in succession 16 points to starboard.*	—
7.45 —	**S.O. 5th B.S.**	**C.-in-C.**	S.L.	**1st B.S. in sight bearing N.**	0730
7.45 —	*S.O. B.C.F.-*	*Battle Cruisers*	Sem.	*Report damage sustained in action*	—
	Princess Royal.	—	—	*Reply : Carpenter's defects : hole in reserve bunker 66 to 82 port at water line, bunker flooded. A upper bunker also flooded through reserve passage. Hole in Admiral's cabin, port side. Armour of B turret shifted. Hole in canteen store and after engine room casing badly damaged by same shot. Hole in X turret at line of deck. Holes in both struts to masts. Several holes in upper deck. All compartments in wake of shots badly splintered X turret large piece punched out of glacis. Armour distorted and turret jammed. A turret left gun breech out of action. Engineers : Fire main pipes. Ship and bunker ventilation trunk badly damaged. At 66 and before 256 Nos. 1 and 2 funnels badly pierced and funnel guys carried away. Gearing of flood valves to B, X and after 4-in. magazine defective. Both after engine room casings completely wrecked.*	0845

Date, Time of Despatch.	From	To	System.	Message.	Time of Origin.
1 JUNE —cont.					
7.45 a.m.	*Princess Royal*—cont.			Boatswains : Main derrick topping lift two guys, fore shroud port side, wire towing pendant, both stump masts topping lift purchases and guys. All screens and covers on upper deck and bridges, nets cut in places, funnel guys.	
				Further reply : Many electrical supply fans, searchlights, navyphones and wiring damaged or destroyed.	1128
	Tiger	—	—	Reply : Principal damage is as follows : Main steam pipe in port turbine room damaged. Right gun of A, left gun of Q damaged and unreliable. Port magazine of Q turret, port 6-in. magazine and shell room flooded. Much damage under fore part forecastle, two large holes just above water line port side.	0825
	New Zealand	—	—	Reply : Unimportant damage to base of X turret. Nothing to interfere with fighting efficiency.	0835
	Inflexible	—	—	Reply : Has sustained no damage	0750
	Indomitable	—	—	Reply : No damage	0840
7.45 —	*Commodore F.*	*Destroyers*	Flags	Alter course in succession 16 points, the ships turning outwards.	—
7.45 —	*S.O. B.C.F.*	*Battle Cruisers*	Flags	Indicate number of officers killed and wounded, and rank of officer left in command. Reply in three hoists. Indicate number of men killed and wounded. Reply in two hoists.	—

	Officers.		
	Killed.	Wounded.	Command.
Inflexible	0	0	1
Indomitable	0	0	1
New Zealand	0	0	1
Tiger	2	0	1
Princess Royal	0	2	1

	Men.	
	Killed.	Wounded.
Tiger	21	38
Princess Royal	18	50
New Zealand	0	0
Inflexible	0	0
Indomitable	0	0

Date, Time of Despatch.	From	To	System.	Message.	Time of Origin.
7.48 —	*S.O. 5th B.S.*	*5th B.S.*	Flags	Alter course together four points to port	—
7.51 —	*Felixstowe*	*Admiralty*	W/T	S.N.O. Harwich from Hornet. Hornet, Mastiff, Matchless, Hind, Druid, Sandfly, Ferret, Beaver, expect to arrive about 0815 and wish to enter.	0715
7.53 —	*Hercules*	*S.O. 1st B.S.*	Sem.	One four-funnelled ship, one Cruiser and Destroyer, bearing S.E. by S. about four miles astern, steering approximately North. Look like British ships.	0750
7.55 —	*Commodore F.*	*Destroyers*	Flags	Alter course in succession to N.N.E.	—
7.55 —	*Fearless*	*Marlborough*	S.L.	Mine on starboard bow	—
7.55 —	**C.-in-C.**	**Dublin**	S.L.	**Demand and reply**	—

Date, Time of Despatch.	From	To	System.	Message.	Time of Origin.
1 JUNE —cont.					
7.56 a.m.	C.-in-C. -	S.O. 5th B.S. -	S.L.	Are you in communication with Warspite? Reply : Barham's W/T cannot get Warspite. Valiant has asked her for information required. Warspite has received signal, but as answer is so weak it cannot be read.	0755 0810
	C.-in-C. -	S.O. 5th B.S. -	S.L.	Further reply from C.-in-C.: I have received her answer. Her position Lat. 56° 39′ N., Long. 1° 43′ E., course West, speed 16 knots at 6.10 a.m.	1000
8.0 —	Engadine -	—	.—	Remarks : Took ship's company off Warrior.	—
8.0 —	S.O. Cruisers	Destroyers -	S.L.	Minotaur's position at 8 a.m. 55° 50′ N., 6° 30′ E. Please pass to screen as they rejoin.	—
8.0 —	C.-in-C. -	Dublin - -	S.L.	Where is Cruiser and two T.B.Ds. you reported in your 0430? Reply : German Armoured Cruiser was lost sight of in fog, in approximate position 55° 28′ N., 6° 32′ E. Position is very approximate because navigating officer has been killed. Submit I may be given 8.0 a.m. position.	0755
	C.-in-C. -	Dublin - -	S.L.	Was she disabled or steaming? Reply : As far as I could see she was not disabled and appeared to be steaming fast.	0816
8.0 —	S.O. B.C.F. -	General -	Flags	Alter course in succession to N. - -	—
8.1 —	S.O. 5th B.S.	5th B.S. -	Flags	Alter course together two points to starboard. Admiral intends to proceed at 16 knots.	—
8.1 —	S.O.3rdL.C.S.	3rd L.C.S. -	S.L.	Alter course in succession to North - -	—
8.2 —	Engadine -	C.-in-C., R.A. Invergordon.	W/T	Warrior completely disabled in tow of Engadine. My course and speed are W.N.W., seven knots. Tug is required urgently. 57° 18′ N., 3° 45′ E.	0500
8.4 —	Marksman -	C.-in-C. -	W/T	Priority. Hawser parted. Shall I sink Sparrowhawk? My position 56° 4′ N., 6° 10′ E. Reply : Is salvage impossible? - -	0801 0855
	Marksman -	C.-in-C. -	W/T	Reply : Sparrowhawk has been sunk having received orders from S.O. 1st B.S.	0915
8.5 —	S.O. Cruisers	Cruisers -	Flags	Indicate percentage of principal fuel remaining on board. Replies :— Minotaur 76 per cent. Hampshire 77 ,, Duke of Edinburgh 70 ,,	—
8.6 —	S.O. 5th B.S.	5th B.S. -	Flags	Alter course together two points to starboard	—
8.7 —	S.O. Cruisers	Cruisers -	S.L.	Report if battlefleet are seen altering course	0805
8.8 —	R.A. Scapa -	Aberdeen -	W/T	For C.-in-C. Weather report. Immingham, Rosyth, Shotley respectively, based on observations at 6 a.m. Wind S.W. moderate (b. 3 or 4), dull (mainly c. and o.), bar. 30.02. Wind West moderate (b. 3 or 4), fair generally (mainly bc. and c.), 29.70. Weather report based on observations at 7 a.m., bar. 30. 22, stationary, temperature 61, wind S.W. light.	0725

Date, Time of Despatch.	From	To	System.	Message.	Time of Origin.
1 JUNE —*cont.*					
8.10 a.m.	Admiralty	Captain S., Maidstone.	W/T	Recall Firedrake and her group of Submarines.	0810
8.10 —	Commodore F.	Destroyers	Flags	*Alter course in succession to E.N.E.*	—
8.10 —	S.O. B.C.F.	S.O. 1st B.C.S.	Sem.	*Can you throw any light as to destruction of Queen Mary ? Reply : It appeared to be an explosion in Queen Mary's magazine due to a salvo hitting.*	0809
8.12 —	S.O. B.C.F.	S.O. 2nd B.C.S.	Sem.	*Can you throw any light as to the cause of destruction of Indefatigable ? Reply : Salvo struck her aft and apparently explosion reached magazine.*	0810
8.12 —	S.O.4thL.C.S.	4th L.C.S.	Flags	*Zigzag 1½ points. First turn to starboard. Admiral intends to proceed 17½ knots.*	—
8.14 —	Captain D13.	S.O. B.C.F.	W/T	My position, course and speed at 8 a.m. 56° 42′ N., 5° 47′ E., South, 20 knots. Request instructions.	0800
8.15 —	Benbow	—	—	Reply : Collect your flotilla and rejoin. Remarks : Passed a large quantity of oil and a cork lifebuoy.	0828 —
8.15 —	**Benbow**	**C.-in-C.**	Flags	**Mine in sight**	—
8.16 —	Biarritz	Lowestoft	W/T	A trawler has just held me up in middle ocean. Is Channel clear? Reply : Channel is clear.	0740
8.17 —	Princess Royal	Lion	Sem.	*Comdr. N. to ditto. At 7.15 a.m. using Lat. 55° 26′ N., Long. 6° 29½ E., obtained intercepts 1¾ miles N. 82 W. Reply : Thank you, I had similar results.*	0745
8.20 —	Admiralty	Captain S., Maidstone.	W/T	Send four fresh Submarines for seven-day period to same stations off Dutch coast as last week. Not to be done by wireless.	0820
				Reply : Propose to send Submarine E.41 as one of the four Submarines if not required for mine-laying.	1008
8.20 —	Warspite	S.O. 5th B.S.	W/T	*Position Lat. 56° 39′ N., Long. 1° 43′ E., course W., speed of advance 16 knots. Condition : Many holes from shell fire, several through armour and below water line, wing engine room practically tight with bulkhead shored, several compartments full, ship on even keel, steering from engine room.* (*Passed to C.-in-C.*)	0610
8.20 —	Badger	S.O. B.C.F.	Sem.	Oil remaining at 8 a.m. :— Tons. Badger - - - 72 Acheron - - - 70 Ariel - - - 76 Attack - - - 60 Hydra - - - 77 Lizard - - - 56 Goshawk - - - 74 Lapwing - - - 74	—
8.22 —	S.O. 5th B.S.	5th B.S.	Flags	*Alter course together two points to port*	—
8.23 —	**C.-in-C.**	**Marksman, S.O. B.C.F.**	W/T	**My position at 8.15 a.m., 55° 54′ N., 6° 10′ E. What will your position be at 8.15 a.m.?**	0800
8.24 —	**C.-in-C.**	**Dublin**	S.L.	**Close**	—

Date, Time of Despatch.	From	To	System.	Message.	Time of Origin.
1 JUNE —*cont.*					
8.25 a.m.	Engadine	—	—	Remarks : Left Warrior and proceeded	—
8.27 —	*S.O.1stB.C.S.*	*Tiger*	Sem.	*Can you pump out your magazine and shell rooms ? Reply : No.*	*0825*
8.29 —	*Commodore T.*	*General*	Flags	*Alter course in succession to N. 42° E.*	—
8.30 —	Fearless	Marlborough	Sem.	I make you to be going about 12½ knots over the ground. Reply : Thank you.	—
8.30 —	**C.-in-C.**	**Oak**	S.L.	**Turn 16 points to port. Inspect wreckage in the oil we have just passed and see if you can get any name of ship.**	**0820**
				Reply : Wreckage is from Destroyer Ardent A lifebuoy was picked up marked Ardent and pieces of recognition laths were seen floating.	**0905**
	C.-in-C.	**Oak**	—	**Do not lose touch. I will turn round in about half-hour's time.**	**0830**
8.30 —	*Commodore F.*	*Destroyers*	Flags	*Alter course in succession to N.E. Admiral intends to proceed at 22 knots.*	—
8.31 —	S.O. B.C.F.	Captain D13 and Narborough.	W/T	My course and speed are N. 20 knots, position 55° 25' N., 6° 46' E., at 8.0 a.m.	0825
8.32 —	**C.-in-C.**	**S.O. 5th B.S., S.O. 1st B.S., S.O. 2nd C.S., Revenge, all Captains D.**	W/T	**My position at 8.15 a.m., 55° 54' N., 6° 10' E., steering N. at 17 knots.**	**0815**
8.33 —	*Commodore F.*	*Destroyers*	Flags	*Alter course in succession to N.E. by N., Admiral intends to proceed at 25 knots.*	—
8.35 —	*Duke of Edinburgh.*	*S.O. 2nd C.S.*	Sem.	*Have lost sight of battlefleet and ships of 5th B.S. They appear to have turned slightly to port.*	*0830*
8.35 —	*S.O. 5th B.S.*	*5th B.S.*	Flags	*Alter course together two points to port. Ships in column to be three cables apart.*	—
8.35 —	Benbow	—	—	Remarks : Firing reported ahead	—
8.36 —	*Commodore F.*	*Kempenfelt*	Flags	*Fleet ahead, inform Opal*	—
8.37 —	S.O. B.C.F.	Badger	S.L.	Detail five Destroyers to screen 2nd Division consisting of Indomitable, New Zealand and Inflexible.	0835
8.40 —	**C.-in-C.**	**General**	Flags	**Reference position 8.15 a.m., 55° 54' N., 6° 10' E.**	—
8.40 —	S.O. B.C.F.	General	Flags	Form divisions in line-ahead, columns disposed abeam to port. Columns to be two miles apart.	—
8.42 —	**Marksman**	**C.-in-C.**	W/T	**My position at 8.15 a.m. was 56° 8' N., 6° 9' E.**	**0834**
8.42 —	*Achates*	*Nonsuch*	W/T	*Indicate your position. Have you seen anything of Phaeton ?*	*0813*
8.43 —	**C.-in-C.**	**C.-in-C., Rosyth.**	W/T	**Warrior in tow of Engadine, send tug**	**0843**
8.45 —	S.O. 1st B.S.	Marksman	S.L.	Proceed and sink Sparrowhawk	—
8.45 —	*Agincourt*	*S.O. 1st B.S.*	Flags	*Attention is called to W.*	—
8.45 —	**S.O. 2nd B.S.**	**C.-in-C.**	S.L.	**Castor and flotilla bears from me S. 50° W.**	**0839**
8.45 —	*S.O. B.C.F.*	*Battle Cruisers*	Flags	*Fleet will be organised in rapid organisation in two Divisions. 1st Division, Lion, Princess Royal, Tiger. 2nd Division, New Zealand, Indomitable, Inflexible.*	—

Date, Time of Despatch.	From	To	System.	Message.	Time of Origin.
1 JUNE —*cont.*					
8.45 a.m.	*Commodore F.*	*Destroyers*	S.L.	*Screen in accordance with No. 9 diagram. 1st Division, A, B, C, D. 2nd Division, E, F, G, H.*	—
8.45 —	*S.O. Cruisers*	*Cruisers*	Flags	*Alter course together two points to port*	—
8.47 —	*Marksman*	*Captain D12*	—	*3½-in. wire parted at 7 knots. Have no wire left, neither has she.*	—
8.47 —	*Commodore F.*	*Destroyers*	Flags	*Alter course in succession to S.S.W. Admiral intends to proceed at 17 knots.*	—
8.47 —	Benbow	—	—	Remarks : Sighted our Destroyers off starboard bow.	—
8.52 —	**C.-in-C.**	**General**	Flags	**Alter course leading ships together rest in succession to S.S.W.**	—
8.54 —	**C.-in-C.**	**S.O. B.C.F.**	W/T	**Dublin is with me. Cruiser she sighted was not disabled.**	0837
8.55 —	*S.O. 4th L.C.S.*	*4th L.C.S.*	Flags	*Alter course together to S.S.W.*	—
8.55 —	**S.O. B.C.F.**	**C.-in-C.**	W/T	**My position 8.15 a.m. was Lat. 55° 29' N., Long. 6° 44' E., steering N. at 20 knots.**	0850
8.56 —	*Commodore F.*	*Kempenfelt*	S.L.	*Spread Destroyers along the front*	—
8.58 —	**C.-in-C.**	**S.O. 4th L.C.S.**	W/T	**Priority. Course S.S.W.**	0855
8.58 —	Orion	C.-in-C.	S.L.	Have just passed considerable wreckage and floating bodies, apparently foreigners.	0827
9.0 —	**S.O. 2nd B.S.**	**C.-in-C.**	S.L.	**At 7 a.m. just before altering course we passed a quantity of empty cylinders painted grey and floating high, also wreckage not of English origin, and some oil. At 8.45 a.m. passed a Carley life-raft, mess stools and broken timber, all obviously English.**	0852
9.0 —	*Commodore F.*	*11th Flotilla*	S.L.	*Destroyers on the port side of Castor form single line-abreast.*	—
9.0 —	*S.O.3rd L.C.S.*	*S.O. B.C.F.*	S.L.	Is speed 18 or 20 knots? Reply : 20 knots.	0900
9.2 —	**C.-in-C.**	**C.-in-C., Rosyth.**	W/T	**Priority. Please send local T.B.Ds. to screen Warspite. Position 6 a.m. 56° 39' N., 1° 40' E., course W., 16 knots.**	0902
9.5 —	*S.O. 5th B.S.*	*5th B.S.*	Flags	*Admiral intends to proceed at 17 knots*	—
9.5 —	*S.O. Cruisers*	*Cruisers*	Flags	*Reform*	—
9.5 —	*Commodore F.*	*11th Flotilla*	S.L.	*Extend your distance from the Admiral*	—
9.6 —	*Shannon*	*S.O.2nd C.S.*	Sem.	*Light Cruisers W., steering S.*	0905
9.8 —	*S.O. Cruisers*	*Cruisers*	Flags	*Admiral intends to proceed at 20 knots*	—
9.10 —	*Gloucester*	*S.O. 3rd L.C.S.*	F.L.	*Narborough, Pelican, Nerissa port bow (Repeated to S.O. B.C.F.)*	0856
9.10 —	*S.O. Cruisers*	*Cruiser*	Flags	*Alter course in succession to S.W. by W.*	—
9.12 —	*Hampshire*	*S.O. 2nd C.S.*	Sem.	*Can no longer see battlefleet*	—
9.15 —	*S.O. 1st B.S.*	*5th Subdivision*	Flags	*Alter course in succession to N.*	—
9.15 —	*Nottingham, Birmingham.*	*S.O. 2nd L.C.S.*	S.L.	*Sound of firing East a long way off*	0905
9.15 —	S.O.2nd L.C.S.	S.O. B.C.F.	S.L. and W/T	Priority. Birmingham reports have heard reports of guns from the East a long way off. (*Received in Iron Duke 9.31 a.m.*)	0915

Date, Time of Despatch.	From	To	System.	Message.	Time of Origin.
1 JUNE —*cont.*					
9.15 a.m.	*Commodore T.*	*1st Division and Lookout.*	Sem.	*Proceed to escort Marlborough whose position at 8.30 a.m. was 54° 41′ N., 5° 10′ E. She is making for M channel, destination Rosyth, speed 14 knots. Our 8.30 position was 52° 40′ N., 3° 2′ E. Get into communication with Marlborough as soon as possible. Three of our Submarines are stationed South of Area 1.*	—
9.16 —	*S.O. 5th B.S.*	*5th B.S.*	Flags	*Admiral intends to proceed at 16 knots*	—
9.16 —	*Fearless*	*Marlborough*	Sem.	I make out you are steering about 5° to the Southward of the signalled course. You appeared to do that during the night as well as when you were steering South.	0915
9.17 —	**Dublin**	**C.-in-C.**	S.L.	**At 6 a.m. I picked up from the water one stoker, a survivor from Tipperary.**	0915
9.17 —	**Admiralty**	**C.-in-C.**	W/T	**At 6.20 Enemy Submarines ordered to close Elbing, position now given Lat. 55° 51′ N., Long. 5° 55′ E.**	0917
9.20 —	*S.O. B.C.F.*	*S.O. 2nd B.C.S.*	S.L.	*Can you give me the exact position of wreck of Indefatigable and time af explosion? Reply: 4 p.m., Lat. 56° 49′ N., Long. 5° 32′ E.*	0915
9.20 —	*Achates*	*Commodore F.*	W/T	*Am searching for Porpoise who is in need of assistance, position 5 a.m. 56° 50′ N., 4° 20′ E., course W., 10 knots.*	0900
9.20 —	*S.O. 5th B.S.*	*5th B.S.*	Flags	*Alter course in succession to S.W.*	—
9.20 —	S.O. B.C.F.	Badger	S.L.	Six Destroyers went to screen 2nd Division when five should only have gone. Reply: Christopher went without orders. I have already recalled her and stationed her at B in JG 3.	0905
9.21 —	Narborough	Canterbury	Sem.	Am I to join Battle Cruiser Squadron now? If so, are they astern of you? Reply: East magnetic 15 miles from us now.	0922
9.21 —	*S.O. Cruisers*	*Cruisers*	Flags S.L.	*Alter course in succession to S.S.W.*	—
9.21 —	**R.A. Scapa**	**Aberdeen**	W/T	**For C.-in-C. from Campania. Ready to proceed. Request instructions.**	0845
9.23 —	Marlborough	—	—	Remarks: Sighted two Submarines three points on the starboard bow.	—
9.23 —	Benbow	—	—	Remarks: Submarine sighted starboard beam of Royal Oak.	—
9.25 —	Faulknor	S.O. 1st B.S.	Sem.	Can Obedient take men which tug is picking up from raft? Reply: Yes.	—
9.30 —	S.O. B.C.F.	Badger	S.L.	1st Flotilla of Destroyers are to be sent home two or three at a time when fuel remaining is only sufficient to reach Rosyth at 15 knots. Report times of parting company beforehand.	0915
9.31 —	Badger	S.O. B.C.F.	Flags	Attention is drawn to N. by W.	—
9.33 —	Colossus	—	—	Remarks: Observed track of oil apparently track of torpedo on port bow.	—
9.34 —	S.O.2ndL.C.S.	S.O. B.C.F.	W/T	My position at 9.25 a.m. Lat. 55° 44′ N., Long. 6° 41′ E.	0930
9.35 —	*Captain D12*	*Marksman*	W/T	*My course N., speed 20 knots*	0925
9.35 —	**C.-in-C.**	**General**	Flags	**Alter course together four points to starboard.**	—

Date, Time of Despatch.	From	To	System.	Message.	Time of Origin.
1 JUNE —*cont.* 9.35 a.m.	Warspite -	—	—	Remarks : Two torpedoes passed ship	—
9.35 —	S.O.3rdL.C.S.	1st L.C.S.	S.L.	My speed is 20 knots	0935
9.35 —	*S.O. B.C.F.* -	*Battle Cruisers*	Flags	*Indicate amount of ammunition unexpended of heaviest gun in armament ? Reply : Lion, 132 common, 132 lyddite 50 A.P., this does not include Q turret. Princess Royal 600, Tiger 420, New Zealand 420, Indomitable 710, Inflexible 750.*	—
9.36 —	Admiralty -	S.O. 3rd B.S.	W/T	3rd B.S. and 3rd C.S. return to harbour and revert to usual notice.	0936
9.40 —	Barham -	—	—	Remarks : Sighted B.C.F. bearing S.E. -	—
9.40 —	*Nonsuch* -	*Captain D4, 11, 12.*	W/T	*I am escorting Acasta to Aberdeen at 10 knots. She is badly damaged. (Received in Iron Duke 9.45 a.m.)*	*0840*
9.42 —	S.N.O. Harwich.	Admiralty -	L/T	Hornet, Hind, Druid, Sandfly, Ferret, Beaver, Matchless, Mastiff, arrived.	—
9.42 —	S.O. B.C.F. -	General	Flags	*Alter course leading ships together the rest in succession to W.S.W.*	—
9.43 —	*S.O. Cruisers*	*Cruisers*	Flags	*Admiral intends to proceed at 17 knots*	—
9.43 —	C.-in-C. -	Destroyers	Flags	**Form Submarine screen ahead when fleet alters course to N. by W. Pass between lines if necessary.**	—
9.45 —	S.O. 5th B.S.	C.-in-C.	S.L.	**Our Battle Cruisers bearing South**	—
9.45 —	S.O. B.C.F.	S.O. 5th B.S.	S.L.	What course are you steering ? Is C.-in-C. in company ; what is his bearing? Reply : Course S.S.W., C.-in-C. bearing W. three miles, speed 16 knots.	—
9.45 —	*Garland* -	*Achates* -	W/T	*My 9 a.m. position 56° 28' N., 2° 4'[E. Indicate Porpoise's position.*	*0905*
9.45 —	Lion -	—	—	Remarks : Battlefleet in sight on port bow	—
9.46 —	C.-in-C. -	General -	Flags	**Alter course together four points to port**	—
9.48 —	S.O.4th L.C.S.	4th L.C.S.	Flags	*Alter course together eight points to starboard.*	—
9.51 —	S.O.2ndL.C.S.	S.O. B.C.F. -	S.L.	Order of 2nd L.C.S., Birmingham, Southampton, Nottingham, from E. to W.	0945
9.52 —	S.O.4thL.C.S.	4th L.C.S.	Flags	*Alter course together three points to port*	—
9.53 —	S.O. 1st B.S.	C.-in-C. -	W/T	**Faulknor, Obedient and Marvel are in company. Marksman destroyed and sank Sparrowhawk. Obedient picked up survivors from raft.** (*Received in Iron Duke 10.50 a.m.*)	0932
9.55 —	S.O. B.C.F.	General	Flags	Alter course leading ships together rest in succession to S.S.W. Admiral intends to proceed at 15 knots.	—
9.55 —	C.-in-C. -	Dublin -	S.L.	**Join Battle Cruiser fleet bearing South from Barham, steering North, 20 knots.**	0945
9.56 —	S.O. B.C.F.	Princess Royal	Sem.	*Can left gun breech of A be repaired ?*	*0955*
9.56 —	Captain D12	Marksman -	W/T	*My course N., speed 20 knots*	*0925*
9.56 —	S.O. 2nd C.S.	Owl -	S.L.	What was it? - Reply : Capsized torpedo craft with red lifebuoys.	0954 0956

Date, Time of Despatch.	From	To	System	Message.	Time of Origin.
1 JUNE —cont.					
9.57 a.m.	Captain D13	Marksman	W/T	*My course and speed are North 20 knots*	*0935*
9.58 —	S.O.3rdL.C.S.	S.O. B.C.F.	S.L.	Gloucester reports Narborough, Pelican and Nerissa in sight.	0913
9.58 —	S.O.4thL.C.S.	4th L.C.S.	Flags	*Alter course together five points to port*	—
9.59 —	S.O. B.C.F.	S.O. 1st, 2nd and3rdL.C.S.	W/T	Alter course leading ships together rest in succession to N. by W.	—
10.0 —	S.O. B.C.F.	Destroyers	S.L.	Take up position as Submarine screen when course is altered to N. by W.	—
10.0 —	**C.-in-C.**	**General**	Flags	**Alter course leading ships together rest in succession to N. by W.**	—
10.0 —	Inconstant	S.O.3rd L.C.S.	S.L.	Have lost touch with Phaeton who is the other side of battlefleet. Reply : Steer N. by E. to regain touch. Reply from Inconstant : I am doing so.	—
10.1 —	C.-in-C.	Dublin	S.L.	**The Battle Cruisers are steering S.**	1000
10.1 —	**S.O.B.C.F.**	**C.-in-C.**	W/T	**Position of wreck of Queen Mary very approximate 56° 44′ N., 5° 49′ E., wreck of Invincible 57° 7′ N., 6° 25′ E., wreck of Indefatigable 56° 49′ N., 5° 32′ E.**	0956
10.2 —	**C.-in-C.**	**S.O.4th L.C.S.**	W/T	*I intend to steer N. by W. at 10 a.m.*	0947
10.5 —	S.O.3rdL.C.S.	3rd L.C.S.	S.L.	*Alter course in succession to N. by W.*	—
10.6 —	S.O.4thL.C.S.	4th L.C.S.	Flags	*Alter course together 16 points to port*	—
10.7 —	Obedient	Captain D12	S.L.	*Am steering N. 30 knots*	—
10.7 —	S.O. B.C.F.	General	Flags	Alter course leading ships together the rest in succession to N. by W.	—
10.7 —	**C.-in-C.**	**S.O.B.C.F.**	W/T	**Consider light cruiser must have been sunk. I want to ascertain if all disabled ships are on the way. Where are New Zealand and Indefatigable? Are all your Light Cruisers and (Destroyers?) accounted for? Sweep up to Lat. 57° 30′ N., Long. 5° 45′ E. on your present line. I will prolong sweep to westward to ensure no disabled ships being there."**	0907
10.8 —	S.O. B.C.F.	13th Flotilla	Flags	Close the Admiral	—
10.10 —	S.O. Cruisers	Cruisers	Flags	*Alter course in succession to N.*	—
10.10 —	**C.-in-C.**	**Light Cruisers**	S.L.	**My course is N. by W.**	—
10.10 —	CommodoreT.	Marlborough	W/T	Laforey and three Destroyers are coming to you. Give Laforey your position, course and speed on D wave.	1000
10.10 —	S.O.3rdL.C.S.	Yarmouth	S.L.	*I am steering N. by E. to regain touch*	1007
10.10 —	S.O. B.C.F.	Narborough	Sem.	Where are the rest of 13th Flotilla?	1008
10.10 —	Minion	Castor	S.L.	*Please give me your position*	—

Date, Time of Despatch.	From	To	System.	Message.	Time of Origin.
1 JUNE *—cont.*					
10.12 a.m.	*S.O.2ndL.C.S.*	*Dublin* - -	S.L.	*Take station West two miles of Nottingham*	—
10.12 —	CommodoreF.	S.O. 2nd B.S.	Sem.	Please give me your reference position Reply : 10 a.m. 55° 50' N., 5° 55' E.	—
10.12 —	*S.O.4thL.C.S.*	*4th L.C.S.* -	Flags	*Alter course together to N. by W. Ships to reform on Comus.*	—
10.13 —	*S.O. Cruisers*	*Cruisers* -	Flags	*Alter course in succession to N. by W.* -	—
10.15 —	S.O. 2nd C.S.	Mischief,Midge	W/T	If you pass a Destroyer bottom up endeavour to sink her.	1015
10.17 —	Warspite -	C.-in-C.,Rosyth	W/T	Two torpedoes missed Warspite in position 56° 31' N., 0° 40' W. Warspite returning to Rosyth with no escort.	0935
10.20 —	*S.O.4thL.C.S.*	*4th L.C.S.* -	Flags	*Zigzag 1½ points. First turn to port, conforming with wing ships.*	—
10.20 —	**R.A. Invergordon.**	**R.A. Scapa** -	W/T	**For C.-in-C. Albion III in charge of two tugs has orders to leave Peterhead and proceed to assistance of Warrior.**	0955
10.21 —	**C.-in-C.** -	**Nonsuch** -	W/T	**What is your position, course and speed? Reply : Taking Acasta in tow. Noon position 57° 16' N., 4° 8' E., course W. ½ N., probable speed six knots.**	1002 1150
10.23 —	*S.O. Cruisers*	*Cruisers* -	Flags	*Admiral intends to proceed at 18 knots* -	—
10.23 —	*S.O. 4th B.S.*	*4th Subdivision*	Flags	*Alter course together 16 points to port* -	—
10.24 —	*Agincourt* -	*S.O. 1st B.S.* -	Flags	*Attention is called to E. by S.* - -	—
10.25 —	*S.O. 5th B.S.*	*5th B.S.* -	Flags	*Admiral intends to proceed at 19 knots* -	—
10.25 —	Castor - -	—	—	Remarks : Buried dead - - -	—
10.27 —	S.O.1stL.C.S.	S.O.3rd L.C.S.	S.L.	Can do 24 knots - - - -	—
10.27 —	Inconstant	S.O.3rd L.C.S.	S.L.	Am in touch with Cordelia and steering N. by W.	—
10.27 —	S.O. B.C.F.	Badger - -	S.L.	Can you account for all 1st Flotilla? - Reply : Yes, except for Defender, who, I think, was struck by fragment of shell yesterday afternoon, and Fearless, who, I think, failed to keep up. Both dropped astern.	1035 1140
10.27 —	*S.O. 4th B.S.*	*4th Subdivision*	Flags	*Alter course together 16 points to port* -	—
10.27 —	**C.-in-C.** -	**C.-in-C.Rosyth**	W/T	**Warrior in tow of Engadine completely disabled, 57° 18' N., 3° 54' E., W.N W, 7 knots.**	0855
10.29 —	*S.O.3rdL.C.S.*	*3rd L.C.S.* -	Flags	*Alter course in succession to N. by W.* -	—
10.30 —	**C.-in-C.** -	**General** -	Flags	**The hands are to be stationed at action stations constantly throughout the day.**	—
10.30 —	*Captain D12*	*Marksman* -	Flags	*Close* - - - - - -	—
10.30 —	S.O.3rdL.C.S.	Cordelia and Galatea.	S.L.	What are Battle Cruisers doing? I have eased to 17 knots. Reply : They are five miles East of Galatea, steering N. by W.	1030
10.30 —	**S.O. 2nd C.S.**	**C.-in-C.** -	W/T	**Destroyer bottom up in 56 8' N., 6 12' E.**	1021
10.30 —	S.O. B.C.F.	Badger - -	S.L.	First two Destroyers can return to their base. Tell 13th Flotilla Destroyers to take their place.	1025

Date, Time of Despatch.	From	To	System.	Message.	Time of Origin.
1 JUNE —*cont.*					
10.31 a.m.	**Blanche**	**C.-in-C.**	S.L.	Three ships accompanied by T.B.Ds. bearing S. by E., steering N., apparently Revenge's division.	1025
10.33 —	Captain D13	S.O. B.C.F.	W/T	My position, course and speed 10.15 a.m. 56° 5′ N., 6° 24′ E., N. by W., at 20 knots. Obdurate, Moresby, Mænad in company.	1015
10.33 —	R.A. Swarbacks Minn.	Admiralty	L/T	Donegal and King Orry sailed	1005
10.35 —	**C.-in-C.**	**Engadine**	W/T	**Priority. What is the position of Engadine and Warrior now?**	1030
10.35 —	S.O.3rdL.C.S.	S.O. B.C.F.	S.L.	Shall we keep to Westward of battlefleet? Reply : No. To the Eastward.	1034
10.35 —	S.O.2ndL.C.S.	S.O. B.C.F.	S.L.	Dublin is stationed West of Nottingham	1030
10.36 —	**Marlborough**	**C.-in-C.**	W/T	**54° 43′ N., 4° 57′ E., two Enemy Submarines on the surface afterwards dived.**	1000
10.37 —	*S.O.2ndL.C.S.*	*Dublin*	S.L.	*What became of Cruiser and two Destroyers reported in your 0430 ? Reply : The German Armoured Cruiser Roon with at least two Destroyers and possibly another Cruiser was seen by myself steering South, but were lost in the fog.*	*1015*
10.38 —	Admiralty	Captain S. Maidstone.	W/T	Retain E. 41. Send three Submarines now and a fourth when available.	1038
10.40 —	**C.-in-C.**	**S.O. 1st B.S., S.O.4thL.C.S., S.O. 2nd C.S.**	W/T	**My position at 10 a.m. Lat. 55° 50′ N., Long. 5° 57′ E., steering N. by W. at 17 knots. Join me.**	1009
10.40 —	Inconstant		—	Remarks : Galatea rejoined 1st L.C.S.	—
10.40 —	*S.O. Cruisers*	*Cruisers*	Flags	*Alter course together one point to port*	—
10.41 —	*Fearless*	*Laforey*	S.L.	*Indicate your position Fearless in company with Marlborough.*	*1045*
10.42 —	*Dublin*	*S.O.2ndL.C.S.*	W/T	*At 6 a.m. this morning nine men rescued from the water. One survivor of Tipperary. I also found Sparrowhawk badly damaged. Efforts were made by the Marksman to tow her, but she was eventually sunk.*	*1030*
10.45 —	S.O. 5th B.S.	Active	S.L.	Take station on starboard bow and zigzag	1046
10.46 —	S.O. 2nd C.S.	Hardy and Mischief.	S.L.	Examine trawler and turn her away from course of fleet.	1045
10.48 —	**C.-in-C.**	**S.O. B.C.F.**	W/T	**How many Destroyers have you in company?** Reply : Eight of 1st Destroyer Flotilla, Christopher, Ophelia and three of 13th Flotilla, making 13 boats. Am sending 1st Destroyer Flotilla base for necessary fuel as they are getting short. 9th Flotilla has returned to fuel. I am short of Fearless and Defender of 1st Destroyer Flotilla. Have asked Captain D13 for account of his flotilla.	**1030** / 1125
10.48 —	S.O. B.C.F.	Captain D13	W/T	Can you account for all your flotilla? Narborough, Nerissa and Pelican are with me. Reply : No.	1045
10.49 —	*S.O.1stL.C.S.*	*1st L.C.S.*	S.L.	*Spread in order of fleet numbers*	*1040*
10.49 —	*S.O. 5th B.S.*	*5th B.S.*	Flags	*Admiral intends to proceed at 17 knots*	—
10.50 —	Warspite	—	—	Remarks : Fired at periscope bearing 175 Red, two rounds 6-in.	—
10.53 —	*S.O. Cruisers*	*Cruisers*	Flags	*Reform*	—

Date, Time of Despatch.	From	To	System.	Message.	Time of Origin.
1 JUNE —*cont.*					
10.55 a.m.	S.O. 1st L.C.S.	S.O. 3rd L.C.S.	S.L.	Battle Cruisers are steering N. by W., last speed given 15 knots. 1st L.C.S. spread West and East in order of fleet numbers.	1050
10.55 —	S.O. 2nd C.S.	Destroyers	Flags	Recall - - - - - - -	—
10.59 —	Marlborough	Fearless, Laforey.	W/T	My position, course and speed at 10.30 a.m., 54° 35′ N., 5° 13′ E., course S.W. by W., 13 knots. Two Enemy Submarines 54° 43′ N., 4° 38′ E., at 10 a.m.	1043
11.0 —	*Captain D12*	*Marksman*	Sem.	*Did you and 2nd Division attack Enemy battlefleet after me this morning ? If so, with what results ? Reply : My attack was spoilt by 12th Flotilla coming down in the middle of second half. In avoiding them I lost second half, so do not know whether they attacked. Enemy then apparently turned away.*	—
11 0 —	Marksman	S.O. 1st B.S.	S.L.	Following survivors now on board Marksman. Ardent, Lieut. Comdr. Marsden; Sparrowhawk, all officers and 51 ratings; Fortune, Artificer Engineer Barnes; Tipperary, Sub.-Lieut. Poulett and 22 ratings (all other Officers including Captain D4 appear to have been lost). Broke, two ratings. About 30 ratings of Sparrowhawk jumped on board Broke last night. (*Passed to C.-in-C. 7 a.m. June 2nd*).	1030
	S.O. 1st B.S.	Marksman	Sem.	Your 1030. Can you ascertain any further details as to how these Destroyers were lost? Has Broke and all her crew been lost also? Reply : I am not sure about Broke, she was badly hit and collided with Sparrowhawk. These losses took place in an attack on Enemy's Battle-Cruisers during first watch. Several torpedoes are believed to have hit.	1120
11 2 —	*S.O. Cruisers*	*Cruisers*	Flags	*Alter course in succession to N. by W.*	—
11.4 —	**C.-in-C.**	**S.O. B.C.F.**	W/T	**When did Queen Mary and Indefatigable go?** **Reply : Indefatigable sank 4 p.m., Queen Mary, 4.30 p.m.**	**1104** **1227**
11.5 —	**C.-in-C.**	**S.O. 2nd C.S.**	S.L.	**Admiral intends to proceed at 16 knots. Form single line-abreast to port, ships in column to be two miles apart. Take station ahead of Admiral six miles.**	—
11.5 —	S.O. B.C.F.	General	Flags	Alter course in succession to N.N.E. Admiral intends to proceed at 18 knots.	—
11.6 —	*S.O. 5th B.S.*	*5th B.S.*	Flags	*Admiral intends to proceed at 16 knots*	—
11.7 —	*S.O. 4th L.C.S.*	*4th L.C.S.*	Flags	*Alter course together to N.W. Reform on Comus.*	—
11.7 —	**C.-in-C.**	**S.O. 2nd C.S.**	S.L.	**My course and speed are N.W., 17 knots**	—
11.7 —	*S.O. Cruisers*	*Cruisers*	Flags	*Admiral intends to proceed at 20 knots*	—
11.8 —	**C.-in-C.**	**General**	Flags	**Alter course leading ships together rest in succession to N.W.**	—

Date, Time of Despatch.	From	To	System.	Message.	Time of Origin.
1 JUNE —*cont.*					
11.8 a.m.	**C.-in-C.**	**Cyclops (for Admiralty).**	W/T	Priority. Harwich force not required except for Destroyers to screen Marlborough. Weather very misty. Am ascertaining no disabled ships are left and returning to base. Whole area swept for disabled Enemy Cruisers without result.	1044
11.9 —	**C.-in-C.**	**S.O. B.C.F.**	W/T	Avoid position of mines - - -	1109
11.9 —	S.O. B.C.F.	S.O. 1st, 2nd and 3rd L.C.S.	W/T	Alter course in succession to N.N.E. Admiral intends to proceed at 18 knots.	1100
11.10 —	S.O. B.C.F.	General	Flags	The hands are to be stationed at action stations constantly throughout the day.	—
11.10 —	Marlborough	—	—	Remarks : Track of torpedo passed Marlborough on port beam 20 to 30 yards from astern.	—
11.12 —	*S.O. Cruisers*	*Cruisers* -	Flags	*Alter course in succession to N.W.* - -	—
11.12 —	*S.O. 3rd L.C.S.*	*Light Cruisers*	S.L.	*Zigzag. Speed of advance 15 knots - -*	—
11.15 —	Badger -	S.O. B.C.F. -	S.L.	Am sending Lizard and Attack now. Propose to send remaining Destroyers as follows : Acheron and Goshawk at 4 p.m., Badger and Lapwing at 5 p.m., Ariel and Hydra at 6 p.m.	1050
11.15 —	*S.O. 4th L.C.S.*	*4th L.C.S.* -	Flags	*Indicate amount of oil fuel remaining on board. Replies :—*	—
				Calliope - 75 per cent.	
				Constance 63 ,,	
				Comus - 69 ,,	
				Royalist - 69 ,,	
				Caroline - 65 ,,	
11.20 —	*S.O. 4th L.C.S.*	*4th L.C.S.* -	Flags	*Zigzag one point. First turn to port*	—
11.20 —	**C.-in-C.**	**Commodore F.**	W/T	Signal names of Destroyers missing from 4th, 11th, 12th Flotilla.	1120
				Reply. : 11th and 12th Flotilla. None missing. Ambuscade reports Tipperary and Fortune blown up. Whereabouts of remainder of 4th Flotilla uncertain. Ambuscade in company with me.	1740
11.20 —	Warspite -	C.-in-C., Rosyth	W/T	Gun range Inchkeith at 2 p.m., outer gate 2.40, inner gate 3.0.	1115
11.20 — (recd.)	**C.-in-C.** -	**S.O.B.C.F.** -	W/T	Avoid position of wrecks with heavy ships unless you are certain that they were not mined.	1100
11.22 —	C.-in-C., Rosyth.	Warspite -	W/T	Two Destroyers of local flotilla being sent now. Three Destroyers of sea-going flotillas proceeding to you as soon as possible.	1100
11.25 —	*Commodore F.*	*Captain D 12 and Broke.*	W/T	*Report names of Destroyers that cannot be accounted for from your flotillas. Ambuscade is with me.*	1125
				Reply from Captain D 12 : Can account for all who were with me but do not know whereabouts of Mischief, who was with Cruisers.	1222
11.25 —	*Malaya* -	*S.O. 5th B.S.*	Sem.	*For information. The base plug of one shell which came from one of Enemy's Battleships is 9-in. in diameter. It would therefore appear that one of them is armed with guns larger than 12-in.*	1117

Date, Time of Despatch.	From	To	System.	Message.	Time of Origin.
1 JUNE —*cont.*					
11.25 a.m.	C.-in-C. -	S.O.B.C.F. -	W/T	Your 0956. Was cause of sinking mines, torpedoes or gunfie? At what time did Queen Mary and Indefatigable go?	
11.27 —	Warspite -	—	—	Remarks : Opened fire four rounds at Submarine.	—
11.28 —	S.O. 1st B.S.	C.-in-C. -	W/T	Have you turned South at all since leaving 0810 rendezvous? Reply : Yes.	1108 1201
11.30 —	Admiralty -	All Ships -	W/T	Owing to mines near Sunk L.V. passage is closed till swept.	1130
11.30 —	S.O. 1st B.S.	Obedient -	S.L.	How many survivors have you and where from? Reply : Rescued men were German bluejackets. They have been taken on board Dutch steamer Texel. Captain informed me that his Government would object to their removal on grounds of neutrality. I did not consider myself justified in removing them by force.	1135 1146
	S.O. 1st B.S.	Obedient -	Sem.	Do you know what ship the German bluejackets belonged? Reply : Boarding officer found the men in an exhausted state and apparently unable to understand English. They had both lost their caps and most of their uniform, consequently name of their ship could not be ascertained, but judging by the size of the raft she must have been at least a Light Cruiser.	1217
11 30 —	*Birmingham*	*S.O.2nd L.C.S.*	S.L.	*Did you hear anyone firing in your direction ? Reply : Southampton fired at a mine.*	*1130*
11.30 —	CommodoreF.	Boadicea -	S.L.	Can you tell me number of Enemy's ships sunk? Reply : No, have heard nothing.	—
11.30 —	Owl - -	S.O. 2nd C.S.	Flags	Permission is requested to let fires die out in boilers not required for 20 knots. Reply : Approved.	—
11.31 —	S.O. B.C.F.	Captain D13 -	W/T	My position at 11.10 a.m. was Lat. 56° 12′ N., Long. 5° 57′ E., steering N.N.E. at 18 knots.	1120
11.31 —	C.-in-C. - -	S.O. 2nd C.S.	S.L.	Do you know anything of Duke of Edinburgh and Black Prince? Reply : Duke of Edinburgh is with me. I know nothing of Black Prince.	1130 1135
11.31 —	S.O. B.C.F.	S.O.2ndL.C.S.	S.L.	What was gunfire? Reply : Floating mine.	1130
11.31 —	C.-in-C. -	S.O. 3rd L.C.S.	S.L.	B.C.F. last seen on my starboard beam. Has Chester been with you? Reply : Passed Chester this morning taking wounded to the Humber.	1130
11.33 —	New Zealand	—	—	Remarks : Passed derelict on starboard beam.	—
11.35 —	Marlborough	Fearless -	Sem.	Please let me know at 12.30 p.m. what course I am steering. I have increased my speed one knot. Reply : I make you to be steering S. 85° W.	— 1235
11.35 —	C.-in-C. -	S.O. 1st B.S.	W/T	Priority. Give position 56 49′ N., 5° 32′ E., a wide berth of 20 miles. Reply : I have already passed this position and I am now 10 miles E.N.E. of it.	1124 1150

Date, Time of Despatch.	From	To	System.	Message.	Time of Origin.
1 JUNE *—cont.*					
11.40 a.m.	Warspite	—	—	Remarks : Sighted periscope right ahead	—
11.40 —	S.O. B.C.F.	Pelican	S.L.	What is wreck? Reply : It is a bow of a British Destroyer.	—
11.44 —	**Marlborough**	**C.-in-C.**	W/T	**54° 23′ N., 5° 7′ E., Enemy Submarine fired torpedo at Marlborough, torpedo passed astern. My course is W., speed 13 knots.**	**1101**
11.45 —	Fearless	Marlborough	W/T	Laforey to Fearless. Position at 11.30 a.m. 53° 49′ N., 3° 36′ E., course N. 22° E., speed 25 knots.	1130
11.45 —	**Canterbury**	**C.-in-C.**	S.L.	**I separated from 3rd B.C.S. after engaging Enemy's Battle Cruisers last night and joined 3rd L.C.S.**	**1140**
11.47 —	C.-in-C., Rosyth.	Warspite	W/T	Where do you wish tugs to meet you? You can proceed straight into dock. Reply : To the West of Beamer Rock	1107 / 1200
11.50 —	*S.O.4thL.C.S.*	*4th L.C.S.*	Flags	*Admiral intends to proceed at 18 knots*	—
11.50 —	C.-in-C. Rosyth.	Warspite	W/T	All arrangements have been made for your ships to enter as requested and defences have been warned.	1133
11.51 —	Canterbury	Bellona	S.L.	It's all right, boys. One shot through us aft and one through our Union Jack.	1150
11.55 —	**S.O. 1st B.S.**	**C.-in-C.**	W/T	**Captain D 12 reports that 12th Flotilla attacked the Enemy's Battle Fleet, 6 Kaiser class and 3 Cruisers at 2 a.m. 1 Battleship blown up.**	**1130**
11.56 —	*S.O.2ndL.C.S.*	*Dublin*	S.L.	*Where is 3rd L.C.S. ? Reply : I have not seen them.*	*1155*
11.56 —	Duke of Edinburgh.	General	Flags	Mine in sight, port quarter	—
11.58 —	Boadicea	Commodore F.	S.L.	Have you any news to give me, please? Who were you fighting? Reply : I took on three German Cruisers last night but was very badly mauled.	—
12.0 noon	*S.O. 4th B.S.*	*4th Division*	Sem.	*Ships of 4th B.S. are to report by semaphore whether they received any hits or suffered any casualties yesterday Wednesday. Replies : Benbow nil, Temeraire nil, Vanguard nil, Bellerophon nil.*	*1200*
12.0 —	Warspite	—	—	Remarks : Two Destroyers sighted	—
12.3 p.m.	*S.O.3rdL.C.S.*	*3rd L.C.S.*	S.L.	*Alter course in succession to N.N.W.*	—
12.5 —	Hercules	*S.O. 1st B.S.*	Sem.	*I cannot keep up this speed much longer. It is practically my full speed and does not admit of cleaning fires. A reduction of one knot would be a very great help.*	*1155*
12.5 —	S.O.3rdL.C.S.	S.O. 1st L.C.S.	S.L.	I am steering N.N.W. which takes me 10 miles W. of westernmost wreck.	1200
12.5 —	Warspite	Destroyers	S.L.	Proceeding at 25 knots	—
12.7 —	Aberdeen	R.A. Scapa	W/T	For C.-in-C. from Rosyth. Steamer entering reports two torpedoes fired at her at 9.35 a.m. in 56° 31′ N., 0° 41′ W.	1151
12.10 —	Foxhound	Lizard	W/T	*My position 56° 04′ N., 6° 02′ E., course N. 74° W., 15 knots.*	*1200*
12.10 —	Warspite	Destroyers	Flags	Proceed at 23 knots	—
12.12 —	S.O. B.C.F.	General	W/T and Flags	Alter course leading ships together the rest in succession to N.E.	1210

Date, Time of Despatch.	From	To	System.	Message.	Time of Origin.
1 JUNE *—cont.*					
12.13p.m.	Fearless	Marlborough -	W/T	Laforey to Marlborough. Noon position 53° 56′ N., 3° 54′ E., course N. 52° E., speed 28 knots.	1108
12.15 —	Owl -	- S.O. 2nd C.S.-	S.L.	The maximum speed at which Hardy can reach Northern base is 15 knots, the remainder 17.	1200
12.15 —	Hardy -	- S.O. 2nd C.S.-	S.L.	Submit I have only sufficient oil fuel for 15 knots leaving a very small margin for safety.	1210
12.17 —	*S.O.1stB.S.*	*5th Subdivision*	Flags	*Alter course in succession to N.W. Admiral intends to proceed at 19 knots.*	—
12.19 —	**C.-in-C.**	**General -**	Flags	**Guides to bear W.S.W. from Guide of fleet.**	—
12.20 —	Warspite -	Destroyers -	Flags	Alter course in succession to W.S.W. -	—
12.21 —	*R.A. 2nd B.S.*	*2nd Division -*	Flags	*Admiral intends to proceed at 17 knots -*	—
12.21 —	*S.O. 2nd B.S.*	*2nd B.S.* -	Flags	*Admiral intends to proceed at 14 knots* -	—
12.23 —	*S.O. 5th B.S.*	*5th B.S.* -	Flags	*Admiral intends to proceed at 19 knots* -	—
12.25 —	**C.-in-C. via Engadine.**	**Warrior** -	W/T	**Two tugs under Yacht Albion are leaving Peterhead to assist you.**	1203
12.25 —	Warspite -	—	—	Remarks : Sighted four Destroyers port bow.	—
12.25 —	*S.O.3rdL.C.S.*	*3rd L.C.S.* -	S.L.	*I am steering N.N.W. to clear dangerous area.*	1225
12.25 —	*S.O. Cruisers*	*Cruisers* -	Flags	*Admiral intends to proceed at 18 knots*	—
12.25 —	Warspite	T.Bs. 24, 26, 28 and 35.	Flags	Zigzag two points - - -	—
12.25 —	*Valiant*	*S.O. 5th B.S.-*	Sem.	*I am informed by Officer in foretop that when you altered course at 9.27, having sighted a Submarine, that he saw the Submarine quite clearly and that you seemed to pass very close to its position, and that although we were in a big oily patch at the time a big circle of oil of quite a different appearance was seen after you had passed over what we consider to be Submarine position.*	1135
12.25 —	S.O. B.C.F. -	Light Cruisers	S.L.	Look out to give positions 56 44′ N., 5° 49′ E., 57° 7′ N., 6° 25′ E., 56 49′ N., 5° 32′ E. a wide berth.	1219
12.27 —	*S.O.2ndB.S.*	*1st Division -*	Flags	*Admiral intends to proceed at 17 knots* -	—
12.30 —	*S.O. Cruisers*	*Cruisers*	Flags	*Spread for look-out duties in the sequence in which ships now are, two miles apart bearing S.W.*	
12.30 —	*S.O. B.C.F.-*	*Battle Cruisers*	Flags and S.L.	*Indicate noon positions :—* *Lion* - *- 56° 24′ N. 6 5′ E.* *Princess Royal - 56° 22′ N. 6 5′ E.* *Tiger* - *- 56° 20′ N. 6 20′ E.* *Indomitable - 56 17′ N. 6 31′ E.* *Inflexible - - 56° 50′ N. 6 15′ E.* *New Zealand - 56° 21′ N. 6 19′ E.*	
12.34 —	Hardy -	S.O. 2nd C.S.	S.L.	Permission to reduce to 15 knots. Reply : Approved. Keep a good look out on W/T.	1231
12.34 —	S.O. 1st L.C.S.	S.O. B.C.F. -	S.L.	Have just passed several bodies in life-belts, as far as can be seen German. The belts are not recognised. Two blue and white pear-shaped mines just passed.	1220

Date, Time of Despatch.	From	To	System.	Message.	Time of Origin.
1 JUNE —*cont.*					
12.35 p.m.	**C.-in-C.**	**General**	Flags	**Columns to be six cables apart**	—
12.35 —	Marlborough	Fearless	W/T	Pass to Laforey. My position, course and speed at noon 54° 25′ N., 4° 52′ E., course W., speed 14 knots.	1225
12.39 —	*Commodore T.*	*General*	Flags	*Alter course in succession to N. 24° E.*	—
12.40 —	*S.O.4thL.C.S.*	*4th L.C.S.*	Flags	*Admiral intends to proceed at 17 knots*	—
12.40 —	Warspite	T.Bs. 24, 26, 28, 35.	Flags	Proceed at 21 knots	—
12.40 —	**C.-in-C.**	**General**	Flags S.L.	**Reference position at noon, 56° 20′ N., 5° 25′ E.**	—
12.40 —	**S.O.2nd C.S.**	**C.-in-C.**	S.L.	**Three of escort Destroyers can just reach northern base at maximum speed 17 knots, Hardy only at 15 knots. Request instructions.**	1220
12.40 —	*S.O. B.C.F.*	*B.C.F.*	S.L. and Sem.	*Make preparations for burying at sea this evening those killed in action. Time will be signalled later.*	1225
12.40 —	Warspite	T.Bs. 24, 26, 28 and 35.	Flags	Alter course together two points to port	—
12.41 —	S.O. B.C.F.	General	S.L. Flags	Reference position noon G.M.T., 56° 24′ N., 6° 5′ E.	1240
12.41 —	*S.O. 5th B.S.*	*5th B.S.*	Flags	*Admiral intends to proceed at 20 knots*	—
12.45 —	Warspite	T.Bs. 24, 26, 28 and 35.	Flags	Alter course together two points to port	—
12.45 —	S.O. 2nd C.S.	Mischief	S.L.	Steer a steady course. Keep just before starboard beam of Minotaur.	—
12.47 —	*S.O. 1st B.S.*	*5th Subdivision*	Flags	*Alter course in succession to W. by S. Admiral intends to proceed at 17 knots.*	—
12.47 —	Inchkeith	Negro, Phœnix 8th Flotilla and Nepean.	W/T	Submarine on surface 32. Yes (see 1.10 p.m. *Warspite to Nepean*.)	1200
12.49 —	**C.-in-C.**	**R.A. Invergordon.**	W/T	**Move Cromarty and fleet-sweeping trawlers to areas 7 and 6 respectively at once. Important to continue search until completed.**	1249
12.50 —	S.O.2ndB.C.S.	S.O. B.C.F.	S.L.	Acheron reports she has just sufficient oil to take her to base at 19 knots in fine weather. *(Passed to Badger.)*	1205
	S.O. B.C.F.	Badger	S.L.	Arrange accordingly, but boats should not leave less than two in company. Reply : Should Acheron and Goshawk proceed to base at once? Pelican and Nerissa have now only sufficient oil to proceed to base at 20 knots.	1256 / 1310
12.50 —	S.O. 2nd C.S.	Midge	S.L.	Steer a steady course. Keep on starboard beam of Minotaur.	—
12.50 —	**S.O.B.C.F.**	**C.-in-C.**	W/T	**Your 0907. New Zealand is here. Indefatigable sunk 10 minutes after engaging Enemy by shell exploding magazine. Queen Mary sunk from same cause. Invincible sunk, probably from same cause, possible might have been a tor-**	1148

Date, Time of Despatch.	From	To	System.	Message.	Time of Origin.
				pedo. All Light Cruisers accounted for. Have not accounted for all Destroyers yet. Nestor, Onslow, Nomad and Turbulent missing. Damage to Enemy consisted in all ships being heavily hit and reduced in speed. One Battle Cruiser was thought to blow up as she disappeared in smoke. Another, undoubtedly Lutzow, was in very bad condition ; when last seen she was closing Enemy Battle Fleet. Information is very scanty as I have been unable to gather in reports.	
12.51 p.m.	S.O. 5th B.S.	5th B.S. -	Flags	Admiral intends to proceed at 16½ knots	—
12.52 —	C.-in-C. -	S.O. B.C.F. - S.O. 1st B.S.	W/T	What is your position, course and speed now? My position at noon, 56° 20' N., 5° 25' E.	1231
	S.O. B.C.F. -	C.-in-C. -	W/T	My position now 56° 32' N., 6° 11' E., course N.E., speed 18 knots.	1230
	S.O. 1st B.S.-	C.-in-C. -	W/T	At 1.30 p.m. my position 57° 5' N., 5° 18' E., course W. ½ S., speed of advance 16 knots.	1332
12.55 —	C.-in-C. -	5th B.S. -	Flags	Take station on present bearing six cables -	—
12.55 —	S.O. 2nd C.S.	Hardy -	S.L.	Are you certain your oil will last you at 15 knots to take you to Northern base? Reply : Hope to get in with about 15 tons left.	1246
12.56 —	Owl -	Captain D13 -	W/T	The speed at which Hardy can reach Scapa Flow is 15 knots.	1220
12.58 —	Galatea -	S.O. B.C.F. -	S.L.	Have just passed Dan Buoy with red flag on my port hand.	—
12.59 —	Rosyth S.S.-	Warspite -	W/T	Submarine on surface 32. Yes 5½ Lux - (see 1.10 p.m. Warspite to Nepean.)	1210
1.0 —	T.B. 25 -	Warspite -	Sem.	What is present course, please? Reply : West by South.	—
1.0 —	Marlborough	General	Flags	Indicate noon position. Reply : Marlborough 54° 25' N., 4° 52' E. ; Fearless 54° 34' N., 5° 0' E.	—
1.0 —	S.O.3rdL.C.S.	S.O. B.C.F. -	W/T	My position now 56° 27' N., 5° 37' E., course N.N.W., speed 18 knots.	1225
1.0 —	S.O. 2nd C.S.	Shannon -	S.L.	Tell Owl to steer a steady course at 18 knots	1256
1.0 —	S.O. 2nd C.S.	Destroyers -	S.L.	Minotaur's noon position 56° 22' N., 5° 26' E.	---
1.3 —	C.-in-C. -	S.O. B.C.F. -	W/T	Have you sufficient Torpedo Boat Destroyers to screen 5th B.S. and B.C.F. to Rosyth? When can squadron join you?	1300
				Reply : Have nine Destroyers now, four of whom must leave at 5 p.m. for base. I hope Champion and three Destroyers will join later. (Received in Iron Duke 2.3 p.m.)	1340
1.3 —	S.O.B.C.S. -	C.-in-C. -	W/T	Your 1104. Indefatigable sank 4 p.m., Queen Mary at about 4.30 p.m. Do not think it was mines or torpedoes, because both explosions immediately followed hits by salvoes.	1227
1.4 —	Commodore F.	Opal -	W/T	Report names of Destroyers of 12th Flotilla in company with you.	1235
1.9 —	Marlborough	General -	Flags	Alter course in succession to S.W.-	—
1.10 —	Commodore F.	Owl and Hardy	S.L.	Hardy proceed independently direct to Scapa calling at Aberdeen for fuel if necessary.	1310

Date, Time of Despatch.	From	To	System.	Message.	Time of Origin.
1 JUNE —*cont.*					
1.10 p.m.	Warspite	Nepean	Sem.	Please give me Inchkeith's 1200, my charts are destroyed, and Rosyth's 1210. Reply: Submarine on surface 12 miles East of Bell Rock, the other, Rosyth 1210 Submarine on surface near Holy Island.	—
1.12 —	Warspite	C.-in-C. Rosyth	W/T	Warspite has casualties as follows: 8 dead, 20 cot cases all suffering seriously from shock.	1312
1.15 —	Warspite	Nepean	Sem.	Keep further ahead - - - -	—
1.15 —	**C.-in-C.**	**General**	Flags	**Alter course leading ships together the rest in succession to N. by W.**	—
1.16 —	*Nessus*	*Commodore F.*	W/T	*Nessus has one boiler out of action. Damage by shell fire.*	*1310*
1.18 —	*S.O. B.C.F.*	*Battle Cruisers*	Sem.	*Ships are to report what boats they have available for service. Reply: Lion— No boats available for service owing to mainmast being shot through. Princess Royal—Two picket boats, one launch, two cutters. Tiger—One picket boat, one motor launch, all pulling boats. Inflexible—All boats. New Zealand—One picket boat, one motor launch, one cutter, two whalers. Indomitable—One steam pinnace, one motor launch, one sailing pinnace, three cutters, three small boats.*	*1317*
1.19 —	Fearless	Marlborough	W/T	Ness to Marlborough. My position 54° 7′ N., 1° 20′ E., steering S. 75° E. Ordered to escort you. Request instructions.	1200
1.19 —	**S.O. 2nd C.S.**	**C.-in-C.**	W/T	**2nd C.S. and Duke of Edinburgh complete with ammunition. Hampshire has expended very little.**	**1300**
1.20 —	Engadine	C.-in-C. Rosyth	W/T	Expect to arrive 7 a.m. 2nd June having on board 35 Officers, 681 men, 24 cot cases, 2 walking cases of Warrior.	1310
1.20 —	T.B. 25	Warspite	Sem.	My orders for T.Bs. to accompany you as far as Elie Fidra Line unless you require me further. Permission to part company there. Reply: Affirmed.	—
1.24 —	**C.-in-C.**	**S.O. 2nd C.S.**	W/T	**How many Destroyers have you with you? Reply: Four Destroyers. Owl senior officer. Proceeding independently to Northern base at 15 knots, their maximum speed at fuel remaining.** (*Received in Iron Duke 2.40 p.m.*)	**1305** **1345**
1.24 —	C.-in-C.	**S.O.M.S., A.C.O. & S.**	W/T	**When Sloops have searched Area 5 they are to continue to hunt Submarines in this area. A.C. Orkney and Shetlands is requested to concentrate trawlers in this area.**	1324
1.25 —	*Ophelia*	*Captain D4*	W/T	*Shark and Acasta are not with Battle Cruisers.*	*1320*
1.25 —	Admiral Rosyth.	Warspite	S.L.	Please tell me if I can render any assistance to you or any other. I hope you bring good news. Reply: We have been attacked by three Submarines to-day Thursday. They are apparently waiting outside.	—

Date, Time of Despatch.	From	To	System.	Message.	Time of Origin.
1 JUNE —*cont.* 1.25 p.m.	*Hampshire* -	*S.O. 2nd C.S.-*	S.L.	*Submit with reference to signal just received to pass to C.-in-C. Iron Duke is not in sight of Hampshire.*	*1310*
1.26 —	Fearless	Laforey	W/T	Make smoke - - - - - -	1337
1.27 —	*Captain D12*	*Mischief*	W/T	*Where are you ?* - - - -	*1240*
1.27 —	**Chester**	**C.-in-C.**	W/T	**Pass to R.A.C. East Coast from Chester. Expect to arrive at Flamborough Head about 2.30 p.m. and outer gate 4.30 p.m. I have no chart and nine other hospital cases.**	1155
1.30 —	*S.O.1stB.C.S.*	*S.O. B.C.F.* -	Sem.	*It is for consideration whether Tiger or Princess Royal should complete with ammunition until examination of engines has been made.*	*1315*
				Reply : Would you prefer that Princess Royal and Tiger did not replenish with any ammunition on arrival ?	*1355*
				Reply : Princess Royal : Yes I think it would be best.	*1340*
1.30 —	S.O. B.C.F. -	General	S.L. and Flags	Alter course leading ships together the rest in succession to N. 16° W.	—
1.30 —	**C.-in-C.**	**S.O. 5th B.S.** -	W/T	**Can you tell me if 5th B.S. did much damage to Enemy force?**	1310
			S.L.	**Reply : There were a fair number of hits but no ship fell out of the line disabled, although one appeared to have speed reduced just when Battleships came up. The Enemy were in a thick haze while 5th B.S. were shown up against a clear horizon. For a great part of action the Enemy could only be distinguished by the flash of their firing. 5th B.S. did not come into action until a considerable time after Battle Cruisers.**	1405
1.30 —	*Shannon*	*S.O. 2nd C.S.-*	S.L.	*Owl is not in visual touch* - -	*1325*
1.30 —	S.O. 5th B.S.	5th B.S.	Flags	*Admiral intends to proceed at 16 knots* -	—
1.30 —	**C.-in-C.**	**General**	Flags	**Guides to bear abeam** - - -	—
1.30 —	Marlborough	Fearless	W/T	Pass to Ness and Laforey from Marlborough. My position at 1 p.m., 54 21' N., 4° 22' E., course West. Speed 14 knots. Close.	—
1.30 —	**C.-in-C.**	**S.O. 2nd C.S.-**	W/T	**My course N. by W. at 1.10 p.m.** -	1325
1.31 —	Fearless	Ness	W/T	Make smoke every two minutes - -	1340
1.31 —	Marlborough	General	Flags	Alter course in succession to West -	—
1.38 —	*S.O.2ndL.C.S.*	*Birmingham, Dublin, Nottingham.*	S.L.	*Indicate amount of coal and oil fuel remaining at noon. Replies : Birmingham—Coal 800 tons, oil 130 tons. Dublin—Coal 860 tons, oil 146 tons. Southampton's coal and oil fuel report—Coal 866 tons, oil 146 tons. Nottingham—638 tons, oil fuel 80 tons.*	*1335*

Date, Time of Despatch	From	To	System.	Message.	Time of Origin.
1 JUNE — cont.					
1.40 p.m.	T.B. 25	Warspite	Flags	Permission is requested to proceed in execution of previous orders. Reply: Affirmed.	—
1.40 —	S.O. Cruisers	Cruisers	S.L.	*Alter course leading ships together rest in succession to N. by W.*	—
1.40 —	Mandate	Commodore F.	W/T	*Your 1325. Full stock of ammunition on board. None expended.*	1330
1.40 —	Scarrow	Calista	W/T	At 2 p.m. Warspite and escort arrives gun range. Keep special vigilance.	1200
1.41 —	**C.-in-C.**	**S.O. 5th B.S.**	W/T and S.L.	**Which ships of your squadron require docking?** **Reply : Warspite, Malaya and probably Barham.**	**1340** **1400**
1.47 —	S.O. 3rd L.C.S.	Light Cruisers	S.L.	*Alter course in succession to N.E.*	—
1.47 —	S.O. 2nd C.S.	Mischief	S.L.	Rejoin your group and tell Owl to proceed independently to Northern base.	—
1.49 —	Commodore T.	General	Flags	*Alter course in succession to N.N.W.*	—
1.49 —	S.O. 1st B.S.	5th Subdivision	Flags	*Alter course together two points to starboard*	—
1.50 —	Marlborough	—	—	Remarks: Sighted large flotilla Destroyers and four Light Cruisers on port quarter.	—
1.50 —	S.O. 2nd C.S.	Mischief	S.L.	Owl is on our starboard quarter	—
1.53 —	Carysfort	—	—	Remarks : Sighted H.M.S. Marlborough	—
1.55 —	Warspite	General	Flags	Proceed at 19 knots	—
1.58 —	Marlborough	—	—	Remarks : Challenged Carysfort	—
1.58 —	Forth	Chester	W/T	From R.A.C. East Coast of England. Your 1155. There is no swept channel. Keep clear of prohibited (?) area off Spurn. Further orders regarding berth will be signalled later.	1325
2.0 —	Marlborough	Fearless	S.L.	I have reduced speed one knot	—
2.0 —	**C.-in-C.**	**S.O. B.C.F.**	W/T	**Do any of your ships require docking?** **Reply : It will only be necessary to list Tiger and Princess Royal in basin. Lion does not require docking. Southampton will require docking to complete repairs but not necessarily immediately.**	**1358** **1721**
2.0 —	Mischief	S.O. 2nd C.S.	S.L.	Does last signal refer to Owl alone or to the 8th group?	—
2.0 —	S.O. Cruisers	Cruisers	S.L.	*Zigzag as ordered in my 0247 of yesterday, Wednesday.*	1350
2.0 —	**C.-in-C.**	**General**	Flags	**Alter course together two points to starboard. Admiral intends to proceed at 16 knots.**	—
2.1 —	S.O. 4th L.C.S.	4th L.C.S.	Flags	*Negative zigzag. Admiral intends to proceed at 18 knots.*	—
2.2 —	**Aberdeen**	**R.A. Invergordon.**	W/T	**For C.-in-C. from Rosyth. Two Submarines on surface reported by patrols in positions 55° 45′ N., 1° 25′ W., 56° 25′ N., 1° 45′ W., both at noon.**	**1335**
2.3 —	S.O. 4th L.C.S.	4th L.C.S.	Flags	*Alter course together two points to starboard*	—

Date, Time of Despatch.	From	To	System.	Message.	Time of Origin.
1 JUNE —*cont*					
2.4 p.m.	*S.O. 1st B.S.*	*5th Subdivision*	Flags	*Alter course together two points to port*	—
2.5 —	**Engadine** -	**C.-in-C., R.A. Invergordon.**	W/T	**Warrior abandoned, crew taken off, Lat. 57° 21′ N., Long. 3° 2′ E., three shackles and 6-in. hawser outboard, proceeding Queensferry. Engadine's position 11 a.m. 57° 10′ N., 2° 17′ E., speed 10·5 knots.**	0830
2.6 —	*Garland* -	*Commodore F.*	W¸T	*I am escorting Porpoise and Contest to Tyne River. Noon position 56° 33′ N., 3° 02′ E.*	1400
2.7 —	*S.O. 4th L.C.S.*	*4th L.C.S.*	Flags	*Alter course in succession N. by W.* -	—
2.7 —	**C.-in-C.** -	**S.O. 2nd C.S.**	W¸T	**Close to within visual signalling distance**	1400
2.10 —	**C.-in-C.** -	**4th L.C.S.** -	W T	**My course was W. by N. at 1.15 p.m.** -	1355
2.11 —	*S.O. 4th L.C.S.*	*4th L.C.S.* -	Flags	*Alter course together two points to starboard*	—
2.13 —	*S.O. Cruisers*	*Cruisers* -	S.L.	*Speed of advance 17 knots* - -	—
2.15 —	Ad. Supt., Newcastle-on-Tyne.	Admiralty -	L.T.	Achilles undocked for emergency, but necessary to re-dock after changing guns to finish bow fitting. This may possibly delay Minotaur one tide or one day.	1157
2.17 —	Marlborough	Commodore T.	S.L.	Marlborough is proceeding to Rosyth. Maximum speed with safety to bulkheads is 13 knots.	1416
				Reply : I am sending four T.B.Ds. to escort you.	1420
2.19 —	*S.O. 1st B.S.*	*5th Subdivision*	Flags	*Alter course together two points to starboard*	—
2.20 —	*Commodore T.*	*General* - -	Flags	*Alter course in succession to N.N.E.* -	—
2.20 —	**C.-in-C.** -	**Commodore F., S.O. 5th B.S.**	S.L.	**Commodore F. to detail two Destroyers to screen Valiant to Rosyth. S.O. 5th B.S. to inform Valiant when Destroyers are detailed. Valiant to exchange positions with S.O. B.C.F. The only Destroyers required are two for Valiant.**	1415
				Reply : Moon and Mounsey - - -	1426
2.20 —	**C.-in-C.** -	**General** -	Flags	**Alter course together two points to port**	—
2.22 —	**C.-in-C.** -	**S.O. 5th B.S.**	S.L.	**Barham and Malaya will proceed with fleet to Scapa and thence to Invergordon for repairs.**	—
2.24 —	**C.-in-C.** -	**Marlborough** -	W/T	**Report to Admiralty details of damage immediately.**	1424
2.25 —	*S.O. 4th L.C.S.*	*4th L.C.S.* -	Flags	*Alter course together to N. by W. and reform on Constance.*	—
2.25 —	Warspite	T.Bs. and Destroyers.	Flags	Proceed in execution of previous orders	—
2.25 —	*Commodore T.*	*General* - -	Flags	*Alter course in succession to E. by N.* -	—
2.25 —	S.O. 2nd L.C.S.	S.O. B.C.F. -	S.L.	Fuel remaining at noon : Nottingham—coal 638, oil 80. Remainder of squadron average coal 800, oil 150.	1420
2.26 —	**C.-in-C.** -	**S.O. 5th B.S.**	S.L.	**Warn Valiant Enemy Submarine is working in approximately 56° 45′ N., 0° 15′ W. Valiant to pass at least 30 miles to Southward of this position.**	1424

Date, Time of Despatch.	From	To	System.	Message.	Time of Origin.
1 JUNE *—cont.*					
2.26 p.m.	*Commodore F.*	*Moon and Mounsey.*	W/T	*When proceed in execution of previous orders is made Moon and Mounsey will proceed and screen Valiant to Rosyth.*	*1426*
2.27 —	*S.O.4thL.C.S.*	*4th L.C.S.*	Flags	*Admiral intends to proceed at 15 knots*	—
2.28 —	**C.-in-C.**	**Admiralty**	W/T	**Have directed Marlborough to report damage direct to Admiralty with a view to her being ordered to dock at Tyne so as to keep Rosyth for Battle-Cruisers and Warspite. Am taking Barham and Malaya to Scapa with a view to repairing at Invergordon later.**	**1428**
2.28 —	*S.O. Cruisers*	*Cruisers*	S.L.	*Alter course together eight points to port*	—
2.30 —	Engadine	S.O. B.C.F.	W/T	Warrior abandoned in 57° 21′ N., 3° 2′ E. Have crew on board proceeding at 10 knots. Position 11 a.m. 57° 10′ N., 2° 17′ E. Expect to arrive Inchkeith 7 a.m.	1420
2.30 —	S.O. B.C.F.	Captain D13	W/T	My position 57° 48′ N., 6° 28′ E., course N. 16° W., speed 18 knots. *(Corrected at 3.15 p.m.)*	1330
2.30 —	Marlborough	General	Flags	Alter course in succession to West. Admiral intends to proceed at 12 knots.	—
2.33 —	S.O.3rdL.C.S.	S.O. B.C.F.	W/T	My position now 56° 49′ N., 5° 15′ E., course N.E., speed 18 knots.	1400
2.34 —	*S.O. 1st B.S.*	*5th Subdivision*	Flags	*Alter course together two points to port*	—
2.35 —	S.O.1stL.C.S.	S.O. B.C.F.	S.L.	Wreck of bow is still above water on my port hand.	1430
2.35 —	Marlborough	—	—	Remarks : H.M.S. Laforey made her pendants.	—
2.35 —	*S.O.4thL.C.S.*	*4th L.C.S.*	Flags	*Zigzag one point. First turn to port conforming with the wing ship.*	—
2.36 —	Fearless	Marlborough	S.L.	Permission to take station astern. Reply : Yes, please.	1435
2.36 —	S.O. B.C.F.	S.O. 1stL.C.S.	S.L.	Fix position of wreck as near as possible	1435
2.40 —	*Commodore F.*	*Broke*	W/T	*Can you account for all Destroyers of 4th Flotilla and are any of them missing ?*	*1250*
2.40 —	**C.-in-C.**	**General**	Flags	**Negative station hands at action stations constantly throughout the day.**	—
2.42 —	*S.O. Cruisers*	*Cruisers*	S.L.	*Alter course together eight points to starboard.*	—
2.42 —	*S.O. 1st B.S.*	*5th Subdivision*	Flags	*Alter course in succession to N. by W.*	—
2.44 —	**C.-in-C.**	**S.O. B.C.F.**	W/T	**Am detaching Valiant to Rosyth. She is undamaged. Propose repairing Malaya and Barham at Invergordon. Warspite has gone to Rosyth. I have warned Valiant of submarines in 56° 45′ N., 0° 12′ W. and 56° 25′ N., 1° 45′ W.**	**1444**
2.45 —	*S.O. Cruisers*	*Cruisers*	S.L.	*Keep within visual signal touch*	—
2.45 —	**S.O. 1st B.S.**	**C.-in-C.**	W/T	**Having run my distance to intercept you I have now turned to N. by W.** *(Not logged as having been received in Iron Duke.)*	**1435**
2.45 —	S.O. 2nd C.S.	S.O. 4th L.C.S.	S.L.	What is bearing of Iron Duke from you, please? Reply : Iron Duke not in sight, I estimate they bear S.S.E. four miles.	1440
2.46 —	Laforey	Marlborough	S.L.	Destroyers in company, Lawford, Laverock and Lookout.	—
2.49 —	*S.O. 1st B.S.*	*5th Subdivision*	Flags	*Alter course together two points to port*	—

Date, Time of Despatch.	From	To	System.	Message.	Time of Origin.
1 JUNE *—cont.*					
2.50 p.m.	**C.-in-C.**	**General**	Flags	**Alter course together two points to starboard.**	—
2.52 —	S.O.2ndB.C.S.	S.O. B.C.F.	S.L.	We have passed many bodies, apparently German, two of which had on red lifebuoys with letters which began with S.M. We also passed foreign whaler with V 29 on her, and can see bow of small vessel sticking up out of the water on our port beam.	1450
2.52 —	**C.-in-C.**	**Commodore F.**	S.L.	**Detach Valiant's screen now. Reply: Submit where will screen find 5th Battle Squadron when proceeding in execution of previous orders. Further reply: Starboard wing column.**	1459
2.52 —	**C.-in-C.**	**Commodore F.**	S.L.	**Send Hardy on independently direct to Scapa, calling at Aberdeen for fuel if necessary.**	1440
2.54 —	S.O.2ndB.C.S.	Ophelia	S.L.	Inspect wreckage on your port bow, and endeavour to destroy wreckage bearing S.W. two miles.	1435
2.55 —	S.O.2ndB.C.S.	Galatea	S.L.	Did you identify wreckage? Reply: I believe it to be the bow of Invincible.	—
2.57 —	Captain D13	S.O. B.C.F.	W/T	My position, course and speed 1 p.m. 57° N., 6° 26′ E., N.E. 18 knots. Moresby and Obdurate returned to base to fuel.	1330
3.0 —	Princess Royal	—	—	Remarks: Passed a lot of oil and three hammocks, a body of a German Officer and German lifebuoy.	—
3.0 —	S.O. 5th B.S.	Barham, Valiant, Malaya.	W/T	*The bodies of all those who were badly damaged before death should be buried at sea, and also others with no special ties.*	1425
3.0 —	Mischief	S.O.4thL.C.S.	Sem.	How does battlefleet bear from you? We have been told to rejoin battlefleet and do not know their position. Reply: Iron Duke at noon 56° 20′ N., 5° 22′ E., N.W. 17 knots, altered course N. by W. at 1315. I estimate she bears S.S.E. from Calliope about four miles.	—
3.1 —	Hercules	S.O. 1st B.S.	W/T	*Peterhead to Nellie Dodds via S.O. Whalers Peterhead patrol. Submarine reported 9.35 a.m. to-day, Thursday, 56° 31′ N., 0° 40′ W.*	1200
3.2 —	Commodore T.	C.-in-C.	W/T	**My position 2.30 p.m. 54° 32′ N., 4° 16′ E., course E. by N., 20 knots. Have sighted Marlborough and despatched escort. Have you any instructions?**	1445
3.4 —	S.O. 1st B.S.	5th Subdivision	Flags	*Alter course together two points to starboard*	—
3.5 —	**C.-in-C.**	**General**	Flags	**Alter course together two points to starboard.**	—
3.5 —	S.O.2ndL.C.S.	S.O. B.C.F.	S.L.	Sounds as of firing S.W.	1515
3.5 —	S.O. B.C.F.	General	Flags	Admiral intends to proceed at 20 knots	—
3.10 —	Commodore F.	Moon and Mounsey.	S.L.	*5th B.S are starboard wing column. Proceed in execution of previous orders.*	—
3.10 —	Vanguard	S.O. 4th B.S.	Sem.	*Eight 12-in guns being loaded with nose fuze shell, submit opportunity may be given to discharge this.*	1445
3.11 —	S.O.3rdL.C.S.	3rd L.C.S.	S.L.	*Alter course in succession to North*	—

Date, Time of Despatch.	From	To	System.	Message.	Time of Origin.
1 JUNE —*cont.*					
3.11 p.m.	*S.O. Cruisers*	*Cruisers*	S.L.	*Speed of advance 14 knots* . . .	—
3.13 —	**C.-in-C.**	**S.O. 4th L.C.S.**	W/T	**My course is N. by W. Keep within visual signal distance.**	1504
3.14 —	S.O.3rdL.C.S.	Cordelia -	S.L.	What is your course? Reply : N. 16° W.	1514
3.14 —	**C.-in-C.** -	**S.O. 1st B.S.**	W/T	**My course is N. by W. advancing 15 knots at 1.15 p.m.**	1501
3.15 —	S.O. B.C.F.	Captain D13 -	W/T	My position 56° 48′ N., 6° 28′ E., course N. 16° W., speed 18 knots.	1330
3.16 —	**C.-in-C.** -	**S.O.s 1st, 2nd, 4th, 5th, B.S., S.O. 4th L.C.S., S.O. 2nd C.S.**	Sem. and W/T	**Carry out the instructions contained in paragraph 5 G.F.G. and T. Order No. 113. Valiant is proceeding to Rosyth and remainder of battle squadrons to Scapa.** (see below)	1515

Replies re ammunition required :—

1st B.S.	A.P.	Lyddite.	Common.
Revenge	101	0	0
Hercules	4	93	0
Agincourt	142	0	0
St. Vincent	84	0	8
Colossus	81	0	12
Collingwood	50	30	0
Neptune	0	21	27
2nd B.S.			
King George	0	0	9
Orion	49	0	0
Monarch	51	0	0
Thunderer	0	0	35
Conqueror	16	0	40
Centurion	19	2	0
Ajax	0	0	6
4th B.S.			
Benbow	40	0	0
Canada	42	0	0
Bellerophon	41	0	21
Vanguard	0	0	15
Superb	0	38	16
Temeraire	0	80	0
Vanguard	0	57	0
5th B.S.			
Barham	135	0	200

4th L.C.S.	For 6-in. guns.		For 4-in. guns.	
	Lyddite.	Common.	Lyddite.	Common.
Calliope	12	2	16	4
Caroline	3	2	0	0
Royalist	2	0	9	0
Comus	0	6	—	17
Constance	0	0	5	5

Date, Time of Despatch.	From	To	System.	Message.	Time of Origin.
3.18 —	S.O.3rdL.C.S.	Cordelia -	S.L.	What is bearing and distance of Battle-Cruisers? Reply : E. by S. about 16 miles.	1515
3.19 —	*S.O. 1st B.S.*	*5th Subdivision*	Flags	*Alter course together two points to starboard*	—
3.20 —	**C.-in-C.** -	**General** -	Flags	**Alter course together two points to port**	—
3.20 —	*S.O. B.C.F.*	*New Zealand*	S.L.	*Keep good look-out for Falmouth joining on port beam.*	1500
3.24 —	*S.O.3rdL.C.S.*	*3rd L.C.S.* -	S.L.	*Alter course in succession to N. 16 W.* -	—

Date, Time of Despatch.	From	To	System.	Message.	Time of Origin.
1 JUNE *—cont.* 3.27 p.m.	*Commodore T.*	*General*	Flags	*Alter course in succession to N. 26° E.*	—
3.28 —	Laforey	Marlborough	Sem.	Submitted Laforey and Lawford are both steering S. 80° W. on this course.	1530
3.30 —	C.-in-C., Rosyth.	Admiralty	L/T	Warspite arrived and proceeding to dock	1458
3.30 —	**C.-in-C.**	**General**	Flags	**Alter course together two points to port**	—
3.34 —	*S.O. 1st B.S.*	*5th Subdivision*	Flags	*Alter course together two points to port*	—
3.35 —	Ariel	S.O. B.C.F.	S.L.	Request permission to part company owing to shortage of fuel at 3.30 p.m. and return to base taking Hydra with me. Request Badger may be informed. Hydra can only reach base at economical speed.	1500
3.35 —	*S.O. 4th L.C.S.*	*4th L.C.S.*	Flags	*Alter course together 16 points to port. Negative zigzag.*	—
3.35 —	S.O. B.C.F.	Badger	S.L.	Ariel and Hydra wish to proceed to base on account of fuel. Send them on.	1534
3.38 —	*S.O. Cruisers*	*Cruisers*	S.L.	*Alter course together four points to starboard. Speed of advance 17 knots.*	—
3.39 —	**C.-in-C.**	**S.O. 5th B.S.**	S.L.	**Barham and Malaya take station astern of 3rd Division now. Give Valiant orders to proceed to Rosyth. Moon and Mounsey are detailed as her screen.**	1458
3.39 —	**C.-in-C.**	**General**	Flags	**Indicate number of killed and wounded (reply to be made in two hoists).**	—

Killed. Wounded.

	Killed	Wounded
Barham	25	34
Malaya	43	53
Colossus	0	4
Castor	12	22
Calliope	9	12

(Wounded includes two Officers, Staff Surgeon and Mate, four men dangerously wounded, six wounded and several slight injuries.)

Remainder	**Nil.**	**Nil.**

Date, Time of Despatch.	From	To	System.	Message.	Time of Origin.
3.40 —	**C.-in-C.**	**S.O. 10th C.S., Donegal.**	W/T	**Reliable report received that commerce raider Moewe and one other raider, or old Cruiser Niobe class, sailed yesterday 31st May and to-day 1st June respectively on raiding cruise. They may act in company. Assume Muckle Flugga patrol in accordance with HF 0042 over 49 of 15th April. Donegal to assume the patrol when the ships of the 10th C.S. are in position.**	1540
3.40 —	*S.O. 5th B.S.*	*Malaya*	Sem.	*Is water confined to compartment stated ? Can Malaya remain out of dock at Scapa for a few days without difficulty ?*	1500
				Reply : Yes, and it is anticipated that water will be confined to present damaged compartments in fine weather at sea or in harbour. At present only slight leaks into adjoining ones.	1615
3.40 —	*Commodore F.*	*All Destroyers*	S.L.	*Indicate at once by W/T number of Officers and men killed and wounded.*	1530
3.43 —	Forth	Chester	W/T	From R.A.C. East coast of England. You will proceed straight into Immingham lock on arrival. Tugs will be ready to assist you. Hospital cases will be discharged from lock.	1427

Date, Time of Despatch.	From	To	System.	Message.	Time of Origin.
1 JUNE *—cont.*					
3.44 p.m.	*S.O. 4th L.C.S.*	*4th L.C.S.*	Flags	*Alter course together eight points to port*	—
3.45 —	Admiralty	Commodore Harwich. V.A. Dover, C.-in-C., Nore.	L/T	Cancel my 543* Harwich, 846* Dover and 137* Nore. *Fleet action imminent.	1545
3.45 —	**Commodore F.**	**C.-in-C.**	S/L	**I understand that Owl, Hardy and Midge have left screen in accordance with orders received from you, but am giving Hardy orders in accordance with your signal 1440.**	**1501**
3.48 —	*Birmingham*	*S.O. 2nd L.C.S.*	S.L.	*Periscope of Submarine in sight* *(Passed to S.O. B.C.F.)*	—
3.48 —	Admiralty	R.A. East Coast	L/T	Have a good hunt for Submarines off Tyne before Marlborough passes, probably at about daylight to-morrow, via M Channel. Do not refer to Marlborough passing by wireless.	1548
3.49 —	*S.O. 1st B.S.*	*5th Subdivision*	Flags	*Alter course together two points to port*	—
3.50 —	**C.-in-C.**	**General**	Flags	**Alter course together two points to starboard.**	—
3.50 —	*S.O. 5th B.S.*	*Valiant*	Flags	*Proceed in execution of previous orders*	—
3.52 —	*S.O. 2nd L.C.S.*	*S.O. B.C.F.*	S.L.	Ophelia bearing W.S.W. six miles	1540
3.56 —	*S.O. 4th L.C.S.*	*4th L.C.S.*	Flags	*Alter course together to N. Form single line-ahead in sequence of fleet numbers.*	—
3.57 —	**C.-in-C.**	**Commanders of Divisions, R.A. Cyclops, R.A. Invergordon.**	Sem. and W/T	**Reference par. 4 G.F.G. and T. Order 113. Ammunition ships are not to be shifted.**	**1355**
4.0 —	**C.-in-C.**	**General**	Flags	**Alter course together two points to starboard.**	—
4.0 —	KingGeorgeV.	—	—	Remarks : 1st Battle Squadron joined up	—
4.0 — -	Marlborough	—	—	Remarks : Ness made her pendants	—
4.0 —	S.O. B.C.F.	Badger	S.L.	I am altering course at 4.15 p.m. for Rosyth at 18 knots till dark, after that you can go on at economical speed. Will that do you? Reply : Yes, thank you.	1600
4.1 —	Badger	S.O. B.C.F.	S.L.	Badger and Lapwing have less than Ariel and Hydra. S.O. 13th Flotilla informs me that Pelican should also go at once.	1540
4.2 —	*S.O. 4th L.C.S.*	*4th L.C.S.*	Flags	*Admiral intends to proceed at 20 knots*	—
4.2 —	S.O. B.C.F.	2nd Division	S.L.	Take station on bearing S. two miles.	—
4.4 —	*S.O. 1st B.S.*	*5th Subdivision*	Flags	*Alter course together two points to starboard*	—
4.5 —	S.O. B.C.F.	Southampton and Galatea.	S.L.	Will you require docking for repairs on arrival? Reply : Southampton will probably require docking for repairs to waterline but not necessarily on arrival.	1540
4.5 —	*S.O. 1st B.S.*	*5th Subdivision*	Flags	*Admiral intends to proceed at 15 knots*	—
4.5 —	S.O. B.C.F.	Galatea	S.L.	Take station on compass bearing S. 89° W. I shall alter course to S. 89° W. at 4.15 p.m.	1603

Date. Time of Despatch.	From	To	System.	Message.	Time of Origin.
1 JUNE —*cont.*					
4.7 p.m.	Engadine	C.-in-C.Rosyth	W/T	Expect to arrive 7 a.m. 2nd June having on board 35 Officers and 681 men of Warrior.	1310
4.7 —	*S.O. 5th B.S.*	*5th B.S.*	Flags	*Admiral intends to proceed at 20 knots*	—
4.8 —	**C.-in-C.**	**Commodore T.**	W/T	**I informed Admiralty that you were not required. There is nothing left to be done. Strengthen Marlborough's screen by two more Destroyers.**	1608
4.8 —	Birmingham	C.-in-C., S.O. B.C.F.	W/T	**Urgent. Submarine's periscope Lat. 57° 19′ N., Long. 5° 59′ E.**	1540
4.10 —	*S.O. 1st B.S.*	*5th Subdivision*	Flags	*The hands are to be stationed at action stations constantly throughout the day.*	—
4.10 —	*S.O. Cruisers*	*Cruisers*	Flags	*Alter course together four points to port*	—
4.10 —	S.O. B.C.F.	S.O. 2nd B.C.S. S.O. 1st, 2nd 3rd L.C.S.	W/T	Alter course leading ships together the rest in succession to S. 89° W. 4.15 p.m.	1600
4.10 —	**C.-in-C.**	**Commodore F.**	S.L.	**Are you in communication with Broke? Where is she?**	1600
				Reply : No, am not in communication with Broke. Last known communication 11 p.m., 31st May with Captain D4.	1700
4.11 —	S.O. B.C.F.	S.O. 1st B.S.	W/T	My position 57° 31′ N., 5° 45′ E., course S. 89° W., speed 18 knots. What is your position, course and speed?	1555
				Reply : My position at 4.30 p.m. Lat. 57° 15′ N., Long. 4° 37′E., course N. by W., advancing 16 knots.	1645
4.12 —	S.O. B.C.F.	S.Os. 1st, 2nd, and 3rdL.C.S.	S.L.	Take station on compass bearing S. 89° W. I shall alter course to S. 89° W. at 4.15 p.m. Spread Light Cruisers at right angles one mile apart. Centre of screen to be two miles ahead on compass bearing S. 89° W.	—
4.15 —	**C.-in-C.**	**S.O. 2nd C.S.**	S.L. and W/T	**Priority. Warrior abandoned in Lat. 57° 10′ N., Long. 2° 17′ E., with towing hawser and cable outboard. Search for her with your Cruisers and if impossible to salve sink her. Two tugs and Yacht Albion left Peterhead to assist p.m. today. If tugs are not required for Warrior send them to tow Acasta. She is in tow of Nonsuch and should be a little to the Eastward of Warrior.**	1545
4.15 —	S.O.2ndL.C.S.	S.O. B.C.F.	S.L.	Birmingham reports : Submarine periscope of no immediate danger to the fleet in sight.	1540
4.15 —	S.O. B.C.F.	General	Flags and S.L.	Alter course leading ships together the rest in succession to S. 89 W.	—
4.16 —	*S.O.3rdL.C.S.*	*3rd L.C.S.*	S.L.	*Alter course in succession to W.*	—
4.18 —	*S.O. 1st L.C.S.*	*Inconstant*	S.L.	*Spread N. one mile from Galatea*	1615
4.19 —	*S.O. 1st L.C.S.*	*Cordelia*	S.L.	*Spread N. one mile from Inconstant*	1620
4.20 —	S.O.4thL.C.S.	Valiant	S.L.	Can you please give me bearing of main body of battlefleet?	—
4.20 —	S.O. B.C.F.	General	Flags	Negative station hands at action stations	—

Date, Time of Despatch.	From	To	System.	Message.	Time of Origin
1 JUNE —cont.					
4.20 p.m	S.O. 5th B.S.	5th B.S.	Flags	Admiral intends to proceed at 16 knots	—
4.21 —	S.O. Cruisers	Cruisers	Flags	Lookouts to be one mile apart	—
4.22 —	S.O.3rdL.C.S.	3rd L.C.S.	S.L.	Form on a line of bearing in the sequence you now are to South.	—
4.23 —	C.-in-C.	General	Flags	**Alter course together two points to port**	—
4.25 —	S.O.4thL.C.S.	4th L.C.S.	Flags	Admiral intends to proceed at 22 knots	—
4.25 —	**S.O. B.C.F.**	**C.-in-C.** Captain D13 S.O.3rd L.C.S.	W/T	**My position 57° 31′ N., 5° 45′ E., course S. 89° W., speed 18 knots.**	1620
4.27 —	**C.-in-C.**	**S.O. 2nd C.S.**	S.L.	**Proceed in execution of previous orders**	1620
4.29 —	S.O. 1st L.C.S.	1st L.C.S.	S.L.	Have you any repairs to require docking? Reply from Inconstant: No, only one small hit with fragment of shell of no importance. I hit what was apparently submerged wreckage, but do not anticipate any damage underwater done. Reply from Cordelia: No	1620 1630 1625
4.30 —	S.O. 1st B.S.	5th Subdivision	Flags	Alter course in succession 16 points to starboard. Admiral intends to proceed at 17 knots.	—
4.30 —	Marlborough	—	—	Remarks: Albatross (T.B.D.) joined up with screen.	—
4.30 —	S.O. B.C.F.	Captain D13	W/T	Return to base	1625
4.30 —	S.O. Cruisers	Cruisers	Flags	Alter course together to W. by N.	—
4.30 —	Galatea	S.O. B.C.F.	S.L.	Position of wreck based on noon position 57° N., 6° 23′ E.	1530
4.32 —	**C.-in-C.**	**Attached Cruisers and Active.**	Flags	**Take station as follows:—** **Active two miles ahead of Admiral.** **4th L.C.S. three miles ahead of Admiral.** **Blanche two miles ahead of Benbow.** **Bellona two miles ahead of Colossus.** **Boadicea two miles ahead of King George V.**	—
4.33 —	S.O. Cruisers	Cruisers	S.L.	Cruisers are to search for Warrior abandoned by Engadine. Duke of Edinburgh is to be prepared to tow her if necessary. Crew were taken off. Look out for Yacht Albion and two tugs.	1625
4.35 —	S.O. B.C.F.	Battle Cruisers	S.L.	Burial service for those who have lost their lives in action will be held at 5.30 p.m. on board ships.	1628
4.35 —	S.O. B.C.F.	Badger	S.L.	On what Destroyer are the survivors of Invincible and Queen Mary?	—
4.40 —	S.O. B.C.F.	Princess Royal, Tiger.	Sem.	Indicate at 6 p.m. what course it is considered Lion is steering. Replies:—	1625
	Princess Royal	S.O. B.C.F.	S.L.	I make Lion's course due W.	1800
	Tiger	S.O. B.C.F.	Sem.	I make Lion's course S. 89° W.	1820
4.42 —	S.O. Cruisers	Cruisers	S.L.	Spread for look-out duties in the sequence in which ships now are two miles apart S. 13 W. from Minotaur. My course is N. 77° W., speed of advance 17 knots.	—
4.45 —	S.O. 1st B.S.	5th Division	Flags	Alter course together two points to starboard	—

Date, Time of Despatch.	From	To	System.	Message.	Time of Origin.
1 JUNE —*cont.*					
4.45 p.m.	Abdiel	C.-in-C. Rosyth	W/T	Preparatory signal for entering Rosyth 7.30 p.m. to-night for oil and 80 service mines.	—
				Reply : Approved and arranged. Proceed to Destroyers trot N. or S. Queensferry.	1835
4.45 —	**C.-in-C.**	**Commodore F.**	S.L.	**Detail T.B.Ds. for subdivisions of B.F. for night. Barham and Malaya will be with 5th subdivision if here, otherwise 6th subdivision.**	**1646**
4.47 —	Admiral, Immingham.	Admiralty	L/T	Chester arrived	1600
4.48 —	**C.-in-C.**	**S.O. 1st B.S., S.O. 4th L.C.S. Commodore F.**	W/T	**Speed of advance 16 knots**	**1637**
4.50 —	S.O. B.C.F.	Valiant	W/T	What is your position, course and speed?	1650
				Reply : My position is Lat. 57° 07′ N., Long. 4° 10′ E., course 251°, speed of advance 17 knots, Moon and Mounsey in company.	1600
4.53 —	*S.O. 1st L.C.S.*	*1st L.C.S.*	S.L.	*Zigzag one point*	—
4.55 —	*S.O. 1st B.S.*	*5th Subdivision*	Flags	*Alter course together two points to port*	—
4.55 —	Admiralty	Admiral, Rosyth.	L/T	Report nature of Warspite's damages and cause.	1655
5.2 —	*S.O. 3rd L.C.S.*	*3rd L.C.S.*	S.L.	*Yarmouth form astern of Falmouth. Gloucester form astern of Birkenhead. Columns to be two miles apart.*	1700
5.2 —	S.O.M.S.	A.C. Orkneys and Shetlands	W/T	Weather conditions improving and favourable for trawlers to sweep.	1700
5.3 —	S.O. 1st L.C.S.	S.O. B.C.F.	S.L.	No ships of 1st L.C.S. require docking as far as can be ascertained. Galatea's armour is bulged out and leaks, but damage is above water-line.	1645
5.5 —	S.O. B.C.F.	General	S.L. and Flags.	Bank fires in boilers not required for 22 knots. Steam for full speed to be at one hour's notice.	—
5.6 —	S.O. 3rd L.C.S.	Canterbury	S.L.	What base are you returning to?	1705
				Reply : I was attached to 3rd B.C.S. for last cruise, after which was being sent to join Commodore T. at Harwich. I got separated from 3rd B.C.S. when Enemy Battle Cruisers engaged them, including Chester and us. We escaped with one 6-in. shot through us aft. I will be short of 500 tons of oil fuel tomorrow noon, also 44 6-in. lyddite and 35 4-in. lyddite. Request you will report circumstances to C.-in-C., and ask for instructions for me. The last base we left was Scapa Flow, where we were working up firing after commissioning. Our proper base is Harwich.	1724
5.10 —	S.O. B.C.F.	General	S.L. and Sem.	1st L.C.S. are firing their 6-in. guns to discharge them.	1707
5.11 —	**C.-in-C.**	**R.A. Scapa**	W/T	**2nd B.S., Duke of Edinburgh, Barham and Malaya returning to Scapa. Arrange mails accordingly.**	**1644**
5.12 —	*S.O. 1st B.S.*	*5th Subdivision*	Flags	*Alter course together two points to starboard*	—

Date, Time of Despatch.	From	To	System.	Message.	Time of Origin.
1 JUNE *—cont.*					
5.14 p.m.	*S.O. B.C.F.-*	*Princess Royal and Tiger.*	Sem.	*Before the service, ships will form in quarter-line to starboard.*	*1710*
5.15 —	**C.-in-C.**	**General**	Flags	**Battlefleet. Let fires die out in boilers not required for 19 knots. Cruisers and Destroyers. Let fires die out in boilers not required for 20 knots.**	—
5.15 —	*Commodore F.*	*Opal*	S.L.	*Is Mischief in company ? Reply : No.*	—
5.18 —	*S.O. 3rd L.C.S.*	*3rd L.C.S.*	S.L.	*Alter course in succession to S. 89° W.*	*1715*
5.18 —	Marlborough	General	Flags	Alter course in succession N. 57° W.	—
5.20 —	*S.O. Cruisers*	*Cruisers*	S.L.	*Zigzag when in station*	*1715*
5.20 —	Hampshire	General	Flags	Submarine in sight	—
5.23 —	*S.O. 1st B.S.*	*5th Subdivision*	Flags	*Alter course together two points to starboard*	—
5.23 —	*S.O. B.C.F.-*	*1st Division Battle Cruisers.*	Flags	*Form single starboard quarter-line*	—
5.23 —	*S.O. B.C.F.-*	*1st B.C.S.*	Sem.	*New Zealand will be firing her guns to discharge them.*	*1720*
5.25 —	S.O. 3rd B.S.	Admiralty	W/T	3rd B.S. and 3rd C.S. arrived at the Swin	1629
5.30 —	**C.-in-C.**	**General**	Flags	**Alter course together two points to starboard. Admiral intends to proceed at 17 knots.**	—
5.30 —	**S.O. 5th B.S.**	**C.-in-C.**	Sem.	**Request that Barham and Malaya may defer oiling until after examination of damage. Reply : Approved.**	1720
5.32 —	**C.-in-C.**	**4th L.C.S.**	S.L.	**Take station ahead three miles. Keep in visual touch.**	—
5.34 —	*S.O. 1st B.S.*	*5th Subdivision*	Flags	*Alter course together two points to port*	—
5.35 —	S.O. B.C.F.	General, Negative Destroyers	Sem. and S.L.	Indicate requirements of coal and oil at 10 a.m. 2nd L.C.S. :— Birmingham and Dublin, 720 tons coal each ; Birmingham and Nottingham 160 tons oil each ; Dublin, 70 tons oil ; Southampton should not complete with fuel until after examination. 1st L.C.S., 1,800 tons oil for squadron :— New Zealand, 1,130 tons coal, 50 tons oil ; Tiger, 1,200 tons coal, 450 tons oil ; Indomitable, 1,200 tons coal, 290 tons oil ; Lion, 1,400 tons coal, 130 tons oil ; Inflexible, 1,200 tons coal, 350 tons oil ; Princess Royal, 1,325 tons coal, 190 tons oil.	1725
5.35 —	*Opal*	*Commodore F.*	S.L.	*Mischief was this morning screening Armoured Cruisers.*	—
5.36 —	*S.O. Cruisers*	*Cruisers*	S.L.	*Nonsuch may be sighted towing Acasta*	*1735*
5.38 —	**C.-in-C.**	**S.O. 1st B.S.**	W/T	**My position at 5 p.m. 57° 24′ N., 4° 9 E., course N. by W., advancing 16 knots. Indicate your position.**	**1707**

Date, Time of Despatch.	From	To	System.	Message	Time of Origin.
1 JUNE *—cont.*					
5.40 p.m.	*Commodore F.*	*Opal*	S.L.	*Report names of 12th Flotilla Destroyers present. Are there any casualties in 12th Flotilla? Reply: Opal, Menace, Munster, Noble, Mary Rose, Narwhal, Nessus, Mindful, Onslaught left us about 5 a.m. after we had joined you. Nessus has six wounded. Onslaught and Obedient, Captain injured, 1st Lieutenant killed. Nonsuch is escorting Acasta to Newcastle.*	—
5.40 —	C.-in-C.	Attached Cruisers.	Flags and S.L.	**Boadicea take station two points before port beam of King George V. 1½ miles. Blanche take station ahead of Colossus 1¼ miles. Bellona take station two points on the starboard bow of Colossus 1½ miles. Active take station ahead of King George V. 1¼ miles. Keep within visual signal distance.**	—
5.41 —	S.O. 2nd C.S.	C.-in-C.	W/T	Hampshire reports Submarine in Lat. 57 10′ N., Long. 3 43′ E.	1725
5.42 —	Marlborough	Admiralty	W/T	All compartments between 76 and 111 stations, starboard, from outer bottom to middle or main deck damaged and flooded. All double bottom compartments between these stations on starboard side, vertical keel damaged and probably double bottom compartments, vertical keel to second longitudinal on port side also damaged. Diesel engine shattered, starboard forward hydraulic pump and air compressor damaged. Boilers and auxiliary machinery in A boiler room not damaged except air blower and Diesel motor oil pump. A boiler room partially flooded but water is being kept under. Right gun A turret fractured.	1708
5.43 —	*S.O. 5th B.S.*	*Valiant*	W/T	*Reference to G.F.G. and T. Order No. 113. Communicate direct to C.-in-C. Rosyth.*	1727
5.45 —	*S.O. 1st B.S.*	*5th Subdivision*	Flags	*Alter course together two points to port*	—
5.45 —	Indomitable-	S.O. B.C.F.	S.L.	Submit Acting E.R.A. 4th Class. Peter Callender, No. 15428, belonging to Indomitable was on board Invincible.	1727
5.45 —	S.O. 5th B.S.	C.-in-C.	S.L.	**Permission is requested for Barham and Malaya to commit bodies of some of those killed in action to the deep at 7 p.m. without easing down. Reply: Approved.**	1740
5.45 —	*S.O.4thL.C.S.*	*4th L.C.S.*	Flags	*Keep closed up*	—
5.48 —	*Tiger*	*S.O. B.C.F.*	Sem.	*Reference R.G.O. 261, paragraph 9. We have 31 men unfit to be landed and 14 other cases of which 10 are cot cases if possible for hospital ship to come alongside.*	1700
5.50 —	C.-in-C.	General	Flags	Alter course together two points to port	—
5.50 —	*S.O.3rdL.C.S.*	*3rd L.C.S.*	S.L.	*Form single line-ahead in sequence of fleet numbers.*	—
5.50 —	Hercules	Revenge	Sem.	*Captain to Captain. Obtained noon position by observation as follows, 57° 18′ N., 5° 30′ E., and Agincourt tells me her noon position was the same within a mile.*	—
5.50 —	C.-in-C.	General	S.L.	**Speed of advance 16 knots**	1725

Date, Time of Despatch.	From	To	System.	Message.	Time of Origin.
1 JUNE —*cont.*					
5.53 p.m	*S.O. 1st B.S.*	*5th Subdivision*	Flags	*Alter course together two points to starboard*	—
5.54 —	*Duke of Edinburgh*	*S.O. 2nd C.S.*-	S.L.	Hampshire reports Submarine report not reliable.	*1750*
5.54 —	**C.-in-C**	R.A. Scapa -	W/T	**Report visibility at 8 p.m., midnight and 4 a.m.**	1727
5.55 —	**S.O.4thL.C.S.**	Active - -	S.L.	Am ordered to keep visual touch with battlefleet. Will you please drop back slightly to give me room?	1755
5.57 —	**C.-in-C.**	**General** -	Flags	**Distance apart of Columns to be eight cables.**	—
5.58 —	**C.-in-C.**	**S.O. B.C.F.** -	W/T	**Have you seen anything?** - - - (*Received by S.O. B.C.F. as Have you seen Aircraft?*)	1751
				Reply : No. Have swept over a large front of at least 30 miles, have seen nothing. I can get no news of Nestor, Onslow, Nomad or Turbulent.	1850
6.0 —	Chester -	—	—	Remarks : Secured to Immingham Dock	—
6.0 —	*Commodore F.*	*Mischief* -	S.L.	*Are you joining screen now? Have you any casualties and have you seen Broke? Reply : I am joining screen. Mischief has no casualties. Reply re Broke—No.*	—
6.0 —	*Commodore T.*	*General* •	Flags	*Alter course in succession to N. by E.* -	—
6.0 —	**C.-in-C.**	**General** -	Sem. and S.L.	**Night disposition : 4th L.C.S. four miles ahead of Flag, Battlefleet LU2 divisions and subdivisions two miles interval. Barham and Malaya will join 5th Subdivision if it is here before dark, otherwise they will be two miles astern of 6th Subdivision. At early dawn leading subdivisions zigzag back, keeping on the proper side of rear subdivision, and rear subdivisions increase speed. Course will be N. 49° W. until altered after daylight. Speed 16 or 17 knots as suited to Destroyers. T.B.Ds. will screen as long as it is sufficiently light. Boadicea two points before outer beam of K. G. V. 11 cables, Bellona two points before outer beam 11 cables of Revenge if present, otherwise Colossus. Blanche and Active two points before the starboard and port beam respectively 11 cables of Iron Duke.**	1750
6.0 —	*Opal* •	*Commodore F.*	S.L.	*Ambuscade tells me that Fortune was blown out of water by three Battleships.*	*1800*
6.0 —	*S.O.4thL.C.S.*	*4th L.C.S.* -	Flags	*Form single line-abreast to port. Speed of advance 16 knots.*	—
6.4 —	Chester -	Admiralty -	L/T	Have arrived at Humber in accordance with orders from R.A. Minotaur. Regret to report loss in general action 31st May, following : Killed, Officers, 2; men, 29; seriously wounded, Officer 1; men, 33; slightly wounded, Officers, 2; men about 14. Damage to ship : Three guns out of action, much damage to upper works, holed in four places above water-line. Engine boilers and all machinery almost intact. No serious damage below water-line. Request address mails to Immingham Dock.	1700

Date, Time of Despatch.	From	To	System.	Message.	Time of Origin.
1 JUNE —*cont.*					
6.5 p.m.	S.O.3rdL.C.S.	Canterbury	S.L.	Take station astern of Gloucester-	1802
6.7 —	*S.O.4thL.C.S.*	*4th L.C.S.*	Flags	*Alter course together four points to starboard*	—
6.10 —	**C.-in-C.**	**General**	Flags	**Alter course together two points to port**	—
6.15 —	Admiralty	R.A. East Coast.	L/T	Forward brief report of damage to Chester as soon as possible. Reply : Chester arrived plates badly holed —two starboard side, station 177, two port side, stations 143 and 58. After-control position completely wrecked. Upper deck badly damaged in places. Side at 72 station above armour holed, bridge damaged, forecastle deck holed. Following guns out of action, P. 1, P. 3, S. 2, S. 4. Six boats damaged and unseaworthy. Nearly all after upper deck fittings damaged. Repairs cannot be effected at Immingham ; they could be done at Hull, but this would delay Destroyers now in hand.	1815
				Further reply from Admiralty : Report what guns and mountings in Chester require replacement, and if any mountings can be repaired in place. Reply : Two 5.5 and one 3-pdr. gun are provisionally condemned and require replacing. Two other 5.5 require examination. No mountings as far as can be seen need replacing, but all require stripping and repairs which could be done in place. One shield to be replaced.	1020
6.15 —	*S.O.2ndL.C.S.*	*Dublin*	S.L.	*What damage ?*	*1807*
				Reply : Damage extensive but not serious. Two armour plates pierced, several holes in ship's side, plating and frames. Main deck and fore bulkhead pierced. Starboard bulkhead 143 shot away. Casing to engine room and several coal shutes pierced. Some damage to cabin doors, boats' davits, voice pipes, chart house, fire main. Considerable damage to seamen's head. Wireless telegraph trunk shot away.	*1845*
6.15 —	S.O. B.C.F.	General	Flags	Form astern and follow in the wake of your divisional Guides.	—
6.16 —	*S.O.4thL.C.S.*	*4th L.C.S.*	Flags	*Alter course together to N. by W.*	—
6.17 —	*S.O.4thL.C.S.*	*4th L.C.S.*	Flags	*Ships in column to be five cables apart*	—
6.20 —	Dublin	S.O. B.C.F.	S.L.	Birkenhead bearing N.W.	1815
6.21 —	Dockyard Rosyth.	Admiralty	L/T	Warspite docked in Dock No. 1 and will be placed on blocks to-night.	1720
6.21 —	**S.O.3rdL.C.S.**	**C.-in-C.**	W/T	**Canterbury in company with me. To what base should she return? My position 57° 19′ N., 4° 27′ E.**	1800
				Reply : Canterbury to proceed to Harwich	1921
6.21 —	*S.O. 1st B.S.*	*Hercules*	Sem.	*What do you make bearing and distance of Iron Duke now ?*	*1820*
				Reply : I make Hercules bearing 342° 16 miles from Iron Duke at 5 p.m.	*1830*

Date, Time of Despatch.	From	To	System.	Message.	Time of Origin.
1 JUNE *—cont.*					
6.23 p.m.	*S.O.3rdL.C.S.*	*3rd L.C.S.*	S.L.	*Speed of advance 18 knots* - - -	—
6.23 —	C.-in-C. -	S.O. B.C.F., S.O. 1st B.S.	W/T	Hampshire reports Submarine in Lat. 57° 10′ N., Long. 3° 43′ E.	1725
6.25 —	C.-in-C. -	General -	Flags	Alter course together two points to starboard.	—
6.26 —	Abdiel -	C.-in-C. Rosyth	W/T	H.M.S. Abdiel expects to arrive within gunshot of Inchkeith 6.20 p.m.	1705
6.28 —	S.O. B.C.F. -	C.-in-C. Rosyth	W/T	Fleet returning to base. Arriving Inchkeith about 8.45 a.m. Request latest swept line and that all available patrols may be sent out to keep Submarines down. I have no Destroyer screen. Further details later.	1810
6.30 —	C.-in-C. -	General -	Sem.	**The bodies of some of those who fell in action in Barham and Malaya will be committed to the deep at 7 p.m. 5 Pendant will be hoisted. Colours will be half-masted at that time.**	1815
6.31 —	S.O. B.C.F. -	Captain D13 -	W/T	Priority. What Destroyers have you missed and what was last news of them?	1830
				Reply : Nomad, Turbulent, Termagant and Nestor did not return after attack on Enemy's Battle Cruisers. Onslow damaged in that attack proceeded to base towed by Defender.	1920
6.35 —	C.-in-C. -	General -	Flags	Assume 2nd organisation - - -	—
6.35 —	*S.O. 5th B.S.*	*5th B.S.* -	Flags	*Admiral intends to proceed at 19 knots* -	—
6.35 —	Admiralty -	Marlborough -	W/T	Report draught of water - - -	1833
				Reply : Marlborough's draught estimated as 39 feet.	2020
				Reply from Admiralty : Proceed to Rosyth for temporary repairs.	2125
6.35 —	C.-in-C. -	5th B.S. -	Flags	Take station astern of St. Vincent - -	—
6.36 —	*S.O.4thL.C.S.*	*4th L.C.S.* -	Flags	*Zigzag one point. First turn to port* -	—
6.45 —	C.-in-C. -	R.A. Scapa -	W/T	Priority. For S.N.O. Blyth. Your 1540, May 31st. Yes.	1831
6.45 —	*S.O. 1st B.S.*	*5th Subdivision*	Flags	*Alter course in succession 16 points to port. Destroyers preserve compass bearings and distances.*	—
6.47 —	C.-in-C. -	R.A. Scapa -	W/T	If Royal Sovereign is not on North shore she is to occupy B 5 berth, Australia C 5 berth.	1800
6.50 —	S.O. B.C.F. -	Badger - -	S.L.	Collect Destroyers, ease down to suitable speed and return to base at 7.30 p.m.	1850
6.50 —	S.O. B.C.F. -	Narborough -	S.L.	Can you give me any information as to the last that was seen of Nestor, Nomad and Onslow?	1835
				Reply : Nomad appeared to be disabled between B.C.F. Nothing was seen of Nestor after she had reported having fired her four torpedoes at Battle Cruisers. Onslow was completely disabled and being towed by Defender. About midnight last night a large Cruiser opened fire in rear of flotilla slightly damaging Petard, several killed and wounded. Turbulent, the last of the line, was not seen again and I fear was totally disabled and sunk.	1900

Date, Time of Despatch.	From	To	System.	Message.	Time of Origin.
1 JUNE *—cont.* 6.50 p.m.	*S.O. 5th B.S.*	*5th B.S.*	Flags	*Admiral intends to proceed at 17 knots*	—
6.50 —	*S.O. 1st B.S.*	*5th Subdivision*	Flags	*Admiral intends to proceed at 15 knots*	—
6.50 —	C.-in-C.	General	Sem.	**If weather is at all thick rear subdivisions are not to open to two miles from leading subdivisions but are to keep close up, the same applies to 5th B.S. if astern of 6th Subdivision.**	1885
6.50 —	Commodore F.	C.-in-C.	S.L.	**With reference to my 1700. I am now in W/T communication with Broke on D wave.**	1805
6.53 —	S.O. B.C.F.	General	Sem. and W/T	**I shall increase speed to 21 knots at 7.30 p.m.**	1853
6.55 —	C.-in-C. Rosyth.	Engadine	W/T	**Enemy Submarines reported at noon to-day in vicinity Firth of Forth. Also Enemy Submarine 1430 in 55° 50′ N., 0° 55′ W.**	1710
6.55 —	S.O. B.C.F.	2nd Division	Sem.	**Take station astern three miles before dark as convenient. I shall proceed at 21 knots at 7.30 p.m.**	1855
6.57 —	Commodore F.	C.-in-C.	S.L.	**Further reply re casualties. Castor— Officers nil, men 12 killed, 23 wounded. Onslaught—Captain injured, 1st Lieutenant killed, and Gunner killed. Obedient—Captain injured, 1st Lieutenant killed. Nessus—6 wounded. Onslaught proceeded to base 5 a.m. to-day. Remainder of Destroyers in company, nil.**	1845
6.58 —	*Mischief*	*Captain D12*	S.L.	*Mischief rejoining 12th Flotilla*	*1850*
7.0 —	Nessus	Bellona	S.L.	**Can you please give me a 6 o'clock position? Reply : 57° 38′ N., 4° 0′ E. at 6 p.m.**	—
7.0 —	*Commodore F.*	*General*	S.L.	*Screens for the night : 1st Subdivision— Ossory, Martial, Magic, Castor, Minion. 2nd Subdivision—Marne, Milbrook, Manners, Kempenfelt, Morning Star. 3rd Subdivision—Mystic, Mons, Mandate, Opal, Oak. 4th Subdivision—Five of 12th. 6th Subdivision—Five of 12th.*	—
7.0 —	S.O. 1st B.S.	C.-in-C.	W/T	**My first position must be erroneous. I now think 57° 59′ N., 3° 43′ E. Am turning Southward to test this.**	1830
7.0 —	C.-in-C.	General	Flags	**Silence and attention**	—
7.5 —	S.N.O. Harwich.	Admiralty	L/T	Submarine E. 53 arrived	—
7.5 —	*Commodore F.*	*Hardy and Owl*	W/T	*Hardy to proceed independently direct to Scapa Flow for fuel.*	*1516*
7.5 —	C.-in-C.	General	Flags	**Alter course leading ships together rest in succession to N. 49° W.**	—
7.7 —	S.O. B.C.F.	S.O. 2nd and 3rd L.C.S.	S.L. and W/T	Close your squadrons in before dark. Stations for the night : 3rd L.C.S. five miles from Lion : 2nd L.C.S., E. five miles from 3rd L.C.S.	1907
7.8 —	*S.O. 1st L.C.S.*	*1st L.C.S.*	S.L.	*Admiral intends to proceed at 21 knots. Negative zigzag.*	—
7.10 —	S.O. B.C.F.	S.O. 1st L.C.S.	S.L.	1st L.C.S. close in before dark and increase distance to five miles ahead. Spread as Submarine screen again at daylight.	1900

Date, Time of Despatch.	From	To	System.	Message.	Time of Origin.
1 JUNE —cont.					
7.10 p.m.	**C.-in-C.** -	**General** - -	Flags	**Divisions separately form single line-ahead in sequence of fleet numbers.**	----
7.15 —	*S.O.3rdL.C.S.*	*Light Cruisers-*	S.L.	*Negative zigzag. Admiral intends to proceed at 19½ knots.*	—
7.18 —	*S.O.4thL.C.S.*	*4th L.C.S.* -	Flags	*Alter course together to N. 49° W. Reform on Comus.*	
7.20 —	**C.-in-C.** -	**General** - -	Flags	**Guides to bear abeam of Guide of fleet. Columns to be 1½ miles apart.**	—
7.20 —	*Hampshire*	*S O. 2nd C.S.-*	S.L.	*Nonsuch and Acasta W. by S. two miles report that they are all right and steaming about 7½ knots.*	*1910*
7.20 —	S.O. B.C.F. -	S.O. 2nd B.C.S.	S.L.	Send your destroyers to Badger at 7.30 p.m.	1918
7.23 —	S.O.2ndB.C.S.	Ophelia and Narborough.	S.L.	Join Badger. Reply from Ophelia : Can you tell me where Badger is? Reply : Close to Lion.	1912
7.25 —	Revenge -	—	—	Remarks : 5th B.S. sighted - - -	—
7.25 —	*S.O. 2nd B.S.*	*1st Division* -	Flags	*Admiral intends to proceed at 14 knots* -	—
7.26 —	**S.O. 5th B.S.**	**C.-in-C.** -	S.L.	**Revenge bearing East from Barham** -	1725
7.30 —	**C.-in-C.** -	**S.Os. of Squadrons, Attached Cruisers, S.O. 4th L.C.S.**	W/T	**Berths in A line : 1 Malaya, 3 Superb, 4 Canada, 6 Barham ; B line : 1 to 4 4th Subdivision, 5 Royal Sovereign ; C line : 1 to 4 6th Subdivision, 5 Australia ; D line : 1 to 4 Revenge, Royal Oak, Hercules, Agincourt ; E line : 2nd Subdivision ; F line : 1st Subdivision ; Y line : 1 to 5 4th L.C.S. ; X lin : 2 to 5 Blanche, Active, Bellona, Boadicea ; Cruisers, Eline : 5, 6 and 7 and F 5 and 6.**	1855
7.30 —	S.O.2ndL.C.S.	S.O. B.C.F. -	S.L.	Dublin's damage just reported extensive. She should not complete with fuel until after examination.	1912
7.30 —	*Commodore T.*	*General* - -	Flags	*Alter course in succession to N.W. by N. Admiral intends to proceed at 18 knots.*	—
7.30 —	S.O. B.C.F. -	General -	Flags	Admiral intends to proceed at 21 knots. Destroyers proceed in execution of previous orders.	
7.30 —	*S.O.3rdL.C.S.*	*Light Cruisers-*	S.L.	*Admiral intends to proceed at 21 knots* -	
7.30 —	**C.-in-C.** -	**S.Os. and R.A.'s of Squadrons, Blanche and Active.**	S.L.	**When divisions are formed columns will remain 1½ miles apart until it gets dark or thick and then open without orders. While divisions are 1½ miles apart Blanche and Active are to be eight cables from Iron Duke.**	1910
7.35 —	*Commodore T.*	*General* - -	Flags	*Alter course in succession to N. 77 W.* -	—
7.35 —	*S.O. 2nd B.S.*	*1st Division* -	Flags	*Admiral intends to proceed at 17 knots* -	—
7.35 —	**C.-in-C.** -	**Commodore F.**	S.L.	**What is Broke's position, has she any other Destroyers in company? Reply : Broke's position at noon, 57° 49' N., 3° 50' E., course N.W., speed 7 knots. She is damaged forward. Should like escort if available.**	1938 / 2045
7.35 —	*S.O.4thL.C.S.*	*4th L.C.S.* -	Flags	*Admiral intends to proceed ta 18 knots* -	—

Date, Time of Despatch.	From	To	System.	Message.	Time of Origin.
1 JUNE *—cont.*					
7.35 p.m.	Bellerophon	C.-in-C. and S.O. 4th B.S.	Sem.	Following received by W/T. C.-in-C. Rosyth to Campania. Enemy Submarines were reported at noon to-day in the vicinity of Firth of Forth, also Enemy Submarines 2.30 p.m. in Lat. 57° 11′ N. (*Long. missed through interference.*)	1710
7.37 —	Lapwing	S.O. B.C.F.	S.L.	Submit have only just got enough oil to go at this speed.	—
7.38 —	Captain D12	Commodore F.	S.L.	*From Broke to Captain D12. My position 1200, 57° 49′ N., 3° 50′ E., course N.W., speed 7 knots. Damage forward, would like escort if available. Can you send escort? I have only three of 12th Flotilla with me screening 5th Division.* (*Passed to C.-in-C.*)	1835
7.40 —	S.O. 4th L.C.S.	4th L.C.S.	Flags	*Admiral intends to proceed at 16 knots*	—
7.40 —	S.O. 1st B.S.	5th Subdivision	Flags	*Admiral intends to proceed at 19 knots*	—
7.40 —	Commodore F.	Minion	S.L.	*Take position midway between E. and F.*	—
7.40 —	S.O. B.C.F.	Captain D13	W/T	Exchange position, course and speed with Badger.	1921
7.42 —	Commodore F.	Broke	W/T	*Indicate your position. What Destroyers have you with you in company?*	1940
7.44 —	Carnoustie S.S	Admiralty	L/T	1st, 7.28 p.m., a large three-funnelled Destroyer. Onslaught on bow, bearing E.S.E., steering S., eight knots. Did not reply to challenge but made following signal. Reply destroyed by gunfire in action. Then vessel was lost in mist going South.	—
7.45 —	S.O. 1st B.S.	Malaya	S.L.	What is course and speed of fleet? Are you ahead or astern of battlefleet? Reply: Fleet in 2nd organisation. Divisions in line-ahead, columns disposed abeam to starboard, columns 1½ miles apart, course N. 49° W., speed 17 knots. Colossus ahead of Barham.	1940
7.49 —	C.-in-C.	S.O. 1st B.S.	W/T	**My position 7 p.m., 57° 53′ N., 3° 50′ E., passing through position 58° 52′ N., 0° 0′ E., at approximately 3 a.m. Keep Northward of this line.**	1912
7.49 —	S.O. 3rd L.C.S.	3rd L.C.S.	F.L.	*I am turning to close Lion*	1940
7.49 —	S.O. 2nd L.C.S.	2nd L.C.S.	S.L.	*My speed is 19 knots*	—
7.50 —	S.O. Cruisers	Cruisers	S.L.	*If Warrior is not seen ships are to turn together eight points to starboard at 8.15 p.m. At 8.45 p.m. ships will turn eight points to starboard again. At 9.15 ships will turn 16 points together and then form single line-ahead on Minotaur in the order from which they spread. Open order, course W. by N. 16 knots. No further signal will be made. Repeat back from out in.*	1948
7.50 —	S.N.O. Harwich.	Admiralty	L/T	Submarines E. 31 and D. 6 arrived	—
7.50 —	S.O. 2nd L.C.S.	2nd L.C.S.	S.L.	*Form single line-ahead in sequence of fleet numbers.*	—

Date, Time of Despatch.	From	To	System.	Message.	Time of Origin.
1 JUNE 7.59 p.m.	—*cont.* C.-in-C. Rosyth.	Admiralty	W/T	Lydiard, Landrail, Liberty arrived -	1900
8.0 —	C.-in-C.	Commodore F.	S.L.	Have you heard anything of Nestor, Onslow, Nomad or Turbulent? Reply: No, nothing heard.	1958
8.0 —	Nonsuch	C.-in-C., Commodore F.	W/T	My 7 p.m. position with Acasta in tow 57° 8′ N., 2° 45′ E., course W., speed 7½ knots.	1845
8.0 —	Abdiel	—	—	Remarks : Abdiel made fast to buoy	—
8.7 —	Naval Centre, Rosyth.	Admiralty	L/T	H.M.S. Termagant reports four Enemy Destroyers steering E. 30 miles from May Island. H.M.S. Termagant losing touch as her speed is reduced to 15 knots. (*Cancelled 10.20 p.m. by following signal :* —Naval Centre, Rosyth, to Admiralty. It is now considered that these were Destroyers of local flotilla.)	—
8.11 —	Laforey	Marlborough	Sem.	Submitted. Could you please give me any details of action as Officers and men are longing to hear news? Reply to Destroyers— Enemy losses known— Roon, one Cruiser, one flotilla leader and two Destroyers sunk or badly damaged. Our losses known are— Warrior abandoned, Acasta and one Light Cruiser badly damaged. Marlborough struck by mine or torpedo. Warspite reduced to 16 knots. Other ships slightly damaged. There were several night actions result not known, but a Light Cruiser was seen to blow up. Enemy torpedo attack failed. Marlborough got some hits on Kaiser and Markgraf. This morning Fearless and Marlborough drove off scouting Zeppelin. Visibility yesterday was four to six miles and very patchy. Touch was lost with Enemy battlefleet at 11.30 p.m., but we heard distant firing during the forenoon to-day. Galatea first reported Enemy Cruisers at 2.20 p.m. and led them towards battlefleet to North-Westward. Enemy turned South 3.45 p.m. and were shortly after engaged by B.C.F. and 5th B.S. Enemy Cruisers joined eight Kaisers about 5 p.m. and turned North. Grand Fleet deployed between B.C.F. and 5th B.S. and opened fire about 8.20 p.m. Eight other German Battleships sighted but were not engaged. Enemy drew off about 8.30 p.m.	1930
8.12 —	S.O. 1st B.S.	C.-in-C.	W/T	Two miles astern of Valiant. What position do you wish me to take up for the night?	1955
				Reply : Request that you will remain there for the night. Form divisions in line-ahead disposed abeam to starboard at early dawn. Ship ahead of you Malaya.	2101

Date, Time of Despatch.	From	To	System.	Message.	Time of Origin.
1 JUNE *—cont.*					
8.15 p.m.	S.O. 1st B.S.	Faulknor	S.L.	Take your Destroyers and form astern of 5th B.S.	—
8.17 —	C.-in-C. Rosyth.	Admiralty	L/T	35 Officers and 685 men survivors from Warrior will arrive Rosyth in Engadine 7 a.m. Friday, 2nd June. Propose to retain them at Rosyth pending further directions.	—
8.17 —	*S.O. 1st L.C.S.*	*1st L.C.S.*	F.L.	*Close in and form single line-ahead by 9.30 p.m.*	2010
8.18 —	**S.O. 2nd C.S.**	**C.-in-C.**	W/T	**Nonsuch and Acasta 1900, 57° 8′ N., 2° 44′ E., about 7·5 knots, all well.**	**2000**
8.20 —	*Opal*	*Commodore F.*	S.L.	*Oak, Opal, Noble, Menace, Munster on starboard side of Iron Duke's column. Ambuscade port side. Mischief, Narwhal Nessus, Mindful, Mary Rose screening Colossus column.*	2010
8.24 —	S.O.3rd L.C.S.	Canterbury	S.L.	C.-in-C. directs you to return to Harwich. You can proceed as soon as convenient. My estimated position at 8 p.m. is 57 8′ N., 3° 43′ E. Have you the necessary charts for channel?	2015
				Reply : Have got necessary charts. Request permission to proceed.	2033
				Reply from R.A. : Approved. Glad to have had your company for a short time. Reply from Canterbury : Many thanks. Glad to have been with you.	2040
8.25 —	*Shannon*	*S.O. 2nd C.S.*	S.L.	*By observation and Engadine's cypher re Warrior's position when abandoned Warrior was 10 miles on Shannon's starboard beam at 7 p.m.*	2010
8.25 —	*Malaya*	*S.O. 5th B.S.*	S.L.	*Owing to the increased motion, oil from damaged bunkers is finding its way into air space of A stokehold and slight leaks to stokehold. The turning about seems to aggravate matters. If possible submit I may not turn too much.*	2010
8.30 —	*Malaya*	*S.O. 5th B.S.*	F.L.	*As a precautionary measure have already drawn fires in A boiler. Malaya can steam about 20 without A.*	1910
8.30 —	Commodore F.	S.O. 2nd B.S.	S.L.	Starboard side will be clear for fleet turning 16 points when flotilla forms astern of 2nd B.S.	2025
8.30 —	**C.-in-C.**	**S.O. 2nd B.S., R.A. 1st B.S.**	S.L.	**Open to two miles**	2025
8.30 —	S.O.4th L.C.S.	4th L.C.S.	F.L.	*When signal to take up night cruising disposition is made 4th L.C.S. will form single line-ahead on Calliope.*	2030
8.34 —	Valiant	C.-in-C. Rosyth	W/T	Expect to arrive at Rosyth between 7 a.m. and 8 a.m. on 2nd of June. Requirements : oil fuel 1,340 tons, one 21-in. R.G.F. torpedo Mark 2***, gyroscope A.D.A. 5 degrees short release and warhead, amatol for same, 15-in. A.P. 289, 15-in. common shell 10, 6-in. lyddite shell 84, 6-in. common shell 8. Request instructions as to returning empties.	1820

Date, Time of Despatch.	From	To	System.	Message.	Time of Origin.
1 JUNE *—cont.*					
8.35 p.m.	Cyclops -	Princetown -	W/T	For information of C.-in-C. by interception. Weather report from Rosyth, Immingham and Harwich respectively. Wind South-West. Weather dull (mainly c. and o.), maximum 29.67. Weather report based on observations at 1 p.m. Wind force at surface of ground, moderate (Beaufort 3 and 4), cloudy, showers, barometer 30.14 falling, temperature 63, wind South-West, force moderate or fresh (Beaufort 4-5)——— (*interference*).	1300
8.37 —	Commodore F.	C.-in-C. -	S.L.	Reports of May 31st. Onslaught unable to steam in tow of Defender. Defender two boilers out of action. Nestor, all torpedoes fired, speed reduced to 17 knots. Garland escorting Achates to Tyne. No other reports.	2020
8.38 —	Christopher	S.O. B.C.F. -	S.L.	Submit I have not enough oil to get in at 21 knots.	1916
8.40 —	S.O. 1st B.S.	S.O. 5th B.S.-	S.L.	I am going 19 knots and have stationed Destroyers astern of 5th B.S. for the night.	—
8.40 —	Cochrane -	S.O. 2nd C.S.-	S.L.	*With reference to Shannon's 2010. I agree with his position.*	2035
8.40 —	**C.-in-C.** -	**S.O. 4th L.C.S.**	W/T	**Take up night stations now** - - -	2025
8.43 —	Aberdeen -	R.A. Invergordon.	W/T	For C.-in-C., from Rosyth. Priority. Termagant reports four Enemy Destroyers steering E. 30 miles from May Island, 7.50 p.m., losing touch.	2022
	S.O. B.C.F. -	C.-in-C. Rosyth	W/T	Re 2022 Aberdeen to R.A. Invergordon. Can any reliance be placed on this report?	2139
	C.-in-C. Rosyth	S.O. B.C.F. -	—	Reply : No, four of local flotilla were in this position painted grey. Please give your 3 a.m. position and course. All available Destroyers be sent to escort.	2250
	S.O. B.C.F. -	C.-in-C. Rosyth	W/T	My position, course and speed at 3 a.m. will be 56° 34′ N., 0° 38′ W., S. 89° W., 21 knots.	0125
8.45 —	Badger -	Captain D13-	W/T	*My position, course and speed 2000, 57° 12′ N., 4° 49′ E., S. 89° W., 13 knots. Destroyers of 13th Flotilla in company. Narborough, Nerissa, Pelican returned to base to oil.*	2025
8.45 —	C.-in-C. Rosyth.	Admiralty -	L/T	Petard and Nicator arrived - - -	2000
8.45 —	**R.A. Scapa**	**Princetown** -	W/T	For C.-in-C. Rosyth reports. With reference to my message K. 68 three or four Submarines appear to be in the vicinity of Firth of Forth. Coastguard wireless.	1515
8.45 —	S.O.2ndB.C.S.	S.O. B.C.F. -	S.L.	Request anchor berths for 2nd Division. Reply : B. 12, B. 13 and B. 14 unless C.-in-C. Rosyth orders otherwise.	1930
8.46 —	Marlborough	General -	Flags	Alter course in succession to West by North.	—
8.50 —	Faulknor -	S.O. 1st B.S. -	S.L.	Submit is Revenge remaining in present position? Reply : Revenge is leading the line and 5th B.S. taking station astern of 5th Subdivision.	—
8.50 —	*S.O. 4thL.C.S.*	*4th L.C.S.* -	F.L.	*Admiral intends to proceed at 17 knots* -	—

Date, Time of Despatch.	From	To	System.	Message.	Time of Origin.
1 JUNE —*cont.* 8.52 p.m.	Valiant	C.-in-C.Rosyth	W/T	Preparatory signal for entering Firth of Forth. One Battleship and two Destroyers expecting to arrive within gun range of Inchkeith 5.15 a.m. Request outer gate at 6 a.m. and that berths be allotted.	1920
8.57 —	S.O. 5th B.S.	S.O. 1st B.S.	S.L.	Permission to form astern of 5th Subdivision as ordered. Reply : Approved.	—
8.59 —	C.-in-C.	R.A. Scapa	W/T	Iron Duke, 1st B.S. less Marlborough, 2nd and 4th B.S. less Emperor of India, Revenge, Royal Oak, 4th L.C.S. Blanche, Bellona, Active require to complete with fuel. Colliers, etc., to proceed alongside on arrival. Approximate amounts required, Battleships 900 tons each, Light and Attached Cruisers 400 tons each.	2026
9.0 —	Marlborough	General	F.L.	At 2150 course will be altered to N. 24° W. without further signal.	—
9.0 —	Caroline	C.-in-C.	F.L.	Your 1830 to Captain D13. We passed some bodies and lifebuoy marked Turbulent at 8 a.m. to-day.	2040
9.2 —	C.-in-C.	R.A. Scapa	W/T	Urgent. For S.N.O. Peterhead. Request trawler unit may be sent to screen H.M.S. Nonsuch towing H.M.S. Acasta disabled to Aberdeen. Position 7 p.m. to-night 1st June 57° 8′ N., 2° 44′ E., course W., 7·5 knots for Aberdeen.	2041
9.4 —	C.-in-C.	S.O. 4th L.C.S.	F.L.	4th L.C.S. increase speed of engines and take station ahead four miles of battlefleet.	—
9.10 —	S.O.4thL.C.S.	4th L.C.S.	F.L.	*Form single line-ahead in sequence of fleet numbers. Admiral intends to proceed at 19 knots.*	—
9.10 —	C.-in-C.	S.O. 2nd B.S.	Sem.	Do not get inside distance : it crowds screen.	2100
9.12 —	C.-in-C.	Commodore F.	S.L.	Am asking for trawler unit to screen Nonsuch.	2042
9.16 —	S.O. 4th B.S.	4th Subdivision	F.L.	*At 9.30 p.m. speed 16 knots without further signal.*	2115
9.18 —	Marlborough	C.-in-C.Rosyth	W/T	Request latest information re swept channels in Firth of Forth. Reply: Outer line Y and Z thoroughly. All main coast lines and approaches.	2025
9.20 —	S.O.2ndL.C.S.	Dublin	W/T	*It is quite possible my W/T will carry away during the night. Look out if necessary for W/T signals to answer calls for me and pass them by visual.*	2115
9.27 —	R.A. Scapa	Aberdeen	W/T	For information of C.-in-C. by interception. H.M.S. Achilles delayed until Sunday 4th June p.m. Addressed to V.A. 2nd C.S., Admiralty, S.N.O. North Shields.	1955
9.29 —	R.A. Scapa	R.A. Invergordon.	W/T	From C.-in-C. Rosyth to C.-in-C. Laurel arrived.	1800
9.30 —	S.O. 2nd C.S.	Cochrane	S.L.	*Keep in open order - - - - -*	*2136*

Date, Time of Despatch.	From	To	System.	Message.	Time of Origin.
1 JUNE —*cont.*					
9.30 p.m.	**C.-in-C.**	S.O.s 1st, 2nd, 4th, 5th, B.S., R.A.s 1st and 2nd B.S., S.O., 4th L.C.S., Commodore F., Captain D12, and attached Cruisers.	W/T	**Admiral intends to proceed at 16 knots**	—
9.30 —	**R.A. Scapa**	R.A. Invergordon.	W/T	**For C.-in-C.　Visibility 10 miles**	**2000**
9.32 —	*Cochrane*	*S.O. 2nd C.S.*	W/T	*Can hear numerous German W/T signals, medium strength.*	*2130*
9.32 —	*S.O. 5th B.S.*	*Malaya*	Sem.	*Would it be possible to steam with B, C and D boiler rooms only ? What speed could Malaya go with two boiler rooms ?*	—
9.39 —	S.O. 2nd B.S.	Commodore F.	Sem.	Drop astern at 9.45 p.m. without further orders.	2135
9.40 —	*Commodore T.*	*General*	F.L.	*Admiral intends to proceed at 14 knots*	—
9.40 —	**Admiralty**	**C.-in-C.**	W/T	**Enemy claim to have destroyed Warspite, Queen Mary, Indefatigable, two Armoured Cruisers with four funnels, two small Cruisers and 10 Destroyers. False reports will shortly be promulgated requiring prompt contradiction. Report losses ascertained and vessels not accounted for.**	**2140**
9.45 —	S.O. 1st B.S.	Bellona	F.L.	Take station astern of St. Vincent	—
9.50 —	*Commodore F.*	*Minion*	S.L.	*Follow me. I shall lead the starboard column*	—
9.50 —	Admiralty	C.-in-C. Rosyth	L/T	Following has been sent to Marlborough. Proceed to Rosyth for temporary repairs. Marlborough's draught is 39 feet. Reply : Following received from Commodore Supt. Rosyth. As it is questionable whether Marlborough with her 39 feet reported draught can be taken into and docked though it might be possible by tipping up basin and alternative is for her to remain and be docked down in dock which has no blocks, it would appear that question of sending her to a floating dock should be considered if one is available. (*Received by Admiralty 1.33 a.m. June 2nd.*)	2150
9.50 —	*S.O. B.C.F.*	*Princess Royal*	F.L.	*Your fore steaming light is burning*	*2100*
9.50 —	*Princess Royal*	*S.O. B.C.F.*	F.L.	*Please show shaded stern light*	*2148*
9.55 —	Admiralty	Dockyard, Rosyth.	L/T	Devonport directed to send at once to Rosyth a Constructive, also an Engineer Officer well acquainted with details of Marlborough to examine defects with you. Report whether men and materials are required from southern yards. Draught of ship reported estimated as 39 feet.	2155
9.56 —	*Commodore T.*	*General*	F.L.	*Keep a look out for Enemy Destroyers*	—

Date, Time of Despatch.	From	To	System.	Message.	Time of Origin.
1 JUNE —*cont.*					
9.56 p.m.	C.-in-C.	Broke	W/T	Burn navigation lights, fleet is closing you	2127
9.59 —	C.-in-C.	Active	W/T	Active to drop astern at daylight and look for Broke, damaged forward. Two Destroyers will be sent when she is located. Take anti-Submarine precaution. Communicate direct with Broke as to her position.	2154
10.0 —	C.-in-C.	Broke	W/T	Active is being sent to you at dawn	2144
10.2 —	*Commodore F.*	*Ossory*	S.L.	*Keep on my port beam*	—
10.5 —	*Broke*	*Commodore F.*	W/T	*My position 2100, 58° 10' N., 2° 46' E., course N. 50° W., speed 7 knots, no ships in company.*	*2123*
10.5 —	Marlborough	Fearless	F.L.	Please let me know at 11 p.m. what you make our mean course?	2150
				Reply : Mean course N. 24° W.	2300
10.5 —	C.-in-C.	S.O. B.C.F.	W/T	Termagant reports four Enemy Destroyers steering E., 30 miles from May Island, 7.50 p.m., lost touch. If true these are probably Minelayers.	2120
10.8 —	*Commodore F.*	*Marshal and Magic.*	S.L.	*Keep well closed up*	—
10.10 —	C.-in-C.	S.O. B.C.F	W/T	Regret to inform you that Caroline reports passing some bodies and lifebuoys marked Turbulent at 8 a.m. to-day 1st June.	2145
10.10 —	*Commodore F.*	*Kempenfelt*	W/T	*I am leading starboard column. Do likewise.*	*2145*
10.13 —	C.-in-C.	Admiralty	W/T	Reference my 1428. No Battle Cruisers require docking, only Marlborough, Warspite, Malaya and probably Barham.	2130
10.15 —	Admiralty	Dockyard, Devonport.	L/T	Direct a Constructive and also an Engineer Officer well acquainted with details of Marlborough to proceed at once to Rosyth to examine defects with Commodore Supt.	2215
10.15 —	C.-in-C.	R.A. 1st B.S.	W/T	Revenge is remaining two miles astern of Malaya for the night.	2128
10.15 —	*S.O.2ndL.C.S.*	*2nd L.C.S.*	S.L.	*Admiral intends to proceed at 21 knots*	—
10.23 —	S.O. 2nd C.S.	C.-in-C.	W/T	My position 10 p.m., Lat. 57° 22' N., Long. 6° 02' E., N. 79° W., 16 knots, turning at 1 a.m. to renew search.	2205
				Reply : Warrior's position a.m. to-day Thursday, 57° 21' N., 3° 2' E., and not as given in my 1545 of to-day Thursday.	2358
10.25 —	C.-in-C. Rosyth.	S.O. B.C.F.	W/T	All arrangements have been made for your ships to enter and defences warned. Lines Y and Z have both been swept twice to-day, Thursday. Swept again at dawn to-morrow, Friday. Patrols disposed around entrances in accordance with Rosyth Secret Memorandum 057/11 of 1916. I will send any available Destroyers of seagoing flotilla to screen you at dawn when your position is known.	2027

Date, Time of Despatch.	From	To	System.	Message.	Time of Origin.
1 JUNE —*cont.*					
10.30 p.m.	Commodore T.	C.-in-C. -	W/T	With reference to message timed 2022 from Aberdeen, my position 8 p.m., 56° 7′ N., 4° 37′ E., course N. 57° W., 15 knots. Propose turning back to intercept Enemy at daylight on meridian of 4° 30′ E.	2205
10.38 —	C.-in-C. Rosyth.	Admiralty -	L/T	Onslaught and Morris arrived - - -	2130
10.40 —	Broke - -	C.-in-C. - -	W/T	Course N. 60° W. I am alright in present weather.	2200
10.41 —	S.N.O. Aberdeen	Admiralty -	L/T	Unity arrived - - -	2230
10.47 —	S.O. 1st B.S.	C.-in-C. -	W/T	I am in my correct night cruising station	2218
10.57 —	R.A. Scapa -	Aberdeen -	W/T	From C.-in-C. Rosyth for C.-in-C. Petard, Nicator and Abdiel arrived.	2015
11.0 —	*S.O.4thL.C.S.*	*4th L.C.S.* -	F.L.	*Admiral intends to proceed at 16 knots* -	—
11.0 —	Admiralty -	Grand Fleet -	W/T	Submarines in the North Sea have been reported as follows: 31st May, 8 a.m., Lat. 57° 36′N., Long. 0° 15′W.; 1st June, Lat. 57° 20′ N., Long. 1° 03′ W.; 31st May, 7 a.m., Lat. 56° 05′ N., Long. 1° 15′W., going South; 1st June, 1 p.m., Lat. 55° 47′ N., Long. 1° 04′ W.; 31st May, 7.30 a.m., Lat.54° 57′ N., Long. 0° 49′ E.; 1st June, p.m., Lat. 54° 04′ N., Long. 1° 28′ E.; 1st June, 10 p.m., proceeding South from Forth; 1st June, 6 p.m., proceeding West from Lat. 56° 00′ N., Long. 6° 03′ E.; 1st June, 5.30 p.m., Lat. 56° 48′ N., Long. 1° 00′ W.; 1st June, 9.30 a.m., Lat. 56° 40′ N., Long. 0° 40′ W.; 1st June, noon, Lat. 56° 26′ N., Long. 1° 43′ W.	2300
11.1	R.A. Scapa -	Aberdeen -	W/T	For C.-in-C. Weather reports. Rosyth— wind W.N.W. moderate, weather dull, sea smooth, barometer 29.65. Shotley— 9 p.m., barometer 30.05, temperature— 64, wind S.W. moderate, weather fair. Immingham—9 p.m., wind W.S.W. moderate or fresh, weather fair, barometer 29.80.	—
11.6 —	R.A. Invergordon.	R.A. Scapa -	W/T	H.M.S. Emperor of India undocked -	1205
11.17 —	C.-in-C. -	Commodore F.	W/T	Priority. Destroyers resume screen -	2311
11.19 —	Canterbury -	C.-in-C. -	W/T	My position 11 p.m. 56° 27′ N., 2° 28′ E., course S. 54° W., 22 knots.	2305
11.23 —	C.-in-C. -	Commodore T.	W/T	Four T.B.Ds. off May Island are local T.B.Ds. If no further news of Enemy return to base.	2323
11.30 —	S.O. 3rd B.S.	Admiralty -	W/T	Permission to proceed into Medway p.m. to-morrow Friday. Reply: Approved.	2300 0800
11.35 —	R.A. Scapa	R.A. Invergordon.	W/T	For C.-in-C. Rosyth reports in Lat. 55° 50′ N., Long. 0° 55′ W., Nicator had torpedo fired at her 2.30 p.m.	1831
11.40 —	Fearless	Marlborough -	W/T	Albatross to Marlborough. Submit I am unable to keep up with you on account of bad weather.	2300

Date, Time of Despatch.	From	To	System.	Message.	Time of Origin.
1 JUNE —*cont.*					
11.43 p.m.	S.O. B.C.F.	C.-in-C.Rosyth	W/T	Preparatory signal for entering Firth of Forth, 18 ships, no Destroyers, wish to enter. Leading ships arrive gun range Inchkeith 6.45 a.m. 5th B.S. and three ships of B.C.F. have been detached since leaving harbour. Indomitable. Inflexible have joined since leaving harbour. Request latest information *re* swept channels.	2315
11.47 —	S.O.3rdL.C.S.	C.-in-C.Rosyth	W/T	Squadron requires to complete with coal on arrival, 600 tons, 4 colliers, 150 tons oil. Ammunition required : ·2 of outfit.	2325
11.50 —	Marlborough	Destroyers	F.L.	Report if you cannot keep up on account of weather.	—
11.55 —	**C.-in-C.**	**Active**	W/T	**Following is received from Broke. My position at 9 p.m. 58° 10′ N., 2° 46′ E., course N. 50° W., speed 7 knots, no ships in company.**	2215
11.57 —	*Commodore F.*	*Destroyers*	W/T	*Form screen according to No. 4 diagram. Admiral intends to proceed at 20 knots.*	—
2 JUNE 12.0 midnight.	*S.O. 2nd C.S.*	*2nd C.S.*	S.L.	*Alter course in succession four points to starboard.*	—
12.0 —	Marlborough	General	F.L.	Alter course in succession to W. Admiral intends to proceed at 10 knots.	—
12.15 a.m.	Marlborough	General	F.L.	Alter course in succession to W.S.W.	—
12.20 —	C.-in-C.Rosyth	Admiralty	L/T	Termagant arrived	0000
12.25 —	Marlborough	General	F.L.	Alter course in succession to S.W. by W.	—
12.28 —	**Marlborough**	**C.-in-C.**	W/T	**Urgent. Position 54° 40′ N., 0° 53′ E., owing to bad weather water is gaining. Making for Flamborough Head at 10 knots.**	0000
				Reply from Admiralty : Approved. R.A. East Coast will be ordered to send tugs to meet you off Flamborough Head. You should go to Humber for temporary repairs.	0125
12.28 —	*Commodore F.*	*Kempenfelt, Opal, Mischief.*	W/T	*Are you resuming screen ? Replies :* Opal, yes. Mischief, screen resumed. Kempenfelt, yes.	0020
12.34 —	**R.A. Scapa**	**R.A. Invergordon.**	W/T	**A 71 for C.-in-C. 249. Submarine reported from Rosyth by Express in 56° 15′ N., 1° 31′ W., at 5.50 a.m., steering W. Coastguard wireless, Aberdeen.**	1956
12.37 —	**C.-in-C.**	**R.A. Invergordon.**	W/T	**Send Soudan and Berbice to Scapa, leaving at daylight.**	0445
12.38 —	**C.-in-C.**	**S.O.M.S.**	W/T	**Priority. Sloops are to return to base, passing Pentland Skerries after 10.30 a.m. Until further orders one Sloop is to be detailed for Noss Head patrol and two detailed to take place of Destroyers which support armed boarding steamers to the eastward during the night.**	2300
12.40 —	*S.O.2ndL.C.S.*	*2nd L.C.S.*	F.L.	*Admiral intends to proceed at 10 knots*	—
12.45 —	Marlborough	C-in-C. Rosyth	W/T	Preparatory signal for entering Firth of Forth. One Battleship, one Light Cruiser, seven Destroyers expect to arrive within gun range of Inchkeith at 1330 tomorrow Friday. Request outer gate and inner gates be opened at 1420 and 1435 respectively. Marlborough's estimated draught 39 feet.	2330

Date, Time of Despatch.	From	To	System.	Message.	Time of Origin.
2 JUNE *—cont.*					
12.47 a.m.	Marlborough	Fearless and Destroyers.	S.L.	Be prepared to come alongside port side of Marlborough to take off ship's company.	0040
12.50 —	*S.O.2ndL.C.S.*	*2nd L.C.S.*	F.L.	*Admiral intends to proceed at 15 knots*	—
1.0 —	*S.O. Cruisers*	*Cruisers*	F.L.	*Alter course in succession four points to starboard.*	—
1.12 —	S.O. B.C.F.	C.-in-C. Rosyth	W/T	Shall require following ammunition *vide* Rosyth Confidential General Order No. 28 :— Lyddite A.P. Common Lion 0 321 0 New Zealand 170 170 76 Indomitable 48 98 29 Inflexible 19 10 58 1st, 2nd and 3rd L.C.S. one quarter. Following ships have wounded *vide* Rosyth Port Order No. 261 :— Lion 3 23 20 Princess Royal 0 38 4 Tiger 31 10 4 Dublin 0 19 0 Southampton 0 55 5 Galatea not ascertained.	2335
1.13 —	*S.O.2ndL.C.S.*	*S.O. B.C.F.and 2nd L.C.S.*	W/T	*My present speed is 15 knots for repairing damage, nothing serious. 2nd L.C.S. proceed at 21 knots, Southampton will follow.*	*0100*
1.14 —	*R.A. 1st B.S.*	*6th Subdivision*	Flags	*Admiral intends to proceed at 18 knots*	—
1.17 —	S.O. B.C.F.	S.O. 1st, 2nd and 3rdL.C.S.	W/T	Report number of hospital cases in ships of 1st and 3rd L.C.S. in accordance with R.P.O. 261, Clause 9. Reply: 1st L.C.S., nil ; 3rd L.C.S., nil ; 2nd L.C.S., Southampton 0, 22, 10; Nottingham, nil ; Dublin 0, 10, 2.	0030
1.17 —	R A. Cyclops	R.A. Invergordon.	W/T	For C.-in-C. Visibility five miles	2400
1.18 —	C.-in-C.	Cyclops	W/T	For S.N.O. Humber. Marlborough in position 54° 40′ N., 0° 53′ E., steering for Flamborough Head, requires assistance to make the Humber. Send powerful tugs to her.	0118
1.20 —	Marlborough via Fearless	Tynemouth Signal Station	W/T	My position 54° 40′ N., 0° 53′ E., making for Flamborough Head. Require assistance of tugs urgently.	0006
1.21 —	C.-in-C.	Active	W/T	My position is 58° 38′ N., 1° 0′ E.	0100
1.27 —	C.-in-C.	Active	W/T	Proceed in execution of previous orders	0124
1.35 —	Lightfoot	Commodore T.	W/T	Submit mistook one of our Destroyers for the Enemy, am rejoining. Please show navigation lights.	0115
1.35 —	Engadine	—	—	Remarks : Arrived Rosyth and anchored	—
1.35 —	S.O. 5th B.S.	R.A. Scapa	W/T	Following require hospital treatment on arrival. Barham, one Officer, 27 men, cot, and six walking cases ; Malaya, 41 cases.	0015
1.35 —	S.O. B.C.F.	S.O.2nd B.C.S., S.O.'s 1st, 2nd, and 3rd L.C.S.	W/T	Prepare to proceed into harbour in following order. 1st L.C.S., 1st Division, 2nd Division of Battle-Cruisers, 3rd L.C.S., 2nd L.C.S. Leading ship to arrive within gun range Inchkeith at 6.45 a.m.	0034

Date, Time of Despatch.	From	To	System.	Message.	Time of Origin.
2 JUNE —*cont.*					
1.35 a.m.	Admiralty -	R.A. East Coast	L/T	Marlborough should be met off Flamborough by tugs with pumping appliances and taken to harbour for temporary repairs. Draught of water 39 feet.	0135
1.40 —	Lookout -	Marlborough -	F.L.	Submit should necessity arise, propose with your approval to go to windward of you and pump out oil to facilitate Destroyers going alongside. Reply ; Thank you, I concur.	—
1.45 —	Albion III. -	R.A. Invergordon.	W/T	Have been unable to find Warrior and am steaming slowly back on Warrior's course. Visibility very poor. *(Received in Iron Duke 4.39 a.m.)*	0145
1.47 —	*S.O.2ndL.C.S.*	*2nd L.C.S.* -	W/T	*Birmingham remain with me. Remainder proceed into harbour.*	*0140*
1.52 —	Marlborough	Fearless -	F.L.	I will be much obliged if you will keep station about 1½ cables to windward of my forebridge so as to reduce seas breaking on us.	0146
1.55 —	Laforey -	Marlborough -	F.L.	Submit could one of the weather boats lay an oil track ahead of you, they have plenty to spare. Reply : Yes, thank you, I shall be much obliged.	0140 / 0150
2.0 —	*S.O. Cruisers*	*Cruisers* -	S.L.	*Alter course in succession four points to starboard.*	—
2.0 —	C.-in-C. Rosyth.	S.O. B.C.F. -	W/T	Arrangements made for your ships to enter. Y and Z channels have both been swept twice to-day, Thursday, and will be swept again at dawn to-morrow, Friday. Patrols disposed round entrance to Firth of Forth in accordance with Rosyth Secret Memorandum 057/11 of April, 1916. I will send any available Destroyers of sea-going flotillas to screen you at dawn when your position is known.	0110
2.5 —	*Laforey* -	*Lance* - -	F.L.	*Lance's division make oil track ahead and weather side of Marlborough.*	—
2.6 —	*Fearless* -	*Marlborough* -	F.L.	I make your speed 12 knots - - -	—
2.7 —	**C.-in-C.** -	**Broke** - -	W/T	**Indicate your position now to Active and C.-in-C.**	**0146**
2.11 —	*S.O.2ndL.C.S.*	*Birmingham* -	W/T	*Present course and speed of Southampton, N. 35° E., 10 knots.*	*0130*
2.12 —	**C.-in-C.** -	**Marlborough** -	W/T	**Priority. Your 0000. S.N.O. Immingham Dock has been informed and directed to send powerful tug.**	**0158**
2.12 —	**C.-in-C.** -	**Canterbury** -	W/T	**Proceed to assistance of Marlborough. At midnight she was in position 54° 40′ N., 0° 53′ E., steering for Flamborough Head at 10 knots.**	**0212**
2.13 —	*Commodore T.*	*General* - -	F.L.	*Alter course in succession to S.W.* - -	—
2.15 —	*S.O. 2nd B.S.*	*R.A. 2nd B.S.*	F.L.	*Commence to come ahead now*	*0215*
2.20 —	Active -	Broke - -	W/T	I am searching for you and shall be in position 58° 27′ N., 1° 40′ E., at 2.45 a.m. *(No answer received by Active.)*	0210
2.30 —	*S.O. B.C.F.* -	*Battle Cruisers*	Flags	*Divisions separately form single line-abreast to port, ships in column to be five cables apart.*	—
2.30 —	*S.O.1stL.C.S.*	*1st L.C.S.* -	F.L.	*Admiral intends to proceed at 18 knots* -	—

Date, Time of Despatch.	From	To	System.	Message.	Time of Origin.
2 JUNE *—cont.*					
2.32 a.m.	*S.O.1stL.C.S.*	*1st L.C.S.*	F.L.	*Alter course in succession to W. by S. Admiral intends to proceed at 16 knots.*	—
2.34 —	Marlborough	Fearless	F.L.	When we make Flamborough Head and swept channel we are proceeding to Humber. On arrival at entrance do you wish to enter the Humber or proceed in accordance with your orders?	0234
				Reply: Thank you, I have no orders, but with your permission I will proceed to base.	0237
2.35 —	**C.-in-C.**	**General**	Flags	**Assume 5th organisation. Form divisions in line-ahead, columns disposed abeam to starboard. Columns to be seven cables apart.**	—
2.35 —	S.O. B.C.F.	1st L.C.S.	S.L.	1st L.C.S. spread on a straight line one mile apart, bearing of centre S. 89° W. two miles.	—
2.36 —	R.A. 2nd B.S.	2nd Division	F.L.	*Admiral intends to proceed at 18 knots*	—
2.40 —	S.O. B.C.F.	General	Flags	Alter course together two points to starboard.	—
2.40 —	*S.O.1stL.C.S.*	*1st L.C.S.*	F.L.	*Admiral intends to proceed at 20 knots*	—
2.40 —	**C.-in-C.**	**Attached Cruisers.**	F.L.	**Take station as follows: Blanche two miles ahead of Iron Duke, Bellona two miles ahead of Revenge, Boadicea two miles ahead of King George V.**	—
2.45 —	Commodore T.	General	Flags	*Admiral intends to proceed at 15 knots*	—
2.45 —	*S.O.4thL.C.S.*	*4th L.C.S.*	Flags	*Ships in column to be five cables apart*	—
2.46 —	**R.A. Scapa**	**R.A. Invergordon.**	W/T	**From C.-in-C. Rosyth for C.-in-C. Engadine arrived.**	**0130**
2.47 —	**C.-in-C.**	**General**	Flags	**Admiral intends to proceed at 15 knots**	—
2.48 —	C.-in-C. Rosyth.	S.O. B.C.F.	W/T	Destroyers for escort are being directed to proceed out on line Y to meet you.	0150
2.49 —	Marlborough	Fearless	F.L.	As my compass is very unreliable would you like to lead Marlborough into anchorage before you proceed to your base? Marlborough draught will be 40 feet.	0245
2.49 —	*S.O.4thL.C.S.*	*4th L.C.S.*	Flags	*Alter course in succession eight points to starboard.*	—
2.50 —	S.O. B.C.F.	General	Flags	Alter course together four points to port	—
2.51 —	*S.O.1stL.C.S.*	*1st L.C.S.*	F.L.	*Zigzag*	—
2.53 —	*S.O.1stL.C.S.*	*1st L.C.S.*	F.L.	*Admiral intends to proceed at 21 knots*	—
2.55 —	**C.-in-C.**	**5th B.S.**	S.L.	**Take station astern of Canada**	—
2.55 —	*S.O.4thL.C.S.*	*4th L.C.S.*	Flags	*Alter course together eight points to port*	—
3.0 —	Marlborough	General	Flags	Alter course in succession to W. by S.	—
3.0 —	S.O. B.C.F.	General	Flags	Alter course together four points to starboard.	—
3.0 —	*S.O.4thL.C.S.*	*4th L.C.S.*	Flags	*Alter course together two points to port*	—
3.0 —	R.A. Scapa	R.A. Invergordon.	W/T	Coal at Scapa 98,800 tons, 34 colliers. Cromarty, 27,100 tons, 11 colliers. Rosyth, 49,778 tons, 21 colliers.	0030

Date, Time of Despatch.	From	To	System.	Message.	Time of Origin.
2 JUNE —*cont.*					
3.0 a.m.	**C.-in-C.** -	**General** -	Flags	**Admiral intends to proceed at 14 knots** -	—
3.0 —	*S.O.2ndL.C.S.*	*Birmingham* -	S.L.	*Keep within easy visual touch at such speed as is safe from Submarines.*	*0250*
3.1 —	*S.O.2ndL.C.S.*	*Birmingham*	S.L.	*My course and speed are W. ½ S. 15 knots*	—
3.5 —	*S.O. Cruisers*	*Cruisers* -	Flags	*Alter course in succession to S. 47° E.* -	—
3.5 —	*S.O. 1st B.S.*	*6th Division* -	Flags	*Admiral intends to proceed at 16 knots* -	—
3.9 —	Marlborough	Lance, Laforey	F.L.	We are going to the Humber. Do you wish to enter the Humber or proceed to your base on arrival at the entrance to Humber?	0304
				Reply from Laforey : I wish to enter and fuel.	0315
				Reply from Lance : I think we will probably require to oil. Reply will be made in one hour's time.	—
3.10 —	S.O. B.C.F. -	General -	Flags	Alter course together four points to port	—
3.15 —	**C.-in-C.** -	**General** -	Flags	**Alter course leading ships together rest in succession to N. 77° W.**	—
3.18 —	*S.O.4thL.C.S.*	*4th L.C.S.* -	Flags	*Admiral intends to proceed at 15 knots* -	—
3.20 —	S.O. B.C.F. -	General -	Flags	Alter course together four points to starboard.	—
3.23 —	*S.O. 2nd B.S.*	*1st Subdivision*	Flags	*Admiral intends to proceed at 11 knots*	—
3.24 —	*S.O. Cruisers*	*Cruisers* -	Flags	*Alter course together two points to starboard*	—
3.25 —	Marlborough	—	—	Remarks : Land ahead - - - -	—
3.27 —	**C.-in-C.**	**General** -	Flags	**Guides to bear abeam of Guide of the fleet. Benbow take Guide of fleet.**	—
3.30 —	*R.A. 2nd B.S.*	*2nd Division* -	Flags	*Admiral intends to proceed at 12 knots* -	—
3.30 —	**C.-in-C.** -	**3rd Division** -	Flags	**Admiral intends to proceed at 17 knots** -	—
3.30 —	S.O. B.C.F. -	General -	Flags	Alter course together four points to port-	—
3.30 —	*S.O.4thL.C.S.*	*4th L.C.S.* -	Flags	*Ships to be 7½ cables apart. Extend your distance from Comus.*	—
3.35 —	*S.O. Cruisers*	*Cruisers* -	Flags	*Alter course together four points to port* -	—
3.36 —	**C.-in-C.** -	**3rd Division** -	Flags	**Admiral intends to proceed at 14 knots** -	—
3.37 —	*R.A. 2nd B.S.*	*2nd Division* -	Flags	*Admiral intends to proceed at 14 knots* -	—
3.40 —	Marlborough	Laforey -	Sem.	Please screen my starboard bow - -	0340
3.40 —	**C.-in-C.** -	**Commodore F.**	S.L.	**What is maximum speed Destroyers can maintain on present course? Reply : 14 knots.**	—
3.40 —	S.O. B.C.F. -	General -	Flags	Alter course together four points to starboard.	—
3.40 —	*S.O.4thL.C.S.*	*4th L.C.S.* -	Flags	*Zigzag one point. First turn to port conforming with wing ships.*	—
3.41 —	**S.O. 5th B.S.**	**C.-in-C.** -	S.L.	**Submitted that a tug, if possible with capstan, may be available to assist Malaya going to buoy, as she will have no steam on capstan.**	0320
				Reply : This will be arranged - -	0358

Date, Time of Despatch.	From	To	System.	Message.	Time of Origin.
2 JUNE *—cont.*					
3.42 a.m.	*S.O. Cruisers*	*Cruisers*	Flags	*Alter course together four points to starboard*	—
.44 —	*S.O. 2nd B.S.*	*1st Division*	Flags	*Admiral intends to proceed at 14 knots*	—
3.45 —	**R.A. Cyclops**	**Aberdeen**	W/T	**For C.-in-C. Submarine reported by Danish steamer steering E.S.E. 10 knots at 5 p.m., 1st, in 55° 22′ N., 1° 22′ W.? Newcastle. Coastguard wireless, Aberdeen.** *(Received in Iron Duke 4 a.m.)*	2221
3.45 —	R.A. Invergordon.	Admiralty	W/T	Hospital ships Soudan and Berbice sailed	0320
3.45 —	*Commodore F.*	*Mystic*	S.L.	*What is maximum speed you can maintain on this course ? Reply : 14 knots.*	—
3.46 —	Marlborough	General	Flags	Alter course in succession to W.S.W.	—
3.46 —	Lydiard	S.O. B.C.F.	W/T	Lydiard and five Destroyers sent for escort. Request what are your course and speed? Reply : My position, course and speed, 56° 19′ N., 1° 9′ W., S. 89° W., 19½ knots.	0300
3.49 —	**C.-in-C.**	**General**	Flags	**Admiral has resumed Guide of the fleet**	—
3.50 —	*S.O.4thL.C.S.*	*4th L.C.S.*	Flags	*Admiral intends to proceed at 14 knots*	—
3.50 —	S.O. B.C.F.	General	Flags	Alter course together four points to port	—
3.52 —	*S.O. Cruisers*	*Cruisers*	Flags	*Alter course together four points to port*	—
3.52 —	Captain D12	S.O. 1st B.S.	S.L.	Speed is too great for Destroyers	0340
3.54 —	Marlborough	General	Flags	Alter course in succession to S.W. by W.	—
3.55 —	*S.O.1stB.C.S.*	*S.O. B.C.F.*	S.L.	*Following received from Tiger : Damage appears more severe than I reported yesterday. Submit I think it inadvisable to coal until ship is clear of water and further examination is made. Reply : Approved.*	*0335*
4.0 —	*S.O. Cruisers*	*Cruisers*	Flags	*Spread in the sequence of Hampshire, Shannon, Minotaur, Duke of Edinburgh, Cochrane four miles apart, bearing N. 43° E.*	—
4.0 —	S.O. B.C.F.	General	Flags	Alter course together four points to starboard.	—
4.0 —	Bonaventure	Marlborough	W/T	Your 0016 received. Tugs are being sent	0230
4.6 —	S.O.3rdL.C.S.	S.O. B.C.F.	W/T	Falmouth will discharge four rounds fused shrapnel at 4 a.m.	0230
4.7 —	*S.O. B.C.F.*	*Tiger*	S.L.	*Keep a look-out for our Destroyers to the Southward. If sighted tell them to close and give them our course and speed.*	*0400*
4.9 —	Marlborough	General	Flags	Alter course in succession to South	—
4.10 —	Marlborough	Grimsby S.S. via Fearless.	W/T	For S.N.O., Immingham Dock. Marlborough, accompanied by Fearless and 10 Destroyers, expect to arrive within gun range of Spurn Point at 0645 and wishes to pass inner defences and western boom. Latest information is requested as to swept channel. Destroyers in need of oil fuel. Marlborough's draught 40 feet. Is mooring buoy available as steam cannot be used for capstan?	0330

Date, Time of Despatch.	From	To	System.	Message.	Time of Origin.
2 JUNE *—cont.*					
				Reply from R.A. East Coast of England. There is not a swept channel. Go to No. 3 peg-top buoy inside Western boom.	0555
4.10 a.m.	S.O. B.C.F.	General	Flags	Alter course together four points to port	—
4.12 —	Fearless	Marlborough	Sem.	Do you wish me to lead you down swept channel? Reply : Yes, please.	0414
4.14 —	Canterbury	Marlborough	W/T	My position 4 a.m. 55° 12′ N., 0° 36′ E., course S. 36° W., 24 knots. What is your position, course and speed?	0400
4.15 —	Fearless	Marlborough	Sem.	We should stand further in shore as swept channel is five miles from Flamborough Head.	—
4.15 —	Peterhead	Sea Ranger	W/T	H.M.S. Acasta is in tow of Nonsuch, not Cruiser Castor.	2210
4.18 —	**R.A. Scapa**	**R.A. Invergordon.**	W/T	**For C.-in-C. Visibility 10 miles**	**0400**
4.20 —	**C.-in-C.**	**General**	Flags	**Admiral intends to proceed at 13 knots**	—
4.20 —	S.O. B.C.F.	General	Flags	Alter course together four points to starboard.	—
4.20 —	**S.N.O. Aberdeen.**	**R.A. Scapa**	W/T	**For C.-in-C. Unity sailed**	**0310**
4.21 —	Lance	Marlborough	Sem.	My division will not require to enter Humber for fuel.	—
4.23 —	Marlborough	General	Flags	Alter course in succession to S.W.	—
4.23 —	*S.O. Cruisers*	*Cruisers*	S.L.	*My course S. 47° E., speed of advance 15 knots. Zigzag when in station.*	—
4.30 —	Fearless	Marlborough	W/T	Canterbury to Marlborough. My position course and speed at 0400 55° 12′ N., 0° 57′ E., S. 61° W., speed 24 knots.	0400
4.30 —	S.O. B.C.F.	General	Flags	Alter course together four points to port	—
4.31 —	S.O. 4th L.C.S.	Cyclops	W/T	Following require hospital treatment on arrival : Calliope, 1 Officer and 8 men, cot cases. Calliope providing cots and bedding.	0430
4.40 —	S.O. B.C.F.	General	Flags	Alter course together four points to starboard.	—
4.41 —	C.-in-C. Rosyth.	Admiralty	W/T	Achates arrived	0421
4.44 —	**S.O. 4th L.C.S.**	**C.-in-C.**	Sem.	**Calliope has four serious cases requiring immediate operation. Request R.A. Scapa may be directed to send hospital boat to Calliope on arrival.**	**0435**
4.46 —	**Marlborough**	**C.-in-C.**	W/T	**My position 4 a.m., 54° 10′ N., 0° 2′ E., course S., 11 knots. Am keeping water under control at present. Expect to arrive Humber 8.30 a.m.**	**0410**
4.50 —	S.O. B.C.F.	General	Flags	Alter course together four points to port	—
4.50 —	Fearless	Marlborough	Sem.	Following received. S.N.O. River Tyne to Fearless. Sending four tugs to Flamborough Head. Cag, fastest tug, should arrive at 10 a.m.	0145
4.54 —	*Commodore T.*	*General*	Flags	*Admiral intends to proceed at 18 knots*	—
4.57 —	St. Abb's Head.	Admiralty	L/T	Valiant and two Torpedo-Boat Destroyers passed N.W.	—
4.58 —	Fearless	Marlborough	Sem.	I am steering a steady S.W. course	—

Date, Time of Despatch.	From	To	System.	Message.	Time of Origin.
2 JUNE —*cont.*					
5.0 a.m.	S.O. B.C.F. -	General	Flags	Alter course together four points to starboard.	—
5.7 —	Commodore T.	General -	Flags	*Admiral intends to proceed at 20 knots* -	—
5.10 —	C.-in-C.	Commodore F.	S.L.	Report when speed can be safely increased. Reply : I consider present speed maximum under present conditions.	0512 0515
5.10 —	S.O. B.C.F. -	General	Flags	Alter course together four points to port	—
5.10 —	Marlborough	Fearless -	S.L.	Please lead down channel - - -	0508
5.11 —	Marlborough	General -	Flags	Alter course in succession to South -	—
5.12 —	C.-in-C.	S.O. 4th L.C.S.	S.L.	Detach a Light Cruiser to assist Active in search for Broke, Active dropped back at 1.30 a.m. Broke 9 p.m. position was Lat. 58° 10′ N., Long. 2° 46′ E., course N. 60° W., 7 knots. Report name of ship detailed. She should communicate with Active. Reply : Constance. (*Calliope passed above to Constance with orders to proceed.*)	0510
5.12 —	C.-in-C.	General -	Flags	Distance apart of columns six cables -	—
5.12 —	Marlborough	Fearless -	S.L.	I have increased 1 knot - - -	—
5.15 —	Flamborough Head.	Admiralty -	L/T	One Battleship, super-dreadnought, one four funnelled Light Cruiser, nine Destroyers. Position, course and speed. E.S.E. 10′ South, 15, apparently British. Challenged and answered. Weather clear.	—
5.19 —	S.O. B.C.F. -	Lydiard -	S.L.	Send four Destroyers to screen 2nd B.C.S., remainder screen 1st B.C.S. My course made good S. 89° W., speed through water 21 knots, zigzagging.	0518
5.20 —	S.O. B.C.F. -	General -	Flags	Alter course together four points to starboard.	—
5.27 —	Valiant -	C. in C. Rosyth	W/T	My 1920. Programme one hour late. Expect to arrive outer gate 7 a.m.	0507
5.28 —	Marlborough	Fearless -	S.L.	I have increased one knot - - -	—
5.30 —	S.O. B.C.F. -	General -	Flags	Alter course together four points to port	—
5.30 —	Active -	C.-in-C. -	W/T	Am unable to get into W/T communication with Broke. Reply : Constance is coming to assist search. Cruiser squadron under R.A. Minotaur being also sent to assist you with Broke.	0530 0600
5.30 —	C.-in-C.	C.-in-C. Rosyth.	W/T	Request information from Engadine whether steps were taken to sink Warrior on abandonment.	0530
5.31 —	Fearless -	Marlborough -	Sem.	Destroyers are asking if oil fuel spray is still required. Reply : Spray not now required. Destroyers take up screening stations.	0531
5.40 —	S.O. B.C.F. -	General -	Flags	Alter course together four points to starboard.	—
5.50 —	S.O. B.C.F. -	General -	Flags	Alter course together four points to port	—

Date, Time of Despatch.	From	To	System.	Message.	Time of Origin.
2 JUNE —*cont.*					
5.55 a.m.	S.O. B.C.F. -	General -	Flags	Let fires die out in boilers not required for 22 knots.	—
5.56 —	*Malaya* -	S.O. 5th B.S.	Sem.	*Besides the 15 men committed to the deep last night Malaya has 32 for burial, also 44 cot cases and two others for hospital.*	*0535*
6.0 —	S.O. B.C.F. -	General -	Flags.	Alter course together four points to starboard.	—
6.1 —	*S.O.2nd L.C.S.*	Birmingham -	S.L.	*My speed is 18 knots*	—
6.4 —	S.O. B.C.F. via Birmingham.	S.O. 2nd L.C.S.	W/T	Priority. Indicate your position. I am sending you four Destroyers as soon as possible.	0603
				Reply : My position, course and speed 56° 35′ N., 0° 53′ W., S. 85° W., 20 knots. Condition is very good. Destroyers not required.	0632
6.5 —	S.O. B.C.F. -	Nepean -	S.L.	When I get to May Island I shall send you with Phœnix and Negro to screen Southampton whose position I will give you.	0608
6.5 —	Lion -	—	—	Remarks : Sighted May Island	—
6.10 —	Galatea -	S.O. B.C.F. -	S.L.	May Island lighthouse S. 86° W. -	0602
6.10 —	S.O. B.C.F. -	General -	Flags	Alter course together four points to port	—
6.10 —	C.-in-C. -	S.O. 1st, 4th and R.A. 1st B.S.	S.L.	**If proceed into harbour is made to 4th or 5th Divisions, the division ordered is to proceed at highest possible speed to base, approaching to Northward of 85° from Old Head from position 40 miles from it, and passing South of Skerries when near. Division being unscreened is to take every precaution against Submarines such as being in open order, line-ahead, quarter-line, and zigzagging about 1½ points after passing through T.B.D. screen.**	0545
6.14 —	Canterbury -	Marlborough -	W/T	My position 6 a.m., course N. 70° E., 10 miles from Flamborough Head, 26 knots.	0605
6.20 —	S.O. B.C.F. -	General -	Flags.	Alter course together four points to starboard.	—
6.22 —	Ipswich -	Admiralty -	W/T	From Talisman, Talisman and two Submarines have been at rendezvous 01 for the last 24 hours. Nothing to report.	0600
6.23 —	Constance -	Active -	W/T	I am ordered to assist you with search. Shall arrive at 58° 32′ N., 0° 20′ E., at 8 a.m.	0600
6.25 —	S.O. B.C.F. -	Destroyers -	Flags	Destroyers form Submarine screen for two columns of Battle Cruisers.	—
6.28 —	S.O. B.C.F. -	Nepean -	S.L.	Had Termagant arrived when you left? Have you heard anything of Onslow and Defender? Reply : Termagant was expected at midnight. I did not see her. I know nothing of Onslow or Defender.	0625
6.30 —	S.O. B.C.F. -	General -	Flags	Alter course together four points to port	—
6.30 —	S.O. B.C.F.-	1st Division -	Flags	*Form single line-ahead in sequence in which ships now are.*	—
6.30 —	C.-in-C. -	S.O. 2nd C.S.	W/T	**If no signs of Warrior by 8 a.m. proceed with cruisers to assist Active in search for Broke who was in Lat. 57° 10′ N., Long. 2° 46′ E. at 9 p.m. last night, injured forward and steering N. 60 W. 7 knots.**	0630

Date, Time of Despatch.	From	To	System.	Message.	Time of Origin.
2 JUNE —*cont.*					
6.32 a.m.	S.O. B.C.F. -	S.O. 1st, 2nd, 3rd L.C.S., 2nd B.C.S.	W/T	Proceed into harbour - - - -	0631
6.34 —	*S.O. 1st L.C.S.*	*1st L.C.S.* -	Flags	*Form single line-ahead in sequence of fleet numbers.*	—
6.35 —	Flamborough Head.	Admiralty -	L/T	One two-funnelled Light Cruiser. Position, course and speed S.E. 7, South, 20. Apparently British. Challenged and answered. Hull informed.	—
6.35 —	*S.O. 3rd L.C.S.*	*3rd L.C.S.* -	Flags	*Alter course in succession to N.W. by W.*	—
6.35 —	S.O. B.C.F. -	General -	Flags	Alter course in succession to W. by S. -	—
6.35 —	*S.O. 2nd B.C.S.*	*2nd Division* -	Flags	*Form single line-ahead* - - - -	—
6.35 —	**C.-in-C.** -	**S.O. 1st B.S.** -	S.L.	**Did you intercept Marlborough?** - **Reply : No** - - - - -	**0626** **0650**
6.36 —	*S.O. 2nd L.C.S.*	*Birmingham* -	S.L.	*My speed is 20 knots* - - - -	*0635*
6.40 —	*S.O. B.C.F.-*	*S.O. 1st B.C.S.* -	Sem.	*I think it desirable for Princess Royal and Tiger to go into basin at next high water. Do you concur ?* *Reply : Yes* - - - - -	*0635* *0645*
6.40 —	**C.-in-C.** -	**Cyclops** - -	W/T	**For R.A. Peterhead. Request Albion and tugs may be directed to look for and assist Acasta in tow of Nonsuch. Position 7 p.m. 1st June 57° 8′ N., 2° 45′ E., course West, 7½ knots.**	**0640**
6.40 —	S.O. B.C.F. -	Lydiard -	S.L.	Can you give me any information as to whereabouts of Onslow, Defender, Nestor or Nomad?	0630
				Reply : Nothing is known of boats mentioned. Turbulent was sunk on night of 31st May.	0700
6.45 —	*S.O. 2nd B.C.S.*	*2nd Division* -	Flags	*Alter course in succession to S. 80° W.* -	—
6.45 —	Lion - -	—	—	Remarks : Six Destroyers joined up -	—
6.50 —	Marlborough	Canterbury -	W/T	Marlborough does not require any more assistance and will arrive at Humber 0800	0643
7.0 —	S.O. B.C.F. -	Nepean - -	S.L.	When I tell you to proceed in execution of previous orders, proceed to pick up Southampton who was in 56° 35′ N., 0° 53′ W., presumably steering for May Island.	0700
7.5 —	S.O. B.C.F. -	Destroyers -	Flags	Proceed in execution of previous orders -	—
7.6 —	**C.-in-C.** -	**R.A. Cyclops, S.N.O. Scapa.**	W/T	**Preparatory signal for entering Scapa Flow via Hoxa Sound. Leading ship expects to arrive at 10 a.m. All hospital drifters muster on arrival. Fleet may be firing lyddite shell now in guns when near base.**	**0705**
7.7 —	*S.O. 3rd L.C.S.*	*Nottingham* -	S.L.	What is wrong with Southampton? - Reply : Southampton stopped to make temporary repairs. Keeping Birmingham with her.	0700 0705
7.20 —	**C.-in-C.** -	**General and Destroyers.**	Sem.	**Opportunity will probably be taken to fire loaded lyddite shell when near Pentland Skerries.**	**0710**
7.28 —	S.O. B.C.F. -	C.-in-C. Rosyth	S.L.	Request crane lighter may come alongside port side as soon as possible to lift roof of Q turret.	0718

Date, Time of Despatch.	From	To	System.	Message.	Tim of Origin
2 JUNE *—cont.*					
7.30 a.m.	C.-in-C.	5th Division	Flags	**Proceed in execution of previous orders** (*into harbour*).	—
7.33 —	S.O.2ndL.C.S.	C.-in-C. Rosyth	W/T	Preparatory signal for entering Firth of Forth. Two ships, Birmingham and Southampton. The leading ship is expected to arrive within gunshot of Inchkeith at 11.15 a.m.	0730
7.39 —	C.-in-C. Rosyth.	Admiralty	L/T	Valiant, Moon, Mounsey, arrived - -	0723
7.41 —	Fearless	Grimsby	W/T	From Marlborough for S.N.O. Tyne. Please cancel my message 0006. Tugs are not now required.	0455
7.42 —	Active	Constance	W/T	My position, course and speed at 8.30 a.m., 58° 20′ N., 2° 22′ E., N. 49° W., 14 knots.	0745
7.45 —	Constance	Active -	W/T	Meet me at 0800, 58° 35′ N., 0° 20′ E. My course is S. 56° E., 18 knots.	0715
7.46 —	**S.O. 5th B.S.**	C.-in-C.	S.L.	**Following wounded requiring hospital treatment. Barham : cot cases, 1 Officer, 25 men ; non-cot, 6 men. Malaya : cot cases, 42 ; non-cot, 2. For burial : Barham, 1 Officer, 3 men ; Malaya, 32 men. Request necessary arrangements may be made for removal of killed and wounded, observing that cots are not available.**	0725
				Reply : If weather permits hospital ships Soudan and Berbice are being ordered to go alongside Barham and Malaya. They should arrive Scapa about noon. If weather is not suitable for going alongside, they will be ordered to anchor near. Arrangements are being made re burials.	1006
7.50 —	R.A. Commanding E. Coast of England.	Marlborough	S.L.	Have you any hospital cases? - - - Reply : No hospital cases - - -	0705 0755
7.51 —	Marlborough	Fearless	S.L.	Proceed as soon as you like. Very many thanks.	0750
7.51 —	**Commodore F.**	C.-in-C. -	Sem.	**I think Destroyers can stand 15 knots** -	0750
7.52 —	S.O.3rdL.C.S.	3rd L.C.S.	S.L.	*Admiral intends to proceed at 18 knots* -	—
7.54 —	S.O. B.C.F. -	General	Flags	Admiral intends to proceed at 18 knots -	—
7.58 —	**S.O.10th C.S.**	C.-in-C.	W/T	**Four Cruisers now on Muckle Flugga patrol. Request two Cruisers be placed S.E. of Iceland.**	0700
7.59 —	S.O. B.C.F. -	General	Flags	Admiral intends to proceed at 15 knots -	—
8.0 —	C.-in-C. -	R.A. 1st B.S., S.O. 4th L.C.S.	S.L.	5th Division pass through 4th L.C.S. -	0755
8.0 —	Fearless	Marlborough -	Sem.	Fearless is very pleased to have seen you safely into harbour and wishes Marlborough a quick recovery from her trouble and a speedy return to the fighting line.	0755
				Reply : Very many thanks from Marlborough. We will be out as soon as we can.	0800
8.0 —	C.-in-C. -	General	Flags	**Admiral intends to proceed at 14 knots** -	—

Date, Time of Despatch.	From	To	System.	Message.	Time of Origin.
2 JUNE —*cont.*					
8.1 a.m.	S.O. B.C.F. -	General	Flags	Admiral intends to proceed at 12 knots	—
8.3 —	Inchkeith	S.O. B.C.F.	S.L.	Defender is towing Onslow, 4 a.m., 56° 38′ N., 0° 45′ W. (*Unreliable.*) Speed four knots. Tug is being sent.	—
8.5 —	S.O. B.C.F. -	General	Flags	Invert the columns from the rear ships passing port side.	—
8.7 —	S.O. 5th B.S.	R.A. Scapa	W/T	Malaya and Barham have 36 Officers and men between them for burial as soon as possible after arrival.	0800
				Reply : Please inform me as soon as possible details of religions distinguishing Officers and men.	0930
8.8 —	C.-in-C. Rosyth.	Admiralty	L/T	Penn and Paladin arrived - - -	0752
8.10 —	**C.-in-C.**	**General**	Flags	**Alter course together two points to starboard.**	—
8.11 —	*S.O. B.C.F.-*	*1st Division*	Flags	*Tiger take Guide of fleet -* - -	—
8.12 —	C.-in-C. Rosyth.	Admiralty	L/T	Moresby arrived - - - -	0744
8.13 —	*S.O. B.C.F.-*	*1st Division*	Flags	*Admiral intends to proceed at 15 knots* -	—
8.13 —	*R.A. 1st B.S.*	*5th Division*	Flags	*Assume open order* - - -	—
8.18 —	*S.O. B.C.F.-*	*1st Division*	Flags	*Admiral intends to proceed at 12 knots* -	—
8.18 —	**C.-in-C.**	**General**	Flags	**Alter course together two points to port**	—
8.20 —	**C.-in-C.**	**R.A. 1st B.S.**	S.L.	**Order your own gate. Report bearing on which you make land, or Skerries.**	**0800**
8.23 —	Admiral Immingham.	Admiralty	L/T	Marlborough, Fearless, Laforey, Lawford, Lance, Lasso, Lookout, Laverock, Lysander, Lark arrived.	—
8.24 —	S.O. Cruisers	Cruisers	S.L.	*Alter course together to West* - - -	—
8.24 —	S.O. B.C.F. -	General	Flags	Admiral intends to proceed at 10 knots. Anchor in the manner previously arranged.	—
8.25 —	*Commodore T.*	*General*	Flags	*Admiral intends to proceed at 22 knots -*	—
8.25 —	Admiral Dover.	Admiralty	L/T	Can normal conditions on patrol lines be resumed? Reply : Yes.	—
8.25 —	*S.O. 4th L.C.S.*	*4th L.C.S.*	Flags	*Admiral intends to proceed at 14 knots* -	—
8.26 —	S.O. B.C.F. -	S.O. 2nd L.C.S.	W/T	If you do not require Destroyers send them to search for Defender towing Onslow in 56° 38′ N., 0° 45′ W., speed four knots. Tug has been sent to them. Nepean is S.O. of Destroyers sent to you.	0815
8.30 —	*S.O. 4th L.C.S.*	*4th L.C.S.*	Flags	*Admiral intends to proceed at 13 knots* -	—
8.30 —	Cordelia	—	—	Remarks : 1st L.C.S. anchored - -	—
8.30 —	**C.-in-C.**	**General**	Flags	**Alter course together two points to port** -	—
8.32 —	*S.O. Cruisers*	*Cruisers*	S.L.	*Negative zigzag* - - - -	—
8.34 —	S.O. B.C.F. -	General	Flags	Have steam for 15 knots at two hours' notice.	—

Date, Time of Despatch.	From	To	System.	Message.	Time of Origin.
2 JUNE —*cont.*					
8.38 a.m.	*S.O. Cruisers*	*Cruisers* -	S.L.	*Cruisers are to search for Broke. Keep a sharp look-out for any boats in case vessel has been abandoned.*	*0820*
8.40 —	**C.-in-C.** -	**General** -	Flags	**Alter course together two points to starboard.**	—
8.40 —	*R.A. 1st B.S.*	*5th Division* -	Flags	*Alter course together 1½ points to starboard*	—
8.44 —	**C.-in-C.** -	**S.O. 2nd C.S.** -	W/T	**Priority. Submarine sighted 4 a.m. to-day, Friday, Lat. 57° 15′ N., Long. 2° 15′ E.**	*0844*
8.45 —	*S.O. Cruisers*	*Cruisers* -	S.L.	*Admiral intends to proceed at 17 knots* -	—
8.47 —	S.O. B.C.F. -	Captain D13 -	W/T	Situation *re* Destroyers. Onslow in tow of Defender in position 56° 38′ N., 0° 45′ W., 4 a.m., speed four knots. Tug has been sent. Turbulent was sunk during the night 31st May. Termagant arrived Rosyth. I fear Nestor and Nomad are lost.	*0825*
				Reply : Am proceeding to search for Defender and Onslow with Mænad in company.	*0945*
8.47 —	**Active** - -	**C.-in-C.** -	W/T	**Have searched as far as 58° 12′ N., 2° 14′ E. I am now searching North. Sea is rapidly rising.**	*0831*
8.50 —	**C.-in-C.** -	**General** -	Flags	**Alter course together two points to starboard.**	—
8.50 —	Constance -	Active - -	W/T	My position at 9 a.m. will be 58° 27′ N., 0° 40′ E. Repeat your position.	*0840*
8.50 —	**Commodore F.**	**C.-in-C.** -	S.L.	**I think Destroyers can manage two more knots.**	*0840*
8.51 —	*R.A. 1st B.S.*	*R.A. Scapa* -	W/T	Preparatory signal for entering Scapa via Hoxa Sound. Four ships are expected to arrive at Nevi Skerry Gate at 10.45 a.m.	*0830*
8.56 —	**C.-in-C.** -	**General** -	Flags	**Alter course together two points to port** -	—
9.1 —	Constance -	Broke - -	W/T	What is your position, course and speed?	*0845*
9.4 —	Submarine G6	Titania -	W/T	Expect to arrive at noon - - -	*0730*
9.5 —	*S.O. 2nd C.S.*	*Shannon* -	S.L. and W/T	*Pass following to Albion and remain on Q wave. S.O. 2nd C.S. to Albion : Search for Warrior abandoned. Proceed to assist Nonsuch, position at 7 p.m. 1st June, 57° 8′ N., 2° 44′ E., course West 7½ knots.*	*0900*
9.5 —	**C.-in-C.** -	**General** -	Flags	**Admiral intends to proceed at 15 knots**	—
9.7 —	*R.A. 1st B.S.*	*5th Division* -	Flags	*Alter course in succession to W. by S.* -	—
9.8 —	**C.-in-C.** -	**S.O. 2nd C.S.** -	W/T	**Priority. Continue searching for Warrior**	—
9.9 —	Falmouth -	—	—	Remarks : 3rd L.C.S. anchored -	—
9.10 —	*S.O. 2nd L.C.S.*	*Nepean* -	S.L.	I do not require your services. You are to search for Defender and Onslow.	*0910*
9.10 —	**S.O. 4th L.C.S.**	**C.-in-C.** -	S.L.	**Have discovered land N.W. by W.** -	—
9.12 —	*S.O. 4th L.C.S.*	*4th L.C.S.* -	Flags	*Admiral intends to proceed at 14 knots* -	—
9.12 —	*R.A. 1st B.S.*	*5th Division* -	Flags	*Alter course together one point to starboard*	—

Date, Time of Despatch.	From	To	System.	Message.	Time of Origin.
2 JUNE —*cont.*					
9.12 a.m.	C.-in-C.	General	Flags	**Alter course together two points to port**	—
9.15 —	*S.O. Cruisers*	*Cruisers*	S.L.	*Submarine sighted in vicinity at 4 a.m. Keep a sharp look out.*	*0915*
9.15 —	C.-in-C.	Commodore F.	S.L.	**Try and get news of Nonsuch and Acasta**	0909
9.19 —	Admiral, Immingham	Admiralty	L/T	Fearless sailed	—
9.20 —	S.O.2nd L.C.S.	Birmingham and Destroyers.	Flags	*Alter course in succession to W.*	—
9.20 —	S.O. 4th L.C.S.	C.-in-C.	Sem.	**Skerries ahead**	0918
9.22 —	C.-in-C.	General	Flags	**Alter course together two points to starboard.**	—
9.23 —	C.-in-C. Rosyth.	Admiralty	L/T	Two additional tugs of power urgently required Rosyth for moving heavy ships. None available at other ports in Scotland. Request two may be sent earliest possible moment.	—
9.24 —	Naval Depôt, North Shields.	Admiralty	L/T	Contest arrived	0900
9.25 —	*S.O. Cruisers*	*Cruisers*	S.L.	*Zigzag. Alter course together to East*	—
9.27 —	Tynemouth	Admiralty	L/T	Contest, Garland, Porpoise, entered Tyne	—
9.27 —	R.A. 1st B.S.	R.A. Scapa	W/T	To confirm my 0830. Leading ship will arrive Nevi Skerry Gate at 10.45 a.m.	0915
9.28 —	C.-in-C. Rosyth.	C.-in-C.	W/T	**Priority. Captain of Warrior reports ship was not sunk when abandoned, but steps were taken as far as possible to make her watertight. Yacht and two tugs from Invergordon are now searching.**	0904
9.30 —	Moss, Copenhagen.	Exchange Telegraph, London.	—	Several circumstances indicate that German Fleet which attacked British in North-Eastern part of North Sea has been put to flight. This afternoon and evening greatest part of German Fleet returned, but dispersed and severely damaged. Politiken states that 11 o'clock this forenoon German torpedo boat appeared outside Ringkoobing, Jutland's West coast. Warships severely damaged unable to proceed. Fifteen minutes later German seaplane arrived, landed near warship and half an hour later disappeared southwards. Three o'clock another German torpedo boat arrived towing damaged warship southwards. Seven o'clock this evening 10 German torpedo boats, of which six severely damaged, passed through Little Belt going very slowly.	—
9.30 —	C.-in-C.	General	Flags	**Admiral intends to proceed at 16 knots**	—
9.30 —	Marlborough	—	—	Remarks : Secured to No. 3 buoy	—
9.35 —	*S.O. Cruisers*	*Cruisers*	S.L.	*Bank fires in boilers not required for 20 knots. Have steam ready for full speed at two hours' notice.*	—
9.35 —	*S.O. Cruisers*	*Cruisers*	S.L.	*Speed of advance 17 knots. Renew search for Warrior.*	*0930*
9.36 —	Scarrou	Albion III.	W/T	Warrior abandoned Lat. 57° 10′ N., Long. 2° 17′ E. (*Remainder jammed.*)	0912
9.36 —	C.-in-C.	Royal Oak	Flags	**Take station astern of Malaya**	—
9.37 —	S.O.2nd L.C.S.	Birmingham	Flags	*Alter course in succession to N. 81° W.*	—

Date, Time of Despatch.	From	To	System.	Message.	Time of Origin.
2 JUNE —*cont.*					
9.40 a.m.	C.-in-C.	General	Sem. and S.L.	Order of entry : 5th, 3rd, 7th, 4th, 6th, 1st and 2nd Subdivisions, Attached Cruisers, 4th L.C.S. 5th, 1st and 2nd Subdivisions South of Skerries, remainder North of Skerries. 4th L.C.S. and Bellona to be ahead screening until 1st and 4th B.S. form single line, then two ships and Bellona turn to starboard and two to port and screen North and South side of line working to the rear. Blanche and Boadicea will go with 2nd B.S. when detached and assist to screen. Ships of subdivisions to take open order by signal from Commanders of subdivisions before passing Skerries. One mile interval between subdivisions.	0900
9.40 —	C.-in-C.	S.O. 1st B.S., S.O. 5th B.S., Royal Oak.	S.L.	Royal Oak will be stationed astern of Malaya before reaching Skerries and is to remain in Flow and anchor in D. 2 berth after 6th Subdivision have anchored.	0920
9.40 —	*Commodore F.*	*Kempenfelt*	S.L.	*Call Nonsuch and Acasta and ask them their positions.*	...
9.40 —	C.-in-C.	Commodore F.	S.L.	Indicate speed Destroyers can do without sustaining damage. Reply : 20 knots.	—
9.41 —	*R.A. 1st B.S.*	*5th Division*	Flags	*Alter course together 1½ points to port*	—
9.45 —	Commodore F.	C.-in-C.	S.L.	Marksman is in touch with Broke, strength 3. Reply : Get her position, course, speed and condition.	—
9.50 —	*Commodore F. via Marksman*	*Broke*	W/T	*What is your position, course and speed, and condition ?*	—
9.50 —	*Marne*	*Commodore F.*	S.L.	*During first night attack of 31st Marne was struck by shell on upper deck, aft deck pierced in two places, damage slight. In second attack Marne fired torpedo. Result of shot not ascertained.*	—
9.53 —	*S.O. 5th B.S.*	*Malaya*	Sem.	*Take station astern of Barham*	—
9.54 —	Naval Depôt, North Shields.	Admiralty	L/T	Garland, Porpoise arrived	0945
9.57 —	Admiralty	C.-in-C. Rosyth	L/T	Marlborough has arrived in Humber for temporary repairs.	0957
10.0 —	C.-in-C.	General	Flags	Alter course leading ships together rest in succession to W.	—
10.0 —	C.-in-C.	2nd B.S., Boadicea, Blanche.	Flags	Proceed in execution of previous orders	—
10.0 —	C.-in-C.	General	Flags	Columns to be eight cables apart	—
10.1 —	C.-in-C.	Malaya	S.L.	You are to remain astern of Barham and Royal Oak astern of you.	0945
10.2 —	A.C. Orkneys and Shetlands.	Napier	W/T	Napier and Marmaduke proceed with all despatch to meet and screen fleet approaching on 80° from S.W. On completion return to Loch Eriboll and meet Australia at 11.30 a.m. 3rd June in position two miles 360° from Cape Wrath and screen her to this base.	0817
10.3 —	*R.A. 1st B.S.*	*5th Division*	Flags	*Alter course together one point to port*	—
10.5 —	S.O. 2nd B.S.	Commodore F.	S.L.	I am turning 16 points, then turning back 13.	—
10.8 —	C.-in-C.	Malaya	Flags	Take up appointed station	—

Date, Time of Despatch.	From	To	System.	Message.	Time of Origin.
2 JUNE —*cont.*					
10.10 a.m.	*S.O. 2nd B.S.*	*1st Division*	Flags	*Alter course in succession 16 points to port*	—
10.10 —	S.O. B.C.F.	Engadine	Sem.	What is position of Warrior? Reply: Warrior abandoned 57° 21′ N., 3° 20′ E., at 7 a.m. 1st June.	1004 1015
	S.O. B.C.F.	Engadine	—	Was Warrior sunk? Reply: Warrior was afloat when I left her. The after part and midship part of upper deck was awash. Captain stated she was making water fast and did not expect her to float for more than one hour.	— 1035
10.10 —	*S.O.4thL.C.S.*	*4th L.C.S.*	Flags	*Negative zigzag*	—
10.11 —	C.-in-C.	R.A. 1st B.S.	W/T	**You can fire the lyddite shell when within six miles of Pentland Skerries if range is clear.**	0920
10.12 —	C.-in-C.	Battleships	Flags	**Expend lyddite shell**	—
10.14 —	Admiralty	Admiral Dover	L/T	Priority. Salvage ship Linnet is to proceed to the Humber immediately. Previous instructions as to proceeding to Gravesend are cancelled. Captain Pomeroy to report at Admiralty.	1014
10.15 —	C.-in-C.	General	Flags	**Assume 2nd organisation**	—
10.16	*S.O.4thL.C.S.*	*4th L.C.S.*	Flags	*Alter course together three points to port*	—
10.16 —	C.-in-C., Rosyth.	Admiralty	L/T	Lion, Tiger, New Zealand, Indomitable, Inflexible, 1st L.C.S., 3rd L.C.S., Nottingham, Dublin, Obdurate arrived.	0925
10.16	*R.A. 1st B.S.*	*5th Division*	Flags	*Assume close order. Admiral intends to proceed 18 knots.*	—
10.17 —	R.A. Scapa	R.A. Invergordon.	W/T	**From S.N.O. Blyth for C.-in-C. Submarine G. 10 arrived. Nothing to report.**	1000
10.17 —	*S.O. B.C.F.*	*S.O. 1st B.C.S. and Tiger.*	W/T	*Please inform me estimated position of wreck of Queen Mary.* *Reply: S.O. 1st B.C.S. Approximate position 56° 50′ N., 5° 52′ E.* *Tiger 56° 57′ N., 5° 50′ E.*	1010 1120 1100
10.17 —	Admiralty	C.-in-C.	W/T	**A sufficient force should be sent out as soon as possible to find Warrior. Captain reports he left her afloat after taking steps to make her as far as possible water-tight.**	1017
10.18 —	Flamborough Head.	Admiralty	W/T	Four Light Cruisers and 10 Destroyers, bearing S.E. 10 miles, steering S., 20 knots. Class indistinguishable owing to haze. Hull informed. Fearless bearing E. three miles, steering N., 15 knots	1142
10.18 —	*S.O.2nd B.S.*	*1st Subdivision*	Flags	*Alter course in succession to S.W. by W.*	—
10.19 —	S.O. B.C.F.	Indomitable, Inflexible.	W/T	Please inform me estimated position of Invincible? Reply: Indomitable 56° 53′ N., 6° 10′ E. Inflexible, 57° 4′ N., 6° 6′ E.	1011 1100 1122
10.19 —	Commodore F.	R.A. Cyclops	W/T	Castor arrives 11.30 a.m. Has 14 hospital cases. Propose to send them in Destroyer.	0930

Date, Time of Despatch.	From	To	System.	Message.	Time of Origin.
2 JUNE —*cont.*					
10.20 a.m	R.A. Scapa -	R.A. Invergordon.	W/T	From C.-in-C. Rosyth for C.-in-C. Moresby, arrived.	0944
10.20 --	C.-in-C.	S.O.M.S. -	W/T	My 2309 of 1st June. Do not pass Pentland Skerries before noon.	0935
10.21 -	C.-in-C. -	4th Subdivision	Flags	Take station astern of 7th Subdivision	—
10.21 --	*S.O.4th B.S.*	*Bellerophon* -	F.L.	*Fleet is now in 2nd organisation. Bellerophon is not in 7th Subdivision.*	*1021*
10.23 --	*S.O. 4th B.S.*	*4th Subdivision*	Flags	*Alter course together 16 points to port* -	—
10.25 --	*R.A. 1st B.S.*	*5th Division* -	Flags	*Alter course in succession to W.N.W.* -	—
10.25 --	C.-in-C. -	5th Subdivision	Flags	Take station astern of 4th Subdivision -	—
10.25 --	*S.O. 2nd C.S.*	*Cochrane* -	S.L.	*Pass following to Albion yacht and remain on Q wave : S.O. 2nd C.S. to Albion. What is your position, course and speed ?*	*1020*
				Reply : 11.30 a.m. 57° 30' N., 0° 0' E., course W. mag., speed 15 knots.	*1150*
10.25 --	S.O. B.C.F. -	S.O. 2nd B.C.S.	W/T	Please inform me of estimated position of Indefatigable. Reply : 56° 48' N., 5° 32' E.	1012
10.26 --	*Commodore F.*	*Broke* -	W/T	*Indicate your position, course and speed* -	*0948*
10.26 --	S.O. B.C.F. -	*Lydiard* -	Sem.	Detail four Destroyers to accompany 3rd L.C.S. and bring in Warrior. Report names to Falmouth and ask her for orders.	1020
10.26 --	S.O. 2nd B.S.	*Commodore F.*	S.L.	Arrange to screen both subdivisions -	1021
10.27 --	*R.A. 2nd B.S.*	*2nd Subdivision*	Flags	*Alter course in succession to S.W. by W. Admiral intends to proceed at 16 knots.*	—
10.27 --	*S.O. 4th B.S.*	*4th Subdivision*	Flags	*Alter course together 16 points to port* -	—
10.27 --	*S.O. 2nd B.S.*	*2nd Subdivision*	Flags	*Take station astern one mile of Erin* - -	—
10.28 --	*S.O.4thL.C.S.*	*4th L.C.S.* -	Flags	*4th L.C.S. take station ahead of Calliope* -	—
10.29 --	S.O. 2nd B.S.	Blanche -	Flags	Join the 2nd Subdivision - - -	—
10.30 --	C.-in-C. -	S.O. 4th L.C.S.	S.L.	Calliope precede Iron Duke into harbour owing to presence of wounded. Only one Light Cruiser to screen on port side.	0945
10.30 --	*S.O.4thL.C.S.*	*4th L.C.S.* -	Flags	*Disregard Senior Officers' motions. Caroline take Junior Officers under your command.*	—
10.30 --	*R.A. 1st B.S.*	*5th Division* -	Flags	*Alter course in succession to N.W. by N.* -	—
	Reuter, Amsterdam.	Reuter-, London.	—	Berlin official Admiralty preliminary report 31st May. High Sea Fleet met considerably superior main portion British battlefleet course afternoon and night between Skager Rack and Horns Reef. Number too heavy for us, successful fighting developed. We destroyed, as till now ascertained, great Battleship Warspite, Battle Cruisers Queen Mary, Indefatigable, two Armoured Cruisers apparently Achilles class, one small Cruiser, new Destroyer leaders (*zerstoererfueherschiffe*) Turbulent, Nestor, Alcaster, great number Destroyers, one Submarine.	—

Date, Time of Despatch.	From	To	System.	Message.	Time of Origin.
2 JUNE	—cont.				
				Number great British Battleships heavily damaged. Among others Battleship Marlborough hit by torpedo. On our side small Cruiser Wiesbaden and Pommern sunk by Enemy (*frauenlat*) and some Torpedo Boats till now unknown. High Sea Fleet to-day returned harbour. Chief Admiralty Staff, (Held) D. Brownrigg.	
10.32 a.m.	*Commodore F. Blake* - -		S.L.	*Send at once for cots and blankets for 14 hospital cases ready for Castor arriving 11.30 a.m.*	—
10.32 --	S.O. B.C.F. -	S.O. 3rd L.C.S.	W/T	Prepare to sail with 3rd L.C.S. and four Destroyers as soon as you are fuelled to bring in Warrior. When will you be ready? Two tugs have been sent already.	1020
				Reply : Hope to get away 2 p.m. Will signal time later. Can we have Oilers at once? There are none here now.	1100
				Further reply from S.O. B.C.F. : When ready bank fires and await orders. Direct Destroyers to do the same.	1105
10.34 —	Dockyard, Rosyth.	Director of Dockyards.	L/T	Princess Royal, Tiger and Southampton being received in basin. No information as to damage yet. Expect large demand for labour.	0805
10.34 —	Canterbury -	S.N.O. Harwich.	W/T	Shall arrive off South Cutler Buoy 1.30 p.m. Permission to enter base.	0945
10.35 —	C.-in-C., Rosyth.	Admiralty -	L/T	Attack and Lizard arrived - - ..	1030
10.35 —	C.-in-C. -	Admiralty -	W/T	V.A.C. B.C.F. reports Queen Mary, Indefatigable blown up by Enemy shell exploding in magazine. Invincible blown up, probably same cause but might be due to mine or Submarine. She was blown in half. Defence similarly blown up. Black Prince unaccounted for and feared sunk. Warrior totally disabled and abandoned after being towed to Lat. 57° 21' N., Long. 3° 2' E., by Engadine. Believed to be still afloat. 2nd C.S. searching for her. Tipperary and Destroyers Turbulent, Fortune, Sparrowhawk and/or Ardent lost, and five or six 4th Destroyer Flotilla are missing. Broke severely damaged making for Scapa Flow. Two Light Cruisers looking for her. Captain D12 reports by signal that his flotilla sank a Battleship Kaiser class in night attack. V.A.C. Battle Cruiser Force reports one Battle Cruiser thought to have been sunk, one severely damaged. Two Light Cruisers known to have been disabled. Enemy's Destroyers were engaged but it is not known yet how many were sunk. Losses of our Battle Cruisers occurred during Battle Cruiser action. Visibility was very low and consequently battlefleet had great difficulty in keeping in touch with Enemy's battlefleet which avoided action, but during the short time	0900

Date, Time of Despatch.	From	To	System.	Message.	Time of Origin.
2 JUNE	*—cont.*				
				in action we apparently inflicted severe damage on some Enemy Battleships. Marlborough only Battleship injured in battlefleet action, injury due to mine or torpedo. Warspite, Barham and Malaya injured before our battlefleet came into action at 6.15 p.m.	
10.35 a.m.	*S.O. 4thL.C.S.*	*4th L.C.S.* -	S.L.	*4th L.C.S. enter after Battle squadrons, remain on screen till after 1st and 4th B.S. form single line-ahead, 2nd Division then turn to port, 1st Division then turn to starboard, screening North and South of line of Battle squadron entering.*	—
10.36 —	R.A. Cyclops-	C.-in-C., R.A. 1st B.S.	W/T	Gate is open - - - - -	1035
10.37 —	C.-in-C. -	General -	Flags	Admiral intends to proceed at 17 knots -	—
10.41 —	S.O. B.C.F. -	C.-in-C. -	W/T	Propose 3rd L.C.S. and four Destroyers as soon as fuelled to bring in Warrior.	1025
10.45 —	*S.O. 2nd B.S.*	*2nd B.S.* -	Flags	*Alter course in succession to W.* -	—
10.45 —	C.-in-C. -	R.A. 1st B.S.-	S.L.	If I catch you off Swona turn to port into Pentland Firth. Go W. of Swona.	1044
10.45 —	*S.O. 5th B.S.*	*7th Subdivision and Royal Oak*	Flags	*Assume open order* - - -	—
10.46 —	Canterbury -	S.N.O. Harwich.	W/T	Require 570 tons of oil fuel, 46 6-in. lyddite shell, 46 4-in. lyddite shell, 64 6-in. cartridges, 78 4-in. Q.F. cartridges, 30 tons fresh water, 5 tons of coal, 700 gallons special mineral lubricating oil.	1005
10.46 —	C.-in-C. -	3rd Subdivision	Flags	Ships in column to be in open order -	—
10.47 —	*S.O. 4th B.S.*	*4th Subdivision*	Flags	*Assume open order* - - -	—
10.48 —	*S.O. 2nd B.S.*	*2nd B.S.* -	Flags	*Admiral intends to proceed at 17 knots* -	—
10.49 —	*S.O. 4th B.S.*	*4th Subdivision*	Flags	*Admiral intends to proceed at 15 knots* -	—
10.51 —	C.-in-C. -	R.A. Cyclops-	W/T	To confirm my 0705. Leading ship Iron Duke expects to arrive 11.30 a.m.	1015
10.51 —	*S.O. 4th B.S.*	*4th Subdivision*	Flags	*Admiral intends to proceed at 13 knots* -	—
10.52 —	Commodore T.	S.N.O. Harwich.	W/T	Expect to arrive in the vicinity 1800. Request instructions as to route.	1045
				Reply : Enter by Sunk L.V. passage. Mine has been destroyed N. 32° E. two miles from Sunk L.V., but area is being thoroughly swept.	1325
10.55 —	*S.O. 1st B.S.*	*5th Subdivision*	Flags	*Assume open order* - - -	—
10.55 —	C.-in-C. -	3rd Subdivision	Flags	Observe very attentively the Admiral's motions.	—
11.0 —	Naval Centre, Hull.	Admiralty -	L/T	Danish steamer Vidar reports sighting Zeppelin 7.20 p.m. 31st May 57° 8' N., 6° 55' E., steering N.W. very fast, marked L24 or L14, had two cars and one look-out bridge on top. 9.45 p.m. 31st May 56° 57' N., 6° 5' E., observed sunken man-of-war with only bow visible above water ; there were metre marks on stem. At same time observed five or six miles W.N.W. of same position	—

Date, Time of Despatch.	From	To	System.	Message.	Time of Origin.
2 JUNE *—cont.*					
				a Cruiser with two masts apparently German burning fiercely. Master picked up in this vicinity seven survivors of (?) G97, three of whom were wounded and one has since died. These men have been landed at Hull and sent to Naval Depot, Immingham.	
11.0 a.m.	C.-in-C.	Berbice	S.L.	Go to Westward until fleet is in harbour.	1100
11.0 —	*S.O. Cruisers*	*Cruisers*	Flags and S.L.	*Alter course together to N.E.*	—
11.0 —	*S.O. 4th B.S.*	*4th Subdivision*	Flags	*Admiral intends to proceed at 15 knots*	—
11.5 —	*S.O. 2nd B.S.*	*2nd B.S.*	Flags	*Assume open order*	—
11.8 —	Admiralty	Admiral, Immingham.	L/T	Admiralty salvage ship Linnet has been ordered to proceed to the Humber. Instructions concerning her are being forwarded. Linnet leaves Dover this forenoon.	1108
11.10 —	*S.O. 2nd B.S.*	*2nd B.S.*	Flags	*Alter course in succession to N. 50° E.*	—
11.10 —	C.-in-C.	S.O. 1st B.S., S.O. 5th B.S., Malaya.	W/T	Owing to strong wind Malaya is not to go to buoy but to anchor in A. 7. Revenge to anchor as already arranged.	1009
11.12 —	Admiral, Dover.	Admiralty	L/T	With reference to Admiralty message timed 1027 of 2nd June. Salvage vessel Linnet leaves Dover for Humber with escort at 11 a.m. to-day Friday.	1100
11.15 —	C.-in-C.	R.A. 1st B.S.	Flags	2nd B.S. is coming South of Skerries. If there is plenty of room come in ahead of them; if not, follow them in. Inform S.O. 2nd B.S.	1110
11.15 —	C.-in-C.	R.A. 4th B.S.	S.L.	Request you will take charge of 3rd Subdivision after passing green buoy.	1102
11.16 —	C.-in-C.	R.A. Cyclops	S.L.	Weather permitting Soudan and Berbice are to be directed to go alongside Barham and Malaya to disembark wounded. If hospital ships cannot go alongside they will be ordered to anchor near Barham and Malaya.	1050
11.17 —	R.A. Cyclops	Commodore F.	W/T	Innan Neb gate is open	1115
11.18 —	*R.A. 1st B.S.*	*5th Division*	Flags	*Alter course together eight points to port*	—
11.19 —	C.-in-C.	R.A. Cyclops	S.L.	Immediate. Orders for hospital ships will be sent on arrival. Ships have following dead on board. Please arrange to have bodies removed from ships as soon as possible. Castor 12 men, Onslaught 2 Officers, Obedient 1 Officer, Calliope 9 men.	1035
11.20 —	C.-in-C.	3rd Subdivision	Flags	Admiral intends to proceed at 15 knots	—
11.22 —	C.-in-C.	Destroyers	Flags	Proceed into harbour	—
11.25 —	*S.O. 4th B.S.*	*4th Subdivision*	Flags	*Admiral intends to proceed at 16 knots*	—
11.28 —	C.-in-C., Rosyth.	Admiralty	L/T	Moon and Mounsey sailed for base	1128

Date, Time of Despatch.	From	To	System.	Message.	Time of Origin.
2 JUNE —cont.					
11.29 a.m.	C.-in-C.	Admiralty	L/T	**Priority. Four Cruisers under R.A. Minotaur are now searching as well as a Yacht and two tugs.**	1129
11.30 —	C.-in-C.	3rd Subdivision	Flags	**Admiral intends to proceed at 13 knots**	—
11.32 —	R.A. 1st B.S.	5th Division	Flags	*Alter course together 16 points to port*	—
11.35 —	S.O. 2nd B.S.	2nd B.S.	Flags	*Alter course in succession to N. 23° W.*	—
11.35 —	S.O. Cruisers	Cruisers	S.L.	*At 11.45 a.m. course will be altered to N. 47° W., speed of advance 16 knots, without further signal.*	1130
11.35 —	R.A. 1st B.S.	5th Division	Flags	*Admiral intends to proceed at 14 knots*	—
11.38 —	Admiralty	Dockyard Sheerness and C.-in-C. Nore.	L/T	Immediate. One of the large paddle tugs at Sheerness is to be despatched at once to Rosyth for moving heavy ships. Matter is most urgent. Report action taken.	—
				Reply : Robust (tug) will leave Sheerness for Rosyth 3 p.m. to-day Friday.	1432
11.40 —	Admiralty	Dockyard Portsmouth and C.-in-C. Portsmouth.	L/T	Immediate. One of the large paddle tugs at Portsmouth is to be despatched at once to Rosyth for moving heavy ships. Matter is most urgent. Report action taken.	—
				Reply : Volcano sails immediately she has completed with coal and provisions, probably about 7 p.m. to-day Friday.	1425
11.40 —	Calliope	—	—	Remarks : Calliope anchored	—
11.40 —	R.A. 1st B.S.	S.O. 2nd B.S.	S.L.	Submit I am following 6th Division in	1135
11.44 —	S.O. B.C.F.	C.-in-C.	W/T	**Unless instructions to the contrary are received from you 3rd L.C.S. will sail 1400 in accordance with my message 1025.**	1128
11.45 —	S.O. 5th B.S.	7th Subdivision	Flags	*Ships in column to be three cables apart. Admiral intends to proceed at 10 knots.*	—
11.45 —	S.O. 2nd L.C.S.	Birmingham	Flags	*Anchor in the manner previously arranged*	—
11.46 —	S.O. 4th B.S.	4th B.S.	Flags	*Admiral intends to proceed at 13 knots*	—
11.50 —	R.A. Cyclops	C.-in-C.	Sem.	**In view of severe weather in Flow suggest Soudan and Berbice anchor in Gutter Sound. Flying Kestrel has been sent to Iron Duke for orders with 45 cots and blankets.**	1130
				Reply : Soudan may anchor in Gutter Sound. Berbice is to anchor near Barham and Malaya in A. 6 and A. 7 berths if she cannot go alongside. As far as possible wounded from Gutter Sound should go to Soudan.	1227
11.50 —	S.O. 4th B.S.	4th Subdivision	Flags	*Anchor in manner previously arranged, starboard anchor, six shackles.*	—
11.52 —	S.O. B.C.F.	1st, 9th and 13th Flotillas.	Sem.	Destroyers fit for sea raise steam and be ready to sail when fuelled to escort injured ships into harbour.	1149
11.52 —	S.O. 4th B.S.	4th Subdivision	Flags	*Admiral intends to proceed at 10 knots*	—
11.53 —	S.O. 4th B.S.	4th Subdivision	Flags	*Assume close order*	—

Date, Time of Despatch.	From	To	System.	Message.	Time of Origin.
2 JUNE	—cont.				
11.55 a.m.	S.O. 2nd B.S.	1st Subdivision	Flag	Admiral intends to proceed at 14 knots. Keep close order.	—
11.58 —	Admiral, Dover.	Admiralty	L/T	May Harwich Destroyers return to Dunkirk?	—
				Reply : Harwich Destroyers are not yet available.	1549
11.59 —	Barham	—	—	Remarks : 7th Subdivision anchored	—
Noon	Malaya	R.A. Scapa	W/T	Officers and men to be buried. Officers : C. of E. 2. Men : C. of E. 17, Wesleyans 3, R.C. 2, not known 5.	1100
12.3 p.m.	Commodore T.	General	Flags	Admiral intends to proceed at 15 knots	—
12.3 —	Superb			Remarks : Anchored	—
12.4 —	S.N.O. Harwich.	Canterbury	W/T	Enter by Sunk passage	1150
12.6 —	S.O. 4th B.S.	4th Subdivision	Flags	Admiral intends to proceed at seven knots	—
12.11 —	R.A. Cyclops	Admiralty	L/T	Iron Duke, Colossus, Collingwood, Neptune, St. Vincent, Barham, Malaya, Superb, Canada, Royal Oak, Calliope arrived.	1130
12.12 —	Commodore T.	General	Flags	Admiral intends to proceed at 22 knots	—
12.15 —	Iron Duke	—	—	Remarks : Secured to buoy	—
12.15 —	C.-in-C.	General	Flags and Sem.	**Have steam for 15 knots at four hours' notice. Senior Officers of squadrons to report if any ships of your squadrons require longer notice for steam.**	—
12.16 —	Captain D13.	S.O. B.C.F.	W/T	Defender is close to Aberdeen. I am returning to base with Mænad. She has 11 survivors on board from Fortune.	1200
12.16 —	Benbow	—	—	Remarks : 4th Subdivision anchored	—
12.18 —	C.-in-C. Rosyth.	Admiralty	L/T	Southampton, Birmingham arrived	1149
12.18 —	Graham, Amsterdam.	Admiralty	L/T	Four Battleships and 11 Destroyers of unknown nationality were seen on 1st June above Terschelling proceeding to N.N.E. about 7 p.m.	—
12.22 —	Admiralty	Ad. Supt. Immingham.	L/T	A Constructive and Engineer Officer well acquainted with details of Marlborough are now proceeding to Humber to consult with you as to repairs of that vessel. Mr. Ollis and Engineer-Admiral Maystone on staff of Director of Dockyards will also consult you respecting repairs to Chester as well as Marlborough.	1222
12.24 —	C.-in-C. Rosyth.	Admiralty	L/T	Goshawk and Acheron arrived	1132
12.30 —	S.O. 1st B.S.	5th Subdivision	Flags	Anchor instantly	—
12.32 —	R.A. Cyclops	Admiralty	L/T	Mystic, Mons, Oak, Ambuscade, Opal, Noble, Menace, Munster, Mandate, Owl, Hardy, Midge arrived.	1200
12.32 —	S.O. 2nd B.S.	1st Division	Flags	Anchor in the manner as previously arranged.	—
12.36 —	Constance	Active	W/T	My position noon was 58° 12′ N., 2° 18′ E., course S. 56° E., speed 18 knots. I intend to steer at 12.45 p.m. N. 33° E. at 15 knots. At 2 p.m. N. 60° W. close to visual signalling distance.	1205

Date, Time of Despatch.	From	To	System.	Message.	Time of Origin.
2 JUNE —*cont.*					
12.38 p.m.	**R.A. Cyclops**	**C.-in-C.** -	Tel.	**Submitted all ammunition ships are allotted as follows : Revenge 76, Barham 15, Hercules 22, St. Vincent 16, Orion 12, Monarch 54, Temeraire 10, Vanguard 1, Collingwood, Isleford.** (*Note.—Made general to ships concerned.*)	1220
12.44 —	**C.-in-C.** -	**Commodore F. Oak and Abdiel.**	Tel.	**Destroyers usual notice for steam** - -	1241
12.45 —	Admiralty -	R.A. East Coast, Captain in Charge Lowestoft.	L/T	Auxiliary patrol vessels can resume normal conditions, and Minesweeping vessels and Sloops may proceed out.	—
12.50 —	Captain Supt. Rosyth.	Lion - -	Sem.	Please signal to me your important defects for seaworthiness so that Dockyard Officers may inspect them and take them in hand.	1235
				Reply : (1) Base of No. 2 funnel very seriously damaged. (2) Canteen flat extensive damage to decks and bulkheads. (3) About two dozen watertight doors and hatches damaged between decks, and a number of skylights and hatches on weather decks. (4) Firemain, brine and fresh water systems damaged. (5) Electrical defects have been shown to your representative. (6) Sick bay extensively damaged, decks and bulkheads perforated, and side armour driven out. (7) Ship's galley and bread troughs entirely destroyed, including decks and bulkheads. (8) Sheet cable holder destroyed, and ship's side and weather deck in vicinity perforated. (9) Mainmast and main derrick shot through. (10) Ship's side and weather deck at 114 station injured. (11) All boats require repair. (12) Blast screens require patching in places. (13) Ship's side plating above 112 station. Stem to 66 perforated by numerous splinters. (14) Net defence rigging and canvas weather screens require renewal in places.	1450
12.50 —	King George V.	—	—	Remarks : Anchored - • - •	—
12.52 —	**C.-in-C.** -	**Commodore F.**	Tel.	**Did Marksman get Broke's position?** - Reply : **Marksman reports unable to pass message to Broke asking her position, etc.**	1250 1330
12.53 —	*R.A. 2nd B.S.*	*2nd Subdivision*	Flags	*Anchor instantly* - - - - -	—
12.55 —	Comus -	—	—	Remarks : Caroline, Comus and Royalist anchored.	—
12.56 —	Gregness -	Admiralty -	L/T	Defender and Onslow arrived. Onslow in tow badly damaged. Achates passing N.	—
1.0 —	*S.O. Cruisers*	*Cruisers* -	S.L.	*Alter course in succession four points to starboard.*	—
1.3 —	C.-in-C. Rosyth.	Admiralty -	L/T	Pelican arrived - - - - -	1250

Date, Time of Despatch.	From	To	System.	Message.	Time of Origin.
2 JUNE 1.8 p.m.	*—cont.* C.-in-C.	General	Sem.	Where possible ships are to complete with fuel to five per cent. above summer stowage.	1247
1.10 —	C.-in-C.	5th Subdivision	Sem.	Report any damage. Have you any casualties?	1310
1.12 —	Naval Depot, North Shields.	Admiralty	L/T	Spitfire arrived 10.30 a.m.	1300
1.19 —	S.O. B.C.F.	Captain D13	W/T	Have sent Negro and Phœnix to look for Defender. If they are not required order them to return to base.	1315
1.25 —	C.-in-C. Rosyth.	Admiralty	L/T	Ariel and Hydra arrived	1305
1.25 —	Active	Constance	W/T	My position noon 58° 27′ N., 1° 12′ E. Will endeavour to sight you about 4 p.m.	1320
1.30 —	Constance	C.-in-C.	W/T	**My position, course and speed at 1400 58° 25′ N., 2° 56′ E., N. 60° W., 15 knots.**	1320
1.36 —	S.O. B.C.F.	Engadine	Sem.	[Check and repeat position of Warrior. Are you sure of latitude? Reply: Position 57° 21′ N., 3° 2′ E. This position was concurred with by Captain and Navigator of Warrior. I had been towing her for 12 hours making for Kinnaird Head.	1310
1.55 —	C.-in-C. Rosyth.	Admiralty	L/T	Narborough, Nerissa, Lapwing, Christopher, Badger, and Ophelia arrived.	1330
2.0 —	S.O. B.C.F.	S.O. 3rd L.C.S.	S.L.	Sail when ready. Position given was correct, *i.e.*, 57° 21′ N., 3° 2′ E. Also look out for certain 1st Flotilla boats which were running out of fuel. Report by wireless the state and position of all met.	1350
2.3 —	Admiralty	Ad. Supt., Immingham Dock Station.	L/T	Chester. Proceed at once with the work of making vessel seaworthy to proceed to another port, reporting as soon as possible time required.	1403
2.5 —	R.A. Cyclops	Admiralty	L/T	King George V., Orion, Ajax, Centurion, Conqueror, Erin, Monarch, Thunderer, Agincourt, Hercules, Vanguard, Benbow, Bellerophon, Temeraire, Revenge, Boadicea, Faulknor, Obedient, Nessus, Martial, Minion, Castor, Mischief, Mindful, Mary Rose, Narwhal, Marksman, Marvel, Ossory, Magic, Morning Star, Marne, Manners, Milbrook, Mameluke, Michael, Napier, Kempenfelt, Blanche, Bellona, Caroline, Royalist, Comus, arrived.	1345
2.5 —	*S.O. Cruisers*	*Cruisers*	S.L.	*Speed of advance 14 knots*	—
2.6 —	S.O. B.C.F.	General	Sem.	Enemy Submarines reported in 56° 44′ N., 1° 55′ E., and 56° 3′ N., 0° 16′ E., at 7.0 a.m. to-day.	1350
2.13 —	Agincourt	C.-in-C.	Sem.	**Ship was only struck by a few splinters of shell. No damage or casualties.**	1405
2.14 —	Admiral, Immingham.	Admiralty	L/T	Earle's Shipbuilding Co. could undertake repairs to Chester without delaying refit of Destroyers, but refit of Killingholme and Tithonus might be slightly delayed.	—

Date, Time of Despatch.	From	To	System.	Message.	Time of Origin.
2 JUNE 2.18 p.m	*—cont.* Commodore F.	C.-in-C. -	Tel.	Onslaught reported that 1st Lieutenant and Gunner were killed and Captain injured, also one gun out of action. Permission was given for her to return to this base yesterday Thursday at 5 a.m. She has not yet arrived. Probably she may have made some other base. Request inquiries may be made.	1415
2.27 —	Admiralty -	S.O. B.C.F. -	L/T	Telegraph brief report of your proceedings	1427
2.47 —	S.N.O. Aberdeen.	Admiralty -	L/T	Onslow arrived - - - - -	1400
2.47 —	Canterbury -	—	—	Remarks : Arrived Harwich - - -	—
2.48 —	Admiral, Immingham.	Admiralty -	L/T	*Re* Marlborough. Principal damage caused by torpedo is between 64 and 92 stations on starboard side, bulkhead on 92 station being damaged and cannot be got at on account of coal bunkers. Thickness of river water prevents examination by diver. Additional shoring of bulkheads and provision of salvage pumps which can be placed on board down below is all that can be done here. If this can be done it is considered that ship can be safely moved to River Tyne in fine weather for docking, but undesirable to risk a longer voyage. Satisfactory salvage pumps not available on Humber. Electrical salvage pumps of 300 tons per hour total capacity preferred. Can these be sent? Ship is at buoy off Immingham.	—
2.55 —	R.A. 1st B.S.-	C.-in-C. -	S.L.	Colossus. 17-in. shell passed through starboard fore superstructure and wrecked after end of it, port side, damaging boat hoisting levers, etc. Many holes in starboard side of fore superstructure from 4-in. shell splinters, several leads of wire cut and one searchlight smashed. Rangefinder B turret out of action, damaged by shell splinter. Fire-main in Captain's cabin cut through. Two men severely wounded, one losing right arm, three slightly wounded. Remaining ships not hit.	1410
3.1 — (recd.)	C.-in-C. -	S.O. B.C.F. -	L/T	Urgent. 4 Cruisers under R.A.C. 7th C.S. have been searching since yesterday but should be glad of the further ships you are sending.	1340
3.5 —	C.-in-C. -	Active -	W/T	Have you located H.M.S. Broke? Report progress.	1338
				Reply : Have thoroughly searched as far as 58° 11′ N., 2° 33′ E., and seen no signs of Broke and have not been in touch with her by W/T. My present position, course and speed 58° 30′ N., 2° 12′ E., N. 50° W., 14 knots. Gale from N.W. with heavy sea.	
3.6 —	S.N.O. Harwich.	Admiralty -	L/T	Canterbury arrived - - - - -	—

Date, Time of Despatch.	From	To	System.	Message.	Time of Origin.
2 JUNE —*cont.*					
3.15 p.m.	S.O. B.C.F.	S.O. 3rd L.C.S.	Sem.	C.-in-C. reports four Cruisers under R.A. 7th C.S. have also been looking for Warrior since yesterday. Chester is believed to be still out. I have no news of her except that she was damaged in action.	1600
3.18 —	Admiralty	Dockyards Portsmouth, Devonport, Chatham, Sheerness.	L/T	Secret. Number of men available will be required temporarily at Rosyth and probably Invergordon. Details will be communicated to you later, but meanwhile all necessary preliminaries should be made for despatch of men at short notice.	1518
3.20 —	S.O. B.C.F.	Indomitable	Sem.	In what position did you last see Chester ? Reply : In 56° 53′ N., 6° 16′ E., at 6 p.m.	1510 1515
3.20 —	**Admiralty**	**C.-in-C.**	L/T	**Have asked V.A. B.C.F. for brief report of engagement as some information must be given to-night. Report from S.O. 5th B.S. is also required. Can you amplify your report in any way?**	**1520**
3.20 —	Admiralty	Dockyard, Rosyth.	L/T	Report as soon as known numbers of Officers and men of various trades required at Rosyth from southern yards for repair of damaged ships. Preliminary notice has been given southern dockyards as to probability of men being needed North.	1520
3.21 —	Admiralty	R.A. Invergordon.	L/T	In case damaged ships should arrive at Invergordon for repair you should report immediately what additional Officers and men of various trades from southern yards you would require, also any materials needed.	1521
3.30 —	Aberdeen	Admiralty	L/T	Unity arrives 5.30 p.m.	—
3.32 —	**Moon**	**C.-in-C., R.A. Invergordon.**	W/T	**Moon and Mounsey will arrive Cromarty 8 p.m.**	**1500**
3.34 —	**S.O. 2nd C.S.**	**C.-in-C.**	W/T	**No signs of Warrior in area 17 miles South, 40 miles North and West and East of her last position. Have seen nothing of Albion and tugs. Good visibility, wind N.W. 6 to 7 somewhat heavy sea. My position at 3 p.m. 57° 53′ N., 2° 45′ E., course N 47° W., advancing 14 knots. Average percentage of coal remaining 55.**	**1501**
4.3 —	Gorleston	Admiralty	L/T	Five Light Cruisers, 10 Destroyers bearing E. eight miles, steaming S. 14 knots.	—
4.6 —	Spurn Head, W.S.S.	Admiralty	L/T	4 p.m. Laforey, Lawford, Lance, Lasso, Lookout, Laverock, Lark, Marlow, sailed.	—
4.7 —	S.O.3rdL.C.S.	S.O. B.C.F.	Sem.	Chester passed 3rd L.C.S. on her way to Humber with wounded.	1520
4.8 —	**C.-in-C.**	**Active**	W/T	**Are you in visual or W/T touch with Broke?**	—
4.17 —	**Revenge**	**C.-in-C.**	S.L.	**Revenge has no damage or casualties**	**1615**
4.20 —	C.-in-C. Rosyth.	Admiralty	L/T	Champion, Mænad, Negro, Napier, Phœnix arrived.	1535
4.20 —	**C.-in-C.**	**Admiralty**	L/T	**Abdiel laid mines on night of 31st—1st in area enclosed by parallel 55° 13′ N. and 55° 2′ N. and meridian 7° 37′ E. and 7° 25′ E.**	—

Date, Time of Despatch.	From	To	System.	Message.	Time of Origin.
2 JUNE —*cont.*					
4.30 —	Active	Constance	W/T	By dead reckoning we passed at 4 p.m. Am now steering N. 60° W., 14 knots. Request instructions.	—
4.46 p.m.	Admiral, Immingham.	Admiralty	L/T	Pensioner Chief Stoker Newcombe of Shark died on board Danish steamer Vidar, Body now at Hull. Request instructions.	—
4.50 —	Carysfort	—	—	Remarks : Harwich Force entered swept channel.	—
4.53 —	C.-in-C.	Active	W/T	**Have you enough fuel to continue search for another 24 hours? Reply : Have sufficient coal for 24 hours at 16 knots, alongside boilers, after which only foremost boiler will be available with coal from reserve bunkers. State of weather prevents any coal being transferred to other boiler rooms.**	**1640**
5.5 —	S.O. B.C.F.	Captain D13 and S.O. 1st Flotilla.	Sem.	Destroyers have steam at two hours' notice. Arrange usual stand by divisions.	1645
5.6 —	S.O. B.C.F.	S.O. 3rd L.C.S. Lydiard.	Sem.	Do not sail. Await orders	1700
5.7 —	C.-in-C. Rosyth.	Admiralty	L/T	Crew of Warrior will have sufficient clothing to travel in by Saturday evening. There is no reserve of bedding or sufficient clothing for kitting up men in this port. Submitted Officers and men of Warrior may be sent to their depôts on Saturday and granted leave after kitting up. Reply : Approved	2030
5.17 —	Nonsuch	Cromarty S.S.	W/T	Acasta and Nonsuch at 5 p.m. 20 miles East of Aberdeen steaming eight knots. All is well. (*Received by C.-in-C. 6.17 p.m.*)	1700
5.35 —	Naval Depôt, North Shields.	Admiralty	L/T	Pigeon expects to pass latitude of May Island 6 p.m.	1700
5.54 —	Dockyard, Rosyth.	Admiralty	L/T	Princess Royal, Tiger and Southampton placed in basin for making seaworthy.	1734
5.58 —	Graham, Amsterdam.	Admiralty	L/T	One British sailor wounded and 51 Germans are due at Ymuiden to-night, picked up by steam trawler. More are likely to follow.	—
6.3 —	C.-in-C. Rosyth.	Admiralty	L/T	Defender arrived	1750
6.9 —	Constance	Active	W/T	My position, course and speed at 6 p.m. 58° 38′ N., 1° 38′ E., S. 56° W., 12 knots. As Broke may be making nearest land steer parallel course to the southward to me.	1740
6.27 —	*Commodore F*	*Magic*	Sem.	*Did you fire any torpedoes Wednesday night? If so, what time? Reply : First torpedo was fired when Castor was fired on. Torpedo apparently went astern. Second torpedo was fired about 11.30 when Castor was fired on by a group of ships, but am unable to say result of this one.*	1824
6.39 —	Peterhead	Albion III.	W/T	Albion to return to Peterhead	1815
6.45 —	S.O. B.C.F.	S.O. 3rd L.C.S. and Lydiard.	S.L.	Sail as ordered forthwith	1850

Date, Time of Despatch.	From	To	System.	Message.	Time of Origin.
2 JUNE 6.52 p.m.	—cont. S.O. 2nd C.S.	Shannon and Hampshire.	S.L.	Constance may be sighted any time after 7 p.m	1850
6.55 —	S.O. 2nd C.S.	C.-in-C.	W/T	My position, course and speed at 6 p.m. 58° 9′ N., 1° 45′ E., N. 47° W., advancing 14 knots, spread, looking out for H.M.S. Broke.	1835
6.55 —	Admiralty	C.-in-C.	L/T	The loss of the Battle Cruisers and Cruisers will necessitate a reorganisation and reduction in the number of squadrons of Battle Cruisers and the Light Cruisers associated with them and Armoured Cruisers. What arrangement do you propose?	1855
7.5 —	C.-in-C.	Admiralty	L/T	Malaya damage consists of two or more holes under water, one 6-in. gun completely out of action, upper deck in the vicinity drooped, superplating in the vicinity badly damaged. Roof plate of turret requires refastening and loading bogey of turret jammed. Extensive wiring and renewal of piping required. Propose to send her Invergordon tomorrow Saturday. Admiral Invergordon informed. Barham Officers' heads completely wrecked. Superstructure cabins port side and Gun room wrecked. Extensive damage main deck, lower deck abreast of forward medical distributing station. All pipes under deck broken and extensive wiring required. All cabins in after cabin flat wrecked and main deck badly damaged. Considered this ship case for Southern Dockyard. Request early reply if she can be taken. Devonport preferred if possible.	—
7.5 —	Minotaur	—	—	Remarks : Challenged and exchanged pendants with Constance.	—
7.7 —	Shannon	S.O. 2nd C.S.	S.L.	Re C.-in-C.'s cypher 0630 of to-day. Was Broke's Latitude 57° 10′ or 58° 10′? Active has searched 58°. Reply : Those instructions were cancelled-	1900 1920
7.10 —	Admiralty	Admiral, Immingham.	L/T	Salvage ship Linnet left Dover 11 a.m. to-day for Humber, speed nine knots. She is fully equipped with all salvage appliances and ample pumping power. Captain Pomeroy, Admiralty Salvage Officer, is proceeding by train with orders to report to you to-morrow morning.	1910
7.10 —	C.-in-C.	Admiralty	L/T	Our losses : Queen Mary, Indefatigable, Invincible, Defence, Black Prince, Sparrowhawk, Ardent, Fortune, Tipperary, Turbulent. Also missing at present : Shark, Nestor, Nomad. Severely damaged : Acasta, Warrior, Broke, Marlborough, Malaya, Warspite. Damaged : Barham. Some Battle Cruisers, Light Cruisers and Destroyers damaged but efficient. Known enemy's losses : One Battleship Kaiser class blown up in Destroyer attack. One Battleship Kaiser class believed sunk by gunfire. One Battle Cruiser, probably Derfflinger, heavily engaged by battlefleet	—

Date, Time of Despatch.	From	To	System.	Message.	Time of Origin.
2 JUNE	—*cont.*			seen to be disabled and stopping. Lutzow seen to be seriously damaged. One Battle Cruiser considered by V.A.C. Battle Cruisers to be blown up. No particulars. One Light Cruiser, six Destroyers seen to sink. At least two more Light Cruisers seen to be disabled. Three other Battleships that were engaged seen to be repeatedly hit. One Submarine rammed and sunk. Fuller report follows.	
7.30 p.m.	Gosling, Gothenburg.	Admiralty -	L/T	Swedish S.S. Balder arrived here to-day with cutter Nomad and smaller boat marked S. 54.	—
7.35 —	Carysfort -	—	—	Remarks : Carysfort secured - - -	—
7.35 —	C.-in-C. -	S.Os. of Squadrons and Commodore F.	Sem. and Tel.	Report when ships under your command are fuelled and ready for action. Replies : 4th L.C.S., with the exception of Constance and one 4-in. gun in Calliope, 7.35 p.m. 4th B.S., midnight. 2nd B.S., 4.45 a.m. 1st B.S., 6 a.m.	1920 / —
7.42 —	C.-in-C. -	S.O. 2nd C.S. -	W/T	Send Hampshire to base - - -	1926
7.50 —	Constance -	S.O. 2nd C.S.-	S.L.	Constance and Active have searched to the north and east, and are now searching towards Peterhead unless you have other instructions for me. Reply : I have no instructions.	1945
8.5 —	Shannon -	S.O. 2nd C.S.	S.L.	*Assuming Broke in a northern position last night and damaged forward she will probably have borne up for Norway or be laying to. Submitted if we are to search for Broke we should make broad sweep towards Skersund and Listor Fiord. By steering S.E. we might get into wireless touch with her.*	1955
8.26 —	Ad. Supt. Newcastle-on-Tyne.	Admiralty -	L/T	Achilles docked. Will be completed and leave 6 p.m. to-morrow Saturday.	1847
8.30 —	Active -	—	—	Remarks : Sighted 2nd C.S. - - -	—
8.33 —	S.N.O. Harwich.	Admiralty -	L/T	Carysfort, Cleopatra, Conquest, Aurora, Undaunted, Lightfoot, Nimrod, Mentor, Miranda, Manly, Myngs, Murray, Milne, Loyal, Leonidas, arrived.	—
8.40 —	C.-in-C. Rosyth.	Admiralty -	L/T	3rd L.C.S., Moorsom, Morris and Liberty sailed.	1955
8.40 —	Minotaur -	—	—	Remarks : Sighted Active bearing N.W. -	—
8.44 —	C.-in-C. Rosyth.	Admiralty -	L/T	Fearless arrived - - - -	2000
8.50 —	C.-in-C. Rosyth.	Admiralty -	L/T	Pigeon arrived - - - -	1958
8.55 —	C.-in-C. Rosyth.	Admiralty -	L/T	Request I may be informed whether any hopes may be held out to inquirers as to fate of Nestor. Reply : Nestor, Nomad and Shark are considered lost.	—
8.58 —	Constance -	Active -	W/T	I intend to steer present course during the night. At 3.30 a.m. N. 11° E. and return to base.	2030
9.0 —	Active -	Cochrane -	S.L.	What is your position, course and speed? Reply : 58° 25' N., 0° 48' E., N. 47° W., 14 knots	—

Date, Time of Despatch.	From	To	System.	Message.	Time of Origin.
2 JUNE —*cont.* 9.1 p.m.	**S.O. 2nd C.S.**	**C.-in-C.**	W/T	Possible position of Broke in Latitude of 57° given in your 0630 has not been searched yet. Request instructions as to future movements.	2052
				Reply : Continue the search for Broke tomorrow Saturday to S. and W. of area already searched by you and return to base by dawn 4th June.	2115
9.6 —	S.N.O. Aberdeen.	Admiralty	L/T	Nonsuch arrived - - - - -	2030
9.11 —	S.O. B.C.F.	S.O. 2nd B.C.S.	F.L.	Have you ascertained whether there are any survivors from Indefatigable?	2048
				Reply : Have been informed a single survivor was picked up. Will endeavour to verify. Have also tried to trace man in hospital and elsewhere.	2110
9.17 —	R.A. Cyclops	Admiralty	L/T	Achates arrived - - - - -	2100
9.20 —	*S.O. Cruisers*	*Cruisers*	F.L.	*Proceed at 12 knots at 10 p.m.* - - -	—
9.22 —	R.A. Cyclops	Admiralty	L/T	Relentless arrived - - - - -	2105
9.35 —	Minotaur	—	—	Remarks : Sighted Submarine on port bow. Submarine made O.L. (?) with arc lamp. 9.38 opened fire. 9.42 Submarine sunk.	—
9.44 —	R.A. Invergordon.	Admiralty	L/T	Moon and Mounsey arrived - - -	2120
9.45 —	**C.-in-C.**	**Admiralty**	L/T	**Battlefleet at four hours' notice and ready for action.**	—
9.47 —	*S.O. B.C.F.*	*S.O. 1st B.C.S.*	Tel.	*Have you ascertained whether there are any survivors from Queen Mary ?*	2145
				Reply : It is understood that four Midshipmen and 13 men were picked up by Laurel.	2215
9.48 —	S.O.2ndB.C.S.	Captain D1 and D13.	F.L.	Request you will inform me if any survivors of Indefatigable were rescued?	2118
				Reply from Captain D1 : I regret to say what I saw I do not think it possible there was a single survivor. There were certainly none rescued.	2210
				Reply from Captain D13 : None of the Destroyers of 13th Flotilla have reported having survivors of Indefatigable on board.	2145
10.13 —	Active	Constance	W/T	My position, course and speed at 9 p.m. 58° 25' N., 0° 48' E., S. 56° W., 12 knots. Am I to follow your instructions in returning to base at 3.30 a.m.	2140
				Reply : Use your own judgment as to returning to base.	2300
10.35 —	*S.O. Cruisers*	*Cruisers*	W/T	*At 11 p.m. alter course together to S. by E., 14 knots, without signal.*	2227
10.40 —	Dunfermline	Admiralty	L/T	Arrangements have been made to place Tiger in No. 2 dock, a.m. to-morrow Saturday. Repairs small.	1957
10.45 —	S.O.3rdL.C.S.	S.O. 2nd C.S.	W/T	My position, course and speed at 10 p.m. 56° 17' N., 2° 17' W., East, 18 knots. Proceeding to search for Warrior and Destroyers unaccounted for. Request area you will search to-morrow Saturday and area already searched so that I may search elsewhere.	2230

Date, Time of Despatch.	From	To	System.	Message.	Time of Origin.
2 JUNE *—cont.*					
				Reply : Area searched 57° 5′ N to 58° N., 2° E. to 4° E., 13 miles N.E. and S.W. of a line through 57° 49′ N., 2° 58′ E., to 0° 30′ E. My position 11 p.m. 58° 49′ N., 0° 5′ W. My course and speed S. by E. 14 knots, sweeping 12 miles either side of this line till 4 a.m. Course will be altered so as to sweep a line parallel to this to the northward and westward.	2335
11.5 p.m.	C.-in-C.	Admiralty	L/T	Submarine sunk by gunfire by **Minotaur** in 58° 32′ N., 0° 20′ E., at 9.35 p.m. 2nd June. *Further message from C.-in-C., 1.4 p.m, June 4th :* After investigation I am convinced that Submarine was E.30. She was uninjured and has arrived at Blyth.	—
11.8 —	S.N.O. Aberdeen.	Admiralty	L/T	Acasta arrived · · · · ·	2120
11.17 —	S.N.O. Harwich.	Admiralty	L/T	Laforey, Lawford, Lookout, Laverock, Lance, Lasso, Lysander, Lark arrived.	—
11.30 —	C.-in-C.	Admiralty	L/T	At 3.50 p.m. on 31st May V.A.C. Battle Cruiser Fleet reported himself engaged with Enemy Battle Cruisers steering about E.S.E., Enemy to the northward. Indefatigable was sunk 10 minutes after commencement of action by shell exploding in magazine. Queen Mary half an hour later, probably same cause. Subsequent to this 5th B.S., which had been in the rear, got into action and shortly afterwards Enemy's battlefleet, which had been reported as in sight by 2nd L.C.S., appeared and V.A. B.C.F. turned round, followed by 5th B.S. I had sent 3rd B.C.S., which was 20 miles ahead of me, to support B.C.F. on learning of the Enemy being in sight, the battlefleet being at this time over 30 miles to the North, steering for the scene of action at 20 knots. 3rd B.C.S. apparently joined B.C.F. about 5 p.m., and Invincible was blown up either by shell in magazine or mine or torpedo. At 5.44 p.m. Cruisers and Light Cruisers ahead of battlefleet were seen to be altering course to port, battlefleet's course then being S.E. by South. The weather was very misty, visibility being about six miles to the westward and less to the eastward Cruisers and Light Cruisers opened fire as they turned, and heavy fire was also heard on the starboard bow and flashes were seen in that direction. There was much doubt as to the situation as the firing was going on all round and nothing was in sight, but at 5.50 p.m. I sighted our Battle Cruisers bearing S.S.W. standing E.S.E. and engaged. I reduced speed to allow the Battle Cruisers to pass ahead of me and	—

Date, Time of Despatch.	From	To	Sys- tem.	Message.	Time of Origin.
2 JUNE 11.30 p.m.	*—cont.* C.-in-C.	Admiralty	L/T— *contd.*	deployed on port wing column, course S.E. by E. Some ships of 1st C.S. had prior to deployment altered course to S.W., apparently to reach western end of battle line. They then got between battlefleet and the Enemy, who were still not in sight from battlefleet and at 6.15 p.m. Defence was hit several times and blew up, a second ship, probably Warrior, being also heavily hit. At 6.14 p.m. Enemy's three-funnel Cruiser with two Destroyers was seen approaching from southward. Iron Duke and other Battleships opened heavy fire at 10,000 yards. She was very heavily hit and passed out of sight. At 6.22 three ships of König class were sighted by Iron Duke bearing about South, range about 11,500 yards. They were heavily engaged by battlefleet and a great many hits were observed. At 6.30 p.m. they all turned to starboard and passed out of sight. At 6.35 p.m. our Battle Cruisers were seen turning to starboard. At 6.44 p.m. battlefleet altered course by 9 Pendant to South. Wreck of Invincible was passed at 7.4 p.m. At 7.2 p.m. Marl-borough, which had previously avoided three torpedoes, was hit by a torpedo or mine. Enemy Battle Cruiser, probably Derfflinger, was seen about this time and heavily engaged by large number of ships and apparently disabled. At 7.15 p.m. an Enemy Destroyer flotilla supported by Cruisers was seen approaching from the westward at about 9,000 yards and battlefleet was turned four points to port when the Destroyers turned to fire. Destroyers were heavily engaged by battlefleet and several were seen to be hit. At 7.35 p.m. battlefleet turned to S.W. to endeavour to regain touch with Enemy, and Enemy's battlefleet were sighted for a few minutes to the westward at 7.55. At 8 p.m. the battlefleet were turned to West by divisions to close but could not get in touch, but the B.C.F. were heard to be firing from a position about six miles ahead of the battlefleet. The battlefleet in the endeavour to close had altered course at intervals from S.E. by E. to West. At 8.22 another Destroyer attack took place and the fleet was turned away, and 4th L.C.S. and flotillas sent to attack Enemy Destroyers. 4th L.C.S. sank at least two Destroyers. At 9 p.m. light being very bad, mist in-creasing, fleet was turned to a course South to pass between Mine Area 1 and Horn Reef in order to intercept Enemy should he return by either Sylt or Ems channels. Flotillas were disposed five	

Date, Time of Despatch.	From	To	System.	Message.	Time of Origin.
2 JUNE 11.30 p.m.	—cont. C.-in-C.	Admiralty	L/T— contd.	miles astern of fleet. At 10 p.m. Abdiel was despatched to lay mines to the southward of Horn Reef L.V. which operation she carried out successfully. During the night, 11th and 4th Destroyer Flotillas became heavily engaged with Enemy's forces of Battle Cruisers and Light Cruisers. 4th Destroyer Flotilla suffered considerably. A large number of torpedoes were fired and several are claimed to have hit. At 2 a.m. 12th Destroyer Flotilla attacked a line of Battleships of the Kaiser class which were steering S.E. by S. The third Battleship in the line was blown up. At 2.30 a.m. 1st June the fleet being then to the southwestward of Horn Reef, course was altered to North to collect the fleet and Destroyers in readiness to renew the action. Visibility three miles. V.A.C. 1st B.S. transferred his flag from Marlborough to Revenge, Marlborough being detached to dock. Our Destroyers did not rejoin till 9.30 a.m. owing to low visibility and uncertainty of positions. A Zeppelin was sighted 3.45 a.m. and driven off by gunfire. The whole of area from the Horn Reef up to position where the action commenced was thoroughly swept by the battlefleet well opened out and B.C.F., the water being traversed several times. A good deal of wreckage was seen but no Enemy's ships, and at 11 a.m. all our disabled ships being then on their way home the fleet steered for bases. The conditions were most difficult on both 31st May and 1st June. The visibility was extremely low to the eastward and at times almost as bad to the westward, but occasionally and particularly when the Battle Cruiser action was taking place the visibility to the westward was distinctly good whilst to the eastward it was very bad. The Enemy had immense advantage in this respect. During Battle Cruiser action the R.A.C. 5th B.S. reports that when he came into action he could only fire at the flashes of the Enemy guns whilst the visibility in the opposite direction was as much as 12 miles. When the battlefleet arrived the Enemy showed no inclination to fight, and the thick mist rendered evasion of action easy. The greater part of the fighting fell to the lot of the B.C.F. and 5th B.S., and I cannot praise too highly the spirit animating the Officers and men of these squadrons and of the whole fleet. It was worthy of the best traditions of the Service. The Destroyer flotillas pressed home their attacks with great determination and	

Date, Time of Despatch.	From	To	System.	Message.	Time of Origin.
2 JUNE 11.30 a.m.	*—cont.* **C.-in-C.**	Admiralty	L/T— *contd.*	success, ably supported by the Light Cruiser squadrons. The battlefleet took the fullest advantage of the few opportunities of engaging which the weather conditions, the short amount of daylight and the Enemy's tactics afforded. I deplore the loss of many gallant Officers and men, but they died, as the wounded are behaving, with the greatest fortitude.	
3 JUNE 12.10 a.m.	S.O. B.C.F.	Admiralty	L/T	Request that an inspector of heavy ordnance be sent to inspect guns of B.C.F.	—
12.16 —	S.O. B.C.F.	Admiralty	L/T	Left base 10.15 p.m. 30th May with Lion, 1st B.C.S., New Zealand, Indefatigable, 5th B.S. less Queen Elizabeth, 1st, 2nd, 3rd L.C.S., Fearless, nine of 1st Destroyer Flotilla, Champion, 10 of 13th Destroyer Flotilla, eight boats of Harwich Force and Engadine. Sighted Enemy Light Cruisers 2.20 p.m. 31st May. Engadine launched seaplane. We sighted five Enemy Battle Cruisers and Destroyers 3.30 p.m. 56° 52′ N., 5° 22′ E. Engaged them at 3.48 p.m., steering E.S.E., bearing N.N.E. parallel courses. 4 p.m. Indefatigable blew up, magazine exploded by shell fire. 4.26 p.m. Queen Mary blew up, same cause. 4.8 p.m. 5th B.S. appeared to engage rear of Enemy. 4.30 p.m. Enemy's Destroyers moved out to attack us and were met by our Destroyers who repelled them and attacked Enemy's Battle Cruisers with torpedo. Nestor and Nomad did not return. Remainder accounted for. 4.38 p.m. 2nd L.C.S. stationed ahead reported Enemy's battlefleet ahead. 4.42 p.m. sighted Enemy's battlefleet and altered course to North. Enemy Battle Cruisers also altered course. 5th B.S. on meeting formed astern and continued engagement. At this time there were distinct signs of Enemy fire being overpowered, and third ship was seen in flames with clouds of smoke and seemed to disappear. We gradually altered course round head of line, which was reduced in speed to N.E. by N. 5.56 p.m. sighted Grand Fleet. 6 p.m. Enemy appeared to be severely hit bearing S.E.; they hauled off to starboard. We conformed. 6.15 p.m. again sighted Enemy's Battleships S.S.W. Defence and Warrior crossed our bows from port to starboard, causing us to haul to port to clear them and to cease firing. 6.21 p.m. 3rd B.C.S. joined from Grand Fleet, taking station ahead of Lion, engaging Enemy's Battle Cruisers who fired on Invincible. She blew up 6.36 p.m., salvo in magazine. Lion proceeding full speed drew ahead	—

Date, Time of Despatch.	From	To	System.	Message.	Time of Origin.
3 JUNE —*cont.* 12.16 a.m.	S.O. B.C.F. -	Admiralty -	L/T— *contd.*	and ordered 3rd B.C.S. to take station astern. Reduced to 18 knots and closed Enemy's van, concentrating heavy fire on leading ship. Forced them to alter course and led battlefleet so that we were between Enemy and his base, steering S.W. in fluctuating light we lost sight of Enemy. 7.58 p.m. ordered 3rd L.C.S. and 1st L.C.S. who were ahead to sweep to westward to locate head of Enemy's line. 8.22 p.m. Enemy re-opened on Light Cruisers. 8.30 p.m. we again sighted and engaged leading Enemy Battle Cruiser, only two being sighted. She was struck by two salvoes, burst into flames with columns of smoke, heavy explosion taking place on board. She disappeared. Enemy Battleships were then sighted and opened fire on us, necessitating our hauling out to port. Minotaur in sight on our port quarter reported Grand Fleet not in sight, so at 9.30 p.m. altered course to South 17 knots in accordance with C.-in-C.'s order, placing Light Cruisers ahead and to starboard to act as a screen. Owing to mist and fighting for some periods at extreme visibility no accurate data of damage to Enemy can be given but considered to be great. Battle Cruisers were not engaged after nightfall. I desire to express my great regret at loss of Rear-Admiral Hood, Captains Sowerby, Prowse and Cay, and the many gallant Officers and men. There were few survivors. Rear-Admiral Hood brought his squadron into action in a most gallant, effective and inspiring manner. His death is a loss to the nation.	
1.4 —	C.-in-C. -	Active, Constance.	W/T	Return to Scapa - - - - -	0104
2.18 —	S.O. B.C.F. -	S.O. 3rd L.C.S.	W/T	3rd L.C.S. should search area S. of 57° 10′ N. and E. of 3° 30′ E. Warrior would probably drift two or three miles an hour to S.E.	0147
4.29 —	Broke - -	S.O. 2nd C.S.-	W/T	Approximate position 3 a.m. 3rd June 56° 21′ N., 0° 12′ E., course W., 6 knots. Will you inform S.N.O. Tyne River Broke arrives damaged 6 p.m. 3rd. Require tug on arrival, also living accommodation and clothing for 160 men. 14 cot cases. (*Passed to C.-in-C., S.O. 3rd L.C.S., Bonaventure.*)	0330
5.19 —	S.O.3rdL.C.S.	C.-in-C. and S.O. B.C.F.	W/T	Torpedo passed under Gloucester 4 a.m. Lat. 56° 48′ N., 0° 33′ E.	0440
6.7 —	C.-in-C. -	S.O. 2nd C.S. -	W/T	Return to base - - - - -	0607
6.10 —	R.A. Cyclops	Admiralty -	L/T	Hampshire arrived - - - - -	0530

Date, Time of Despatch.	From	To	System.	Message.	Time of Origin.
3 JUNE *—cont.* 8.57 a.m.	Talisman	Admiralty	W/T	Submarines at rendezvous nought one have been attacked by Enemy Submarines. Submarines have dived. Talisman has left vicinity but will be within W/T touch of Submarines.	0845
				Reply : Return to base at once	1055
9.7 —	Immingham-	Admiralty	L/T	Survivors state Shark was in action with Enemy's Battle Cruisers and Destroyers for an hour from 6 p.m. Engines and steering gear disabled about 6.15 p.m. All guns out of action except one by 6.30 p.m. Ship sunk by torpedo from Enemy's Destroyer 7 p.m. They think they are only survivors. Torpedo-man states torpedo from Shark hit four-funnel German Cruiser but does not know whether ship sank. Report by letter follows.	—
11.20 —	North Shields	Admiralty	L/T	Officer commanding Spitfire reports that he torpedoed a four-funnel Cruiser German of the Königsberg class and that she was seen to heel over.	1050
11.46 — (recd.)	C.-in-C.	S.O. B.C.F.	L/T	**I trust you are well. Please accept my sincere congratulations on the action of the forces under your Command under the difficult and disadvantageous conditions of light and weather which existed for you. The heavy losses which I deeply deplore appear to be largely due to those conditions, and your ships inflicted very severe damage to the Enemy although the great defensive strength of their ships saved more from becoming total losses. Words cannot express my deep sympathy with relatives and friends of the gallant officers and men who have gone under.**	1030
				Reply. Many thanks for your kind and sympathetic telegram and for congratulations which I am conveying to ships here. Thank you I am well.	1235
1.7 p.m.	Immingham-	Admiralty	L/T	Marlborough fore part damaged to 66 station. Damage to starboard side from 66 to 111, centre of damage about 90 bulkhead, outer and inner bottom apparently destroyed in wake. Water in following compartments : starboard wings and bunkers from 66 to 111 and watertight compartments 66 to 90 starboard, all of which are full up to main or middle deck. Outer parts of 90 bulkhead destroyed. Starboard longitudinal bulkhead "A" boiler room badly bulged and weakened, with after door so distorted as to admit considerable quantities of water into boiler room, and it is considered these bunkers are fully open to the sea. Bulkhead has been shored as much as possible. Propose vessel be docked in Tyne floating dock if possible to effect temporary repairs to bulkhead and outer bottom	—

Date, Time of Despatch.	From	To	System.	Message.	Time of Origin.
3 JUNE	—*cont.*			before proceeding elsewhere for permanent repairs. Nothing has been done with ship's divers owing to strong tide and muddiness of river. Draught of water forward 33 ft. 6 in., aft 31 ft. 0 in. List to starboard $2\frac{3}{4}°$ with about 200 tons of trimming water port side. Previous to trimming, list was $6\frac{1}{2}°$. Ship's Officers, Admiralty Officers and yard concur. Vessel will be ready to proceed to Tyne Sunday night for docking Monday morning.	
1.20 —	C.-in-C.	Admiralty and C.-in-C. Devonport.	L/T	Barham will leave p.m. to-day Saturday for Devonport. Following is damage as ascertained. Two holes in embrasure plating starboard side abreast forward 6-in. gun. Main deck plating starboard side abreast B turret and over medical store and distributing station will require complete renewal in places. Beams and brackets in vicinity of connecting deck to barbette buckled. Auxiliary W/T cabinet wrecked, requires complete renewal. Exhaust fans and trunking to oil driven generating room and hydraulic engine room between main deck and upper deck will require renewal. All ventilating fans, heaters, etc., supplying mess deck and all brine pipes, electric leads, voice pipes underneath upper deck in vicinity require replacing. Middle deck in medical distributing station, voice pipes, electric leads, etc., under middle deck in lower conning tower flat require renewal in places. Hatch to medical store requires renewal. 82 bulkhead perforated in places and buckled slightly between main deck and upper deck. Starboard side new watertight door required. Officers' heads on forecastle deck level aft completely shattered. All trunks, ventilation and aerial, in vicinity completely wrecked. Gun room and cabin port side of upper deck wrecked. Trunk to wing engine room, ventilator and ventilation trunks and fans in vicinity badly damaged. Holes in upper and main deck between 184 and 186 stations port side. Pipes under and ventilation fan D 65 and trunking in vicinity require renewal. All cabins between 237 station and Admiral's dining cabin completely gutted. All pipes, wiring, etc., ventilation trunking in this flat will require renewal. Shot hole in ship's side in this vicinity, and large holes in middle and main deck. Cabins between these stations on middle deck will require renewal. Side frames and brackets connecting to main deck under badly buckled and distorted. No apparent damage to side armour plates. Request all material possible be hastened.	1320

Date, Time of Despatch.	From	To	System.	Message.	Time of Origin.
3 JUNE —*cont.* 2.40 p.m.	C.-in-C.	Admiralty	L/T	Urgent. **My report of action should be corrected as follows. The three torpedoes were avoided by Marlborough at 8 p.m., not prior to 7.2 p.m. These torpedoes were probably from Enemy's Destroyers. Rear divisions of battlefleet were engaged with Enemy's battlefleet for considerable time between 7 and 8 p.m., although Enemy was only visible from van for short period. Submit communications to press** *re* **Enemy's casualties and our own, and general history of action, may be amended to agree with my reports of the action. Last night's communiqué magnifies ours and minimises Enemy's casualties, and gives somewhat false impression of action generally.**	—
3.6 —	C.-in-C	Admiralty	L/T	**Barham sails to-day Saturday for Devonport by Minch and Irish Sea. Two Destroyers from Scapa will screen her as far as the Smalls. It is submitted that they may be relieved there at 3.30 a.m., Monday, 5th June, by two Destroyers from the Southern Command to screen her to Devonport.**	—
3.10 —	C.-in-C.	S.N.O. Tyne	L/T	**Your 1050. Konigsberg had only 3 funnels report time, position, and class of ship torpedoed by Spitfire. Reply. Spitfire reports about 7 p.m., 31st May, position unknown, 4 tall funnels, attacked from N.W., torpedoes seen to hit.**	1510 2252
4.11 —	S.O. B.C.F.	S.O. 3rd L.C.S.	W/T	What is your position, course and speed? Reply : My position, course and speed 56° 28′ N., 5° 13′ E., course S.E., 16.	1450 1530
4.49 —	Dublin	Bonaventure	W/T	Landrail and Termagant now screening me to Tyne are ordered to proceed from there to Harwich. Should they keep to War Channel from Tyne to Sunk L.V. If not, request route.	1425
4.28 —	Newton S.S.	Admiralty	L/T	3rd, 3.30 p.m. Position, course and speed Dublin and two T.B.Ds. N.E. nine miles, South 18. Four Destroyers with Broke now proceeding W., 14 knots.	—
4.56 —	Admiralty	C.-in-C.	L/T	**Following from H.M. the King. I am deeply touched by the message which you have sent me on behalf of the Grand Fleet. It reaches me on the morrow of a battle which has once more displayed the splendid gallantry of the Officers and men under your command. I mourn the loss of brave men, many of them personal friends of my own, who have fallen in their country's cause. Yet even more do I regret that the German High Seas Fleet, in spite of its heavy losses, was enabled by the misty weather to evade the full consequences of an**	—

Date, Time of Despatch.	From	To	System.	Message.	Time of Origin.
3 JUNE —*cont.*					
				encounter they have always professed to desire, but for which when the opportunity arrived they showed no inclination. Though the retirement of the Enemy immediately after the opening of the general engagement robbed us of the opportunity of gaining a decisive victory, the events of last Wednesday amply justify my confidence in the valour and efficiency of the fleets under your command.	
5.45 p.m.	Tynemouth. W.S.S.	Admiralty	L/T	Dublin entered Tyne. Landrail, Termagant passed station South.	—
6.15 —	Admiralty	R.A. East Coast and S.N.O. Tyne.	L/T	Marlborough should proceed to Tyne tomorrow evening if ready.	1815
6.30 —	R.A. Cyclops	Admiralty	L/T	Minotaur, Cochrane, Shannon, Duke of Edinburgh arrived.	—
7.0 —	S.O. B.C.F.	General	S.L.	Following telegram received from C.-in-C. G.F. begins : Please accept my sincere congratulations on the action of the forces under your command, under the difficult and disadvantageous conditions of light which existed for you. Your ships inflicted very severe damage to the Enemy. Words cannot express my deep sympathy with relatives and friends of the gallant Officers and men who have gone under. Ends. I wish to add my own congratulations to those of our C.-in-C. and my great sympathy with relatives and friends of those who died so gloriously. I am even prouder than ever of my command. No Admiral could have wished to be better served. Thank you.	1940
7.47 — (recd.)	C.-in-C.	S.O. B.C.F.	L/T	Please direct Captain of Warrior to report whether all secret and confidential matter was removed from Warrior or destroyed.	1910
9 — (recd.)	Admiralty	S.O. B.C.F.	L/T	Can you give probable names of Enemy's Battle Cruisers on 31st May ? Did you identify Von der Tann or was a new vessel there ?	
10.10 p.m.	S.O. B.C.F.	Battle Cruisers	F.L.	*Please inform me what Battle Cruisers you identified and the sequence in which they were formed. State which you engaged and their positions in the line. This is to identify what Enemy Battle Cruisers were present. Reply as early as possible.*	2135
	Princess Royal	—	—	Reply : *Lutzow, Derfflinger, Seydlitz, Moltke, Von der Tann. At the commencement Princess Royal concentrated on leading ship.*	0700
	Tiger	—	—	*Hindenburg, Lützow, Derfflinger, Seydlitz, Moltke. Engaged Seydlitz, fourth ship in the line, until Queen Mary sank, then Derfflinger, third ship.*	0815

Date, Time of Despatch.	From	To	System.	Message.	Time of Origin.
3 JUNE—*cont.*	*Indomitable*	—	—	*In action at 6.30 p.m. Seydlitz, Derfflinger and another. We engaged Derfflinger. In action at 8.30 p.m. Seydlitz and either Derfflinger or a Battleship. We engaged Seydlitz.*	
	Inflexible	—	—	*Cannot identify any German Battle Cruiser. It is considered that Inflexible was only engaged with German Dreadnought Battleships and Light Cruisers.*	—
11.20 p.m. (recd.)	C.-in-C.	S.O. B.C.F.	L/T	What Battle Cruisers are fit for action at present ?	2305
				Reply. Ships ready for immediate service New Zealand, Indomitable, Inflexible. Ships whose fighting efficiency is impaired and whose seaworthiness is not complete, Lion, Princess Royal, Tiger. These could fight in emergency.	0006
4 JUNE 12.5 a.m. (recd.)	C.-in-C.	S.O. B.C.F.	L/T	Warrior's report 31st May just received. Call on Captain to report exact condition of ship when abandoned and chances of her remaining afloat in the heavy weather which prevailed on 1st June.	2340
12.38 —	C.-in-C.	S.O. 3rd L.C.S.	W/T	Report area searched yesterday	0005
				Reply to C.-in-C. and S.O. B.C.F.: Area enclosed by following lines will be completed 8 a.m. from 57° 5′ N., 3° E., 76 miles E. by S., 20 miles S. by W., 50 miles S.E., 30 miles S.W., 120 miles N.W. Bow of Destroyer, nationality unknown, found 56° 25′ N., 6° 40′ E.	0125
8.35 —	C.-in-C.	S.O. 3rd L.C.S.	W/T	Priority. Search between Lat. 57° 0′ N., 57° 30′ N., Long. 4° 0′ E., 5° 0′ E.	0835
9.25 — (recd.)	C.-in-C.	S.O. B.C.F.	L/T	Ask Captain of Warrior when he last saw Black Prince and what her position was then with reference to Battle Fleet.	0910
9.40 —	S.O. B.C.F.	Admiralty	L/T	From reports of ships present it appears that German Battle Cruisers engaged were Lützow, Moltke, Derfflinger, Von der Tann and one new vessel of greater displacement than Lützow. Visibility made identification extremely difficult.	—
10.22 —	S.O. 3rd L.C.S.	C.-in-C.	W/T	My position 56° 15′ N., 3° E. Have just commenced unsearched strip extending 55 miles E. by S. Propose subject to your approval complete and then search area ordered, finishing 2000 instead of 1600. Reply : Approved.	0930
11.44 — (recd.)	C.-in-C.	S.O. B.C.F.	L/T	Urgent. Priority. For Captain of Warrior. Hasten reply to my 1910 and 2340 of 3rd June. Telegraph details of sinking of Enemy's Light Cruiser reported in your letter from Engadine, dated 31st May also whether position	1120

Date, Time of Despatch.	From	To	System.	Message.	Time of Origin.
4 JUNE —*cont.*				given in which Warrior was abandoned is considered to be accurate.	
				Reply. Captain of Warrior reports Cyphers thrown overboard, also Signal Books in use.* . . . Written statement follows. When abandoned stem of ship was 2 or 3 feet above water, stern about normal draught, every sea washing over upper deck, at least 2 feet of water on main deck, decks and bulkheads terribly shattered by shell fire and no longer water-tight. Ship settling down, stability gone, consider no chance of remaining afloat in increasing heavy weather prevailing, probably sank in 2 or 3 hours at most. Black Prince last seen 5.50 p.m. 31st May, position F or G. I received unconfirmed report that Black Prince or Duke of Edinburgh was seen to sink 10 minutes after Defence. At 5.45 p.m. Defence and Warrior fired on Enemy Light Cruiser Russian type for about half hour at 13,500 to 5,500 yards. She was seen to sink about 6.30 p.m. bearing about S.S.E. from Warrior and S.S.W. from Lion. Warrior was abandoned about 15 miles North (magnetic) from position given.	1701
2.0 p.m.	C.-in-C.	S.O. 3rd L.C.S.	W/T	Return to base on completion of search	1400
3.20 —	C.-in-C.	Admiralty	L/T	Priority. Urgent. I suggest claim for victory on the part of the Germans should be met by the immediate publication in the press of the fact that the British fleet remained on and to the southward of the scene of action during the greater part of 1st June looking for the Enemy.	—
4.25 —	C.-in-C.	Naval Depôt, N. Shields.	L/T	Your 2252, 3rd June. Was Spitfire with remainder of 4th Flotilla at the time she attacked the 4-funnelled cruiser? If not, what was her position relative to remainder of Flotilla? Was cruiser alone or was she in company with other vessels? If so, what class were they, and how many? Is there any possibility of ship attacked being a British 4-funnelled Armoured Cruiser?	1625
				Reply. Spitfire reports position unknown owing to loss of bridge, times approximate was next astern of Tipperary, in line of Destroyers believed in station 5 miles astern of Battle Fleet, about 11 p.m. 31st May, when attacked by 4 Enemy Cruisers from N., which sank Tipperary. Spitfire fired torpedo at 2nd in line, seen to hit, Enemy listed badly, believed sunk. Had 4 very tall funnels. Commanding Officer emphatic on vessel being Enemy. Spitfire just after rammed port bow to	0100 5/6 16

* Part omitted refers to disposal of secret documents only.

Time Time of Despatch.	From	To	System.	Message.	Time of Origin.
4 JUNE —*cont.*				port bow Enemy's Cruiser with 3 perpendicular funnels, 1 red band on every funnel, 2 cranes. Spitfire carried off 20 feet Enemy's side plating, about 11.30 p.m. Enemy's Battle Cruiser with 2 funnels far apart passed close astern of Spitfire, steering between S. and W., observed on fire between funnels and on forecastle.	
5.10 p.m.	C.-in-C.	Admiralty	L/T	Can you telegraph any information as to general appearance of Wiesbaden class of German Light Cruiser, particularly whether she has three or four funnels?	—
6.45 —	C.-in-C.	Admiralty	L/T	I hope to be able to wire more definite information as to German losses to-night Sunday.	—
8.0 —	Office of Chief Censor, Admiralty.	Press Bureau	—	The Secretary of the Admiralty makes the following announcement. Until the C.-in-C. has had time to consult the Officers engaged, and to write a full despatch, any attempt to give a detailed history of the naval engagement, which began on the afternoon of the 31st May and ended in the morning hours of the 1st June, would evidently be premature, but the results are quite plain. The Grand Fleet came in touch with the German High Seas Fleet at 3.30 on the afternoon of the 31st May. The leading ships of the two fleets carried on a vigorous fight, in which Battle Cruisers, fast Battleships and subsidiary craft all took an active part. The losses were severe on both sides; but when the main body of the British fleet came into contact with the German High Seas Fleet, a very brief period sufficed to compel the latter, who had been severely punished, to seek refuge in their protected waters. This manœuvre was rendered possible by low visibility and mist; and although the Grand Fleet were now and then able to get into momentary contact with their opponents no continuous action was possible. They continued the pursuit until the light had wholly failed, while the British Destroyers were able to make a successful attack upon the Enemy during the night. Meanwhile Sir John Jellicoe, having driven the Enemy into port, returned to the main scene of action and scoured the seas in search of disabled vessels. By noon the next day (1st June) it became evident that there was nothing more to be done. He returned, therefore, to his bases 400 miles away, refuelled his fleet, and in the evening of the 2nd June was again ready to put to	—

Date, Time of Despatch.	From	To	System.	Message.	Time of Origin.
4 JUNE—*cont.*					
				sea. The British losses have already been fully stated, and there is nothing to add to or subtract from the latest account published by the Admiralty. The Enemy losses are less easy to determine. That the accounts they have given to the world are false is certain, and we cannot yet be sure of the exact truth. But from such evidence as has come to our knowledge the Admiralty entertain no doubt that the German losses are heavier than the British, not merely relatively to the strength of the two fleets, but absolutely. There seems to be the strongest ground for supposing that included in the German losses are two Battleships, two Dreadnought Battle Cruisers of the most powerful type, two of the latest Light Cruisers (Wiesbaden and Elbing), a Light Cruiser of the Rostock type, the Light Cruiser Frauenlob, at least nine Destroyers and Submarine.	
10.50 p.m.	C.-in-C.	Admiralty	L/T	Priority. Urgent. After careful examination of evidence of eye-witnesses from battlefleet I beg to report that following German vessels were sunk during day action of 31st May and Destroyer attacks night of 31st May—1st June. Battleships and Battle Cruisers, three certain, one being Battleship Kaiser class ; probably two more. Light Cruisers, five certain. Destroyers, six certain. Submarine, one certain. *(Repeated to S.O. B.C.F.)*	2248
5 JUNE 9.28 p.m.	Captain S., Harwich.	Admiralty	L/T	Submarines E. 55, E. 26, D. 1 returned from Horn Reef. Nothing to report.	2105
6 JUNE 12.54 a.m.	Admiralty	C.-in-C.	L/T	From Sir Douglas Haig. The Army in France sends through me the assurance of their whole-hearted admiration of your gallant and successful action in the North Sea. While deploring the losses amongst our brave comrades in the Grand Fleet, we all hope the Navy will yet have its heart's desire of a fight to a finish, of which the Enemy's discretion has again robbed you.	—
2.0 p.m.	C.-in-C.	Admiralty	L/T	I request that immediate steps be taken to prevent the publication of such statements as those in articles in issue of "Weekly Dispatch," dated 4th June, headed "The Lesson of it all." Such articles are most hurtful to discipline and morale, and discouraging to the Officers and men of the fleet. Other newspapers plainly indicate the time at which fleet sailed, and its bases. It is not possible to conduct operations successfully under such conditions. A censorship such as is imposed by War Office on news from land front should be at once adopted.	—

Date, Time of Despatch.	From	To	System.	Message.	Time of Origin.
6 JUNE *—cont.* 9.0 p.m.	Admiralty	C.-in-C.	L/T	The article in "Weekly Dispatch" had not been submitted for censorship. The other articles which indicate time and date of sailing were printed in defiance of censorship after having been cut out of the Press Association's message, which it is believed supplied all the offending papers. The cases are now in hands of Director of Public Prosecutions. The censorship on naval matters is virtually the same as that on military matters, but in the event of a naval battle it has been thought wise to give as wide a latitude as possible to the press, relying on their not abusing the indulgence. The experience of this occasion will, of course, be borne in mind.	—

APPENDIX III.

REPORT BY THE COMMANDER-IN-CHIEF OF THE GERMAN HIGH SEA FLEET ON THE BATTLE OF JUTLAND.

Berlin 1916.

LIST OF GERMAN PLANS TO ACCOMPANY THE
REPORT BY THE COMMANDER-IN-CHIEF OF THE HIGH SEA
FLEET ON THE BATTLE OF JUTLAND.

APPENDICES I.–VII. CHARTS.

*German Plan I.—Plan of intended Operations on 31 May 1916.
    ,,   II.—Submarine Patrol Areas.
    ,,   III.—The Advance on 31 May.
    ,,   IV.—Battle Cruiser Action.
    ,,   V.—Movements of German High Sea Fleet and approximate
                  Position of British Fleet in the Battle of Jutland on
                  31 May.
    ,,   VI.—Diagrams of important Phases of the Battle of Jutland.
    ,,   VII.—The Return of the Main Fleet, 31 May–1 June.

NOTE.—All times in this report are German (summer time) time, *i.e.*, two hours in advance of Greenwich Mean Time.

The Germans appear to use the words " armoured cruiser " and " battle cruiser " indiscriminately; the literal translation has been adopted.

INTERIM REPORT BY THE COMMAND OF THE HIGH SEA FORCES ON THE BATTLE OF THE SKAGERRAK

Commander-in-Chief
    of the
High Sea Forces.

July 4, 1916.

Your Royal and Imperial Majesty's humble servant has the honour to report on the operation of 31 May and 1 June, and the Battle of the Skagerrak, as follows :

A. *THE OBJECT UNDERLYING THE OPERATION.*

The operation against Lowestoft on 23 and 24 April of this year had the effect which our war plan intended it to have.

The enemy justly considered it as a challenge, and was clearly not disposed to submit a second time to a similar blow without opposition. He began to rouse himself. We heard of fresh groupings of his naval forces at the various bases on the East Coast, and of repeated cruises by considerable portions of his Fleet in the northern part of the North Sea.

This situation suited our plans, and I decided to utilize it to the full by making a renewed advance with our whole Fleet as soon as the refit of the SEYDLITZ was complete.

The temporary suspension of the Submarine Warfare against Commerce permitted of the co-operation of all submarines which were ready for sea.

* Seven German Plans will be found in case containing charts.

In the middle of May, therefore, I despatched all submarines to sweep through the northern portion of the North Sea, and to take up positions off the enemy's main bases: *i.e.*, Humber, Firth of Forth, Moray Firth and Scapa Flow, from 23 May onwards, and then to compel the enemy to put to sea, by making an advance with our Fleet, and to give battle under conditions favourable to us.

I hoped by these dispositions to bring the submarines into action and at the same time to utilize them for reconnaissance purposes.

Two operations were prepared, one, an advance in a North-Westerly direction against the English Coast, the other, an advance in a Northerly direction into the Skaggerak.

For the North-Westerly advance, extended scouting by airships was indispensable, as it would lead into an area where we could not let ourselves be drawn into an action against our will.

There was less danger of this in the Northerly advance, for the coast of Jutland afforded a certain cover against surprise from the East, and the distances from the enemy's bases were greater. Aerial reconnaissance, although desirable here also, was not absolutely necessary.

The advance towards the North West promised to be the more effective, and was therefore considered first; consequently all airships were kept in readiness for the operation from 23 May onwards.

Unfortunately the weather was unfavourable for the undertaking. The Fleet waited in vain from 23–30 May for weather favourable for aerial scouting.

The weather on 30 May showing no signs of change, and it being impossible to keep the submarines off the enemy ports any longer, I decided to abandon the North-Westerly advance, and to carry out that towards the North, if necessary, without the assistance of airships.

B. *THE PLAN OF OPERATION.*

The Senior Officer of Scouting Forces, Vice-Admiral Hipper, was ordered to leave the Jade at 4 a.m. on 31 May, with the I and II Scouting Groups, the 2nd Leader of Destroyers in the REGENSBURG and the II, VI and IX Destroyer Flotillas, and to push on to the Skagerrak, keeping out of sight of Horns Reef and the Danish Coast, to show himself before dark off the Norwegian coast, so that the British would receive news of the operation, and to carry out a cruiser and commerce warfare during the late afternoon and the following night off and in the Skagerrak.

The Main Fleet, consisting of the I, II and III Squadrons, IV Scouting Group, 1st Leader of Destroyers in the ROSTOCK and the remainder of the Destroyer Flotillas, was to follow at 4.30 a.m., to cover the Scouting Forces during the operation, and to meet them on the morning of 1 June.

The detached submarines were informed by wireless that the enemy forces might put to sea on 31 May and 1 June.

German Plans I–II. German Plan I shows the intended operation. German Plan II shows the areas to be swept by the submarines and their distribution off the enemy's harbours.

The Naval Corps (Flanders) gladly undertook to block the British Naval Ports in the Hoofden in a similar manner.

C. *THE COURSE OF THE OPERATION.*

1. *Up to the encounter with the enemy.*

The Channel swept by our Mineseeking Forces to the West of Amrum Bank, through the enemy minefields, enabled the High Sea Forces to reach the open sea in safety.

See German Plan III The Advance. Scouting by airship was at first not possible on account of the weather.

At 7.37 a.m. "U. 32" reported 2 heavy ships 2 cruisers and several destroyers about 70 miles east of the Firth of Forth, on a South-Easterly course.

At 8.30 p.m. (*sic*) the wireless "decoding" station Neumünster reported that 2 large war vessels or squadrons with destroyers had left Scapa Flow.

At 8.48 a.m. " U. 66 " reported having sighted, about 60 miles East of Kinnaird Head, 8 enemy heavy ships, light cruisers and destroyers on a North-Easterly course.

The reports gave no indication of the enemy's intentions. The difference in the composition of the individual units and their divergent (*sic*—Trans.) courses did not show that they intended to co-operate or to advance against the German Bight, or that their movements had any connection whatsoever with our operation.

The reports received did not, therefore, cause us to modify our plans, but only led us to hope that we might succeed in bringing a part of the enemy's Fleet to action.

Between 2 and 3 p.m., L. 9, L. 16, L. 21, L. 23 and L. 14 ascended in succession for the purpose of long-distance reconnaissance in the sector between North and West from Heligoland.

They did not succeed in taking part in the action which developed soon afterwards, nor did they observe anything of our Main Fleet or of the enemy, nor did they hear anything of the engagement, although L. 14, according to her own reckoning, was over the scene of action at 10 p.m.

The ELBING, the cruiser on the western wing of the Senior Officer of Scouting Forces' screen, despatched the leaderboat of the IV Destroyer Half-flotilla to examine a steamer. At 4.28 p.m. this destroyer reported having sighted some single enemy ships about 90 miles west of Bovberg.

Figure 1.

Screen of the Senior Officer of Scouting Forces.

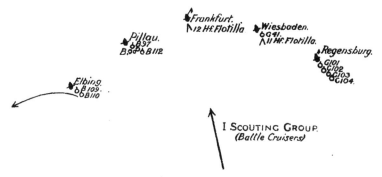

On sighting our forces, the enemy (8 light cruisers of the CAROLINE class) altered course at once to the North. Our cruisers gave chase, with the result that at 5.20 p.m. the Senior Officer of Scouting Forces sighted two columns of large ships steering about East bearing about West; they were soon recognised to be 6 battle cruisers—3 LIONS, 1 TIGER, 2 INDEFATIGABLES—and light forces.

The Senior Officer of Scouting Forces recalled the II Scouting Group, which was to the North of him in chase of the enemy, and proceeded to attack.

The enemy deployed towards the South and formed line of battle. The Senior Officer of Scouting Forces followed this movement (which was exceedingly welcome, as it afforded us the possibility of drawing the enemy on to our Main Fleet); he advanced in quarter line to within effective range, opening fire at 5.49 p.m. at a range of about 13,000 metres (14,217 yards).

2. *The first phase of the Battle : the Cruiser Action.*

The action took place on a South-Easterly course, its exact progress is shown in German Plan IV.

The Senior Officer of Scouting Forces kept the enemy at an effective distance. His guns were well laid. Hits were registered on all the enemy ships.

By 6.13 p.m. the armoured cruiser INDEFATIGABLE, the last ship in the line, was sunk with a violent explosion by the fire of the VON DER TANN.

The gunnery superiority, and advantageous tactical position were distinctly on our side, until, at 6.19 p.m. a new squadron, consisting of 4 or 5 ships of the QUEEN ELIZABETH class, with a considerable superiority in speed, appeared from a North-Westerly direction, and took part in the action with an opening range of about 20,000 metres (21,872 yards).

This rendered the position of our cruisers critical.

The new opponent fired with remarkable rapidity and accuracy, the accuracy being partly due to the impossibility of returning his fire.

At 6.26 p.m. the distance between the opposing armoured cruisers was about 12,000 metres (13,123 yards), and between our armoured cruisers and the QUEEN ELIZABETHS about 18,000 metres (19,685 yards).

Of the Flotillas under the orders of the Senior Officer of Scouting Forces, only the IX Flotilla was at this time in a position from which an attack could be launched.

The 2nd Leader of Destroyers (Commodore Heinrich) in REGENS-BURG, with some boats of the II Flotilla, proceeding at utmost speed, was about abreast of the van of the Senior Officer of Scouting Forces. The cruisers of the II Scouting Group, with the remainder of the Flotillas, were compelled by the QUEEN ELIZABETHS to haul off to the East, and, therefore, in spite of taxing their engines to the utmost, had not been able to reach their position in the van of the armoured cruisers.

In view of the situation, the 2nd Leader of Destroyers ordered the IX Flotilla to proceed to relieve the pressure on the battle cruisers. This Flotilla was already proceeding to attack on its own initiative, in pursuance of orders given by its Senior Officer, Commander Goehle.

Figure 2.

Phase of the battle at 6.26 p.m

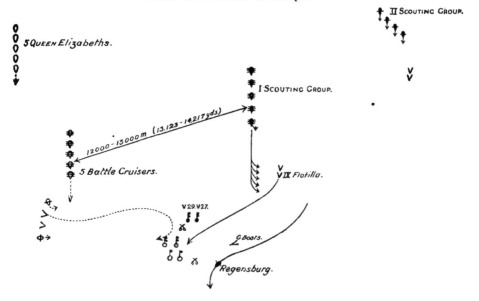

At about 6.30 p.m. the IX Flotilla advanced to the attack under heavy enemy fire. Twelve torpedoes were fired at the enemy line at a range of 9,500–8,000 metres (10,389–8,749 yards).

It was not possible to **bring off** the attack nearer to the enemy, as, simultaneously with the advance of the IX Flotilla, 15 to 20 British destroyers, supported by light cruisers, advanced to counter-attack and to repel our destroyers.

A destroyer action resulted at very close range (1,000–1,500 metres) (1,093–1,640 yards). The REGENSBURG, with those boats of the II Flotilla which were with her, and the medium calibre guns of the armoured cruisers, took part in the conflict. The enemy turned away after about 10 minutes.

On our side V. 27 and V. 29 were sunk by heavy shell fire. The crews of both boats were rescued under enemy fire by V. 26 and S. 35.

On the enemy's side, 2, possibly 3, destroyers were sunk and 2 others so badly damaged that they were left behind and subsequently fell **victim** to the Main Fleet.

The enemy made no attempt to save the crews of their boats.

During the destroyer attack, the British armoured cruisers were effectively held by the large calibre guns of the I Scouting Group. The latter successfully evaded a large number of enemy torpedoes (observed by the IX Flotilla) by edging away a few points.

Towards 6.30 p.m. a violent explosion was observed on the third enemy armoured cruiser QUEEN MARY. When the clouds of smoke dispersed the enemy cruiser had disappeared.

Whether her destruction was caused by the guns, or by a torpedo from the armoured cruisers, or by a torpedo from the IX Flotilla is uncertain. It was probably the work of the guns.

In any case the attack by the IX Flotilla resulted in the temporary cessation of the enemy's fire.

The Senior Officer of Scouting Forces made use of this and ordered the armoured cruisers to turn in succession to a North-Westerly course, thereby ensuring **that he would be** at the head of the cruisers in the next phase of the action.

Immediately after the torpedo **attack,** the German **Main Fleet** appeared on the scene just in time to bring help to the Scouting Forces, which were engaged with the enemy in considerably superior strength.

3. *The second phase of the Battle : the Chase.*

The Main Fleet was in the order K. 312*, the Fleet Flagship leading the I Squadron, course North, speed 14 knots, distance apart of ships 700 metres (3½ cables), distance apart of Squadrons 3,500 metres (19 cables), the destroyers screening the Squadrons against submarines, the light cruisers surrounding and screening the Main Fleet.

At 4.28 p.m., when about 50 miles west of Lyngvig, the first information was received of the sighting of enemy light forces, and at 5.35 p.m. the first report came to hand that enemy heavy forces were in sight. The distance between the Senior Officer of Scouting Forces and the Main Fleet was at this time about 50 miles.

On receipt of this report, line of Battle K. 312* was closed up, and the order " Clear for Action " given.

The report received at 5.45 p.m. from the Senior Officer of Scouting Forces, that he was engaged with 6 enemy armoured cruisers on a South-Easterly course, showed that we had succeeded in bringing some of the enemy to action and in drawing them on to our Main Fleet.

The task of the Main Fleet was now to relieve the materially weaker armoured cruisers as quickly as possible, and to endeavour to cut off a premature retreat of the enemy.

---

* *Admiralty Note.—* ? Keillinie 312—Single Line ahead in the sequence 3rd Squadron, 1st Squadron, 2nd Squadron.

For the latter reason I altered course to North-West at 6.05 p.m., increased to 15 knots, and, a quarter of an hour later, altered course to West in order to bring the enemy between two fires.

Whilst this alteration of course of the Main Fleet was in progress, the II Scouting Group reported that a British Squadron of 5 battleships was joining in the action.

The position of the I Scouting Group, which was now opposed by 6 armoured cruisers and 5 battleships, might become critical.

In consequence everything depended on effecting a junction with the I Scouting Group as soon as possible : I therefore altered course back to North.

At 6.32 p.m. sighted the ships in action.

At 6.45 p.m. the III and I Squadrons were able to open fire, and the Senior Officer of Scouting Forces placed himself and his ships at the head of the Main Fleet.

German Plan VI[1].—Phase of the Battle at 6.55 p.m.

The enemy's light forces turned immediately towards the West, and as soon as they were out of range, towards the North.

It is doubtful whether they suffered any damage from the fire of our battleships in this short time.

The British armoured cruisers turned in succession to North-West. The QUEEN ELIZABETHS followed in their wake, and thus covered the cruisers, which had suffered severely.

At 6.49 p.m., while the Squadrons were passing each other, the Senior Officer of the VI Flotilla, Commander Max Schultz, attacked with the XI Half-Flotilla. The result could not be observed.

The next phase of the battle became a chase : our Scouting Forces endeavouring to keep on the heels of the enemy battle cruisers, and our main body on those of the QUEEN ELIZABETHS.

With this purpose in view our main body proceeded at utmost speed, and, divisions separately, turned towards the enemy as far as North-West.

In spite of this, the enemy's armoured cruisers succeeded in getting out of range of the I Scouting Group soon after 7 o'clock.

The QUEEN ELIZABETHS were also able to increase their lead to such an extent that they could only be kept under fire by the I Scouting Group and the V Division. The hope that one of the pursued ships would be so badly disabled as to fall to the Main Fleet was not realised, although the shots fell well; at 7.30 p.m. it was clearly observed that a ship of the QUEEN ELIZABETH class turned away, after having been hit several times, and withdrew from the battle with diminished speed and with a heavy list to port. The ship was not observed to sink.

In the meantime the ships of the Main Fleet were only able to sink 2 modern destroyers (Nestor and Nomad), which had been disabled during the attack of the IX Flotilla and subsequently overtaken. Their crews were made prisoners.

German Plan VI[2].—Phase of the Battle at 7.15 p.m.

As at 7.20 p.m. the fire of the I Scouting Group and of the ships of the V Division seemed to slacken, I was under the impression that the enemy was succeeding in escaping, and therefore issued an order to the Senior Officer of Scouting Forces, and therewith the permission to all vessels, for the " general chase."

In the meantime the visibility, which had hitherto been good, became less so. The wind had backed from North-West through West to South-West. Smoke from cordite and funnels hung over the water and obscured all view from North to East.

Our own Scouting Forces were only visible for a few seconds at a time

As a matter of fact, the Senior Officer of Scouting Forces had been outflanked by enemy battle cruisers and light forces by the time he received the order for the " general chase," and under their pressure he was forced to turn to the North. He was unable to report this, as intended, for a short time previously the main and auxiliary W/T stations in his Flagship (LÜTZOW) had been put out of action by a heavy shell.

The decrease of fire at the head of the line was only due to the setting sun making it more and more difficult and finally practically impossible to range and to spot.

When, therefore, at 7.40 p.m. the enemy's light forces, grasping the situation, made a torpedo attack against our armoured cruisers, the Senior Officer of Scouting Forces had no alternative but to edge away, and, finally, to order his force to alter course to South-West, and to get into closer touch with our Main Fleet, he being unable to reply effectively to the enemy's fire.

4. *The third phase of the Action : the Battle.*

About the same time the pressure from ahead on the van of the Main Fleet caused it to bear away in an Easterly direction.

At 7.48 p.m., therefore, the signal " Form on the van " was made, the ships formed into line; the speed was temporarily reduced to 15 knots, in order to give the divisions which had been proceeding at utmost speed an opportunity to re-establish close order, the Fleet having become somewhat extended.

While these operations of the Main Fleet were in progress, the II Scouting Group, under Rear-Admiral Boedicker, got into action with a light cruiser of the CALLIOPE class, which he set on fire. Shortly before 8 p.m. the II Scouting Group encountered several light cruisers of the " Town " class and several battleships, including the AGINCOURT. The haze over the water made it impossible to estimate the whole strength of the enemy. The scouting group was at once caught under heavy fire, to which it replied; it fired torpedoes, and then turned away towards its own Main Fleet. The result could not be observed, as a smoke screen had to be developed at once for the protection of the cruisers. In spite of the smoke screen, the WIESBADEN and PILLAU were heavily hit. The WIESBADEN (Captain Reiss) was unable to proceed and remained stopped under the enemy's fire.

German Plan VI[3].—*Phase of the Battle 7.42–8 p.m.*

The Senior Officers of the XII Half Flotilla and IX Flotilla, which had been astern of the cruisers, recognising the seriousness of the situation, proceeded to attack. Fire was opened on both Flotillas from a line of numerous battleships steaming North-West; the destroyers approached to 6,000 metres (6,561 yards) and then fired 6 torpedoes each at the enemy battleships. In this case also it was impossible to observe the result, for dense clouds of smoke concealed the enemy immediately after turning away.* Both flotillas, however, thought they might claim success, as the attack was made under favourable conditions.

At about this time the British Main Fleet, under Admiral Jellicoe, must have joined Admiral Beatty's forces, which had been pursued up to now.

This resulted in heavy fighting from about 8.10–8.35 p.m. in the van of the Main Fleet round the disabled WIESBADEN. In this action the ships also were able to use their torpedoes.

The QUEEN ELIZABETHS, and perhaps Beatty's battle cruisers, attacked from a North-North-Westerly direction. (It appears, however,

---

* It is not clear in the German whether their destroyers or the British battleships turned away.—Trans

from statements made by prisoners, that the battle cruisers took no part in the battle after 7 p.m.)   A new squadron of armoured cruisers (3 INVINCIBLES and 4 WARRIORS), besides light cruisers and destroyers, attacked from the North, and the enemy's battle squadrons attacked from the North-East to East.

German Plan VI[4].—*Phase of the Battle at 8.16 p.m.*

It was principally the I Scouting Group and the leading ships of the III Squadron that had to repulse the attack.   During this attack the armoured cruisers were forced to turn away so sharply, that at 8.35 p.m. I was obliged to turn the line by a " Battle turn " to starboard together, to West.

German Plan VI[5].—*Phase of the Battle at 8.35 p.m.*

While our line was being inverted, two boats of the III Flotilla (G. 88 and V. 73) and the leader boat of the I Flotilla (S. 32) attacked. The remainder of the III Flotilla had broken off their attack, having been recalled by the 1st Leader of Destroyers.   The latter had issued this order on observing the slackening in the enemy's fire, which convinced him that the enemy had turned away, and that the Flotilla, which would be urgently required later on in the action, was being launched into a void.   Owing to the embarrassment of the van, the boats of the remaining flotillas were not able to attack.   Some of them (IX and VI Flotillas) were just returning from the 8 p.m. attack.

Immediately after the inversion of the line the enemy temporarily ceased firing, partly because they lost sight of us in the smoke screen developed by the destroyers for the protection of our line, and particularly of our armoured cruisers, but mainly no doubt, on account of the appreciable losses they had suffered.

The following ships were definitely seen to sink : A ship of the QUEEN ELIZABETH class (name not known); a battle cruiser (INVINCIBLE); two armoured cruisers (BLACK PRINCE and DEFENCE); a light cruiser and two destroyers (one of which was marked 04).

The following ships were heavily damaged, some being set on fire : one armoured cruiser (WARRIOR) which subsequently sank; three light cruisers and three destroyers.

On our side only V. 48 was sunk; WIESBADEN rendered not under control; and LÜTZOW so badly damaged that the Senior Officer of Scouting Forces was forced to leave the ship about 9 p.m. under enemy fire and transfer to MOLTKE.

On this account the Command of the I Scouting Group devolved till 11 p.m. on the Commanding Officer of the DERFFLINGER (Captain Hartog)

The remaining armoured cruisers and van ships of the III Squadron had suffered too, but they kept their station in the line.   After the enemy had been obliged to cease firing at our line, which was proceeding West, they attacked the already badly damaged WIESBADEN.   It could be clearly seen that the ship defended herself bravely against over-whelming odds

It was as yet too early to assume "night cruising order."   The enemy could have compelled us to fight before dark, he could have prevented our exercising our initiative, and finally he could have cut off our return to the German Bight.

There was only one way of avoiding this : to deal the enemy a second blow by again advancing regardless of consequences, and to bring all the destroyers to attack.

This manœuvre would necessarily have the effect of surprising the enemy, upsetting his plans for the rest of the day, and, if the attack was powerful enough, of facilitating our extricating ourselves for the night. In addition this afforded us the opportunity of making a final effort to succour the hard-pressed WIESBADEN, or at least to rescue her crew.

Consequently, at 8.55 p.m. the line was again turned to starboard on to an Easterly course, the armoured cruisers were ordered to attack the head of the enemy's line as fiercely as possible, all flotillas were given the order to attack, and instructions were issued to the 1st Leader of Destroyers (Commodore Michelsen) to transfer the crew of the WIESBADEN to his boats.

The action brought about by this movement soon developed similarly to that of 8.35 p.m., except that our van was still further embarrassed.

German Plan VI[7].—*Phase of the Battle at 9.17 p.m.*

The destroyers sent to the WIESBADEN had to abandon their attempt to rescue the crew. The WIESBADEN and the advancing boats were under such heavy fire that the Senior Officer of the Flotilla considered it useless to risk the latter. While turning away, V. 73 and G. 88 fired a total of 4 torpedoes at the QUEEN ELIZABETHS

The fire directed against our line was mainly concentrated on the armoured cruisers and the V Division. These ships suffered very severely, as they were able to distinguish little more of the enemy than the flashes of his salvoes, whereas they themselves apparently offered good targets.

The conduct of the armoured cruisers is especially deserving of the highest praise. Although a number of their guns were unable to fire and some of the ships themselves were severely damaged, they nevertheless advanced recklessly towards the enemy, in compliance with their orders.

The handling of the III Squadron (Rear-Admiral Behncke) and the behaviour of the ships of the V Division were equally praiseworthy. They and the armoured cruisers bore the brunt of the battle, thereby making it possible for the flotillas to attack with effect

The boats of the VI and IX Flotillas, which were in the van with the cruisers, were the first to attack. The III and V Flotillas, stationed with the Main Fleet, followed suit.

The II Flotilla was held back for the time being by its Senior Officer, in order to prevent it from advancing into a void in the rear of the VI and IX Flotillas. This measure was justified by subsequent events. The I Half Flotilla and a few boats of the VI and IX Flotillas were occupied in screening the damaged LÜTZOW. There was no further opportunity for the approaching VII Flotilla to attack.

As the VI and IX Flotillas approached, they drew on themselves the heavy fire hitherto directed against the armoured cruisers. They were able, however, to approach to within 7,000 m. (7,658 yards) of the centre of the curved line of battleships, consisting of more than 20 units proceeding on courses from East-South-East to South, and to attack under favourable conditions. During the attack S. 35 was hit amidships by a heavy shell and sank at once.

All the remaining boats returned and laid a thick smoke screen between their own fleet and the enemy, in order to protect the van of the Main Fleet, which was being severely pressed.

The purpose of the advance was gained by this destroyer attack.

At 9.17 p.m. a "battle turn" together was therefore made, the line proceeding first on a Westerly course and then altering by a turn in succession to South-West, South and finally South-East, in order to counter the enveloping movement of the enemy, whose van already bore South-East, and to keep a line of retreat open for us.

Shortly after our turn, the enemy ceased fire.

The enemy must have turned away during the attack by the VI and IX Flotillas, as the III and V Flotillas only sighted light forces, and therefore had no opportunity of attacking.

The casualties sustained by the enemy in this phase of the battle cannot be given. Up to the present the only information received is that the MARLBOROUGH was struck by a torpedo. However, it may be taken for certain that other successes were obtained.

Our armoured cruisers and the ships in the van of the III Squadron had suffered severely. Nevertheless, all ships were able to keep station in the "night cruising order" at the high speed of 16 knots; even the LÜTZOW was proceeding at medium speed when she was seen last at 9.30 p.m., abreast of the Fleet Flagship.

5. Movements and actions during the night.

The reports made by the flotillas, regarding the strength of the enemy sighted by them, made it certain that we had been in action against the whole British Fleet.

It might be taken for granted that the enemy would endeavour to force us to the Westward by attacks with strong forces during the hours of dusk, and by destroyer attacks during the night, in order to force us to give battle at daybreak. They were strong enough to do so.

Should we succeed in checking the enemy's enveloping movement and reaching Horns Reef before them, we should retain the initiative for the next morning.

With this object in view, all destroyer flotillas had to be used for attacking during the night, even at the risk of having to do without them in the new engagements which might be expected at dawn. The Main Fleet itself had to make for Horns Reef, in close order, by the shortest route, and to maintain this course in defiance of all attacks of enemy.

German Plan VII.

Orders to this effect were issued. At the same time the Leader of Submarines ordered all submarines in Borkum Roads to advance to the North.

The Senior Officers of the Destroyer Forces stationed the flotillas on a line East-North-East and South-South-West, that is in the direction from which the enemy's Main Fleet was expected to pursue.

A large number of the boats had already expended their torpedoes during the day actions; some had been left behind to protect the severely damaged LÜTZOW; some were retained by their Senior Officers in order to have them at their disposal in case of need. Thanks to this decision it was possible to rescue the crews of the ELBING and ROSTOCK later on.

Only the II, V, VII and portions of the VI and IX Flotillas therefore advanced to attack. The boats had various night actions with light forces of the enemy; they saw nothing of his Main Fleet. At daybreak L. 24 sighted a portion of the Main Fleet in the "Jammerbucht."* The enemy had, therefore, drawn off to the North after the battle.

The II Flotilla, to which the Northern part of the sector was allotted, was forced away by cruisers and destroyers, and returned viâ The Skaw. The 2nd Leader of Destroyers allowed it to use its discretion regarding this route.

The remaining flotillas assembled at dawn with the Main Fleet.

Before it became quite dark, the Main Fleet had a short but serious encounter with the enemy. At 10.20 p.m., while the I and II Scouting Groups were endeavouring to take station ahead, they were subjected to heavy fire from a South-Easterly direction. Only the flashes of the enemy's salvoes could be seen. The ships which were already severely damaged received further hits without being able to make any serious reply to the fire. They, therefore, turned away and took up a position on the disengaged side, pushing themselves between the II and I Squadrons

---

* Note.—Jammer Bight in the Skagerrak.

German Plan VI⁸.—*Sketch for* 10.30 *p.m.*

The van of the I Squadron followed the movement of the cruisers, whereas the II Squadron (Rear-Admiral Mauve) continued on its course, thus drawing the enemy's fire. As the II Squadron recognised that light conditions made a reply impossible, it edged away in order to draw the enemy towards the I Squadron. The enemy did not pursue, but ceased firing.

At about the same time the IV Scouting Group (Commodore von Reuter) was in action under identical conditions with 4–5 cruisers, including ships of the HAMPSHIRE class.

Bearing in mind that the van of the Main Fleet in particular would be called upon to repulse enemy attacks, and in order to have the main strength in the van at daybreak, the II Squadron was ordered to take station astern. The I Scouting Group became the rearguard, the II Scouting Group became the vanguard, and the IV Scouting Group was entrusted with the screening of the starboard side.

The battle squadrons therefore proceeded in the following order: I Squadron, Fleet Flagship, III Squadron, II Squadron, the I and III Squadrons in inverse order. WESTFALEN (Captain Redlich) was leading ship of the line.

During the night the enemy attacked practically uninterruptedly from the East with light forces, and at times also with heavy forces.

The II and IV Scouting Groups, and particularly the ships of the I Squadron (Vice-Admiral Schmidt) had to repulse these attacks. The result was excellent.

At 2.0 a.m. an armour cruiser of the CRESSY class (name not known), entirely misjudging the situation, approached the rear ships of the I Squadron and the Fleet Flagship to within 1,500 metres (1,645 yards). In a few minutes she was set on fire by our guns and sank, 4 minutes after fire was opened, with terrific explosions.

According to careful estimation 1 armoured cruiser, 1 light cruiser and 7 destroyers were sunk during the night, and several light cruisers and destroyers were badly damaged.

Our losses were the FRAUENLOB, POMMERN and V. 4. The ROSTOCK and ELBING had to be abandoned and blown up. The FRAUENLOB (Captain Hoffman, Georg) was hit by a torpedo at 12.45 a.m. while the IV Scouting Group were in action with 4 cruisers of the "Town" class. According to the statement of some of the few survivors, she sank soon afterwards, fighting to the last. The POMMERN (Captain Bölken) was torpedoed at 4.20 a.m., and blew up with a tremendous explosion. V. 4 ran on an enemy mine at 4.50 a.m. The crew were saved.

At 1.30 a.m. the ROSTOCK and ELBING became engaged with destroyers, on the port side abreast of the van of the I Squadron; they were at last compelled to turn away from the enemy's torpedoes and break through the line of the I Squadron in order not to hamper the fire of our battleships.

During this manœuvre the ROSTOCK was hit by a torpedo, while the ELBING collided with the POSEN.

Both cruisers were unable to manœuvre. The ROSTOCK remained afloat until 5.45 a.m., and was then blown up, on hostile cruisers being sighted, after the entire crew including the wounded had been transferred to boats of the III Flotilla. The crew of the ELBING were also taken on board a boat of the III Flotilla, only the Commanding Officer, the executive officer, the torpedo officer and a cutter's crew remaining on board in order to keep the ship afloat as long as possible. On hostile forces being sighted at 4 a.m., the ELBING had to be blown up too. The crew who had remained on board escaped in the cutter, were picked up later by a Dutch trawler and returned home *via* Holland.

The LÜTZOW was kept afloat until 3.45 a.m. Towards the end the ship was navigated from the after bridge. All attempts to stop the water from rushing in were in vain, the fore part of the ship had suffered too severely. Finally the ship had about 7,000 tons of water in her. The forecastle was flooded up to the truck of the Jack staff. The propellers revolved out of water. The ship had to be abandoned. The crew, including all the wounded, were transferred to the destroyers G. 40, G. 37, G. 38 and V. 45, and the LÜTZOW was sunk by a torpedo. The 4 destroyers had altogether 1,250 men of the LÜTZOW on board. On two occasions they encountered enemy cruisers and destroyers, and on both occasions they attacked under the leadership of the Senior Commanding Officer (Lieutenant-Commander Beitzen, Richard), and successfully fought their way back to the German Bight. During the last action the engines of G. 40 were hit, and she had to be taken in tow.

When the Main Fleet received information of this, the 2nd Leader of Destroyers in the REGENSBURG turned back and met the tow. S. 32, leader boat of the I Flotilla (Lieutenant-Commander Fröhlich), was hit at 1 a.m. by a heavy shell in the boiler room and was temporarily disabled. However, by feeding the boilers with sea water, the Commanding Officer succeeded in reaching Danish territorial waters. Destroyers which had been sent out then towed her home through Nordmanns Deep.

6. *The situation on the morning of 1st June.*

During the night, L. 11, L. 13, L. 17, L. 22 and L. 24 ascended to make an early reconnaissance.

At 5.10 a.m. L. 11 reported a group of 12 British battleships, numerous light forces and destroyers on a Northerly course about the middle of the line Terschelling–Horns Reef, and, immediately afterwards, 6 large enemy battleships and three battle cruisers to the North of the first-mentioned group. The airship came under heavy fire, but kept in touch. Shortly after having been sighted, the enemy altered course to the West and were lost to sight in thick weather.

At 4 a.m. L. 24 sighted a flotilla of enemy destroyers and about 6 submarines 50 miles West of Bovberg. The airship was fired at and replied by dropping bombs; then scouting further to the North, she discovered at 5 a.m., in the Jammerbucht, a group of 12 large battleships and numerous cruisers, which were proceeding South at high speed. It was impossible to keep touch and to reconnoitre further, as the clouds were only 800 m. (2,624 feet) above the water.

At daybreak the Main Fleet itself saw nothing of the enemy. The weather was so thick that one could hardly see the length of a squadron.

The reports received from the armoured cruisers showed that the I Scouting Group could no longer fight a serious action. The ships in the van of the III Squadron must also have lost in fighting value.

Of the fast light cruisers only the FRANKFURT, PILLAU, and REGENSBURG were at my disposal.

Owing to the bad visibility, further scouting by airships could not be counted on. It was, therefore, hopeless to try and force a regular action on the enemy reported to the South. The consequences of such an encounter would have been a matter of chance. I therefore abandoned any further operations and gave the order to return to base.

On the way back, when to the West of List, the OSTFRIESLAND ran on a mine, in a minefield which we knew nothing of and which apparently had been laid by the enemy shortly before. The ship was able to enter harbour under her own steam.

Several submarine attacks on our returning Main Fleet were unsuccessful, thanks partly to the watchfulness of our aircraft, which joined the Main Fleet off List and accompanied it to the estuaries.

All ships and destroyers returned to the estuaries during the course of the day.

Special mention must be made of the bringing in of the severely damaged SEYDLITZ (Captain von Egidy). It is due to the admirable seamanship of the Commanding Officer and his crew that the ship was able to reach harbour.

The submarines which left the Ems were ordered to look for the ELBING and for the damaged ships of the enemy. The submarines off the English ports were ordered to make every endeavour to remain on their stations for one day more.

At 6.20 p.m. U. 46 met a damaged ship of the IRON DUKE class (MARLBOROUGH) about 60 miles north of Terschelling. She fired a torpedo, but missed. Of the submarines which lay off the enemy's harbours, U.B. 21 hit an enemy destroyer on 31 May, and U. 52 one on 1 June. Owing to hostile counter-measures the sinking in neither case was observed.

D. *THE LOSSES ON EITHER SIDE.*

According to a careful appreciation of the observations made by us, the enemy losses were :—

1 large battleship of the QUEEN ELIZABETH class	28,500 tons.
3 battle cruisers (QUEEN MARY, INDEFATIGABLE, INVINCIBLE)	63,000 „
4 armoured cruisers (BLACK PRINCE, DEFENCE, WARRIOR, and one of the CRESSY class)	53,700 „
2 light cruisers	9,000 „
13 destroyers	15,000 „
Total	169,200 „

Our losses were :—

1 battle cruiser (LÜTZOW)	26,700 tons.
1 old battleship (POMMERN)	13,200 „
4 light cruisers (WIESBADEN, ELBING, ROSTOCK, FRAUENLOB)	17,150 „
5 destroyers	3,680
Total	60,730 „

The losses of the enemy are, practically without exception, total losses, whereas we were able to rescue the crews of the LÜTZOW, ELBING, ROSTOCK, and half the crews of the destroyers.

We expended 3,596 heavy shells, 3,921 medium and 2,962 small calibre shells and 107 torpedoes.

E. *SUMMARY.*

The success obtained is due to the fact that our Squadron and Flotilla Leaders were filled with zeal for battle, and realised the object of the undertaking, and to the excellent work performed by the ships' companies, who were imbued with the greatest martial ardour.

Its achievement was only rendered possible by the quality of our ships and armament, the fact that the peace training of the units was conscious of its object, and by the conscientious training carried out in individual ships

The large amount of experience gained will be exploited with the greatest care.

The battle has proved that in building up our Fleet, and in the development of the individual types of our ships, we have been guided by correct strategical and tactical views, and that we should, therefore, continue on the same lines.

All arms have borne their share in this result, the decisive factor was, however, both directly and indirectly, the long range heavy armament of the LARGER VESSELS. It caused the greater part of the known losses inflicted on the enemy, and it enabled the flotillas to carry out a successful attack against the enemy's Main Fleet. The above observation in no way detracts from the merit of the flotillas, whose attack on the enemy battlefleet was finally successful in enabling us to break away completely from the enemy.

The LARGE WAR VESSEL, battleship and cruiser, is and remains, therefore, the foundation of Sea Power, and should be further developed by enlarging the calibre of the guns, increasing the speed and perfecting the armour above and below water.

F. THE FURTHER CONDUCT OF OUR NAVAL WAR.

In conclusion I have the honour respectfully to report to Your Majesty that, with the exception of the DERFFLINGER and SEYDLITZ, the High Sea Fleet will be ready for further battles by the middle of August.

Should the future operations take a favourable course, it may be possible to inflict appreciable damage on the enemy; but there can be no doubt that even the most favourable issue of a battle on the high seas WILL NOT COMPEL ENGLAND to make peace in THIS war. The disadvantages of our geographical position compared with that of the Island Empire, and her great material superiority, cannot be compensated for by our Fleet to a degree which will enable us to overcome the blockade instituted against us, or to overpower the Island Empire herself, even if all our submarines are fully available for military purposes.

A victorious termination of the war within measurable time can only be attained by destroying the economic existence of Great Britain, namely, by the employment of submarines against British commerce.

In the conviction that it is my duty, I must continue respectfully to dissuade Your Majesty from adopting any modified form of this warfare, because it would mean reducing this weapon to an anomaly and because the results would probably not be in proportion to the risk incurred by the boats. Further, even with the most conscientious care on the part of the Commanding Officers, it will be impossible to avoid incidents in British waters where American interests are so prevalent, which will force us to humiliating concessions, unless we are able to prosecute the submarine campaign in its acutest form.

(Signed)   SCHEER.

To His Majesty
    the Emperor and King.

Admiralty Note.—The German original of this report was found in an officer's cabin of one of the ships scuttled at Scapa.

APPENDIX IV.

No. 339/H.F. 0034.

" Iron Duke,"

SIR,   30th October 1914.

THE experience gained of German methods since the commencement of the war make it possible and very desirable to consider the manner in which these methods are likely to be made use of tactically in a fleet action.

2. The Germans have shown that they rely to a very great extent on submarines, mines and torpedoes, and there can be no doubt whatever that they will endeavour to make the fullest use of these weapons in a fleet action, especially since they possess an actual superiority over us in these particular directions.

3. It therefore becomes necessary to consider our own tactical methods in relation to these forms of attack.

4. In the first place, it is evident that the Germans cannot rely with certainty upon having their full complement of submarines and minelayers present in a fleet action, unless the battle is fought in waters selected by them, and in the Southern area of the North Sea. Aircraft, also, could only be brought into action in this locality.

5. My object will therefore be to fight the fleet action in the Northern portion of the North Sea, which position is incidentally nearer our own bases, giving our wounded ships a chance of reaching them, whilst it ensures the final destruction or capture of enemy wounded vessels, and greatly handicaps a night destroyer attack before or after a fleet action. The Northern area is also favourable to a concentration of our cruisers and torpedo craft with the battlefleet; such concentration on the part of the enemy being always possible, since he will choose a time for coming out when all his ships are coaled and ready in all respects to fight.

6. Owing to the necessity that exists for keeping our cruisers at sea, it is probable that many will be short of coal when the opportunity for a fleet action arises, and they might be unable to move far to the Southward for this reason.

7. The presence of a large force of cruisers is most necessary, for observation and for screening the battlefleet, so that the latter may be manœuvred into any desired position behind the cruiser screen. This is a strong additional reason for fighting in the Northern area.

8. Secondly, it is necessary to consider what may be termed the tactics of the actual battlefield.

The German submarines, if worked as is expected with the battlefleet, can be used in one of two ways :—

    (a) With the cruisers, or possibly with destroyers.
    (b) With the battlefleet.

In the first case the submarines would probably be led by the cruisers to a position favourable for attacking our battlefleet as it advanced to deploy, and in the second case they might be kept in a position in rear, or to the flank, of the enemy's battlefleet, which would move in the direction required to draw our own Fleet into contact with the submarines.

9. The first move at (a) should be defeated by our own cruisers, provided we have a sufficient number present, as they should be able to force the enemy's cruisers to action at a speed which would interfere with submarine tactics.

The cruisers must, however, have destroyers in company to assist in dealing with the submarines, and should be well in advance of the battlefleet; hence the necessity for numbers.

10. The second move at (b) can be countered by judicious handling of our battlefleet, but may, and probably will, involve a refusal to comply with the enemy's tactics by moving in the invited direction. If, for instance, the enemy battlefleet were to turn away from an advancing

Fleet, I should assume that the intention was to lead us over mines and submarines, *and should decline to be so drawn.*

11. I desire particularly to draw the attention of their Lordships to this point, since it may be deemed a refusal of battle, and, indeed, might possibly result in failure to bring the enemy to action as soon as is expected and hoped.

12. Such a result would be absolutely repugnant to the feelings of all British Naval Officers and men, but with new and untried methods of warfare new tactics must be devised to meet them.

I feel that such tactics, if not understood, may bring odium upon me, but so long as I have the confidence of their Lordships I intend to pursue what is, in my considered opinion, the proper course to defeat and annihilate the enemy's battlefleet, without regard to uninstructed opinion or criticism.

13. The situation is a difficult one. It is quite within the bounds of possibility that half of our battlefleet might be disabled by under-water attack before the guns opened fire at all, if a false move is made, and I feel that I must constantly bear in mind the great probability of such attack and be prepared tactically to prevent its success.

14. The safeguard against submarines will consist in moving the battlefleet at very high speed to a flank before deployment takes place or the gun action commences.

This will take us off the ground on which the enemy desires to fight, but it may, of course, result in his refusal to follow me.

If the battlefleets remain within sight of one another, though not near the original area, the limited submerged radius of action and speed of the submarines will prevent the submarines from following without coming to the surface, and I should feel that after an interval of high speed manœuvring, I could safely close.

15. The object of this letter is to place my views before their Lordships, and to direct their attention to the alterations in pre-conceived ideas of battle tactics which are forced upon us by the anticipated appearance in a fleet action of submarines and minelayers.

16. There can be no doubt that the fullest use will also be made by the enemy of surface torpedo craft.

This point has been referred to in previous letters to their Lordships, and, so long as the whole of the First Fleet Flotillas are with the Fleet, the hostile destroyers will be successfully countered and engaged.

The necessity for attaching some destroyers to Cruiser Squadrons, alluded to in paragraph 9, emphasizes the necessity for the junction of the 1st and 3rd Flotillas with the Fleet before a fleet action takes place.

17. It will, however, be very desirable that *all* available ships and torpedo craft should be ordered to the position of the fleet action as soon as it is known to be imminent, as the presence of even Third Fleet Vessels after the action or towards its conclusion may prove of great assistance in rendering the victory shattering and complete.

The Channel Fleet should be accompanied by as many destroyers, drawn from the Dover or Coast patrols, as can be spared.

I trust that their Lordships will give the necessary orders on the receipt of information from me of an impending fleet action.

18. In the event of a fleet action being imminent, or, indeed, as soon as the High Sea Fleet is known to be moving Northward, it is most desirable that a considerable number of our oversea submarines should proceed towards the Fleet, getting first on to the line between the Germans and Heligoland in order to intercept them when returning. The German Fleet would probably arrange its movements so as to pass Heligoland at dusk when coming out and at dawn when returning, in order to minimise submarine risk. The opportunity for submarine attack in the Heligoland Bight would not therefore be very great, and from four to six submarines would be the greatest number that could be usefully

employed there. The remainder, accompanied by one or two light cruisers, taken, if necessary, from the Dover patrol, should work up towards the position of the fleet, the light cruisers keeping in wireless touch with me.

I have the honour to be, Sir,

Your obedient servant,

J. R. JELLICOE,

Admiral.

The Secretary
   of the Admiralty]

M. 03177/14.

Admiralty,

7th November 1914.

SIR,
      I HAVE laid before My Lords Commissioners of the Admiralty your letter of the 30th ultimo, No. 339/H.F. 0034, and I am commanded by them to inform you that they approve your views, as stated therein, and desire to assure you of their full confidence in your contemplated conduct of the Fleet in action.

2. My Lords will, as desired, give orders for all available Ships and Torpedo Craft to proceed to the position of the Fleet Action on learning from you that it is imminent.

I am, Sir,

Your obedient Servant,

W. GRAHAM GREENE.

The Commander-in-Chief,
   H.M. Ships and Vessels,
      Home Fleets.